t Marinas, It's a Sure
ign of Savings

k for the sign of BoatU.S. Marina Discounts!

900 marinas nationwide offer valuable discounts to BoatU.S. Members, many
h include fuel, repairs, and overnight slips in addition to haul-out, launch ramp,
out and more. Just look for the BoatU.S. sign; its your key to savings. To locate
as that participate in the discount program, log-on to BoatUS.com/marinas.

et the discounts, you've got to be a Member. Call 800-395-2628 today!

- 25% OFF Transient Slip Rentals
- 10¢ Off Per Gallon Fuel
- Up to 15% OFF Repairs

BoatU.S. COOPERATING MARINAS — FLORIDA & BAHAMAS, AL, MS, LA, TX

A EAST COAST

nd Yacht Basin
nd, (904) 277-4615

Marina
, 749-4407

Hi-Lift
305) 931-2550

Marina
305) 935-4295

eral Yacht Club
veral, (321) 784-2292

rtin's Marina
(863) 983-3151

e Service
(863) 673-1460

Boat Repair
) 403-1848

anding Lake Crescent
, (386) 698-2485

Marina
e, (305) 258-4092

Marina
, (954) 893-0004

at Marine Service Center
h, (954) 924-9444

Works
, (954) 925-6336

e, Inc.
86) 738-0010

formance Center
h, (561) 272-0066

lub at Delray Beach
h, (561) 272-2700

Marina
ale, (954) 527-1829

Yachting Center
ale, (954) 764-2233

auderdale/New River
ility
ale, (954) 828-5423

ity Marina
800) 619-1780

Marina-Fort Pierce
72) 466-7300

ht Club
72) 464-1734

n Marina & Lodge
(386) 467-2002

arine Service
(954) 989-9997

over Marina
, (305) 230-3034

Yacht Center
) 588-9911

ht Center
e, (904) 384-5577

rina
, (904) 223-4757

ng/Pier 68 Marina
e, (904) 765-9925

ne
Beach, (904) 249-8200

n & Marina
ch, (772) 334-0936

nd Marina
ch, (772) 229-2811

cks Marina, LLC
) 746-3312

ark Marina
e, (305) 361-1281

Marine Service
, (863) 676-6657

Lighthouse Point Marina
Lighthouse Point, (954) 941-0227

Paradise Marine
Melbourne, (321) 255-9553

Sundance Marina
Melbourne, (321) 242-7140

Harbortown Canaveral Marina
Merritt Island, (321) 453-0160

Matheson Hammock Marina
Miami, (305) 665-5475

Metro Parks
Miami, (305) 755-7861

North Beach Marina
Miami, (305) 758-8888

Pelican Harbor Marina
Miami, (305) 754-9330

Sea Isle Marina & Yachting Center
Miami, (305) 377-3625

UK Sailmakers, Miami
Miami, (305) 858-3000

Bill Bird Marina
Miami Beach, (305) 947-3525

Sebastian Inlet Marina
Micco, (772) 664-8500

North Palm Beach Marina
N. Palm Beach, (561) 626-4919

Old Port Cove Marina
N. Palm Beach, (561) 626-1760

Fleming Island Marina
Orange Park, (904) 269-0027

Everglades Adventures RV & Sailing
Resort
Pahokee, (561) 924-7830

Crystal Cove Marine Services, LLC
Palatka, (386) 328-4000

Holiday Inn Marina
Palatka, (386) 328-3481

Barnacle Busters
Palm Beach Gardens, (561) 625-4484

Palm Coast Marina
Palm Coast, (386) 446-6370

Manatee Cove Marina
Patrick AFB, (321) 494-7455

Aqua Toy Store
Pompano Beach, (954) 784-9011

Aquamarina Hidden Harbour
Pompano Beach, (954) 941-0498

Sands Harbor Marina
Pompano Beach, (954) 942-9100

Yacht Management Marina
Pompano Beach, (954) 941-6447

Adventure Yacht Harbor
Port Orange, (386) 756-2180

New Port Cove Marine Center
Riviera Beach, (561) 844-2504

Boat Tree Marina
Sanford, (407) 322-1610

Monroe Harbour Marina
Sanford, (407) 322-2910

River's Edge Marina
St. Augustine, (904) 827-0520

Finest Kind Marina
Stuart, (772) 223-4110

Mariner Cay Marina
Stuart, (772) 287-2900

River Forest Yachting Center
Stuart, (772) 287-4131

Sailfish Marina
Stuart, (772) 283-1122

Stuart Corinthian Yacht Club
Stuart, (772) 221-1900

Winston Yacht Club, Inc.
Sunny Isles Beach, (305) 932-0720

Jib Yacht Club and Marina
Tequesta, (561) 746-4300

Kennedy Point Marina
Titusville, (321) 383-0280

FLORIDA KEYS

Hawk's Cay Resort and Marina
Duck Key, (305) 743-9000

Treasure Harbor Marine
Islamorada, (305) 852-2458

Anchorage Resort & Yacht Club
Key Largo, (305) 451-0500

Garden Cove Marina
Key Largo, (305) 451-4694

Molasses Reef Marina
Key Largo, (305) 451-9411

Pirate Hat Marina
Key Largo, (305) 731-0060

Safe Harbor Marina
Key West, (305) 294-9797

Dolphin Marina & Lodging
Little Torch Key, (305) 872-2685

Little Palm Island
Little Torch Key, (800) 343-8567

Black Ghost Outfitting & Guest House
Marathon, (305) 743-4118

Mangrove Marina
Tavernier, (866) 626-4768

FLORIDA WEST COAST

Galati Marine, Inc.
Anna Maria, (941) 778-0755

Water Street Hotel & Marina
Apalachicola, (850) 653-3700

DeSoto Marina Inc. & Nav-A-Gator
Grille
Arcadia, (941) 627-3474

Jug Creek Marine
Bokeelia, (239) 283-3331

Back Bay Marina of Southwest
Florida
Bonita Springs, (239) 992-2608

Boat Surplus
Bradenton, (941) 755-7797

Cortez Fishing Center
Bradenton, (941) 795-7796

Rivertown Boat Works & Marina
Bradenton, (941) 761-2662

Twin Dolphin Marina
Bradenton, (941) 747-8300

Bradenton Beach Marina
Bradenton Beach, (941) 778-2288

Tarpon Point Marina
Cape Coral, (239) 549-4900

Chokoloskee Island Park
Chokoloskee, (239) 695-2414

Clearwater Bay Marine
Clearwater, (727) 443-3207

Clearwater Municipal Marina
Clearwater, (727) 462-6954

Cortez Cove Marina
Cortez, (941) 761-4554

Aquamarina Twin Rivers Marina
Crystal River, (352) 795-3552

Crystal River Watersports/Days Inn
Crystal River, (352) 795-7033

Pete's Pier, Inc
Crystal River, (352) 795-3302

Harborwalk Marina
Destin, (850) 337-8250

Royal Palm Marina
Englewood, (941) 475-6882

Fisherman's Cove Marina
Freeport, (850) 835-2035

City of Ft. Myers Yacht Basin
Ft. Myers, (293) 321-7080

Gulf Harbour Marina
Ft. Myers, (239) 437-0881

Jacks Marine
Ft. Myers, (239) 694-2708

Legacy Harbour Marina
Ft. Myers, (239) 461-0775

Fort Myers Beach Marina
Ft. Myers Beach, (239) 463-9552

Sunrise Marina & Yacht Club
Ft. Walton Beach, (850) 362-0232

Emerald Coast Yachts, Inc
Gulf Breeze, (888) 204-0241

Snapper Marina
Hernando Beach, (352) 596-2952

Anclote Village Marina, Inc.
Holiday, (727) 937-9737

Holmes Beach Marina
Holmes Beach, (941) 778-2121

Islands Cove Marina
Holmes Beach, (941) 779-0401

Wolfgang Schulz Marine Engine
Service
Holmes Beach, (941) 778-2873

Homosassa Riverside Resort
Homosassa, (800) 442-2040

Magic Manatee Marina
Homosassa, (352) 628-7334

Port Hudson Marina, LLC
Hudson, (727) 869-1840

Holiday Inn Harbourside Marina
Indian Rock Beach, (727) 595-9484

Pelican Bend Marina
Isles of Capri, (239) 394-3452

Largo Intercoastal Marina, LLC
Largo, (727) 595-3592

Madeira Beach Municipal Marina
Madeira Beach, (727) 399-2631

Elkham Marine Services
Marco Island, (239) 601-2979

The Marina at Factory Bay
Marco Island, (239) 389-2929

Marquardt's Marina
Mexico Beach, (850) 648-8900

River Forest Yachting Center - Moore
Haven
Moore Haven, (863) 612-0003

Prosperity Pointe Marina
N. Ft Myers, (239) 995-2155

Marinatown Yacht Harbor
N. Ft Myers, (239) 997-2767

Boathouse Grill & Marina
Naples, (239) 530-0000

Cocohatchee River Marina
Naples, (239) 566-2611

Fishfinders at Vanderbilt Beach
Marina
Naples, (239) 597-2063

Gulf Shores Marina
Naples, (239) 774-0222

Naples Boat Club
Naples, (239) 430-4994

Naples City Dock
Naples, (239) 213-3070

Bluewater Bay Marina
Niceville, (850) 897-2821

Bob's Boat Yard
Osprey, (941) 966-2552

Regatta Pointe Marina
Palmetto, (941) 729-6021

Riviera Dunes Marina
Palmetto, (941) 723-9595

Panama City Marina
Panama City, (850) 872-7272

Sun Harbor Marina
Panama City, (850) 785-0551

Treasure Island Marina
Panama City Bch, (850) 234-6533

Bahia Mar Marina
Pensacola, (850) 432-9620

Holiday Harbor Marina, Inc.
Pensacola, (850) 492-0555

Palafox Pier and Yacht Harbor
Pensacola, (850) 432-9620

Pelicans Perch Marine & Boatyard
Pensacola, (850) 453-3471

Pineland Marina
Pineland, (239) 283-3593

Mobile Marine Mechanic, Inc.
Port Charlotte, (941) 625-5329

Sunset Landing Marina
Port Richey, (727) 849-5092

Captain's Cove Marina
Port Saint Joe, (850) 227-3357

Port St. Joe Marina
Port St. Joe, (850) 227-9393

Saint Marks Yacht Club
Saint Marks, (850) 925-6606

Sarasota Cay Club Resort Marina
Sarasota, (941) 355-2781

Turtle Beach Marina
Sarasota, (941) 349-9449

Yow's Marine Services, Inc.
Sarasota, (941) 957-1366

Pasadena Marina
South Pasadena, (727) 343-4500

York Road Marina
St. James, (239) 283-1149

Captian Levi's Fiberglass Boat Repair
& Detailing
St. Petersburg, (727) 391-7639

Great American Marine
St. Petersburg, (727) 343-6520

Marina Outpost
St. Petersburg, (727) 384-3474

Salt Creek Boat Works, Inc.
St. Petersburg, (727) 821-5482

River Haven Marina
Steinhatchee, (352) 498-0709

Sea Hag Marina
Steinhatchee, (352) 498-3008

UK Sailmakers Gulfcoast
Tampa, (813) 250-1968

American Boat Works
Tarpon Springs, (727) 942-4152

Anclote Harbors
Tarpon Springs, (727) 934-7616

Belle Harbour Marina
Tarpon Springs, (727) 943-8489

The Landing at Tarpon Springs
Tarpon Springs, (727) 937-1100

Turtle Cove Marina
Tarpon Springs, (727) 934-2202

John's Pass Marina
Treasure Island, (727) 360-6907

Crow's Nest Marina
Venice, (941) 484-7661

BAHAMAS

Bluff House Marina
Abaco, (800) 745-4911

Sunrise Resort & Marina
Freeport, GBI, (242) 352-6834

Marsh Harbour Marina & Yacht Club
Marsh Harbour, Abaco, (242) 367-2700

Paradise Harbour Club & Marina
Nassau, (242) 363-2992

ALABAMA

Delta Port Marina
Coden, (251) 767-3443

Pirates Cove Marina
Elberta, (251) 987-1223

Eastern Shore Marine, Inc.
Fairhope, (800) 458-7245

Bon Secour Lodge
Gulf Shores, (334) 968-7814

Homeport Marina
Gulf Shores, (251) 968-4528

Nelson Boat Yard, Inc
Gulf Shores, (251) 968-7974

Turner Marine Yacht Sales
Mobile, (251) 476-1444

Bear Point Marina
Orange Beach, (251) 981-2327

Hudson Marina
Orange Beach, (334) 981-4127

MISSISSIPPI & LOUISIANA

Bay Marina
Bay St. Louis, MS (228) 466-4970

Tiki Restaurant and Marina
Gautier, MS (228) 497-1591

Fort Bayou Marina
Ocean Springs, MS (228) 875-9438

Mariner's Village Marina
Mandeville, LA (985) 626-1517

Quantum New Orleans
New Orleans, LA (985) 283-4058

Rigolet's Marina
New Orleans, LA (504) 662-5002

TEXAS

Fiberglass TAC/BBM Boat Mfg
Bacliff, (281) 339-1511

Tempest Marine Services
Brazoria, (979) 233-0700

Watergate Yachting Center
Clear Lake Shores, (281) 334-1511

Corpus Christi Municipal Marina
Corpus Christi, (361) 826-3980

West Bay Marina
Galveston, (409) 737-3636

Serendipity Resort
Palacios, (361) 972-5454

St. Christopher Haven Marina
Port O'Connor, (361) 983-4841

Cove Harbor North
Rockport, (361) 729-6661

Fulton Harbor
Rockport, (361) 729-6661

Rockport Harbor
Rockport, (361) 729-6661

Quantum Gulf Coast
Seabrook, (281) 474-4168

Seabrook Shipyard
Seabrook, (281) 474-2586

Tops-N-Towers
Seabrook, (281) 474-4000

**Not all discounts
offered at all marinas,
visit BoatUS.com
for details.**

Over Half a Million Members Know, It Pays to Belong!

DOZIER'S WATERWAY GUIDE
THE CRUISING AUTHORITY

F O U N D E D   I N   1 9 4 7

Waterway Guide publishers, staff and family enjoy a day on the water to watch the Blue Angels perform over Annapolis.

Publisher	**JACK DOZIER** jdozier@waterwayguide.com
Associate Publisher	**CRAIG DOZIER** cdozier@waterwayguide.com
General Manager	**CHUCK BAIER** cbaier@waterwayguide.com
Editor	**SUSAN LANDRY** slandry@waterwayguide.com
Editorial Assistant	**TERRY GRANT** tgrant@waterwayguide.com
Web & News Editor	**TED STEHLE** tstehle@waterwayguide.com
Director of Marketing	**DENIELLE T. D'AMBROSIO** denielle@waterwayguide.com
Production Artist	**REESA KUGLER** rkugler@waterwayguide.com
Web Coordinator	**MIKE SCHWEFLER**
Marketing Associate	**DEBI DEAN** ddean@waterwayguide.com
Book Sales	**LESLIE TAYLOR** ltaylor@waterwayguide.com
Accounts Manager	**ARTHUR CROWTHER** accounts@waterwayguide.com
Administrative Assistant	**MARGIE MOORE**
Shipping & Receiving	**KEVIN GRAVES**

Cover: An aerial view of Government Cut, Miami.
WATERWAY GUIDE PHOTOGRAPHY
Cape Florida Lighthouse on Key Biscayne.
Photo Credit: Laura Rivas.
Day out on the water.
Photo Credit: Susan Landry.

EDITORIAL OFFICES
York Associates, LLC
326 First Street, Suite 400
Annapolis, MD 21403
Send Correspondence to: P.O. Box 4219
Annapolis, MD 21403, 443-482-9377

BOOK SALES:
www.WaterwayGuide.com
800-233-3359

CORPORATE & ACCOUNTING OFFICES
Waterway Guide/Skipper Bob Publications
Dozier Media Group
P.O. Box 1125, Deltaville, VA 23043

CONTRIBUTORS

- Chris Caldwell • Jay Corzine
- Kay Gibson • Mark Gonsalves
- Pepper Holmes • Gil Johnson
- Carl Jordan • Rick Kennedy
- Robert Linder • Diane & Michael Marotta
- Peter Mitchell • Alan Pereya
- Kip & Larry Putt • Jim Quince
- Jody Reynolds

ADVERTISING SALES
GENERAL ADVERTISING
INQUIRIES
CRAIG DOZIER
cdozier@waterwayguide.com

CRUISING EDITORS

CHESAPEAKE BAY EDITION
JACK & CRAIG DOZIER

ATLANTIC ICW EDITION
BUD & ELAINE LLOYD
JACK & CRAIG DOZIER

NORTHERN EDITION
LARRY & RUTH SMITHERS
BUD & ELAINE LLOYD

BAHAMAS EDITION
JANICE BAUER CALLUM
ROBERT WILSON

SOUTHERN EDITION
GEORGE DANNER
BUD & ELAINE LLOYD

GREAT LAKE EDITION
BOB KUNATH
WALLY MORAN
TED & AUDREY STEHLE

 Member of National Marine Manufacturers Association – Printed In Canada

Navigating Your Guid

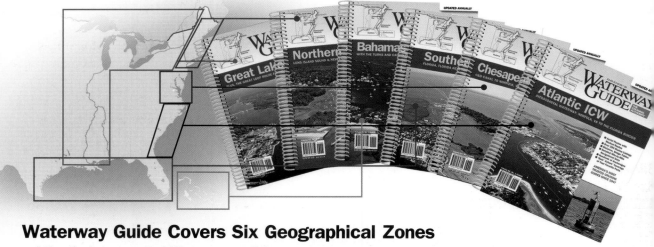

Waterway Guide Covers Six Geographical Zones

- **Atlantic Intracoastal Waterway edition:** Intracoastal Waterway to Florida
- **Chesapeake Bay edition:** Delaware Bay and Chesapeake Bay through Norfolk, VA
- **Southern edition:** Florida and the Gulf Coast to the Mexican border
- **Bahamas edition:** The Bahamas Islands and the Turks and Caicos Islands
- **Great Lakes edition:** Great Loop Cruise and the Great Lakes
- **Northern edition:** New Jersey through Maine

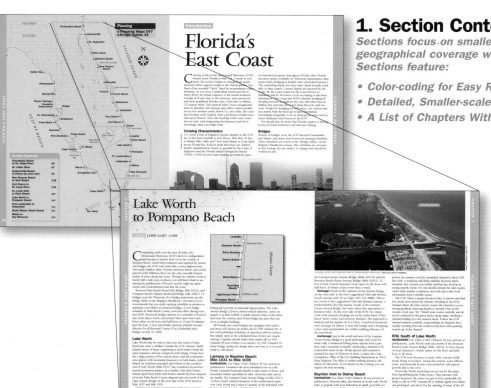

1. Section Contents

Sections focus on smaller areas of geographical coverage within the regions. Sections feature:

- *Color-coding for Easy Reference*
- *Detailed, Smaller-scale Maps*
- *A List of Chapters Within Each Section*

2. Chapters

Chapters focus on even smaller coverage areas within the sections. Chapter information include

- *Aerial Photos With Marked Routes*
- *Navigational Reports*
- *Dockage and Anchorage Information*
- *Goin' Ashore Features on Towns Along the Way*

Marina Listings and Locator Charts

Southern Guide covers hundreds of marinas with the following information:

- *Clearly Labeled Charts*
- *Marina Locator Arrows*
- *Marina Amenities*
- *Phone Numbers*
- *Internet and Wireless Internet Capabilities*
- *Fuel, Services and Supplies*
- *GPS Coordinates and Bold Type for Advertising Sponsors*

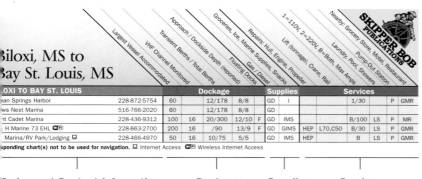

Biloxi, MS to Bay St. Louis, MS		Dockage				Supplies			Services				
BILOXI TO BAY ST. LOUIS													
Ocean Springs Harbor	228-872-5754	60		12/178	8/8	GD	I			1/30		P	GMR
Crows Nest Marina	516-766-2020	60		12/178	8/8	GD						P	GMR
Point Cadet Marina	228-436-9312	100	16	20/300	12/10	F	GD	IMS			B/100	LS	P	MR
H Marine 73 EHL WiFi	228-863-2700	200	16	/90	13/9	F	GD	GIMS	HEP	L70,C50	B/30	LS	P	GMR
Marina/RV Park/Lodging	228-466-4970	50	16	10/75	5/5		GD	IMS	HEP		B	LS	P	GMR

Corresponding chart(s) not to be used for navigation. Internet Access WiFi Wireless Internet Access

Marina and Contact Information *(advertising partners are bolded)* — **Dockage** — **Supplies** — **Services**

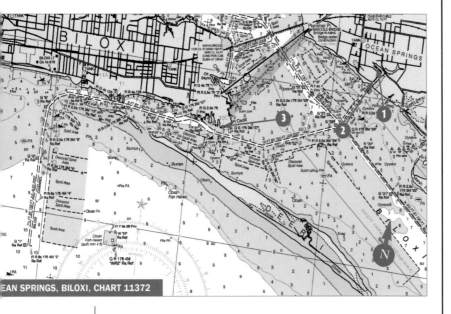

OCEAN SPRINGS, BILOXI, CHART 11372

Clearly labeled marina locator charts help tie it all together.

Skipper's Handbook

A whole section on useful boating references.

Bridges and Distances

Tables give you bridge opening times and mileage between points.

Goin' Ashore

Quick-read features on ports and towns you'll visit along the way.

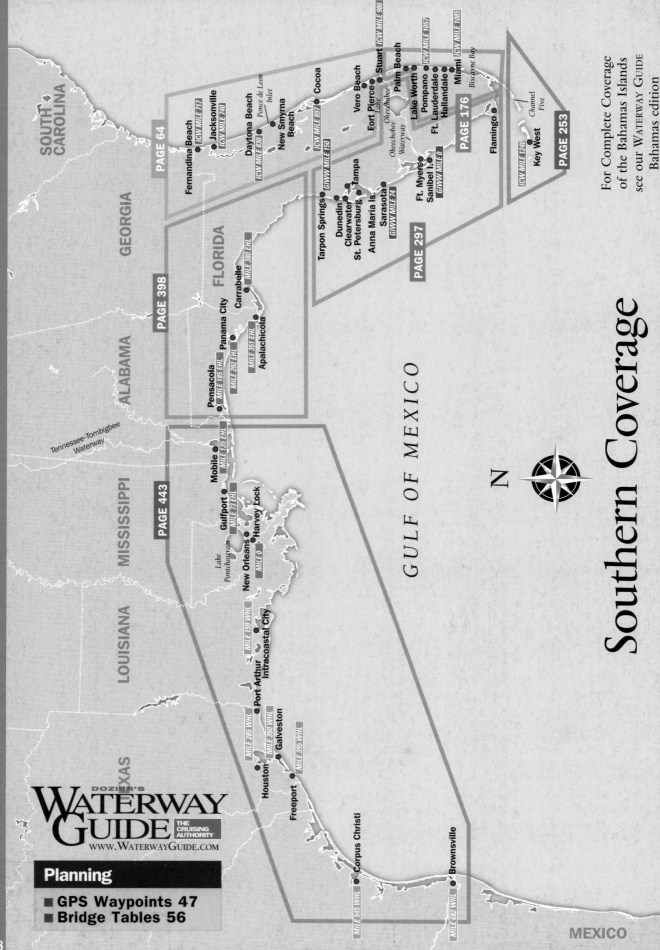

CONTENTS

Southern Coverage

SOUTH CAROLINA

GEORGIA

ALABAMA

MISSISSIPPI

LOUISIANA

TEXAS

FLORIDA

MEXICO

N

GULF OF MEXICO

Tennessee-Tombigbee Waterway

Lake Pontchartrain

PAGE 64

PAGE 398

PAGE 443

PAGE 297

PAGE 176

PAGE 253

Fernandina Beach — *ICW MILE 717*
Jacksonville — *ICW MILE 740*
Daytona Beach — *ICW MILE 830*
Ponce de Leon Inlet
New Smyrna Beach
Cocoa — *ICW MILE 897*
Vero Beach
Fort Pierce — *ICW MILE 966*
Stuart
Palm Beach — *ICW MILE 1015*
Lake Worth — *ICW MILE 1057*
Pompano
Ft. Lauderdale
Hallandale — *ICW MILE 1085*
Miami — *ICW MILE 1095*
Biscayne Bay
Flamingo
Channel Five
Key West — *ICW MILE 1240*

Tarpon Springs — *GIWW MILE 150*
Dunedin
Clearwater
Tampa
St. Petersburg
Anna Maria Is.
Sarasota — *GIWW MILE 74*
Ft. Myers — *GIWW MILE 0*
Sanibel I.

Lake Okeechobee
Okeechobee Waterway

Carrabelle — *MILE 380 EHL*
Panama City — *MILE 292 EHL*
Apalachicola — *MILE 351 EHL*
Pensacola — *MILE 185 EHL*
Mobile — *MILE 135 EHL*
Gulfport — *MILE 73 EHL*
Harvey Lock — *MILE 0*
New Orleans — *MILE 159 WHL*
Port Arthur
Intracoastal City — *MILE 285 WHL*
Houston
Galveston — *MILE 350 WHL*
Freeport — *MILE 395 WHL*
Corpus Christi — *MILE 545 WHL*
Brownsville — *MILE 682 WHL*

For Complete Coverage of the Bahamas Islands see our WATERWAY GUIDE Bahamas edition

DOZIER'S
WATERWAY GUIDE
THE CRUISING AUTHORITY
WWW.WATERWAYGUIDE.COM

Planning
- GPS Waypoints 47
- Bridge Tables 56

8

Contents

VOLUME 64, NO. 3

DOZIER'S
WATERWAY GUIDE®
THE CRUISING AUTHORITY

A DOZIER MEDIA GROUP PUBLICATION

Florida's Upper East Coast

Cruising south on the Intracoastal Waterway (ICW), mariners enter Florida at Mile 714. A study in contrasts, the scenery begins its change from nearly deserted, white-capped sounds to the claustrophobic confines of the crowded "ditch" lined by mountainous condominiums. As you cross Cumberland Sound and the St. Marys River, the broad expanses of the marsh-bordered Georgia ICW give way to the narrower, more protected and more populated Florida route.

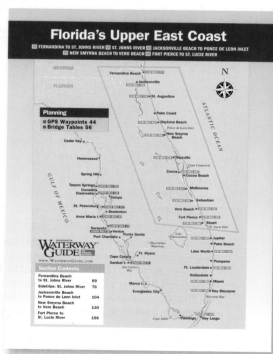

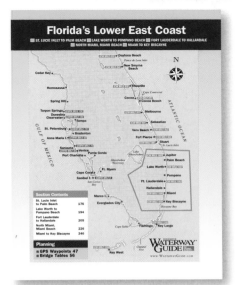

The Florida Keys

Extending in a sweeping southwesterly curve from Miami and the mainland, the Florida Keys offer the cruising boater an environment unlike other Waterway areas. In many ways, the Keys resemble the islands of the Bahamas. However, a main highway and a total of 18.94 miles of bridges tie them together.

Florida's Lower East Coast

Once you pass Vero Beach, you are positioned midway between the upper and lower reaches of the Indian River. As the river widens, the dredged channel begins to straighten out for the 13 miles south to Fort Pierce. The project depth along this stretch is 12 feet, but the controlling depth is 8 feet or less.

The Florida Keys

Extending in a sweeping southwesterly curve from Miami and the mainland, the Florida Keys offer the cruising boater an environment unlike other Waterway areas. In many ways, the Keys resemble the islands of the Bahamas. However, a main highway and a total of 18.94 miles of bridges tie them together.

Contents

Florida's West Coast

Zoologically and geographically, Florida's lower west coast differs substantially from the east. The cruising, too, is entirely different. The sophistication, glamour and luxury so prevalent on the east coast comes in more measured doses here. The pace is slower, the atmosphere more relaxed and the amenities somewhat more limited and spaced farther apart, but the cruising is superb.

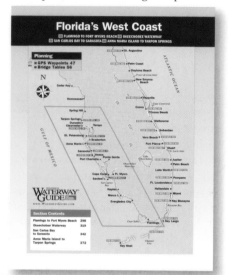

Florida's Upper Gulf Coast

Florida's Panhandle, stretching from Carrabelle or Apalachicola on the eastern end to Pensacola and Perdido Bay on the west, is sometimes called the Forgotten Coast. It can be reached in one of three ways: From the east, either directly across 130 to 170 miles of the Gulf of Mexico or skirting the Big Bend area just offshore; or from the west from Mobile Bay, from which many Midwestern cruisers come, down the river route.

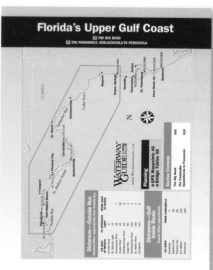

Gulf Coast

The area west from Florida along the Gulf Coast historically has been described as the playground of the South. The region is known for its miles of pure white beaches, scenic landscapes and historic towns. This trip can challenge your boating skills. Expect to encounter a variety of conditions, ranging from open water on Mobile Bay and Mississippi Sound to narrow, sometimes cramped, canals and waterways. Lagoons and bayous often alternate with long and sometimes tedious land cuts.

CONTENTS

Blue Sky and Calm Seas Ahead

In a very real way, our Guides are a barometer of future boating activity. As a planning tool, they are purchased well in advance of departing on a cruise, so we read the increases in our sales and increases in visits to our Web site during 2010 as favorable leading indicators of increased boater activity in the future. As further proof of this forecast, our advertising sponsors - the people who help support our research and production staff in our mission to provide you with the most accurate and timely navigation and cruising information - sense this improvement and have reacted with increased spending to attract our readers and rebuild their marine businesses. These are the same marinas and businesses, run by people like you and I, that we all rely on to support our boating lifestyle.

All of us who venture out on the water know we will experience a storm eventually. We prepare for it, endure it and then feel a sense of relief when the wind begins to calm, and we see clear sky ahead. The "perfect storm" – economic, political and weather - we have been going through recently was especially severe and caught most people by surprise. But now, our mood at WATERWAY GUIDE is upbeat as the indicators tell us that this latest storm is subsiding, and the sky ahead is clearing.

Economic forecasters, like weather forecasters, have unique job security – they get paid whether their forecast is right or wrong. The recession has altered retirement accounts and, for many cruisers, that has meant a change in cruising plans, even boat ownership itself. From an economic perspective, the political climate has not helped those who worked and saved to have the means to join the boating/cruising lifestyle. Business owners, managers and professionals who, as a group, make up a large percentage of boaters have been reluctant to invest further due to new certainties and uncertainties. But there is sunshine on the horizon, and as it returns, confidence and spirits are being boosted leading to a return to a healthy and active boating environment.

And the weather - well perhaps Al Gore is right (although Tipper apparently doesn't think so). And I'm not convinced either. Following a winter of extreme cold and windy weather,

Pictured (from left): John Dozier, Ned Dozier, Associate Publisher Craig Dozier and Publisher Jack Dozier, with Scooter and Molly.

we now have a summer of extreme heat. Unusual yes, but certainly not unprecedented. Learning from the past, even long before there were records, we know there have been both long term and short term cyclical swings in the weather which caused both temperature and water level to either rise or fall far above or below today's "normal" levels. Are we the cause of the current cycle? Perhaps partly, but who or what caused past climate cycles before there were politicized government grants to study and make a determination on such events? One of the advantages of being older is witnessing the recent past. I clearly remember government funded scientific studies declaring in the 1960s that human activities were causing a gradual clouding and cooling of the earth that would lead us to the next great Ice Age. This garnered lots of attention and grant revenue at the time.

The good news – and there is always good news - is that the things we have control over are short term swings, or relatively so. The economy will recover through the hard work and resourcefulness of the American business community and individuals. Politics and its effect on our lives will swing back to the center. The weather, as always, will be mostly fair with a little foul thrown in.

Boaters are an optimistic group. That is both fortunate and necessary. Optimism helped us achieve our dreams, and it is what has gotten us through this latest storm. We know we can either solve the problems or, on our own, work our way through them. Keep your course to the clear sky ahead, and enjoy your time on your boat.

See you on the water!

Jack Dozier,
Publisher

Waterway Guide Lady docked at Staniel Cay Yacht Club in the Exumas.

Cruising Editors

Janice Bauer Callum

Janice Bauer Callum

Janice Bauer Callum and her husband, George, have been sailing together for 45 years. George has a much longer sailing history. In his youth, he sailed the eastern seaboard with his family onboard their 8-meter *Gracious,* and crewed for numerous Chicago to Mackinac races, as well as taught sailing for the Michigan City Yacht Club. Over the years, Janice and George have cruised and raced the Great Lakes, the East Coast, the Caribbean and the Bahamas. When they weren't cruising or racing their sloop *Morning Glory* with their three children, Treavor, Heather and Dayne, they were racing windsurfers. Janice was a District Chairperson for the International Windsurfing Class Association for whom she organized races for thousands of sailors and qualified them for the first Olympic sail boarding competition in Los Angeles.

Since their retirement in 2000, Janice and George have been docked on the beaches of Mexico and sailed their Hallberg-Rassy Rasmus, *Calamus,* from the Tennessee-Tombigbee Waterway up and down the eastern seaboard and the ICW to the Bahamas, where they sail several months every year. For the short time that they are not onboard Calamus, they are at their small ranch on Lake Calamus in Burwell, Nebraska—home of the oldest (and only) Windsurfing Rodeo.

George E. Danner

George Danner

An avid boater whose home port is Galveston Bay, TX, George Danner is WATERWAY GUIDE's cruising editor for the ICW from Mississippi to Brownsville, TX. He began serious cruising several years ago by trailering his 26-foot Monterey express cruiser to Chesapeake Bay, Key West, Destin, FL and the Carolina coast from Charleston to Hilton Head Island. Now with a 2006 Silverton 34C, *La Mariposa,* recently added to the fleet, George focuses on Gulf excursions from Galveston to Mississippi and southern trips to Corpus Christi and South Padre Island. The western Gulf region is home to some of the finest cruising grounds in the country, and the Danner family frequently explores its coastal waters for new land and sea-based adventures. Out of the water, George is president of a corporate strategy consulting firm in Houston.

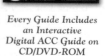

CRUISING EDITORS

Bob and Carol Kunath

Bob and Carol Kunath have owned about a dozen sail and power-boats over the past 40 years. They've ranged from small lake open boats to those equipped for offshore shark and tuna fishing, and sail and powerboats on Lake Michigan where they have been cruising for the past fifteen years. During those years they have cruised extensively throughout Lake Michigan and the North Channel of Lake Huron. Both are Past Commodores of the Bay Shore Yacht Club in Illinois, and members of the Waukegan, IL Sail and Power Squadron, where Bob has served as an officer and instructor, and the Racine Yacht Club. He has also contributed to *Latitudes and Attitudes*, the USPS national magazine *Ensign*, and holds a USCG Master's license. During 2005 Bob and Carol completed a two-year cruise of the Great Loop in their Pacific Seacraft 38T trawler, *Sans Souci*, logging 9,000 miles on the Loop and many side trips. Recently they have resumed cruising all of Lake Michigan, but have plans to expand that area, perhaps back into the rivers of the Midwest or canals of Canada. Bob has also been a seminar presenter at West Marine Trawlerfest, U. S. Power Squadron and AGLCA events, sharing their knowledge of Lake Michigan and cruising. For the past five years Bob and Carol have, as Cruising Editors for *Waterway Guide*, covered Eastern and Western Lake Michigan including Green Bay and Door County for that publication. Bob and Carol also recently updated and revised *Skipper Bob's Lake Michigan, 2010 edition.*

Bob and Carol Kunath

Bud and Elaine Lloyd

Bud and Elaine Lloyd, are the cruising editors for South Florida, the Keys and Okeechobee Waterway. After being long-time sailors (they had several sailboats over the years), the Lloyds decided that in order to do the type of cruising they dreamed of they needed a trawler. Diamond Girl is a 36-foot 1990 Nova/ Heritage East Sundeck. From their home port of Long Beach, California, they cruised all over Southern California and parts of Mexico extensively for over 30 years. After retiring from the printing business in 2005, they decided that it was time to get serious about fulfilling a life-long dream of cruising the Chesapeake Bay and ICW. So in December 2005, they put Diamond Girl on a ship and sent her to Ft. Lauderdale, Florida. They have now been cruising on the East Coast for almost 5

Bud and Elaine Lloyd

years and have found the experience even more rewarding than they ever imagined. They have made several trips up and down the ICW, have spent the summers cruising on the Chesapeake Bay, and have made numerous crossings of the Okeechobee Waterway. Bud and Elaine are full-time liveaboard cruisers and can't wait to see what awaits them over the next horizon. Now the WATERWAY GUIDE has given them the opportunity to write about what they enjoy most…cruising!

Wally Moran

Wally Moran, WATERWAY GUIDE's cruising editor for Georgian Bay, the North Channel, the St. Marys River and Lake Huron, is a former newspaper publisher who has sailed these favored cruising grounds since honeymooning there in 1978. His more recent travels have taken him from Chesapeake Bay to Tampa Bay, then back to Canada via Lake Huron and Lake Erie, the Erie Barge Canal, the Hudson River, Chesapeake Bay, the Intracoastal Waterway and offshore. Wally's next planned cruise will see his completion of the Great Loop into the Gulf of Mexico and on into the Caribbean, before returning to Canada. Wally sails his Dufour 34 *Gypsy Wind* throughout the Georgian Bay area, which he assures WATERWAY GUIDE readers is the "best freshwater boating in the world" and encourages all boaters to visit.

Wally Moran

Larry and Ruth Smithers

Larry and Ruth Smithers are cruising editors for WATERWAY GUIDE's Northern edition from Cape Cod through Maine. They have boated in various capacities since the early 1970s. Serious passionate boating gripped them with the acquisition of *Back Dock,* their 56-foot Vantare pilothouse motoryacht. They quickly discovered that work got in the way of boating. Bidding their land life adieu they sold their practice, leased out their home in Wisconsin, packed up and moved aboard to cruise full time in pursuit of high adventure and sunsets worthy of the nightly celebratory conch horn serenade. The Smithers have completed the Great Loop, cruised the Bahamas and, as always, look forward to continue exploring new territories.

Larry and Ruth Smithers

Larry spent the first half of his working career in the international corporate world and the last as a chiropractor. He is now retired, a U.S. Coast Guard-licensed captain and can proudly recite the pirate alphabet. Ruth's career was in public accounting. She retired to become a stay-at-home mother, which ultimately evolved into being a professional volunteer and dilettante. She enjoys basket making and her role as "Admiral."

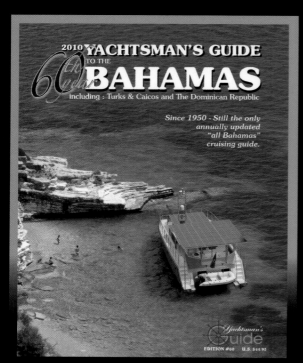

Audrey and Ted Stehle

Audrey and Ted Stehle

Audrey and Ted Stehle are WATERWAY GUIDE's cruising editors for the inland rivers and the Tenn-Tom Waterway, from Chicago to Mobile Bay, for the Great Lakes 2011 Guide.

They began boating as sailors in the early 1970s on the Chesapeake Bay, and then switched to power after retirement. In addition to extensive cruising of Chesapeake Bay and its tributaries, they have traveled the ICW to Florida many times, completed the Great Loop, cruised the Ohio, Tennessee and Cumberland rivers and made six trips on the Tenn-Tom Waterway. Their Californian 45 is presently on Chesapeake Bay, but plans call for returning it to Kentucky Lake to resume cruising the Cumberland and Tennessee rivers. When not cruising, the Stehles reside in Cincinnati, OH to be near their children and grandchildren, and engage in volunteer work.

Robert Wilson

Robert Wilson

Robert Wilson has been cruising in the Bahamas from his homeport in Brunswick, GA for the past nine years. He and his wife, Carolyn, began sailing on Lake Lanier, just north of Atlanta, GA, shortly after they met 25 years ago. Robert is a former employee benefits consultant, and is a Past Commodore of the Royal Marsh Harbour Yacht Club in Abaco. Together, they have written extensively about their sailing adventures throughout the Bahamas on their 38-foot Island Packet, *Gypsy Common*. Their current boat, *Sea Island Girl*, is a North Pacific 42 pilothouse trawler, which they cruised in the Pacific Northwest along the coast of British Columbia, before shipping the boat to Florida to continue cruising throughout the Bahamas aboard their new trawler.

When not cruising, the Wilsons reside in Atlanta, GA, where Carolyn teaches pre-school, and Robert continues consulting and writing. Robert is WATERWAY GUIDE's cruising editor for the northern Bahamas. ∎

Things To Know Before You Go

There are many reasons we go cruising, but they can all be summed up in one word: adventure. The thought of casting off those dock lines with a fully provisioned boat and a reasonably blank calendar is intoxicating indeed. Exploring waters like the Florida Keys and the Intracoastal Waterway (ICW) can take a lifetime. Luckily, we have that.

For ICW boaters, the ultimate experience is the long-range cruise—the one that continues through several seasons, allowing you to follow the fair weather, from north to south and back again. (Boaters lucky enough to enjoy this lifestyle are often referred to as "snowbirds.") About two weeks into "sweater weather" on the Chesapeake Bay—much like migratory waterfowl—these cruisers are preparing to head for the warmer climes of North Carolina and ports farther south.

Wise skippers schedule their 1,090-mile voyage between Norfolk and Miami so that they neither catch up with the mosquitoes nor get caught by snow. A workable schedule involves dropping Maine astern by the first of September and reaching the Chesapeake by the end of the month, just in time to enjoy the fall foliage. By the time October arrives, the Annapolis boat shows get into full swing. After that, it is a good idea to leave Norfolk—and what can be wet, nasty weather—behind you.

Once you have arrived in the Carolinas, the boat will be safe from ice for a time, should you need to leave it moored or docked, while you regroup or return home for a visit. Serious snowbirds, however, will be well into Georgia or Florida long before it is time to prepare their Thanksgiving dinners.

The Time Factor

A trip down the Intracoastal Waterway between Fernandina and Miami can take a week, a month or as long as you choose. It all depends on how fast you go, which route you choose and how long you decide to linger along the way.

If you plan to keep moving under power almost every day—stopping each evening to enjoy the amenities of a marina or anchorage—the following running times are fairly typical. In about 10 days (barring weather or mechanical delays), you can run from the Georgia/Florida border to Miami. Most ICW cruisers take longer, stopping along the way to explore coastal towns and take in the sights, however. You can also run along the coast and make the trip in three to four days.

Visit Florida

It is smart to allow time along the way for sightseeing, resting, waiting out bad weather or making repairs to the boat. Of course, the boat's features and the skipper's temperament will determine whether the pace is fast or slow. Sailboats averaging 5 to 8 knots can cover the same number of miles on a given day as a powerboat that cruises at 20 to 25 knots. The only difference is that the sailboat's crew will have a much longer day underway.

Those who are eager to reach southern waters can cruise the length of the Florida coast in a week or two, while others who want to poke around in the Waterway's scores of harbors and gunkholes can spend a month without seeing everything.

First-Aid Basics

A deep cut from a filet knife is normally not a big deal at home where medical help is close at hand, but on the Waterway (where you may be a long way from help), you will need to be able to patch yourself up until you can get to an emergency clinic or hospital emergency room. Adequate first-aid kits are essential, along with a medical manual that you can understand quickly; the standard reference is "Advanced First-Aid Afloat" by Dr. Peter F. Eastman. Good first-aid kits can be found at most marine supply stores and better pharmacies or drug stores.

Cruisers who take medication should make sure their current prescription has plenty of refills available so supplies can be topped off along the way. Additionally, make sure crew members are aware of any medication you are on in case you become injured and unable to answer questions regarding your health.

All safety equipment—harnesses, life preservers, jack lines, medical kit, etc.—should be in good working condition, within easy reach and ready at a moment's notice. All aboard—crew and guests—should know where to find the emergency equipment. In addition to having the proper first-aid gear aboard, all aboard should be versed in basic "first responder" procedures including CPR and making a May-Day call on the VHF radio.

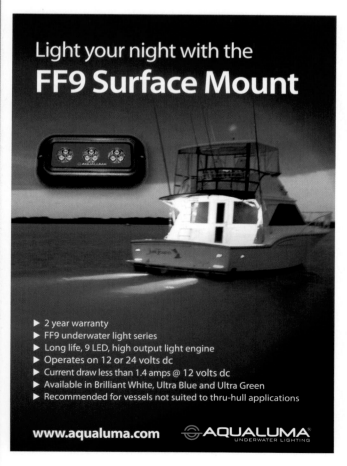
Check out our Goin' Ashore sections of this guide; they are equipped with contact information for local hospitals and emergency clinics. Most importantly, if someone's life is in imminent danger, make a May-Day call on VHF Channel 16. This is the best way to get quick help. Making a 911 call on your cell phone is also an option, but not one you should count on because of variable coverage by cellular providers.

A Note on Clean Marinas

The next time you pull into your favorite ICW facility, you might want to look around for some indication of it being a designated Clean Marina. Many states around the country— including those covered in this edition of WATERWAY GUIDE— have launched programs in recent years aimed at making marina owners and boaters more aware of how their activities affect the environment. In order for one's marina to be designated a "Clean Marina," the facility's owner has to take a series of steps prescribed by that state's respective program, anything from making sure tarps are laid down when boat bottoms are worked on, to providing pump-out facilities. (The steps were derived from an Environmental Protection Agency document presented to states across America.)

The underlying principle behind these voluntary, incentive-based programs is this: If the waters we cruise are not clean, then we will cruise elsewhere and the marine businesses in the polluted areas will suffer. The programs represent a nice coupling of economics and environmental management that is catching on with marina owners and boaters alike. So if you see the Clean Marina designation at your favorite facility, rest assured they are doing the right thing for the environment; if not, ask why.

■ THINGS YOU WILL NEED

To minimize time spent waiting for spare parts—which can be considerable in some areas WATERWAY GUIDE recommends that cruising mariners take along certain equipment.

Spare Parts

For the engine, bring spare seals for the raw-water pump and an extra water-pump impeller, along with V-belts, points and plugs for gas engines (injectors for diesel engines), a fuel pump and strainer, a distributor cap, fuses, lube oil and filter cartridges. Also, carry a list of service centers for your type of equipment, and bring the engine manual and the parts list.

Other things to bring: spare deck cap keys, a head-repair kit, fresh water pump repair kit, spare hose clamps, lengths of hose and an extra container of fuel. (Keep in mind that, if you want to anchor out, fueling up during the day when there are no crowds at the fuel docks is a good idea.)

Carry a good tool kit with varying sizes of flat- and Phillips-head screwdrivers, socket wrenches (metric and standard), pliers, etc. Remember that all the spare parts in the world are fairly useless without a proper bag of tools aboard to install them with.

For Docking and Anchoring

Your docking equipment should include a minimum of four bow and stern lines made of good, stretchy nylon (each about two-thirds the length of your boat—longer if you would like an extra measure of convenience) and two spring lines (1.5 times the length of your boat) with oversized eyes to fit over pilings. If you have extra dock lines, consider bringing them along with your shore power cord and a shore power adapter or two.

For anchoring, the average 30-foot boat needs 150 to 200 feet of 7/16- to 1/2-inch nylon line with no less than 15 feet of 5/16-inch chain shackled to a 20- to 30-pound plow-type or Bruce anchor – or a 15-pound Danforth-type anchor. Storm anchors and a lunch hook are also recommended. Larger yachts should use 7/8-inch nylon and heavier chain. While one anchor will get you along, most veteran cruisers carry both a plow and fluke-type anchor to use in varying bottom conditions. Ground tackle is always the subject of debate and every skipper has their own ideas of how much chain versus rode and the type of anchor.

Consult a good reference like Chapman's Piloting or West Marine's "West Advisor" articles (available online) if you are unsure about proper anchoring techniques, and make sure that you master them before setting off down the Waterway.

Tenders and Dinghies

A dinghy is needed if you plan to anchor out, gunkhole or carry an anchor to deeper water when kedging off a shoal. Inflatable dinghies are popular, but they require an outboard motor to get them around easily. On the other hand, rowing a hard dinghy is excellent exercise. Check registration laws where you plan to spend any length of time, as certain states, including Florida and Maryland, have become very strict in enforcing dinghy registration.

Always chain and lock your dinghy when you leave it unattended – even if it is tied off to your boat, as more than one Waterway cruiser has woken to a missing dinghy while at anchor on the Waterway. Outboard engines should always be padlocked to the transom of your dinghy or on a stern rail, as they are often targets of thieves.

Keeping Comfortable

Another consideration when equipping your boat for a cruise is temperature control inside the cabin. Many powerboats—particularly trawlers—are equipped with an air conditioner for those hot, steamy nights. Others can get away with fans and wind socks. When considering heating options for your boat, select something that is not going to suck your batteries dead—and, even more important, something that is safe. Many reliable and safe marine propane heaters are available nowadays for those cruising late into the fall season. If you plan to spend a lot of time in northern waters, a built-in diesel heater may fit the bill.

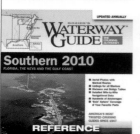

Since the weather can turn chilly, or even downright cold, in the Carolinas during autumn, and Georgia or northern Florida any time in winter, most experienced ICW cruisers have full cockpit enclosures to guard the crew from the elements.

Battling the Sun and Bugs

Cruisers in an open cockpit need the protection of a dodger, an awning, or a bimini top, not to mention sunscreen and a hat. In fact, many hard-core cruisers have an enclosure that surrounds the entire cockpit. Whatever your method, take measures to make sure you are not out in the elements unprotected all day if you can avoid it.

You will want a good quality sunscreen lotion or spray on board with you if you have any intention of enjoying the topside portion of your boat. Bug screens for hatches, ports and companionways are a must, as you will want to have the boat open for adequate cross ventilation in warm weather.

Glare off the water can be a major contributor to fatigue. Consider purchasing a quality pair of sunglasses, and make sure that they are polarized, as this feature removes annoying reflected light from your view. They also help prevent long-term damage to your eyes and vision.

Navigating Essentials

Charts for coastal piloting belong at the helm station, not in the cabin, so a clipboard or spray-proof plastic case comes in handy. Many ICW veterans like to use the spiral bound chart "kits" that feature small-scale charts laid out in order according to the Waterway route. Since the local conditions change constantly, use only the latest charts, and keep them updated with the U.S. Coast Guard's Local Notices to Mariners, which are available online at www. navcen.uscg.gov/lnm. For planning, many charts and nautical publications (Coast Pilots, light lists, tide tables) can be downloaded free of charge via the Internet. See the Skipper's Handbook section for more detail on how to access this valuable information with your computer.

Many cruisers are now equipping themselves with the latest GPS chart plotters and computer-driven electronic gizmos, and while convenient, they are not a requirement for cruising the ICW. Radar is a wonderful aid, not only to "see" markers and other vessels, but also to track local storms; perhaps half of all ICW boats have it. Single-Sideband (SSB) and amateur (ham) radio are excellent for long-range communications, but you can get by without either one on the Waterway. You will not want to cruise the Waterway without a depth sounder; this item is almost essential.

You should learn how to operate all of your navigation electronics inside and out before you rely on them for navigation. A dense fogbank is no place to figure out how your navigation equipment works. As always, you should have paper charts available as backup in case your electronic unit malfunctions.

A VHF marine radio is the cruiser's lifeline to the Coast Guard, marinas and other boats and is also necessary for contacting ICW bridges. Mount yours at the helm or keep a handheld unit there. Many manufacturers now offer a RAM (remote access microphone) option, which allows the skipper to use the hand unit and control the radio from the helm.

Most cruisers carry mobile (cellular) telephones, but you cannot count on coverage everywhere, as these systems are optimized for land users. See the "VHF Radio" section of the Skipper's Handbook (located at the front of the book) for more detail on VHF radio operation and regulations.

Have a compass adjuster swing (calibrate) your steering compass before departure so you can run courses with confidence. Also carry a good hand-bearing compass or binoculars with a built-in compass for getting bearings to fixed marks or points ashore.

Considerations for Sailboaters

Sailors sometimes worry about travel on the ICW, but unless your mast is higher than 65 feet, or the keel draws more than 7 feet, the trip is entirely possible, and likely easy. Boats that have less than a 6-foot draft usually have few problems, while 5 feet or less is optimum. Truth of the matter is that more sailboats than powerboats are usually seen transiting the ICW.

The Julia Tuttle Bridge in Miami has a 56-foot fixed vertical clearance, many Gulf Coast bridges have 50-foot vertical clearances, and one bridge across Florida's Okeechobee Waterway is just 49 feet (although a local marina will heel over taller boats, using 55-gallon drums of water as ballast, to slip underneath it). While overhead power lines are generally quite high, be sure to allow several feet of extra clearance to prevent arcing to the mast. See our bridge tables in the Skipper's Handbook (following this section) for overhead clearances, opening schedules and mile marker locations.

Sailors obviously cannot pace motorboats on plane, but they do have the option of using occasional fair winds to enjoy the quieter ride and save some fuel, often simply by unrolling the jib. Rules forbid sailing through a drawbridge unless a sailboat is without power; notify the bridge tender if this is the case. There may be some good-natured ribbing when a sailboat pulls up to the fuel dock and tops off with five gallons instead of 500.

The Money Issue

Everyone is concerned about money, but when you are a long-range cruiser, the issue becomes a bit more complicated. Luckily, cruisers today can get by with much less cash than in the past. Almost all banks have ATMs. Many grocery stores and drugstores (and even fast food restaurants) accept ATM and Visa or MasterCard check cards. Remember that most banks will honor the cash advance feature of Visa cards and the MasterCard. In addition, American Express offices will accept a cardholder's personal check in payment for Travelers Checks and will also dispense cash to cardholders.

Most marinas, especially the large ones, accept major credit cards and oil company credit cards for dockage, fuel and marine supplies. Most restaurants, motels and grocery stores will also accept major credit cards. Credit card statements also serve as excellent records of expenses while traveling.

A majority of banks now offer online banking services that allow you to pay your bills remotely via the Internet. With online banking, you can pay bills, set up new payees, transfer funds, check your balances – and much more. You can also set up recurring payments on an "auto-pay" system that pays your bills automatically every month, or when your payee sends your bank an "e-bill."

Do be careful where you conduct your online banking sessions from, however. Many public marina computers "remember" passwords and forms (handy for a thief looking to steal your identity or your money), and many marina Internet WiFi (wireless) connections are not totally secure. Best to use your own computer that is hooked up to a terrestrial network with your own secure firewall running.

Getting Your Mail

Your incoming mail can be sent to General Delivery in towns where you plan to put in and stay awhile. Many ICW veterans have friends or family at home check their mail and occasionally forward it to them in the next town they plan to pull into. Tell the sender to write "Hold for Arrival" on the envelope, along with your name and your boat's name. Notify the post office that you want your mail held. They will hold first-class mail or forward it to another post office on receipt of a change-of-address card.

The United States Postal Service is now offering a service called Premium Forwarding that is designed to work in tandem with their Priority Mail program. There are also many companies that specialize in forwarding mail and paying bills for Waterway cruisers. Simply enter "mail forwarding, bill services" into your favorite Internet search engine, and many choices should show up for you.

Check the Skipper's Handbook section following this one for mail-drop locations along the ICW, as well a complement of specific details on getting your mail and paying bills.

Waterway Guide Web Updates

WATERWAY GUIDE has recently upgraded its Web site (www.WaterwayGuide.com) to provide boaters with the most up-to-date cruising information available, including fuel prices. These Web site upgrades strongly focus on reader interaction. WATERWAY GUIDE offers cruisers three portals to help plan their trips or report back on what they have just experienced: "Navigation Updates" offers the most up-to-date information available on such items as Waterway conditions, changing bridge schedules and hazards to navigation; "Waterway News" reports events, marina updates and general ICW information; and "Cruiser Comments" lets boaters post their own observations and experiences from the Waterway. Best of all, these three portals are broken into easy-to-follow regions, so navigating WATERWAY GUIDE's Web site is even easier than navigating the Waterway. ∎

Skipper's Handbook

A Guide to Cruising Essentials

Coast Guard

The Coast Guard stands watch at all times to aid vessels of all sizes and the persons on board. The Coast Guard activities listed below cover the areas included in this edition of WATERWAY GUIDE The intermediate command level between districts and stations is now called a "Sector" (formerly a "Group"). In some areas, you can quickly reach the Coast Guard by dialing *CG on a cellular phone. If you have a question of a non-emergency nature, the Coast Guard prefers that you telephone the nearest station. As always, if there is an emergency, initiate a May Day call on VHF Channel 16. The following Coast Guard district offices cover the areas in this book:

SEVENTH COAST GUARD DISTRICT, Brickell Plaza Federal Building, 909 S.E. First Ave., Miami, FL 33131. 305-415-6860. *www.uscg.mil/d7*

■ Florida East Coast

SECTOR JACKSONVILLE:

Station Mayport: South side of St. Johns River, at the south end of the Mayport waterfront. 904-564-7613.

Station Ponce de Leon Inlet: At the south side of the entrance to the inlet. 386-428-9085.

Station Port Canaveral: In the northeast corner of west basin, 1,000 yards from mid-channel. 321-868-4200.

SECTOR MIAMI:

Station Fort Pierce: South side of inlet, 1.2 miles west of the outer end of the south jetty. 772-464-6100.

Station Lake Worth Inlet: On the mainland a half-mile north of the Riviera Beach/Singer Island Bridge. 561-844-4470.

Station Fort Lauderdale: East side of ICW at Mile 1066.8, in Port Everglades. 954-927-1611.

Station Miami Beach: On the north side of Miami Harbor Channel, 1.2 miles northwest from outer end of the north jetty. 305-535-4368.

■ Florida Keys

SECTOR KEY WEST:

Station Islamorada: Located at the southwest end of Plantation Key at Mile Marker 86, at Venetian Shores. 305-664-4404.

Station Marathon: On the north side of Vaca Key, 1.1 miles east of Knight Key Channel. 305-743-6388.

Station Key West: At Pier D2, Trumbo Point Naval Annex. 305-292-8856.

EIGHTH COAST GUARD DISTRICT, Hale Boggs Federal Building, 500 Poydras Street, New Orleans, LA 70130. 504-589-6225. *www.uscg.mil/d8*

Additional Resources   U.S. Coast Guard *www.uscg.mil*

■ Florida West Coast and Gulf Coast

SECTOR ST. PETERSBURG:

Station Fort Myers Beach: Northeast corner under the Matanzas Bridge. 239-463-5754.

Station Cortez: Near the east end of the Cortez Road Bridge. 941-794-1261.

Station St. Petersburg: West side of Tampa Bay, 1.3 miles north of Coquina Key. 727-896-2816.

Station Sand Key: Clearwater, east side St. Joseph Sound entrance. 727-596-8666.

Station Yankeetown: Approximately four miles above the mouth of Withlacoochee River. 352-447-6900.

SECTOR MOBILE:

Station Destin: On eastern side of Santa Rosa Island at the western end of the Destin Bridge. 850-244-7147.

Station Panama City: Located on the southwest side of Alligator Bayou. 850-234-4228.

Station Pensacola: Located at the Naval Air Station. 850-453-8282.

■ Alabama

SECTOR MOBILE:

Station Mobile: West end of Arlington Channel. 251-441-5960.

Station Dauphin Island: On eastern tip of the island. Open seasonally. 251-861-7241.

■ Mississippi

SECTOR MOBILE:

Station Pascagoula: East side of the Pascagoula River, about one mile above the entrance. 228-769-5601.

SECTOR NEW ORLEANS:

Station Gulfport: Northwest side of small-craft harbor. 228-865-9754.

■ Louisiana

SECTOR NEW ORLEANS:

Station New Orleans: Bucktown area, on Lake Pontchartrain. 504-846-6181.

Station Venice: West side of Tiger Pass. 985-534-2332.

Station Grand Isle: Just inside Barataria Pass, at northeast end of Grand Isle. 985-787-2136.

■ Texas

SECTOR HOUSTON-GALVESTON:

Station Sabine: West side of Sabine Pass, 5.6 miles north/northwest of Sabine Pass East Jetty Light. 409-971-2195.

Station Galveston: East side of Galveston Channel, about four miles west of Galveston Jetty Light and Houston Ship Channel. 409-766-5633.

Station Freeport: Entrance channel to Freeport at Surfside Jetty. 979-233-7551.

SECTOR CORPUS CHRISTI:

Station Port O'Connor: North bank of the ICW in Port O'Connor. 361-983-2617.

Station Port Aransas: On the northeast end of Mustang Island, located at the east end of Corpus Christi Channel. 361-749-5217.

Station Corpus Christi: At Hangar 41, Naval Air Station. 361-939-6212.

Station Port Isabel: South end of South Padre Island, at Brazos Santiago Light. 956-761-2668.

904   U.S. COAST GUARD

Port Security Procedures

Florida is cruise ship country. To a lesser extent, so are the ports around the Gulf of Mexico. Combine that with numerous military and strategic industrial facilities and you have a target-rich environment for terrorism that stretches from Jacksonville, FL to Brownsville, TX. Note that while the many gambling vessels hereabouts may not be considered "cruise ships" under the strict definition, they may be covered as such under a port's security plan.

Since September 11, 2001, the U.S. Coast Guard and other law enforcers have increased their presence at ports, near military vessels and throughout the length of the Intracoastal Waterway. The Coast Guard—now a division of the U.S. Department of Homeland Security—requires that all recreational boaters make themselves aware of local security zones, permanent and temporary, before leaving the dock. Cruise ships, military vessels and tankers carrying hazardous materials constitute temporary security zones, and furthermore, the rules apply whether they are dockside or under way.

Any violation of the security zones is punishable by civil penalties of up to $27,500 per violation, while criminal penalties call for imprisonment for up to six years and fines reaching $250,000. Ignorance of the security zones is no excuse. Having said that, because the regulators could not foresee every eventuality when mandating an 100-yard no-enter zone around moving vessels, law-abiding boaters sometimes find themselves unable to comply with the letter of the law, without, say, hitting a jetty. In such cases, common sense and good communication should prevail.

Homeland Security officials are always considering measures to better protect maritime targets. Federal agencies are seriously considering a national scheme to license all boaters as well as mandating the onboard installation of expensive identification transponders called AIS or automatic identification systems. It should be no surprise that boaters have responded negatively, ridiculing the proposal as an expensive, invasive and ineffective burden.

Government officials view the recreational boating community as an ally. We can do our part—and perhaps stave off draconian licensing and surveillance measures—by becoming familiar with a Coast Guard program called America's Waterway Watch. Think of it as a neighborhood watch program for the Waterways.

It is not the intent of America's Waterway Watch to spread paranoia or to encourage spying on one another, and it is not a surveillance program. Instead, it is a simple deterrent to potential terrorist activity. The purpose of the program allow boaters and others who spend time along the water to help the authorities counter crime and terrorism.

To report suspicious behavior, call the National Response Center at 877-249-2824. For immediate danger to life or property, call 911, or call the Coast Guard on Marine VHF-FM Channel 16. To learn more about the program, visit www.americaswaterwaywatch.org.

At the end of this section are listed the ports and places that require a little forethought and vigilance on your part. Following the steps in the action plan below will help ensure a trouble-free journey and keep you and your crew out of the headlines.

Prepare:

■ Before you leave, check the current charts for the area in which you will be traveling, and identify any security areas. Security zones are highlighted and outlined in magenta with special notes regarding the specific regulations pertaining to that area.

■ The Coast Guard Maritime Safety Line, 800-682-1796, has information from more than 30 Coast Guard Port Captains from the Mississippi River to the Atlantic Ocean. This toll-free hotline line has up-to-date information on local Waterways and ports, openings, closures and restrictions.

■ Check the latest Local Notice to Mariners (available online at www.navcen.uscg.gov/lnm/default.htm—posted at some marinas), and identify any potential security areas that may not be shown on the chart.

■ Listen to VHF Channel 16 for any Sécurité alerts from the Coast Guard for the area you will be cruising (departing cruise ships, Naval vessels, fuel tankers, etc.) prior to departure.

■ Talk to boaters in your anchorage or marina that just came from where you will be traveling. They will most likely have tips and suggestions on any potential security zones or special areas they encountered on their way.

Stay Alert While Underway:

■ Mind the aforementioned outlined magenta security areas noted on your charts.

■ Look for vessels with blue or red warning lights in port areas, and if approached, listen carefully, and strictly obey all instructions given to you.

■ Keep your VHF radio switched to Channel 16, and keep your ears tuned for bulletins, updates and possible requests to communicate with you.

■ Avoid commercial port operation areas, especially those that involve military, cruise-line or petroleum facilities. Observe and avoid other restricted areas near power plants, national monuments, etc.

■ If you need to pass within 100 yards of a U.S. Naval vessel for safe passage, you must contact the U.S. Naval vessel or the Coast Guard escort vessel on VHF Channel 16.

■ If government security or the U.S. Coast Guard hails you, do exactly what they say, regardless of whether or not you feel their instructions have merit.

Sensitive Southern Port Areas

Fernandina Beach—Nuclear submarines use the St. Marys entrance en route to their base at Kings Bay, GA. When this happens, area security is so tight that all other traffic may be halted while the sub passes through.

Jacksonville—Jacksonville has a strong military presence with a carrier battle group homeported at the Mayport Naval Base. Cruise ships have also begun to operate from the Port of Jacksonville along the St. Johns River.

Cape Canaveral—Third busiest cruise ship port in the world. Security zones around the home of NASA are tied to satellite and space shuttle launches.

Port of Palm Beach—The fourth busiest port in Florida.

Port Everglades—Second busiest cruise ship port in the world. Ft. Lauderdale's port area and cruise ship terminal is at the intersection of the ICW and the entrance, an area of strong current and dense recreational boating traffic.

Miami—Busiest cruise ship port in the world. Cruise ships and commercial vessels are often berthed on the docks lining the south side of the Government Cut channel. When present, so are armed Coast Guard patrol craft.

Key West—A regular stop for cruise ships from other Florida ports.

Tampa—Florida's largest port is home to four cruise ships. Note that the Sunshine Skyway Bridge has a 100-foot security zone around each dolphin and bridge support structure.

Galveston—Ship traffic here is enormous, including tankers and cruise ships. While not as busy a cruise ship base as Florida ports, it still ranks eleventh in the world.

Corpus Christi—Crude oil in, gasoline out; this busy port supports area refineries.

Additional Resources

Department of Homeland Security
www.dhs.gov

U.S. Coast Guard
www.uscg.mil

Local Notice to Mariners
www.navcen.uscg.gov/lnm

Atlantic Intracostal Waterway Association
www.atlanticintracoastal.org

America's Waterway Watch
www.americaswaterwaywatch.org

Courtesy: U.S. Army Corps of Engineers

Rules Of The Road

It is all about courtesy. Much like a busy highway, our Waterways can become a melee of confusion when people don't follow the rules of the road. But unlike Interstate 95 and its byways, the Florida and Gulf Coast Waterways aren't fitted with eight-sided stop signs or the familiar yellow, green and red traffic lights. You will need to rely on your own knowledge to safely co-exist with fellow boaters and avoid collisions.

Most heated Waterway encounters can be avoided by simply slowing down, letting the other boat go first and biting your tongue, regardless of whether you think they are right or wrong. Pressing your agenda or taking out your frustrations with the last bridge tender you encountered normally leads to unpleasantness. When in doubt, stand down, and get out of the other guy's way. The effect on your timetable will be minimal.

Anyone planning to cruise our Waterways should make themselves familiar with the rules of the road. "Chapman Piloting: Seamanship and Small Boat Handling" and "The Annapolis Book of Seamanship" are both excellent on-the-water references with plentiful information on navigation rules. For those with a penchant for the exact regulatory language, the Coast Guard publication "Navigation Rules: International-Inland" covers both international and U.S. inland rules. (Boats over 39.4 feet are required to carry a copy of the U.S. Inland Rules at all times.) These rules are also available online here: *www.navcen.uscg.gov/mwv/navrules/navrules.htm.*

The following is a list of common situations you will likely encounter on the Waterways. Make yourself familiar with them, and if you ever have a question as to which of you has the right-of-way, let the other vessel go first.

Resources

The Coast Guard publication "Navigation Rules—International-Inland" is available at most well-stocked marine stores, including West Marine (*www.westmarine.com*) and Bluewater Books and Charts (*www.bluewaterweb.com*). These establishments normally stock the aforementioned Chapman's and Annapolis Seamanship books also.

Passing or being passed:

■ If you intend to pass a slower vessel, try to hail them on your VHF radio to let them know you are coming.

■ In close quarters, BOTH vessels should slow down. Slowing down normally allows the faster vessel to pass quickly without throwing a large wake onto the slower boat.

■ Slower boats being passed have the right-of-way, and passing vessel must take all actions necessary to keep clear of these slower vessels

At opening bridges:

■ During an opening, boats traveling with the current go first and generally have the right-of-way.

■ Boats constrained by their draft, size or maneuverability (dredges, tugs and barges) also take priority.

■ Standard rules of the road apply while circling or waiting for bridge opening.

Tugs, freighters, dredges and naval vessels:

■ These beasts are usually constrained by draft or their inability to maneuver nimbly. For this reason, you will almost always need to give them the right-of-way, and keep out of their path.

■ You must keep at least 100 yards away from any Navy vessel. If you cannot safely navigate without coming closer than this, you must notify the ship of your intentions over VHF (Channel 16).

■ Keep a close watch for freighters, tugs with tows and other large vessels while offshore or in crowded ports. They often come up very quickly despite their large size.

■ It is always a good practice to radio larger vessels (VHF Channel 1 or 16) to notify them of your location and your intentions. The skipper of these boats are generally appreciative of efforts to communicate with them. This is especially true with dredge boats on the ICW.

In a crossing situation:

■ When two vessels under power are crossing and a risk of collision exists, the vessel that has the other on her starboard side must keep clear and avoid crossing ahead of the other vessel.

■ When a vessel under sail and a vessel under power are crossing, the boat under power is usually burdened and must keep clear. The same exceptions apply as per head-on meetings.

■ On the Great Lakes and western rivers (Mississippi River system), a power-driven vessel crossing a river shall keep clear of a power-driven vessel ascending or descending the river.

Power vessels meeting one another or meeting vessels under sail:

■ When two vessels under power (sailboats or powerboats) meet "head-to-head," both are obliged to alter course to starboard.

■ Generally, when a vessel under power meets a vessel under sail (not using any mechanical power), the powered vessel must alter course accordingly.

■ Exceptions are: Vessels not under command, vessels restricted in ability to maneuver, vessels engaged in fishing (and by that the rules mean commercial fishing) or those under International Rules, such as a vessel constrained by draft.

Two sailboats meeting under sail:

■ When each has the wind on a different side, the boat with the wind on the port side must keep clear of the boat with the wind on the starboard side.

■ When both have the wind on the same side, the vessel closest to the wind (windward) will keep clear of the leeward boat.

■ A vessel with wind to port that sees a vessel to windward, but cannot determine whether the windward vessel has wind to port or starboard, will assume that windward vessel is on starboard tack and keep clear.

Naval vessels under escort always have the right of way. (U.S. Coast Guard)

Bridge Types

Swing Bridges:
Swing bridges have an opening section that pivots horizontally on a central hub, allowing boats to pass on one side or the other when it is open.

Lift Bridges:
Lift bridges normally have two towers on each end of the opening section that are equipped with cables that lift the road or railway vertically into the air.

Pontoon Bridges:
A pontoon bridge consists of an opening section that must be floated out of the way with a cable to allow boats to pass.

Bascule Bridges:
This is the most common type of opening bridge you will encounter. The opening section of a bascule bridge has one or two leaves that tilt vertically on a hinge like doors being opened skyward.

Bridge Basics

Life on the Intracoastal Waterway (ICW) and Gulf Intracoastal Waterway (GIWW) often revolves around bridge openings, and with scores of bridges between Fernandina Beach, FL and Brownsville, TX, you will likely encounter one or more a day. A particular bridge's schedule can often decide where you tie up for the evening or when you wake up and get under way the next day.

The handy bridge tables, farther ahead in this section, are an essential resource for planning your day's travel. Because many bridges restrict their openings during morning and evening rush hours, to minimize inconvenience to vehicular traffic, you may need to plan an early start or late stop to avoid getting stuck waiting for a bridge opening. Take a few minutes before setting out to learn whether bridge schedules have changed; changes are posted in the Coast Guard's Local Notice to Mariners reports, which can be found online at *www.navcen.uscg.gov/lnm*.

The easiest way to hail a bridge is via VHF radio. Bridges in most states use VHF Channel 13, while bridges in Florida, Georgia and South Carolina monitor VHF Channel 09. Keep in mind that bridge tenders are just like the rest of us—everyone has their good and bad days. The best way to thwart any potential grumpiness is to follow the opening procedures to the letter, and act with professionalism. This will almost always ensure a timely opening.

Bridge Procedures:

■ First, decide if it is necessary to have the drawbridge opened. You will need to know your boat's clearance height above the waterline before you start down the ICW. Drawbridges have "Clearance Gauges" to show the closed vertical clearance with changing water levels, but a bascule bridge typically has 3 to 5 feet more clearance than what is indicated on the gauge at the center of its arch at mean low

tide. Bridge clearances are also shown on NOAA charts.

■ Contact the bridge tender well in advance (even if you can't see the bridge around the bend) by VHF radio or phone. Alternatively, you can sound one long and one short horn blast to request an opening. Tugs with tows and U.S. government vessels may go through bridges at any time, usually signaling with five short blasts. A restricted bridge may open in an emergency with the same signal. Keep in mind bridge tenders will not know your intentions unless you tell them.

■ If two or more vessels are in sight of one another, the bridge tender may elect to delay opening the bridge until all boats can go through together.

■ Approach at slow speed, and be prepared to wait, as the bridge cannot open until the traffic gates are closed. Many ICW bridges are more than 40 years old, and the aged machinery functions slowly.

■ Once the bridge is open, proceed at no-wake speed. Keep a safe distance between you and other craft, as currents and turbulence around bridge supports can be tricky.

■ There is technically no legal right-of-way (except on the Mississippi and some other inland rivers), but boats running with the current should always be given the right-of-way out of courtesy. As always, if you are not sure, let the other guy go first.

■ When making the same opening as a commercial craft, it is a good idea to contact the vessel's captain (usually on VHF Channel 13), ascertain his intentions and state yours to avoid any misunderstanding in tight quarters.

■ After passing through the bridge, maintain a no-wake speed until you are well clear and then resume normal speed.

VHF Communications

Skippers traveling the ICW use their VHF radios almost every day to contact other vessels and bridge tenders, make reservations at marinas, arrange to pass other vessels safely and conduct other business. WATERWAY GUIDE has put together the following information to help remove any confusion as to what frequency should be dialed in to call bridges, marinas, commercial ships or your friend anchored out down the creek.

Channel Usage Tips

■ VHF Channel 16 (156.8 MHz) is by far the most important frequency on the VHF-FM band. It is also the most abused. Channel 16 is the international distress, safety and hailing frequency.

■ The Coast Guard recommends that boaters normally keep tuned to and use Channel 16, but no conversations of any length should take place there—its primary function is for emergencies only.

■ VHF Channel 09 is mostly used as a hailing channel and is intended to keep traffic off of Channel 16. Bridges in Florida should be hailed on VHF Channel 09.

■ Federal Communications Commission (FCC) regulations require boaters to maintain a watch on either Channel 09 or 16 whenever the radio is turned on and not being used to communicate on another channel.

■ Since the Coast Guard does not have the capability of announcing an urgent marine information broadcast or weather warning on Channel 09, its use is optional. The Coast Guard recommends that boaters normally keep tuned to and use Channel 16.

■ Recreational craft typically communicate on Channels 68, 69, 71, 72 or 78A. Whenever possible, avoid calling on Channel 16 altogether by prearranging initial contact directly on one of these channels. No transmission should last longer than three minutes.

■ The radio-equipped bridges covered in this edition use Channel 13, except in the state of Florida, which uses Channel 09.

■ The Coast Guard's main working channel is 22A, and both emergency and non-emergency calls generally are switched to it in order to keep 16 clear. Calling the Coast Guard for a radio check on VHF Channel 16 is prohibited.

■ The Bridge-to-Bridge Radio Telephone Act requires many commercial vessels, including dredges and tugboats, to monitor Channel 13. Channel 13 is also the frequency most used by bridges outside the state of Florida.

■ The Coast Guard has asked the FCC to eliminate provisions for using Channel 09 as an alternative calling frequency to Channel 16 when it eliminates watch keeping on Channel 16 by compulsory-equipped vessels.

VHF Channels

09—Used for radio checks and hailing other stations (boats, shoreside operations). Also used to communicate with drawbridges in Florida.

13—Used to contact and communicate with commercial vessels, military ships and drawbridges. Bridges in Alabama, Mississippi, Louisiana and Texas monitor 13.

16—Emergency use only. May be used to hail other vessels, but once contact is made, conversation should be immediately switched to a working (68, 69, 71, 72, 78A) channel.

22—Used for U.S. Coast Guard safety, navigation and Sécurité communications.

68, 69, 71, 72, 78A—Used primarily for recreational ship-to-ship and ship-to-shore communications.

VHF Channel 16—
In Case of Emergency

MAYDAY—The distress signal MAYDAY is used to indicate that a station is threatened by grave and imminent danger and requests immediate assistance.

PAN PAN—The urgency signal PAN PAN is used when the safety of the ship or person is in jeopardy.

SÉCURITÉ—The safety signal SÉCURITÉ is used for messages about the safety of navigation or important weather warnings.

Resources

U.S. Coast Guard VHF Channel Listing:
www.navcen.uscg.gov/marcomms/vhf.htm

FCC VHF Channel Listing:
www.wireless.fcc.gov/marine/vhfchanl.html

Hurricanes

With visions of hurricanes Isabel, Rita, Wilma and Katrina still fresh in the country's collective minds, more folks are tuned into turbulent tropical weather than ever. Hurricanes can create vast swaths of devastation, but ample preparation can help increase your boat's chances of surviving the storm.

While all coastal areas of the country are vulnerable to the effects of a hurricane (especially from June through November), the Gulf Coast, Southern and Mid-Atlantic states typically have been the hardest hit. And even cities far from the ocean, such as Annapolis, MD, aren't immune to the damages these storms cause, either—WATERWAY GUIDE's offices were inundated with more than 4 feet of water from Hurricane Isabel in September 2003.

Hurricane Conditions

■ According to the National Weather Service, a mature hurricane may be 10 miles high with a great spiral several hundred miles in diameter. Winds are often well above the 74 mph required to classify as hurricane strength—especially in gusts.

■ Hurricane damage is produced by four elements: tidal surge, wind, wave action and rain. Tidal surge is an increase in ocean depth prior to the storm. This effect, amplified in coastal areas, may cause tidal heights in excess of 15 to 20 feet above normal. Additionally, hurricanes can produce a significant negative tidal effect as water rushes out of the Waterways after a storm.

Storm Intensity

Saffir-Simpson Categories
■ **Category 1** . . . . . . 74–95 mph
■ **Category 2** . . . . . 96–110 mph
■ **Category 3** . . . . 111–130 mph
■ **Category 4** . . . . 131–155 mph
■ **Category 5** . . . . . . .155+ mph

■ The most damaging element of a hurricane for boaters is usually wave action. The wind speed, water depth and the amount of open water determine the amount of wave action created. Storm surges can transform narrow bodies of water into larger, deeper waters capable of generating extreme wave action.

■ Rainfall varies; hurricanes can generate anywhere from 5 to 20 inches, or more, of rain. If your boat is in a slip, you have three options: If it is in a safe place, leave it where it is; move it to a refuge area; or haul it and put it on a trailer or cradle.

■ The National Weather Service reports that wind gusts can exceed reported sustained winds by 25 to 50 percent. So, for example, a storm with winds of 150 mph might have gusts of more than 200 mph.

■ Some marinas require mandatory evacuations during hurricane alerts. Check your lease agreement, and talk to your dockmaster if you are uncertain. After Hurricane Andrew, Florida's legislature passed a law prohibiting marinas from evicting boats during hurricane watches and warnings. Boaters may also be held liable for any damage that their boat does to marina piers or property; check locally for details.

■ Rivers, canals, coves and other areas away from large stretches of open water are best selected as refuges. Your dockmaster or fellow mariners can make suggestions. Consult your insurance agent if you have questions about coverage.

■ Many insurance agencies have restricted or cancelled policies for boats that travel or are berthed in certain hurricane-prone areas. Review your policy and check your coverage, as many insurance companies will not cover boats in hurricane-prone areas during the June through November hurricane season. Riders for this type of coverage are notoriously expensive.

Preparing Your Boat

■ Have a hurricane plan made up ahead of time to maximize what you can get done in amount of time you will have to prepare (only 12 hours in some cases). You won't want to be deciding how to tie up the boat or where to anchor when a hurricane is barreling down on you. Make these decisions in advance.

■ Buy hurricane gear in advance (even if there is no imminent storm). When word of a hurricane spreads, local ship stores run out of storm supplies (anchors and line, especially) very quickly.

■ Strip every last thing that isn't bolted down off the deck of the boat (canvas, sails, antennas, bimini tops, dodgers, dinghies, dinghy motors, cushions, unneeded control lines on sailboats—everything), as this will help reduce windage and damage to your boat. Remove electronics and valuables, and move them ashore.

■ Any potentially leaky ports or hatches should be taped up. Dorades (cowls) should be removed and sealed up with their deck caps.

■ Make sure all systems on board are in tip-top shape. Fuel and water tanks should be filled, bilge pumps should be in top operating condition and batteries should be fully charged.

■ You will need many lengths of line to secure the boat—make certain it is good stretchy nylon (not Dacron). It is not unusual to string 600 to 800 feet of dock line on a 40-foot-long boat in preparation for a hurricane.

■ If you can, double up your lines (two for each cleat), as lines can and will break during the storm. Have fenders and fender boards out, and make sure all of your lines are protected from chafe.

cont'd

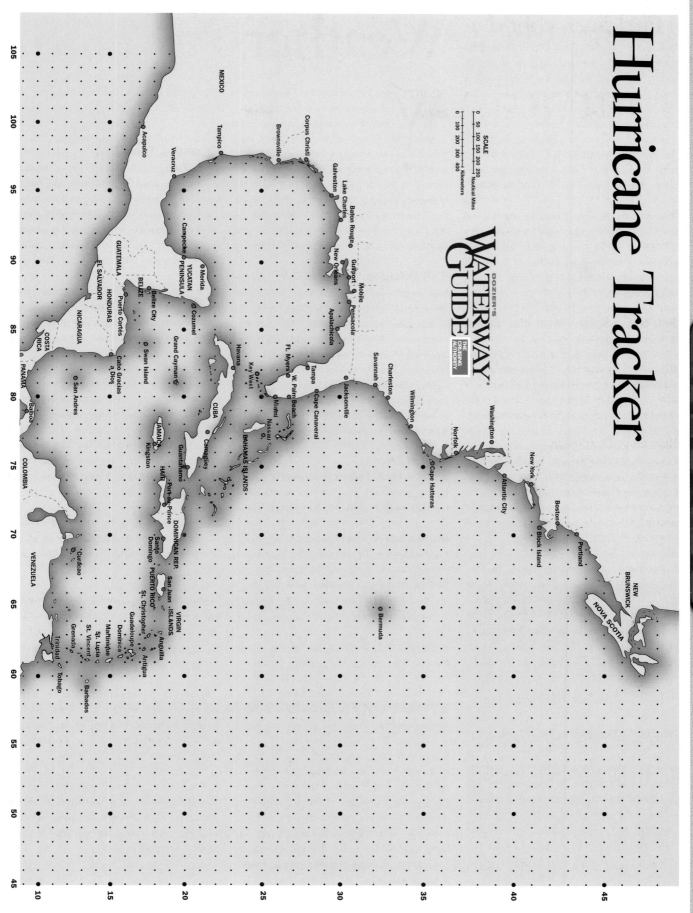

Hurricane Tracker

Hurricanes, cont'd.

■ If you are anchored out, use multiple large anchors; there is no such thing as an anchor that is too big. If you can, tie to trees with a good root system, such as mangroves or live oaks. Mangroves are particularly good because their canopy can have a cushioning effect. Be sure mooring lines include ample scope to compensate for tides 10 to 20 feet above normal. Keep in mind that many municipalities close public mooring fields in advance of the storm.

■ Lastly, do not stay aboard to weather out the storm. Many people have been seriously injured (or worse) trying to save their boats during a hurricane. Take photos of the condition in which you left your boat and take your insurance binder with you.

Returning Safely After the Storm

■ Before hitting the road, make sure the roads back to your boat are safe for travel. Beware of dangling wires, weakened docks, bulkheads, bridges and other structures.

■ Check your boat thoroughly before attempting to move it. If returning to your home slip, watch the waters for debris and obstructions. Navigate carefully, because markers may be misplaced or missing. If your boat is sunk, arrange for engine repairs before floating it, but only if it is not impeding traffic. Otherwise, you will need to remove it immediately.

■ Contact your insurance company right away if you need to make a claim.

Resources

NOAA Hurricane Resource Center:
www.hurricanes.noaa.gov

National Hurricane Center:
www.nhc.noaa.gov

BoatU.S. Hurricane Resource Page:
www.boatus.com/hurricanes

WATERWAY GUIDE Navigation Updates:
www.waterwayguide.com

VHF-FM Broadcasts/NOAA Weather Radio VHF Frequencies

WX1 .... 162.550 MHz
WX2 .... 162.400 MHz
WX3 .... 162.475 MHz
WX4 .... 162.425 MHz
WX5 .... 162.450 MHz
WX6 .... 162.500 MHz
WX7 .... 162.525 MHz

Weather

While large portions of the Intracoastal Waterway are protected from harsh weather, skippers should always check the latest forecasts before casting off their lines or weighing anchor (especially if hopping offshore).

Staying out of bad weather is relatively easy if you plan ahead. The National Weather Service (NWS) provides mariners with continuous broadcasts of weather warnings, forecasts, radar reports and buoy reports over VHF-FM and Single Side Band (SSB) radio. Reception range for VHF radios is usually up to 40 miles from the antenna site, though Florida stations are frequently heard in the near Bahamas. There are almost no areas on the U.S. coast where a good quality, fixed-mount VHF cannot pick up one or more coastal VHF broadcasts. Also, there is no substitute for simply looking at the sky, and either stay put or seek shelter if you don't like what you see.

SSB Offshore Weather

SSB reports are broadcast from station NMN Chesapeake, VA and from station NMG, New Orleans, LA. The broadcasts are not continuous, so refer to the latest schedules and frequency lists (see below) to catch them. SSB reports provide the best source of voice offshore weather information. Two major broadcasts alternate throughout the day. The High Seas Forecast provides information for mariners well offshore, including those crossing the North Atlantic Ocean. Coastal cruisers will be more interested in the Offshore Forecast, which includes information on waters more than 50 miles from shore. The forecast is divided into various regions. Mid-Atlantic cruisers will be most interested in Hudson Canyon to Baltimore Canyon, Baltimore Canyon to Hatteras Canyon, Hatteras Canyon to 31N Latitude, and the southwest North Atlantic south of 31N latitude and west of 65W longitude.

On the Web:

■ **NOAA National Weather Service:** www.nws.noaa.gov. This site provides coastal and offshore forecasts for the continental U.S. and nearby waters, including Puerto Rico and the U.S. Virgin Islands, weather maps, station reports and marine warnings.

■ **NOAA Marine Weather Radio:** www.weather.gov/om/marine. Provides coverage areas and frequencies for VHF weather radio products in all 50 states.

■ **National Hurricane Center:** www.nhc.noaa.gov. Tropical warnings, advisories and predictions are available here. There is also access to historical data relating to hurricanes and tropical weather. Weatherfax schedules are available online.

■ **National Data Buoy Center:** http://seaboard.ndbc.noaa.gov. This site provides near-real-time weather data from buoys and light stations.

Weather Frequencies

UTC	CHESAPEAKE, VA NMN FREQUENCIES (kHz)	NEW ORLEANS, LA NMG FREQUENCIES (kHz)
0330 (Offshore)	4426.0, 6501.0, 8764.0	4316.0, 8502.0, 12788.0
0515 (High Seas)	4426.0, 6501.0, 8764.0	4316.0, 8502.0, 12788.0
0930 (Offshore)	4426.0, 6501.0, 8764.0	4316.0, 8502.0, 12788.0
1115 (High Seas)	6501.0, 8764.0, 13089.0	4316.0, 8502.0, 12788.0
1530 (Offshore)	6501.0, 8764.0, 13089.0	4316.0, 8502.0, 12788.0
1715 (High Seas)	8764.0, 13089.0, 17314.0	4316.0, 8502.0, 12788.0
2130 (Offshore)	6501.0, 8764.0, 13089.0	4316.0, 8502.0, 12788.0
2315 (High Seas)	6501.0, 8764.0, 13089.0	4316.0, 8502.0, 12788.0

(UTC, or Coordinated Universal Time, is equivalent to Greenwich Mean Time)

Lightning

They don't call Florida the Lightning Capital of the World for nothing. Florida averages more than ten deaths and thirty injuries from lightning every year, according to Prof. William Becker of the University of Florida. Approximately fifty percent of the deaths and injuries occur to individuals involved in recreational activities, and nearly forty percent of those are water-related: boating, swimming and fishing. Ewen Thomson, another Florida-based lightning expert, has spent his career studying the effects of lightning on boats, and he is considered the world's leading authority in his field.

Using 2000-2003 statistics from BoatU.S. insurance, Thomson says that .54 percent of all cruising sailboats were struck by lightning during that period. In Florida, the rate was about double that, or slightly more than one in a hundred. For catamarans the nationwide figure was 1.2 percent per year, so in Florida the rate was probably 2.4 percent per year for catamarans, according to Thomson. His own research suggests that the probability of a boat being struck by lightning in Tampa Bay is as high as 4 percent in any given year.

"Research shows that boaters die when current flows through the brain causing cardiopulmonary arrest," Thomson says. "Not all lightning victims die, of course. Besides burns and hemorrhaging, survivors initially may suffer headaches, ringing in the ears, dizziness, nausea, vomiting and seizures. Lingering disabilities include depression, personality change, memory loss, difficulty processing information and impotence."

Thunderstorms in Florida and over its coastal waters are a daily occurrence from March to October. Even with the best weather reports, along with constant and accurate observations of climactic conditions, boaters can still be caught in open waters in a thunderstorm. Then, with or without a lightning protective system, it is critical to take additional safety precautions to protect the boat's personnel.

Lightning experts often recommend that boaters go ashore at the onset of a thunderstorm, but such advice is impractical for cruisers who are living aboard as they transit Southern Waterways. Otherwise, University of Florida researchers recommend these generic precautions:

■ Stay in the center of the cabin. If no enclosure (cabin) is available, stay low in the boat. Don't be a "stand-up human" lightning mast.

■ Keep arms and legs in the boat. Do not dangle them in the water.

■ Discontinue fishing, waterskiing, Scuba diving, swimming or other water activities when there is lightning or even when weather conditions look threatening. The first lightning strike can be a mile or more in front of an approaching thunderstorm cloud.

■ Shut off and do not use or touch the major electronic equipment, including the radio, throughout the duration of the storm.

■ If possible, lower, remove or tie down the radio antenna and other protruding devices if they are not part of the lightning protection system.

■ To the degree possible, avoid making contact with any portion of the boat connected to the lightning protection system. Never be in contact with two components connected to the system at the same time. Example: The gear levers and spotlight handle are both connected to the system. Should you have a hand on both when lightning strikes, the possibility of electrical current passing through your body from hand to hand is great. The path of the electrical current would be directly through your heart.

It would be desirable to have individuals aboard who are competent in cardiopulmonary resuscitation (CPR) and first aid. Many individuals struck by lightning or exposed to excessive electrical current can be saved with prompt and proper artificial respiration and/or CPR. There is no danger in touching persons after they have been struck by lightning.

If a boat has been, or is suspected of having been, struck by lightning, check out the electrical system and the compasses to ensure that no damage has occurred. As suggested above, one way to prevent death, injury or damage to equipment is a well designed lightning protection system. Experts such as Thomson and the marine industry are working to develop standards that will do just that, but at this writing, most cruising vessels either have no protection or systems that work slightly better than placebo.

Starting from the top of the vessel, Thomson recommends installing air terminals (lightning rods) attached to other system components with heavy gauge cable hidden inside the boat's structure. Typically, Thomson looks for existing metal structures, such as a bimini frame and deck rails on a powerboat or the metal bow and stern pulpits or toe rails on sailboats. Ideally these structural conductors are as far outboard as possible.

Lightning protection systems of the past relied on bonding a vessel's metal fittings and equipment to a so-called grounding plate mounted on the bottom of the vessel. Ewen said such a system falls short in salt water and was "hopelessly inadequate" in dissipating lightning in fresh water. He recommends that special terminals be installed to augment the grounding plate.

Thomson developed "Siedarc" terminals after his research showed that the area just above the waterline was where vessels frequently suffered damage from lightning "sideflashes." Sideflashes are sparks carrying hundreds of thousands of volts of electricity, which cause damage, injury and possibly death. "If lightning can be thought of as having a preference," Thomson said, "that preference is to escape from a vessel at or near the waterline."

Besides preventing loss of life or injury, a lightning protection system can avert thousands of dollars worth of damage to sensitive marine electronics.

The system works by creating, in effect, a "Faraday cage" around the boat and its occupants. This is named after inventor Michael Faraday, who in 1836 discovered that an enclosure of conducting materials shielded its contents from electrical effects, a finding that can be used to protect against lightning.

Resources

Ewen M. Thomson, PhD,
www.marinelightning.com

Charles Industries, manufacturer of a portable marine defibrillator,
www.charlesindustries.com

Going Aground

SKIPPER'S HANDBOOK

"**E**ither you have gone aground or you lie," say the old salts, meaning that sooner or later every boat touches bottom. Of late, cruisers transiting the Intracoastal Waterway (ICW) have found this to be particularly true because of chronically insufficient government funds for dredging.

That said, most of the Waterway is lined with soft, forgiving mud (save for some coastal inlet and river areas that are typically sand), so going aground may be an inconvenience, but it is rarely dangerous, let alone life-threatening. Still, it is wise to have a plan of action and basic familiarity with the tried-and-true techniques for getting unstuck from the muck.

To avoid trouble, a prudent mariner will invest a few minutes in research before leaving the dock. For the latest updates on ICW dredging and shoaling, visit *www.waterwayguide.com* and click on the "Navigation Updates" and "Cruising News" sections. These pages are updated daily with the latest shoaling and dredging updates, which are fed to our main office by WATERWAY GUIDE's intrepid cruising editors and cruisers like yourself.

What to do First

■ Throttle back immediately, and put the engine into neutral. If under sail, douse and properly stow all sails to avoid being blown farther onto the shoal.

■ Assess the situation. Look back where you came from (it had to be deep enough or you wouldn't be here) and in all other directions for landmarks that might tell you exactly where you are.

■ Determine next the direction to deeper water so you can plan your escape. A quick glance at the GPS and a chart often reveals where you have gone wrong and where the deepest water is relative to your location.

■ When all else fails, it is not a bad idea to sound around the boat with your boat hook (or a fishing rod in a pinch) to determine on which side of the boat is the deeper water. Some skippers carry a portable depth sounder that can work from the dinghy during occasions like this.

■ Determine the state of the tide, especially if you are in an area with a wide range. If it is dropping, you must work fast. If it is rising, you will have some help getting the boat off.

How to Break Free

■ In less severe situations, you may be able to simply back off the bar, but begin gently to avoid damaging the propeller(s).

■ If the tide is low and rising, it may be best to simply set an anchor on the deep side and wait to be floated free. If it is falling, and you have a deep-keel boat, be sure that the hull will lie to the shallower side of the shoal so the incoming tide does not fill the cockpit.

■ Sailboats usually come off after turning the bow toward deep water and heeling over to reduce the draft. Placing crewmembers out on the rail works, too. Leading a halyard to the dinghy and pulling gently can provide tremendous leverage for heeling the boat also.

■ Keeping wakes to a minimum is common courtesy on the Waterway, but a boat aground can actually benefit from the rising motion of a good wake to free itself from the bottom. One commonly used technique is to radio a passing powerboater and actually request a wake. As the waves lift the boat aground, the helmsman should apply throttle and turn toward deeper water. (Passing powerboats should never create wake without a request for assistance from the vessel aground.)

■ A powered dinghy can also be used to tow a boat off a shoal. If you know where the deep water is, you can tie a line off to the bow, and pivot the boat into deeper water.

■ Kedging, or pulling off with an anchor, is the next logical step. Use the dinghy to carry an anchor (or float it on a life jacket and push it ahead of you while wading—wearing one yourself) as far into deep water as possible. Then use a winch, windlass or your own muscle to pull the boat into deeper water. You may need to repeat the process a few times, resetting the anchor in progressively deeper water until the boat is free of the bottom.

■ The U.S. Coast Guard long ago ceased towing recreational vessels, but if you are aground and in imminent danger (e.g., aground in a dangerous inlet and taking on water), you may make an emergency request for assistance. Simple ICW groundings in calm weather with no immediate danger do not warrant a call to the Coast Guard.

■ If you need outside help from a commercial towboat or Good Samaritan, be sure both of you understand in advance exactly what you plan to do. Fasten the towline to a secure cleat at the bow, and stand well clear of the end when it comes taut, as it can snap with deadly force.

Resources

WATERWAY GUIDE (Navigation Updates): *www.waterwayguide.com*
Atlantic Intracoastal Waterway Assn.: *www.atlintracoastal.org*
TowBoatU.S.: *www.boatus.com/towing*
Sea Tow: *www.4seatow.com*

Getting Your Mail and Paying Bills

One of the most anxiety-inducing issues cruisers face is how to keep their financial life in order while on an extended journey. Luckily, most banks today offer some sort of online banking that allows you to pay your bills with simple Internet access, and post offices will usually hold forwarded mail for transient boaters. With the advent of online banking and new forwarding services from the United States Postal Service (USPS), keeping on top of your bills and important mail need not be a huge hassle.

Options for Mail

General Delivery

■ Use general delivery when you have a person (or "mail forwarder") collecting the mail for you at home while you are away.

■ It works the best when you are on the move. Your mail forwarder can send bundles of your mail to different post offices ahead of your arrival as you move along the coast. The post office will generally hold these for 10 days.

■ The mail should be addressed as follows:
Your Name
Boat Name
General Delivery
City, State, ZIP Code
"Hold for Arrival" printed on both sides

Premium Forwarding Service

The USPS is now offering a new service called Premium Forwarding that is designed to work in tandem with their Priority Mail program.

■ Once a week, normally on Wednesday, all of your mail is bundled in Priority Mail packaging and sent to you at a single specified temporary address.

■ Premium Forwarding includes most mail that standard forwarding does not normally include, like magazines, catalogs and yes, junk mail.

■ Mail can be sent to a general delivery address (as long as that post office accepts general delivery mail, of course).

■ There is an enrollment fee of $10, and each subsequent weekly Priority Mail shipment costs $10.40. The USPS bills a credit or debit card for each week's delivery fee.

■ Once you pick a temporary forwarding address, it cannot be changed as you and your boat move around. Premium Forwarding is designed for people who will be at a fixed temporary address for at least two weeks.

Standard Forwarding Service

■ Standard mail forwarding will automatically send your mail to a specified address (general delivery addresses included) at no extra charge.

■ Each piece of mail is sent individually, versus the Premium Forwarding service, which sends a single bundle of mail each week on Wednesdays.

■ Does not include magazines, periodicals or junk mail.

Hold Mail

■ You can have your mail held at your home post office from 3 to 30 days and retrieve it when you return.

Paying Bills

■ There are several companies (many online) that will handle paying your bills or forwarding your mail while you are away. Probably the best known is St. Brendan's Isle, which services more than 3,000 cruisers from its offices in Green Cove Springs, FL. NATO in Sarasota, FL has also been in business and assisting cruisers in getting their mail for decades.

■ If you aren't already doing it and your bank offers it, consider participating in online banking. You can set it up so many of your bills are automatically paid out of your checking account each month.

■ If you have a company that does not work with your bank's online bill pay service, see if they will take a credit card number and have them bill that every month.

■ Many companies will take credit card numbers over the phone for payment.

Mail Drops

The following post offices receive and hold mail for transient boaters, are conveniently located (unless otherwise noted) and will hold mail for as long as 10 days.

Priority mail generally takes about three or four days to reach you, and the post office may require photo identification, so be prepared.

Have your mail forwarder address your mail as follows:

Your Name, Boat Name
General Delivery
City, State, Zip Code

"Hold for arrival" should be printed prominently in several places on the mailing and a return address always included. If you are expecting more mail, leave a forwarding address with the post office when you move on. Forwarded mail often takes a week or more to arrive at the next destination.

State	Address	ZIP Code
■ Alabama		
Demopolis	100 W. Capitol St	36732
■ Florida		
Apalachicola	20 Ave. D, Ste. 101	32320
Atlantic Beach	1001 Mayport Road	32233
Carrabelle	93 Tallahassee St.	32322
*Clearwater	100 S. Belcher Road.	33765
Cocoa	600 Florida Ave., Ste. 101	32922
Daytona Beach (Attn: General Delivery)	220 N. Beach St.	32114
Fernandina Beach	401 Centre St.	32034
*Fort Myers (Miracle Mile Station)	3954 Broadway	33901
*Fort Pierce (Downtown Station)	1717 Orange Ave.	34950
Key West (Main Post Office)	400 Whitehead St.	33040
Lantana	201 W. Ocean Ave.	33462
Marathon	5171 Overseas Highway.	33050
Miami (Flagler Station)	500 NW 2nd Ave.	33101
*Naples (Main Post Office)	1200 Goodlette Road N.	34102
*New Smyrna Beach	301 Mission Drive	32168
East Palatka	134 W. McCormick Road	32131
Palm Beach	95 N. County Road	33480
Panama City (Downtown Station)	421 Jenks Ave.	32401
St. Augustine South (Belks)	2121 U.S. Highway 1 S., Ste. B	32086
*St. Petersburg (Main Post Office)	3135 1st Ave. N.	33730
Sanford	401 E. 1st St.	32771
*Sanibel	650 Tarpon Bay Road.	33957
*Stuart	801 S.E. Johnson Ave.	34994
Tampa (Commerce Retail Station)	401 N Ashley Drive	33602
Tarpon Springs	850 E. Lime St.	34689
Venice	350 W. Venice Ave.	34285
*Vero Beach	2050 13th Ave OFC	32960
■ Louisiana		
Madisonville	100 Covington St.	70447
*New Orleans (Main Post Office)	701 Loyola Ave.	70113
■ Mississippi		
*Columbus	524 Main St.	39701
*Iuka	801 W. Eastport St	38852
Biloxi	135 Main St	39530
Gulfport (Downtown Station)	2421 13th St.	39501
■ Texas		
*Galveston	601 25th St.	77550
Port O'Connor	611 W. Adams St.	77982

* Post office not within walking distance of the waterfront.

Onboard Waste and No-Discharge Zones

Up until the late '80s, many boaters simply discharged their untreated sewage overboard into the water. After a revision to the Clean Water Act was passed in 1987, the discharge of untreated sewage into U.S. waters within the three-mile limit was prohibited. Shortly thereafter, pump-out stations became a regular feature at marinas and fuel docks throughout the Intracoastal Waterway (ICW).

Simply stated, if you have a marine head installed on your vessel and are operating in coastal waters within the U.S. three-mile limit (basically all of the waters covered in the Guide you are now holding), you need to have a holding tank, and you will obviously need to arrange to have that tank pumped out from time to time.

Government regulation aside, properly disposing of your waste is good karma. While your overboard contribution to the Waterway may seem small in the grand scheme of things, similar attitudes among fellow boaters can quickly produce unsavory conditions in anchorages and small creeks. The widespread availability of holding tank gear and shoreside pump-out facilities leaves few excuses for not doing the right thing.

No-Discharge Zones

■ No Discharge means exactly what the name suggests. No waste, even waste treated by an onboard Type I marine sanitation device (MSD), may be discharged overboard. All waste must be collected in a holding tank and pumped out at an appropriate facility.

■ There are three No-Discharge Zones in the coastal waters that this guide covers, and all of them are in the state of Florida: The waters of the Florida Keys National Marine Sanctuary, the waters within the city of Key West and the waters around the town of Destin on the Florida Gulf Coast.

■ If you plan to travel outside the coverage area for this guide, keep in mind that there are some areas (e.g. Lake Champlain, Ontario municipalities) that forbid overboard discharge of any waste, including gray water from showers or sinks. Familiarize yourself with local regulations before entering new areas to ensure you don't get hit with a fine.

The Law

■ If you have a marine head onboard and are operating on coastal waters within the U.S. three-mile limit (basically all of the waters covered in the Guide you are now holding), you need to have an approved holding tank or Type 1 MSD.

■ All valves connected to your holding tank or marine head that lead to the outside (both Y-valves AND seacocks) must be wire-tied in the closed position. Simply having them closed without the wire ties will not save you from a fine if you are boarded.

■ You may discharge waste overboard from a Type 1 MSD (Lectra-San, Groco Thermopure) in all areas except those designated as No-Discharge Zones. A Type I MSD treats waste by reducing bacteria and visible solids to an acceptable level before discharge overboard.

■ While small and inconvenient for most cruisers, "Port-A-Potties" meet all the requirements for a Type III MSD, as the holding tank is incorporated into the toilet itself.

Pump-Out Station and Holding Tank Basics

■ Many marinas along the ICW are equipped with pump-out facilities, normally located at the marina's fuel dock. Check the included marina listing tables throughout this Guide—they list the availability of pump-out services at each facility. Most marinas charge a fee for the service.

■ Several municipalities and local governments on the ICW have purchased and staffed pump-out boats that are equipped to visit boats on request, especially those at anchor. Radio the local harbormaster to see if this service is available in the area you are visiting. There is normally a small fee involved.

■ You will want to keep an eye out on your holding tank level while you are transiting the Waterway, especially if you are getting ready to enter an area where you many not have access to proper pump-out services for a few days. Plan a fuel stop or marina stay to top off the fuel and water tanks, and empty the other, before you set out into the wild.

Marine Sanitation Devices

■ **Type I MSD:** Treats sewage before discharging it into the water. The treated discharge must not show any visible floating solids and must meet specified standards for bacteria content. Raritan's Lectra-San and Groco's Thermopure systems are examples of Type I MSDs. Not permitted in No-Discharge Zones.

■ **Type II MSD:** Type II MSDs provide a higher level of waste treatment than Type I units, and are larger as a result. These units are usually found on larger vessels due to their higher power requirements. Not permitted in No-Discharge Zones.

■ **Type III MSD:** Regular holding tanks store sewage until the holding tank can either be pumped out to an onshore facility or at sea beyond the U.S. boundary waters (three miles offshore).

Resources

BoatU.S. Listing of No-Discharge Zones: *www.boatus.com/gov/f8.asp*

EPA Listing of No-Discharge Zones: *www.epa.gov*

Federal Clean Vessel Act Information: *http://federalaid.fws.gov/cva/cva.html*

Charts and Publications

Charts are a must-have for any passage on the Intracoastal Waterway (ICW). Charts are a two-dimensional picture of your boating reality—shorelines, channels, aids to navigation and hazards. Even in an age of electronic chartplotters, most experts agree that paper charts have value and should be carried as a back-up. ICW charts incorporate an extremely helpful feature, a magenta line that traces the Waterway's path. Some cruisers call it "The Magenta Highway."

The Internet Age

With widespread availability of the Internet, most all of the publications you will need are available for download from the government in Adobe Portable Document File (PDF) format free of charge. While this is handy, keep in mind that the electronic versions are mainly for reference and planning purposes, as they are not readily accessible while you are at the helm underway.

Once you download them, Coast Pilots and Light Lists can be printed, but since each edition weighs in at about 350-plus pages, they are best viewed online. If you think you will be accessing one of these volumes frequently, buy the bound version from your chart agent.

Most of NOAA's chart catalog is now available for viewing online. Since you can't print these charts, they are best used for planning and reference purposes. Many ICW cruisers hop on their laptops the evening before their next departure and use these online charts to plan out the following day's travel, since they are up-to-date the moment you view them.

NOAA Charts

■ For the ICW, you will primarily use harbor and small-craft charts. Small craft charts are the small, folded strip charts that cover the ICW-centric portion of the coast. Harbor charts, as the name suggests, cover smaller Waterways and ports.

■ NOAA Charts are updated and printed by the government on regular schedules—normally every one to two years. (Each new printing is called an edition.)

■ Third-party companies often reproduce NOAA charts into book/chart kit form. Many veteran ICW cruisers use these, as they have all the charts laid out in page order, which means you don't have to wrestle with large folded charts at the helm. Keep in mind that even the latest versions of these charts need to be updated with the Local Notice to Mariners to be timely and accurate.

■ Changes to the charts between printings are published in the U.S. Coast Guard Local Notice to Mariners, which is available exclusively online at *www.navcen.uscg.gov/lnm*.

■ A disadvantage of printed NOAA Charts is that the version on the shelf at your local store may be a year old or more. For the sake of accuracy, it is necessary to check back through the Local Notice to Mariners and note any corrections, especially for shoal-prone areas.

■ NOAA's complete chart catalog is also available for viewing as a planning or reference tool online at *http://ocsdata.ncd.noaa.gov/OnLineViewer*.

■ Even if you have electronic charts on board, you should always have a spare set of paper charts as a backup. Electronics can and do fail. What's more, electronic viewing is limited by the size of the display screen, whereas a paper chart spread over a table is still the best way to realize "the big picture."

Print-on-Demand Charts

■ Print-on-Demand charts are printed directly by the chart agent at the time you purchase the chart. The charts are the ultimate in accuracy, as they are corrected with the Local Notice to Mariners on a weekly basis.

■ Print-on-Demand charts are water-resistant, and there are two versions with useful information in the margins, including tide tables, emergency numbers, frequencies, rules of the road, etc. One version is for recreational boaters and one for professionals.

■ Print-on-Demand charts are available through various retailers, including Bluewater Books and Charts and West Marine.

Local Notice to Mariners

■ Each week, the U.S. Coast Guard publishes corrections, urgent bulletins and updates in the Local Notice to Mariners. One example of this is the removal or addition of a navigational mark. Serious boaters will pencil such changes directly on the charts as they are announced.

■ Local Notices to Mariners are now available online at *www.navcen.uscg.gov/lnm*.

Light Lists

■ Light Lists provide thorough information (location, characteristics, etc.) on aids to navigation such as buoys, lights, fog signals, day-beacons, radio beacons and RACONS. For the Southern region, use volumes 3 and 4.

■ Light Lists can now be downloaded in PDF format free of charge from the U.S. Coast Guard by visiting the Web site at *www.navcen.uscg.gov/pubs/LightLists/LightLists.htm*.

■ Alternatively, you can order or purchase bound copies of Coast Pilots from your chart agent.

Coast Pilots

■ The U.S. Coast Pilot is a series of nine books providing navigational data to supplement the National Ocean Service (NOS) charts. Subjects include navigation regulations, outstanding landmarks, channel and anchorage peculiarities, dangers, weather, ice, routes, pilotage and port facilities.

■ For the areas covered in the Southern edition of WATERWAY GUIDE, use volumes 4 and 5.

■ Coast Pilots can be downloaded free of charge from NOAA by visiting *http://nauticalcharts.noaa.gov/nsd/coastpilot.htm*.

■ You can order Coast Pilots from your chart agent if a bound copy is more convenient for your use.

Tides and Currents

■ Tide tables give predicted heights of high and low water for every day in the year for many important harbors. They also provide correction figures for many other locations.

■ Tidal current tables include daily predictions for the times of slack water, the times and velocities of maximum flood and ebb currents for a number of Waterways, and data enabling the navigator to calculate predictions for other areas.

■ Tide tables and tidal current tables are no longer published by NOS; several private publishers print them now, and many chart agents carry them.

■ Additionally, tide and tidal current tables are available for viewing online at *http://tidesandcurrents.noaa.gov*.

Launch Ramps

Lists of public launch ramps operated by government agencies, both state and local, can be obtained for the states covered in the Southern 2011 WATERWAY GUIDE by writing the various state governments.

■ **Alabama Department of Conservation and Natural Resources**
64 North Union St.
Suite 468
Montgomery, AL 36130
www.dcnr.state.al.us

■ **Mississippi Department of Wildlife, Fisheries and Parks**
1505 Eastover Drive
Jackson, MS 39211-6374
www.mdwfp.com

■ **Louisiana Department of Culture, Recreation and Tourism**
P.O. Box 94361
Baton Rouge, LA 70804
www.crt.state.la.us

■ **Texas Parks And Wildlife Department**
4200 Smith School Road
Austin, TX 78744
www.tpwd.state.tx.us

The vast number of public ramps in Florida prohibits the state government from publishing an official listing. Anyone needing information on public ramps should contact:

■ **Florida Department of Environmental Protection**
Division of Recreation and Parks
3900 Commonwealth Blvd.
Tallahassee, FL 32399
www.dep.state.fl.us/parks

Insurance

Not all Yacht Insurance Policies are Created Equal

There is no such thing as a standard yacht insurance policy. Take a look at your policy, and you will find that your policy falls into one of two basic types. If your policy lists "named perils" like fire, wind, and lightning, then your policy is a "named perils" policy. Only the fortuitous perils listed in the policy are covered. Nothing else is covered. If your policy has language that sounds like it covers all fortuitous risks, then you are fortunate to have an "all risk" policy. It covers all fortuitous risks, except for the exceptions. Watch out, the exceptions are numerous, and this is where the insurance company lists what risks are not covered. Every "all risk" policy has different exceptions, some more numerous than other.

Another big difference in yacht policies is the type of value the boat is insured for. Some policies insure the boat for market value. That means that you may pay premium based on a boat value of 350,000, but if there is a total loss, and the current market value is only $275,000. That is all you will collect. On the other hand, if your policy insures your yacht on an agreed "declared value" basis, if your yacht is insured for $350,000 and there is a total loss, you get the $350,000, with no questions asked about the value of your boat.

There are certain questions you should ask your insurance agent before you buy your insurance. What is the insurance company's attitude about paying claims? Isn't that the reason that you are buying the insurance? Are they eager to help you get your boat fixed as soon as possible – or do they act as if you have done something wrong? Will they drop you at renewal, or increase your premium if you had a claim? There are actually insurance companies who look for long term relationships and commitments with their clients, and they want to get your boat fixed as soon as possible when you have a claim. The terms and conditions of your policy may be negotiable. If there is a clause that you don't like, ask about the options you have, or if the clause can be deleted. You may be pleasantly surprised.

Cary Wiener is president of Pantaenius America Ltd., a yacht insurance agency licensed in all of the United States dedicated to the yachting industry with its own special yacht insurance policy. Pantaenius America is part of the renowned worldwide Pantaenius group. He is also a maritime lawyer, having represented ship-owners for over 30 years. He has published numerous articles and books on maritime law.

CARY ROBERT WIENER
President

Pantaenius America Ltd.
500 Mamaroneck Avenue
Harrison, New York. 10528
914 - 381 - 2066
www.pantaenius.com

Photo Courtesy: Gary Reich.

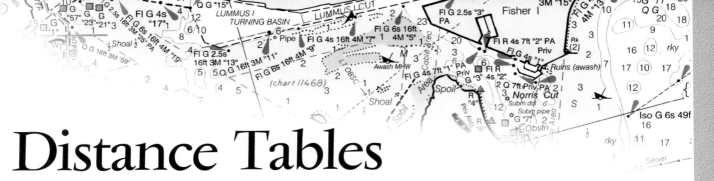

Distance Tables

Inside-Route Distances:
Fernandina Beach to Key West

STATUTE MILES (upper-right triangle) / **NAUTICAL MILES** (lower-left triangle)

Locations (in order along the diagonal):

1. Fernandina Beach, Fla. — 30°40.3' N., 81°28.0' W.
2. Jacksonville, Fla. — 30°19.2' N., 81°39.0' W.
3. St. Augustine, Fla. — 29°53.6' N., 81°18.5' W.
4. Marineland, Fla. — 29°40.1' N., 81°13.0' W.
5. Daytona Beach, Fla. — 29°12.6' N., 81°00.7' W.
6. New Smyrna Beach, Fla. — 29°01.7' N., 80°55.1' W.
7. Titusville, Fla. — 28°37.3' N., 80°47.9' W.
8. Cocoa, Fla. — 28°21.3' N., 80°43.1' W.
9. Eau Gallie, Fla. — 28°07.9' N., 80°37.1' W.
10. Melbourne, Fla. — 28°05.0' N., 80°35.5' W.
11. Vero Beach, Fla. — 27°39.0' N., 80°22.4' W.
12. Fort Pierce, Fla. — 27°27.5' N., 80°19.3' W.
13. Salerno, Fla. — 27°08.8' N., 80°11.6' W.
14. Stuart, Fla. — 27°12.2' N., 80°15.6' W.
15. Port Mayaca, Fla. — 26°59.1' N., 80°36.8' W.
16. Clewiston, Fla. — 26°45.6' N., 80°55.2' W.
17. Moore Haven, Fla. — 26°50.0' N., 81°05.3' W.
18. Fort Myers, Fla. — 26°38.9' N., 81°52.3' W.
19. Jupiter, Fla. — 26°56.8' N., 80°05.4' W.
20. Port of Palm Beach, Fla. — 26°46.1' N., 80°03.0' W.
21. Fort Lauderdale, Fla. — 26°06.8' N., 80°07.2' W.
22. Port Everglades, Fla. — 26°05.6' N., 80°07.0' W.
23. Miami, Fla. — 25°47.0' N., 80°11.0' W.
24. Tavernier, Fla. — 25°00.7' N., 80°31.3' W.
25. Matecumbe Harbor, Fla. — 24°51.1' N., 80°44.5' W.
26. Marathon, Fla. — 24°42.2' N., 81°06.7' W.
27. Flamingo, Fla. — 25°08.5' N., 80°55.4' W.
28. Key West, Fla. — 24°33.7' N., 81°48.5' W.

STATUTE MILES (upper triangle — distances from each row to each subsequent location)

From	2	3	4	5	6	7	8	9	10	11	12	13	14	15	16	17	18	19	20	21	22	23	24	25	26	27	28
1	41	60	79	114	130	162	181	198	201	235	249	273	278	310	336	349	406	289	302	348	350	373	435	453	486	491	527
2		56	75	109	124	158	176	193	197	230	244	268	274	305	331	344	402	284	297	344	345	368	430	449	481	486	522
3			18	53	68	101	120	137	140	174	188	212	217	248	275	288	344	227	241	287	289	312	373	392	425	430	466
4				35	51	83	102	119	122	157	170	194	199	230	257	270	327	209	222	269	270	293	356	374	407	412	448
5					16	48	67	84	87	121	135	159	165	196	222	235	292	175	188	235	236	259	321	339	372	377	413
6						32	52	68	72	106	120	144	150	181	207	220	276	159	173	219	220	243	305	323	356	362	397
7							20	36	39	74	87	112	116	147	174	188	244	127	139	186	188	211	273	291	323	329	365
8								16	21	54	68	92	98	129	155	168	224	107	121	167	168	191	253	273	304	311	346
9									3	38	52	76	81	112	138	152	208	91	104	151	152	175	237	257	288	293	329
10										34	47	71	77	108	135	148	205	87	100	147	148	171	234	252	284	290	326
11											14	38	44	75	101	114	170	53	67	113	114	137	199	219	250	257	292
12												24	30	61	87	100	157	39	53	99	100	123	185	205	236	243	278
13													9	40	67	81	137	20	32	79	80	104	166	185	216	222	258
14														31	58	70	128	25	38	85	86	109	171	190	222	228	264
15															26	40	96	56	69	116	117	141	203	221	253	259	295
16																13	70	83	96	143	144	167	229	247	280	285	321
17																	56	96	108	155	156	180	242	261	292	298	334
18																		152	166	212	213	236	298	318	349	356	390
19																			14	60	61	84	146	166	197	204	239
20																				47	48	71	133	152	184	190	226
21																					1	24	86	106	137	144	178
22																						23	85	105	136	142	177
23																							62	82	113	120	154
24																								22	54	60	96
25																									33	40	75
26																										39	48
27																											84

NAUTICAL MILES (lower triangle — distances from each location to preceding locations)

To	1	2	3	4	5	6	7	8	9	10	11	12	13	14	15	16	17	18	19	20	21	22	23	24	25	26	27
2	36																										
3	53	49																									
4	69	65	16																								
5	99	95	46	30																							
6	113	108	59	44	14																						
7	141	137	88	72	42	28																					
8	157	153	104	89	58	45	17																				
9	172	168	119	103	73	59	31	14																			
10	175	171	122	106	76	63	34	18	3																		
11	204	200	151	136	105	92	64	47	33	29																	
12	216	212	163	148	117	104	76	59	45	41	12																
13	237	233	184	169	138	125	97	80	66	62	33	21															
14	242	238	189	173	143	130	101	85	70	67	38	26	8														
15	269	265	216	200	170	157	128	112	97	94	65	53	35	27													
16	292	288	239	223	193	180	151	135	120	117	88	76	58	50	23												
17	303	299	250	235	204	191	163	146	132	128	99	87	70	61	34	11											
18	353	349	299	284	254	240	212	195	181	178	148	136	119	111	83	61	49										
19	251	247	197	182	152	138	110	93	79	76	46	34	17	22	49	72	83	132									
20	262	258	209	193	163	150	121	105	90	87	58	46	28	33	60	83	94	144	12								
21	303	299	249	234	204	190	162	145	131	128	98	86	69	74	101	124	135	184	52	41							
22	304	300	251	235	205	191	163	146	132	129	99	87	70	75	102	125	136	185	53	42	1						
23	324	320	271	255	225	211	183	166	152	149	119	107	90	95	122	145	156	205	73	62	21	20					
24	378	374	324	309	279	265	237	220	206	203	173	161	144	149	176	199	210	259	127	116	75	74	54				
25	394	390	341	325	295	282	253	237	223	219	190	178	161	165	192	215	227	276	144	132	92	91	71	19			
26	422	418	369	353	323	309	281	264	250	247	217	205	188	193	220	243	254	303	171	160	119	118	98	47	29		
27	427	423	374	358	328	315	286	270	255	252	223	211	193	198	225	248	259	309	177	165	125	123	104	52	35	34	
28	458	454	405	389	359	345	317	301	286	283	254	242	224	229	256	279	290	339	207	196	155	154	134	83	65	42	73

Photo Courtesy: Susan Landry.

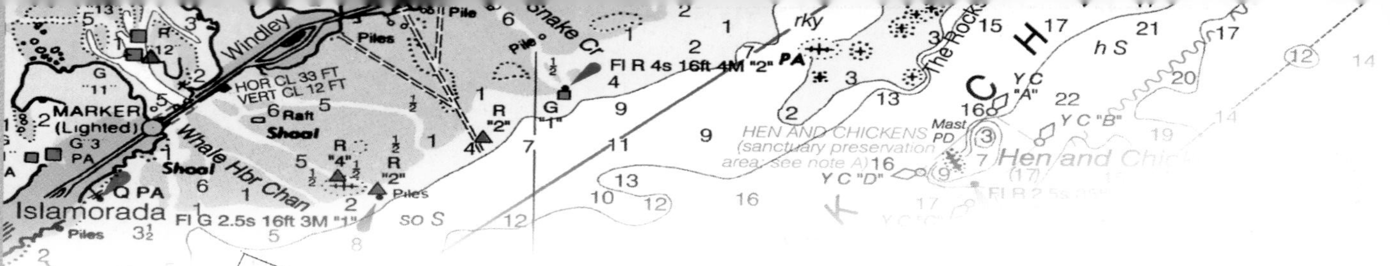

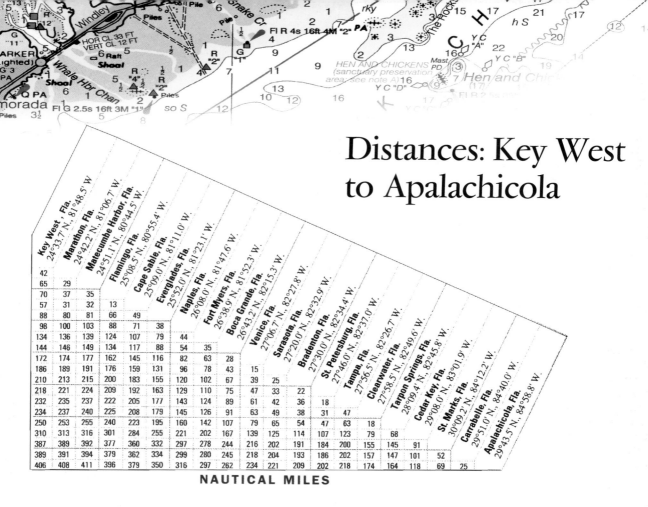

Distances: Key West to Apalachicola

	Key West, Fla. 24°33.7' N., 81°48.5' W.	Marathon, Fla. 24°42.2' N., 81°06.7' W.	Matecumbe Harbor, Fla. 24°51.1' N., 80°44.5' W.	Flamingo, Fla. 25°08.5' N., 80°55.4' W.	Cape Sable, Fla. 25°09.0' N., 81°11.0' W.	Everglades, Fla. 25°52.0' N., 81°23.1' W.	Naples, Fla. 26°08.0' N., 81°47.6' W.	Fort Myers, Fla. 26°38.9' N., 81°52.3' W.	Boca Grande, Fla. 26°43.2' N., 82°15.3' W.	Venice, Fla. 27°06.7' N., 82°27.8' W.	Sarasota, Fla. 27°20.0' N., 82°32.9' W.	Bradenton, Fla. 27°30.0' N., 82°34.4' W.	St. Petersburg, Fla. 27°46.0' N., 82°37.0' W.	Tampa, Fla. 27°56.5' N., 82°26.7' W.	Clearwater, Fla. 27°58.5' N., 82°49.6' W.	Tarpon Springs, Fla. 28°09.4' N., 82°45.8' W.	Cedar Key, Fla. 29°08.0' N., 83°01.9' W.	St. Marks, Fla. 30°09.2' N., 84°12.2' W.	Carrabelle, Fla. 29°51.0' N., 84°40.0' W.
Marathon	42																		
Matecumbe Harbor	65	29																	
Flamingo	70	37	35																
Cape Sable	57	31	32	13															
Everglades	88	80	81	66	49														
Naples	98	100	103	88	71	38													
Fort Myers	134	136	139	124	107	79	44												
Boca Grande	144	146	149	134	117	88	54	35											
Venice	172	174	177	162	145	116	82	63	28										
Sarasota	186	189	191	176	159	131	96	78	43	15									
Bradenton	210	213	215	200	183	155	120	102	67	39	25								
St. Petersburg	218	221	224	209	192	163	129	110	75	47	33	22							
Tampa	232	235	237	222	205	177	143	124	89	61	42	36	18						
Clearwater	234	237	240	225	208	179	145	126	91	63	49	38	31	47					
Tarpon Springs	250	253	255	240	223	195	160	142	107	79	65	54	47	63	18				
Cedar Key	310	313	316	301	284	255	221	202	167	139	125	114	107	123	79	68			
St. Marks	387	389	392	377	360	332	297	278	244	216	202	191	184	200	155	145	91		
Carrabelle	389	391	394	379	362	334	299	280	245	218	204	193	186	202	157	147	101	52	
Apalachicola, Fla. 29°43.5' N., 84°58.8' W.	406	408	411	396	379	350	316	297	262	234	221	209	202	218	174	164	118	69	25

NAUTICAL MILES

Distances: Apalachicola to Brownsville

STATUTE MILES

	Port St. Joe, Fla. 29°49.1' N., 85°18.8' W.	Panama City, Fla. 30°08.2' N., 85°37.6' W.	Fort Walton Beach, Fla. 30°24.0' N., 86°36.7' W.	Pensacola, Fla. 30°24.0' N., 87°13.0' W.	Mobile, Ala. 30°41.5' N., 88°02.2' W.	Pascagoula, Miss. 30°21.9' N., 88°33.8' W.	Biloxi, Miss. 30°23.5' N., 88°52.0' W.	Gulfport, Miss. 30°21.4' N., 89°05.6' W.	New Orleans, La. 29°57.0' N., 90°03.7' W.	Houma, La. 29°35.9' N., 90°42.6' W.	Morgan City, La. 29°41.3' N., 91°12.7' W.	Lake Charles, La. 30°13.1' N., 93°15.5' W.	Orange, Tex. 30°04.0' N., 93°43.3' W.	Beaumont, Tex. 30°04.6' N., 94°05.2' W.	Port Arthur, Tex. 29°49.5' N., 93°57.6' W.	Galveston, Tex. 29°18.5' N., 94°48.1' W.	Houston, Tex. 29°45.0' N., 95°17.4' W.	Texas City, Tex. 29°22.7' N., 94°53.2' W.	Freeport, Tex. 28°56.3' N., 95°20.4' W.	Port O'Connor, Tex. 28°26.5' N., 96°24.4' W.	Rockport, Tex. 28°01.1' N., 97°02.9' W.	Aransas Pass, Tex. 27°53.9' N., 97°08.0' W.	La Quinta, Tex. 27°52.6' N., 97°15.7' W.	Corpus Christi, Tex. 27°48.8' N., 97°24.0' W.	Port Mansfield, Tex. 26°33.4' N., 97°25.6' W.	Port Isabel, Tex. 26°03.6' N., 97°12.8' W.	Port Brownsville, Tex. 25°57.1' N., 97°24.0' W.
Apalachicola, Fla. 29°43.5' N., 84°58.8' W.	31	59	129	173	246	255	274	285	348	410	447	604	618	647	640	707	751	708	749	825	877	885	898	905	985	1021	1036
Port St. Joe		41	113	155	230	239	258	268	331	392	430	587	602	629	624	689	734	690	732	809	861	868	881	887	968	1003	1018
Panama City			71	114	189	197	216	227	290	351	389	545	560	588	582	648	693	649	690	766	819	826	840	846	926	962	977
Fort Walton Beach				43	117	127	145	157	219	280	318	474	489	518	511	578	623	579	620	696	748	755	769	774	855	892	907
Pensacola					84	93	112	122	185	246	284	441	456	484	478	544	589	545	587	663	715	722	735	741	822	858	872
Mobile						67	85	97	159	220	258	415	429	458	451	518	563	519	560	636	688	696	709	716	796	832	847
Pascagoula							37	47	110	171	209	366	381	409	403	468	513	470	511	587	640	647	661	666	747	783	797
Biloxi								32	96	157	194	351	366	394	388	453	498	456	496	573	625	632	646	651	732	769	783
Gulfport									76	138	175	333	348	375	368	435	480	436	478	554	605	613	626	633	713	749	764
New Orleans										61	99	255	270	299	292	359	404	360	402	478	529	536	550	556	636	673	688
Houma											38	194	209	237	231	297	342	299	339	417	468	475	489	495	575	612	626
Morgan City												157	171	200	193	260	305	261	303	379	430	437	451	457	537	574	589
Lake Charles													37	66	59	125	170	127	168	244	296	304	316	322	404	440	455
Orange														30	24	90	135	92	132	209	261	268	282	288	368	405	419
Beaumont															30	97	142	98	139	215	267	274	288	293	375	411	426
Port Arthur																67	112	68	109	185	237	244	258	264	345	381	396
Galveston																	55	12	46	122	174	182	194	200	281	318	333
Houston																		55	97	173	224	232	245	252	333	368	383
Texas City																			51	128	180	186	200	206	287	323	338
Freeport																				81	132	140	153	160	241	276	291
Port O'Connor																					52	60	72	78	159	196	211
Rockport																						10	23	30	110	146	161
Aransas Pass																							14	20	100	136	151
La Quinta																								17	98	133	148
Corpus Christi																									102	138	153
Port Mansfield																										38	53
Port Isabel																											15

	Apalachicola	Port St. Joe	Panama City	Fort Walton Beach	Pensacola	Mobile	Pascagoula	Biloxi	Gulfport	New Orleans	Houma	Morgan City	Lake Charles	Orange	Beaumont	Port Arthur	Galveston	Houston	Texas City	Freeport	Port O'Connor	Rockport	Aransas Pass	La Quinta	Corpus Christi	Port Mansfield	Port Isabel
Port St. Joe	27																										
Panama City	51	36																									
Fort Walton Beach	112	98	62																								
Pensacola	150	135	99	37																							
Mobile	214	200	164	102	73																						
Pascagoula	222	208	171	110	81	58																					
Biloxi	238	224	188	126	97	74	32																				
Gulfport	248	233	197	136	106	84	41	28																			
New Orleans	302	288	252	190	161	138	96	83	66																		
Houma	356	341	305	243	214	191	149	136	120	53																	
Morgan City	388	374	338	276	247	224	182	169	152	86	33																
Lake Charles	525	510	474	412	383	361	318	305	289	222	169	136															
Orange	537	523	487	425	396	373	331	318	302	235	182	149	32														
Beaumont	562	547	511	450	421	398	355	342	326	260	206	174	57	26													
Port Arthur	556	542	506	444	415	392	350	337	320	254	201	168	51	21	26												
Galveston	614	599	563	502	473	450	407	394	378	312	258	226	109	78	84	58											
Houston	653	638	602	541	512	489	446	433	417	351	297	265	148	117	123	97	48										
Texas City	615	600	564	503	474	451	408	396	379	313	260	227	110	80	85	59	10	48									
Freeport	651	636	600	539	510	487	444	431	415	349	295	263	146	115	121	95	40	84	44								
Port O'Connor	717	703	666	605	576	553	510	498	481	415	362	329	212	182	187	161	106	150	111	70							
Rockport	762	748	712	650	621	598	556	543	526	460	407	374	257	227	232	206	151	195	156	115	45						
Aransas Pass	769	754	718	656	627	605	562	549	533	466	413	380	264	233	238	212	158	202	162	122	52	9					
La Quinta	780	766	730	668	639	616	574	561	544	478	425	392	275	245	250	224	169	213	174	133	63	20	12				
Corpus Christi	786	771	735	673	641	622	579	566	550	483	430	397	280	250	255	229	174	219	179	139	68	26	17	15			
Port Mansfield	856	841	805	743	714	692	649	636	620	553	500	467	351	320	326	300	244	289	249	209	138	96	87	85	89		
Port Isabel	887	872	836	775	746	723	680	668	651	585	532	499	382	352	357	331	276	320	281	240	170	127	118	116	120	33	
Port Brownsville	900	885	849	788	758	736	693	680	664	598	544	512	395	364	370	344	289	333	294	253	183	140	131	129	133	46	13

NAUTICAL MILES

Customs

For the purposes of returning to the United States after cruising abroad, there are two sets of rules. One set of rules applies everywhere; the other accords a significant advantage to skippers who make landfall at ports in South Florida, if they had the forethought to register under the Local Boater Option.

U.S. Customs and Border Protection launched the program in October 2006 to benefit vessels arriving at ports from Daytona Beach southward to Key West and up to Tampa. This swath of South Florida takes in most of the arrivals by cruisers coming home from the Bahamas, Caribbean and Mexico.

Whether participating in the Local Boater Option or not, the master of a vessel arriving from abroad must immediately telephone Customs and be ready to answer questions with ship's papers and passports at hand. The federal government requires that U.S. citizens traveling to Bermuda, Canada, Mexico, the Bahamas and Caribbean nations carry valid passports. In the past, cruisers could use other forms of identifications, such as a birth certificate, because that satisfied requirements by the Bahamas and other destination countries. The more stringent U.S. requirement is part of the general effort to tighten border security since 9/11.

For vessels arriving between Sebastian Inlet and Key West, the 24-hour numbers to call are 800-432-1216 or 800-451-0393. For other arrivals, use the telephone numbers listed in the table on this page. (During good weather windows and or at the end of a busy weekend, such as Memorial Day or July Fourth, you may experience long periods on hold before reaching an officer.)

After reporting by telephone, the captain and crew will be assigned an arrival number and instructed to present themselves at the nearest Customs office for a face-to-face inspection, unless they have pre-registered under the Local Boaters Option.

To register under this program, which is free of charge, U.S. citizens and permanent residents must present themselves at one of the four enrollment centers in Florida with passports and ship's papers. Enrollment should include a vessel's crew as well as captain. Customs has established enrollment centers at the Port of Miami, West Palm Beach, Port Everglades in Ft. Lauderdale and Key West.

Once enrolled in the program, arriving boaters who telephone Customs on arrival will most likely receive vessel clearance over the phone and will not be required to present themselves in person. This expedited process only applies to vessels arriving from Daytona Beach and southward to Key West, and as far north as Tampa. More than 7,000 persons have registered under the Local Boater Option.

Elsewhere in Florida, as well as Alabama, Missisippi, Lousiana and Texas, all arrivals will be required to present themselves in person for inspection. Customs and Border Protection was using South Florida as a test area to work out the details of the Local Boater Option and fully expects to expand the program to other areas. So even if you are planning to use ports outside South Florida, it might behoove you to telephone Customs before shoving off, just in case the initiative has been expanded since publication.

The Local Boater Option does not replace a requirement that any vessel returning from abroad have a current Customs decal, if that vessel is 30 feet or longer. The cost of the decal is $27.50. Customs encourages boaters to purchase the decal online, which can be done by going to the agency's Web site (www.cbp.gov), clicking on the Travel tab and following the links.

Another legacy of 9/11 is that boaters who have not left U.S. waters are required to submit to the same procedures as those returning from abroad if they have had "contact" with any foreign vessel "hovering" in U.S. waters. According to Customs Officer Angel Marquez, hovering means a foreign vessel that is approaching a U.S. port, hove-to or anchored and waiting for permission to enter. Contact, he said, means personal contact, not an exchange of VHF radio messages. Examples of contact would be boarding the foreign vessel or exchanging goods. "Passing a can of beer from one boat to another is contact," he said.

Designated Ports of Entry

■ FLORIDA

(Call 800-432-1216 or 800-451-0393 to report arrivals from Ft. Pierce south and around the coast up to and including Ft. Myers):

City	Telephone
Fernandina Beach	904-261-6154
Ft. Pierce/St. Lucie (airport)	772-461-1733
Jacksonville/St. Augustine	904-360-5020
Daytona Beach (airport)	386-248-8043
Port Canaveral	321-783-2066
Melbourne (airport)	321-674-5796
West Palm Beach	561-844-4393
Ft. Lauderdale/Port Everglades	954-761-2000
Port of Miami	305-536-4758
Key West	305-296-5411
Ft. Myers (airport)	239-561-6205
Sarasota	941-359-5040
Port Manatee	813-634-1369
St. Petersburg	727-536-7311
Tampa	813-712-6000
Panama City	850-785-4688
Pensacola	850-476-0117
West Palm Beach	561-848-6922

■ GULF STATES

(Report to individual stations):

City	Telephone
Mobile, AL	251-441-5111
Pascagoula, MS	228-762-7311
Gulfport, MS	228-863-6350
New Orleans, LA	504-623-6600
Morgan City, LA	985-632-8182
Lake Charles, LA	337-439-5512

■ TEXAS

City	Telephone
Port Arthur/Sabine	409-727-0285
Houston/Galveston	409-766-3581
Freeport	979-233-3004
Corpus Christi	361-888-3352
Brownsville	956-542-6201
Lake Amistad/Del Rio	830-774-4345
Roma	956-849-1678

GPS Waypoints

The following list provides selected waypoints for the waters covered in this book. The latitude/longitude readings are taken from government light lists and must be checked against the appropriate chart and light list for accuracy. Some waypoints listed here are lighthouses and should not be approached too closely as they may be on land, in shallow water or on top of a reef. Many buoys must be approached with caution, as they are often located near shallows or obstructions. The positions of every aid to navigation should be updated using the Coast Guard's Local Notices to Mariners, which are available online at www.navcen.uscg.gov/lnm.

The U.S. Coast Guard will continue to provide Differential GPS (DGPS) correction signals for those who need accuracy of 10 meters or less, though most GPS receivers now come with an internal capability for receiving differential signals.

Prudent mariners will not rely solely on these waypoints to navigate. Every available navigational tool should be used at all times to determine your vessel's position.

■ Florida East Coast

LOCATION	LAT.	LON.
St. Marys Entrance Lighted Buoy STM	N 30° 42.900'	W 081° 14.650'
St. Johns Lighted Buoy STJ	N 30° 23.583'	W 081° 19.133'
St. Augustine Lighted Whistle Buoy STA	N 29° 54.917'	W 081° 15.283'
Ponce de Leon Inlet Lighted Bell Buoy 2	N 29° 04.767'	W 080° 53.483'
Cape Canaveral App. Chnl. Lig. Buoy 8	N 28° 23.867'	W 080° 33.433'
Fort Pierce Inlet Lighted Buoy 2	N 27° 28.650'	W 080° 15.417'
St. Lucie Entrance Lighted Buoy 2	N 27° 10.017'	W 080° 08.383'
Lake Worth Inlet Lighted Buoy LW	N 26° 46.367'	W 080° 00.600'
Boca Raton Inlet North Jetty Light 2	N 26° 20.167'	W 080° 04.183'
Hillsboro Inlet Entrance Lighted Buoy HI	N 26° 15.133'	W 080° 04.467'
Port Everglades Lighted Buoy PE	N 26° 05.500'	W 080° 04.767'
Bakers Haulover Inlet Jetty Light	N 25° 53.933'	W 080° 07.183'
Miami Lighted Buoy M	N 25° 46.100'	W 080° 05.000'

■ Florida Keys

LOCATION	LAT.	LON.
Biscayne National Park N. Lig. Buoy N	N 25° 38.733'	W 080° 05.367'
Fowey Rocks Light	N 25° 35.433'	W 080° 05.800'
Triumph Reef Light 2TR	N 25° 28.267'	W 080° 06.917'
Pacific Reef Light	N 25° 22.267'	W 080° 08.517'
Carysfort Reef Light	N 25° 13.317'	W 080° 12.683'
Elbow Reef Light 6	N 25° 08.667'	W 080° 15.500'
Molasses Reef Light 10	N 25° 00.717'	W 080° 22.583'
Davis Reef Light 14	N 24° 55.550'	W 080° 30.167'
Alligator Reef Light	N 24° 51.100'	W 080° 37.133'
Tennessee Reef Light	N 24° 44.767'	W 080° 46.933'
Coffins Patch Light 20	N 24° 40.550'	W 080° 57.500'
Sombrero Key Light	N 24° 37.667'	W 081° 06.650'
Big Pine Shoal Light 22	N 24° 34.117'	W 081° 19.550'
Looe Key Light 24	N 24° 32.800'	W 081° 24.150'
American Shoal Light	N 24° 31.500'	W 081° 31.167'
Pelican Shoal Light 26	N 24° 30.367'	W 081° 35.983'
Stock Island Approach Channel Light 32	N 24° 28.483'	W 081° 44.533'
Key West Ent. Lighted Whistle Buoy KW	N 24° 27.683'	W 081° 48.033'
Key West NW Chan. Ent. Lig. Bell Buoy 1	N 24° 38.867'	W 081° 53.967'
Sand Key Light	N 24° 27.233'	W 081° 52.650'
Cosgrove Shoal Light	N 24° 27.467'	W 082° 11.100'
Twenty-Eight Foot Shoal Light	N 24° 25.800'	W 082° 25.533'
Halfmoon Shoal Light WR2	N 24° 33.500'	W 082° 28.433'
Rebecca Shoal Light	N 24° 34.733'	W 082° 35.117'
Dry Tortugas Light	N 24° 38.000'	W 082° 55.233'
New Ground Rocks Light	N 24° 40.000'	W 082° 26.650'
Ellis Rock Light	N 24° 38.950'	W 082° 11.033'
Smith Shoal Light	N 24° 43.100'	W 082° 55.300'

Florida Bay and West Coast

LOCATION	LAT.	LON.
Bullfrog Banks Light BB	N 24° 50.733'	W 081° 20.567'
Arsenic Bank Light 1	N 24° 52.250'	W 080° 53.017'
East Cape Light 2	N 25° 05.000'	W 081° 04.967'
Northwest Cape Light 4	N 25° 12.833'	W 081° 11.750'
Little Shark River Entrance Light 1	N 25° 19.350'	W 081° 09.233'
Broad Creek Light 6	N 25° 26.317'	W 081° 12.200'
Lostmans River Light 8	N 25° 32.567'	W 081° 14.983'
Pavilion Key Light 10	N 25° 40.917'	W 081° 21.400'
Cape Romano Shoals Light	N 25° 41.300'	W 081° 38.783'
Indian Key Pass Light 1	N 25° 47.983'	W 081° 28.067'
Coon Key Light	N 25° 52.900'	W 081° 37.933'
Capri Pass Light 2	N 25° 58.500'	W 081° 46.267'
Gordon Pass Shoal Light	N 26° 05.483'	W 081° 48.683'
San Carlos Bay Light SC	N 26° 25.133'	W 081° 57.550'
Sanibel Island Light	N 26° 27.183'	W 082° 00.850'
Charlotte Harbor Ent. Lig. Bell Buoy 2	N 26° 39.850'	W 082° 19.567'
Venice Inlet Light 1	N 27° 06.767'	W 082° 28.217'
Big Sarasota Pass Light 1	N 27° 15.567'	W 082° 33.767'
New Pass Entrance Light NP	N 27° 18.917'	W 082° 35.883'
Longboat Pass Approach Light LP	N 27° 25.850'	W 082° 41.850'
Southwest Channel Ent. Lig. Bell Buoy 1	N 27° 32.333'	W 082° 48.600'
Tampa Bay Lighted Buoy T	N 27° 35.317'	W 083° 00.717'
Pass-A-Grille Entrance Light PG	N 27° 40.583'	W 082° 46.017'
Johns Pass Light JP	N 27° 46.500'	W 082° 48.033'
Clearwater Pass Channel Light 1	N 27° 58.267'	W 082° 50.850'
Anclote Anchorage South Ent. Light 1	N 28° 08.283'	W 082° 51.950'
Anclote River Entrance Light 1	N 28° 10.383'	W 082° 49.533'
Anclote Anchorage North Ent. Light 2	N 28° 15.050'	W 082° 52.900'
Homosassa Bay Entrance Light 2	N 28° 41.433'	W 082° 48.650'
Crystal River Lighted Buoy 2	N 28° 47.517'	W 082° 58.583'
Withlacoochee River Entrance Light 1	N 28° 58.133'	W 082° 49.717'
Cedar Keys Main Channel Light 1	N 29° 04.000'	W 083° 04.550'

Florida Bay and West Coast (continued)

LOCATION	LAT.	LON.
Cedar Keys NW Channel App. Light 2	N 29° 08.483'	W 083° 07.850'
Suwannee River, Alligator Pass Light 2	N 29° 14.583'	W 083° 11.783'
Suwannee R., McGriff Pass Daybeacon 1	N 29° 18.583'	W 083° 12.017'
Steinhatchee River Light 1	N 29° 39.383'	W 083° 27.433'
St. Marks River Lighted Buoy SM	N 30° 04.300'	W 084° 10.800'
Carrabelle Channel Lighted Bell Buoy 2	N 29° 44.550'	W 084° 39.200'
St. George Island W Jetty Lig. Buoy 1	N 29° 36.167'	W 084° 57.217'
St. Joseph Bay Lig. & Ent. Rg. A Rear Lig.	N 29° 55.100'	W 085° 22.833'
St. Andrew Bay Ent. Lig. Whistle Buoy SA	N 30° 05.500'	W 085° 46.433'
Choctawhatchee Bay Ent. Lig. Whi. By CB	N 30° 22.250'	W 086° 30.900'
Pensacola Bay Ent. Lig. Gong Buoy 1	N 30° 16.267'	W 087° 17.550'

Alabama

LOCATION	LAT.	LON.
Perdido Pass Ent. Lig. Whistle Buoy PP	N 30° 15.517'	W 087° 33.400'
Mobile Entrance Lighted Horn Buoy M	N 30° 07.517'	W 088° 04.117'

Mississippi

LOCATION	LAT.	LON.
Petit Bois Island Obstruction Light 2	N 30° 13.400'	W 088° 29.200'
Horn Island Pass Lig. Whistle Buoy HI	N 30° 08.500'	W 088° 34.667'
Dog Keys Pass Lighted Gong Buoy 1	N 30° 12.933'	W 088° 47.450'
Gulfport Ship Chan. Lig. Whistle Buoy GP	N 30° 07.167'	W 088° 52.667'

Louisiana

LOCATION	LAT.	LON.
Chandeleur Light	N 30° 02.800'	W 088° 52.700'
Old Harbor Island Lighted Buoy 1	N 29° 46.600'	W 089° 03.717'
Miss. R., Gulf Outlet App. Lig. Horn Buoy NO	N 29° 26.400'	W 088° 56.800'
Pass a Loutre N Pass Lig. Bell Buoy 2	N 29° 14.283'	W 088° 57.467'
South Pass Lighted Bell Buoy 2	N 28° 58.717'	W 089° 06.517'
Southwest Pass Ent. Lig. Whistle Buoy SW	N 28° 52.650'	W 089° 25.917'
Barataria Pass Lighted Whistle Buoy BP	N 29° 13.967'	W 089° 54.117'
Belle Pass Entrance Lighted Bell Buoy 2	N 29° 04.267'	W 090° 13.667'

■ Louisiana (continued)

LOCATION	LAT.	LON.
Cat Island Pass Ent. Lig. Whistle Buoy CI	N 29° 00.217'	W 090° 33.917'
Point Au Fer Reef Light	N 29° 22.333'	W 091° 23.067'
Atchafalaya Channel Ent. Lig. Bell Buoy A	N 29° 10.000'	W 091° 33.900'
Sabine Bank Channel Lig. Whistle Buoy SB	N 29° 25.017'	W 093° 40.017'

■ Texas

LOCATION	LAT.	LON.
Galveston Bay Ent. Lig. Whistle Buoy GA	N 29° 09.483'	W 094° 25.900'
Freeport Ent. Lighted Whistle Buoy FP	N 28° 52.617'	W 095° 14.150'
Colorado River W Jetty Entrance Light 1	N 28° 35.467'	W 095° 59.067'
Matagorda Ship App. Lig. Wh. Buoy MSC	N 28° 25.300'	W 096° 05.217'
Aransas Pass Ent. Lig. Whistle Buoy AP	N 27° 47.567'	W 096° 57.367'
Pt Mansfield Chan. Ent. Lig. Wh. Buoy PM	N 26° 33.867'	W 097° 15.383'
Brazos Santiago Pass Ent. Lig. Wh. By BS	N 26° 03.933'	W 097° 06.583'

■ Bahamas

LOCATION	LAT.	LON.
Memory Rock Light	N 26° 56.800'	W 079° 06.800'
Indian Cay Light	N 26° 43.000'	W 079° 00.100'
Settlement Point Light	N 26° 41.500'	W 078° 59.900'
Freeport, Pinder Point Light	N 26° 31.500'	W 078° 46.400'
Great Stirrup Cay Light	N 25° 49.700'	W 077° 54.000'
Nassau, Paradise Island Light	N 25° 05.200'	W 077° 21.100'
Great Isaac Light	N 26° 01.800'	W 079° 05.400'
North Rock Light	N 25° 48.100'	W 079° 15.700'
North Bimini Island Light	N 25° 43.700'	W 079° 18.000'
Gun Cay Light	N 25° 34.500'	W 079° 18.800'
South Riding Rock Light	N 25° 13.800'	W 079° 09.000'

Skipper's Notes

Tide Tables

Fernandina Beach, Amelia River, Florida, 2010

Times and Heights of High and Low Waters

July

Day	Time (h m)	Height (ft)	Height (cm)
1 Th	0525 1128 0519* 1134*	0.2 2.6 0.5 3.0	6 79 15 91
2 F	0600 1212* 0607*	0.3 2.6 0.6	9 79 18
3 Sa	1213 0636 1259* 0700*	2.8 0.3 2.7 0.7	85 9 82 21
4 Su ◑	1255 0715 0148* 0758*	2.6 0.3 2.8 0.8	79 9 85 24
5 M	0143 0758 0240* 0900*	2.4 0.3 2.9 0.8	73 9 88 24
6 Tu	0236 0846 0335* 1003*	2.3 0.2 3.1 0.7	70 6 94 21
7 W	0333 0938 0429* 1102*	2.3 0.1 3.4 0.5	70 3 104 15
8 Th	0432 1032 0522* 1157*	2.3 0.0 3.6 0.3	70 0 110 9
9 F	0529 1126 0614*	2.4 -0.2 3.8	73 -6 116
10 Sa	1248 0624 1221* 0704*	0.1 2.6 -0.3 4.0	3 79 -9 122
11 Su ●	0136 0718 0115* 0754*	-0.1 2.7 -0.5 4.2	-3 82 -15 128
12 M	0224 0811 0209* 0843*	-0.2 2.9 -0.5 4.2	-6 88 -15 128
13 Tu	0311 0904 0304* 0932*	-0.4 3.1 -0.5 4.1	-12 94 -15 125
14 W	0357 0958 0400* 1022*	-0.5 3.3 -0.4 3.9	-15 101 -12 119
15 Th	0445 1053 0458* 1112*	-0.5 3.4 -0.3 3.6	-15 104 -9 110
16 F	0533 1151 0559*	-0.4 3.5 -0.1	-12 107 -3
17 Sa	1205 0623 1251* 0705*	3.3 -0.4 3.5 0.2	101 -12 107 6
18 Su ◐	0100 0715 0153* 0814*	3.0 -0.2 3.5 0.3	91 -6 107 9
19 M	0201 0811 0257* 0925*	2.7 -0.1 3.5 0.4	82 -3 107 12
20 Tu	0305 0910 0400* 1032*	2.5 0.0 3.5 0.4	76 0 107 12
21 W	0410 1009 0458* 1133*	2.4 0.0 3.5 0.4	73 0 107 12
22 Th	0511 1106 0552*	2.4 0.1 3.6	73 3 110
23 F	1225 0605 1158 0640*	0.3 2.4 0.1 3.6	9 73 3 110
24 Sa	0112 0654 1246* 0723*	0.3 2.5 0.1 3.6	9 76 3 110
25 Su	0153 0737 0129* 0803*	0.2 2.6 0.1 3.6	6 79 3 110
26 M ○	0230 0818 0210* 0840*	0.2 2.7 0.1 3.5	6 82 3 107
27 Tu	0305 0856 0250* 0914*	0.2 2.7 0.1 3.4	6 82 3 104
28 W	0338 0934 0329* 0948*	0.2 2.8 0.2 3.3	6 85 6 101
29 Th	0409 1011 0408* 1021*	0.2 2.8 0.3 3.1	6 85 9 94
30 F	0440 1049 0449* 1056*	0.2 2.9 0.5 3.0	6 88 15 91
31 Sa	0512 1128 0533* 1132*	0.3 2.9 0.6 2.8	9 88 18 85

August

Day	Time (h m)	Height (ft)	Height (cm)
1 Su	0546 1211* 0621*	0.3 2.9 0.7	9 88 21
2 M	1212 0624 1259* 0716*	2.6 0.3 3.0 0.8	79 9 91 24
3 Tu ◑	1259 0709 0154* 0818*	2.4 0.3 3.1 0.8	73 9 94 24
4 W	0153 0802 0253* 0925*	2.3 0.3 3.2 0.8	70 9 98 24
5 Th	0255 0901 0354* 1029*	2.3 0.2 3.4 0.6	70 6 104 18
6 F	0400 1003 0454* 1127*	2.4 0.1 3.7 0.4	73 3 113 12
7 Sa	0503 1105 0550*	2.6 -0.1 3.9	79 -3 119
8 Su	1219 0602 1204* 0643*	0.2 2.8 -0.3 4.1	6 85 -9 125
9 M	0109 0658 0101* 0733*	-0.1 3.1 -0.5 4.2	-3 94 -15 128
10 Tu ●	0156 0752 0157* 0822*	-0.3 3.4 -0.6 4.2	-9 104 -18 128
11 W	0242 0845 0252* 0911*	-0.4 3.6 -0.6 4.1	-12 110 -18 125
12 Th	0328 0938 0348* 1000*	-0.5 3.8 -0.4 3.9	-15 116 -12 119
13 F	0414 1032 0445* 1050*	-0.5 3.9 -0.2 3.6	-15 119 -6 110
14 Sa	0502 1127 0545* 1143*	-0.4 3.9 0.0 3.2	-12 119 0 98
15 Su	0553 1226* 0648*	-0.2 3.8 0.3	-6 116 9
16 M ◐	1239 0647 0128* 0757*	2.9 0.0 3.6 0.5	88 0 110 15
17 Tu	0141 0746 0234* 0907*	2.7 0.2 3.5 0.6	82 6 107 18
18 W	0248 0850 0340* 1014*	2.5 0.3 3.5 0.6	76 9 107 18
19 Th	0355 0954 0440* 1113*	2.5 0.4 3.5 0.6	76 12 107 18
20 F	0456 1053 0534*	2.5 0.4 3.5	76 12 107
21 Sa	1203 0549 1145 0620*	0.6 2.6 0.3 3.5	18 79 9 107
22 Su	1245 0634 1231* 0701*	0.5 2.7 0.3 3.5	15 82 9 107
23 M	0122 0714 0113* 0737*	0.4 2.9 0.2 3.5	12 88 6 107
24 Tu ○	0156 0752 0152* 0811*	0.3 3.0 0.2 3.5	9 91 6 107
25 W	0227 0827 0229* 0844*	0.3 3.1 0.3 3.4	9 94 9 104
26 Th	0257 0902 0306* 0916*	0.3 3.2 0.3 3.3	9 98 9 101
27 F	0326 0936 0344* 0948*	0.3 3.2 0.4 3.1	9 98 12 94
28 Sa	0356 1012 0423* 1021*	0.3 3.3 0.5 3.0	9 101 15 91
29 Su	0427 1049 0504* 1057*	0.4 3.3 0.6 2.8	12 101 18 85
30 M	0502 1131 0551* 1138*	0.4 3.3 0.7 2.7	12 101 21 82
31 Tu	0543 1220* 0644*	0.5 3.3 0.8	15 101 24

September

Day	Time (h m)	Height (ft)	Height (cm)
1 W ◑	1226 0632 0116* 0747*	2.5 0.5 3.3 0.9	76 15 101 27
2 Th	0124 0730 0220* 0854*	2.5 0.5 3.4 0.8	76 15 104 24
3 F	0231 0836 0326* 0959*	2.5 0.4 3.6 0.7	76 12 110 21
4 Sa	0340 0944 0428* 1057*	2.7 0.2 3.8 0.5	82 6 116 15
5 Su	0445 1050 0526* 1150*	2.9 0.0 3.9 0.2	88 0 119 6
6 M	0544 1151 0620*	3.3 -0.2 4.1	101 -6 125
7 Tu	1238 0639 1249* 0710*	0.0 3.6 -0.4 4.1	0 110 -12 125
8 W ●	0125 0732 0145* 0800*	-0.2 4.0 -0.5 4.1	-6 122 -15 125
9 Th	0211 0824 0240* 0848*	-0.4 4.2 -0.4 3.9	-12 128 -12 119
10 F	0256 0915 0334* 0937*	-0.4 4.3 -0.3 3.7	-12 131 -9 113
11 Sa	0343 1008 0429* 1027*	-0.3 4.3 -0.1 3.4	-9 131 -3 104
12 Su	0431 1101 0527* 1120*	-0.2 4.1 0.2 3.2	-6 125 6 98
13 M	0522 1159 0628*	0.0 3.9 0.4	0 119 12
14 Tu	1217 0618 0100* 0734*	2.9 0.3 3.7 0.6	88 9 113 18
15 W ◐	0121 0721 0206* 0842*	2.7 0.5 3.5 0.8	82 15 107 24
16 Th	0230 0829 0313* 0947*	2.6 0.6 3.4 0.8	79 18 104 24
17 F	0337 0936 0414* 1043*	2.6 0.7 3.4 0.8	79 21 104 24
18 Sa	0436 1035 0506* 1130*	2.7 0.6 3.4 0.7	82 18 104 21
19 Su	0525 1127 0551*	2.9 0.6 3.4	88 18 104
20 M	1209 0608 1212* 0630*	0.6 3.0 0.5 3.4	18 91 15 104
21 Tu	1243 0646 1253* 0705*	0.5 3.2 0.4 3.4	15 98 12 104
22 W	0115 0722 0131* 0739*	0.4 3.4 0.4 3.4	12 104 12 104
23 Th ○	0145 0756 0208* 0812*	0.4 3.5 0.4 3.3	12 107 12 101
24 F	0215 0830 0245* 0844*	0.4 3.6 0.4 3.2	12 110 12 98
25 Sa	0245 0904 0322* 0918*	0.4 3.6 0.4 3.1	12 110 12 94
26 Su	0316 0939 0401* 0953*	0.4 3.7 0.5 3.0	12 113 15 91
27 M	0350 1018 0442* 1031*	0.5 3.6 0.6 2.8	15 110 18 85
28 Tu	0428 1101 0529* 1114*	0.5 3.6 0.7 2.7	15 110 21 82
29 W	0512 1151 0623*	0.6 3.6 0.8	18 110 24
30 Th	1206 0606 1249* 0724*	2.6 0.6 3.5 0.9	79 18 107 27

October

Day	Time (h m)	Height (ft)	Height (cm)
1 F ◑	0107 0709 0153* 0828*	2.6 0.6 3.6 0.8	79 18 110 24
2 Sa	0216 0819 0300* 0931*	2.7 0.5 3.6 0.6	82 15 110 18
3 Su	0326 0931 0403* 1027*	3.0 0.4 3.7 0.4	91 12 113 12
4 M	0430 1039 0502* 1119*	3.3 0.2 3.8 0.2	101 6 116 6
5 Tu	0528 1141 0556*	3.7 0.0 3.9	113 0 119
6 W	1207 0622 1239* 0647*	-0.1 4.1 -0.2 3.9	-3 125 -6 119
7 Th ●	1254 0713 0133* 0737*	-0.2 4.4 -0.3 3.8	-6 134 -9 116
8 F	0140 0804 0227* 0826*	-0.3 4.5 -0.3 3.7	-9 137 -9 113
9 Sa	0226 0853 0319* 0915*	-0.3 4.6 -0.2 3.5	-9 140 -6 107
10 Su	0313 0944 0412* 1005*	-0.2 4.4 0.0 3.3	-6 134 0 101
11 M	0402 1036 0507* 1057*	0.0 4.2 0.3 3.0	0 128 9 91
12 Tu	0453 1130 0604* 1154*	0.2 4.0 0.5 2.8	6 122 15 85
13 W	0549 1229* 0705*	0.5 3.7 0.7	15 113 21
14 Th ◐	1256 0651 0132* 0808*	2.7 0.7 3.4 0.8	82 21 104 24
15 F	0203 0759 0235* 0908*	2.7 0.8 3.3 0.9	82 24 101 27
16 Sa	0308 0907 0335* 1001*	2.7 0.9 3.2 0.8	82 27 98 24
17 Su	0405 1008 0427* 1045*	2.8 0.8 3.1 0.8	85 24 94 24
18 M	0454 1101 0512* 1123*	3.0 0.7 3.1 0.7	91 21 94 21
19 Tu	0536 1147 0552* 1158*	3.2 0.6 3.1 0.5	98 18 94 15
20 W	0614 1229* 0629*	3.4 0.5 3.1	104 15 94
21 Th	1230 0650 0108* 0704*	0.5 3.6 0.5 3.1	15 110 15 94
22 F	0102 0725 0146* 0739*	0.4 3.7 0.4 3.1	12 113 12 94
23 Sa ○	0135 0800 0224* 0815*	0.3 3.8 0.4 3.0	9 116 12 91
24 Su	0208 0836 0302* 0851*	0.3 3.9 0.4 2.9	9 119 12 88
25 M	0244 0914 0343* 0929*	0.3 3.9 0.4 2.9	9 119 12 88
26 Tu	0322 0955 0426* 1011*	0.3 3.9 0.5 2.8	9 119 15 85
27 W	0405 1041 0514* 1059*	0.4 3.8 0.6 2.7	12 116 18 82
28 Th	0453 1132 0606* 1154*	0.4 3.7 0.6 2.7	12 113 18 82
29 F	0550 1228* 0703*	0.5 3.6 0.6	15 110 18
30 Sa ◑	1257 0656 0130* 0803*	2.8 0.5 3.5 0.5	85 15 107 15
31 Su	0205 0809 0235* 0901*	2.9 0.5 3.5 0.4	88 15 107 12

November

Day	Time (h m)	Height (ft)	Height (cm)
1 M	0313 0922 0338* 0956*	3.2 0.4 3.5 0.2	98 12 107 6
2 Tu	0415 1030 0437* 1048*	3.6 0.2 3.5 0.0	110 6 107 0
3 W	0512 1132 0533* 1138*	3.9 0.1 3.4 -0.2	119 3 104 -6
4 Th	0605 1229* 0626*	4.2 -0.1 3.4	128 -3 104
5 F	1226 0656 0123* 0716*	-0.3 4.4 -0.2 3.3	-9 134 -6 101
6 Sa ●	0114 0745 0215* 0806*	-0.3 4.5 -0.2 3.3	-9 137 -6 101
7 Su	0101 0734 0205* 0755*	-0.3 4.5 -0.1 3.1	-9 137 -3 94
8 M	0149 0823 0255* 0844*	-0.1 4.3 0.0 3.0	-3 131 0 91
9 Tu	0237 0912 0345* 0935*	0.0 4.1 0.2 2.9	0 125 6 88
10 W	0327 1002 0437* 1028*	0.2 3.8 0.4 2.7	6 116 12 82
11 Th	0419 1054 0530* 1125*	0.5 3.5 0.6 2.6	15 107 18 79
12 F	0517 1149 0624*	0.7 3.2 0.7	21 98 21
13 Sa ◐	1225 0620 1245* 0716*	2.6 0.8 3.0 0.7	79 24 91 21
14 Su	0126 0725 0141* 0805*	2.7 0.9 2.9 0.7	82 27 88 21
15 M	0222 0829 0233* 0849*	2.8 0.9 2.8 0.6	85 27 85 18
16 Tu	0312 0925 0322* 0929*	3.0 0.8 2.7 0.5	91 24 82 15
17 W	0356 1015 0406* 1007*	3.2 0.7 2.7 0.4	98 21 82 12
18 Th	0437 1101 0448* 1044*	3.4 0.5 2.7 0.3	104 15 82 9
19 F	0516 1143 0528* 1121*	3.6 0.4 2.7 0.2	110 12 82 6
20 Sa	0554 1223* 0608* 1159*	3.7 0.3 2.7 0.1	113 9 82 3
21 Su ○	0633 0103* 0647*	3.8 0.2 2.7	116 6 82
22 M	1238 0713 0144* 0728*	0.1 3.9 0.2 2.7	3 119 6 82
23 Tu	0120 0755 0227* 0811*	0.0 3.9 0.2 2.7	0 119 6 82
24 W	0203 0839 0311* 0857*	0.0 3.9 0.2 2.7	0 119 6 82
25 Th	0251 0925 0358* 0948*	0.1 3.8 0.2 2.7	3 116 6 82
26 F	0343 1016 0448* 1044*	0.1 3.7 0.2 2.8	3 113 6 85
27 Sa	0442 1110 0540* 1146*	0.2 3.5 0.2 2.9	6 107 6 88
28 Su ◑	0547 1208* 0635*	0.3 3.3 0.1	9 101 3
29 M	1252 0659 0110* 0731*	3.1 0.3 3.2 0.0	94 9 98 0
30 Tu	0157 0812 0213* 0826*	3.3 0.3 3.0 -0.1	101 9 91 -3

December

Day	Time (h m)	Height (ft)	Height (cm)
1 W	0259 0921 0314* 0921*	3.6 0.2 2.9 -0.2	110 6 88 -6
2 Th	0357 1024 0413* 1013*	3.8 0.1 2.9 -0.3	116 3 88 -9
3 F	0451 1121 0508* 1104*	4.0 -0.1 2.9 -0.3	122 -3 88 -9
4 Sa	0542 1214* 0600* 1154*	4.1 -0.1 2.8 -0.3	125 -3 85 -9
5 Su ●	0631 0103* 0650*	4.2 -0.2 2.8	128 -6 85
6 M	1242 0718 0151* 0738*	-0.3 4.1 -0.1 2.8	-9 125 -3 85
7 Tu	0129 0804 0236* 0825*	-0.2 4.0 -0.1 2.7	-6 122 -3 82
8 W	0216 0849 0321* 0911*	-0.1 3.8 0.0 2.7	-3 116 0 82
9 Th	0302 0934 0405* 0958*	0.1 3.5 0.2 2.6	3 107 6 79
10 F	0350 1018 0448* 1047*	0.3 3.3 0.3 2.5	9 101 9 76
11 Sa	0440 1102 0531* 1139*	0.4 3.0 0.4 2.5	12 91 12 76
12 Su	0534 1148 0615*	0.6 2.8 0.4	18 85 12
13 M ◐	1232 0634 1237* 0658*	2.6 0.7 2.5 0.4	79 21 76 12
14 Tu	0127 0737 0129* 0743*	2.6 0.7 2.4 0.4	79 21 73 12
15 W	0220 0840 0222* 0828*	2.8 0.7 2.3 0.4	85 21 70 12
16 Th	0310 0937 0314* 0914*	3.0 0.6 2.3 0.3	91 18 70 9
17 F	0357 1028 0404* 0959*	3.2 0.5 2.3 0.1	98 15 70 3
18 Sa	0442 1114 0452* 1044*	3.4 0.3 2.3 0.0	104 9 70 0
19 Su	0526 1159 0538* 1130*	3.6 0.1 2.4 -0.2	110 3 73 -6
20 M	0609 1242* 0623*	3.7 0.0 2.5	113 0 76
21 Tu ○	1215 0653 0125* 0708*	-0.3 3.8 -0.1 2.6	-9 116 -3 79
22 W	0102 0738 0208* 0755*	-0.4 3.9 -0.2 2.7	-12 119 -6 82
23 Th	0150 0823 0252* 0844*	-0.4 3.9 -0.3 2.8	-12 119 -9 85
24 F	0241 0910 0337* 0936*	-0.4 3.8 -0.3 2.9	-12 116 -9 88
25 Sa	0335 0959 0424* 1031*	-0.3 3.6 -0.3 3.0	-9 110 -9 91
26 Su	0434 1050 0513* 1130*	-0.1 3.3 -0.3 3.1	-3 101 -9 94
27 M	0538 1146 0605*	0.0 3.0 -0.3	0 91 -9
28 Tu ◑	1233 0648 1246* 0701*	3.2 0.1 2.8 -0.3	98 3 85 -9
29 W	0138 0801 0150* 0758*	3.3 0.2 2.5 -0.3	101 6 76 -9
30 Th	0242 0912 0255* 0857*	3.4 0.1 2.4 -0.3	104 3 73 -9
31 F	0343 1016 0358* 0955*	3.5 0.0 2.4 -0.3	107 0 73 -9

Heights are referred to mean lower water which is the chart datum of sounding. All times are local. Daylight Saving Time has been used when needed.

Fernandina Beach, Amelia River, Florida, 2011

Times and Heights of High and Low Waters

January

Day	Time (h m)	Height (ft)	Height (cm)
1 Sa	0613 1212* 0624*	6.5 -0.3 5.4	198 -9 165
2 Su	1215 0707 0106* 0717*	-0.7 6.6 -0.4 5.5	-21 201 -12 168
3 M	0108 0756 0155* 0806*	-0.8 6.7 -0.5 5.5	-24 204 -15 168
4 Tu ●	0156 0842 0239* 0852*	-0.7 6.6 -0.6 5.5	-21 201 -18 168
5 W	0241 0925 0321* 0935*	-0.6 6.5 -0.5 5.5	-18 198 -15 168
6 Th	0323 1004 0400* 1016*	-0.5 6.2 -0.4 5.4	-15 189 -12 165
7 F	0404 1042 0437* 1056*	-0.2 6.0 -0.2 5.4	-6 183 -6 165
8 Sa	0444 1119 0515* 1135*	0.1 5.7 -0.1 5.3	3 174 -3 162
9 Su	0526 1156 0554*	0.3 5.4 0.1	9 165 3
10 M	1216 0612 1234* 0635*	5.2 0.6 5.1 0.2	158 18 155 6
11 Tu	1258 0703 0116* 0721*	5.2 0.8 4.9 0.3	158 24 149 9
12 W ◐	0145 0759 0204* 0811*	5.2 0.9 4.7 0.3	158 27 143 9
13 Th	0238 0857 0258* 0904*	5.2 0.9 4.6 0.2	158 27 140 6
14 F	0337 0954 0357* 0958*	5.4 0.8 4.6 0.1	165 24 140 3
15 Sa	0438 1049 0458* 1052*	5.6 0.5 4.7 -0.2	171 15 143 -6
16 Su	0536 1143 0554* 1146*	5.9 0.3 5.0 -0.5	180 9 152 -15
17 M	0630 1235* 0647*	6.2 -0.1 5.3	189 -3 162
18 Tu	1238 0720 0123* 0738*	-0.8 6.6 -0.5 5.6	-24 201 -15 171
19 W ○	0129 0808 0210* 0827*	-1.1 6.8 -0.8 5.9	-34 207 -24 180
20 Th	0219 0856 0255* 0916*	-1.4 7.0 -1.1 6.1	-43 213 -34 186
21 F	0307 0943 0339* 1006*	-1.5 7.0 -1.3 6.3	-46 213 -40 192
22 Sa	0356 1031 0425* 1057*	-1.4 6.9 -1.3 6.4	-43 210 -40 195
23 Su	0448 1119 0513* 1149*	-1.2 6.6 -1.2 6.4	-37 201 -37 195
24 M	0543 1209* 0604*	-0.9 6.3 -1.0	-27 192 -30
25 Tu	1243 0643 0101* 0700*	6.3 -0.5 5.9 -0.8	192 -15 180 -24
26 W ◑	0141 0747 0157* 0800*	6.2 -0.2 5.5 -0.6	189 -6 168 -18
27 Th	0244 0852 0258* 0901*	6.1 0.0 5.2 -0.4	186 0 158 -12
28 F	0351 0955 0404* 1003*	6.0 0.1 5.1 -0.4	183 3 155 -12
29 Sa	0457 1056 0508* 1102*	6.0 0.0 5.1 -0.3	183 0 155 -9
30 Su	0557 1154 0607* 1159*	6.1 -0.1 5.2 -0.4	186 -3 158 -12
31 M	0650 1246* 0659*	6.2 -0.2 5.4	189 -6 165

February

Day	Time (h m)	Height (ft)	Height (cm)
1 Tu	1252 0737 0134* 0746*	-0.4 6.3 -0.3 5.5	-12 192 -9 168
2 W	0140 0820 0216* 0830*	-0.5 6.3 -0.4 5.6	-15 192 -12 171
3 Th ●	0223 0859 0254* 0910*	-0.5 6.2 -0.4 5.7	-15 189 -12 174
4 F	0303 0936 0329* 0948*	-0.4 6.1 -0.4 5.7	-12 186 -12 174
5 Sa	0341 1012 0403* 1025*	-0.2 5.9 -0.3 5.7	-6 180 -9 174
6 Su	0418 1046 0437* 1101*	0.0 5.6 -0.2 5.6	0 171 -6 171
7 M	0455 1121 0511* 1138*	0.2 5.4 0.0 5.6	6 165 0 171
8 Tu	0535 1157 0548*	0.5 5.2 0.2	15 158 6
9 W	1218 0620 1236* 0631*	5.5 0.7 5.0 0.3	168 21 152 9
10 Th	0101 0712 0121* 0721*	5.5 0.8 4.8 0.4	168 24 146 12
11 F ◐	0151 0810 0212* 0817*	5.4 0.9 4.7 0.3	165 27 143 9
12 Sa	0250 0911 0312* 0917*	5.5 0.8 4.7 0.2	168 24 143 6
13 Su	0355 1010 0418* 1017*	5.6 0.7 4.8 0.0	171 21 146 0
14 M	0500 1108 0521* 1117*	5.9 0.4 5.1 -0.3	180 12 155 -9
15 Tu	0600 1203* 0620*	6.3 0.0 5.6	192 0 171
16 W	1214 0654 1255* 0714*	-0.7 6.7 -0.5 6.0	-21 204 -15 183
17 Th	0109 0745 0144* 0806*	-1.1 6.9 -0.9 6.5	-34 210 -27 198
18 F ○	0202 0834 0230* 0857*	-1.4 7.1 -1.2 6.8	-43 216 -37 207
19 Sa	0253 0923 0316* 0948*	-1.5 7.1 -1.4 7.0	-46 216 -43 213
20 Su	0343 1011 0402* 1039*	-1.4 7.0 -1.4 7.1	-43 213 -43 216
21 M	0434 1100 0450* 1131*	-1.2 6.7 -1.3 7.0	-37 204 -40 213
22 Tu	0528 1150 0541*	-0.8 6.4 -0.9	-24 195 -27
23 W	1225 0626 1242* 0637*	6.8 -0.4 6.0 -0.6	207 -12 183 -18
24 Th ◑	0121 0728 0137* 0737*	6.5 0.0 5.6 -0.2	198 0 171 -6
25 F	0223 0832 0238* 0841*	6.2 0.3 5.3 0.0	189 9 162 0
26 Sa	0329 0935 0343* 0944*	6.0 0.4 5.2 0.2	183 12 158 6
27 Su	0434 1034 0447* 1044*	6.0 0.4 5.2 0.2	183 12 158 6
28 M	0534 1130 0546* 1141*	6.0 0.3 5.4 0.2	183 9 165 6

March

Day	Time (h m)	Height (ft)	Height (cm)
1 Tu	0626 1220* 0637*	6.1 0.2 5.6	186 6 171
2 W	1234 0711 0106* 0723*	0.1 6.2 0.0 5.8	3 189 0 177
3 Th	0121 0752 0146* 0804*	0.0 6.2 -0.1 6.0	0 189 -3 183
4 F ●	0203 0830 0223* 0842*	-0.1 6.2 -0.1 6.1	-3 189 -3 186
5 Sa	0242 0906 0257* 0919*	-0.1 6.1 -0.1 6.2	-3 186 -3 189
6 Su	0318 0942 0330* 0955*	0.0 6.0 -0.1 6.2	0 183 -3 189
7 M	0353 1016 0402* 1030*	0.1 5.8 0.0 6.2	3 177 0 189
8 Tu	0429 1051 0435* 1106*	0.3 5.6 0.2 6.1	9 171 6 186
9 W	0506 1126 0510* 1144*	0.5 5.4 0.3 6.0	15 165 9 183
10 Th	0547 1205* 0551*	0.7 5.3 0.5	21 162 15
11 F	1226 0635 1248* 0640*	5.9 0.9 5.1 0.6	180 27 155 18
12 Sa ◐	0114 0732 0138* 0739*	5.9 1.0 5.1 0.6	180 30 155 18
13 Su	0311 0933 0337* 0943*	5.9 1.0 5.1 0.5	180 30 155 15
14 M	0416 1035 0444* 1048*	5.9 0.8 5.3 0.3	180 24 162 9
15 Tu	0525 1134 0552* 1151*	6.2 0.5 5.6 0.0	189 15 171 0
16 W	0628 1230* 0654*	6.5 0.1 6.2	198 3 189
17 Th	1252 0726 0124* 0751*	-0.4 6.8 -0.4 6.7	-12 207 -12 204
18 F	0150 0819 0215* 0845*	-0.8 7.1 -0.8 7.2	-24 216 -24 219
19 Sa ○	0245 0910 0304* 0937*	-1.1 7.2 -1.1 7.6	-34 219 -34 232
20 Su	0337 1000 0352* 1029*	-1.2 7.2 -1.3 7.7	-37 219 -40 235
21 M	0428 1051 0439* 1121*	-1.2 7.1 -1.2 7.7	-37 216 -37 235
22 Tu	0519 1141 0528*	-0.9 6.8 -0.9	-27 207 -27
23 W	1213 0611 1232* 0618*	7.5 -0.5 6.5 -0.5	229 -15 198 -15
24 Th	0106 0707 0124* 0714*	7.2 -0.1 6.2 -0.1	219 -3 189 -3
25 F	0201 0807 0218* 0814*	6.8 0.3 5.8 0.3	207 9 177 9
26 Sa ◑	0259 0909 0316* 0918*	6.4 0.6 5.6 0.7	195 18 171 21
27 Su	0400 1009 0418* 1022*	6.2 0.7 5.5 0.8	189 21 168 24
28 M	0503 1106 0521* 1122*	6.0 0.8 5.6 0.8	183 24 171 24
29 Tu	0601 1158 0618*	6.0 0.7 5.7	183 21 174
30 W	1218 0652 1246* 0708*	0.8 6.0 0.6 6.0	24 183 18 183
31 Th	0110 0737 0130* 0753*	0.7 6.1 0.4 6.3	21 186 12 192

April

Day	Time (h m)	Height (ft)	Height (cm)
1 F	0157 0818 0211* 0834*	0.5 6.1 0.3 6.5	15 186 9 198
2 Sa	0239 0857 0248* 0913*	0.4 6.2 0.2 6.7	12 189 6 204
3 Su ●	0318 0935 0323* 0950*	0.3 6.1 0.2 6.7	9 186 6 204
4 M	0355 1012 0357* 1026*	0.3 6.0 0.2 6.7	9 183 6 204
5 Tu	0430 1048 0430* 1102*	0.4 5.9 0.3 6.7	12 180 9 204
6 W	0505 1124 0504* 1139*	0.5 5.8 0.4 6.6	15 177 12 201
7 Th	0542 1201* 0540*	0.6 5.6 0.5	18 171 15
8 F	1218 0622 1241* 0622*	6.5 0.8 5.5 0.6	198 24 168 18
9 Sa	0100 0709 0125* 0712*	6.4 0.9 5.5 0.7	195 27 168 21
10 Su	0149 0804 0215* 0812*	6.4 1.0 5.5 0.8	195 30 168 24
11 M ◐	0243 0904 0313* 0918*	6.3 0.9 5.6 0.7	192 27 171 21
12 Tu	0345 1004 0419* 1025*	6.3 0.7 5.8 0.6	192 21 177 18
13 W	0452 1102 0526* 1130*	6.4 0.4 6.2 0.3	195 12 189 9
14 Th	0557 1159 0630*	6.6 0.1 6.8	201 3 207
15 F	1232 0657 1254* 0729*	-0.1 6.8 -0.3 7.3	-3 207 -9 223
16 Sa	0131 0752 0147* 0824*	-0.4 7.0 -0.7 7.8	-12 213 -21 238
17 Su	0227 0846 0239* 0917*	-0.7 7.1 -0.9 8.0	-21 216 -27 244
18 M ○	0321 0938 0328* 1010*	-0.8 7.1 -1.0 8.1	-24 216 -30 247
19 Tu	0412 1030 0417* 1102*	-0.8 7.0 -0.8 8.0	-24 213 -24 244
20 W	0502 1121 0506* 1154*	-0.6 6.8 -0.5 7.7	-18 207 -15 235
21 Th	0553 1213* 0557*	-0.2 6.5 -0.1	-6 198 -3
22 F	1246 0647 0105* 0651*	7.4 0.2 6.2 0.4	226 6 189 12
23 Sa	0138 0743 0157* 0750*	7.0 0.5 6.0 0.8	213 15 183 24
24 Su	0231 0841 0252* 0852*	6.5 0.8 5.8 1.1	198 24 177 34
25 M ◑	0326 0938 0349* 0955*	6.2 0.9 5.8 1.3	189 27 177 40
26 Tu	0422 1030 0447* 1054*	6.0 0.9 5.8 1.3	183 27 177 40
27 W	0517 1119 0542* 1148*	5.9 0.9 6.0 1.2	180 27 183 37
28 Th	0608 1205* 0632*	5.9 0.8 6.3	180 24 192
29 F	1239 0655 1249* 0718*	1.1 5.9 0.6 6.5	34 180 18 198
30 Sa	0126 0739 0131* 0801*	0.9 5.9 0.5 6.8	27 180 15 207

May

Day	Time (h m)	Height (ft)	Height (cm)
1 Su	0210 0821 0211* 0841*	0.7 6.0 0.4 6.9	21 183 12 210
2 M	0251 0902 0249* 0921*	0.6 6.0 0.4 7.0	18 183 12 213
3 Tu ●	0329 0942 0326* 0959*	0.5 6.0 0.4 7.0	15 183 12 213
4 W	0406 1022 0402* 1038*	0.5 5.9 0.4 7.0	15 180 12 213
5 Th	0443 1101 0439* 1118*	0.5 5.8 0.4 6.9	15 177 12 210
6 F	0521 1141 0518* 1159*	0.6 5.7 0.5 6.9	18 174 15 210
7 Sa	0603 1223* 0602*	0.7 5.7 0.6	21 174 18
8 Su	1243 0649 0109* 0654*	6.8 0.7 5.7 0.7	207 21 174 21
9 M	0131 0742 0200* 0754*	6.7 0.7 5.8 0.8	204 21 177 24
10 Tu ◐	0223 0839 0257* 0900*	6.6 0.6 6.0 0.8	201 18 183 24
11 W	0321 0937 0400* 1007*	6.5 0.4 6.3 0.6	198 12 192 18
12 Th	0423 1034 0505* 1111*	6.5 0.2 6.7 0.4	198 6 204 12
13 F	0527 1131 0609*	6.5 -0.1 7.1	198 -3 216
14 Sa	1213 0629 1226* 0708*	0.1 6.6 -0.4 7.6	3 201 -12 232
15 Su	0113 0727 0121* 0805*	-0.1 6.7 -0.6 7.9	-3 204 -18 241
16 M	0210 0823 0214* 0859*	-0.3 6.7 -0.7 8.0	-9 204 -21 244
17 Tu ○	0304 0917 0306* 0952*	-0.5 6.7 -0.7 8.0	-15 204 -21 244
18 W	0355 1010 0356* 1044*	-0.4 6.6 -0.5 7.9	-12 201 -15 241
19 Th	0444 1102 0445* 1135*	-0.3 6.5 -0.3 7.6	-9 198 -9 232
20 F	0534 1153 0535*	0.0 6.3 0.1	0 192 3
21 Sa	1224 0623 1243* 0626*	7.2 0.2 6.1 0.6	219 6 186 18
22 Su	0112 0715 0133* 0722*	6.8 0.5 6.0 1.0	207 15 183 30
23 M	0200 0807 0223* 0821*	6.5 0.7 5.9 1.3	198 21 180 40
24 Tu ◑	0247 0859 0314* 0921*	6.1 0.8 5.8 1.4	186 24 177 43
25 W	0336 0948 0407* 1018*	5.8 0.8 5.9 1.5	177 24 180 46
26 Th	0427 1035 0459* 1111*	5.7 0.8 6.1 1.4	174 24 186 43
27 F	0518 1120 0551*	5.6 0.7 6.3	171 21 192
28 Sa	1202 0609 1205* 0639*	1.3 5.6 0.6 6.5	40 171 18 198
29 Su	1250 0657 1249* 0725*	1.1 5.6 0.5 6.7	34 171 15 204
30 M	0137 0744 0132* 0809*	0.9 5.7 0.4 6.9	27 174 12 210
31 Tu	0220 0828 0215* 0852*	0.7 5.8 0.3 7.0	21 177 9 213

June

Day	Time (h m)	Height (ft)	Height (cm)
1 W ●	0302 0912 0256* 0934*	0.6 5.8 0.2 7.1	18 177 6 216
2 Th	0342 0955 0337* 1016*	0.4 5.8 0.2 7.1	12 177 6 216
3 F	0421 1038 0418* 1059*	0.4 5.8 0.2 7.1	12 177 6 216
4 Sa	0502 1123 0501* 1143*	0.3 5.8 0.2 7.0	9 177 6 213
5 Su	0544 1209* 0548*	0.3 5.9 0.3	9 180 9
6 M	1228 0631 1257* 0641*	6.9 0.3 6.0 0.4	210 9 183 12
7 Tu	0115 0721 0149* 0741*	6.8 0.2 6.1 0.5	207 6 186 15
8 W	0206 0816 0244* 0846*	6.6 0.1 6.3 0.6	201 3 192 18
9 Th ◐	0301 0913 0344* 0951*	6.5 0.0 6.6 0.5	198 0 201 15
10 F	0400 1009 0447* 1054*	6.3 -0.2 6.9 0.4	192 -6 210 12
11 Sa	0502 1106 0551* 1155*	6.2 -0.3 7.2 0.2	189 -9 219 6
12 Su	0605 1202* 0651*	6.2 -0.4 7.4	189 -12 226
13 M	1255 0705 1258* 0749*	0.0 6.2 -0.5 7.6	0 189 -15 232
14 Tu	0152 0802 0153* 0843*	-0.1 6.3 -0.6 7.7	-3 192 -18 235
15 W ○	0246 0857 0246* 0935*	-0.2 6.3 -0.5 7.7	-6 192 -15 235
16 Th	0337 0950 0337* 1026*	-0.2 6.2 -0.4 7.5	-6 189 -12 229
17 F	0425 1041 0425* 1114*	-0.2 6.2 -0.1 7.2	-6 189 -3 219
18 Sa	0511 1131 0513* 1159*	0.0 6.1 0.2 6.9	0 186 6 210
19 Su	0556 1218* 0601*	0.2 5.9 0.6	6 180 18
20 M	1243 0642 0104* 0651*	6.6 0.4 5.9 1.0	201 12 180 30
21 Tu	0124 0728 0149* 0745*	6.2 0.6 5.8 1.2	189 18 177 37
22 W	0206 0814 0235* 0841*	5.9 0.7 5.8 1.4	180 21 177 43
23 Th ◑	0250 0901 0323* 0936*	5.6 0.7 5.9 1.5	171 21 180 46
24 F	0337 0948 0413* 1030*	5.4 0.7 6.0 1.4	165 21 183 43
25 Sa	0428 1034 0506* 1121*	5.3 0.6 6.1 1.3	162 18 186 40
26 Su	0521 1121 0558*	5.3 0.6 6.3	162 18 192
27 M	1211 0614 1208* 0649*	1.1 5.3 0.4 6.6	34 162 12 201
28 Tu	0100 0705 1255* 0737*	0.9 5.4 0.3 6.8	27 165 9 207
29 W	0147 0754 0142* 0824*	0.7 5.6 0.2 7.0	21 171 6 213
30 Th	0232 0842 0229* 0909*	0.5 5.7 0.0 7.1	15 174 0 216

Heights are referred to mean lower water which is the chart datum of sounding. All times are local. Daylight Saving Time has been used when needed.

Fernandina Beach, Amelia River, Florida, 2011

Times and Heights of High and Low Waters

July

Day	Time (h m)	Height (h)	Height (cm)
16 F ●	0316 0929 1018 0954*	0.2 6.6 -0.8 6.9	6 177 -24 219
17 Sa	0444 1105 0450* 1130*	0.1 6.0 -0.2 6.6	3 180 -6 201
18 Su	0525 1148 0534*	0.2 5.8 0.6	6 180 18
19 Tu	1209 0605 0619*	6.3 0.3 5.9 0.9	192 9 180 27
20 Tu	1248 0645 0112* 0706*	6.0 0.5 5.5 1.2	183 15 180 37
21 W	0727 0154* 0757*	5.7 0.7 5.9 1.3	174 18 180 40
22 Th	0207 0812 0239* 0851*	6.6 0.5 5.7 1.4	201 15 174 43
23 Sa ○	0251 0859 0324* 0945*	5.3 0.7 5.9 1.4	162 21 180 43
24 Su	0341 0948 0411* 1038*	5.2 0.7 6.0 1.3	158 21 183 40
25 Tu	0435 1038 0516* 1130*	5.5 0.6 6.2 1.2	168 18 189 37
26 Tu	0532 1129 0612*	5.5 0.5 6.4	158 15 195
27 W	1222 0628 0113* 0705*	1.0 5.4 0.5 6.7	30 165 15 204
28 Th	1222 0721 0113* 0755*	0.7 5.6 0.3 6.9	21 171 9 210
29 Sa	0201 0812 0239* 0843*	0.7 5.9 0.0 6.9	21 180 0 210
30 Sa ○	0247 0902 0253* 0930*	-0.2 6.4 -0.2 7.3	-6 192 -6 223
31 Su	0332 0902 0342* 1017	-0.2 6.5 -0.4 7.3	-6 198 -12 223
1 F ●	0316 0929 1016 0954*	0.1 5.9 -0.3 7.2	3 180 -9 219
2 Sa	0358 1016 0369* 1040*	-0.1 6.0 -0.2 7.2	-3 183 -6 219
3 Su	0440 1104 0446* 1125*	-6.1 6.0 -0.2 6.8	-18 180 -6 216
4 M	0524 1153 0535*	-0.2 6.1 -0.1	-6 189 -3
5 Tu	1212 0610 1243* 0629*	7.0 -0.2 5.9 0.1	213 -6 192 3
6 W	0100 0700 0135* 0728*	6.8 0.0 5.7 0.3	207 0 174 9
7 Th	0150 0753 0230* 0831*	6.6 0.2 5.5 0.4	201 6 168 12
8 F ◐	0243 0850 0329* 0936*	6.3 0.3 5.5 0.8	192 9 168 24
9 Sa	0341 0948 0431* 1038*	5.9 0.4 5.6 0.9	180 12 171 27
10 Su	0442 1045 0535* 1139*	6.0 0.3 5.9 0.7	183 9 180 21
11 M	0546 1143 0637*	5.9 0.4 6.1	180 12 186
12 Tu	1238 0647 1240* 0734*	7.2 0.2 5.9 0.6	219 6 180 18
13 W	0135 0745 0136* 0827*	5.9 0.1 6.0 0.7	180 3 183 21
14 Th	0228 0839 0345* 0917*	6.0 0.0 6.2 0.7	183 0 189 21
15 F ○	0317 0930 0319* 1004*	-0.1 6.3 -0.2 7.1	-3 192 -6 216

August

Day	Time (h m)	Height (h)	Height (cm)
16 Tu	0416 1043 1105*	-0.5 6.6 -7.2	-15 201 219
17 W	0500 1134 0522* 1153*	6.6 -0.4 6.9	201 -18 207 -12 210
18 W	0547 1226* 0616*	-0.6 6.1 -0.2	-18 186 -6
19 F	1242 0637 0119* 0714*	6.8 -0.5 6.9 0.1	207 -15 210 3
20 Sa	0133 0731 0214* 0816*	6.6 -0.4 6.9 0.3	201 -12 210 9
21 Su ○	0227 0829 0313* 0920*	6.3 -0.3 6.9 0.5	192 -9 210 15
22 Th	0324 0929 0416* 1023*	6.0 -0.2 6.9 0.5	183 -6 210 15
23 Sa	0426 1029 0521* 1123*	5.9 -0.1 6.8 0.5	180 -3 207 15
24 Su	0500 1128 0624*	5.8 0.1 6.9	177 3 210
25 Th	0212 0810 0244* 0900*	6.3 -0.3 6.9 0.5	192 -9 210 15
26 Sa	0259 0857 0337* 0956*	5.7 -0.2 6.9 0.5	162 -6 210 15
27 Sa	0354 0958 0521* 1051*	5.3 -0.2 6.9 0.5	162 -6 210 15
28 Su	0453 1054 0535* 1145*	5.4 -0.4 6.9 1.0	165 -12 210 30
29 Th	0553 1237 0632*	5.6 0.7 6.7	171 21 204
30 Tu	0128 0651 0141* 0815*	6.3 0.2 6.2 1.3	192 6 189 40
31 W	0217 0837 0253* 0904*	6.1 0.1 6.1 1.4	186 3 186 46

September

Day	Time (h m)	Height (h)	Height (cm)
1 Sa	0523 1157 0556*	0.6 6.4 1.1	18 195 34
2 Su	1215 0814 0101* 0637	5.7 5.7 0.5 1.3	174 174 18 40
3 M	1255 0639 0119* 0724*	5.6 0.6 6.3 1.3	171 18 192 40
4 Su ○	0137 0727 0205* 0818	6.3 0.3 6.2 1.5	192 9 189 46
5 M	0222 0258* 0916*	5.9 0.3 5.9 1.5	180 9 180 46
6 Th	0318 0356* 1013*	5.4 0.4 6.0 1.5	165 12 183 46
7 W	0419 0458* 1109*	5.6 0.5 6.5 0.8	171 24 198 6
8 Th	0524 0558*	5.9 0.7 6.7	180 21 204
9 F	0623 1222* 0654*	6.1 0.4 6.8	186 18 207 21
10 Sa	0720 0107* 0747*	6.0 0.3 7.0	180 12 213
11 Tu	0814 0215* 0838*	5.6 0.2 7.4	171 6 226
12 M ○	0907 0324* 0948*	5.6 0.4 7.4	171 12 226
13 Tu	0959 0416* 1031*	5.3 0.7 7.3	162 21 223
14 W	1053 0504* 1112*	5.6 0.6 7.1	171 24 216
15 Th	0501 1147 0544* 1138*	6.6 0.6 6.9 -0.3	201 27 210 -9

October

Day	Time (h m)	Height (h)	Height (cm)
16 Su	0526 1206* 0607*	6.9 -0.5 7.6 0.1	210 -15 232 3
17 M	0606 1248* 0652*	-0.4 7.3 0.4	-3 223 12
18 Tu	0653 0134* 0743*	6.3 -0.3 7.0 0.3	192 -9 213 9
19 W	0748 0225* 0840*	6.1 -0.2 6.7 0.3	186 -6 204 9
20 Th	0852 0321* 0938*	5.9 -0.1 6.5 0.7	180 -3 198 21
21 F	0956 0422* 1035*	5.8 0.4 6.4 0.7	177 12 195 18
22 Sa	1100 0524* 1130*	6.1 0.4 6.5 0.3	186 12 198 6
23 Su	0558 1201* 0624*	6.6 0.3 6.5	201 9 198
24 M	0657 0100* 0720*	0.2 6.3 0.6	-6 192 18
25 Tu	0753 0157* 0814*	0.0 6.0 0.7	-15 183 21
26 W ●	0209 0941 0343* 0959*	-0.2 6.1 -0.9 7.0	-6 186 -27 213
27 Th	0300 0343* 0959*	-1.0 6.8 -0.8 6.9	-30 207 -24 213
28 F	0350 0416* 1052*	-1.0 6.8 -0.8 6.8	-30 207 -24 207
29 Sa	0440 1129 0526* 1145*	-0.9 7.0 -0.8 6.6	-27 213 -24 201
30 Su	0531 1223* 0620*	-0.9 7.8 -0.6	-27 238 -18
31 M	1239 0625 0117* 0716*	6.4 -0.7 7.1 -0.2	195 -21 216 -9

November

Day	Time (h m)	Height (h)	Height (cm)
16 W	0529 1209* 0614*	6.1 0.6 0.5	186 18 207 15
17 Th	1233 0624 0135* 0708*	5.9 0.7 6.4 0.7	180 21 195 21
18 F	0126 0727 0151* 0805*	5.8 0.6 6.1 0.7	177 27 186 21
19 Sa	0225 0833 0250* 0903*	5.8 0.5 5.9 0.6	177 15 180 18
20 Su	0329 0938 0353* 1000*	5.9 0.6 6.1 0.6	186 30 189 18
21 Su	0435 1041 0456* 1056*	6.1 0.6 6.2 0.5	186 27 189 15
22 Tu	0537 1142 0556* 1152*	6.3 0.7 7.0 0.8	192 21 213 -24
23 W	0635 1240* 0652*	6.4 0.7 6.5	226 -18 195
24 Th ●	1247 0735 0135* 0747*	7.8 -1.1 7.5 -0.5	238 -34 229 -15
25 F	0135 0825 0228* 0841*	7.8 -1.2 7.8 -0.9	238 -37 238 -27
26 Sa	0232 0845 0318* 0934*	7.5 -1.2 7.7 -0.8	229 -37 235 -24
27 Su	0322 0924 0408* 1026*	6.9 -1.1 7.5 -0.6	210 -30 229 -18
28 M	0412 1002 0458* 1118*	7.2 -1.1 7.2 -0.4	219 -21 219 -12
29 Tu	0503 1152 0549*	-0.9 7.0 -0.3	-27 213 -9
30 W	1209 0558 1240* 0642*	6.1 -0.7 6.5 0.4	186 -21 198 12

December

Day	Time (h m)	Height (h)	Height (cm)
16 F	1214 0606 1234* 0640*	5.5 0.0 5.9 -0.2	168 0 186 -6
17 Sa	0106 0708 0126* 0736*	5.7 0.1 5.9 -0.3	174 3 180 -9
18 Su ○	0203 0813 0219* 0834*	5.8 0.9 6.1 -0.4	177 27 186 -12
19 M	0307 0919 0326* 0934*	6.1 0.9 5.6 -0.6	186 9 171 -18
20 Tu	0415 1023 0432* 1032*	6.3 0.7 5.6 -0.8	192 3 171 -24
21 W	1124 0535* 1131*	6.6 0.6 5.7 -1.0	201 -12 174 -30
22 Th	0621 1223* 0635*	6.9 0.8 5.8	210 -18 177
23 F	1228 0719* 0131* 0735*	-1.2 7.2 -0.8 6.0	-37 219 -24 183
24 Sa ●	0123 0812 0212* 0825*	-1.3 7.3 -0.9 6.0	-40 223 -27 183
25 Su	0216 0903 0301* 0916*	-1.3 7.2 -1.0 6.0	-40 219 -30 183
26 M	0305 0952 0347* 1006*	-1.1 7.0 -0.9 5.9	-34 213 -27 180
27 Tu	0353 1039 0434* 1054*	-0.8 6.7 -0.7 6.1	-24 204 -21 177
28 W	0441 1123 0518* 1141*	-0.5 6.4 -0.4 6.3	-15 195 -12 171
29 Th	0530 1206* 0603*	-0.2 6.3 -0.1 6.3	0 180 -3
30 F	1226 0622 1248* 0651*	5.5 0.4 5.5 0.1	168 12 168 3
31 Sa	0112 0718 0132* 0739*	5.3 0.2 5.1 0.2	162 6 155 6

Heights are referred to mean lower water which is the chart datum of sounding. All times are local. Daylight Saving Time has been used when needed.

SKIPPER'S HANDBOOK

Miami, Government Cut, Florida, 2010

Times and Heights of High and Low Waters

Heights are referred to mean lower water which is the chart datum of sounding. All times are local. Daylight Saving Time has been used when needed.

Miami, Government Cut, Florida, 2011

Times and Heights of High and Low Waters

January

Day	Time (h m)	Height (ft)	Height (cm)
1 Sa	0608 1147 0613*	2.5 0.2 2.3	76 6 70
2 Su	1208 0700 1238* 0705*	-0.4 2.5 0.1 2.4	-12 76 3 73
3 M	1257 0747 0126* 0753*	-0.4 2.5 0.0 2.4	-12 76 0 73
4 Tu ●	0143 0830 0211* 0837*	-0.4 2.5 0.0 2.4	-12 76 0 73
5 W	0227 0911 0254* 0919*	-0.3 2.5 0.0 2.3	-9 76 0 70
6 Th	0309 0949 0336* 1000*	-0.3 2.4 0.0 2.3	-9 73 0 70
7 F	0350 1025 0416* 1040*	-0.2 2.4 0.0 2.2	-6 73 0 67
8 Sa	0430 1101 0456* 1121*	0.0 2.3 0.0 2.1	0 70 0 64
9 Su	0510 1138 0537*	0.1 2.1 0.1	3 64 3
10 M	1203 0551 1216* 0620*	2.0 0.2 2.0 0.1	61 6 61 3
11 Tu	1248 0637 1257* 0706*	1.9 0.4 1.9 0.2	58 12 58 6
12 W ◐	0139 0728 0143* 0758*	1.9 0.4 1.9 0.2	58 12 58 6
13 Th	0235 0825 0236* 0853*	1.8 0.5 1.8 0.1	55 15 55 3
14 F	0336 0925 0335* 0949*	1.9 0.5 1.8 0.0	58 15 55 0
15 Sa	0437 1022 0437* 1043*	1.9 0.4 1.9 -0.1	58 12 58 -3
16 Su	0535 1116 0536* 1135*	2.1 0.3 2.0 -0.3	64 9 61 -9
17 M	0628 1206* 0631*	2.2 0.1 2.1	67 3 64
18 Tu	1224 0717 1255* 0724*	-0.4 2.4 0.0 2.3	-12 73 0 70
19 W ○	0113 0804 0142* 0814*	-0.6 2.5 -0.2 2.4	-18 76 -6 73
20 Th	0201 0849 0229* 0904*	-0.6 2.6 -0.4 2.5	-18 79 -12 76
21 F	0249 0934 0317* 0954*	-0.7 2.7 -0.5 2.6	-21 82 -15 79
22 Sa	0337 1020 0406* 1045*	-0.6 2.6 -0.6 2.6	-18 79 -18 79
23 Su	0428 1106 0457* 1138*	-0.5 2.6 -0.6 2.5	-15 79 -18 76
24 M	0521 1155 0551*	-0.3 2.5 -0.5	-9 76 -15
25 Tu	1234 0618 1247* 0650*	2.4 -0.2 2.3 -0.5	73 -6 70 -15
26 W ◑	0134 0720 0145* 0752*	2.3 0.0 2.2 -0.4	70 0 67 -12
27 Th	0238 0826 0248* 0857*	2.2 0.1 2.1 -0.3	67 3 64 -9
28 F	0346 0932 0355* 1001*	2.1 0.2 2.0 -0.3	64 6 61 -9
29 Sa	0453 1035 0500* 1100*	2.1 0.2 2.0 -0.3	64 6 61 -9
30 Su	0552 1133 0559* 1154*	2.2 0.1 2.1 -0.3	67 3 64 -9
31 M	0644 1224* 0651*	2.2 0.0 2.1	67 0 64

February

Day	Time (h m)	Height (ft)	Height (cm)
1 Tu	1243 0729 0110* 0737*	-0.4 2.3 -0.1 2.2	-12 70 -3 67
2 W	0127 0809 0152* 0819*	-0.4 2.3 -0.1 2.2	-12 70 -3 67
3 Th ●	0208 0846 0232* 0858*	-0.4 2.3 -0.2 2.2	-12 70 -6 67
4 F	0247 0920 0309* 0935*	-0.3 2.3 -0.2 2.2	-9 70 -6 67
5 Sa	0324 0954 0344* 1012*	-0.2 2.2 -0.2 2.2	-6 67 -6 67
6 Su	0359 1027 0419* 1049*	-0.1 2.2 -0.2 2.1	-3 67 -6 64
7 M	0434 1101 0454* 1128*	0.0 2.1 -0.1 2.0	0 64 -3 61
8 Tu	0510 1136 0531*	0.1 2.0 -0.1	3 61 -3
9 W	1209 0548 1213* 0612*	1.9 0.2 1.9 0.0	58 6 58 0
10 Th	1255 0634 1256* 0702*	1.9 0.3 1.8 0.0	58 9 55 0
11 F ◐	0149 0729 0148* 0801*	1.8 0.4 1.7 0.0	55 12 52 0
12 Sa	0251 0834 0251* 0905*	1.8 0.4 1.7 0.0	55 12 52 0
13 Su	0358 0941 0400* 1008*	1.8 0.4 1.8 -0.1	55 12 55 -3
14 M	0502 1043 0508* 1107*	2.0 0.2 1.9 -0.3	61 6 58 -9
15 Tu	0559 1139 0609*	2.2 0.0 2.1	67 0 64
16 W	1201 0650 1230* 0704*	-0.4 2.3 -0.2 2.4	-12 70 -6 73
17 Th	1253 0738 0119* 0757*	-0.6 2.5 -0.4 2.5	-18 76 -12 76
18 F ○	0142 0825 0208* 0847*	-0.7 2.6 -0.6 2.7	-21 79 -18 82
19 Sa	0232 0910 0256* 0937*	-0.7 2.7 -0.8 2.8	-21 82 -24 85
20 Su	0321 0956 0345* 1027*	-0.6 2.7 -0.8 2.7	-18 82 -24 82
21 M	0411 1043 0436* 1119*	-0.5 2.6 -0.8 2.6	-15 79 -24 79
22 Tu	0503 1132 0529*	-0.3 2.5 -0.6	-9 76 -18
23 W	1213 0558 1225* 0627*	2.5 -0.1 2.3 -0.5	76 -3 70 -15
24 Th ◑	0111 0659 0122* 0730*	2.3 0.0 2.2 -0.3	70 0 67 -9
25 F	0215 0804 0226* 0836*	2.1 0.2 2.0 -0.2	64 6 61 -6
26 Sa	0323 0912 0335* 0942*	2.0 0.3 1.9 -0.1	61 9 58 -3
27 Su	0430 1017 0443* 1043*	2.0 0.2 2.0 -0.1	61 6 61 -3
28 M	0530 1114 0542* 1137*	2.1 0.2 2.0 -0.1	64 6 61 -3

March

Day	Time (h m)	Height (ft)	Height (cm)
1 Tu	0621 1204* 0633*	2.1 0.1 2.1	64 3 64
2 W	1224 0704 1248* 0717*	-0.2 2.2 0.0 2.2	-6 67 0 67
3 Th	0107 0741 0128* 0757*	-0.2 2.2 -0.1 2.3	-6 67 -3 70
4 F ●	0146 0816 0204* 0834*	-0.2 2.3 -0.2 2.3	-6 70 -6 70
5 Sa	0222 0850 0239* 0910*	-0.2 2.3 -0.2 2.3	-6 70 -6 70
6 Su	0257 0923 0312* 0945*	-0.1 2.3 -0.2 2.3	-3 70 -6 70
7 M	0330 0956 0344* 1021*	0.0 2.2 -0.2 2.3	0 67 -6 70
8 Tu	0403 1029 0417* 1059*	0.0 2.2 -0.1 2.2	0 67 -3 67
9 W	0436 1103 0452* 1138*	0.1 2.1 -0.1 2.1	3 64 -3 64
10 Th	0513 1140 0532*	0.3 2.0 0.0	9 61 0
11 F	1223 0557 1222* 0621*	2.0 0.4 1.9 0.0	61 12 58 0
12 Sa ◐	0115 0651 0114* 0720*	1.9 0.4 1.9 0.1	58 12 58 3
13 Su	0315 0857 0320* 0929*	1.9 0.5 1.9 0.1	58 15 58 3
14 M	0422 1007 0433* 1037*	2.0 0.4 1.9 0.0	61 12 58 0
15 Tu	0527 1113 0544* 1140*	2.1 0.2 2.1 -0.1	64 6 64 -3
16 W	0627 1211* 0647*	2.3 0.0 2.3	70 0 70
17 Th	1238 0720 0105* 0745*	-0.3 2.4 -0.3 2.6	-9 73 -9 79
18 F	0132 0810 0156* 0838*	-0.4 2.6 -0.5 2.8	-12 79 -15 85
19 Sa ○	0223 0859 0245* 0929*	-0.5 2.7 -0.7 2.9	-15 82 -21 88
20 Su	0312 0946 0334* 1019*	-0.5 2.8 -0.8 3.0	-15 85 -24 91
21 M	0402 1033 0423* 1109*	-0.5 2.8 -0.8 2.9	-15 85 -24 88
22 Tu	0452 1121 0514*	-0.4 2.7 -0.7	-12 82 -21
23 W	1200 0544 1211* 0607*	2.8 -0.2 2.6 -0.5	85 -6 79 -15
24 Th	1252 0638 0104* 0704*	2.6 0.0 2.4 -0.3	79 0 73 -9
25 F	0148 0738 0201* 0806*	2.4 0.2 2.2 -0.1	73 6 67 -3
26 Sa ◑	0249 0842 0303* 0912*	2.2 0.3 2.1 0.1	67 9 64 3
27 Su	0353 0949 0411* 1018*	2.1 0.4 2.0 0.1	64 12 61 3
28 M	0457 1052 0517* 1118*	2.1 0.4 2.0 0.2	64 12 61 6
29 Tu	0556 1148 0617*	2.1 0.3 2.1	64 9 64
30 W	1211 0645 1236* 0707*	0.2 2.1 0.2 2.2	6 64 6 67
31 Th	1258 0728 0118* 0750*	0.1 2.2 0.1 2.3	3 67 3 70

April

Day	Time (h m)	Height (ft)	Height (cm)
1 F	0140 0806 0157* 0830*	0.1 2.3 0.0 2.4	3 70 0 73
2 Sa	0218 0842 0233* 0907*	0.1 2.3 -0.1 2.4	3 70 -3 73
3 Su ●	0254 0917 0307* 0944*	0.1 2.3 -0.1 2.5	3 70 -3 76
4 M	0329 0952 0340* 1020*	0.1 2.3 -0.1 2.5	3 70 -3 76
5 Tu	0402 1027 0413* 1057*	0.1 2.3 -0.1 2.4	3 70 -3 73
6 W	0436 1102 0447* 1136*	0.2 2.2 -0.1 2.4	6 67 -3 73
7 Th	0511 1138 0523*	0.3 2.2 0.0	9 67 0
8 F	1216 0549 1217* 0605*	2.3 0.3 2.1 0.0	70 9 64 0
9 Sa	0101 0634 0102* 0655*	2.2 0.4 2.1 0.1	67 12 64 3
10 Su	0151 0729 0157* 0754*	2.2 0.4 2.0 0.1	67 12 61 3
11 M ◐	0248 0833 0302* 0902*	2.1 0.4 2.0 0.2	64 12 61 6
12 Tu	0350 0941 0413* 1011*	2.2 0.3 2.1 0.1	67 9 64 3
13 W	0453 1045 0522* 1115*	2.2 0.1 2.3 0.0	67 3 70 0
14 Th	0553 1144 0626*	2.4 -0.1 2.5	73 -3 76
15 F	1214 0649 1239* 0725*	-0.1 2.5 -0.3 2.7	-3 76 -9 82
16 Sa	0109 0742 0132* 0819*	-0.2 2.7 -0.5 2.9	-6 82 -15 88
17 Su	0202 0833 0222* 0911*	-0.3 2.8 -0.7 3.0	-9 85 -21 91
18 M ○	0253 0922 0312* 1001*	-0.3 2.8 -0.7 3.0	-9 85 -21 91
19 Tu	0343 1012 0403* 1051*	-0.3 2.8 -0.7 3.0	-9 85 -21 91
20 W	0433 1101 0454* 1141*	-0.2 2.7 -0.6 2.8	-6 82 -18 85
21 Th	0525 1151 0546*	0.0 2.6 -0.4	0 79 -12
22 F	1232 0619 1243* 0642*	2.7 0.1 2.4 -0.2	82 3 73 -6
23 Sa	0124 0716 0138* 0741*	2.5 0.2 2.3 0.0	76 6 70 0
24 Su	0219 0817 0237* 0843*	2.3 0.3 2.2 0.2	70 9 67 6
25 M ◑	0316 0919 0339* 0945*	2.2 0.4 2.1 0.3	67 12 64 9
26 Tu	0413 1018 0442* 1043*	2.1 0.4 2.1 0.4	64 12 64 12
27 W	0508 1111 0540* 1136*	2.1 0.3 2.1 0.4	64 9 64 12
28 Th	0558 1159 0631*	2.1 0.2 2.2	64 6 67
29 F	1223 0643 1241* 0716*	0.4 2.1 0.1 2.3	12 64 3 70
30 Sa	0106 0725 0121* 0758*	0.3 2.2 0.0 2.4	9 67 0 73

May

Day	Time (h m)	Height (ft)	Height (cm)
1 Su	0146 0805 0158* 0838*	0.3 2.3 0.0 2.4	9 70 0 73
2 M	0224 0844 0235* 0917*	0.3 2.3 -0.1 2.5	9 70 -3 76
3 Tu ●	0300 0922 0310* 0957*	0.2 2.3 -0.1 2.5	6 70 -3 76
4 W	0336 1001 0346* 1036*	0.2 2.3 -0.1 2.5	6 70 -3 76
5 Th	0412 1039 0423* 1117*	0.3 2.3 -0.1 2.5	9 70 -3 76
6 F	0451 1120 0503* 1159*	0.3 2.2 -0.1 2.4	9 67 -3 73
7 Sa	0533 1203* 0547*	0.3 2.2 0.0	9 67 0
8 Su	1244 0620 1252* 0638*	2.4 0.3 2.2 0.0	73 9 67 0
9 M	0132 0714 0147* 0736*	2.3 0.3 2.2 0.1	70 9 67 3
10 Tu ◐	0225 0815 0249* 0841*	2.3 0.3 2.2 0.2	70 9 67 6
11 W	0321 0918 0356* 0947*	2.3 0.1 2.3 0.2	70 3 70 6
12 Th	0421 1021 0503* 1052*	2.3 0.0 2.4 0.1	70 0 73 3
13 F	0521 1120 0606* 1152*	2.4 -0.2 2.6 0.1	73 -6 79 3
14 Sa	0620 1216* 0705*	2.5 -0.4 2.7	76 -12 82
15 Su	1248 0716 0110* 0801*	0.0 2.6 -0.5 2.8	0 79 -15 85
16 M	0142 0810 0202* 0853*	-0.1 2.6 -0.6 2.9	-3 79 -18 88
17 Tu ○	0234 0902 0253* 0944*	-0.1 2.7 -0.6 2.9	-3 82 -18 88
18 W	0324 0952 0343* 1033*	-0.1 2.7 -0.6 2.9	-3 82 -18 88
19 Th	0415 1042 0434* 1121*	-0.1 2.6 -0.5 2.8	-3 79 -15 85
20 F	0506 1132 0525*	0.0 2.5 -0.3	0 76 -9
21 Sa	1209 0558 1222* 0617*	2.6 0.1 2.4 -0.1	79 3 73 -3
22 Su	1257 0651 0113* 0711*	2.5 0.2 2.3 0.1	76 6 70 3
23 M	0144 0746 0206* 0807*	2.3 0.3 2.1 0.3	70 9 64 9
24 Tu ◑	0233 0842 0301* 0904*	2.2 0.3 2.1 0.4	67 9 64 12
25 W	0322 0936 0357* 1000*	2.1 0.3 2.0 0.4	64 9 61 12
26 Th	0412 1027 0453* 1052*	2.0 0.3 2.0 0.5	61 9 61 15
27 F	0503 1115 0547* 1142*	2.0 0.2 2.1 0.5	61 6 64 15
28 Sa	0552 1200* 0637*	2.0 0.1 2.2	61 3 67
29 Su	1227 0640 1242* 0723*	0.4 2.1 0.0 2.3	12 64 0 70
30 M	0110 0726 0123* 0808*	0.4 2.1 0.0 2.3	12 64 0 70
31 Tu	0152 0810 0203* 0851*	0.3 2.2 -0.1 2.4	9 67 -3 73

June

Day	Time (h m)	Height (ft)	Height (cm)
1 W ●	0231 0854 0242* 0934*	0.3 2.2 -0.2 2.5	9 67 -6 76
2 Th	0311 0937 0322* 1016*	0.2 2.3 -0.2 2.5	6 70 -6 76
3 F	0351 1020 0403* 1059*	0.2 2.3 -0.2 2.5	6 70 -6 76
4 Sa	0433 1105 0446* 1142*	0.2 2.3 -0.2 2.5	6 70 -6 76
5 Su	0518 1152 0533*	0.1 2.3 -0.2	3 70 -6
6 M	1226 0607 1242* 0624*	2.5 0.1 2.3 -0.1	76 3 70 -3
7 Tu	0113 0700 0137* 0721*	2.4 0.0 2.3 0.0	73 0 70 0
8 W	0202 0757 0236* 0822*	2.4 0.0 2.3 0.1	73 0 70 3
9 Th ◐	0256 0857 0339* 0927*	2.3 -0.1 2.3 0.1	70 -3 70 3
10 F	0353 0958 0444* 1030*	2.3 -0.2 2.4 0.2	70 -6 73 6
11 Sa	0454 1058 0548* 1131*	2.3 -0.3 2.5 0.1	70 -9 76 3
12 Su	0555 1156 0648*	2.4 -0.4 2.6	73 -12 79
13 M	1229 0655 1251* 0745*	0.1 2.4 -0.5 2.7	3 73 -15 82
14 Tu	0124 0751 0145* 0838*	0.0 2.5 -0.6 2.7	0 76 -18 82
15 W ○	0216 0845 0236* 0928*	0.0 2.5 -0.5 2.7	0 76 -15 82
16 Th	0307 0936 0326* 1015*	0.0 2.5 -0.5 2.7	0 76 -15 82
17 F	0357 1024 0414* 1100*	0.0 2.5 -0.4 2.6	0 76 -12 79
18 Sa	0445 1111 0502* 1143*	0.0 2.4 -0.3 2.5	0 73 -9 76
19 Su	0533 1158 0550*	0.0 2.3 -0.1	0 70 -3
20 M	1225 0621 1244* 0637*	2.4 0.1 2.2 0.1	73 3 67 3
21 Tu	0107 0709 0130* 0726*	2.3 0.1 2.1 0.2	70 3 64 6
22 W	0148 0758 0219* 0817*	2.2 0.2 2.0 0.4	67 6 61 12
23 Th ◑	0231 0847 0310* 0910*	2.1 0.2 2.0 0.5	64 6 61 15
24 F	0317 0938 0403* 1003*	2.0 0.2 2.0 0.5	61 6 61 15
25 Sa	0407 1027 0459* 1055*	1.9 0.2 2.0 0.5	58 6 61 15
26 Su	0500 1116 0555* 1145*	1.9 0.1 2.0 0.5	58 3 61 15
27 M	0555 1203* 0648*	2.0 0.0 2.1	61 0 64
28 Tu	1233 0648 1248* 0737*	0.4 2.0 -0.1 2.3	12 61 -3 70
29 W	0118 0738 0133* 0824*	0.4 2.1 -0.2 2.4	12 64 -6 73
30 Th	0202 0827 0216* 0910*	0.3 2.2 -0.2 2.5	9 67 -6 76

Heights are referred to mean lower water which is the chart datum of sounding. All times are local. Daylight Saving Time has been used when needed.

Miami, Government Cut, Florida, 2011

Times and Heights of High and Low Waters

July

Day	Time h m	Height ft	Height cm	Day	Time h m	Height ft	Height cm
1 F ●	0246 0914 0300* 0954*	0.2 2.3 -0.3 2.5	6 70 -9 76	16 Sa	0336 1005 0353* 1035*	0.0 2.5 -0.2 2.6	0 76 -6 79
2 Sa	0330 1001 0344* 1037*	0.1 2.4 -0.3 2.6	3 73 -9 79	17 Su	0420 1048 0437* 1113*	0.0 2.4 -0.1 2.5	0 73 -3 76
3 Su	0414 1049 0430* 1121*	0.0 2.4 -0.3 2.6	0 73 -9 79	18 M	0503 1130 0519* 1151*	0.0 2.4 0.0 2.4	0 73 0 73
4 M	0501 1138 0518*	-0.1 2.5 -0.3	-3 76 -9	19 Tu	0545 1211* 0601*	0.1 2.3 0.1	3 70 3
5 Tu	1205 0549 1229* 0610*	2.6 -0.2 2.5 -0.2	79 -6 76 -6	20 W	1227 0627 1253* 0643*	2.3 0.1 2.2 0.3	70 3 67 9
6 W	1251 0642 0123* 0705*	2.5 -0.2 2.4 0.0	76 -6 73 0	21 Th	0105 0709 0137* 0728*	2.2 0.2 2.1 0.4	67 6 64 12
7 Th	0140 0738 0220* 0805*	2.5 -0.2 2.4 0.1	76 -6 73 3	22 F	0145 0755 0224* 0816*	2.1 0.2 2.1 0.5	64 6 64 15
8 F ◐	0233 0837 0322* 0908*	2.4 -0.3 2.4 0.2	73 -9 73 6	23 Sa ◑	0228 0844 0316* 0910*	2.0 0.3 2.0 0.6	61 9 61 18
9 Sa	0331 0939 0426* 1012*	2.3 -0.3 2.4 0.2	70 -9 73 6	24 Su	0317 0937 0413* 1006*	2.0 0.3 2.0 0.7	61 9 61 21
10 Su	0434 1041 0532* 1114*	2.3 -0.3 2.4 0.2	70 -9 73 6	25 M	0413 1031 0513* 1103*	2.0 0.2 2.1 0.6	61 6 64 18
11 M	0538 1140 0634*	2.3 -0.3 2.5	70 -9 76	26 Tu	0513 1125 0612* 1156*	2.0 0.2 2.2 0.5	61 6 67 15
12 Tu	1213 0640 1237* 0731*	0.2 2.3 -0.4 2.5	6 70 -12 76	27 W	0613 1216* 0706*	2.1 0.0 2.3	64 0 70
13 W	0109 0737 0131* 0823*	0.1 2.4 -0.4 2.6	3 73 -12 79	28 Th	1246 0709 0104* 0756*	0.4 2.2 -0.1 2.5	12 67 -3 76
14 Th	0201 0830 0221* 0910*	0.1 2.4 -0.4 2.6	3 73 -12 79	29 F	0134 0802 0151* 0842*	0.3 2.4 -0.2 2.6	9 73 -6 79
15 F ○	0250 0919 0308* 0954*	0.0 2.5 -0.3 2.6	0 76 -9 79	30 Sa ●	0220 0852 0238* 0927*	0.1 2.5 -0.3 2.7	3 76 -9 82
				31 Su	0306 0942 0325* 1011*	0.0 2.6 -0.3 2.8	0 79 -9 85

August

Day	Time h m	Height ft	Height cm	Day	Time h m	Height ft	Height cm
1 M	0352 1031 0412* 1056*	-0.2 2.7 -0.3 2.8	-6 82 -9 85	16 Tu	0429 1100 0447* 1114*	0.1 2.6 0.2 2.6	3 79 6 79
2 Tu	0439 1120 0501* 1141*	-0.3 2.8 -0.2 2.8	-9 85 -6 85	17 W	0506 1138 0524* 1149*	0.2 2.5 0.4 2.5	6 76 12 76
3 W	0528 1212* 0553*	-0.3 2.8 -0.1	-9 85 -3	18 Th	0543 1217* 0601*	0.3 2.4 0.5	9 73 15
4 Th	1228 0621 0105* 0647*	2.7 -0.3 2.7 0.1	82 -9 82 3	19 F	1225 0622 1258* 0641*	2.4 0.3 2.4 0.6	73 9 73 18
5 F	0118 0717 0202* 0747*	2.6 -0.2 2.6 0.2	79 -6 79 6	20 Sa	0103 0703 0143* 0725*	2.3 0.4 2.3 0.7	70 12 70 21
6 Sa ◐	0213 0818 0304* 0850*	2.5 -0.2 2.5 0.4	76 -6 76 12	21 Su ◑	0146 0751 0234* 0818*	2.2 0.5 2.2 0.8	67 15 67 24
7 Su	0313 0922 0410* 0956*	2.4 -0.1 2.5 0.4	73 -3 76 12	22 M	0235 0847 0332* 0919*	2.2 0.5 2.2 0.9	67 15 67 27
8 M	0419 1026 0516* 1101*	2.4 0.0 2.5 0.4	73 0 76 12	23 Tu	0334 0948 0435* 1023*	2.2 0.5 2.2 0.8	67 15 67 24
9 Tu	0525 1128 0619*	2.4 0.0 2.5	73 0 76	24 W	0439 1048 0536* 1122*	2.2 0.4 2.4 0.7	67 12 73 21
10 W	1201 0628 1225* 0715*	0.4 2.4 0.0 2.6	12 73 0 79	25 Th	0543 1145 0633*	2.3 0.3 2.5	70 9 76
11 Th	1255 0725 0117* 0804*	0.3 2.5 0.0 2.6	9 76 0 79	26 F	1215 0643 1237* 0724*	0.6 2.5 0.1 2.7	18 76 3 82
12 F	0145 0815 0205* 0848*	0.3 2.6 0.0 2.7	9 79 0 82	27 Sa	0105 0738 0127* 0812*	0.3 2.7 0.0 2.9	9 82 0 88
13 Sa ○	0230 0901 0248* 0928*	0.2 2.6 0.0 2.7	6 79 0 82	28 Su	0153 0830 0216* 0858*	0.1 2.9 -0.1 3.0	3 88 -3 91
14 Su	0312 0942 0330* 1005*	0.1 2.6 0.0 2.7	3 79 0 82	29 M ●	0240 0921 0304* 0943*	-0.1 3.1 -0.1 3.1	-3 94 -3 94
15 M	0351 1022 0409* 1040*	0.1 2.6 0.1 2.6	3 79 3 79	30 Tu	0327 1010 0352* 1029*	-0.2 3.2 -0.1 3.1	-6 98 -3 94
				31 W	0416 1101 0442* 1116*	-0.3 3.2 0.0 3.1	-9 98 0 94

September

Day	Time h m	Height ft	Height cm	Day	Time h m	Height ft	Height cm
1 Th	0506 1152 0534*	-0.3 3.1 0.1	-9 94 3	16 F	0504 1144 0524* 1150*	0.4 2.7 0.7 2.6	12 82 21 79
2 F	1205 0559 1246* 0629*	3.0 -0.2 3.0 0.3	91 -6 91 9	17 Sa	0539 1225* 0602*	0.5 2.6 0.9	15 79 27
3 Sa	1258 0656 0144* 0729*	2.9 0.0 2.9 0.5	88 0 88 15	18 Su	1228 0619 0109* 0645*	2.5 0.6 2.6 1.0	76 18 79 30
4 Su ◐	0155 0759 0245* 0834*	2.7 0.1 2.7 0.6	82 3 82 18	19 M	0111 0706 0200* 0737*	2.4 0.7 2.5 1.0	73 21 76 30
5 M	0258 0905 0352* 0942*	2.6 0.3 2.7 0.7	79 9 82 21	20 Tu ◑	0202 0803 0257* 0840*	2.4 0.7 2.5 1.1	73 21 76 34
6 Tu	0405 1012 0458* 1048*	2.6 0.3 2.6 0.7	79 9 79 21	21 W	0304 0909 0359* 0947*	2.4 0.7 2.5 1.0	73 21 76 30
7 W	0513 1115 0600* 1147*	2.6 0.4 2.7 0.6	79 12 82 18	22 Th	0411 1015 0501* 1050*	2.5 0.7 2.6 0.8	76 21 79 24
8 Th	0615 1211* 0653*	2.6 0.4 2.7	79 12 82	23 F	0518 1116 0558* 1146*	2.6 0.5 2.8 0.6	79 15 85 18
9 F	1238 0709 0100* 0739*	0.5 2.7 0.3 2.8	15 82 9 85	24 Sa	0619 1211* 0651*	2.8 0.4 2.9	85 12 88
10 Sa	0124 0756 0145* 0820*	0.5 2.8 0.3 2.8	15 85 9 85	25 Su	1237 0716 0103* 0740*	0.4 3.1 0.3 3.1	12 94 9 94
11 Su	0205 0838 0225* 0857*	0.4 2.8 0.4 2.8	12 85 12 85	26 M	0127 0809 0154* 0828*	0.1 3.3 0.2 3.2	3 101 6 98
12 M ○	0244 0917 0304* 0932*	0.3 2.9 0.4 2.8	9 88 12 85	27 Tu ●	0215 0900 0243* 0916*	-0.1 3.4 0.1 3.3	-3 104 3 101
13 Tu	0320 0954 0340* 1006*	0.3 2.9 0.4 2.8	9 88 12 85	28 W	0303 0950 0332* 1004*	-0.2 3.5 0.1 3.3	-6 107 3 101
14 W	0355 1030 0415* 1039*	0.3 2.9 0.5 2.7	9 88 15 82	29 Th	0353 1041 0422* 1053*	-0.2 3.5 0.2 3.3	-6 107 6 101
15 Th	0429 1107 0450* 1114*	0.4 2.8 0.6 2.7	12 85 18 82	30 F	0444 1133 0514* 1144*	-0.2 3.4 0.4 3.2	-6 104 12 98

October

Day	Time h m	Height ft	Height cm	Day	Time h m	Height ft	Height cm
1 Sa	0538 1226* 0610*	0.0 3.2 0.5	0 98 15	16 Su	0506 1159 0533*	0.6 2.8 0.9	18 85 27
2 Su	1238 0636 0123* 0710*	3.0 0.2 3.1 0.7	91 6 94 21	17 M	1201 0546 1243* 0616*	2.6 0.6 2.7 1.0	79 18 82 30
3 M	0137 0739 0224* 0816*	2.9 0.4 2.9 0.8	88 12 88 24	18 Tu	1246 0634 0132* 0708*	2.5 0.7 2.7 1.0	76 21 82 30
4 Tu ◐	0240 0846 0328* 0924*	2.8 0.5 2.8 0.9	85 15 85 27	19 W	0139 0730 0226* 0810*	2.5 0.8 2.6 1.0	76 24 79 30
5 W	0348 0953 0432* 1029*	2.7 0.6 2.7 0.8	82 18 82 24	20 Th ◑	0241 0836 0325* 0916*	2.5 0.8 2.6 0.9	76 24 79 27
6 Th	0455 1055 0531* 1125*	2.7 0.7 2.7 0.8	82 21 82 24	21 F	0348 0944 0424* 1019*	2.6 0.7 2.7 0.7	79 21 82 21
7 F	0555 1150 0622*	2.7 0.7 2.8	82 21 85	22 Sa	0455 1048 0522* 1117*	2.8 0.7 2.8 0.5	85 21 85 15
8 Sa	1214 0647 1237* 0707*	0.7 2.8 0.7 2.8	21 85 21 85	23 Su	0557 1146 0617*	3.0 0.5 3.0	91 15 91
9 Su	1257 0732 0120* 0746*	0.6 2.9 0.6 2.8	18 88 18 85	24 M	1210 0654 1240* 0710*	0.2 3.2 0.4 3.1	6 98 12 94
10 M	0137 0812 0159* 0823*	0.5 3.0 0.6 2.9	15 91 18 88	25 Tu	0102 0749 0132* 0801*	0.0 3.4 0.3 3.2	0 104 9 98
11 Tu	0214 0849 0236* 0858*	0.4 3.0 0.6 2.9	12 91 18 88	26 W ●	0152 0841 0222* 0851*	-0.2 3.5 0.2 3.3	-6 107 6 101
12 W ○	0249 0926 0312* 0933*	0.4 3.0 0.7 2.9	12 91 21 88	27 Th	0242 0932 0313* 0941*	-0.2 3.5 0.2 3.3	-6 107 6 101
13 Th	0323 1002 0346* 1008*	0.4 3.0 0.7 2.8	12 91 21 85	28 F	0333 1023 0404* 1032*	-0.2 3.5 0.3 3.2	-6 107 9 98
14 F	0356 1040 0420* 1044*	0.5 3.0 0.8 2.8	15 91 24 85	29 Sa	0424 1114 0456* 1125*	-0.1 3.4 0.4 3.1	-3 104 12 94
15 Sa	0430 1118 0455* 1121*	0.5 2.9 0.9 2.7	15 88 27 82	30 Su	0518 1207* 0551*	0.0 3.2 0.5	0 98 15
				31 M	1219 0615 0101* 0650*	3.0 0.2 3.1 0.6	91 6 94 18

November

Day	Time h m	Height ft	Height cm	Day	Time h m	Height ft	Height cm
1 Tu	0117 0715 0157* 0754*	2.8 0.4 2.9 0.7	85 12 88 21	16 W	0511 1208* 0547*	0.5 2.6 0.7	15 79 21
2 W ◐	0218 0820 0255* 0858*	2.7 0.6 2.7 0.8	82 18 82 24	17 Th	1222 0606 1258* 0645*	2.5 0.6 2.6 0.7	76 18 79 21
3 Th	0321 0924 0354* 0959*	2.6 0.7 2.7 0.8	79 21 82 24	18 F ◑	0122 0709 0152* 0748*	2.5 0.6 2.6 0.6	76 18 79 18
4 F	0425 1025 0450* 1054*	2.6 0.8 2.6 0.7	79 24 79 21	19 Sa	0226 0815 0249* 0850*	2.5 0.6 2.6 0.4	76 18 79 12
5 Sa	0524 1119 0541* 1142*	2.6 0.8 2.6 0.6	79 24 79 18	20 Su	0332 0921 0348* 0950*	2.7 0.6 2.7 0.2	82 18 82 6
6 Su	0516 1107 0526* 1125*	2.7 0.8 2.6 0.5	82 24 79 15	21 M	0435 1021 0447* 1046*	2.8 0.5 2.8 0.0	85 15 85 0
7 M	0601 1150 0608*	2.8 0.7 2.7	85 21 82	22 Tu	0535 1118 0544* 1140*	3.0 0.4 2.9 -0.2	91 12 88 -6
8 Tu	1205 0642 1230* 0647*	0.4 2.8 0.7 2.7	12 85 21 82	23 W	0631 1212* 0638*	3.1 0.3 3.0	94 9 91
9 W	1243 0722 0108* 0726*	0.4 2.9 0.7 2.7	12 88 21 82	24 Th	1233 0724 0105* 0732*	-0.3 3.2 0.2 3.0	-9 98 6 91
10 Th ○	0119 0800 0145* 0804*	0.3 2.9 0.7 2.7	9 88 21 82	25 F ●	0124 0816 0156* 0824*	-0.4 3.3 0.1 3.0	-12 101 3 91
11 F	0154 0838 0220* 0842*	0.3 2.9 0.7 2.7	9 88 21 82	26 Sa	0216 0906 0247* 0915*	-0.4 3.2 0.2 3.0	-12 98 6 91
12 Sa	0229 0917 0256* 0920*	0.3 2.9 0.7 2.6	9 88 21 79	27 Su	0307 0956 0339* 1007*	-0.3 3.1 0.2 2.9	-9 94 6 88
13 Su	0305 0957 0332* 1000*	0.3 2.8 0.7 2.6	9 85 21 79	28 M	0359 1045 0432* 1059*	-0.1 3.0 0.3 2.8	-3 91 9 85
14 M	0343 1038 0412* 1042*	0.4 2.8 0.7 2.5	12 85 21 76	29 Tu	0452 1135 0526* 1152*	0.1 2.8 0.4 2.6	3 85 12 79
15 Tu	0424 1122 0456* 1129*	0.4 2.7 0.8 2.5	12 82 24 76	30 W	0547 1224* 0623*	0.3 2.7 0.4	9 82 12

December

Day	Time h m	Height ft	Height cm	Day	Time h m	Height ft	Height cm
1 Th	1247 0645 0115* 0721*	2.5 0.4 2.5 0.5	76 12 76 15	16 F	1206 0546 1231* 0622*	2.4 0.2 2.5 0.2	73 6 76 6
2 F ◐	0145 0745 0206* 0818*	2.4 0.6 2.4 0.5	73 18 73 15	17 Sa	0103 0645 0122* 0721*	2.4 0.3 2.4 0.1	73 9 73 3
3 Sa	0243 0843 0258* 0912*	2.3 0.7 2.3 0.5	70 21 70 15	18 Su ◑	0204 0750 0218* 0823*	2.4 0.3 2.4 0.0	73 9 73 0
4 Su	0341 0938 0349* 1002*	2.3 0.7 2.3 0.4	70 21 70 12	19 M	0310 0855 0319* 0925*	2.4 0.3 2.4 -0.2	73 9 73 -6
5 M	0435 1029 0439* 1048*	2.3 0.7 2.3 0.3	70 21 70 9	20 Tu	0415 0959 0422* 1026*	2.5 0.3 2.4 -0.3	76 9 73 -9
6 Tu	0525 1116 0527* 1131*	2.4 0.6 2.3 0.2	73 18 70 6	21 W	0518 1059 0524* 1123*	2.6 0.2 2.5 -0.4	79 6 76 -12
7 W	0611 1159 0612*	2.5 0.6 2.3	76 18 70	22 Th	0617 1156 0622*	2.7 0.1 2.6	82 3 79
8 Th	1212 0654 1240* 0655*	0.2 2.5 0.5 2.4	6 76 15 73	23 F	1218 0711 1250* 0718*	-0.5 2.8 0.0 2.6	-15 85 0 79
9 F	1251 0736 0119* 0738*	0.1 2.6 0.5 2.4	3 79 15 73	24 Sa ●	0110 0802 0141* 0810*	-0.6 2.9 -0.1 2.7	-18 88 -3 82
10 Sa ○	0129 0817 0157* 0819*	0.0 2.6 0.4 2.4	0 79 12 73	25 Su	0201 0850 0232* 0901*	-0.5 2.8 -0.1 2.7	-15 85 -3 82
11 Su	0207 0857 0235* 0901*	0.0 2.7 0.4 2.4	0 82 12 73	26 M	0251 0937 0321* 0949*	-0.5 2.8 -0.1 2.6	-15 85 -3 79
12 M	0245 0938 0314* 0943*	0.0 2.6 0.4 2.4	0 79 12 73	27 Tu	0339 1021 0409* 1037*	-0.3 2.7 -0.1 2.5	-9 82 -3 76
13 Tu	0325 1019 0355* 1028*	0.0 2.6 0.3 2.4	0 79 9 73	28 W	0427 1105 0458* 1124*	-0.2 2.5 0.0 2.4	-6 76 0 73
14 W	0407 1100 0439* 1115*	0.0 2.6 0.3 2.4	0 79 9 73	29 Th	0516 1147 0546*	0.0 2.4 0.1	0 73 3
15 Th	0454 1144 0528*	0.1 2.5 0.2	3 76 6	30 F	1212 0605 1230* 0636*	2.2 0.2 2.2 0.1	67 6 67 3
				31 Sa	0101 0657 0114* 0728*	2.1 0.3 2.1 0.2	64 9 64 6

Heights are referred to mean lower water which is the chart datum of sounding. All times are local. Daylight Saving Time has been used when needed.

Tampa, St. Petersburg, Florida, 2010

Times and Heights of High and Low Waters

July

Day	Time (h m)	Height (ft)	Height (cm)	Day	Time (h m)	Height (ft)	Height (cm)
1 Th	0609 1212* 0613*	0.5 6.2 1.1	15 189 34	16 F	1206 0630 1249* 0700*	7.9 -0.8 7.5 -0.2	241 -24 229 -6
2 F	1232 0646 1258* 0656*	6.4 0.6 6.2 1.3	195 18 189 40	17 Sa	0102 0721 0147* 0800*	7.5 -0.6 7.6 0.2	229 -18 232 6
3 Sa	0116 0726 0145* 0744*	6.2 0.7 6.4 1.5	189 21 195 46	18 Su ◐	0157 0816 0244* 0903*	7.1 -0.3 7.6 0.5	216 -9 232 15
4 Su ◑	0201 0811 0232* 0840*	6.0 0.7 6.5 1.6	183 21 198 49	19 M	0252 0914 0340* 1007*	6.8 -0.1 7.5 0.6	207 -3 229 18
5 M	0248 0902 0320* 0941*	5.9 0.7 6.8 1.5	180 21 207 46	20 Tu	0346 1013 0436* 1108*	6.5 0.1 7.5 0.7	198 3 229 21
6 Tu	0338 0956 0410* 1043*	5.9 0.6 7.0 1.3	180 18 213 40	21 W	0442 1111 0532*	6.4 0.2 7.5	195 6 229
7 W	0431 1052 0504* 1142*	5.9 0.4 7.3 1.0	180 12 223 30	22 Th	1204 0537 1205* 0626*	0.6 6.3 0.2 7.5	18 192 6 229
8 Th	0526 1147 0558*	6.0 0.1 7.6	183 3 232	23 F	1256 0631 1256* 0716*	0.6 6.3 0.3 7.5	18 192 9 229
9 F	1238 0622 1243* 0653*	0.6 6.2 -0.2 8.0	18 189 -6 244	24 Sa	0144 0722 0144* 0802*	0.5 6.4 0.3 7.5	15 195 9 229
10 Sa	0132 0718 0138* 0746*	0.3 6.5 -0.5 8.3	9 198 -15 253	25 Su	0228 0808 0229* 0844*	0.4 6.5 0.3 7.5	12 198 9 229
11 Su ●	0225 0811 0232* 0838*	-0.1 6.7 -0.8 8.5	-3 204 -24 259	26 M ○	0310 0852 0311* 0923*	0.3 6.5 0.4 7.4	9 198 12 226
12 M	0316 0904 0325* 0928*	-0.5 7.0 -0.9 8.6	-15 213 -27 262	27 Tu	0348 0933 0351* 1000*	0.3 6.6 0.5 7.2	9 201 15 219
13 Tu	0405 0957 0418* 1020*	-0.7 7.2 -0.9 8.5	-21 219 -27 259	28 W	0425 1013 0428* 1037*	0.3 6.6 0.7 7.0	9 201 21 213
14 W	0454 1052 0511* 1112*	-0.9 7.4 -0.8 8.2	-27 226 -24 250	29 Th	0459 1053 0506* 1113*	0.4 6.6 0.9 6.8	12 201 27 207
15 Th	0542 1150 0604*	-0.9 7.5 -0.5	-27 229 -15	30 F	0533 1133 0543* 1151*	0.5 6.6 1.1 6.5	15 201 34 198
				31 Sa	0608 1215* 0623*	0.5 6.6 1.3	15 201 40

August

Day	Time (h m)	Height (ft)	Height (cm)	Day	Time (h m)	Height (ft)	Height (cm)
1 Su	1232 0646 1259* 0708*	6.3 0.6 6.7 1.4	192 18 204 43	16 M ◐	0134 0749 0221* 0840*	7.1 0.1 7.7 0.8	216 3 235 24
2 M	0116 0730 0147* 0801*	6.1 0.7 6.8 1.5	186 21 207 46	17 Tu	0229 0847 0318* 0944*	6.7 0.4 7.5 1.1	204 12 229 34
3 Tu ◑	0205 0820 0238* 0901*	6.0 0.7 6.9 1.6	183 21 210 49	18 W	0325 0949 0414* 1045*	6.5 0.7 7.4 1.1	198 21 226 34
4 W	0257 0917 0333* 1007*	6.0 0.7 7.2 1.4	183 21 219 43	19 Th	0420 1049 0510* 1140*	6.4 0.8 7.3 1.1	195 24 223 34
5 Th	0354 1019 0430* 1111*	6.0 0.5 7.4 1.1	183 15 226 34	20 F	0515 1144 0604*	6.4 0.8 7.3	195 24 223
6 F	0454 1120 0530*	6.2 0.2 7.8	189 6 238	21 Sa	1230 0609 1235* 0653*	1.0 6.5 0.7 7.4	30 198 21 226
7 Sa	1210 0554 1220* 0629*	0.7 6.5 -0.2 8.1	21 198 -6 247	22 Su	0116 0659 0121* 0737*	0.8 6.7 0.7 7.5	24 204 21 229
8 Su	0107 0654 0117* 0725*	0.3 6.9 -0.5 8.5	9 210 -15 259	23 M	0158 0744 0205* 0818*	0.7 6.8 0.7 7.5	21 207 21 229
9 M	0200 0750 0214* 0818*	-0.2 7.3 -0.8 8.7	-6 223 -24 265	24 Tu ○	0238 0826 0246* 0855*	0.5 7.0 0.7 7.5	15 213 21 229
10 Tu ●	0252 0845 0309* 0909*	-0.6 7.7 -1.0 8.8	-18 235 -30 268	25 W	0315 0905 0326* 0931*	0.5 7.1 0.7 7.3	15 216 21 223
11 W	0341 0938 0402* 0959*	-0.9 8.0 -1.0 8.6	-27 244 -30 262	26 Th	0350 0942 0403* 1005*	0.4 7.2 0.8 7.1	12 219 24 216
12 Th	0430 1032 0455* 1051*	-1.0 8.1 -0.8 8.3	-30 247 -24 253	27 F	0425 1018 0440* 1039*	0.5 7.2 1.0 6.9	15 219 30 210
13 F	0517 1128 0547* 1144*	-0.9 8.1 -0.5 7.9	-27 247 -15 241	28 Sa	0459 1054 0517* 1113*	0.6 7.1 1.1 6.6	18 216 34 201
14 Sa	0605 1225* 0641*	-0.7 8.0 0.0	-21 244 0	29 Su	0534 1133 0556* 1152*	0.7 7.1 1.3 6.4	21 216 40 195
15 Su	1238 0655 0123* 0738*	7.5 -0.3 7.8 0.4	229 -9 238 12	30 M	0613 1217* 0640*	0.8 7.1 1.5	24 216 46
				31 Tu	1236 0656 0108* 0730*	6.3 0.9 7.1 1.6	192 27 216 49

September

Day	Time (h m)	Height (ft)	Height (cm)	Day	Time (h m)	Height (ft)	Height (cm)
1 W ◑	0129 0747 0204* 0831*	6.2 1.0 7.2 1.7	189 30 219 52	16 Th	0301 0921 0348* 1016*	6.6 1.3 7.3 1.5	201 40 223 46
2 Th	0227 0847 0303* 0938*	6.2 0.9 7.4 1.5	189 27 226 46	17 F	0356 1023 0442* 1111*	6.5 1.4 7.2 1.4	198 43 219 43
3 F	0328 0953 0404* 1044*	6.3 0.7 7.7 1.2	192 21 235 37	18 Sa	0450 1120 0534* 1159*	6.6 1.3 7.3 1.3	201 40 223 40
4 Sa	0430 1059 0506* 1145*	6.6 0.4 8.0 0.8	201 12 244 24	19 Su	0543 1210* 0622*	6.8 1.2 7.3	207 37 223
5 Su	0533 1201* 0606*	7.0 0.0 8.3	213 0 253	20 M	1243 0632 1256* 0706*	1.1 7.0 1.1 7.4	34 213 34 226
6 M	1241 0634 0100* 0703*	0.3 7.5 -0.4 8.6	9 229 -12 262	21 Tu	0123 0717 0139* 0747*	0.9 7.3 1.0 7.5	27 223 30 229
7 Tu	0135 0731 0156* 0756*	-0.2 8.0 -0.7 8.8	-6 244 -21 268	22 W	0202 0758 0220* 0825*	0.7 7.5 0.9 7.4	21 229 27 226
8 W ●	0226 0825 0251* 0847*	-0.6 8.4 -0.8 8.8	-18 256 -24 268	23 Th ○	0239 0836 0300* 0901*	0.6 7.7 0.9 7.3	18 235 27 223
9 Th	0315 0917 0345* 0936*	-0.8 8.7 -0.8 8.6	-24 265 -24 262	24 F	0316 0912 0338* 0935*	0.6 7.7 0.9 7.2	18 235 27 219
10 F	0404 1009 0436* 1026*	-0.8 8.7 -0.6 8.3	-24 265 -18 253	25 Sa	0352 0947 0416* 1008*	0.6 7.7 1.0 7.0	18 235 30 213
11 Sa	0451 1102 0528* 1118*	-0.7 8.6 -0.2 7.8	-21 262 -6 238	26 Su	0428 1022 0454* 1042*	0.7 7.7 1.1 6.8	21 235 34 207
12 Su	0539 1158 0620*	-0.3 8.3 0.2	-9 253 6	27 M	0505 1100 0534* 1120*	0.8 7.6 1.2 6.6	24 232 37 201
13 M	1212 0628 1256* 0714*	7.4 0.1 8.0 0.8	226 3 244 24	28 Tu	0546 1145 0618*	0.9 7.5 1.4	27 229 43
14 Tu	0109 0720 0154* 0812*	7.0 0.6 7.7 1.2	213 18 235 37	29 W	1207 0631 1238* 0709*	6.4 1.0 7.5 1.5	195 30 229 46
15 W ◐	0205 0818 0252* 0915*	6.7 1.0 7.4 1.5	204 30 226 46	30 Th	0104 0724 0138* 0808*	6.4 1.1 7.5 1.6	195 34 229 49

October

Day	Time (h m)	Height (ft)	Height (cm)	Day	Time (h m)	Height (ft)	Height (cm)
1 F ◑	0206 0826 0240* 0914*	6.4 1.1 7.6 1.5	195 34 232 46	16 Sa	0327 0948 0405* 1031*	6.6 1.8 7.0 1.6	201 55 213 49
2 Sa	0310 0934 0342* 1020*	6.7 0.9 7.8 1.1	204 27 238 34	17 Su	0420 1047 0456* 1119*	6.7 1.7 7.0 1.4	204 52 213 43
3 Su	0413 1041 0443* 1120*	7.0 0.6 8.1 0.7	213 18 247 21	18 M	0511 1139 0544*	6.9 1.5 7.1	210 46 216
4 M	0516 1145 0543*	7.5 0.2 8.3	229 6 253	19 Tu	1203 0600 1226* 0630*	1.1 7.2 1.3 7.1	34 219 40 216
5 Tu	1216 0616 1244* 0640*	0.2 8.1 -0.2 8.5	6 247 -6 259	20 W	1244 0645 0110* 0713*	0.9 7.5 1.1 7.2	27 229 34 219
6 W	0109 0712 0140* 0733*	-0.3 8.6 -0.4 8.6	-9 262 -12 262	21 Th	0124 0727 0153* 0753*	0.7 7.8 1.0 7.2	21 238 30 219
7 Th ●	0200 0805 0234* 0824*	-0.6 8.9 -0.6 8.5	-18 271 -18 259	22 F	0203 0807 0234* 0831*	0.6 7.9 0.9 7.1	18 241 27 216
8 F	0249 0856 0327* 0913*	-0.7 9.1 -0.6 8.3	-21 277 -18 253	23 Sa ○	0242 0844 0314* 0907*	0.5 8.0 0.8 7.0	15 244 24 213
9 Sa	0338 0946 0417* 1002*	-0.6 9.0 -0.4 8.0	-18 274 -12 244	24 Su	0322 0920 0354* 0942*	0.5 8.0 0.8 6.9	15 244 24 210
10 Su	0425 1037 0507* 1052*	-0.4 8.7 0.0 7.6	-12 265 0 232	25 M	0401 0957 0435* 1018*	0.5 8.0 0.9 6.8	15 244 27 207
11 M	0513 1130 0556* 1145*	0.0 8.4 0.5 7.2	0 256 15 219	26 Tu	0442 1037 0517* 1100*	0.6 7.9 1.0 6.6	18 241 30 201
12 Tu	0600 1226* 0647*	0.5 7.9 0.9	15 241 27	27 W	0526 1124 0603* 1150*	0.6 7.8 1.1 6.5	18 238 34 198
13 W	1240 0650 0123* 0741*	6.9 1.0 7.5 1.4	210 30 229 43	28 Th	0613 1219* 0653*	0.8 7.7 1.2	24 235 37
14 Th ◐	0137 0744 0219* 0838*	6.6 1.4 7.3 1.6	201 43 223 49	29 F	1249 0707 0119* 0750*	6.5 0.9 7.7 1.2	198 27 235 37
15 F	0232 0845 0313* 0937*	6.5 1.7 7.1 1.7	198 52 216 52	30 Sa ◑	0152 0809 0221* 0852*	6.6 0.9 7.7 1.0	201 27 235 30
				31 Su	0256 0917 0321* 0956*	6.9 0.8 7.7 0.8	210 24 235 24

November

Day	Time (h m)	Height (ft)	Height (cm)	Day	Time (h m)	Height (ft)	Height (cm)
1 M	0358 1026 0421* 1055*	7.3 0.6 7.8 0.4	223 18 238 12	16 Tu	0332 0959 0400* 1017*	6.8 1.7 6.5 1.0	207 52 198 30
2 Tu	0459 1129 0520* 1151*	7.8 0.3 7.9 0.0	238 9 241 0	17 W	0421 1050 0449* 1102*	7.1 1.4 6.6 0.8	216 43 201 24
3 W	0558 1228* 0617*	8.2 0.0 7.9	250 0 241	18 Th	0509 1138 0536* 1145*	7.3 1.2 6.6 0.6	223 37 201 18
4 Th	1244 0654 0124* 0711*	-0.3 8.6 -0.3 8.0	-9 262 -9 244	19 F	0554 1223* 0620*	7.6 0.9 6.7	232 27 204
5 F	0136 0747 0218* 0802*	-0.5 8.9 -0.4 7.9	-15 271 -12 241	20 Sa	1229 0637 0107* 0702*	0.4 7.8 0.7 6.7	12 238 21 204
6 Sa ●	0226 0837 0309* 0851*	-0.6 8.9 -0.4 7.8	-18 271 -12 238	21 Su ○	0112 0718 0151* 0741*	0.2 8.0 0.5 6.7	6 244 15 204
7 Su	0215 0826 0258* 0839*	-0.5 8.8 -0.2 7.5	-15 268 -6 229	22 M	0156 0758 0234* 0820*	0.1 8.1 0.4 6.7	3 247 12 204
8 M	0302 0914 0346* 0927*	-0.2 8.5 0.1 7.2	-6 259 3 219	23 Tu	0240 0839 0318* 0901*	0.0 8.1 0.4 6.7	0 247 12 204
9 Tu	0348 1003 0432* 1017*	0.1 8.1 0.4 6.9	3 247 12 210	24 W	0325 0923 0402* 0946*	0.0 8.1 0.3 6.6	0 247 9 201
10 W	0433 1055 0518* 1109*	0.5 7.7 0.8 6.6	15 235 24 201	25 Th	0411 1011 0448* 1038*	0.0 7.9 0.4 6.6	0 241 12 201
11 Th	0519 1148 0605*	1.0 7.3 1.2	30 223 37	26 F	0500 1105 0537* 1137*	0.2 7.8 0.4 6.6	6 238 12 201
12 F	1203 0607 1240* 0655*	6.4 1.4 7.0 1.4	195 43 213 43	27 Sa	0554 1202* 0631*	0.3 7.6 0.4	9 232 12
13 Sa ◐	1257 0701 0131* 0747*	6.4 1.7 6.7 1.5	195 52 204 46	28 Su ◑	1239 0655 0101* 0729*	6.8 0.5 7.5 0.4	207 15 229 12
14 Su	0150 0801 0221* 0840*	6.4 1.8 6.6 1.4	195 55 201 43	29 M	0141 0801 0200* 0830*	7.0 0.6 7.4 0.2	213 18 226 6
15 M	0241 0902 0311* 0930*	6.6 1.8 6.5 1.3	201 55 198 40	30 Tu	0242 0909 0259* 0930*	7.3 0.5 7.3 0.0	223 15 223 0

December

Day	Time (h m)	Height (ft)	Height (cm)	Day	Time (h m)	Height (ft)	Height (cm)
1 W	0342 1014 0357* 1027*	7.7 0.3 7.2 -0.2	235 9 219 -6	16 Th	0337 1008 0404* 1018*	6.7 1.4 5.9 0.7	204 43 180 21
2 Th	0441 1113 0455* 1122*	8.0 0.0 7.2 -0.4	244 0 219 -12	17 F	0429 1102 0455* 1108*	6.9 1.1 6.0 0.4	210 34 183 12
3 F	0538 1209* 0551*	8.2 -0.2 7.2	250 -6 219	18 Sa	0519 1152 0546* 1157*	7.2 0.8 6.1 0.1	219 24 186 3
4 Sa	1215 0631 0102* 0643*	-0.5 8.4 -0.3 7.2	-15 256 -9 219	19 Su	0608 1241* 0633*	7.5 0.5 6.3	229 15 192
5 Su ●	0106 0721 0152* 0732*	-0.5 8.4 -0.3 7.1	-15 256 -9 216	20 M	1246 0654 0128* 0718*	-0.2 7.8 0.2 6.5	-6 238 6 198
6 M	0155 0809 0239* 0819*	-0.5 8.2 -0.2 7.0	-15 250 -6 213	21 Tu ○	0134 0739 0215* 0802*	-0.4 8.0 -0.1 6.6	-12 244 -3 201
7 Tu	0241 0854 0324* 0904*	-0.3 8.0 -0.1 6.8	-9 244 -3 207	22 W	0221 0824 0300* 0847*	-0.6 8.1 -0.3 6.7	-18 247 -9 204
8 W	0325 0939 0407* 0950*	0.0 7.7 0.2 6.6	0 235 6 201	23 Th	0309 0910 0345* 0934*	-0.7 8.1 -0.4 6.8	-21 247 -12 207
9 Th	0407 1024 0447* 1037*	0.3 7.3 0.4 6.4	9 223 12 195	24 F	0357 0958 0431* 1027*	-0.7 8.0 -0.5 6.9	-21 244 -15 210
10 F	0448 1110 0528* 1126*	0.7 7.0 0.7 6.3	21 213 21 192	25 Sa	0448 1050 0519* 1124*	-0.6 7.8 -0.5 6.9	-18 238 -15 210
11 Sa	0531 1157 0609*	1.0 6.6 0.9	30 201 27	26 Su	0541 1144 0609*	-0.3 7.5 -0.4	-9 229 -12
12 Su	1216 0616 1244* 0653*	6.2 1.3 6.3 1.0	189 40 192 30	27 M	1223 0639 1241* 0704*	7.0 0.0 7.2 -0.3	213 0 219 -9
13 M ◐	0106 0708 0132* 0742*	6.2 1.6 6.1 1.1	189 49 186 34	28 Tu ◑	0123 0743 0138* 0803*	7.1 0.2 6.9 -0.2	216 6 210 -6
14 Tu	0156 0808 0221* 0834*	6.3 1.7 6.0 1.0	192 52 183 30	29 W	0223 0851 0237* 0905*	7.2 0.3 6.6 -0.2	219 9 201 -6
15 W	0246 0910 0312* 0926*	6.5 1.6 5.9 0.9	198 49 180 27	30 Th	0324 0957 0336* 1006*	7.3 0.3 6.5 -0.2	223 9 198 -6
				31 F	0424 1057 0435* 1103*	7.4 0.1 6.4 -0.3	226 3 195 -9

Heights are referred to mean lower water which is the chart datum of sounding. All times are local. Daylight Saving Time has been used when needed.

Tampa, St. Petersburg, Florida, 2011

Times and Heights of High and Low Waters

Heights are referred to mean lower water which is the chart datum of sounding. All times are local. Daylight Saving Time has been used when needed.

Tampa, St. Petersburg, Florida, 2011

Times and Heights of High and Low Waters

July

Day	Time	Height (ft)	Height (cm)
1 F ●	0451 0705 0156* 1001*	1.4 1.3 2.6 -0.3	43 40 85 -9
2 Sa	0510 0759 0241* 1038*	1.3 1.3 2.6 -0.3	40 40 85 -9
3 Su	0530 0858 0329* 1115*	1.5 1.2 2.7 -0.2	46 37 82 -6
4 M	0553 1002 0421* 1151*	1.5 1.2 2.6 -0.2	46 37 79 -6
5 Tu	0620 1112 0518*	1.7 1.0 2.6	52 30 79
6 W	0605 1201 0552*	1.8 0.9 2.6	55 27 79
7 Th	0650 1229 0624*	0.2 0.9 2.0	6 28 61
8 F ○	1228 0650 0624*	0.5 0.5 1.7	15 61 52
9 Sa	0104 0726 0153* 0746*	0.8 0.8 1.7	24 67 15
10 Su	0139 0806 0322* 0934*	1.0 0.9 2.4 0.5	30 73 15
11 M	0213 0852 0448* 1145*	1.0 2.4 0.3	30 73
12 Tu	1041 0707*	2.6 -0.1	79 -3
13 W	1139 0800*	2.7 -0.3	82 -9
14 Th	1233 0846*	2.8 -0.3	85 -9
15 F ○	0420 0624 0123* 0925*	1.4 1.3 2.7 -0.2	43 40 85 -6
16 Sa	0452 0820 0252* 1028*	1.6 1.2 2.6 0.0	49 37 79 0
17 Su	0506 0934 0333* 1055*	1.6 1.2 2.8 0.1	49 37 85 3
18 M	0521 1008 0416* 1122*	1.7 1.1 2.3 0.1	52 34 70 3
19 Tu	0541 1103 0501* 1148*	1.8 1.0 2.1 0.5	55 30 64 15
20 W	0605 1201 0552*	1.9 0.9 1.8	58 27 58
21 Th	1216 0633 0653*	0.7 2.0 1.7	21 61 52
22 F	1245 0707 0813*	0.9 2.1 1.5	27 64 46
23 Sa ●	0114 0747 0335* 1007*	1.0 2.2 0.6 1.5	30 67 18
24 Su	0142 0834 0452*	1.2 2.3 0.5	37 70 15
25 M	0928 0600*	2.4 0.3	73 9
26 Tu	1027 0656*	2.5 0.1	76 3
27 W	1125 0743*	2.6 0.0	79 0
28 Th	0322 0627 0121* 0901*	1.5 1.4 2.7 0.0	46 43 83 0
29 F	0338 0700 0109* 0901*	1.5 1.3 2.7 -0.1	46 40 83 -3
30 Sa ●	0353 0918 0332* 1009*	1.5 1.3 2.8 -0.1	46 40 85 -3
31 Su	0408 0818 0246* 1009*	1.6 1.1 2.8 0.0	49 34 85 0

August

Day	Time	Height (ft)	Height (cm)
1 M ●	0426 0914 0336* 1042*	1.7 1.0 2.7 0.2	52 30 82 6
2 Tu	0447 1012 0429* 1113*	1.8 0.8 2.6 0.4	55 24 79 12
3 W	0513 1114 0527* 1143*	2.0 0.7 2.2 0.7	61 21 67 21
4 Th	0545 1223 0635*	2.2 0.6 1.9	67 18 58
5 F	1212 0622 0141* 0804*	1.0 2.0 0.5 1.6	30 61 15 49
6 Sa ○	1238 0708 0309* 1019*	1.2 2.0 0.4 1.4	37 61 12 43
7 Su	1258 0804 0439*	1.3 1.9 0.5	40 58 15
8 M	0914 0557*	1.8 0.1	55 3
9 Tu	1032 0659*	1.9 0.0	58 0
10 W	1143 0747*	2.1 0.0	64 0
11 Th	0306 0557 0133* 0826*	1.6 1.5 2.7 0.1	49 46 82 3
12 F	0320 0700 0133* 0858*	1.4 1.4 2.7 0.1	43 43 82 3
13 Sa ●	0333 0743 0215* 0924*	1.7 1.2 2.6 0.3	52 37 79 9
14 Su	0344 0835 0254* 0948*	1.8 1.1 2.6 0.3	55 34 79 9
15 M	0355 0918 0332* 1009*	1.9 0.9 2.4 0.5	58 27 73 15
16 Tu	0409 1000 0411* 1031*	1.7 1.0 2.3 0.7	52 30 82 6
17 W	0447 1043 0453* 1053*	1.8 0.8 1.7 0.9	55 24 52 12
18 Th	0450 1130 0539* 1116*	2.0 0.7 1.9 1.0	61 21 67 21
19 F	0519 1244 0635* 1140*	2.2 0.8 1.9	67 18 58
20 Sa	0554 0127* 0749*	1.0 0.5 1.6	30 15 49
21 Su ○	1204 0636 0244* 0951*	1.3 2.4 0.6 1.4	40 73 18 43
22 M	1222 0730 0407*	1.4 2.6 0.5	43 79 9
23 Tu	0839 0522*	2.6 0.1	79 3
24 W	0957 0621*	2.5 0.3	76 0
25 Th	0159 0427 0110* 0709*	1.6 1.5 2.6 0.2	49 46 79 6
26 F	0213 0543 0133* 0750*	1.6 1.5 2.7 0.1	49 46 82 3
27 Sa	0228 0642 0108* 0826*	1.7 1.4 2.7 0.1	52 43 82 3
28 Su	0244 0735 0200* 0859*	1.8 1.1 2.6 0.3	55 34 79 9
29 M	0301 0826 0251* 0930*	1.9 0.9 2.7 0.5	58 24 82 15
30 Tu	0320 0917 0343* 0959*	2.6 0.4	76 0
31 W	0344 1010 0438* 1025*	2.0 0.4 2.3 0.6	64 12 70 18

September

Day	Time	Height (ft)	Height (cm)
1 M	0413 1108 0539* 1050*	2.5 0.3 1.9 1.2	76 9 64 37
2 F	0447 1212 0654* 1112*	2.6 0.4 1.7	79 12 52
3 Sa	0528 0127* 0845* 1126*	2.7 0.5 1.5	82 15 46
4 Su	0619 0254*	2.7 0.3	82 9
5 M	0726 0423*	2.6 0.5	79 15
6 Tu	0859 0537*	2.5 0.3	76 15
7 F	0137 0342 0342* 0633*	1.7 1.6 2.5 0.3	52 49 76 9
8 M	0146 0524 0524* 0715*	1.8 1.5 2.4 0.4	55 46 76 12
9 F	0200 0629 0629* 0749*	1.8 1.2 2.6 0.5	55 40 76 15
10 Sa	0215 0718 0138* 0817*	1.9 1.1 2.6 0.6	58 34 76 18
11 Th	0259 0759 0103* 0839*	2.0 0.8 2.4 0.7	61 24 73 21
12 F	0237 0836 0251* 0900*	2.1 0.6 2.0 0.9	64 18 61 27
13 W	0249 0914 0333* 0918*	2.2 0.5 1.9 1.0	67 15 58 30
14 Th	0251 1006 0452* 0937*	2.4 0.4 1.8 1.1	73 15 64 34
15 F	0324 1101 0559* 0952*	2.5 0.4 1.7 1.5	76 12 61 40
16 Su	0349 1104 0533* 1018*	2.5 0.3 1.9 1.3	79 9 64 37
17 Sa	1152 0744* 1101*	2.6 0.4 0.4 1.7	79 15 49
18 Tu	0456 1251* 0744* 1101*	2.7 0.5 1.6 1.5	82 15 49 46
19 W	0541 0202*	2.6 0.5	79 15
20 Tu ○	0640 0323*	2.5 0.3	76 15
21 F	0759 0436*	2.4 0.5	73 15
22 Sa	1226 0807 0535*	1.7 1.6 0.4	52 49 0
23 Su	1243 0444 0535*	1.8 1.5 0.4	55 46 12
24 Sa	0101 0551 0624*	1.9 1.2 0.5	58 40 15
25 Tu	0118 0646 0107* 0740*	2.0 1.0 2.6 0.6	61 30 79 18
26 M	0729 0203* 0812*	2.0 0.8 2.4 0.7	61 24 73 21
27 W	0158 0825 0258* 0841*	2.8 0.4 1.9 1.1	85 12 58 34
28 F	0223 0914 0354* 0908*	2.9 0.3 1.7 1.5	88 9 52 46
29 Sa	0251 1006 0452* 0931*	2.7 0.1 1.8 1.4	82 3 64 43
30 Su	0324 1101 0559* 0952*	2.8 0.0 1.9 1.5	85 0 58 46

October

Day	Time	Height (ft)	Height (cm)
1 Sa	0402 1202* 0727* 1007*	2.9 0.1 1.7 1.6	88 3 52 49
2 Su ○	0446 0113*	2.8 0.2	82 6
3 M	0541 0232*	2.7 0.3	82 9
4 Tu ○	0658 0350*	2.5 0.4	76 12
5 W	0848 0455*	2.3 0.5	70 15
6 Su	1220 0426 0033* 0546*	1.9 1.6 2.3 0.5	58 49 70 15
7 F	1237 0542 0626*	1.7 1.3 0.6	52 40 21
8 Tu	1254 0635 0611*	1.8 1.0 0.8	55 30 24
9 W	0110 0717 0138* 0725*	2.1 0.9 2.2 0.9	64 27 67 27
10 Th	0124 0754 0222* 0747*	2.4 0.6 2.1 1.1	73 18 64 34
11 F	0137 0827 0302* 0807*	2.6 0.3 1.9 1.3	79 9 58 40
12 Sa	0151 0859 0339* 0825*	2.8 0.0 1.9 1.3	85 0 58 40
13 Su	0210 0937 0416* 0842*	2.8 -0.3 1.7 1.5	85 -9 52 46
14 M	0233 1007 0454* 0901*	2.7 -0.1 1.8 1.4	82 3 55 43
15 W	0255 1046 0538* 0922*	2.7 0.2 1.7 1.5	82 6 52 46
16 Su	0336 1132 0635* 0946*	2.7 0.2 1.6 1.5	82 6 49 46
17 M	0416 1227* 0754* 1016*	2.6 0.2 1.5	79 6 46
18 Tu	0505 0131*	2.7 0.3	82 9
19 W	0606 0239* 1033*	2.4 1.7	73
20 Th	0121 0750 0043* 1103*	2.0 1.2 2.1 1.8	61 37 64 55
21 F	0322 0911 0441* 1127*	1.6 2.3 2.2 1.9	49 67 58
22 Sa	0446 1044 0542* 1151*	1.2 1.3 2.0	37 67 21
23 Su	0549 1202* 0611*	0.8 2.2 0.7	24 67 21
24 Tu	0110 0643 0110* 0648*	2.1 0.9 2.2 0.9	64 27 67 30
25 Tu	1239 0733 0719*	2.4 0.1 1.1	73 3 34
26 M	0822 0312*	2.8 -0.3	85 -9
27 W	0133 0947 0412* 0747*	2.8 -0.3 1.9 1.4	85 -9 58 43
28 Th	0211 1032 0514* 0812*	2.9 -0.4 1.7 1.5	88 -12 52 46
29 Sa	0250 1055 0556* 0856*	2.6 -0.3 1.9 1.4	79 -9 58 43
30 Su	0332 1152 0713* 0913*	2.9 0.0 1.7 1.5	88 0 52 46
31 M	0420 1252*	2.7 0.0	82 0

November

Day	Time	Height (ft)	Height (cm)
1 Tu	0518 0155*	2.5 0.2	76 6
2 W ○	0635 0257* 1039*	2.2 0.3 1.7	67 9 52
3 Th	0244 0824 0353* 1102*	1.5 1.4 2.5 1.8	46 43 55
4 F	0427 1012 0440* 1125*	1.2 1.4 2.6 1.8	37 43 55
5 Sa	0534 1136 0521* 1147*	0.9 1.4 2.1	27 55 24
6 Su	0523 1143 0607* 1107*	0.6 1.0 1.2	18 55 18
7 M	0604 1239 0626* 1125*	0.3 0.9 2.3	9 55 70
8 Tu	0641 0129* 0551* 1144*	0.1 2.7 1.4 2.4	3 82 73
9 W	0715 0214* 0613*	0.0 1.7 1.3	0 52 40
10 Th ○	1205 0748 0255* 0632*	2.5 -0.1 1.4	76 -3 43
11 F	1249 0822 0333* 0650*	2.6 -0.2 1.4	79 -6 43
12 Sa	1259 0858 0411* 0653*	2.6 -0.2 1.4	79 -6 43
13 Su	0133 0937 0453* 0713*	2.6 0.0 1.5	79 0 46
14 M	0211 1020 0541* 0820*	2.6 -0.2 1.8	79 -6 46
15 Tu	0255 1108 0634* 0919*	2.6 -0.1 1.7	79 -3 52
16 W	0347 1200* 0724* 1048*	2.5 0.0 1.5 1.4	76 0 46 43
17 Th	0450 1255* 0806*	2.2 0.1 1.6	67 3 49
18 F ○	1237 0824 0449* 0842*	1.3 1.4 2.0 1.7	46 61
19 Sa	0218 0755 0241* 0914*	1.0 1.8 0.4 1.9	37 55 18
20 Su	0338 0938 0328* 0946*	0.7 0.7 2.1	27 55 24
21 M	0442 1107 0411* 1018*	0.3 1.6 0.3 2.3	9 49 9 70
22 Tu	0539 1239* 0449* 1052*	0.3 0.3 2.3	9 9 70
23 W	0631 0134* 0522* 1128*	0.1 -0.1 1.2 2.5	3 -3 37 76
24 Th	0728 0231* 0552*	-0.6 1.3	-18 40
25 F ●	1207 0811 0350* 0621*	2.8 -0.7 1.3	85 -21 40
26 Sa	1249 0859 0436* 0653*	2.6 -0.7 1.3	79 -21 40
27 Su	0133 0947 0529* 0733*	2.6 -0.5 1.3	79 -15 40
28 M	0219 1034 0614* 0832*	2.6 -0.6 1.3	79 -18 40
29 Tu	0309 1121 0653* 0954*	2.6 -0.2 1.4	79 -6 43
30 W	0405 1207* 0727* 1136*	2.5 -0.1 1.4	76 -3 43

December

Day	Time	Height (ft)	Height (cm)
1 Th	0513 1252* 0800*	1.8 0.2 1.6	55 6 49
2 F ○	0123 0645 0136* 0832*	1.0 0.4 1.7	30 46 52
3 Sa	0255 0806 0203* 0903*	0.8 0.5 1.8	24 40 55
4 Su	0405 1017 0303* 0933*	0.5 0.5 2.0	15 40 61
5 M	0459 1140 0343* 1003*	0.2 1.0 0.3 2.1	6 30 64
6 Tu	0544 1248* 0420* 1032*	-0.1 1.3 0.2 2.2	-3 34 67
7 W	0625 0146* 0452* 1101*	-0.3 2.0 1.1 2.3	-9 43 67
8 Th	0704 0235* 0520* 1133*	-0.4 2.2 1.1 2.3	-12 37 70
9 F	0740 0316* 0546*	-0.5 2.5 1.2	-15 37
10 Sa ○	1206 0816 0350* 0615*	2.4 -0.5 1.3	73 -15 40
11 Su	1242 0851 0418* 0652*	2.5 -0.5 1.3	76 -15 40
12 M	0121 0928 0444* 0738*	2.4 -0.5 1.3	73 -15 40
13 Tu	0204 1006 0511* 0835*	2.4 -0.5 1.4	73 -15 34
14 W	0251 1045 0541* 0943*	2.3 -0.4 1.0	70 -12 30
15 Th	0344 1126 0613* 1103*	2.1 -0.3 0.9	64 -9 43 27
16 F	0448 1208* 0648*	1.8 0.0 1.6	55 0 49
17 Sa	1232 0607 0136* 0726*	1.0 0.5 1.7	30 46 52
18 Su ○	0202 0748 0035* 0805*	0.8 0.6 1.8	24 40 55
19 M	0324 0946 0218* 0847*	0.5 0.8 2.0	15 24 61
20 Tu	0435 1136 0303* 0932*	0.2 1.0 2.1	6 30 64
21 W	0537 0106* 0342* 1019*	-0.1 1.3 0.9 2.2	-3 34 34 67
22 Th	0632 0217* 0425* 1107*	-0.3 2.1 1.1 2.2	-9 43 37 67
23 F	0723 0311* 0511* 1156*	-0.4 2.0 1.1 2.3	-12 37 34 70
24 Sa ●	0809 0349* 0601*	-0.5 2.3 1.2	-15 37
25 Su	1244 0852 0418* 0656*	2.5 -0.8 1.2	76 -24 34 37
26 M	0131 0931 0441* 0755*	2.4 -0.7 1.0	73 -21 30
27 Tu	0218 1006 0503* 0858*	2.5 -0.5 1.0	73 -15 27
28 W	0305 1040 0526* 1006*	2.0 -0.3 0.8	61 -9 24
29 Th	0356 1112 0552* 1119*	2.0 -0.4 1.0	70 -12 30
30 F	0454 1144 0622*	1.8 -0.4 0.7	55 -3 43 21
31 Sa	1239 0608 0217* 0655*	0.6 1.2 0.9 1.6	18 37 9 49

Heights are referred to mean lower water which is the chart datum of sounding. All times are local. Daylight Saving Time has been used when needed.

ICW Bridges:

ICW Bridges:
Florida's East Coast and the Keys

KEY: Statute miles from Norfolk
Bridge: Schedule / Openings SR=State Route
Drawbridge clearances are closed, vertical, in feet. *=Except federal holidays

FLORIDA BRIDGES MONITOR ((())) CHANNEL 09

720.7 `5'` **Kingsley Creek RR Bridge:** Open, except when train is approaching.

720.7 `65'` **Kingsley Creek Twin Bridges (SR A1A):** (Fixed)

739.2 `24'` **Sisters Creek:** Opens on signal. (Replacement with a high-level fixed bridge has been recommended, but funding has not been established.) 800-865-5794.

742.1 `65'` **Wonderwood Drive (twin):** (Fixed)

744.7 `65'` **Atlantic Beach:** (Fixed)

747.5 `65'` **Jacksonville Beach McCormick Bridge (U.S. 90):** (Fixed)

749.5 `65'` **Pablo Creek (Butler Blvd. SR 202):** (Fixed)

758.8 `65'` **Palm Valley (SR 210):** (Fixed)

775.8 `65'` **Vilano Beach/Usina Bridge (SR A1A):** (Fixed)

777.9 `25'` **St. Augustine Bridge of Lions (SR A1A):** Mon.-Fri.* (year-round), 7 a.m. to 6 p.m., opens on the hour and half-hour, but does not open 8 a.m., noon and 5 p.m. Wknd & hldy, 7 a.m. to 6 p.m., opens on the hour and half-hour. (Temporary bypass bridge in use with 90-foot vertical clearance when up. Completion of work on new bridge scheduled for 2010 and removal of temp. bridge within one year.) 800-865-5794. (Note: Clearance maybe less than charted.)

780.3 `65'` **State Road 312:** (Fixed)

788.6 `25'` **Crescent Beach (SR 206):** Opens on signal. 800-865-5794.

803.0 `65'` **Palm Coast Parkway:** (Fixed)

810.6 `65'` **Flagler Beach:** (Fixed)

816.0 `15'` **Bulow (L.B. Knox Bridge):** Opens on signal. 386-441-0777.

824.9 `65'` **Ormond Beach (SR 40):** (Fixed)

829.1 `65'` **Daytona Beach-Seabreeze Twin Bridges:** (Fixed)

829.7 `22'` **Daytona Beach-Main Street:** Opens on signal. 386-239-6477.

830.1 `65'` **Daytona Beach-Intl. Speedway Blvd.:** (Fixed)

830.6 `21'` *Barge Removing 6/16* **Daytona Beach-Memorial (Twin):** Year-round, Mon.-Sat.*, no openings 7:45 a.m. to 8:45 a.m., 4:45 p.m. to 5:45 p.m., but opens at 8:15 a.m. and 5:15 p.m. 386-239-6540.

835.5 `65'` **Port Orange (SR A1A):** (Fixed)

845.0 `24'` **Coronado Beach (George Musson Memorial Bridge):** Year-round daily, 7 a.m to 7 p.m., opens on the hour and at :20 and :40 past the hour. 386-424-2024.

846.5 `65'` **Harris Saxon Bridge:** (Fixed)

869.2 `27'` **Allenhurst (Haulover Canal) Bridge (SR A1A):** Opens on signal. 321-867-4859.

876.6 `7'` **Jay Jay/NASA Railroad Bridge:** Normally open; closes only when train is approaching (infrequent).

878.9 `9'` *65'* **Titusville (Max Brewer Bridge) (SR 402):** Year-round, Mon.-Fri.*, no openings 6 a.m. to 7:15 a.m., 3:15 p.m. to 4:30 p.m. Construction of a new, high-level fixed bridge began summer 2009 with completion in late 2011. 321-264-5068.

885.0 `27'` **Addison Point (SR 405) (NASA Causeway Bridge):** Year-round, Mon.-Fri.*, no openings 6:30 a.m. to 8 a.m., 3:30 p.m. to 5 p.m. 321-867-7200.

894.0 `65'` **City Point (Twin):** (Fixed)

897.4 `65'` **Cocoa (SR 528) (Twin):** (Fixed)

909.0 `65'` **Palm Shores Pineda Causeway:** (Fixed)

914.4 65' **Eau Gallie (SR 518):** (Fixed)

918.2 65' **Melbourne (SR 516):** (Fixed)

943.3 65' **Wabasso:** (Fixed)

951.9 66' **Vero Beach (SR 60):** (Fixed)

953.2 65' **Vero Beach 17th Street:** (Fixed)

964.8 26' **Fort Pierce North Bridge (SR A1A):** Opens on signal. 772-468-3993.

965.8 65' **Fort Pierce South Bridge (SR A1A):** (Fixed)

981.4 65' **Jensen Beach Causeway (SR 707A):** (Fixed)

984.9 65' **Sewalls Point-Ernest Lyons Bridge (SR A1A):** (Fixed)

995.9 25' **Hobe Sound Highway Bridge (SR 708):** Opens on signal. 772-546-5234

1004.1 25' **Jupiter Highway Bridge (CR 707):** Opens on signal. 561-746-4261. Hail as "707 Bridge."

1004.8 26' **Jupiter Federal Bridge (U.S. 1):** Opens on signal. 561-746-4907.

1006.2 35' **Indiantown Road (SR 706):** 24 hrs daily, opens on the hour and half-hour. 561-746-7114.

1009.3 35' **Juno Beach-Donald Ross Bridge:** 24 hrs daily, opens on the hour and half-hour. 561-626-3030.

1012.6 24' **PGA Boulevard:** 24 hrs daily, opens on the hour and half-hour. 561-624-3684.

1013.7 25' **North Palm Beach-Parker Bridge (U.S. 1):** 24 hrs daily, opens at :15 and :45 past the hour. 561-624-4175.

1017.2 65' **Riviera Beach - Jerry Thomas Memorial Bridge (SR A1A):** (Fixed)

1021.8 17' **West Palm Beach-Flagler Memorial (SR A1A):** 24 hrs daily, opens at :15 and :45 past the hour. 561-833-7339.

1022.6 21' **West Palm Beach-Royal Park (SR 704):** 24 hrs daily, opens on the hour and half-hour. 561-655-5617.

1024.7 14' **West Palm Beach-Southern Boulevard (SR 98/ 700/80):** 24 hrs daily, opens at :15 and :45 past the hour. 561-833-8852.

1028.8 35' **Lake Worth-Lake Ave. (SR 802):** Opens on signal. 561-540-2516.

1031.0 13' **Lantana-E. Ocean Ave.:** 24 hrs daily, opens on the hour and half-hour. 561-582-2320.

1035.0 21' **Boynton Beach-E. Ocean Avenue (SR 804):** Opens on the hour and half-hour. 561-733-0214.

1035.8 25' **Woolbright Rd.-S.E. 15th St.:** Opens on signal. 561-732-6461.

1038.7 9' **Delray Beach-George Bush Boulevard:** 24 hrs daily, opens on signal. 561-276-5948.

1039.6 12' **Delray Beach-Atlantic Avenue (SR 806):** 24 hrs daily, opens at :15 and :45 past the hour. 561-276-5435.

1041.1 30' **Delray Beach-Linton Boulevard:** 24 hrs daily, opens on the hour and half-hour. 561-278-1980.

1044.9 25' **Boca Raton-Spanish River Road:** 24 hrs daily, opens on the hour and half-hour. 561-395-5417.

1047.5 19' **Boca Raton-Palmetto Pk. Rd. (SR 798):** 24 hrs daily, opens on the hour and half-hour. 561-392-5903.

1048.2 9' **Boca Raton-Camino Real:** 24 hrs daily, opens on the hour and at :20 and :40 past the hour. 561-395-7132.

1050.0 21' **Deerfield Beach-Hillsboro Boulevard (SR 810):** 24 hrs daily, opens on the hour and half-hour. 954-428-1090.

1053.9 13' **Hillsboro Inlet (to ocean):** Year-round daily, 7 a.m. to 6 p.m., opens on the hour and :15, :30 and :45 past the hour. 954-943-1847.

1055.0 15' **Pompano Beach-N.E. 14th Street:** Year-round, 24 hrs daily, opens at :15 and :45 past the hour. 954-942-6909.

1056.0 15' **Pompano Beach-Atlantic Boulevard (SR 814):** Year-round, 24 hrs daily, opens on the hour and half-hour. 954-941-7119.

SKIPPER'S HANDBOOK

1059.0 **15'** **Lauderdale-by-the-Sea—Commercial Blvd. (SR 870):** Year-round, 24 hrs daily, opens on the hour and half-hour. 954-772-3987.

1060.5 **22'** **Fort Lauderdale-Oakland Park Boulevard:** 24 hrs daily, opens at :15 and :45 past the hour. 954-566-3711.

1062.6 **25'** **Fort Lauderdale-Sunrise Blvd. (SR 838):** 24 hrs daily, opens on the hour and half-hour. 954-564-6986.

1064.0 **24'** **Fort Lauderdale-Las Olas Boulevard:** Year-round, 24 hrs daily, opens at :15 and :45 past the hour. 954-463-0842.

1065.9 **55'** **Fort Lauderdale-S.E. 17th St. Bridge (SR A1A):** Year-round, 24 hrs daily, opens on the hour and half-hour. 954-524-7783.

1069.4 **22'** **Dania Beach Boulevard (SR A1A):** Year-round, 24 hrs daily, opens on the hour and half-hour. 954-922-7833.

1070.5 **22'** **Hollywood-Sheridan Street:** 24 hrs daily, opens at :15 and :45 past the hour. 954-923-2597.

1072.2 **25'** **Hollywood Beach Boulevard (SR 820):** 24 hrs daily, opens on hour and half-hour. 954-922-3366.

1074.0 **31'** **Hallandale Beach Blvd. (SR 824):** Year-round, 24 hrs daily, opens at :15 and :45 past the hour. 954-456-6630.

1076.3 **65'** **Golden Beach-N.E. 192nd Street:** (Fixed)

1078.0 **30'** **Sunny Isles-N.E. 163rd Street (SR 826):** Year-round, Mon.-Fri.*, 7 a.m. to 6 p.m., opens at :15 and :45 past the hour. Wknd & hldy, 10 a.m. to 6 p.m., opens at 15: and :45 past the hour.

1080.0 **32'** **Bakers Haulover Inlet (to ocean):** (Fixed)

1081.3 **16'** **Bay Harbor-Broad Causeway:** Year-round, 8 a.m. to 6 p.m., opens at :15 and :45 past the hour.

1084.6 **25'** **Miami-79th Street JFK Causeway (West Span):** Opens on signal. 305-758-1834.

1087.2 **56'** **Julia Tuttle Causeway-36th St. (I-195):** (Fixed)(Note: Bridge is less than standard ICW vertical clearance.)

1088.6 **12'** **Miami-Venetian Causeway (West):** Year-round, Mon.-Fri. 7 a.m. to 7 p.m. Opens on the hour and half-hour. Opens on request Saturday, Sunday and federal holidays. 305-358-6258.

1088.8 **65'** **Miami-MacArthur Causeway Bridge (i-395):** (Fixed)

1089.3 **65'** **Miami-Dodge Island Highway:** (Fixed)

1089.3 **22'** **Miami-Dodge Island Railway:** Normally open.

1089.3 **26'** **Miami-Dodge Island Highway (Old):** Normally open.

1091.6 **65'** **Miami-Powell/Rickenbacker Causeway:** (Fixed)

1126.9 **65'** **North Key Largo-Card Sound:** (Fixed)

1134.1 **65'** **Jewfish Creek (U.S. 1):** (Fixed)

Bridges and Locks: Okeechobee Waterway

KEY: **Miles West Of Atlantic ICW Intersection**
Vertical Clearance **Bridge:** Schedule / Openings
SR=State Route. Drawbridge clearances are closed, vertical, in feet. *=Except federal holidays

3.4 **65'** **Stuart-Evans Crary Sr. Bridge (SR A1A):** (Fixed)

7.3 **65'** **New Roosevelt Bridge (U.S. Highway 1):** (Fixed)

7.4 **7'** **Railroad (FEC):** Open except when train approaching.

7.4 **14'** **Old Roosevelt Bridge:** Opens on signal. Does not open if adjacent railroad bridge is closed. 561-692-0321.

9.5 **54'** **Palm City (SR 714):** (Fixed)

14.0 **56'** **Interstate 95:** (Fixed)

14.5 **55'** **Thomas B. Manuel (Twin):** (Fixed)

15.1 **St. Lucie Lock:** Operating hours are 6 a.m. to 9:30 p.m. Normally make fast at south side. Radio ahead for current opening schedules: Drought restrictions in effect during 2009.

17.1 `56'`	**State Road 76A:** (Fixed)	

28.1 `55'`	**Indiantown (SR 710):** (Fixed)

28.5 `7'` **Indiantown Railway Bridge:** Year-round daily, 6 a.m. to 10 p.m., opens on signal, 10 p.m. to 6 a.m., opens with three hours' advance notice.

38.0 `7' Down- 49' Up` **Port Mayaca Railroad (Lift Bridge):** Normally open, not tended, operated by train crew when needed. Vertical clearance may vary with lake level.

38.8 `55'` **U.S. Highways 98 & 441:** (Fixed)

38.9 **Port Mayaca Lock:** Operating hours are 6 a.m. to 9:30 p.m. Normally make fast at south side. Radio ahead for current opening schedules: Drought restrictions in effect during 2009.

60.7 `11'` **(Rim Route) Torry Island Bridge (SR 717):** Year-round, Mon.-Thu., 7 a.m. to 6 p.m., opens on signal, but not at night. Fri.-Sun., 7 a.m. to 7 p.m., opens on signal, but not at night. (Swing bridge, slow, hand-operated.)

78.0 **Moore Haven Lock:** Operating hours are 6 a.m. to 9:30 p.m. Normally make fast at north side. Radio ahead for current opening schedules: Drought restrictions in effect during 2009.

78.3 `5'` **Moore Haven Railroad:** Year-round daily, 6 a.m. to 10 p.m., opens on signal. 10 p.m. to 6 a.m., does not open. (Swing bridge, slow, hand-operated.)

78.4 `55'` **Moore Haven (U.S. 27):** (Fixed)

93.5 **Ortona Lock:** Operating hours are 6 a.m. to 9:30 p.m. Normally make fast at north side. Radio ahead for current opening schedules: Drought restrictions in effect during 2009.

103.0 `28'` **La Belle (SR 29):** Daily, 6 a.m. to 10 p.m.; opens on signal, except no openings 7 a.m. to 9 a.m. and 4 p.m. to 6 p.m. 10 p.m. to 6 a.m., opens on three hours notice.

108.2 `9'` **Fort Denaud:** Year-round daily, 6 a.m. to 10 p.m., opens on signal. 10 p.m. to 6 a.m., opens with three hours notice.

116.0 `23'` **Alva:** Year-round daily, 6 a.m. to 10 p.m., opens on signal, 10 p.m. to 6 a.m., opens with three hours' notice.

121.4 **W.P. Franklin Lock:** Operating hours are 6 a.m. to 9:30 p.m. Normally make fast at south side. Radio ahead for current opening schedules: Drought restrictions in effect during 2009.

126.3 `27'` **Olga (SR 31):** Year-round daily, 6 a.m. to 10 p.m., opens on signal. 10 p.m. to 6 a.m., opens on three hours notice.

128.9 `55'` **Interstate 75:** (Fixed)

129.9 `5'` **Beautiful Island Railway Bridge:** Opens on signal. Span overhangs channel when open; vertical clearance is 55 feet open.

134.6 `56'` **Edison Bridges:** (Fixed)

135.0 `55'` **Caloosahatchee Bridge:** (Fixed)

138.6 `55'` **Mid Point Memorial Bridge:** (Fixed)

142.0 `55'` **Cape Coral (Twin Bridges):** (Fixed)

148.9 **Gulf ICW—Mile 0**

151.0 `70'` **Punta Rassa (Sanibel Causeway):** "A"

Bridges: Florida's West Coast

KEY:	Statute Miles from GIWW Mile 0
Vertical Clearance	**Bridge:** Schedule / Openings

SR=State Route. Drawbridge clearances are closed, vertical, in feet. *=Except federal holidays

`55'` **Goodland:** (Fixed)

`55'` **Marco Island:** (Fixed)

`65'` **Fort Myers Beach (Matanzas Pass):** (Fixed)

`23'` **Big Carlos Pass (SR 865):** Year-round daily, no openings 7 p.m. to 8 a.m.

`70'` **Sanibel Causeway-"A":** (Fixed)

`9'` **Sanibel Causeway-"B":** (Fixed)

`26'` **Sanibel Causeway-"C":** (Fixed)

9' **Matlacha Pass (SR 78):** Year-round, Mon.-Sat., 8 a.m. to 10 a.m. and 3 p.m. to 7 p.m., opens on signal; does not open at other times. Year-round, Sun., 7 a.m. to 10 a.m. and 3 p.m. to 7 p.m., opens on signal; does not open at other times.

45' **Punta Gorda (U.S. 41):** (Fixed)

34.3 **9'** **Boca Grande Swing Bridge:** Year-round, Mon-Fri*, 7 a.m. to 6 p.m., opens on the hour and half-hour. Wknd & hldy, 7 a.m. to 6 p.m., opens on the hour, :15, :30 and :45 past the hour.

43.5 **26'** **Manasota Key (Tom Adams Bridge) (SR 776):** Opens on signal.

49.9 **26'** **Manasota:** Opens on signal.

54.9 **25'** **Venice-Airport (Circus Bridge) (U.S. 41 South):** Opens on signal.

56.6 **30'** **Venice Avenue:** Year-round, Mon.-Fri.*, 7 a.m. to 4:30 p.m. opens at :10, :30, and :50 past the hour, no openings 4:35 to 5:35 p.m.

56.9 **30'** **Hatchett Creek (U.S. 41):** Year-round, Mon.-Fri.*, 7 a.m. to 4:20 p.m., opens on the hour and every :20 thereafter, no openings 4:25 to 5:25 p.m. Wknd & hldy, 7:30 a.m. to 6 p.m., opens on the hour and every :15 thereafter.

59.3 **14'** **Nokomis/Casey Key (Albee Bridge):** Opens on signal.

63.0 **9'** **Blackburn Point:** Opens on signal.

68.6 **18'** **Stickney Point (SR 72):** Year-round, Mon.-Fri, 6 a.m. to 10 p.m., opens on the hour and every :20 thereafter. (May have more clearance then Charted)

71.6 **25'** **Sarasota-Siesta Key:** Year-round, Mon.-Fri.*, 7 a.m. to 11 a.m. opens on signal, opens on the hour and every :20 thereafter until 6 p.m.

73.6 **65'** **Ringling Causeway (SR 789):** (Fixed)

23' **New Pass (SR 789) (to Gulf):** Year-round, 7 a.m. to 6 p.m., opens on the hour and every :20 thereafter.

16' **Longboat Pass (SR 789) (to Gulf):** Year-round, opens on signal.

87.4 **22'** **Cortez (SR 684):** May 16 to Jan. 14, 6 a.m. to 7 p.m., opens on the hour and every :20 thereafter. Jan. 15 to May 15, 6 a.m. to 7 p.m., opens on the hour and half-hour.

89.2 **24'** **Anna Maria Island (SR 64):** May 16 to Jan. 14, 7 a.m. to 6 p.m., opens on the hour and every :20 thereafter. Jan. 15 to May 15, 6 a.m. to 7 p.m., opens on the hour and half-hour.

99.0 **175'** **Sunshine Skyway-Main Spans (I-275):** (Fixed)

110.5 **65'** **Maximo Point:** (Fixed)

10' **Tampa-Garrison Channel (East & West Access):** (Fixed) Privately built bridges. Charts show 10-foot fixed vertical clearances, but reports indicate about 5 feet of additional clearance on the west span. Approach with caution.

15' **Hillsborough River-Platt Street:** Year-round daily, opens on signal with two hours' notice.

40' **Twin Highway:** (Fixed)

15' **Brorein Street:** Year-round daily, opens on signal with two hours' notice.

11' **Kennedy Boulevard:** Year-round daily, opens on signal with two hours' notice.

7' **Cass Street:** Year-round daily, opens on signal with two hours' notice.

12' **Laurel Street:** Year-round daily, opens on signal with two hours' notice.

40' **U.S. 275:** (Fixed)

43' **Old Tampa Bay-Gandy Bridge:** (Fixed)

44' **Old Tampa Bay-W. Howard Frankland Bridge:** (Fixed)

40' **Courtney Campbell Parkway:** (Fixed)

18' **Pinellas Bayway "A" Cats Point:** (Fixed)

11' **Pinellas Bayway "B" Bird Key (SR 679):** Opens on signal.

113.0 **25'** **Pinellas Bayway "E" Southern (SR 679):** Weekends and federal holidays: 9 a.m. to 7 p.m., opens on the hour, and at :30 past the hour.

SKIPPER'S HANDBOOK

114.0 `25'` **Pinellas Bayway Northern "C":** Year-round daily, 7 a.m. to 7 p.m., opens on the hour and every :20 thereafter.

117.7 `23'` **St. Petersburg Beach (Corey Causeway):** Year-round, Mon.-Fri.*, 8 a.m. to 7 p.m., opens on the hour and every :20 thereafter. Wknd & hldy, 10 a.m. to 7p.m., opens on the hour and every :20 thereafter.

118.9 `21'` **Treasure Island Causeway:** Year-round daily, 7 a.m. to 7 p.m., opens on the hour and every :15 thereafter. 11 p.m. to 7 a.m., 10 minutes notice required.

`74'` **Johns Pass (to Gulf):** (Fixed)

122.8 `25'` **Madeira Beach (Welch Causeway SR 699):** Year-round, wknd & hldy, 9:30 a.m. to 6 p.m., opens on the hour and every :20 thereafter.

126.0 `20'` **Park Boulevard (SR 248):** Opens on signal.

129.3 `25'` **Indian Rocks Beach (CR 694):** Opens on signal.

131.8 `75'` **Belleair Causeway:** (Fixed)

`74'` **Clearwater Pass (to Gulf) (SR 183):** (Fixed)

136.0 `74'` **Clearwater Memorial Causeway (SR 60):** (Fixed)

141.9 `24'` **Dunedin-Honeymoon Island:** Opens on signal.

Bridges: GIWW, East of Harvey Lock

KEY: Statute Miles from GIWW Mile 0
Vertical Clearance **Bridge:** Schedule / Openings
SR=State Route. Drawbridge clearances are closed, vertical, in feet. *=Except federal holidays

361.4 `65'` **Apalachicola-St. George Island (SR G1A):** (Fixed)

351.4 `65'` **Gorrie Memorial (U.S. 98/319):** (Fixed)

347.0 `11'` **Railroad (swing bridge):** Open except when train approaching.

329.3 `65'` **White City (SR 71):** (Fixed)

`75'` **Port St. Joe (U.S. 98):** (Fixed)

315.4 `65'` **Overstreet (SR 386):** (Fixed)

295.4 `50'` **Panama City-Dupont Bridge (U.S. 98):** (Fixed)

284.6 `65'` **Hathaway (U.S. 98):** (Fixed)

271.8 `65'` **West Bay Creek (SR 79):** (Fixed)

250.4 `65'` **Choctawhatchee Bay (U.S. 331/SR 83):** (Fixed)

234.2 `64'` **Mid-Bay:** (Fixed)

`49'` **Destin (to Gulf):** (Fixed)

223.1 `50'` **Brooks-Fort Walton Beach (U.S. 98):** (Fixed)

206.7 `50'` **Navarre Causeway (SR 87):** (Fixed)

189.1 `65'` **Pensacola Beach Twin Bridges (SR 399):** (Fixed)

`50'` **Pensacola: Bay Bridge:** (Fixed)

AL, MS & LA BRIDGES MONITOR (((VHF))) CHANNEL 13

`65'` **Bayou Chico (Barrancas Avenue):** (Fixed)

171.8 `73'` **Gulf Beach (SR 292):** (Fixed)

`54'` **Perdido Pass Channel (to Gulf):** (Fixed)

158.7 `73'` **Foley Beach Express Bridge:** (Fixed)

154.9 `73'` **Portage Creek Twin Bridges (SR 59):** (Fixed)

`73'` **Mobile Bay-Dog River (SR 163):** (Fixed)

127.8 `83'` **Dauphin Island:** (Fixed)

`8' Down - 73' Up` **Bayou La Batre Lift Bridge (SR 188):** Daily, no openings 8 p.m. to 4 a.m. Mon.-Sat.*, no openings 6:30 a.m. to 8:30 a.m., 2 p.m. to 5 p.m.

`8'` **Pascagoula-Singing River (CSX Railroad Swing Bridge):** Opens on signal.

`80'` **Highway (U.S. 90):** (Fixed)

`95'` **Biloxi Bay (U.S. 90):** (Fixed)

`14'` **Biloxi Bay Railway:** Opens on signal.

60' Biloxi-Interstate 110 Twin Bridges: Opens on six hours' notice.

13' Bay St. Louis-Railway: Opens on signal.

85' Bay St. Louis (U.S. 90): (Fixed)

11' Rigolets-Railroad Swing Bridge: Opens on signal.

66' Rigolets-Ft. Pike Highway (U.S. 90): (Fixed)

65' Pte. aux Herbes (I-10): (Fixed)

13' and 4' Highway (SR 11) and Railroad bridges: Open on signal.

13.0 **137'** Paris Road: (Fixed)

7.5 Inner Harbor Navigation Canal (to Mississippi River)

7.5 **0' Down - 156' Up** Florida Avenue and Southern Railway Lift Bridge: Mon.-Fri.*, no openings 6:30 to 8:30 a.m. and 3:30 to 6:45 p.m.

6.7 **40' Down - 156' Up** North Claiborne Ave. (Judge Seeber Lift Bridge) (SR 39) : Mon.-Fri.*, No openings 6:30 a.m. to 8:30 a.m. and 3:30 p.m. to 6:45 p.m.

6.2 **0'** St. Claude Avenue (SR 46): Mon.-Fri.*, No openings 6:30 a.m. to 8:30 a.m. and 3:30 p.m. to 6:45 p.m.

5.8 Mississippi River

2.5 **150'** New Orleans-Crescent City Connection: (Fixed)

0 Harvey Lock

6.5 Inner Harbor Industrial Lock (to Lake Pontchartrain)

0' Gentilly Highway and Railroad: Open on signal.

115' Interstate 10: (Fixed)

50' Down - 120' Up Chef Menteur Highway Lift Bridge (U.S. 90): Mon.-Fri.*, no openings 7 a.m. to 8:30 a.m., 5 p.m. to 6:30 p.m.

44' Lakeshore Bascule and Railroad Bridges: Opens on signal.

22' Lake Pontchartrain Causeway (from N. Orleans): (Fixed)

50' Lake Pontchartrain Causeway (from N. Orleans): (Fixed)

22' Lake Pontchartrain Causeway (from N. Orleans): (Fixed)

42' Lake Pontchartrain Causeway (from N. Orleans): Mon.-Fri.*, No openings 5:30 a.m. to 9:30 a.m. and 3 p.m. to 7 p.m., all other times opens on three hours advance notice. 504-835-3116 (Police dispatch).

22' Lake Pontchartrain Causeway (from N. Orleans): (Fixed)

Bridges: GIWW, West of Harvey Lock

KEY: Statute Miles from GIWW Mile 0

Vertical Clearance **Bridge:** Schedule / Openings
SR=State Route. Drawbridge clearances are closed, vertical, in feet. *=Except federal holidays

LA & TX BRIDGES MONITOR 〈〈📻〉〉 CHANNEL 13

0.1 **9'** Harvey Route Railroad: Opens on signal

0.1 **7'** Harvey Route Highway (SR 18): Opens on signal.

0.8 **95'** Harvey Route Highway Twin Bridges: (Fixed)

2.8 **45'** Harvey Route Lapalco Boulevard: Mon.-Fri.*, no openings 6:30 a.m. to 8:30 a.m., 3:45 p.m. to 5:45 p.m.

1.0 AA **100'** Algiers Alternate (AA) Route Highway Bridge (SR 407): (Fixed)

3.7 AA **2' Down - 100' Up** Missouri Pacific Railroad Lift Bridge: Normally open.

3.8 AA **40' Down - 100' Up** (A.A.) Belle Chasse Highway Lift Bridge (SR 23): Mon.-Fri.*, no openings 6 a.m. to 8:30 a.m., 3:30 p.m. to 7 p.m.

11.9 `73'`	**Crown Point Highway:** (Fixed)	
35.2 `73'`	**Larose Highway:** (Fixed)	
35.6 `35' Down - 73' Up`	**Larose-Bourg Cutoff Lift Bridge (SR 1):** Opens on signal.	
49.8 `0'`	**Bayou Blue Pontoon Bridge (SR 316):** Opens on signal.	
54.4 `73'`	**Houma-Prospect Boulevard (SR 3087):** (Fixed)	
57.6 `73'`	**Houma-Park Avenue:** (Fixed)	
57.7 `73'`	**Houma-Main Street:** (Fixed)	
58.9 `4' Down - 70' Up`	**Southern Pacific Railroad Lift Bridge:** Opens on signal.	

59.9 `40'` **Bayou DuLarge (SR 315):** Mon.-Fri.*, no openings 6:45 a.m. to 8:30 a.m., 11:45 a.m. to 12:15 p.m., 12:45 p.m. to 1:15 p.m., and 4:30 p.m. to 6 p.m.

93.0 **Bayou Boeuf Lock**

94.3 **Cable Ferry:** Daily, Operates from 5:30 a.m. to 10:30 p.m.

113.0 `73'` **North Bend (SR 317):** (Fixed)

129.7 **Cable Ferry:** Daily, operates 24 hours a day.

134.0 `73'` **Cypremort Bridge (SR 319):** (Fixed)

163.0 **Leland Bowman Lock**

170.3 `73'` **Forked Island:** (Fixed)

178.4 **Cable Ferry:** Daily, operates during daylight hours.

219.8 `73'` **Gibbstown:** (Fixed)

231.5 `0'` **Grand Lake Pontoon Bridge (SR 384):** Mon.-Fri.*, no openings 6 a.m. to 8 a.m. and 2 p.m. to 4 p.m.

238.0 `0'` **Black Bayou Pontoon Bridge (SR 384):** Mon.-Fri.*, no openings 6 a.m. to 8 a.m. and 2 p.m. to 4 p.m.

238.2 **Calcasieu Lock**

243.8 `50' Down - 135' Up` **Ellender Lift Bridge (SR 27):** Requires four hours' notice to open. 800-752-6706.

254.1 **Cable Ferry:** Do not attempt to pass a moving cable ferry.

286.3 `136'` **Port Arthur (SR 73/87):** (Fixed)

288.8 `73'` **Highway (SR 87):** (Fixed)

319.3 `73'` **High Island:** (Fixed)

356.0 `12'` **(Alternate Route) Pelican Island Railroad/ Highway Bridge:** Mon.-Fri.*, no openings 7 a.m. to 8:30 a.m., noon to 1 p.m., 4:15 p.m. to 5:15 p.m. (75-foot overhang when open).

357.2 `7'` **RR Bridge:** Opens on signal.

357.3 `74'` **Gulf Freeway (two bridges, I-45):** (Fixed)

393.8 `73'` **Surfside Beach (SR 232):** (Fixed)

397.6 `73'` **Freeport Bridge (SR 1495):** (Fixed)

418.0 `0'` **Pontoon Bridge (Farm Road 457):** (Fixed)

440.7 `73'` **Matagorda Bridge (Farm Road 2031):** Opens on signal.

533.1 `48'` **Aransas Pass (SR 361):** (Fixed)

552.7 `73'` **John F. Kennedy Causeway Park Road 22:** (Fixed)

665.1 `73'` **Port Isabel Causeway Park Road 100:** (Fixed)

666.0 `0'` **Port Isabel–Long Island Pontoon Bridge:** Mon.-Fri.*, 5 a.m. to 8 p.m., opens for recreational craft only on the hour.

Florida's East Coast

Cruising south on the Intracoastal Waterway (ICW), boaters enter Florida at Mile 714. A study in contrasts, the scenery begins its change from nearly deserted, white-capped sounds to the claustrophobic confines of the crowded "Ditch" lined by mountainous condominiums. As you cross Cumberland Sound and the St. Marys River, the broad expanses of the marsh-bordered Georgia ICW give way to the narrower, more protected, and more populated Florida route. From here to Miami, 375 statute miles (326 nautical miles) away, navigational aids are plentiful, and marinas and urban centers proliferate as you continue south. Below St. Lucie Inlet, the coastline becomes truly tropical, with a profusion of palm trees and exotic flowers. Here, the bustling Gold Coast comes into its own, with burgeoning development and fewer anchorages than you might wish.

U.S. Army Corps of Engineers (USACE) project depths on the ICW are 12 feet from Norfolk, VA to Fort Pierce, FL, Mile 965; 10 feet to Miami, FL, Mile 1085; and 7 feet from Miami to Cross Bank across Florida Bay. Keep in mind that these are ideal depths, maintained as closely as possible by the USACE and the Florida Inland Navigation District (FIND). (FIND receives state funding provided by taxes on waterfront property throughout Florida; thus, Florida has more money available for Waterway maintenance than states where dredging is funded only with federal money.) The controlling depth, the least water depth actually available, is what counts. Current depths are reported by the USACE, by the Coast Guard (in the Local Notice to Mariners) and by WATERWAY GUIDE according to the latest information. The USACE and FIND schedule dredging of shoaling sections throughout the year, and what was too shallow last year may be 12 feet deep this year, and vice versa. Funds for dredging are still scarce; use caution, and stay armed with the most up-to-date information.

You should also be aware that Florida requires a fishing license for both freshwater and saltwater fishing.

Dozens of bridges cross the ICW between Fernandina Beach and Miami, and many have restricted opening schedules. Unfortunately, there seems to be no consistency about restricted hours. Some are restricted for different hours in specific months, some are closed during rush hours and some open on the quarter-hour, half-hour or even at 20 minutes and 40 minutes past the hour. To add to the confusion, the restrictions are constantly changing. Just because a bridge opened on a certain schedule last season does not mean it is still on that same schedule. (See the Skipper's Handbook section in the front of the Guide for the current schedules at publication.)

Though the bridge information was correct at the time it was reported—after checking Coast Pilots, the Federal Register and Local Notice to Mariners—some bridge information here may have already changed by the time of publication. Check locally to verify bridge schedules before your transit.

Florida ICW bridges monitor VHF Channel 09, designated by the Federal Communications Commission as the "bridge tender channel." ICW bridges in other states (except South Carolina and Georgia) still answer on VHF Channel 13, as do the locks in the Okeechobee. In Florida waters, it is a good idea to monitor both the bridge channel and VHF Channel 16—one on your ship's radio and one on a handheld radio, if your main set doesn't have a dual-watch capability—to monitor oncoming commercial traffic and communications with the bridge tender.

The proper horn signal for a bridge opening is one prolonged blast (four to six seconds) and one short blast (approximately one second). Bridge operators sound this signal when ready to open the bridge, and then usually the danger signal, five short blasts, when they are closing the bridge. The operator of each vessel is required by law to signal the bridge tender for an opening, even if another vessel has already signaled.

When using VHF, always call bridges by name, and identify your vessel by name and type (such as sailing vessel or trawler). If you are unable to raise the bridge using VHF radio, use a horn signal. (For further information, see the Coast Pilot 4, Chapter Two: Title 33, Navigation Regulations, Part 117, Drawbridge Regulations.) If the gates do not come down and the bridge does not open after repeated use of the radio and the horn, call the Coast Guard and ask them to call the bridge tender on the land telephone line, or you may be able to call the bridge directly. Phone numbers for many bridges are given in the Skipper's Handbook, although some of the numbers are not for the actual bridge tender, but for a central office that manages that bridge, such as the Florida Department of Transportation's Northeast Region. Its hotline number is posted on all drawbridges in its jurisdiction (800-865-5794). Some bridges are not required to open in high winds. If you encounter a bridge that won't open, it is prudent to drop the hook in a safe spot until the situation is resolved.

Most bridges carry a tide board to register vertical clearance at the center of the span. In Florida, however, the tide board figure (and the one noted on the chart) is generally for a point five feet toward the channel from the bridge fender. In the case of arched bridges, center channel clearance is frequently higher than the tide gauge registers. So check your chart and the tide boards and, unless it specifically notes that vertical clearance is given "at center," you may be able to count on a little extra height at mid-channel, under the arch of the bridge. Some bridges may bear signs noting extra height at center in feet.

With a few exceptions, the ICW between Fernandina and Miami is protected from strong winds and is usually free of rough water. Tidal heights range from more than 7 feet at Fernandina to about 1.5 feet at Key West. Currents up to 4 knots may be encountered between Fernandina and Haulover Canal, especially at inlets. Lesser currents up to about 2 knots occur from Haulover Canal to Miami.

The Florida ICW is well-marked and easy to follow. Keep track of your position by checking off markers on the chart as you pass. Take a little extra care where inlet, river and ICW channels meet; a few moments' study of the chart ahead of time will prevent confusion in those areas where a buoy system changes direction.

Much of Florida's eastern ICW is narrow and shoal-bordered, with scattered anchorages. As the population continues to increase, favorite anchorages are becoming more crowded. Good anchorages are still available if you plan ahead. Using an anchor light is important and required by law, and some places will give you a ticket for not having one on at night. Marina dockage faces much the same space shortage, so you should reserve ahead or plan to arrive early at your chosen marina during the winter cruising season. Most dockmasters make every effort to find room for one more, and the friendliness of the boating community usually makes up for the crowded conditions.

In 2004 and 2005, the hurricanes that hit the Florida coastline caused damage from Fernandina Beach to Pensacola. Many marinas sustained significant damage. Most facilities have fully recovered while some have permanently closed or sold out to developers. Before cruising in Florida, call the marinas of your intended destinations and make reservations early.

Many retirees who have sold their homes are cruising the East Coast and the islands on a more or less full-time schedule. In Florida, governments at every level regard liveaboards as a problem. Florida law does not distinguish between a resident of the state who lives and works there, has their mail delivered to the marina, has the marina address on their driver's license, votes there, and lives on a boat instead of a house versus a transient who lives and votes somewhere else but happens to want to winter in Florida on their boat.

The widely held, if unofficial view is that the first category of people rarely move their boats, pump bilge and black water overboard, allow boats to deteriorate, create nuisance problems for "real" local residents, don't pay property taxes, etc. So the state, counties and local municipalities have acted to curtail liveaboards more and more aggressively. In Florida, merely describing yourself as a "liveaboard" changes your status under the law. Florida municipalities along the Intracoastal Waterway have adopted restrictive anchoring regulations, and then employed the heavy hand of waterborne law enforcement to intimidate out-of-staters. These regulations have come about because wealthy landowners resent the sight of

North Fernandina Beach. (Not to be used for navigation.) Photo Courtesy of Mike Kucera.

vessels anchored in front of their properties (not to mention the far more legitimate concern about abandoned and derelict vessels).

State law defines a liveaboard boat as "any vessel used solely as a residence or any vessel represented as place of business, a professional or other commercial enterprise or a legal residence." For cruisers, the operative phrase is *represented as a legal residence*. Maritime lawyers and WATERWAY GUIDE editors suggest that cruising boaters who might otherwise call themselves "liveaboards" should adopt the term "full-time cruisers," or just "cruisers." That shifts the burden to the local authorities, forcing them to prove a boat is a residence.

Boating, however, injects about $18 billion into the Florida economy each year, so officials at the state level began to fret at the mounting publicity about anchoring disputes and police harassment. In 2005, the state of Florida called "time out" and rewrote the law, forbidding the locals from restricting "non-liveaboards in navigation." Cities like Ft. Lauderdale and Miami had imposed time constraints on anchoring and Vero Beach had flat out prohibited it within their waters. However, in 2009, the State of Florida, after many lawsuits, passed legislation (327.02) that stated, "that local governmental authorities are prohibited from regulating the anchoring outside of such mooring fields of vessels other than liveaboard vessels..." That is not to say that municipalities may not try to enforce old regulations, but unless you are anchored within a designated mooring field, or you are impeding navigation, you are legal as long as you are a "cruising" and not a "liveaboard" vessel.

Documented vessels without a state registration in full force-and-effect must also obtain a Florida registration and display the validation decal on the vessel while using Florida waters. There is no grace period.

This situation will only occur if your home state does not require registration of documented vessels, or you are returning from a long cruise down-island and have not been renewing your registration.

Any documented or state-registered vessels in Florida longer than 90 days must be registered with a county tax collector, unless the owner can document that the vessel is under repair at a bonafide yacht yard. Owners may retain their out-of-state registration number if planning to return to their home state within a reasonable period of time.

Registering your boat in Florida has tax consequences. The "use" component of Florida's sales and use tax law provides uniform taxation of items purchased out of state, but stored or used in Florida. A credit for lawfully imposed taxes paid to another state, a U.S. territory or the District of Columbia is permitted. Credit is not given for taxes paid to another country. For boats, the state sales tax rate is six percent, and individual counties may tack on extra.

If a boat is purchased in a state that has a sales tax rate of four percent, the owner may be required to pay an additional two percent when the boat is brought into Florida. Beware: A boat that remains in Florida for more than 90 consecutive days or more than 183 days in a one-year period is presumed taxable, unless it qualifies for another exemption.

As boats compete for space and traffic increases along the ICW, local agencies have set up Idle-Speed/No-Wake Zones. Such speed limits protect shorelines, wildlife, shore facilities and berthed boats from wake damage and help cut down on boating accidents. Idle speed means putting the engine in gear with no increase in throttle, while taking care to maintain control of the vessel. Other areas have Slow-Speed Zones where minimum wake is required, while others may have a limit on wake height. Read the signs. In crowded areas (such as Fort Lauderdale and Miami), especially on weekends and holidays when less experienced boaters are on the water, always slow down, and keep alert. Manatee zones have speed restrictions that are strictly enforced. Many are seasonal, and the posted signs may be difficult to read, so keep an eye out for them.

When yachtsmen think of Florida, they usually envision balmy breezes, endless sunshine and consistently warm weather. That is true more often than not, but moderate to heavy frosts occur frequently in northern and central Florida and sometimes extend to the toe of the peninsula.

From autumn to spring, Florida is under the influence of an eastward-flowing cycle of cold and warm fronts. An arriving cold front is heralded by a shift in the prevailing east wind to the south, then to the southwest. Here, the front may hang motionless for a few hours or a day, and the weather can become warm and reminiscent of summer.

Then the wind moves abruptly into the northwest, often accompanied by heavy black cloud banks, line squalls and rain. With clearing, the wind may remain northerly for several days, bringing cold, windy and sparkling bright weather. The wind shifts back to the east—sometimes suddenly, sometimes gradually—bringing warmer air, some cloudiness, a breeze and "normal" Florida weather. Sometimes the wind will stubbornly stay northeasterly for two or three days at 15 to 25 knots.

Frequently, the cycle turns full circle within three or four days. Fast or slow, the pattern repeats itself all winter. Cold fronts demand respect and caution, as northers can bring severe weather with rough seas and strong winds. Cold snaps in northern Florida can freeze dock lines and hoses and cause unexpected damage. Monitor NOAA weather forecasts from a variety of sources regularly, especially in December and January.

Florida's summer is tropical, with temperatures in the 90s and high humidity, usually accompanied by a refreshing sea breeze. June and September are the rainiest months, with lots of sunshine between showers. Mosquitoes and sandflies may be bothersome, particularly around swampy, wooded or mangrove-fringed areas. Insect screens are a necessity. Winds are generally light to moderate from the east, a phenomenon that makes crossing the Gulf Stream to the Bahamas comparatively easy.

Remember, though, that June through November is hurricane season. Listen to the NOAA broadcasts on the weather stations of your VHF radio each day. The colorful graphics of local television news also can be useful, as well as the many available online weather sources.

Morning mist is common during the winter months along both coasts of central and northern Florida. Pea-soup "sea fog" can occur from fall through spring in northeast Florida any time warm calm weather settles over cool ocean waters. It appears as a low dark cloud over the ocean that gently rolls in to engulf the coast and sometimes lasts all day. It should be respected.

One of the biggest weather threats in Florida is lightning, which is a daily afternoon occurrence in the warmer months. That is how Florida earned its nickname as "The Lightning Capital of the World." Refer to the Skipper's Handbook section in the front of this guide for a full treatment of this dangerous phenomenon. ■

Fort Clinch. (Not to be used for navigation.) Photo Courtesy of Mike Kucera.

Florida's Upper East Coast

☐ **FERNANDINA TO ST. JOHNS RIVER** ☐ **ST. JOHNS RIVER** ☐ **JACKSONVILLE BEACH TO PONCE DE LEON INLET**
☐ **NEW SMYRNA BEACH TO VERO BEACH** ☐ **FORT PIERCE TO ST. LUCIE RIVER**

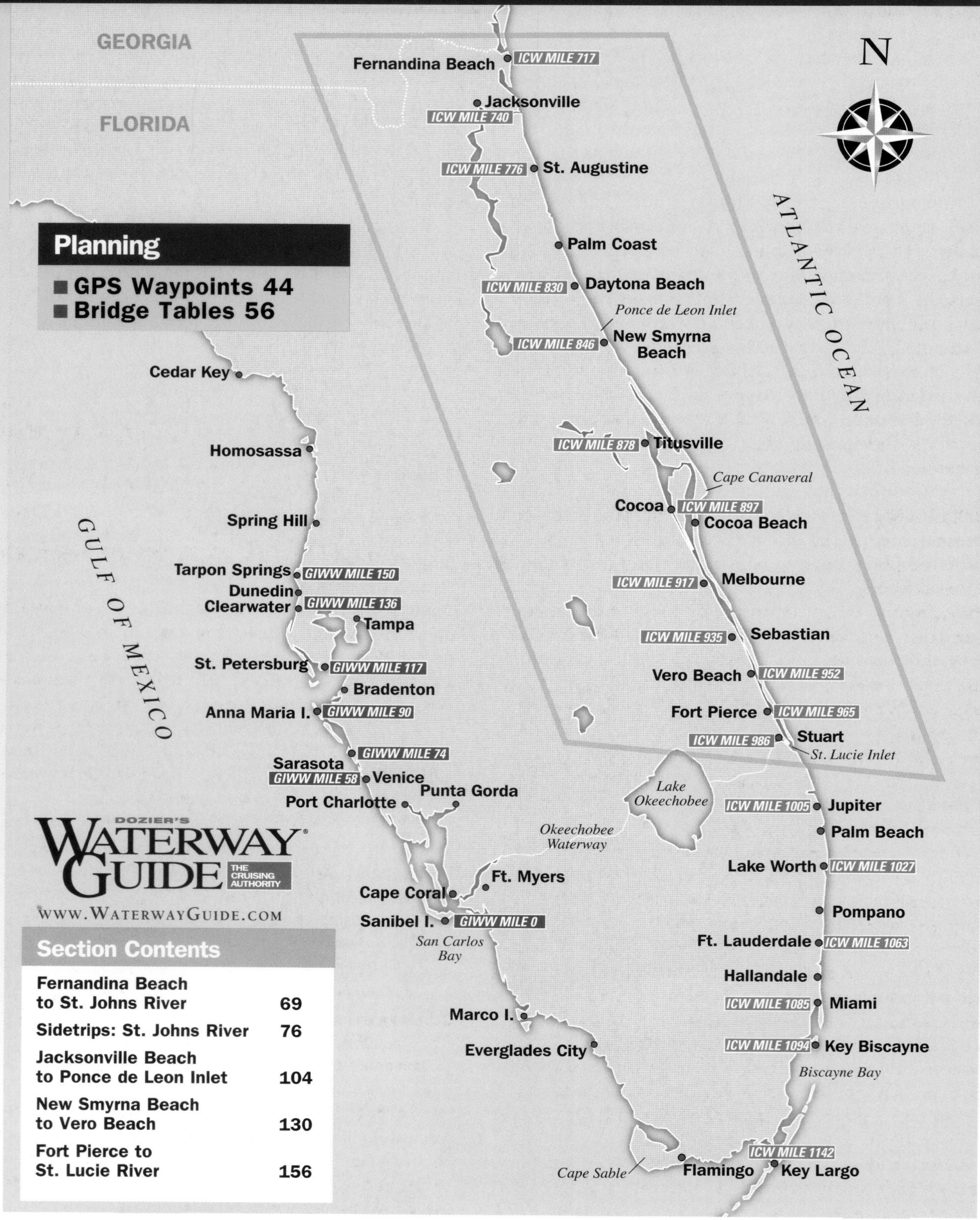

GEORGIA

FLORIDA

N

Fernandina Beach ● ICW MILE 717

Jacksonville ●
ICW MILE 740

ICW MILE 776 ● St. Augustine

ATLANTIC OCEAN

Palm Coast ●

ICW MILE 830 ● Daytona Beach
Ponce de Leon Inlet

ICW MILE 846 ● New Smyrna Beach

Planning
■ **GPS Waypoints 44**
■ **Bridge Tables 56**

Cedar Key ●

Homosassa ●

ICW MILE 878 ● Titusville
Cape Canaveral

Cocoa ● ICW MILE 897
● Cocoa Beach

Spring Hill ●

Tarpon Springs ● GIWW MILE 150
Dunedin ●
Clearwater ● GIWW MILE 136

ICW MILE 917 ● Melbourne

● Tampa

ICW MILE 935 ● Sebastian

GULF OF MEXICO

St. Petersburg ● GIWW MILE 117

Vero Beach ● ICW MILE 952

● Bradenton

Anna Maria I. ● GIWW MILE 90

Fort Pierce ● ICW MILE 965

ICW MILE 986 ● Stuart
St. Lucie Inlet

GIWW MILE 74

Sarasota ●
GIWW MILE 58 ● Venice
Port Charlotte ● Punta Gorda

Lake Okeechobee

ICW MILE 1005 ● Jupiter

DOZIER'S
WATERWAY GUIDE THE CRUISING AUTHORITY

Okeechobee Waterway

● Palm Beach

WWW.WATERWAYGUIDE.COM

Lake Worth ● ICW MILE 1027

Cape Coral ● ● Ft. Myers
Sanibel I. ● GIWW MILE 0
San Carlos Bay

● Pompano

Ft. Lauderdale ● ICW MILE 1063

Hallandale ●

ICW MILE 1085 ● Miami

Marco I. ●

Everglades City ●

ICW MILE 1094 ● Key Biscayne
Biscayne Bay

Cape Sable

ICW MILE 1142

Flamingo ● ● Key Largo

Fernandina Beach to St. Johns River

CHARTS 11488, 11489, 11490, 11491, 11502, 11503

As you cross the St. Marys River and enter the state of Florida, you will notice a change in the characteristics of the Intracoastal Waterway (ICW). Georgia's long, open sounds and wide rivers gradually transform into a series of creeks and rivers connected by narrow land cuts. The ICW crosses several navigable inlets that no doubt attracted the early explorers. The first settlers built strategic, profitable ports along these protected inside waters. Today's cruisers use improved and connected passages that link many of these original settlements.

NAVIGATION: Use Chart 11489. The St. Marys Entrance is deep, wide, jettied and well-marked, but exercise caution when going through, as the jetties become submerged at mid-tide. It is a relatively easy entry and exit point, conveniently located just off the ICW. The short offshore jump from here to the St. Johns River at Mayport (near Jacksonville), or to the inlet at St. Augustine, bypasses the sometimes shallow, shifting channels at Nassau Sound, and a northerly leg to St. Simons will cut out the meandering shallows found in Cumberland Sound and Jekyll Creek. Both the St. Johns and the St. Simons inlets do involve long entry channels and strong currents to return to the ICW; be careful, and try to plan exits and entries with a slack current or fair tide.

The active Kings Bay Naval Submarine Base, located in Cumberland Sound north of the junction of the St. Marys River, continues to be the reason for frequent dredging and renumbering of buoys, beginning where the ICW joins the head of Cumberland Sound, and continuing to the ocean inlet. The channel is consequently quite deep and was again dredged in summer 2008. The St. Marys Entrance Channel buoys, offshore of the entrance, were eliminated several years ago. The buoy that formerly was "10" is now flashing red buoy "2," and every buoy in Cumberland Sound up to the head of Kings Bay was renumbered accordingly. ICW daybeacon numbering remains unchanged. Your older charts may not show this change.

When passing from Cumberland Dividings into Cumberland Sound, there is a tricky spot in the ICW channel just south of green daybeacon "75" (Mile 707.8 just east of Kings Bay). Heading south, alter course westward to favor red daybeacon "76," leaving it close to starboard, and then continue south in the channel, avoiding the charted 4- to 5-foot-deep shoal to port. Also be sure to leave green daybeacon "79" well to port heading south. You will probably see a Navy patrol boat as you pass Kings Bay entering Cumberland Sound. *Here, the green markers will be left to starboard southbound out of Cumberland Sound to the Florida line until you pick up quick flashing green buoy "1" in the Amelia River near Mile 715.*

The ICW fronts the Kings Bay Naval Submarine Base near Mile 708, and Navy security patrols carefully monitor traffic from both directions, especially when submarines are passing through Cumberland Sound and St. Marys Entrance. They will ask you to move outside of the channel if a submarine is in the vicinity. Patrol boats respond on VHF Channel 16. The submarines travel at high speeds in open water, creating very large wakes. For more information on security zones around U.S. Naval vessels, see the "Port Security Procedures" section found in the Skipper's Handbook in the front of this guide.

On the Amelia River at Mile 718 past the Fernandina Beach waterfront, swing wide between red daybeacons "14" and "16," and favor the north side between red daybeacons "16" and "18" due to 6-foot depths on the magenta line between the two. Red daybeacon "18" appears to be too far to the west, but head toward it to give the shoal at the bend marked by flashing green "1" a wide berth, both

Fernandina Beach, FL

Looking east at the St. Marys Entrance and Cumberland Sound. Fernandina Beach is to the right.
(Not to be used for navigation.) WATERWAY GUIDE PHOTOGRAPHY

above and below. After passing flashing green "1," swing to the east side of the channel as indicated by the magenta line on the chart. The shoal making out here from the west side is about 6 feet or less at low water, as noted by our cruising editor in late 2009.

Fernandina Beach–Mile 716

Florida's northernmost city, Fernandina Beach, is on Amelia Island east of the ICW. Discovered in 1562 by the French explorer Jean Ribault, who named it Isle de Mai, the Spanish settled the island in 1567. They renamed it Santa Maria, established a mission and built Fort San Fernando. In 1702, the British captured the island and gave it the name that finally stuck: Amelia, in honor of King George II's daughter. Amelia Island has enjoyed a colorful history. In its earlier years, pirates and smugglers used it as their stronghold, and during Prohibition, rum-runners continued the tradition. Eight different flags have flown over Amelia Island, among them the standard of the conquistadors and the French Huguenots, the British Union Jack and the Stars and Bars of the Confederacy. The island is the only place in the United States to have been claimed by so many governments.

Dockage: At Mile 715.3 is the entrance to Egans Creek (east of the Waterway), which leads to Tiger Point Marina and Boat Works, the first marina you will encounter as you enter Florida from the north and Amelia Island's only natural deepwater marina. Tiger Point is also a full-service repair yard with approach depths of 6.5 to 7 feet. Diesel fuel (no gas) can be found at Florida Petroleum

and possibly transient dockage. It is usually best to dock alongside Florida Petroleum's fixed dock during higher tides. Many commercial vessels fuel up here, so there may be a wait.

The Fernandina Harbor Marina is located at Mile 716.7. Dredging of the interior part of this marina was completed in 2007, so transient dockage is available on both sides of the floating face dock as well as at several slips on the interior of the marina. It is still a good idea to call ahead for reservations, as this is a popular stop. Fernandina Harbor Marina also has gas and diesel fuel, pump-out, a laundry facility, an on-site restaurant and restrooms/showers.

About a block from Fernandina Harbor Marina is a small store that carries limited staples, but serious grocery shopping at Winn-Dixie and Publix is about two miles away and requires a cab. The historic downtown district, next to the waterfront, has several restaurants, taverns and gift shops. The Tourist Information Center can provide a helpful map.

Anchorage: Fernandina Harbor Marina has installed 20 moorings in the anchorage area across the channel from their marina. Seven are reserved for transient boaters who call ahead, while most are available on a first-come, first-served basis. The mooring fee includes dinghy dockage, use of the marina showers, trash disposal and a free pump-out at the dock. The mooring area is marked with yellow buoys, but anchoring is still permitted outside the marked area. Anchored boats may use the dinghy dock and showers for a modest fee.

Looking west over Egans Creek & ICW in Fernandina. (Not to be used for navigation.) Photo Courtesy of Mike Kucera.

If you choose to anchor, take care that your swinging circle does not extend into the channel or the mooring area. Also make sure that you have adequate scope on your anchor for the varying depths. Caution is advised, as sunken boats have been present in this area in the past, and their debris may still be on the bottom. Several sunken boats have been observed outside of the channel between red daybeacons "14" and "16." Boats have been observed anchoring up the Amelia River in Bells River and also in Lanceford Creek. These anchorages should be approached with caution, as the chart contours show varied depths with snags and mud banks. The tidal range is greater than 7 feet, and tidal currents run up to 2 knots here. Although it is a relatively short dinghy ride to the marina dinghy dock, the anchorage and mooring areas are open to winds, wakes and considerable tidal current. Always display anchor lights, as commercial and other traffic can be heavy at all hours.

At Mile 719.5, entering the Amelia River and the ICW from the east, Jackson Creek provides 7-foot depths at mean low water, although its entrance is recently reported to have shoaled to 4 feet. Like all anchorages in the area, it has swift tidal currents. It is relatively narrow, and the north side should be favored to avoid the charted shoal. The Amelia River breaks off to the west of the Waterway at Mile 719.8 with 6- to 7-foot depths at mean low water. Although it is preferred over Jackson Creek to the north, it is also quite narrow. Enter slowly with the depth sounder on. Use of two anchors in a Bahamian moor might be wise due to the narrowness and swift currents in either of these anchorages.

GOIN' ASHORE:
FERNANDINA BEACH, FL

The downtown historic district, a 50-block section surrounding Centre Street, is an attractive and popular gingerbread seaport dating from the 1850s, when Florida's first cross-state railroad ran from Fernandina to Cedar Key (the railroad tracks still run past the waterfront with occasional traffic). The area is listed on the National Historic Register and is worth a visit. The old train depot is a satellite office for the Chamber of Commerce and serves as the Tourist Information Center. Several restaurants, specialty shops, a pharmacy and banks are within walking distance of the waterfront, including the Palace Saloon (117 Centre St., 904-491-3332), Florida's oldest tavern. The Beech Street Grill (801 Beech St., 904-277-3662) serves creative dinner specials, complemented by their extensive wine list. There is piano music nightly, and Sunday brunch is served from 11:00 a.m. to 2 p.m. Dine inside or out at Espana Restaurant and Tapas (22 S. 4th St., 904-261-770) specializing in dishes from Spain and Portugal. Brett's Waterway Cafe is located at Fernandina Harbor Marina. You can't find a better view in town (1 S. Front St., 904-261-2660). 29 South is getting great reviews. Find them 2 blocks from the waterfront (29 S. 3rd St., 904-277-7919). An old favorite in town is Marina Seafood Restaurant, located just across the street and the railroad tracks from the marina (101 Centre St., 904-261-5310).

For lodging, the Hampton Inn and Suites is located right on the waterfront in the middle of all of the great

Fernandina Beach, FL

Fernandina Beach Area, FL

FERNANDINA BEACH AREA		Largest Vessel Accommodated	VHF Channel Monitored	Approach / Dockside Depth (reported)	Transient Berths / Total Berths	Floating Docks	Gas / Diesel	Groceries, Ice, Marine Supplies, Snacks	Repairs: Hull, Engine, Propeller	Lift (tonnage), Crane, Rail	1=110V, 2=220V, B=Both, Max Amps	Laundry, Pool, Showers	Pump-Out Station	Nearby: Grocery Store, Motel, Restaurant
				Dockage				**Supplies**			**Service**			
1. Tiger Point Marina 715.5 🖵	904-277-2720	55	16/11	4/50	7/8	F		M	HEP	L35	B/50	S		
2. Florida Petroleum Corp. 716.5	904-261-3200 x117	285	16	3/13	50/30	D					B/50			GMR
3. **FERNANDINA HARBOR MARINA 716.7** 🖵(WIFI)	**904-491-2090**	**150**	**16/68**	**60/101**	**18/8**	**F**	**GD**	**GIMS**			**B/100**	**LS**	**P**	**MR**
4. Oyster Bay Harbour	904-491-4773	PRIVATE SLIPS												
5. Amelia Island Yacht Basin 721 🖵(WIFI)	904-277-4615	110	16/72	30/135	5.5/7	F	GD	IMS	HEP	L36	B/50	LS	P	GMR

Corresponding chart(s) not to be used for navigation. 🖵 Internet Access (WIFI) Wireless Internet Access

downtown shopping and eateries (19 S. 2nd St.,). There are also a number of bed and breakfasts in the downtown district. The Addison on Amelia (614 Ash St., 904-277-1604) provides an elegant setting to soothe the weary traveler. The Williams House (103 S. 9th St., 904-277-2328) is mere blocks from the downtown district in one direction and the Atlantic beaches in the other.

For shopping, try French Market Antiques (203 Centre St., 904-491-0707), Old World Traditions (206 Centre St., 904-277-9627), Fantastic Fudge (218 Centre St., 904-277-4801) or Del Pesco Fine Art (13 N 4th St., 904-491-7710). There is a surprising amount of shops and restaurants in this small town, too numerous to mention all of them, so take the time to explore all of the side streets.

With local attractions such as Fort Clinch State Park, Cumberland Island National Seashore, Amelia Island State Park and the island itself, Fernandina makes a pleasant stopover. Luxury resorts such as the Ritz Carlton and Amelia Island Plantation at the south end of the island draw tourists and conferees from afar, and new housing development in the area is attracting a wave of new residents. There is an area of strip malls and large stores of the popular home improvement, drug and department variety usually found in booming residential areas, just off-island, near Yulee. When exploring beyond the downtown Fernandina Beach area, however, you will need to arrange for transportation.

South of the historic area, you can see white smoke from the chimneys of two paper mills in Fernandina Beach. Although the huge paper mills are still busy, better emissions controls have improved the quality of the air and water. A sizable commercial fishing fleet, consisting mainly of shrimp boats, lies docked above and below the marina. A commercial dock to the north accommodates freighters and containerships.

Mile 720 to Mile 735

NAVIGATION: Use Chart 11489. Just southwest of the Jackson Creek entrance to the Amelia River (near Mile 720), the ICW turns south and leaves the Amelia River for Kingsley Creek. The Kingsley Creek Railroad Swing Bridge (5-foot closed vertical clearance, normally open

ADDITIONAL RESOURCES

- ■ CITY OF FERNANDINA BEACH, 904-277-7305, www.fbfl.us
- ■ FERNANDINA BEACH ONLINE, www.fbfl.us
- 🚩 NEARBY GOLF COURSES
  Fernandina Beach Municipal Golf Course, 2800 Bill Melton Road, Fernandina Beach, FL 32034, 904-277-7370
- ⚕ NEARBY MEDICAL FACILITIES
  Baptist Medical Center Nassau
  1250 S. 18th St., Fernandina Beach, FL 32034, 904-321-3500

except for train traffic) and twin fixed high-level highway bridges carrying U.S. A1A (65-foot vertical clearances) span the ICW at Mile 720.7. The high-level bridges here are unofficially considered to be among the "lowest" of the 65-foot bridges on the ICW; expect no more than 64 feet at high tide. If in doubt, check the clearance boards, and go through at half tide. With the wide tidal range (7 feet), currents can be unexpectedly strong here.

Although the railroad bridge is usually open, trains hauling logs to the area's two paper mills can delay your journey. The bridge gives no warning when it is going to close, and it does not have a VHF radio. If you are in this area and you hear train whistles, be aware that the bridge could close as you approach it. After passing beneath the bridges, you could see either a wide expanse of water or mud flats on either side of the channel, depending on the state of the tide.

Dockage: Amelia Island Yacht Basin, in a cove just north of the bridges to the east past green daybeacon "13," is a full-service marina with haul-out capabilities that welcomes transients. The narrow channel leading to the marina may look questionable, but locals report good depths, particularly after a dredging project a few years ago increased low-tide depths to 5.5 feet. Contact marina personnel on VHF Channel 16 for current channel depths.

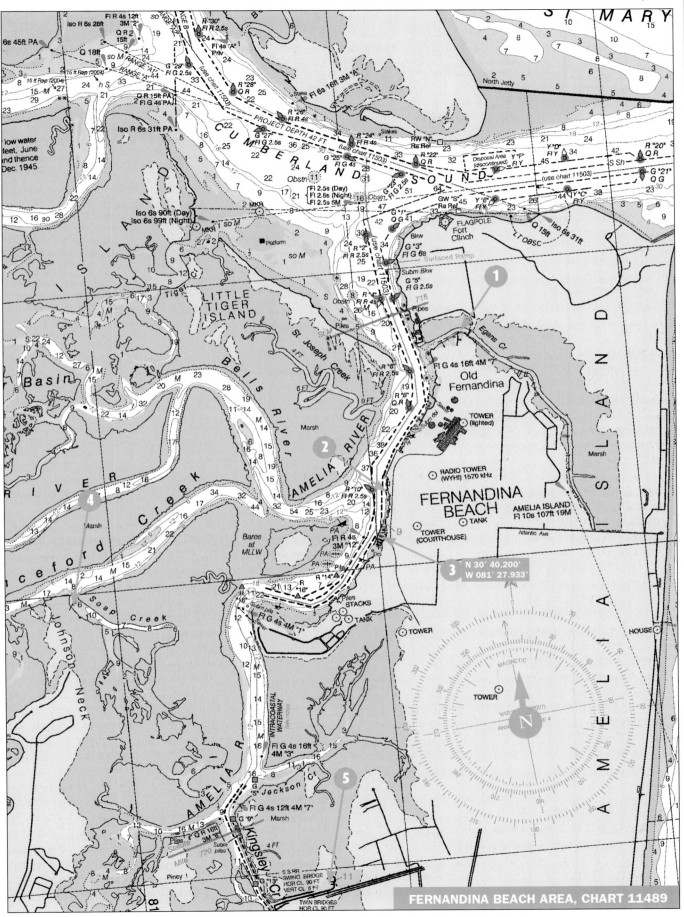

FERNANDINA BEACH AREA, CHART 11489

Fort George Island, FL

Amelia Island Yacht Basin is a good choice in strong winds when other marinas may be too exposed, but transient space fills quickly in bad weather, so call ahead. A variety of local restaurants are a short cab ride away. Their transient space has increased from 20 to 30 slips.

Amelia City to Fort George River— Mile 725 to Mile 735

NAVIGATION: Use Chart 11489. South from the bridges to flashing red "14," shoaling reduces depths along the west side of the channel to 5- to 8-foot depths. In the ICW channel at green daybeacon "21" and flashing red "24," just north of the entrance to Alligator Creek, the narrow channel makes a sharp sweep to the east. Unwary skippers will find two-foot depths outside of the channel at flashing red "24," green daybeacon "25" and red daybeacon "26." From red daybeacon "26" to flashing red "28," follow the magenta line on the chart, and avoid the shoaling and submerged pilings to starboard.

Just past flashing red "28" (about Mile 724), you will pass Amelia City, a small waterside hamlet tucked into a bend on the east side of the river. You will see bulkheads, some private docks and a few houses. Inside of the marsh, past the bulkhead area, are more houses.

The shallowest part of the South Amelia River is between red daybeacon "34" and red daybeacon "36." Although charted at 8 feet in January 2009, there is around 6 feet of water at extreme low tide. Favor the green side between red daybeacon "34" and flashing green "37." Head toward red daybeacon "36" to follow the magenta line, rounding red daybeacon "38" and green daybeacon "39." The charted 7- to 8-foot depths are the best you will get through here. Follow the magenta line on your chart carefully around red daybeacon "42," then favor green daybeacon "43" rather than flashing red "44."

There was dredging during spring and summer 2006 between South Amelia River (in Nassau Sound) quick flashing red "46" and south to Sisters Creek flashing red "74." Beyond quick flashing red "46" there had been a temporary red nun "46A" in place for many years (shown on some older charts as red daybeacon "46A"). Following this dredging, red nun buoy "46A" was removed. The charted red daybeacon at the entrance to the cut just north of Mile 730 has been renumbered "46A," according to the January 2009 edition of the chart.

Since this is such a changeable area, remember to be on the alert for shoaling and the possibility that there may be additional aids in place when you make passage here. New charts do not have a magenta line drawn along the route across Nassau Sound. The current may be very strong, so watch your set and drift; slow boats may have to crab across. The swing bridge across Nassau Sound's ocean inlet, at the southern end of Amelia Island, is still in place (15-foot vertical clearance), but closed to traffic and has been replaced with a fixed bridge.

Anchorage: As the chart clearly shows, the ICW channel hugs the Amelia Island shore just south of Amelia City. There is an anchorage just north of Mile 726 off the

entrance to Alligator Creek. Enter by turning to the northeast between red daybeacon "36" and flashing green "37." However, be careful; its entrance is shallow, carrying only 6-foot depths at low water, and then increasing to 8-foot depths off Alligator Creek. Tugboats have been observed taking a shortcut through this anchorage area at high tide.

■ LOWER AMELIA ISLAND

The lower portion of Amelia Island is home to a large and lovely resort community, Amelia Island Plantation. The resort still hosts several major annual tennis tournaments. No dockage is available on the premises, however. The closest place to stay is Amelia Island Yacht Basin near Mile 721, described earlier. The island is also the site of an oceanfront Ritz-Carlton Hotel.

Sawpit Creek and Gunnison Cut— Mile 730 to Mile 735

NAVIGATION: Use Chart 11489. Between Miles 730 and 735 (at Mile 735 the ICW meets the Fort George River), shorelines close in somewhat as the channel runs through narrow land cuts and two natural creeks. The dredging of Sawpit Creek in 2006 corrected the persistent shoaling in the vicinity of flashing green "49" for a while, but it is back. It is a good idea to favor the deep natural channel along the west (red) side of the ICW when rounding the bend marked by flashing green "49." Sawpit Creek and Gunnison Cut lead to Sisters Creek and the St. Johns River crossing. A January 2010 survey shows 3- and 4-foot depths on the green side of the channel at mean low water.

Fort George Island—Mile 735 to Mile 740

NAVIGATION: Use Chart 11489. East of the ICW channel, Fort George Island makes an attractive side trip, with its Indian mounds, wildlife sanctuary and lush jungle growth. The area of shoaling between green daybeacon "73" and flashing red "74," reported at 7 feet, was dredged in 2006, but the January 2010 survey conducted by the Army Corps of Engineers indicates that shoaling has again encroached upon this area. We recommend against cruising on the Fort George River because of shoaling in the marked channel, a fixed bridge with a 15-foot vertical clearance and a shoaled inlet. The once-popular anchorage here is reported to be shoaled to the point that it can no longer be recommended. If possible, explore this unspoiled natural area by land.

GOIN' ASHORE: FORT GEORGE ISLAND, FL

From a land base, you can do some sightseeing ashore at Kingsley Plantation, which is open to the public. An Englishman built the first house on this site in 1763. When the Spanish took possession of the area in the 1790s, ownership passed to the improbably named Don Juan McQueen.

Born in Philadelphia and bred in Charleston, SC, McQueen had served as a courier for George Washington during the Revolutionary War. After the war, McQueen became a Spanish subject and plantation owner. In 1813, the land came into the hands of Zephaniah Kingsley, who was born in Bristol, England but reared in a Quaker household in Charleston. Kingsley, a slave trader and planter, built the plantation into an empire, and his house still stands. Park guards welcome visiting boaters. Entrance to the plantation grounds is free, but there is a small fee for guided tours of the buildings.

Also of interest to visit by land are the state parks at beautiful and remote Big and Little Talbot islands.

ADDITIONAL RESOURCES

■ Florida State Parks, www.floridastateparks.org

⛳ NEARBY GOLF COURSES
Mill Cove Golf Club, 1700 Monument Road,
Jacksonville, FL 32225, 904-646-4653
www.millcovegolf.com

⚕ NEARBY MEDICAL FACILITIES
St. Vincent's Medical Center
1 Shircuff Way, Jacksonville, FL 32204, 904-308-7300

■ TO ST. JOHNS RIVER

South of the ICW junction with the Fort George River, the ICW route runs a straightforward path through Sisters Creek to the St. Johns River. As you travel along some sections of Sisters Creek, you may see the superstructures of large ships headed up or down the St. Johns River. The suspension bridge at Dames Point, at the western end of Blount Island, can be used as a landmark when you are headed south. Favor the east bank just south of flashing red "82," because shoaling has created water depths of 6 to 8 feet along the west bank. Opening of the Sisters Creek Bridge (Mile 739.2, 24-foot closed vertical clearance) is unrestricted, but you may have to wait; the tender usually waits for several boats before opening the span. Watch for crosscurrents at the bridge. A high-level fixed replacement bridge is planned by 2013. A sign on the bridge warns of heavy traffic at the intersection of Sisters Creek and the St. Johns River.

The city of Jacksonville operates boat ramps and small-boat facilities on both sides of the bridge, which causes congestion, particularly on weekends. The old slips that were part of Sisters Creek Marina, on the creek to the north of the ramps, are in disrepair, and there is no other dockage for transients in this area.

SISTERS CREEK BRIDGE Mile 739.1
WATERWAY GUIDE PHOTOGRAPHY

Sisters Creek/St. Johns River Intersection
NAVIGATION: Use Chart 11489. The pilots and captains of large vessels in this area always announce their approach and intentions at the Sisters Creek and St. Johns River intersection via Sécurité warning. Listen on VHF Channel 16. Smaller vessels in the area should answer them back if in close proximity, and stay clear of these large vessels.

At this point, the St. Johns River is narrow, compared to some of its broad expanses south of Jacksonville. Crossing can present problems to lightly powered vessels, given the strong currents (2 to 3 knots on the ebb), obstructed visibility and continuous commercial traffic. Observe markers closely until you are safely into the ICW land cut beyond the St. Johns River. Do not attempt to pass

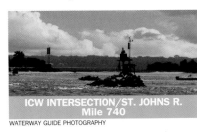
ICW INTERSECTION/ST. JOHNS R. Mile 740
WATERWAY GUIDE PHOTOGRAPHY

between what appears to be islets downriver from the land cut entrance; there are rocks between them. Keep in mind that large oceangoing vessels have the right of way, so watch out for them while transiting the St. Johns River. Also, remember that the shipyard on the east side of the Sisters Creek entrance to the St. Johns River creates a blind spot for small boats heading into the river.

The land cut from this point southward through the Jacksonville Beach area is well-marked, but at low tide, the dredged channel is narrow. Follow the markers carefully to stay on the channel's centerline, and be prepared to squeeze over for tugs with barges. On weekends and holidays, small boats often anchor in the land cut just beyond the river crossing. The current in the land cut below the St. Johns River flows toward the river on the ebb and can be very strong. Eddies may be present between red nun buoy "2" and flashing green "1," requiring close attention to the helm. When entering the channel, favor the green daybeacons until you reach red daybeacon "8."

Cruising Options
The splendid St. Johns River, which winds its way from Mayport to Sanford, is described in the following chapter. Cruisers continuing south on the ICW will find their course resuming in the chapter titled "Jacksonville to Ponce de Leon Inlet." ■

WATERWAY GUIDE advertising sponsors play a vital role in bringing you the most trusted and well-respected cruising guide in the country. Without our advertising sponsors, we simply couldn't produce the top-notch publication now resting in your hands. Next time you stop in for a peaceful night's rest, let them know where you found them—WATERWAY GUIDE, The Cruising Authority.

Sidetrips: St. Johns River, FL

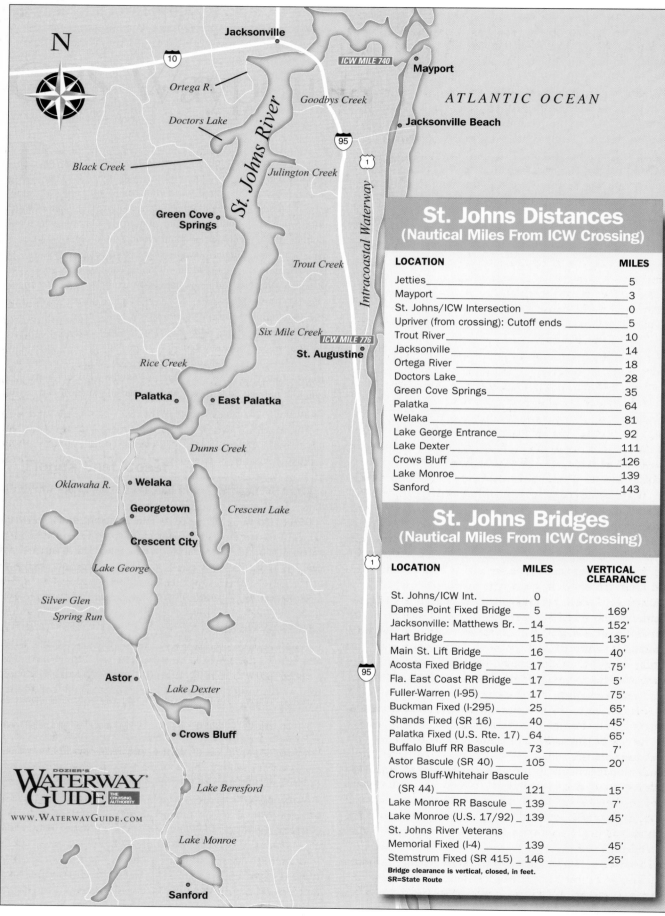

St. Johns Distances
(Nautical Miles From ICW Crossing)

LOCATION	MILES
Jetties	5
Mayport	3
St. Johns/ICW Intersection	0
Upriver (from crossing): Cutoff ends	5
Trout River	10
Jacksonville	14
Ortega River	18
Doctors Lake	28
Green Cove Springs	35
Palatka	64
Welaka	81
Lake George Entrance	92
Lake Dexter	111
Crows Bluff	126
Lake Monroe	139
Sanford	143

St. Johns Bridges
(Nautical Miles From ICW Crossing)

LOCATION	MILES	VERTICAL CLEARANCE
St. Johns/ICW Int.	0	
Dames Point Fixed Bridge	5	169'
Jacksonville: Matthews Br.	14	152'
Hart Bridge	15	135'
Main St. Lift Bridge	16	40'
Acosta Fixed Bridge	17	75'
Fla. East Coast RR Bridge	17	5'
Fuller-Warren (I-95)	17	75'
Buckman Fixed (I-295)	25	65'
Shands Fixed (SR 16)	40	45'
Palatka Fixed (U.S. Rte. 17)	64	65'
Buffalo Bluff RR Bascule	73	7'
Astor Bascule (SR 40)	105	20'
Crows Bluff-Whitehair Bascule (SR 44)	121	15'
Lake Monroe RR Bascule	139	7'
Lake Monroe (U.S. 17/92)	139	45'
St. Johns River Veterans Memorial Fixed (I-4)	139	45'
Stemstrum Fixed (SR 415)	146	25'

Bridge clearance is vertical, closed, in feet.
SR=State Route

Sidetrips on the St. Johns River

The St. Johns River flows north for 248 miles from the heart of central Florida to the Atlantic Ocean at Mayport. For about 20 miles inside the ocean entrance, recreational vessels share the river with big ships churning upstream to the international port of Jacksonville. From the intersection of the St. Johns River and the Intracoastal Waterway (ICW) at ICW Mile 739.5, you may meet several types of commercial vessels - from freighters, tankers and containerships to tugs, towing barges and even cruise ships. Upriver from Jacksonville, commercial traffic consists largely of tugs and barges.

With its Atlantic Ocean access, the St. Johns River and the ICW are within easy reach, and the Jacksonville area is a prime playground for boaters. The city of Jacksonville offers good restaurants, museums, a zoo, a National Football League team (Jacksonville hosted the Super Bowl in 2005) and plenty of full-service marinas.

Vessels with very shallow-drafts (or better yet, use a dinghy) can reach the Jacksonville Zoo and Gardens. Turn off the main St. Johns River channel between flashing red buoys "64" and "66" into the Trout River, and then pick up red daybeacon "2" and green daybeacon "3," which mark the Trout River channel. The zoo's floating concrete "T" dock is located on the north bank of the Trout River, just northeast of the Highway 17 Bridge, about three-quarters of a mile off the St. Johns River. (For more information about the zoo, call 904-757-4463.) Zoo officials report the depth at the dock to be between 1 and 2 feet at low tide, and there are no plans to dredge.

Residential areas with many private piers line the shore south of Jacksonville to the Green Cove Springs area. The trees are carefully preserved, making it difficult to see the houses. The river is less developed and more scenic farther south; part of the river is a wildlife sanctuary, and many skippers make this beautiful trip an annual cruise.

If you are not in a hurry while heading south in the fall or going north in the spring, stop and take a cruise south "up" the river. Unfortunately, exploring the most beautiful part of the St. Johns River is limited to boats able to pass under the Shands Bridge (45-foot fixed vertical clearance) south of Green Cove Springs at Red Bay Point, about 40 miles southwest of the ICW. There are plans afoot to replace the old 45-foot bridge with a new 65-foot fixed span. Stay tuned. Sanford is a good place to spend the winter, and many yachtsmen leave their boats there for an extended period.

The river boasts infinitely varied scenery. It is as broad in places as a great bay, sometimes placid, sometimes wild, with pockets of civilization scattered sparsely along its shores. Narrow and winding in other places, its subtropical vegetation and heavy stands of trees grow right down to the water's edge—its sloughs, creeks, loops and backwaters are often choked with water hyacinths. Fortunately, restraining fences and bulkheads help keep most of this floating vegetation out of the channel.

One reason for the popularity of the St. Johns River is its fishing. The river, its lakes and its tributaries comprise what is widely known as the "Bass Capital of the World," and the evidence suggests that its reputation is well-deserved. Florida requires fishing licenses for freshwater and saltwater (license not required for those under 16 or over 65, or certified as totally and permanently disabled).

Hundreds of creeks and small rivers, deep or shoal, flow into the St. Johns River and all have something to offer. Without a good outboard-powered dinghy, you will miss a lot in this area. The same dinghy that transports the casual fisherman upstream to discover new challenges can also enhance the cruiser's pleasure in discovering the quiet and scenic anchorages along the St. Johns River's upper reaches. Here, too, is a proliferation of bird life: Osprey, turkey vultures, pelicans, anhinga, terns, cranes, herons, egrets, bald eagles, cormorants, ducks and many songbirds are visible along the river.

The upper (southern) portion of the St. Johns River supports many varieties of freshwater fish. From November through March, the great manatees (sea cows)—protected by law—live along certain stretches. There are manatee zones along all banks of the St. Johns River in Duval and Clay counties, including Doctors Lake. In summer and warm winters, the creeks and sloughs are home to alligators sleeping in the sun along the banks. Shoreside development includes state parks, fish camps (both primitive and luxurious) and a few proper marinas, some large and some small. None of humanity's intrusions detract from the overall scene, but rather all blend so well that they seem like natural outgrowths of river life.

Cruising Conditions

Between Mayport and Sanford, the St. Johns River is deep and easy to cruise, because the channel is maintained for commercial craft. The relatively few shoals are well-marked. Overhead clearance is set at 45 feet by two fixed bridges (the first is south of Green Springs at Red Bay Point and carries a 45-foot vertical clearance), but follow charts carefully, and keep an eye on the depth sounder. If the chart looks doubtful, go marker-to-marker. Several unmarked shoal spots extend toward the channel between Palatka and the Buffalo Bluff Railroad Bridge (7-foot closed

vertical clearance), near Murphy Island. The Coast Guard reports that the overhead power cable just north of the Astor Bridge has less than the charted 50-foot clearance, but does not give an exact figure.

Snags are seldom a problem in main channels of the St. Johns River, but approach side streams and sloughs carefully. Keep an eye out for trap markers as well. These markers vary from commercially produced floats to those improvised with plastic soda bottles. Some markers are fouled with vegetation (almost impossible to see), the current pulls some under and some are black in color. The size of the traps varies from the conventional crab traps to huge contraptions that almost require a derrick to haul them.

In the narrow snakelike reaches beyond Lake George, it is safest to stay in the center of the channel, although depths tend to hold close toward the riverbanks. Constant passage of fuel barges headed to and from the port of Sanford helps keep the channel clear.

The St. Johns River is used year-round by recreational craft. On weekends and holidays, especially when the weather is good, the river carries heavy traffic. You will see everything from mid-sized cruisers and small runabouts to bass boats and personal watercraft, all in a great hurry to reach their destinations. No-Wake Zones abound, especially in the Astor/Blue Springs area, where the rules are strictly enforced. Maintain only steerageway here (even sailboats producing little wake), as it is a manatee area. Be particularly observant from November through mid-April, when the manatees are in residence. Marine patrol vessels often stand by to enforce regulations.

Dealing with River Currents

Skippers of sailboats with auxiliary power or low-powered motor cruisers should check their tidal current tables before starting upriver to Jacksonville from the ICW or Atlantic Ocean entrance. River currents meeting strong ocean tides can create tricky conditions. Be aware of the differences in tidal current times, and note that slack water does not necessarily coincide with high or low tide. The ebb in the river can run 2 to 3 knots, making a slow passage for underpowered boats. The tidal current tables give corrections to the fixed bridge (45-foot vertical clearance) at Red Bay Point in Green Cove Springs. This location is upriver (south) of Green Cove Springs. The average maximum flood given is 0.9 knots, and the average maximum ebb, 0.6 knots. The next location is Tocoi, approximately 15 nautical miles upriver, where the current is described as "weak and variable."

Current past Tocoi can be strongly influenced by the water level in the upper (southern) part of the river, as it flows south to north. It can be strong enough to make docking across the current difficult for underpowered or deep-keeled vessels.

Looking west over the St. Johns River Entrance. (Not to be used for navigation.) WATERWAY GUIDE PHOTOGRAPHY

River Tides

Tides are given in the tide tables to Welaka, 66 nautical miles south of Jacksonville. The corrections, based on Mayport (Atlantic Ocean entrance), are all ratios that must be used as a multiplier. The spring range (full and new moon) at Mayport can exceed 5 feet and, at Palatka, is around 1.5 feet. Wind and rainfall can affect depth (and, of course, current), especially on the upper reaches. If you plan to cruise and gunkhole widely, it would be advisable to carry a lead line or long boat pole to supplement your depth sounder. Sounding into areas where charts may not indicate all the shoals may be advisable.

■ ST. JOHNS ENTRANCE

NAVIGATION: Use Charts 11489 and 11491. The St. Johns Entrance is one of the safest and easiest gateways from the Atlantic Ocean. Ocean freighters use it, as do fishing skiffs. Recreational boats make it a point of entry and departure for passages along the coast, coming into and leaving marinas at Mayport (two miles upriver) and on the Intracoastal Waterway (ICW) five miles upriver.

The ocean approach landmark is St. Johns Light, standing 83 feet above the shore, a mile south of the St. Johns River north jetty. The light shines from a square white tower and is easy to spot from the ocean. The St. Johns River red-and-white sea buoy, flashing Morse (A) "STJ," located three miles east of the jetties, guides boaters into the marked inlet channel. Other landmarks include a tower at Jacksonville Beach and a water tank (painted in a red-and-white checkerboard design) at the Mayport Naval Air Station. Other water tanks line the beaches to the south.

Mayport, on the St. Johns

NAVIGATION: Use Chart 11489. Inside the jetties, the St. Johns River runs unobstructed and naturally deep past the Mayport Basin, which is usually occupied by enormous naval craft. The basin is off-limits to recreational craft, except in extreme emergencies.

Dockage: The town of Mayport, three miles inside the entrance jetties on the south side of the river, is an important commercial and sportfishing center that provides dockage for cruising boats. Mayport is a good place to lay over before you start your cruise up the St. Johns River, as supplies are readily available here. The St. Johns Boat Company is located a mile and a half from the ICW on the north side of the river across from Mayport and offers haul-out service with a 100-ton lift and a 300-ton railway. Large vessels can be accommodated at the docks, and there is a do-it-yourself as well as full-service work yard for vessels of all sizes. Also on this side of the river is Morningstar Marina at Ft. George. This marina provides transient dockage as well as dry storage for vessels up

St. Johns River, FL

			Largest Vessel Accommodated	VHF Channel Monitored	Transient Berths / Total Berths	Approach / Dockside Depth (reported)	Floating Docks	Gas / Diesel	Groceries, Ice, Marine Supplies, Snacks	Repairs: Hull, Engine, Propeller	Lift (tonnage), Crane, Rail	1=110v, 2=220v, B=Both, Max Amps	Laundry, Pool, Showers	Pump-Out Station	Nearby: Grocery Store, Motel, Restaurant

MAYPORT, TROUT RIVER

			Dockage				Supplies			Service					
1. Morningstar Marinas at Ft. George Island ⌨ WiFi	904-251-0050	70	16/10	/5	41/26	F	GD					/50		P	R
2. St. Johns Boat Company WiFi	904-251-3707	200	16	/5	10/10				HEP	L100,R		B/100		P	R
3. Morningstar Marinas at Mayport ⌨	904-246-8929	200	16	10/10	30/30	F	GD	IMS	EP			B/50	LS	P	GR
4. Seafarer's Marina	904-765-8152	95	16	5/75	13/13			IM				1/50	LS	P	GMR

Corresponding chart(s) not to be used for navigation. ⌨ Internet Access WiFi Wireless Internet Access

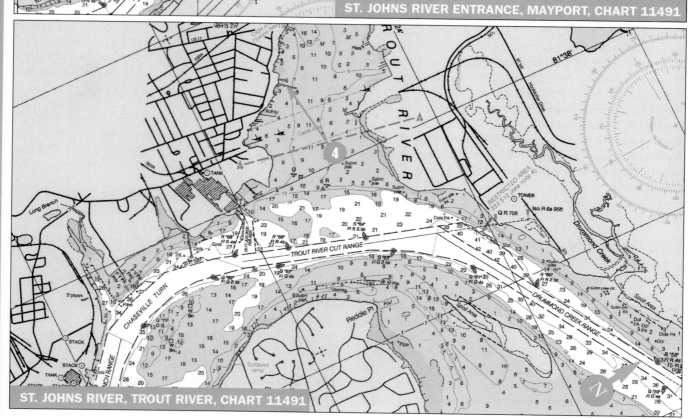

ST. JOHNS RIVER ENTRANCE, MAYPORT, CHART 11491

ST. JOHNS RIVER, TROUT RIVER, CHART 11491

to 45 feet. On the south side of the river, Morningstar Marinas at Mayport (formerly Jacksonville Marina) provides fuel and excellent local seafood. From there, take a ferry ride across the St. Johns River to Fort George Island, or spend hours watching the constant activity of the commercial fleet and the sportfishing boats. The Coast Guard station is at the south end of the Mayport waterfront. A luxury residential and marina project (Ft. George Harbour) is near the inlet.

■ THE ST. JOHNS RIVER FROM THE ICW

Southbound on the ICW, the Waterway crosses the St. Johns River just west of Mile Point, about five miles from the St. Johns Entrance and a little more than a mile west of Mayport. At that point, the ICW leaves Sisters Creek and enters Pablo Creek at red nun buoy "2" (Mile 740) for the run south.

Dockage: On the northeast corner of the intersection of the ICW and the St. Johns River is Atlantic Marine and Dry Dock, a bustling shipbuilding and repair yard for ferries, gambling boats and large oceangoing tugs, as well as vessels of every size and description.

Fort Caroline, on the St. Johns

About 1.7 miles west of the ICW, on the south side of the river (opposite flashing red buoy "34") at St. Johns Bluff, a national park features a re-creation of French-built Fort Caroline. The French (who discovered the St. Johns River in May 1562 and called it Riviere de Mai) established North America's first Protestant settlement in 1564. They built Fort Caroline to secure their landholdings, but the Spanish, who had established St. Augustine, temporarily defeated them. Under Spanish rule it was called Fort San Mateo, but the French retook it two years later and restored its original name.

Fort Caroline is worth visiting, but the current is strong and the water, even close in, can carry 45-foot depths. It is best to rent a car in Jacksonville and drive to the fort. Do not attempt to anchor by Blount Island and then dinghy across to the fort. There is no place to land a dinghy, and the steep banks are home to rattlesnakes and water moccasins.

■ UPRIVER TO JACKSONVILLE

NAVIGATION: Use Chart 11491. This chart covers the mouth of the St. Johns River on the Atlantic Ocean to the Ortega River just past downtown Jacksonville. The route to Jacksonville is a big-ship channel, well-marked and simple to run. It generally follows the wide, natural course of the river. For the most part, deep water prevails alongside the marked channel, there are no intricate ranges and the next light or marker ahead is always within sight. Even for slow sailboats, the trip is less than a day's travel and your

efforts will be rewarded. While currents gradually decrease upriver, the flow runs up to 3 knots at first and, near the downtown Jacksonville bridges, can be a major factor. Plan your trip for a fair current by calculating slack before flood and maximum flood at Mile Point (at flashing red buoy "22") on the St. Johns River to get an interval of time to arrive at the ICW crossing.

Coast Pilot Volume 4 points out four critical traffic areas on the St. Johns; commercial vessels must give a Sécurité call on VHF Channel 13 to avoid meeting one another at these points. These areas are the junction of the St. Johns River and the ICW, Dames Point Turn, Trout River Cut and Commodore Point. Recreational boats do not need to make a Sécurité call—you will have enough maneuvering room to stay out of the way—but monitor VHF Channel 13 so you will know whether you will be meeting a big ship or a tug with tow.

East of Sisters Creek and the ICW, the channel enters wide and straight Dames Point-Fulton Cutoff, dredged to eliminate a bend in the St. Johns River's natural course. The impressive high-level bridge across the St. Johns River and Mill Cove is officially named the Napoleon Bonaparte Broward Bridge, but is known by locals as the Dames Point Bridge (169-foot fixed vertical clearance above the main channel).

Mainly a complex of wharves, warehouses and a container terminal, Blount Island (created by dredge spoil) is on the north side of the Dames Point-Fulton Cutoff chan-

nel. Although the loop behind the island is deep, three low bridges (5-, 8- and 10-foot fixed vertical clearances) prevent a complete circuit.

Anchorage: You may anchor off Little Marsh Island east of Blount Island and across the old St. Johns River Channel, but stay clear of the channel by Blount Island. Watch for trap markers, and do not interfere with the private docks along Little Marsh Island. Use this anchorage only if necessary; there is no place to go ashore here. You will find 7- to 10-foot depths. A much better anchorage is approximately 10 miles up the St. Johns River, behind Exchange Island and just before the Matthews Bridge (152-foot fixed vertical clearance). Back River pierces Blount Island from the Dames Point-Fulton Cutoff Channel; it is entirely commercial. Recreational craft should not attempt to anchor, sightsee or fish in the channel.

Broward and Trout Rivers, off the St. Johns

The unmarked Broward River requires local knowledge and is blocked off by a wharf extending 500 yards from shore. Many local boats use the Trout River just two miles beyond, which is the Waterway leading to the Jacksonville Zoo. It has twin daybeacons at the entrance, red "2" and green "3," central depths of 10 feet and a twin-span bridge upstream with a controlling fixed vertical clearance of 29 feet. The Sal Swing Bridge just beyond it, has a 2-foot

closed vertical clearance. A short distance up the Trout River to port before the bridges is the Seafarer's Marina with some transient dockage.

◼ JACKSONVILLE, ON THE ST. JOHNS

NAVIGATION: Use Chart 11491. Along the St. Johns River from the ICW (between flashing red buoy "24" and flashing green buoy "25"—near Mile 739.5) all the way to the Hart Bridge at Commodore Point (just past flashing green buoy "79"), the posted speed limit in the channel is 25 mph. Manatee zones are designated as Slow-Speed/Minimum-Speed or Idle-Speed/No-Wake Zones from the channel to shore. A No-Wake Zone lies from the Hart Bridge to the Interstate 95 (Fuller-Warren) Bridge. The St. Johns River is consistently patrolled, and speed limits are strictly enforced. The river is brackish all the way to Palatka, and, when these waters are very warm, wooden boats may have trouble with putty bugs, which can be just as destructive as Teredo worms.

From the ICW crossing at Mile 740, the river generally winds in an east-west direction until it broadens at Hendricks Point in South Jacksonville and turns south. At first, most of the development is on the western shore,

Jacksonville, FL

ST. JOHNS RIVER		Dockage					Supplies		Service				
		Largest Vessel Accommodated	VHF Channel Monitored	Transient Berths / Total Berths	Approach / Dockside Depth (reported)	Floating Docks	Gas / Diesel	Groceries, Ice, Marine Supplies, Snacks	Repairs: Hull, Engine, Propeller	Lift (tonnage), Crane, Rail	1=110V, 2=220V, B=Both, Max Amps	Laundry, Pool, Showers	Pump-Out Station	Nearby: Grocery Store, Motel, Restaurant
1. Arlington Marina	904-743-2628	50	16/68	6/30	16/5	F	GD	I		L30,R	B/50	S		GR
2. Metropolitan Park Marina	904-630-0839	72-Hour Complimentary Docking									B/50		P	GMR
3. The Jacksonville Landing **WiFi**	904-353-1188	72-Hour Complimentary Docking			F			IS			1/30			R
4. River City Brewing Co. & Marina **WiFi**	904-398-7918	150	16	10/62	18/13	F	GD				B/50	LS		GMR

Corresponding chart(s) not to be   **used for navigation.** ⌨ Internet Access **WiFi** Wireless Internet Access

JACKSONVILLE, CHART 11491

south of the Ortega River, ranging from summer cabins and elegant homes to large commercial complexes. The heavily industrialized riverfront (with the largest deep-water harbor on the southern Atlantic coast) begins just off the Trout River, back at flashing red buoy "64," while residential areas are across the river.

Bridges: The St. Johns River runs wide and deep past the yards and wharves. About 12 miles past the Dames Point Bridge (169-foot fixed vertical clearance), the first of the downtown bridges appears: two high-level structures about a half-mile apart. First is the red Matthews Bridge (152-foot fixed vertical clearance), followed by the green Hart Bridge (141-foot fixed vertical clearance). Note that tugs and barges cross the river channel at all hours of the day and night, so be cautious. For more information about

navigating through Jacksonville, contact the Mayport Coast Guard Operations Center, 24 hours a day, at 904-247-7312 or on VHF Channel 16. There is also a Local Notice to Mariners broadcast on VHF Channel 22A at 8:15 a.m. and 6:15 p.m. daily.

After the Hart Bridge, the four remaining Jacksonville bridges are within less than a mile of each other. From east to west the bridges are the Main Street Lift Bridge (blue, 40-foot closed vertical clearance), the twin Acosta bridges (75-foot fixed vertical clearances), the Florida East Coast Railroad Bascule Bridge (black, 5-foot closed vertical clearance) and the 75-foot-high Interstate 95 Fuller Warren fixed bridge, which replaced the demolished Fuller-Warren Bascule Bridge. The remaining drawbridge responds on VHF Channel 09 (as do all Florida draw

Sidetrips: St. Johns River, FL

Looking west-northwest over Jacksonville and the St. Johns River. The Hart Bridge is visible in the foreground.
(Not to be used for navigation.) WATERWAY GUIDE PHOTOGRAPHY

spans). The railroad bridge is usually open, except when a train is expected. Trains cross relatively frequently, all at slow speed.

It is common to meet barge traffic in the area of these bridges; contact the tugboat skippers on VHF Channels 13 or 16 so they can tell you how to stay out of their way. After you pass the Fuller-Warren Bridge, the river widens. The next bridge is approximately eight miles upriver, located past the Naval Air Station. The Buckman Bridge is a twin-span high-level bridge that carries eight lanes of Interstate 295. Its fixed vertical clearance is reported at 65 feet.

Dockage: Jacksonville Landing, a festival-type marketplace located on the north waterfront, offers 72-hour complimentary dockage on a first-come, first-served basis. There is no electricity or water available, but cleats are plentiful, and rafting is permitted. Recreational craft must not get in the way of the sightseeing boats or the busy water taxis, however.

The city of Jacksonville operates the 75-slip Metropolitan Park Marina on the north bank of the river near Alltel Stadium and the tent-like pavilion of Metropolitan Park. This facility is intended for public use and does not charge for dockage except during special events such as football games and concerts. The floating docks now have power (30 and 50 amp service available via a self-service kiosk), water and pump-out

facilities. Transients may tie up here, on a space-available basis, for up to 72 hours. The docks are in a park that is open only from sunrise to sunset, so when the park is closed, they lock the area and you will be unable to enter or leave. The city dockmaster monitors VHF Channel 72 only during special events, but you can reach him at 904-630-0839. Upgrades to the marina were funded by a partnership with various state and local agencies, to the tune of almost 1.5 million dollars.

A little farther away is a shipyard for big ships; one or more are often here for repairs. Soon, the delightful aroma of roasting coffee, coming from the Maxwell House Coffee Co., may fill the air.

Anchorage: You can anchor near the Matthews Bridge, between Exchange Island and the Arlington waterfront, behind the City Limits Range. Holding ground is best to the east and north of the bridge in 9 to 11 feet of water. A tug racing to its next assignment or a recreational boat speeding in the main channel might jostle you here. Approximately a quarter-mile north of the anchorage is a dock for tugs. In this comfortable anchorage, you may see the college rowing teams practicing, honing their skills against the swift current. With the wind out of the north, you might elect to anchor in 8 to 20 feet of water on the southern side of the Matthews Bridge, in the lee of Exchange Island.

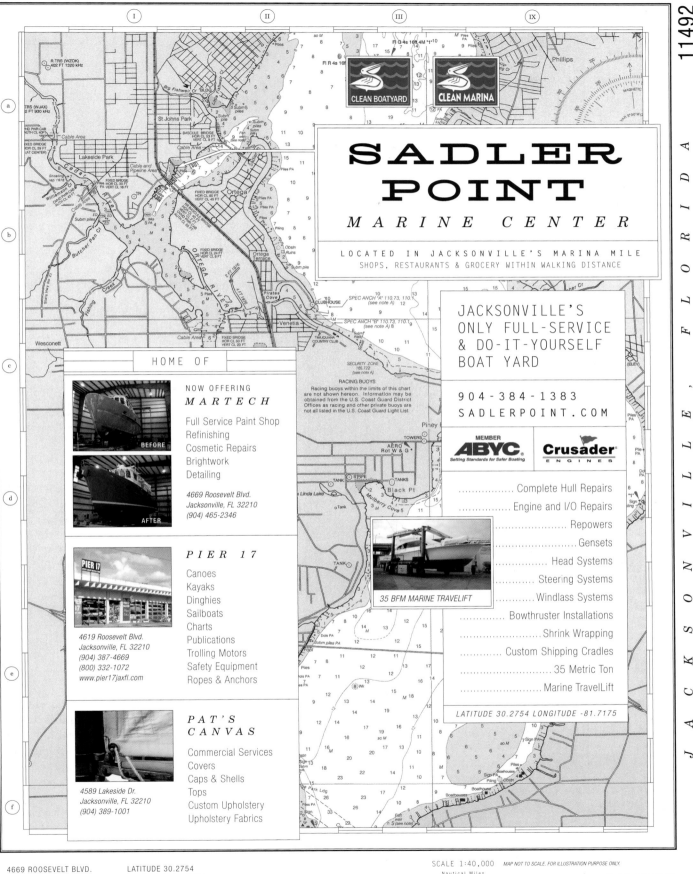

Ortega River, Jacksonville, FL

ORTEGA RIVER		Largest Vessel Accommodated	VHF Channel Monitored	Transient Berths / Total Berths	Approach / Dockside Depth (reported)	Floating Docks	Groceries, Ice, Marine Supplies, Snacks	Gas / Diesel	Repairs: Hull, Engine, Propeller	Lift (tonnage), Crane, Rail	1=110v, 2=220v, B=Both, Max Amps	Laundry, Pool, Showers	Pump-Out Station	Nearby: Grocery Store, Motel, Restaurant
			Dockage				**Supplies**				**Service**			
1. The Marina at Ortega Landing 💻 WiFi	904-387-5538	70	16/68	/192	6/6	F		I			B/200	LPS	P	GR
2. Ortega Yacht Club Marina WiFi	904-389-1199	60	16/8	4/99	7/6	F		I			B/50	LS		GR
3. Pier 17 Marine Inc.	**904-387-4669**	**MARINE STORE - SUPPLIES/CHARTS**												GR
4. Sadler Point Marine Center	**904-384-1383**	50	16	/65	6/8			M	HEP	L25	B/50	S	P	GR
5. Huckins Yacht Corp.	**904-389-1125**	80	16	/20	6/6				HEP	L77	B/50			GR
6. Cedar Point Marina	904-772-1313	60	16	/23	6/6	F					B/50	S		GMR
7. Lambs Yacht Center Inc. 💻 WiFi	**904-384-5577**	120	16/8	12/240	8/7		GD	IMS	HEP	L100, R	B/50	S	P	GR
8. Florida Yacht Club	904-387-1653	70	16	Reciprocal Privileges							B/50	PS		MR

Corresponding chart(s) not to be used for navigation. 💻 Internet Access WiFi Wireless Internet Access

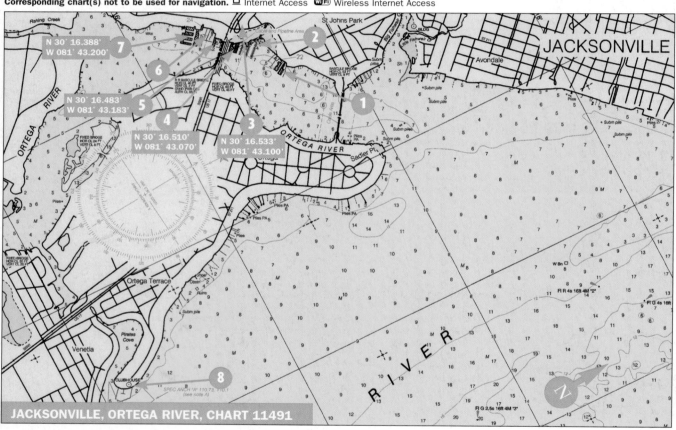

JACKSONVILLE, ORTEGA RIVER, CHART 11491

Chart callouts:
- 7: N 30° 16.388' W 081° 43.200'
- 5: N 30° 16.483' W 081° 43.183'
- 4: N 30° 16.510' W 081° 43.070'
- 3: N 30° 16.533' W 081° 43.100'

GOIN' ASHORE:
JACKSONVILLE, FL

Following the Civil War, Jacksonville became a popular winter resort. Visitors arriving by steamboats and railroad enjoyed the mild winters, fine restaurants and hotels until Henry Flagler extended the railroad south to Palm Beach and then Miami in the 1890s. Then, these early snowbirds went with the rails. In the early 1900s, Jacksonville promoted its mild climate, low labor cost and easy rail access to become the "Winter Film Capital of the World," with more than 30 studios. In the 1920s, local politicians forced the studios to go elsewhere, and Hollywood was born.

Sidetrips: Ortega River, FL

Looking northeast over the Ortega River, with the St. Johns River and Jacksonville in the background.
(Not to be used for navigation.) WATERWAY GUIDE PHOTOGRAPHY

Beyond the busy commercial area, the Jacksonville waterfront is delightful. Tranquil riverside parks and open space line the waterfront. The city's riverfront redevelopment project includes both banks of the river. Jacksonville Landing, a festival-type marketplace, complements the Southbank Riverwalk; both are popular attractions. On the north waterfront, with 72-hour complimentary dockage, Jacksonville Landing (904-353-1188) features outdoor entertainment, a variety of dining options and more than 40 specialty shops.

Southbank offers dock space, restaurants, shopping and recreation. Near River City Marina on the south bank, between the Main Street and Acosta bridges, begins the lovely Southbank Riverwalk, a mile-long boardwalk, offering many restaurants and shops. A maritime museum is on the riverbank next to the fountain and the marina. The Museum of Science and History is well worth a visit, particularly if you have children aboard. The museum features a planetarium, dinosaur replica, jaguar exhibit, a holozone virtual reality game and displays depicting Florida pioneer life. The neighboring park features a fountain with a computer-controlled light and water show. Across the river, you will see one of the tallest buildings in Florida, with windows that are kept clean by an automatic washer that travels up and down on tracks.

Alltel Stadium, also known as the Gator Bowl, is located past the second bridge (the green-colored Hart Bridge) on the north side. The stadium is home to the Jacksonville Jaguars, the college postseason Gator Bowl Classic and the annual Georgia-Florida football game, often described as the world's largest outdoor cocktail party. Also on the north shore near Alltel Stadium and the transient docks is Metropolitan Park, with its striking tent-like outdoor auditorium, a popular site for concerts and festivals.

For provisioning, Winn-Dixie (777 N. Market St., 904-353-6810) is located just 10 blocks north of the waterfront. For changing crews or a quick trip home, Jacksonville International Airport, 10 miles north of the city, has commercial air service to all major cities.

ADDITIONAL RESOURCES

- Museum of Science and History, 904-396-6674
  www.themosh.org

- Jacksonville Convention and Visitors Bureau,
  800-733-2668, **www.visitjacksonville.com**

- **NEARBY GOLF COURSES**
  Hyde Park Golf Club, 6439 Hyde Grove Ave.
  Jacksonville, FL 32210
  904-786-5410

- **NEARBY MEDICAL FACILITIES**
  St. Vincent's Medical Center
  1 Shircliff Way, Jacksonville, FL 32204, 904-308-7300

Ortega River, off the St. Johns

The hub of Jacksonville's marine industry, the Ortega River (pronounced "or-TEE-ga") is in a residential area three miles southwest of the Fuller-Warren Bridge.

NAVIGATION: Use Chart 11491. The best way to enter the Ortega River is to head due south from the Fuller-Warren (I-95) Bridge. Heading south, delay your westward turn until you pass flashing red "2" and the white daybeacon marking the shoal extending south off Winter Point. There is no light or daybeacon at the mouth of the Ortega River. With the old light missing, be sure to mind the charted obstructions and pilings north of Sadler Point. Depths here are 5 to 6 feet in the river (with shallower spots), but watch the depth sounder, and proceed slowly, especially if you have a draft of 5 feet or more. The tidal range is about 1 foot. Check for local information on depths and markers before entering the Ortega River.

For deepest water, give a wide berth to the shoal off Sadler Point, and line up for the Ortega River Bascule Bridge (9-foot closed vertical clearance) after you are clear of the shallow water. Because of its low clearance in an area of high marine traffic, the Ortega River Bridge, a 1920s-vintage classic, is the most frequently opened drawbridge in Florida (about 15,000 openings per year).

The water is relatively consistent beyond the second bridge, with 4- to 5-foot depths at mean low water. A fixed highway bridge (45-foot vertical clearance) and a railroad bascule (2-foot closed vertical clearance) cross the Ortega River about three-quarters of a nautical mile past the Ortega River Bascule Bridge.

Dockage: The Ortega River has an almost solid wall of yards, marinas and boatbuilders on the northwest bank, notably Sadler Point Marina, Lambs Yacht Center, Huckins Yachts, Ortega Yacht Club Marina and The Marina at Ortega Landing. The Marina at Ortega Landing is the first marina to starboard when heading upstream and is now part of a residential development. Next upstream is the Ortega Yacht Club Marina, which has transient slips and all fuels. Just before the railroad bridge to starboard is Sadler Point Marina, which, along with dockage, offers a full service and do-it-yourself boatyard with a 35-ton Travelift. Sadler Point also has some covered slips available. They pride themselves on being environmental stewards. Immediately to starboard past the railroad bridge is Huckins Yacht Corp., known for its beautiful custom yachts. Frank Pembroke Huckins was instrumental in designing the famous PT boats of World War II. The company was originally located at what is now the Maxwell House Coffee Co. near the Jacksonville waterfront. After the war, the company moved to its present location on the Ortega River. The full-service Lambs Yacht Center is also located past the railroad bridge with transient slips, all fuels, extensive repair capabilities and a lifts for haul-outs. Lamb's also offers wet storage under sturdy concrete sheds and is convenient to grocery and other shopping.

The southwest shore is entirely residential, with private docks and wooded plots. The only problem in finding a

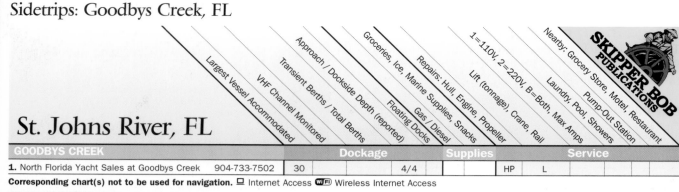

St. Johns River, FL

GOODBYS CREEK		Largest Vessel Accommodated	VHF Channel Monitored	Transient Berths / Total Berths	Approach / Dockside Depth (reported)	Floating Docks	Groceries, Ice, Marine Supplies, Snacks	Gas / Diesel	Repairs: Hull, Engine, Propeller	Lift (tonnage), Crane, Rail	1=110V, 2=220V, B=Both, Max Amps	Laundry, Pool, Showers	Pump-Out Station	Nearby: Grocery Store, Motel, Restaurant
		Dockage					**Supplies**				**Service**			
1. North Florida Yacht Sales at Goodbys Creek	904-733-7502	30			4/4					HP		L		

Corresponding chart(s) not to be used for navigation. 🖳 Internet Access 📶 Wireless Internet Access

ST. JOHNS RIVER, GOODBYS CREEK, CHART 11492

berth may be choosing among the yards and marinas, many of which welcome transients. Pier 17 Marine is nearby and has a large inventory of marine supplies and charts. The Roosevelt Mall, four or five blocks from the waterfront, has a large variety of shore amenities (restaurants, groceries, theaters and shops). There is also convenient city bus service here that runs to downtown Jacksonville.

Anchorage: A few boats can anchor, with care, in the open spaces between the various boatyards and marinas. This is a busy area, so minimizing your swinging room will be important. Keep clear of the channel, and set an anchor light at night. Naturally, you should get permission from dock owners before you tie up your dinghy.

◼ UPRIVER TO PALATKA

NAVIGATION: Use Chart 11492. With a few exceptions, the St. Johns River seems to transform itself into a lake immediately beyond the Ortega River, with widths averaging a couple of miles or more for most of the 47 miles to Palatka. This section is great for sailing, although strong

winds out of the north or south can kick up quite a chop. Deep water stretches from shore to shore, providing plenty of room for a sailor to make long, pleasant reaches.

Even when the going is tranquil, it is wise to run compass courses for each lengthy reach between the daybeacons and lights, making sure you always have a good idea of your position. This country is great for fishing and crabbing, but the bobbing floats of the commercial crabber's pots—some of which are dark and difficult to see—are numerous enough to warrant close attention.

Dockage: About two nautical miles past the entrance to the Ortega River, at Pirates Cove on the western shore, is the Florida Yacht Club, one of the country's oldest (charted, to starboard in a protected lagoon), open only to members and their guests. The club may accept guests that are members of reciprocating yacht clubs; call ahead for details. They offer an on-site restaurant, a pool and showers.

Anchorage: Beyond Goodbys Creek, on the eastern side of the river, you can anchor in Plummers Cove between Beauclerc Bluff and the Buckman Bridge, also known locally as Three Mile Bridge (65-foot fixed vertical clearance). The entrance is straightforward. Just avoid the shoal

St. Johns River, FL

DOCTORS LAKE, JULINGTON CREEK		Largest Vessel Accommodated	VHF Channel Monitored	Transient Berths / Total Berths	Approach / Dockside Depth (reported)	Floating Docks	Groceries, Ice, Marine Supplies, Snacks	Gas / Diesel	Repairs: Hull, Engine, Propeller	Lift (tonnage), Crane, Rail	1=110V, 2=220V, B=Both, Max Amps	Laundry, Pool, Showers	Pump-Out Station	Nearby: Grocery Store, Motel, Restaurant
1. Villas Continental & Yacht Club Marina	904-264-2467	65		/86	5/4						B/50	LPS		GMR
2. Doctors Lake Marina	904-264-0505	60					G	I		HE		B/50	LS	P	
3. Fleming Island Marina ⌨	904-269-0027	50		/114	7/7	F		IM	HEP	L25,C	1/30	S		GMR
4. Mandarin Holiday Marina	904-268-1036	50	16/68	5/150	6/6	GD	GIMS	HEP	L15	1/30			P	GMR
5. The Marina at Julington Creek	904-268-5117	47	16/09	/103	6/5	G	IMS	E	L	B/50			P	R

Corresponding chart(s) not to be used for navigation. ⌨ Internet Access 📶 Wireless Internet Access

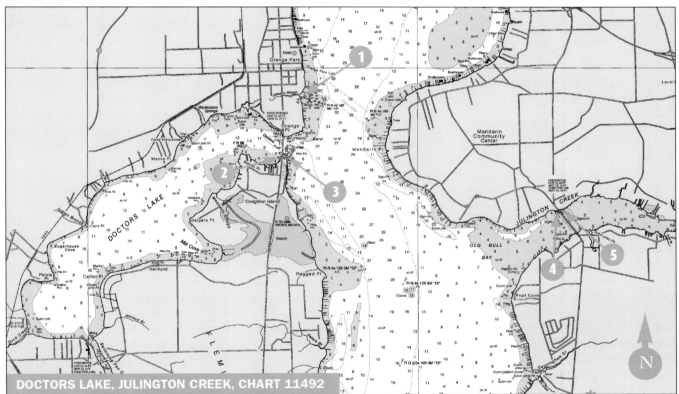

DOCTORS LAKE, JULINGTON CREEK, CHART 11492

off Beauclerc Bluff, which is marked by green daybeacon "9." Go in at the approximate middle of the "entrance," dodging the trap markers that sometimes pepper both the entrance and interior. Note shoaling along the shoreline, and sound your way in. This is not a cozy anchorage, but it is adequate in calm conditions or lacking any alternative. Anchor in depths of 6 to 8 feet—the holding is good in mud. The anchorage is wide open to the west, and you will hear some noise from the naval air station across the river at Piney Point. Remember that all along the St. Johns River, remnants of old docks, some submerged, can be hazardous. Most of these are charted, but still warrant a close lookout.

Doctors Lake, off the St. Johns

NAVIGATION: Use Chart 11492. About two miles south of the Buckman Bridge (65-foot fixed vertical clearance), on the west side of the St. Johns River, is Doctors Lake, four miles long and deep in many places (7- to 10-foot depths) almost to the banks. The lake is beautiful and protected, and its wooded shores are dotted with homes, many with their own docks. The entrance to Doctors Lake, spanned by a 37-foot fixed vertical clearance bridge, is marked by red daybeacon "2" off Orange Point, which was moved farther away from shore toward the channel. Stay clear of the shoaling on both sides of Doctors Inlet, and steer toward the middle of the entrance.

Dockage: On the south side of Doctors Inlet before the bridge, Fleming Island Marina handles boats of all sizes with a full-service yard (25-ton lift for haul-outs) and well-maintained docks and common areas. Transients are welcome at the new floating docks. Eight miles of newly constructed paths for walking and bicycling provide access to restaurants, laundry, pharmacies and a grocery. Enter the marina (7-foot approach and dockside depths) from the north and follow the private markers.

Green Cove Springs, Trout Cr., Palatka, FL

GREEN COVE SPRINGS, TROUT CR., PALATKA		Largest Vessel Accommodated	VHF Channel Monitored	Transient Berths / Total Berths	Approach / Dockside Depth (reported)	Floating Docks	Gas / Diesel	Groceries, Ice, Marine Supplies, Snacks	Repairs: Hull, Engine, Propeller	Lift (tonnage), Crane, Rail	1=110V, 2=220V, B=Both, Max Amps	Laundry, Pool, Showers	Pump-Out Station	Nearby: Grocery Store, Motel, Restaurant
				Dockage				**Supplies**		**Service**				
1. Reynolds Park Yacht Center 💻 WiFi	904-284-4667	400	16	10/70	12/10	F		M	HEP	L60,C	B/100	LS	P	R
2. Holland Marine	904-284-3349	50		/15	10/10	F		M	HEP	L25, C	1/50			GMR
3. GREEN COVE SPRINGS MARINA 💻	**904-284-1811**	100	16/68	/20	14/11	F		IM	P	L30	1/30	LS		GMR
4. Pacetti Marina & Campground 💻	904-284-5356		13/69	10/30	6/7		G	GIM				LS		MR
5. Outback Crab Shack at Six Mile Marina	904-522-0500				5.5/15					DOCK & DINE				
6. Crystal Cove Resort Marina	386-328-4000						GD	M	HEP			S		MR
7. Quality Inn & Suites Riverfront 💻	386-328-3481	100		21/21	25/8			IS			B/50	LPS		GMR
8. BOATHOUSE MARINA 💻	**386-328-2944**	60	16	4/40	8/8		GD	IS			B/50	LS	P	GMR
9. Gibson Dry Docks	386-325-5502	50		/20	6/6					L20				GMR

Corresponding chart(s) not to be used for navigation. 💻 Internet Access WiFi Wireless Internet Access

Doctors Lake Marina is located just inside the bridge on the south shore of Doctors Inlet with transient slips, gas, laundry and showers/restrooms.

Anchorage: If you can clear the 37-foot fixed vertical clearance bridge and decide to anchor out in Doctors Lake, do so with care because the holding ground in some places is poor. The bottom is covered with very fine, soft silt, and even the best of anchors will not set well. We advise: In west through northwest winds, anchor above Peoria Point in Sugarhouse Cove; in strong northerly winds, try close in to the shore between Macks Point and Indigo Branch; in heavy easterly weather, try the mouth of Mill Cove. In all places, be certain to power down on your hook and check it frequently. Respect the charted submerged piling areas. Do not anchor in the middle of the lake except in an emergency; it is far too exposed.

Almost directly across the St. Johns River from Doctors Lake is Julington Creek, broad and unobstructed as far as a fixed bridge (15-foot vertical clearance). The creek is shoaling, so sound your way in, and check the depth of your swinging arc if you choose to anchor here. Above the opening, the creek shoals quickly to 4-foot depths or less, especially on the north side. For larger boats, Old Bull Bay at Julington Creek's mouth is a good anchorage with shelter from north through southeast winds. This attractive area is especially good for dinghy exploration. You will find 7- to 8-foot depths on a line between the points of land and 4 to 6 feet closer to the bridge.

Black Creek, off the St. Johns

Black Creek empties into the St. Johns River about three miles north of Green Cove Springs on the western bank of the St. Johns River just north of Wilkies Point. A fixed bridge at the entrance has a vertical clearance of 30 feet, and upstream is another with a fixed vertical clearance of 20 feet. An overhead cable with an authorized vertical clearance of 47 feet also crosses the creek about two miles above the first bridge. If you can get under all of these (or have your mast unstepped at a nearby marina), you can cruise upriver to the headwaters and the town of Middleburg, which rivals St. Augustine as one of the nation's oldest settlements. A grocery store is a pleasant walk from the Middleburg waterfront, but there are no transient docks.

Black Creek is deep, placid, unspoiled and offers a microcosm of the world's subtropical rivers. If you make the trip in late spring or summer, don't be surprised if you disturb a slumbering alligator along the banks.

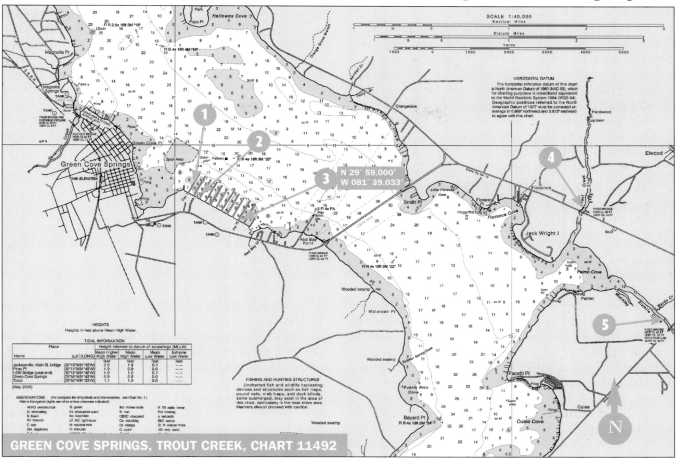

GREEN COVE SPRINGS, TROUT CREEK, CHART 11492

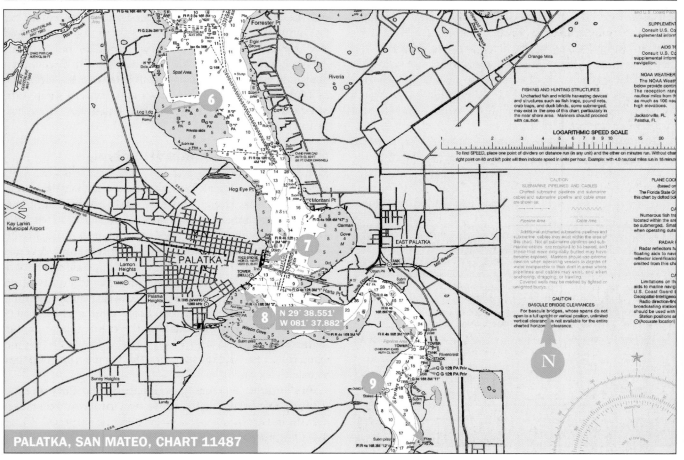

PALATKA, SAN MATEO, CHART 11487

Sidetrips: Green Cove Springs, FL

Upriver on the St. Johns

Continuing on the St. Johns River upriver from Black Creek, both banks offer coves with safe overnight spots. Most of these are obvious on the charts. You need only select a cove on the east or west bank, depending upon the wind direction at the time of your arrival. Most of the bottom here is sticky black mud, good holding for a well-set hook. Usually a current sets with the tide as far as Lake George. South of the lake, the weak current sets downstream (northward).

■ GREEN COVE SPRINGS TO PALATKA

The town of Green Cove Springs is on a very shallow, pretty cove off the St. Johns River. Here, the long piers of a World War II Navy facility jut out into the river. These piers clearly show up on the chart for the area.

Green Cove Springs took its name from the sulfur mineral spring found here. Long reputed to have medicinal qualities, the waters attracted many famous visitors in the late 1800s and early 1900s. Today, visitors will find the spring in the midst of a city park fringed with fine old homes. St. Mary's Episcopal Church, built in the late 19th century, is an elegant riverfront structure with an unusual architectural feature: fire-escape doors beneath the stained-glass windows along the sides of the building.

NAVIGATION: Use Chart 11492. The 45-foot fixed vertical clearance bridge that sets overhead clearance for the upper St. Johns River is located south of Green Cove Springs, running across the river between Red Bay and Smith points. When transiting the Green Cove Springs area, stick to the marked channel to avoid both charted shoals and possible submerged obstructions. Also, watch for trap markers that might be at the edge of the channel or between the bridge fenders.

Dockage: Green Cove Springs Marina offers transient dockage. If they do not have any space available at the dock, a mooring may available; call ahead for details. Green Cove Springs is a well-protected spot for safe long-term storage, and they have just added additional space for 500 more boats for storage. They also have on site approved contractors for painting, mechanical, electrical repair, bottom work and canvas, as well as a marine supply store. Holland Marine (formerly Ortega River Boatyard), open at the old Navy pier Slip Six, may sometimes have transient slips available. Governors Creek, just north of the town, has a boat ramp and fishing pier. Watch for the charted overhead power lines (30-foot vertical clearances) and fixed bridges (8- and 11-foot vertical clearances heading upstream respectively) if you enter.

Anchorage: Boats may anchor across from the Reynolds Park piers between Popo Point and the Smith Point (Shands) Bridge on the eastern shore of the river. Note the shoal water south of Hallowes Cove, as well as the 3-foot-deep spot northeast of flashing red "20." Floating plastic jugs or life preservers sometimes mark this shallow spot. Enter well southeast of flashing red "20," avoiding the charted cable area. Protection is good only from the northeast, but holding is excellent in 7 to 10 feet of water. About four miles upriver (south) from the Shands Bridge, a scenic cove on the west side of the river is located south of Bayard Point and north of another unmarked shoal northeast of Clark Creek. Depths are 9 to 10 feet in this cove, which is protected from the northwest and offers good holding in sandy mud. Sound your way in while dodging the trap markers that are often set here.

Trout Creek, off the St. Johns

Southeast of Green Cove Springs, Trout Creek enters the St. Johns River on the north side of Palmo Cove, around the east end of Jack Wright Island. Trout Creek is a popular anchorage, but note that there is a fixed bridge about a half-mile up the creek. The official listed vertical clearance is 14 feet at high water, but it actually has a 17-foot vertical clearance. Trout Creek is a deep and gorgeous stream, with controlling depths of 7 feet well above the bridge.

Palmo Cove, Sixmile Creek, off the St. Johns

Opposite Trout Creek on Palmo Cove is Sixmile Creek, which contains one of the area's most famous and popular watering holes, the Outback Crab Shack at Six Mile Marina (904-522-0500). The family-owned and operated restaurant features fresh seafood, live music on weekends and one of the world's longest floating docks, about a quarter-mile long. Still, on busy weekends, it is often impossible to find space except by rafting up and joining the crowd. Charted depths indicate depths of at least 4 feet in Palmo Cove approaching the creek, where depths immediately increase to 13 to 14 feet. However they go back down to 4 feet just before the fixed bridge (12-foot vertical clearance).

Anchorage: Boats may anchor in Palmo Cove in 7 to 10 feet of water with good protection from every direction but the west.

South to Palatka

The 65-foot fixed bridge at Palatka is a 25-mile-long journey south along the river's wooded and narrow banks from the Shands Bridge at Green Cove Springs. Fish weirs (stakes) and numerous trap markers populate the river hereabouts. Heading south from Green Cove Springs, the first of six ranges starts about eight miles past the Shands Bridge. As you proceed south, all are back ranges (look astern) except one. A power plant with twin towers is across the river from Forrester Point, approximately four miles north of the Palatka Bridge—it is charted and highly visible. Approaching the power plant, some of the local navigational aids may be partially obscured by bird nests.

◼ PALATKA

....

NAVIGATION: Use Chart 11487. South from the Shands Bridge, the river is marked from flashing red "22" to flashing green "31" at the first range. This one leads into the second, which takes you past Ninemile Point and in turn leads you into the third range, which passes south of Verdiere Point. Set a course eastward to the final three ranges heading southward to the massive towers of a high-tension line (60-foot vertical clearance, with 91-foot clearance over the channel) that crosses the river. Beam winds, particularly from the west, can be very strong here, so keep dead on the ranges unless you have a shallow draft. **Palatka's high and low tides occur about 7.25 and 8.5 hours, respectively, after Mayport's tides.** The water depth in the channels ranges from 8 to 12 feet at mean low tide. The tidal range is about a foot.

Dockage: North of Palatka, about a mile west of flashing green "41," the Crystal Cove Marina has a motel and Corky Bell's Seafood Restaurant. A set of daybeacons will lead shoal-draft boats to the marina. Gasoline, diesel and a few transient slips are available, with 6-foot depths at the approach and 4-foot depths at the docks. Call ahead to 386-328-4000 for information and dock reservations.

The Quality Inn and Suites Riverfront, just to the north of the Memorial Bridge, has transient dockage for boats up to 100 feet, showers, laundry, a pool and restaurants nearby. Be careful on your approach, but once close to the docks, depths are 8 feet. Past the bridge to starboard is the city of Palatka's dock, with dockside depths of 6 feet. Space is available on a first-come, first-served basis for boats up to 60 feet. Only household current (15-amp 110-volt) is available, and there are no showers, water or other amenities. A sign on the shore end of the dock gives the Palatka City Hall phone number and police department number. Shopping and restaurants are a few blocks away.

Boathouse Marina, south of the town dock, offers transient slips, restrooms, showers and a laundry. Dockage with electricity and pump-out facilities are available and plans for a fuel dock are in the works. Head for the dock approximately midway between flashing green "1" and flashing red "2." Depths of 7 to 8 feet are reported. The

town is just three blocks away. In the summer, on most Saturday evenings, the town sponsors concerts in the waterfront amphitheater.

South of Palatka, just east of flashing red "12," is Gibson Dry Docks, a repair facility that allows owners to do their own work.

Anchorage: There is some anchoring room south of the bridge, on the west side of the river between the bridge and the city dock. Numerous commercial piers were once located on the southwest side and many of the old pilings have been removed, but some remain; be cautious. Sound your way in and use an anchor light at night, making sure to stop well off the channel to clear tug and barge traffic. Stay to the north to avoid shoal areas. Holding ground is fair in mud and silt.

You can also anchor north of Palatka along the east shore near the power cables below Cow Creek, or in Carman Cove by Maritoni Point, just east of flashing green "47." Sound your way in. The holding is good in mud. Note that both anchorages are wide open to northwest through southeast winds.

Avoid Wilson Cove, which is situated south of the bridge on the west side of the river. The old sawmill here was removed years ago, but the abandoned wrecks, stumps and sunken logs make passage treacherous. On the north shore of Devils Elbow, opposite flashing red "6," is a dock with 6 to 8 feet of water, formerly known as the "Burger King" (now closed) dock. Although it is reportedly possible to tie here, it is not recommended. There is a dock next door where boats can tie up at Gator Landing. Across the street are a large hardware store, a drugstore and a grocery. Down the street to the left are a fresh fruit stand and a bait shop.

GOIN' ASHORE: **PALATKA, FL**

Called the "Gem City on the St. Johns," Palatka was a winter playground for President Grover Cleveland, James Mellon and other influential people in the late 1800s. With excellent rail service, the town's commerce prospered through the tourism, lumber and citrus industries. With the "Great Freezes" of 1895 and the increased popularity of Jacksonville, Palatka's golden era ended and only the lumber industry remained strong. Today, a state-of-the-art paper mill here produces a half-million tons of paper products each year.

Palatka retains the ambience of an old river town. A city park along the riverfront has picnic shelters, boat ramps and restrooms, and brick-paved residential streets run beneath grand old oaks hung with Spanish moss. The Mug Race, the largest inland sailboat race in the country, is held annually the first Sunday in May and runs from Palatka to Jacksonville. The Rudder Club of Jacksonville sponsors this race, featuring more than 400 racing and cruising sailboats. The elegant 1854 Bronson-Mulholland House, also known as Sunny Point, located at 100 Madison St., is open to the public for tours on Tuesday, Thursday and Sunday afternoons. The town holds its annual Azalea Festival in March and the Low Country River Boil and Oyster Roast in July.

Sidetrips: Palatka, FL

A long walk from the marinas south of the bridge is Ravine Gardens State Park. Begun in 1933, the 182-acre state park is built around natural ravines. The nature trails wander among thousands of azaleas and other ornamental plants growing near streams and ravines. There are picnic grounds and jogging trails. The park is open daily from 8 a.m. to sundown. For more information, call 386-329-3721.

ADDITIONAL RESOURCES

■ Putnam County Chamber of Commerce,
www.putnamcountychamber.org

⚑ **NEARBY GOLF COURSES**
Palatka Golf Club, 1715 Moseley Ave.,
Palatka, FL 32177, 386-329-0141
www.palatkagolfclub.com

⚕ **NEARBY MEDICAL FACILITIES**
Putnam Community Medical Center
611 Zeagler Drive, Palatka, FL 32177, 386-328-5711

■ UPRIVER TO SANFORD

Past the Palatka Bridge, the St. Johns River puts on its most beautiful face, reminiscent of the quiet, winding Waccamaw River, just north of Georgetown, SC. For 80 miles, the scenery varies, and you can enjoy an array of villages, towns and anchorages. A number of aids to navigation, that do not appear on some chart editions, mark shoals or other hazards, and bird nests change the apparent shape or obscure the numbers of some markers. All the way to Lake Monroe, osprey architecture (nest building) on the daybeacons grows more profuse, so look carefully.

Much of the area is undeveloped and excellent for bird-watching. Bald eagles are sometimes close enough to photograph without a telephoto lens, anhingas (snakebirds) sit and dry their wings, manatees swim nearby and alligators sleep in the sun along the shore. Fishing is good, but remember that you need a Florida license if you are between 16 and 65 years old.

NAVIGATION: Use Charts 11487 and 11495. From here, upriver to Welaka, about 20 gorgeous miles away, the relatively narrow St. Johns River has navigational aids and adequate depths for barge traffic. Fish traps, stakes, submerged pilings and shoaling, usually along the banks, require your attention at all times, so follow the markers carefully, cruise slowly and take no shortcuts. At the foot of Murphy Island is winding Dunns Creek, a wilderness stream with a controlling depth of 4 feet. It leads through eight miles of untamed country to Crescent Lake (about 10 miles long with depths of 7 to 13 feet). The creek itself has several very sharp turns, but both Dunns Creek and Murphy Creek make for lovely gunkholing.

Once past the common mouths of Murphy and Dunns creeks, proceed marker to marker. Two shoals extend from Murphy Island almost into the south side of the channel. The bottom here is hard sand, so know your boat's position at all times. Favor the north side of the river just before and at flashing green "23" to avoid shoaling and submerged pilings. At Buffalo Bluff, near green daybeacon "27," a bascule railroad bridge (7-foot closed vertical clearance) is normally open, but closes 20 to 30 minutes before trains arrive, several times a day. The bridge tender responds on VHF Channel 09 and is usually on duty during the day. When approaching Welaka from red daybeacon "42A" to flashing red "52," check your chart, and watch the depth sounder carefully for shoals in mid-river; some are marked, but many are not.

Anchorage: Porters Cove, approximately 3.3 miles upriver from the Palatka Bridge, has good protection from the west, and fair protection from the northwest and southwest. The cove, with wooded banks, is between the overhead power cables at Rivercrest and flashing red "12" on the west side of the river. Sound your way in to anchor in 8- to 10-foot depths. The plentiful osprey nests here have Spanish moss woven into the usual twigs and sticks.

A snug anchorage is in Murphy Creek where it crosses Dunns Creek. Enter in the middle of the Dunns Creek mouth at Rat Island between pilings and trap markers. Watch the depth sounder and proceed slowly; you should find at least 5 feet in the channel, but depths are far less outside. Murphy Creek is to starboard about a half-mile ahead and has pilings on both sides. Anchor anywhere past the pilings in 7- to 20-foot depths. Trap markers are the only signs of civilization here among the pristine wooded banks.

Browns Landing, approximately 7.5 miles south of Palatka, has a good anchorage. Leave the channel between flashing red "16" and red daybeacon "18" and head north. Holding is good in 10- to 14-foot depths. Watch for the shoal marked by red daybeacon "18."

About 1.5 miles south of Dunns Creek on the St. Johns River, a good spot lies in the first bend of the S-turn leading to the bascule railroad bridge (7-foot closed vertical clearance). When headed south, the HALF-MILE sign (small, white and illegible) is between green daybeacon "25" and flashing red "26." You must make the northwest turn before you see the bridge. You have to get closer still before you will spot the draw, on the southeast (port) side close to shore. You will find 14 to 17 feet of water and plenty of swinging room in the space between the daybeacon and the southeast shore. Keep clear of the fish traps just inshore to the south, and set an anchor light.

A comfortable anchorage lies between the land and the northeast side of the most northern of the Seven Sisters Islands. Enter opposite flashing red "28," favoring the landward side. Watch the depth sounder and stay away from the shoal area off the islet's upper tip. This anchorage is well-protected and quiet, in spite of houses along the northeast shore. Note the charted 6-foot spot at the entrance to this creek.

Just before the never-to-be-completed Cross-Florida Greenway (Canal) is Stokes Landing and Stokes Island.

Stokes Landing features several boatyards, one of which maintains tugs, but from time to time, handsome mega-yachts are hauled for repairs here, looking out of place in the isolated, jungle-like setting. Behind Stokes Island, you will find 8- to 9-foot depths.

A couple of miles beyond the Buffalo Bluff Railroad Bridge (Chart 11495), the entrance to the canal is to star-board, marked by red-green "C," opposite Trout Island. Before going through the canal, west of green daybeacon "33A," check locally for depths and the operating hours of the Buckman Lock. On the other side of the lock is Rodman Reservoir, also known as Lake Ocklawaha, cre-ated from the Ocklawaha River. Here, you will find boat ramps, camping, picnic sites and excellent pan fishing. This section and a nine-mile canal on the west coast at Yankeetown were the only two portions of the Cross-Florida Barge Canal completed before public opposi-tion, caused by environmental concerns and right-of-way problems, halted the project in 1971. Controlling depth is reported to be 7 feet, though the chart says 12 feet. Numerous navigational aids mark the completed section of the canal from the St. Johns River to the Ocklawaha River and through the Rodman Reservoir. Contact the Office of Greenways and Trails at 352-236-7143 for the latest canal conditions and bridge and cable clearances.

Between the Buffalo Bluff Railroad Bridge and Welaka, the early morning sun and ground fog might make it dif-ficult to see the markers. Also, the bird nests built on the pilings obscure some marker numbers along the way. This avian architecture, from a distance, can change the shapes of triangles into squares.

Welaka to Lake George

Now a sleepy hamlet, Welaka was once a bustling steam-boat depot for the transportation of wood, produce and tourists. Ulysses S. Grant was a passenger on the steam-boat that made the trip from Welaka up the Ocklawaha River to its headwaters at Silver Springs, one of Florida's early tourist attractions. Nowadays, elegant antique steam-boats rendezvous here. Welaka is also home to one of the river's upscale fishing, vacation and conference resorts, the Floridian Sports Club.

NAVIGATION: Use Chart 11495. Welaka is a good stopover area, with an anchorage by Turkey Island. There is a sign on the riverbank in front of a Welaka condominium near red daybeacon "46" that says: JACKSONVILLE 77, SANFORD 67. The number of trap markers here varies, but you will usu-ally find room to anchor. In this section of the St. Johns River, trap setters are about as likely to set their traps in the channel as out of it. The area off flashing green "43" is shoaling, as is the area off the islets between Turkey Island and the mainland. A shoal is also developing from a bar at flashing green "45," as well as around the islets at the entrance. Enter approximately midway between the light and the islets; depths are charted at 12 feet or better, but watch the depth sounder carefully. Anchor inside, past the islets by Turkey Island in depths of 8 to 17 feet. Holding

is good in mud, although roaring bass boats might awaken you early here. Just south of Welaka, at flashing red "52," the Ocklawaha River flows into the St. Johns River, car-rying water that originally surfaced at Silver Springs, a popular tourist attraction near Ocala. Follow the straight channel carefully from red daybeacon "54" to flashing red "58" since it is narrow, with shoaling on both sides.

Stay in the channel between red daybeacon "64" and flashing green "65," as there are 3-foot depths on both sides. South of Welaka to Lake George, a good part of the channel is dredged. Pay attention to markers, watch for lateral drift and keep the depth sounder on, because it is easy to get out of the channel. In spots, depths are only 2 to 3 feet on both sides.

Dockage: Acosta Creek Harbor, at flashing red "42," is built around a charming old Florida river house, and offers transient and long-term dockage, showers, laundry, a swimming pool, a marina store and guest accommoda-tions. The marina also has dry storage and is a full-service or do-it-yourself yard. Several restaurants dot the river within a couple of miles of the marina. There is a new town dock in Welaka with good water depths, but no services. This is a good place to stop to visit the Welaka Maritime Museum as well as the Welaka National Fish Hatchery and Aquarium, where striped bass are hatched and grown for reintroduction to other rivers.

Anchorage: A good secluded anchorage where, if you are lucky, you can see deer feeding on water hyacinths, is in the curve of the St. Johns River, east and behind Buzzards Point, in 13 feet of water. Entering from the west, turn off the channel halfway between flashing green "59" and red daybeacon "60," avoiding the charted 6-foot shoal. Leaving the anchorage, follow the water's edge in 13 feet of water until a course due south brings you to flashing green "61A," avoiding the 3-foot shoal to starboard. The anchor-age is protected in northerly and easterly winds.

Another pretty spot to drop the hook is upriver, 1.5 miles south of Little Lake George in Fruitland Cove, on the St. Johns River's eastern shore. You will find good shelter here from north through east winds, and the many houses along the shore prevent any feeling of isolation. Watch the depth sounder and anchor out of the channel by flashing green "63" in 8 to 11 feet of water. Note the cable area

CHAPTER 2

SIDETRIPS ON THE ST. JOHNS RIVER

St. Johns River, Welaka, Georgetown, FL

WELAKA AREA, GEORGETOWN		Largest Vessel Accommodated	VHF Channel Monitored	Approach / Dockside Depth (reported)	Transient Berths / Total Berths	Floating Docks	Groceries, Ice, Marine Supplies, Snacks	Gas / Diesel	Repairs: Hull, Engine, Propeller	Lift (tonnage), Crane, Rail	1=110V, 2=220V, B=Both, Max Amps	Laundry, Pool, Showers	Pump-Out Station	Nearby: Grocery Store, Motel, Restaurant
				Dockage				**Supplies**			**Service**			
1. Acosta Creek Harbor WiFi	386-467-2229	80	16/69	4/40	16/12			M	HEP	L30	B/50	LPS	P	
2. Georgetown Marina, Lodge & RV Park	386-467-2002	60	16/68	7/7	12/5.5	GD	IMS				B/50	LS	P	MR

Corresponding chart(s) not to be used for navigation. ⌨ Internet Access WiFi Wireless Internet Access

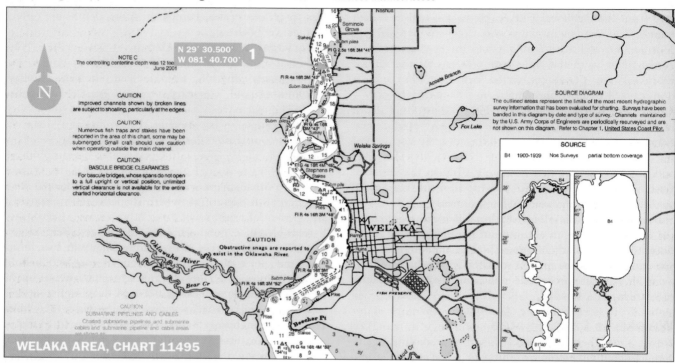

WELAKA AREA, CHART 11495

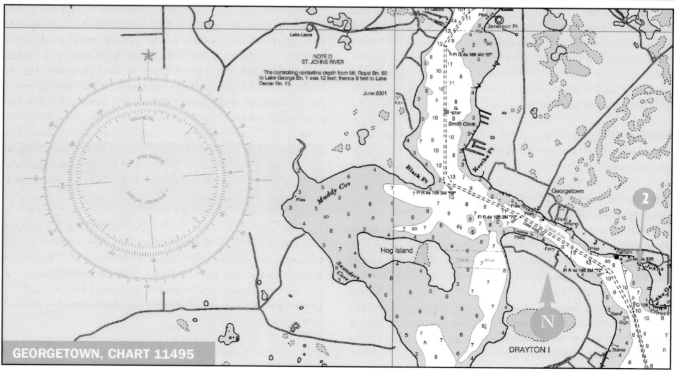

GEORGETOWN, CHART 11495

shown on the chart. Just past flashing green "65" near Jenerson Point, a Victorian home with a matching boathouse graces the east bank of the river.

Two ferries cross the channel in this area. The Fort Gates Ferry is about four miles south of Welaka; it crosses just south of the overhead power cable between Buzzards Point and Mount Royal. The second ferry is eight miles south of Welaka, at Georgetown; it provides the only vehicular connection between the mainland and Drayton Island. These antique ferries serve unpaved roads.

Across the St. Johns River from Porky's, a well-known bar, fish camp and restaurant in Georgetown, is one of the river's more intriguing sites. Tied up on Drayton Island is a once-elegant, 100-foot-long 1924 Matthews motoryacht. Her wooden hull was covered with white cement by her present owners, who have lived aboard this gorgeous, if fading, vessel for 15 years.

Lake George, along the St. Johns

NAVIGATION: Use Chart 11495. The first of the large lakes in the St. Johns River, Lake George is 75 nautical miles south of Jacksonville. This 10-mile-long lake, five miles wide with a straight, deep channel, can be rough when winds are strong up or down its length. The lake is the site of a Navy bombing range. As the charts show, the range runs parallel to the channel along three sets of pilings and encompasses much of the eastern half of the lake. The rim is marked by tall pilings, while shorter pilings mark the target area. It should be avoided.

Markers for the channel across the lake are easy to see. A range on the north end of the lake at Lake George Point leads back to the St. Johns River. A range at the southern end of Lake George leads through a hyacinth fence to the dredged channel across the Volusia Bar. The fence looks like a long set of bridge fenders; the channel is between the fenders, while outside it are rocks and declining depths. The area is posted as a Slow-Speed/Manatee Zone. Once through Lake George, you will enter yet another beautiful part of the river, continuing toward Lake Monroe. Much of the area is undeveloped and part of a wildlife sanctuary.

Dockage: In Georgetown on the north side of Lake George, the Georgetown Marina, Lodge and RV Park has a few transient slips, gas and diesel fuel, laundry, showers and a pump-out station. Groceries, a restaurant and lodging are nearby.

Astor to Hontoon Landing, along the St. Johns

NAVIGATION: The river then deepens towards Astor, about four miles south of Lake George. Fishing camps and waterside restaurants surround the bascule bridge (20-foot closed vertical clearance). For seafood, locals recommend the Blackwater Inn and William's Landing Pub (closed Mondays) just south of the bridge on the west side. The restaurant dockage can handle vessels in the 40-foot range, but dock bow-in to get depths at your stern of 4 to 5 feet.

Astor enforces its no-wake law strictly, so be sure to slow down between the signs. The bridge is a single-span bascule that monitors VHF Channels 09 and 16; it hangs over the channel when open. The overhead power cable north of the bridge is reported by the Coast Guard to have less than its charted 50-foot vertical clearance, but an exact measurement was not given.

Waterfront homeowners with docks and boat slips in the Astor area have rigged various devices—PVC pipes, float lines, fences, etc.—to keep water hyacinths from building up and choking access to the river. Without such devices, the docks become surrounded by plant life and look as if they were constructed inland.

Manatee regulations upriver from Astor are strictly enforced. From here to Lake Monroe, keep an eye out for bald eagles, anhingas, ibises, herons and egrets. In the cool months, alligators migrate south to Lake Harney, but if the winter is warm, chances are you will find many of them in the river.

Dredged cuts have eliminated many turns in the St. Johns River channel. Bars block entrance to many of the oxbows that show deep water inside. Overhanging foliage sometimes obscures daybeacons here, adding confusion to some of the cuts where the natural course of the river makes abrupt turns off the channel (with some turns actually wider than the channel itself). The markers are there, however, so go slowly, pay attention and enjoy the beauty of this special place.

As the crow flies, Lake Dexter is four miles south of Astor and less than 20 miles from Lake Monroe. On the river, however, it is more like 30 miles through a wilderness broken only by a few convenient marinas. The route is well-marked, but losing concentration will put you aground quickly.

There are No-Wake Zones on both sides of the Whitehair Bascule Bridge (15-foot closed vertical clearance), and self-appointed shoreside wake monitors that are located immediately south of the bridge can be particularly vocal if your wake fails to meet their specifications. A Manatee Zone, enforced year-round, begins just downriver of flashing green "53" and extends all the way to flashing green "81" south of Blue Springs. Please use common sense and common courtesy.

Dockage: North of the Whitehair Bridge, you will find the Boat Show Marina, with a lounge, snack bar, floating docks and repair services. A strong current perpendicular to the slips adds challenge to docking, but the marina personnel are very helpful.

Anchorage: The unnamed loop known locally as Catfish Bend, between red daybeacons "36" and "38" and just north of Crows Bluff, has good holding and protection in about 17 feet of water. Sound your way in. The area is largely undeveloped and beautiful; you might see an alligator. If you do not have time for the entire trip to Sanford, Crows Bluff is a good place to turn around and start back downriver (north).

Hontoon Dead River, off the St. Johns

Real wilderness lies on the Hontoon Dead River, whose mouth is about three miles away from the Whitehair Bridge and just opposite the end of Beresford Peninsula. Be sure to bring along a camera and fishing gear.

Hontoon State Park is at the apex of the curve marked by flashing green "53." The park offers picnic tables, grills, spotless showers, a nature trail and an observation tower. The park docks are on the north end of Hontoon Island, along the St. Johns' western shore next to the river's marked entrance. This spot is especially popular on summer weekends. Boats drawing 5 feet or less can tie up over soft mud at the ends of the two T-docks, but there is only room for two or three. Small outboard boats and pontoon boats can get inside. At the nearby Hontoon Landing Resort and Marina, you can get gasoline or rent houseboats, pontoon boats and runabouts. There is also transient dockage, along with lodging and a store.

Fishermen, campers and picnickers frequently use the free pedestrian ferry, which crosses the river from the island to the mainland. The pay telephone is next to the ranger's office. The park has a leash law, ostensibly to prevent your pet from falling prey to an alligator. You might also see manatees in the area.

Hontoon Landing to Lake Monroe, along the St. Johns

It is a 13-mile-long journey from Hontoon Landing to Lake Monroe. The winding river has narrow channels, land cuts, water hyacinths and snags, but there are good navigational aids. This Waterway is extremely beautiful, with an abundance of birds, turtles and manatees.

Blue Springs State Park is just south of flashing green "71." The stream from Blue Springs to the St. Johns River is roped off to protect the manatees that reside there during the cool months. Just above the stream is an observation platform dock with a dinghy-friendly beach alongside. The springs are worth exploring. Hontoon Island Park and Blue Springs State Park are independent of each other, but share a common manatee area that is carefully monitored by the marine patrol. If you are moving too fast (and even auxiliary sailboats sometimes do), you could get a ticket or a warning.

At flashing red "96," the narrow entrance to the Wekiva River is almost totally obscured by water hyacinths. Although a boat with a 5-foot draft can be taken several miles up, the Wekiva River's entrance is tricky; explore it only with local knowledge.

The river continues to meander five miles more from the Wekiva River to the three bridges just before Lake Monroe. Just before the bridges is a power plant with multiple overhead cables crossing the river. The last two cable crossings, significantly lower than the others, have vertical clearances of 49 feet, according to the latest chart.

Dockage: The Port of Sanford is on the south side just before the railroad bridge. This location offers spectacular bird- and turtle-watching. The Boat Tree Marina is located in the large basin just before the bridges. They may offer transient dockage, but call ahead to check.

Anchorage: South of Hontoon Island at Starks Landing is a good anchorage in the little-used river loop behind the island off the western bank. Enter at the north end by flashing green "69" and proceed slowly, as this is a manatee refuge. An area charted as having 23-foot depths may have less than 5 feet of water. The bottom is soft mud, and you should set an anchor light. You can dinghy to the beach just past the entrance of the springs. Sanford is only a few hours run from here, even for slow boats.

Emanuel Bend, a favorite anchorage for locals, is across from the Wekiva River, between green daybeacons "95" and "97." Both ends are navigable, but the south end is very narrow and may be full of hyacinths and overhanging trees. Campers may be on the island. Depths are less than the chart indicates. At Butchers Bend, enter at either end, with 7.5-foot depths at the north entrance at flashing green "109" and 6-foot depths at the south at green daybeacon "111." This very pretty spot is popular with locals and fishermen. There may be alligators, so be cautious in allowing pets or children to swim.

Lake Monroe

NAVIGATION: Use Chart 11498. The last run, to Lake Monroe, is almost straight. Just before the lake, you come to a railroad bascule bridge with a 7-foot closed vertical clearance; call the tender on VHF Channel 09. Next come two fixed spans (45-foot vertical clearances). The old swing bridge just east of the railroad bascule is gone except for the section extending from the south bank, which is now a fishing pier. The boat ramp immediately after this section of old bridge can generate significant congestion in the river channel. Boaters attempting to enter Lake Monroe had reported that depths were less than those charted, most likely due to a persistent drought that affected water levels in Central Florida in 2009. That was not an issue at press time.

From the second fixed bridge, follow the channel markers carefully to the channel junction at flashing red "8." The channel headed toward the north leads to the power plant across the lake at Enterprise; the one to the southeast goes to Sanford. Stay out of the area to the northeast between the two channels; the spar buoys mark sunken trees used to attract fish. Red daybeacon "10" is next, followed by junction marker "RG." Now, it gets complicated: One channel heads south and then along the shore, and the other channel heads southeast toward the marina. Go from red daybeacon "12" to flashing green "5." This number is related to no other lights nearby. The Coast Guard placed two daybeacons, green "1" and red "2," almost to the north, in line with flashing green "5." Visiting boaters and even locals find them confusing. The numbers "1" and "2" cannot be read from "5," but circle to port closely around "5" and head between "1" and "2," as the depth is at least 6 feet. A shoal with only a few feet of water extends from the corner of the mole almost to a line drawn between flashing green "5" and red daybeacon "2." Proceed paral-

St. Johns River, Hontoon Landing Area, FL

HONTOON LANDING AREA		Largest Vessel Accommodated	VHF Channel Monitored	Approach / Dockside Depth (reported)	Transient Berths / Total Berths	Floating Docks	Gas / Diesel	Groceries, Ice, Marine Supplies, Snacks	Repairs: Hull, Engine, Propeller	Lift (tonnage), Crane, Rail	1=110V, 2=220V, B=Both, Max Amps	Laundry, Pool, Showers	Pump-Out Station	Nearby: Grocery Store, Motel, Restaurant
				Dockage				Supplies			Service			
1. St. Johns River Marina	386-736-6601	70	16	12/170	12/10	F		M	HEP	L	B/50	S	P	GMR
2. Hontoon Landing Resort & Marina	386-734-2474	58	88	2/50	12/6	G	GIMS				B/50	PS	P	GMR
3. Hontoon Island State Park	386-736-5309	50		40/40	17/6	F	IS				1/30	S		M

Corresponding chart(s) not to be used for navigation. 🖥 Internet Access 📶 Wireless Internet Access

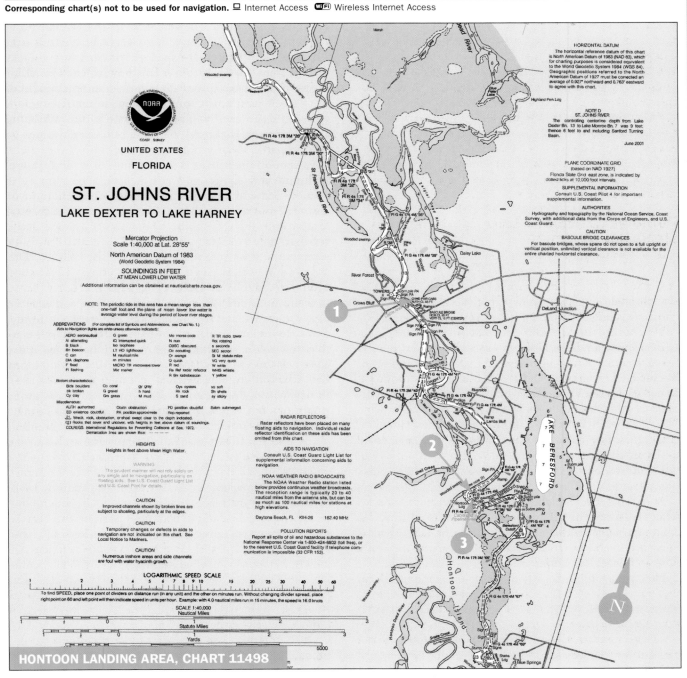

HONTOON LANDING AREA, CHART 11498

Sidetrips: Sanford, FL

lel to the shore to red daybeacon "4." The last daybeacon before the marked channel to Monroe Harbour Marina's east entrance is red daybeacon "6." Do not pass between red daybeacon "6" and the shore, because the water is shallow. Leave red daybeacon "6" to the west (starboard), and follow the marked channel into the marina.

QUICK FACT:

Sanford, the county seat of Seminole County, has a population estimated to be about 50,000. An older agricultural and resort area, the city is situated beside beautiful Lake Monroe, one of a series of lakes that eventually form the St. John River.

The ancient inhabitants were the Timucuan Indians. War and disease decimated the tribe by 1760, and eventually the Seminoles occupied the area. Although Florida was acquired from Spain in 1821, the Seminole Wars went on for many years. Development did not begin until 1842, when the town of Mellonville was established. Florida gained statehood in 1845, and Mellonville became the county seat. The planting of orange groves began in earnest, and in 1869 a fruit packing plant was established there.

Henry Sanford bought 12,500 acres west of Mellonville and established the community of Sanford. With the arrival of the railroad, development came rapidly during the late 1800s. Mellonville was absorbed by Sanford in 1883, and in that year, President Chester Arthur vacationed for a week at the Sanford House, a hotel built on the shores of Lake Monroe.

Freezing weather ruined the citrus crops in 1895, and after that, the farmers in the area started growing vegetables. Celery was first planted in 1896, and well into the 1970s the city nicknamed itself Celery City. During World War II, the Federal Government established a major Naval Air Station at Sanford, which, at its peak, was home to nearly 2,000 military personnel. The base closed in 1968, and the property was eventually converted into the Orlando Sanford International Airport.

When Walt Disney World opened in 1971, the economy began to shift strongly to tourism and residential development centered around Orlando. Because of Sanford's long history as a trade center, the city retains many beautiful older homes and commercial buildings. With streets shaded by live oaks with Spanish moss, and its location on Lake Monroe with access to the St. John River, it has marinas offering access to Jacksonville and the Intracoastal Waterway. Sanford's old downtown shopping area is about 4 blocks long and 2 blocks wide with Magnolia Square in the center and boasts many very nice shops and restaurants. Parking is free, and a new river walk and many Bed & Breakfasts are within walking distance.

■ SANFORD

At one time, Sanford was an important river port, but the only commercial traffic now is an infrequent fuel barge. Here, you enter civilization again with businesses, stores, motels and accommodations for cruising boats. Sanford, once the center of a big celery-producing area, now harvests up to four crops a year of various garden produce, including citrus fruit.

Dockage: Sanford's municipal marina, known as Monroe Harbour Marina, is within easy walking distance of downtown, with most everything you need for an enjoyable cruise. Located next to the Marina Hotel (which provides dockage for overnight guests) and Fitzgerald's, a lively nightspot, the marina offers dockage for transient boats, but seems primarily intended for locals. The marina places short-term transients in either the east or west basin; you will not see the entrance to the west basin until you are almost on it. From flashing red "5," run parallel to the mole, and the opening appears to starboard. Make a right-angle turn into the basin. A deep spot off the marina is the turning basin for *Romance*, a dining and sightseeing cruise boat. The skipper is friendly and willing to give advice either by VHF radio or ashore. Transient boats should avoid the charted channel leading into the west basin. The entrance channel has a reported depth of 5 feet.

GOIN' ASHORE: SANFORD, FL

Downtown Sanford has been renovated and is eager to please. Quaint shops and restaurants line the brick streets, all an easy walk from the nearby marinas. Many people consider this area an excellent place to spend the winter. It is a good place to use as a base for visiting the Central Florida Zoo (which is on the waterfront, but a bit too far to walk), Disney World, Epcot Center, Sea World and other Florida attractions, but you will need to rent a car or take public transportation. If you visit in spring, however, be prepared for an invasion from Florida's legendary love bugs and the ubiquitous deerfly.

ADDITIONAL RESOURCES

■ City of Sanford, www.sanford.fl.gov

⚑ **NEARBY GOLF COURSES**
Mayfair Country Club, 3536 Country Club Road, Sanford, FL 32771, 407-322-2531

⚕ **NEARBY MEDICAL FACILITIES**
Central Florida Regional Hospital
1401 W. Seminole Blvd., Sanford, FL 32771
407-321-4500

Sanford Area, FL

SANFORD AREA		Largest Vessel Accommodated	VHF Channel Monitored	Transient Berths / Total Berths	Approach / Dockside Depth (reported)	Floating Docks	Groceries, Ice, Marine Supplies, Snacks	Gas / Diesel	Repairs: Hull, Engine, Propeller	Lift (tonnage), Crane, Rail	1=110V, 2=220V, B=Both, Max Amps	Laundry, Pool, Showers	Pump-Out Station	Nearby: Grocery Store, Motel, Restaurant
		Dockage					**Supplies**				**Service**			
1. Boat Tree Marina ⬚ WiFi	407-322-1610	70	16	/645	16/12	F	G	GIMS	HEP	L25	B50	LPS	P	MR
2. Monroe Harbour Marina ⬚ WiFi	407-322-2910	80	16	5/236	6/6	F	G	IM	HEP	L35	B50	LS	P	GMR
3. Sanford Boat Works & Marina & Yacht Club	407-322-6613	70	16	2/169	8/6	F	GD	MS	HEP	L25	B50	LPS	P	R

Corresponding chart(s) not to be used for navigation. ⬚ Internet Access 📶 Wireless Internet Access

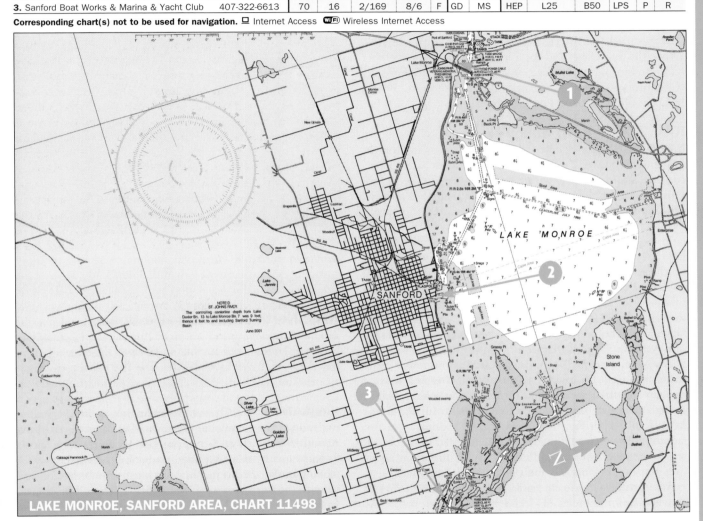

LAKE MONROE, SANFORD AREA, CHART 11498

Indian Mound Slough, off the St. Johns

Just south of the city, a short dredged cut leads from Lake Monroe to Indian Mound Slough, crossed by the Osteen Bridge (25-foot fixed vertical clearance). Lights here are difficult to see, and the U.S. Army Corps of Engineers has reported encroaching shoals. The channel usually has 5.5 feet, but this level may drop during dry spells. The shallowest part is between flashing red "2" and green daybeacon "5" to the south of Mothers Arms; proceed slowly and cautiously until in the Government Cut. The obstructions near green daybeacon "5" are tree stumps.

Beyond Indian Mound Slough, the St. Johns River system is wild, natural and unimproved, and cruising is restricted to outboards with shallow drafts. Numerous cattle ranches are here, and the area is excellent for bird-watching.

Cruising Options

From Sanford we return you coastward to Jacksonville Beach and the ICW leg south to Daytona Beach and Ponce de Leon Inlet. Mariners wishing to head north on the ICW should procure the WATERWAY GUIDE ICW edition, which picks up in St. Marys, GA, just over the Florida border. ■

....

WATERWAY GUIDE is always open to your observations from the helm. E-mail your comments on any navigation information in the guide to: editor@waterwayguide.com.

Jacksonville Beach to Ponce de Leon Inlet

CHARTS 11485, 11486, 11488, 11489, 11490, 11491

The Jacksonville Beach region is part of what Floridians call the "First Coast," because it was settled first. It vigorously competes with the Gold Coast, the Sun Coast and the Treasure Coast for developer and tourist dollars. The area begins a parade of shoreside communities such as Atlantic Beach, Neptune Beach, Jacksonville Beach and Ponte Vedra Beach.

ICW: Mile 740 to Mile 745

NAVIGATION: Use Chart 11489. After crossing the St. Johns River at Mile 740, the Intracoastal Waterway (ICW) continues along Pablo Creek toward Jacksonville Beach. Follow the markers carefully to stay on the narrow, dredged channel's centerline, and be prepared to squeeze over for tugs with barges. Small boats often anchor in the land cut just beyond the river crossing on weekends and holidays. The current in the cut flows toward the river on the ebb and can be very strong—up to 3 knots on the ebb and 2.5 knots on the flood, even without spring tides. Eddies between red nun buoy "2" and flashing green "1" at the entrance to Pablo Creek require close attention to the helm. When entering the channel, favor the green markers until you reach red daybeacon "8."

The new Wonderwood Bridge (charted on newer chart editions, absent on others) is situated at Mile 742.1, with slightly less than the charted 65 feet of vertical clearance at high tide. The 65-foot-high (also less on higher tides) Atlantic Beach Bridge (Mile 744.7) is the gateway to the Jacksonville Beach region. The large enclosed basin on the west side, just south of the Atlantic Beach Bridge, is a private marina for the surrounding condominium owners.

Anchorage: On the east side of the ICW at Mile 744.8, between flashing green "17" and green can buoy "19," is a wide and surprisingly deep stream. A number of boats are permanently moored here, and there appears to be little space for transient anchorage. If you choose to try to anchor here, enter only from the north, with an eye out for shoaling on the south side, and anchor behind the island. Leftover mooring anchors may still be on the bottom, so be wary of snags and set the hook well against the swift current. This is not an "A-plus" anchorage, but will do in a pinch if you need an evening layover.

ATLANTIC BEACH BRIDGE
Mile 744.7

WATERWAY GUIDE PHOTOGRAPHY

ICW: North of Jacksonville Beach

⚠ **THE FOLLOWING AREA REQUIRES SPECIAL ATTENTION DUE TO THE STRENGTH OF CURRENTS AT THE ATLANTIC BEACH BRIDGE.**

NAVIGATION: Use Chart 11489. Shoaling continues on the east side of the channel at green can "19," just north of the Atlantic Beach Bridge. Green can "19" is sometimes difficult to locate, as often it is pulled under by the current. After passing under the bridge, hug the west side of the channel close to the private marina, where depths should be around 15 feet. Eddies sometimes form above, under and below the bridge. Green can "19A," shown south of the bridge on older charts, has been removed.

The narrow, well-marked channel at the Atlantic Beach Bridge has ebb currents up to 6 knots at new and full moons, in synchrony with the St. Johns River. It is easy to lose control here and there is not much horizontal clearance. A number of fishermen work this area in small—often very small—boats. The Coast Pilot says: "On the flood, the current in the channel flows southward and at right angles to the bridge at an average velocity of 3.4 knots at strength. On the ebb, the current flows northward and sets about 15 degrees to the right of the axis of the channel at an average velocity of 5.2 knots at strength. The currents at a distance of 100 yards either

Looking west over Jacksonville Beach and the McCormick Bridge. (Not to be used for navigation.) WATERWAY GUIDE PHOTOGRAPHY

Jacksonville Beach, FL

Jacksonville Beach, FL

SKIPPER BOB PUBLICATIONS

| | | Approach / Dockside Depth (reported) | VHF Channel Monitored | Transient Berths / Total Berths | Largest Vessel Accommodated | Groceries, Ice, Marine Supplies, Snacks | Gas / Diesel | Repairs: Hull, Engine, Propeller | Lift (tonnage), Crane, Rail | 1=110V, 2=220V, B=Both, Max Amps | Laundry, Pool, Showers | Pump-Out Station | Nearby: Grocery Store, Motel, Restaurant |

JACKSONVILLE BEACH		Dockage				Supplies				Service			
1. PALM COVE MARINA 0.5 W OF 747 ⬜ WIFI	904-223-4757	90	16/69	25/221	6/6	F	GD	GIMS	HEP	L35	B/50	LPS	P GMR
2. BEACH MARINE 747 ⬜ WIFI	904-249-8200	125	16/68	40/350	6/6	F	GD	GIMS	HEP	L10	B/100	LS	P GMR

Corresponding chart(s) not to be used for navigation. ⬜ Internet Access WIFI Wireless Internet Access

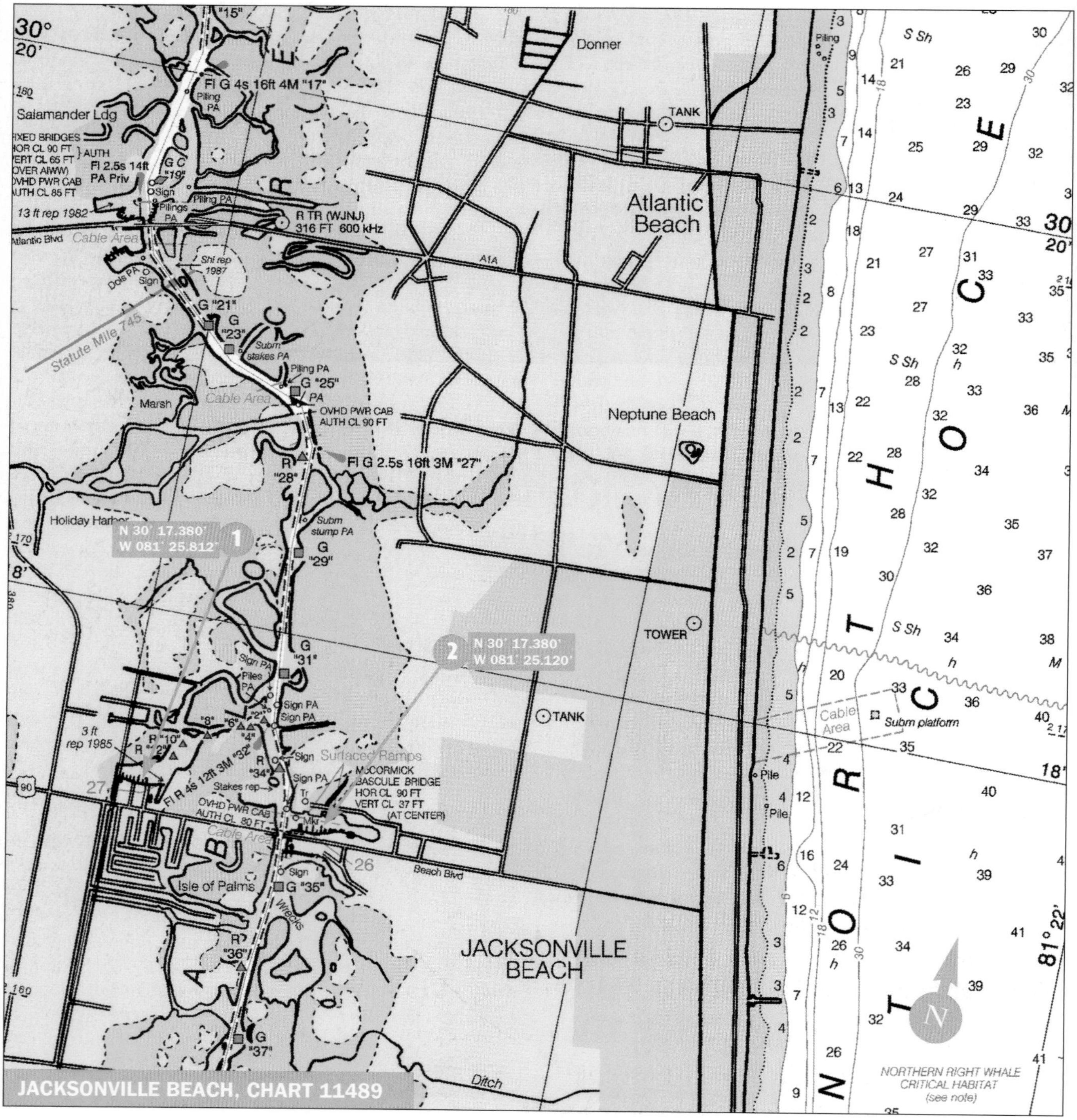

JACKSONVILLE BEACH, CHART 11489

Jacksonville's Finest Full-Service Facility

Palm Cove Marina *is proud to present:* the largest dry storage facility with the finest wet slip accommodations on Jacksonville's Intracoastal Waterway. We also provide a successful environment for 15 onsite businesses. Unique amenities such as a pool, very competitive ethanol free fuel prices, travel lift, full marine service and the friendliest staff in the business set us apart.

- Pool • Laundry
- Competitively priced Ethanol free fuel
- Newly dredged channel Full Marine service,
- 35 ton travel lift
- Ship Store
- Restaurant • Wi-Fi
- Complete shopping within 1 block
- Lounge & Showers
- Transient dockage
- Pump out

Palm Cove Marina

Located at Marker 32 on the
Intracoastal Waterway
N.W. of the McCormick Bridge

14603 Beach Boulevard • Jacksonville, FL 32250
Dockmaster 904-223-4757 • Dry Storage 904-223-1336
Service 904-821-0992
Fax 904-223-6601
www.palmcovemarina.com
e-mail pcm@palmcovemarina.com

BoatU.S. COOPERATING MARINA

CLEAN MARINA

We Monitor
VHF Channel 16

Jacksonville Beach, FL

side of the bridge are much weaker with practically no turbulence and give no warning of the strong current at the bridge."

END SPECIAL CAUTION AREA.

South, to Jacksonville Beach

NAVIGATION: Use Chart 11489. By the time you read this, the old McCormick Bascule Bridge (Mile 747.5, 37-foot closed vertical clearance) should be completely removed. The final phase of construction of a replacement high-level fixed bridge was completed in late 2009. There had been construction delays and daylong closures of the ICW for about 3 years. The second span of the new bridge was built in the same location as the old bridge. Our cruising editor noted, in early 2010, that the finishing touches were being done on the fender system under the center span.

Watch for strong currents, especially on the ebb (although they are not as strong as the currents through the Atlantic Beach Bridge). Also, boats exiting Beach Marine can sometimes cause unanticipated congestion here.

Jacksonville Beach—Mile 748

Ponce de Leon landed here in the 1500s in his search for the Fountain of Youth, and Jacksonville Beach has been a lively resort community ever since. This popular stopover, with its beautiful beach, offers a full range of services, stores and restaurants, and makes a convenient central base for side trips to Fernandina Beach, Forts Clinch and Caroline, Kingsley Plantation or the city of Jacksonville.

The proximity of the airports at Jacksonville and Daytona makes this a fine layover and fitting-out port. Many mariners cruise south to this point in the fall, leave their boats and fly home for business. When the cold weather arrives up north, they return to their boats and continue their journeys southward.

Opened in 1986, the Mayo Clinic Jacksonville was the first extension of the Mayo Clinic beyond Rochester, MN. Long known for its quality health care, Mayo provides medical diagnosis, treatment and surgery, and offers a comprehensive physical examination in one day. The clinic is an eight-story white tile building just off Butler Boulevard (not far from the marinas) on San Pablo Road. For more information, call 904-953-2000.

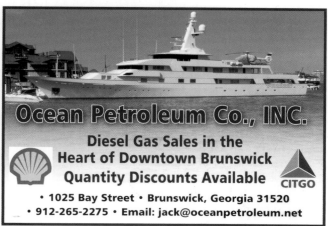

Dockage: North of the McCormick Bridge, at flashing red "32," is a small creek on the west side leading to Lake Cusic, which is unnamed on the chart. Stay to the middle of the privately marked entrance which has 6-foot depths at mean low water. The Palm Cove Marina (formerly Jacksonville Yacht Basin) has fuel (gas and diesel) and wet and dry storage. This 200-slip marina also features clean bathrooms, a restaurant, a ship's store, electronics service, a Travelift, pump-out station and transient dockage at floating docks for boats up to 70 feet. Convenient shopping is just down the street from Palm Cove Marina, as are rental cars and public transportation to explore the nearby Jacksonville area.

Beach Marine (also to the north, but on the east side of the Waterway) has floating docks, a restaurant, transient slips, gas and diesel fuel and a repair yard in a large enclosed basin. This full-service marina has excellent amenities and a helpful staff. The approach and dockside depths here are reported to be greater than 7 feet at low tide, with 12-foot depths available at high tide—the result of dredging. The turning basin at the east end of the marina has ample space for large boats. The beach is about two miles away, shopping is over the bridge to the west, and rental cars and public transportation to Jacksonville are nearby.

Palm Valley Cut: Mile 747 to Mile 759

NAVIGATION: Use Chart 11489. From the McCormick Bridge, the channel is well-marked, and the tidal range is about 5 feet. South of the Pablo Creek Bridge (65-foot fixed vertical clearance) at Mile 749.5, the route enters 10-mile-long Palm Valley Cut. There is a high-rise condominium development with a private boat basin just south of the Pablo Creek Bridge on the west side of the ICW. The current may give your vessel a strong sideways push, and shoals are encroaching from the west side just south of Mile 750 at the intersection of Pablo and Cabbage creeks.

Just beyond, is the straight Palm Valley Cut. Near the south end of the cut, the Waterway passes under the 65-foot high-rise Palm Valley Bridge at Mile 758.8. Just past this bridge are the headwaters of the Tolomato River (Mile 760), which lead to St. Augustine. The only marker in Palm Valley Cut (red daybeacon "2") is just before the bridge; stay in the middle of the channel or favor the east side if depths start to decrease suddenly. There are numerous small floats along Palm Valley Cut that appear to be near the centerline. The deeper water is to the east of these floats.

On the east side of the Waterway is the Harbour Island at Marsh Landing development, featuring home sites, new homes and private docks directly on the ICW and around a manmade harbor. Skippers, as always, are responsible for their own wakes. The narrow Palm Valley Cut, from the Marsh Landing area to just south of the Palm Valley Bridge (fixed, 65-foot vertical clearance), is a No-Wake Zone. Proceed with appropriate caution. The east side of Palm Valley Cut is residential. Watch for debris, manatees and alligators in this popular fishing spot and mind the depth sounder.

Recent residential development with docks is evident on parts of the western shore at the southern end, although most of it is still beautifully wild and wooded. Dredging of the southern part of Palm Valley Cut cleared out some of the problem shoaling areas, which are holding 10- to 12-foot depths. Depths are around 7 to 8 feet in the northern part of the cut. Deeper water is usually generally found toward the docks on the east side of the cut. Dredging of the northern part of Palm Valley Cut occurred during late 2009 and early 2010 so expect depths there to be near the controlling depth of 12 feet once again.

ICW: Mile 760 to Mile 776

NAVIGATION: Use Charts 11489 and 11485. At Mile 760, the ICW enters the headwaters of the Tolomato River, which flows south to meet the Matanzas River at the St. Augustine Inlet. The dredged channel between Mile 760 and Mile 765 provides a deepwater route through the marshes and side waters. There is an uncharted wreck outside of the channel east of red daybeacon "10."

The river deepens below Pine Island (just north of Mile 765), and the ICW begins to follow its natural deep channel. From Mile 765 to Mile 770, pay close attention to the chart, as shoaling extends into the channel at flashing green "27." Give the marker a wide berth and stay toward the west bank.

Although problems have diminished recently, there is occasional shoaling near Capo Creek. Between green daybeacon "29" and red daybeacon "30," favor the east side of the channel. Above green daybeacon "33," a shoal extends toward the channel—give that marker a wide berth. South of green daybeacon "33," keep to the western side and give a wide berth to flashing red "44" just before Mile 770 (Chart 11485 picks up here). Beware of the shoal that extends from flashing green "45," below Mile 770; it juts out from the upper point of the Guana River and extends northward along the east bank.

For a little adventure, take a dinghy ride up the Guana River to a dam about three miles upstream, which is part of the Guana-Tolomato-Matanzas Rivers National Estuarine Research Reserve, a network of 55,000 acres of protected marsh, waters and wetlands in Flagler and St. Johns counties. Anchor your vessel at the mouth of the river, off the Waterway, taking care to avoid the charted submerged piling, but do not leave it unattended. Once at the dam, the beach is just across the highway.

USINA-VILANO BRIDGE
Mile 775.8

WATERWAY GUIDE PHOTOGRAPHY

Be alert for strong sideways currents at the junction of the Guana River and the ICW, which also may drag trap floats underwater. About a mile south of the Guana River on the west side, you will pass an airport. The route is well-marked, wide and deep to the Usina-Vilano Beach Bridge (Mile 775.8, vertical clearance 65 feet), except for a shoal that extends into the channel at flashing green "49." Keep a sharp eye out for this marker and the next green light (flashing green "51"), because they both have a tendency to blend in with the buildings and docks on the eastern side of the ICW channel. There may be strong currents at an angle at the Usina-Vilano Bridge, and some cruisers report that the clearance may be less than 65 feet at high tide.

Dockage: Several restaurants with dockage for patrons are north of the Usina-Vilano Bridge on the east side of the Waterway. Tying up at Cap's, the popular restaurant in the vicinity of flashing green "51," can be very rough, especially on busy summer weekends. Pass this area with no wake, as there are usually boats at the dock, sometimes rafted several deep.

Anchorage: Shoaling continues to be a problem at the Pine Island anchorage at Mile 765, particularly on the south side, and boats frequently go aground here. A sometimes-present line of crab pot markers usually indicates the shoal line on the southern side of the anchorage; it is deeper toward the north shore, but there is not much swinging room. The current is minimal, and holding and protection are excellent; however, it can be very buggy when there is no wind. Enter just south of green daybeacon "25" and favor the north bank. Mind the depth and allow for the full range of tide in your entire swinging circle. Shoals and submerged obstructions make the entrance north of the island between green daybeacon "21" and flashing green "23" almost impassable. The farther you anchor from the ICW, the less you will be affected by wakes of passing boats.

■ ST. AUGUSTINE—MILE 776

 THE FOLLOWING AREA REQUIRES SPECIAL ATTENTION DUE TO SHOALING OR CHANGES TO THE CHANNEL

NAVIGATION: Use Chart 11485. **Use the Fernandina Beach Tide Tables. For high tide, subtract 20 minutes; for low tide, subtract 5 minutes.** A dredged private basin at a condominium development south of flashing red "54" on the Tolomato River has two entrances on the east side of the river. Watch for shoaling in the vicinity of green daybeacon "57," north of the Usina-Vilano Bridge.

There is no magenta line on the chart for the area between Mile 775 and Mile 780 because there is continuous shoaling, as well as frequent changes to the marking system in the area. Study the chart before you get to the Usina-Vilano Bridge and note that red nun buoy "58" and flashing red "58A" do not appear on the most recent chart (Edition 35, dated 8/1/2007), and have not for a number of years, as this is such a changeable area. It may be different when you pass through.

The ICW channel south of the Usina-Vilano Bridge is deceptively close to the beach (east) side as it approach-

St. Augustine, FL

Looking south over the ICW route with the St. Augustine Inlet to the left and St. Augustine to the right. (Not to be used for navigation.)

es St. Augustine Inlet. Honor all markers in place south of the bridge at the time of your arrival. In May 2010, these markers included flashing green "57A," quick flashing red buoy "60" and flashing green buoy "59," which is opposite and very close to the beach. There is a shoal that is bare at low tide south and west of flashing green "57A" which catches many unwary transient boaters each year. Favor the green side of the channel between flashing green "57A and "59," and be sure to honor red buoy "60" to starboard when heading south.

After passing between flashing green buoy "59" and quick flashing red buoy "60," the ICW channel turns sharply to the west to pass between the first set of Matanzas River markers (flashing green "1" and red nun buoy "2") just inside St. Augustine Inlet. Be careful to distinguish the inlet markers from the ICW markers. Also be careful not to confuse the marked channel into Salt Run for the ICW channel. Call one of the local towing services for advice if you are unable to sort out the numerous markers.

Commercial and sportfishing boats use the St. Augustine Inlet regularly; get local information, but avoid this spot in rough conditions. Shoaling is common and the markers are frequently moved and may not be accurate, although the inlet is dredged on a regular basis. (Our editor has used this inlet in a deep draft boat and found it to be very straightforward.) Waves break dangerously close to the dredged channel, especially at low tide with ebb current against an onshore wind. There are nearly always breakers on the shallows

on each side of the inlet, which looks intimidating even when the channel is flat calm. In January 2010, the St. Augustine Inlet was surveyed at around 12 to 15 feet deep at low tide at the outside bar. However, remember that this channel is subject to change at any time. When entering the inlet and heading northbound on the ICW, it is important to run a sufficient distance past the tip of the beach on the north side of the inlet channel before turning into the ICW channel.

The local marinas, especially Camachee Cove Yacht Harbor, and towing services SeaTow and TowBoatU.S., have updated information on possible shoaling.

END SPECIAL CAUTION AREA.

Heading south, before you reach the Bridge of Lions, you will see a tall white cross and then a fort, Castillo de San Marcos (charted). Closer to town, the twin spires of the Catholic cathedral appear, making an interesting skyline. Beyond the inlet, on the Conch Island (east) side, the ICW channel turns sharply west, sweeps wide around Anastasia Island's northern tip and then turns up the Matanzas River and under the Bridge of Lions (Mile 777.9, 25-foot closed vertical clearance). This bridge, one of the most attractive on the ICW, was completed in 1927. It underwent extensive repairs over a five year period beginning in 2005. You will not likely see any construction equipment on scene at the bridge. A temporary lift bridge that was built to transport vehicular traffic while the old bridge was being rehabilitated has been removed.

The Bridge of Lions operates on the same schedule as always. (Monday through Friday, it opens on the hour and half-hour between 7 a.m. and 6 p.m., but it does not open at 8 a.m., noon or 5 p.m. On weekends and holidays, it opens on the hour and half-hour between 7 a.m. and 6 p.m.) The bridge rehabilitation project was completed and the bridge officially re-opened on March 17, 2010. There were still some construction closures in April 2010, but all construction was expected to be completed at press time in summer 2010. The cost of this extensive project was $76 million. The goal was to improve the bridge's safety while preserving its historic value.

BRIDGE OF LIONS
Mile 777.9
WATERWAY GUIDE PHOTOGRAPHY

Dockage: The number of berths available to transients in St. Augustine reflects its long-standing popularity as a port of call. Several elaborate marine complexes cater to cruising boats. Immediately north of the Usina-Vilano Bridge on the west side of the ICW, Camachee Cove Yacht Harbor is the center of the huge Camachee Island complex. In recent years, Camachee Cove has renovated its central docking area and transient dockage, as well as a large number of its permanent slips. Six fueling stations are operational, and much fueling can be done from individual slips. Call ahead for docking instructions. This full-service marina is the home of the Northeast Florida Marlin Association. The enclosed basin offers excellent protection and is surrounded by 20 businesses offering every imaginable service for boaters, including a boatyard for haul-out and repairs and an award-winning restaurant, the Kingfish Grill. The newly opened deli, Waterside Market, serves breakfast and lunch and sells basic groceries. Bulkheads and jetties on both sides of Camachee Cove's entrance help prevent shoaling and protect the outside slips. The entrance channel was dredged in 2008. The marina has floating docks, two boaters' lounges, updated showers and restrooms, three laundry facilities and a well-stocked ship's store. Downtown St. Augustine is a couple of miles away, and the marina provides two courtesy cars for touring the town or for re-provisioning.

Also located in the complex is Camachee Yacht Yard, where most any repair can be handled with trained on-site technicians, 50-ton lift and every possible repair.

Conveniently located south of the inlet, on Salt Run, is the Conch House Marina Resort, a recently renovated and expanded marina complete with a tropical motif, thatched roofs, motel rooms, a seafood restaurant, a pub with live music, a pool and floating docks.

There is also dockage on both sides of the Waterway south of the Bridge of Lions, and all the facilities near the bridge are convenient to the city's restaurants and historic attractions. The St. Augustine Municipal Marina, south of the bridge on the west side, offers transient dockage

ST. AUGUSTINE LIGHT
Mile 776.5
WATERWAY GUIDE PHOTOGRAPHY

and convenient fuel. Consider the direction of the current when docking here, as well as construction equipment at the Bridge of Lions. Anchored vessels may land dinghies at a floating dock for a fee. A ship's store, boaters lounge and modern laundry and shower facilities are available. The Anchorage Inn and Marina (standing by on VHF Channel 16) offers dockage on the east side of the ICW just south of the Bridge of Lions.

The San Sebastian River, which branches off the Matanzas River at Mile 780, has a number of marine businesses, including the Luhrs/Mainship factory and associated docks. Exercise caution when docking anywhere on this river, as the current is swift. There are two service yards on the river. St. Augustine Marine Center is located near green daybeacon "13" and handles all the commissioning for the Luhrs/Mainship factory. Its lift is capable of handling large multihulls, and its railway can handle large wooden boats and other vessels not suitable for a Travelift. Oasis Boatyard and Marina offers full-service or do-it-yourself repairs, with extensive lift capacity. Rivers Edge Marina is just

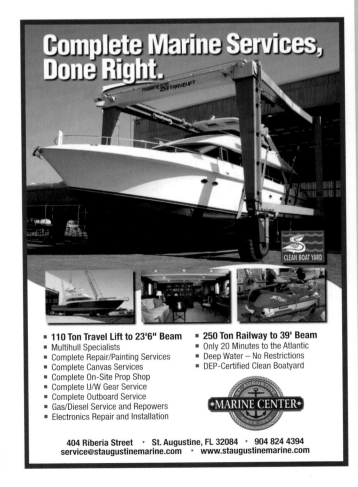

St. Augustine, FL

ST. AUGUSTINE				Dockage			Supplies		Service					
		Largest Vessel Accommodated	VHF Channel Monitored	Transient Berths / Total Berths	Approach / Dockside Depth (reported)	Floating Docks	Groceries, Ice, Marine Supplies, Snacks	Gas / Diesel	Repairs: Hull, Engine, Propeller	Lift (tonnage), Crane, Rail	1=110V, 2=220V, B=Both, Max Amps	Laundry, Pool, Showers	Pump-Out Station	Nearby: Grocery Store, Motel, Restaurant
1. Camachee Cove Yacht Harbor 775.7 ☐ WiFi	904-829-5676	125	16/68	40/260	7/7	F	GD	GIMS	HEP	L50, C	B/100	LPS	P	GMR
2. Camachee Yacht Yard 775.7	904-823-3641	65	16			F			HEP	L50, C	B/50	LS	P	GMR
3. Kingfish Grill 775.7	904-824-2111	90	16	5/5	8/8	F		GIMS						GMR
4. Conch House Marina .6 W of 776.6 WiFi	904-824-4347	200	16/69	45/200	6/6	F	GD	GIMS	HEP		B/100	LPS	P	GMR
5. Anchorage Inn Marina & Fish Camp 777.7 WiFi	904-826-0010	125	16	16/30	20/12	F		GIMS			B/50	LPS		
6. St. Augustine Municipal Marina 777.7 ☐ WiFi	904-825-1026	280	16/71	62/77	20/20	F	GD	IMS			B/100	LS	P	GMR
7. Fish Island Marina 779.8	904-471-1955	150	16	8/45	21/21	F	D				1/30	S		GMR
8. St. Augustine Marine Center .8 NW of 780 WiFi	904-824-4394	150	16	/50	10/6	F		M	HEP	L110,C,R	B/100	S	P	GMR
9. Oasis Boatyard & Marina 1.2 NW of 780	904-824-2520	60		/25	16/16	F		IMS	HP	L50	1/30	L		GMR
10. Rivers Edge Marina 1.8 NW of 780 WiFi	904-827-0520	130	16/71	15/130	13/13	F	GD	GIMS	HEP		B/100	LPS	P	GMR
11. The Marine Supply & Oil Co. 1.8 NW of 780	904-829-2271						GD	M						

Corresponding chart(s) not to be used for navigation. ☐ Internet Access WiFi Wireless Internet Access

a half mile south of downtown St. Augustine at green daybeacon "29." The marina is a short walk away from food and marine supply stores, as well as stores offering beer, wine and spirits.

There is a new high-and-dry storage marina, Cat's Paw, on the south side near the mouth of San Sebastian River (around red daybeacon "8"), but it is not for transients. There is also a dry storage/condominium residen-

tial development called Ancient City Marina going up (slowly) beyond the Luhrs/Mainship docks (around red daybeacon "24"), south side, adjacent to Route 1 at the old Sebastian Harbor.

Anchorage: The city of St. Augustine is currently placing moorings in that have been used as anchorages, including Salt Run. Once the moorings are in place, anchoring within the field boundaries will be prohibited. In the past,

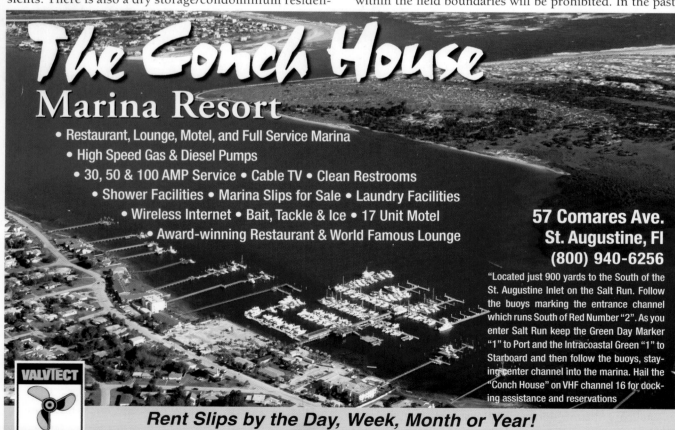

NOTE D
Due to continuous shoaling between mile marker 775 and 780 the IAWW magenta course line is not being charted.

SAN SEBASTIAN RIVER
The controlling depth of the improved channel from the junction with the Intracoastal Waterway to the Kings Street Bridge was 8 ft for a mid-width of 50 feet.

Feb 1996

ST. AUGUSTINE, CHART 11485

St. Augustine, FL

boaters wishing to visit St. Augustine could anchor either north or south of the Bridge of Lions at Mile 778. These popular anchorages were nearly always full. Additional daybeacons were added to better define the channel on both sides of the Bridge of Lions. These are red daybeacon "6A" and green daybeacon "7" on the north side of the bridge and red daybeacon "8" on the south side. Do not anchor in the channel. There is some room to anchor to the east by green daybeacon "7."

Holding is best, although still rather poor, north of the bridge; boats often drag anchor south of the bridge, just from the tide change. Set your anchor well in either area and expect to swing on the current. The anchorage north of the bridge can be very uncomfortable or even untenable in strong northeasterly wind. With the moorings in place, it will be difficult to find sufficient room in which to anchor outside of the designated field. This north mooring field will be designated San Marcos and will have 28 mooring balls.

When anchoring south of the bridge, be certain to anchor south of the waterfront restaurant to avoid the infamous underwater cable that crosses the northern end of the anchorage. Also be aware that there may be debris on the bottom from hurricanes and derelict boats that have sunk at anchor, here and in the north anchorage as well. The debris has reportedly been removed, but there may still be wreckage on the bottom. Also, be aware that the area around red daybeacon "10" at the southern limit of the southern anchorage is continuing to shoal, and that red daybeacon "10A" has been added to better mark the channel there. All of this information will be moot as you will likely have to take a mooring. The Menendez mooring field will have 70 mooring balls and looks to take up most of the existing anchoring space south of the bridge.

Dinghy dockage is available at daily, weekly or monthly rates from St. Augustine Municipal Marina and will be included in the daily mooring fee. The Municipal Marina will be managing the moorings. It is a moderate walk east across the Bridge of Lions to reach Stewart's, a well-stocked small grocery store selling local fruits and vegetables, excellent meat and off-the-boat fresh shrimp and other seafood. It is well worth the walk, especially since the other grocery stores require land transportation. Stewart's does not take credit cards, however, only cash or checks.

You can reach the Salt Run anchorage (Mile 777 just off the St. Augustine Inlet) by following the private channel markers of the Conch House Marina Resort. Once past the marina, you will spot two clusters of anchored and moored boats, the first to the west of the marked channel and the second to the east. The second one, with 7- to 8-foot depths, is better and will likely still have some room to anchor after the moorings are installed. As with the other anchorages around St. Augustine, be careful of debris on the bottom. Salt Run is peaceful but crowded, though depths may be shallower than shown on the chart (about 6.5-foot mean low water depths have been reported at the entrance channel). The north and south Salt Run mooring fields will have 80 total moorings available.

In recent years, a few local and transient boats have been observed anchoring in the San Sebastian River, but this is not a good anchorage for a variety of reasons: the only deep water is directly in the narrow dredged channel, the reversing current here is very swift, and there is a sizeable fleet of shrimp trawlers that use the commercial docks upriver as their base, coming and going at all hours.

A city-financed pump-out boat operates out of Conch House Marina Resort in Salt Run. It visits the Salt Run and Bridge of Lions (north and south) anchorage areas on Thursdays only, weather permitting. There is no charge for pump-outs on the moorings, although vessels pumped out in marinas or at anchor will be charged.

GOIN' ASHORE: **ST. AUGUSTINE, FL**

Founded in 1565 as a Spanish military outpost, St. Augustine is the oldest continuously occupied European settlement in the United States. Traces of the city's Spanish heritage are everywhere, and a Spanish Quarter where conquistadors once strolled is re-created for the 21st-century visitor. Tourists can inspect the battlements and dungeons of Castillo de San Marcos National Monument, built in 1672, and wander the narrow old streets of San Agustin Antiquo, which depict Spanish Colonial life. The grounds and exterior of Castillo de San Marcos are free and available for touring. Walking from the old town gates across from Castillo de San Marcos, you will quickly encounter the oldest wooden schoolhouse in the United States, the Spanish Quarter's Living History Museum, and the National Greek Orthodox Shrine. Along St. George Street, three blocks from the city marina, there are many specialty shops and restaurants.

Superb examples of 19th-century Spanish Renaissance architecture can be seen nearby. Flagler College occupies the buildings and grounds of Henry Flagler's luxurious Ponce de Leon Hotel, built in 1888. Tours are scheduled several times a day to view the original Tiffany stained glass windows, fountains, mosaics and sculpture in the beautifully restored hotel building that now serves as the college offices and main dormitory. Across King Street from Flagler College are the Lightner Museum (1948 restoration of the Alcazar Hotel, also built by Henry Flagler, 1887) and the Casa Monica Hotel (built in 1888 and restored in 1999), with its upscale restaurant and martini bar, 95 Cordova (at 95 Cordova St., 904-810-

6810). Columbia Restaurant at St. George and Hypolita streets is one of the oldest and best-regarded Cuban restaurants in Florida. Scarlett O'Hara's (70 Hypolita St., 904-824-6535) features an oyster bar, excellent conch fritters and reasonably priced drinks. The Bunnery (904-829-6166) on St. George Street, specializing in fresh-baked pastries, is popular for breakfast and lunch. Don't miss a tour and wine tasting at the San Sebastian Winery on King Street. The Marine Industries Association of North East Florida (MIANEF) sponsors the St. Augustine Boat Show; look for future announcements at www.mianef.org.

ADDITIONAL RESOURCES

- St. Augustine, FL, **www.oldcity.com**
- St. Augustine Visitors Bureau, **www.visitoldcity.com**

⚑ **NEARBY GOLF COURSES**
Royal St. Augustine Golf & Country Club, 301 Royal St. Augustine Parkway, St. Augustine, FL 32094, 904-824-4653, **www.royalstaugustine.com**

☤ **NEARBY MEDICAL FACILITIES**
Flagler Hospital, 400 Health Park Blvd., St. Augustine, FL 32086, 904-819-5155

◼ MATANZAS TO ORMOND BEACH: MILE 780 TO MILE 825

Matanzas River
NAVIGATION: Use Chart 11485. A mile south of St. Augustine on the Matanzas River at Mile 780.3, two 65-foot fixed vertical clearance highway spans (state Route 312) cross the river and the current is swift here. The Matanzas River channel is deep but narrow, so follow the array of markers carefully until the dredged cut takes over south of Matanzas Inlet.

To Matanzas Inlet
NAVIGATION: Use Chart 11485. About three miles south of the St. Augustine high-rise bridges is a beautiful, recently renovated example of Queen Anne-style architecture, near red daybeacon "28" on the west side of the Waterway. Charted as "CUP" (meaning cupola), the structure is private property; do not go ashore.

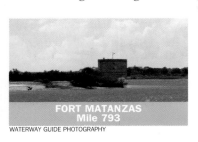

FORT MATANZAS
Mile 793
WATERWAY GUIDE PHOTOGRAPHY

Several markers along the stretch should be given a wide berth to avoid shoals. At red daybeacon "30," steer wide toward the east side of the channel to avoid the encroaching shoals from the west bank. Just north of Crescent Beach, at Mile 789, tides from St. Augustine and Matanzas inlets meet. From here, you run a dredged channel most of the next 80 miles to the Indian River. At Crescent Beach, you will encounter the Crescent Beach Bascule Bridge (Mile 788.6, 25-foot closed vertical clearance), which opens on signal. The bridge tender is particularly helpful and accommodating; there are no clearance boards, but a sign states that you have 3 feet of additional vertical clearance at the center. Sailboats have run aground on both sides of the narrow channel, however. From the bridge, keep your wake at a minimum for the next three miles. At Mile 792.2, shoaling extends into the channel, and red daybeacon "80" (at the beginning of the Matanzas Inlet area discussed below) needs a wide berth.

Matanzas Inlet Area

 THE FOLLOWING AREA REQUIRES SPECIAL ATTENTION DUE TO SHOALING OR CHANGES TO THE CHANNEL

NAVIGATION: Use Chart 11485. Approach the Matanzas Inlet area with caution and only after asking a local tow service for the latest information, as this is always a particularly tricky portion of the ICW. There are four green can buoys numbered "81A," "81B," "81C" and "81D," marking the east side of the channel just north of Fort Matanzas and one red nun buoy, "80A," marking the west side. There is no magenta line here, as the channel shifts frequently. Dredging of the ICW channel is scheduled for fall 2010 through spring 2011. The depth is reported to be around 12 feet throughout most of the channel. Channel markers may be different than charted when you pass through as this channel fills in and changes regularly despite frequent dredging. If it has been a few years since dredging, remember that the natural flow of water usually rules here, and the natural channel is usually close to the dunes on the west side. Honor the floating markers that are in place. Our cruising editors noted less then 5-foot depths here in May 2010 between red nun "80A" and green can "81A" mid-channel at mean low water. Other boaters passing through this area in spring 2010 have advised to hug the red markers ("80," "80A" and "80B") going through this area. Hopefully the dredging project scheduled for late 2010 will alleviate this chronic problem for a while.

END SPECIAL CAUTION AREA.

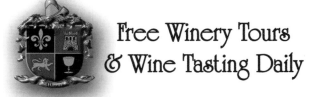

Palm Coast, FL

PALM COAST		Dockage					Supplies			Service			
		Largest Vessel Accommodated	VHF Channel Monitored	Transient Berths / Total Berths	Approach / Dockside Depth (reported)	Floating Docks	Gas / Diesel	Groceries, Ice, Marine Supplies, Snacks	Repairs: Hull, Engine, Propeller	Lift (tonnage), Crane, Rail	1=110V, 2=220V, B=Both, Max Amps	Laundry, Pool, Showers	Pump-Out Station	Nearby: Grocery Store, Motel, Restaurant
1. Newcastle Marine 800.7	386-447-0999	YACHT MANUFACTURER												
2. Rhodes Marine Services 801.4	386-446-5588	32			/8	F		M	EP					
3. PALM COAST MARINA 802.9 WiFi	386-446-6370	100	16	15/100	8/10		GD	GIMS			B/100	LS	P	GMR
4. THE MARINA AT HAMMOCK BEACH RESORT 803 WiFi	386-597-5030	125	16	150/209	8/7	F		GIMS			B/100	LPS	P	GMR

Corresponding chart(s) not to be used for navigation. ⌨Internet Access WiFi Wireless Internet Access

PALM COAST, CHART 11485

At the north end of Rattlesnake Island, you will see the stark remains of Fort Matanzas, once a Spanish outpost and now a national monument. You can reach the fort via a small National Park Service ferry that runs between Anastasia Island and Rattlesnake Island. Its terminal is just north of the inlet, and it is an easy drive from St. Augustine. Boats often anchor overnight off the ICW in the inlet channel just to the north of the fort.

Marineland—Mile 796

Marineland Marina has been closed for a number of years. Marineland's oceanarium has reopened, but is only accessible by land. The facility has new dolphin tanks and there have been many other improvements. Call 904-471-1111

for more information. Current operating hours are 8:30 a.m. to 4:30 p.m. daily, except Thanksgiving and Christmas.

The current between Marineland and the ICW crossing of the Matanzas River can be strong enough to pull trap markers underwater, but it decreases as you proceed toward Palm Coast.

ICW: Mile 797 to Mile 803

Marshland alternates with forests along the banks of the Matanzas River here as you pass through a part of the Guana-Tolomato-Matanzas National Estuarine Research Reserve, south of Marineland on the east side of the ICW. You will likely encounter kayak tour groups here during warmer weather; give them a slow, no-wake pass out of

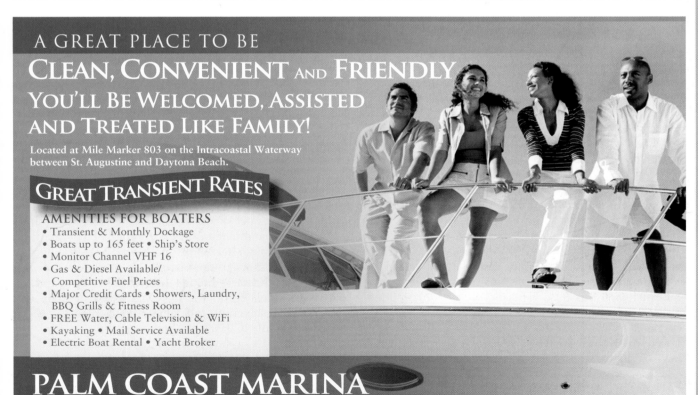

Palm Coast, FL

courtesy. At Mile 800.7, the small, but well-known yard of Newcastle Marine, builders of large expedition-style yachts, is on the east side. This cut seems eerie and almost desolate in places, so it comes as a surprise when, farther down the cut on the west side, several wide, rip-rapped channels appear. This is the community of Palm Coast, accessible via its three canals. The large planned residential community includes six miles of beach and Waterway frontage. Across from Palm Coast on the east side of the ICW is another cleared area, Ginn Hammock Beach, with residential lots and some new houses, canals, a large condominium building and a large marina basin.

NAVIGATION: Use Chart 11485. Locals report shoaling at Mile 797, on the west side of the channel just past flashing red "90," and additional shoaling from flashing red "94" to red daybeacon "104." Red daybeacon "92" has been repositioned to mark deeper water. WATERWAY GUIDE cruising editors have confirmed depths as low as 7 feet between red daybeacon "92" and flashing red "94" and again between flashing red "94" and red daybeacon "96." Depths of 8 feet were also reported north of red daybeacon "100." There was also reported to be a shoal encroaching from the west at red daybeacon "110" in summer 2010. Depths were found to be 5 to 6 feet near mean low water.

Dockage: At Mile 803, a canal leads westward to the Palm Coast Marina. Once inside, favor the south side of the channel. The staff here welcomes transient yachts of all sizes, and the dockmaster allows the office to serve as a mail drop. Gas and diesel fuels are available here. The old Harborside Inn at the Palm Coast Marina has been removed, and the first phase of the new Palm Coast Resort has been built in its place.

The Marina at Hammock Beach is in the large separate dredged basin directly across the ICW from the Palm Coast Marina, where the chart shows "Bon Terra." This marina offers transients the full range of amenities available at the Club at Hammock Beach. Transportation is provided 24 hours a day. On-site amenities, such as a pool and fitness center, are also now available to transient boaters. This is a huge private condominium and residential community, with its own dredged basin and private slips.

If you leave these marinas on a slow boat (less than 10-knot speed) at the start of the ebb tide, you can ride the current all the way to Ponce de Leon Inlet. There is a fixed, high-level toll bridge, Palm Coast Parkway Bridge (Mile 803.0, 65-foot fixed vertical clearance) just south of the entrance to the Palm Coast Marina.

ICW: Mile 804 to Mile 809

NAVIGATION: Use Chart 11485. Between Mile 804 and Mile 807, you will notice a narrow interconnecting canal on the east side of the Waterway. This was part of the original ICW and gives an idea of the size of some earlier sections.

At Mile 805, on the west side of the ICW, is Grand Haven, a country club community. For several miles south of Palm Coast Marina, condominiums with community docks and boat lifts, golf courses and private homes line both sides of the ICW. The west side of the ICW down to Mile 809 is currently undergoing residential development, with many docks extending out toward the ICW. Not all of the docks are in deep water, however, and boaters should not assume that, just because there is a dock, the water is deep enough. Stay in the center of the channel, especially south of the high-rise bridge at Palm Coast, near the long series of docks on the west side.

There is a shoal making off from the St. Joe Canal at red daybeacon "110" to the south of these docks. This daybeacon has been placed here to mark this shoal and is not shown on current charts (Edition 35 from August 2007 at press time in summer 2010).

Exposed rocks line both sides of the long Fox Cut from green daybeacon "1" to green daybeacon "5." Red daybeacons "2" and "4" and flashing green "3" mark rocks that extend to the edge of the channel. A ramp, dock and launch facility have been dug out of the west side of the Waterway at flashing green "3" and red daybeacon "4." This is a Slow-Speed/No-Wake Zone. Stay to the center of the channel when passing the ramp. Rocks intermittently line the ICW's west side close to shore at the residential construction, just south of the ramp, down to the entrance to the cement plant anchorage at Mile 809.

ICW: Mile 809 to Mile 818

NAVIGATION: Use Chart 11485. The Flagler Beach Bridge (65-foot fixed vertical clearance) crosses the Waterway at Mile 810.6. Expect shoals near the bridge along the edges of the channel. A 7-foot-deep shoal was observed immediately south of the bridge. There is a busy ramp on the south side of the bridge; pass at idle speed. Between the Flagler Beach Bridge and the L.B. Knox Bridge (Mile 816.0, 15-foot closed vertical clearance, opens on signal) five miles south, the channel is lined with trap markers on both sides, and some floats are in the channel itself. A dock development on the east side of the Waterway, just north of the Flagler Beach Bridge, is a recent addition, although the docks have been empty of boats ever since it was built, and its entrance was roped off. By the time you pass through here, slips might be available.

At Mile 812.4, red daybeacon "20" was moved to the bend in Smith Creek, and red daybeacon "20A" was added at the previous location of "20." Marine construction and associated residential development are underway on the west side of the ICW in this area.

At Mile 814, a small, marked side channel leads to a state park and a ramp. This is the beginning of a Manatee Zone, with a 30-mph speed limit in the channel (25 mph at night) and slow speed required outside the ICW channel.

At Mile 816, expect congestion at the boat ramp at the L.B. Knox Bridge. Clearance is only 15 feet, but the bridge opens on signal. South of the bridge, the channel

Looking north over Daytona Beach and its four bridges. (Not to be used for navigation.) WATERWAY GUIDE PHOTOGRAPHY

shoals along the east side from flashing red "2" to flashing green "7." Now the Waterway enters the headwaters of the Halifax River, which gradually widens in its reach to Daytona. The channel, straight and well-marked, follows closely along the eastern bank and passes attractive homes. There is a negligible tidal range here. Just north of the Ormond Beach Bridge (Mile 824.9, 65-foot fixed vertical clearance), the channel gradually shifts toward the middle of the river.

Anchorage: At Mile 809, a side channel carrying less than 6-foot depths at its entrance, with 11-foot depths inside, leads west to a charted cement plant, which has been closed for some time. A Sea Ray factory here generates a great deal of boat traffic during the day; this activity is reported to begin early in the morning. Enter near the center of the channel; watch the depth sounder and ease toward the north shore. Once past the un-navigable side channels, you can move back to the middle. Anchor on the south side above the side channels, or past the boat factory; No Trespassing signs make it clear that you may not go ashore. Holding is reported to be marginal here. There are several homes with docks on the south side at the entrance, and the north side is currently undergoing residential and golf course development.

Tomoka Basin—Mile 819

Tomoka State Park, along the riverbanks of the Tomoka River, was once home to the Timucua Indians. Today, you can walk beneath the same ancient oaks that shaded their huts nearly 400 years ago or explore the marshes and tidal creeks by dinghy. Fishing, hiking, picnicking and bird watching also are popular.

NAVIGATION: Use Chart 11485. The first wide bight to the west at Mile 818.5 is, like most of the Halifax River's off-channel waters, too thin for all but shoal-draft vessels.

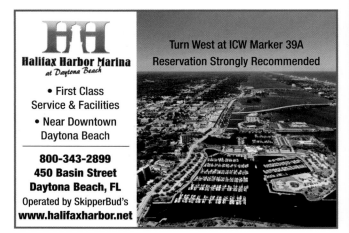

Daytona Beach to Ponce de Leon Inlet, FL

DAYTONA BEACH TO PONCE DE LEON INLET		Largest Vessel Accommodated	VHF Channel Monitored	Approach / Dockside Depth (reported)	Transient Berths / Total Berths	Floating Docks	Gas / Diesel	Groceries, Ice, Marine Supplies, Snacks	Repairs: Hull, Engine, Propeller	Lift (tonnage), Crane, Rail	1=110V, 2=220V, B=Both, Max Amps	Laundry, Pool, Showers	Pump-Out Station	Nearby: Grocery Store, Motel, Restaurant
				Dockage				**Supplies**			**Service**			
1. Loggerhead Club & Marina-Daytona Bch 829	386-523-3100	75	16/79	10/85	6/6		GD	GIMS			B/50	LPS	P	R
2. Halifax Harbor Marina 830.7	386-671-3601	100	16/71	/550	8/8	F	GD	IMS			B/50	LS	P	MR
3. Halifax River Yacht Club 830.7	386-255-7459	150	16/68	3/38	7/5						B/50	LS		R
4. West Marine Retail Store 830.7	386-226-9966	MARINE SUPPLIES						M						GMR
5. Aquamarina Daytona 831.5 [wifi]	386-252-6421	200	16	40/			GD	IMS	HEP	L	B/50	LS	P	GMR
6. Seven Seas Marina & Boatyard 835.5	386-761-3221	50	16	10/40	6/10		GD	IM	HP	L30,C	B/100	LS		GMR
7. Adventure Yacht Harbor Inc. 837 [wifi]	386-756-2180	65	16/18	6/150	6/7		GD	IMS	EP		B/50	LS	P	GMR
8. Inlet Harbor Restaurant & Marina .8 SE of 839.5	386-767-3266	125	06	12/84	9/15	F	GD	GIMS	E	L10	B/100	LS	P	R
9. Sea Love Boat Works Inc. 1.3 SE of 839.5	386-761-5434	90	16/7	1/3	8/8		D	IM	HEP	L70	B/200	S		GR
10. Light House Boatyard & Marina 839.5	386-767-0683	80	16/11	8/28	6/8		GD	IM	HP	L50	B/50	S		GMR

Corresponding chart(s) not to be used for navigation.   ⌧ Internet Access   (WiFi) Wireless Internet Access

If you can follow the array of stakes and nudge your way in through the very shoal Tomoka Basin, the Tomoka River itself is deep quite a bit farther upstream.

For deeper-draft boats, the five-mile-long passage from Tomoka Basin to the Ormond Beach Bridge (Mile 824.9, 65-foot fixed vertical clearance) calls for close attention to markers. Stick to the middle on this stretch because the east and west sides shoal and the water is shallow outside the channel. Depths are generally 8 feet during mean low water at mid-channel in this area, although shoaling to 4 feet has been reported at the edge of the channel near red daybeacon "20" south of the Ormond Beach Bridge. The open water of the Halifax River above the Ormond Beach Bridge is a popular windsurfing area. On a blustery day expect to see several windsurfers crisscrossing the channel.

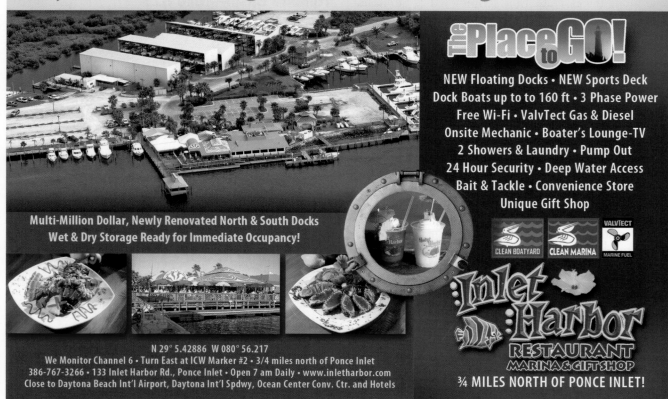

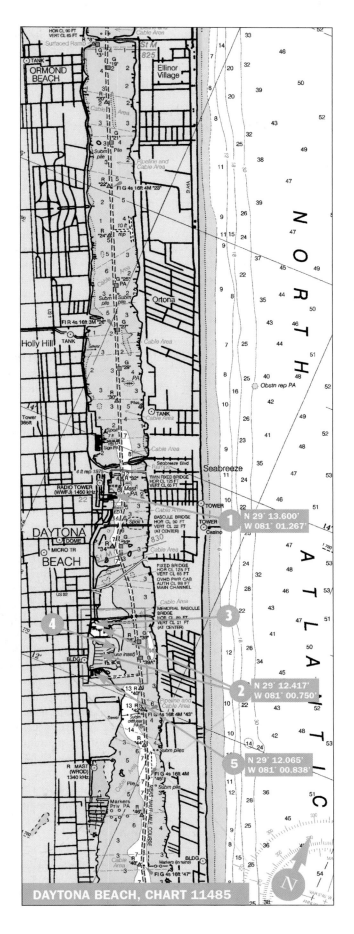

DAYTONA BEACH, CHART 11485

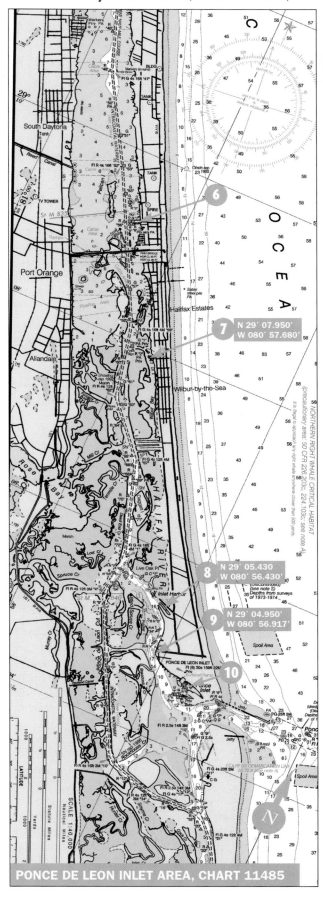

PONCE DE LEON INLET AREA, CHART 11485

Daytona Beach, FL

Ormond Beach—Mile 825

NAVIGATION: Use Chart 11485. **Use the Fernandina Beach Tide Tables. For high tide, add 3 hours and 17 minutes; for low tide, add 4 hours and 31 minutes.** The tidal range in this area is less than one foot. The Ormond Beach Bridge (state Route 40, 65-foot fixed vertical clearance) looms overhead at Mile 824.9. Slow speed is required in this area for the manatee zone. Local festivals are often held on the nearby grounds of the Casements, the former summer home of John D. Rockefeller, which houses museum exhibits. It is now owned and maintained by the city. A high-rise condominium, visible from the Waterway, has replaced the old landmark Ormond Hotel. The city has developed extensive parklands along the banks of the Halifax near the bridge. These riverfront areas are pleasant spots for walkers and picnickers, but there are no docks. Late in November, Ormond Beach hosts an antique car rally, featuring a gaslight parade of old cars. It commemorates the birth of auto racing, which began here on the broad, smooth beach.

◼ DAYTONA BEACH— MILE 830

While the official tourist season for this northern Florida "summer resort" runs from Memorial Day to after Labor Day, Daytona Beach is popular all year long. In spring and fall, boats on the north-south run stop over, and in winter and summer, its mild climate attracts yachtsmen and tourists from other areas that are too hot or too cold. Skippers often stop at Daytona Beach either to have work done at the area's good repair yards or just to lay over for a while to enjoy its many nearby attractions. The ICW waterfront on the west side in Daytona Beach is becoming dotted with large new condominium buildings. Most conspicuous of these are the twin towers with associated docks in the works at the former Aloha Publix complex on the north side of the Seabreeze Bridge.

NAVIGATION: Use Chart 11485. Daytona Beach has four bridges: the Seabreeze Bridge (twin-span high-rise, 65-foot fixed vertical clearance) at Mile 829.1; the Main Street Bridge (22-foot closed vertical clearance) at Mile 829.7; the International Speedway Bridge (65-foot fixed vertical clearance) at Mile 830.1 and Memorial Bridge (21-foot closed vertical clearance) at Mile 830.6—the

DAYTONA BEACH MEM. BRIDGE
Mile 830.6

WATERWAY GUIDE PHOTOGRAPHY

only one with opening restrictions (the Main Street Bridge opens on signal). The Memorial and Main Street bridges respond to sound signal as well as VHF calls on Channel 09. The Memorial Bridge does not open Monday through Saturday (except on Federal holidays) between the hours of 7:45 a.m. and 8:45 a.m. and 4:45 p.m. and 5:45 p.m., except for openings at 8:15 a.m. and 5:15 p.m.

Dockage: Marinas and yacht yards line the shore on the west side of the Waterway from north of the city all the way to Ponce de Leon Inlet. The Loggerhead Club & Marina-Daytona Beach (formerly Caribbean Jack's Marina), south of the Seabreeze Bridge, offers transient dockage and a convenient fuel dock. The restaurant on premises remains Caribbean Jack's. The municipal Halifax Harbor Marina, south of Memorial Bridge in an enclosed basin, is convenient to downtown Daytona. Enter Halifax Harbor Marina through the marked entrance channel just west of ICW green daybeacon "39A." The marina boasts 550 slips, a 10-acre park, excellent amenities, nearby restaurants and shopping. They also have gas and diesel fuel, a free pump-out service and a store. The city bus stop is an easy walk away. Just south, the former Daytona Marina and Boatworks is now called Aquamarina Daytona which is open 24/7 for fuel and dockage. The gold dome you see is a Chart House Restaurant.

Anchorage: The anchorages both above and below the Seabreeze Bridge were still active in 2010. The anchorage south of the Seabreeze Bridge is deeper, but there is

SEA LOVE MARINA & BOAT WORKS

SLIPS AVAILABLE • 30 TO 200AMP POWER
ESCORT SERVICE TO AND FROM SEA LOVE MARINA AND BOAT WORKS AVAILABLE FROM TOW BOAT US LOCATED ON SITE.

Sea Love Boat Works, Inc.
Located at Down The Hatch Restaurant and Deck Bar, the Area's Finest Dockside Dining

Down The Hatch Restaurant
4894 Front Street
Ponce Inlet, FL 32127
386-761-4831

- Hull and Bottom Painting
- Marine Supplies and Paint
- Wood and Fiberglass Repair
- Propeller, Shaft & Rudder Repair
- On-Call Mechanic
- Custom Fabrication
- On-Site Top-Side Paint Specialist
- On-Call Coast Guard Certified Welder

LARGEST LIFT CAPACITY IN CENTRAL FLORIDA

yachtpaint.com

70 TON TRAVELIFT • UP TO 23' BEAM
MONITORING VHF CHANNELS 7 & 16
• DIESEL FUEL

386-761-5434 • www.sea-love-boat-works.com
Less Than 1 Mile North of Ponce de Leon Inlet (Daytona Beach)
4877 Front Street, Ponce Inlet, FL 32127

Daytona Beach, FL

scattered debris on the bottom. This area is a Slow-Speed/No-Wake Zone. The anchorage north of the Seabreeze Bridge shallows up quickly, and it is a cable area. Signs on each shore mark their locations, but they are difficult to pick out from the water. The sign on the western shore is just south of the twin condos on the site of the old Aloha Publix complex. This anchorage is also at one end of a 25-mph Manatee Zone, so wakes from passing boats can be a problem. This entire anchorage area seems to be generally shoaling, but it is still handy when you arrive late in the day from St. Augustine.

The chart doesn't show it, but there is a cozy anchorage east of the Waterway in the vicinity of the charted 11-foot depths at Mile 830.7. To reach it, turn east off the Waterway immediately south of the Memorial Bridge. Using the yacht club's green daybeacons "3" and "5" as a back range, slowly go east to within 100 to 150 feet of shore; if you stay on the range, you should find at least 6 feet of water over the bar. At this point, turn south along the shore to find a slot of water 9 to 13 feet deep, about 100 feet from shore. The shoal on the channel side of this anchorage is less than 3 feet deep at mean low water. It provides fine protection from northeast to southeast winds. Many boats also anchor in the deep water pocket northwest of red daybeacon "44," although depths are said to be less than those charted. Avoid the cable area if you stop here. It has been reported that the Daytona police sometimes enforce an anchoring limit of five days in city waters, but the 2009 law prohibits such a limit.

GOIN' ASHORE:
DAYTONA BEACH, FL

Three miles west of the Waterway, Daytona Beach International Airport provides scheduled service to most cities. The airport area is also home to Embry-Riddle Aeronautical University, which specializes in aviation-related degrees that usually lead to airline careers. On the western edge of town, Daytona International Speedway (the "World's Finest and Fastest") is where the nation's top drivers and automobiles compete in the Daytona 500 every February and the famous 24 Hours of Daytona endurance race. Daytona Beach also has several golf courses, a noted school for baseball umpires, an impressive Corvette car museum and a large weekly flea market.

College students famously (or infamously, depending on the viewpoint) celebrate spring break at Daytona Beach; bus tours to Disney World leave from here; and visitors can catch jai alai matches, greyhound racing and exhibition baseball games. Bike Week (the Harley-Davidson, black-leather crowd) happens in March, before the spring break revelers arrive. If you are interested in motorcycles, you will be able to see everything from spectacular customized bikes to high-speed racers on the streets or at the Harley-Davidson dealer, the largest in the country.

Daytona's 23 miles of beach were once a proving ground for automobile engines in the early 1900s. Automobile pioneers like Louis Chevrolet and Henry Ford found the hard-packed sand, gentle slope and wide expanse of beach to be the perfect venue for auto racing. Today, the beach remains popular with motorists, though they are restricted to a leisurely 10-mph pace and must pay an access fee. Automobile racing moved inland to Daytona International Speedway in 1959 as cars became faster and crowds of spectators grew larger.

Daytona Beach, however, is much more than automobile racing. Within walking distance from the marinas, the Old Daytona Beach Street is totally renovated with pedestrian walkways, riverfront parks and plenty of shops and restaurants. The municipal library is just north of Halifax Harbor. The Main Street Pier, Oceanfront Boardwalk and the Coquina Clock Tower are historic landmarks. The Halifax Historical Museum (252 S. Beach St., 386-255-6976) presents Daytona Beach from a historical perspective. The Museum of Arts and Sciences (325 S. Nova Rd., 386-255-0285) features interactive exhibits of Florida history, African culture, Chinese and American artwork and laser shows in the planetarium. From

ADDITIONAL RESOURCES

■ Daytona Beach Area Convention & Visitors Bureau, 800-544-0415, www.daytonabeach.com

■ Visit Daytona, www.daytonavisit.com

⛳ **NEARBY GOLF COURSES**
Daytona Beach Golf Club, 600 Wilder Blvd., Daytona Beach, FL 32114, 386-671-3500

NEARBY MEDICAL FACILITIES
Halifax Health Medical Center, 303 N. Clyde Morris Blvd., Daytona Beach, FL 32114, 386-254-4000

March through October, the Daytona Beach Bandshell (250 N. Atlantic Ave., 386-671-8250) sponsors a concert series with a variety of music from jazz and big band to rhythm and blues.

Port Orange—Mile 835

NAVIGATION: Use Chart 11485. Stay in the channel between Daytona and Port Orange, as there are many shoals just outside. Be particularly wary of the spot between red daybeacons "42" and "44" and from "46" to "48," marked on the chart as part of a measured nautical mile course. At Mile 835.5, about halfway between the city and Ponce de Leon Inlet, the twin spans of the Port Orange Bridge (65-foot fixed vertical clearance) carry state Route A1A across the ICW. Current is swift here, and the narrow channel can be congested, especially on weekends. Tide boards at full-moon high tide sometimes show a center-span clearance of 63 feet. Our cruising editor encountered 7-foot shoals mid-channel between green daybeacons "57" to "61."

Just below the Port Orange Bridge, a small mangrove island on the west side of the ICW channel is a nesting ground for pelicans, egrets and cormorants during the spring. The nesting birds are prevalent above and below the Port Orange Bridge down to Ponce de Leon Inlet. If you should see any, confine your activity to watching only, and do not disturb the nests.

The course south from Port Orange passes through a dredged cut that is crowded with fishermen in small outboard craft, so watch your wake. There was a shoal reported to be in the channel on the west side between red daybeacons "68" and "70" in the vicinity of Tenmile Creek. Green daybeacon "69" has been relocated to mark the deeper water, and depths are now reported to be around 9 feet at the edge of the channel. Red daybeacon "68A" has been added here to further define the deeper water. There is a condo with private docks on the east side of the ICW between green daybeacon "71" and red daybeacon "72." Its entrance channel is marked with a rather large red nun buoy and green can buoy, which can be confusing for both north and southbound ICW travelers. Do not confuse these for the floating ICW markers marking the beginning of the Ponce de Leon Cut just to the south after flashing green "1."

Dockage: A short distance below the Port Orange Bridge on the east side of the Waterway past red daybeacon "58" is Adventure Yacht Harbor. They offer covered and open slips, gas and diesel and an on-site restaurant. Look for the marked entry channel.

■ PONCE DE LEON INLET —MILE 840

 THE FOLLOWING AREA REQUIRES SPECIAL ATTENTION DUE TO SHOALING OR CHANGES TO THE CHANNEL

NAVIGATION: Use Chart 11485. The Ponce de Leon Inlet area begins north of Mile 840. Just west of the inlet, the Ponce de Leon Cut portion of the ICW is pro-tected, but subject to shoaling, especially at its north and south ends. This area, from red daybeacon "72" through green daybeacon "41," at the New Smyrna Beach Harris-Saxon Bridge (65-foot fixed vertical clearance), was dredged between April and December 2008. Ponce de Leon Inlet itself and the north and south channels were dredged in spring 2010.

From flashing green "1" to red daybeacon "6," on the north end of Ponce de Leon Cut, shoals are a constant problem. Our cruising editor observed 9-foot depths here at mean low water. Several buoys in this area are moved as needed and may not match what is printed on your chart. Green can buoys "3" and "3A" and red nun buoys "2" and "2A" mark the channel in addition to the fixed markers. The most recent chart shows no magenta line here, as the shoals and markers change so frequently.

On the south side of the Ponce de Leon Cut area of the ICW, there has, at times, been a shoal of varying depths extending across the entire ICW channel between red daybeacon "18" and floating green over red (where the older chart showed green daybeacon "19") as well as at red daybeacon "20," so give the marker a wide berth and favor the east bank. This area is subject to change and may be marked differently when you arrive. Our cruising editor found 10-foot depths at mean low water in the channel here, but reports of 4-foot depths mid-channel near red daybeacon "18" were reported in May 2010.

Like most Atlantic inlets, Ponce de Leon Inlet shifts and shoals. A hydrographic survey resulted in a major construction project and new jetties, but you should use Ponce de Leon Inlet to access the ocean only with up-to-date local knowledge. It is shallow and open to the east, so southeast swells can be treacherous, even in moderate winds. The Coast Guard has been reporting shoaling in Ponce de Leon Inlet Channel into the ocean since March 2006, when temporary markers were placed to mark the deepest water, however, dredging of this inlet was completed in May 2010.

The floating markers indicated on the chart in the North Channel of Ponce de Leon Inlet, where it branches from the Waterway at ICW red nun "2" and green can "3," are in place. Locals frequently use the North Channel, but you may want to call the Corps of Engineers or the Coast Guard for the latest information about its depths. It is shoal and confusing where it joins the inlet channel.

The South Channel to Ponce de Leon Inlet is marked and sees daily Coast Guard, commercial and recreational boat usage. The Coast Guard reports shoaling in the vicinity of temporary green cans "7A" and "7B," marking the shoal on the east side of the turn from the jetty into the South Channel. Conditions may be very different by the time you may want to run this inlet; seek local knowledge. Hopefully the dredging in May 2010 has at least temporarily alleviated the problems in this area.

Ponce de Leon Inlet, FL

Looking west from the ocean through Ponce de Leon Inlet, with its historic red lighthouse to the right. (Not to be used for navigation.)

WATERWAY GUIDE PHOTOGRAPHY

The North Channel and Rockhouse Creek are not included in periodic dredging because they are not authorized federal channels. The controlling depth for entering the anchorage area at Rockhouse Creek is around 7 feet. The entrance is close to the north bank of the creek. The marsh island on the southeast side of the creek is now a Florida Inland Navigation District (FIND) disposal site for dredge material.

When entering Ponce de Leon Inlet from the ocean, your best bet is to wait for a local commercial or charter boat and follow it if you are unfamiliar with the inlet. These boats come in around 4:30 p.m. With any swell running or ebb current against onshore wind, it could be very difficult, and the shoaling and frequent change of markers may make it unsafe for you, your crew and your vessel. At other times, call TowBoatU.S. or Lighthouse Boatyard at the inlet on the VHF and ask for assistance through the entrance. This marina is especially friendly to transients and makes an effort not to turn anyone away. Knowledgeable locals warn that those unfamiliar with the area should never attempt to enter this inlet at night, as the lights from the nearby airport can be easily confused with the channel and jetty lights.

END SPECIAL CAUTION AREA.

Dockage: Sea Love Boat Works, a mile east of Mile 840 on the North Channel of the inlet, offers transient berths, diesel fuel and almost any type of repair. Their 70-ton Travelift can haul boats with up to a 23-foot beam.

Down the Hatch Seafood Company, a popular local restaurant, is located at Sea Love. Lighthouse Boatyard, a mile to the south and adjacent to the inlet, has transient dockage, gas and diesel fuel and some repair services. Inlet Harbor Marina at the north end of the North Channel offers transient dockage and pump-out service. They have an award-winning restaurant on-site with daily music as well as a bait and tackle and gift shops.

Anchorage: All the side creeks in this area—North Channel, Spruce Creek, the unnamed side creek to the east and south of Spruce Creek, and Rockhouse Creek—are now designated No-Wake Zones to protect the manatee population. Rockhouse Creek is a popular weekend anchorage and a congested small-boat passage. The spoil island on the southeast side of Rockhouse Creek and adjacent to the ICW was scheduled to receive much of the spoil from recent dredging, but it was instead used to refurbish the beach oceanside of the inlet.

The historic Ponce de Leon Inlet Lighthouse is open to the public and provides a stunning panoramic view of the area. It is open daily except Thanksgiving and Christmas.

Cruising Options

For navigational information on the ICW south of the inlet, refer to the next chapter, "New Smyrna Beach to Vero Beach." The next opportunity going south to leave the ICW and go offshore is the Canaveral Barge Canal at Mile 894, east to Canaveral Inlet. ∎

New Smyrna Beach to Vero Beach

CHARTS 11472, 11474, 11476, 11478, 11481, 11484, 11485

At about Mile 840, the Intracoastal Waterway (ICW) begins its departure from the Halifax River and enters the Ponce de Leon Cut north of Ponce de Leon Inlet, joining with the Indian River North just below the inlet. Strong tidal currents often run up and down the land cut and occasionally may give your vessel a sideways push.

NAVIGATION: Use Chart 11485. **Use the Miami Harbor Entrance Tide Tables. For high tide at Ponce Inlet, add 5 minutes; for low tide, add 33 minutes.** Expect to encounter shoaling around Rockhouse Creek, and stay on the southwest (red marker) side of that bend for the deepest water. Coming in from Ponce de Leon Inlet (see the cautions in the previous chapter), the safest route to the ICW is the South Channel leading to New Smyrna Beach, the Indian River North and Mosquito Lagoon farther south on the ICW.

The charted floating markers for the North Channel from Ponce de Leon Inlet are on station, and the channel is always active with traffic. From the west side of North Channel to the George Musson Memorial Bridge at Coronado Beach (Mile 845.0, 24-foot closed vertical clearance, restricted opening schedule) is a strictly enforced No-Wake Zone, as is the intersection of the ICW and the South Channel. Favor the east side of the ICW channel from Ponce de Leon Inlet's South Channel to the George Musson Memorial Bridge at Mile 845.

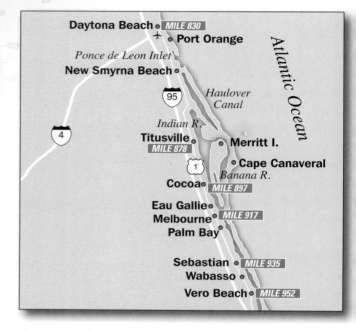

GEORGE MUSSON MEMORIAL BRIDGE, Mile 845
WATERWAY GUIDE PHOTOGRAPHY

HARRIS SAXON BRIDGE Mile 846.5
WATERWAY GUIDE PHOTOGRAPHY

Dredging between red daybeacon "72" (just north of Mile 840) and green daybeacon "41" (just north of the Harris Saxon Bridge at New Smyrna, Mile 846.5) was completed in late 2008. This project included the entire Ponce de Leon Cut areas, as well as the ICW stretch from the South Channel to the Harris Saxon Bridge (Mile 846.5). Conditions described are current as of May 2010, but may be different when you go through the area, as conditions are ever-changing here. Check the Coast Guard Local Notice to Mariners and our Web site for updates. One of

the areas where dredge spoil was deposited is the island on the southeast side of the Rockhouse Creek anchorage, which has given some additional wind protection from that direction.

There is a shoal-prone area in the channel between red daybeacon "18" and the marker where the chart indicates green daybeacon "19" had 9-foot depths. Give red daybeacon "20" a wide berth, and favor the east bank to avoid shoals that extend into the channel from the mainland along the curved approach to the George Musson Memorial Bridge.

The George Musson Memorial Bridge (Mile 845.0, 24-foot closed vertical clearance) is hydraulic and relatively slow in opening; a current complicates the approach. The bridge opens on the hour, 20 minutes after the hour and 40 minutes after the hour, from 7 a.m. to 7 p.m., seven days a week.

New Smyrna Beach, on the ICW

South of the George Musson Memorial Bridge at Mile 845.0, continue to favor the eastern shore until the channel swings toward New Smyrna Beach, and watch for shoaling at the curve between flashing greens "33" and "35." The former shoal off flashing green "35" has been dredged, and water depths are no less than 9 feet at mean low water off red daybeacon "34." The chart will help you spot the turn to the west.

Sheephead Cut, Mile 845.5, is a more direct marked channel between Chicken Island and Bouchelle Island;

Looking north over New Smyrna Beach and the ICW. (Not to be used for navigation.) WATERWAY GUIDE PHOTOGRAPHY

a green-red junction daybeacon indicates the eastern tip of Chicken Island. The preferred channel is the ICW route around the north side of Chicken Island. The other channel, also with about 9-foot depths, leads through Sheephead Cut and meets the ICW and another green-red junction daybeacon at the west end of Chicken Island. If you are considering avoiding the possibility of shoals on the ICW route at red daybeacon "34" by cutting through Sheephead Cut, check with the local towing services or Coast Guard Station Ponce de Leon Inlet for the latest updates on depths. In the past few years before the latest dredging, there was conflicting information as to which was deeper as the channels are subject to shoaling, but both routes carried adequate depths, according to our cruising editor.

New Smyrna Beach's harbor comes up suddenly beyond flashing red "38," which marks the turn toward the Harris Saxon Bridge (Mile 846.5, 65-foot fixed vertical clearance). Do not cut corners off the Waterway where green daybeacons "37" and "39" and a white "DANGER" daybeacon mark a shoal; also honor green can "39A," which is not shown on current charts. The ICW channel has only 7-foot depths at low tide just off the New Smyrna Yacht Club close to flashing green "45." The tiny anchorage area south of flashing green "45" is deeper and holds a few permanently moored boats.

Dockage: You may find space at the newly renovated New Smyrna Beach City Marina inside the basin off the ICW at flashing red "38" northwest of the Harris Saxon

Bridge. The harbor and marina are only a block from the downtown area. Farther north, the Riverview Hotel and Marina, just south of the George Musson Memorial Bridge, stands beautifully restored after years of abandonment. You can use its dock (limited space) to dine at Riverview Charlie's or to stay overnight. Farther south, the New Smyrna Yacht Club, on an island west of the ICW and south of the Harris Saxon Bridge, welcomes members of clubs that are listed in the American Registry of Yacht Clubs. (They do not offer reciprocity to Florida Yacht Club members.) There is no overnight docking allowed at the park docks just northwest of the Harris Saxon Bridge. The northernmost dock is reserved for the water taxi.

New Smyrna Beach, FL

New Smyrna Beach, FL

NEW SMYRNA BEACH		Dockage					Supplies				Service			
		Largest Vessel Accommodated	VHF Channel Monitored	Approach / Dockside Depth (reported)	Transient Berths / Total Berths	Floating Docks	Gas / Diesel	Groceries, Ice, Marine Supplies, Snacks	Repairs: Hull, Engine, Propeller	Lift (tonnage) Crane, Rail	1=110v, 2=220v, B=Both, Max Amps	Laundry, Pool, Showers	Pump-Out Station	Nearby: Grocery Store, Motel, Restaurant
1. Riverview Hotel & Marina 845 🖥WiFi	386-428-5858	50		/8	15/15			I			B/100	LPS		GMR
2. North Causeway Marine 846.4	386-427-5267	60		2/35	8/10		GD	GIMS	HEP	L	B/50			GMR
3. NEW SMYRNA BEACH CITY MARINA 846.5	**386-409-2042**	**65**	16	**7/42**	**8/10**	F		I			**B/50**	LS	P	**GMR**
4. Fishing Cove Marina 846.6	386-428-7827	60		2/18	8/8	F	G	IMS	E	L				GMR
5. Night Swan Intracoastal B & B 847 🖥WiFi	386-423-4940	32		3/6	12/8	F								GMR
6. Smyrna Yacht Club 847	386-427-4040	57	16	4/74	/4	F					B/50	PS	P	MR

Corresponding chart(s) not to be used for navigation. 🖥 Internet Access WiFi Wireless Internet Access

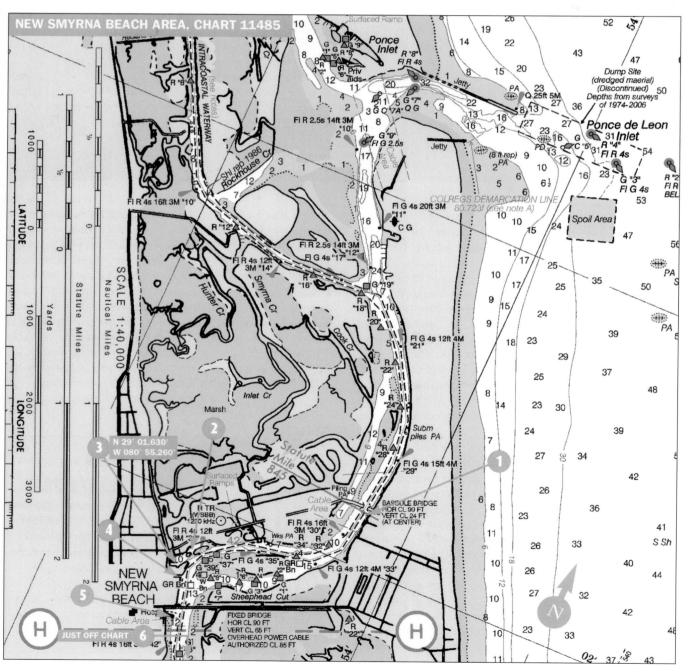

NEW SMYRNA BEACH AREA, CHART 11485

Anchorage: Sheephead Cut runs close to Chicken Island. There is only space for three or four smaller boats to anchor on the south side of the channel between green daybeacon "1" and just beyond green daybeacon "3" (between the markers and the condominium docks on Bouchelle Island). Show an anchor light, and make sure that you will not swing into the channel or the docks at the tidal change; this is a very small, tight anchorage. Local boats use the channel heavily at all hours.

GOIN' ASHORE:
NEW SMYRNA BEACH, FL

The downtown area of New Smyrna Beach begins only a block from the Municipal Marina, and one of the first things a visitor will see is a bakery, followed by an assortment of restaurants and shops. Anyone interested in a little sightseeing should take in the New Smyrna Sugar Mill ruins, about three miles from the harbor. Built in the early 1800s with coquina stones (a natural limestone formed of broken shells and corals), the mill processed sugarcane into granular sugar that was shipped north. Molasses, a processing by-product, went south for rum production. In 1835, the Seminole Indians, who had been driven out of the region, returned to raid and burn all 10 of the area's mills. The local sugar industry never recovered.

Directly across the street from Municipal Marina is a park of historical interest. A plaque commemorates the Greeks who first settled the area. Two markers give separate stories regarding the impressive foundations of what was originally the Turnbull Palace. One mentions the destruction of one of the several buildings by two Union gunboats.

The Marine Discovery Center (located on the ICW at the North Causeway east of the marinas) is a nonprofit educational center offering history and sunset tours as well as eco-tours of the New Smyrna area. They also provide information about city-owned water taxi service to the restaurants and lighthouse at Ponce Inlet. Call 386-428-4828 for information about both. Water taxis make the run every two hours, beginning at 11 a.m. daily, except on Saturdays, when they start at 9 a.m.

Those who want to explore the New Smyrna Beach area should consider using the bus system. Pick up a schedule from any bus. The local car rental agency will pick up customers at the marinas—inquire with the marina office where you are staying. Less than two miles away, the wide sandy beaches offer a relaxing day of sunbathing, swimming, water sports and surf fishing. A summer concert series in the gazebo at Riverside Park features local bands and musicians. The city's Atlantic Center for the Arts (1414 Art Center Ave., 386-427-6975) hosts many exhibitions by world-renowned and local artists. The New Smyrna Beach Museum of History (120 Sams Ave., 386-478-0052) has interpretive exhibits of local culture and history.

ICW: South to Mosquito Lagoon

The Harris Saxon Bridge (Mile 846.5) has a 65-foot fixed vertical clearance. The city has built an attractive park at the northwest end of this bridge with a boardwalk, fishing pier and three small docking areas. The park bulkhead takes up the entire area between the condominiums at the marina and the Harris Saxon Bridge.

NAVIGATION: Use Chart 11485. For about the next 10 miles, the ICW runs down a straight, dredged channel between the mainland and a jumble of small islets that support several fishing camps along with the usual Florida waterfront housing on the west side. Keep an eye out for kayaks and small fishing boats here; they frequently anchor in the channel or too close to the edge. Luckily for them, a good deal of this area is a No-Wake Zone, from Mile 852.8 to Mile 858.4. There is shoaling near flashing red "42," and shoaling continues to be a problem from red daybeacon "50" to flashing green "69," with some spots holding less than 8-foot depths. Shoaling is most noticeable between red daybeacon "64" and green daybeacon "67," where 7-foot depths were observed. This is an area of frequent manatee sightings, so proceed cautiously anytime you see a circular disturbance on the surface of the water.

Mosquito Lagoon, off the ICW: Mile 855 to Mile 870

Mosquito Lagoon (an open, shallow expanse of water) can only be explored by dinghy or shallow-draft boat. The same conditions that make this water popular for mosquitoes and deer flies also create an ideal feeding and breeding ground for sport and commercial fish, including redfish, sea trout and mullet. Crabs, clams and shrimp thrive among the dense aquatic grass beds. Flocks of white pelicans and the small fishing boats that fill Mosquito Lagoon attest to the abundance of fresh seafood. Swimming toward a common destination, the birds herd fish together by flapping their wings on the water. Before the fish can escape, the pelicans gobble them up.

Haulover Canal, FL

NAVIGATION: Use Chart 11485. Eight-foot deep spots are numerous in the channel, but outside, depths decrease suddenly. A Manatee No-Wake Zone exists from red daybeacon "64" at Mile 852.8 to green daybeacon "9A" at Mile 858.4. Shoaling has been reported between green daybeacons "25" and "29" in Mosquito Lagoon. There also is shoaling near green daybeacon "35," which is just past mile 865.

If visibility is good, you may see a large building in the distance to the south as you reach the middle of Mosquito Lagoon. This is the Space Shuttle hangar, or vehicle assembly building (VAB) at the Kennedy Space Center. Closer to the Space Center are gantries and perhaps a rocket being readied for launch. In clear weather, the giant VAB is visible for distances of 20 miles or more.

Stay in the middle of the channel, and don't hug markers too closely, as some areas at the channel edges are shallow. Proceed slowly, keep an eye on the depth sounder and watch your wake to avoid damaging other boats near the channel.

Uncharted spoil banks line the outside of the dredged Mosquito Lagoon channel. If you choose to exit the channel to anchor, seek local knowledge or do so carefully, so that if there is a spoil bank just outside the channel, you hit it at slow speed. There are few places deep enough for ICW travelers to anchor for the night.

Seventy-two hours before any launches, the southern end of Mosquito Lagoon (on an imaginary line from Haulover Canal east to three miles out in the Atlantic Ocean) will be off limits to all watercraft. Security boats from the Coast Guard and Kennedy Space Center patrol these waters during this restricted time and levy fines to unauthorized boats entering this zone. This security zone does not include the ICW route.

Anchorage: Some areas of Mosquito Lagoon are deep enough for shallower draft vessels to anchor outside of the channel. These should be approached with caution, as shallow spoil banks often line the eastern edges of the channel. Two anchoring areas are east of green daybeacon "19" in the 6- to 7-foot deep area and southeast of red daybeacon "24" in the 10-foot-deep charted area, however the area of deeper water is quite small. Vessels report the best passage by entering the first anchorage from south of green daybeacon "19" and the second anchorage from north of red daybeacon "24."

Haulover Canal—Mile 869

NAVIGATION: Use Chart 11485. This mile-long rocky cut (with jettied entrances) provides easy passage from Mosquito Lagoon to the Indian River on the opposite side of Merritt Island. The Allenhurst Haulover Canal Bridge (27-foot closed vertical clearance) crosses the canal at Mile 869.2 and opens promptly on request. If the bridge tender does

HAULOVER BRIDGE
Mile 869.2

WATERWAY GUIDE PHOTOGRAPHY

VISIT FLORIDA

QUICK FACT:

KENNEDY SPACE CENTER VISITOR COMPLEX

Some lucky mariners cruising Florida's central east coast could be in for a spectacular sky show if their journey happens to coincide with any launches. Marinas and anchorages in the Titusville area are excellent viewing sites. Tours of the space center provide a close-up view of Space Shuttle Launch Pads A and B, the massive Vehicle Assembly Building, and the 365-foot *Saturn V* moon rocket. Because the launch site is in a secured area, visitors must board buses for two-hour tours. The first tour blasts off at 9:45 a.m., with continuous departures every 15 minutes and the last tour starting at 2:45 p.m. For updated launch information, check the schedule at www.KennedySpaceCenter.com. The last shuttle launch for Discovery was scheduled for September 2010.

But even if the timing is not right to witness an actual launch, Kennedy Space Center's Visitor Complex is worth a stopover. Twin IMAX theaters show two space movies on the five-and-a-half-story big screens. The *Explorer* is a full-sized replica of the space shuttles *Atlantis, Discovery and Endeavour,* and Galaxy Center is a 61-foot model of one module from the international space station. Other attractions include the Astronauts Memorial and the massive Space Mirror, which tracks the movement of the sun, using reflected sunlight to illuminate the names cut through the monument's surface. The Gallery of Manned Spaceflight displays authentic *Mercury, Gemini* and *Apollo* capsules. The visitor complex opens daily at 9 a.m., closing only on Christmas Day and certain launch days. For more information, contact the Visitors Center at 321-449-4444; Kennedy Space Center Visitor Complex, Mail Code: DNPSS, SR405, Kennedy Space Center, FL 32899.

not respond to VHF Channel 09, use a horn signal (one long, one short) to request an opening. Be aware that there are shallow areas at both entrances to the Haulover Canal.

Although the current can run swiftly here, the tidal range is minimal. Strong winds may lower or raise the river and canal levels by as much as 2 feet. The ramp on the inside of the basin (southwest of the Haulover Canal Bridge) is always busy with small fishing boats. The entire Haulover Canal is a Slow-Speed/Minimum Wake Zone, protecting the numerous (and usually visible) resident manatees that feed just below the surface. Wildlife abounds on shore, which is overgrown with vegetation. Keep a lookout for herons, egrets, alligators, manatees and small fishing boats.

On weekends, both Mosquito Lagoon and Haulover Canal are congested with small boats of every type and description, many dangerously overloaded. The small fishing boats often have as many as three people standing up to cast at the edge of the channel or under the bridge. Fortunately, much of the congested area is a Slow-Speed Manatee area, thus preventing wakes that could capsize these tiny boats.

Anchorage: The basin on the southwest side of the Haulover Canal Bridge is too small to even consider as an anchorage for most cruising boats, although a small boat with a shallow draft on a short scope may fit.

Indian River, along the ICW

NAVIGATION: Use Chart 11485. A straight, dredged channel extends from Haulover Canal's western mouth across the flats of the upper Indian River. This channel tends to shoal along both sides, although depths are usually well-maintained in the center.

Depths in this area are holding between 8 and 9 feet. Navigate cautiously, and avoid being pushed out of the channel by beam winds. Flashing green "1" and red daybeacon "2" are the first two aids to navigation you will encounter heading southwest out of the Haulover Canal. After reaching these markers, two huge white tanks (charted as "TANK [NW OF TWO]") on the Indian River's west bank line up with the less visible red markers on the channel's north side and may be used to aid in navigation. When steering for the tanks, keep an eye on the markers ahead and astern, watching for leeway. A wide variety of birds inhabit the spoil islands to the north of the channel, so keep a close lookout for pelicans, cormorants and anhingas here. White pelicans are even more numerous here than on Mosquito Lagoon.

Even off the marked channel, the lower Indian River is wide and deep for most of the 120 miles to the St. Lucie River and Inlet. There is usually 65 feet of vertical clearance at most of the fixed bridges across the Indian River, but exercise care after any periods of heavy rain.

The tideboards have been replaced in the last few years on the fixed high-rise bridges in the Indian River. Observe these carefully, especially if your mast is close to the limit. Several stretches allow sailboats to hoist their canvas in the right conditions, and powerboaters to relax—although you should still remain watchful for shoal areas and trap markers. The channel is dredged from Haulover Canal to past Cocoa, but outside the channel, depths vary widely.

Cape Canaveral Area— Mile 878 to Mile 943

In what has come to be known as the Space Coast Area (Mile 878 to Mile 943), the coastal topography changes from a slender barrier strip to a broad stretch of land, which forms Cape Canaveral. Inside the cape area, the waters divide around Merritt Island, forming Indian River on the mainland side and Banana River on the east side. This section of the Indian River is a pleasure to navigate, though strong winds from the north or south may kick up an uncomfortable chop.

NAVIGATION: Use Chart 11485. There are numerous bridges, both high-span and restricted, that cross the Indian River. If a closed bridge delays your passage, waiting boats will probably have plenty of room to maneuver. You may even want to consider anchoring off the channel, as depths along the river accommodate most boats. In fall, when days shorten, anchoring is preferable to entering a strange harbor at night. Watch closely for interesting sights along the banks of the river; this will add to the pleasure of the cruise. In other areas farther south, the Indian River is too wide to see much ashore.

Titusville—Mile 878

Titusville, a good port from which to visit Disney World and the other theme parks in the Orlando area, is an important agricultural center for the Florida citrus industry. Its protected harbor has a well-marked entry channel that normally carries 7-foot depths. As soon as you enter the harbor, depths increase. Anchoring is prohibited in the harbor because of a lack of space. Boaters anchored nearby (outside the harbor) may tie up at the dinghy dock and use the showers for a fee.

NAVIGATION: Use Chart 11485. North of Titusville, the (Jay-Jay) NASA Railroad Bridge crosses the ICW at Mile 876.6 with a 7-foot closed vertical clearance. The bridge is normally left in the open position unless a train is approaching, which is infrequent. When a train is approaching, the green flashing "go-ahead" signals shift to flashing red, and a siren sounds. The siren continues for the next eight minutes, after which the bridge closes, the train crosses, and then the bridge reopens. The siren does not stop until the bridge has been reopened and the signals have reverted to green.

About two miles south of the NASA Railroad Bridge, Titusville's Max Brewer Bridge (state Route 402) crosses the ICW at Mile 878.9 with a 9-foot closed vertical clearance. The Titusville/Max Brewer

MAX BREWER BRIDGE
Mile 878.9

WATERWAY GUIDE PHOTOGRAPHY

Titusville, FL

Indian River, FL

		Largest Vessel Accommodated	VHF Channel Monitored	Transient Berths / Total Berths	Approach / Dockside Depth (reported)	Floating Docks	Gas / Diesel	Groceries, Ice, Marine Supplies, Snacks	Repairs: Hull, Engine, Propeller	Lift (tonnage), Crane, Rail	1=110v, 2=220v, B=Both, Max Amps	Laundry, Pool, Showers	Pump-Out Station	Nearby: Grocery Store, Motel, Restaurant
TITUSVILLE					**Dockage**			**Supplies**			**Service**			
1. Titusville Municipal Marina 878.3 🖳	321-383-5600	165	16	35/195	8/8	F	GD	GIMS			B/50	LS	P	GMR
2. Westland Marina 878.3	321-267-1667	55		/75	9/9			IM	HEP	L50	B/50	S		GMR
3. Kennedy Point Yacht Club & Marina 883 🖳 WiFi	321-383-0280	70	16/71	10/125	6/7			GIMS			B/50	LPS	P	MR

Corresponding chart(s) not to be used for navigation. 🖳 Internet Access WiFi Wireless Internet Access

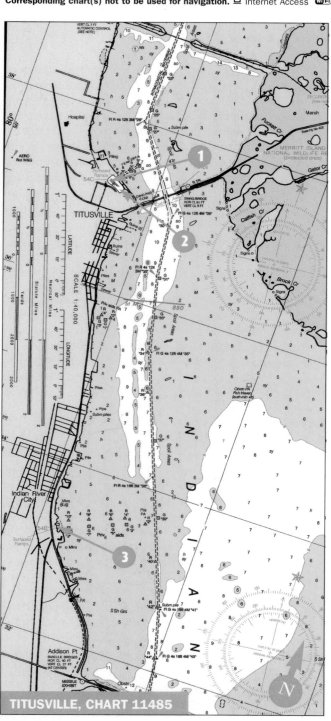

TITUSVILLE, CHART 11485

Bridge is a swing highway bridge and has restricted openings. All year, Monday through Friday, the bridge does not open from 6 a.m. to 7:15 a.m. and from 3:15 p.m. to 4:30 p.m. The Titusville/Max Brewer Bridge is being replaced with a 65-foot high-rise bridge. Construction began in May 2009 and is supposed to be complete in spring 2011.

Stay well inside the channel between the Titusville/Max Brewer Bridge and the Addison Point/NASA Causeway Bridge; there is shoaling to depths as shallow as 6 feet in spots, especially from green daybeacon "33" to south of red daybeacon "34" where the channel narrows. If you do leave the channel to watch a NASA launch, proceed carefully and use your depth sounder. About six miles below Titusville, the Addison Point/NASA Causeway Bridge (state Route 405, Mile 885.0, 27-foot closed vertical clearance) crosses the channel and has restricted hours. The bridge does not open from 6:30 a.m. to 8 a.m. and from 3:30 p.m. to 5 p.m., Monday through Friday. Note that the Haulover, Max Brewer and NASA Causeway bridges close for space center launches. The times are announced on VHF Channels 09 and 22A.

At about Mile 888.5, there is a large power plant on the west side of the Waterway with power cables crossing the ICW in a northeasterly direction. These cables have a charted height of 85 feet over the main channel.

Dockage: Two marinas are located in the Titusville basin. The first is the friendly Titusville Municipal Marina, which welcomes transients and offers gas and diesel fuels. The Titusville Municipal Marina went through a major renovation in 2008. Transient dockage and fuel are available, and the old floating docks have been replaced with fixed docks of the same number and size as before. The second facility in the Titusville basin is Westland Marine, which offers a do-it-yourself boatyard. Groceries, fast food, a West Marine and other stores are within short walking distance from the basin. A few miles south on the Indian River, at green daybeacon "39," you will see a marked entrance channel leading to Kennedy Point Marina and Yacht Club with limited accommodations.

Anchorage: It is possible to anchor outside the marked channel leading to the Titusville Basin north of the Titusville/Max Brewer Bridge (Mile 878.9), but sound your way along when looking for a spot to set the hook. Be aware that this area can be uncomfortable in strong winds, and wakes from the ICW can be a problem. The city

Looking northeast over Port Canaveral and the Canaveral Barge Canal. (Not to be used for navigation.)

marina is friendly to anchored boats. The City of Titusville plans to place a large mooring field in the area where boats now anchor. The field is still in the planning phase, so it may be several years before moorings will be available to transient boaters.

Just south of Titusville, at about Mile 883 (opposite Indian River City on the mainland), you will see a large charted area of deeper water with depths of 7 to 8 feet to the east of the ICW. This anchorage is an excellent spot to watch space center launches. Give the charted spoil areas a wide berth, and then sound your way over toward Merritt Island. The holding is good, but this anchorage offers no protection from wind or choppy water. If you sound your way in far enough, wakes from channel traffic are almost entirely eliminated, although other boats moving around in the anchorage may give you a good rolling. This spot is about five miles from the launch site and more than a mile from the ICW.

Addison Point Bridge, better known as NASA Causeway Bridge (Mile 885.0, 27-foot closed vertical clearance, opening schedule discussed earlier in this chapter), and subsequent bridges that cross the Indian River, can provide a safe overnight anchorage from all wind directions. Simply choose the side that will be sheltered from the wind. Note, however, that the spoil areas and shoals shown on the chart (and those not shown on the chart) seem to be expanding. Some spoil islands were washed away during hurricanes and are now shoals. If you leave the channel to seek out protection behind a bridge causeway, go slowly, and keep an eye on your depth sounder.

Canaveral Barge Canal—Mile 894

East of the ICW channel, just north of the City Point twin fixed bridges (Mile 894.0, 65-foot fixed vertical clearances), look for markers indicating the entrance to the Canaveral Barge Canal, which cuts through Merritt Island

to the Banana River and Canaveral Inlet, and then to the Atlantic Ocean. (Chart 11478 shows the route toward the ocean in detail.) Green daybeacons "13," "11A" and "11" are at the entrance to the barge canal. Use caution, and check for local information on depths in the dredged canal.

Canaveral Barge Canal, FL

Looking east over Merritt Island and the Canaveral Barge Canal. (Not to be used for navigation.) WATERWAY GUIDE PHOTOGRAPHY

Our cruising editor advises that there were 8-foot depths or greater throughout the canal in early 2010. The eight-mile-long journey from the ICW to the Atlantic Ocean includes a three-mile-long cut through Merritt Island with one restricted bridge, a crossing of the Banana River and passage through Canaveral Lock and twin bascule bridges with rush-hour closures.

The Christa McAuliffe Drawbridge (State Route 3, Mile 1.0, 21-foot closed vertical clearance) opens on the hour and half hour from 6 a.m. to 10 p.m. daily, but is closed between 6:15 a.m. and 8:15 a.m. and from 3:10 p.m. to 6:59 p.m., Monday through Friday, except federal holidays. The state Route 401 twin bascule bridges (25-foot closed vertical clearance) at Mile 5.5 open on signal during the day, except it is closed from 6:30 a.m. to 8:00 a.m. and from 3:30 p.m. to 5:15 p.m., Monday through Friday, except federal holidays. Both bridges require a three-hour advance notice to open between 10:00 p.m. and 5:59 a.m. Assuming the canal has adequate depths, the trip is worth the effort. The canal has traffic from local recreational boaters and cruise ships at Port Canaveral. Expect congestion near the two sets of boat ramps near the port.

Canaveral Lock (321-783-5421), operating year-round from 6 a.m. to 9:30 p.m., is the largest navigation lock in Florida and is designed to reduce tidal currents and prevent hurricane tides from entering the Banana River. The lift of the lock is 3 to 4 feet depending on the tide stage. Contact the lock tender on VHF Channel 13 for instructions, and set your fenders in place before entering the lock. Be forewarned that the cleats are inadequate and placed 100 feet apart, making it difficult to secure fore and aft when locking through.

Dockage: The Canaveral Barge Canal contains several excellent marinas for cruising boats.

Harbortown Marina Canaveral is conveniently located in a basin one mile west of the Banana River with gas and diesel fuel, transient slips, lift for haul-outs, long term dry storage, on-site restaurant, a laundry, pool and showers.

Cape Marina, located at Canaveral Inlet, with easy access from both the ocean and the ICW, offers transient dockage, haul-out, repairs, do-it-yourself area, high speed fuel pumps, pump-out, nearby restaurants, laundry and a marine store.

Sunrise Marina welcomes transients to its floating docks and offers full-service repairs, gas and diesel fuel and easy ocean access.

Ocean Club at Port Canaveral, with its associated service facility Scorpion Marine/Port Canaveral Marine, opened in 2008. It is located west of Cape Marina. There are floating transient slips 40 to 110 feet in length. They offer high-speed fuel service, complete marina amenities and a large clubhouse. The 100-ton lift is wide enough for large catamarans.

Kennedy Space Center is the main attraction in Port Canaveral. The popular visitor center includes space flight exhibits, IMAX movies and a trip to the launch complex. The Cove, located near the marinas, is a waterfront recreational area with beaches, several restaurants, casino ships and specialty shops.

Anchorage: At the City Point Bridge just south of the entrance to the Canaveral Barge Canal, you can enter on the southwest side and anchor behind the causeway in 7- to 8-foot depths with good holding. Anchorage is also possible west of the lock, just below the spoil island where 7-foot depths may be found. Boats with clearances less than 36 feet can anchor in 7-foot depths south of the fixed bridge in the Banana River.

Canaveral Barge Canal and Indian River, FL

SKIPPER BOB PUBLICATIONS

MERRITT ISLAND AND INDIAN RIVER		Largest Vessel Accommodated	VHF Channel Monitored	Transient Berths / Total Berths	Approach / Dockside Depth (reported)	Floating Docks	Gas / Diesel	Groceries, Ice, Marine Supplies, Snacks	Repairs: Hull, Engine, Propeller	Lift (tonnage), Crane, Rail	1=110V, 2=220V, B=Both, Max Amps	Laundry, Pool, Showers	Pump-Out Station	Nearby: Grocery Store, Motel, Restaurant
				Dockage				**Supplies**			**Service**			
1. Harbor Square Marina 1.5 E of 893.6	321-453-2464	70	16	10/120	13/7		D	IM	HP		B/50	LS	P	GMR
2. Harbortown Marina Canaveral 4E of 893.6 ☐ WiFi	321-453-0160	72	16/10	20/275	7/7		GD	IMS	HEP	L70	B/50	LPS	P	GM
3. Cocoa Village Marina 897.5 WiFi	321-632-5445	150	16/68	24/117	7/7			I			B/100	LS	P	GMR
4. Banana River Marine Service	321-452-8622	50		2/60	4.5/4.5			MS	HEP	L35	B/50	LS	P	GMR
5. Coastal Marine Repair Inc.	321-453-1885	60		2/60	4.5/4.5			MS	HEP	L35	B/50	LS	P	GR
6. Sunrise Marina 8.6 E of 893.6	321-783-9535	98	16	3/21	20/8	F	GD	IMS	E	L12	B/50			MR
7. Cape Marina 7 E of 893.6 ☐ WiFi	321-783-8410	130	16/68	/114	12/12	F	GD	IMS	HEP	L80	B/50	LS	P	GMR
8. Port Canaveral Yacht Club 6.9 E of 893.6	321-784-2292	65	16/68	/50	40/10	F				C	B/50	LS		R
9. Ocean Club at Port Canaveral 6.7 E of 893.6	321-635-8883	110	16	/75	14/12		GD	IMS			B/100	LS	P	R
10. Scorpion Marine/Port Canaveral Marine	321-784-5788	120	16		15/15	F	GD	IMS	HEP	L15,C110		LPS	P	R

Corresponding chart(s) not to be used for navigation. ☐ Internet Access WiFi Wireless Internet Access

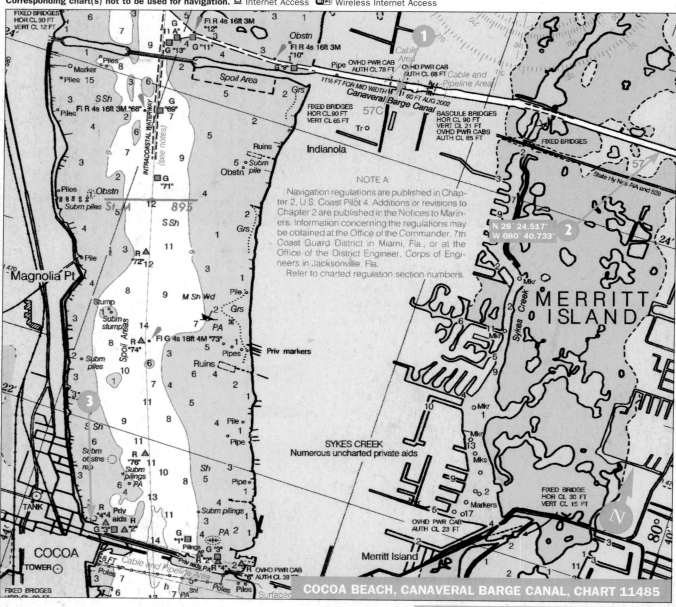

NOTE A
Navigation regulations are published in Chapter 2, U.S. Coast Pilot 4. Additions or revisions to Chapter 2 are published in the Notices to Mariners. Information concerning the regulations may be obtained at the Office of the Commander, 7th Coast Guard District in Miami, Fla., or at the Office of the District Engineer, Corps of Engineers in Jacksonville, Fla.
Refer to charted regulation section numbers.

COCOA BEACH, CANAVERAL BARGE CANAL, CHART 11485

PORT CANAVERAL CHART ON PAGE 142

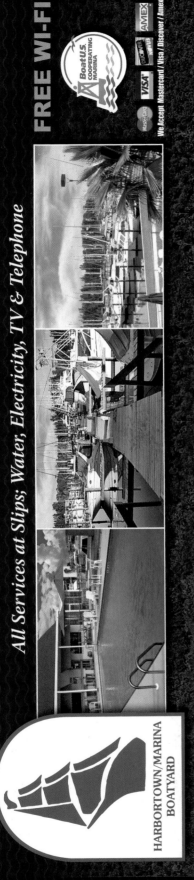

Port Canaveral, FL

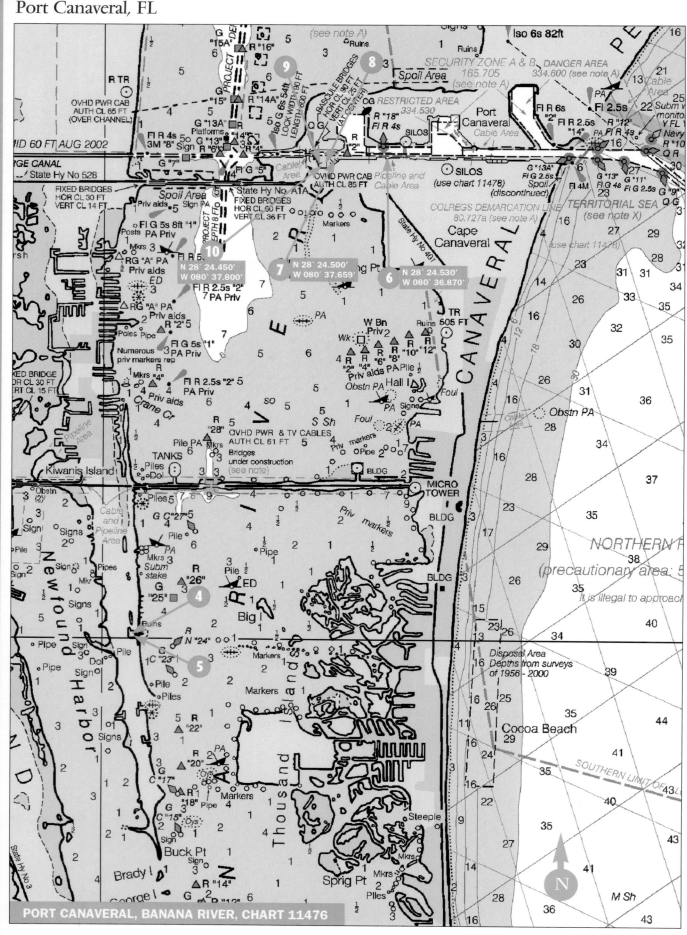

PORT CANAVERAL, BANANA RIVER, CHART 11476

Banana River

Mariners should be aware that a "No Motor Zone" (NMZ) and manatee sanctuary have been established north of the power lines that run east to west over the Banana River to the NASA Causeway. Vessels fitted with a propeller (even stowed) are not allowed in this area.

Once you have transited the Canaveral Barge Canal across to the Banana River, you will see a north-south and an east-west channel. The south channel leads to two facilities, but only vessels that can clear the 36-foot fixed vertical clearance bridge will be able to reach them. The north channel is well-marked and offers anchorage possibilities south of the NMZ discussed above, while the south channel is harder to follow and more shallow, with 4- to 5-foot depths in places. The southern portion of the Banana River can also be entered from the Indian River at Dragon Point and green daybeacon "1" at ICW Mile 914. Facilities here are covered in the Eau Gallie/Melbourne section, just ahead.

Cocoa, on the ICW—Mile 897

NAVIGATION: Use Chart 11485. The Cocoa twin fixed bridges (65-foot vertical clearances) cross the ICW at Mile 897.4.

Dockage: The former Whitley Bay Marina has new docks and is now named Cocoa Village Marina. Many of the slips have been sold, but there is usually plenty of space for transients. Call ahead for reservations. The new two-story office and clubhouse facilities are located east of the tall condominium building. Pay close attention to the daybea-

cons marking the channel parallel to the bridge. Extensive dredging within the marina was completed, and all slips are at least 6 feet deep. This marina is convenient to the attractions, shops and restaurants of Historic Cocoa Village.

Anchorage: You can anchor west of the channel just off the town or east of the channel. Sound your way into either spot to a suitable depth, avoiding the charted cable and pipeline area. The most popular anchorage is south of the bridge on the west side, where you should find 6 to 9 feet. On the west bank is Lee Wenner Park and a surfaced ramp, where you might be able to tie the dinghy at the long fixed dock. The former "free dock" for larger boats is no longer available. Nearby, you will find a shopping center, a hardware store and a marine store.

At Mile 904.5, on the east shore of the Indian River, is "The Point." Just north is a residential stretch of shoreline that provides a pleasant setting for an anchorage that is protected from northeast to southeast winds, with good holding in 9- to 11-foot depths. Don't be alarmed if you hear peacocks yelling "help" on shore.

GOIN' ASHORE:
COCOA, FL

On the inland side of the Waterway, a water tower with a large American flag painted on it serves as a landmark for Cocoa. The Historic Cocoa Village Association operates a visitor information center at 216 Florida Ave., where visitors can obtain information on local attractions and events, and also car rentals, if needed. There is a library two blocks north of Cocoa Village Marina on Indian River Drive, with Internet access available for checking e-mail.

From Cocoa, you can rent a car to visit Disney World (60 miles away) or the Kennedy Space Center. Cocoa has almost everything, including a redevelopment of "Old Cocoa" in remembrance of Florida from the 1920s to the 1950s. A non-profit organization, Cocoa Main Street, was formed to ensure and enhance the preservation of Historic Cocoa Village. In fact, the restored town center was chosen as the location for a movie set in 1960s Key West. Clustered near a beautifully landscaped plaza, quaint antique buildings house the Cocoa Village Playhouse, art galleries, craft shops, boutiques and several good restaurants. Black Tulip draws repeat business from miles around. Across the street, Mama D's Deli and Bakery serves up homemade Italian delicacies, and Café Margaux is equally delightful. Murdock's Bistro offers great food and a bit of history. Its eclectic decor was created largely from many beautiful architectural pieces salvaged from the old landmark Brevard Hotel on the west bank of the Indian River, just south of the high-rise bridge. An eight-story residential condominium complex is on the former hotel site.

Within walking distance of the waterfront, a multi-building hardware complex, S. F. Travis & Co., can provide mariners with some of those hard-to-get gadgets and tools. On the east side of the Indian River, attractions include other fine restaurants, a dozen theaters, an 80-store mall, supermarkets and space center exhibits—but you will probably choose to take a cab there. Lovely beaches are just eight miles away.

Eau Gallie, FL

Indian River, FL

PALM SHORES, EAU GALLIE AREA	Phone	Largest Vessel Accommodated	VHF Channel Monitored	Transient Berths / Total Berths	Approach / Dockside Depth (reported)	Floating Docks	Groceries, Ice, Marine Supplies, Snacks	Repairs: Hull, Engine, Propeller	Gas / Diesel	Lift (tonnage), Crane, Rail	1=110V, 2=220V, B=Both, Max Amps	Laundry, Pool, Showers	Pump-Out Station	Nearby: Grocery Store, Motel, Restaurant
		Dockage					**Supplies**			**Service**				
1. Sundance Marine 910.8 🖥 WiFi	321-242-7140	55		2/78	7/5.5		IM	E			B/50	LS		R
2. Anchorage Yacht Basin 1.1 E of 914.5	321-773-3620	150		10/100	6/6		GIMS		GD	C	B/50	LS		GMR
3. Telemar Bay Marina 1.8 E of 914.5	321-773-2468	110	16	20/210	9/9		GIMS	EP	GD	L40	B	LS	P	GMR
4. Eau Gallie Yacht Basin 915 🖥	321-242-6577	60	16	2/60	8/8		IMS				B/50	LS	P	GMR
5. Waterline Marina 915 🖥 WiFi	321-254-0452	80	16	8/92	8/7						B/50	LS	P	GMR
6. Eau Gallie Boat Works 915	321-254-1766	60	16		6/6			HEP		L30,C,R	B/50			GMR

Corresponding chart(s) not to be used for navigation. 🖥 Internet Access WiFi Wireless Internet Access

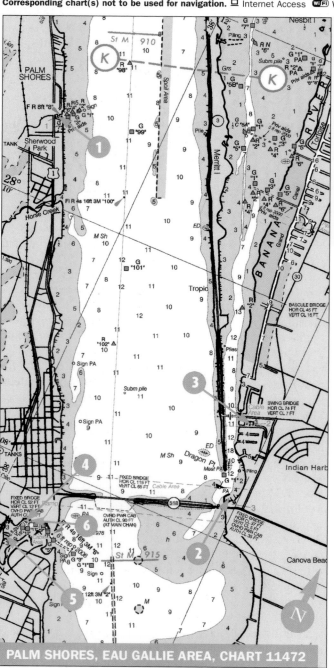

PALM SHORES, EAU GALLIE AREA, CHART 11472

ADDITIONAL RESOURCES

- Florida's Space Coast, **www.space-coast.com**
- Cocoa Beach Area Chamber of Commerce, **www.cocoabeachchamber.com**

NEARBY GOLF COURSES
Cocoa Beach Country Club, 5000 Tom Warriner Blvd., Cocoa Beach, FL 32932, 321-868-3361

NEARBY MEDICAL FACILITIES
Cape Canaveral Hospital, 701 W. Cocoa Beach Causeway, Cocoa Beach, FL 32931, 321-799-7111

Palm Shores, on the ICW—Mile 909

NAVIGATION: Use Charts 11485 and 11472. The stretch to Palm Shores from Cocoa presents a few problems, including the ever-present trap markers that sometimes stray into the channel. The U.S. Army Corps of Engineers reports continuous shoaling between flashing green "77" and green daybeacon "81" south of the Cocoa Bridge, with no new dredging planned until new disposal areas for dredge spoil are established. The controlling depth through this stretch was last reported to be 7 feet. Favor the western side of the channel, but watch for trap markers. Do not attempt anchoring outside flashing green "83," as it is shoaling here. At Mile 909.0, the Palm Shores Pineda Causeway Bridge (65-foot fixed vertical clearance) crosses the Waterway. South of the bridge, starting about Mile 910, the channel tends to shoal. The best water can be found along or even outside the western edge.

Below the Palm Shores Bridge, the channel is wide. A charted spoil area extends to the south from the bridge along the east side for approximately 2.5 miles. The only craft that may have problems are sailboats attempting to tack back and forth across the river.

Dockage: On the west side of the Waterway, Sundance Marina, formerly Diamond 99 Marina, has a charted, marked entry at about Mile 911. The controlling depth for the marina is reported to be around 5 feet (depending on

Looking northeast over Eau Gallie. (Not to be used for navigation.) WATERWAY GUIDE PHOTOGRAPHY

wind and rainfall; tidal rise and fall in this area is negligible). Call ahead for updated information.

Anchorage: You may observe a number of boats anchored both above and below the Palm Shores (Pineda Causeway) Bridge on the west side of the Indian River. This is not a recommended anchorage for transient boaters.

■ EAU GALLIE/MELBOURNE— MILE 914 TO MILE 918

Once two distinct towns, each with its own harbor and facilities, these communities have merged under the name of Melbourne to form the "metropolis" of the Space Coast. However, old-timers and itinerant mariners still think of them as separate harbors. The current edition of Chart 11472 no longer mentions Eau Gallie, but the point that once featured a big stucco dragon is still referred to as Dragon Point. The dragon, destroyed by storms, is reportedly going to be reconstructed.

EAU GALLIE BRIDGE
Mile 914.4

WATERWAY GUIDE PHOTOGRAPHY

Eau Gallie, on the ICW—Mile 914

NAVIGATION: Use Chart 11472. Eau Gallie, at Mile 914 on the east side of the Indian River, has long been a popular port with facilities that match a harbor several times its size. Many skippers leave their boats here for extended periods, catch a plane from Melbourne International Airport, and then return to cruise farther. At Mile 914, you will pass the east side of the old swing bridge that now serves as a fishing pier, replaced by the Eau Gallie high-rise bridge (Mile 914.4, 65-foot fixed vertical clearance).

The mouth of the Banana River is located inside Dragon Point, north of the bridge and east of the ICW. To enter, round green daybeacon "1" off Dragon Point on the north side of the entrance, but keep at least 100 feet south of that daybeacon. Use the remaining tail of what was once a huge green stucco dragon (four people could fit in its mouth) as a landmark. You can see it clearly as you approach. Groundings on Dragon Point's rocky rim occur frequently. Reports are that the charted shoal building up from the bridge is well south of green daybeacon "1." It is a sandy shoal, and it would be better to ground there than on Dragon Point's rocks. If you do hit the rocks, edge off backwards. Do not try to go over them. Manatees or porpoises sometimes welcome boaters to this area.

The old Mathers Swing Bridge over the Banana River (north and on the inside of Dragon Point/Merritt Island) was upgraded with a new swing bridge with 7-foot vertical clearance at mean low water. It opens on request and monitors VHF Channel 09.

Dockage: Several full-service marinas are located above and below the Eau Gallie Bridge and east and west of the Waterway. On the east side of the Indian River in the

Melbourne, FL

Looking northwest into Melbourne Harbor. (Not to be used for navigation.) WATERWAY GUIDE PHOTOGRAPHY

mouth of the Banana River, two marinas are available. On the south shore, just north and east of the high-rise bridge, is Anchorage Yacht Basin. The entrance is straightforward, but you should check for current depths with Anchorage Yacht Basin before entering the channel.

Telemar Bay Marina is located just south of the Mathers Bridge and includes a full-service yard and a ship's store. Shopping is located within long walking distance of Telemar Bay Marina. It may be possible to leave a dinghy at the park beach adjacent to the bridge. Traffic is very heavy on this road. Between the Anchorage Yacht Basin and Telemar Bay is the Eau Gallie Yacht Club.

Eau Gallie Yacht Basin, located on the west side of the Indian River in a basin south of the Eau Gallie Causeway Bridge, is charming and offers good protection with an easy-to-enter, well-maintained recently dredged entrance. Depths are 8 feet in both the entrance and marina. Favor the seawall to starboard as you enter, swing past the park and dock at the facilities ahead. The Eau Gallie Boat Works, a "boutique boatyard," is just beyond and features a large marine railway as well as an open-ended lift on rails. Waterline Marina, associated with a condominium development, is at the head of the basin. It is a short walk from the Eau Gallie Yacht Basin or Eau Gallie Boat Works through quaint streets to the historical restored downtown area of Eau Gallie, with its restaurants, shops, antiques, galleries and a farmers' market on Saturdays. There is a West Marine and post office within longer walking distance. The former Intracoastal Marina, with its well-marked channel at Mile 917, is closed and is expected to be rebuilt as a private marina associated with the new condos planned on its former site.

Anchorage: Between Dragon Point and the Mathers Swing Bridge on the Banana River (off the ICW), you can anchor in 10- to 18-foot depths with good holding. No tide will worry you here, but the current must be taken into account. Depths vary with wind and rain, and wakes can be considerable (although numerous No-Wake signs have resulted in some improvement). Be careful not to interfere with the entrances to the yacht club or the marinas. There is a coquina outcropping on the west side, almost from Dragon Point to the bridge. In case the anchor or chain tangles and cannot be freed, the marina to the north by the bridge can provide a diver to help you.

The city of Indian Harbour Beach claims jurisdiction over the waters on the east side of the Banana River, from Lansing Island to Poinciana Drive. According to the city, anchoring is banned, except in emergency situations. Boaters should check for local information before anchoring here. Many transients anchor on the west side of Dragon Point in suitable weather to avoid the crowds inside the harbor. The marinas in the lower Banana River do not allow dinghy dockage, even for a fee. Recent charts show wrecks with masts on both the west and east sides of Dragon Point.

Some vessels have been observed anchoring in the Eau Gallie Basin on the southwest side of the Eau Gallie Causeway Bridge. There is little space outside the channel, and the holding is poor.

Melbourne, on the ICW—Mile 917

The quiet, pleasant town of Melbourne sits midway between Jacksonville Beach and Florida's Gold Coast. It is home port to the Florida Institute of Technology's big research vessels, on the port side of the harbor entrance.

NAVIGATION: Use Chart 11472. Two high-level spans (both have 65-foot vertical clearances) cross the Waterway

Indian River, FL

MELBOURNE		Dockage					Supplies		Service					
		Largest Vessel Accommodated	VHF Channel Monitored	Transient Berths / Total Berths	Approach / Dockside Depth (reported)	Floating Docks	Gas / Diesel	Groceries, Ice, Marine Supplies, Snacks	Repairs: Hull, Engine, Propeller	Lift (tonnage), Crane, Rail	1=110V, 2=220V, B=Both, Max Amps	Laundry, Pool, Showers	Pump-Out Station	Nearby: Grocery Store, Motel, Restaurant
1. Melbourne Harbor Marina 918.5 🖳	321-725-9054	130	16/68	25/100	5.5/8		GD	IMS			B/50	LS	P	GMR
2. Pelican Harbor Marina Inc. 921.2	321-956-0960	43		3/56	4/5			IMS			1/30			MR
3. Palm Bay Marina 921.2	321-723-0851	40	73	3/60	3/3		G	IM	HEP	L5	1/30	S		

Corresponding chart(s) not to be used for navigation. 🖳 Internet Access (WiFi) Wireless Internet Access

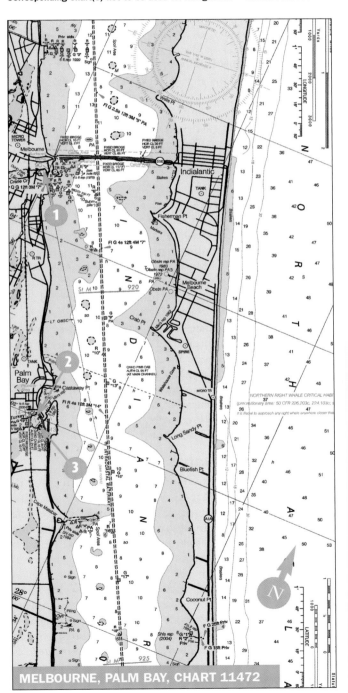

MELBOURNE, PALM BAY, CHART 11472

at Mile 918.2. Melbourne's landlocked harbor is easily approached just south of the bridges. To enter the basin from the Waterway, turn west at red daybeacon "6," and then follow the markers until you are close to shore. The channel turns sharply to starboard, then leads to the enclosed basin.

Dockage: The Melbourne Harbor Marina is to starboard at the head of the basin mentioned above, and the yacht club is to port. The marina offers most anything you would need, including all types of repairs, a Chart House restaurant and a popular tiki bar and grill next to the dock office. The harbor and channel are dredged to a controlling depth of 8 feet, although the depth is reported to be between 6 and 7 feet between red daybeacon "6" and flashing green "7."

Downtown Melbourne is a short walk from Melbourne Harbor Marina. Here, you will find a quaint restored historical area with shops, restaurants, antiques stores and art galleries. Both Melbourne and Eau Gallie historical downtown areas have monthly art walks, seasonal farmers markets and entertainment.

GOIN' ASHORE:
Melbourne, FL

Melbourne, FL has long been a destination for cruisers transiting the ICW. For those heading south in the fall and winter, it feels like you have finally arrived in Florida. For the most part, you have left the cold north winds behind you, and palm trees start becoming more the rule and not the exception. Melbourne is also the site of such happenings as the annual Melbourne (Seven Seas Cruising Association) SSCA Gam in early November. It draws many boaters, and their dollars, to the local economy. The weekend long festivities allow boaters to sample the hotel accommodations, restaurants and sights that Melbourne has to offer.

Settlers began to arrive in the Melbourne area in the late 1800s. Peter Wright, the areas' most noted settler, used to sail regularly up and down the Indian River to deliver mail to other settlers living along the river between Titusville and Malabar. This area provided the best of both worlds to folks looking for a place to call their own—fertile land and water access. Melbourne and its sister, Eau Gallie, grew up side-by-side, each on either side of the Indian River. They remained as individual cities until voters decided in 1969 to consoli-

Wabasso, FL

date them into what is now the City of Melbourne. How did Melbourne get its name? An early settler, John Hector, came to North America from Melbourne, Australia and became the first postmaster. But he wanted a different name. Mrs. R.W. Goode is the one that suggested the name Melbourne and after drawing straws, Melbourne won.

If you are on the mainland in Melbourne and looking for dinner and music, try Matt's Casbah at 801 E. New Haven Ave. (321-574-1099). Matt's offers a bar, interesting seafood dishes, as well as beef and pork all prepared with creativity. They also offer live music on Wednesday, Friday and Saturday. The Mainstreet Pub, just down the street from Matt's at 705 E. New Haven Ave. (321-723-7811) has a full bar and a very affordable menu. They, too, offer music on Friday and Saturday nights with a live D.J. Walk off your meal by checking out the Christmas Cottage, Coins and Curiosities, Get Fired Out Pottery, the Giftique and the Indian River Soap Co. All of these great shops and additional galleries are also located on E. Haven Ave. Hotels are also located nearby to accommodate your guests that don't wish to stay aboard.

ADDITIONAL RESOURCES

- The official Web site of the City of Melbourne, FL
  www.melbourneflorida.org
- Melbourne's Main Street page
  www.downtownmelbourne.com
- Melbourne International Airport, www.mlbair.com

⛳ **NEARBY GOLF COURSES**
Crane Creek Reserve, 475 W. New Haven Ave.
Melbourne, FL 32910, 321-674-5716

⚕ **NEARBY MEDICAL FACILITIES**
Melbourne Medical Center, 15 E. Hibiscus Blvd.
Melbourne, FL 32901, 866-415-2419

Palm Bay, along the ICW—Mile 925

NAVIGATION: Use Chart 11472. Just past Mile 925, the channel slants a bit toward the west. You will enter a dredged channel with less than 6 feet of water on both sides in most places, so stay in the middle. The spoil islands are eroding on the north side. The one nearest North Rocky Point is a pelican rookery.

The spoil island between red daybeacons "18" and "20" is very small with a long sandy shoal spit to its west. With frequent bends, the ICW channel passes west of Grant Farm Island (Mile 930), the only inhabited spoil island in the Indian River, accessible only by boat. From here on, proceed cautiously, and be careful not to stray outside the channel, where the water may be only a few feet deep. You may have to strain to make out the markers, which seem to blend into the shoreline. Also be alert for uncharted oyster beds and trap markers on both sides of the ICW. The lower part of Grant Farm Island is a rookery used mainly by ibises and egrets.

Anchorage: Because of the beaches on their west sides, the two spoil islands accessed by heading west off the ICW just north of red daybeacon "20" at Mile 925 are favorite local anchoring spots. On less crowded weekdays, Waterway travelers often use this area for overnight anchorage. Depths are slightly less than shown on the chart. Shoals extend westward from these islands and are usually marked with pipes or stakes. This anchorage continues to be popular with cruisers in spring 2010.

■ MICCO TO WABASSO— MILE 933 TO MILE 943

Micco, on the ICW—Mile 933

Dockage: Several marinas welcome cruising boats in this area. At Mile 934 is Sebastian River Marina and Boatyard, where renovated wet and dry slips are offered for sale, and owners' amenities are expected to be available. There is space for transient boaters, and a "Hurricane Club" offers its members dry storage with secure anchors to the pavement.

Sebastian Inlet Marina, with floating docks, offers full service and fuel. There are two entrance channels to the marinas on the west side of Mile 937.5, one on the north side of the spoil island and one to its south. The northern entrance leading to Capt'n Butchers Bait, Ice and Fuel and to Fins Marina (formerly Sembler Marina) is reported to carry 6-foot depths from the ICW to the marinas. Fins Marina reports that it has 6-foot depths inside the marina.

The southern entrance leads to Capt. Hiram's Resort, Restaurant, Bars, Marina and Key West Inn, a popular spot with locals. Transients are welcome, and gas and diesel fuel are available.

Anchorage: Anchorage for shallow-draft vessels may be available off Capt. Hiram's Resort, with approximately 5-foot depths at mean low water. There are a number of permanently moored vessels here.

ICW, South to Wabasso— Mile 935 to Mile 943

NAVIGATION: Use Chart 11472. Sebastian Inlet, at Mile 936, is crossed by a fixed bridge with a 37-foot vertical clearance and is used by local boats to reach the ocean. Constant shoaling necessitates careful piloting. Cruisers should heed the charted cautionary note here: Swift cross-currents and the resulting shifting channel make navigation difficult without up-to-date local information. The channel from the ICW to Sebastian Inlet was last dredged in summer 2007. A 3,000-foot long by 100-foot wide and 9-foot deep channel provides access to the ocean, but as with all ocean inlets, a cautious approach is warranted, as shoaling is ever-present and continuous. The currents in this area can also affect travel on the ICW. Our cruising editor reports that this stretch had been dredged to 12

Looking west through Sebastian Inlet. Use local knowledge here. (Not to be used for navigation.) WATERWAY GUIDE PHOTOGRAPHY

feet at mean low water in early 2010, however, stay in the middle of the channel whenever possible.

Wabasso, on the ICW—Mile 943

NAVIGATION: Use Chart 11472. The dredged ICW channel runs straight for 10 miles to Wabasso. At Wabasso, 25 miles south of Melbourne, small wooded islands suddenly crowd the narrowing river and create a maze through which the channel twists and turns. Observe markers carefully. Expect

WATERWAY GUIDE PHOTOGRAPHY

sporadic spots of shoaling between the Sebastian area and Vero Beach. Now the heavily congested areas are temporarily behind you as you enter one of the Indian River's most attractive stretches. At Mile 943.3, the Wabasso fixed bridge, vertical clearance 65 feet, crosses the Waterway (although 64-foot vertical clearance has been observed on the tide boards recently). There is a new private basin associated with a residential community on the northwest side of the Wabasso Bridge. More and more developments and private homes are springing up along the stretch between Wabasso and Vero Beach, including new condominiums. Be on the lookout for manatees and other wildlife. Some of the islands in this area are rookeries for a variety of bird species. South of the Wabasso Bridge, on the west side of the ICW, are the

Sebastian, FL

Indian River, FL

SEBASTIAN AREA		Dockage				Supplies		Service				
		Largest Vessel Accommodated	VHF Channel Monitored	Approach / Dockside Depth (reported)	Transient Berths / Total Berths	Floating Docks	Groceries, Ice, Marine Supplies, Snacks	Gas / Diesel	Repairs: Hull, Engine, Propeller	Lift (tonnage), Crane, Rail	1=110V, 2=220V, B=Both, Max Amps	Laundry, Pool, Showers	Pump-Out Station	Nearby: Grocery Store, Motel, Restaurant
1. SEBASTIAN RIVER MARINA & BOATYARD 934 📶	772-664-3029	100	16/68	4/70	6/6		GD		HEP	L40	B/50	S	P	GMR
2. Sebastian Inlet Marina 934.3 📶	772-664-8500	45	16	4/250	5/5	F	GD	IMS	E	L16	B/50	S	P	GMR
3. Capt'n Butchers Marina 937.2	772-589-2552	60	16	2/25	5/5		GD	IS			B/50	L		MR
4. Fins Marina 937.5	772-589-4843	80	16	10/100	6/6		GD	I			B/50	S	P	GMR
5. Capt. Hiram's Resort 937.7 📶	772-589-4345	50	16	14/46	5/5		GD	IS			B/50	LPS	P	GMR

Corresponding chart(s) not to be used for navigation. 🖥 Internet Access 📶 Wireless Internet Access

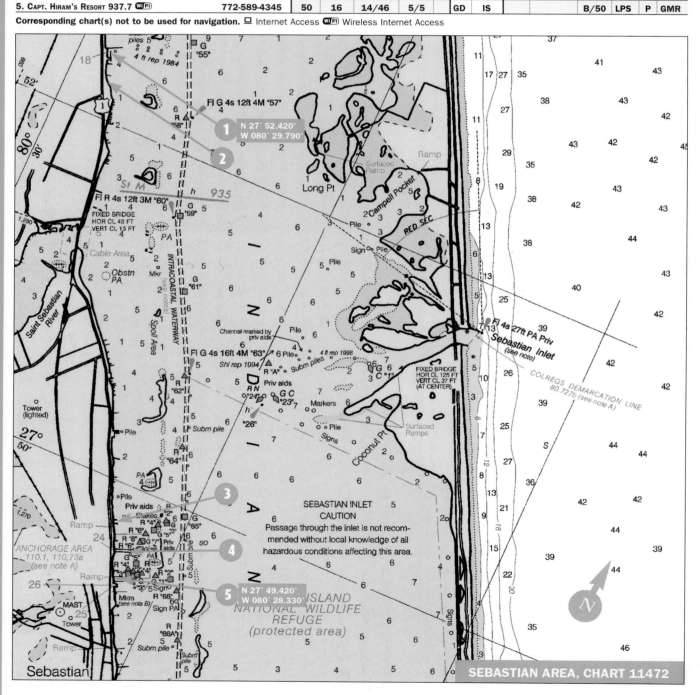

SEBASTIAN AREA, CHART 11472

Vero Beach, FL

Vero Beach, FL

VERO BEACH	Largest Vessel Accommodated	VHF Channel Monitored	Transient Berths / Total Berths	Approach / Dockside Depth (reported)	Floating Docks	Gas / Diesel	Groceries, Ice, Marine Supplies, Snacks	Repairs: Hull, Engine, Propeller	Lift (tonnage), Crane, Rail	1=110V, 2=220V, B=Both, Max Amps	Laundry, Pool, Showers	Pump-Out Station	Nearby: Grocery Store, Motel, Restaurant
			Dockage			**Supplies**			**Service**				
1. LOGGERHEAD CLUB & MARINA—VERO BEACH 948.5 **WiFi** 772-770-4470	75	16	8/124	6/6		GD	IMS			B/50	LPS	P	GMR
2. VERO BEACH CITY MARINA 952 ⌨ **WiFi** 772-231-2819	118	16/66	18/88	8/10		GD	IMS	HEP		B/50	LS	P	GMR
3. Vero Marine Center Inc. 952 772-562-7922	30	16	/49	3/3		M	E	L3	1/30	S		R	

Corresponding chart(s) not to be used for navigation. ⌨ Internet Access **WiFi** Wireless Internet Access

VERO BEACH AREA, CHART 11472

Looking northeast over Vero Beach basin. (Not to be used for navigation.) WATERWAY GUIDE PHOTOGRAPHY

docks of the Environmental Learning Center. Jones Fruit Dock, at Mile 945.7, is a vestige of old Florida. Be sure to slow down when passing it, especially if any smaller boats are tied along the face dock.

Dockage: At Mile 948.5, north of Vero Beach, on the west side of the Waterway, a charted, marked channel leads to the docks of Loggerhead Club and Marina (formerly Grand Harbor Marina), an elaborate development with condominiums, golf, tennis and handsome waterfront homes. Check entrance depths with the marina; deeper-draft boats may have some difficulty with the dredged channel at times.

Anchorage: Shallower-drafted boats, such as catamarans, have been observed at anchor behind the spoil island just south of Pine Island near Mile 946.4. The entrance to this anchorage is reported to be between that spoil island and flashing red "112." After proceeding in a northwesterly direction, anchor between the spoil island and Hole in the Wall Island. Charted depths are only 3 to 4 feet in this area.

■ VERO BEACH—MILE 952

Just past some sizable islands, you will see Vero Beach (Mile 952), a boating center and stopover with a variety of facilities on both sides of the Indian River, above and below the Vero Beach Bridge (state Route 60, Mile 951.9, 65-foot fixed vertical clearance). This is the beginning of the more densely populated areas of Florida, and the number of boats increases accordingly. Keep well inside the marked channel when passing through the bridge, and maintain a firm hand on the helm, as winds and current can be strong here.

VERO BEACH/BARBER BRIDGE (SR 60) Mile 951.9

WATERWAY GUIDE PHOTOGRAPHY

QUICK FACT:

PELICAN ISLAND, EAST OF THE ICW

North of Wabasso and to the east of the ICW sits Pelican Island. In 1903, President Theodore Roosevelt set aside this three-acre island as a bird sanctuary. At one time, the demand for plumes in ladies' hats had so escalated the hunting of birds nesting here that their survival was uncertain. Today, Pelican Island, the first national wildlife refuge, continues to serve as a haven for ibises, egrets, double-crested cormorants, blue herons and brown pelicans. The Pelican Island National Wildlife Refuge extends from below Sebastian Inlet to just above the Wabasso Bridge at Mile 943. For information on visiting Pelican Island, contact the Merritt Island National Wildlife Refuge. Information is also posted on a sign off the ICW, north of marker "69." Check www.fws.gov/pelicanisland for more information on local access to Pelican Island.

A little more than a mile below the Vero Beach Bridge is another high-rise bridge, the Seventeenth Street Bridge, with a 65-foot fixed vertical clearance at Mile 953.2. Between the bridges on the west side is a power plant, which is a favorite spot for manatees to lounge. You must maintain a slow speed from November 15 through April 30, according to a posted sign, except when in the channel.

NAVIGATION: Use Chart 11472. **Use the Miami Harbor Entrance Tide Tables. For high tide, add 2 hours, 56 minutes; for low tide, add 3 hours 41 minutes.** There is shoaling into the channel between red daybeacons "128" and "130" north of Vero Beach. Red daybeacon "128A" has been placed to help guide mariners through this area. Shoaling from red daybeacon "136" to the Vero Beach Bridge occurs in several spots within the channel, reducing depths to 5 or 6 feet on the edges of the channel. Stay mid-channel to avoid these shoals. Just north of the Vero Beach (state Route 60) Bridge, markers to the east lead up the old ICW route past the city park to Vero Beach City Marina. Enter the harbor by turning between flashing green "139" and the bridge, and then go in parallel to the bridge until you have lined up the channel markers. Be mindful of the strong current, and compensate for the set. There is shoaling off of the mangrove island to the north at the entrance, so do not get too close to it while compensating for the effects of the current. Outside of the channel that leads into the marina and mooring field, you will encounter 4-foot depths or less.

As you continue south along the ICW and pass under the two bridges, stick to mid-channel as edges of the channel shoal quickly for a mile or so south of the bridges. From north of Vero Beach at red daybeacon "120" to green daybeacon "149," the Manatee Speed Zone is enforced year-round.

Dockage: Inexpensive and well-protected city-owned moorings are available in both the north and south basins, and Vero Beach City Marina is between the two mooring fields.

Only 37 of the 57 moorings are rentals, which can make it quite crowded in the busy season. Each mooring is assigned by the dockmaster of the Vero Beach City Marina (reservations recommended). Even if moorings are reserved, boaters may still have to share them; boats traveling together are encouraged to make arrangements to raft together. Otherwise, the first boat at a mooring is asked to put out fenders and accept whatever raft is assigned. Ashore at the municipal marina, showers are available. Trash disposal and use of the dinghy dock are complimentary for moored boats. Crews of moored boats enjoy the use of a comfortable lounge, laundry and picnic area. There is a free shuttle bus that runs Monday through Saturday, with new longer hours and improved service.

Vero Beach's popular north basin offers some tranquility. NO-WAKE signs are posted, improving comfort. Vero Beach City Marina, a little park-like area, offers transient dockage, gas and diesel fuel, a ship's store and boat repairs.

The marina has acquired adjacent property and now can offer additional slips at floating docks. They also offer an area for dry storage. A lengthy, but worthwhile, dinghy ride up peaceful Bethel Creek leads to a small shopping area with good stores and a deli. South of the Vero Beach Bridge, a marked, charted channel leads east to the Quail Valley River Club Marina, for members only.

Anchorage: Anchoring anywhere in Vero Beach had been illegal. However, since the passage of the 2009 legislation, the city can no longer prohibit anchoring, except within the designated mooring field. Unfortunately, most of the areas outside the channel and near the mangrove islands above and below Vero Beach are shallow, so you would likely not be able to anchor there.

GOIN' ASHORE:
VERO BEACH, FL

The area was first settled in the mid-1800s. The construction of Flagler's railroad in the late 1890s, helped the local fishermen and farmers get their products north to the East Coast. In the early 1900's, Drainage Districts were created to drain the wetlands and make them habitable. Citrus became a bumper crop, as well as cattle ranching and timber farming. The town of Vero itself was laid out, canals were dredged and a power plant was installed in 1918. The town continued to grow. Then a bridge was built to connect the island to the mainland in 1919 and the town decided to start attracting tourists, which it does to this day. Vero Beach started out as a part of Ft. Pierce, but in 1925, then representative Anthony Young proposed a bill that would create Indian County to have Vero Beach removed from the control of Ft. Pierce. His bill passed 23 to 9.

Vero Beach is a favorite with cruisers. Many who plan to leave, don't. Hence its nickname, "Velcro Beach." Its affluent ocean resort section is close to the ICW, but the city itself remains a couple of miles inland. More than just a resort town, Vero Beach processes much of the Indian River citrus crop before shipping it to points around the country. In Vero Beach proper, visitors enjoy stores and restaurants that rival those of the Gold Coast cities to the south. The Center for the Arts is within walking distance of the city marina and the Vero Beach Yacht Club.

A great many dining choices await you in Vero Beach. Shutters at the Disney Vero Beach Resort offers casual family dining for breakfast, lunch and dinner (9250 Island Grove Terrace, 772-234-2180). The Riverside Café (3341 Bridge Plaza Drive, 772-234-5550) has food, music and a Happy Hour 7 days a week and overlooks the Indian River Lagoon. Or dine at The Sea Grill at the Surf Club Hotel while gazing at the beachfront pool (4700 N. A1A, 772-231-1600).

Shells & Things (3119 Ocean Drive, 772-234-4790) sells "ocean inspired treasures," jewelry, gifts and things to make your boat or home beachy. For a little history on the local citrus industry from the days of the Spanish explorers through present day, try the Indian River Citrus Museum at the Heritage Center (772-770-2263). The McLarty Museum (13180 N. SR A1A, 772-589-2147) displays items salvaged from the Spanish Plate Fleet of 1715. And don't miss the McKee Botanical Gardens (350 US Highway 1, 772-794-0601) to view its collection of indigenous flora and fauna.

ADDITIONAL RESOURCES

 Vero Beach, **www.verobeach.com** or **www.covb.org**

 NEARBY GOLF COURSES
Quail Valley Golf Club, 2345 Highway A1A
Vero Beach, FL 32963, 772-492-2020

NEARBY MEDICAL FACILITIES
Indian River Medical Center, 1000 36th St.,
Vero Beach, FL 32960, 772-567-4311

Cruising Options

Boaters proceeding south will next encounter Fort Pierce. It has a number of marine facilities, and its deep ocean inlet provides access to run outside to points south or as a gateway east to the Bahamas Islands. ■

WATERWAY GUIDE advertising sponsors play a vital role in bringing you the most trusted and well-respected cruising guide in the country. Without our advertising sponsors, we simply couldn't produce the top-notch publication now resting in your hands. Next time you stop in for a peaceful night's rest, let them know where you found them—WATERWAY GUIDE, The Cruising Authority.

Fort Pierce to St. Lucie River

CHARTS 11428, 11472, 11474, 11475

Once you pass Vero Beach, you are positioned midway between the upper and lower reaches of the Indian River. As the river widens, the dredged Intracoastal Waterway (ICW) channel begins to straighten out for the 13 miles south to Fort Pierce. The project depth along this stretch is 12 feet, but the actual controlling depth is 8 feet or less.

Some of the spoil islands scattered along this stretch are blanketed in the spring by nesting pelicans, cormorants, herons and egrets. Enjoy watching them, but do not disturb the nests. In winter, the area from the Vero Beach Bridge south to the high-rise 17th Street Bridge becomes a protected area for manatees. They like the warm water discharged by the neighboring power plant. You will see the plant's three stacks near the bridge on the west side. You can also keep a lookout for manatees farther south at the southern Fort Pierce Bridge; this is another favorite lounging area for the gentle creatures—nature's couch potatoes.

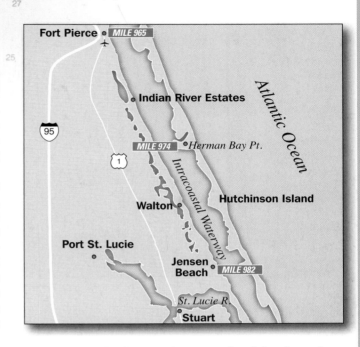

FORT PIERCE—MILE 965

NAVIGATION: Use Chart 11472. **Use the Miami Harbor Entrance Tide Tables. For high tide, add 49 minutes; for low tide add 1 hour, 1 minute.** From Vero Beach at Mile 952 to Fort Pierce at Mile 965, the ICW continues south along the Indian River. In Vero Beach, shoaling exists in spots from flashing green "139" to red daybeacon "142," and from green daybeacon "149" to flashing green "153," reducing water depths to 5 or 6 feet along the edges of the channel. Watch the depth sounder, and stay in the middle of the channel to avoid shallow water and spoil banks outside the channel. There is also shoaling in spots from flashing green "157" to green daybeacon "165," with depths of less than 8 feet.

From green daybeacon "155" to green daybeacon "173," the Manatee Speed Zone varies from seasonal to year-round. The zones are posted on the markers. The stretch past Harbor Branch at Mile 960 is a strictly enforced Idle Speed/No-Wake Zone.

At Mile 964.8, the North Bridge at Fort Pierce (bascule, 26-foot closed vertical clearance) opens on signal. A half-mile south of Taylor Creek (Mile 965.1) is the intersection of the Intracoastal Waterway (ICW) and Fort Pierce Inlet. Just beyond the intersection, at Mile 965.8, is the South Bridge at Fort Pierce (65-foot fixed vertical clearance, state Route A1A). Watch for shoaling between red daybeacon "184" and red daybeacon "186" on the eastern edge of the channel between the North Bridge and the inlet. Use caution, and follow the aids to navigation closely in this area.

There is also shoaling on the west side of the channel just to the north of the South Bridge at the edge of the turning basin where our cruising editor found 7 feet at mean low water in January 2010.

Use the Miami Harbor Entrance Tide Tables. For high tide, subtract 31 minutes; for low tide, subtract 18 minutes. The Fort Pierce Inlet is wide and deep with two stone jetties, an inner channel (30-foot depths) and a turning basin (28-foot depths). The channel is marked with ranges and buoys (both lighted and unlighted). Tidal currents in the inlet are strong, averaging 3 to 4 knots. Where the inlet channel crosses the ICW down to the Fort Pierce South Bridge (Mile 965.8), strong crosscurrents exist with a set to southward on the flood and northward on the ebb.

Note: Tidal ranges are 3 feet at the jetties and 1.5 feet in the Indian River near the city marina. In the entrance channel, the large shallow area inside the north jetty is a popular weekend hangout for local boaters. In the area of Peter Cobb Bridge (South Bridge, Mile 965.8), the Idle-Speed/No-Wake Manatee Zone is poorly marked but strictly enforced.

Many cruising boats make Fort Pierce Inlet their exit or entry port for an outside run. Deep-sea fishing is a big attraction here because of the safe, deep inlet and its proximity to the Gulf Stream.

Dockage: Just north of the Fort Pierce North Bridge, on the west side, is Riverside Marina and Boat Works, a large, mainly do-it-yourself yard and dry storage area with some transient dockage available—call ahead.

Immediately south of the Fort Pierce North Bridge is Taylor Creek. This well-marked creek is the home of

Fort Pierce, FL

Looking west over Fort Pierce Inlet. (Not to be used for navigation.) South Florida Water Management District

Harbortown Marina-Ft. Pierce, a large full-service marina and boatyard. The marina basin and entrance has been dredged, but call ahead to check depths if you have a deep-draft boat. Dinghy dockage is available for a fee. Offering a warm welcome to transients, Harbortown has a jetty-protected harbor that eliminates currents. There is also a pool and a good restaurant on the property. Also located on Taylor Creek is Cracker Boy Boat Works, with a do-it-yourself repair yard.

South of the South Bridge (65-foot fixed vertical clearance) is Fort Pierce City Marina's dredged marked entrance channel, which has been relocated to the north very close to the bridge. Older charts show the former entrance, which is farther south, but is now shoaled in. Transient dockage is available in the rebuilt inner basin with 137 slips. Call the City Marina on VHF Channel 16 for entrance channel information and docking instructions. It has two fueling areas, one that lies just inside the basin on the south side with both diesel and gas, and one on the next T-head to the west, for diesel fuel only. The fuel docks are located out of the current.

Every Saturday, year-round, a farmer's market at the improved waterfront park adjacent to the marina features fresh produce, baked goods, arts and crafts and live entertainment. Our cruising editor claims it is the best he has seen. The nearby downtown area's library, restaurants and shops are within walking distance. The popularity of this downtown area and its marina continues to expand with numerous fishing tournaments throughout the year, a variety of festivals and a synchronized music and light show at Christmas and between Memorial Day and July Fourth.

Anchorage: Previously, boaters were limited to 96 hours of continuous anchorage anywhere in the city of Fort Pierce and 14 days in St. Lucie County. Again, those restrictions are no longer valid with the passage of Florida Statute 327.02 in 2009. There is an anchorage between the Ft. Pierce North Bridge and the Taylor Creek channel, to the west of the ICW channel off Harbortown Marina, although depths are reported to be less than the charted 8 feet. Some boats also anchor on the north side of the commercial basin, where there are 10- to 20-foot depths, although this is not recommended.

There are two anchorage areas on the east side of the ICW south of the South Bridge at Fort Pierce. The first is just to the south of green daybeacon "9" off Causeway Island in the privately marked entrance channel to Faber Cove. This channel branches off the ICW at Mile 967, near red daybeacon "188." The shallowest place in this channel is at the entry where the chart shows 7-foot depths, but our cruising editor reported 5-foot depths here. The spoil island at red daybeacon "2" on the south side of the privately marked channel was reduced to a broad shoal during hurricanes of the past few years.

If the anchorage area south of green daybeacon "9" is crowded, you may want to sound around the edges with the dinghy first, because the boundary of deep water is different than shown on the chart. Causeway Island has been developed as a condominium project with its own enclosed boat basin, and the area is now not as attractive for anchoring as it once was. The second anchorage is in Faber Cove. Follow the channel markers east toward Thumb Point. Green daybeacon "15" marks the entrance to the cove, but you may have trouble crossing the charted shoal which now reaches across the entire channel at green daybeacon "13." Faber Cove is reported to have shoaled to around 3.5 feet in some areas.

DISCOVER Harbortown Marina

WHITICAR
MARINE SERVICES NORTH
772.460.0660

RESTAURANT

RETAIL SHOPS

BOATYARD

HARBORTOWN MARINA-FORT PIERCE
INDIAN RIVER AND TAYLOR CREEK, OFF ICW

1936 Harbortown Drive, Fort Pierce, FL 34946
P 772-466-7300, 772-466-0947
F 772-466-0962
www.harbortownmarina-fortpierce.com
dockmaster@harbortownmarina-fortpierce.com

NEARBY

TRANSPORTATION: On-site car rentals, courtesy bicycles
AIRPORT: St. Lucie International, 2 miles
PHARMACY: CVS across street
MEDICAL: Emergency Room, 5 miles; AED on-site
VETERINARIAN: Numerous vets within 2-5 miles
GOLF: Two 18-hole courses within 5 miles
TENNIS: 3 public courts within 2-5 miles
NOTEWORTHY: Mangrove Island protects marina

APPROACH & DOCKING

Harbortown Marina-Fort Pierce is located at mile marker 965, west of ICW red "184" at the confluence of Taylor Creek with the Indian River, and directly in from Fort Pierce Inlet (no bridges). Taylor Creek joins the ICW perpendicularly from the west at red "184," and our main transient and fuel docks are on Taylor Creek.

WHAT TO EXPECT...

DOCKAGE RATE: $2.00/ft./night; $12/ft./annually
CREDIT CARDS: MC, Visa, Amex, Discover
HOURS: 7:00am-7:00pm (Call ahead for after-hour accommondations)
TRANSIENT/TOTAL SLIPS: 40/320
VHF MONITOR/WORKING: 16/68
DEPTH MLW: Controlling depth 9 feet
TIDE RANGE: 1.5 feet
LOA MAX: 160 feet
DOCKS: 8 fixed, 1 floating
ELECTRIC: 30/50/100-amp, single and 3-phase
FUEL: High- and low-speed Diesel, Gas
PUMP-OUT: Provided at Fuel Dock
HEADS/SHOWERS: Multiple units
LAUNDRY: Coin machines on-site

POOL/GRILLS: Heated Pool, Pavilion with grills
INTERNET/WIFI: Yachtspots Wi-Fi
CABLE: (13 Channels) provided at no charge
PET FRIENDLY: Pet walking areas, mitts provided
SHIPS STORE: Whiticar Marine Store, IRBW Store
MEETING FACILITIES: Outdoor Pavilion & Rest.
REPAIRS: Indian River Boatworks & Whiticar
LIFT/TONS: 50- and 150-ton lifts on-site
STORAGE: 320 wet slips, 150 dead storage
YACHT BROKERAGE: FL Coast Marine, Whiticar YS, Classic Yachts
RESTAURANT: Harbor Cove Waterfront on-site
GROCERIES: Publix across street
NEAREST TOWN: Located in Port of Fort Pierce

DESCRIPTION OF FACILITIES

CLEAN BOATYARD

The marina was carved from a huge spoil island, with the outer edge of the spoil, now grown in with mangroves, left as a protective barrier. Nine piers host more than 320 wet slips and alongside dockage ranging in size from 25 to 125 feet. Amenities include a boater's lounge, heated pool, waterfront restaurant, cable TV, Wi-Fi and laundry, along with a picnic pavilion, fish cleaning stations, a fuel dock and boatyard with 50- and 150-ton straddle lifts. BoatU.S. member discounts apply.

Causeway Island and Fort Pierce, FL

SKIPPER BOB PUBLICATIONS

FORT PIERCE AREA	Phone	Largest Vessel Accommodated	VHF Channel Monitored	Transient Berths / Total Berths	Approach / Dockside Depth (reported)	Floating Docks	Gas / Diesel	Groceries, Ice, Marine Supplies, Snacks	Repairs: Hull, Engine, Propeller	Lift (tonnage), Crane, Rail	1=110v, 2=220V, B=Both, Max Amps	Laundry, Pool, Showers	Pump-Out Station	Nearby: Grocery Store, Motel, Restaurant
				Dockage			**Supplies**		**Service**					
1. Pelican Yacht Club 1 E of 965.6 ☐ WiFi	772-464-2700	95	16	/92	6/6		GD	GIMS			B/50	LPS	P	GMR
2. Ft. Pierce Inlet Marina .8 E of 965.6	772-464-8451	70		/42	7/7						B/50	LS	P	GMR
3. RIVERSIDE MARINA 964.1 ☐ WiFi	**772-464-5720**	100	16	5/70	6/6			M	HEP	L70	B/50	S	P	GMR
4. HARBORTOWN MARINA-FORT PIERCE 965 ☐ WiFi	**772-466-7300**	145	16/68	40/320	10/6		GD	IMS	HEP	L150,C	B/100	LPS	P	GMR
5. Cracker Boy Boat Works 965.1	772-465-7031		16		8/7			M	HEP	L70,C	B/50	S		GMR
6. Taylor Creek Marina 965.1	772-465-2663	40	68	5/600	8/3	F	G	IMS	HEP	L	1/30			GR
7. Ft. Pierce City Marina 966.5 ☐ WiFi	772-464-1245	80	16/09	15/182	7/7		GD	GIMS			B/50	LS	P	GMR
8. Harbour Isle Marina .8 E of 966.2	772-461-9049	100	16/69	10/63	8/8	F					B/100		P	GMR

Corresponding chart(s) not to be used for navigation. ☐ Internet Access WiFi Wireless Internet Access

GOIN' ASHORE: FORT PIERCE, FL

Founded as a military base during the Seminole War, Fort Pierce today is the center of the Indian River citrus industry. During World War II, its wide, gently sloping beaches provided the perfect grounds for U.S. servicemen training for amphibious assaults. Today, the beaches are still sometimes used for training Navy SEALS, but they mostly attract vacationers intent on relaxing. Within the city limits, visitors can wander through the Savannas, a large wilderness recreation project. Just north of the Fort Pierce Inlet, swimming, surfing and picnicking draw tourists and locals alike to the state recreation area.

Fort Pierce has several notable attractions. The Manatee Observation and Education Center (480 N. Indian River Drive, 772-466-1600, ext. 3333) features hands-on exhibits and boat tours to explore the manatees, Florida's "Gentle Giants," and other sea creatures such as dolphins, pelicans and terns. The area visitors center is next to the Manatee Center. The Navy SEAL Museum (3300 N. Highway A1A, 772-595-5845) illustrates the training and missions of the Navy frogmen. The St. Lucie County Marine Center (420 Seaway Drive, 772-462-3474) provides a portal to the underwater world of the Indian River Lagoon, which extends 156 miles from Ponce de Leon Inlet to Jupiter. This diverse estuary is home to more than 3,000 species of organisms.

For a tropical dining experience with a waterfront view, the Original Tiki Bar and Restaurant (772-461-0880), a local favorite at the Fort Pierce City Marina, offers fresh seafood, full bar service and live music on weekends. Ian's Tropical Grill (1205 N.E. Dixie Highway, 772-334-4563) has upscale casual dining and great seafood. Downtown services, such as the public library, the post office, banks, a general store, a deli, cafés, a bakery and art galleries, are near the City Marina. Publix and Winn Dixie Supermarkets and West Marine are a short bus ride away.

ADDITIONAL RESOURCES

■ City of Fort Pierce, 772-460-2200,
www.cityoffortpierce.com

⚑ NEARBY GOLF COURSES
Indian Hills Golf Course, 1600 S. Third St., Fort Pierce, FL 34950, 772-461-9620

⚕ NEARBY MEDICAL FACILITIES
Lawnwood Regional Medical Center & Heart Institute 1700 S. 23rd St., Fort Pierce, FL 34950, 772-461-4000

Hutchinson Island, Along the ICW

NAVIGATION: Use Chart 11472. Hutchinson Island stretches 22 miles between Fort Pierce Inlet and St. Lucie Inlet, on the ocean (east) side of the Waterway. Shoaling to 8 feet or less may occur along this stretch, first on both sides of green daybeacon "189" in the channel, and at about Mile 973.5, where private markers to Big Mud Creek head off to the east. (Do not mistake private green daybeacon "1," in shallow water up Big Mud Creek, for an ICW marker.) Shoaling is extending intermittently from red daybeacon "198" to the area past the overhead power cables (90-foot authorized overhead clearance at main channel) near green daybeacon "205." (The shallowest depth reported by our cruising editor was around 6.5 feet at red daybeacon "200," red daybeacon "206" and green daybeacon "207.") Other chronic shoal

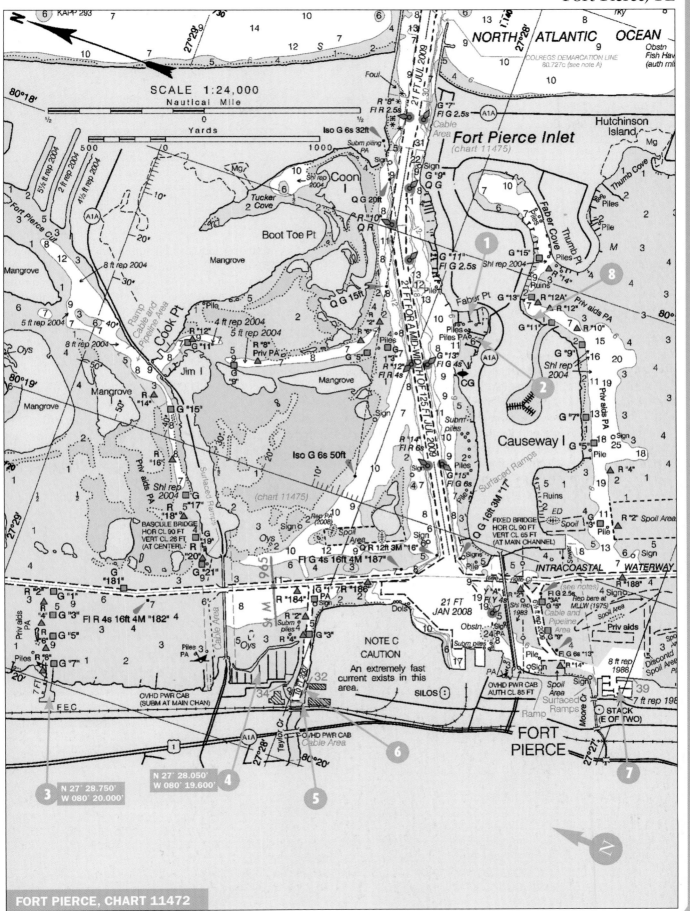

NORTH ATLANTIC OCEAN

Fort Pierce Inlet
(chart 11475)

Hutchinson Island

Thumb Cove

Faber Cove

Coon I

Tucker Cove

Boot Toe Pt

Mangrove

Causeway I

Cook Pt

Jim I

Mangrove

Mangrove

Oys

Mangrove

BASCULE BRIDGE
HOR CL 90 FT
VERT CL 26 FT
(AT CENTER)

FIXED BRIDGE
HOR CL 90 FT
VERT CL 65 FT
(AT MAIN CHANNEL)

INTRACOASTAL WATERWAY

Oys

Oys

NOTE C
CAUTION
An extremely fast
current exists in this
area.

SILOS

OVHD PWR CAB
(SUBM AT MAIN CHAN)

FEC

OVHD PWR CAB
Cable Area

OVHD PWR CAB
AUTH CL 85 FT

Spoil
Area

Surfaced
Ramps

STACK
(E OF TWO)

FORT
PIERCE

N 27° 28.750'
W 080° 20.000'

N 27° 28.050'
W 080° 19.600'

SCALE 1:24,000
Nautical Mile

Yards

FORT PIERCE, CHART 11472

Hutchinson Island, Jensen Beach, FL

HUTCHINSON ISLAND, JENSEN BEACH		Largest Vessel Accommodated	VHF Channel Monitored	Approach / Dockside Depth (reported)	Transient Berths / Total Berths	Floating Docks	Groceries, Ice, Marine Supplies, Snacks	Gas / Diesel	Repairs: Hull, Engine, Propeller	Lift (tonnage), Crane, Rail	1=110V, 2=220V, B=Both, Max Amps	Laundry, Pool, Showers	Pump-Out Station	Nearby: Grocery Store, Motel, Restaurant
		Dockage					**Supplies**				**Service**			
1. Nettles Island Marina 979.5 ☐ WiFi	772-229-2811	100	16	10/65	8/9		GD	GIMS	EP		B/100	LS	P	GMR
2. Conchy Joe's Seafood Restaurant 981.1	772-334-1130	25		/5	2.5/2.5									GMR
3. Sun Dance Marina North 982.2	772-334-1416	45	16/10	8/10	8/4	F	G	GIM	HEP	L8	1/30			GMR
4. Four Fish Marina & Inn	772-334-0936	90	16	15/35	8/5	F	GD	GIMS	HEP	L50	B/50		P	GMR
5. HUTCHINSON ISLAND MARRIOTT BEACH RSRT/MAR 985 ☐ WiFi	772-225-3700	125	16/10	20/77	7/6		GD	GIMS			B/50	LPS	P	MR

Corresponding chart(s) not to be used for navigation. ☐ Internet Access WiFi Wireless Internet Access

spots are near the Jensen Beach Bridge and just past the ICW crossing of the St. Lucie River at the "Crossroads." (See the "St. Lucie Inlet to Palm Beach" chapter for details.)

Nearby, at Mile 975, the St. Lucie Power Plant stands on Herman Bay Point at Big Mud Creek, on the east side of the Indian River. Here, several high-level (90-foot authorized vertical clearance at channel crossing) cables cross to the mainland. Four miles farther on, on the east side at Mile 979, you should spot Nettles Island (the skinny part of the island is at Mile 977), with a trailer and marina complex built around canals. The charted depth off the ICW here is 5 to 6 feet with shallow, unmarked spoil banks.

Visitors can reach Hutchinson Island via three long causeways, which connect the mainland to the beaches.

The first is the 65-foot fixed South Bridge at Fort Pierce (Mile 965.8), and farther south is the 65-foot fixed Jensen Beach Causeway at Mile 981.4. The third route to the beaches on Hutchinson Island is the 65-foot vertical clearance Sewalls Point Bridge. A large pier, a park, a picnic area and a playground lie on the northwest side of the Jensen Beach Causeway. Currents along this run will be affected by whichever inlet is nearer—Fort Pierce Inlet to the north or St. Lucie Inlet to the south.

Dockage: Nettles Island Marina is located on the east side of Nettles Island. Its entrance channel leads easterly from the ICW at Mile 979.2 between flashing red "214" and green daybeacon "215" and is marked by private green daybeacon "1."

HUTCHINSON ISLAND, JENSEN BEACH, CHART 11472

■ JENSEN BEACH TO ST. LUCIE INLET

Below Fort Pierce, the Indian River is deceptively wide; you will see many birds walking along the shoals outside of the channel. The ICW route, which follows the deep natural channel, continues to narrow here, so be sure to keep markers lined up ahead and astern.

Dockage: Around the Jensen Beach Causeway, the first of the many marine facilities in and around Stuart start to appear. Thatched-roof Conchy Joe's Seafood Restaurant is located just north of the Jensen Beach Causeway on the west side of the ICW. Call for dockage availability for dinghies and boats drawing less than two feet (dockage is reserved for dining patrons). Follow the well-marked channel carefully; the bottom is soft. Sundance Marina North, just south of the bridge on the mainland, offers floating docks and boat repairs.

At Mile 982.8 is the Four Fish Marina and Inn, situated off a marked channel on the west side of the ICW. Four Fish has a 50-ton lift and marine repairs. Outrigger Harbor Marina's marked channel is just before red daybeacon "224." The marina has a limited number of transient slips, fuel and an on-site restaurant, the Dolphin Bar and Shrimp House, overlooking the ICW.

Located to the east of the ICW on Hutchinson Island, at Mile 985.0 just past the Sewalls Point Bridge, the Hutchinson Island Marriott Beach Resort and Marina offers short- and long-term transient dockage, gas and diesel fuel, a laundry, a pool and restrooms/showers, along with full use of the resort facilities and a golf course.

Anchorage: From about Mile 981 to Mile 982, north and south of the Jensen Beach Causeway, you will find two good, though unprotected, anchorages on the west side of the ICW. Pick your anchorage according to the wind. Tidal range here is only a foot. The area of deep water in the north anchorage is fairly small as there are less than the charted depths. There is a waterfront park area, as well as Conchy Joe's Seafood Restaurant, with a dinghy dock, adjacent on the northwest side of the Jensen Beach Causeway. You will find depths of at least 7 feet in the south anchorage, but it is often crowded with boats, some of which stay permanently. Keep clear of the charted pipeline and cable areas on both sides of the bridge. To reach the south anchorage, make your turn westward midway between red daybeacon "220" and green daybeacon "221," and then double back toward the Jensen Beach Causeway. Protection is good here only in westerly to northwesterly winds and gets quite bumpy in winds from the south.

ICW: Mile 981 to Mile 988

Martin County begins just south of Mile 980. Except for hospitals, zoning restrictions allow buildings a maximum of just four stories. Local captains returning from the Bahamas are said to locate St. Lucie Inlet by merely aiming midway between the high-rise buildings of St. Lucie County to the north and the high-rises of Palm Beach County to the south.

Manatee Pocket, FL

MANATEE POCKET (MILES FROM ICW MILE 987.8)		Largest Vessel Accommodated	VHF Channel Monitored	Dockage				Supplies			Service					
				Transient Berths / Total Berths	Approach / Dockside Depth (reported)	Floating Docks	Gas / Diesel	Groceries, Ice, Marine Supplies, Snacks	Repairs: Hull, Engine, Propeller	Lift (tonnage), Crane, Rail	1=110v, 2=220v, B=Both, Max Amps	Laundry, Pool, Showers	Pump-Out Station	Nearby: Grocery Store, Motel, Restaurant
1. Whiticar Boat Works Inc. 1.5	772-287-2883	70	09	/15	6/6				M	HEP	L50	B/50			GMR
2. SAILFISH MARINA OF STUART .8 🖳	**772-283-1122**	**95**	**16**	**4/35**	**9/8**		**GD**	**IMS**	**HEP**	**L50**	**B/50**	**LS**	**P**	
3. Finest Kind Marina 1	772-223-4110	85	16/73	2/16	9/7	F	GD	GIMS			B/50	S		R
4. MARINER CAY MARINA 1.1	**772-287-2900**	**50**	**16**	**5/48**	**6/6**		**GD**	**I**			**B/50**	**LPS**	**P**	
5. PIRATE'S COVE RESORT & MARINA 1.8 🖳	**772-223-9216**	**90**	**68**	**10/20**	**7/6**		**GD**	**IMS**			**B/50**	**LPS**	**P**	**GMR**
6. THE HINCKLEY YACHT SERVICES 1.8 🖳📶	**772-287-0923**	**115**	**16/09**	**/80**	**7/7**			**M**	**HEP**	**L150**	**B/200**	**S**	**P**	**GMR**
7. Stuart Corinthian Yacht Club 1.9	772-221-1900	45		2/23	8/5						B/50	S		R
8. A.J. Boatyard 2.2	772-286-5339	60		/13	/6	F		M	P	L	B/50	S		GMR
9. Manatee Marina 2.2	772-288-2888	53	16	4/50	7/5		GD	IMS	HEP	L16	B/50			GMR
10. FINZ WATERFRONT GRILL	**772-283-1929**	DOCK & DINE												

Corresponding chart(s) not to be used for navigation. 🖳 Internet Access 📶 Wireless Internet Access

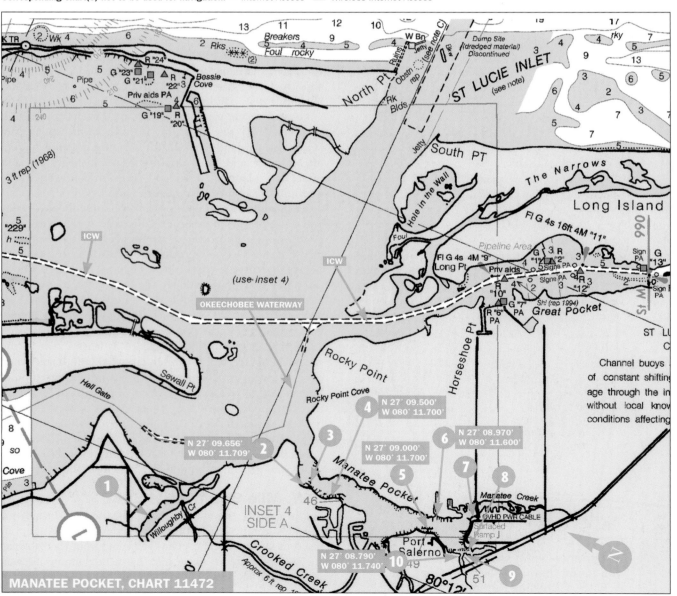

MANATEE POCKET, CHART 11472

The Crossroads: At the St. Lucie Inlet, Mile 988, the intersection of the ICW and the St. Lucie River (Mile Zero on the Okeechobee Waterway route to Florida's West Coast) is locally referred to as the Crossroads. Mariners should be on the alert for shoaling in this constantly shifting area. Markers in the inlet are uncharted, as they are constantly moved according to shoaling. Markers can be particularly confusing where the Waterways intersect. Remember, treat buoys marking the St. Lucie River entrance as red-right-returning. In the ICW, red-right-returning is southbound on Florida's east coast down to the Keys.

The St. Lucie Inlet Crossroads—Mile 988

> ⚠ **THE FOLLOWING AREA REQUIRES SPECIAL ATTENTION DUE TO SHOALING OR CHANGES TO THE CHANNEL**

NAVIGATION: Use Chart 11472. When crossing the St. Lucie River on the ICW, be careful of crosscurrents that can result in westerly or easterly sets depending on flood or ebb tides. Allow for the crosscurrents when turning from the ICW into the St. Lucie River or vice versa.

The 16-foot-high flashing red "240" (ICW marker) at the Crossroads channel marks the beginning of the St. Lucie River and the Okeechobee Waterway westbound. Red daybeacon "2" and flashing green "3," about .3 miles south, mark the continuation of the ICW south. You will find them southerly past the white daybeacon on the west side of the ICW reading DANGER—SHOAL, which should be left well to starboard when southbound.

If turning west toward Stuart and the Okeechobee Waterway, flashing red buoy "2" and green can buoy "3," southwest of flashing red "240," are the first markers in the St. Lucie River. In winter 2010, shoaling to 5 feet at mean low water was found between a bar between these two markers, however a dredge was on scene and the minimum depths are now reported to be at least 8 feet at mean low water in May 2010. The nuns and cans have been moved to mark the deeper water. If heading east out the St Lucie Inlet at the crossroads, green daybeacon "17," to the east of the ICW, is the first marker you will encounter.

An invisible line at the St. Lucie River separates Florida's Treasure Coast from the Gold Coast. Here, you have a choice of routes: continue down the ICW to the resort areas of southern Florida; move outside via the St. Lucie Inlet and cruise down the Atlantic Ocean (faster, avoiding the ever-increasing number of Slow-Speed/Minimum-Wake manatee and boating safety zones and the numerous restricted bridges); or travel along the St. Lucie River and down the South Fork through the Okeechobee Waterway to Fort Myers and Florida's West Coast, if your draft is shallow enough to do so and you can pass under a 49-foot bridge. (See the "Okeechobee Waterway," Chapter 14, in this guide for more information, and check our Web site, www.waterwayguide.com, for the latest lake depths.)

Though protected by jetties and a detached breakwater, St. Lucie Inlet can be dangerous for small boats and inexperienced mariners. The inlet was dredged and re-marked in early 2009, and depths of 10 feet or greater are shown on the April 2009 survey, although this could change at any time. Seek local knowledge by calling one of the local towing service operators, a dockmaster at one of the marinas inside or the Coast Guard. The entrance buoys are not charted because of constant shifting of the channel. Currents typically run 3 to 4 knots through the inlet. For two hours after high and low tides, currents continue to flow. The easiest entrance is during slack water, when virtually no current exists. As with any ocean inlet on the east coast, a strong ebb tide against an easterly wind will produce high, closely spaced waves in the inlet, especially in shallow ones like St. Lucie.

> **END SPECIAL CAUTION AREA.**

Manatee Pocket, off the ICW

Although strictly considered a point along the Okeechobee Waterway, Manatee Pocket is little more than a half mile from the ICW and is often visited by cruisers traveling north and south on the Waterway. Considered an all-weather anchorage, it is a delightful boating area where you can usually find dockage. Except in a few spots near shore, depths are a uniform 5 to 6 feet, with a soft mud bottom. Take care that your anchor sets well in the mud. The most popular anchorage is in the bay between Mariner Cay Marina and Pirate's Cove Resort & Marina. A sign at the entrance to Manatee Pocket that alerts boaters that anchoring here is limited to 72 hours may still be in place. If anyone approaches you, make sure you have a copy of Florida Statute 327.02 on board. Remember, the entire Manatee Pocket is an Idle-Speed/No-Wake Zone, which also includes dinghies.

Port Salerno, a small town at the head of Manatee Pocket, features several restaurants, a post office, an auto-parts store and a grocery store. Included in the Pirate's Cove Resort & Marina complex just south of the anchorage are a restaurant and sportfishing charter boats. Farther on is Finz Waterfront Grill, providing dockage and shore power. Also within walking distance is a large West Marine store. Just beyond the Pirate's Cove Resort & Marina docks is a tiny waterfront pier distinguished by a sign that says MOORING LIMITED TO ONE HOUR. It can be used by dinghies from boats anchored in Manatee Pocket, or by craft up to about 40 feet if dinghies are not blocking the end of the pier. Walk up the pier, turn left and follow the street up to the traffic light at Dixie Highway. Within three blocks you will find the post office, a bank, restaurants, a barber shop, groceries and stores selling fishing gear and bait.

Manatee Pocket is also home to the Chapman School of Seamanship, which offers courses and programs for recreational boaters, along with its vocational offerings in the maritime field. Bargain hunters looking for a good used boat may want to check out Chapman's collection of 75 to 100 boats donated to the school. The Chapman Web site, www.chapman.org, contains course offerings and a list of the donated boats offered for sale, plus information about the new maritime library and maritime artifacts collection.

Dockage: Sailfish Marina of Stuart, the first marina on the right when entering Manatee Pocket, is the closest marina to the St. Lucie Inlet and offers transient dockage, gas and diesel fuel, a bait and tackle shop, fishing charters and a full-service boatyard. Farther in on the right, Mariner Cay Marina accepts transients and has gas and diesel fuel, a laundry, pool, restrooms/showers and pump-out service. Next is Pirate's Cove Resort & Marina, which offers transient space, gas and diesel fuel, shore power and pump-out service at its hotel and restaurant resort. Manatee Marina, farther down toward the end of Manatee

Pocket, also accepts transients and offers a full range of mechanical, electrical and hull repairs on-site. Hinckley Yacht Services, on the opposite side, offers repair service and a 150-ton lift.

■ ST. LUCIE RIVER

NAVIGATION: Use Chart 11428. **For Stuart, use the Miami Harbor Entrance Tide Tables. For high tide, add 2 hours, 13 minutes; for low tide, add 3 hours, 30 minutes.** From its intersection with the Atlantic ICW at Mile 987.8 and Mile Zero of the Okeechobee Waterway, the St. Lucie River heads westward before turning to the north for a few miles at Okeechobee Mile 0.5. Note the shoal area shown on the chart between the ICW and the St. Lucie River's Hell Gate (at flashing green "17"). The dredged channel splits these extensive shoals inside Sewalls Point (where tides, incidentally, run about an hour behind Stuart), so follow the markers carefully as you enter. Aids to navigation are often relocated, and additional ones established, to mark the best water—take time to observe all aids, and do not become confused if they do not exactly match your chart.

Tidal range is only about a foot, but the strong current bears watching, although it loses force as you proceed up the St. Lucie River. Dredging took place in the St. Lucie River near Manatee Pocket in early 2010. Be particularly alert for large wakes when traveling between the Crossroads area (where the St. Lucie River meets the ICW) and the entrance to Manatee Pocket. This short, but narrow, stretch is often crowded with powerboats speeding to or from the ocean via the St. Lucie Inlet. Deep water in the channel starts past Manatee Pocket.

Where the St. Lucie River opens up and the long finger of Sewalls Point stretches downstream on the east side, the high ground is heavily wooded, with estates, both large and small, along the landscaped terrain. Boats infrequently anchor on the southwest side of Sewalls Point, between Hell Gate and almost to the point. Depths hold close to the shore, but make sure that your anchor is set—currents tend to run swiftly here. The west side is equally attractive, residential and fronted by many private docks where property owners berth their vessels. Additional navigational aids, red daybeacons "6A" and "12A," were added within the last few years to better mark the shoaling along the natural channel, and are not shown on older charts.

Traveling upriver, green daybeacon "23" and flashing green "23A," just east of the Roosevelt Bridge (65-foot fixed vertical clearance), can be difficult to locate. Skippers should take special care to locate these markers before getting too close to the bridge.

Four bridges cross the St. Lucie River along the six miles between Manatee Pocket and downtown Stuart. First is the St. Lucie River Bridge (65-foot fixed vertical clearance) at Sewalls Point (the town), carrying state Road A1A. The channel runs just west of the highest point on the bridge. Four miles farther up the St. Lucie River, the remaining three bridges are clustered together within a distance of 800 feet: the Roosevelt Bridge (65-foot fixed vertical clearance); a railroad bascule bridge with a 7-foot closed vertical clearance; and the remaining half of the old Roosevelt bascule bridge with a 14-foot closed vertical clearance. The railroad bridge, just west of the Roosevelt Bridge, is normally open but closes automatically when a train approaches. The railroad bridge has a horizontal clearance (width) of only 50 feet, compared to the old Roosevelt Bridge's horizontal clearance of 80 feet. With little in the way of a turning basin prior to the old Roosevelt bascule bridge, and with marine traffic and currents running, passage through the two bridges can be tricky, especially from the wider Roosevelt to the narrower railroad bridge. Exercise care.

Dockage: Loggerhead Club & Marina (formerly Harborage Yacht Club and Marina) is open for business across the river from Stuart with 150 slips at floating docks. Slips are available for transients and long-term rentals. Amenities include a fuel dock, pump-out facilities, ships store, restrooms, a clubhouse, Captain's lounge, two pools and an on-site restaurant.

Anchorage: Just north of the St. Lucie River Bridge, in Hoggs Cove, protection is good from northerlies and easterlies. Watch the charted rocky shoal off Pisgah Hill, and set the anchor in 7 to 9 feet of water. If you plan an early morning start to the east, it is better to anchor here rather

Stuart, Palm City FL

ST. LUCIE RIVER–NORTH & SOUTH FORK		Largest Vessel Accommodated	VHF Channel Monitored	Dockage			Supplies		Service					
				Transient Berths / Total Berths	Approach / Dockside Depth (reported)	Floating Docks	Gas / Diesel	Groceries, Ice, Marine Supplies, Snacks	Repairs: Hull, Engine, Propeller	Lift (tonnage), Crane, Rail	1=110v, 2=220v, B=Both, Max Amps	Laundry, Pool, Showers	Pump-Out Station	Nearby: Grocery Store, Motel, Restaurant
1. St. Lucie Marine 7.0	772-692-2000	50		/20	6/5			IM	HP	L30	B/50	S	P	GMR
2. Loggerhead Club & Marina - Stuart 7.2 WiFi	772-692-4000	90	16	24/151	8/6		GD	GIS			B/100		P	GR
3. Sandpiper Marina WiFi	772-335-7875	100	16	6/61	8/8		GD	GIMS	HEP		B/50	LPS		MR
4. Harbor Inn & Marina 7.8	772-692-1200	65	16	1/79	10/8						B/50	P		MR
5. Waterway Marina 7.7	772-220-2185	65		/5				S			B/50	S	P	GMR
6. Allied Marine Group/Britt Point Marine 7.5 ☐	772-692-1122	130		/60	7/7			M	HEP	L60	B/50			R
7. Sunset Bay Marina & Anchorage 8 WiFi	772-283-9225	120	16	60/198		F	GD	GIMS			B/50	LS	P	R
8. Martin County Marina 9	772-221-8198	30	5	2/2	6/5	F	G	IM	HEP			LS		
9. Monterey Inn and Marina 9.6 WiFi	772-283-3500	40		6/12	6/5			I			B/50			MR
10. Riverwatch Marina 9.6	772-286-3456	80	16	4/28	6/5	F	GD	IMS	HEP	L60	B/50	S		GMR

Corresponding chart(s) not to be used for navigation. ☐ Internet Access WiFi Wireless Internet Access

than in Stuart past the Roosevelt Bridge. Here, you will have the sun in your eyes for a shorter time. The early sun can also make spotting aids to navigation difficult.

St. Lucie River, North Fork

A turn to the right, after passing through the old Roosevelt Bridge, takes you off the Okeechobee Waterway and up the North Fork of the St. Lucie River. This can be a very pleasant side trip if your cruising schedule allows you the time.

Dockage: Located on the North Fork of the St. Lucie River just inside Britt Point (due east of green daybeacon "5"), Waterway Marina welcomes transients with a wide variety of services aimed at providing a comfortable stay for its guests. Just to the north, Harbor Inn & Marina features a pool and The Deck Restaurant. In the same area is Britt Point Marina. A mile or so to the northwest, just beyond Greenridge Point, is the Club Med Sandpiper Resort, where cruisers are welcome.

Anchorage: A bit farther north is Kitching Cove, which provides a fine anchorage in 6 to 7 feet of water. At the north end of the anchorage, take a scenic dinghy trip to the headwaters of the river.

Stuart, on the St. Lucie River

From the Okeechobee Waterway, Stuart, tucked back along the St. Lucie River, is barely visible, yet it is as well-equipped as almost any port on the Atlantic coast, and contains a sizable winter boat colony. Marine facilities and shore activities are a vital part of the community, and protection is good.

Dockage: Before reaching the Palm City Bridge, Martin County Marina is visible on the starboard side. It has gasoline, but limited dockage. A channel marked by private daybeacons leads in from the Waterway.

Across from Palm City, just north of the Palm City Bridge (54-foot fixed vertical clearance), a marked channel leads into Riverwatch Marina, with 6-foot depths in the approach channel and 5-foot depths in the docking basin. Limited transient dockage is available for boats up to 50 feet. On both sides of the eastern end of the Palm City Bridge are the facilities of Bassett Boat Co. (also known as MarineMax), a dealer for Hatteras and Sea Ray. This is a full-service boatyard, but there are few slips for transient use unless they are being used in connection with service.

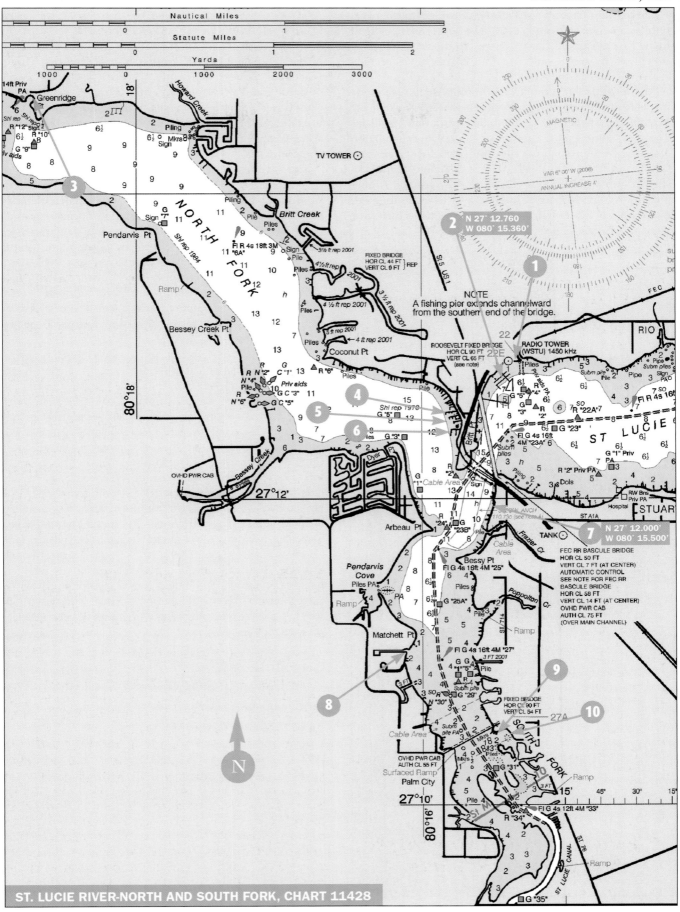

ST. LUCIE RIVER-NORTH AND SOUTH FORK, CHART 11428

Stuart, FL

Three miles beyond the Palm City Bridge and between red daybeacons "40" and "40A," the south fork of the St. Lucie River bears off the Waterway to the east. This is an exceptionally scenic side trip that is navigable for most cruising boats all the way to the Route 76 Bridge.

Anchorage: The popular Southpoint Anchorage mooring field in Stuart closed, but in early 2009, Sunset Bay Marina & Anchorage opened beautiful new facilities. There are somewhat fewer moorings available than before (70 or so). The remaining moorings have been relocated farther south. Facilities ashore are available to moored vessels, including dinghy docking, showers and limited parking. Other amenities include a cruisers lounge and grill area, and an on-site restaurant, Sailor's Return, provides hearty fare.

GOIN' ASHORE: **STUART, FL**

The countryside surrounding Stuart provides a little bit of everything for which Florida is noted: citrus, winter vegetables, flowers and cattle. The city itself acts as the business and distribution center for the area. As the Martin County seat, Stuart has most of the facilities found in an urban center, including Martin Memorial Hospital, which accepts emergency patients at its own dock (4-foot depths alongside).

The region's agricultural importance notwithstanding, the emphasis throughout the area has gradually shifted from farming to sportfishing. Although Stuart's claim to being the "Sailfish Capital of the World" is sometimes disputed by other Florida cities, no one would deny that both its outside and inside waters provide outstanding fishing. Charter boats sail daily out of Stuart, Manatee Pocket and other nearby ports. Stuart has gained further prominence as a center of custom sportfishing boatbuilding. Several yards still build fine wooden yachts. A visit to one of these facilities makes an interesting diversion, and the boats are magnificent.

Downtown Stuart's facelift and revitalization has been a boon for residents and tourists. The restored Lyric Theater (59 S.W. Flagler Ave., 772-286-7827) features plays and concerts, and once-abandoned city blocks have been transformed into gift shops, art galleries and trendy restaurants. The Barn Theatre (2400 S.E. Ocean Blvd., 772-287-4884) performs comedies and musicals year-round. The Courthouse Cultural Center (80 S.E. Ocean Blvd., 772-287-6676) sponsors galleries, juried shows and art festivals featuring local and international artists. The Stuart Heritage Museum (161 S.W. Flagler Ave., 772-220-4600) features exhibits and memorabilia of the history and culture of Stuart and Martin County. Some local favorites for dining include the Flagler Grill (47 S.W. Flagler Ave., 772-221-9517) for casual fare, and Arthur's Dockside, with food from 11 a.m. to 10 p.m. (11 p.m. on weekends) and entertainment at 9 p.m. (131 S.W. Flagler Ave., 772-219-3625), for seafood with waterfront views. The post office, the library, banks and other services are nearby.

■ ST. LUCIE CANAL

NAVIGATION: Use Chart 11428. The Okeechobee Waterway departs the South Fork of the St. Lucie River near this point and continues as the start of the St. Lucie Canal with the St. Lucie Lock at Mile 15 of the Okeechobee Waterway. Check for local information regarding the Okeechobee Waterway if you plan to proceed through any of the locks. During continuing severe drought conditions in 2008, the controlling navigational draft available for Okeechobee Route 1 was around 4 feet. However, in 2010, the lake levels provide channel depths across the lake of approximately 8.5 feet. Before planning a crossing, check current levels, which are available at www.waterwayguide. com. Route 2 was open in spring 2010, but the U.S. Army Corps of Engineers warned that those who take this route do so at their own risk. The water depths there are reported by our cruising editor to be 6 feet.

You can find navigation and lock schedule information at www.saj.usace.army.mil. Conditions can change, especially if tropical storms or hurricanes pass over Lake Okeechobee.

The canal carrying the Okeechobee Waterway up to the lake itself is deep and easy to traverse. You pass under the fixed 56-foot vertical clearance high-level bridge, Interstate 95 and the Florida Turnpike (Thomas B Manuel) Bridge with a 55-foot fixed vertical clearance, at approximately Mile 14. American Custom Yachts (772-221-9100), another large full-service boatyard and custom builder, is located on the south shore between the bridges. It has limited space for transients, and berths are exposed to the wakes of passing vessels. Its facilities have nearly doubled in size, but it is still more of a facility at which you would stop only if you needed repairs or other services.

St. Lucie Lock. (USACE)

St. Lucie Canal, FL

ST. LUCIE CANAL			Dockage				Supplies		Service				
		Largest Vessel Accommodated	VHF Channel Monitored	Transient Berths / Total Berths	Approach / Dockside Depth (reported)	Floating Docks	Gas / Diesel	Groceries, Ice, Marine Supplies, Snacks	Repairs: Hull, Engine, Propeller	Lift (tonnage), Crane, Rail	1=110V, 2=220V, B=Both, Max Amps	Laundry, Pool, Showers	Pump-Out Station	Nearby: Grocery Store, Motel, Restaurant
1. Riviera Yachts of the Americas Inc. 13.8	772-403-1060	85			7/7				HEP	L40	B/50			
2. American Custom Yachts Inc. 14.5	772-221-9100	126	16/68	/23	8/8		GD	MS	HEP	L150,C	B/100			
3. RIVER FOREST YACHTING CENTER 16	**772-287-4131**	150	16	10/28	10/9				HEP	L55	B/100	S	P	

Corresponding chart(s) not to be used for navigation. 🖥 Internet Access 📶 Wireless Internet Access

ST LUCIE CANAL, CHART 11428

Dockage: River Forest Yachting Center is located west of the St. Lucie Lock and offers transient dockage, boat repairs and a pump-out station. This facility specializes in storage with its massive climate-controlled indoor storage building for boats up to 60 feet, and its Hurricane Club that offers reserved storm storage ashore in either a wet or dry slip.

Cruising Options

WATERWAY GUIDE now returns the cruiser to the ICW for the trip south in the next chapter, "St. Lucie Inlet to Palm Beach." Those wishing to continue their journey on the Okeechobee Waterway should refer to the "Okeechobee Waterway" Chapter 14, which continues the cross-Florida journey from the St. Lucie Lock to Fort Myers. ■

WATERWAY GUIDE advertising sponsors play a vital role in bringing you the most trusted and well-respected cruising guide in the country. Without our advertising sponsors, we simply couldn't produce the top-notch publication now resting in your hands. Next time you stop in for a peaceful night's rest, let them know where you found them—WATERWAY GUIDE, The Cruising Authority.

QUICK FACT:

SHRIMPING ON THE ICW IS REWARDING AND FUN

Few cruisers take advantage of the Florida ICW's great gifts to man—shrimp. Florida law allows anyone with a fishing license and a dip net to harvest a five-gallon bucket of shrimp per day, which is a lot of shrimp. You can also use a cast net, but that takes a bit more practice. The average cruiser could master the dip net technique in fairly short order.

Timing and location are key to catching ICW shrimp. Beginning in early December, shrimp start running in the areas from Daytona Beach to the Sebastian Inlet. In Miami, one of the best shrimping periods is February. In fact, walk by the docks of the Miami Boat Show at the Marriott Hotel during the night, and you will likely see some of the exhibitors dipping nets into the fast-moving current. With all the amenities of cosmopolitan Miami at night, these folks choose to have fun catching their supper.

Not only do the shrimp move at night, but they are said to be thickest at around the time of the full moon. Water temperature may also play a role, the cooler the better.

Shrimpers set up lights on the docks to attract the shrimp, then scoop them into their nets. It is best to have work gloves to protect against their spiny shells, as the shrimp flip around trying to escape.

Shrimping is usually done at the dock, but there is no reason why the swim platform of an anchored vessel wouldn't make a good location, all else being equal. During peak periods, shrimpers can make their five-gallon limit (heads on) in just a few hours. ■

PDPHOTO.ORG

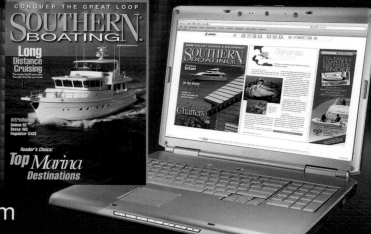

Florida's Lower East Coast

■ ST. LUCIE INLET TO PALM BEACH ■ LAKE WORTH TO POMPANO BEACH ■ FORT LAUDERDALE TO HALLANDALE
■ NORTH MIAMI, MIAMI BEACH ■ MIAMI TO KEY BISCAYNE

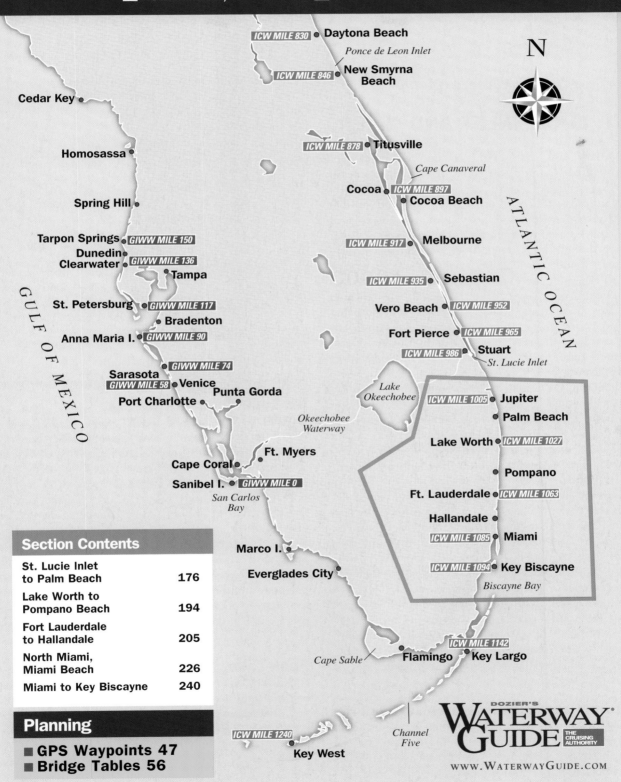

N

ICW MILE 830 Daytona Beach
Ponce de Leon Inlet
ICW MILE 846 New Smyrna Beach

Cedar Key

Homosassa

ICW MILE 878 Titusville
Cape Canaveral

Spring Hill

Cocoa *ICW MILE 897*
Cocoa Beach

Tarpon Springs *GIWW MILE 150*
Dunedin
Clearwater *GIWW MILE 136*
Tampa

ICW MILE 917 Melbourne

St. Petersburg *GIWW MILE 117*

ICW MILE 935 Sebastian

Bradenton

Vero Beach *ICW MILE 952*

Anna Maria I. *GIWW MILE 90*

Fort Pierce *ICW MILE 965*

GIWW MILE 74

ICW MILE 986 Stuart
St. Lucie Inlet

Sarasota
GIWW MILE 58 Venice
Punta Gorda
Port Charlotte

Lake Okeechobee

ICW MILE 1005 Jupiter
● Palm Beach

Okeechobee Waterway

Lake Worth ● *ICW MILE 1027*

Ft. Myers

● Pompano

Cape Coral
Sanibel I. *GIWW MILE 0*
San Carlos Bay

Ft. Lauderdale ● *ICW MILE 1063*

Hallandale ●

ICW MILE 1085 Miami

ICW MILE 1094 Key Biscayne

Marco I.

Everglades City

Biscayne Bay

G U L F   O F   M E X I C O

A T L A N T I C   O C E A N

Section Contents

Planning

■ **GPS Waypoints 47**
■ **Bridge Tables 56**

ICW MILE 1142
Cape Sable Flamingo ● Key Largo

ICW MILE 1240
Key West

Channel Five

DOZIER'S
WATERWAY GUIDE THE CRUISING AUTHORITY

WWW.WATERWAYGUIDE.COM

St. Lucie Inlet to Palm Beach

CHARTS 11428, 11466, 11472, 11474

■ ST. LUCIE INLET AND RIVER

NAVIGATION: Use Chart 11472. In the previous chapter see highlighted "Caution" for additional details on the St. Lucie Crossroads.

As you cross the St. Lucie Inlet, traveling on the Intracoastal Waterway (ICW), pay strict attention to your course, and keep a firm hand on the helm (and note, too, that even though the St. Lucie Inlet was dredged in early 2009, you should seek local knowledge before attempting to use it). The junction of the river, ICW and inlet creates strong, contrary currents. If yours is a lightly powered vessel, it is important to watch your track to avoid being swept off course by the tidal current—look behind you as well as ahead. Do not get confused by the buoys and daybeacons marking the St. Lucie Inlet, St. Lucie River and the ICW.

The center of the Crossroads is located just past flashing red "240" (an ICW marker—leave to starboard heading south on the ICW), after which you will see St. Lucie River flashing red buoy "2," indicating the start of the St. Lucie River route west. Leave it to starboard if you are turning west up the river to Stuart and the Okeechobee (i.e., red-right-returning).

On the east side of the ICW, the incoming St. Lucie Inlet markers end with green daybeacon "17" near the junction with the ICW (leave to port as you continue south on the ICW). The first aid to navigation on the southbound continuation of the ICW is a daybeacon with white dayboards, reading DANGER SHOAL (leave it well to starboard), followed by red daybeacon "2" and flashing green "3." Manatee Speed Zones occur with increasing frequency south of St. Lucie Inlet. Most commonly, speed zones in the ICW channel will be 25 mph; outside the channel, speed zones will be Slow-Speed/Minimum-Wake to shore. Be alert, however, to whether the posted speed zone includes or excludes the channel and if it is seasonal.

Great Pocket, South of Horseshoe Point

NAVIGATION: Use Chart 11472. When entering Great Pocket past Horseshoe Point, watch for shoaling and use caution in the area. Long docks and piers are on both sides of Great Pocket, but are not shown on the chart. The eastern docks are part of a state park, and those to the west belong to a condominium complex.

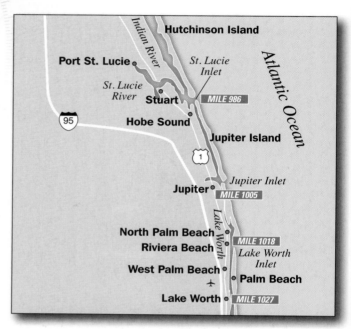

St. Lucie Inlet State Park, South of St. Lucie Inlet

A bit of wilderness is preserved just south of the inlet in the St. Lucie Inlet State Park and adjoining Reed Wilderness Seashore Wildlife Refuge at the north end of Jupiter Island. A small floating dock and a long pier with slips for smaller boats are near the north end of the park. Depths here average 4 feet. Tie off carefully and use fenders, as powerboats often pass without slowing, causing heavy wakes. A small charge is collected on the honor system for use of the park, which is accessible only by boat. From the dock, an elevated wooden walkway with restrooms and picnic pavilions at either end cuts through the mangrove swamp to the ocean about a half mile away. You may swim, fish or beach comb at the beautiful ocean beach. Dogs are allowed on the walkway, but not on the beach.

Peck Lake, Along the ICW

NAVIGATION: Use Chart 11472. Low dunes, uninhabited beaches and sparkling ocean waters may beckon, but if you draw more than 5 feet, anchoring in Peck Lake poses a challenge. Peck Lake, east of the channel, has depths of 6 to 12 feet, but only in a narrow strip from the ICW to close to shore. Deep water for entrance from Peck Lake is located close to flashing green "19," on the south side. Take it slowly, and head in on a course of 060 toward the DANGER sign. Once anchored, a dinghy ride to shore brings

Looking west over St. Lucie Inlet and the Crossroads. (Not to be used for navigation.)

South Florida Water Management District

you to within a stones throw over the dunes to a beautiful, unspoiled Atlantic Ocean beach. This park area is for daytime use only, and the portion north of the crossover path is closed in the spring and early summer months to protect nesting least terns (*sterna antillarum*, the smallest of the American terns). South of this path, the beach is available for walking, swimming or sunbathing.

A platform structure, apparently for collecting weather data, has been erected in Peck Lake just off the beach. When temperatures are above 60 degrees, with little or no wind, sand gnats (commonly called "no-see-ums") can be a problem. The anchorage at Peck Lake is often busy during the week and becomes even more crowded on weekends. There was a sunken boat observed by our cruising editor in the southern area of the Peck Lake anchorage. Even when wrecks are removed, there is the possibility of debris remaining on the bottom, so exercise caution when choosing an anchoring spot.

Dockage: On the west side of the ICW, just across from Peck Lake, is the Loblolly Marina. Do not be scared off by the two PRIVATE signs; transient and long-term dockage are available here in a very protected basin. Loblolly can accommodate vessels up to 110 feet. They offer wireless Internet, laundry facilities and showers/restrooms.

Manatee Zone, Along the ICW

A Manatee Zone is posted from green daybeacon "21" in Peck Lake to the Hobe Sound Bridge (Mile 995.9), which includes areas both outside and inside the channel.

North of green daybeacon "21," the Manatee Zone does not include the ICW channel, and has a 25-mph speed limit in the channel only. This speed limit goes past the Peck Lake anchorage, at flashing green "19," which is very close to the ICW channel and can be subject to large wakes, although most boaters are usually courteous enough to slow for the anchored boats here.

Some Manatee Speed Zones are seasonal (winter months), while others are year-round. Assume that restrictions are year-round if no specific dates appear on the sign.

■ HOBE SOUND—
MILE 996 TO MILE 1000

The Jove Indians, whose name the Spanish pronounced "Ho-bay," gave Hobe Sound its name. A highly exclusive area, sometimes compared with Palm Beach, Hobe Sound shows off many of its grand mansions and manicured lawns along the eastern shore of the channel. The Hobe Sound National Wildlife Refuge dominates the western shore of the sound at about Mile 997, and its natural wilderness contrasts strikingly with the sculptured lawns on the eastern shore.

NAVIGATION: Use Chart 11472. At the northern end of Hobe Sound, the Hobe Sound Highway Bascule Bridge, with a charted closed vertical clearance of 21 feet at center, crosses the ICW at Mile 995.9 and opens on signal. Both sides of the well-marked channel through Hobe Sound have good depths, but do not stray too far, and give points a wide berth.

Hobe Sound is heavily populated with both Slow-Speed/Minimum-Wake and Idle-Speed/No-Wake Zones to protect the manatees. These friendly, slow-moving creatures frequent the area from November through March, so keep them in mind as you transit the sound. Much of the ICW channel itself is exempt from these speed restrictions, but check posted warnings to be certain. In one area, for example, signs on daybeacons cite different speed restrictions for craft larger and smaller than 35 feet.

Anchorage: Because there is a 25-mph speed limit in the Hobe Sound channel, almost all anchorages here are susceptible to annoying boat wakes. In easterly winds, craft drawing less than 4 feet will find an attractive anchorage just off the western shore of Harbor Island. Sound your way in, and set the hook well. Three anchorages also are usable west of the ICW channel between red daybeacons "38" and "44" north of Mile 1000. Follow your chart carefully. In the daytime, passing vessels and water skiers may throw some wake your way, but nights are generally peaceful. Do not be surprised by a routine boarding from local marine police, and be sure to show an anchor light. In Jupiter Sound, a poor anchorage, protected from boat wakes by a nearly continuous spoil bank, is just south of red daybeacon "54." This crowded anchorage is hard to enter and exit, due to a proliferation of private moorings and derelict boats. White spherical buoys mark the northern entrance, which carries 6.5-foot depths. The former southern entrance has shoaled badly.

■ JUPITER—MILE 1002

NAVIGATION: Use Chart 11472. The Waterway leads into Jupiter Sound, where the estates of Hobe Sound give way to only slightly more modest homes. Nearby spoil areas and shoals demand careful attention to the marked channel—stay in bounds. Special caution is required in the vicinity of Hell Gate, Mile 1002, where shoaling extends into the channel north of red daybeacon "52." A submerged obstruction lies north of flashing green "53," just off the channel. Several small marinas and high-and-dry facilities are on the western shore of Jupiter Sound. The Jupiter Highway Bridge (Hail as 707 Bridge) at Mile 1004.1 (25-foot closed vertical clearance) opens on signal. If your vessel is lightly powered, do not get caught by the swift current here while waiting for the bridge. Contact the bridge tender early, and allow for the set of the current.

Dockage: The JIB Yacht Club and Marina is just south of this bridge on the east side of the ICW. This marina, with 6-foot approach and dockside depths, offers gas and diesel fuel and limited transient dockage.

Jupiter Inlet

NAVIGATION: Use Chart 11472. **Use the Miami Harbor Entrance Tide Tables. For high tide, subtract 10 minutes; for low tide, subtract 9 minutes.** Notable for its red brick lighthouse and aquamarine-colored waters, Jupiter Inlet fights a constant battle with shifting sand. Cited by the Coast Guard as "not navigable without local knowledge," despite dredging, the inlet channel is often unsafe for all but small boats with local knowledge. If you are tempted to try and run the inlet, be sure to get reliable and up-to-the-minute information before doing so. A useful source of additional information is the Web site for the Jupiter Inlet District Commission (561-746-2223, www.jupiterinletdistrict.org). They have a live Web cam that reports current weather and sea conditions and allows you to observe the inlet conditions at any time.

Jupiter Inlet leads to the confluence of Jupiter Sound to the north, Lake Worth Creek to the south and Loxahatchee River to the west. A short jetty protects the inlet entrance from the north, and a steel barricade extends halfway into the inlet from the south bank. The mouth of the inlet has strong currents, eddies, turbulence and breaking seas over sandbars that extend from the south side of the inlet offshore towards the northeast. Jupiter Inlet has a mean tidal range of 2.5 feet.

ICW Mile 1004 to Mile 1014

NAVIGATION: Use Chart 11472. **Use the Miami Harbor Entrance Tide Tables. For high tide, add 28 minutes; for low tide add 1 hour and 5 minutes.** At Mile 1004, at the intersection of the ICW and Jupiter Inlet, the route south begins a sharp reverse S-curve, first to starboard (west) into the Jupiter Inlet/Loxahatchee River, then under the Jupiter Federal Bridge (Mile 1004.8, U.S. 1, 26-foot closed vertical clearance, opens on signal), then to port (south) out of the Loxahatchee into Lake Worth Creek. There has been consistent shoaling over the years at Mile 1004 at red nun buoy "2" at the turn into Jupiter Inlet. The area was last dredged in 2009. Depths remain good with 12-foot depths at red nun buoy "2," decreasing to 8-foot depths at the Jupiter Federal Bridge.

The channel bustles with boats of all sizes, and the shore gleams with one-story condominiums and houses set among beautifully manicured lawns. Do not let your eye stray too far from mid-channel, and check the depth and boat speed frequently. This patrolled stretch is a marked Idle-Speed/No-Wake Zone, channel included.

The chart's magenta line follows the northern side of the river channel through the Jupiter Federal Bridge (U.S. 1) at Mile 1004.8, and then makes a sharp turn south just before reaching the state Route Alternate A1A Bridge over the Loxahatchee River to enter Lake Worth Creek. Follow the buoys, watch inlet currents and make the final turn to port cautiously. You will not see the opening southbound into the creek until you are almost on it, and boats coming from the south will not be visible until after you have begun the final swing.

Joseph R. Melanson of www.skypic.com

Atlantic Ocean

Jupiter Inlet (Use Local Knowledge)

ICW

Looking east over Jupiter Inlet and the ICW. (Not to be used for navigation.)

Location: situated at Loblolly, a distinguished private residential community on the west shore of Peck's Lake at Hobe Sound between Palm Beach and Stuart, Florida; forty minutes north of Palm Beach International Airport.

Convenience: close by Stuart offers complete marine services; the St. Lucie Inlet is only 3 bridgeless miles north for access in minutes to some of the world's greatest game fishing, cruising, and sailing waters.

LOBLOLLY MARINA

Facilities: secure, safe, and able to accommodate craft up to 110 feet in length. Surge protected 30, 50 and 100 amp electrical service, telephone, and softened water. Restrooms, showers, wireless internet service, and laundry facilities. A limited number of slips are available to transients and on an annual or seasonal basis.

7407 S.E. Hill Terrace, Hobe Sound, Florida 33455   Telephone (772) 546-3136 • ktine@loblollyinfo.com
New Yacht Club Facility Opening Fall 2009. A Limited Number of Memberships Are Available.
We monitor Channel 16 • ICW MM 992.2

Hobe Sound, Jupiter Area, FL

JUPITER AREA		Largest Vessel Accommodated	VHF Channel Monitored	Transient Berths / Total Berths	Approach / Dockside Depth (reported)	Floating Docks	Gas / Diesel	Groceries, Ice, Marine Supplies, Snacks	Repairs: Hull, Engine, Propeller	Lift (tonnage), Crane, Rail	1=110V, 2=220V, B=Both, Max Amps	Laundry, Pool, Showers	Pump-Out Station	Nearby: Grocery Store, Motel, Restaurant
				Dockage				**Supplies**				**Service**		
1. Loblolly Marina 992.2 ▢ WiFi	772-546-3136	130	16/10	5/79	6/8			I			B/100	LS	P	
2. Jupiter Hills Lighthouse Marina 1002.2 WiFi	561-744-0727	65	16	/12	15/5	F			P		B/50	L	P	M
3. Blowing Rocks Marina 1002.2 WiFi	561-746-3312	70	16	2/60	6/5		GD	IMS	HEP		1/50	S	P	GMR
4. Jupiter Pointe Club & Marina 1002.8	561-746-2600	55	16/65	/15	6/6	F	G	IS	HP	L	B/50	S		GMR
5. JIB Yacht Club Marina 1004.2 ▢ WiFi	561-746-4300	70	16	4/40	8/8		GD	IMS			B/100	LPS	P	GMR
6. Jupiter Seasport Marina 1004.8	561-575-0006	60	16	/42	15/8		GD	IMS	HEP		1/50	LS		MR
7. Loggerhead Club & Marina—Jupiter 1006.8	561-747-8980	100	16	5/31	7/6	F	GD	IMS	EP			PS	P	GR
8. Admiral's Cove Marina 1007 ▢ WiFi	561-745-5930	130	16	/74	8/8	F	GD	IMS	P		B/100	LPS	P	GMR
9. The Bluffs Marina 1008 WiFi	561-627-6688	155					GD				B/100			
10. Loggerhead Club & Marina—Palm Bch Gardens 1009 WiFi	561-627-6358	120	16	10/140	8/8		GD	GIMS			B/100	LS	P	GMR

Corresponding chart(s) not to be used for navigation. ▢ Internet Access   WiFi Wireless Internet Access

JUPITER FEDERAL BRIDGE
Mile 1004.8
WATERWAY GUIDE PHOTOGRAPHY

Be equally vigilant when heading north. The corner where the Loxahatchee River and Lake Worth Creek join is blind, whether you are heading north or south. Either way, the route appears to dead-end in a false lead created by the state Route Alternate A1A Bridge (25-foot fixed vertical clearance) and a railroad bascule bridge beside it (4-foot closed vertical clearance, normally open except during train traffic) crossing the Loxahatchee River.

The Loxahatchee River, Florida's only designated wild and scenic river, is shallow beyond the bridges. It is virtually un-navigable for craft drawing more than 3.5 or 4 feet and any craft requiring overhead clearance greater than 25 feet, but it is definitely worth exploring. It is marked by private aids to navigation. You may be able to dock at the Jupiter marinas and investigate by dinghy. Several miles of the Loxahatchee River's main northwest fork border the 11,500-acre Jonathan Dickinson State Park, which offers great freshwater and saltwater fishing, canoeing, hiking, bicycling, picnicking, camping and guided tours of the Loxahatchee.

The ICW through Lake Worth Creek is actually a relatively straight dredged channel through the creek's watershed. The entire length is lined with homes, and boat traffic can be heavy, especially on weekends. Much of the length below Mile 1007 does not have speed restrictions. The Indiantown Road Bridge (state Route 706, 35-foot closed vertical clearance) crosses the Waterway at Mile 1006.2 and has restrict-

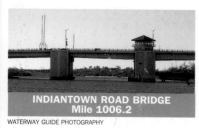

INDIANTOWN ROAD BRIDGE
Mile 1006.2
WATERWAY GUIDE PHOTOGRAPHY

ed openings. The bridge opens on the hour and half-hour 24 hours a day, seven days a week. The shallow anchorage north of the Indiantown Road Bridge on the east side of the ICW is full of small boats permanently moored, along with a public boat ramp and a floating hot dog stand on weekends in season. This is an enforced No-Wake Zone.

The Donald Ross Bridge (35-foot closed vertical clearance) at Mile 1009.3 opens on the hour and half-hour. Farther south, both the PGA Boulevard and Parker (U.S. 1) bridges, about a mile apart, have restricted openings at all times. The PGA Boulevard Bridge (Mile 1012.6, 24-foot closed vertical clearance) opens on the hour and half-hour 24 hours daily. The Parker Bridge (Mile 1013.7, 25-foot closed vertical clearance) opens at 15 and 45 minutes past the hour 24 hours daily. The well-developed area in the mile or so between the PGA and Parker bridges, and including the "North Palm Beach Waterway" (a canal, splitting off to the west of the ICW), is a well-justified Slow-Speed/Minimum-Wake Zone. The No-Wake Zone continues to the opening into Lake Worth at Mile 1014.2.

Dockage: The Jupiter Yacht Club, on the east side at Mile 1006.5, is a private club. A little farther south on the west side is Loggerhead Club & Marina-Jupiter, primarily a high-and-dry marina with floating docks, most of which are private. A few transient slips are usually available, but call ahead.

At Mile 1007.8, Admiral's Cove Marina offers upscale marina and shoreside amenities, including five restaurants, an Olympic-size swimming pool and a clubhouse with a spa, fitness center, tennis and golf.

The Bluffs Marina and Loggerhead Club & Marina-Palm Beach Gardens (formerly Frenchman's Marina) are just north and south of the Donald Ross Bridge, respectively. Both are in protected basins off the ICW. Loggerhead normally can accommodate transient boats. From Mile 1011 to Mile 1018, 16 marinas and boatyards, offering all kinds of marine services and repairs, lie on the ICW channel and Lake Worth.

ST. LUCIE INLET TO PALM BEACH

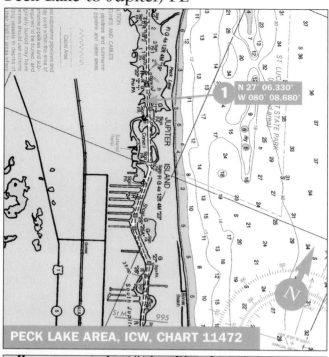

PECK LAKE AREA, ICW, CHART 11472

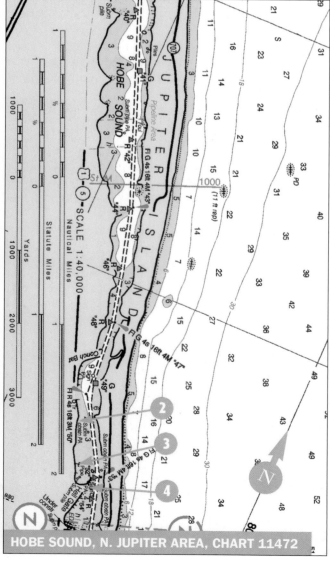

HOBE SOUND, N. JUPITER AREA, CHART 11472

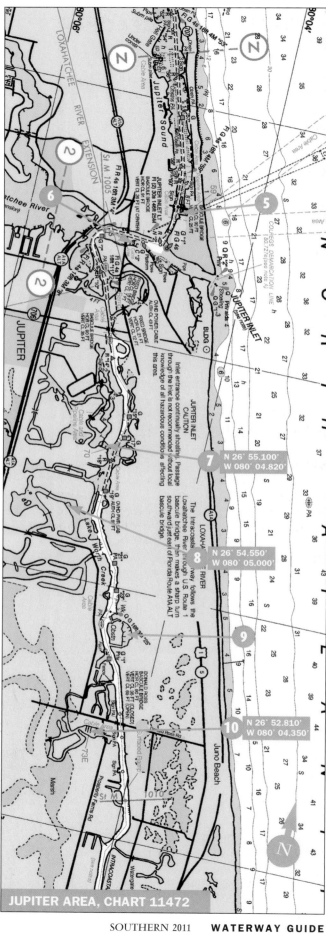

JUPITER AREA, CHART 11472

NORTH PALM BEACH— MILE 1012

A concentration of marinas is located on the ICW stretch from just north of the PGA Boulevard Bridge in North Palm Beach to Palm Beach. All are convenient to the area's famous shopping, from The Gardens Mall in Palm Beach Gardens to Worth Avenue in Palm Beach.

Dockage: North of the PGA bridge, Soverel Harbour Marina is a sizable facility that welcomes transients. Gas and diesel fuel are available next door at PGA Marina. Soverel Harbour Marina is also next door to Seminole Boat Yard for any necessary haul-out or yard work. Carmine's Italian Restaurant and Gourmet Market is on-site at the marina.

The PGA Bridge area is restaurant junction, with the River House Restaurant (American cuisine featuring seafood and steaks) on the west bank and Seasons 52 on the east bank north of the bridge, while south of the bridge are Panama Hatties ("Floribbean" seafood) on the east bank and Waterway Café (salads and seafood) on the west bank. Traffic can be congested from boats docking at the restaurants.

LAKE WORTH/NORTH PALM BEACH—MILE 1014

NAVIGATION: Use Chart 11472. At Mile 1014, just past the Parker Bridge (U.S. 1), the Waterway enters the open waters of Lake Worth proper. The lake is long and broad, but shallow, except for the ICW channel. Do not confuse the ICW markers leading south with those splitting off to the east and then north to hospitable Old Port Cove Marina and the extreme upper end of Lake Worth (and then to Little Lake Worth), a separate body of water (see below). Lining both shores of Lake Worth are boating-oriented towns and cities with marinas that include all the resort amenities.

Some of Lake Worth is a Manatee Zone with Slow-Speed/Minimum-Wake restriction, but with a few exceptions, most of the ICW channel is exempt from these restrictions and enjoys a 25-mph speed limit. Limited stretches of Idle-Speed/No-Wake Zones appear at bridges and adjacent to marinas. Carefully observe restricted speed limits, where they prevail. Lake Worth is crowded with boats, marinas and private docks, so damage from wakes can be severe.

Dockage: Just south of the Parker Bridge to starboard, North Palm Beach Marina (owned by Old Port Cove Holdings, the owners of Old Port Cove Marina across the Waterway) has floating docks and a convenient fuel dock with pump-out right on the ICW. To reach Old Port Cove Marina, after entering Lake Worth proper, turn off the ICW to the east, following the private green daybeacons, then head north around the Old Port Cove townhouses and condominiums. You will spot the entrance off to port shortly after passing green daybeacon "7." Hail Old Port Cove Marina on VHF Channel 16, and someone will direct you to a slip. The marina offers fuel and all amenities, as well as a pump-out boat to service your vessel at your slip. Renovations were completed with floating docks and updated electrical connections to accommodate vessels up to 200 feet. A restaurant is on-site at Old Port Yacht Club.

Anchorage: Some cruisers have reported adequate depths for anchoring in the lagoons off the North Palm Beach Waterway. They are reached by turning to starboard at the bend just before Parker Bridge. The canal is charted at 7 feet with 6-foot depths in the first basin and 8 feet in the second, both of which will be to starboard. This is a very fine residential community. In the

Palm Beach skyline from the Intracoastal Waterway. ©ISTOCKPHOTO/crowman

Riviera Beach, FL

North Palm Beach, Rivera Beach, FL

NORTH PALM BEACH		Largest Vessel Accommodated	VHF Channel Monitored	Transient Berths / Total Berths	Approach / Dockside Depth (reported)	Floating Docks	Gas / Diesel	Groceries, Ice, Marine Supplies, Snacks	Repairs: Hull, Engine, Propeller	Lift (tonnage), Crane, Rail	1=110V, 2=220V, B=Both, Max Amps	Laundry, Pool, Showers	Pump-Out Station	Nearby: Grocery Store, Motel, Restaurant
				Dockage				Supplies			Service			
1. E & H Boat Works/The Ways Boat Yard 1011.7	561-622-8582	80	16	/10	10/5			MS	HEP	L70,CR	B/50	S		GMR
2. Seminole Boat Yard 1011.9	561-622-7600	100	16	9/9	6/6			GIMS		L100,C	B/100	S		GR
3. SOVEREL HARBOUR MARINA 1011.9 ☐ⓌⒾⒻⒾ	561-691-9554	75	16	10/141	12/12	F		GIMS			B/50			GMR
4. PGA Marina 1011.9	561-626-0200	150		5/25	8/8	F	GD	GIMS	HEP	L	B/50			GMR
5. Harbour Point Marina 1012.1	561-622-6890			PRIVATE (NO TRANSIENTS)										
6. NORTH PALM BEACH MARINA 1013.7 ☐ⓌⒾⒻⒾ	561-626-4919	150	16/8	10/107	10/8	F	GD	GIMS			B/100	LS	P	GR
7. OLD PORT COVE MARINA 1014 ☐ⓌⒾⒻⒾ	561-626-1760	200	16/8	20/300	8/15	F	D	IMS			B/100	LS	P	GMR
8. Lake Park Harbor Marina 1016.2 ⓌⒾⒻⒾ	561-881-3353	75	16	20/103	6/8	F	GD	GIMS			B/50	LS	P	GMR
9. LOGGERHEAD CLUB & MARINA—RIVIERA BEACH 1017	561-840-6868	47	DRY STORAGE		6/6	F	GD	IMS		L20				
10. NEW PORT COVE MARINE CENTER 1017.4 ☐	561-844-2504	70	16/8	5/350	7/8	F	GD	IMS	E		B/50	LS	P	GR
11. CANNONSPORT MARINA 1017.5 ☐ⓌⒾⒻⒾ	561-848-7469	120	16	/50	12/12		GD	IMS			B/100	LPS	P	GMR
12. Buccaneer Marina 1017.6	561-842-1620	80	16/68	/16	12/12		GD				B/50	LP		GMR
13. Sailfish Marina 1017.7 ☐ⓌⒾⒻⒾ	561-844-1724	110	16/68	40/92	8/8	F	GD	GIMS			B/50	LPS		GMR
14. Riviera Beach Yacht Center 1017.8 ☐ ⓌⒾⒻⒾ	561-863-4126	150	16	/40	8/8	F	GD	IMS	HEP	L150	B/100	S	P	GMR
15. Riviera Beach Municipal Marina 1018	561-842-7806	200	16/11	30/145	11/8		GD	GIMS			B/50	LS	P	GMR
16. Cracker Boy Boat Works 1018.1 ☐	561-845-0357	100	16		16/16			M	HEP	L100	B/50	S		R

Corresponding chart(s) not to be used for navigation. ☐ Internet Access ⓌⒾⒻⒾ Wireless Internet Access

past, anchoring required a permit, but that is not presently required with the passage of Florida Statute 327.02. However, no landing is permitted.

Just after clearing the Parker Bridge (U.S. 1) and passing North Palm Beach Marina to starboard, enter Lake Worth and immediately turn off the ICW to port. Follow the green daybeacons off to the east, then north around Old Port Cove, and then follow the daybeacons to the extreme (northern) head of Lake Worth. You can drop the hook in 10- to 14-foot depths and have plenty of swinging room. You may find a handy place to land the dinghy at the east abutment of the A1A Bridge (8-foot fixed vertical clearance) over the cut between Lake Worth and Little Lake Worth. Dinghies have been stolen here, so it is best to chain your skiff to the chain-link fence, and make sure your outboard is also locked down. Groceries, marine supplies and extensive shopping areas are nearby. Boaters who anchor on the east side of Old Port Cove in Lake Worth are not bothered by restrictions on anchoring. The west side, close to Old Port Cove Marina, had been subject to a four-day limit, with fee and registration requirements. Get local knowledge here before anchoring.

■ RIVIERA BEACH— MILE 1017

NAVIGATION: Use Chart 11472. Lake Worth is broad in the first stretch leading to the Jerry Thomas Memorial Bridge (Blue Heron Boulevard, 65-foot fixed vertical clearance) at Mile 1017.2. The channel is narrow, but a 25-mph speed limit holds in the channel, with Slow-Speed/Minimum-Wake outside the channel to shore. A Slow-Speed/Minimum-Wake Zone was established in the ICW channel in 2008, in the vicinity of the Lake Park Harbor Marina south to Blue Heron Bridge. In a strong crosswind, watch the set of your course.

Just through the bridge, you must make a decision. Directly ahead is Peanut Island. If you plan to continue south on the ICW, you will alter course to starboard, following the ICW around Peanut Island on the west side. If you plan to exit through Lake Worth Inlet, a shorter route makes a turn to port (east) picking up red daybeacon "8" (leave to port) and green daybeacon "9" (leave to starboard); carefully follow the relatively narrow channel in past Singer Island and its marinas to flashing red "8," marking the northerly rim of the Lake Worth Inlet. In the channel past Singer Island, favor the easterly side and keep your eye on the depth sounder, as 2- and 3-foot shoals appear just past the green daybeacon channel markers to starboard (west). There is a shoal

Lake Worth, FL

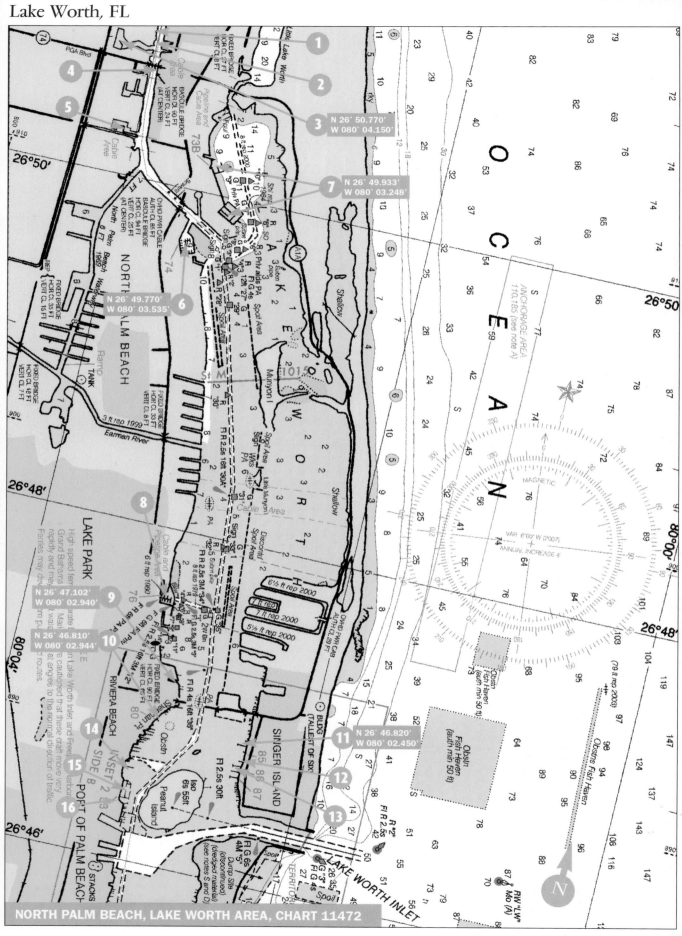

NORTH PALM BEACH, LAKE WORTH AREA, CHART 11472

Lake Worth Inlet, FL

PORT OF PALM BEACH

Looking east toward Lake Worth Inlet, Peanut Island and the Port of Palm Beach. (Not to be used for navigation.)

encroaching into the channel at green daybeacon "1," and a 6-foot spot is in the center of the channel just to its port. From there, you alter course to port (leaving flashing red "8" to starboard) to clear the inlet. If draft is an issue, a safer and more prudent course would be to follow the ICW to the turning basin, then head out toward the inlet.

Dockage: Lake Park Harbor Marina, north of the Riviera Beach Bridge, offers transient dockage at new floating docks, laundry and a pump-out station. The next marina facility south is the Loggerhead Club and Marina—Riviera Beach at Marina Grande, on the west side just above the Riviera Beach Bridge. It is conspicuous for its two towers and huge dry storage facility. South of the Riviera Beach Bridge, marine facilities are abundant on both shores, north and south of Lake Worth Inlet. On the mainland western shore, beginning at Riviera Beach, are repair yards capable of handling boats of any size. New Port Cove Marine Center, the first encountered here, has dry storage space, 45 slips in the water and engine repair services. They can accommodate vessels up to 70 feet at their docks.

The Riviera Beach Yacht Center is located just off the ICW south of New Port Cove Marine Center. The yard can facilitate just about any repair with its huge 150-ton lift and staff of capable mechanics. Gas and diesel fuel are available at the fuel dock at the Riviera Beach Municipal Marina, the next facility heading south on the ICW channel, opposite Peanut Island. Farther south, Cracker Boy Boat Works also has repair services and do-it-yourself facilities with a 100-ton lift on-site.

On the eastern shore, the resort area of Singer Island is crowded with houses, motels, docks and restaurants. Cannonsport Marina, with newly rebuilt docks, is the northernmost facility. It caters to sportfishing vessels, but transient slips are available, as are gas and diesel fuel. There is a strong current at both marinas on Singer Island, so exercise care while docking.

Sailfish Marina Resort, located just inside Lake Worth Inlet on Singer Island, offers a full-service marina with 8-foot dockside depths (but shallower water on the approach both from the north at the bridge and the south at the inlet), plus all amenities, including children's programs. Giant "jacks," a type of schooling fish, patrol the docks at Sailfish Marina. During the afternoon, while fishermen clean their catch, the school waits patiently for leftovers at the cleaning tables. It is quite a spectacle and worth watching.

Peanut Island, on the ICW

NAVIGATION: Use Chart 11472. All of Peanut Island continues to be developed as a park and environmental restoration project. It is very popular locally and is usually surrounded with many small boats anchored all around, especially on weekends. Island facilities now include picnic shelters and restrooms, and a new dredged boat basin on its northwest side for dinghy tie up. There are kayaking lagoons and scenic outlooks along the walkways. Native vegetation has replaced the casuarina trees (invasive Australian pines) that used to cover the island. Water taxis regularly transport visitors to the new docks on the east side. The former Coast Guard Station and JFK Bomb Shelter on the south side of

Peanut Island are now part of the Palm Beach Maritime Museum and open for tours.

Water taxi service is available in Lake Worth, primarily to take visitors from Sailfish Marina and Phil Foster Park, at the Singer Island side of the Riviera Beach Bridge, to the park at Peanut Island, and for sightseeing on the Palm Beach shoreline. The water taxis will transport boaters to shore as their schedules allow. Call the water taxi on VHF Channel 16.

■ LAKE WORTH INLET— MILE 1018

Wide, well-marked and jettied, Lake Worth Inlet boasts a deep straightforward ship channel that is one of the easiest to enter on the Atlantic coast. The meandering Gulf Stream is closer here than at any point in the United States (sometimes as close as a mile offshore, but usually out about 8 to 12 miles), and both commercial and recreational craft give the inlet heavy use. Its location, approximately midway between two other easy-to-navigate inlets, Fort Pierce (60 miles north) and Port Everglades (53 miles south), makes it popular with boaters who prefer to travel offshore. Some shoaling lies close in on the north side of the entrance channel, but it is frequently dredged. About one mile west, inside the Lake Worth Inlet, the Port of Palm Beach handles commercial cargo, ranging from construction supplies to seafood, to tropical fruit and cruise ships.

Lake Worth is a favorite point of departure for boats bound to and from the Bahamas Islands. If you are arriving here from a foreign port, the owner/operator of a U.S. vessel must call 800-432-1216 or 800-451-0393 immediately, whether at anchor, a private home or a marina. These numbers are available 24 hours a day. An arrival number is assigned and all persons aboard have 24 hours to go in person to the Homeland Security Customs and Border Patrol office that they instruct you to visit (this procedure is for both Customs and Immigration clearance). Foreign yachts must call the same number from the first place that the vessel docks.

Boaters in Florida, that frequently check in from other countries, can now apply for a Local Boaters Option Card (LBO) and ID number so that the physical trip to Customs and Border Protection (CBP) office is no longer necessary. You have to make an appointment in advance at one of these offices and secure a personal interview (with your vessel information and passports) to qualify for the Local Boaters Option Pilot Program. The CBP is encouraging participation in the LBO program.

NAVIGATION: Use Chart 11472. **Use the Miami Harbor Entrance Tide Tables. For high tide, subtract 21 minutes; for low tide, add 4 minutes.** The Coast Guard establishes fixed and moving security zones at the Port of Palm Beach for the protection of passenger vessels (cruise ships), vessels carrying cargoes of a particular hazard and vessels carrying hazardous gases. A moving security zone activates when such a vessel passes red and white buoy "LW" when entering the port, and becomes a fixed zone when the ship is docked. These zones cover the waters within 100 yards all around the subject vessels, and no craft can enter without prior permission. Patrol craft may be contacted on VHF Channel 16 for the status of these security zones.

Anchorage: There are at least six anchorages in the vicinity of Lake Worth Inlet. Anchor lights should be used in all Lake Worth anchorages. These anchorages include:

■ Just northeast of the Riviera Beach Bridge in 8- to 13-foot depths over the "Discontinued Spoil Area." There are a number of derelict boats and a few sunken ones here. Beware of wreckage on the bottom.

■ Just northwest of the ICW, between red daybeacon "40" and green daybeacon "41," derelict boats are anchored very close together. This anchorage is not recommended for transient boaters.

■ Just southeast of the turning basin marked by flashing green lights "11" and "13" in 9 to 13 feet of water; avoid the "cable area" shown on the chart. This area is subject to tidal currents from the inlet, so observe proximity of other anchored vessels and their anchor set.

■ A half-mile south of the inlet along the east shore of Lake Worth, just southwest of Palm Beach at red daybeacon "6." Avoid the charted spoil and cable areas here. There are numerous permanently moored vessels in this area. Depths are 8 to 12 feet.

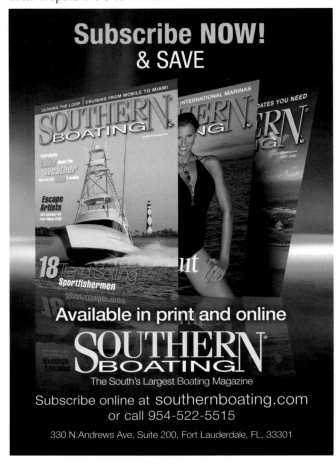

The Palm Beaches, FL

West Palm Beach & Palm Beach, FL

WEST PALM BEACH & PALM BEACH		Largest Vessel Accommodated	VHF Channel Monitored	Approach / Dockside Depth	Transient Berths / Total Berths	Floating Docks	Gas / Diesel	Groceries, Ice, Marine Supplies, Snacks	Repairs: Hull, Engine, Propeller	Lift (tonnage), Crane, Rail	1=110V, 2=220V, B=Both, Max Amps	Laundry, Pool, Showers	Pump-Out Station	Nearby: Grocery Store, Motel, Restaurant
						Dockage			**Supplies**			**Service**		
1. Rybovich Marina 1019.5 🖵	561-844-1800	275	16	20/150	14/14	F	GD	IMS	HEP	L300,C,R	B/100	S	P	GMR
2. Palm Beach Yacht Club Marina 1022.9	561-655-1944	130	16/68	5/45	13/13		GD	IM			B/100	LS		GMR
3. PALM HARBOR MARINA 1022 🖵 WiFi	800-435-8051	250	16	50/198	11/11	F	GD	IMS			B/200	LS	P	GR
4. TOWN OF PALM BEACH TOWN DOCKS 1024.5 🖵	561-838-5463	195	16/69	10/87	9/12			S			B/100	S	P	GR

Corresponding chart(s) not to be used for navigation. 🖵 Internet Access WiFi Wireless Internet Access

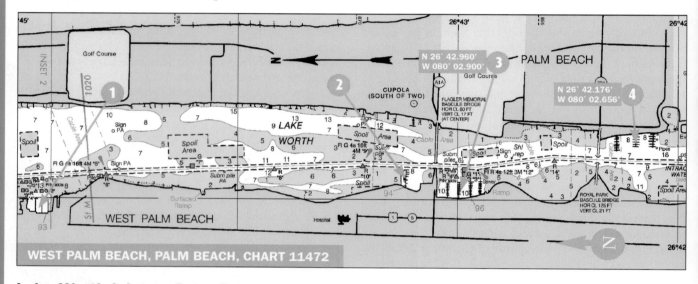

WEST PALM BEACH, PALM BEACH, CHART 11472

Lake Worth Inlet to Palm Beach— Mile 1018 to 1021

NAVIGATION: Use Chart 11472. South of the inlet and Peanut Island, Lake Worth is open, the Waterway channel is well-marked and maintained, and patches of deep water appear along the eastern Palm Beach shore.

Palm Beach, with its opulent, lushly landscaped homes, private docks and luxurious yachts, can be viewed up close via an inshore side channel leading from the inlet south almost to the first bascule bridge, Flagler Memorial at Mile 1021.8 (17-foot closed vertical clearance). Only the northern extremity of this side channel is marked. South of the last red marker, daybeacon "6," the channel close to the Palm Beach shore is wide and deep, but the scattered, unmarked shoal and spoil areas toward the center of Lake Worth require local knowledge. At low water, boats with a draft of 5 feet or less can rejoin the ICW north of the Flagler Bridge. The safest route across Lake Worth is to maintain a southwesterly course from the Palm Beach side south of red daybeacon "6" across the lake, but make sure you reach the ICW before flashing green "5," as 3-foot charted shoals lie south and east of it, just outside of the channel.

As with all other Palm Beach County bridges, openings are restricted 24 hours a day, seven days a week, year-round, on both the Flagler Bridge (Mile 1021.8, 17-foot closed vertical clearance) and the Royal Park Bridge (Mile 1022.6, 21-foot closed vertical clearance). The Flagler Bridge opens at 15 and 45 minutes past the hour. The Royal Park Bridge opens on the hour and half-hour.

West Palm Beach—Mile 1022

The West Palm Beach shore of Lake Worth is given over to marinas, boatyards and yachting amenities. In other places, any one of these would be outstanding in size, quality of work and service. Here, though, mariners can be overwhelmed by the choices. Not all the services available here are confined to the waterfront. A phone call or a short walk can put you in touch with just about every known kind of boat specialist—sailmakers, electronic sales and services, boat designers, boat maintenance and cleaning and diving services. Supplies of all kinds are close at hand.

Dockage: Just before Mile 1020, privately maintained green daybeacon "1" marks the entrance to Rybovich Super Yacht Marina, with expanded floating service docks, fuel, showers and boat repair for boats up to 275 feet. This is a megayacht service facility. There are low-level condominium buildings to the south of the marina, and resort facilities and amenities include a fitness center, captains lounge and a pool. Restaurants and entertainment are just a taxi ride away.

A WORLD-CLASS DESTINATION
IN THE HEART OF THE PALM BEACHES.

INCREDIBLE LOCATION
INCOMPARABLE FACILITIES
IMPECCABLE STYLE

PALM HARBOR MARINA
THE PALM BEACHES, FLORIDA

400 North Flagler Drive, Suite A
West Palm Beach, Florida 33401

For information on Palm Harbor
Marina call (800) 435-8051 or visit
www.PalmHarbor-Marina.com

Guests and crew will find the new Palm Harbor Marina ideally located in the heart of the Palm Beaches. Palm Beach International Airport, the Atlantic Ocean, the world famous Breakers Hotel, renowned golf courses and Worth Avenue shopping are nearby. The vibrant nightlife of Clematis Street, restaurants, boutique shopping and City Place are a short stroll from your slip.

- 200 slips for yachts up 250'
- State-of-the-art custom concrete floating dock system
- Dockage and golf cart porter service
- Single and three-phase power with surge protection
- High-speed diesel and gasoline pumps
- Free WiFi, basic cable and telephone
- Private clubhouse and fitness center

Beginning Fall 2010 the Intracoastal will be dredged at 10' near the Good Samaritan Medical Center

Seasonal and Annual Grand Opening Rates Now Available

Slips Available from 50' to 250' | Reserve Yours Today! | (800) 435-8051   PalmHarbor-Marina.com

Palm Beach, FL

■ PALM BEACH— MILE 1018 TO MILE 1030

Across Lake Worth from West Palm Beach, Palm Beach remains a winter ocean resort of elegance and charm. Worth Avenue deserves a visit, with its collection of famous boutiques, jewelers, art galleries, restaurants and antiques stores. Grand old hotels such as the Brazilian Court and the Breakers have been renovated and still set the standard for this historically significant resort. One pleasant way to see Palm Beach is to have lunch or dinner at one of the numerous fine restaurants, such as Taboo at 221 Worth Ave. Then, have a leisurely stroll around town to take in the sights.

Dockage: Just below the Flagler Memorial Bridge at red daybeacon "2," on the west shore in West Palm Beach, Palm Harbor Marina has transient berths, all fuels and the usual amenities. Downtown West Palm Beach and City Place, an upscale outdoor mall surrounding an open-air plaza with live entertainment, shopping, theaters, restaurants, groceries and art galleries, are all nearby. It is a festive commercial and cultural district. A free trolley runs from Clematis Street in West Palm Beach to City Place.

On the east (Palm Beach) side, the Town of Palm Beach Docks, just south of the Royal Park Bridge, are a pleasant and convenient place to stay. (Complimentary dockage is not to exceed four hours for lunch during the daytime hours of 8 a.m. to 5 p.m. There is no complimentary dockage offered after 5 p.m.) There is a minimum charge for overnight stays, regardless of boat length. Palm Beach

Docks can accommodate vessels up to 250 feet and provide all of the amenities one could want including pump-out, security, wireless Internet and shower/restrooms.

Bridges: One more bridge connects the mainland and Palm Beach. The Southern Boulevard Bridge (Mile 1024.7, 14-foot closed vertical clearance) opens at 15 and 45 minutes past the hour daily, 24 hours a day.

Cruising Options

After leaving Palm Beach, the ICW leads boaters through Lake Worth into the narrow land cut that continues south to Fort Lauderdale and Miami. For details on the next leg, turn to the following chapter, "Lake Worth to Pompano Beach." Mariners who plan to head offshore to the Bahamas should turn to the Bahamas coverage in our separate Bahamas edition. WATERWAY GUIDE provides full information on crossing the Gulf Stream, customs regulations and island hopping, cruising and anchoring throughout the Bahamas. ■

WATERWAY GUIDE advertising sponsors play a vital role in bringing you the most trusted and well-respected cruising guide in the country. Without our advertising sponsors, we simply couldn't produce the top-notch publication now resting in your hands. Next time you stop in for a peaceful night's rest, let them know where you found them—WATERWAY GUIDE, The Cruising Authority.

The Secret is Out!
At the Palm Beach Town Docks, all the magic of Palm Beach is at the end of your dock!

Since the 1940's, The Town of Palm Beach's Town Docks have provided the yachting public space for both power and sailing yachts. The historical Brazilian, Australian and Peruvian Docks are tucked away at the west end of the avenues for which they are named and at the foot of world famous Worth Avenue.

The finest beaches, restaurants, hotels and shopping are just walking distance from your slip. Adjacent to this public marina is Lake Drive Park which marks the southern terminus of the Town's gorgeous six-mile-paved jogging and biking Lake Trail.

Completed in 1998, the Town Dock's total renovation provides state of the art docking, electric, security and sewage pump-out facilities. The Town Docks offer accommodations for yachts up to 250 feet and ten foot draft. Security, showers, heads, free parking, CATV, WI-FI, ice and docking assistance are available daily. Come and avail yourselves of what the only public marina on Palm Beach has to offer. We look forward to being of service to you, your guests and crew.

- *3 Miles South of Palm Beach Inlet*
- *10 Minutes from Palm Beach International Airport*
- *Annual, Seasonal and Transient Dockage Available*
- *Florida D.E.P. Clean Marina Designation*
- *Monitoring Channel 16*

Town of Palm Beach Town Docks
500 Australian Avenue Docks
Palm Beach, FL 33480
(561)838-5463 (561)227-6345
email: jluscomb@townofpalmbeach.com

Lake Worth to Pompano Beach

CHARTS 11466, 11467, 11469, 11472

Continuing south over the next 30 miles, the Intracoastal Waterway (ICW) alters its configuration and becomes a narrow land cut in the vicinity of Boynton Beach. Lined with residences and spanned by numerous bridges, the ICW truly looks like a water highway here. Two small, shallow lakes, Wyman and Boca Raton, and a brief stretch of the Hillsboro River are the only naturally formed bodies of water along this route. Though the Atlantic Ocean is barely half a mile away in places, you will find it hard to see among the proliferation of houses, motels, high-rise apartments and condominiums that line the route. On weekends especially, boat traffic can be heavy, and wakes bounce back and forth between bulkheads on each side. It is a fascinating trip to observe South Florida waterfront living firsthand, but it is in stark contract to the wilderness-lined ICW farther north.

Between Palm Beach's Royal Park Bridge, Mile 1022.6, and Pompano Beach's Atlantic Boulevard Bridge, Mile 1056, 13 bridges cross the Waterway. (For bridge restrictions, see the Bridge Tables in the Skipper's Handbook section located in the front of this book.) WATERWAY GUIDE recommends that you study opening schedules in advance to minimize your delays at restricted bridges. Restricted bridges in Palm Beach County operate 24 hours a day, seven days a week, year-round. Most open twice each hour, either on the hour and half-hour or 15 and 45 minutes past the hour, except the Camino Real Bridge at Mile 1048.2, which opens on the hour, then 20 minutes past and 40 minutes past the hour. Broward County bridges operate on a similar schedule, opening either on the hour and half-hour or 15 and 45 minutes past the hour.

Lake Worth

Lake Worth may be wide in this area, but south of Palm Beach, the water is shallow outside the ICW channel. Small islands (many of them originating as dredge spoil banks) break the open expanses and are overgrown with foliage. Estates border a large portion of the eastern shore, and tall condominiums appear with increasing frequency on both banks. John's Island, an Audubon-managed spoil island in the southern end of Lake Worth (Mile 1027), has completed an environmental restoration project on a smaller scale than Peanut Island. Spoil from John's and Peanut islands has been deposited in the Palm Beach County disposal area just north of the Lake Avenue Bridge on the west side of the ICW, between Mile 1027 and Mile 1029.

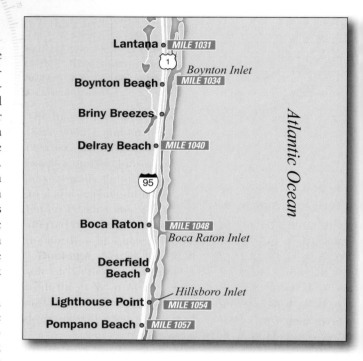

Small water-oriented communities, with many amenities for yachtsmen, are located all along Lake Worth. The first of these, the town of Lake Worth, has small shops, restaurants and art galleries. A large municipal beach and a 1,000-foot-long fishing pier provide recreational opportunities. The Lake Avenue Bridge (35-foot closed vertical clearance, opens on signal) is at Mile 1028.8. A public launch ramp on the mainland near the western end of this bridge has piers that can serve as dinghy landings.

All Florida east coast bridges are equipped with radios, and most will answer an initial call on VHF Channel 09. A few with published schedules of operation will not answer, but simply open at the scheduled times if they see vessels waiting. Captains should make their initial call on VHF Channel 09 and, if there is no answer, try VHF Channel 16, a horn signal or, as a last resort, a phone call (check the Bridge Tables in the Skipper's Handbook section located in the front of this book for phone numbers).

Lantana to Boynton Beach— Mile 1031 to Mile 1035

NAVIGATION: Use Chart 11467. Lantana is the next mainland town on Lake Worth. The Lantana-Ocean Avenue Bridge, at Mile 1031.0 (13-foot charted closed vertical clearance), is the southernmost span over Lake Worth and connects Lantana on the mainland with Hypoluxo

Lantana to Boynton Beach, FL

LANTANA TO BOYNTON BEACH		Largest Vessel Accommodated	VHF Channel Monitored	Transient Berths / Total Berths	Approach / Dockside Depth (reported)	Floating Docks	Gas / Diesel	Groceries, Ice, Marine Supplies, Snacks	Repairs: Hull, Engine, Propeller	Lift (tonnage), Crane, Rail	1=110v, 2=220v, B=Both, Max Amps	Laundry, Pool, Showers	Pump-Out Station	Nearby: Grocery Store, Motel, Restaurant
		Dockage					**Supplies**			**Service**				
1. Loggerhead Club and Marina-Lantana 1030.2	561-582-4422	45	16	2/350	6/5		G	IMS	EP	L7.5	1/50	S		GMR
2. Murrelle Marine 1030.4	561-582-3213	55	16	/35	4.5/5			IMS	HEP	L50	B/50	S		
3. Loggerhead Club and Marina-South Lantana 1030.5 [WiFi]	561-721-3888	120	16	12/80	7/7			IMS			B/50	PS		GR
4. Palm Beach Yacht Center 1032.7	561-588-9911	80	16	10/100	6/6		GD	IMS	HEP	L80	B/50	S	P	GMR
5. Gateway Marina 1033.1	561-588-1211	30	68	/211	6/6	F	G	IMS	HEP	L	1/30			

Corresponding chart(s) not to be used for navigation. 🖥 Internet Access [WiFi] Wireless Internet Access

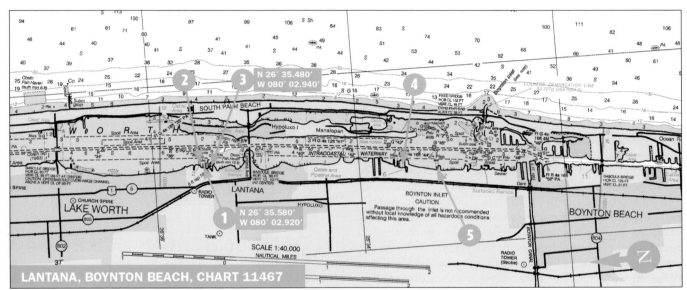

LANTANA, BOYNTON BEACH, CHART 11467

Looking north over Boynton Inlet and the Intracoastal Waterway. (Not to be used for navigation.)

Joseph R. Melanson of skypic.com

Boynton Inlet, FL

Island and South Palm Beach on the ocean side. The bridge tender at Mile 1031.0 identifies the bridge as the Lantana-Ocean Avenue Bridge, distinguishing it from the Boynton Beach-Ocean Avenue Bridge four miles south. Both the Lantana-Ocean Avenue Bridge (Mile 1031.0) and the Boynton Beach-Ocean Avenue Bridge (Mile 1035.0, 21-foot closed vertical clearance) open on the hour and half-hour, 24 hours a day, seven days a week

Dockage: North of the Lantana-Ocean Avenue Bridge, on the west side, is the Loggerhead Club and Marina-South Lantana with 70 wet slips (561-721-3888). This is just south of the Loggerhead Club and Marina—Lantana, a predominantly dry-slip marina, but with a few transient slips.

South of the Lantana-Ocean Avenue Bridge, the route enters the approaches to Boynton Inlet. On the west side of the ICW, two repair yards with transient dockage are in the yacht basin (Palm Beach Yacht Center and Gateway Marina). The approach is marked and has depths of 4 to 6 feet.

A seafood restaurant with dockage for diners is near the Boynton Beach-Ocean Avenue Bridge, and a shopping center and supermarket are within walking distance of the waterfront.

Anchorage: Just to the south and west of the Lantana-Ocean Avenue Bridge is a good anchorage with room for many craft. Commercial fishing boats operate from a pier here, and a restaurant is nearby. Anchoring used to be limited to 96 consecutive hours in any 30-day period, and a permit was required for stays of 18 hours or more. Contact the Code Compliance Office of the City Building Department at 318 S. Dixie Highway to see if this rule still applies since the passage of Florida Statute 327.02. The office is within walking distance; ask ashore for directions. If you anchor in the evening, you can register the next morning.

Boynton Inlet to Delray Beach

NAVIGATION: Use Chart 11467. Boynton Inlet, also known as South Lake Worth Inlet, is popular with local fishermen, but it is narrow, shallow and crossed by a fixed bridge with an 18-foot vertical clearance. The Coast Guard does not recommend passage through the inlet without complete local knowledge of all the hazardous conditions that exist. Jetties protect the entrance, and the unmarked channel is about 100 feet wide. A retaining wall helps stabilize Boynton Inlet's shoreline, but currents run swiftly, and bad tidal rips develop in strong easterly winds. No one should attempt the inlet except under ideal weather conditions and with up-to-date local information from a reliable source.

The ICW, where it passes Boynton Inlet, is narrow and shallow, inside and outside the channel. Shoaling in the ICW channel where the inlet current crosses the channel is a continuing problem, reducing depths in the vicinity of red nun buoy "46." This area both north and south of red nun buoy "46" was last dredged in 2008, so check locally for information on depths and/or marking before you pass through. Watch your course carefully, and do not be confused by the green buoys (quite large) marking a channel

leading in to the western shore. Follow the ICW channel markers carefully, as groundings are frequent here, usually resulting from the current at Boynton Inlet pushing vessels out of the channel.

ICW, South of Lake Worth

NAVIGATION: Use Chart 11467. Lake Worth ends just north of the Boynton Beach-Ocean Avenue Bridge (Mile 1035.0, 21-foot closed vertical clearance), which opens on the hour and half-hour at all times.

The ICW now becomes a canal, with concrete bulkheads lining its borders. Along this stretch, town follows town, and beautiful homes surrounded by subtropical growth add to the view.

From Lake Worth south, keep an eye out for the many Slow-Speed/Minimum-Wake Zones. They increase with greater frequency the closer you get to Fort Lauderdale. Be ready to call on VHF Channel 09 or whistle signal (two blasts: one prolonged, one short) for the opening of many of the 28 bridges that span the channel between Lake Worth and Government Cut at Miami Beach. Schedule a little extra time for the southward trip to allow for restricted openings, occasional bridge malfunctions and No-Wake Zones.

The Woolbright Road (Southeast 15th Street) Bridge (25-foot closed vertical clearance) is a bascule bridge connecting Boynton Beach with Ocean Ridge. The bridge crosses the Waterway at Mile 1035.8 and opens on signal.

■ DELRAY BEACH—MILE 1040

NAVIGATION: Use Chart 11467. **Use the Miami Harbor Entrance Tide Tables. For high tide, add 1 hour, 24 minutes; for low tide, add 2 hours, 7 minutes.** At Mile 1038, a charted shoal (less than 4.5-foot depths) encroaches on the western edge of the ICW at red daybeacon "52A." There is some shoaling in spots along the channel just south of Lake Roger to the north side of Lake Wyman and again in the channel on the south side of Lake Wyman. The first Delray Beach bridge you will encounter is the George Bush Boulevard Bridge (Mile 1038.7, 9-foot closed vertical clearance). The George Bush Bridge opens on signal at all times.

The second bridge in Delray Beach is the Atlantic Avenue Bridge (Mile 1039.6, 12-foot closed vertical clearance). The bridge opens at 15 and 45 minutes past the hour, 24 hours a day, seven days a week.

The Linton Boulevard Bridge (Mile 1041.0, charted 30-foot closed vertical clearance—27 feet is more realistic) opens on the hour and 30 minutes past the hour, 24 hours a day, seven days a week. Approximately 0.6 miles south of this bridge, at Mile 1041.7, steer well clear of the white buoy marked Rocks well out from the western shore of the ICW.

Dockage: Boating amenities at Delray Beach range from municipal slips (usually full of long-term rentals—reported five-year waiting list) to restaurants with their own dockage and full-service marinas and repair shops.

The Yacht Club at Delray Beach, located at Mile 1039.9 on the east side of the ICW, accepts transients with facilities including a laundry, Internet access and close proximity to the shopping district along Atlantic Avenue. They have 44 slips and can accommodate vessels up to 130 feet. Fuel delivery can be arranged.

Just north of the Atlantic Avenue Bridge (Mile 1039.6, 12-foot closed vertical clearance) is a city park complex (lawn bowling, shuffleboard, etc.) on the mainland (western) side of the ICW. Complimentary daytime dockage is available at the park (two-hour limit, no overnight docking) and there is a convenient and inexpensive pump-out station (a sign advises 4-FOOT DEPTH at mean low water) south of the bridge. Farther south, the Delray Harbor Club Marina offers transient space, a heated pool and a full fuel dock. Pass this fuel dock at idle speed.

Anchorage: At about Mile 1042, the round basin to the west of the Waterway, known locally as Pelican Harbor, has been a 24-hour anchorage only by order of the town of Delray Beach. The basin has 5-foot depths at the entrance and 6-foot depths inside. Poor holding has been reported, due to a very soft bottom. If you are planning to anchor here for more than 24 hours, check to see if you still need to get a permit from the city manager at City Hall (100 N.W. First Ave.), as the passage of the 2009 law should not require you to do so.

From Delray Beach south to Fort Lauderdale, smaller boats, and those bothered by the constant buffeting of the irregular, choppy sea caused by wakes, might consider traveling on weekdays when traffic is lighter. Wakes on this narrow channel retain their energy between opposing bulkheads, bouncing back and forth for some time after the passing of the craft that caused them. If the weather permits, you may just want to make the outside run from Lake Worth South to avoid the numerous bridges and boat wakes.

GOIN' ASHORE:
DELRAY BEACH, FL

Settled by Michigan farmers in 1895, Delray Beach is a mixture of new developments, fine older homes and other reminders of a gentler, more leisurely Florida.

In 1906, Japanese immigrants came to the area and established the Yamato Colony midway between Delray Beach and Boca Raton. Until 1940, the colony harvested winter vegetables and pineapples. The Morikami Museum and Japanese Gardens, founded by one of the original settlers, commemorate the history and culture of the colony. The adjoining park, with its Oriental gardens, is the site of tea ceremonies and several annual Japanese festivals. Call 561-495-0233 for directions.

The Old School Square Cultural Art Center (51 N. Swinton Ave., 561-243-7922), a National Historic Site, comprises architecturally significant school buildings restored to become the Crest Theatre, Cornell Museum and the Vintage Gymnasium. With a permanent art gallery in its lobby, the Crest Theatre sponsors a variety of concerts, musicals and dance and cabaret performances. The Cornell Museum includes four galleries

Delray Beach to Pompano Beach, FL

		Dockage					Supplies			Service				
	Phone	Largest Vessel Accommodated	VHF Channel Monitored	Transient Berths / Total Berths	Approach / Dockside Depth (reported)	Floating Docks	Gas / Diesel	Groceries, Ice, Marine Supplies, Snacks	Repairs: Hull, Engine, Propeller	Lift (tonnage), Crane, Rail	1=110V, 2=220V, B=Both, Max Amps	Laundry, Pool, Showers	Pump-Out Station	Nearby: Grocery Store, Motel, Restaurant
DELRAY BEACH														
1. Yacht Club at Delray Beach 1039.8 WiFi	561-272-2700	130	16	6/44	6.5/6.5						B/100	LS		GMR
2. Delray Beach Municipal Marina 1039.8	561-243-7136	55		/24	/10			I			B/50	LS	P	GR
3. Delray Harbor Club Marina 1040.5 WiFi	561-276-0376	200	16/11	7/43	8/8	F	GD	IMS			B/100	PS		GMR
BOCA RATON AND DEERFIELD BEACH														
4. Boca Raton Resort & Club 1048.2	561-447-3475	175	16	20/32	12/10			GIS			B/100	LPS		GMR
5. Marina One	954-421-2500							M	E					R
6. Cove Restaurant and Marina 1050.1	954-427-9747	200	16/9	/31	7/7		GD	GIMS			B/50	L		GMR
HILLSBORO INLET AREA, POMPANO BEACH														
7. Lighthouse Point Yacht/Racquet Club 1052.2 WiFi	954-942-7244	100	16/68	/78	10/8			IS			B/50	LPS	P	GR
8. Lighthouse Point Marina Inc. 1053.7	954-941-0227	90	16	10/100	7/7		GD	IMS			B/50	LPS	P	GMR
9. Yacht Management Marina WiFi	954-941-6447	85	16	5/24	12/5				HEP				P	P
10. Merritt's Boat and Engine Works 1054.8	954-941-0118	100			10/8			M	HP	L100				MR
11. Aquamarina Hidden Harbour 1054.8 WiFi	954-941-0498	43		3/3		F	GD	IMS	HEP	L75	B/30		P	
12. Sands Harbor Resort & Marina 1056.2	954-942-9100	100	16	40/50	10/10		GD	IMS			B/50	LPS	P	GMR

Corresponding chart(s) not to be used for navigation. ⌨ Internet Access 📶 Wireless Internet Access

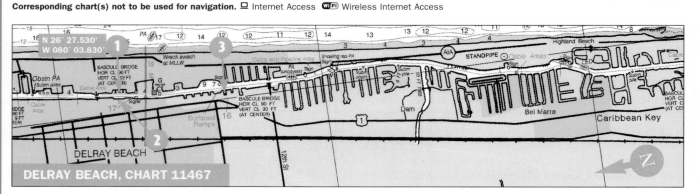

DELRAY BEACH, CHART 11467

N 26° 27.530'
W 080° 03.830'

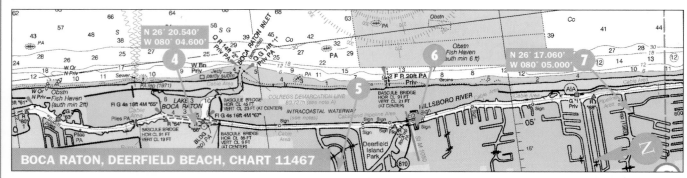

N 26° 20.540'
W 080° 04.600'

N 26° 17.060'
W 080° 05.000'

BOCA RATON, DEERFIELD BEACH, CHART 11467

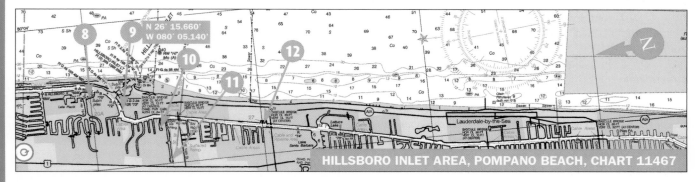

N 26° 15.660'
W 080° 05.140'

HILLSBORO INLET AREA, POMPANO BEACH, CHART 11467

with rotating exhibits, lecture series and artist showcases. The Vintage Gymnasium is a popular venue for town festivals and community events. The adjacent Entertainment Pavilion features concerts and movies under the stars.

Atlantic Avenue, the city's main street, features many historic and restored buildings and more than 150 boutiques and galleries close to the ICW. In the historic downtown Pineapple Grove district, the Ocean City Lumber Company has new life as a shopping, dining and entertainment center. The avenue leads to the ocean, where surfers attack the waves, and sunbathers bask on the wide sandy beaches. The Delray Beach Playhouse (950 N.W. Ninth St., 561-272-1281), next to Lake Ida, produces several comedies, musicals and Broadway plays each season. Town services such as the post office, library, banks and downtown shopping and restaurants are a few blocks from The Yacht Club at Delray Beach.

ADDITIONAL RESOURCES

- Greater Delray Beach Chamber of Commerce, 561-278-0424, **www.delraybeach.com**
- City of Delray Beach, 561-243-7000, **www.mydelraybeach.com**
- **NEARBY GOLF COURSES**
  Delray Beach Golf Club, 2200 Highland Ave., Delray Beach, FL 33445, 561-243-7380, **www.delraybeachgolfclub.com**
- **NEARBY MEDICAL FACILITIES**
  Delray Medical Center, 5352 Linton Blvd., Delray Beach, FL 33484, 561-498-4440

■ BOCA RATON—MILE 1045

NAVIGATION: Use Chart 11467. **Use the Miami Harbor Entrance Tide Tables. For high tide, add 23 minutes; for low tide, add 1 hour, 7 minutes.** The Spanish River Road Bridge (Mile 1044.9, 25-foot closed vertical clearance) opens on the hour and 30 minutes past the hour, 24 hours a day. About a mile to the south, the ICW crosses broad, shallow Lake Wyman through a narrow, well-marked channel favoring the eastern shore. If you stray from the channel, unmarked shoals call for extra caution. Be on the lookout for skiers and swimmers in the water.

About five miles south of Delray Beach, the ICW route leads into Lake Boca Raton through a cut lined with beautiful homes. Before entering the lake, the ICW passes under Palmetto Park Road Bridge (19-foot closed vertical clearance) at Mile 1047.5. The bridge opens on the hour and half-hour. This bridge crosses a narrow opening through which strong currents stream. If your vessel is lightly powered, when running with the current be sure to avoid being carried into the bridge or being carried by eddies into the concrete walls and docks along the sides. During weekends and particularly in-season, many small boats mill around the boat ramp next to the southwestern bridge abutment at Silver Palm Park, adding to the confusion.

Boca Raton, FL

Joseph R. Melanson of skypic.com

Looking east over Boca Raton Inlet and the low-clearance Camino Real bascule bridge. (Not to be used for navigation.)

The ICW then passes through Lake Boca Raton on its western side and continues south through the Camino Real Bridge (Mile 1048.2, 9-foot closed vertical clearance). It opens on the hour, and at 20 and 40 minutes past the hour 24 hours daily. This is the only restricted bridge in Palm Beach County that opens more than twice an hour, attesting to the large number of boats passing through. This is also the southernmost bridge in Palm Beach County.

When heading south through the Palmetto Park and Camino Real bridges, keep in mind that the current usually reverses in the ICW as it passes the Boca Raton Inlet. It is nothing even a lightly powered vessel can't handle, but be aware of it, particularly on an incoming tide. The Camino Real Bridge can be quite busy, particularly on weekends in-season.

The ICW channel through Lake Boca Raton is an Idle-Speed/No-Wake Zone, and the local marine police make a point to strictly enforce it. It is busy with tour boats and water taxis ferrying passengers between the Boca Raton Resort & Club and its private beach.

The Boca Raton Inlet is not recommended for passage without local knowledge of the conditions present. The tall, pink Boca Raton Resort and Club is a landmark visible from many miles offshore. The inlet's entrance has short jetties marked by private lights, and depths change throughout due to shoaling and shifting sandbars. The inlet channel and markers are not charted, and transit is considered dangerous. The Boca Inlet Bridge (23-foot closed vertical clearance) crosses the inlet and opens each quarter-hour from 7 a.m. to 6 p.m., or on signal at other times.

Dockage: The Boca Raton Resort and Club is located at Mile 1048. This first-class hotel is a local landmark and offers dockage with a 50-foot minimum charge. At Mile 1050, Cove Marina has transient dockage with a 7-foot-deep approach and offers gas and diesel fuel.

Anchorage: Just south of the Palmetto Park Bridge (Mile 1047.5), a small anchorage is located at the northeastern end of Lake Boca Raton. Enter north of flashing green "65," and anchor in 8-foot depths north and east of the charted shoal areas. An unmarked channel runs through the anchorage area and along the eastern shore to the Boca Raton Inlet. There is heavy traffic in the area, especially on weekends.

GOIN' ASHORE: **BOCA RATON, FL**

First discovered by Ponce de Leon, the area is shown on 16th-century Spanish charts as Boca de Ratones, by different accounts meaning "mouth of the harbor of the hidden rocks" or "Thieves Inlet." Over the centuries, the name was transmogrified into Boca Raton, which people have wrongly taken to mean "Rat's Mouth."

Local lore tells of treasure buried near Boca Raton Inlet by Edward Teach, alias Blackbeard the Pirate. The man who left the most lasting mark on the area, however, was the eccentric architect Addison Mizner. In 1925, he bought 6,000 acres and set out to build a dream city to outshine Venice with its splendor. The Waterway route through Lake Boca Raton hugs the western shore and passes within view of the resort Mizner designed and built. After Mizner went spectacularly bankrupt, the resort became a millionaires-only club. In 1942, the U.S. Army took it over and used it as a radar training school. Now, the entire complex encompasses the private Boca Raton Resort and Club.

"Downtown Boca" along Federal Highway and East Palmetto Park features upscale shopping, art galleries and street parties with local musicians. Located on Second Street and Federal Highway, Mizner Park is a unique mixed-use development of more than 40 shops, restaurants, a cinema, an amphitheater, offices and townhomes.

The Boca Raton Museum of Art (501 Plaza Real, 561-392-2500) has more than 4,000 works ranging from pre-Columbian to the modern masters. The Children's Museum (498 Crawford Blvd., 561-368-6875) displays children's art from the Americas in a historic wooden building. Caldwell Theatre Company (7901 N. Federal Highway, 561-241-7432) produces current Broadway hits, musicals and revivals. The Boca Raton Resort and Club (501 E. Camino Real, 561-447-3000) offers a great place to stroll the grounds, dine in one of several fine restaurants, enjoy the many shops and spend a night away from the boat.

■ DEERFIELD BEACH/ LIGHTHOUSE POINT

NAVIGATION: Use Chart 11467. The ICW leaves Lake Boca Raton through the Camino Real Bridge at Mile 1048.2, described earlier. It then enters another straight section

---

ADDITIONAL RESOURCES

■ City of Boca Raton, 561-393-7700,
www.ci.boca-raton.fl.us

■ Boca Raton Chamber of Commerce, 561-395-4433,
www.bocaratonchamber.com

NEARBY GOLF COURSES
Red Reef Executive Golf Course, 1221 N. Ocean Blvd., Boca Raton, FL 33432, 561-391-5014

NEARBY MEDICAL FACILITIES
Boca Raton Community Hospital, 800 Meadows Road, Boca Raton, FL 33486, 561-995-7100

---

with many canals, followed at Mile 1050 by the Hillsboro River with its many bridges and speed restrictions. Manatee Zones and Boating Safety Zones are frequent and often overlap. Where they do, the more restrictive limitation applies. Some are seasonal (November 15 through March 31); some are year-round; some are weekends only; some are for the full width of the water; and some are more restrictive within a specified distance from the shore. The official signs are well-placed and repeated at intervals, and some vary in only small details. You must keep a sharp lookout and read each sign carefully. The speed and wake limits are vigorously enforced by state, county and municipal police boats.

Hillsboro Inlet, FL

Looking north over Hillsboro Inlet and Pompano Beach. (Not to be used for navigation.)

Deerfield Beach is the next city, closely followed by the Lighthouse Point area, Hillsboro Inlet and Pompano Beach proper. A maze of man-made canals shoots off the ICW in all directions, and from here southward, virtually all land routes end up at the water.

Near Deerfield Beach, the Hillsboro Drainage Canal enters the ICW from the west at Mile 1049.9. During times of high flow from the canal, currents dangerous for lightly powered boats exist in the ICW, about 100 yards from the Hillsboro Boulevard Bridge. Southbound boats approaching the bridge should not proceed past the canal until the bridge is fully open, and should maintain adequate headway to avoid being pushed into the east bridge fender by the canal crosscurrents. There is a reported rock charted adjacent to the ICW channel just south of the Hillsboro Drainage Canal.

Deerfield Island Park is on the west side of the ICW. On the south side of the island, a short distance up the Hillsboro Drainage Canal, the park's boat dock can accommodate dinghies and small runabouts up to about 16 feet. There is no anchorage nearby, but there is a yacht club farther up the canal, and Cove Marina and Restaurant lies just on the south side of the bridge. The park has picnic areas and nature walks.

In Florida, all moveable bridges, including those in Broward County (from Deerfield to Hallandale, Mile 1074), monitor VHF Channel 09. For cruisers with cellular phones, all bridge signs in Broward County list the bridge telephone numbers, along with the VHF channel monitored. (Broward County has 10-digit dialing; you must dial the area code, 954, before dialing the phone number listed on the bridge.)

Note: All ICW bridges in Broward are on schedules 24 hours a day, seven days a week, year-round, except during the annual Air and Sea Show the first weekend in May (Las Olas and East Sunrise will be the only bridges affected). Other special events that may require deviations from schedules are announced in Local Notice to Mariners.

The Hillsboro Boulevard Bridge (state Route 810, Mile 1050.0, 21-foot closed vertical clearance) opens on the hour and half-hour at all times. From the bridge to Mile 1052 (south of red daybeacon "68"), shoaling exists along the edges of the channel.

Lighthouse Point, on the ICW
NAVIGATION: Use Chart 11467. Following the almost straight line of the Hillsboro River, the channel through the Lighthouse Point area is easy to run. The water is deep almost to the shore, and full-service marinas featuring everything from fuel, repairs and restaurants to swimming pools and tennis courts are convenient to the nearby Hillsboro Inlet. Marinas here tend to be located in snugly protected basins close to the Waterway, but sufficiently removed to avoid wakes from inlet traffic. An Idle-Speed/No-Wake Zone exists from just south of the Deerfield Beach-Lighthouse Point border at red daybeacon "68" to south of Hillsboro Inlet at flashing

green "73," where the speed restriction becomes Slow-Speed/Minimum-Wake. Shoaling is reported on both sides of red daybeacon "68B."

The array of canals off the western side of the ICW channel can be confusing to the newcomer. Be sure you have the latest edition of Chart 11467 (edition 41 dated June 2008 at press time in summer 2010).

Dockage: At Mile 1052.0, the Lighthouse Point Yacht and Racquet Club accepts transients and offers a restaurant, lounge and fitness center. The Lighthouse Point Marina, at Mile 1053.7, offers a full-service fuel dock, a pool, laundry and shower facilities. Yacht Management Marina, just inside Hillsboro Inlet, offers transient dockage up to 65 feet, a pool, 24-hour security and easy ocean access.

Hillsboro Inlet, South of Lighthouse Point
NAVIGATION: Use Chart 11467. **Use the Miami Harbor Entrance Tide Tables. For high tide at Hillsboro Inlet Coast Guard Station, subtract 16 minutes; for low tide add 3 minutes.** At Hillsboro Inlet, the 136-foot-tall lighthouse for which the area is named has one of the most powerful beacons on the coast (visible from 28 miles at sea). The fast-operating Hillsboro Inlet Bridge (13-foot closed vertical clearance), spanning the inlet approach from the ICW, is restricted between 7 a.m. and 6 p.m., opening on the hour and at 15, 30 and 45 minutes past the hour. Note that this bridge is not on the ICW proper. The current runs swiftly beneath the bridge. Wait for the bridge to open completely before you start your passage.

Although Hillsboro Inlet's shoals shift rapidly, dredging

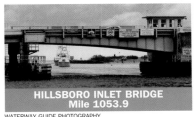

**HILLSBORO INLET BRIDGE
Mile 1053.9**
WATERWAY GUIDE PHOTOGRAPHY

is frequent, and local boats and the large fleet of charter fishing and head boats heavily travel the passage here. The outer channel was dredged to 20-foot depths in the last couple of years, which resulted in controlling depths seaward from the jetties of 15 feet, and 8 feet from the jetties to the bridge. Swells and/or tidal rip on the ebb against an easterly wind will decrease the available depth from 8 feet. Under good weather conditions, boats with 5-foot drafts or less can run the inlet safely by observing the constant flow of local boats going in and out. With any swell from the east, passage becomes hazardous. Local reports indicate to proceed all the way to the red-and-white sea buoy "HI" before turning south, to avoid shoals. A rock jetty extends southeast from the north side of the inlet and is submerged at the outer end. It is wise to seek local knowledge before running this inlet.

Just south of Hillsboro Inlet, the Waterway swings wide around a projecting point that builds out from the eastern shore. South from the inlet, for the next mile and a half, shoaling occurs in spots along the edges of the channel. The speed limit is Slow-Speed/Minimum-Wake to just

before the next bridge, where an Idle-Speed/No-Wake Zone begins. Beyond that bridge, a sign lists the complex speed restrictions that prevail for the next 2.5 miles.

■ POMPANO BEACH— MILE 1056

NAVIGATION: Use Chart 11467. Two bascule bridges cross the ICW in Pompano Beach, both with 15-foot closed vertical clearance. The northernmost, the Northeast 14th Street Bridge, crosses the Waterway at Mile 1055. The bridge opens at 15 and 45 minutes past the hour. The Atlantic Boulevard Bridge, at Mile 1056, opens on the hour and half-hour. Both bridges monitor VHF Channel 09.

Dockage: Pompano Beach has abundant boating services on protected side canals or in enclosed basins along the Waterway. Almost anything the yachtsman might want in the way of service, supplies, convenience or outright luxury is available in the immediate area. Just north of the Northeast 14th Street Bridge, Merritt Boat Works is a major yacht yard. No dockage is available for transients. Just before the Atlantic Boulevard Bridge, the Sands Harbor Resort & Marina provides transient dockage, gas and diesel fuel, a pool, showers and laundry facilities. On the far side of Lettuce Lake, the Ramada Inn Pompano offers dockage and some amenities.

Anchorage: Anchoring in Lake Santa Barbara (approximately Mile 1057.0) on the west side of the ICW is still possible. The local marine police do not encourage it, but can not forbid it (refer them to Florida Statute 327.02). Apparently, shoreline property owners complain that some cruising boats stay for weeks. Wakes from Waterway traffic make this an uncomfortable anchorage and charted depths of 6 to 7 feet are not reliable. Anchoring is possible in Lettuce Lake on the east side of the ICW, but not recommended since the lake is wide open to heavy and fast ICW traffic. It has 7- to 12-foot depths.

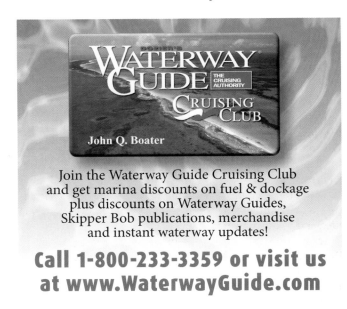

Pompano Beach, FL

GOIN' ASHORE:
POMPANO BEACH, FL

Pompano Beach means fishing. After all, even its name was inspired by one of the more popular species found in its waters. When some native folks served a group of survey-ors who were mapping the area the local game fish, they wrote the name of the fish, "pompano," on their map—and the name has stuck to the spot ever since. Pompano Beach has much to offer besides fishing. Visitors ashore can browse at one of the shopping centers back-to-back at the Atlantic Boulevard Bridge, or dine at one of the many restaurants. Sports such as golf, tennis, diving, swimming and surfing are readily available. Pompano Park (1800 S.W. Third St., 954-972-2000) features harness racing, poker tournaments and fine American cuisine at the Top of the Park.

In April, the Pompano Beach Seafood Festival brings together arts and crafts, non-stop live entertainment and great seafood. During the summer, "Music Under the Stars" sponsors a variety of free concerts throughout the city. The Pompano Beach Amphitheater (1806 N.E. Sixth St., 954-946-2402) presents a variety of national musical acts year-round.

ADDITIONAL RESOURCES

■ City of Pompano Beach, 954-786-4600

■ Greater Pompano Beach Chamber of Commerce, 954-941-2940, www.pompanobeachchamber.com

⚑ **NEARBY GOLF COURSES**
Pompano Beach Golf Course, 1101 N. Federal Highway, Pompano Beach, FL 33060, 954-786-4142

℞ **NEARBY MEDICAL FACILITIES**
Solantic Walk-in Urgent Care, 1161 S. Federal Highway, Pompano Beach, FL 33062, 954-580-4001

Cruising Options

Ahead to the south lies a true yachting center, Fort Lauderdale, the Venice of America. In settled weath-er, shoal-drafters who desire an offshore run can exit the Waterway at Hillsboro Inlet and rejoin it at Port Everglades. Or check our Bahamas edition for headings from either Hillsboro Inlet or Port Everglades that will take you to Grand Bahama or Bimini. ■

....

WATERWAY GUIDE is always open to your observations from the helm. E-mail your comments on any navigation information in the guide to: editor@waterwayguide.com

Boats docked along the Waterway. Photo Courtesy of Chuck Baier

Fort Lauderdale to Hallandale

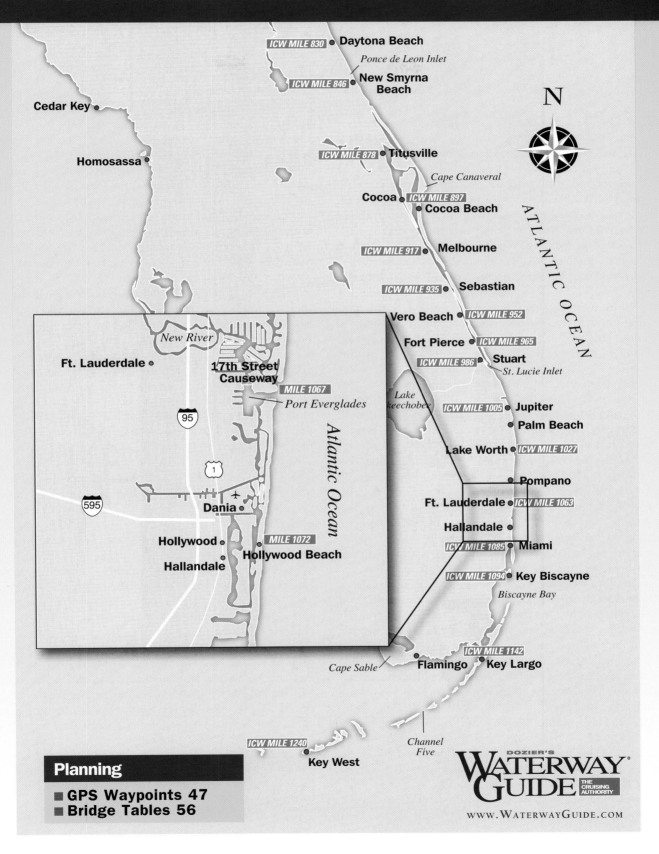

ICW MILE 830 ● Daytona Beach

Ponce de Leon Inlet

ICW MILE 846 ● New Smyrna
Beach

Cedar Key ●

Homosassa ●

ICW MILE 878 ● Titusville

Cape Canaveral

Cocoa ● ICW MILE 897
● Cocoa Beach

Melbourne

ICW MILE 917 ● Melbourne

ICW MILE 935 ● Sebastian

Vero Beach ● ICW MILE 952

Fort Pierce ● ICW MILE 965

ICW MILE 986 ● Stuart
St. Lucie Inlet

N

ATLANTIC OCEAN

Lake Okeechobee

ICW MILE 1005 ● Jupiter

● Palm Beach

Lake Worth ● ICW MILE 1027

● Pompano

Ft. Lauderdale ● ICW MILE 1063

Hallandale ●

ICW MILE 1085 ● Miami

ICW MILE 1094 ● Key Biscayne

Biscayne Bay

ICW MILE 1142

Cape Sable ● Flamingo ● Key Largo

ICW MILE 1240

Key West

Channel Five

Inset map

New River

Ft. Lauderdale ●

17th Street
Causeway

MILE 1067
— Port Everglades

95

Atlantic Ocean

1

595

Dania ●

Hollywood ●

Hallandale ●

MILE 1072

Hollywood Beach ●

Planning

■ GPS Waypoints 47
■ Bridge Tables 56

DOZIER'S
WATERWAY
GUIDE THE CRUISING AUTHORITY

WWW.WATERWAYGUIDE.COM

Fort Lauderdale to Hallandale

CHARTS 11466, 11467, 11469, 11470

■ FORT LAUDERDALE

Nearly 300 miles of canals, channels and waterways make their way through the Fort Lauderdale area, and at least half are navigable by virtually any size recreational craft. Often referred to as the "Yachting Capital of the World," the city lies about halfway between the Palm Beaches and Miami. With the Atlantic Ocean surf to the east and the traffic-laden Intracoastal Waterway (ICW) running north and south, the city is conspicuously water-oriented. The New River and its tributaries cut through the center of town, and artificial side canals run almost everywhere.

Well-known as a yachting center, Fort Lauderdale harbors more recreational boats than any other port in Florida. The number of registered vessels in Broward County is more than 53,000—the third highest of any county in Florida. Not surprisingly, the marine industry—marinas, boatyards and builders, yacht and charter brokers and marine services—ranks second only to tourism, generating about $11 billion in gross marine sales in Broward County annually. Marine and related industries employ more than 134,500 people in Broward County.

Although the entire city of Fort Lauderdale has the look of a huge yachting center, most boating amenities and services are concentrated in three main areas: the ICW, the New River and the Dania Cut-off Canal. Jostling each other for room is a collection of marinas, yacht services, sailmakers, boatyards, sales organizations, dinghy manufacturers, marine-supply stores and other useful facilities. Interior decorators, electronics experts, hairdressers, air-conditioning firms, bankers, boutiques and gourmet shops all consider themselves boating specialists and depend on the yachting trade for patronage. Skippers can tie up at on-the-water restaurants and shopping centers for shoreside dining, shopping or strolling.

The Marine Industries Association of South Florida (MIASF), a trade association for recreational boating, has a membership base of more than 800 marine-related businesses. Its helpful publications, Broward Safe Boating Guide and the Marine Guide, with its membership roster, are available from the MIASF office. Call MIASF at 954-524-2733 or 800-BOAT-001 for information on almost any marine matter, or visit their Web site at www.miasf.org.

Fort Lauderdale is an important commercial harbor. The straight, deep inlet at Port Everglades forms an excellent big-ship terminal and commercial port, handling millions of tons of ocean cargo each year. The cruise ship terminals in the port often have as many as eight or 10 of the largest cruise ships, including the *Queen Mary II*, in port at one time. Anyone cruising these waters will encounter cruise ships, tankers, freighters and military vessels.

NAVIGATION: Use Charts 11467 and 11470. **Use the Miami Harbor Entrance Tide Tables. For high tide at Bahia Mar, subtract 5 minutes; for low tide add 33 minutes.** For the eight miles from Pompano Beach to Port Everglades, the boater faces five bridges, scores of canals and rows of homes, small and large, on both sides of the ICW. For all practical purposes, the Fort Lauderdale area begins at Mile 1059, two miles south of Pompano, just past Lauderdale-by-the-Sea.

The initial ICW stretch is straight (with no need for aids to navigation), densely populated and heavily traveled. The channel then zigzags north of the Sunrise Boulevard Bridge and past Coral Ridge Yacht Club and Sunrise Harbor Marina, with associated condominiums to the west. Speed restrictions in open stretches differ for weekends and weekdays, and there are a number of short Idle-Speed/No-Wake Zones. In one three-mile segment, there are almost 60 side canals, many with offshoots of their own, and each is lined with gorgeous houses, most with boats in front of them.

To the east, on the ocean side of the Waterway, 180-acre Hugh Taylor Birch State Recreation Area stretches for three-quarters of a mile north of the Sunrise Boulevard Bridge (Mile 1062.6, 25-foot closed vertical clearance, opens on the hour and half hour) opposite the yacht club and marina. A pleasant, wooded oasis, the park provides the perfect spot for a sailor's holiday, rental canoes on a quiet lagoon, a swimming beach or a tropical picnic. Unfortunately, the park has no docks on the Waterway. Local marine police frequently patrol the Waterway here and vigorously enforce the speed limit.

South of the Sunrise Boulevard Bridge, the route is less straight, and markers reappear. Stay close to the western bank until you reach the first aid to navigation, flashing green "3," where the channel heads southeast. At the second aid, flashing green "5," the channel turns back southwest. Be careful to give the mainland point opposite flashing green "5" a wide berth. Before you make your turn, be sure to locate the next marker (flashing red "8"), as shoals extend out on both sides and too wide a swing will put you hard aground. An Idle-Speed/No-Wake Zone begins north of flashing red "8," north of the Las Olas Boulevard Bridge.

Bridges: Between Mile 1059 and Mile 1064 are four bridges, all restricted. The first, the Commercial Boulevard Bridge (Mile 1059.0, 15-foot closed vertical clearance), opens on the hour and half-hour. The Oakland Park

Boulevard Bridge (Mile 1060.5, 22-foot closed vertical clearance) opens at 15 and 45 minutes past the hour. The Sunrise Boulevard Bridge (Mile 1062.6, 25-foot closed vertical clearance) opens on the hour and half-hour. The Las Olas Bridge (Mile 1064, 24-foot closed vertical clearance) opens at 15 and 45 minutes past the hour. Special closures are in effect at the Sunrise and Las Olas bridges during the first weekend of May each year during the annual Air and Sea Show.

Dockage: More than a half-dozen restaurants (Charley's Crab [954-561-4800] and Shooters Waterfront Café USA [954-566-2855] among them), just above and below the Oakland Park Boulevard Bridge have docks for their customers. On weekends, several of the livelier drinking and dining spots on the east side have boats rafted out into the ICW, six or more deep. Just north of the Sunrise Boulevard Bridge are the Coral Ridge Yacht Club and the Sunrise Harbor Marina for megayachts.

There is an area of privately rented slips about a half-mile north of the Las Olas Bridge and west of the ICW at Mile 1063.5. To reach the long-term dockage areas at Isle of Venice and Hendricks Isle, turn west off of the ICW at Middle River between flashing green lights "3" and "5."

These canals are the last three straight north-south canals in the Nurmi Isles section. Hendricks Isle is the westernmost large isle; Isle of Venice is the next one east. Many properties rent slips on these two islands. Most are long-term rentals, but some properties rent slips on a daily basis. The various docks are different sizes and provide different shoreside amenities and they are priced accordingly.

The best way to find a slip here is to stop elsewhere temporarily, and then visit the area to check dock availability. During the winter season, slips here may be hard to find. All liveaboard docks here are equipped with a direct pump-out hose to each slip, which must be hooked up to each vessel's holding-tank deck fitting. "Y" valves must be locked, and flow-through treatment devices cannot be used. With new condominium development in this area, there is considerably less liveaboard dockage space than in the past.

Heading south, the Las Olas Marina is located on the east side of the ICW both north and south of the Las Olas Boulevard Bridge (Mile 1064.0,

LAS OLAS BRIDGE
Mile 1064

WATERWAY GUIDE PHOTOGRAPHY

BAHIA MAR TOWER
Mile 1064

WATERWAY GUIDE PHOTOGRAPHY

SE 17TH ST. CAUSEWAY BRIDGE
Mile 1065.9

WATERWAY GUIDE PHOTOGRAPHY

charted 24-foot closed vertical clearance, opens at 15 minutes and 45 minutes past the hour). This facility, operated by the city of Fort Lauderdale, offers dockage on both sides of the bridge, with larger slips on the north side and smaller ones on the south side. Ashore is a comfort station with restrooms, showers, laundry, dockmaster's office, a police station and a conference area. The piers feature security gates, vacuum pump-out at each slip and typical hookups of water, shore power and cable TV. There are floating docks right at the bridge for small boats and dinghies to tie up to visit the beach for the day, and lockers are available in the building there. Parking is available in designated areas. The Las Olas Marina is convenient to the beautiful beach strip with its shops, entertainment and resort hotels.

Anchorage: A cove along the west shore, immediately south of the Las Olas Bridge, offers the only designated anchorage within Fort Lauderdale's city limits. The anchorage and mooring area contains 10 city-owned moorings, which are available on a first-come, first-served basis. There is space for a few boats to drop the hook outside of the mooring area, but you must stay at least 500 feet from the moorings. There is no longer a 24-hour limit to your stay. Boats anchored on the outside close to the channel are subject to the current's effect.

The old moorings were removed and replaced with new equipment during summer 2007. The city dockmaster, whose office stands by on VHF Channels 09 and 16, will come by to collect. Phone ahead at 954-828-7200 for more information about availability. Any one vessel may rent moorings for no more than 30 days during a calendar year, and discounts may not be applied to mooring fees. Anchored vessels are requested not to block access to the docks at private residences adjacent to the Las Olas mooring area. White and orange buoys have been placed along the south boundary of the moorings to warn visitors not to anchor here. All landing of dinghies is done at the Las Olas Marina on the opposite (east) side of the ICW from the anchorage. Showers, laundry and trash disposal are available there for moored boats.

Miracle Mile, at Fort Lauderdale

Between the Las Olas Bridge (24-foot closed vertical clearance) and the Southeast 17th Street Bridge (55-foot closed vertical clearance), Fort Lauderdale's famous Miracle Mile sprawls out before you. The Miracle Mile (actually spanning about two miles) has two concentrated areas of marinas, one at either end, close to the bridges. Canals branch off in all directions, lined by spectacular homes with yachts docked at their doors. Many of these residences have been "remodeled" or expanded in size numerous times. Multimillion-dollar homes are often torn down here to make room for even more expensive homes.

Ashore, the changes on the Fort Lauderdale oceanfront between Bahia Mar (site of the Fort Lauderdale International Boat Show, one of the world's largest) and Sunrise Boulevard are a definite improvement. The busiest part of this beachfront is limited to one-way north-

QUICK FACT:

History of Fort Lauderdale

For at least 5,000 years, people have been drawn to Fort Lauderdale. The prehistoric peoples of South Florida, known as the "Glades Culture," and the early historic period peoples of the area, the Tequesta, enjoyed the abundance of natural resources available along Fort Lauderdale's New River. By 1763, the last of these aboriginal peoples had left the area. The Seminole Indians settled here between the 18th and 19th centuries. White settlers, most of whom farmed and fished for a living, first arrived in the area in the 1890s. They named their settlement after a fort that Maj. William Lauderdale had built there in 1838, during the Second Seminole War.

Although brief, Florida's period as a British possession occurred during a historically significant 20 years. The northern Colonies staged a revolution during Florida's time under the Union Jack, but Florida remained loyal, becoming a sanctuary for Tories.

After the war, the Treaty of 1783 returned Florida to Spanish domain, and the second Spanish era began. Around the same time, the Seminole Indians, who separated from the Creek Nation, claimed the Everglades as their home. The English and the Indians were not the only ones arriving in the area; the Spanish were busy claiming territories, but not settling here. To ensure its domain, Spain granted a large tract of land near the Miami River to a nobleman, who introduced yet another group into the area when he imported African slaves as field hands.

Florida became a U.S. territory in 1821, and this time the Spanish left permanently. The new nation encouraged its citizens to homestead, and by 1835, about 50 people had established a settlement along the New River. In 1836, a series of insurrections staged by the Seminoles led to full-scale war. In 1838, Maj. William Lauderdale and his 223 Tennessee volunteers were posted to the area and built a fort, which was named in their commander's honor. However, the Seminoles proved formidable enemies, and the wars continued for nearly 20 years. In 1839, the third Fort Lauderdale was built along the beach, not far from what is now Bahia Mar.

In 1845, Florida was admitted into the Union, and Fort Lauderdale started to develop. The East Coast Canal Company dredged a coastal barge canal that eventually connected the natural waterways. With the completion of a main road, stagecoach transportation connected the New River with northern cities. Henry Flagler extended his railroad from Jacksonville to Miami and, in exchange for right-of-way through Fort Lauderdale, agreed to establish a railroad station there. The first train arrived in 1896.

In 1906, Gov. Napoleon Bonaparte Broward, convinced that farming the Everglades was possible, promoted his plan to build a series of canals to drain the land and "feed the nation." News of the undertaking attracted land speculators who, having bought up thousands of acres, publicized a huge land lottery. The 143 residents of Fort Lauderdale, anticipating the arrival of thousands of new citizens, incorporated the town in 1911. However, when buyers discovered that the land was a huge swamp, mostly underwater, the land boom collapsed. Shortly thereafter, the entire downtown area burned to the ground.

In one of the little ironies of history, Broward's idea to reclaim swampland became a reality, albeit on a smaller scale. This quite literally made Fort Lauderdale. Residents, remaining after the land bust, dredged canals to drain the low swamps and piled the dredged muck along the shoreline. The land formed by the spoil became the site of today's luxury waterfront homes and yacht docks. As the draining of the Everglades began and the land slowly emerged, farming doubled—and then tripled. The business district began to rebuild, and cargo and passenger service started operating from the North New River Canal to Lake Okeechobee.

Broward County became more affluent. Tourists came to sample the tropical climate, and with Prohibition, rumrunners smuggled their wares from the Caribbean and Bahamas. The rich and powerful vacationed in Fort Lauderdale, too. Warren G. Harding, Franklin D. Roosevelt and Henry Ford came for the yachting, fishing and golf. Charter fishing fleets flourished, and sightseeing boats took to the waves. With the influx of tourists, another land boom began and, once again, speculators drove land prices sky-high.

The devastating hurricane of 1926 ended Fort Lauderdale's second land boom. The wholesale destruction of lives and property threw the area into an economic slump just three years before the Great Depression hit the rest of the nation. In the 1930s and early 1940s, the Great Homestead Act, passed by the Florida legislature, spurred a modest resurgence of home building. Federal work projects built U.S. Route 1, Port Everglades and its inlet and completed the ICW.

During World War II, Fort Lauderdale served as a major naval base and military training center. After the war, many returning servicemen settled there.

bound traffic and features bike trails, sidewalks and landscaping, all creating an attractive setting. Beach Place, an oceanfront multilevel shopping and entertainment complex with a Marriott resort, is drawing crowds, as are the numerous restaurants and nightclubs both north and south of Las Olas Boulevard. A large number of high-rise luxury condominium resorts, quite conspicuous from offshore, now line the strip between Sunrise and Las Olas Boulevards. These promise new upscale shopping and dining experiences in their lower floors as well.

NAVIGATION: Use Chart 11470. Between the Las Olas and Southeast 17th Street bridges, and farther south beyond the Dania Beach Boulevard Bridge (Mile 1069.4, 22-foot closed vertical clearance, opens on the hour and half hour), there are nearly continuous Slow-Speed/Idle-Speed Zones.

Just as the marinas here resemble little cities within a main city, the Waterway acts as their highway, and dense bow-to-stern traffic has become the rule rather than the exception. As on any crowded highway, watch out for Sunday drivers shooting out from all directions, crossing your bow, even tailgating.

The waters can churn feverishly from all the comings and goings. Some skippers travel only on weekdays to avoid the heavy weekend traffic between Pompano Beach and Miami.

Port Everglades is a major cruise ship port, and traffic is heavy in the area. If approaching from the south, the ICW channel may be difficult to pick out along the east side of the turning basin.

The Southeast 17th Street Causeway Bridge at Mile 1065.9 has a vertical clearance of 55 feet and opens on the hour and half-hour as needed. Vessels waiting on the south side for the bridge openings should stay clear of the turning basin and cruise ship berths, as well as government patrol boats.

Dockage: Although jam-packed with permanent year-round or seasonal boats, most marinas reserve some space for transients, so the visiting cruiser is almost certain to find a berth at one place or another. At the height of the season, you must reserve a berth in advance of arrival.

The first concentration of marine facilities southbound begins at the Las Olas Bridge on the eastern side of the ICW (the western side is residential except for the small anchorage and mooring area just south of the bridge). Going south, the marinas that appear are: the Las Olas Marina, just north and south of the bridge; the Hall of Fame Marina; and the large Bahia Mar Yachting Center, which has completed a major reconstruction, reconfiguration and conversion to floating slips on the north and south sections of the marina, as well as rebuilding an easy-access fuel dock.

The marinas offer virtually everything—from the basics such as berths, fuel, dockside water, electricity and marine supplies—to the fantastic. You will find swimming pools, on-the-boat telephone service, valet and maid service, catering and provisioning, cable television, tennis courts and beach access. Bahia Mar even boasts a literary landmark as one of its many attractions. Slip F-18 has been dedicated to John D. MacDonald's character Travis McGee. The plaque, which formerly marked the slip where Travis McGee docked his houseboat, *The Busted Flush*, is now on display in the dockmaster's office.

Water taxis stand by on VHF Channel 68 and will pick up or drop off passengers at locations throughout Fort Lauderdale, along both the ICW and the New River. The water taxis (954-467-6677) charge $13 for an all-day pass ($10 if over 65), offering unlimited stops and rides for the whole day. Details on fares, routes and stops are at www.watertaxi.com. Service to South Beach, Miami Beach's Art Deco District, usually runs on Thursday through Monday, but call to check availability.

A relatively short land-taxi ride away are two West Marine stores—at 2300 S. Federal Highway (an expanded "superstore" with adjacent Marine Services store) and 1201 N. Federal Highway. Most stores will special-order any type of equipment from the local boating businesses or from manufacturers. You can pick the equipment up yourself or have it delivered to the store. Boat Owners Warehouse (BOW), located on state Route 84 a few blocks west of South Federal Highway, offers competitive prices, knowledgeable help and special ordering from an extensive network of local marine suppliers.

The second concentration of marinas begins just north of the Southeast 17th Street Causeway Bridge. Heading south on the west side of the ICW, the Lauderdale Yacht Club has a narrow marked entrance channel through shallows. Next on the western side is the Lauderdale Marina, which has an easily accessed and popular fuel dock, directly on the ICW. Boaters should try to come in against the current, take up as short a space as possible and fuel up quickly. There is often a line of boats waiting, especially on weekends. TowBoatU.S. boats are based here.

If you don't feel like going to a fuel dock, let Peterson Fuel Delivery come to you. They offer their customers tanker direct prices and can fuel your vessel wherever you are in the Fort Lauderdale/Miami-Dade area.

The next facility south on the west side, directly on the ICW, is the former Marriott Portside-turned-Fort Lauderdale Grande, now the updated Hilton Fort Lauderdale Marina, an LXR luxury marina. Across the ICW on the east side is another LXR marina, The Hyatt Regency Pier Sixty Six Resort & Marina. Pier Sixty-Six offers resort amenities and a fuel dock.

Just south of the Southeast 17th Street Causeway Bridge on the east side is Sails Marina, formerly the Best Western Marina Inn and Yacht Harbor. The docks were redone, and updated utilities and amenities were installed. This marina is part of a planned new shoreside development.

Marine Police boats are active in the vicinity of the Lauderdale Marina and the 17th Street Causeway Bridge. It is necessary to maintain the slowest possible speed through this area to avoid a warning or ticket. Do not be tempted to speed up to make the bridge.

Marinas, restaurants, condominiums, a huge dry storage marina and marine services also line the 15th Street Canal, the first canal on the west side of the ICW just north of the Southeast 17th Street Causeway Bridge. A luxurious marina, the Boathouse of Fort Lauderdale, offering both wet and dry slips for sale or lease, is on the south side about halfway down the canal.

The canal has a public boat ramp and runs parallel to the busy shopping strip along Southeast 17th Street. The Southport Raw Bar at the end of the canal is a popular spot to visit by dinghy. From here, it is an easy walk down Cordova Road to the Harbor Shops shopping center on the south side of Southeast 17th Street where Bluewater Books and Charts, Publix and various other shops and restaurants are located.

Fort Lauderdale, FL

PETERSON FUEL DELIVERY
1-866-404-FUEL

FORT LAUDERDALE		Largest Vessel Accommodated	VHF Channel Monitored	Approach / Dockside Depth (reported)	Transient Berths / Total Berths	Floating Docks	Gas / Diesel	Groceries, Ice, Marine Supplies, Snacks	Repairs: Hull, Engine, Propeller	Lift (tonnage), Crane, Rail	1=110V, 2=220V, B=Both, Max Amps	Laundry, Pool, Showers	Pump-Out Station	Nearby: Grocery Store, Motel, Restaurant
				Dockage			**Supplies**			**Service**			
1. Coral Ridge Yacht Club 1062.3 WiFi	954-566-7886	100	16	3/58	10/4						B/200	PS	P	GMR
2. Sunrise Harbor Marina 1062.3	**954-667-6720**	200	16/11	6/22	9/8	F					**B/100**		P	GMR
3. Las Olas Marina/Mooring Field 1063.4 ⬜WiFi	954-828-7200	200	16	60/60	12/10	F		I			B/100	LS	P	GMR
4. Hall of Fame Marina 1063.8 ⬜WiFi	**954-764-3975**	130	16/08	41/41	9/9			I			B/100	LPS	P	GMR
5. Bahia Mar Beach Resort & Yachting Ctr 1064.4 ⬜WiFi	**954-764-2233**	250	16	150/245	13/8	F	GD	GIMS			B/200	LPS	P	GMR
6. Hyatt Regency Pier Sixty-Six Resort & Marina 1066.5 WiFi	**954-728-3578**	300	16	70/142	16/16		GD	GIMS			B/200	LPS		GMR
7. The Sails Marina 1067 WiFi	954-525-3484	300	16	24/24	25/25		GD	I			B/50		P	GMR
8. Hilton Fort Lauderdale Marina 1066.5	**954-527-6781**	300	16/71	33/33	20/10			IS			B/50	LPS	P	GMR
9. Cable Marine East 1066.4	954-462-2822	65	16/09	/12	20/15				HEP	L40	B/50			GMR
10. Lauderdale Marina 1066.2 ⬜WiFi	**954-523-8507**	160	16	10/60	10/10	F	GD	IMS	HEP	L35	B/50	S	P	GMR
11. Lauderdale Yacht Club 1066.0	**954-524-5500**				5/5									
12. Boathouse of Fort Lauderdale	**866-397-9993**		SLIPS FOR SALE OR LEASE AVAILABLE											

Corresponding chart(s) not to be used for navigation. ⬜ Internet Access WiFi Wireless Internet Access

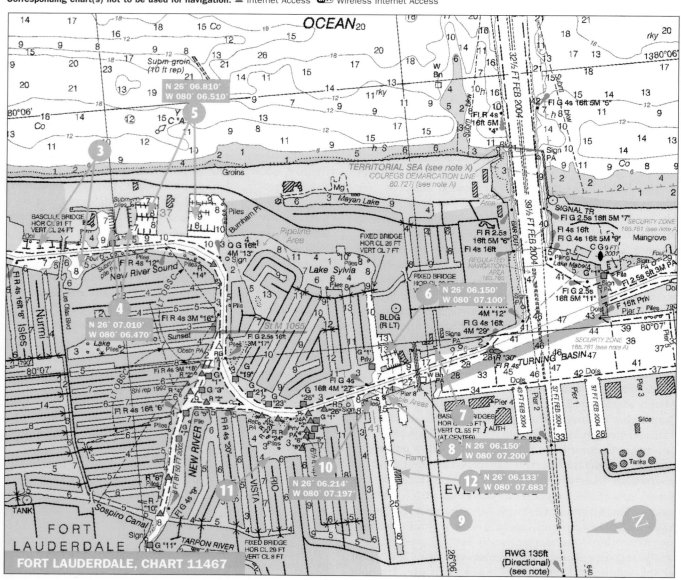

FORT LAUDERDALE, CHART 11467

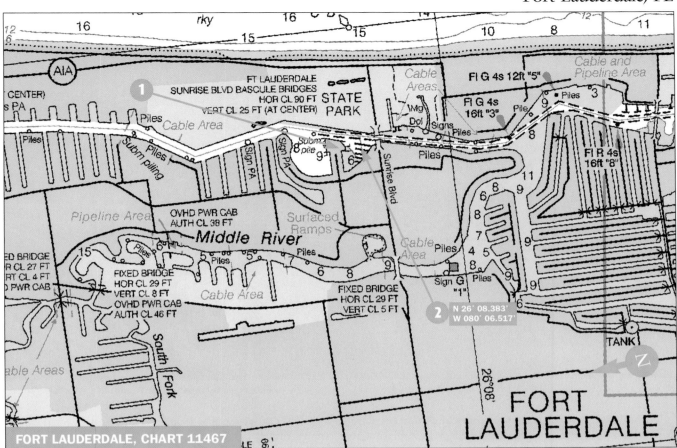

FORT LAUDERDALE, CHART 11467

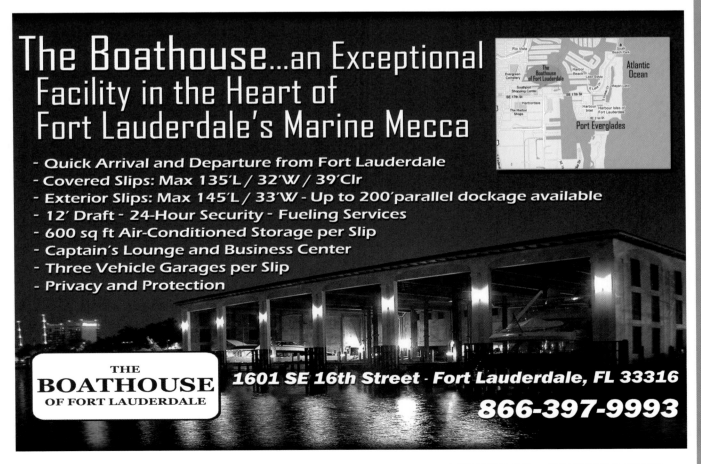

Miracle Mile, FL

Looking north Fort Lauderdale's Miracle Mile and the Intracoastal Waterway. (Not to be used for navigation.) WATERWAY GUIDE PHOTOGRAPHY

Within short walking distance from the Southport Raw Bar is also a hardware store, the Quarterdeck Restaurant and several dive shops. There is an Office Depot in the Southport Shopping Center and a CVS Pharmacy at the southeast corner of Federal Highway and Southeast 17th Street. The Bimini Boatyard Restaurant (954-525-7400) on the south side of the canal and 15th Street Fisheries Restaurant (954-763-2777) at the Lauderdale Marina are popular eateries in this area. Northport Marketplace, adjacent to the Convention Center and port facilities on the southwest side of the Southeast 17th Street Causeway Bridge, was redeveloped as a marine marketplace. Several relatively new hotels are in this vicinity, as well. If entering the port area by car, you should be aware that Eisenhower Boulevard is a secure area with road blocks at each end from the vicinity of the Convention Center to its intersection with state Route 84, and out almost to South Federal Highway.

Anchorage: To enter the anchorage area in Lake Sylvia, head east past the southwestern corner of Bahia Mar Marina, cut well inside flashing green "13," then hug the eastern sea wall when approaching the entrance channel into the lake. Continue to stay close to the sea wall until you are clearly into the lake. You will pass a large condominium building and private residences with docks as you head south. Stay close to the docks on the east side until about two-thirds of the way into the entrance channel, then move into the middle of the channel and enter the lake. The last stretch of the entrance, where you head into the middle of the canal, has an uneven bottom and is about 7 feet deep at low tide. Luxurious homes surround the anchorage. The previous 24-hour limit imposed on anchoring no longer

applies. On weekends, Lake Sylvia is full of local boats, many rafted for the night. It is also one of two legal waterskiing areas in the city (the other is in the Middle River). There is no place here to land a dinghy.

New River, at Fort Lauderdale— Mile 1065

The gently curving, meandering New River bisects the heart of Fort Lauderdale and serves as another major yacht-service area. Long before the Miracle Mile stretch emerged, the New River was Fort Lauderdale's yachting center, with

NEW RIVER/FT. LAUDERDALE ENT. Mile 1065

WATERWAY GUIDE PHOTOGRAPHY

some of the finest facilities for building, repair, haul-out and storage on the entire East Coast. Even if you don't need anything, it is worth taking a trip—by your boat, dinghy or one of the regularly scheduled sightseeing craft—just to see the contrast of the old and new Fort Lauderdale. In the past several years, there has been major construction of high-rise condominiums and apartment buildings near the river—downtown Fort Lauderdale is becoming a place to live and work.

Depending on the tide, small boats with less than 10 feet of overhead clearance and drawing less than 2 feet can make the full circuit of the New River, South New River Canal and the Dania Cut-off Canal and rejoin the ICW just south of Port Everglades. The entire trip is 11.7 miles with 2.2 miles from the ICW to Cooley's Landing, 1.7 miles to the Interstate 95 Bridge on the South New River Canal,

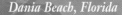

New River, FL

4.8 miles to the Interstate 95 Bridge on the Dania Cut-off Canal and three miles to the ICW. (The Fort Lauderdale Historical Society's fascinating booklet, "Fort Lauderdale's Waterways and Along Its Banks," can be purchased at the Fort Lauderdale History Center, 219 S.W. Second Ave., Fort Lauderdale, FL 33301, 954-463-4431.)

NAVIGATION: Use Chart 11470. **Use the Miami Harbor Entrance Tide Tables. For high tide at the Andrews Ave. Bridge, add 15 minutes; for low tide add 51 minutes.** Entrance to the New River depends on the direction you travel. The mouth is forked, and its two openings merge obliquely with the ICW at two different points. Check your chart carefully, and see the detailed directions below.

New River Approach, From the North

Heading south, the route to the New River follows the ICW around a sharp turn to the west past flashing red "16." Just beyond, the channel splits. Care should be taken when you pass red-and-green junction daybeacon "A." To go up the New River, leave the marker to port; to continue down the ICW channel, leave it to starboard. The water is shallow immediately behind this daybeacon, and boats going up the New River frequently run aground by passing it on the wrong side. Leave it to port and, heading west, watch for daybeacons "1" through "4." There is a white-and-orange DANGER daybeacon marking the charted shoal,

as well as one marking the shoal on the opposite side of the ICW from the New River entrance.

New River Approach, From the South

Heading north, the ICW is basically a straight line from the Southeast 17th Street Causeway Bridge to flashing red "20," where the Waterway channel starts a turn to the east, but a secondary channel continues northward to the mouth of the New River. If bound for the New River from the ICW heading north, vessels should leave flashing red "20" to starboard.

After passing the light, favor the bulkhead-lined western shore just opposite red daybeacon "2" until you have made the turn into the river's buoy system. Aids to navigation on the New River route, after passing red and green junction daybeacon "A" or flashing red "20," follow the normal red-right-returning rule for the river itself (river aids to navigation do not have the yellow squares or triangles of ICW aids).

When traveling the southern approach to the New River, watch the chart closely, and sort out the confusing transposition of buoys and colors before trying the entrance. Once inside the river's mouth, the buoy pattern is easy to follow.

Bridges on the New River

Some New River bridges have restricted openings. The first span, Southeast Third Avenue Bridge (16-foot

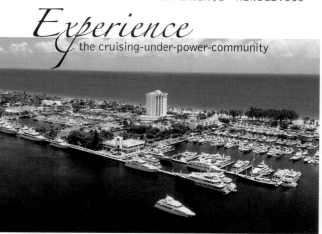

closed vertical clearance), opens on signal, except from 7:30 a.m. to 9:00 a.m., and from 4:30 p.m. to 6:00 p.m., Monday through Friday.

ANDREWS AVENUE BRIDGE
WATERWAY GUIDE PHOTOGRAPHY

The Andrews Avenue Bridge (21-foot closed vertical clearance) opens on signal, except from 7:30 a.m. to 9:00 a.m., and from 4:30 p.m. to 6:00 p.m., Monday through Friday.

The FEC Railroad Bridge (4-foot closed vertical clearance, normally open except for train traffic) operates semi-automatically; the operator has override capabilities even though electronic controls have been installed. The U.S. Army Corps of Engineers is making an effort to develop more reliable service at this bridge; call 800-342-1131, ext. 209, to report any delay of more than 10 minutes. There is a clock on the bridge that counts down the time remaining before opening.

The William H. Marshall Memorial Bridge (20-foot closed vertical clearance) connects Fourth Avenue on the south with Seventh Avenue on the north; the draw opens on signal except from 7:30 a.m. to 9:00 a.m., and from 4:30 p.m. to 6:00 p.m., Monday through Friday.

The strong tidal current should be considered when transiting the New River, because there is always congestion, especially at the bridges and along the Las Olas Riverfront dining and entertainment area.

The New River forks beyond the William H. Marshall Memorial Bridge into the North Fork and the South Fork of the New River. The North Fork is residential and has only one bridge (a hand-operated swing). The South Fork is residential for a distance, but becomes commercial where it makes a sharp turn to the west at Pier 17 and River Bend Marina. Several bridges cross the South Fork.

The Davie Boulevard Bridge (21-foot closed vertical clearance) does not open Monday through Friday from 7:30 a.m. to 9:00 a.m., and from 4:30 p.m. to 6:00 p.m.

Next are the twin Interstate 95 spans with 55-foot fixed vertical clearances, followed by a railroad bridge (2-foot closed vertical clearance) with a draw tender. The railroad bridge remains open except when trains are approaching. Here, there is also a fixed 55-foot vertical clearance railroad bridge for Tri-rail passenger trains. However, freight trains must still use the old bascule bridge. You may encounter strong currents near the twin bridges and around the nearby railroad bridges; turning room is limited. Extra caution is needed here.

Most large boats do not go any farther than the New River's other restricted span, the state Route 84 Bridge (21-foot closed vertical clearance) on South New River Canal. Its span opens only with 24-hour advance notice. The telephone number is 954-776-4300 (Department of Transportation). This is one of the few bridges in Fort Lauderdale not equipped with a VHF radio (the bridge is unmanned).

New River, FL

Looking east over the New River and I-95. (Not to be used for navigation.) WATERWAY GUIDE PHOTOGRAPHY

Cruising up the New River

NAVIGATION: Use Chart 11470. Just beyond its mouth, the New River wanders lazily through a short stretch edged by fine lawns and some of the area's older, grander and more gracious homes. Entering the commercial area, you pass over south Florida's only traffic tunnel, which carries U.S. Highway 1 beneath the river. This area was Fort Lauderdale's original business district, and its first boating center. Long before World War II, the wooded riverbanks were lined with docks, much as they are today.

A Slow-Speed/Minimum-Wake Zone is in effect along the New River between the ICW and Tarpon Bend, where the Tarpon River branches off to the south. The last New River marker, red daybeacon "12," marks a hard shoal extending into the channel at Tarpon Bend. Deep-draft vessels should not hug this too closely as they make the hard turn around it. The bottom is a rock ledge. After red daybeacon "12," keep to the middle of the river. Minimum depths are around 8 feet, but there are plans to dredge it to accommodate the megayachts needing to get to the facilities upriver. Above Tarpon Bend, the New River is an Idle-Speed/No-Wake Zone.

Beyond the William H. Marshall Memorial Bridge (20-foot closed vertical clearance), the river branches, and the principal channel takes the South Fork into another opulent residential section. The water is brown and murky, tinted by the Everglades' cypress swamps, which drain into an inland link in the river. Floating water hyacinths, coconuts and other debris appear frequently. Occasionally, you will spot the broad back of a manatee or the bulging eyes of an alligator.

Dockage: At the New River Downtown Docks, the city offers dockage along the river available on a first-come, first-served basis, or by reservation a few days in advance. The New River Downtown Docks are located in the heart of downtown, a short distance upriver from the beginning east of the Southeast Third Avenue Bridge and extending intermittently to the William H. Marshall Memorial Bridge at Cooley's Landing. There are 100 slips, for both transients and long-term rentals, on both sides of the river, offering full services and an excellent view of passing river traffic. Many of the slips were renovated and have state of

New River– Mile 1065, FL

NEW RIVER–MILE 1065		Largest Vessel Accommodated	VHF Channel Monitored	Transient Berths / Total Berths	Approach / Dockside Depth (reported)	Floating Docks	Gas / Diesel	Groceries, Ice, Marine Supplies, Snacks	Repairs: Hull, Engine, Propeller	Lift (tonnage), Crane, Rail	1=110V, 2=220V, B=Both, Max Amps	Laundry, Pool, Showers	Pump-Out Station	Nearby: Grocery Store, Motel, Restaurant
				Dockage				**Supplies**			**Service**			
1. Cooley's Landing Marina 🖳	954-828-4626	50	16/09	/30	10/6			I			B/50	LS	P	GMR
2. Riverfront Marina	954-527-1829	40	16	/300	10/6		GD	GIMS	HEP	L7.5			P	GMR
3. New River Downtown Marina 🖳	954-828-5423	130	16/09	80/100	25/12	CITY DOCKS					B/100			GMR
4. River Bend Marine Center **WiFi**	954-523-1832	80		20/65	10/8			GIS	HEP	L70,C	B/50	S		GMR
5. **LAUDERDALE MARINE CENTER**	**954-713-0333**	**175**	**16**	**99/110**	**10/12**	F		**IMS**	**HEP**	**L70,C**	**B/100**	**LS**	**P**	**GMR**
6. Jackson Marine Sales	954-792-4900	75			8/8			M	HEP	L70				GMR
7. Marina Mile Yachting Center	954-522-6262	150		10/35	12/10	F			HEP	L70	B/255			GMR
8. **MARINA BAY MARINA RESORT** 🖳**WiFi**	**954-791-7600**	**150**	16/68	50/168	12/45	F					**B/200**	**LPS**		**MR**
9. **YACHT HAVEN PARK & MARINA**	**954-583-2322**	**100**			12/6						**B/50**	**LPS**		**MR**
10. Rolly Marine Service Inc. **WiFi**	954-583-5300	150			9/9			IMS	HP	L200, C40	B/200	S		
11. Cable Marine West **WiFi**	954-587-4000	120	16	/75	12/12			M	HEP	L80	B/100			GMR
12. Billfish Marina 🖳	954-587-6226	110	16	45/45	14/9				HEP	L70	B/50			MR
13. Pipewelders Marine Inc.	954-587-8400	80			10/7	TUNA TOWERS DAVITS OUTRIGGERS					B/30			
14. New River Marina	954-584-2500			/15	13/7			M	HEP	L80	B/50			GMR
15. Marina Road Boat Yard	954-321-1010	65		/4					HEP	L30				
16. Bradford Marine Inc. 🖳**WiFi**	954-791-3800	175	78A	60/105	10/10				HEP	L300	B/200	S		GMR
17. Roscioli Yachting Center Inc. 🖳**WiFi**	954-581-9200	150		75/75	10/10				HEP	L265	B/100			GMR

Corresponding chart(s) not to be used for navigation. 🖳 Internet Access **WiFi** Wireless Internet Access

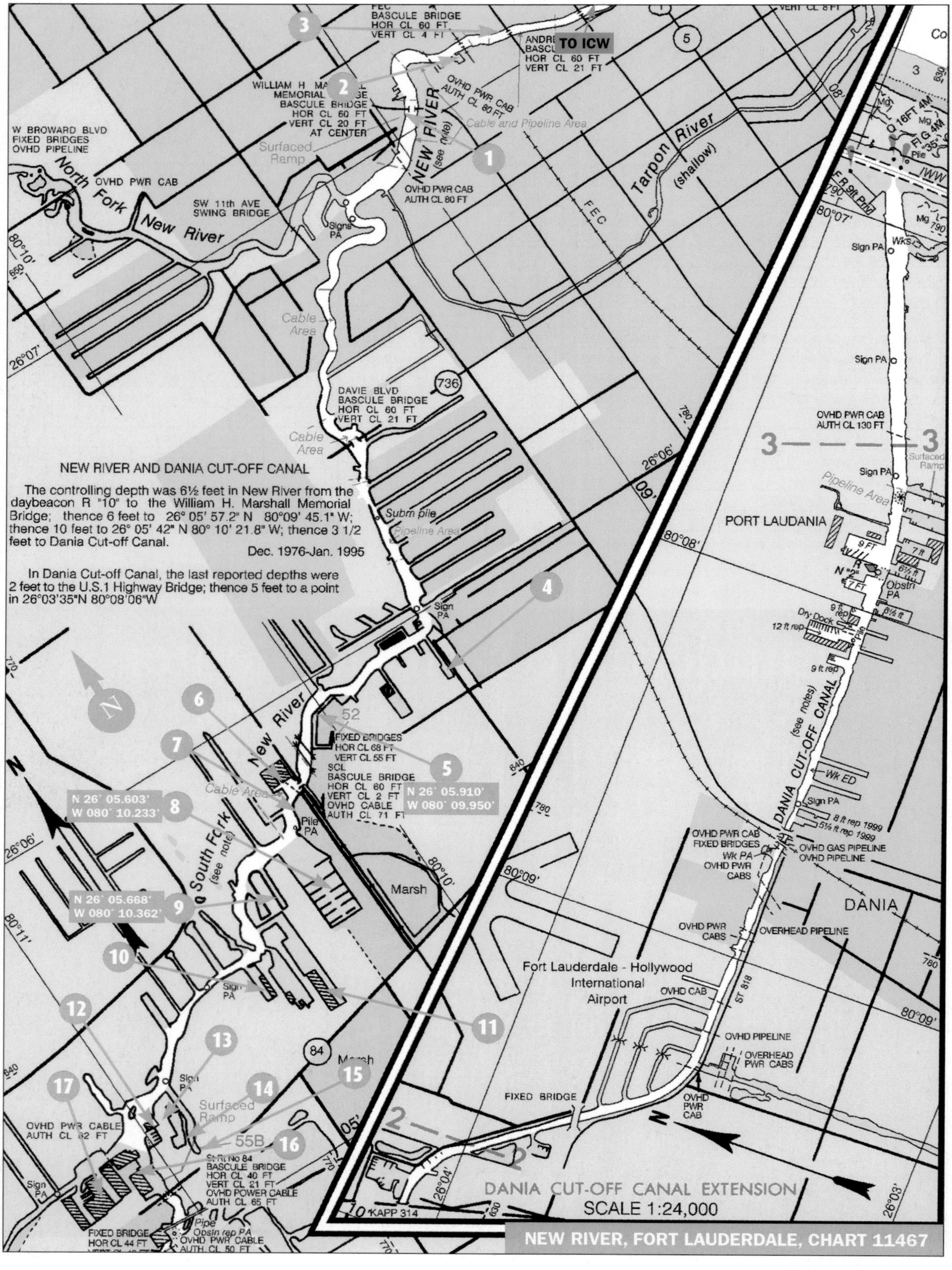

FEC
BASCULE BRIDGE
HOR CL 60 FT.
VERT CL 4 FT

③

ANDRE
BASC
TO ICW
HOR CL 60 FT
VERT CL 21 FT

5

Co

WILLIAM H MA
MEMORIAL
BASCULE BRIDGE
HOR CL 60 FT
VERT CL 20 FT
AT CENTER

②

OVHD PWR CAB
AUTH CL 80 FT

Cable and Pipeline Area

16 FT 4M
Mg
FLG 4M
Pile

①

NEW RIVER (see note)

Tarpon River
(shallow)

Mg
790

FEC

80°07'

Sign PA

WkS

W BROWARD BLVD
FIXED BRIDGES
OVHD PIPELINE

North Fork

OVHD PWR CAB

New River

SW 11th AVE
SWING BRIDGE

Sign
PA

OVHD PWR CAB
AUTH CL 80 FT

Sign PA

80°10'

660

26°07'

26°06'

OVHD PWR CAB
AUTH CL 130 FT

3

3
Surfaced
Ramp

Cable
Area

DAVIE BLVD
BASCULE BRIDGE
HOR CL 60 FT
VERT CL 21 FT

736

Pipeline Area

Sign PA

PORT LAUDANIA

9 FT

Cable
Area

NEW RIVER AND DANIA CUT-OFF CANAL

The controlling depth was 6½ feet in New River from the
daybeacon R "10" to the William H. Marshall Memorial
Bridge; thence 6 feet to 26° 05' 57.2" N 80°09' 45.1" W;
thence 10 feet to 26° 05' 42" N 80° 10' 21.8" W; thence 3 1/2
feet to Dania Cut-off Canal.

Dec. 1976-Jan. 1995

In Dania Cut-off Canal, the last reported depths were
2 feet to the U.S.1 Highway Bridge; thence 5 feet to a point
in 26°03'35"N 80°08'06"W

Subm pile

Pipeline Area

80°08'

80°08'

26°06'

7 FT

N "2"
R

7 FT

Obstn
PA

Dry Dock
9 ft

6½ FT

8¼ FT

12 ft rep

9 ft red

Sign
PA

④

⑥

52

FIXED BRIDGES
HOR CL 68 FT
VERT CL 55 FT
SCL
BASCULE BRIDGE
HOR CL 60 FT
VERT CL 2 FT
OVHD CABLE
AUTH CL 71 FT

⑤

N 26° 05.910'
W 080° 09.950'

Wk ED

Sign PA

8 ft rep 1999
5½ ft rep 1999

⑦

N 26° 05.603'
W 080° 10.233'

⑧

Cable Area

New River

Pile
PA

South Fork (see note)

N 26° 05.668'
W 080° 10.362'

⑨

26°06'

80°11'

⑩

Sign
PA

Marsh

80°10'

DANIA CUT-OFF CANAL (see notes)

OVHD PWR CAB
FIXED BRIDGES
Wk PA
OVHD PWR
CABS

OVHD GAS PIPELINE
OVHD PIPELINE

DANIA

OVHD PWR
CABS

OVERHEAD PIPELINE

⑪

Fort Lauderdale - Hollywood
International
Airport

OVHD CAB

OVHD PIPELINE

⑫

⑬

84

Marsh

⑮

OVERHEAD
PWR CABS

⑰

Sign
PA

⑭

Surfaced
Ramp

80°09'

FIXED BRIDGE

OVHD PWR
CAB

OVHD PWR CABLE
AUTH CL 62 FT

55B

⑯

Sign
PA

St Rd No 84
BASCULE BRIDGE
HOR CL 40 FT
VERT CL 21 FT
OVHD POWER CABLE
AUTH CL 65 FT

2

26°03'

DANIA CUT-OFF CANAL EXTENSION
SCALE 1:24,000

KAPP 314

FIXED BRIDGE
HOR CL 44 FT
Pipe
Obstn rep PA
OVHD PWR CABLE
AUTH CL 50 FT

NEW RIVER, FORT LAUDERDALE, CHART 11467

the art electrical hookups and pump-out connections for individual slips. Numerous towering condominiums line both sides of the New River adjacent to many of the docks, starting east of the Southeast Third Avenue Bridge and continuing to the William H. Marshall Memorial Bridge. Continuing the theme of Riverwalk on the north side of the river, beautiful landscaping, sculpture and brick walkways line the south side of the New River as well, along the renovated dockage area. The city dockmaster's office (954-828-5423) is on the south bank, just east of the Andrews Avenue Bridge. These docks are convenient to shopping and historical, business and cultural centers and the popular entertainment and dining areas along Riverwalk, Las Olas Boulevard and the Himmarshee Historical District. There is a Publix supermarket just two blocks south of the bridge on Andrews Avenue.

Cooley's Landing Marina, another city-owned marina on the New River, is located in a park on the north bank, with 30 slips located on both sides of the William H. Marshall Bridge. Dockage here is for vessels less than 50 feet in length. This popular location, with less river traffic, offers water, shore power, cable TV and pump-out at each slip, using a do-it-yourself portable pump-out tank, in addition to laundry, shower and restroom facilities. It is also convenient to shopping and the cultural centers. Cooley's Landing is open seven days a week from 8 a.m. to 5 p.m. If docking at Cooley's, time your arrival close to slack water for best maneuverability, as the current can be rather brisk.

Most cruisers thoroughly enjoy this river dockage. Water traffic is heavy on weekends, and extra fendering is desirable, although wake action is not nearly so noticeable as might be expected. The variety of watercraft is seemingly endless, and the sights and sounds of this traffic are fascinating. Las Olas Boulevard, just a short walk from slips on the north bank of the New River Downtown Docks and a bit farther from Cooley's Landing, offers excellent restaurants, gourmet food shops, fashionable boutiques and specialty shops. On the south side of the New River, just above the railroad bridge and across from the River House Restaurant, is the Riverfront Marina, the only fuel stop in this stretch.

A two-mile stretch of yacht yards, service shops and freshwater storage begins less than a mile above the Davie Boulevard Bridge, on the New River's South Fork. The channel accommodates deep-draft vessels to the storage and yacht-repair yards up to the Interstate 95 bridges (55-foot fixed vertical clearances).

The facilities include River Bend and Lauderdale Marine Center, a full-service facility for larger yachts, that has expanded eastward to take in the property between it and River Bend. This, the largest marine facility in the U.S., boasts a 50-acre complex that can haul and repair vessels up to 170 feet and 330 tons. Located farther along the South Fork past the I-95 and railroad bridges on the west side, is the Ft. Lauderdale Boat Club. Jackson Marine Sales still operates the service and repair facility; however, no fuel is sold there.

The Marina Bay Marina Resort, located on the southern shore shortly after passing under the I-95 bridges and through the second railroad bridge, offers full amenities plus floating villas, a pool, tennis courts, clubhouse and restaurant. The amenities include exercise, Internet and movie rooms, plus a coffee lounge. It has a country club atmosphere and is "pet friendly." Another Idle-Speed/ No-Wake Zone on the New River extends about 500 yards on either side of the bridge.

Yacht Haven Park and Marina accommodates vessels up to 100 feet and offers laundry and shower facilities. Expect redevelopment of the shoreside facilities here in the near future. Billfish Marina, located along the South Fork of the New River, offers transient dockage, boat repairs and a 70-ton lift.

Bradford Marine and the expanded facilities at Roscioli Yachting Center are also located in the same area. This area is accessed from state Route 84 (near the I-95 exchange) in the area known as Marina Mile. A dry storage marina, Marina Road Boat Yard, is above the Route 84 Bridge.

South New River Canal, Back to the ICW

NAVIGATION: Use Chart 11467. The "south fork" of the South Fork, the South New River Canal, leads to the southwest. Although narrow, it holds good depths, but a 50-foot-high cable south of the boatyards limits vertical clearance here.

The canal passes under the state Route 84 Bridge (21-foot closed vertical clearance) and then joins the Dania Cut-off Canal two miles south. This passage along the south fork of the South Fork is surrounded by wilderness and swamp, has a 2-foot controlling depth and is suited for small boat exploration only. East of this junction is another water-control gate. Rising like a guillotine, it allows vessels with less than 10-foot vertical clearances to pass beneath its dripping blade.

Note: Chart 11467 (in the New River Extension and Dania Cut-Off Canal Extension insets) notes that in the Dania Cut-Off Canal, the lastest reported depths were 2 feet west of the U.S. 1 Highway Bridge (no fixed vertical clearance is given on the chart, but it is observed to have a vertical clearance of around 10 feet). Various fixed bridges have limited vertical clearances that are not shown on the chart, but 10 feet is the controlling height west of Dania. The route then proceeds eastward past several marinas and several large yards to Port Laudania, where small freighters and cargo ships dock. Shortly thereafter, the Dania Cut-Off Canal joins the ICW in Dania Sound. Typically, the Dania Cut-off Canal is entered from the ICW, proceeding to the west; see the coverage of Dania Beach (in the following pages) for a description of the canal.

Dockage: Boaters' Park, on the north side of the Dania Cut-off Canal, has docks, picnic tables and restrooms for boaters on small vessels (with low clearances).

GOIN' ASHORE: **FORT LAUDERDALE— NEW RIVER, FL**

Fort Lauderdale, an important destination port on the ICW, has many onshore attractions and superb boating amenities. Located on the north bank between the river docking areas is the Broward County Performing Arts Center, a commanding presence on the New River at the heart of historic Sailboat Bend. The Arts and Science District also features the Museum of Discovery and Science, the Historical Society Museum, the Museum of Art and the IMAX Theater. Tom Jenkins' Bar-B-Q (954-522-5046), a local favorite for years, is located a few blocks south of the river on Federal Highway. Adventuresome travelers can take the shuttle bus to the Tri-Rail Terminal just west of I-95 off Broward Boulevard, three miles from the New River dockage area. The Tri-Rail makes connections to towns with marinas from West Palm Beach to Miami. The city bus terminal, located near the river, provides excellent transportation anywhere in Broward County. Rental car agencies with competitive rates are conveniently located.

On the north side of the New River, just east of the FEC Railroad Bridge, is a large shopping and entertainment complex, Las Olas Riverfront, with a dazzling array of shops and restaurants.

The Himmarshee Historic District, inland and adjacent to this area, features numerous restaurants and shops in a restored historical setting. Nightly live entertainment at the gazebo, a 23-screen cinema with new releases, restaurants ranging from casual to fine cuisine and extraordinary martini bars are all part of this festive riverfront. Riverfront Cruises depart from the dock on a regular basis for tours of the New River, ICW and Port Everglades. Public parking is available at the county parking garage across from Las Olas Riverfront after 11 a.m. on weekdays and all day on Saturdays and Sundays. The Sun Trolley offers inexpensive ($0.50 in exact change for each trip) transportation around the downtown area and to the beach (every 10 minutes on weekends) as well as several other routes for similar fares (or free to the Tri-Rail). Information is available at 954-761-3543 and at www.suntrolley.com.

Riverwalk, located on the north side of the New River, connects the area from the Southeast Third Avenue Bridge to the Broward Center for the Performing Arts. Special events include a Jazz Brunch—held the first Sunday of every month in the Bubier Park area of Riverwalk—New Year's Eve fireworks, Arts and Crafts Festivals and a St. Patrick's Day celebration.

ADDITIONAL RESOURCES

■ Greater Fort Lauderdale Convention and Visitors Bureau, 800-227-8669, **www.sunny.org**

■ Riverwalk Fort Lauderdale, **www.goriverwalk.com**

⚑ **NEARBY GOLF COURSES**
Plantation Preserve Golf Course & Club, 7050 W. Broward Blvd., Plantation, FL 33317, 954-585-5020, **www.plantation.org/golf/**

☤ **NEARBY MEDICAL FACILITIES**
Broward General Medical Center, 1600 S. Andrews Ave., Fort Lauderdale, FL 33316, 954-355-4400, **www.browardhealth.org**

Port Everglades, FL

Looking southwest over the bustling Port Everglades complex and inlet. (Not to be used for navigation.) Len Kaufman/Broward County

Port Everglades—Mile 1066

Port Everglades is the third busiest cruise-ship port in the world, with more than three million passengers expected in 2010. A modern deepwater harbor, it is the third of Fort Lauderdale's important boating areas. Ashore, expensive waterfront homes overlook the endless stream of cruise ships, recreational craft, tankers, freighters and warships constantly parading through the inlet. Nearly 150 warships, both domestic and foreign, visit the port every year. Port Everglades is now off limits to private vehicular traffic, with police guards at each entrance.

Security Zones: The Coast Guard establishes a moving security zone for the protection of passenger vessels (cruise ships), vessels carrying cargoes of particular hazard and vessels carrying liquefied hazardous gas, when such a vessel passes buoy "PE" to enter the port. Approaching closer than 100 yards to such a vessel is prohibited without prior permission.

The Coast Guard also has established a fixed security zone for Port Everglades for the protection of passenger vessels (cruise ships) and vessels carrying cargoes of particular hazard. When such vessels are docked in the port, boat traffic may still proceed along the ICW, provided that they stay to the east of law enforcement craft and cruise ship tenders being used to mark the transit lane. When such vessels are not docked, boats may use the ICW without restriction.

Occasionally, all traffic may be halted temporarily while ships are docking or undocking. Patrol craft may be contacted on VHF Channel 16 for the status of these security zones.

NAVIGATION: Use Charts 11470 and 11467. When approaching the port, the most prominent objects are four stacks painted red and white and equipped with red aircraft lights. For the weary mariner searching for the port from offshore, the stacks are a welcome sight indeed.

Warning: Keep clear of large-vessel traffic in the busy inlets, especially Port Everglades, Government Cut and Lake Worth. Huge commercial ships cannot maneuver

Dania Beach to Hollywood, FL

DANIA BEACH TO HOLLYWOOD		Largest Vessel Accommodated	VHF Channel Monitored	Approach / Dockside Depth (reported)	Transient Berths / Total Berths	Floating Docks	Gas / Diesel	Groceries, Ice, Marine Supplies, Snacks	Repairs: Hull, Engine, Propeller	Lift (tonnage), Crane, Rail	1=110V, 2=220V, B=Both, Max Amps	Laundry, Pool, Showers	Pump-Out Station	Nearby: Grocery Store, Motel, Restaurant
1. Sun Power Diesel 1 W of 1068.6	954-237-2200	100		2/13	20/10	F		IMS	E		R	B/50		GMR
2. Harbour Towne Marina 1 W of 1068.6	**954-926-0300**	200	16/11	35/165	14/7	F	GD	GIMS	HEP	L88	B/100	LS	P	GMR
3. Playboy Marine Center 1 W of 1068.6	954-920-0533	65	16	3/3	10/10			IM		L88,C18	B/50	S		
4. Royale Palm Yacht Basin 1 W of 1068.6	954-923-5900	100	78	30/60	7/7				HEP	L50	B/50	LS		GMR
5. Derecktor Shipyards 1 W of 1068.6	954-920-5756	184		/36	14/14	F	GD	MS	HEP	L150,C60,R	B/200	S		GMR
6. Associated Marine Technologies 1 W of 1068.6	954-926-0308	112	16/71		6/6				HEP	L90	B/150			
7. Hollywood Municipal Marina 1072.1	954-921-3035	115	16	15/55	7/7		GD	I			B/100	LS	P	GMR
8. Loggerhead Club & Marina-Hollywood 1072.5	**954-457-8557**	120	16	15/190	15/8			GIMS			B/100	LPS	P	GMR

Corresponding chart(s) not to be used for navigation. 🖥 Internet Access 📶 Wireless Internet Access

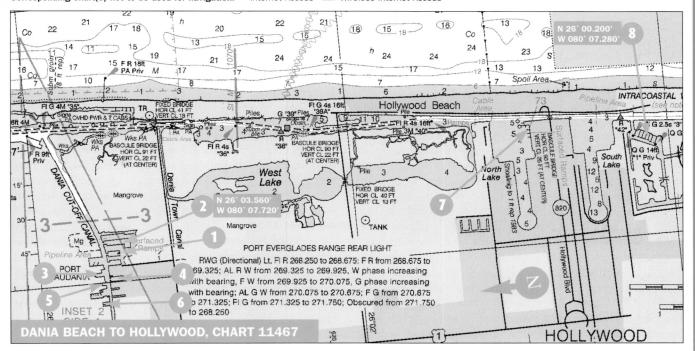

DANIA BEACH TO HOLLYWOOD, CHART 11467

easily, much less dodge small boats. The Coast Guard has established a Slow-Speed Zone in the Port Everglades Entrance Channel from the outer end of the jetties to the turning basin and ICW. The Coast Guard strictly enforces this Slow-Speed Zone.

The entire port area has deep water, with the exception of the northeastern corner outside the marked ICW channel. Deepwater docking extends to the south along the ICW to the Dania Cut-off Canal. At the point where the Waterway crosses the ship channel, keep the inlet and Waterway buoys sorted out in your mind. Remember that Waterway markers have a yellow triangle or square above the numerals.

Vessels southbound on the ICW follow the arrow-straight course of the chart's magenta line as it heads across the turning basin into the channel leading south from the southeastern corner where the Fort Lauderdale Coast Guard Station is located. After passing close to the

Coast Guard Station, be careful to avoid the mangroves and partially-submerged rocks outside of the channel on the eastern side of the ICW, while keeping the required distance from the cruise ships usually berthed on the mainland side, and paying close attention to the Slow-Speed/Minimum-Wake Zones.

One of the best and safest in Florida, Port Everglades Inlet itself is well-marked with flashing buoys along the entrance channel. Currents average .7 knots with a tidal range of 3.1 feet in the turning basin. The port and inlet may be crowded with both commercial and recreational traffic.

The inlet is a popular take-off point for cruisers heading for the Bahamas, as well as fishermen heading out to the nearby Gulf Stream, and skippers cruising north and south along the coast to escape the bridges and speed restrictions. It is also popular with ICW boaters hankering for different scenery.

Dania Beach, FL

Important Note: Vessels with mast heights over 56 feet that are headed south of Miami's Julia Tuttle Causeway (Mile 1087.2) have no choice but to go outside at Port Everglades. These vessels can then rejoin the ICW via Miami's Government Cut at Dodge Island.

The Outside Run to Miami

NAVIGATION: Use Charts 11467 and 11466. In ordinary weather, the run outside—north or south—is easy, safe and pleasant. Proceeding out the wide, straight channel, you will find good depths. The waters are reportedly clear of obstruction out beyond the jetties and inlet buoys.

On the south side, the good water extends well inshore, so many boaters turn south just beyond flashing green "5." On the north side, however, a submerged breakwater and a large spoil area parallel the ship channel and obstruct navigation. The local small craft that often run along the beach inside the spoil area (which sometimes surfaces at low tide) follow a hazardous course. Newcomers and those aboard larger boats should stay clear of this area by standing offshore past the jetty and flashing red buoy "2."

Southbound boats can travel safely within a quarter to a half mile of the beach, outside the breakers, all the way to Miami. This route keeps you inshore of the Gulf Stream, with its approximately 2-knot northerly set. Going north, stand out to sea to take advantage of the free push. Boats equipped with GPS will easily recognize the Gulf Stream by the increase in speed over the bottom or a sudden tendency to drift off course to the north.

The NOAA Weather Stations (Miami, WX-1, serves this area) broadcast the location of the inshore edge of the Gulf Stream from 4 p.m. to 8 p.m. on Mondays, Wednesdays and Fridays, and from 4 a.m. to 8 a.m. on Tuesdays, Thursdays and Saturdays in the fall and winter. NOAA Weather is not giving Gulf Stream hazards and locations in periods of warm weather because satellite photographs do not distinguish between water and air temperatures. The western edge of the Gulf Stream ranges from as close as a mile offshore to more than 10 miles; the width of the Gulf Stream is also stated in the WX broadcasts. The Gulf Stream really moves water. A sailboat can travel along at a good clip going south in the stream and stay in the same place all day. Sometimes southbound boats may be lucky enough to find a counter current running close to the shoreline.

Broward County has placed buoys at 50 locations of interest in the offshore waters of Broward County for scuba divers and snorkelers. To protect the coral from damage, these buoys should be used as moorings, instead of dropping anchor. Call 954-519-1270 for more information.

Dania Beach—Mile 1069

Named for its early Danish settlers, the city of Dania Beach was once the "Tomato Capital of the World." Visitors today can enjoy the beach, the 800-foot-long fishing pier and a remarkable collection of antiques shops. Or they can take

in the luxurious Dania Jai Alai Palace and perhaps place a few bets. The Dania Marine Flea Market has returned to the Dania Jai Alai Palace parking lot and is held annually in March. Check online at www.daniamarinefleamarket.com for information and dates.

NAVIGATION: Use Chart 11467. The area from Port Everglades Inlet to the next bridge south along the ICW is a manatee protection Slow-Speed/Minimum-Wake Zone. Take special care opposite the power plant, where the warm discharge water frequently attracts manatees. The area is well-marked with signs, and speed limitations are rigidly enforced, especially during weekends and the winter season. Leaving Port Everglades, observe the buoys and, if in doubt, favor the mainland. The eastern side is shallow and marshy with rocks outside the channel. The expanding port complex now extends to the Dania Cut-off Canal south of the inlet at Mile 1069.4.

The Dania Cut-off Canal area is a busy marine service center. Businesses here include well-equipped yards, modern marinas, boatbuilders and marine service specialists. Harbour Towne Marina is host to a large collection of yacht brokers and marine service shops such as engine, electronics, canvas and other repair shops, including Sun Power Diesel, which has relocated from the New River to this marina. In addition to good protection, the canal offers a rare treat for this part of the coast: There are no bridges on the Waterway between the canal and Port Everglades so boats berthed on the canal have unimpeded access to the inlet and ocean. Moreover, it is the nearest dockage to the Fort Lauderdale-Hollywood International Airport for those arriving and departing by air.

The Dania Cut-off Canal is an interesting Waterway to explore. Consult the New River text earlier in this chapter for a detailed description of the round-trip route from the New River and Fort Lauderdale counter-clockwise around to the ICW. Remember to watch your depths if you take this route. When approaching the canal from either direction along the ICW, keep a sharp lookout for high-speed traffic swinging out of the canal into the Waterway.

Just north of the Dania Beach Boulevard Bridge, on the ocean (east) side of the ICW, the former commercial complex has been redeveloped as SeaTech, an ocean engineering research facility of Florida Atlantic University. The Dania Beach Boulevard Bridge (Mile 1069.4, 22-foot vertical clearance) opens on the hour and half-hour.

Dockage: Along the Dania Cut-off Canal, several marinas offer transient dockage and boat repair, including Harbour Towne Marina, Royale Palm Yacht Basin, Playboy Marine, Broward Marine and Derecktor-Gunnell. SeaFair Marina, just off the Waterway on the east side behind an 18-foot clearance bridge, does not accept transients.

Hollywood Beach—Mile 1072

South of Dania Beach and the Dania Cut-Off Canal starts an area that has become almost a suburb of Fort Lauderdale and Miami. From Hollywood and Hallandale begins the built-up area all along the ICW of waterside condominiums and luxurious homes. Pay attention to the many No-Wake Zones, as they are well-policed.

NAVIGATION: Use Chart 11467. South of Dania Beach, the ICW cuts through several broad natural areas where the water is spread thinly, and the dredged channel is narrow. Pay careful attention to navigational markers and your depth sounder. The Sheridan Street Bridge (Mile 1070.5, 22-foot closed vertical clearance), which opens at 15 and 45 minutes past the hour, has a dogleg approach. The channel cuts across from the east close to the western shore before passing under the bridge. Be sure not to stray out of the charted, marked channel. Shoaling near green daybeacon "39" leaves depths at about 6 feet. Stay clear of the submerged pilings along the east shore at flashing green "39A."

The speed limit within the ICW channel is 25 mph (with a Slow-Speed/Minimum-Wake Zone buffer within 50 feet of shore) until reaching an Idle-Speed/No-Wake Zone about a quarter-mile south of the Sheridan Street Bridge, which continues past the next bridge, the Hollywood Boulevard Bridge (Mile 1072.2, 25-foot closed vertical clearance), which opens on the hour and half-hour. Farther south, Slow-Speed/Minimum-Wake Zones will alternate with 25-mph limits within the ICW channel and more Idle-Speed/No-Wake Zones. Watch carefully for regulatory signs, and read them carefully. In some areas, the ICW channel is exempt; in others, different speeds apply on weekends and/or seasonally, and other restrictions may apply.

Dockage: South of the Sheridan Street Bridge, the eastern shore is lined with casual restaurants complete with tie-up locations on the bulkhead for dining customers. The only local marina is Ruffy's. The Hollywood Municipal Marina lies at the southeast corner of North Lake (Mile 1072.2). The marina maintains 15 slips for transients and sells gas and diesel fuel. Call ahead if you wish to dock here. Although South Lake (south of Hollywood Beach Boulevard Bridge) has reportedly been dredged, North Lake has not. Controlling depths in the middle of the lake at large are reportedly as little as 1.5 to 2.5 feet. If docking at Hollywood Municipal Marina, stay close to the docks, as the minimum depth alongside is reportedly 6.5 feet at mean low water.

At red daybeacon "42," just south of the Hollywood Boulevard Bridge (Mile 1072.2, 25-foot closed vertical clearance), the Loggerhead Club and Marina offers a wealth of amenities. In addition to the conventional water and shore power, the facility offers slip-side cable TV, a vacuum pump-out system for each slip and wireless Internet access throughout the marina. The facility offers a lounge with Internet access, telephone service, a TV and daily newspapers. Air-conditioned restrooms and show-ers offer separate toilets and private dressing rooms. Also, coin-operated laundry facilities are conveniently located in the marina office building. Pool and health club facilities are located nearby; the health club offers gym equipment, tennis courts and a spa. A ship's store offers cold drinks, ice and snacks, as well as maintenance and repair items. Complimentary bicycles are also available. Hollywood's proximity to Fort Lauderdale makes these marinas fine alternatives when berths are hard to find.

Just a short walk from the Hollywood Municipal Marina, across the Hollywood Boulevard Bridge, is beautiful Hollywood Beach and a three-mile stretch of Oceanwalk along the beach, with restaurants and out-door dining. A few miles west (a 45-minute walk) on U.S. Route 1 in downtown Hollywood you will find extensive shopping and a historic, re-created old town with a new family oriented park in the center of Hollywood Circle. A short distance north of the bridge, on the east side of the ICW, is an excellent Greek restaurant, Opa Taverna, with happy hour from 4 p.m. to 7 p.m. every day.

Anchorage: Near the Sheridan Street Bridge, anchorage is available both north and south of the bridge along the east shore. The little cove with the beach at the north anchorage is within the boundaries of a park where anchoring is prohibited. Therefore, be sure you drop your anchor a bit north of the cove for 7-foot depths. On the south side, there is a snug anchorage for one or two boats north of the line of docks along the edge of the Waterway in 9- to 11-foot depths.

A short distance south of the Hollywood Boulevard Bridge is South Lake. Although the chart still shows depths of 4 and 5 feet, dredging has increased controlling depths to 28 feet and as much as 40 feet; investigate with caution. There is room for a number of boats, and the holding is good, but you may be rolled by the wake of passing boats on the ICW.

Hallandale—Mile 1074

South of Hollywood is Hallandale, with the Hallandale Beach Boulevard Bridge (Mile 1074.0, 31-foot closed vertical clearance). It opens at 15 and 45 minutes past the hour.

At this point, the channel is well-marked, relatively straight and bordered by high-rises leading through this growing suburban area to North Miami and Greater Miami. ∎

....

Waterway Guide advertising sponsors play a vital role in bringing you the most trusted and well-respected cruising guide in the country. Without our advertising sponsors , we simply couldn't produce the top-notch publication now resting in your hands. Next time you stop in for a peaceful night's rest, let them know where you found them—Waterway Guide, The Cruising Authority.

North Miami, Miami Beach

CHARTS 11466, 11467, 11468, 11469

Miami, as a whole, is a cultural conglomerate. Its aura represents the business influence of the New York metropolitan area, the Spanish cultural attributes of Havana and Latin America and the vibrant nature of the West Coast entertainment industry. It also represents the source from which the migration north through Fort Lauderdale, Boca Raton, the Palm Beaches and as far north as Jupiter stems. It is the initiator of the sprawl of "Megalopolis," which now stretches from the northern edges of the Keys to Martin County, and is still growing and spreading.

The tourism boom that originated in Miami has never faded, and the invention of the South Beach area of Miami Beach with its art deco flavor has caused the label of "celebrity capital of South Florida" to stick. Miami has successfully retained the golden image that it never truly lost.

For help in locating dockage, check WATERWAY GUIDE's marina listings in this chapter. Visiting boaters may also call the Marine Council at 305-569-1672 for information on the local marine and tourism industry.

WATERWAY GUIDE's coverage of the Greater Miami area is divided into two chapters. This "North Miami/Miami Beach" chapter deals with the upper Miami mainland, the Intracoastal Waterway (ICW) from Dumfoundling Bay just north of Bakers Haulover Inlet to MacArthur Causeway, the various crossover passages from the mainland to Miami Beach, and then Miami Beach itself. The "Miami to Key Biscayne" chapter, immediately following, covers the downtown and harbor areas and Government Cut, the main big-ship access to Miami Harbor. It also includes Virginia Key, Dinner Key, Key Biscayne, Coconut Grove, Coral Gables and Biscayne Bay, all of which could be considered part of the Florida Keys, but in reality are normally considered part of the approach to the Keys. Boca Chita is considered the official start of the Florida Keys by water and Key Largo by land.

ICW ROUTE— MILE 1074 TO MILE 1085

NAVIGATION: Use Chart 11467. From the Hallandale Beach Boulevard Bridge to south of Sunny Isles, boaters must comply with the IDLE-SPEED/NO-WAKE (minimum steerage) and SLOW SPEED/MINIMUM-WAKE (5 knots) signs (except for one brief passage in the middle of Dumfoundling Bay, where signs

indicate a 25-mph speed limit in the channel). The Hallandale Beach Boulevard Bridge (state Route 824, Mile 1074.0, 31-foot closed vertical clearance) opens at 15 and 45 minutes past the hour, 24 hours daily.

The Golden Beach (Northeast 192nd Street) Bridge crosses the Waterway at Mile 1076.3 with a 65-foot fixed vertical clearance. South of Golden Beach, the ICW, especially well-marked along here, enters the Miami area. Dumfoundling Bay is a broad, open and generally shallow body of water with a few deeper patches along its eastern shore. There is no anchorage room here; it is all a cable area. At Dumfoundling Bay's southern end, the marked route crosses over to the western shore. To the north of the Maule Lake entrance, there is a shoal marked by a privately maintained white daybeacon— give it a wide berth.

From Dumfoundling Bay, the ICW enters Biscayne Creek, with the community of Sunny Isles on the eastern shore. The Sunny Isles Bridge (Mile 1078.0, state Route 826), a twin-bascule bridge with a 30-foot charted closed vertical clearance, links that community to the mainland. It is restricted Monday through Friday, year-round, from 7 a.m. to 6 p.m., opening at 15 and 45 minutes past the hour. On weekends and federal holidays from 10 a.m. to 6 p.m., the bridge opens at 15 and 45 minutes past the hour. An anchorage is located just north of the bridge in the bay on the east side of the ICW. Just south of the bridge, on the east side, are boating facilities with fuel docks.

When you observe that the tidal current is speeding up along the Waterway route, you are nearing Bakers Haulover Inlet.

Looking north over North Miami, with Bakers Haulover Inlet to the right. (Not to be used for navigation.) WATERWAY GUIDE PHOTOGRAPHY

Dockage: The Turnberry Isle Marina Yacht Club and the Loggerhead Club & Marina, across from Golden Beach, both accept transients. Turnberry Isle Marina Yacht Club offers full amenities—wireless Internet, showers and laundry, 24-hour security and floating docks. Diesel fuel is available at their convenient fuel dock. They can accommodate vessels up to 180 feet at their attractive facility, which includes an inviting dockside pool. They are conveniently located just off the ICW.

Loggerhead Club & Marina, also located just off the ICW is in a large, but protected harbor. They can accommodate vessels up to 120 feet and have numerous amenities including a Captain's Lounge, waterfront dining and great shopping nearby. Every imaginable convenience of the Aventura area is at your doorstep.

At Mile 1077, a straight, narrow and deep canal cuts westward off the ICW to Maule Lake and the Williams Island Marina, which offers full resort amenities and dockage in a well-protected harbor. At Williams Island, you can go to the spa or gym, or play tennis then have a dip in one of the pools. Enjoy breakfast, lunch or dinner at the café. Williams Island can accommodate a 150-foot vessel with up to 7-foot draft.

Just north of Bakers Haulover Inlet is Haulover Beach Park Marina with fuel and transient dockage; call ahead for space availability. At the park, there are charter fishing boats, tennis courts, a nine-hole golf course and a beautiful ocean beach.

Bakers Haulover Inlet—Mile 1080

⚠️ **THE FOLLOWING AREA REQUIRES SPECIAL ATTENTION DUE TO SHOALING OR CHANGES TO THE CHANNEL**

NAVIGATION: Use Chart 11467. Northernmost of Miami's entrances from the Atlantic Ocean, this passageway is heavily used by fishermen and local boats, and since it was dredged a few years ago, it has become a popular and easily accessible inlet to the ocean. The only limitation being a fixed bridge with a 32-foot vertical clearance.

Coming in from the Atlantic, Bakers Haulover Inlet is marked by a quick-flashing white light on the south jetty and

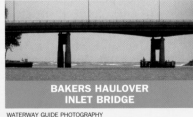

BAKERS HAULOVER INLET BRIDGE
WATERWAY GUIDE PHOTOGRAPHY

is spanned by a fixed bridge (32-foot vertical clearance). Jetties are short here, and currents are strong. The inlet can become especially nasty when wind and current oppose. Government Cut, a clear, well-marked inlet only 8.3 nautical miles to the south, is Miami's big-ship entrance and would normally be your inlet of choice. Heading south on the ICW to reach Bakers Haulover Inlet, turn to port out of the ICW at red daybeacon "4A" and take a bearing on the entrance to the inlet, a straight shot.

North Miami & North Miami Beach, FL

NORTH MIAMI/NORTH MIAMI BEACH		Largest Vessel Accommodated	VHF Channel Monitored	Approach / Dockside Depth (reported)	Transient Berths / Total Berths	Floating Docks	Gas / Diesel	Groceries, Ice, Marine Supplies, Snacks	Repairs: Hull, Engine, Propeller	Lift (tonnage), Crane, Rail	1=110V, 2=220V, B=Both, Max Amps	Laundry, Pool, Showers	Pump-Out Station	Nearby: Grocery Store, Motel, Restaurant
		Dockage					**Supplies**			**Service**			
1. Loggerhead Club & Marina—Aventura 1075.2 ⌨	305-935-4295	120	16	12/99	20/10			GIS			B/100		P	GMR
2. Turnberry Isle Marina Yacht Club ⌨ (WiFi) 1075.8	305-933-6934	180	16	20/117	30/8	F	D	IS			B/100	LPS	P	GMR
3. Aquamarina Hi Lift 1077.3	305-931-2550	40		/9		F	G	IMS	HEP	L				
4. Williams Island Marina 1076.6 ⌨ (WiFi)	305-937-7813	160	16/10	/99	10/7	F		I			B/100	PS	P	R
5. Haulover Beach Park Marina 1079.7	305-947-3525	90		/150	8/8		GD	IMS			B/50	S	P	R
6. Keystone Point Marina 1.3 W of 1080.9	305-940-6236	110	16/09	10/26	8/10	F	GD	IMS	HEP	L23	1/50		P	GMR

Corresponding chart(s) not to be used for navigation. ⌨ Internet Access (WiFi) Wireless Internet Access

The shoaling problem on the ICW channel west of Bakers Haulover Inlet, Mile 1080, south of red daybeacon "6A," is legendary. Periodically it is dredged, and like clockwork, it fills back in. In spring 2010, there were four green can buoys marked "7," "7A," "7B" and "7C," which directed you towards the red side of the channel to avoid the shoaling. Watch for a strong set to the west with flood tide and to the east with the ebb.

Follow these buoys even if it appears that they are leading you to one side of the normal channel. Shoal depths of 3.5 to 4 feet at mean low water are being reported at press time summer 2010. There is a Slow Speed/Minimum-Wake restriction along this entire area.

END SPECIAL CAUTION AREA.

Anchorage: One of the finest overnight anchorages along this section of the ICW lies across the Waterway from Bakers Haulover Inlet at Mile 1080. The only drawback is its entrance. According to reports, at high tide you should turn cautiously northwest off the ICW, approximately 75 feet north of red daybeacon "6A," and then slowly head directly toward the large, green, rounded roof of the Florida International University athletic building (approximately 305 degrees magnetic).

To pass safely between the 3-foot-deep bar to port and the 4-foot-deep spoil area to the north, use your chart's large-scale inset on side B. If you encounter depths of less than 8 feet within the first couple of hundred feet, you are beginning to stray out of the channel. Inside this virtually undeveloped deepwater basin are serene anchorages protected from all wind directions with depths charted at 7 to 16 feet. The bottom is quite soft (there may be debris in some places); make sure that your anchor is well-set. Visiting boaters are not permitted ashore on the university's property.

On the mainland opposite Bakers Haulover Inlet is the start of North Miami. Here, in protected New Arch Creek, are a number of boating amenities, repair yards and stores that are eager to serve transient mariners. There is a well-marked approach channel leading west from ICW red daybeacon "12."

Upper Biscayne Bay

NAVIGATION: Use Chart 11467. Use the Miami Harbor Entrance Tide Tables. For high tide at Baker's Haulover Inlet, add 57 minutes; for low tide, add 1 hour 37 minutes. The upper bay is extremely shallow, and the ICW cuts diagonally across it from northeast to southwest down to the 79th Street Causeway. The channel is narrow but well-marked, favoring the eastern shore until it passes under Broad Causeway. The Broad Causeway Bridge (Mile 1081.3, 16-foot closed vertical clearance) is the first of five restricted Miami spans. The span opens at 15 and 45 minutes past the hour, year-round, between 8 a.m. and 6 p.m.

A variety of routes wait south of Broad Causeway. Threading between markers, passing under or through various bridges and causeways, the mariner can stay with the ICW to Miami and the Keys, or leave the ICW, via any of several routes, to explore Miami Beach.

From Broad Causeway to Government Cut, smaller boats with a maximum vertical clearance requirement of less than 35 feet can follow an alternate route southward, called the Miami Beach Channel, thereby avoiding the heavy ICW traffic and delays at bridges with restricted openings. This relatively well-marked channel runs south along the eastern coast of Biscayne Bay (the western shore of Miami Beach) to Government Cut. Land for homes was created by pumping sand up from Biscayne Bay's bottom and depositing it behind bulkheads. As a consequence, minimum depths of 6 to 7 feet lie almost anywhere near the shore, except where indicated on the chart. The open bay outside the ICW channel, on the other hand, has depths of only 1 to 3 feet.

There are four bridges along the Miami Beach Channel. The 79th Street Causeway East, 25-foot closed vertical clearance, opens on signal. The Julia Tuttle Bridge East has a 35-foot fixed vertical clearance. The Venetian Causeway East Bridge (5-foot closed vertical clearance) has restricted hours. The bridge opens on signal, except from November 1 through April 30, Monday through Friday, from 7:15 a.m. to 8:45 a.m., and then again from 4:45 p.m. to 6:15 p.m.; the draw does not open during these hours. If any vessels are waiting to pass, the draw opens when signaled at 7:45 a.m., 8:15 a.m., 5:15 p.m. and 5:45 p.m. These restrictions are still in place,

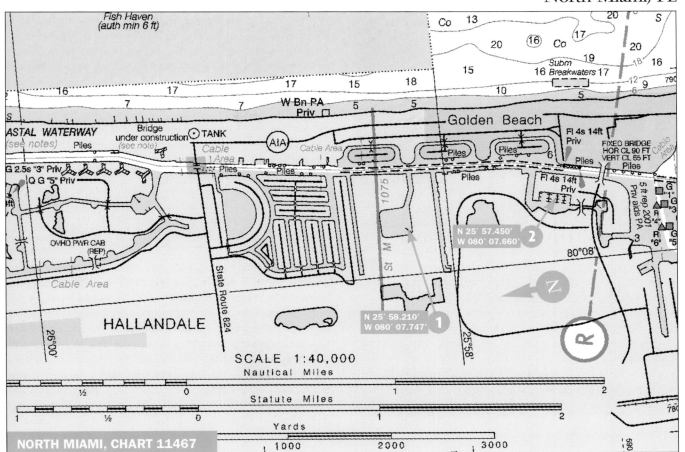

NORTH MIAMI, CHART 11467

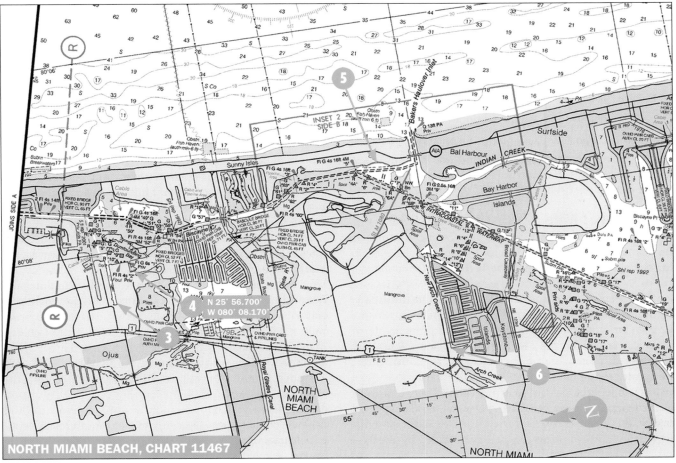

NORTH MIAMI BEACH, CHART 11467

Miami Beach, FL

Looking west over Bakers Haulover Inlet and its 32-foot fixed bridge. (Not to be used for navigation.) WATERWAY GUIDE PHOTOGRAPHY

although rumors of a change in the schedule have been floating around for some time; make sure to check with the bridge tender for the current schedule. The draw opens on signal on Thanksgiving Day, Christmas Day, New Year's Day and Washington's Birthday. The Miami Channel now becomes the Meloy Channel and the final bridge is the MacArthur Causeway Bridge (35-foot fixed vertical clearance at the eastern end).

WATERWAY GUIDE next covers the main ICW route as far south as MacArthur Causeway, the fifth of the six causeways (north to south) linking Miami and Miami Beach, and then describes the approaches to Miami Beach and the famed resort area itself.

ICW Route: Mile 1085 to Mile 1090

NAVIGATION: Use Chart 11467. Continuing south from Broad Causeway, follow your chart scrupulously, observing the markers and staying strictly to the charted magenta line. The channel runs diagonally across Biscayne Bay to the western shore and the 79th Street Causeway (Mile 1084.6, 25-foot closed vertical clearance opens on signal). Be sure to indicate that you want the "western" span when calling the 79th Street Causeway on VHF Channel 09; there is another span of the 79th Street Causeway to the east.

Just south of the western span of the 79th Street Causeway is the marked entrance to Little River, which has facilities that offer various services for transients. South of Little River, the ICW—now narrow and surrounded by shoals—

continues relatively straight to the Julia Tuttle Causeway Bridge (Mile 1087.2). This is the fixed bridge (56-foot fixed vertical clearance) that sets limiting overhead clearance for the inside passage from Fort Lauderdale to Miami. A few extra feet may be gained at low tide, but study the tide gauge before starting through.

The next pair of bridges (the Venetian and MacArthur causeways) are only a short distance apart. The Venetian Causeway (western span), at Mile 1088.6, has a 12-foot closed vertical clearance at center and operates on a restricted schedule. Monday through Friday, from 7 a.m. to 7 p.m., the bridge opens on the hour and half hour. Saturdays, Sundays and federal holidays, the bridge opens on request. The MacArthur Causeway is a pair of bridges with 65-foot fixed vertical clearances at Mile 1088.8.

Although well-marked, it is wise to take particular care navigating the ICW at the MacArthur Causeway, as the markers here can be confusing. Just north of the causeway, channel markers lead off from the ICW to enter the Main Ship Channel of Government Cut. (No small-boat traffic is allowed when the cruise ships are in, and marine police diligently patrol the entrance.) Once through the MacArthur Causeway Bridge, markers indicate the route southeast to Fishermans Channel, south of Dodge Island.

Dodge Island Railway and Highway bridges cross the Waterway at Mile 1089.3. The highway bridge has a 65-foot fixed vertical clearance, and the railroad and old highway draw spans have 22- and 26-foot closed vertical clearances, respectively. Both draw spans are usually

ALL THE ESSENTIALS. ALL THE ESSENCE.

Located directly on The Intracoastal Waterway, Turnberry Isle Marina Yacht Club delivers everything you and your vessel require. Beyond what is essential, you'll enjoy the things that make our marina a cut above the rest. A crew that is as attentive as your own. Impeccable facilities. Plus a location that offers safe haven with convenient access via Bakers Haulover Inlet and is surrounded by the shops of Aventura Mall, the beaches, world-class dining and more. The essentials meet the essence of ocean travel at Turnberry Isle Marina Yacht Club.

yachts up to 180'
•
30-, 50- and 100-amp service, single and 3-phase
•
24-hour security
•
private pool
•
two phone lines, mail
•
showers, ice, laundry
•
wireless internet access
•
annual, seasonal, transient

Turnberry Isle Marina Yacht Club

19735 TURNBERRY WAY, AVENTURA, FLORIDA 33180
TEL 305.933.6934 • FAX 305.933.6908
MARINA@TURNBERRYISLE.COM • WWW.TURNBERRYISLEMARINA.COM

left in the open position. Once you pass these bridges, Fishermans Channel is the alternate route east to reach Government Cut (as well as Miami Beach Marina) when the Main Ship Channel is closed.

Dockage: Pelican Harbor Marina lies just north of the Venetian Causeway (west). It has excellent facilities and easy access to Miami. Call ahead if you need dockage at this popular facility. Farther south of the 79th Street Causeway is Palm Bay Club and Marina, which offers deepwater slips to 120 feet, 24-hour security, tennis courts, a pool, restrooms/showers, gas and diesel fuel and pump-out service at its fuel dock.

Cross-Routes to Miami Beach

The routes between the ICW and the Miami Beach Channel, each paralleling one or another of the causeways that connect the mainland to the ocean islands, are all readily apparent on the chart. While most are safe, they still call for close attention to the chart, buoys and depth sounder.

Broad Causeway

NAVIGATION: Use Chart 11467. The northernmost crossover to Miami Beach appears just below Broad Causeway. (In reality, this is the beginning of the alternate route southward, designated as the Miami Beach Channel, described earlier.) At green daybeacon "15," bear a bit east of south off the ICW toward flashing red "2" (leave to starboard), which then leads to the short, marked channel at the tip of

Biscayne Point. Passing through the narrow channel marked by green daybeacons "3" and "5" to port and red daybeacons "4" and "6" to starboard, steer for red daybeacon "8" at the western tip of Normandy Isle, commonly accepted as the boundary of Miami Beach. Here, you will come upon deep water, but do not try to circumnavigate the island unless you use a dinghy. A fixed bridge with a 5-foot vertical clearance connects the island to the ocean beach.

At the East 79th Street Causeway (the second crossover) connecting Normandy and Treasure islands (25-foot closed vertical clearance, opens on signal, be sure to include "east" in your call for an opening), this route meets the second crossover (see below). If you are using this route to Indian Creek, on the eastern shore of Miami Beach, steer east passing north of La Gorce and Allison islands and through the bascule bridge connecting Allison Island with the beach island. If you are continuing down Miami Beach Channel, steer south between flashing green "11" to port and red daybeacon "12" to starboard to the next eastern terminus of the third cross-over, the Julia Tuttle Causeway, which is not recommended without local knowledge.

79th Street Causeway, North—Mile 1083.5

NAVIGATION: Use Chart 11467. This route leaves the ICW three-quarters of a mile north of the causeway (also known as the John F. Kennedy Causeway) and heads between markers and across a spoil area toward Harbor Island. It then passes along the unmarked north side of Treasure Island to deeper water off Normandy Isle. Here, it joins the Miami Beach Channel (described above). South and east of the next bridge (79th Street Causeway—East) is the entrance to Indian Creek (described below).

Shoaling has been reported at the eastern end of Treasure Island, between the island and red daybeacon "8" off Normandy Isle. Give a good berth to the daybeacon, and you will find the best water along the Treasure Island shore. To be certain, wait for half tide or better. Even at dead low water, depths of at least 8 feet are available near and at the 79th Street Causeway. Although charts indicate a channel with controlling depths of 7 feet and more north of the Julia Tuttle Causeway (the next causeway south), local knowledge is required.

Julia Tuttle Causeway—Not Recommended Without Local Knowledge

Leaving the ICW at green daybeacon "39," a channel parallels the north side of the Julia Tuttle Causeway. The channel runs just north of a few 2- to 3-foot-deep shoal areas along the causeway. The only aid-to-navigation identifying the channel is green daybeacon "25" marking the 35-foot vertical clearance fixed bridge (Julia Tuttle—East Bridge) over the Miami Bridge Channel on the eastern shore of Biscayne Bay. Thus, without local knowledge, this east-west crossover is not recommended.

Upper Biscayne Bay & Miami Beach, FL

MIAMI BEACH		Dockage				Supplies					Service			
		Largest Vessel Accommodated	VHF Channel Monitored	Transient Berths / Total Berths	Approach / Dockside Depth (reported)	Floating Docks	Gas / Diesel	Groceries, Ice, Marine Supplies, Snacks	Repairs: Hull, Engine, Propeller	Lift (tonnage), Crane, Rail	1=110V, 2=220V, B=Both, Max Amps	Laundry, Pool, Showers	Pump-Out Station	Nearby: Grocery Store, Motel, Restaurant
1. North Beach Marina 1084.8	305-758-8888	30		DRY STORAGE ONLY						IMS	HP	L9	1/30	R
2. Gator Harbor West 2 E of 1084.8	305-754-2200	45		/20	6/6						B/100	L		GMR
3. North Bay Landing Marina .5 E of 1083.8	305-861-5343	120	16/68	/118	8/8		G	GIMS			B/100	LPS	P	GMR
4. Pelican Harbor Marina .3 E of 1084.8	305-754-9330	50	16/68	10/98	6/6		GD	IMS			B/50	S	P	
5. Palm Bay Club & Marina .5 W of 1085.3 🖥️Ⓦ🄵🄸	305-751-3700	150	16/68	10/50	9/9		GD	GIS			B/100	LPS	P	GM
6. Wyndham Resort Miami Beach	305-532-3600	200	16/09	/200	7/7						B/50			MR
7. Fontainebleau Resort & Towers	305-538-2022	140		4/23	7/7						B/100	PS		MR
8. Sunset Harbour Yacht Club Ⓦ🄵🄸 2 E of 1088	305-398-6800	150	16/11	25/125	10/9			GI			B/100	LPS	P	GMR
9. Miami Beach Marina 1089 3 E of 1089 Ⓦ🄵🄸	305-673-6000	250	16/68	100/400	13/12	F	GD	GIMS			B/100	LPS	P	GMR

Corresponding chart(s) not to be used for navigation. 🖥️ Internet Access Ⓦ🄵🄸 Wireless Internet Access

MIAMI BEACH, CHART 11467

Venetian Causeway, North and South

NAVIGATION: Use Chart 11467. The next two crossings between the ICW and Miami Beach are north and south of the Venetian Causeway. Both routes are safe and easy, with the one on the north being slightly deeper. This causeway jumps over a series of small islands to Belle Isle, the oldest island in Biscayne Bay and the closest to Miami Beach. The two cross-routes skirt the islands' northern and southern extremities.

To cross to the north of the Venetian Causeway, turn east from the ICW at flashing green "49." (There is also a private white marker with a sign for Sunset Harbour Yacht Club, which you leave to starboard. Use Inset 3 on the chart.) The channel is relatively well-marked, though some daybeacons may be missing. The channel leads directly to the Miami Beach Channel and Sunset Harbour Yacht Club on Miami Beach. (See a description of this marina below under "Miami Beach" and "Dockage.")

Miami Beach, FL

SUNSET HARBOUR
YACHT CLUB

Looking east over Biscayne Bay. (Not to be used for navigation.) WATERWAY GUIDE PHOTOGRAPHY

Anchorage: Good anchorages lie west and south of the small island with the Flagler Monument (south of the eastern span of the Venetian Causeway). Approach these via the Miami Beach Channel or the cross-bay route south of the Venetian Causeway (on the northern side of the entrance channel with 6-foot depths). Depths in the anchorage run up to 8 feet, so most recreational craft can drop the hook comfortably. Check your chart carefully to avoid cable and pipeline areas.

MacArthur Causeway

NAVIGATION: Use Chart 11467. The final cross-bay passage is along the main ship channel to the end of the MacArthur Causeway. The southernmost approach to Miami Beach is spanned by a 35-foot fixed bridge (U.S. Route 41/A1A) near the U.S. Coast Guard base at the inner end of Government Cut at Meloy Channel.

■ MIAMI BEACH

No matter which route you take to Miami Beach, be sure to allow ample time for sightseeing once you get there. Essentially a creation of the tourism industry, Miami Beach and its islands are mostly man-made. Its hip, vibrant image, now punctuated by the popularity of Latin

music, thrives in the Art Deco District, with its numerous hotels and acclaimed restaurants, as well as the trendy South Beach area. So many people in the entertainment industry have moved here that it has been dubbed "Hollywood East." Some of the world's most flamboyant hotels and residences grace the nine miles of beach here, and visitors will find unlimited entertainment, spectacular water views and thousands of graceful coconut palms. If you travel with a pet aboard, you will find that virtually all the sidewalk restaurants are extremely pet-friendly.

Indian Creek Side Trip

Indian Creek is a narrow body of water that splits off Miami Beach proper and the beach. It skirts down across the road from many of the lavish hotels in Miami Beach's Bar Harbor area. Several of the hotels maintain dockage on the bulkhead, such as the Fontainbleau Hilton, but you should definitely call ahead to ensure space.

NAVIGATION: Use Chart 11467. Going south on the Miami Beach Channel, you can leave the route at red daybeacon "10" south of Normandy Isle and go east to the beginning of Indian Creek. Be sure to stay within the charted deep water, and enter between La Gorce Island and Normandy Isle. From this point, head south on the eastern side of Allison Island to Indian Creek's only drawbridge (charted closed vertical clearance 11 feet, but tide gauges indicate only 8 feet), which opens on signal. The Coast Guard has proposed to temporarily change the opening schedule, allowing the bridge to remain closed

Looking north over Miami Beach. (Not to be used for navigation.) WATERWAY GUIDE PHOTOGRAPHY

during certain periods when it undergoes rehabilitation. Make sure to check with the bridge tender for the current schedule. In Indian Creek itself, favor the eastern shore; shoaling occurs along parts of the western bank of the creek.

Dockage: Although Miami Beach has many docks, plan your stops ahead and, if possible, call for reservations. The area is packed with boats. A tip to remember when you are searching for accommodations is not to overlook anything except the private clubs. You never know when and where you may find a vacant berth for at least an overnight stay. Indian Creek is chock-full of hotel and condominium docks, and South Miami Beach is making more room for transients.

Back on Biscayne Bay, Sunset Harbour Yacht Club—reachable via the Miami Beach Channel or the northern Venetian Causeway route (see above)—offers slips for lease or sale. Transient space is also available, but be sure to call ahead to check availability. The slips at this equity yacht club offer telephone and satellite television hookups, wireless Internet access, pump-out service and more. A large condominium complex rounds out Sunset Harbour.

A major supermarket, drugstore, post office and a city bus stop are less than three blocks away. The Lincoln Road Mall (16th Street), a pedestrian-only street mall with numerous art galleries, shops, restaurants, theaters and the home of the New World Symphony Orchestra, is

within easy walking distance of Sunset Harbour, as is the Miami Beach Convention Center, principal location of the Miami International Boat Show.

Farther south on Meloy Channel (the southern end of Miami Beach Channel), just opposite the Coast Guard base, Miami Beach Marina offers electricity, water, telephones, cable television, fuel, bait and fishing supplies. A well-known restaurant, Monty's Restaurant and Raw Bar (305-672-1148), at Miami Beach Marina, offers excellent food and service, in both a swimming pool/raw bar setting and upstairs in a fine food restaurant. The location also has many restaurants within walking distance, including Joe's Stone Crab (305-673-0365) and Smith & Wollensky (305-673-2800) in the South Beach area.

Anchorage: Make a turn east at ICW flashing green "49" immediately north of the Venetian Causeway Bridge (west). Proceed about two miles, and drop the anchor just off the Sunset Harbour Channel (privately maintained daybeacons and lights), or go about two miles more to a relatively small, well-protected bight along the Miami Beach shoreline routinely used as an anchorage. (Due to increased usage, this anchorage has recently expanded and spilled over into Biscayne Bay on the other side of the channel.) Located directly south of Sunset Harbour Yacht Club and north of the easternmost Venetian Causeway fixed bridge, this anchorage shows charted depths of 7 to 11 feet over a mud bottom. Wakes, from passing vessels, particularly on weekends, can be disturbing. There is a public park with docks, a launch ramp and a Miami Beach

Police Marine Patrol station on the east shore of this anchorage. Boaters leave their dinghies tied up at the docks outside the launch ramp, but the docks are unattended. If you continue south on the ICW and pass through the Venetian Causeway Bridge (west) then immediately turn east following close to the northern shoreline, you will come into a large bay near the Miami Yacht Club docks and find good anchorage. Farther east there are numerous opportunities to anchor, in 7 to 10 feet of water, with better protection between the small islands all the way to the South Beach area, which was previously discussed.

GOIN' ASHORE:
SOUTH BEACH, FL

Ocean Drive on South Beach, from about Fifth Street to 14th Street in the heart of the Art Deco District, is home to numerous shops and restaurants. Freshly painted hotels feature sidewalk cafés. From an outdoor table, diners can gaze across a broad public beach to the ocean. The News Cafe, open 24-hours a day, offers good food, reasonable prices and unparalleled opportunities for people-watching. Grillfish, at the corner of Collins and Espanola, as its name implies, offers a variety of fresh seafood.

A basic supermarket is at Fifth Street and Collins Avenue, and a gourmet market and cafe, The Epicure, is at Alton Road and 10th Street. And if you can't wait three hours for a table at Joe's Stone Crab, either get a "to go" order or walk the extra block south to Smith & Wollensky. This southern branch of the famous New York eatery has first-class steak and seafood.

Cruising Options

Government Cut and Miami proper are treated in the following chapter, "Miami to Key Biscayne." Bimini is a short 42-mile hop away, and the Keys are at your back door from here. Just chart your course, pick your weather and go. ■

WATERWAY GUIDE advertising sponsors play a vital role in bringing you the most trusted and well-respected cruising guide in the country. Without our advertising sponsors, we simply couldn't produce the top-notch publication now resting in your hands. Next time you stop in for a peaceful night's rest, let them know where you found them—WATERWAY GUIDE, The Cruising Authority

Miami to Key Biscayne

A major commercial and recreational port, Greater Miami bustles with activity on land and water. Study your charts carefully before attempting to transit this busy and sometimes confusing area. You will find many excellent, expensive marinas with substantial amenities. You will also find less fancy, but somewhat more economical ones. For dockage information, check WATERWAY GUIDE's marina listings in this chapter. Visiting boaters may also call the Marine Council at 786-586-4688 for information on the local marine and tourism industry.

This segment begins at the MacArthur Causeway (Mile 1088.8) heading south and covers the Port of Miami and Government Cut, slightly overlapping the previous chapter. Coverage then continues with the Miami mainland and the Miami River, Virginia Key, Key Biscayne and middle Biscayne Bay, concluding with a brief description of the outside run north or south from Government Cut.

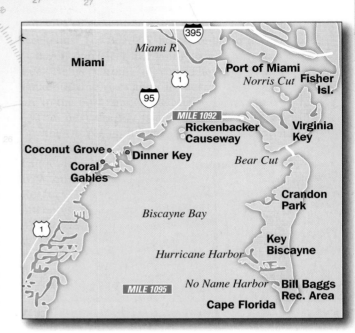

Miami Proper

NAVIGATION: Use Chart 11467. The oldest causeway across Biscayne Bay, MacArthur Causeway (Mile 1088.8) is mostly an earthen dike, built of sand dredged from the bordering big-ship channel. At its western end, the Intracoastal Waterway (ICW) runs beneath a span of the MacArthur Causeway with a 65-foot fixed vertical clearance. (If traveling north on the ICW, be aware that the next fixed bridge, part of the Julia Tuttle Causeway at Mile 1087.2, only has a 56-foot fixed vertical clearance.) Most drawbridges in Miami-Dade County have radios, but the bridge tenders do not always answer, especially if the bridge has a set schedule. Florida bridges operate on VHF Channel 09.

Watson Park lies east of the MacArthur Causeway Bridge (West), on the northeast corner of the ICW and the wide and deep Miami Main Channel to the Atlantic Ocean. The entire western part of Watson Park is the home of the famed Parrot Jungle and Gardens. The 18.6-acre park features an Everglades exhibit, serpentarium (snake facility), children's area with petting zoo, animal barn, playground, water play areas, baby bird and plant nurseries, picnic pavilions, two amphitheaters, jungle trails and aviaries. Also on Watson Park are a commercial marina and two private boating clubs.

The Main Channel runs east-southeast past Watson Park to port, with the Port of Miami to starboard on Dodge Island. It then runs straight past the Coast Guard station and Miami Beach Marina to the north opposite the eastern end of Dodge Island, then out through Government Cut to the ocean.

Security Zones: The Coast Guard has established security zones for the protection of passenger vessels, such as cruise ships, and for vessels carrying cargo of particular hazard, such as liquefied or compressed flammable gases. When such a vessel passes buoy "M," entering the port, no private vessel may approach it closer than 100 yards without prior permission.

On the south side of the Port of Miami Main Channel are the Dodge Island ship terminal facilities. A fixed security zone has been established for the entire Main Channel. When there are no subject vessels docked in the security zone (i.e., cruise ships or those containing hazardous materials), there are no restrictions and the channel may be freely used. When there is one such vessel docked, passage along the channel is limited to the northern side with law enforcement craft and cruise ship tenders marking the prohibited waters. If there are two or more of the defined vessels docked, the channel is closed, and craft must use Fishermans Channel (see below) to travel to and from the ocean. Patrol craft can be contacted on VHF Channel 16 for information on the status of these security zones at any given time.

Extending from the Main Channel to the sea, Government Cut inlet is deep, well-marked and easy to run in any weather. Stay within the channel until you are well clear of the jetties. Small local boats often shortcut the channel to avoid the current, but to keep clear of the subsurface rocks outside the channel. Strangers should exercise prudence, continuing well past flashing red buoy "8" and flashing green buoy "9." Two ranges mark the center of the outer channel.

Miami, FL

Looking west over Government Cut to Dodge Island, the Port of Miami and the ICW. (Not to be used for navigation.) WATERWAY GUIDE PHOTOGRAPHY

■ PORT OF MIAMI

NAVIGATION: Use Chart 11467. South of the MacArthur Causeway Bridge (Mile 1088.8, 65-foot fixed vertical clearance), the ICW crosses north and south across the Port of Miami's turning basin and goes under the three bridges connecting the west end of Dodge Island with the city of Miami. The first bridge, the Dodge Island Highway Bridge at Mile 1089.3, is a fixed highway bridge with a 65-foot fixed vertical clearance. The Dodge Island Railway Bridge (22-foot closed vertical clearance) is normally open, except for scheduled rail traffic. The old highway bridge (26-foot closed vertical clearance), no longer used, is now left in the open position.

Fishermans Channel—Mile 1089

NAVIGATION: Use Chart 11467. **Use the Miami Harbor Entrance Tide Tables.** In the process of upgrading the Dodge Island shipping center, Fishermans Channel—the alternate route to and from Government Cut along the south side of Lummus and Dodge islands—has been extensively dredged and modified. The channel is wide, and depths of 22 feet or more extend from the east end of Lummus Island to the west end of Dodge Island. Watch out for frequent dredging operations in this area. Through the short passage from the west end of this channel to the ICW, controlling depth is about 10 feet at mean low water, but make sure you identify the markers carefully.

Biscayne Bay pilots report that recent dredging in and around the Port of Miami has affected currents in the harbor. Both flood and ebb are stronger than published predictions.

Outward bound, just follow the buoys. Long-passage cruisers sometimes follow Fishermans Channel as far as Fisher Island and anchor off its southern side, off the western tip, clear of traffic, in order to get an early start at the Atlantic.

Dockage: Miami offers a wide variety of marine amenities. Among them, the Sea Isle Marina and Yachting Center lies off the ICW just north of the Venetian Causeway West Bridge, in front of a large hotel complex. It has excellent facilities and easy access to downtown Miami. Call ahead for dockage at this popular facility.

Miamarina at Bayside offers transient and long-term dockage, a laundry, and showers/restrooms, but no fuel. Miamarina at Bayside is the home of Strictly Sail, the in-the-water sailboat show portion of the annual Miami International Boat Show. Transportation from Miamarina is readily available to any location in the Greater Miami area. It is a three-block walk south or west to catch the MetroMover, which connects with MetroRail. Bus service is available only a block away, and water taxis depart from the marina for various destinations on Miami Beach and Key Biscayne.

For additional dockage, as described in the previous chapter, Sunset Harbour Yacht Club is located on the shores of Miami Beach, just a short hop across the Venetian Causeway's northern channel to the marina. Just 2 blocks north and one block east from the yacht club, there is a Publix supermarket, a liquor store and several small cafés. The South Beach area is within walking distance (about a mile to a mile and a half) or just a short cab ride away, as is Joe's Stone Crab Restaurant (305-673-0365, about two miles). There is a usable dinghy dock south of the yacht club next to the harbor police office.

Looking southwest over Watson Island and the MacArthur Causeway. (Not to be used for navigation.) Joseph R. Melanson of www.skypic.com

Miami River—Mile 1090

One of Miami's principal boating-service areas is along the Miami River, which flows out of the Everglades to divide the city. The Miami River extends four miles between its mouth, at Mile 1090 on the ICW, and the head of navigation at 36th Street. Boating services along its banks include custom builders, yacht brokers and boat dealers, sales and service agents, propeller specialists and sailmakers. Along with these are completely equipped haul-out, repair and storage yards.

NAVIGATION: Use Chart 11467. South of the Dodge Island bridges, the ICW runs south in deep water for about a half mile to the mouth of the Miami River on the west bank, between Bay Front Park and Claughton Island. Favor the starboard (western) shore all the way past Bay Front Park, and then execute a sharp turn to starboard into the river's mouth. Give green daybeacons "1" and "3" (the river's only markers) a wide berth and favor the starboard side upon entry. They indicate the shoal water off Claughton Island.

Miami River's controlling depth is 14 feet at mean low water up to the Northwest 27th Avenue Bridge and then 9 feet up to the 36th Street Dam. Boats proceeding upriver should lower outriggers and antennas. If land traffic is heavy (and it usually is), bridge tenders will enforce the law.

The stated controlling depths hold on Miami River's more important side branches—South Fork (three miles from the river's mouth) and Tamiami Canal (one mile farther on). Both shoot obliquely off to the southwest, and like the main river, each has its own series of boatyards and marine installations. Tamiami Canal, a drainage ditch

that parallels the Tamiami Trail to the northwest almost across Florida, is navigable for 6-foot draft (8 feet at high tide) vessels as far as a low limiting fixed bridge over Northwest 37th Avenue.

In addition to the vast array of recreational craft and amenities to serve them, the Miami River carries considerable commercial traffic. Tugs working in pairs maneuver to place the big oceangoing vessels that line the last mile or so of the river. Give these ships plenty of room.

Bridges: A dozen bridges cross the Miami River and, except for two structures (fixed vertical clearances 75 feet), they all have restricted openings. They remain closed year-round from 7:30 a.m. to 9 a.m., and from 4:30 p.m. to 6 p.m. weekdays, except federal holidays. A pending change would add an additional closed period from 12:05 p.m. to 12:59 p.m., but would exclude tugs and tugs towing vessels from all closure periods.

You can follow such an exempt vessel up or down the river, and take advantage of its openings, but do not forget to make your own signal to the bridge tender.

Most Miami River clearance gauges show the clearance at the fenders instead of the center of the span; there may be a sign indicating the additional clearance available at the center.

The first bridge going upriver is the Brickell Avenue Bridge, 23-foot closed vertical clearance at the center. Closed vertical clearances for the other bridges in sequence up the Miami River (with type of bridge in parentheses) are: South Miami Avenue, 21 feet (bascule); Southwest Second Avenue, 11 feet (bascule); South Miami Avenue, 75 feet (fixed); Southwest First Street, 18 feet (bascule); West Flagler Street, 35 feet

Miami Harbor & Miami River, FL

MIAMI HARBOR & MIAMI RIVER		Largest Vessel Accommodated	VHF Channel Monitored	Transient Berths / Total Berths	Approach / Dockside Depth (reported)	Gas / Diesel	Groceries, Ice, Marine Supplies, Snacks	Repairs: Hull, Engine, Propeller	Lift (tonnage), Crane, Rail	1=110V, 2=220V, B=Both, Max Amps	Laundry, Pool, Showers	Pump-Out Station	Nearby: Grocery Store, Motel, Restaurant
				Dockage		**Supplies**			**Service**				
1. Miami Yacht Club 1088.7 🖥️📶	305-377-9877	40		2/40	6/6		IMS		L2	1/30	PS		GR
2. Sea Isle Marina & Yachting Center 1088.5 📶	**305-377-DOCK**	**150**	**16**	**140/220**	**9/14**	**GD**	**GIMS**			**B/50**	**LPS**	**P**	**GMR**
3. Miamarina at Bayside 1090 🖥️	305-579-6955	190	16/18	45/135	14/10		I			B/100	LS	P	GMR
4. Norseman Shipbuilding Corp.	305-545-6815	95		/25	15/10			HEP	L100,C	B/50			GMR
5. Anchor Marine, LLC	305-545-6348	50					M	EP	L15				GMR
6. Merrill-Stevens Dry Dock	305-324-5211	225		/15	16/10	GD	M	HP	L70	B/100			GMR
7. Miami Yacht & Engine Works	305-325-0233	85			12/10	D		HEP	L75	B/50	S		GMR
8. Austral International Marina	305-325-0177			5/5	6/6		MS	HEP	L30	B/50	S		GMR
9. Florida Detroit Diesel Allison	305-638-5300						M	E	C				R
10. Agra Yacht Service	305-635-6945	82			7/7		M	HEP	L70	B/50			MR
11. Allied Marine	305-633-9761	120	78/09		8/8		M	HP	L	B/100			MR
12. Jones Boat Yard Inc.	305-635-0891	275			15/15		MS	HEP	L60				
13. Epic Marina 1090 📶	305-400-7489	305	16	20/20	17/8					B/200	P	P	MR

Corresponding chart(s) not to be used for navigation. 🖥️ Internet Access 📶 Wireless Internet Access

(bascule); Northwest Fifth Street, 12 feet (bascule); Northwest 12th Avenue, 22 feet (bascule); highway bridge, 75 feet (fixed); Northwest 17th Avenue, 17 feet (bascule); Northwest 22nd Avenue, 25 feet (bascule); Northwest 27th Avenue, 21 feet (bascule); and a railroad bridge just before the dam, 6 feet (bascule). There is one bridge (fixed, 8 feet) over the South Fork, and a swing bridge with 6 feet (erroneously charted as bascule), crossing the Tamiami Canal.

Whenever a big event takes place at Orange Bowl Stadium, home of the University of Miami Hurricanes football team, extra closures are usually imposed. If you plan to go upriver, check ahead of time for bridge restrictions. All closures for the regularly scheduled events at the

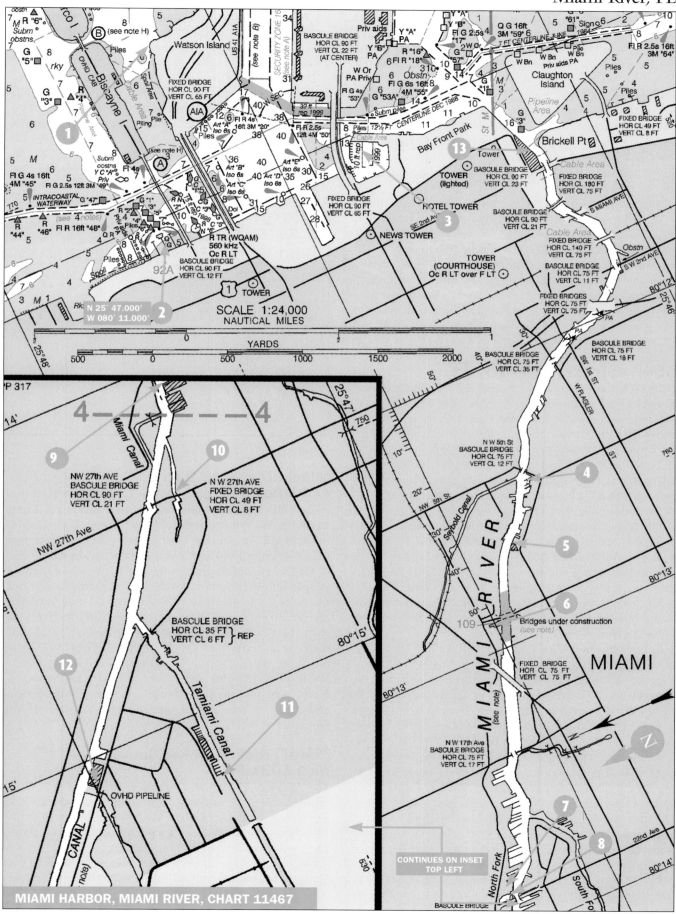

MIAMI HARBOR, MIAMI RIVER, CHART 11467

Miami, FL

Orange Bowl, from August through January, are posted online in the Local Notice to Mariners (www.navcen.uscg.gov/lnm) starting in late July; they are repeated a week or two before the event dates. These closures usually last only about two hours.

Dockage: There are many facilities for the cruising boater on the Miami River, although only a few cater to transients. Epic Marina, at the mouth of the river, offers transient dockage to large motoryachts. Richard Bertram and Company and Jones Boatyard are both located on the Tamiami Canal and accept transient guests. Jones Boatyard also has gas and diesel fuel available.

Anchorage: North of the Venetian Causeway, depart the ICW, and head east toward the islands where you will find plenty of anchorage possibilities. You can also continue east along the islands until you arrive at Belle Isle, where you will want to turn to port and continue past two more islands. Enter the canal between the second and third island (where there is no bridge), turn to starboard, and then continue west until you arrive into Sunset Lake, where you can anchor in 8 feet of water in a very protected setting.

GOIN' ASHORE: **MIAMI, FL**

Miami is a major city with a culturally diverse population and an appetite for action. Some call it "the new capital of Latin America." Its dog-racing tracks are world-famous; its airport is one of the world's major installations; and its jai alai fronton is the largest in Florida. Golf courses, theater and an abundance of hotels, restaurants and nightclubs provide visitors with a kaleidoscope of opportunities for entertainment. Major athletic events are staged year-round. Yacht clubs conduct sailing regattas on Biscayne Bay almost every weekend.

The city's name, and the river's, is an Anglicization of the Indian Mayami, meaning "sweet water." The first settlement, built in 1836, was Fort Dallas, a stronghold in the Seminole War and an early command of William Tecumseh Sherman, the Ohio general of Civil War fame. Soon after came Brickell's Indian trading post, then trappers, fishermen, farmers and the swarm of northern tourists who followed in the wake of Julia Tuttle and Henry Flagler.

Some deem the Miami River the most historic spot in all of southeast Florida. At its mouth were three settlements: a Tequesta Indian village, a slave plantation and an army fort. To the south was William Brickell's trading post; to the north, Julia Tuttle's home. It was there that Tuttle convinced Henry Flagler in 1895 to bring his railroad southward from Palm Beach—the defining event that created the city of Miami.

Miami River crosses cultures while embracing history and architecture. Up the river a bit, past freighters bound for Haiti and Central America, is José Martí Park. The East Little Havana neighborhood, now also known as Little Managua, was Tent City three decades ago, when it was an encampment for Mariel refugees. Much earlier, it was an Indian village. A number of industrial landmarks testify to Miami River being a working river in the truest sense for more than a century.

Just south of the Dodge Island bridges is Bay Front Park, built where an Indian village once stood. Its 62 acres of luxuri-

ant landscaping include broad promenades lined with beautiful sculpture, a light tower where laser light shows are presented weekly and a bandshell with concerts—some free, some requiring tickets—on an irregular year-round schedule.

The shoreside facilities are excellent, and the restaurants, shops and entertainment of the adjacent Bayside complex will prove popular for skippers and crew alike. In addition to overnight slips, hourly daytime dockage is available at reasonable rates at Miamarina. The Historical Museum of South Florida's River Tour and other sightseeing vessels also leave from Miamarina. Within walking distance of Bay Front Park, west on Third Street to Second Avenue, then a short distance south, is a small, but well-stocked grocery.

ADDITIONAL RESOURCES

■ Greater Miami Convention and Visitors Bureau, 800-933-8448, www.miamiandbeaches.com

⚐ NEARBY GOLF COURSES
Crandon Golf Key Biscayne, 6700 Crandon Blvd., Key Biscayne, FL 33149, 305-361-9129
www.crandongolfclub.com

℞ NEARBY MEDICAL FACILITIES
Mercy Hospital, 3663 S. Miami Ave., Miami, FL 31133, 305-854-4400
www.mercymiami.com

Middle Biscayne Bay

NAVIGATION: Use Chart 11467. Cruising south of the Powell/Rickenbacker Causeway is easier if you use Chart 11465 (ICW—Miami to Elliot Key). Although the scale is the same on both charts, Chart 11465 covers a larger area (as far as Elliot Key) and makes navigation simpler.

Skippers southbound along the main ICW channel should follow the chart closely and take time to sort out the buoys. On the Waterway east of the mouth of the Miami River, several channels (described earlier), all with their own markers, meet and intersect. An abrupt turn to starboard at quick flashing green "59" just northeast of the tip of Claughton Island (Mile 1090) is the prime trouble spot. Beware of the confusion of buoys and the surrounding shoal water. Slow down, and take your time picking out the navigational aids for your particular course.

Powell/Rickenbacker Causeway— Mile 1091.6

The William M. Powell Causeway (65-foot fixed vertical clearance) will probably be referred to as "the Powell/Rickenbacker" or just "Rickenbacker" for some time to come. The older structure is dwarfed alongside its modern replacement and remains in use as a fishing pier.

South of the Powell/Rickenbacker Causeway, Biscayne Bay changes character, becoming broad, relatively deep (average 10 feet) and lovely. Sailing regattas are held in these waters

Looking southeast from Coconut Grove over Dinner Key and its three marinas. (Not to be used for navigation.) WATERWAY GUIDE PHOTOGRAPHY

nearly every weekend, while fishing, swimming, waterskiing and cruising are everyday, all-day, all-year activities. Cruisers will find this part of Biscayne Bay especially inviting. The deep, open water makes a pleasant change from the narrow confines of much of the ICW.

Dockage: Virginia Key is at the east end of the causeway, and at its western tip is a marina with transient slips and a nearby restaurant. The key's main attraction is the famous Seaquarium.

Bear Cut is on the southeast side of Virginia Key, between that key and Key Biscayne. It is unmarked at its northeastern end, except for red daybeacon "2," which provides an outlet to the ocean for smaller boats from Crandon Park Marina that can pass under the Bear Cut Bridge (16-foot fixed vertical clearance).

Anchorage: A well-protected anchorage lies just inside the Miami Marine Stadium, which closed after Hurricane Andrew damaged it in 1992. Marine Stadium Marina is located here and has gas and diesel fuel. This is primarily a "high and dry" storage facility. On the south side of the entrance is Rickenbacker Marina, with slips, fuel and other facilities; rental moorings are located just outside the entrance.

Just south of the Powell/Rickenbacker Causeway, on the mainland side, the Villa Vizcaya Museum and Gardens (the Dade County Art Museum) are open to the public, but there is no dockage, even for a dinghy. In case of an emergency, just south is an emergency dock belonging to Mercy Hospital. It has depths of 4 feet at mean low water and 6 feet at high tide, and provides a telephone, restricted to emergency use only.

Dinner Key, in Biscayne Bay

The major center of boating activity for the southern sector of Biscayne Bay is Dinner Key, served by a 1.5-mile-long, well-marked channel on the western mainland shore. It was once a seaplane base—first for the enormous Pan American clippers flying to the Caribbean and South America, and later for the U.S. Coast Guard.

Dockage: The 582-slip Dinner Key Marina offers full services, including water, electricity, cable TV and telephone, but no fuel. Nearby, an attractive restaurant features an exhibit of artifacts and pictures from the days when the Pan Am clippers operated.

Dinner Key's location puts boaters within walking distance of the popular Coconut Grove area with its galleries and cafes. Visit CocoWalk for an open-air shopping and entertainment center experience. Most of the private marinas and yacht clubs in the area offer reciprocal agreements for members of other recognized yacht clubs. Be sure to call ahead, because space may be tight.

A short distance north of Dinner Key Marina is the Coral Reef Yacht Club, which uses the same entrance channel from Biscayne Bay as the marina. Members of other yacht clubs may be able to arrange brief transient dockage; call ahead before reaching the club.

Anchorage: After ten years of trying to get permits, the City of Miami finally acquired permission to install a mooring facility adjacent to Dinner Key Marina. As of November 2009, Dinner Key Marina, located on the western bank of Biscayne Bay, has a mooring field of 225 mooring balls. The new facility

Biscayne Bay, FL

BISCAYNE BAY		Largest Vessel Accommodated	VHF Channel Monitored	Transient Berths / Total Berths	Approach / Dockside Depth (reported)	Floating Docks	Gas / Diesel	Groceries, Ice, Marine Supplies, Snacks	Repairs: Hull, Engine, Propeller	Lift (tonnage), Crane, Rail	1=110V, 2=220V, B=Both, Max Amps	Laundry, Pool, Showers	Pump-Out Station	Nearby: Grocery Store, Motel, Restaurant
		Dockage						**Supplies**		**Service**				
1. Mercy Hospital 1093	305-285-2768	60			/5			EMERGENCY	ONLY	DOCKAGE				
2. Grove Isle Marina ⌨ 1093	305-858-4753	120	16	/85	8/12	F		I	EP		B/100	PS	P	MR
3. Coral Reef Yacht Club 1094	305-858-1733	54	12	/102	6/6	F		I		C	B/100	PS	P	GMR
4. Bayshore Landing Marina (WiFi) 1094	305-854-7997	95	16/11	1/200	5/6			I			B/50	LPS	P	GMR
5. Grove Key Marina 1094	305-858-6527				18/8		GD	IMS	HEP	L12	1/30		P	GMR
6. Dinner Key Marina 1095 ⌨	305-579-6980	110	16	58/580	8/7			IS			B/100	LS	P	GMR
7. Matheson Hammock Marina 1097	305-665-5475	50		/243	5/5	F	GD	IS			B/50	PS	P	R
8. Black Point Marina 1106	305-258-4092	50	16	10/200	4/6	F	GD	IMS			B/50		P	GR
9. LOGGERHEAD CLUB & MARINA-SOUTH MIAMI 1106	**305-258-3500**	**40**	**16**	**/299**	**8/12**	**F**		**IS**	**EP**				**P**	**GMR**
10. Homestead Bayfront Marina 1111	305-230-3033	48	16	174	7/7		GD	GIS		L	B/50	PS	P	GMR

Corresponding chart(s) not to be used for navigation. ⌨ Internet Access (WiFi) Wireless Internet Access

will add to the service of the marina guests and provide many amenities. Included in the cost of the mooring are pump-out service and a water taxi service that will take you into the marina, which is very close to the attractions of Coconut Grove. A coin-operated laundry, showers, a customer lounge and a dinghy dock are included in the daily fee. You can also come in to take on water. Vehicle and bicycle parking, along with trash pickup and recycling are available as well. You can usually spot several transients, some waiting for favorable weather to cross to the Bahamas. Anchoring is still possible outside of the mooring field to the north (on the opposite side of the channel) and to the east in 7 to 9 feet of water.

Coconut Grove

For years, the U.S. Sailing Winter Sail Training Center has been at Coconut Grove's Kennedy Park. Equipped with a 40-foot-wide ramp and a pair of two-ton capacity hoists, as well as good weather and good winds virtually all winter long, the center proves invaluable to those training for the Olympics, and the various one-design classes holding midwinter regattas here.

Unlike the rest of Miami, low-key and restful Coconut Grove preserves much of the ambience of traditional Florida. All the usual daily necessities—laundries, supermarkets, restaurants, post office, library, bank, drugstores—are only a short distance from the marinas, as are art galleries, antiques and gift shops, boutiques and craft shops catering to tourists.

For a reminder of the early days, take in Coconut Grove's lovely secluded lanes, pioneer homes and old estates. Or take in a brisk game of tennis at the free courts here, and then dine at one of the fine restaurants in town.

Coral Gables, South of Coconut Grove

NAVIGATION: Use Charts 11467 and 11465. Located directly south of Coconut Grove, Coral Gables has its own waterway with a well-marked entrance and a 5-foot controlling depth at mean low water. Since bridges on both branches of this waterway are fixed (most offer about a 12-foot vertical clearance), you will likely have to explore by dinghy. The canals interconnect, wind through residential sections and finally exit to the bay just north of Coral Gables' wide Tahiti Beach.

Dockage: About four miles south of Coconut Grove is Matheson Hammock Park, a county park, beach and marina (Matheson Hammock Marina). It is one of South Florida's few remaining natural areas, with native forest and a lagoon-type atoll beach. This marina has slips for transients, fuel, a restaurant, sandy beach and other amenities. Approach depth is 5.5 feet at mean low water, with 5-foot depths dockside. Farther south is Black Point Marina with transient dockage at floating docks, gas and diesel fuel and on-site supplies. Loggerhead Club & Marina, located in the same protected basin as Black Point Marina, provides transient dockage, an on-site restaurant, the Ocean Grill, a Captain's Lounge with coffee and popcorn and a ship's store. They also have both diesel and gas and pump-out facilities. Continuing south is Homestead Bayfront Marina, with similar facilities to Black Point Marina.

Key Biscayne—Mile 1094

Across Biscayne Bay from Coconut Grove is Key Biscayne, site of southern Florida's first town, founded in 1839. It was also headquarters for a band of renegades who lured ships onto the reefs and "salvaged" their cargo. Today, the Key is made up of two unusual parks. The northern end is taken up by Dade County's Crandon Park, the southern by Bill Baggs Cape Florida State Park.

Crandon Park

Occupying the northern end of Key Biscayne at Mile 1094, this county park boasts a marina (Crandon Marina), boat ramp, two miles of ocean beach (named among the top 10 beaches in the nation) and excellent picnic grounds; nearby is the International Tennis Center and an excellent golf course. Bus service is available to the city. Transient boats are welcome on a space-available basis.

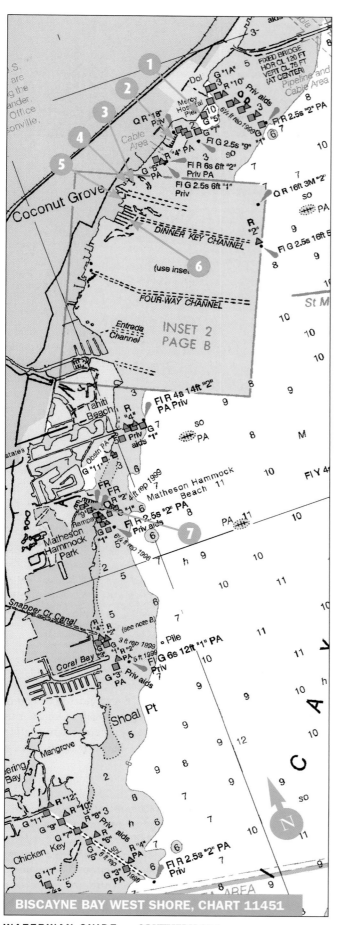

BISCAYNE BAY WEST SHORE, CHART 11451

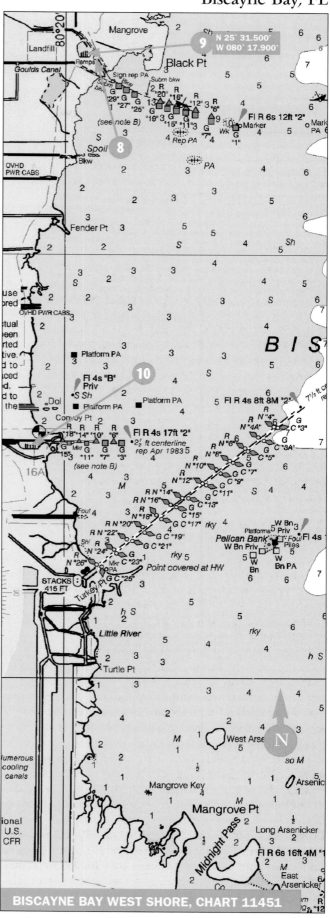

BISCAYNE BAY WEST SHORE, CHART 11451

Key Biscayne, FL

KEY BISCAYNE		Largest Vessel Accommodated	VHF Channel Monitored	Transient Berths / Total Berths	Approach / Dockside Depth (reported)	Floating Docks	Gas / Diesel	Groceries, Ice, Marine Supplies, Snacks	Repairs: Hull, Engine, Propeller	Lift (tonnage), Crane, Rail	1=110V, 2=220V, B=Both, Max Amps	Laundry, Pool, Showers	Pump-Out Station	Nearby: Grocery Store, Motel, Restaurant
		Dockage					**Supplies**			**Service**				
1. Rickenbacker Marina Inc. 1091.5	305-361-1900	85	16	2/198	8/6		G	IMS	HEP		B/50	LS	P	R
2. Crandon Marina 1.9 E of 1092	305-361-1281	50	16/68	10/228	6/6	F	GD	GIMS			B/50	L	P	GMR
3. Marine Stadium Marina 1091.5	305-361-3316	43 DRY STORAGE ONLY			8/10		GD	GIMS	HEP	L9				R

Corresponding chart(s) not to be used for navigation. 💻 Internet Access 📶 Wireless Internet Access

KEY BISCAYNE AREA, CHART 11465

Dockage: The Crandon Marina complex includes a restaurant, laundry, gas and diesel fuel and pump-out. It is best approached from Biscayne Bay by a privately marked natural channel that leads northeastward from the shoal light (flashing white, four seconds) off West Point (near where flashing green "73" was formerly located). The marina also has moorings available in its protected cove with easy access marina amenities..

Anchorage: Two of the most popular harbors among boaters waiting for favorable weather to cross over to the Bahamas are Hurricane Harbor, near the southwest corner of Key Biscayne, and No Name Harbor, around the point from Hurricane Harbor and in the state park (see below).

No Name Harbor has shore access; Hurricane Harbor does not. There is a fee to anchor overnight in No Name Harbor—Hurricane Harbor is free. When the wind is out of the east, a third strategy is to simply anchor in the lee of the west side of Key Biscayne, just north of Hurricane Harbor's entrance.

At the head of No Name Harbor, the Boaters' Grill offers a menu of appetizers, light meals, deli take-out along with beer and wine. Also available are clean restrooms, inexpensive showers and a pay phone; the laundry is not always operational. Cleats along the seawall make going ashore much simpler. There are no fenders along the raw concrete seawall, so you should rig your own fenders in advance. A pump-out station is located on the southern side of the harbor, near the entrance. There is no seawall protection here either, so rig your own fenders in advance. There is a small fee for daily tie-ups, but overnight stays along the wall are prohibited. In 2010, overnight anchorage was still available for a fee. Envelopes are provided for depositing the fees in an honor-system box. There is room for about 25-plus boats. The bottom is hard mud in 10 to 12 feet of water, and holding is good with wind protection from all directions except due west (and that is still not too bad).

Bill Baggs Cape Florida State Park

At the southern end of Key Biscayne is Bill Baggs Cape Florida State Park, named after the late Miami newspaper editor who championed the fight to designate this area a state park. With more than a mile of ocean beach, the park is set in a wilderness of tropical growth. There are bike paths and running trails in a beautiful tropical setting here; this is a great place to get off the boat and stretch your legs, but will require a walk or bike from Hurricane or No Name harbors. Don't forget your camera, though, because there are numerous opportunities for beautiful shots.

The oldest structure in Miami-Dade County is the 95-foot-high Cape Florida Lighthouse. The original light was built in 1825 and has survived numerous hurricanes, an 1836 Seminole Indian attack that resulted in a fire and the harsh effects of the environment. Refurbished that same year, its replacement was in service until 1878, when Fowey Rocks Light, whose position five miles offshore enabled it to better guide deep-draft ships that had to stand far out to sea, took over. The structure was restored to its authentic 1855 condition and is now maintained and charted as a private aid to navigation, flashing a white beam that is visible seven miles out to sea.

The Run Offshore From Miami

Coming up on the outside from the south, northbound boats that want to enter inshore waters can take either Cape Florida Channel or Biscayne Channel, once they have passed Fowey Rocks Light, or they can continue on to Government Cut. The Miami GPS Differential Beacon (nominal range 75 miles) is located on Virginia Key near the west end of the fixed bridge across Bear Cut.

The run north, outside from Government Cut, is spectacular and offers the best available view of the Miami Beach skyline.

The run south from Government Cut offers some interesting coastline as well, leading past Virginia Key and Key Biscayne to the next entry from the ocean at Cape Florida. At Key Biscayne's southern end is the restored Cape Florida Lighthouse (described earlier).

Coming down along the ocean side of Key Biscayne, southbound boats should stand offshore on the run from Miami. Take a heading due south from the entrance buoys off Government Cut's Outer Bar Cut to pick up Biscayne Channel Light (better known locally as Bug Light), the 37-foot-high spidery pipe structure (flashing white every four seconds) marking the seaward entrance of Cape Florida and Biscayne channels. Coming in, at flashing red

"6," you have a choice of two channels leading to Biscayne Bay. Depths in the shared entrance channel to the Cape Florida Channel and the Biscayne Channel are charted at 7 feet at mean low water over the bar.

From the sea, the right-hand, northern fork is the Cape Florida Channel leading past the prominent lighthouse and the lovely palm-fringed beach. The chart clearly identifies the deepwater passage along the curving shoreline, indicating also the two shoal spots situated between one- and two-tenths of a mile southwest of the shore.

Hug the shore along the curving concrete bulkhead of the park property to clear the charted shoals, marked by green daybeacon "1." At the inner end, bear off to leave red daybeacon "2" and flashing red "4" to starboard. From the outside, this is the easiest route to No Name Harbor, the area's most popular jump-off point for mariners awaiting favorable weather for a Bahamas passage.

The southern route, which is better marked and deeper than the unmarked Cape Florida Channel, is known as Biscayne Channel. It is wide, straight, well-marked and easy to run. Depths in the channel range from 11 to 16 feet. Even so, the channel is sometimes limited by its entrance depth from the ocean. At its western end, the channel produces good fishing during flood tide.

Additional detail for Miami southbound is in the following chapter describing Hawk Channel, which is the outside route to the Keys. It also covers the inside, ICW route to the Middle Keys.

Cruising Options

Cruisers are now in an ideal position to head east to the Bahamas or continue south into the fabled Florida Keys. ■

....

WATERWAY GUIDE is always open to your observations from the helm. E-mail your comments on any navigation information in the guide to: editor@waterwayguide.com.

Cape Florida Lighthouse. Photo Courtesy of Laura Rivas.

KEY WEST FUN

Discover a city where real estate titles date back to the Kings of Spain. Stroll the palm-lined streets and discover gingerbread mansions, tin-roofed conch houses, the John Audubon House and Ernest Hemingway's home. Walk in the footsteps of Thomas Edison, Lou Gehrig, Harry Truman and Tennessee Williams.

Gaze at the fabled treasure of the galleon Atocha. Discover tomorrow's fine art treasures by Key West's well-known and unknown artists. In Key West, you can visit these and a host of other attractions by taking advantage of convenient public transportation, taxis, pedi-cabs, tour trains, trolleys, bicycles or even your own two feet.

With its balmy weather and crystal blue skies, the island is famous among the outdoors set for its diving, fishing, water sports and golfing at the nearby Key West Golf Club, a course designed by Rees Jones. But only in Key West would the sun shine the brightest when it sets. Everyone gathers for the never planned, always varied, Sunset Celebration on the Mallory Dock.

The southernmost point in Key West, FL.
©IstockPhoto/HengkyYasin

Once the sun is safely tucked away by jugglers, mimes, musicians and street artists, the city moves to a different beat. A night beat. The streets, filled with sidewalk cafes, open-air bars, legendary pubs and world-class restaurants, come alive. Gourmets and gourmands alike treat their palates to island specialties. Drama, musicals and comedy flourish on their stages.

As you enjoy these sights, you will discover that modern Key West is a warm-hearted place where all are welcome. However you choose to see the town, you will discover that old town Key West is one of America's true architectural and botanical treasures. On even the tiniest lanes, the locals have faithfully restored old wooden homes and adorned them with lush tropical trees and flowers.

New restaurants and stores are popping up in the historic Bahama Village neighborhood, which was settled in the 19th Century by Bahamian immigrants. Hemingway loved coming here to mix with the hard-working locals at boxing matches and arm-wrestling contests.

You will be certain to notice the roosters roaming free in the streets and alleys of Key West—either walking with you, or waking you with a noisy crow.

The island's seafaring tradition lives on at the renovated Historic Seaport district, known locally as the Key West Bight. Dozens of shrimp boats once called this harbor home.

These days, "the Bight" is a popular place to arrange a day on the water, whether you are a diver, snorkeler, fisherman or eco-tourist. Others come just to stroll along the harbor walk or dine at one of the many restaurants.

Key West is fun, rich in history, and well worth several days of your cruise.

Key West Rooster.
©IstockPhoto/Vasina

Introduction

The Florida Keys

Extending in a sweeping southwesterly curve from Miami and the mainland, the Florida Keys offer the cruising mariner an environment unlike any other Waterway area. In many ways, the Keys resemble the islands of the Bahamas. However, a main highway and 42 bridges (a total of 18.94 miles of bridges) tie them together. West of Marathon, Seven Mile Bridge, which is actually 6.77 miles, is the longest; the Harris Gap Channel Bridge is the shortest at 108 feet and the Jewfish Creek Bridge is the newest. The original, built in 1944, was replaced when the $93 million 65-foot-high bridge opened in May 2008. The highway runs from the tip of the Florida peninsula to Key West, the nation's southernmost city. Farther west, the Marquesas and the Dry Tortugas provide the challenge of remote and unconnected islands, accessible only by water or air. Tourism and fishing support the numerous communities lining U.S. 1 South, known as the Overseas Highway.

With outstanding natural and artificial underwater reefs, fishermen, snorkelers and Scuba divers have found a tropical paradise along the southeastern or ocean side of the Keys. The northern and northwestern sides are a fisherman's heaven and the gateway to the Everglades National Park.

Spaniards were the first white settlers in this area, and while they formally called the Keys "Los Martires" ("The Martyrs" because of their peculiar and twisted shapes), their generic word "cayos" led to the term Americans have adopted. The Indians were in the Keys before the Spaniards, of course, but they didn't quite have their Department of Homeland Security up and operating efficiently, so they were displaced by immigrants. It is an age-old story.

The Conch Republic

On April 23, 1982, the United States Border Patrol established a military-style roadblock on U.S. 1 at Florida City. The Border Patrol stopped all northbound highway traffic at a place motorists know as The Last Chance Saloon and searched for illegal aliens and drugs. The ensu-

ing well-publicized traffic jam—traffic stretched back for 19 miles—supposedly stymied the Key's tourism industry. This may be a myth, though. The traffic jam only influenced people departing the Keys, and those people were probably out of money anyway. Why would anyone want to leave the Keys if they still had money left to be spent?

Citizens of the Keys (called "Conchs") elected to secede from the Upper 48. With tongue in cheek, but with a serious gleam in their eyes, they selected a flag, designated their boundaries and became the "Conch Republic." It proclaimed its independence, declared war on the United States and then immediately surrendered, applying for foreign aid. The roadblock was discontinued after several days, and the economy was saved. Today, the tradition of the Conch Republic revolution continues with a yearly celebration, in April, and appointment of various Conch Ambassadors. To many Key West locals, both natives and transplants alike, the event symbolizes both the intense individualism of the island's people and the keen sense of humor that they enjoy.

Routes through the Keys

Below Miami, two different, but equally interesting, routes are available for the cruise along the Keys to Key West and beyond to the Dry Tortugas. One follows the Intracoastal Waterway (ICW) "inside" through Florida Bay; the other, deeper passage on the "outside" is the Hawk Channel route.

ICW to Florida Bay

The well-marked, but shoal-draft, ICW channel down to Florida Bay, northwest and north of the main chain of islands, is well-protected in all but the worst weather.

While a hard chop built up from strong winds can provide a wet ride, most cruising boats should experience no difficulties making this passage. Because of numerous shoal depth areas and the possibility that a strong northerly can literally blow the water out, pay strict attention to navigational aids and the course of the charted magenta line. Better yet, pay more attention to the weather you expect to encounter. If it is going to be bad, stay

Introduction: The Florida Keys

put. Many boats will leave "tracks" somewhere along this route. This is usually just stirred-up, powdery sand. Should you go aground, it is generally not too difficult to regain deeper water unless, of course, you plow your way in at fairly high speed. There are towing services available (expensive); both the Coast Guard and its Auxiliary monitor VHF Channel 16 and have stations along the way. They are not permitted to tow except in a life threatening situation, but they can provide assistance such as contacting a commercial towing service should you have trouble making direct contact.

Be advised, though, that if you run aground in the Keys and hit coral heads, coral reefs or seagrass beds, you are going to end up paying a large fine for your transgression. Count on it. And that is in addition to what it costs you to get your boat out of trouble and repaired. Take care not to damage this fragile ecosystem.

Hawk Channel Offshore

The deepest and most viable route for vessels with a draft of 5 feet or more is Hawk Channel, running from Miami to Key West. Not "officially" part of the ICW, it lies southeast and south of the Keys, taking the form of a somewhat protected "channel" running between the line of Keys and the Florida Reef (actually a series of reefs paralleling the islands).

With a controlling depth of 9 feet at mean low water, and in the lee of the Keys themselves, it is generally rather well-protected from winter northerlies and affords even more protection the farther down the Keys you go. In ordinary weather, it is a pleasant sail or an easy run for the entire length of the Keys.

The prevailing southeasterly winds can provide a nice boost for a long reach under sail. With numerous breaks in the outer reef, however, it can offer its share of rough water, should the wind be strong from the southern or southwestern quarter.

During the winter season (November through April), lobster or crab pots marked by floats of all descriptions are everywhere along both routes. Most ICW cruisers should be prepared to dive to clear their own shafts and check their props. As for navigation, GPS and radar are both extremely useful, but a reliable compass and an accurate depth sounder are just as necessary. An autopilot has its place, particularly along the Hawk Channel route, but you still must watch for and dodge the crab pots, as well as other vessels.

To Florida's West Coast

Two routes are available to leave the ICW and traverse Florida Bay westward for Cape Sable and points north along Florida's west coast. The first begins at ICW Mile 1173, north of Long Key and skirting shoals on and surrounding Old Dan Bank (use Charts 11449 and 11452). The so-called "Yacht Channel" is well-marked and protected. However, it abounds in charted, but otherwise unmarked, shoal patches of 5 to 6 feet in depth (less in a significant blow from the north and less still for vessels straying even marginally off

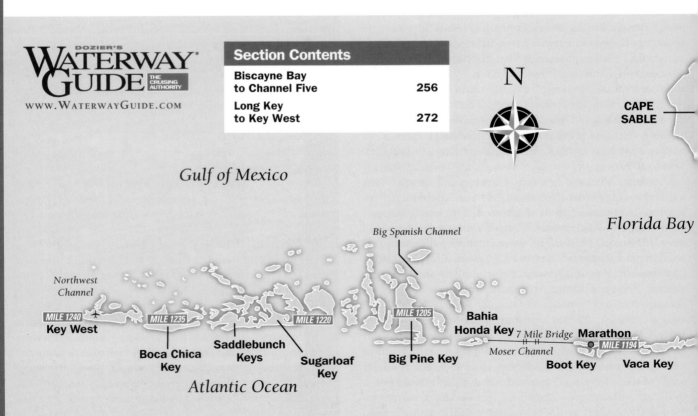

DOZIER'S
WATERWAY GUIDE
THE CRUISING AUTHORITY
WWW.WATERWAYGUIDE.COM

N

CAPE SABLE

Gulf of Mexico

Florida Bay

Big Spanish Channel

Northwest Channel

MILE 1240
Key West

MILE 1235

MILE 1220

MILE 1205

Bahia Honda Key 7 Mile Bridge **Marathon**

MILE 1194

Moser Channel

Boca Chica Key

Saddlebunch Keys

Sugarloaf Key

Big Pine Key

Boot Key   **Vaca Key**

Atlantic Ocean

course). This route is not recommended for boats drawing over 4 feet or for travel in poor light.

A second route begins just west of ICW Mile 1190, due north of Marathon (use Chart 11453). Deeper-footed vessels will need to look out for shoals surrounding Rachel Bank to begin a course of 003 degrees magnetic in 7- to 11-foot depths direct to flashing red "2," located 2.2 miles south of East Cape Sable.

Note: The best-marked route to the north consists of six markers along Moser Channel between the bridge and Bullard Bank. Older chart editions do not show these markers. Be sure to use the 35th edition of Chart 11442, and the 17th edition of Chart 11449 when traveling in this area (the latest charts available in summer 2010.) At Bullard Bank, you can head directly to the aforementioned flashing red "2" off East Cape Sable. At light "2," there is well-marked and relatively straightforward access either easterly to Flamingo in the heart of Everglades National Park or northwesterly, roughly paralleling the Three Nautical Mile Line along the west coast to visit Little Shark River or the Thousand Islands.

However, please consider what your final destination is before you pick the route to use. If you have a vessel big enough to cruise along offshore, then heading for East Cape is just adding extra miles to your trip. Basically, if the weather is right and you are seriously heading north from the Seven Mile Bridge, you may not want to go anywhere near the tip of Florida. In that case, we suggest that you consider a course of 337 degrees magnetic and a distance of 136 miles that will bring you in proximity of land up around Boca Grande Channel.

Connections Between the ICW Inside Route and the Hawk Channel Outside Route

There are only three major routes between the ICW and Hawk Channel. The first, Cape Florida/Biscayne Channels (treated as one), at ICW Mile 1096, is the northern crossover from Biscayne Bay to the Atlantic. The others, Channel Five at ICW Mile 1170 and Moser Channel at ICW Mile 1195, are under bridges with 65-foot vertical clearances along U.S. Route 1. Several other channels with mixed limitations exist. All receive individual treatment in the text.

Prevailing Winds

An intelligent mariner needs to be particularly aware of the winds while navigating in the Keys. There are, for example, a number of marinas located along the "top" of the Keys. By that, we mean the Florida Bay side. These marinas will have higher water readings when the wind blows out of the north and lower depths when the wind is southeasterly. For marinas on the Hawk Channel side of the Keys, the opposite is true. If one considers the water that embraces the Keys, no matter which side, to be a moveable entity, then one will allow for it being where you want it to be or not where you want it to be and make allowances. If it is windy, and you are not sure how the depths are going to play out for you, stay put.

Note: A list of Keys anchorages appears at the end of the second Keys chapter, "Long Key to Key West." ∎

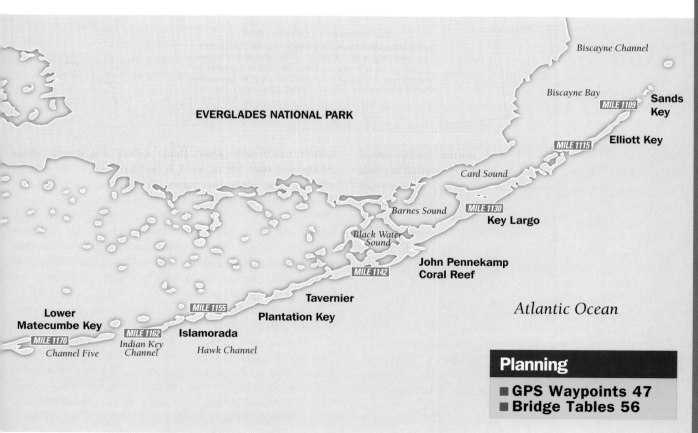

Biscayne Bay to Channel Five

CHARTS 11442, 11445, 11448, 11449, 11451, 11452, 11453, 11462, 11463, 11464, 11465, 11467

For boats that draw no more than 4.5 feet and can take the occasional short, hard chop of shallow water, the Intracoastal Waterway (ICW) route through bays, sounds and, ultimately, Florida Bay, provides a relatively protected and interesting passage all the way to Marathon and beyond to Bahia Honda. The inside route to Marathon has a wide variety of marinas and shore facilities, plus a variety of anchorages for different wind and weather conditions.

If continuing on to Key West from Marathon, there are two options: crossing over to Hawk Channel in the Atlantic at Moser Channel, or going through Big Spanish Channel southwest of Marathon, into Florida Bay and running down the northern edge of the remaining keys. If winds are blowing from the north or northeast at more than 10 to 15 knots, Hawk Channel, on the south and sheltered side of the Keys, will be the more comfortable route heading southwest, as the westerly curve of the keys can provide more protection. The route through Big Spanish Channel involves navigating shifting shoals and will take a bit longer, but in southerly or southeasterly winds it will be the more protected route heading southwest. A word to the wise is advisable here: there are no marine facilities on the Florida Bay side between Big Spanish Channel and Key West.

Let us add this caveat, too. When you are down in the Florida Keys, your travel is totally weather dependent. There is plenty of good weather here and a lot to enjoy. Waiting for good travel weather is smart boating especially in the Keys.

Note: Locations ashore (not on the Waterway proper) in the Keys are commonly referred to by the mile markers along U.S. Route 1, with "Mile Zero" at Key West. The Keys are also unique in that there are many different, distinct areas requiring a great variety of charts. We will refer to charts with their appropriate titles and the most current edition numbers for a given cruising area. We then refer to the proper chart by number only when discussing specific locations within that area.

■ INSIDE ROUTE—ICW

NAVIGATION: Use Charts 11467 and 11451. Chart 11451 provides the most comprehensive coverage to Marathon. But it is a small-craft chart and not the most convenient to handle.

Heading south, after passing beneath the Powell/Rickenbacker Causeway (65-foot fixed vertical clearance) at Mile 1091.6, you pass Virginia Key to the east. Immediately following is Key Biscayne (with a yacht club, two interesting parks with marinas described in the previous chapter and several anchorages). Here, you enter lower Biscayne Bay and Biscayne National Park. Up to eight miles wide and about 28 nautical miles long, lower Biscayne Bay is a cleaner, different body of water than all the other bays along this coast.

Just below Key Biscayne, to the east, you will see the remaining seven houses of Stiltsville, an eclectic group of get-away homes that now belong to the National Park Service. They are visible along the reef. To the west lies Dinner Key (Mile 1094) with a cluster of friendly marine services, including yacht clubs, marinas, a boatyard, a restaurant and a new mooring field with 225 moorings, (see details in the previous chapter).

After a straight run for approximately 16 statute miles, the ICW route passes through the well-marked, but narrow channel at Featherbed Bank (Mile 1108). Biscayne National Park boundary flashing yellow lights "B" and "C" lie exactly on the ICW route and serve as helpful intermediate checkpoints on this long run. East of the ICW channel near Mile 1107 is a side channel marked by daybeacons and lights, with 6-foot controlling depths. It

Distances
Inside Route—ICW (Miles from Miami)

LOCATION	STATUTE MILES
Miami (Mile 1090)	0
Angelfish	30
Jewfish Creek	43
Tavernier	60
Islamorada	69
Channel Five	80
Marathon	102
Moser Channel	107
Harbor Key Bank Light	128
Northwest Channel	147
Key West	154

(Moser Channel to Key West via Hawk Channel is 40 statute miles.)

Looking east over Boca Chita Key, which lies just 16 miles south of Key Biscayne. (Not to be used for navigation.) WATERWAY GUIDE PHOTOGRAPHY

runs past several small islands and past Boca Chita Key, then close in to Sands and Elliott keys. Take care in both channels because of shoaling.

Dockage: Two marinas operated by Miami-Dade County, Black Point Marina and Homestead Bayfront Park Marina, are on the mainland side to the west, south of Featherbed Bank Cut. Both marinas were covered in Chapter 10 Under the Coral Gables section.

Biscayne National Park

NAVIGATION: Use Charts 11451 and 11463. Some of the northern keys, accessible only by boat or airplane, are privately owned. Elliott Key, about three miles east of ICW Mile 1113, is part of Biscayne National Park and, as such, is open to the public. During summer months with prevailing winds from the southeast, Elliott Key plays host to hundreds of boats. Dockage is available for boats up to about 26 feet at the park center, midway down the key. There are slips for 60 small craft and two dinghy landings. There is no approach channel to the boat basin, and depths may be as little as 2 feet; cruising craft habitually join the crowd by anchoring well-offshore. Do not go in too close, and keep an eye out for storm systems during the summer. During the winter, far fewer boats will visit this beautiful island, because frequent northerlies make anchoring here risky and downright uncomfortable. Biscayne National Park prohibits all personal watercraft ("jet skis").

Graced with a hardwood jungle and a shell-laden ocean beach, Elliott Key is the largest of the 25 keys encompassed by Biscayne National Park. Campsites and picnic grounds are available through the park rangers at the visitor center.

Showers and restrooms are located in a building a short distance from the boat basin; drinking-quality water is available from a faucet there, but not at the slips. Pets must be on an attended leash that is no longer than six feet in length. Visitors are requested not to feed wildlife. There is overnight dockage available, but daytime visits are free. An automated machine collects dockage fees (half price

Boca Chita Lighthouse, Boca Chita Key, FL. ©IstockPhoto/GatorL

Biscayne Bay, FL

BISCAYNE BAY	VHF Channel Monitored	Largest Vessel Accommodated	Approach / Dockside Depth (reported)	Transient Berths / Total Berths	Floating Docks	Gas / Diesel	Groceries, Ice, Marine Supplies, Snacks	Repairs: Hull, Engine, Propeller	Lift (tonnage), Crane, Rail	1=110V, 2=220V, B=Both, Max Amps	Laundry, Pool, Showers	Pump-Out Station	Nearby: Grocery Store, Motel, Restaurant
			Dockage				**Supplies**				**Services**		
1. Elliott Key Harbor 3.1 E of 1112.0 305-230-1144		35		2/6									S
2. Boca Chita Key 3 E of 1106 305-230-7275													

Corresponding chart(s) not to be used for navigation. 🖥 Internet Access 📶 Wireless Internet Access

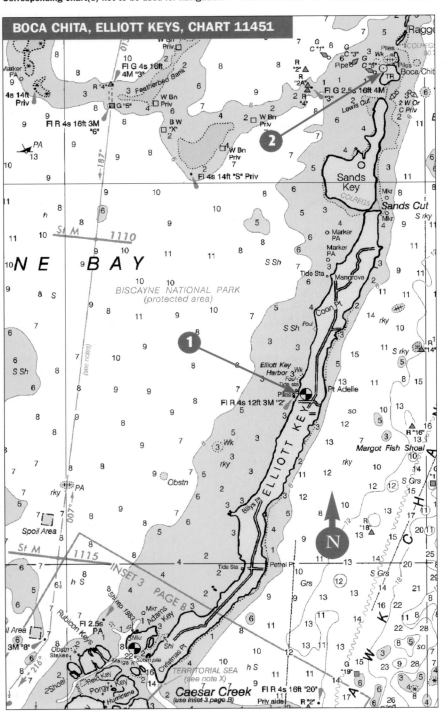

BOCA CHITA, ELLIOTT KEYS, CHART 11451

for holders of National Park Service or Golden Access passes), which is sort of a "reverse ATM" that accepts coins and bills up to $20. The rest of the 181,500-acre park (including much of Biscayne Bay) includes portions of the ocean reef and numerous shipwreck sites.

Dockage: Just north of Sands Key is Boca Chita Key. Here the National Park Service operates a facility for cruising boats, providing alongside dockage for 25 to 30 craft. A channel with at least 5-foot depths begins a half mile north of Sands Key Light (flashing green "3") and runs straight in toward the middle of Boca Chita Key. The channel is marked with three pairs of daybeacons. Neither drinking water nor showers are available, although there are restrooms available ashore. Boats with pets onboard are not permitted to dock, even if the animal remains on the boat. The same fee applies for overnight dockage here as at Elliott Key.

Anchorage: Just north of Elliott Key is Sands Key, a popular anchorage, despite poor holding on a grassy bottom. At the southeastern end of Elliott Key is Caesar Creek (southeast of Mile 1116) with a shallow entrance marked by Park Service buoys. Caesar Creek winds around tiny Adams Key (facilities ashore for day use only) and with a southern spur leading to an anchorage between Rubicon and Reid keys; it meanders past Elliott Key and out toward Hawk Channel. It is a pretty passage, but not for yachtsmen in cruising-sized boats, unless the yachtsman is very skilled.

Following the park markers, boats with less than a 4-foot draft can reach Hawk Channel. For more information, contact Biscayne National Park at 9700 S.W. 328th St., Homestead, FL 33033, 305-230-7275.

Card Sound

NAVIGATION: Use Charts 11451 and 11463. After traversing Featherbed Bank and altering course to approximately 192 degrees magnetic for about eight statute miles, you will find flashing red "8." At this point, you will alter course to about 221 degrees magnetic (just to the west of Rubicon Keys and Caesar Creek) for the straight, three-statute-mile, well-marked, but narrow channel run through 3- and 4-foot shoals to the pass through Cutter Bank and into Card Sound (at about Mile 1119).

Once in Card Sound, you will pass numerous fishing channels between the adjacent keys to the east. One is Angelfish Creek, heavily used for passage between the ICW and Hawk Channel. Angelfish Creek is considered questionable by some as a crossover from the ICW to Hawk Channel due to a 5-foot-deep rocky ledge at the eastern, or Hawk Channel end, of the creek. See the "Hawk Channel" section for more detail. The crossover from Hawk Channel can be quite convenient for cruisers heading north in a rising northerly, as it takes you inside protected waters before you leave Hawk Channel and face exposure to the Atlantic waters just south of Miami's Government Cut.

Dockage: Located on Key Largo, if you qualify as a member or a sponsored guest, the Ocean Reef Club (305-367-2611) offers sportfishing, golf, restaurants, lodging and shopping in an idyllic setting. The club once welcomed transients here, but it is now back to a "members and sponsored guests only" policy. The Secret Service has called Ocean Reef Club one of the most secure communities in the United States, and several past presidents have vacationed here. Richard Nixon liked to come here with his friend Bebe Rebozo, who was a member.

Anchorage: Just past Mile 1120, the entrance to Angelfish Creek, in Card Sound, is a well-known rendezvous and anchoring spot under the lee of small Pumpkin Key. Popular with locals as a hurricane hole, Waterway cruisers frequently congregate here, some waiting to cross the Gulf Stream to the Bahamas by exiting the bays via Angelfish Creek and others just to enjoy a quiet stop en route.

Barnes Sound

NAVIGATION: Use Charts 11451 and 11463. From Cutter Bank Pass, set a course of 233 degrees magnetic for about 5.4 statute miles to flashing green "17," which leads to the pass through Card Bank to Little Card Sound (Mile 1125). A 65-foot fixed vertical clearance bridge at Mile 1126.9 serves as the next landmark. This is the first of two highway bridges leading to the Keys from the mainland.

The channel under the bridge is marked and dredged, but it shallows rapidly upon entering Barnes Sound, so follow your markers closely. Once you are through the channel to flashing red "26" in Barnes Sound, good depths (6 to 8 feet) run the straight 4.5 nautical miles or so to the end of Barnes Sound and the Jewfish Creek channel leading to Blackwater Sound. The bottom is grassy and offers relatively poor holding. Depending on wind direction, the chop can build and Barnes Sound can get sloppy.

Dockage: Inside, where Manatee Creek was dead-ended by construction of the Overseas Highway (U.S. Route 1) decades ago, Manatee Bay Marine (at Mile 112.5 on the highway) operates a working yard, with full-time mechanics and a 60-ton lift. The facility normally reserves dockage for repair customers. Transients looking for dockage in this laid-back and out-of-the-way location may find them at one of the three mini-marinas just east of Manatee Bay Marine. Cruisers anchored out can make arrangements for dinghy landings and other services here.

Anchorage: During the winter season, you will likely encounter commercial stone crabbing or lobster boats, in addition to the usual menagerie of sportfishermen and ICW cruisers. About two-thirds of the way down Barnes Sound (Mile 1132), two channels are visible to the west. The second leads to what is known locally as Port Laura at Manatee Creek, about a mile north of Division Point. Numerous boats typically anchor off this channel, making it easier to spot. Controlling depth of the channel is about 5 feet at mean low water, depending on the wind-driven tide.

Jewfish Creek

NAVIGATION: Use Charts 11451 and 11463. At about Mile 1133, you enter the well-marked, deep Jewfish Channel. From here on, you really are in the Keys. Jewfish Creek itself is a favorite fishing spot, and small boats often congregate in the area. The numerous anchored or slow-trolling small fishing boats occupying this narrow channel require a close watch and a fast hand on the throttle to slow to Idle-Speed/No-Wake when encountering these smaller vessels. The route leads to the Jewfish Creek Bridge, Mile 1134.1 The original bascule bridge, built in 1944, was recently replaced by a 67-foot, $93-million beauty. Opened in May 2008, this structure saves time and money for boaters as well as land travelers. Marina facilities and an anchorage area are available after you pass through the span.

Dockage: Immediately south of the bridge, on the western side, is the well-known Gilbert's Family Paradise Island Resort, with a long wooden wharf along the channel for easy access to the gasoline and diesel pumps. The motel, pool and other areas have been renovated. Boaters have access to the resort's restrooms, showers, pool and coin-operated laundry machines. A pay phone and newspapers are available.

On the east side of the channel, the Anchorage Resort & Yacht Club has concrete piers available to transients, with 30- and 50-amp shore power. The resort has a large pool and hot tub, restrooms and showers, laundry, gas grills, cable TV hookups and shoreside hotel rooms. Fuel is not available. Key Largo lies to the east, and offers many sites of historical, geological and romantic interest in its 30-mile length. Some sites are close to marinas, but if this is a first visit, it is best to arrange for land transportation. Marina Del Mar welcomes transients and offers laundry and shower facilities.

Private watercraft are rented locally, so be prepared to navigate carefully and defensively here. The local radio sta-

Jewfish Creek, FL

Looking south-southwest over Jewfish Creek. (Not to be used for navigation.) WATERWAY GUIDE PHOTOGRAPHY

tion in this area is WCTH-FM 100.3, offering up-to-date local information and music.

Anchorage: Boats are often seen anchoring just to the south of the bridge near green daybeacon "37." Charted depths outside of the channel in the immediate vicinity are 5 to 6 feet. This anchorage is exposed to wakes and winds from any westerly quadrant.

Blackwater Sound—Mile 1135

NAVIGATION: Use Charts 11451 and 11464. Leaving Jewfish Creek at flashing red "38" and setting a course of 224 degrees magnetic will take you the three statute miles to the entrance to Dusenbury Creek and Tarpon Basin (Mile 1139). In Blackwater Sound to the west lies the Everglades National Park with its vast expanses of water and mangrove forests. All of the keys within the park are restricted from landings except where specifically designated and charted by park authorities. The fishing on the expansive shallow flats here is outstanding, but catch and licensing regulations are in effect here and enforcement is strict.

To the east of flashing green "41" lies Key Largo, with several good spots to drop the hook in a weedy bottom with fair holding. A small marina is located just north of a dredged canal, which leads to Largo Sound on the ocean side. Subject to strong currents, the canal is restricted to boats able to run in the 4 feet of water available and clear the two 14-foot fixed vertical clearance

bridges. It is nevertheless an interesting side trip by tender if you cannot make it any other way. Hawk Channel is accessible from Largo Sound (see the "Hawk Channel" section for more detail).

On to Florida Bay

NAVIGATION: Use Charts 11451 and 11464. From Blackwater Sound, the ICW snakes through mangrove-lined Dusenbury Creek (Mile 1138), where roseate spoonbills occasionally can be seen. The birds look for food by making sweeping motions with their flat bills. They are pink in color and rather pretty. Tarpon Basin is next; if you draw more than 3 feet, pay close attention to channel markers, and take it slowly. Our cruising editor draws 4 feet and found plenty of depth when staying in the channel.

Pay particular attention to red daybeacon "42" through flashing red "48," and hug them closely while making the hard turn to starboard. The water here is clear most of the time, so keep your head up, out of the cockpit. Although charts show 5- to 6-foot depths, depth sounders may register 2.5- to 3-foot depths in certain spots just off the channel. At flashing red "48," steer directly for red daybeacon "48A," and then on to flashing red "50." Narrow Grouper Creek is marked by red daybeacon "52" and exits between green daybeacon "53" and red daybeacon "52A." Flashing red "54" leads into Buttonwood Sound.

Anchorage: A once-favored anchorage, the bottom of Tarpon Basin is said to have grown over with grass. Unless you have either an excellent grass hook or can find one of the widely spaced clear spots, holding will be poor, but you will find a dinghy dock at MM1140 at the Government Center. Boaters are allowed to tie up here to gain shore access.

In Buttonwood Sound, to the south of Baker Cut, you will find the Upper Keys Sailing Club. This is a private sailing club, but if you get permission, you may be able to stop here for a short time and wander down to town, which isn't more than a half-mile walk. If you have to pay a small fee to use the facilities, it is worth it. Nearby is a liquor store, a Wendy's, some good restaurants and several stores. If you drop a hook in Tarpon Basin, you owe it to yourself to get local knowledge about the mangrove tunnels that you can explore from the comfort of your dinghy.

Buttonwood Sound

 THE FOLLOWING AREA REQUIRES SPECIAL ATTENTION DUE TO SHOALING OR CHANGES TO THE CHANNEL

NAVIGATION: Use Charts 11451 and 11464. Buttonwood Sound (Mile 1141) starts the area of 5-foot controlling depths along the ICW. Deeper water is sometimes inexplicably found to either side of the channel. Nevertheless, adhere strictly to the magenta line on the chart unless you maintain constant watch of your depth sounder or you have obtained local knowledge. Pay close attention to your exact location in relation to ICW markers, both forward and astern. Groundings are frequent for unwary boaters. Although the normal 1-foot tidal range may not warrant concern, strong winds can create considerable alterations in depth, making the water difficult to read, and may blow a boat just enough off course to make a difference.

END SPECIAL CAUTION AREA.

Pigeon Key to Cowpens Cut

NAVIGATION: Use Charts 11451 and 11464. Leaving Buttonwood Sound, the ICW continues its shallow course through a well-marked, but narrow channel (Baker Cut) into Florida Bay at Mile 1144. Shoal spots lie on either side of the channel. After you have passed Pigeon Key and, a bit later, swing to starboard to avoid a little (unnamed) island that will be to your right, you will pass red daybeacon "64A" to starboard. Paying careful attention to your chart, you can head south from here to a little bay with private markers. The water depths just off the channel are 6 feet, then shallow to 4 feet as you get closer to shore. If you are in need of re-supply, and can find a place to land the dinghy, there is a shopping center with a supermarket very close by. The area is labeled "Community Hbr" on the chart. You may call Mangrove Marina for specific navigation. Mangrove Marina welcomes transients with fuel, pump-out, wireless Internet and haul-out services.

If you get chased out of the little bay by northerly conditions, you could always go into Tavernier Creek and access the shopping center from there. Tavernier Creek is deep, but the limiting factors are the fixed highway bridge with its vertical clearance of 15 feet and the strong current that runs through here. Tavernier Creek Marina, north of the bridge, is big and sells fuel.

The area just beyond Cowpens Cut can be confusing when you arrive at flashing red "78" (Mile 1153.7). For some reason, the Coast Guard believes that the ICW ends here. The yellow squares and triangles no longer appear on aids to navigation, and the daybeacons and lights appear in a different section of the Light List. On the other hand, NOS/NOAA considers the ICW to continue on to Key West. The magenta line continues on charts, and the mileage continues to increase. Coverage in the Coast Pilot chapter on the ICW also continues to Key West.

Plantation Key Area

NAVIGATION: Use Charts 11451 and 11464. At Mile 1156, Snake Creek leads off to the southeast. Its channel is marked with flashing red "12" at the northern end; note that the aids here are numbered from the ocean side. This channel with a drawbridge (27-foot closed vertical clearance) provides access to Hawk Channel on the ocean side, but the channel on the ocean side of the bridge has shoaled, and the passage is not recommended for the faint of heart or the unskilled. Only use this channel when you have good light and visibility. Coast Guard Station Islamorada may be able to provide depth information.

From Cotton Key at ICW red daybeacon "80" (Mile 1158) to Steamboat Channel, the Waterway passes through what is perhaps the shallowest part of the entire route. Remember, touching a sandy bottom at slow speeds is rarely dangerous, but at high speeds, can do considerable damage to your props. There just isn't enough water here to take any chances—care is recommended. Marker floats for lobster and stone crab traps fill the channel and surrounding water in season so be careful about fouling your propeller shaft. During the off-season (May 15 to October 15), all traps and floats are supposed to be removed. Navigation is much simpler then, but some stray traps do remain, requiring a sharp lookout.

Dockage: Cowpens Cut through Cross Bank (Mile 1153) leads into the Plantation Key area. Cowpens was named for the pens used to hold manatees, which were used for food. Boats drawing up to 5 feet can visit Plantation Yacht Harbor Marina, but call ahead to the marina for an update on the status of the entry channel depths. Transient slips, gas and diesel fuel, a laundry, pool and restrooms/showers are available here. Plantation Yacht Harbor Marina offers protection from all but hurricane-force winds. The village of Islamorada owns this facility and they keep it in excellent condition. This is a very nice place to stop for a while. In addition to the docks, it has a soccer pitch, tennis courts, a swimming pool, a doggie park, basketball courts, a saltwater swimming beach and a baseball diamond, not to mention a place to jog.

Key Largo, FL

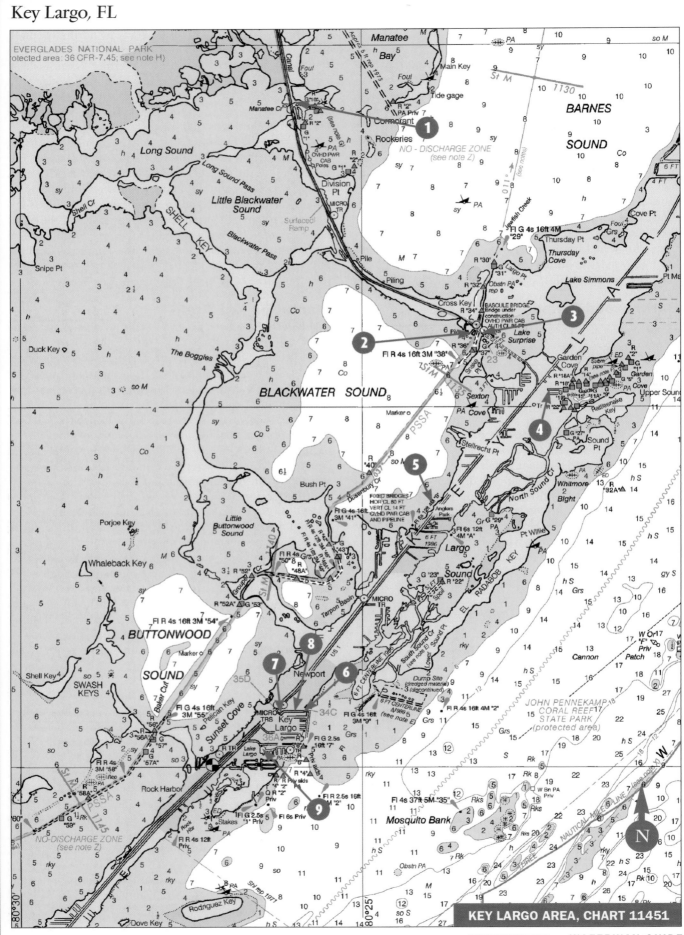

KEY LARGO AREA, CHART 11451

Key Largo to Plantation Key, FL

WG

Nearby: Grocery Store, Motel, Restaurant
Pump-Out Station
Laundry, Pool, Showers
1=110V, 2=220V, B=Both, Max Amps
Lift (tonnage), Crane, Rail
Repairs: Hull, Engine, Propeller
Groceries, Ice, Marine Supplies, Snacks
Gas / Diesel
Floating Docks
Approach / Dockside Depth (reported)
Transient Berths / Total Berths
VHF Channel Monitored
Largest Vessel Accommodated

KEY LARGO TO PLANTATION KEY			Dockage				Supplies			Services			
1. Manatee Bay Marine Inc. 3.4 NW of 1131.5	305-451-3332	50	16/72	/45	4.5/6			M	HEP	L70,C	1/15	S	P	R
2. Gilbert's Resort Marina 1134 **WiFi**	305-451-1133	105	16	/40	11/11		GD	IMS			B/50	LPS		GMR
3. Anchorage Resort - (Yacht Club) Condo 1134 **WiFi**	305-451-0500	180	16/09	/20	6/8			I			B/50	LPS		MR
4. Garden Cove Marina	305-451-4694	40	16/78	6/14	4/14	F	G	IM	EP	LR	1/30			GMR
5. The Marina Club at Black Water Sound 1136.5	305-451-3726	35	16		4/4	F	G	IM	E	L		S		GMR
6. Key Largo Harbor	305-451-0045	80	16		4/10		GD	IM	HP	L80	B/50			
7. Key Largo Resort Marina ▭**WiFi**	305-453-7171	65	16	50/77	4.5/18			IS			B/50	LPS		MR
8. Ocean Divers	305-451-1113	50	16		5/20		GD	I						GMR
9. Pilot House Marina **WiFi**	305-451-3452	70	16	10/30	4/4.5		GD	I			B/100	LS		R
10. Blue Waters Marina 1.3 SE of 1149.7	305-853-5604	60		/20	4.5/20						B/50	LS		GMR
11. Curtis Marine Inc. 1.3 SE of 1149.7	305-852-5218	60		1/20	4.5/14			M			B/50	LS		GMR
12. Mangrove Marina 1.3 S of 1150.0 **WiFi**	305-852-8380	70	16	120/130	5/5		GD	IMS	HEP	L60	B/50	LS	P	GMR
13. Tavernier Creek Marina 1.4 SE of 1151.7	305-852-5854	38		4/36	5/5		G	GIMS	HEP	L6	1/30			GR
14. PLANTATION YACHT HARBOR MARINA 1.8 S OF 1154.6	**305-852-2381**	**80**	**16**	**7/83**	**5/5**		**GD**	**I**			**B/50**	**LPS**	**P**	**MR**
15. Smuggler's Cove Marina 1157	305-664-5564	50	79	8/26	5/6		GD	GIMS	E		B/50	S		MR

Corresponding chart(s) not to be used for navigation. ▭ Internet Access **WiFi** Wireless Internet Access

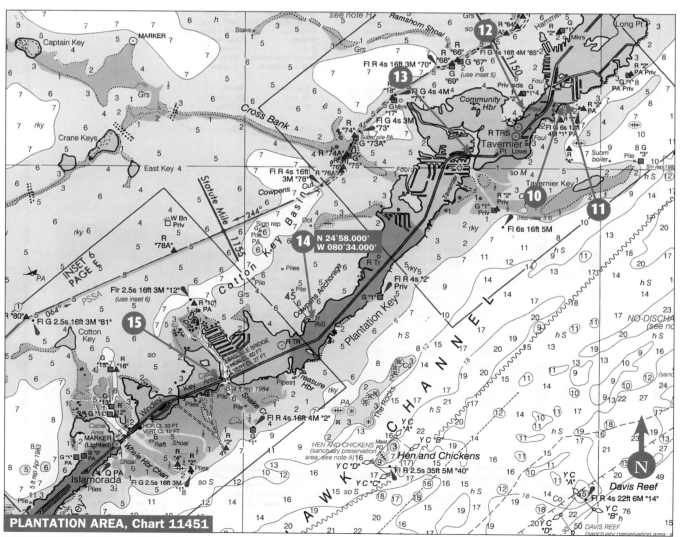

PLANTATION AREA, Chart 11451

Plantation Key, FL

Looking over Plantation Yacht Harbor Marina. (Not to be used for navigation.) Photo Courtsey of Plantation Yacht Harbor Marina.

If westbound, to get to Plantation Yacht Harbor Marina from flashing red "78," continue toward red daybeacon "78A" for one nautical mile; eastbound, from red daybeacon "78A," proceed toward flashing red "78" for about one nautical mile. Then alter course to about 150 degrees magnetic and proceed about one nautical mile toward shore. You will spot a red and white horizontally striped lighthouse at the end of the marina's breakwater. Leave it to starboard, hang a sharp starboard turn around the lighthouse and move up the marked channel to the marina. The former Dockside Restaurant is now the Village Hall, with offices and meeting rooms. No food service is currently available, but good restaurants are nearby.

All of the recreational amenities are available to marina visitors free or for a nominal charge for those not using the marina. The marina is popular with cruisers, so call ahead for reservations. Dockage rates vary by season; there is no minimum number of days.

Upper Matecumbe Key, Islamorada
NAVIGATION: Use Charts 11451 and 11464. **Use the Miami Harbor Entrance Tide Tables. For high tide, add 2 hours 45 minutes; for low tide, add 4 hours.** The village of Islamorada (Spanish for "Purple Island"), on the third largest island in the Keys, may be reached on a southeasterly course from red daybeacon "84" prior to entering Steamboat Channel. Locals use an anchorage with 5-foot depths at mean low water.

The reception of weather information in the Middle Keys has improved with the establishment of a transmitter on Teatable Key on Channel WX-5 (162.450 MHz). The local radio station is WCTH-FM 100.3. On TV, Channel 17 is the

Plantation Key to Lower Matecumbe Key, FL

PLANTATION KEY TO LOWER MATECUMBE KEY		Largest Vessel Accommodated	VHF Channel Monitored	Transient Berths / Total Berths	Approach / Dockside Depth (reported)	Floating Docks	Gas / Diesel	Groceries, Ice, Marine Supplies, Snacks	Repairs: Hull, Engine, Propeller	Lift (tonnage), Crane, Rail	1=110V, 2=220V, B=Both, Max Amps	Laundry, Pool, Showers	Pump-Out Station	Nearby: Grocery Store, Motel, Restaurant
			Dockage				**Supplies**			**Services**				
1. Holiday Isle Resort & Marina 1157.5	305-664-2321	110	16	19/56	4.5/6		GD	GIMS			B/50	LPS	P	MR
2. Lorelei Rest./Islamorada Yacht Basin 1160.2	305-664-2692	45	16	2/	4.5/4.5						B/50			GMR
3. Coral Bay Marina 1160.2 WiFi	305-664-3111	60	16	10/35	6/6			M	HEP	L50	B/50	LS	P	GMR
4. Caribee Boat Sales & Marina 1160.2	305-664-3431	38			5.5/5.5		G	IM	HEP	L				GMR
5. World Wide Sportsman/Bayside Marina	305-664-3398	40	16	4/40	3/3.5		GD	IMS			B/50	S	P	GMR
6. Watermark Marina of Islamorada 1161.0	305-664-8884	55			5/4		G			L35	B			MR
7. Bud 'n' Mary's Fishing Marina 1162.1	305-664-2461	50	77	10/35	4.5/4.5		GD	GIM	HP	L	B/50			MR
8. Caloosa Cove Marina & Resort 1169.5	305-664-4455	70	16	5/40	6/6		GD	GIMS			B/50	LPS		MR

Corresponding chart(s) not to be used for navigation. 🖵 Internet Access   WiFi Wireless Internet Access

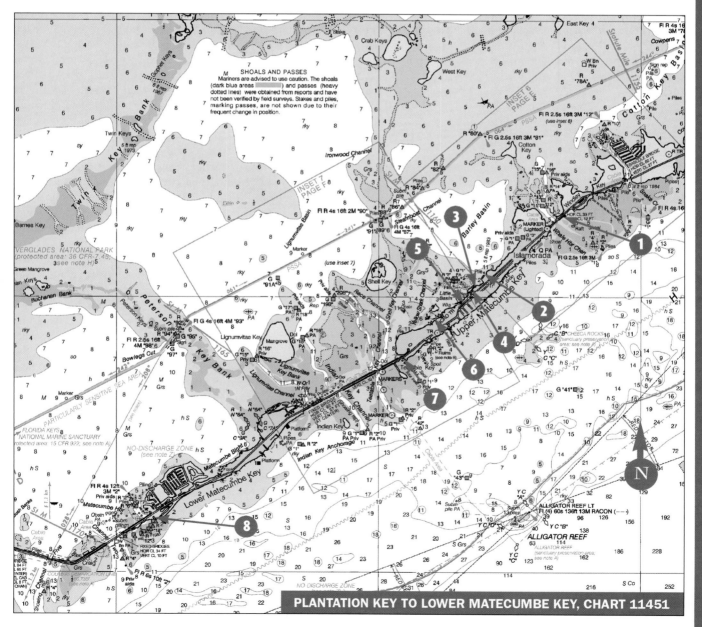

PLANTATION KEY TO LOWER MATECUMBE KEY, CHART 11451

NOAA Channel, repeating the same weather reports available on VHF weather channels.

Dockage: From red daybeacon "84," steering a course of 150 degrees magnetic and keeping your eye dead ahead on the charted tall radio tower, you will pass through a local mooring area offshore from Lorelei's Restaurant (305-664-2692) and arrive at a set of white stakes, marking the entrance to Coral Bay Marina. Turning to starboard, follow their path to a relatively small 35-slip marina equipped with a 50-ton Travelift, exceptional mechanics and 10 transient slips. Although the slips are weathered, all the shore power hookups (30- and 50-amp) and TV cable hookups are like new and the folks are friendly and accommodating.

Just northeast of Coral Bay Marina is a tight, well-protected yacht basin (4-foot controlling depth at mean low water) beside the Lorelei Restaurant and Cabana Bar (highway mile marker 82). The casual outdoor bar and restaurant is a magnet for locals, cruisers and land-based tourists, and it is the place to be at sunset. The restaurant has been rebuilt since Hurricane Wilma, which did considerable damage, and it is a fun place to spend "happy hour" or the evening with live music and good food.

GOIN' ASHORE:
UPPER MATECUMBE KEY, FL (OLD ISLAMORADA)

Welcome to the heart of Islamorada. The Monroe County, FL village of Islamorada, incorporated on Nov. 4, 1997, stretches 18.2 miles, from the Channel Two Bridge at Keys Mile Marker 72.8 to the Tavernier Creek Bridge at Keys Mile Marker 91. (Note that the highway Mile Markers or MM do not correspond to the Waterway Statute Miles. Also, addresses are given as "bayside" or "oceanside," depending on which side of Overseas Highway, (U.S. 1) they fall.) As an incorporated village, Islamorada includes Lower Matecumbe, Lignumvitae, Indian, Teatable, Upper Matecumbe, Wilson, Windley and Plantation Keys. But, prior to incorporation, Upper Matecumbe Key was Islamorada…the "Purple Island." On foot or by bicycle, Upper Matecumbe Key is a manageable 4.8 miles centered roughly on the World Wide Sportsman—MM 81.2 and its excellent Islamorada Fish Company Restaurant and

Seafood Market, inviting Zane Gray Long Key Lounge and Bayside Marina.

On Upper Matecumbe Key, along U.S. Route 1 (Overseas Highway), you will find a small but good and well-stocked market, a large hardware store with a marine supply section, a marine supply and equipment store, a Post Office, book store, two well-stocked liquor stores, several banks with 24-hour ATMs, numerous restaurants, retail shops and hotel/motels. For the length of the Key, both sides of U.S. Route 1 have pedestrian/bike paths that are paved for most of their length and the paths make walking and biking on the Key pleasant, easy and safe. The nearest full-size supermarket is the Winn Dixie in Tavernier—MM 92 and the nearest 24/7 medical care is the Mariners Hospital, also in Tavernier.

Working north from the World Wide Sportsman; immediately adjacent to the Sportsman, on the bayside, are the Morada Bay Beach Café with Mediterranean cuisine and a small boat/dinghy dock on the Little Basin, and Pierre's Restaurant featuring excellent modern French cuisine and an extensive wine list (dinners only, reservations a must). Directly across Rt. 1, on the oceanside, are two more excellent fine dining restaurants: Chanticleer South, a branch of the well-respected French restaurant Chanticleer on Nantucket Island (again, dinner only, reservations strongly recommended) and Kaiyo, with Asian-fusion cuisine, a good wine list and sushi bar. Continuing north, in quick succession are Two Martinis' Fine Wine and Spirits, the Islamorada Restaurant and Bakery (the famous "Bobs Bunz"), the Islamorada Library, Tower of Pizza, Caribee Boat Sales, with a decent marine supply store, the Trading Post Market and Deli—MM 81.5, really a small, well-stocked supermarket, and, directly behind the Trading Post (with a foot path connecting them), the Coral Bay Marina.

At MM 81.7, Hooked on Books, a small independent book seller with an excellent collection of books about the Keys, the Everglades and Florida, is on the oceanside, and on the bayside, are the Ichthyophile with pottery, art, videos and books about fish and fishing, and the Angelika Clothing Company with an extensive line of quality women's beach and resort wear. Next, at MM 82 bayside, at the large mermaid sign, is the Lorelei Restaurant and Cabana Bar with good food (breakfast, lunch and dinner), reputedly the best happy hour on the Key, live entertainment seven nights a week and, for boaters, a marina and dinghy dock—the place to be at sunset, crowded and alive. Within the next mile are Mangrove Mike's Café, family dining breakfast, lunch and dinner (voted the best breakfast in Islamorada—try the white chocolate chip, macadamia pancakes), the Whistle Stop Sports Bar, Pub and Grill and (next door) well-stocked liquor store, a large hardware store (with a marine section), the History of Diving Museum (open 10 a.m. to 5 p.m. daily) and the Islamorada Chamber of Commerce and Visitors Center. Then at the top of the Key, oceanside, are two resorts with marinas and multiple restaurants, one on each side of the Whale Harbor Channel. On the south side of the channel, on Upper Matecumbe Key, is the Whale Harbor Inn and Marina with Wahoo's Bar and Grill and Braza Lena, a Brazilian Churrascaria (steakhouse), both are excellent. North of the channel, and on Windley Key, is the Holiday Isle Beach Resort and Marina with Jaw's Raw Bar.

Distances
Outside Route—Hawk Ch. (Miles from Miami)

LOCATION	STATUTE MILES	NAUTICAL MILES
Miami (Government Cut)	0	0
Miami (Cape Florida)	8	6.9
Fowey Rocks Light	14	12.0
Angelfish Creek	28	24.0
South Sound Creek	51	44.0
Tavernier	63	54.7
Islamorada	70	60.8
Channel Five	82	71.0
Duck Key	92	79.9
Marathon (Sisters Creek)	102	88.6
Moser Channel	109	94.7
Key West	151	131.0

(Moser Channel to Key West via Hawk Channel is 40 statute miles.)

Channel Five, crossed by a fixed bridge with a 65-foot vertical clearance. (Not to be used for navigation.) WATERWAY GUIDE PHOTOGRAPHY

Although most of the things of interest to a cruising boater lie north of the World Wide Sportsman, to the south, between the Sportsman and Bud and Mary's Fishing Marina there are a number of retail shops, art galleries and restaurants. Notable are the Redbone Galleries specializing in fine original angling and island art, the Green Turtle Inn featuring fresh seafood, the Midway Café and Coffee Bar, exactly what the name implies, coffee beans are roasted on site, the Lazy Days Restaurant with a menu dominated by fresh local seafood and spectacular ocean views, MM 79.9, and, for a change from seafood and island fare, try the Outback Steakhouse at the Hampton Inn, MM 80.

To go ashore on Upper Matecumbe Key from the bayside, visit the marina at the Lorelei Restaurant, MM 82, the Coral Bay Marina, MM 81.5, or the Bayside Marina at The World Wide Sportsman, MM 81.2 (in the Little Basin); or anchor in the Lorelei Anchorage, off the Lorelei Restaurant and Marina and the entrance to the Coral Bay Marina, or in the Little Basin off The World Wide Sportsman (if you draw less then 3.5 feet). Dinghies from anchored boats are welcome at the Lorelei Dinghy Dock, at The World Wide Sportsman and at the Morada Bay Beach Café's small boat dock (in the Little Basin adjacent to The World Wide Sportsman). The Coral Bay Marina does not have a dinghy dock; when the office is open dinghies can, with permission and space permitting, tie up in front of the office for an hour or two. In addition, Bud and Mary's Fishing Marina, at the southwest tip of the Key, can be accessed from the Bay through the Shell Key Channel or the Indian Key Channel.

From the Ocean/Hawk Channel side, go to the ends of the key. On the oceanside of the fixed Whale Harbor Channel Bridge at the northeast end of Upper Matecumbe Key, both the Holiday Isle Resort & Marina (north end of the bridge) and the Whale Harbor Inn & Marina (south end of the bridge) welcome visiting boaters. In calm conditions or with light winds

from the west through to the north-northeast, it is possible for vessels drawing up to 5 feet to anchor on the sand off the Whale Harbor Inn, this is not a particularly good or a recommended anchorage; but if you do anchor here, you and your dinghy are welcome in the marina at the Whale Harbor Inn. At the southwest end of Upper Matecumbe Key, Bud and Mary's Fishing Marina welcomes boats that can negotiate the 33-foot fixed vertical clearance Teatable Key Channel Bridge.

ADDITIONAL RESOURCES

■ History of Upper Matecumbe Key,
www.keyshistory.org/uppermatkey.html

⛳ **NEARBY GOLF COURSES**
Key Colony Beach Golf & Tennis, 460 Eighth St.,
Key Colony Beach, FL 33051, 305-289-1533
www.keycolonybeach.net

⚕ **NEARBY MEDICAL FACILITIES**
Mariners Hospital, 91500 Overseas Highway,
Tavernier, FL 33070, 305-434-3000
www.baptisthealth.net

Lignumvitae Basin

NAVIGATION: Use Charts 11451 and 11464. Lying between Steamboat Channel (Mile 1161) and Bowlegs Cut (Mile 1165), Lignumvitae Basin offers good depths for substantial keels and fair-weather anchorages in the lees of Shell Key and Lignumvitae Key to the south. These two keys, bordered by the three navigable channels between Upper and Lower Matecumbe keys and historic Indian Key (at the south end of Indian Key Channel), are all now a part of the Lignumvitae Key Management Area. Indian Key has small boat docks, and the pier at Lignumvitae Key can accom-

Outside Route, Hawk Channel, FL

modate medium-size cruising craft (4-foot depths) at both locations, although no docking is permitted after 5 p.m., and no pets are allowed ashore.

A visit to the Lignumvitae State Botanical Site is worthwhile. Rangers conduct tours at 10 a.m. and 2 p.m. except on Tuesdays and Wednesdays, when the site is closed. At 18 feet above sea level, Lignumvitae Key is the highest of the Keys; it is named for one of the hardest woods in the world, "the tree of life."

All channels in the management area are well-marked, but only Indian Key Channel offers significant fixed vertical clearance (27 feet). The shallow turtle-grass flats in this area are also clearly marked. The flats are all closed to boats with internal combustion engines (gas or diesel, inboard or outboard). State law enforcement officers police the area, and violators (particularly those who have damaged the grass with their props) are subject to stiff fines. Five heavy moorings (complimentary) have been established on the northwest sides of both Lignumvitae Key and Shell Key. Additional moorings are available west of Indian Key, though they are unprotected from prevailing southeasterly winds.

As a historical aside, Indian Key was the first county seat of Dade County. My, how things change. Indian Key doesn't have a soul living on it. And Miami-Dade? Just a few folks call it home now.

Channel Five

NAVIGATION: Use Charts 11451 and 11449. Leaving Bowlegs Cut through Peterson Key Bank at Mile 1165, cruisers have the option of continuing on the ICW inside, or crossing over to the Hawk Channel (ocean) passage outside. Hawk Channel is reached through the second major crossover point: deep, well-marked Channel Five, crossed by a fixed bridge with a 65-foot vertical clearance. To reach Channel Five from green daybeacon "97" (near Mile 1165), steer about 210 degrees on a course to the south-southwest for five miles. This will bring you to a point just north of the bridge.

Please pay attention to this caveat when using Channel Five, however: The channel itself is spottily marked. There are a couple of marks south of the Channel Five Bridge—red daybeacon "4," flashing red "2" and green daybeacon "1." After passing under the bridge, take those marks in the order given, if heading for Hawk Channel. There is a prominent shoal to port south of the bridge. The red aids mark its westernmost edge.

There are no marks indicating the best water to the north of the bridge. Pay attention. Heading straight for the center span should keep you out of trouble.

From the bridge, if you are heading south, plot your course southwesterly to flashing red "44," which, when left to starboard, puts you into Hawk Channel. At that point, alter course westerly to 247 degrees magnetic.

To continue on the ICW inside from Mile 1165 and Bowlegs Cut, steer a course of 246 degrees magnetic to flashing green "1," about six nautical miles west, just north of Old Dan Bank.

■ OUTSIDE ROUTE— HAWK CHANNEL

In westerly through northerly winds of 15 knots or more, Hawk Channel may provide a more protected passage along the Keys than the ICW route. Access outside to Hawk Channel from Miami and Miami Beach is through Government Cut. From just below Miami in Biscayne Bay, the Florida Channel/Biscayne Channel (treated as one) provides a more protected route. In winter, northerlies frequently become northeasters (20 knots or more) for several days, and give Hawk Channel a lumpy, irregular following sea. It only abates where the Keys bend to the west.

Well-found and appropriately crewed sailboats will get a great sleigh ride. Powerboats, depending on size, may find it a wet and uncomfortable passage. Obviously, knowledgeable skippers with larger boats equipped with stabilizers and autopilots should not have difficulties.

Hawk Channel is relatively wide; nevertheless, navigation should be precise, because the aids to navigation are frequently far apart and difficult to spot. Compass courses should be the rule, as well as following prudent piloting practices. GPS will be extremely useful in this passage, particularly during times of poor visibility.

You should take a cautious attitude when planning daily runs, and plan to complete each day's run well before dark. As in the Bahamas, night passages are not recommended. Fortunately, both anchorages and marinas can be found at reasonable intervals throughout the Keys.

In heavy easterly weather, beam seas are the rule, amplified by current and counter-current in the stretches abeam the numerous gaps in the Florida reef. Sailboats might like this weather, but powerboats may wish to sit it out or move inside to the ICW.

When winds slacken and veer to the southeast and south, conditions quiet down. With slack winds, sailboats may motorsail or make short close-hauled runs. Powerboats may still roll, but the journey will be generally enjoyable.

Distances within this section and the anchorage portion are measured in statute miles from the south side of Government Cut, almost parallel with ICW Mile 1090. Use them as a rough guide only.

Hawk Channel

NAVIGATION: Use Charts 11468, 11465, 11463 and 11451. Chart 11451 provides the most comprehensive coverage to Marathon, but it is a small-craft chart. The other charts listed provide different perspectives on the navigation routes discussed.

To enter Hawk Channel from Government Cut, you must go seaward through Outer Bar Cut past the spoil areas. Or if you are familiar with the area, cut between the range markers just south of the jetty. Either way, bear in mind there is a 3-foot shoal area extending out from Cape Florida. Keep red daybeacon "2," outside of Bear Cut just past Virginia Key, well off to starboard. You might do well to set a southeasterly course to pass about one mile inside Fowey Rocks Light (flashing white every 10 seconds) and the red daybeacon "2" and green daybeacon "3" marking the start of Hawk Channel. The channel markers, as with the ICW, generally follow red-right-southbound. Some variation has crept in with recent storms and channel changes, so navigate carefully using the latest charts. (The latest edition of 11451 in Summer 2010 is the 34th from October 2009.)

The second route from below the Powell/Rickenbacker Causeway gives a choice of the Cape Florida or Biscayne channels. Both of these converge at 12-foot flashing red "6" south of Cape Florida's lighthouse. Vessels using Biscayne Channel from the west must pass between the two daybeacons (green "7" and red "8") just before flashing red "6." The cluster of houses amidst the reefs south of Biscayne Channel is Stiltsville, whose landmark homes are part of Biscayne National Park. When going to seaward in either channel, remember that green markers are to starboard until you reach green flashing "1."

From here to Hawk Channel, between red daybeacon "2" and green daybeacon "3," at ICW Mile 1098 west of Fowey Rocks, swing well east of the shoals south of Biscayne Channel green flashing "1," red flashing "2" and the flashing white light on a 37-foot skeleton tower. From this point to Channel Five is approximately 74 statute miles. (Unlike the ICW, NOAA charts show no magenta line or mile markers on Hawk Channel. All mile indications here refer to approximate comparable ICW mile markers.)

Slower boats may want to plan short runs between anchorages or marine facilities along the way. If you are sightseeing, you may want to do the same. To the west as you pass Fowey Rocks Light are the first of the small keys projecting above the ancient reef between the ocean and Biscayne Bay. About three miles on, the Ragged Keys appear, followed closely by Boca Chita, Sands and Elliott keys (described near the beginning of this chapter). At Bowles Bank Light (flashing red "8"), the channel bends to the south-southwest as the westward curve of the Florida Keys commences.

Caesar Creek

NAVIGATION: Use Charts 11451 and 11463. At the southwest end of Elliott Key, Caesar Creek (ICW Mile 1116) is the first crossover to the ICW that is open to shallow-draft vessels. The channel is well-marked, but narrow, and bounded by 1- to 2-foot depths at low tide; use caution when transiting this area. Caesar Creek also provides a tight little anchorage at its western end. Flashing red "20" is at the entrance to the Park Service's marked channel. The channel is charted with at least 7 feet at mean low water and has a low point of 4 feet on the bayside. Enter in the early morning when the water is easy to read.

Angelfish Creek—Mile 1118

NAVIGATION: Use Charts 11451 and 11463. Local skippers use well-marked Angelfish Creek, about three nautical miles south of Caesar Creek, to cross over from ocean to bay and back. For all but deep-draft vessels, it is fairly simple. But if you have a deep keel, stay well out until the channel markers line up before you enter. Just inside the entrance from Hawk Channel is a rocky ledge with 5-foot depths at low water.

Keep dead center in Angelfish Creek at low tide, and maintain enough speed to prevent leeway. Do not enter if another boat is coming out; you need to stay on the centerline. Once inside, the controlling 5-foot depth creates no problem, and you can often find deeper water. Depths of 7-foot-plus along this passage are the rule rather than the exception. Side creeks offer anchorages, but the bottom is rocky, and currents are strong. You may want to continue through Angelfish Creek and anchor in the lee of Pumpkin Key.

Dockage: South of the oceanside entrance to Angelfish Creek is the previously mentioned Ocean Reef Club. It is a private club that accepts only members and sponsored guests. Other facilities along the Hawk Channel side cater to transients, though many are oriented primarily to sportfishermen. Average approach depths are 5 feet to many of these privately marked channels.

John Pennekamp Coral Reef State Park

NAVIGATION: Use Charts 11451 and 11463. At green daybeacon "23," you cross the northwest boundary of the 25-mile John Pennekamp Coral Reef State Park.

To reach the park's land attractions by boat, enter through South Sound Creek on the southwest side of Largo Sound, about midway down Key Largo (ICW Mile 1141), and less than two miles to the north of Mosquito Bank flashing green "35." Flashing red "2" marks the entrance. The channel carries 6-foot depths, but 5-foot depths are reported in Largo Sound. Dive and sightseeing boats use this channel frequently, so be prepared to move, but not too far, because 3-foot depths have been reported out of the channel. Because of the narrow channel and blind turns, commercial vessels make a Sécurité call on VHF Channel 16 before entering it. Listen for such calls, and make your own if appropriate.

Vessels with drafts of 4 feet or less and overhead clearances of 14 feet or less can cross over from Blackwater Sound to Largo Sound via a rock cut that connects the southernmost corner of Blackwater Sound with the western shore of Largo Sound. (The shallowest water lies at the beginning and end of the cut.) If you cannot get your big boat through here, it makes a great dinghy trip. Bear in mind that a strong current runs through here.

The underwater park contains 178 square nautical miles of coral reef, sea grass beds, mangrove swamps and the larger of two living reefs that lie in Florida waters. Tropical fish live around the coral and there are shipwrecks, making an underwater paradise for Scuba divers and snorkelers. Only hook-and-line fishing is permitted.

Dockage: The John Pennekamp Coral Reef State Park's marina consists of nine full-service slips with power, water, showers and pump-out. Call the dockmaster on VHF Channel 16 or 305-451-6325 to check availability.

Park activities include glass-bottom boat tours, scuba gear rentals and instruction, boat rentals, a 47-site campground and a visitors center with a 30,000 gallon saltwater aquarium.

Port Largo Canal, FL

Looking northwest over Tavernier Creek (4-foot depths), suitable for dinghies and small vessels.
(Not to be used for navigation.) WATERWAY GUIDE PHOTOGRAPHY

Anchorage: Although overnight anchoring is prohibited in Largo Sound, about a dozen moorings (white mooring balls) are located in the southwest corner of the sound, near the park headquarters. Simply tie up to an empty one, and dinghy over to the dockmaster's office (in the dive center) to check in.

Port Largo Canal and Lagoon

If you are interested in exploring and have the freedom of shoal draft and low overhead limitations, a dredged canal with 4-foot depths and strong currents leads from the northwest corner of Largo Sound into Blackwater Sound and the ICW. Narrow and restricted by two fixed bridges with 14-foot vertical clearances, small fishing and dive boats mostly use the canal.

A number of restaurants, hotels and marine facilities lie along the Port Largo Canal located north of Rodriguez Key (ICW Mile 1145) on Key Largo. A north-northwesterly heading from flashing red "2" will help guide you into the difficult-to-find mouth of the canal. A useful landmark is the gray house located on the point just left of the canal entrance.

The lagoon is deep, but the outside channel carries only 5 feet. Passing large vessels in the canal can be difficult; pay attention to Sécurité calls. There is a 90-degree turn in this canal that the locals call "Crash Corner." Block ice is available from Key Largo Harbor, and a nearby shopping center has a grocery store, drugstore and bookstore.

Anchorage: About a mile north of Rodriguez Key is the Rock Harbor anchorage. Be aware of which way the wind will be blowing. Depths behind Rodriguez average 7 to 8 feet, and the holding is good over grass and sand. This is a good stop for boats preparing to cross to the Bahamas or heading on to Marathon.

Tavernier Key to Lower Matecumbe Key

NAVIGATION: Use Charts 11451 and 11464. At about the point where Tavernier Key is joined to Key Largo, another charted channel leads due north at ICW Mile 1150. (See section E, inset 5, of Chart 11451.) Well-equipped Tavernier Creek Marina provides all kinds of boat services and has a rigging shop for sailboats. A 15-foot vertical clearance fixed bridge crosses the channel, however, preventing access for sailboats from the south.

Below Key Largo, Hawk Channel leads from the charted Triangles, marked by green daybeacon "39" (at about ICW Mile 1150), west of Molasses Reef, about nine statute miles southwest to Hen and Chickens flashing red "40." The unmarked shoal known as "The Rocks," with depths of 3 feet at mean low water, lies northwest of flashing red "40." Take care in navigating as these rocks have created problems for daydreaming sailors.

Snake Creek to Channel Five

NAVIGATION: Use Charts 11451 and 11464. Snake Creek (ICW Mile 1157), at the east end of Windley Key, is a limited crossover to the ICW that leads off to the northwest below "The Rocks." The marked channel is reportedly shallow, with 4-foot depths or less at the entrance, though small boats and the Coast Guard use it. Just beyond Snake Creek Channel at the western end of Windley Key is Whale Harbor Channel, privately marked and maintained. Whale Harbor Channel leads into a basin with 5-foot approach depths just before the bridge. Holiday Isle Resort and Marina offers sportfishing activities, and there are motel rooms, restaurants and many bars ashore. Whale Harbor Channel continues under a 12-foot fixed vertical clearance bridge to the ICW side.

Teatable Key

NAVIGATION: Use Charts 11451 and 11449. Tiny and picturesque Teatable Key (ICW Mile 1163), once a navy base and now a private island, lies on the Hawk Channel side of the southwest end of Upper Matecumbe Key. On Teatable Key, there is a VHF-FM continuous weather transmitter broadcasting on Channel WX-5 (162.450 MHz). This greatly improves the reception of weather information in the Middle Keys.

Dockage: Behind Teatable Key to the east, a privately maintained channel (controlling depth 4.5 feet) leads to Bud 'n' Mary's Marina, one of the oldest and most active sportfishing centers in the Florida Keys. Rental skiffs and guided fishing charters are available, as well as transient dockage. Call ahead for reservations.

Indian Key

The Florida Park Service maintains historic Indian Key, which lies farther west, off the eastern tip of Lower Matecumbe Key. Indian Key is open to public visits from 8 a.m. to sunset. Once a thriving village, county seat and local center for the "wrecking" trade, Indian Key is now an archaeological curiosity of house and warehouse foundations and impressive brick cisterns, spaced along a thoughtfully placed grid of streets and avenues. Two-foot depths alongside a small dock limit access. You can anchor along the southeast side of Indian Key or pick up the pennant of one of the several courtesy mooring buoys there, but approach Indian Key only from the ocean side, and expect Atlantic swells from the southeast even in settled weather as the reef is not deep enough here to break up the swells.

Teatable Key and Indian Key Channels

Between the two small keys lie two channels to the bay side: Teatable Key Channel and Indian Key Channel. A fixed bridge with a 10-foot vertical clearance limits access to Teatable Key Channel. Indian Key Channel is also a simple run all the way to ICW Mile 1163 northwest of the Lignumvitae Key State Botanical Site (mentioned in the ICW section of this chapter). This would be considered a major crossover if it were not for the 27-foot fixed vertical clearance bridge.

Lower Matecumbe Key

Lower Matecumbe Key is the midpoint in the run from Fowey Rocks to Key West. At its western tip, Channel Two, with a 10-foot fixed vertical clearance bridge, is a restricted crossover. Robbie's of Islamorada (www.robbies.com) is a major sportfishing marina with supplies, boat rentals and charters, and the Hungry Tarpon Restaurant (www.hungrytarpon.com) is at the head of a privately marked channel running south from the ICW at Mile 1175, a couple of nautical miles past Channel Five.

Channel Five—ICW Mile 1172

About a nautical mile west of Channel Two is the second major crossover to the ICW, Channel Five. It is a relatively deep, all-weather passage with a 65-foot fixed vertical clearance bridge that joins the ICW at about Mile 1170. From this point, you are on your final leg to Key West. ■

Manatee. Photo Courtesy of Susan Landry.

Long Key to Key West

CHARTS 11438, 11439, 11441, 11442, 11445, 11146, 11447, 11448, 11451, 11452, 11453

As mentioned in the previous chapter, at Mile 1166, just beyond Bowlegs Cut, cruisers bound for Marathon or Key West via the Intracoastal Waterway (ICW) have the choice of crossing over to the Hawk Channel route via Channel Five (crossed by a 65-foot fixed vertical clearance bridge) or continuing on the ICW. To take the Hawk Channel route, pass through the Channel Five Bridge and continue on, leaving red daybeacon "4" and flashing red "2" to port and green daybeacon "1" to starboard. From there, leave flashing red "44" to starboard, and then take a southwesterly course heading parallel to Long Key and the Long Key Viaduct (23-foot fixed vertical clearance at the center of each arch). Cruisers using Hawk Channel to come down the Keys can use Channel Five to cross over to Florida Bay and the West Coast.

NAVIGATION: Use Charts 11451, 11448, 11449, 11453 and 11442. From Channel Five to Moser Channel (Seven Mile Bridge), the next major crossover to Hawk Channel, the ICW route has depths of 7 to 9 feet. On approaching Old Dan Bank (Mile 1173), boats bound for the west coast of Florida will have their first opportunity to depart the ICW for the passage north to the west coast of Florida via the Yacht Channel, which cuts across Florida Bay.

This 23-mile-long marked route northwest to East Cape is comfortably deep for most cruising boats, but requires compass courses and careful navigation. Markers are spaced from three to seven miles apart, and near-route shoals will snare the inattentive. (See the Florida Keys section for information about East Cape and Flamingo.)

"Back country" fishing is renowned in this area, but be sure to have a current Florida fishing license, and know the Florida Fish and Wildlife Conservation Commission catch limits enforced by state officers. There is an excellent anchorage off Sandy Key, south of East Cape Sable. Boats drawing less than 4.5 feet can follow the marked channel to Flamingo, where there is a marina in the heart of Everglades National Park. (For more information, see the "Flamingo to Fort Myers Beach" chapter found later in this Guide.)

ICW Inside Route—Mile 1180 to Mile 1197 (Seven Mile Bridge)

NAVIGATION: Use Charts 11451, 11449 and 11453. Back on the ICW, Long Key—roughly south of Old Dan Bank—is the home of Long Key State Park (305-664-4815), a 300-acre wild area with a campground, numerous picnic tables and grills. The ICW passes west of Old Dan Bank on a course of 246 degrees magnetic for about six statute miles in good depths to Channel Key Pass, the passage between the shoals of Channel Key Bank (Mile 1179).

Long Key Viaduct (23-foot fixed vertical clearance) lies to the southeast before passing through Channel Key Pass. Powerboaters with local knowledge frequently use it en route to Duck Key and the marina at Hawk's Cay Resort on the Hawk Channel (i.e., oceanside).

Grassy Key Bank (Mile 1182) projects northerly from long, low Grassy Key. At this point, if you plan to stop at Marathon, you can take the shortcut to Marathon on the ICW side. Plot a course between Bamboo Key and the shoal to its northwest. Skirt Stirrup Key, then take a bearing on Rachel Key, passing between Rachel Key and the marked shoal on Rachel Bank. Thereafter, you should have depths of at least 7 feet until quite close to shore.

At this point, you can pick from among the many marinas lining the north shore of Marathon, or (if you have sufficient clearance to pass under the 19-foot fixed vertical clearance of the Seven Mile Bridge) follow on around Knight Key and south through Knight Key Channel (Mile 1194) to find flashing green "1," marking the entrance to the channel to Boot Key Harbor, between Knight Key and Boot Key.

Dockage: Cruisers with deep-draft access (up to 8 feet) may want to overlook the shortcut and remain on the ICW route. Some of the "old standbys" on the north side of Marathon (Vaca Key) are no more. Faro Blanco Marine Resort (bayside) at Mile 1193 is one of them. Faro Blanco was severely damaged by Hurricane Georges in 1998, but in 2005 when Hurricane Wilma came along and added more destruction, Faro Blanco could stand no more and has been closed ever since. The docks on the Florida Bay side were destroyed, and most of the houseboats on the oceanside were sunk. Much of what was once was Faro Blanco—rooms, restaurants and amenities—has been torn down altogether. New construction appears to be ongoing. One day, presumably, something nice will come of all this, but not anytime soon.

There have been some turnovers in the yacht docking business in Marathon, too, but names and facilities have not changed much. The marinas that line the western entrance to Boot Key Harbor are all intact, Faro Blanco Oceanside being an exception. As conditions change with the seasonal hurricanes, you can get up-to-date information on all the marinas in the Marathon area by visiting www.bootkeyharbor.com/bkh_marinas.htm.

Those with drafts of less than 4.5 feet may want to try the excellent facilities at the nearby Banana Bay Resort Marina. This marina was ravaged by Hurricane Wilma, but it is back on its feet. The motel proper got the first infusion of money after Wilma and the marina experienced the second transfusion. It is a small marina, but that is part of its distinct charm. You will get to know your neighbors.

Members of the Florida Council of Yacht Clubs and the American Registry of Yacht Clubs will be welcome at the Marathon Yacht Club (305-743-6739), depending on slip availability. Full-service repairs and first-class carpentry work are available nearby at Keys Boat Works. Enjoy a meal at the Yacht Club's dining room.

Seven Mile Bridge to Northwest Channel

NAVIGATION: Use Charts 11451, 11453 and 11448. The famous Seven Mile Bridge begins its passage west at the western end of Marathon, immediately crossing Knight Key Channel (15-foot minimum fixed vertical clearance—two spans). Though frequently used by powerboaters, the preferred passage through the spans is not well-marked. Currents run swiftly with either tide, and the monofilament lines of numerous anglers dangle in profusion from the old bridge above for about half the distance into Knight Key Channel from shore. If you do choose this route, once through to the oceanside, keep well clear of the shoal extending west of Knight Key.

The next, and preferred, passage, Moser Channel (Mile 1197), is the primary passageway and the last major crossover from the inside route (the next crossover has a bridge with a 20-foot fixed vertical clearance) to Hawk Channel. Over Moser Channel, the hump of the "new" Seven Mile Bridge has a 65-foot fixed vertical clearance. Here, about a mile west of Pigeon Key, the channel is deep and well marked. Once through the channel, take a charted course of 242 degrees magnetic toward Key West.

Prior to reaching Seven Mile Bridge, at Bethel Bank (Mile 1194), you will note a split in the chart's magenta track, which is clearly shown on Chart 11451. The southern route leads closer to Moser Channel, and then continues west past Little Money Key and the massive RV resort on Ohio Key. It then bends southward, following the northern shore of Bahia Honda Key, leading to the U.S. 1 fixed bridge (20-foot vertical clearance) at Mile 1205 over the last crossover from the ICW to Hawk Channel. If you are cruising the Florida Keys in a boat that can get under a bridge with 20-foot vertical clearance, you have a few more options than most. The other ICW route continues on a more northerly route to Big Spanish Channel heading for Florida Bay, the Gulf of Mexico and the northwest passage to Key West.

This northwestern route to Key West from Bethel Bank continues past Bahia Honda into the National Key Deer Wildlife Refuge. The route, shown best on Chart 11448, then bends north just past green daybeacon "29" at about mile 1204, steering a course of about 300 degrees magnetic. At this point, you are in the well-marked Big Spanish Channel route to the Gulf and then to Key West via the Northwest Channel. Markers have been changed and added to this area, requiring use of only the most recent chart editions (at press time Summer 2010, Edition 15, August 2006). A shoal north of Cutoe Key sets the controlling depth of 5 feet at mean low water between red daybeacon "42" and green daybeacon "43." The channel then continues for about three more nautical miles to Harbor Key Bank flashing green "57" (Mile 1218), where it opens into the Gulf of Mexico.

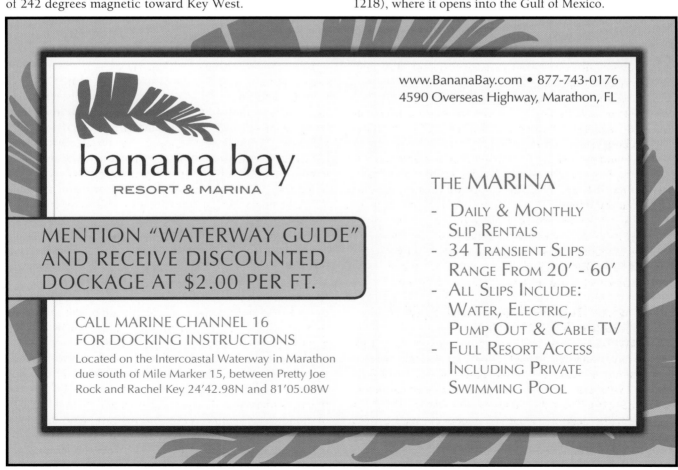

Marathon, FL

Around the corner, so to speak, from flashing green "57" is water of 7 feet with a deeper channel cutting back to the southeast through the flats. This might be a nice place to hang out when the weather is good and forecasted to stay that way. You are off the beaten track, but close enough to it to get under way again with no trouble. The fishing in the deeper channel could be great.

At this point you should shift to Chart 11442. From Harbor Key Bank Light, a course of 250 degrees magnetic will carry you to flashing green bell buoy "1," marking the Northwest Channel to Key West (N 24° 38.880'/W 081° 53.960'). In navigating to the marker, be sure to avoid low keys about two miles offshore in depths up to 26 feet. Without local knowledge, the Calda Channel and various other short-cuts are not recommended. Harbor areas are covered in the separate "Key West" section of this chapter. The keys afford protection in winds from the south and east, but Hawk Channel is a better route when northerly winds are expected.

Hawk Channel Route

NAVIGATION: Use Charts 11451, 11449 and 11453. Opposite Channel Five in Hawk Channel, at flashing red "44," your course to Vaca Key and Marathon is relatively clear in the range of 247 to 258 degrees magnetic to East Washerwoman Shoal at flashing green "49."

Dockage: On Hawk Channel, abeam Channel Five, it is about 10 nautical miles to Hawk's Cay Resort on Duck Key (Mile 1180). Heading south in Hawk Channel, at flashing red "44," follow a heading of about 255 degrees magnetic to the eight entry daybeacons that guide you into the Duck Key moat. Once inside the channel entrance, turn to the right and, at Idle Speed/No-Wake, enjoy the deep water and house tour on your way to the marina at Hawk's Cay Resort. The area in front of the dolphin and seal pens has shoaled somewhat; vessels drawing more than 5 feet should wait for a rising tide. If your assigned slip lies across the marina, skirt the slips clockwise, and avoid the center shoals. A swift crosscurrent can cause problems when docking here; check with the marina staff, and use caution.

Marina guests enjoy a ship's store with basic grocery items (including beer and wine), fuel, pump-out at the fuel dock, coin-operated laundry, pools and restrooms/showers. There is a putting green at Hawk's Cay, and guests can play a round on the 18-hole golf course of the Sombrero Country Club in Marathon.

To the west of Duck Key (see also Chart 11453) you will find Grassy, Crawl, Little Crawl, Deer and Fat Deer keys. Driftwood Marina has a 60-ton Travelift, a 10-ton forklift along with repair and storage facilities. Fat Deer Key is fronted by Coco Plum Beach, which is well-marked by a 14-story-high condominium tower, Bonefish Towers, an excellent landmark from Hawk Channel (and the highest building in all of the Florida Keys). Bonefish Towers (at about Mile 1187), lies at the eastern edge of the deep channel leading to the Key Colony Beach basin. Just inside the cut to starboard, the small, but well-protected, man-made harbor of the Bonefish Marina can accommodate deep-draft vessels and may have a transient slip or two available. It is a private condo marina. Farther down the (No-Wake) channel to the left, just after you enter the basin, Key Colony Beach Marina can usually accommodate transient vessels with drafts of up to 6 feet. Both diesel fuel and gasoline are available here, and this location puts you in the heart of the city of Key Colony Beach.

Shops, restaurants, hotels and some of the Keys' best ocean beaches are within walking distance. Within a short cab ride are restaurants regarded as among the best in the Middle Keys. Some are situated on nearby Grassy Key. The five-star Hideaway Café (open daily, serving until 11 p.m., courtesy transportation provided, 305-289-1554) is tucked within the comfortable Rainbow Bend Resort (www.rainbowbend.com). The Key Colony Inn is just down the street from the marina and has great seafood and Italian dishes.

Vaca Key/Marathon/Boot Key Harbor

NAVIGATION: Use Charts 11451 and 11453. Continuing west in Hawk Channel past Key Colony Beach, Vaca Key lies off to starboard. The closest gateway to it and the community of Marathon lies where Vaca Key and Boot Key meet at Sister Creek, just northwest of East Washerwoman Shoal, marked by flashing green "49" at Mile 1192. The creek entrance, with 5-foot mean low water depths, is marked by flashing red "2." Boot Key Harbor, one of the best and most heavily populated harbors in the Keys, lies just beyond the head of the creek.

Sister Creek is lined on one side with residential developments, docks and canals. On the Boot Key side, there are three radio stations that are owned by the Keys Radio Group, hidden in the mangroves. The tower used to transmit the signal for Radio Martí is actually elsewhere in Marathon. Radio programming is still broadcasting to Cuba 24 hours a day, but the Cuban government continues to broadcast interference. This signal battle has been going on now for 30 years. Since the demise of the Boot Key Bridge, the only way to the island is by boat.

Skippers of vessels with drafts over 5 feet will prefer to enter Boot Key Harbor via the east-west channel between Boot Key and Vaca Key. Boot Key Channel is approached from Hawk Channel (heading west) by a turn due north, once Sombrero Key Light is directly abeam to port. Four miles north of Sombrero Key, you will find the channel's entry markers, flashing green "1" and red daybeacon "2," situated just south of Knight Key. These are supplemented by additional daybeacons leading to an abundance of marine facilities along Boot Key Channel and in the harbor beyond. Strictly observe the posted SLOW-SPEED/MINIMUM-WAKE ZONE in this busy area. This channel carries 7 feet at mean low water.

Dockage: Immediately to port when entering Boot Key Channel's MINIMUM-WAKE ZONE, Marathon Marina and Boat Yard has easy access and deepwater slips. Marathon Marina and Boat Yard offers full-service repair work for both power and sail vessels and features a 60-ton lift which is going to be replaced with a larger lift. In 2010, they are

Looking west over Boot Key Harbor and the city of Marathon. (Not to be used for navigation.) WATERWAY GUIDE PHOTOGRAPHY

Long Key to Marathon, FL

LONG KEY TO MARATHON KEY	Phone	Largest Vessel Accommodated	VHF Channel Monitored	Dockage				Supplies			Services				
				Transient / Total Berths	Approach / Dockside Depth	Floating Docks	Gas / Diesel	Groceries, Ice, Marine Supplies, Snacks	Repairs: Hull, Engine, Propeller	Lift (tonnage), Crane, Rail	1=110V, 2=220V, B=Both, Max Amps	Laundry, Pool, Showers	Pump-Out Station	Nearby: Grocery Store, Motel, Restaurant
1. Hawks Cay Resort Villas Marina 📺 1180	305-743-7000	110	16	52/85	5/5		GD	GIMS			B/50	LPS	P	GMR
2. Driftwood Marina 1187.3	305-289-0432		16		4/18	F		M	HP	L60	B/50	S		GMR
3. Bonefish Marina 1187.0 (WiFi)	305-743-7015	55		18/48	8/			I			B/50	LS	P	G
4. Key Colony Beach Marina 1187.0	305-289-1310	120	6	10/40	10/6		GD	IMS			B/50		P	GMR
5. Outta The Blue Marina 1187.3	305-289-0285	48		5/10	8/12			IM	HEP	L60	B/50		P	GMR
6. Sombrero Resort & Marina 1192.0 (WiFi)	305-289-7662	70	16	70/70	10/15			I			B/50	LPS	P	GMR
7. Sombrero Marina Dockside 1192.0 (WiFi)	305-743-0000	90	16	/57	7/16			IS			B/100	LS	P	GMR
8. Boot Key Harbor City Marina 1193 (WiFi)	305-289-8877	60	16	12/238	10/20	F		IS			B/50	LS	P	GMR
9. Marathon Boat Yard Marine Center 1193.0 📺(WiFi)	305-743-6341	70	16	/20	8/10			M	HEP	L60	B/50	LS	P	GMR
10. Burdines Waterfront 1193	305-743-5317	50	16	21/21	10/7		GD	GIMS				LS		GMR
11. Pancho's Fuel Dock 1193	305-743-2281	90	16	3/20	8/8		GD	GIMS			B//50	S		GMR
12. Marathon Marina & Boat Yard 1193	305-743-6575	110	16	60/118	9/11		GD	IMS	HEP	L50	B/50	LS	P	MR
13. Capt. Pip's Marina & Hideaway/Porkys Bayside (WiFi)	305-743-4403		16		5/5			I						GMR
14. Banana Bay Resort & Marina 1193 📺(WiFi)	305-743-3500	60	16	33/33	5/7			I			B/50	PS	P	GMR

Corresponding chart(s) not to be used for navigation. 📺 Internet Access (WiFi) Wireless Internet Access

in the process of upgrading all of their facilities. The fuel dock has been upgraded. They have built a new fitness room with the latest equipment and have improved and enlarged the laundry. They will be constructing a swimming pool as well as adding 12 new slips. All of this was to be completed before the end of summer 2010. The restaurant (Lazy Days South) has been upgraded and will offer slips for boaters dining there. Lazy Days offers a very good menu and has the best views of sunsets in the area.

A west-end dining option is a half-mile stroll to the end of Knight Key. Here, you will find the 7-Mile Grill close to the old trestle bridge with ancient Emerson fans still whirling away in a 1950s time warp. It is open weekends and additional days that vary with the season. Breakfast here, on a warm winter's day, is to die for.

Immediately beyond Marathon Marina is Pancho's Fuel Dock, followed by Burdine's Restaurant and Marina. The store stocks a professional fishing tackle inventory.

The Boot Key Bascule Bridge, as of 2010, is in a permanently open position and the span will be removed.

The automobile access to the small island has been terminated. Be aware, though, that the overhead cables here are 65 feet high and will remain.

Immediately after passing through the bridge, you will see the entry channel to the very well-protected Marathon Boat Yard Marine Center to your left. Marathon Boat Yard has a 60-ton Travelift and a paint tent. They are proud of their "Clean Boat Yard" designation and their quality workmanship. Boaters will also have access to their certified diesel, air-conditioning and refrigeration technicians.

West Marine has a new and enlarged store next door to the Marathon Boat Yard Marine Center (not to be confused with Marathon Marina and Boat Yard). There used to be a dinghy dock in the boat yard, but in spring 2010, we discovered that it no longer exists. Marine supplies are also available at Tugboat Marine (discount prices and good service); Home Depot (with boating supplies); Inflatable Boats of the Florida Keys (repairs and service for most major brands and retail sales); and the local NAPA auto parts store, which stocks a large variety of marine engine parts.

On the same side, farther into the harbor, is the Boot Key Harbor City Marina. There is seawall tie-ups for several boats, but no slips; basic utilities are available, but with few luxuries. There has been a major enlargement to the dinghy docks. There is still an area for hard dinghies only and one for soft dinghies, but the number of docks have doubled. Water is available for a modest charge, but there is no fuel service. The laundry room has been upgraded and improved along with the heads and showers. The boaters lounge not only boasts of wireless Internet, but also has TV viewing areas with theater-style seating. Pump-outs are available at the marina, and a pump-out boat services the harbor area. The marina office administers the moorings described below. The dockmaster and other marina personnel are very friendly and helpful.

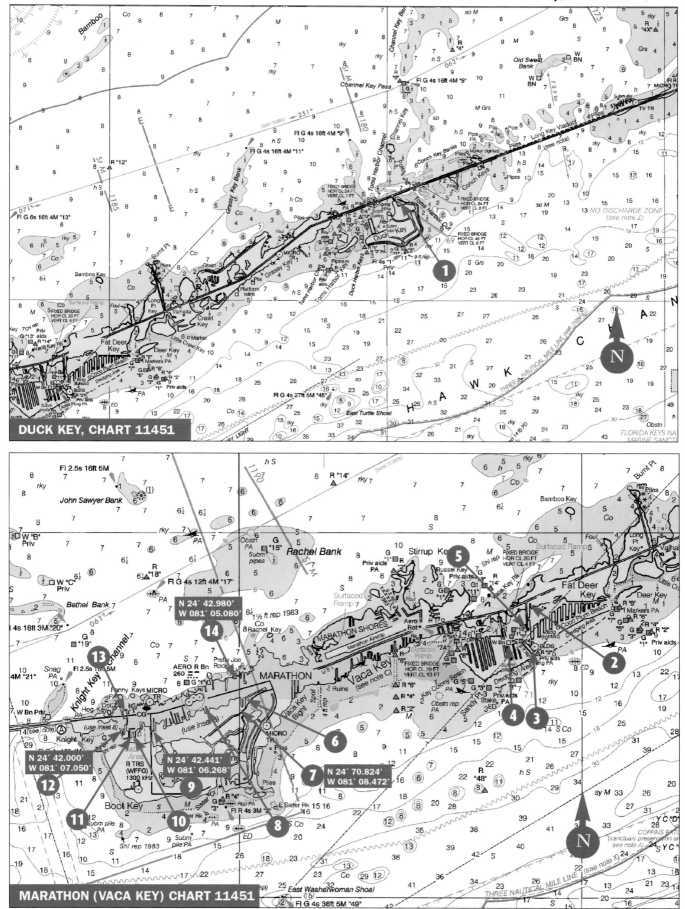

DUCK KEY, CHART 11451

MARATHON (VACA KEY) CHART 11451

Marathon, FL

The Sombrero Marina Dockside offers deep-draft slips and useful services geared toward the liveaboard population of Boot Key. Dockage is available by the day, week, month or year, though some slips are available for sale. There is a large transient population at the marina. For a fee, you can have dinghy tie-up privileges (nearest to complete shopping), a bike rack, message services and water. Showers are also available. The Dockside Lounge will lend you a handheld VHF radio for contacting vessels while ashore. The lounge has live entertainment nightly and is home to Boot Key Harbor's lively collection of characters. The deck outside the bar has been covered over with canvas and tarps and makes the area habitable on rainy days or during days when the sunlight is blistering.

Sombrero Resort and Marina is a 74-slip marina at the end of Boot Key Harbor that can handle vessels up to 65 feet. The amenities include a swimming pool, restaurant, tiki bar, showers and laundry.

Anchorage: Finding a place to anchor in Boot Key Harbor can be a challenge from Thanksgiving through March. You can anchor on the south side of the western approach channel, either on the west side of the bridge or on the east side. The Boot Key Harbor City Marina has established a mooring field that has helped to reduce the number of derelict boats. You can reach them by calling 305-289-8877 or hail them on VHF Channel 16. They do not take reservations, but if you appear in person, you can go on a waiting list if they are full. Currently, there are 226 moorings and 15 of them will take 60-foot boats; the balance of 215 are for boats 45 feet and under. The mooring rates are on a daily, weekly or monthly basis and include showers, weekly pump-out and dinghy dock privileges. More information is available from www.cimarathon.fl.us.

You can also anchor outside of the harbor in the lee of Boot Key in 8 to 9 feet on a line between red daybeacon "2" and Sombrero Key Light. Shoal draft vessels can work their way closer to shore in the charted 5-foot area. This anchorage is comfortable in northeast through southeast winds, but you will want to move around to the north side of Marathon for any strong winds out of the south or southwest.

GOIN' ASHORE: **MARATHON, FL**

At the head of Boot Key Harbor (via the channel skirting the north side of Sombrero Resort and Lighthouse Marina), re-provisioning possibilities abound, most of them clustered along U.S. Route 1, within walking distance of the inner harbor boat basin and Sombrero Beach Road. West of Sombrero Beach Road, you will find a Publix supermarket; Bank of America (with outside ATM); the post office; Marathon Liquor & Deli (Mile Marker 50), with a huge selection of beers, wines and liquor and perhaps the best gourmet deli selection in the Keys; and Home Depot.

East of Sombrero Beach Road are fast food restaurants, a K-Mart, a Winn-Dixie supermarket and the Marathon

Airport (305-289-6060, Mile Marker 52). Several national car rental services operate from the airport. A bike ride on Sombrero Beach Road leads to one of the finest public beaches in the Keys.

Fresh local seafood is available at Capt. Cliff's Seafood. Via dinghy, Capt. Cliff's is located at the end of the channel on the west side of Burdine's Marina. While you are at Burdine's, stop at their upstairs restaurant and try one of their many delicious menu items. And don't forget Lazy Days at the Marathon Marina and Boat Yard. A "must try" lobster Reuben sandwich is available at The Keys Fisheries located at mile marker "49" on the north side of U.S. Route 1. A boat selling ice makes daily runs in the harbor; another offers pump-out service.

For diversions ashore, consider the Museums of Crane Point Hammock (home of the Museum of Natural History of the Florida Keys and the Florida Keys Children's Museum; U.S. Route 1 at Mile Marker 50.5, across from K-Mart; open 9 a.m. to 5 p.m., Monday through Saturday; noon to 5 p.m. Sunday (305-743-9100). The Natural History Museum's nature trails wind through a tropical palm forest, canopied with now-threatened Florida thatch palms and a typical hardwood hammock setting, loaded with black ironwood, Jamaican dogwood, gumbo limbo, buttonwood, Strangler fig and other trees and shrubs native to the area.

The longer (half-mile) trail leads to the Crane House, surrounded by exotic specimen trees and is open to the Gulf of Mexico with spectacular views. The museum building displays artifacts from pre-Columbian Indian inhabitants, shipwrecked Spanish cannons, simulated underwater environments and interactive touch tanks for an up-close and personal experience with the sea.

On a calm day, try a dinghy excursion, walk or bike trip to explore the traditional Conch-style structures of Pigeon Key (Old Overseas Highway, two miles west of the east end of Seven Mile Bridge; Tuesday through Sunday, 9 a.m. to 5 p.m.). Built in 1909 by railroad magnate Henry Flagler as a construction camp for the final push of his Florida East Coast Railway from Vaca Key to Key West, the settlement has since had several incarnations (fishing camp, park, movie set and marine biology center). Nevertheless, the characteristic architecture of the early period is the real deal. Most recently, the island has been taken over by the Pigeon Key Foundation for restoration as a National Historic Site and development as an environmental education center. Whether landing by dinghy, on foot or bike (via a two-mile stretch of the old highway bridge), there is a small admission fee. You can also take a trolley-style shuttle from the mainland, which runs on the hour. This trip is well worth your time. Don't forget to look over the side of the bridge on your trip out to see giant spotted eagle rays swimming between the bridge spans or the tarpon holding themselves steady in the strong current.

The Dolphin Research Center, located on Grassy Key seven miles east of Marathon, is a not-for-profit organization that provides education about dolphins. They have interactive dolphin encounters, swimming with the dolphins, dolphin demonstrations and more. They can be reached at 305-289-0002.

ADDITIONAL RESOURCES

 Monroe County Tourist Development Council, 1-800-FLA-KEYS, **www.fla-keys.com/marathon**

 NEARBY GOLF COURSES
Key Colony Beach Golf & Tennis, 460 Eighth St., Key Colony Beach, FL 33051, 305-289-1533
www.keycolonybeach.net

NEARBY MEDICAL FACILITIES
Fishermen's Hospital, 3301 Overseas Hwy., Marathon, FL 33050, 305-743-5533
www.fishermanshospital.com

■ SEVEN MILE BRIDGE TO SUGARLOAF KEY—MILE 1197 TO MILE 1225

West-southwest of Vaca Key (Marathon) and Boot Key lies the famed Seven Mile Bridge, whose channels are discussed in the previous ICW portion of this chapter. It is the third and last major crossover in the Keys between Hawk Channel and Florida Bay for boats requiring the 65-foot vertical clearance of Moser Channel (Mile 1199).

NAVIGATION: Use Chart 11445. You will see the Seven Mile Bridge as you head southwest, once you pass Sombrero Key Light to port. The old Bahia Honda Bridge (Mile 1207), at Bahia Honda Key's western end, is a national historic monument that is slowly disintegrating into the water. The bridge has a section removed so that sailboats can pass through to the cove between the old bridge and the new twin bridges (20-foot fixed vertical clearance). Do not make your approach from the southeast; stay west of the little island half a nautical mile off the tip of Bahia Honda Key to avoid the shifting sand shoals. There is plenty of water (9-plus feet mean low water), but be aware of the currents under the bridge. The Coast Guard reports hanging debris underneath the Bahia Honda Bridge; use caution when traversing the area.

Anchor off the state park, and go ashore to enjoy two of the nicest beaches in the Keys. The palm-rimmed beach on the western edge is sheltered and roped off for swimming. A park concession stand is nearby. A beach across the road looks out on Hawk Channel. Bring shoes or aqua socks to hike the nature trail that winds along the shore of a tidal lagoon; you will see tropical plants and beautiful birds here.

Dockage: Transients can find dockage in the well-protected boat basin at the state park on Bahia Honda (entrance from the north side of Bahia Honda). There is plenty of water in the harbor, but the entrance is shallow (controlling depth of 3.5 feet at mean low water with an average tidal range of a little over a foot; favor the east side of the channel on entry). With 19 transient slips inside the man-made harbor (if your vessel can take the

Newfound Harbor, FL

Bahia Honda, Newfound Harbor, Little Torch Keys, FL

BAHIA HONDA, NEWFOUND HARBOR, LITTLE TORCH KEYS		Dockage				Supplies		Services			
		Largest Vessel Accommodated	VHF Channel Monitored	Transient Berths / Total Berths	Approach / Dockside Depth (reported)	Groceries, Ice, Marine Supplies, Snacks	Gas / Diesel · Repairs: Hull, Engine, Propeller · Lift	1=110V, 2=220V, B=Both, Max Amps	Laundry, Pool, Showers	Pump-Out Station	Nearby: Grocery Store, Motel, Restaurant
1. Bahia Honda State Park & Marina 1205	305-872-3210	50	16/10	19/19	3.5/4.5		GIS	1/30	S	P	G
2. Little Palm Island 1215	305-872-2524	120	16/09	14/14	6/5		I	B/100	PS		MR
3. Dolphin Marina 1215	305-872-2685	50	16/09	/14	4/10	GD	IS	1/30			

Corresponding chart(s) not to be used for navigation. 🖳 Internet Access 📶 Wireless Internet Access

draft restrictions), there is usually space available, with hot showers included.

Continuing west past Bahia Honda Key, you will see the Newfound Harbor Keys, about 4.5 miles due north of the superb diving sites of Looe Key National Marine Sanctuary. The relatively well-marked and well-protected Newfound Harbor Channel has become an increasingly popular anchorage area with depths of 6 to 21 feet at mean low water in sand and grass. On entry, give flashing red "2" a wide berth to starboard to avoid shoaling that extends about 75 yards west of this mark.

Little Palm Island Resort and Spa, a secluded and very luxurious resort on Little Palm Island (westernmost of the Newfound Harbor Keys and called Little Munson on some charts), is located at the mouth of Newfound Harbor Channel, off to starboard as you enter the channel, and is accessible only by boat or seaplane. Location footage for the movie "PT-109" was filmed here. The resort's French restaurant is open to visiting mariners and can be reached at 305-872-2551. We recommend that visiting mariners dress appropriately—collared shirt for the men as a minimum with slacks and slacks or a dress for women. Sunday brunch is served from 11 a.m. to 2:30 p.m. Dockage is complimentary while dining, or you can anchor to the northeast and use your dinghy. Reservations are required. No children under 16 years of age are allowed here.

Farther into Newfound Harbor, just beyond the U.S. Route 1 bridge, waterside dining can be found at Parrotdise Waterfront Bar & Grille (305-872-9989) on Little Torch Key, open from 11 a.m. daily. The Little Palm launch goes to Dolphin Marina and Parrotdise is just a .25-mile walk away. Dockage is available for boats that can clear the bridge.

With some ingenuity, you may be able to locate a dinghy landing on Big Pine Key near the east end of the bridge over Pine Channel. This may mean just tying to a mangrove tree. From here, complete re-provisioning is possible about a mile east at the island's full-size Winn-Dixie store.

If you can locate transportation (and decent directions), No Name Pub (305-872-9115, on No Name Key, just west of the bridge crossing Bogie Channel to No Name Key) is a funky and unique Keys classic considered a Florida Keys landmark since 1935. Pizza is the main event, and folks drive miles for it. There is good reason.

On the west side of Pine Channel, the canal nearest the Overseas Highway leads to Dolphin Marina, with a controlling depth of 3.5 feet at mean low water. Both gasoline and diesel fuel are available here. Dolphin Marina is the departure point for the Little Palm Island ferry service. The boats used are classics.

Anchorage: Heading west again, Niles Channel offers a reasonably well-protected anchorage between Ramrod Key and Summerland Key. Anchor between red daybeacons "4" and "6" in 7 to 10 feet of water. Be careful to avoid a couple of 2- and 3-foot shoals here. The area is also not well-protected from southerlies. Farther west, before Loggerhead Keys and due north of flashing red "50A," a marked shoal-draft channel with the entrance marked by green daybeacon "1" leads to sheltered, though relatively shallow Kemp Channel, between Cudjoe and Summerland keys. This channel only carries 4 to 5 feet.

Back in Hawk Channel, about two miles west of Key Lois, another marked channel (controlling depth 3.5 feet mean low water) leads to the protection of Pirate's Cove on the east side of Sugarloaf Key. From there, those with minimal draft requirements can make passage for the deep but protective basin of Cudjoe Marina. Shoreside restrooms are available, but there are no other amenities except ample fishing and diving supplies and a restaurant next door. If you can get in here, however, and the weather is turning abysmal, this is a great place to hide.

■ SUGARLOAF KEY TO KEY WEST

NAVIGATION: Use Charts 11445, 11442 and 11441. Hawk Channel narrows past the marked and lighted Ninefoot Shoal (Mile 1224) and passes safely north of West Washerwoman Shoal to Key West. From the western end of Sugarloaf, the Saddlebunch Keys extend for about three miles to the start of the Boca Chica Key complex. Here, about two miles past flashing red "56," the deep, well-marked Boca Chica Channel (Mile 1235) leads into the basin and mooring area of the Boca Chica Naval Air Station. This facility is open to retired and active-duty members of the armed forces. Rental moorings, ice, showers and limited snacks are available.

NEWFOUND HARBOR, LITTLE TORCH KEYS, CHART 11445

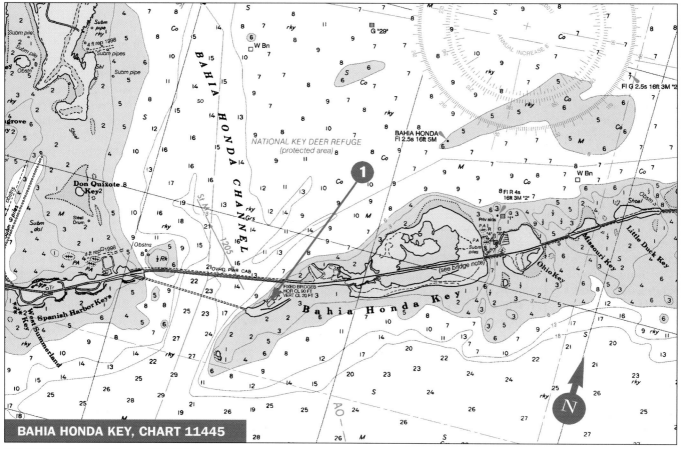

BAHIA HONDA KEY, CHART 11445

Sugarloaf Key, FL

Immediately west of Boca Chica Channel is an unnamed, but charted channel leading into Stock Island. Several boatbuilders, boat storage and fishing docks are here, also the Kings Pointe Marina, formerly home to a number of liveaboards and long-range cruisers, as well as tournament sportfishing boats. The marina, for the most part, has become a dockominium, with most of the slips having been sold. But many are available as transient slips. Discretion suggests calling ahead for availability. Gasoline and diesel fuel, restrooms and showers and coin-operated laundry machines are available.

Nearby the Hogfish Bar and Grill (www.hogfishbar. com) is a unique open-air restaurant and bar. It is famous for its hogfish sandwich, cold beer, local flavor and entertainment. Either on the marina premises or in the immediate vicinity, you will find a Yamaha dealer and repair shop, a 5-Star PADI diving center, Accurate Marine Electronics and Key West Sail & Canvas. Re-provisioning from this location will require a cab ride.

Key West Harbour Yacht Club and Marina (at the site of the former Peninsular Marine Services) is an oasis at the tip of Stock Island. The marina offers transients slips in a resort atmosphere. Amenities include a five-star restaurant on-site, pool, exercise facilities, pump-out at each slip, non-ethanol fuel and a beach.

A little farther west on Stock Island is Robbie's Marina. Traditionally, Robbie's has been heavily involved in repair and refurbishing of large, commercial vessels, as well as megayachts. The long-range plan is to become a megayacht marina handling vessels from as small as 50 feet, to 100 to 300 feet, meeting the growing need for large vessel dockage. It seems to be accomplishing this goal.

Past Stock Island, the towers and radomes of Key West International Airport appear to starboard along with many waterfront hotels and condominiums. At the southwesterly tip of Key West, off Whitehead Spit (Mile 1241), you can cut inside, leaving to port flashing red "12," which marks the eastern side of the Main Ship Channel from the ocean. Turn sharply to starboard, steering for flashing green "13," leaving it to port as you turn northwestward up the well-buoyed Main Ship Channel.

■ KEY WEST

Early Spanish explorers originally called this last in the chain of Florida Keys "Cayo Hueso" (KAI-o WAY-so), "Bone Island," after the piles of Native American skeletons originally found there. Later, British-Bahamian settlers developed the present designation, which was at once descriptive geographically and easier on the English tongue.

Since 1821, when the Spanish reluctantly ceded Florida to the United States, Key West has undergone transitions of far greater magnitude than its name change. Historically, this island served as a haven for pirates and wreckers (and later, America's anti-piracy fleet), as the vibrant seat of the U.S. cigar manufacturing industry and

as a major Navy base and Coast Guard drug interdiction center. The Coast Guard mission today is centered on Homeland Security, with keeping Cubans from arriving illegally in the United States with dry feet as a secondary function (according to U.S. policy, once they step ashore, a Cuban migrant may stay).

No matter what the military buzz of the moment is, Key West is the sunny, end-of-the-line destination for tourists and travelers of all descriptions. Lots of them come down Route 1. Thousands more ooze their way off cruise ships that dock at the Key West waterfront and discharge humans in various "resort wear" outfits that might cause some raised eyebrows on Park Avenue. Some local Key West outfits, however, make the tourists look tame. As quintessential Key West troubadour Michael McCloud sings of those who drift into the Schooner Wharf Bar where he plays, "Ya get bimbos and bozos and bikers and boozers, daytime drunks and three-time losers. Ya get the room full of rednecks and fancy-dressed fellas, busloads of bluehairs and dirtbags and sailors."

Casual sailing duds substitute for more formal attire almost anywhere. Jimmy Buffett tunes, smoke from hand-made cigars and frangipani blossoms lightly fill the air; tourist shops and raucous bars are juxtaposed to what are surely some of the finest open-air restaurants and most tastefully preserved period architecture in America. Key West is difficult to categorize and easily misunderstood. It is a unique and irresistible magnet to yachtsmen, long-distance cruisers and sportfishermen. For them, Key West offers amenities and attractions of virtually every level and description.

NAVIGATION: Use Charts 11441 and 11447. The entrance to Key West from the Atlantic Ocean side is relatively straightforward, yet the abundance of buoys in the area can confuse a first-time visitor, particularly at night. We strongly recommend that first-timers do not attempt a night passage, particularly through the Northwest Channel Entrance from the Gulf of Mexico. The Main Ship Channel guides the deepest-draft commercial vessels in from the Atlantic Ocean on a well-marked path leading just west of north from lighted red-and-white whistle buoy "KW" on a range to the prominent (and lighted) red-and-white water tank on the western end of the island. The channel takes an abrupt dogleg to the northwest at quick flashing red buoy "8," and then another dogleg (about a mile farther), this time to the north, between flashing green buoy "9" and quick flashing red buoy "12." Entrance for boats southbound on Hawk Channel should be made at the first elbow in the Main Ship Channel.

From the Gulf of Mexico side, enter Key West via the deep and well-marked Northwest Channel. If you are arriving at night with the experience we have suggested above, you will see the lights of the microwave antennas on shore long before you pick up the flashing buoys of Smith Shoal Light. Again, a night approach is not recommended here.

The Northwest Channel (shown best on Chart 11441) begins at flashing green bell buoy "1." At this point, steer a course for red nun "2," leaving it to starboard and continuing between quick-flashing green buoy "3" to port and red nun "4" to starboard. Both are located to bring you safely inside between two submerged jetties, east and west. The eastern jetty is awash at high tide. Then, continue on down the well-marked channel to the Main Ship Channel at flashing green buoy "19." Continuing on Chart 11447, a sharp turn to the northeast here will bring you to flashing red "24" and the Key West Bight. Only highly experienced navigators should attempt this channel at night.

If you decide to explore the wonders of the water, you can take a leisurely seven-mile-long boat ride southeast of Key West to Sand Key. At Sand Key, you can secure your boat to one of 21 mooring balls made available at this natural shallow reef.

Dockage: The Westin Key West Resort & Marina (formerly the Truman Annex) is located just off the main channel to starboard as you enter the harbor. Access to the marina may be limited because cruise ships dock on the outside pier. The only downside to this location is when the wind and waves are up. Waves slip in from the open channel, around the breakwater, adding substantially to the already abundant action from passing watercraft. In these conditions, you may want the greater protection of docking opportunities within Key West Bight.

To reach Key West Bight, continue in the Main Ship Channel until just before flashing red buoy "24," then turn right, heading to flashing red "2" and quick flashing red "4" to starboard at the end of the seawall. The spacious floating docks (finger slips port and starboard) of the Galleon Resort & Marina lie immediately to starboard on rounding the seawall. Adjacent to the Historic Seaport Harbor Walk, which now extends all the way to the restaurants and shops on the southeast side of the bight, the Galleon Marina is a popular spot. Reservations are recommended far in advance during high season, and especially for regatta weeks and Fantasy Fest (a 10-day party in October with thousands of costumed revelers). Galleon Resort & Marina has 90 slips and can accommodate vessels to 150 feet in length. Amenities include a pool, private beach, exercise room and sauna. The marina is breakwater shielded from wakes.

Immediately next door, A&B Marina has a long floating pier with diesel fuel at its head and a shopping complex at its foot. Daily dockage, including water and shore power, is available. While a few slips have floating fingers, many boats are moored perpendicular to the main dock, secured with bowlines to pilings. A&B Marina has numerous long-term rentals and limited transient dockage. Next to the marina office, White Tarpon Groceries and Spirits has a basic selection of dry goods and snacks along with a better-than-average assortment of wines, beers and liquors.

Next door to Tarpon's is the Damn Good Food Deli, which is open until midnight in case of a late-night snack attack. They open at 6 a.m. In Key West Bight, they deliver. The Commodore Waterfront Restaurant (305-294-9191) offers something of a contrast to the area's dominant seafood offerings (though the chef here also prepares seafood entrees). Situated between the A&B and Galleon marinas, Alonzo's Oyster Bar (305-294-5880, open 11 a.m. to 11 p.m.)

Key West, FL

is under the same management as the justly famous Turtle Kraals across the bight. Superb house specialties such as white diablo clam chili and roasted mussels could keep you from exploring as many Key West restaurants as you might like. Upstairs, the A&B Lobster House (305-294-5880, open 6 p.m. to 11 p.m.) serves up Florida's famous crustacean and plenty of steak (reservations are recommended). The next stop along the Harbor Walk is the Conch Republic Seafood Company (305-294-4403), famous for its baked oysters callaloo, featuring indoor and outdoor dining. The Harbor Walk connects virtually all marine facilities, restaurants, bars, shops and an excellent market that cluster around the bight.

On the south side of the bight is the Historic Seaport at Key West Bight, a.k.a. Key West Bight Marina, identified by the CHEVRON sign at the easily accessible fuel dock, as well as the cluster of schooners available for harbor cruises. The marina can accommodate deep-draft boats (up to 12-foot drafts) in any of its 33 transient slips. Access to the marina shower and bathhouse is included, and both gas and diesel are available at the fuel dock. The marina operates one of the dinghy docks on the island for those anchored out or on moorings outside the bight. The dinghy dock rates at time of publication were $6 per day or $80 monthly.

Immediately shoreward of the marina's fuel dock, Turtle Kraals Restaurant (305-294-2640) is justly famous for its colorful seafood preparations Floribbean-style and its tower bar. Bahamian or blues music fills the air here nightly.

Next door, the Waterfront Market makes complete re-provisioning available at the water's edge, literally a few paces from the Key West Bight dinghy landing at the Historic Seaport. The market has a large deli, fresh seafood and meat selection, gourmet dry goods and international specialties, an impressive supply of fresh produce, bakery items and a serious selection of beers and wines.

A half-block west of the market, alongside Schooner Wharf (where several of the wharf's namesakes have long been berthed), you will learn where it is the boaters go: the Schooner Wharf Bar. This is the one that comes up in sailing magazine articles and in late-night discussions among trans-ocean cruisers when talk turns to the best bars in the world. Something of a cross between an open-air beach shanty and an old wooden vessel, this is where some of Key West's very best musicians sing and play. Sunset Ale flows abundantly, big black dogs have the run of the place, and sailing, diving and drinking yarns spin freely.

At the southeast end of the inner harbor, Conch Harbor Marina is dead ahead as you enter the bight, rounding flashing red "4" at the end of the breakwater, and easily identified by the large TEXACO sign (both gasoline and diesel fuel available). Most slips are reserved well in advance and reservations must be made via a faxed form. Among the 40 slips is a shoreside complex, with Dante's Raw Bar Restaurant. Pump-out is available at the fuel dock and at several of the slips. Just across the Harbor Walk from the marina's main dock, the Half Shell Raw Bar (305-294-7496) has seafood selections in tempting variety.

A bit farther afield, via the marked channel around the north end of Fleming Key, additional transient dockage is available at City Marina at Garrison Bight, which has dockage on both sides of the 18-foot vertical clearance fixed bridge carrying Route 1 north (North Roosevelt Boulevard). This should not be confused with Garrison Bight Marina, just across the bight, which is primarily used by local small-boat fishermen, many of them utilizing the marina's ample dry storage capability. Limited transient slips are also available at the Key West Yacht Club nearby. Spencer's Boat Yard is also at this location with its lift and repair capabilities. This is the only lift in Key West proper. The others are out on Stock Island. The chart depicts 50-foot-high power lines at the opening of the bight, but the yacht club and others claim they have 60 feet of vertical clearance. If vertical clearance is a consideration, call ahead, wait for low tide and then make your own decision.

If a bad blow out of the north is predicted, the previously mentioned King's Pointe Marina or Sunset Marina on Stock Island are well-protected choices.

To get away from the party atmosphere of downtown Key West and Duval Street, and for a change in latitude, try Sunset Marina on the north end of Stock Island. From the main Key West Channel, pass the entrance to Key West Bight on a northeast heading past the Coast Guard Station. If your clearance allows, pass through the Fleming Key Bridge (18-foot fixed vertical clearance). If the clearance of the bridge is a problem, swing north around Fleming Key and into Garrison Bight.

After leaving the bridge behind (if you had enough clearance to pass under), turn sharply to port just short of green daybeacon "19," steering a course north then northeast, avoiding the 3- to 5-foot shoal areas to starboard in a sizable anchorage just west of Sigsbee Park. To the northeast of Sigsbee Park, pick up red daybeacon "36," and follow it very carefully to the east in the approximately one-mile, narrow, but well-marked channel to Sunset Marina. If you can not pass under the bridge, follow the marked channel around Fleming Key, then head southeast toward red daybeacon "36" off the northeastern end of Sigsbee Park after passing flashing green "17" and avoiding the 6-foot shoal area if you are a deeper draft vessel.

An alternative is to call Sunset Marina and they will send a small pilot boat to guide you into their marina. Here you will find a well-fitted-out resort marina, with 30- and 50-amp shore power, a full marine service shop, water, diesel fuel and gasoline, both central and portable slip-side pump-out facilities, Internet access, fax services and a short walk to The Key West Golf Club, a public golf course. Hurricane Joe's Bar and Seafood Grill, with excellent conch and calamari dishes, is also a short walk to just across Route 1, or, if conditions permit, you can dinghy the short distance. Fresh catches of tuna, wahoo, grouper and dolphin are also served alongside traditional non-seafood meals.

Anchorage: If you are short on money, and time spent going to and from your boat is not a consideration, Key West abounds with anchorage possibilities, though many locations afford only modest protection from fast-shifting winds and swift currents. The holding southwest of Wisteria Island (known locally as Christmas Tree Island) is poor.

A better choice is just west of Fleming Key, but the reversing current is particularly strong here, making careful watches during the first turn of the tide a virtual necessity. Remember to take into consideration the number of anchors, swinging radius and windage of surrounding vessels. Fresh winds against the tides regularly make for some interesting float patterns; keep an eye out for other vessels that may wander too close to your vessel.

Both the Wisteria Island and Fleming Key anchorages are relatively close to Old Town and the Key West Bight Marina dinghy dock. Just inside the breakwater protecting the bight, turn to starboard in front of the Chevron sign, past the first dock, then turn to port toward the Waterfront Market. Turn again to port as you approach the seawall. The dinghy dock is located immediately in front of Turtle Kraals Restaurant. The fee for tying up your dinghy is payable to the Key West Bight Marina.

Northwest of Wisteria Island, the current is reportedly less troublesome, but this area is wide open to winter winds from the north and is also a long dinghy ride into Key West Bight. When the water is rough in any of the anchorages, the passage across the main channel to and from town in a small underpowered dinghy can be wet and dangerous. An alternative is Key West Water Taxi (monitoring VHF Channel 68) with launch service available between the anchorages and its docks on the Harbor Walk at the foot of Williams Street.

An alternative to the first two anchorages is in the area just to the north of the mooring field and Sigsbee Park. There are good depths of 7 to 9 feet and good holding. Make sure you are outside of the mooring field buoys. From here, you can access the second dinghy dock at Garrison Bight and pay your fee to the Garrison Bight Marina. This anchorage is exposed to the north, but has much less current and boat wakes than the others. Even in strong northerly winds, the shallow water between here and the Gulf cuts down most of the swells just leaving you with wind waves.

Key West is a federal No-Discharge Zone (no waste, even that which has been treated, is allowed to be discharged overboard). The city has established a mooring field east of Fleming Key, charging daily and monthly rates. There were a total of 149 rental moorings in this area in summer 2010. A pump-out service for boats on moorings, anchored or in marinas is provided by City Marina Pump-Out (305-809-3981 or VHF Channel 16), service available Monday through Saturday 8 a.m. to 4 p.m.

Key West, FL

KEY WEST		Largest Vessel Accommodated	VHF Channel Monitored	Transient Berths / Total Berths	Approach / Dockside Depth (reported)	Floating Docks	Gas / Diesel	Groceries, Ice, Marine Supplies, Snacks	Repairs: Hull, Engine, Propeller	Lift (tonnage), Crane, Rail	1=110V, 2=220V, B=Both, Max Amps	Laundry, Pool, Showers	Pump-Out Station	Nearby: Grocery Store, Motel, Restaurant
		Dockage					**Supplies**		**Services**					
1. Key West Harbour Yacht Club & Marina 🖳 WIFI	305-292-3121	110	16	20/100	6.5/7	F	GD	GIMS	HEP	L	B/100	LPS	P	MR
2. King's Pointe Marina 1237 WIFI	305-294-4676	80	16	20/113	10/15		GD	IMS		L7	B/50	LS	P	GMR
3. Robbie's Marine 1237	305-294-1124	300	16	20/120	14/14		GD	MS	HEP	L100,C	B/100	S		GMR
4. Key West Yacht Club 1243	305-296-3446	70	16	3/64	6/9			I			B/50	S		MR
5. City Marina at Garrison Bight 1243	305-809-3981	50	16	10/250	7/6	F					B/50	LS	P	GMR
6. Spencer's Boat Yard 1243	305-296-8826	55			4/6			M	HEP	L60	B/50			GMR
7. Garrison Bight Marina 1243	305-294-3093	28			4/6		G	GIMS	EP	STORAGE			GMR
8. A & B Marina 1243 🖳	305-294-2535	130	16	40/50	30/12	F	D	GIMS			B/100	LS	P	GMR
9. Galleon Marina 1243 WIFI	305-292-1292	150	16	80/90	20/9	F		GIMS			B/50	LPS	P	GMR
10. Weston Key West Resort & Marina 1243	305-292-4375	500	16	25/44	37/14	F		IS			B/50	LPS	P	GMR
11. Key West Bight Marina 1243	305-809-3984	200	16	30/145	20/10		GD	GIMS	EP		B/100	LPS	P	MR
12. Conch Harbor Marina 1243 🖳 WIFI	305-294-2933	185	16	20/40	30/12		GD	IMS			B/100	LPS	P	GMR
13. Sunset Marina Key West Inc. 1239 🖳 WIFI	305-296-7101	100	16	25/163	6.5/9	F	GD	GIMS	EP	L14	B/50	LS	P	G

Corresponding chart(s) not to be used for navigation. 🖳 Internet Access WIFI Wireless Internet Access

GOIN' ASHORE: KEY WEST, FL

In the past three decades, the city of Key West has undergone a noticeable transformation from a tiny tourist and fishing curiosity into a luxurious, moneyed resort. Nowhere is this more evident than in the aggressive but controlled development of quality hotels, Key West-styled condominiums, proudly restored wooden homes, historic sites and inventive new restaurants. But despite all these developments, Key West is still Key West.

Within an easy walk from the major marinas and public dinghy landing, Old Town serves up a savory variety of re-provisioning and dining possibilities, along with tasteful (and not-so-tasteful) shops, sights, watering holes, dives and other local color. Pick up a free Key West map, available at most marinas and many shops.

Sugar Apple Natural Foods (917 Simonton St., 305-292-0043), a vegan deli, is your source for herbs, homeopathic remedies, vitamins, literature and hard to find items for a healthy lifestyle.

Peppers of Key West (602 Greene St., 305-295-9333) carries an extraordinary selection of hot sauces. It is recommended that you have a beverage with you to accompany the free samples of tasty hot sauces. At the Blond Giraffe Key Lime Pie Factory, you can watch extraordinary key lime pies being made and enjoy a tasty slice of pie with cream, meringue or chocolate topping either on-site or as take-out (five Key West locations). They have been so successful that they have opened stores on Front Street Duval, Green and Truman Ave.

The Pirate Soul Museum (524 Front St., 305-292-1113) has a collection of pirate artifacts including what may be the world's only authenticated pirate treasure chest. The tour concludes in the Pirate Soul Shoppe, and you can eat at the Rum Barrel restaurant and hoist a mug of grog. The Coffee Plantation (713 Caroline St., 305-295-9808) is a coffee house and Internet café (wireless Internet available). You can use their computers or your own, print, fax, burn a CD and check your e-mail while having coffee and a pastry.

For the boat, within a block of Harbor Walk, Key West Marine Hardware (818 Caroline St., 305-294-3519) is an unusually well-stocked chandlery. Nearby West Marine (725 Caroline St., 305-295-0999) has the usual catalog selection of supplies, but the fact that it is close to Key West Bight makes it extremely handy. If you will be frequenting West Marine for this and that, tie up at the City Marina at Key West Bight; it is by far the closest. Fill your propane tanks at Suburban Propane on Catherine Street. Key West Island Bookstore (on Fleming) has a large and well-organized collection of used paperbacks at bargain prices and an extensive collection of new books on Florida and the Keys. The Restaurant Store (1111 Eaton St.) is jam-packed with a huge selection of culinary items, likely including that just-right galley utensil.

Then there are bars, bars and more bars. As the "Conch Republic National Anthem" has it, this is where "Drinking is considered a sport." The bars are numerous, diverse and even semi-historical, including Sloppy Joe's Bar (201 Duval St.) of Ernest Hemingway fame, which seems always abuzz with live music and youthful dancers. There is more of that at Hog's Breath Saloon (400 Front St.), serving the saloon's own medium-weight beer on tap, along with lunch and dinner daily. Margaritaville (500 Duval St.) is awash in Jimmy Buffett memorabilia, and you can buy the famed cocktail along with Buffett clothing, CDs and other items. Finnegan's Wake Irish Pub & Eatery (320 Grinnell St.) offers a pleasant and dark reprieve from the neon glare of Duval Street. It is just what an Irish public house ought to be—plenty of Guinness and Black and Tan—along with Irish music and hearty pub fare, served into the wee hours.

The sunset celebration at Mallory Square is still a draw, whether it is your first or 100th visit to Key West. Now, spread between the area behind the Westin Resort and

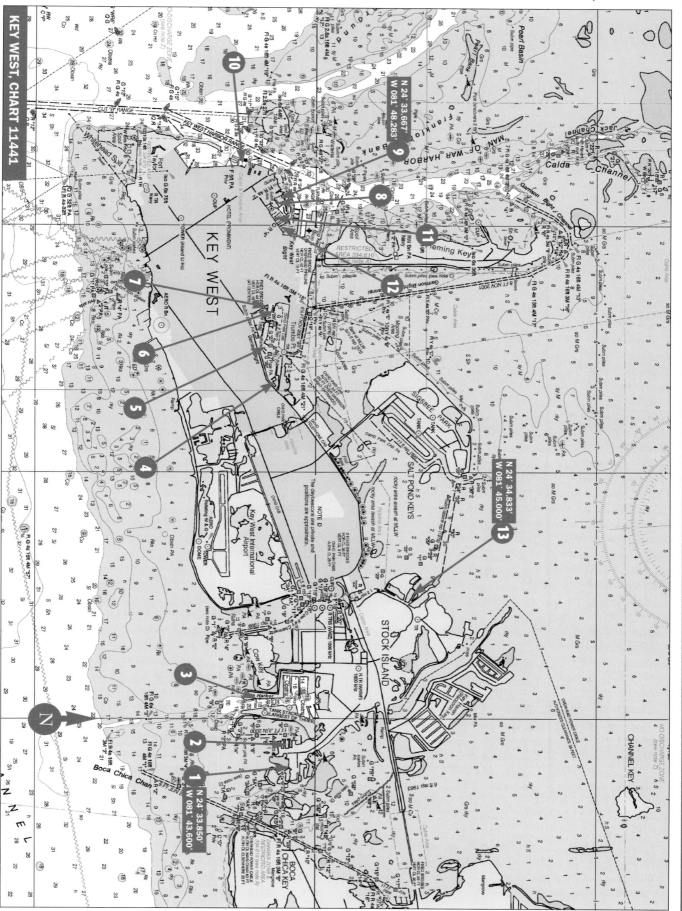

KEY WEST, CHART 11441

KEY WEST

N 24°33.667'
W 081°48.283'

N 24°34.833'
W 081°45.000'

N 24°33.850'
W 081°43.600'

Looking northeast over Key West, with Mallory Square area on the left. (Not to be used for navigation.) WATERWAY GUIDE PHOTOGRAPHY

the old square, you will find two evenings' worth of sunset entertainment. Wander through the crowd and enjoy performances of trained cats that leap (most reluctantly) through hoops of fire, acrobatic musicians, pig acts, mimes, contortionists, sword swallowers, bicycle tricksters and other oddities. There are always tempting concoctions to snack on while waiting for the sunset.

On your way to or from Mallory Square, don't miss the Key West Memorial Sculpture Garden. Bronze busts of the island's historic figures portray a colorful and intriguing past. Financed entirely (more than $700,000) by individual memorials etched in the bricks of the garden walkway, the tour is free. It is simply a knockout.

The restaurant selection in this relatively small, end-of-the-road town rivals that of any major American port city. Local residents from as far away as Key Largo will travel the full length of the Overseas Highway for lunch in Key West in preference to a shorter run to Miami. Close to the inner harbor, the oldest restaurant in Key West, Pepe's Café (305-294-7192, 806 Caroline St., no reservations accepted), has served everyone from Ernest Hemingway and Harry Truman to Carl Hiaasen and Bob Dylan. There is a reason. Pepe's is a magnet for those searching for the best in seafood (mahi-mahi with caper butter sauce, for example) served in a relaxed but intimate garden setting. Open from 6:30 a.m. to 11 p.m. daily, its breakfasts are legendary, as are Pepe's platters of fresh Apalachicola Bay oysters served later in the day.

A top-end favorite, also close to the docks, is Bagatelle (115 Duval St., 305-296-6609), serving lunch and dinner daily, where a creative, tropical flare permeates the menu and the seafood chowder is superb.

Kelly's Caribbean Bar, Grill & Brewery (301 Whitehead St., 305-293-8484) serves delicious beef, poultry and seafood at reasonable prices. Sit in their outdoor courtyard under the shade trees and get lightly misted on those hot summer days while you wait for your meal. Kelly's is also a significant historic landmark as the first Pan Am Airlines ticket was sold out of the building that houses the restaurant.

Unpretentious Camille's Restaurant (1202 Simonton St., 305-296-4811, no reservations accepted) is a local favorite.

MAIN SHIP CHANNEL

MALLORY SQUARE

OLD TOWNE AREA

PIER HOUSE

GALLEON RESORT
AND MARINA

HYATT HOTEL
& RESTAURANT

MARKER 24

ENTRANCE

RED MARKER 4

Key West's Luxurious Resort Marina

The Galleon MARINA

Marina guests enjoy the pool, fitness center, sauna, outdoor spa, sundecks and the harbor view tiki bar.

The Galleon's breakwater shielded floating docks have been engineered for maximum protection and security (24 hrs.) for your vessel. The Galleon provides Old Towne Key West's finest accommodations for yachts up to 135 ft. Guests not staying on board may find luxurious two bedroom, two bath suites with complete kitchens at the dockside Galleon Resort...all near the exciting nightlife of famous Olde Towne Key West. A full watersports program...small boat and jet skis, as well as mopeds and bicycles. Our Harbourmaster is on duty 24 hours, 7 days a week monitoring channel 16. Plenty of fresh water at no extra charge, 50 amp electricity, cable TV, telephones and 9 ft. of water dockside. A warm welcome awaits you!

619 Front Street, Key West, FL 33040. For additional information call Toll free: 1-800-6MARINA or 305-292-1292

Key West, FL

The ingredients are strictly fresh, the preparation gourmet and the prices at budget level. Mangoes (700 Duval St., 305-292-4606) has spacious outdoor seating under a canopy of trees right in the hub of the "Duval scene." Yet that seems an ocean away from this verdant oasis, with tropical-style food to match. La Trattoria (524 Duval St., 305-296-1075 reservations recommended) has been described as an "upscale SoHo-style New York bistro," making it hard to imagine you are in the laid-back Keys and not either there or in Venice. Locals flock to it for the authentic taste of old Italy. Here is a chance for them to "get off the rock" (escape the Keys) without actually leaving.

Louie's Backyard (700 Waddell Ave., 305-294-1061, reservations advised) is actually a backyard—right on the Atlantic Ocean. Indoor and spectacular outdoor seating is arranged in a series of terrace levels, descending to the sea. Louie's is widely regarded as having the best and most innovative cuisine in the Florida Keys, and that says a lot in this league. Prices are high, but customers come away satisfied.

For a complete change of pace, try Blue Heaven (729 Thomas St., 305-296-8666, open daily for breakfast, lunch and dinner; limited reservations for dinner). Most of the seating is outside under a tropical canopy. Something of a hippie throwback and the inspiration for Jimmy Buffett's 1995 song, "Blue Heaven Rendezvous," casual would overstate the formality of the place by some measure. Key West's famous (some would say infamous) free-range descendants of Cuban fighting cocks roam the grounds in flocks, pecking for scraps under Blue Heaven's picnic-style tables. However, if you like (or think you might) Caribbean-vegetarian cuisine—served with a festive spirit in the open air—this is the place. And the price is right.

For seriously authentic and inexpensive Cuban cuisine, El Siboney (900 Catherine St., 305-296-4184) is consistently recommended as the place to go. Ropa vieja (shredded beef), boliche (Cuban pot roast) and paella are well represented here. There are ample sides of yucca, black beans and platanos, with rice pudding or flan for dessert. You will not find better Cuban food, period.

Except for the new resort hotels, the concrete, plastic and glass-cluttered strip malls on U.S. Route 1 and the condominiums on Smathers Beach, architecture is "Conch Island" style and itself worth a serious walking tour. Otherwise, tourist attractions abound (all with fees), such as Ernest Hemingway's home (907 Whitehead St.), Tennessee Williams' house (1413 Duncan St.) and President Harry S. Truman's Little White House (111 Front St.).

Be sure to stop by the Southernmost Point in the Continental United States, a multi-striped buoy on Whitehead Street. Point of fact, though, this is not the Southernmost Point in the Continental United States. The Southernmost Point in the Continental United States is a deserted beach at East Cape, at the tip of Florida, nine miles from the nearest human habitation at Flamingo. Because Key West is an island, it is not part of the continental United States. It is part of the contiguous 48 States. Demonstrations about this incongruity by the Whitehead Street marker are useless. Make-believe is what Key West is all about anyway.

Another option is the tourist-laden, but informative, Conch Train Tour (board at the corner of Duval and Front streets).

Those interested in tropical flora shouldn't miss Nancy Forrester's Secret Garden (1 Free School Lane, off Simonton Street between Fleming and Southard streets, 305-294-0015, 10 a.m. to 5 p.m. daily during the winter season). Over the years, Nancy Forrester and her friends have converted an old derelict lot into a botanical treasure trove of rare palms and tropical forest plants—as much an art form as a garden.

ADDITIONAL RESOURCES

- Key West Paradise, **www.keywest.com**
- Key West Travel Guide, **www.keywesttravelguide.com**

NEARBY GOLF COURSES
Key West Golf Club, 6450 E. College Road, Key West, FL 33040, 305-294-5232, **www.keywestgolf.com**

NEARBY MEDICAL FACILITIES
Lower Keys Medical Center, 5900 College Rd., Key West, FL 33040, 305-294-5531

■ TO THE DRY TORTUGAS

Seventy miles from the nearest settlement in Key West, the Dry Tortugas are the westernmost of the Florida Keys, the most remote and, in some respects, the most fascinating and beautiful. The Marquesas Keys lie in the path to the Tortugas, only 24 miles west of Key West. They make an excellent stop to break up the trip to the Dry Tortugas. Other than the Marquesas, there are no intermediate anchorages and, west of Key West, there are no facilities or supplies of any kind.

Because of erratic, and sometimes severe, weather in the area (unpredicted fronts packing high winds are not that unusual), passage to the Dry Tortugas requires planning for the unexpected and packing everything—water, food, fuels, clothing and all other supplies—for a trip of substantially longer duration than anticipated. Schedules are not recommended. Weekend trippers, Caribbean-bound cruisers and fishermen alike frequently find themselves holed up for a week or more in the modestly protected harbor off Garden Key in persistent 25- to 35-knot winds attending stalled fronts in the Gulf of Mexico or off the Cuban coast.

If weather conditions are less than ideal, a trip to the Dry Tortugas should be postponed. In all conditions, boats bound for the Dry Tortugas should be equipped, at a minimum, with a VHF radio, depth sounder and GPS unit. Careful checking with NOAA radio forecasts before and during such a trip is essential for your safety. Once at Garden Key, the National Park Service posts daily NOAA weather reports at its docks. Before departure from Key West, skippers should also check with the Coast Guard for the current Local Notice to Mariners, no longer available in print form, but available online, at no cost, at www.navcen.uscg.gov. In addition to changes in aids to navigation in the area, you should check on any military operations in the restricted area west of the Marquesas Keys. The Coast Guard can be reached on VHF Channels 16 and 22A in Key West. Despite these cautions, with careful preparation, a voyage to the Dry Tortugas can be most rewarding. But if you think you won't bother to really get ready for this trip, don't go.

The Routes

One route runs south of the Marquesas, and the other, to the north. The southern route via West Channel, then west past Man Key and then Boca Grande Key, permits easy access to the best anchorage in the Marquesas. Check your charts for shoal areas, and stay clear of both keys.

Approach Mooney Key from the southeast. The northern route via Northwest Channel leads out past Harbor Key Bank and then west. You can switch channels if you change your mind and head through the north-south Boca Grande Channel, approximately two miles west of Boca Grande Key and identified by green daybeacon "1" to the north and red daybeacon "2" to the south. Or, stop off and anchor to the west of Boca Grande Key near green daybeacon "17" in 10 to 16 feet at mean low water.

The Marquesas

An interesting stopover with a fairly well-sheltered lagoon, the Marquesas are made up of numerous small keys arranged in the shape of a South Seas atoll. Chart 11439 shows Mooney Harbor, with its entrance between Gull and Mooney keys and room for several boats. Don't count on getting in here, though. Use binoculars to look for an entrance. If you have a high tide, an overhead sun and can find a way in, then you might want to try it. Some promising looking entrances might be between the two large islands to the southeast marked "mangrove" on the chart. Two other potential entrances on the south side to the west of Mooney Harbor Key might provide enough depth. A third possibility exists on the western side of the atoll. Only very shoal draft vessels should attempt entry, and be prepared to get yourself off the bottom if you run aground. You are likely out of VHF range for assistance here. Otherwise skip it. If you need or want to stop here, try to figure out the winds and then anchor in the lee of the Marquesas. An anchorage on the southwestern side of the atoll is comfortable in winds from an easterly quadrant. Depths of 9 to 10 feet can be found fairly close to shore.

Enjoy dinghying through the maze of passages in the atoll, but do not go ashore. This is a marine sanctuary and signs on the shore prohibit you from landing. This area is known for the famous Spanish treasure ship, the Atocha, which sank just to the west of the Marquesas in the Quick Sands. Many boat captains from Key West bring their clients here to bonefish or to angle for tarpon and permit.

Marquesas to Dry Tortugas

NAVIGATION: Use Charts 11439 and 11438. Heading west from either the anchorage or the lagoon, after clearing the shoals to the south of west of the Marquesas, use Halfmoon Shoal and Rebecca Shoal Light as waypoints. Mind your

depth sounder as you leave the shallows east of the light. On the northern route, the same suggestion applies, but you do have some markers along the shallows south of your course. The marker on the western edge of New Grounds Shoal (flashing four seconds, 19 feet high) can also serve as a waypoint before passing Rebecca Shoal. From the light, you pass over deep water. As you approach the eastern edge of the Dry Tortugas, you can pick out Bush Key and Garden Key with Fort Jefferson dominating the island landscape.

The approach for long-distance cruisers from the north is best made due south on the meridian W 082° 52.00, passing immediately abeam of lighted boundary buoy "I" (yellow) to a point about one-quarter mile east of the red and green daybeacon at Middle Ground. From there, head to red daybeacon "6" and Northwest Channel. Skip the eastern channel, as you cannot count on it. Vessels approaching from the south are advised to use Southwest Channel east of Loggerhead Key and marked initially by green can "1." At red daybeacon "6," Garden Key's southerly entry channel requires an abrupt turn to starboard to follow the closely spaced markers on both sides of the deep channel into the anchorage.

A solid isthmus between Bush Key and Garden Key comes and goes. The latest corrected charts we examined while preparing this section of the WATERWAY GUIDE indicate that the isthmus has returned (edition 13, January 2008). Hurricane Charley, which went right over Fort Jefferson in 2004, took out parts of it, but whatever vagrant currents created it also appear able to keep the land bridge viable. We would suggest that you buy print-on-demand charts if you are vitally interested in the latest on the channels in and out of the Garden Key anchorage beside Fort Jefferson.

Anchorage: Best anchorage is found in front of (to the east) the deteriorated steamship docks at Garden Key's southern end. There is variable holding here in 13 to 28 feet of water. Be careful; outside the channel, charted depths are about a foot. It is best to search out a sandy spot, then make sure your anchor is set well and securely buried with an anchor dive. In this relatively confined and exposed area, there are nearly always at least half a dozen boats on the hook, often more than twice that number during a blow. Park regulations restrict overnight anchoring to within one nautical mile of Garden Key. During nesting season, you may want to anchor away from Bush Key to avoid the nighttime noise of the sooty terns.

Prior to making the passage you should carefully check your charts and aids to navigation against the latest weekly Local Notice to Mariners from the Coast Guard, available online at www.navcen.uscg.gov/lnm. You can download and print out the latest weekly report in its entirety.

GOIN' ASHORE: **DRY TORTUGAS, FL**

First charted by Spanish explorer Ponce de Leon and named for the turtles gathering there, the Dry Tortugas became U.S. territory in 1821 with the purchase of Florida from Spain. Situated on the rim of the Gulf Stream at the pivot point of trade routes to the Mississippi River and Gulf

The Dry Tortugas, FL

Coast, the Dry Tortugas were quickly recognized for their navigational and strategic importance. Garden Key soon became the site of a substantial lighthouse. A quarter-century later, construction began on a mighty fortress there. But the technologies of seamanship and national defense changed before the fort was completed. Chief among them was the invention and use of rifled cannon shot, which went through the sides of masonry forts like they were made of cookie dough.

Today the eerie presence of massive, but never-finished Fort Jefferson still dominates Garden Key, but its importance is historical. The working lighthouse, long since moved to Loggerhead Key to the west, also appears as a sentinel from the past. Contemporary value of this island group is found in its pristine natural beauty—the unpolluted clarity of its waters and sparkling live reef systems, and the raucous wonder of thousands of nesting seabirds.

In 1992, the entire area, bound by an elliptical circuit of 10 large yellow buoys, was dedicated as the Dry Tortugas National Park. Touring Fort Jefferson on your own is an option, but you will learn much more if you take one of the ranger-guided tours. The rangers share many interesting and unusual facts that will enhance your visit and understanding of life at the fort. The largest of the forts of last century's American coastal defense perimeter (eight-foot-thick brick walls, standing 50 feet high to support three gun tiers and surrounding a 17-acre quad), it is also one of the most well-preserved.

Though construction began in 1846 and continued for 30 years thereafter, the challenges of a poor foundation base to support its weight, the effects of salt air on iron gun bay doors and reinforcement rods, malaria and repeated yellow fever epidemics and advances in weaponry combined to frustrate its completion. Nonetheless, the six interconnected bastions and moated walls are all in place, nearly complete and fully open to inspection, along with many of the original cannons, mortars and other implements of 19th-century war. The masonry work in this fort, if you know anything about it, is a thing to behold. It appears as if brain surgeons constructed the granite spiral staircases.

Though the fort was never directly involved in hostilities, it was an infamous federal prison during the Civil War and for some time thereafter. The Union used it to imprison deserters. Its most famous inmate was Dr. Samuel Mudd, the Maryland physician convicted for complicity in the assassination of President Abraham Lincoln because of his role in setting the broken leg of Lincoln's assassin, John Wilkes Booth. Two years after Dr. Mudd's tireless efforts to fight the yellow fever epidemic that overwhelmed the fort's garrison in 1867, he was pardoned. The cells he occupied can be seen today.

Persistent disease epidemics and a damaging hurricane prompted the Army to abandon the fort in 1878. Thereafter, it found few uses of any kind, beyond a brief stint as a Navy coaling station, which is remembered only by its fueling of the USS Maine on its fatal voyage to Cuba in 1898. In 1935, President Franklin D. Roosevelt proclaimed the vacant fortress a national monument.

Bush Key, just across the channel from Fort Jefferson, has been a protected refuge for the sooty tern since 1908, after egg hunters had all but decimated the species. Sooties by the thousands, along with numerous brown and black noddies, nest on Bush Key beginning in February—and are strictly off-limits to human visitors from then until completion of the nesting season in October. Frigatebirds have established a rookery on Long Key immediately to the south, and roseate terns regularly nest on Hospital Key to the north. Boaters are required to stand well off these keys during the nesting season. Careful snorkeling, Scuba diving and recreational fishing are encouraged on the unspoiled coral reefs throughout the park; however, spearfishing, taking of lobsters and commercial fishing are prohibited. Good dive/snorkeling sites can be found on the Windjammer site off Texas Rock and near White Shoal.

On arrival at the Dry Tortugas, it is best to check in at the National Park Service Visitor Center (in Fort Jefferson) for a copy of the park's brochure with maps and regulations and the latest weather report. The Park Service has restrooms at its docks (with no wash basins or other running water) and beach space for dinghy landings. The park is a No-Discharge Zone and, time permitting, park rangers may check your vessel's Y-valve. If your holding tank is not functioning, they will tie-wrap the valve and insist that you use the restrooms on the dock. There are picnic tables, a few charcoal grills and a beautiful sandy beach at the fort's south end. Everything you require must be brought with you, and all trash must be carted back to your boat.

If you are short on time, but still curious about the Dry Tortugas, take one of the high-speed ferries from Key West or the seaplane tour. A trip out here on your own boat, however, is the way to do it. You will never forget it.

ADDITIONAL RESOURCES

■ Dry Tortugas National Park, **www.nps.gov/drto**

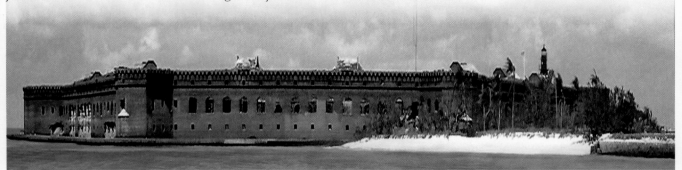

Fort Jefferson. WATERWAY GUIDE PHOTOGRAPHY

Anchoring in the Keys

Carry a couple types of anchors on board with you as no one anchor will fit every situation. A two-anchor Bahamian moor is recommended when strong reversing tidal currents are present or when an anchorage is tight and swinging room is limited, but only if everyone is on two anchors.

Ordinary anchorages require a burying-type anchor such as a plow. When the bottom gets grassy, when hard marl or coral lie under a shallow layer of powdery sand or when coral and rock line an area, then a good, solid, hooking anchor or kedge is best.

Mileage indicated here is in statute miles, and no effort has been made to tell you how far off the channel the anchorage is located. You should be able to find these spots easily on your chart. Each of these anchorages has been visited or observed by a WATERWAY GUIDE contributor. There are other places, though, where a prudent boater can anchor. Let us know how these anchorages are, or if you find other good ones—visit us online at www.waterwayguide.com and follow the "Submit" link.

ICW ROUTE

Ragged Keys (Mile 1106). East of the ICW, 7-foot approach, 8 feet to shoal west of Keys. Holding fair to good in grassy mud. Limited protection from northeast through southeast.

Sands Key (Mile 1108). East of the ICW, 6-foot approach, 5 feet in area west of northern portion of the key. Holding fair to good in grassy mud. Protected from south to northeast.

Elliott Key (Mile 1109 to Mile 1114). East of the ICW, 5-foot approach, 5 feet to shoal anywhere along west side of the key. Holding fair to good depending on rocky to grassy mud bottom. Protection from northeast through southeast.

Caesar Creek (Mile 1115). East of the ICW, anchorage open to both routes. Four-foot approach from ICW; 12 feet in best area between Rubicon and Reid keys. Holding good; Bahamian moor recommended on mud and some grass. Well-protected.

Angelfish Creek (Mile 1120). East of the ICW, anchorage open to both routes. Five-foot approach from both ends. Anchorage in side creeks north of channel is 5 feet deep. Holding mixed: some rocky areas, some hard. Strong currents; Bahamian moor recommended. Well-protected.

Pumpkin Key (Mile 1122). East of the ICW, 9-foot approach, 7 feet to shoal anywhere in lee of key depending on winds. Holding fair to good in grassy mud with some rocks.

Steamboat Creek in Card Sound (Mile 1125). East of the ICW, 9-foot approach, 7 feet to shoal north and in mouth of creek off Jew Point. Holding good in grassy mud. Protection only from southwest to east.

Manatee Bay in Barnes Sound (Mile 1132). West of the ICW, 5-foot approach and 5 feet to shoal in area near marked channel leading into Manatee Creek. Holding good in hard bottom. Protection fair to good except in strong winds from north to northwest.

Sexton Cove (Mile 1135). East of the ICW, 7-foot approach, 6-foot depth to shoaling close in. Holding fair in grass and hard bottom with some rocks. Protection from northwest through southeast.

Stellrecht Point (Mile 1136). Southeast of the ICW, 7-foot approach, 6 feet to shoal just south of the point. Holding fair to good in grassy mud. Protected from north through southwest.

Sunset Cove, Buttonwood Sound (Mile 1142). Southeast of the ICW, 5-foot approach, 4 feet or less close in, 5 feet near Pelican Key and near Upper Keys Sailing Club docks. Holding fair to good. Protection from east through south and to west. From the north, close in to the key.

Butternut Key (Mile 1146). Northwest of the ICW, 6-foot approach, 5 feet near eastern Butternut Key just north of marker "60." Holding fair in soft bottom. Protection only from northwest to north.

Tavernier Community Harbor (Mile 1150). South of the ICW, 5-foot approach, 5 feet outside basin, 4 feet inside. Holding poor to fair in dense, grassy bottom. Protection fair to good in all but strongest north winds.

Cowpens (Mile 1155). Southeast of the ICW, 5-foot approach and depth. Numerous spots to anchor in Cowpens anchorage area. Fair to good holding in soft bottom, some grass. Protection from east through west, depending on exact anchoring spot.

Upper Matecumbe Key (Mile 1160). South of the ICW, 6-foot approach and 5 feet in the anchorage off of the restaurant/bar. Protection from south and southeast. Holding fair in soft bottom.

Lignumvitae Key (Mile 1164). Southeast of the ICW, 7-foot approach to either side of key. DO NOT ANCHOR; use the heavy moorings provided. Protection is dependent on being in the lee of the key.

Long Key Bight (Mile 1170). On ocean side of Channel Five Bridge, 9-foot approach, shoaling to 5 feet at center. Anchor as far in as draft allows. Holding good, some grass. Protection good from all but east winds.

Rachel Key (Mile 1190). Southwest of the ICW, south of Rachel Bank, 7-foot approach, 5 feet in area southwest of Rachel Key and southeast of charted shoal. Holding fair to good in sand and grass. Protection fair to good depending on exact anchorage.

Boot Key Harbor (Mile 1195). East of the ICW, accessible through Knights Key Channel or Moser Channel, then east to Boot Key Channel. See details in anchorages for Hawk Channel route.

Bahia Honda area (Mile 1205). Southwest of the ICW in charted cove, 7-foot approach, 7 feet to shoal inside 6-foot line. Holding fair in grassy mud. Protection from east through southwest only. You can, with care, anchor just outside the park basin in 8 feet if you can get under the 20-foot clearance at the bridge.

Key West (Chart 11447). Anchorages in the Key West area are limited. However, enterprising yachtsmen are continually finding new ones. The best accepted one is Wisteria Island at Mile 1245. It is the northernmost of the two small islands off Key West Bight. Anchorage is north or east, as south of the island the holding is poor. Seven-foot-depth approach, with 7 feet to shoal near shore. West of Fleming Key is another alternative. Note: The anchorage is adjacent and contiguous to the harbor and is exposed to the wash and wake of passing vessels. Holding is good in fairly hard bottom. Protection from east and south, with shoals providing wave reduction from the north. Or proceed around the north end of Fleming Key and anchor north of the mooring field and off of Sigsbee Park.

HAWK CHANNEL ROUTE

(Mileage in statute miles from Government Cut, parallel to ICW Mile 1090.)

Caesar Creek (Mile 1118). Anchorage open to both routes. Seven-foot approach from Hawk Channel, 4 feet from ICW. Anchorage best between Rubicon and Reid keys. Twelve-foot depth, holding good. Bahamian moor recommended. Well-protected.

Angelfish Creek (Mile 1122). Anchorage open to both routes. Five-foot approach from both channels. Anchorage in side creeks north of channel. Five-foot depth, holding

mixed, some hard and some rocky areas. Strong currents, Bahamian moor recommended. Well-protected.

Largo Sound (Mile 1141). Five-foot approach, some 5-foot depths near the channel, but 3 feet is the norm. Holding fair, some grass, well-protected.

Rodriguez Key (Mile 1145). Seven-foot approach, 7 feet or less close in. Anchor in lee as required for protection. Holding good. Note wrecks north of key and shoal to the west.

Rock Harbor (Mile 1144). Seven-foot approach, anchor as close in as draft will permit. Protection from north to northeast. Mandalay Restaurant (cash only) has a dinghy beach.

Tavernier Key (Mile 1150). Six-foot approach, less close in. Anchor in Tavernier Harbor area. Holding good. Some protection from northwest to north, southwest through south.

Whale Harbor (Mile 1158). Five-foot approach, 5 feet in anchorage. Anchor in lee relative of keys to north and to small key to southwest near marker "5A." Holding fair, some grass. Protection fair northwest through east. Note shoals.

Indian Key (Mile 1165). Seven-foot approach, 7 feet or less at anchorage close in. Anchor on southeast side of key in lee. Holding good in sand and sea grass. Protection fair from northwest through northeast.

Long Key Bight (Mile 1172). Nine-foot approach, shoaling to 5 feet in center. You can anchor as far in as draft allows. Holding good in some sea grass. Good protection from all but due east.

Boot Key Harbor (Mile 1193). Five-foot approach from Sister Creek, 7-foot approach from Boot Key Channel. Eleven feet to shoaling near head of harbor. Holding good. Bahamian moor suggested. Good protection for 360 degrees except in severe east-northeast winds. Little room to anchor outside of mooring field.

Bahia Honda Key (Mile 1207). Ten-foot approach, 9 feet and less close in between bridges. Holding fair to good. Bahamian moor suggested. Fair to good protection.

Newfound Harbor (Mile 1215). Seven-foot approach, 9 feet and less close in toward highway bridge. Holding good. Fair to good protection in all but worst southerly winds.

Niles Channel (Mile 1215). Seven-foot approach, depths of 7 to 21 feet in sand and grass. Holding fair to good in mud and grass. Fair to good protection in all but worst winds from the south.

Saddlebunch Harbor (Mile 1228). Five-foot approach through narrow channel between Saddlebunch Keys and Pelican Key. Anchor in 7 to 8 feet of water just inside. Holding fair. Buoy your anchor. Fair to good protection.

Key West (Mile 1241). See ICW route.

Florida's West Coast

◻ **FLAMINGO TO FORT MYERS BEACH** ◻ **OKEECHOBEE WATERWAY**
◻ **SAN CARLOS BAY TO SARASOTA** ◻ **ANNA MARIA ISLAND TO TARPON SPRINGS**

Photo Courtesy of Susan Landry and WATERWAY GUIDE.

Florida's West Coast

☐ FLAMINGO TO FORT MYERS BEACH ☐ OKEECHOBEE WATERWAY
☐ SAN CARLOS BAY TO SARASOTA ☐ ANNA MARIA ISLAND TO TARPON SPRINGS

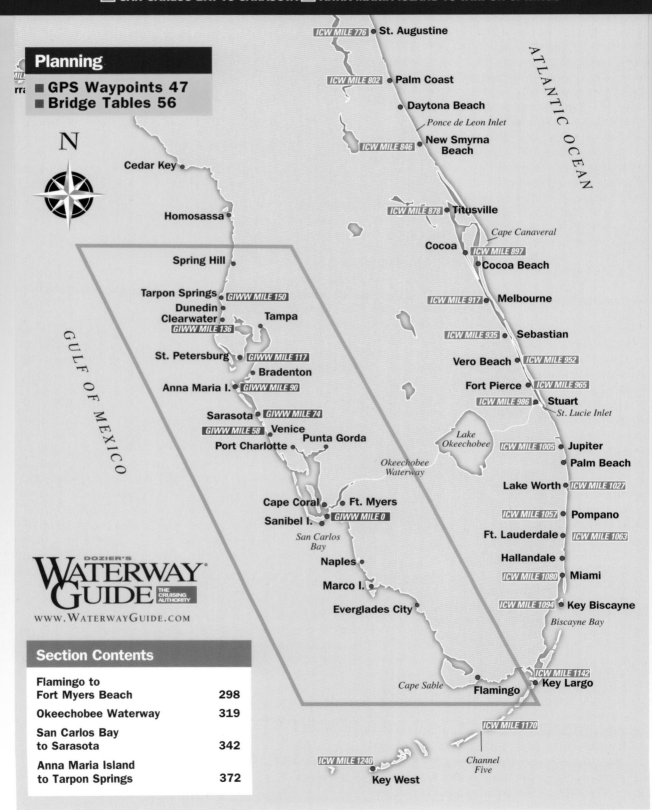

Planning

- GPS Waypoints 47
- Bridge Tables 56

N

DOZIER'S
WATERWAY GUIDE THE CRUISING AUTHORITY
WWW.WATERWAYGUIDE.COM

ICW MILE 776 St. Augustine
ICW MILE 802 Palm Coast
Daytona Beach
Ponce de Leon Inlet
ICW MILE 846 New Smyrna Beach
ICW MILE 878 Titusville
Cape Canaveral
Cocoa ICW MILE 897
Cocoa Beach
ICW MILE 917 Melbourne
ICW MILE 935 Sebastian
Vero Beach ICW MILE 952
Fort Pierce ICW MILE 965
ICW MILE 986 Stuart
St. Lucie Inlet
Lake Okeechobee
ICW MILE 1005 Jupiter
Palm Beach
Lake Worth ICW MILE 1027
ICW MILE 1057 Pompano
Ft. Lauderdale ICW MILE 1063
Hallandale
ICW MILE 1080 Miami
ICW MILE 1094 Key Biscayne
Biscayne Bay

ATLANTIC OCEAN

Cedar Key
Homosassa
Spring Hill
Tarpon Springs GIWW MILE 150
Dunedin
Clearwater
GIWW MILE 136
Tampa
St. Petersburg GIWW MILE 117
Bradenton
Anna Maria I. GIWW MILE 90
Sarasota GIWW MILE 74
GIWW MILE 58 Venice
Port Charlotte Punta Gorda
Cape Coral Ft. Myers
Sanibel I. GIWW MILE 0
San Carlos Bay
Naples
Marco I.
Everglades City

GULF OF MEXICO

Okeechobee Waterway

Cape Sable Flamingo
ICW MILE 1142 Key Largo
ICW MILE 1170
ICW MILE 1240 *Channel Five*
Key West

Introduction

Florida's West Coast

Zoologically and geographically, Florida's lower west coast differs substantially from the east. The lower east coast is crowded with people and cultures and, except for the Keys, represents a mega-city stretching from Biscayne Bay to Palm Beach. The cruising, too, is entirely different. The sophistication, glamour and luxury so prevalent on the east coast comes in more measured doses on the west coast. The pace is slower, the atmosphere more relaxed and the amenities somewhat more limited and spaced farther apart, but the cruising is superb. From the swampy wilderness of the Everglades to the long sweep of Sanibel and Captiva islands, from picturesque fishing villages to the bustling big-city ports in Tampa Bay to the quaint, restaurant-laden Greek sponge center of Tarpon Springs, Florida's southwestern waters have much to offer.

The lower half of the coast is alternately wild and developed. At the bottom of the peninsula, the Ten Thousand Islands guard the swampland of the Everglades. Up the coast, the shoreline develops into sandy beach backed by a solid wall of pine and tropical hardwood jungle.

At San Carlos Bay, the tropical barrier islands emerge. Deep water moves in closer toward shore, and resort communities begin to appear. The Gulf Intracoastal Waterway (GIWW) begins at Mile Zero at the mouth of the Caloosahatchee River, where the Okeechobee Waterway ends.

Now the west coast begins to somewhat resemble the east, with increased boat traffic, houses, marinas and shore activity. From as far south as Naples up the coast to Clearwater, the mangroves increasingly give way to extensive shoreside development.

Cruising Conditions

Cruising waters through much of the lower half of Florida's west coast are protected. The GIWW—for the most part either a dredged channel behind barrier islands or a passage shielded from the Gulf of Mexico—begins at the mouth of the Caloosahatchee River and runs 150 statute miles north to Anclote Keys through a narrow channel. Outside the marked route, shoals are everywhere, similar to the ICW on Florida's east coast.

Though they might seem worse to the inexperienced, most tidal currents are less than 2 knots here. At 1 to 3 feet, the tidal range is relatively small, and water depths tend to be governed more by wind than by tide. When winds blow from the northeast, the water is driven out of the bays, while strong winds from the southeast and southwest push water in. Under northeast wind conditions, there is generally less water in the bays than the chart shows. Be especially wary when a spring low tide combines with a fresh northeast breeze.

From time to time, your skill at navigating a compass course will be tested as you follow the course offshore into the Gulf proper. The occasionally capricious weather may surprise you with a severe and sudden storm. Be prepared with the latest charts and weather advisories, and make sure your boat and equipment are in top shape.

Florida's West Coast— Gulf Intracoastal Waterway

Florida's West Coast Waterway provides the same type of protection from inclement weather as the Atlantic ICW and, like its East Coast counterpart, the GIWW varies in nature with location. In some areas, the GIWW is serpentine with many sharp bends and turns; in other places, it runs in open straightaways. No matter its course, the GIWW still requires navigational vigilance, so keep the following precautions in mind:

■ Look astern as often as ahead, and keep markers lined up fore and aft to maintain your course in-channel.

■ Stay to mid-channel as often as possible, and be alert to side currents that may cause lightly powered vessels to drift off course and out of the channel.

■ Slow down in any area where shoaling is likely, especially if your boat draws more than 3 feet. West coast bottoms tend to commonly consist of soft mud or sand. Grounding at slow speed will do less damage than running full-tilt onto a shoal. ■

Flamingo to Fort Myers Beach

CHARTS 11426, 11427, 11429, 11430, 11431, 11432, 11433, 11451, 11452

The wild and undeveloped Everglades swampland, beginning at Flamingo, provides a glimpse into nature that is both amazing and educational. Heading north toward the desolate Ten Thousand Islands, cruisers will continue to wonder if they are still in Florida, but it is this very diversity that makes cruising the west coast such a draw for the adventuresome.

For approximately 130 statute miles from Flamingo to Fort Myers Beach, the cruising skipper first travels off Cape Sable's East, Middle and Northwest capes, along the edge of the wild, primitive and beautiful Ten Thousand Islands region, and then through the impromptu continuation of the Intracoastal Waterway (ICW) behind the green mangrove curtain from the Ten Thousand Islands region to the Goodland/Marco Island area. At that point the cruising skipper has the choice of moving offshore at Marco Island, or following the winding eight-mile stretch of the ICW from Marco Island to Naples and finally out to the Gulf of Mexico. From there, the skipper runs the shoreline to San Carlos Bay and the official start, Mile Zero, of the Gulf Intracoastal Waterway (GIWW) at its juncture with the Okeechobee Waterway, crossing Florida to the east.

Routes to and From Flamingo

NAVIGATION: Use Chart 11451. The combination of Hurricanes Katrina and Wilma set Flamingo back substantially as the unique overnight stopover it had become. As of summer 2010, the Flamingo Marina was open (it had been closed because of damage received in 2005 Hurricane Wilma). The channel into the marina has been dredged, but is still shallow. Boats drawing more than 3.5 to 4 feet should be cautious. Before you venture into Flamingo, we suggest that you call ahead (239-695-3101) for current information and conditions. Taking it slow and easy is recommended when exploring this area.

The key to reaching Flamingo (with the aforementioned caveats in mind), either for a daytime visit or an anchorage, is locating flashing red "2," which is 1.95 nautical miles on a course of 178 degrees magnetic from East Cape, on Cape Sable. The approaches to flashing red "2" are either from the Keys, via Yacht Passage, directly from Key West across Florida Bay (both covered in the "Florida Keys" section), or from the north, skirting the edges of Everglades National Park on the west coast of Florida.

To reach Flamingo, you will travel approximately eight miles east-by-northeast from flashing red "2," passing four markers to flashing green "9," which starts off the marked entry to Flamingo-proper. You will then turn north-northeast for a little over a mile in the narrow but well-marked channel to the Flamingo basin. Follow the markers carefully; depths outside the channel are 1 to 2 feet at mean low water. Play the tides if your draft is over 3 feet—the chart shows 4.5 feet in the entry channel, but the date of the sounding data is quite old.

Dockage: Controlling depths are 4.5 feet inside the basin at Flamingo with a soft muddy bottom. For helpful resources in planning your visit, such as activity schedules, trail guides, a backcountry trip planner, natural history and much more, visit the home page of the Everglades National Park Web site at www.nps.gov/ever or call Park Services at 305-247-7700.

North from East Cape Sable

NAVIGATION: Use Charts 11451, 11431 and 11429. From Flamingo, retrace your entry route and round East Cape Sable heading north. You will encounter thousands of lobster and crab pot markers if you leave the marked boundaries of Everglades National Park.

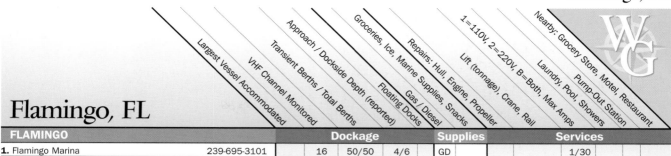

Flamingo, FL

FLAMINGO		Dockage			Supplies	Services	
1. Flamingo Marina	239-695-3101	16	50/50	4/6	GD		1/30

Column headers (diagonal): Largest Vessel Accommodated / VHF Channel Monitored / Transient Berths / Total Berths / Approach / Dockside Depth (reported) / Floating Docks / Gas / Diesel / Groceries, Ice, Marine Supplies, Snacks / Repairs: Hull, Engine, Propeller / Lift (tonnage), Crane, Rail / 1=110V, 2=220V, B=Both, Max Amps / Laundry, Pool, Showers / Pump-Out Station / Nearby: Grocery Store, Motel, Restaurant

Corresponding chart(s) not to be used for navigation. 💻 Internet Access 📶 Wireless Internet Access

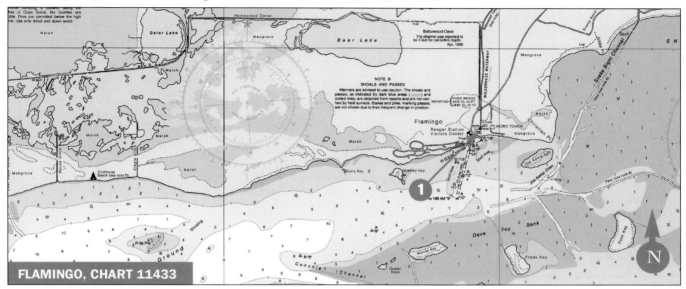

FLAMINGO, CHART 11433

Pay close attention to your chart and the depth sounder. If you are so equipped, enter appropriate waypoints into your GPS, and plot your course around Middle and Northwest capes inside the park boundaries. If you are planning to head for Cape Romano, Marco Island or Naples, set your course to remain well offshore. Remember to stay well south of the finger shoals, about 12 miles below Cape Romano.

A closer-to-shore, but slower route will provide many rewards. If the winds are light and the weather pleasant, you can anchor off the beach between East and Middle capes and dinghy ashore. The area provides excellent beachcombing opportunities, but this lures few to people go here.

Remember, however, the weather caveat for this area. The winter season's stronger winds and frontal storms arrive with ample warning from the northwest through north and finally the northeast. When you clear the East Cape, if the winds are strong from the northwest, seas can increase rapidly. The farther out into the Gulf of Mexico you go, the worse it will get.

Heading toward Cape Romano and its long shoals, your exposure is from the entire northern sector. "Holing up" in a blow is recommended. Even in the summer, squall lines and even high winds from the prevailing south easterlies can stir things up. NOAA weather reports on VHF WX2 or WX3 should keep you informed so you can make the passage safely.

TEN THOUSAND ISLANDS

Passing Cape Sable a half-mile offshore and then paralleling the coast still inside the occasional park markers brings you into the Ten Thousand Islands. This area stretches for about 56 nautical miles to Cape Romano. Primitive, remote and uninhabited, these islands form the coastline of the Everglades National Park.

Heading north from East Cape (Chart 11431), enjoy the beautiful beaches if your schedule and weather permit. Anchor off the beach and dinghy ashore. The Middle Cape Canal just north of Middle Cape is reported to be a good fishing spot, but you will need a freshwater license if you intend to take the rod into Lake Ingraham.

Little Shark River

NAVIGATION: Use Charts 11431 and 11432. About six miles above the Northwest Cape, pick up the marked entrance to the Little Shark River off the point just south of Ponce de Leon Bay.

Little Shark River is a gateway to the inner regions of the park and can provide access to the Wilderness Waterway connecting Flamingo and Everglades City. This route is not recommended for vessels requiring more than 18 feet of clearance nor those that have high cabins and/or windscreens because of the narrow channels and overhanging foliage in some areas. Those drawing more than 4 feet need

Everglades City, FL

Looking southwest over Everglades City. (Not to be used for navigation.) WATERWAY GUIDE PHOTOGRAPHY

not apply. However, if you are looking to wait out nasty northerly weather, getting a hook down in Little Shark River and out of the waves is good for anyone. The water is deep, and the scenery is beautiful. Mariners have been waiting out bad weather here for many years.

Marked channels lead into coffee-colored wide and shallow bays, or up narrow rivers through and past hundreds of islands and winding Waterways. Many cruising boats anchor in the first mile or so of the Little Shark River, which is protected by a 60-foot-high mangrove forest. Remember, navigating this type of course requires knowing where you are at all times; it is easy to get lost.

Anchorage: Anchoring in the Little Shark River is pretty straightforward—10 to 12 feet of water and a good solid mud bottom with plenty of swing room. There is a strong current, so make sure your anchor is well set. If your boat is not screened in, keep plenty of bug repellent handy. In fact, keep some handy even if you do have screens. Those with keen eyes can spot alligators along the banks or in the water. At night, a flashlight shone into the wilderness will usually reveal dozens of little red eyes that belong to alligators. This is a definite "no swimming" area.

The pelicans work this area quite often and are fun to watch. A crab line dropped overboard and carefully hauled in will supply the galley with a magnificent meal. Fishing is good, but licenses are required, and limits must be carefully observed. Leave the area as you find it.

Everglades City

Everglades City's early life, dating back more than 1,000 years to the age of the coastal mound dwellers, was based on trade, fishing and shellfishing. With the arrival of early settlers, it gradually evolved into a shipping port for produce and seafood. Seafood is still a major economic factor in the area, but is following the decline of the produce market. There was a time, back in the 1970s, when commercial fishermen in this area tapped into a market that had nothing to do with fish, and many of them had become abnormally wealthy. Locals used to say that a good fisherman, who knew all the ins and outs of the trade, was usually wearing so much gold jewelry around his neck that it would drown him if he fell overboard from his mullet skiff.

In July 1983, federal agents sealed off the only road out of Everglades City and arrested 28 people. They were also seeking 13 others. It was the culmination of a two-year crackdown on smuggling that had led to the seizure of about 350,000 pounds of marijuana and the arrests of 94 people. One suspect, former Justice David McCain of the Florida Supreme Court, was sought on charges of conspiring to import marijuana. Those were heady times in Everglades City.

Unique to Everglades City is the Rod & Gun Club. Once a rambling, private, wood frame home, it is now a delightful hotel right on the Barron River, and it is

Everglades City to Gullivan Bay, FL

EVERGLADES CITY TO GULLIVAN BAY		Largest Vessel Accommodated	VHF Channel Monitored	Transient Berths / Total Berths	Approach / Dockside Depth (reported)	Floating Docks	Gas / Diesel	Groceries, Ice, Marine Supplies, Snacks	Repairs: Hull, Engine, Propeller	Lift (tonnage), Crane, Rail	1=110V, 2=220V, B=Both, Max Amps	Laundry, Pool, Showers	Pump-Out Station	Nearby: Grocery Store, Motel, Restaurant
				Dockage				**Supplies**			**Services**			
1. Rod and Gun Club 💻	239-695-2101	100	16	17/17	5.5/5.5			IMS			B/50	PS		GMR
2. Port of the Islands Marina 💻📶	239-821-2885	60	16	70/90	5/6	F	GD	IMS			B/50	LPS	P	MR

Corresponding chart(s) not to be used for navigation. 💻 Internet Access 📶 Wireless Internet Access

worthy—if you have the time—of a trip all the way in from Indian Key just to see it, dine here and maybe, stay overnight. You will be in touch with another era entirely. Lots of people whose names you may recognize have been here. For openers, try Presidents Roosevelt, Truman, Eisenhower, Hoover and Nixon. From Hollywood, actors John Wayne, Burt Reynolds, Sally Field, Sean Connery, Danny Glover and Joe Pesci. Novelist Ernest Hemingway visited here. So did Mick Jagger of the Rolling Stones, and Burl Ives and Gypsy Rose Lee.

Since heavy insecticide spraying has been virtually eliminated in the Everglades National Park, mosquitoes have become almost as important a consideration as weather. They swarm continually in warm weather. If you plan to anchor in this area, opt for spots that garner what breeze there is, and keep plenty of bug spray on hand.

NAVIGATION: Use Charts 11429 and 11430. North of the Little Shark River, it is advisable to follow the markers out and farther offshore to transit the wide and shallow mouth of Ponce de Leon Bay. Prudence would indicate staying outside the three-mile limit. For about 33 nautical miles, only channels among the islands break the coast. Some are deep enough to attract shoal-draft boats and increasing numbers of skippers seeking more remote anchorages and good fishing.

These unmarked channels require careful, experienced navigation. One remote ranger station can be spotted on the north shore of one channel, but no other sign of civilization will be evident beyond park boundary signs until you reach a mark offshore of Everglades City. At this point, you find the 16-foot-high flashing white light "IK," about 3.5 nautical miles off flashing green "1" at Indian Key, which leads into the marked channel to Everglades City. Flashing green "1" is difficult to pick out from offshore; try using GPS coordinates to guide you in.

Dockage: Up the Barron River, The Rod and Gun Club, built by the late Barron G. Collier, has dockage for 17 transients up to 100 feet, with limited facilities. Slips offer 30- and 50-amp/220-volt shore power. Water, ice and marine supplies also are available. The old clubhouse is well worth a visit, and a bike ride to nearby Chokoloskee Island is a good diversion. There is a general store and post office there that is out of another age entirely.

If you head a bit farther upriver (sailboats go left around the island to avoid the power lines), you will pass a number of seafood houses prior to arriving at the Barron River Marina, part of an RV campground. If you are low on cash, the town's ATM is just a few blocks away inside a convenience store.

Everglades City has all the basics: a market, hardware store and post office. This town is a far different place than most communities along the Waterway. Nightlife is whatever or whomever you have brought along. Everglades City is also the northern terminus of the Everglades Wilderness Waterway.

Those desiring the amenities of a full-service resort in a primeval setting will find them seven miles (as the crow flies) farther west of Everglades City at Port of the Islands Resort and Marina, located at the head of the shallow Faka Union River. After exiting Indian Key Pass (the entry you followed into Everglades City from the Gulf), turn northwest to find green daybeacon "3" off Gomez Point at the tip of Panther Key. This marks the entrance to the five-mile-long mangrove-fringed channel on the Faka Union River to Port of the Islands.

The channel is well-marked by daybeacons, beginning with green daybeacon "3" and red daybeacon "4." Controlling depths in the channel are 3 feet at mean low water, so you may have to wait for tides to pass through. Call ahead on VHF Channel 16 to verify available space and for advice on tide and channel conditions. Most of the passes and Waterways, other than Indian Key Pass, have numerous sandbars and shoals. The small-boat operator can be a good source of information for side trips and excursions off the main channels.

Anchorage: If you do not want to go all the way up to Everglades City, and would rather drop the hook, you can anchor shortly after entering Indian Key Pass. Anchor northwest of flashing green "7" in Russell Pass where you will have at least 7-foot depths at mean low water. For more wind protection, you can proceed farther up Russell Pass to where it opens up to starboard and find 7- to 8-foot depths. Make sure you avoid the uncharted pocket to starboard or you could find yourself on the bottom at low tide. Consider two anchors, as currents can be swift.

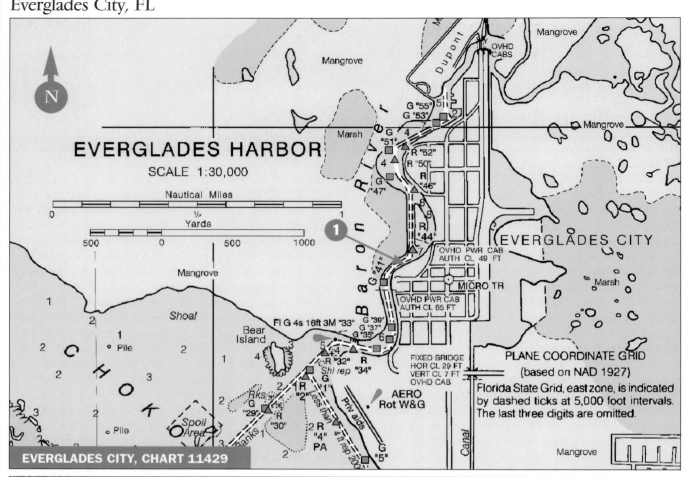

EVERGLADES HARBOR

SCALE 1:30,000

Nautical Miles

Yards

EVERGLADES CITY, CHART 11429

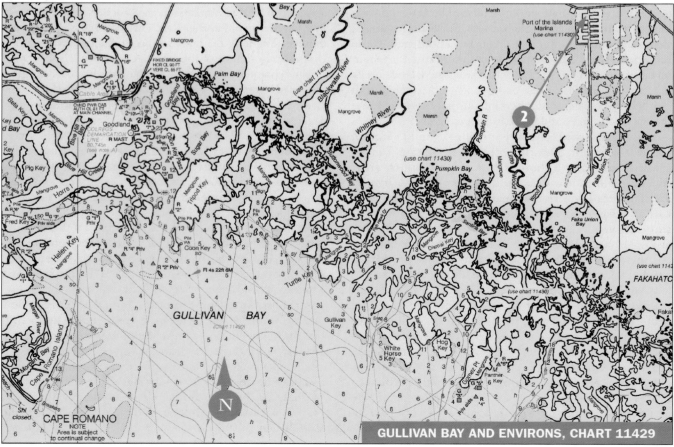

GULLIVAN BAY AND ENVIRONS, CHART 11429

■ EVERGLADES CITY TO MARCO ISLAND

Two routes are available to travel from the Ten Thousand Islands area to Marco Island and beyond: the Inland Passage and the Outside Passage.

Inland Passage

NAVIGATION: Use Chart 11430. If your draft is 4 feet or less and height above water is less than 55 feet, you may save some time by taking the inside and protected route to Marco Island. Vessels with slightly deeper drafts may take this route if they have the flexibility to schedule their trip at high tide.

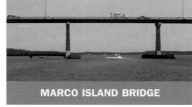

MARCO ISLAND BRIDGE

WATERWAY GUIDE PHOTOGRAPHY

The route begins about six miles west of Faka Union Bay at the head of Gullivan Bay off Coon Key where Coon Key Light, a 22-foot-high flashing white light, marks the entrance to Coon Key Pass. Stay well east of the light (400 to 500 yards), and head north up the east side of Coon Key to pick up red daybeacon "2" (on the west side of Tripod Key), and then through well-marked Coon Key Pass (heading north, leave red markers to starboard) to the village of Goodland, which is east of Marco Island. The route is a bit lean in spots, with the shoals (4-foot charted depths) on the east side of the Marco Bridge (55-foot fixed vertical clearance) being the major concern. Fortunately, the bottom is reported to be soft mud. Local boats frequently use this passage (some at high speed), so ask for current conditions, then make your own decision.

Dockage: Situated on a small peninsula of a large island and marsh complex, the village of Goodland is a laid-back fishing town with good but unpretentious restaurants, fishing supplies and some groceries.

The Calusa Island Yacht Club (west of Coon Key Pass red daybeacon "6") welcomes transients to its docks and can accommodate vessels up to 60 feet. The marina facilities are located in quiet mangrove surroundings and include a ship's store, showers, a laundry, fuel and a boat yard with repair facilities. Next door, Walker's Coon Key Marina has slips, and Moran's Barge Marina at the foot of the Goodland Bridge also has transient spots available for smaller vessels.

On Sunday afternoon, be sure to catch the show at Stan's Idler Hour Restaurant. An unusual mix of locals and the Marco Island condominium crowd blend into the weekly festival that includes the "Buzzard Lope" dance.

Other restaurant options include the Little Bar, a deceptively top-end establishment that may require reservations, the Old Marco Lodge Crab House or Moran's. There is also a local fish market that sells to the public. The fixed 55-foot bridge sets the vertical clearance for the rest of the route.

Anchorage: You can anchor just before green daybeacon "3" in 7 to 10 feet of water, or across the channel from green daybeacon "7" in 8- to 10-foot depths and dinghy to town. As of spring 2010, red daybeacon "8" was missing, so pay close attention to your instruments, and stay in deep water.

Goodland to Marco Island

NAVIGATION: Use Chart 11430. This section of the Waterway and the Big Marco River require considerable care, even for those who have traveled it before. Local knowledge, which is available at Goodland or over the VHF radio, can help. Markers are moved when necessary to reflect shifting shoals and may not be exactly where the chart shows them. Many prefer a rising tide for obvious reasons.

After entering Coon Key Pass, between Coon and Tripod keys, follow the well-marked channel into Goodland keeping the red markers to starboard. The first navigation challenge is when you approach red daybeacon "6." Make sure you give this marker a very wide berth because of a sand bar that extends well into the channel to starboard. After you have passed Goodland, you will notice (as mentioned above) that daybeacon "8" is missing. At red daybeacon "10," you will need to make a sharp turn to starboard, staying close to the marker, and very soon you will make a turn to port to pass under the Interstate 92 bridge (55-foot vertical clearance). Our cruising editor draws 4 feet and did not have a problem in spring 2010 one hour before high tide. Maintain a close watch on the depth sounder, and use a pre-set alarm, if available. It is also a good idea to study your charts and GPS carefully after you have gathered some local knowledge. It is very doable, just pay close attention to your depth sounder and charts.

After passing under the bridge, you will find deeper water for a short time. Just beyond daybeacon "16," there is a very shallow area when approaching daybeacon "18." Once past "18" the water deepens again. When you pass green daybeacon "25," make sure you do not head straight for the bridge open span. You will need to veer to port and head for daybeacon "26." Don't be fooled by what the smaller boats are doing because it gets extremely shallow if you go straight. It looks as though you are going completely off track because daybeacon "26" is almost to shore on the west side of the river. Leave red daybeacon "26" to starboard, and run parallel to the bridge a short distance until you can turn to port through the center passage span. As you pass under the bridge, to the east is a string of small islands which are bird sanctuaries for thousands of pelicans, egrets and cormorants.

Just past the bridge, the daybeacons change sides; now you will have green to starboard and red to port, until you reach the Gulf of Mexico. Big Marco Pass is too shallow for passage. Capri Pass is marked and tricky, but usually quite passable.

Whether you plan to access the inside route, prior to reaching the Gulf, or you plan to take the outside route, pay special attention to the markers. Be sure to avoid the shoal beyond green daybeacon "11" as you head west.

Marco Island, FL

Looking east over Marco Island. (Not to be used for navigation.) WATERWAY GUIDE PHOTOGRAPHY.

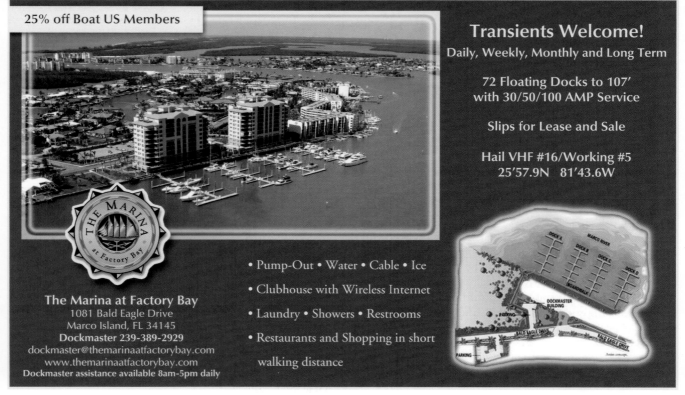

Goodland, Marco Island, FL

MARCO ISLAND		Largest Vessel Accommodated	VHF Channel Monitored	Transient Berths / Total Berths	Approach / Dockside Depth (reported)	Floating Docks	Gas / Diesel	Groceries, Ice, Marine Supplies, Snacks	Repairs: Hull, Engine, Propeller	Lift (tonnage), Crane, Rail	1=110V, 2=220V, B=Both, Max Amps	Laundry, Pool, Showers	Pump-Out Station	Nearby: Grocery Store, Motel, Restaurant
				Dockage				**Supplies**			**Services**			
1. Walker's Coon Key Marina	239-394-2797	60	16	5/40	8/6	F	GD	IMS	HEP	L35	1/30	LS		GMR
2. CALUSA ISLAND YACHT CLUB & MARINA	**239-394-2076**	75	16/5	25/100	5/6	F	GD	IMS	HEP	L50	B/50	LS	P	GMR
3. Morans Barge Marina	239-642-1920	UNDERGOING RENOVATIONS												
4. MARINA AT FACTORY BAY 🖥	**239-389-2929**	107	16	/71	14/14	F		I			B/200	LS	P	GMR
5. SNOOK INN	**239-394-3313**	60		20/20		RESTAURANT DOCKS								GMR
6. Marco River Marina Inc. 🖥	239-394-2502	130	16/09	20/100	7/8	F	GD	GIMS	HEP	L35	B/100	LS	P	GMR
7. MARCO ISLAND MARINA 🖥 📶	**239-642-2531**	110	16/11	15/120	7/7	F		I			B/100	LPS	P	GR
8. The Tarpon Club South	239-394-5643	40	16	/100	4/5	F	G	M			1/50			R
9. The Tarpon Club North	239-394-9666	50	16/09	/100	4.5/5	F	GD	IM			1/50			R
10. Esplanade Marina	239-394-6333	60	16/11	11/77	6/6	F		IMS			B/50	LS	P	GMR

Corresponding chart(s) not to be used for navigation. 🖥 Internet Access 📶 Wireless Internet Access

When you reach quick flashing green "9," you jog slightly to starboard. If you plan to continue into the Gulf, be aware that Coconut Island was totally obliterated by Hurricane Wilma and today is what appears to be a sand bar. It is still on the charts, but don't be fooled. The area is well-marked, so just pay close attention to the markers.

If you plan to proceed to Naples via the inland route, make a turn to starboard around quick flashing green "9"

(north), and move carefully into the Calhoun Channel, where the rules of the road shift back to red to starboard, green to port.

In short, where the Waterway crosses the Big Marco River channel, the markers are somewhat confusing. Pay attention and sort them out for the route you are taking. If you are heading south, or if you are approaching Capri Pass from the south, make sure you chart a course to 16-foot-high flashing red "2" and the 16-foot flashing white light to stay clear of the shoaling near Big Marco Pass.

Outside Passage

NAVIGATION: Use Chart 11429. To reach Marco Island from Everglades City, or farther south outside in the Gulf, you must pass outside the shoals of Cape Romano and well offshore of the cape itself. Charts record isolated depths (mean low water) of as little as 1 and 3 feet as far out as the three-mile limit. Your course should take you at least three to four miles west of Cape Romano if coming from the south or north. Use your GPS and enter a good stand-off waypoint south of the finger shoals. If using radar, Cape Romano will be prominently displayed, as you lay offshore to avoid it.

The shoals extend out from Big Marco Pass and the southern end of Marco Island. As mentioned before, to reach Marco Island, do not take Big Marco Pass; take Capri Pass instead, which is about one mile due east of flashing red "2." As mentioned above, the charted Coconut Island is no longer there, so pay attention when you get to red day-beacon "6" and continue into the pass with caution. There is plenty of room, but it does get busy on weekends.

There are some "mystery towers" out in the Gulf of Mexico. Twenty years or so ago, when they first went in, no one seemed to know what they were for, including the United States Coast Guard. "Towers? What towers?" People who thought they knew all about unwanted government intrusion into personal business were sure the towers were put there to keep track of drug smugglers. That wasn't the case.

Marco Island, FL

MARCO ISLAND AREA, CHART 11430

The towers in the lower Gulf, between Cape Romano and the Dry Tortugas, and in the upper Gulf near Apalachicola are what are called air combat information towers. Military pilots train doing practice dogfights high up in the heavens in the general area of the towers. The planes carry transponders, and the signals from the planes are recorded by the towers and sent back to a central location. As the planes "fight," their airspeed, altitude and attitude are constantly monitored. Then, when the pilots get back to base, they can replay the dogfight on a TV screen to see how the mission went and where they can improve—your tax dollars at work.

The only thing that may startle you if you are near these towers is that sometimes the jets break the sound barrier and you will get a sonic boom. It sounds like an artillery shell going off down the block with a crack sharp enough to make you jump every time.

Dockage: If you are looking for quiet surroundings, Marco Island Marina, on the south side next to the Marco Island-Bear Point Bridge, is a good spot. The entrance, approximately 3 miles from Capri Pass, past the stanchion of power lines, is well-marked and has 8-foot approach depths. Amenities include showers, an excellent slip-side pump-out facility, water, shore power (30- and 50-amp), cable TV and a guest card for the full-service restaurant at the adjacent yacht club. From the facility, a walk of less than a mile leads to a Publix, a Walgreen's Pharmacy and other shopping amenities.

The Marina at Factory Bay is the closest and deepest marina upon entering Capri Pass heading up the Big Marco River past Collier Bay. Bear to starboard past flashing red "14" and the Snook Inn Restaurant; the Marina at Factory Bay is just around the corner. Hail the dockmaster for assistance tying up and to arrange a long-term or transient stay at comfortable floating slips seven days a week. The marina has pump-out service, shore power, water and cable TV on the docks. Showers/restrooms, a laundry and wireless Internet are available at the shoreside clubhouse. Restaurants and stores are within walking distance.

Marco River Marina is close by in the southwestern corner of Factory Bay, and may be hailed on VHF Channel 16 for reservations and directions. The Snook Inn, a landmark for more than 25 years, offers dockage for patrons and waterfront dining inside or out at the tiki bar. You can find it just west of the Marina at Factory Bay.

Anchorage: Protected anchorages and good holding are available in both Smokehouse Bay and Factory Bay. Smokehouse Bay is tricky to get into, but once inside, it is well-protected (360 degrees). When entering the channel, just past daybeacon "12," turn to starboard and enter a shallow, but well-marked pass into Smokehouse Bay. Once you work your way into the channel, proceed to daybeacon "7" and then enter the anchorage. There is 10 feet of water and very good holding. Grocery shopping is easily accessed by going through the low bridge at the end of the anchorage, then to port to the convenient dinghy dock.

Factory Bay also has good holding with 10 to 12 feet of water. A sand bar splits the bay, but there is plenty of water around the edge. Anchor in the southeast side by red daybeacons "2" and "4." Enjoy a pleasant anchorage.

GOIN' ASHORE:
MARCO ISLAND, FL

The earliest known settlers of Marco Island arrived sometime around 1500 B.C. The Calusa Indians, followed by the Spanish and, later, the Seminole Indians, called this area home. Today, Marco Island is a destination resort of the first magnitude. It is the largest and northernmost of the Ten Thousand Islands, and offers both land and sea travelers a variety of possibilities for rest, recreation and re-provisioning.

Purchasing his first tract of land in the early 1920s, Barron Collier began a grand development plan, which included relocating all the existing pioneer homes to Goodland so they would not interfere with his extensive undertaking. He was unsuccessful, however, in his attempt to purchase land from an unrelated family headed by William Collier. William Collier's former holdings comprise the old island buildings that help Marco Island retain its homestead character. They include the Old Marco Inn and several homes that now house restaurants.

In 1964, the heirs of Barron Collier sold their Marco Island holdings to the Deltona development company, which actively pursued retirees and vacationers. For easier access, a toll bridge was built linking the north end of the island to the mainland. At that time, the beachside Voyager Inn (now part of Marriott's Marco Island resort) was the only building on the beach. During

Marco Island, FL

the development of Marco Island by the Deltona Corporation, which was owned by the Mackle Brothers, the daughter of one of the brothers, Barbara Mackle, was kidnapped in suburban Atlanta, where she was a student at Emory University. The kidnappers forced her into their car at gunpoint and took her to a rural area where they buried her in a fiberglass box equipped with an air pump, ventilation pipes, water laced with sedatives and a light. She was "buried alive" for 83 hours. Her father, Robert Mackle, paid a $500,000 ransom, and the kidnappers told him where to find his daughter, who was rescued alive. The kidnappers were later caught.

Today, Marco Island offers hotels, condominiums, apartments, homes, a full range of services and dozens of restaurants and shops. The subtropical climate, natural beauty and easy Gulf access attract growing numbers of visitors.

ADDITIONAL RESOURCES

■ Marco Island Area Chamber of Commerce,
www.marcoislandchamber.org

⚑ **NEARBY GOLF COURSES**
Hideaway Beach Golf Course, 250 South Beach Drive, Marco Island, Florida 34145, 239-394-5555
www.hideawaybeachclub.org

℞ **NEARBY MEDICAL FACILITIES**
Marco Healthcare Center, 40 Heathwood Drive, Marco Island, FL 34145, 239-394-8234

■ MARCO ISLAND TO NAPLES

NAVIGATION: Use Chart 11430. If you choose to go outside for this 8.2-mile-long stretch, it is a fairly straightforward passage along the face of Marco Island to the well-marked, but slightly tricky channel entrance to Gordon Pass.

A rock jetty on the south side of Gordon Pass extends 100 yards into the Gulf of Mexico. Favor the south side of the channel along the jetty. With onshore winds and outgoing tide, it can be challenging for slow or underpowered vessels. Once inside, do not run green daybeacons "7" to "7A" as a straight line. Take it wide to the right to avoid the shoal off the northern spit (it is visible at low tide).

Hamilton Harbor fuel dock has gas and diesel east of flashing red "20." Continuing upriver, Naples City Dock has a fuel dock with gas, diesel and pump-out service. Naples Boat Club, at red daybeacon "40," has an 8 a.m. to 5 p.m. full-service fuel dock with complimentary pump-out service for anyone who needs it. Naples Boat Club also offers shore power, repairs and laundry and shower facilities.

The Inside Route

NAVIGATION: Use Chart 11430. From Capri Pass to just past Little Marco Island on the ICW route, the channel shown on the chart bears the following warning: "Improved channels shown by broken lines are subject to shoaling, particularly at the edges." There are spots, particularly at daybeacon "30A," where the water gets very shallow. Pay strict attention to the channels and don't

Naples, FL

NAPLES		Largest Vessel Accommodated	VHF Channel Monitored	Transient Berths / Total Berths	Approach / Dockside Depth (reported)	Floating Docks	Groceries, Ice, Marine Supplies, Snacks	Gas / Diesel	Repairs: Hull, Engine, Propeller	Lift (tonnage), Crane, Rail	1=110V, 2=220V, B=Both, Max Amps	Laundry, Pool, Showers	Pump-Out Station	Nearby: Grocery Store, Motel, Restaurant
				Dockage			Supplies		Services					
1. Hamilton Harbor Yacht Club	239-775-0506	60	16	3/36	7/7	F	GD	IS			B/50	S	P	R
2. Southpointe Marina at Windstar	239-774-0518	70	16/12	/72	5/5									
3. Naples Yacht Club	239-262-7301	130	16	4/92	8/6	F	GD	I			B/50	PS	P	GMR
4. Naples City Dock	239-213-3070	120	16	11/84	9/9		GD	IS			B/100	LS	P	GMR
5. Olde Naples Seaport	239-643-0042	100	16	10/30	8/7	F		I	HEP		B/50	LS	P	GMR
6. Naples Boat Club	239-263-2774	110	16	20/47	8/8	F	GD	IMS	HEP	L70	B/100	LPS	P	GMR
7. Marine Max of SW FL LLC	239-262-1000	65	16		6/6			M	HEP	L70	B/50			MR
8. Brookside Marina	239-774-3200	35	16	3/110	4/4	F	G	IMS	HEP		B/50			
9. The Marina at Naples Bay Resort	239-530-5134	90	16	/97	5.5/5.5	F	GD	IMS			B/70	LPS	P	GMR
10. Naples Sailing & Yacht Club	239-774-0424	65	16	8/80	4/4	F		I			B/50	PS		MR

Corresponding chart(s) not to be used for navigation. ⌨ Internet Access (WIFI) Wireless Internet Access

stray. This is a very pretty pass and shouldn't be missed if your draft allows.

About halfway along (red daybeacon "46"), you pass Rookery Bay, a major wildlife sanctuary, and will likely encounter local fishing boats. Anchorages, while severely restricted because of the shoal sides, are available in several spots along the route, including Rookery Channel.

Whether you are returning from a trip south or just starting out, Naples is a good place to pick up or dis-charge crew. The airport (or a rental car) is a quick cab ride away.

Dockage: Dock space is usually available at Naples' numerous marinas, though local marina operators recommend calling ahead for slip or mooring reservations, particularly during the peak periods (holidays and weekends). Hamilton Harbor, convenient to Gordon Pass, is the first facility to starboard as you turn north for Naples. They offer some transient slips, fuel, showers and pump-out facilities.

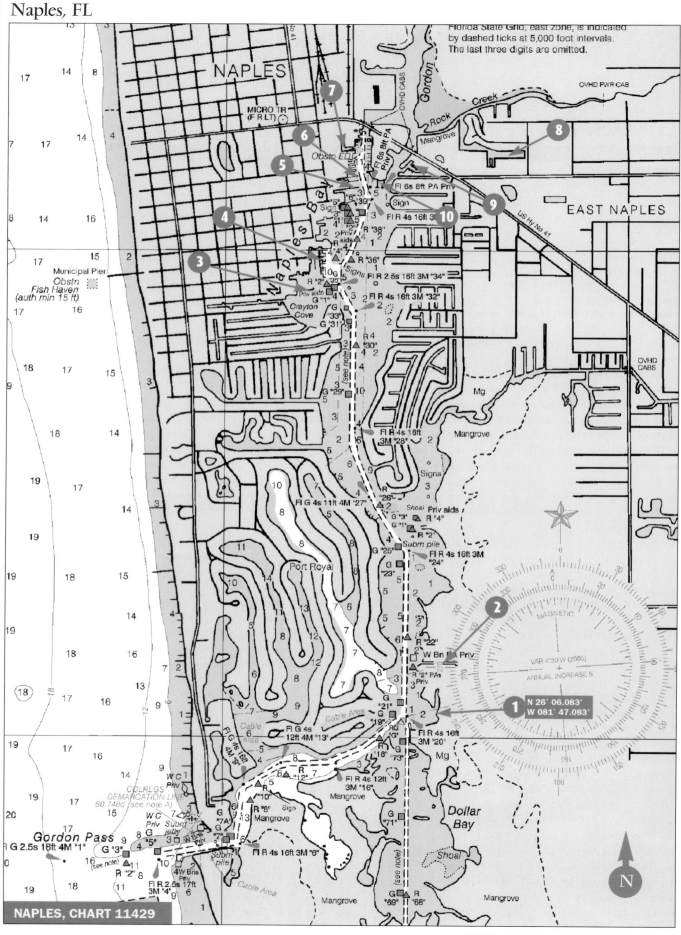

Florida State Grid, east zone, is indicated by dashed ticks at 5,000 foot intervals. The last three digits are omitted.

NAPLES

EAST NAPLES

Municipal Pier
Obstn
Fish Haven
(auth min 15 ft)

Crayton Cove

Port Royal

Gordon Pass

Dollar Bay

NAPLES, CHART 11429

Looking north over Gordon Pass. (Not to be used for navigation.) Photo Courtesy of Sam Harris.

Naples City Dock, beginning just to the west of green daybeacon "35" and extending to the north, has 79 slips. In 2010, the mooring balls, controlled by the Naples City Dock, are once again open and usable. There are a total of 12 moorings in two well-protected coves. Rental of the moorings includes use of a bathhouse and laundry facilities. The Dock Restaurant offers casual, open-air dining overlooking the harbor.

If you continue north on the Gordon River (beware of the shoal 200 feet northwest of red daybeacon "36"), the next marina on the west bank is Olde Naples Seaport, now a private "dockominium." When owners are away, the dockmaster rents slips to last-minute transients.

Naples Boat Club, next door to Olde Naples Seaport, is an exceptional facility that welcomes transients to its full-service marina, with a fuel dock in a convenient location on Naples Bay at red daybeacon "40." Naples Boat Club also offers complimentary pump-out service.

The marina at Naples Bay Resort offers dockage, gas and diesel, a laundry, pool, showers and a restaurant. Both the Naples Sailing and Yacht Club and the Naples Yacht Club offer reciprocity to members of other recognized yacht clubs and may have transient space available.

Anchorage: Anchorage areas abound, but you will need to be careful where you go off the marked channel, as it becomes very shallow. After entering Gordon Pass, turn north between red daybeacons "10" and "12." A charted bar with 4-foot depths crosses the entrance. At the first canal to starboard enter and anchor in a well-protected cove in 9-foot depths amongst very beautiful homes. A second option is to proceed into Gordon Pass to green daybeacon "21," turn to port, and then again to port into the first cove. You will be well-protected from all sides in 7-foot depths.

GOIN' ASHORE: **NAPLES, FL**

The Naples Trolley, which stops throughout Old Naples, picks up passengers at its terminal several blocks away from both the Naples City Dock and the Naples Boat Club on Sixth Avenue. On 12th street, the Naples Ships Store not only has a broad selection of nautical gift ideas, but also a large inventory of marine hardware and supplies. In the same strip of stores, Napoli on the Bay has pizza and espresso (10:30 a.m. to 10 p.m.), and a gourmet store that specializes in citrus shipping. Nearby are a beauty salon, delicatessen, Mermaids at the Cove (serving breakfast and lunch, opens at 8 a.m.), an upscale restaurant and gift and clothing stores. Wynn's Market, located on Tamiami Trail N (closed on Sundays), is about 1.4 miles away.

On the west end of Sixth Avenue South is Tin City, a funky waterside shopping spot that occupies an old oyster-processing plant. It includes 40 shops, two restaurants (one, CJ's Boardwalk Bar & Grill, serves a memorable sautéed calamari salad) and a café.

Public tennis courts are four blocks away in Cambier Park. The Naples Beach Club provides a courtesy van for golfers who want to play its 18-hole course overlooking the Gulf of Mexico.

West Marine can be reached by dinghy. Pass under the eastern highway bridge and follow Rock Creek to the first canal on the right. Ask Brookside Marina (located in front of the West Marine store) for permission to tie up while you shop.

If you are having electronics problems, you will find speedy turnaround service at Naples Marine Electronics in Village Plaza on Davis Boulevard. While waiting for your gear to be repaired, check out the used book options at the Book Exchange located in the same plaza. Or unpack your golf clubs and play a round. Known as the "Golf Capital of the World," the Naples/Marco Island area boasts more than 53 courses.

Wiggins Pass, Naples. (Not to be used for navigation.) Photo Courtesy of Sam Harris.

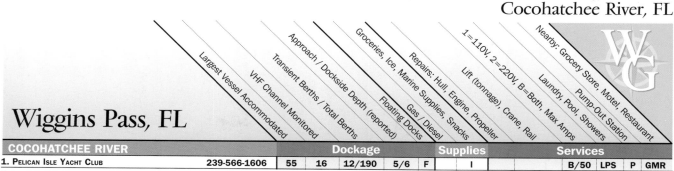

Wiggins Pass, FL

	Largest Vessel Accommodated	VHF Channel Monitored	Transient Berths / Total Berths	Approach / Dockside Depth (reported)	Floating Docks	Groceries, Ice, Marine Supplies, Snacks	Gas / Diesel	Repairs: Hull, Engine, Propeller	Lift (tonnage), Crane, Rail	1=110V, 2=220V, B=Both, Max Amps	Laundry, Pool, Showers	Pump-Out Station	Nearby: Grocery Store, Motel, Restaurant
COCOHATCHEE RIVER				**Dockage**				**Supplies**			**Services**		
1. PELICAN ISLE YACHT CLUB 239-566-1606	55	16	12/190	5/6	F			I		B/50	LPS	P	GMR

Corresponding chart(s) not to be used for navigation. ☐ Internet Access 📶 Wireless Internet Access

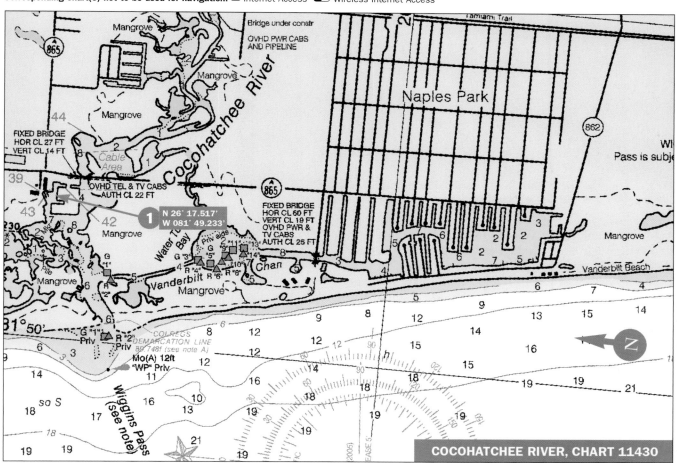

COCOHATCHEE RIVER, CHART 11430

■ GORDON PASS TO FORT MYERS BEACH

NAVIGATION: Use Charts 11430 and 11427. There is no inside route between Naples and Fort Myers Beach, so to reach Fort Myers Beach, you must either exit Gordon Pass or continue offshore if that is how you came from Marco Island. Plan to stay about a couple of miles off the beach. In good weather, which locals say is almost always the case, the Gulf of Mexico is calm and easy to transit. In winter months, when the winds are often out of the northwest or north, it can get ugly. If the winds are northwest at more than 12 knots, you may want to tarry a while in Naples.

Judge your own vessel's capabilities, as winter winds commonly range from 10 to 15 or even 20 knots, with higher gusts. Such winds raise seas, which may be no problem heading south with following seas, but can make for a very wet ride heading north. Pick your weather correctly and it should be no problem. Any time a frontal system passes through, no matter what time of year, you can expect rough ride on this leg.

About 5.7 miles north of Gordon Pass, narrow Doctors Pass has, at times, served as a harbor of refuge. The area is marked and frequently dredged. Favor the center of Doctors Pass. Local knowledge from area boaters might be helpful, but in any case, there are no services for transients in Outer Doctors Bay or beyond.

Dockage: Seven and a half miles farther north, Wiggins Pass admits vessels drawing 4 feet or less. Daybeacons lead from Wiggins Pass for a distance of just under a half-mile into the Cocohatchee River. Once through Wiggins

Big Carlos Pass, FL

Looking west over Big Carlos Pass. (Not to be used for navigation.) Photo Courtesy of Sam Harris.

Pass, controlling channel depths to the marina are 4 to 5 feet. Pelican Isle Yacht Club, located just inside Wiggins Pass, offers all amenities and transient dockage. Without local knowledge of the privately maintained markers beyond red daybeacon "12," it is best to call ahead for instructions on VHF Channel 16.

If you are hugging the coastline about a mile offshore, note where the shoal projects out on the north side of Big Carlos Pass. If you are trying to reach Estero Bay and Fort Myers Beach, you can enter here if you know the present location of the channel, or can find a lead-in boat to follow. Although charts indicate controlling depths of 4 to 6 feet, the channel reportedly carries about 8 feet of water. Although constantly shifting, it reportedly follows the contour of Lovers Key on approach from the south. It is best to call ahead to nearby Fish Tale Marina or Estero Bay Boat Tours (VHF Channel 79) for an update on directions and controlling depths.

Estero Bay

NAVIGATION: Use Chart 11427. Once inside the Big Carlos Pass Bascule Bridge (23-foot closed vertical clearance, closed from 7 p.m. to 8 a.m. daily), daybeacons guide your passage either north or south through the natural and historic beauties of Estero Bay.

Controlling depths in the marked channel south of Big Carlos Pass to New Pass are reported to be 4 feet at mean low water with a 2.5-foot tidal range. New Pass is unmarked and impassable to the Gulf of Mexico. Shoal markers warn of 2-foot mean low water depths. Keep a close watch for the numerous pots set in these waters, each attached by a warp to a trap set for the Atlantic blue crab.

GOIN' ASHORE:
ESTERO BAY, FL

Established as Florida's first aquatic preserve in 1963, Estero Bay's 12.5-mile-long estuary, rookery and fisherman's paradise is protected from further development. American bald eagles, brown and white pelicans, American oyster catchers, black skimmers, anhinga "water turkeys," ibises, great blue herons, egrets, double-crested cormorants and a large variety of terns and gulls are all regulars here. It is a rare occasion when a dinghy exploration (or guided tour) will not spot at least one of Estero Bay's resident dolphin pods and, during the summer months at low water, a manatee or two. Black mullet leap from these waters continuously while many other varieties of fish (snook, redfish, sheepshead, mackerel and snapper) tend to their business less ostentatiously below.

Historically, this area was the geographic center of the Calusa Indian tribe, which lived here in harmony with this aquatic environment for some 2,000 years. The Calusas developed a thriving civilization of more than 100,000 people by building up their land for residence and worship by the bucketful—with shells gathered from "oyster bars," laboriously piled on protective mounds reaching as high as 60 feet. After marauding Spanish explorers and European diseases took their toll, however, nothing was left of them save their impressive shell mounds. The largest and highest is Mound Key (now a state park), approximately two miles northeast of Big Carlos Pass and an easy dinghy ride from suitable anchorage (in 7- to 9-foot depths) on the back side of Black Island.

ADDITIONAL RESOURCES

■ Estero Bay Preserve State Park, 239-992-0311
www.floridastateparks.org/esterobay

Looking southeast over Matanzas Pass to Fort Myers Beach on Estero Island to the right. (Not to be used for navigation.)

■ BIG CARLOS PASS TO FORT MYERS BEACH

Two routes to Fort Myers Beach are the Inside Passage, if you have already been visiting Estero Bay, or the Outside Passage up the Gulf from Big Carlos Pass.

Inside Passage

NAVIGATION: Use Chart 11427. Once you are past the shoals on entering Big Carlos Pass, the inside route north to Fort Myers Beach is well-marked from Big Carlos Pass along the northeast side of Estero Island to Matanzas Pass and the north side of Fort Myers Beach. The Fish Tale Marina is located about a mile north of the bascule bridge (23-foot closed vertical clearance) and at the end of the wide canal leading west from green daybeacon "59."

From there, it is a matter of carefully watching the many markers blazing the trail to Matanzas Pass and the facilities along the northern shore of Fort Myers Beach.

Outside Passage

NAVIGATION: Use Chart 11427. From Big Carlos Pass, chart a course for the Morse (A) 16-foot-high marker "SC." From that point, you should be able to pick out 16-foot flashing red "2" approximately one mile to the north-northwest. Be careful: Shoals move around here a bit, but from that point, you should be able to pick out the well-marked entrance channel leading off from San Carlos Bay into Matanzas Pass, making a 90-degree turn behind the northwestern hook of Estero Island.

Currents are sometimes swift, depending on the tide, and an endless stream of fishing boats of all sizes utilize the channel that runs between Estero Island and San Carlos Island.

Dockage: Heading south after entering Matanzas Pass, the first marina you will find is Moss Marine's well-lighted complex of white buildings, highly visible to starboard, adjacent to daybeacon "17." Transient berths are available, but make advance reservations, particularly during the winter months. Transients enjoy full amenities, such as showers, mobile pump-out, a ship's store, laundry, repair services, cable television and phone hook-up with voicemail.

A large casino boat berths here and marina guests that choose to cruise pay only the departure fee. Public access to the Gulf beach, a fishing pier and a variety of restaurants—predominantly outdoor sidewalk tables, with both fast food and more sturdy fare such as Greek saganaki and grilled octopus—are within walking distance.

Directly opposite Moss Marine, the Fort Myers Beach Marina is likely to have slips available for visitors. Next door, by the Bridge Restaurant, Gulfstar Marine also has transient slips. Just to the south, Gulf Marine has a 150-ton lift, on-site prop shop, on-site welding and fabrication and a large variety of full service repairs and refit services. Olsen Marine Service next door has a 37-ton lift and a variety of marine service and repair capabilities.

At the far end of the harbor (beyond the shrimp fleet) is Salty Sam's Marina, where you can get gas and diesel fuel or tie up for a bite at the Parrot Key Caribbean Grill. A short distance up the northern channel, Hurricane Bay Marine offers full-service repairs.

Fort Myers Beach also has 70 mooring balls available for boats up to 60 feet in length. Matanzas Inn Marina manages the mooring field for the city. Call the harbormaster at 239-463-9258 for an assignment and current prices.

Fill your propane tank at Bal Gas, east of the bridge on the north side near the shrimper fleet. If you seek

Fort Myers Beach, FL

FORT MYERS BEACH		Largest Vessel Accommodated	VHF Channel Monitored	Transient Berths / Total Berths	Approach / Dockside Depth (reported)	Floating Docks	Gas / Diesel	Groceries, Ice, Marine Supplies, Snacks	Repairs: Hull, Engine, Propeller	Lift (tonnage), Crane, Rail	1=110V, 2=220V, B=Both, Max Amps	Laundry, Pool, Showers	Pump-Out Station	Nearby: Grocery Store, Motel, Restaurant
		Dockage					**Supplies**		**Services**					
1. Pink Shell Beach Resort & Spa	239-463-8633	80	16/71	15/	15/5			IS			120	P		GMR
2. Moss Marine 🖥 WiFi	**239-765-6677**	**170**	**16**	**35/40**	**10/8**		GD	IMS			B/50	LS	P	GMR
3. Matanzas Inn Marina 🖥	800-462-9258	50		16/16	12/8							LS		MR
4. Ft. Myers Beach Marina 🖥	239-463-9552	45	16/07	/27	17/8		GD	IM	EP		B/50	LPS	P	GMR
5. Olsen Marine Service Inc.	**239-463-6750**	**55**	**16**		**6/6**			M	HEP	L37,C	B/50	S		GMR
6. Gulf Marine Ways & Supply	239-463-6166	130		/2	10/10			M	HEP	L150,C	B/50			GMR
7. Salty Sam's Marina WiFi	239-463-7333	225	16	50/130	14/12	F	GD	IMS	HEP	L13	B/50	LS	P	GMR
8. Fish Tale Marina	239-463-3600	60	16/09	/100	4/8	F	G	IMS	HEP	L15	B/50	LS	P	GMR
9. Santa Maria Resort	239-765-6700	36		28/40	6/5						1/30			GMR
10. Waterside at Bay Beach WiFi	239-765-6400	60		/42	10/8	F					1/50	PS	P	GMR

Corresponding chart(s) not to be used for navigation. 🖥 Internet Access WiFi Wireless Internet Access

music in an outdoor setting, dinghy over to the Bridge Restaurant. Sunday evenings you will find young and wish-they-were-young bopping together to a local reggae band.

Because of the amenities and pleasant ambience, the relatively spacious harbor at Fort Myers Beach has become home to a fair number of liveaboards. Beyond the facilities immediately surrounding the harbor, a drive several miles west of the bridge (on San Carlos Boulevard) will take you to major shopping, re-provisioning and resupply opportunities, including two large supermarkets, the Book Center (for an outstanding collection of well-organized new and used books), a massive Ace Hardware and restaurants to suit almost any culinary fancy. During "the season," the red trolleys run and facilitate exploring and shopping.

Bonita Bills, on the east side of the harbor and south of the bridge, is a favorite restaurant/bar with good food and a free dinghy dock and entertainment. When the shrimp boat is docked at their T-Dock, take advantage of buying fresh shrimp, at reasonable prices, right from the boat.

Cruising Options

Fort Myers Beach is a pivotal location for vessels making passages farther north up the west coast of Florida or south along the coast to Flamingo and the Keys. Or you can pick up the across-Florida Okeechobee Waterway and cruise all the way to its east coast terminus at the ICW in Stuart. This is a genuine nautical crossroads. The city of Fort Myers is included in our coverage of the Okeechobee Waterway, which connects Florida's east and west coasts. ∎

Fort Myers Beach, FL

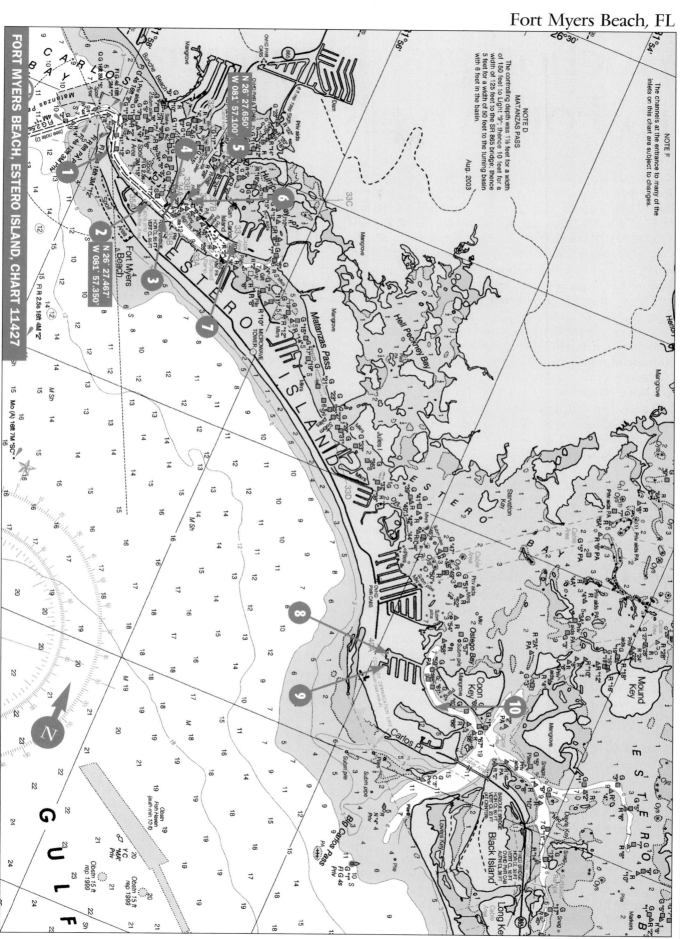

FORT MYERS BEACH, FL

FORT MYERS BEACH, ESTERO ISLAND, CHART 11427

NOTE F
The channels at the entrance to many of the inlets on this chart are subject to changes.

NOTE D
MATANZAS PASS
The controlling depth was 1½ feet for a width of 150 feet to Light "9"; thence 10 feet for a width of 125 feet to the SR 865 bridge; thence 5 feet for a width of 50 feet to the turning basin with 6 feet in the basin.
Aug. 2003

N 26° 27.650'
W 081° 57.100'

N 26° 27.467'
W 081° 57.350'

Anchorages: Flamingo to Fort Myers Beach

Outside Flamingo Basin. Prior to the hurricane damage, there was a fine anchorage area just outside Flamingo Basin. We suggest calling either Everglades National Park (305-242-7700) or the Flamingo Marina itself (239-695-3101) to determine current status. The approach and anchoring area provides a minimum of 4 feet. Anchor north of red "18" between the channel and bulkhead, but be sure not to get too close to the channel. The holding is good in mud, but there is only limited space available. This anchorage is really just for those who are awaiting high tide to enter the park's marina basin. The area is well-protected except from the south, but bugs can be a problem in-season.

Between Middle Cape and East Cape. The anchorage offers 10 feet, but depths decrease as you approach the beach. Holding is good in hard sand. Protection is good from the north and northeast only. Watch out for bugs during offshore winds.

Little Shark River. Drop the hook in the bend north of red "4." You will find 7 feet in the approach and 10 feet in the anchorage. Holding is good in soft to hard mud, and protection is good in practically all winds. It can be buggy on warm, quiet nights.

Note: There are numerous protected and interesting anchorages up the Little Shark River. Currents can be strong, but holding is generally good. Protection is good in practically all winds, but bugs can be a problem during calm periods.

Gullivan Bay Area. This area to the east of Cape Romano is a gunkholer's paradise. To the west of Panther Key and in Dismal Key Pass are two anchorages that provide plenty of quiet and solitude. Watch the tidal flow, and anchor accordingly.

Indian Key Pass Area. This is located east up Russell Pass past marker "7." There is 7 feet in the approach and 8-plus feet in the anchoring area. The holding is good, but there are some shell banks. Protection is generally good in all wind directions. Currents are an issue so consider two anchors.

Keewaydin Island Area/Rookery Channel. You will find 7 feet in the approach and 5 feet in the anchorage area. Holding is good in a hard bottom, but currents can be fairly strong. Protection is generally good in all wind directions. Watch out for bugs during warm, calm periods. Abeam of red "44," tie up the dinghy securely at the beach, being aware of the wakes of passing boats. From here, you can walk a path to good shelling and beachcombing.

Gordon Pass Area. This spot is located off the channel north of marker "12." Look for 5-plus feet in the approach and 8-plus feet in the anchorage. Currents can be strong. Holding is good in sand and mud. Protection is generally good in all wind directions. After turning north into the pass, favor the western side and then take the third and most eastern stream. It is surrounded by houses and offers a well-protected anchorage in 8 to 10 feet of water. Do not anchor in the charted cable area.

Marco Island. Go up the Big Marco River to Factory Bay, northeast of Marco River Marina. You will find good holding in 6 to 8 feet of water. Get permission to leave your dinghy at the marina, and visit the big marine store, grocery store, drugstore, hardware store and restaurants nearby. WARNING: The marina locks its gate in the evening. Or anchor in Smokehouse Bay for 360 degree protection and easy access to shopping.

Fort Myers Beach. Fort Myers Beach has 70 mooring balls available for boats up to 60 feet in length. Matanzas Inn Marina manages the mooring field for the city. Call the harbormaster at 239-463-9258 for an assignment. There is limited room to anchor outside of the mooring field.

Anchorages. Photo Courtesy of Susan Landry.

Bridges/Distances
(From Okeechobee Waterway Mile 0)

LOCATION	MILES	CLEARANCE
St. Lucie / ICW Int.	0	
Stuart: Evans Crary Sr. Bridge (A1A)	3.4	65
New Roosevelt (U.S. 1) Bridge	7.3	65
FEC Railroad Bridge	7.4	7
Old Roosevelt Bridge	7.4	14
Palm City Bridge (SR 714)	9.5	55
I-95 Fixed Bridge	14	56
Florida Turnpike Fixed Bridge	14.5	55
St. Lucie Lock	15.1	**
SR 76A Fixed Bridge	17.1	55
Indiantown Fixed Bridge (SR 710)	28.1	54
Indiantown Railroad Bridge	28.5	*7
Port Mayaca: RR Lift Bridge	38	
—Down		7
—Raised		49
U.S. 98 & U.S. 411 Fixed Bridge	38.8	55
Port Mayaca Lock	39	**
Lake Okeechobee	39	
Rim Route: Pahokee	50.6	
Torry Island Bridge (SR717)	61	**11
Direct Route: Clewiston	64	
Rim Route: Belle Glade	65	
Rim Route: Clewiston	75.7	
Moore Haven Lock	78	**
Moore Haven RR Bridge	78.3	5
U.S. 27 Fixed Bridge	78.5	55
Ortona Lock	93.5	
La Belle (SR 29) Bridge	102.9	*28
Fort Denaud Bridge	108.2	9

Bridges/Distances
(From Okeechobee Waterway Mile 0)

LOCATION	MILES	CLEARANCE
Alva Bridge	116	23
W.P. Franklin Lock	121.4	**
Olga (SR 31) Wilson Pigott Bridge	126.2	27
I-75 Fixed Bridge	128.9	55
Beautiful Island RR Bridge	129.9	5
Fort Myers: Edison Twin Brs.	134.5	56
Caloosahatchee Fixed Bridge	135	55
Mid Point Memorial Fixed Bridge	138.6	55
Cape Coral Twin Fixed Bridge	142	55
Gulf Intracoastal Waterway Mile 0	148.9	
Punta Rassa (Sanibel Causeway) "A"	151	70

Bridge clearance is vertical, closed, in feet.
All bridges bascule or swing type unless noted.

* Restricted openings   ** Closed at night

Cape Canaveral

Melbourne

Atlantic Ocean

Lake Kissimmee

95

1

Fort Pierce

Kissimmee R.

Kissimmee Waterway

Okeechobee

Stuart

MILE 0

ST. LUCIE
LOCK

MILE 15

Lake
Istokpoga

Indiantown

MILE 40

St. Lucie Canal

PORT MAYACA
LOCK

Port Mayaca

Lake Okeechobee

MILE 55

W. Palm Beach

Pahokee

MOORE HAVEN
LOCK

MILE 78

MILE 65

Clewiston

Belle Glade

Lake Worth

Lake
Harbor

1

Punta Gorda

75

Caloosahatchee R.

MILE 103

ORTONA
LOCK

Olga

LaBelle

MILE 121

Alva

FRANKLIN
LOCK

Fort
Myers

MILE 144

Cape
Coral

Fort Myers Beach

Captiva Island

Pine I. Sd.

Charlotte Hbr.

GIWW MILE 0

Sanibel Island

Boca Raton

Fort Lauderdale

95

75

1

Gulf of Mexico

DOZIER'S
WATERWAY
GUIDE
THE CRUISING AUTHORITY
WWW.WATERWAYGUIDE.COM

Okeechobee Waterway

CHARTS 11427, 11428

The Okeechobee Waterway is considered by many to be the dividing line between Central Florida and South Florida. When traveling from the north, this is where you will begin to see greater changes in the climate and vegetation, and even in the people—more "Northerners," either seasonal "snowbirds" or full-time transplants, and a decided increase in the Hispanic culture.

Opened in 1937, the Waterway offers a chance to see rural Florida, with small towns much as they were early in the last century. The scenery varies as the passage progresses from east to west from river to canal, to lake, to canal, and back to river again. On the Okeechobee Waterway, ranches and big commercial farms alternate with moss-hung wilderness, while bustling boomtowns coexist alongside sleepy villages that popped up long before Miami was built. With its backwaters and "bywaters," its islands and coves, and its flora and fauna, the Caloosahatchee River was once the only way to get from the Gulf of Mexico to Central Florida, via small steamers and freighters. Some still consider the Caloosahatchee (76.6 miles) the most scenic part of the Okeechobee Waterway, thanks to the old river's off-channel oxbows. Small cruise ships now occasionally make the trip.

For the boater, the Okeechobee Waterway and Lake Okeechobee provide quite a transition from the pace of busy coastal cities to the tranquility of Florida's heartland. The Waterway is also a tremendously efficient route from the east coast to the west coast of Florida, the only alternative being the long trek down around the Keys and up across Florida Bay, or vice versa. The Okeechobee Waterway is 154 or 165 statute miles (134 or 144 nautical miles), from the Atlantic Ocean to the Gulf of Mexico, depending on whether you take Route 1 across Lake Okeechobee (8.6-foot depths in spring 2010) or the Rim Route (6.0-foot depths in spring 2010; use at your own risk because of debris) along the lake's southern shore. The Waterway can be divided into three distinct sections:

1. From Mile Zero (the intersection of the Okeechobee Waterway and the Atlantic ICW at St. Lucie Inlet) down the South Fork of the St. Lucie River to the St. Lucie Canal to Lake Okeechobee.
2. Lake Okeechobee itself (either the "Open-Water Route" directly across the lake, or the "Rim Route" along the lake's southern shore).
3. From Clewiston through the Caloosahatchee Canal and down the Caloosahatchee River to the end of the Okeechobee Waterway in San Carlos Bay, at Mile Zero of the Gulf Intracoastal Waterway (GIWW) heading north.

On Lake Okeechobee, a skipper has the choice of t[wo] routes for crossing. The first, Route 1, is an open-wa[ter] crossing (39 statute, 34 nautical miles, 8.6-foot controlli[ng] depths at publication), and the second, Route 2 which [is] also referred to as the Rim Route (50 statute, 44 nau[ti]cal miles, 6.0-foot depths at publication; use at your o[wn] risk), follows the shoreline south from Port Mayaca, on [the] eastern shore, before entering the tree-protected rim ca[nal] and running past Clewiston to Moore Haven.

Cruising Characteristics

Chart 11428 covers the area from the intersection with [the] Atlantic ICW to Fort Myers, and Chart 11427 contin[ues] down the Caloosahatchee River to the Gulf Intracoas[tal] Waterway (GIWW) and the Gulf of Mexico. From t[his] point, cruisers have the option of moving north on [the] GIWW to the Sun Coast, outside in the Gulf to the [Big] Bend or the Panhandle, or south to southwest Florida a[nd] the Keys.

Caution: Much of Chart 11428 is at a scale of 1:80,0[00;] this is different from the charts adjoining at either e[nd,] 11472 and 11427, both at 1:40,000, the usual Waterw[ay] scale. Chart 11428 has two insets at its eastern end and o[ne] where it reaches Lake Okeechobee, plus an extension at [the] western end—all of these are at various larger scales.

Navigating Locks

The water level in Lake Okeechobee is higher than a[ny]where on the Atlantic Ocean or Gulf ICW. Whether y[ou] are headed east or west, you ascend through the locks [to] Lake Okeechobee, and then descend after you leave. [The] Waterway has five modern, spacious and well-hand[led] locks and more than 20 bridges, ranging from electron[ically] controlled to hand-operated. Normally, locks oper[ate] between 6 a.m. and 9:30 p.m., but check ahead for curr[ent] lock-through schedules.

Locking through is simple compared to procedu[res] necessary in the northeastern U.S. canal systems. L[ock] personnel furnish all necessary lines, and regular fend[ers] will suffice when locking through. Allow approxima[tely] 15 minutes once inside a lock. The Okeechobee Waterw[ay] locks are easier to transit when you are the only b[oat] locking through, and the lock attendant will give you [the] windward dock line first when winds are strong. Gu[sty] winds can set up a surge in the locks, so use caution. [The] attendant also might warn you that you could be lock[ing] through with a manatee or an alligator. Lockmasters [on] the Okeechobee are usually helpful and courteous.

Note: The U.S. Army Corps of Engineers requires boat operators to turn off radar units during lockage to avoid exposing lock personnel to possible radiation risks. It is recommended, however, that engines be left running.

When you reach the dolphins and the sign ARRIVAL POINT before each lock, contact the lockmaster on **VHF Channel 13**. Give your vessel's name and direction, and request lockage. At that time, they will inform you of the current lockage status and estimate your wait time. It could be as long as 45 minutes to an hour in the unusual case where they have just started locking through from your side. The lockmaster will also instruct you as to port- or starboard-to, indicating which side of the lock to steer to and how to arrange your fenders; see the Bridge Tables in the Skipper's Handbook section for the side normally used. The lockmaster will then indicate for you to enter when the traffic light is green.

If you receive no response on VHF, sound two long and two short blasts. (Not a part of the Waterway, Clewiston Lock is used to leave the Waterway and reach the facilities at Clewiston; it is the only lock without a VHF radio.) At each lock, for the smallest of craft, there is a pull-cord hanging down by a sign marking its location. The green light is your signal to enter the lock. The lockmaster will then hand you, or drop to you, a bow line and a stern line, or the lines will be hanging down from the top of the lock's sidewall, and you will have to steer to them and pick them up (in this case, keep a boathook handy).

When your boat enters at the lower level and is to be raised in the lock, take care that the line does not hit you in the face when it is dropped by the lockmaster. Be prepared for moderate turbulence as water rushes in or out of the lock. Two people can safely handle a small or medium-sized boat, but an extra pair of hands is always useful on large boats. Single-handing through the locks is not safe and is strongly discouraged.

Check when you are doing your pre-cruise planning, and recheck again at the first lock, to make sure the entire Waterway is open. Maintenance on the locks is normally done each summer, and through-passage from the East Coast to the Gulf Coast may not be possible for as long as several months. During such times, Lake Okeechobee may be accessible from one side or the other, but not both. During a drought, lockage may be restricted depending on water supply. Call the Corps of Engineers at Clewiston (863-983-8101) for information or go to the Internet at www.saj.usace.army.mil and use the "Coastal Navigation" selection from the menu, followed by the link to "Navigation Projects and Studies."

Depths and Clearances

The depth of water in Lake Okeechobee can vary widely as a result of rainfall onto the drainage area to the north and the lake itself. As a result of an ongoing drought, the level fell to a record low of 3.36 feet in mid-2007—the lowest level ever recorded—but lake levels had recovered to 8.6 feet in early 2010, due to hurricanes in 2008 and a tropical storm in 2009. The Corps of Engineers and the South Florida Water Management District manage the level of the lake. There are a variety of ecological, environmental and economic reasons for various levels, and some of them conflict with others.

The depths charted in Lake Okeechobee are based on a datum of 12.56 feet. If skippers know the lake level, they can determine the difference between the datum and the current level and modify the charted depths accordingly. Depths in the sections between dams on either side of the lake vary slightly with lake level changes, but the differences are seldom enough to affect navigation.

The Port Mayaca Railroad Bridge, Mile 38.0, sets the 49-foot controlling vertical clearance of the Waterway. If you have any questions about clearance, call the Corps of Engineers at Clewiston (863-983-8101). Sailboaters can have their mast un-stepped at Stuart, or wait and have it done at the Indiantown Marina, which is closer to the Port Mayaca Bridge.

Navigating the Okeechobee Waterway

With the exception of a lake crossing in imperfect weather, passage along the Okeechobee Waterway is easy, piloting is simple and navigational aids are adequate for daytime running. Aids to navigation are numbered in several sequences from east to west all the way across; even-numbered red aids are on the starboard side (as they are southbound along the Atlantic ICW). Conversely, leave red aids to port eastbound on the Waterway, as you would when northbound on the ICW. Reservations are recommended at marinas on the Okeechobee Waterway.

Nighttime navigation is not recommended, because shoals and deadheads (partially submerged objects) are obscured. Fortunately, ample facilities and occasional anchorages make after-dark travel unnecessary. Some of the bridges operate daily from 6 a.m. to 10 p.m., and require a minimum of three hours notice to open at other times. Phone numbers are posted on each bridge; calls are best made during normal office hours. You can use adjacent dolphins for tie-ups. Anchoring in approach areas to some of the locks is also possible, and the lockmasters can provide local knowledge concerning depths and conditions. As mentioned before, aids to navigation are the same as the ICW pattern: going west, keep red aids to navigation to starboard, green ones to port; yellow squares and triangles are shown on dayboards and buoys.

Currents are not a problem in the Okeechobee Waterway, except for the turbulence that occurs when locks are opened. Average tides at the mouth of the St. Lucie River are 1.1 feet; 1.3 feet at Fort Myers; and 2.4 feet at Punta Rassa (at the western end of the Okeechobee Waterway) near Mile Zero of the GIWW heading north.

Weather

Central Florida weather is generally benign. In winter, the prevailing wind is north to northeast, as opposed to summer, when wind is normally east to southeast, with very little rain except when cold fronts from the north pass through. Summer days are calm in the mornings,

St. Lucie River—North & South Fork, FL

ST. LUCIE RIVER—NORTH & SOUTH FORK		Largest Vessel Accommodated	VHF Channel Monitored	Transient Berths / Total Berths	Approach / Dockside Depth (reported)	Floating Docks	Gas / Diesel	Groceries, Ice, Marine Supplies, Snacks	Repairs: Hull, Engine, Propeller	Lift (tonnage), Crane, Rail	1=110V, 2=220V, B=Both, Max Amps	Laundry, Pool, Showers	Pump-Out Station	Nearby: Grocery Store, Motel, Restaurant
1. St. Lucie Marine 7.0	772-692-2000	50		/20	6/5			IM	HP	L30	B/50	S	P	GMR
2. Loggerhead Club & Marina - Stuart 7.2 (WiFi)	772-692-4000	90	16	24/151	8/6		GD	GIS				B/100		P	GR
3. Sandpiper Marina (WiFi)	772-335-7875	100	16	6/61	8/8		GD	GIMS	HEP			B/50	LPS		MR
4. Harbor Inn & Marina 7.8	772-692-1200	65	16	1/79	10/8							B/50	P		MR
5. Waterway Marina 7.7	772-220-2185	65		/5				S				B/50	S	P	GMR
6. Allied Marine Group/Britt Point Marine 7.5	772-692-1122	130		/60	7/7			M	HEP	L60	B/50			R
7. Sunset Bay Marina & Anchorage 8 (WiFi)	772-283-9225	120	16	60/198		F	GD	GIMS				B/50	LS	P	R
8. Martin County Marina 9	772-221-8198	30	5	2/2	6/5	F	G	IM	HEP				LS		
9. Monterey Inn and Marina 9.6 (WiFi)	772-283-3500	40		6/12	6/5			I				B/50			MR
10. Riverwatch Marina 9.6	772-286-3456	80	16	4/28	6/5	F	GD	IMS	HEP	L60	B/50	S		GMR

Corresponding chart(s) not to be used for navigation. ⌨ Internet Access (WiFi) Wireless Internet Access

with occasional patchy fog; winds pick up at about 10 a.m. Afternoons often bring showers and thunderstorms, particularly late in the day, so it is a good idea to plan on getting in early. Hurricanes do occur in season, June through November.

Since Lake Okeechobee is the second largest freshwater lake located wholly in the continental United States. (Lake Michigan is the largest), it can get nasty. You should know which forecasts cover the area. The continuous NOAA marine weather comes from West Palm Beach and Fort Myers on VHF Channel WX-3, and from Belle Glade on WX-2.

■ ST. LUCIE RIVER

NAVIGATION: Use Chart 11428. From its intersection with the Atlantic ICW at Mile 987.8 and Mile Zero of the Okeechobee Waterway, informally known as the "Crossroads," the St. Lucie River heads west before turning to the north for a few miles at Mile 0.5. At this turn is the entrance to Manatee Pocket, described in the chapter "Fort Pierce to St. Lucie River."

Note the shoal area shown on the chart between the ICW and the St. Lucie River's Hell Gate. The dredged channel splits these extensive shoals inside Sewalls Point, so follow the markers carefully as you enter. Aids to navigation are often relocated, and additional ones established, to mark the best water—take time to observe all aids, and don't become confused if they do not exactly match your chart. Tidal range is only one foot, but the strong current bears watching, although it loses force as you proceed up the St. Lucie River. Be particularly alert for large wakes when traveling between the Crossroads and the entrance to Manatee Pocket. This short, but narrow stretch is often crowded with powerboats speeding to or from the ocean via the St. Lucie Inlet. Deep water in the channel starts past Manatee Pocket.

Where the St. Lucie River opens up, and the long finger of Sewalls Point stretches downstream on the east side, the high ground is heavily wooded, with estates, both large and small, along the landscaped terrain. Boats infrequently anchor on the southwest side of Sewalls Point, between Hell Gate and almost to the point. Depths hold close to the shore, but set your anchor well—currents tend to run swiftly here. The west side is equally attractive, residential and fronted by many private docks where property owners berth their vessels.

Traveling upriver, green daybeacon "23" and flashing green "23A," just east of the Roosevelt Bridge (65-foot fixed vertical clearance), can be difficult to locate. Because the shoal that these mark has a habit of attracting boats new to the area, skippers should take special care to locate these markers before getting too close to the bridge.

Bridges: Four bridges cross the St. Lucie River along the six miles between Manatee Pocket and downtown Stuart. First is the Evans Crary Bridge, carrying state Road A1A (Mile 3.4, 65-foot fixed vertical clearance). The channel is just west of the highest point on the bridge. Four miles farther up the St. Lucie River, the remaining three bridges are clustered together within a distance of 800 feet. They include the 65-foot fixed vertical clearance high-rise Roosevelt Bridge (Mile 7.3), a railroad bascule bridge (Mile 7.4) with a 7-foot closed vertical clearance, and the remaining half of the old Roosevelt Bascule Bridge (Mile 7.4, 14-foot closed vertical clearance). The railroad bridge, just east of the Roosevelt Bridge, is normally open, but closes automatically when a train approaches. The railroad bridge has a horizontal clearance of only 50 feet, compared to the old Roosevelt Bridge's horizontal clearance of 80 feet. In traffic, with currents running, passage through the two bridges can be tricky, especially from the wider fixed Roosevelt Bridge to the narrower railroad bridge—exercise care.

Dockage: On the north side of the St. Lucie River, right before the bridges, is the convenient Loggerhead Club & Marina with transient dockage, gas and diesel fuel and pump-out service.

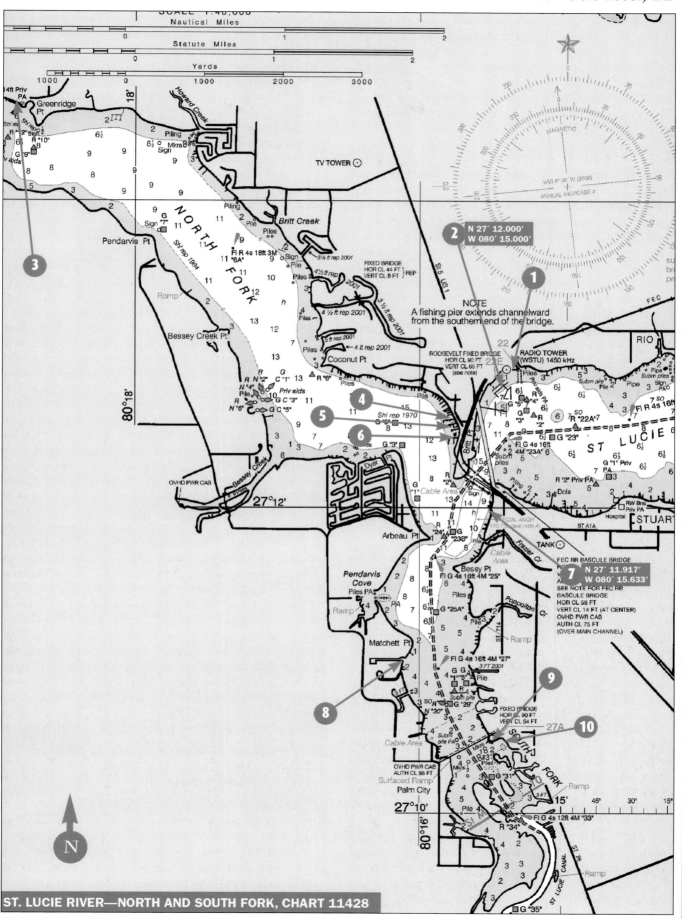

ST. LUCIE RIVER—NORTH AND SOUTH FORK, CHART 11428

Stuart, FL

Anchorage: Just north of the St. Lucie River Bridge, in Hoggs Cove (Mile 4.5), protection is good from northerlies and easterlies. Watch the shoal off Pisgah Hill, and anchor in 7 to 9 feet. If you plan an early-morning start eastward, it is better to anchor here rather than in Stuart past the Roosevelt Bridges. Here, you will have the sun in your eyes for a shorter time. The early sun also makes spotting aids to navigation difficult.

St. Lucie River, North Fork

A turn to the right, after passing through the old Roosevelt Bridge, takes you off the Okeechobee Waterway and up the North Fork of the St. Lucie River. This can be a very pleasant side trip if your cruising schedule allows you the time.

Dockage: Located on the North Fork of the St. Lucie River just inside Britt Point (due east of green daybeacon "5"), Waterway Marina welcomes transients with a wide variety of services aimed at providing a comfortable stay for its guests. Just to the north, Harbor Inn & Marina features a pool and The Deck Restaurant. In the same area is Britt Point Marina. A mile or so to the northwest, just beyond Greenridge Point is the Club Med Sandpiper Resort, where cruisers are welcome.

Anchorage: A bit farther north is Kitching Cove, which provides a fine anchorage in 6- to 7-foot depths. At the north end of the anchorage, take a scenic dinghy trip to the headwaters of the river.

Stuart, on the St. Lucie River

From the Okeechobee Waterway, Stuart, tucked back along the St. Lucie River, is barely visible, yet it is as well-equipped as almost any port on the Atlantic coast and contains a sizable winter boat colony. Marine facilities and shore activities are a vital part of the community, and protection is good.

Dockage: Sunset Bay Marina, at the shore side of the mooring field, has been refurbished and offers restrooms, showers, laundry facilities, a dayroom lounge with TV and a marina store. The fuel dock with pump-out station is open from 7 a.m. to 6 p.m.

Before reaching the Palm City Bridge, just before red nun "30," Martin County Marina is visible on the starboard side. It has gasoline but limited dockage. A channel marked by daybeacons leads in from the Waterway.

Across from Palm City, just upriver from the 54-foot fixed vertical clearance Palm City Bridge (Mile 9.5), a marked channel leads into Riverwatch Marina, with 5-foot depths in the channel and 4.5-foot depths in the basin. Limited transient dockage is available for boats up to 50 feet. On both sides of the eastern end of the Palm City Bridge sit the facilities of Bassett Boat Co. (also known as MarineMax), dealer for Hatteras and Sea Ray. This is a full-service boatyard, but there are a few slips for transient use in connection with service.

Three miles beyond the Palm City Bridge and between red daybeacons "40" and "40A," the South Fork of the St. Lucie River bears off the Waterway to the east. This is an exceptionally scenic side trip that is navigable for most cruising boats all the way to the Route 76 Bridge.

Anchorage: Just upriver from the Roosevelt hand railroad bridges is Sunset Bay Marina and Anchorage (formerly Southpoint Anchorage). Check in with the harbormaster after picking up a mooring and pay the fee, which is the same for all sizes of craft, and includes free wireless Internet coverage for the mooring field. Dinghy dockage is available along a new long floating dock or along the wall on Frazier Creek, a bit farther upriver. You can not anchor in the mooring area, but you may anchor across the river in Pendarvis Park.

Three blocks east of the dock is the beautifully restored downtown area of old Stuart, with shops and restaurants. To reach the nearest shopping center, which has a supermarket, dinghy into Frazier Creek (at the south end of the anchorage) and tie up to the seawall in Shepard Park. From here, it is a five-block walk south along Route 1. Call 772-283-1814 for the schedule of the inexpensive "Community Coach" that services the area on weekdays.

GOIN' ASHORE: **STUART, FL**

The countryside surrounding Stuart provides a little bit of everything for which Florida is noted: citrus, winter vegetables, flowers and cattle. The city itself acts as the business and distribution center for the area. As the Martin County seat, Stuart has most of the facilities found in an urban center, including Martin Memorial Hospital, which accepts emergency patients at its own dock (4-foot depths alongside).

The region's agricultural importance notwithstanding, the emphasis throughout the area has gradually shifted from farming to sportfishing. Although Stuart's claim to being the "Sailfish Capital of the World" is sometimes disputed by other Florida cities, no one would deny that both its outside and inside waters provide outstanding fishing. Charter boats sail out of Stuart, Manatee Pocket and other nearby ports. Stuart has gained further prominence as a center of custom sportfish boatbuilding. Several yards still build fine wooden yachts. A visit to one of these facilities makes an interesting diversion, and the boats are magnificent.

Downtown Stuart's facelift and revitalization has been a boon for residents and tourists. The restored Lyric Theater hosts plays and concerts, and abandoned city blocks have been transformed into gift shops, art galleries and trendy restaurants. Some favorites are the Flagler Grill (47 S.W. Flagler Ave., 772-221-9517), Luna Italian Restaurant (49 S.W. Flagler Ave., 772-288-0550) and the Osceola Street Cafe (26 S.W. Osceola St., 772-283-6116).

ADDITIONAL RESOURCES

■ Martin County Convention & Visitors Bureau, **www.martincountyfla.com**

■ Guide to Stuart, Florida, **www.stuartfla.com**

⚑ NEARBY GOLF COURSES
Martin County Golf and Country Club, 2000 S.E. St. Lucie Blvd., Stuart, FL 34996, 772-287-3747

⚕ NEARBY MEDICAL FACILITIES
Martin Memorial Medical Center, 200 S.E. Hospital Ave., Stuart, FL 34950, 772-287-5200

ST. LUCIE CANAL

NAVIGATION: Use Chart 11428. The Okeechobee Waterway departs the South Fork of the St. Lucie River near this point and continues as the start of the St. Lucie Canal with the lock at Okeechobee Waterway Mile 15.

The canal is deep and easy-to-traverse. You pass under two fixed high-level bridges, the 56-foot vertical clearance Interstate 95 and the 55-foot vertical clearance Florida Turnpike (Thomas B. Manuel) Bridge at Mile 14.5. American Custom Yachts, a large, full-service boatyard and custom builder, is located on the south shore between the bridges. It has limited space for transients, and berths are exposed to the wakes of passing vessels. Its facilities have nearly doubled in size, but it is still more of a facility at which you would stop only if you needed repairs or other services.

St. Lucie Lock—Mile 15

NAVIGATION: Use Chart 11428. The lock operates on demand from 6 a.m. to 9:30 p.m. Radio ahead to the lock or contact the Corps of Engineers for current schedules before your departure, however. WATERWAY GUIDE also lists important updates to navigation at www.waterwayguide.com.

This first lock of the system lifts you approximately 13 feet. When approaching the No-Wake Zone entrance area, check the light system. If the light is red and a call on VHF Channel 13 or 16 does not get a response, give two long and then two short blasts, then wait well downstream in the standby area to avoid the discharge from the dam and lock. Many boats arrive at the lower side of this lock and then turn around and go back without locking through, so the lockmaster does not assume, even if he sees you arrive, that you wish to lock through. You must call him via VHF or horn. On each side of each lock, there is a sign marked ARRIVAL POINT. Enter slowly on the green signal, and be prepared to accept lines fore and aft from the lockmaster. As the water level rises, maintain your position with care.

Additional information may be obtained from the lockmaster for the route ahead. A Corps of Engineers map of the Okeechobee Waterway shows government recreational areas for public use. A note of caution: The Waterway plays host not only to many varieties of fish but also to manatees (an endangered species), alligators and turtles of all sizes. The manatees frequently are "locked through," so take extra care if they are reported in the area.

Dockage: Immediately west of the St. Lucie Lock is a group of eight slips for boats up to 35 feet, offering picnic and playground areas and nature trails. Four of the slips are first-come, first-served, and advance reservations can be made for the other four slips (877-444-6777). Reservations must be made at least 72 hours before arrival. Stays are limited to two weeks. If you do stay at these slips, be sure to go to the visitor center just east of the lock for interesting and instructive exhibits.

Less than a mile farther on along the south shore of the St. Lucie Canal, a new yachting facility is completed and ready for dockage. River Forest Yachting Center is located on a nine-acre complex, designed to provide safe, protected yacht hurricane storage, both indoor and out, for part-time Florida residents. A unique feature is a 45,000-square-foot, climate-controlled warehouse for long-term storage of boats up to 65 feet. Alongside dockage is available for vessels up to 100 feet, with up to 100-amp shore power; transients are welcome if space is available. An interesting feature is a Hurricane Club, wherein for an annual fee, when a hurricane threatens, your vessel will be hauled and secured to the ground. For information, call 772-287-4131. The project has received a warm welcome from the boating community. There is also a brand new facility which has been completed and is ready for use on the Caloosahatchee River side of the Waterway at LaBelle.

Anchorage: Directly across the Waterway from the Corps of Engineers slips, at the entrance to a narrow bay, is a quiet overnight anchorage for one boat.

Indiantown—Mile 29

The small community of Indiantown, less than a mile north of the canal, has a post office, medical center, markets, banks and casual restaurants. Also near the canal is Owens Grove, selling excellent fruit and fresh-squeezed juices. The grove has a small gift shop, a company of freely roaming peacocks and the Cracker House, a Florida pioneer farm home that can be toured. The Seminole Country Inn and Restaurant was built in 1925 by S. Davis Warfield, a railroad executive, and was used by his niece, Wallis Warfield Simpson, on her honeymoon with the Duke of Windsor, explaining why Main Street in Indiantown is named Warfield Boulevard.

NAVIGATION: Use Chart 11428. Approaching Indiantown from the east, you will pass under the Indiantown Bridge (55-foot fixed vertical clearance) at Mile 28.1. At Okeechobee Waterway Mile 28.5 is the Indiantown Railway Bridge with a 7-foot closed vertical clearance. The operator may anticipate you, but if it is closed, call on VHF Channel 09. If a train is approaching, you may be delayed, as the train always has the right-of-way. The bridge opens on signal between 6 a.m. and 10 p.m. and requires a three-hour notice to open between 10 p.m. and 6 a.m. Less than a mile east of these bridges, on the north side of the canal, is a park with a boat ramp and a posted No-Wake Zone.

Dockage: A short distance beyond the railroad bridge is Indiantown Marina. For those intending to cross Lake Okeechobee via the direct route, this is the last marina until Clewiston, which is 35 miles away. Although Indiantown is a large marina (with a long-term dry-storage lot), it has very few transient slips. The staff is very accommodating and friendly. The owners have really spruced up the marina with new landscaping, and it has become a very pleasant and relaxing stop. Skippers planning to overnight here should call ahead for reservations. In addition to mast un-stepping, the marina staff has developed a

St. Lucie Canal, FL

ST. LUCIE CANAL		Largest Vessel Accommodated	VHF Channel Monitored	Transient Berths / Total Berths	Approach / Dockside Depth (reported)	Floating Docks	Gas / Diesel	Groceries, Ice, Marine Supplies, Snacks	Repairs: Hull, Engine, Propeller	Lift (tonnage), Crane, Rail	1=110v, 2=220v, B=Both, Max Amps	Laundry, Pool, Showers	Pump-Out Station	Nearby: Grocery Store, Motel, Restaurant
		Dockage					**Supplies**			**Services**				
1. Riveria Yachts of the Americas Inc. 13.8	772-403-1060	85			7/7				HEP	L40	B/50			
2. American Custom Yachts, Inc. 14.5	772-221-9100	126	16/68	/23	8/8		GD	MS	HEP	L150,C	B/100			
3. RIVER FOREST YACHTING CENTER 16	**772-287-4131**	**150**	**16**	**10/28**	**10/9**				**HEP**	**L55**	**B/100**	**S**	**P**	
4. Indiantown Marina 29 🖥 📶	772-597-2455	120	16	10/	8/8	F	GD	GIMS	HEP	L30	B/50	LS	P	GMR

Corresponding chart(s) not to be used for navigation. 🖥 Internet Access 📶 Wireless Internet Access

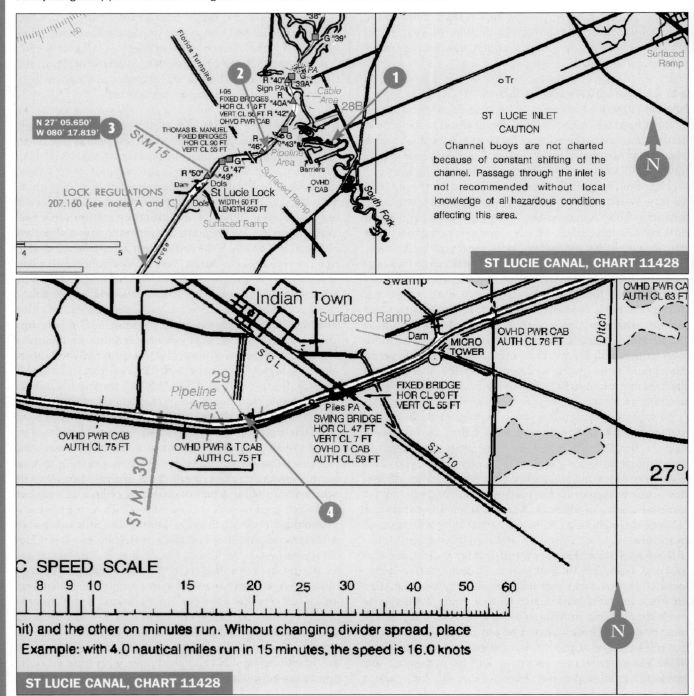

ST LUCIE CANAL, CHART 11428

ST LUCIE CANAL, CHART 11428

unique way to get sailboats with masts up to 53 feet high under the 49-foot-high Port Mayaca Bridge; they simply heel the boat over by placing several 55-gallon drums of water along the deck.

■ PORT MAYACA

NAVIGATION: Use Chart 11428. At Mile 38.0, the Port Mayaca Railroad Lift Bridge (49-foot open vertical clearance, 7-foot vertical clearance when closed) sets the controlling overhead clearance for the Okeechobee Waterway. Elsewhere, at least 54 feet of overhead clearance can be carried. Be sure to stay south of red daybeacon "52," as a ledge of rocks and submerged pilings runs from the marker to the northern bank of the canal. The highway bridge (U.S. Highway 98 and 441, mile 38.8) has a 55-foot fixed vertical clearance, and the lock is just a short distance ahead, serving as the entrance to the lake. Mooring dolphins provide the only place to make fast before reaching the lock, but they may be in use by barges.

At certain water levels, the Port Mayaca lock is open at both ends, and on the flashing (or steady) green (or yellow) light, you may proceed through cautiously. If you have any questions, contact the lockmaster on VHF Channels 16 or 13. Eastbound boats may experience some difficulty with adverse winds and resulting seas. Under these conditions, entering the lock and making fast can be tricky. Until the lock is closed, waves tend to ricochet from wall to wall. Heading westbound is considerably easier, but if the winds are brisk, be prepared for a choppy exit.

Anchorage: Be warned that anchoring beyond the lock is also precarious. A layover elsewhere would be a better plan. In times of normal lake levels, a small cove immediately south of the lock's east fenders may be used as an anchorage, if necessary, for vessels up to 5 feet in draft, but there is a shallow area in the center of this cove. The bottom is very soft and holding is poor. Ask the lockmaster for information concerning this cove.

■ LAKE OKEECHOBEE

Lake Okeechobee is the second-largest freshwater lake located wholly in the continental United States (after Lake Michigan). Likened to a saucer full of water, Lake Okeechobee is shallow, with normal depths from 7 to 11 feet, depending on the season and annual rainfall; in periods of prolonged drought, it has fallen to below 8 feet. For up-to-date information on lake depths, call the Corps of Engineers office in Clewiston at 863-983-8101. During periods of strong winds, the lake becomes choppy and turbulent with short, hard seas typical of shallow water.

Originally the headwaters of the Everglades, which author Marjorie Stoneman Douglas called "the river of grass," Lake Okeechobee is now the centerpiece of South Florida's water-resource system. The lake is completely enclosed by an impressive levee system, officially named

the Herbert Hoover Dike. The result of two disastrous hurricanes in the 1920s, when the lake was literally blown out of its banks (the larger of the hurricanes killed more than 1,500 people in Belle Glade on the southern rim of Lake Okeechobee in 1928), the dike's construction began during the Hoover administration.

Bass fishermen and their specialized boats frequent the known "holes" and wrecks. Pan fishermen are along the edges, in drainage canal entrances, near the locks and in the crannies of the many spoil islands along the southern rim. Seasonal tournaments bring out hordes of amateurs and professionals. The Corps of Engineers currently has a multi-million-dollar project to "restore" the Kissimmee River, which feeds into the lake on its north side, to its previous natural course, thus undoing the multi-million-dollar project that straightened the riverbed and added locks and dams. This will be good for the environment, but will greatly reduce the river's availability for boating.

Crossing Lake Okeechobee

Chart 11428 shows the two accepted routes across Lake Okeechobee. The Open Water Route (the most direct) is discussed first. Consideration of the Rim, or southern shore, Route follows.

The Open Water Route (Route 1)—Mile 40 to Mile 65

The Open Water Route is normally an enjoyable run, and Clewiston is a worthwhile stopover point. The controlling depth for Route 1 by specific lake level can be determined by subtracting 6.06 feet from the published lake level. If the lake level and season are right, expect to see hundreds of beautiful white pelicans bunched together on the half-dozen offshore spoil islands that line the Clewiston approach channel. Unlike brown pelicans, which plunge-dive from high above the water for their meals, white pelicans scoop up fish by merely submerging their heads and necks while swimming.

NAVIGATION: Use Chart 11428. Actually crossing the southern portion of Lake Okeechobee, this 25-mile-long passage departs from the Port Mayaca channel in a southwesterly direction. The first run of 15 miles has one aid to navigation, flashing red "6," about seven miles out, to help you compensate for a slight magnetic anomaly in this area, which might affect your compass. About three miles out from the Port Mayaca Lock, there is a visible wreck to starboard. Do not be led off course. Your GPS chartplotter or radar could be useful on this stretch if visibility is less than optimum.

As you approach flashing green "7" on the eastern edge of Rocky Reef, note what appears to be a cluster of markers and the remains of a platform. Sort things out beforehand and follow the chart's magenta line carefully. After clearing the cut through the reef, stick to the charted course. The apparent shortcut due west, an auxiliary floodway channel, is reportedly shoal and obstructed with large boulders (particularly noticeable at low lake levels).

Big Sawgrass Marsh, FL

BIG SAWGRASS MARSH		Dockage				Supplies		Services		
	Largest Vessel Accommodated	VHF Channel Monitored	Approach / Dockside Depth (reported)	Transient Berths / Total Berths	Floating Docks	Gas / Diesel	Groceries, Ice, Marine Supplies, Snacks	Repairs: Hull, Engine, Propeller	Lift (tonnage), Crane, Rail	1=110V, 2=220V, B=Both, Max Amps	Laundry, Pool, Showers	Pump-Out Station	Nearby: Grocery Store, Motel, Restaurant
1. Okee-Tantie Campground & Marina	863-763-2622	40		2/51	6/6	F	G	GIMS			1/30		R

Corresponding chart(s) not to be used for navigation. 🖥 Internet Access 📶 Wireless Internet Access

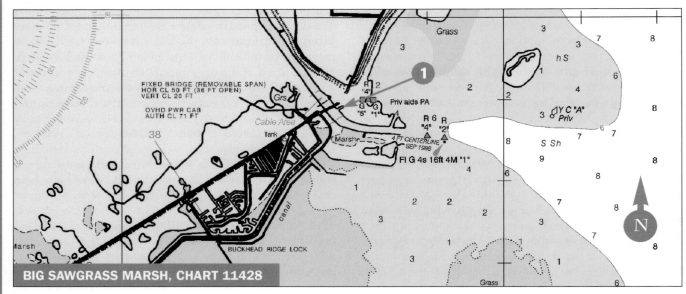

BIG SAWGRASS MARSH, CHART 11428

Entering the Clewiston approach channel, marked by a private concrete cylinder and numerous lights and daybeacons, is simple. Westbound, green daybeacon "1" is difficult to spot. If the water level is low or the winds are brisk, pay strict attention to course-keeping; this is where the controlling depth for Route 1 applies. The channel is lined on both sides with rocks and spoil areas here. Exercise special care in the area between red daybeacons "4" and "6." This is another area in which the use of your GPS chartplotter will come in handy.

Close in to Clewiston, be aware that fishnets and traps are a way of life here, and their small markers are sometimes difficult to see. Some of the fishermen in high-speed bass boats or skiffs also add to the annoyance, but Clewiston, which bills itself as the "Sweetest Town in America," due to its role in sugarcane production, is a real pleasure to visit.

Directly before reaching the Clewiston Lock, the channel makes a hard 90-degree turn to the northwest. There are no nearby channel markers on this northwesterly stretch, and a sign on the levee pointing to Moore Haven is difficult to read. The intersection can be confusing, but don't go through the lock unless you wish to visit Clewiston. The Clewiston Lock is not equipped with a VHF radio, but if lake levels are not unusual, the lock is often left open. If the traffic light is green, proceed through. If you wish passage and the lockmaster does not wave to you, use two long and two short blasts of your horn or whistle.

The Corps of Engineers in Clewiston (863-983-8101) has more information on scheduled maintenance and lock operations.

On an eastbound trip from Clewiston, the Port Mayaca entrance markers may be hard to pick out. On the charted course, power company stacks are clearly visible at the port, and a heading directly toward them will bring you almost directly to the channel entrance. Previously taken GPS readings will simplify matters.

The Rim Route (Route 2)— Mile 40 to Mile 75

Special Note About Lake Okeechobee Drought Conditions

At the time of publication, the Rim Route was open (with a depth of 6 feet), but the Corps of Engineers warned that boaters use Route 2 at their own risk. While the channel is marked, there are submerged obstructions and uncharted shoals to contend with.

NAVIGATION: Use Chart 11428. If you are not pressed for time, or if the lake crossing is questionable due to weather, Route 2, the Rim Route (10 miles longer), can be an interesting alternative. While open to Lake Okeechobee for about 15 miles, the exposure is from west through north. Unless winds are from this quadrant (and in the small-craft advisory category), this part of the passage should be a pleasant one.

Lake Okeechobee— Rim Route, FL

LAKE OKEECHOBEE—RIM ROUTE		Dockage						Supplies			Services			
		Largest Vessel Accommodated	VHF Channel Monitored	Transient Berths / Total Berths	Approach / Dockside Depth (reported)	Floating Docks	Gas / Diesel	Groceries, Ice, Marine Supplies, Snacks	Repairs: Hull, Engine, Propeller	Lift (tonnage), Crane, Rail	1=110v, 2=220v, B=Both, Max Amps	Laundry, Pool, Showers	Pump-Out Station	Nearby: Grocery Store, Motel, Restaurant
1. LOGGERHEAD CLUB & MARINA-LAKE OKEECHOBEE 50.5	561-924-7832	70	16	25/84	8/8	F	GD	GIMS	EP		1/50	LS	P	GMR
2. Slim's Fish Camp 61	561-996-3844	60	09	10/66	8/8	F	G	GIS	E		1/50	LS		GMR
3. Roland Martin's Marina & Resort 75.6 WiFi	863-983-3151	130	16/68	130/130	8/7	F	GD	IMS			B/50	LPS	P	GMR

Corresponding chart(s) not to be used for navigation. 🖳 Internet Access WiFi Wireless Internet Access

From Mile 55 on to Clewiston, where it joins Route 1, and farther to the Caloosahatchee Canal entrance, the course stays between the mainland levees surrounding Lake Okeechobee and the regular and spoil islands lining the rim. Depths vary according to lake levels and wind conditions; the controlling depth for this route can be determined by subtracting 8.66 feet from the official lake level. The shallowest stretch is the easternmost four miles; beyond, depths increase significantly. Other than Pahokee and Clewiston, the only stopping points along the way are a small fish camp and possibly pilings or dolphins.

Pahokee—Mile 50.6
A small farming-oriented village, Pahokee reportedly got its name from the early American Indian inhabitants who called the area Payahokee ("grassy waters").

NAVIGATION: Use Chart 11428. The local harbor can be reached from red entrance daybeacon "2," which is opposite red channel daybeacon "62." If the wind is strong from the northwest or north, waves from Lake Okeechobee will be reflected back from the breakwater and, combining with the incoming waves, can result in an uncomfortable, or even dangerous, situation for boats in the channel as they pass the breakwater. Near red daybeacon "78," Mile 54, there is a charted, straight, well-marked channel that leads out through the shallows bordering the Rim Route to the "deep" water of the lake.

Dockage: A marked channel leads to the Loggerhead Club & Marina's Lake Okeechobee Outpost. This property was rebuilt and reopened in 2009. Vessels up to 100 feet can be accommodated at floating docks and water, power and pump-out facilities are provided at each slip. Both gas and diesel are also available. The Camp Store on-site sells ice and snacks. The town, about three blocks away, offers groceries, two hardware stores, a bank, a drugstore and friendly inhabitants.

Anchorage: Five miles or so farther on, the Waterway is shielded behind spoil and natural islands in the lee of Kreamer Island, where you will find an anchorage. In fact, this protected stretch extending to just beyond Hurricane Gate 4 is considered the best area on the route for a secure anchorage. The "gate" is normally closed.

The casuarina trees (Australian Pines) that used to line the east side are now dead and leafless, victims of the

Corps of Engineers project to destroy all invasive, non-native vegetation. (This condition persists throughout the Rim Route as far as Moore Haven and lends a forlorn, desolate flavor to the route.) The west side of the gate, outside the immediate channel, is the recommended side for anchoring. Feel your way gently over the bottom and use a Bahamian moor (two anchors set in opposite directions) to reduce swinging.

Torry Island/Belle Glade—Mile 60.7
The Torry Island Bridge from Belle Glade has only an 11-foot closed vertical clearance at normal lake levels. The fixed span just west of the swing span has a vertical clearance of 13 feet, which may be an advantage if you only require 12 feet of clearance. This bridge is hand-operated, and it takes awhile for the operator to get in place to open the span, so be sure to call ahead on VHF Channel 09. Hours are from 7 a.m. to 6 p.m. Monday through Thursday, and 7 a.m. to 7 p.m. Friday through Sunday (fishing days). The bridge remains closed at night. Some anchoring room is west of the bridge if you want an early start. But note that early risers also include many small-boat fishermen who rarely show concern for anchored craft.

Belle Glade is a farming community whose WELCOME TO BELLE GLADE highway signs add, HER SOIL IS HER FORTUNE. The fish camp has some provisions, and you can probably find a way to get into the town area proper (nearly two miles distant), where you will find a community golf course, a small airfield and numerous stores.

This section of the Okeechobee Waterway from Mile 55 to Mile 75.7 (Clewiston) has always been one of the more interesting stretches on the trip. Hyacinths and water lettuce grow in profusion, sometimes even clogging the channel. If you must pass through them, do it slowly. Should you clog your prop and rudder, back down and then push ahead. Occasionally, the Rim Route will be closed to navigation because of vegetation in the water. These closures will be announced in Local Notice to Mariners; call 863-983-8108 for up-to-date information.

Belle Glade to Clewiston— Mile 60.7 to Mile 75.7
From Belle Glade, the Waterway first heads south for several miles, and then angles northwest past such communities as Bean City and Lake Harbor. A road parallels the

Lake Okeechobee, FL

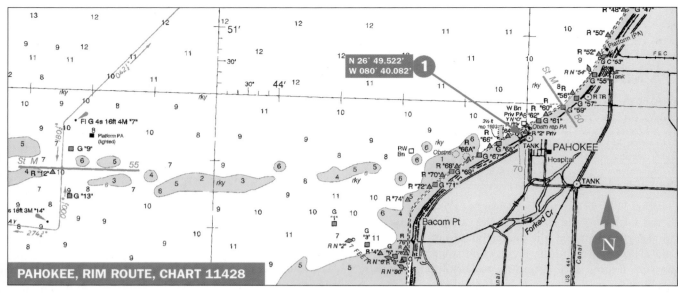

PAHOKEE, RIM ROUTE, CHART 11428

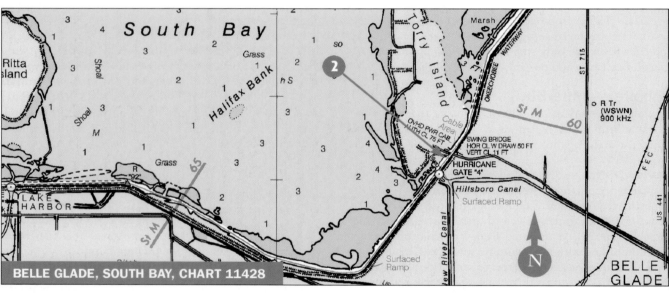

BELLE GLADE, SOUTH BAY, CHART 11428

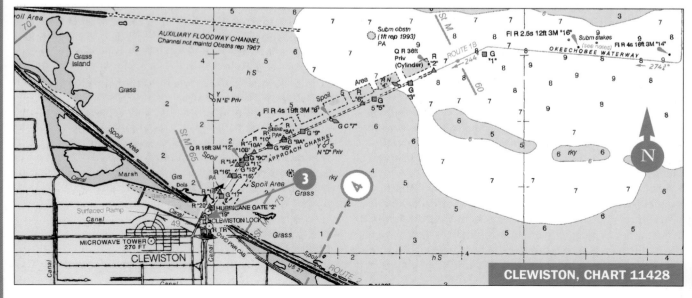

CLEWISTON, CHART 11428

Waterway most of the way, but you will not see it, since it is behind the ubiquitous levee. Where the Waterway turns westward at Mile 62.5, there is a charted small lagoon lakeward of the channel; this can be a fair-weather anchorage for several boats.

Hurricane Gate 3 at about Mile 67 is usually closed. Islands, both natural and spoil, still offer protection from winds off the lake, although if the water level is high, it can get a bit unpleasant, though not dangerous. There are markers along the way: Red daybeacon "94" is at Mile 70, and the channel is narrow and straightforward. As you approach Clewiston (Mile 75.7), be alert for small fishing boats anchored off the channel.

■ CLEWISTON—MILE 75.7

NAVIGATION: Use Chart 11428. Route 1 joins Route 2 at this juncture—a point about halfway between Stuart and Fort Myers. Mileage from this point on is based on the lesser "cross-lake" figure of Mile 65; the rim mileage of 75.7 stops here. A hurricane gate and a lock 50 feet wide by 60 feet long, operated by a contractor for the South Florida Water Management District (SFWMD), allow access through the levee into Clewiston Harbor. This lock is not equipped with a VHF radio, so contact with the lockmaster must be made visually (waving is the method of choice) or by whistle signals, two long and two short. (But as mentioned before, if the lake is at normal levels, the lock is often left open and clear for traffic; watch the traffic light to see if it is green or red.) After entering the lock, grab a couple of the lines hanging from the top of the chamber and hold on. Lock personnel may help with the lines, but the change in water level as the lock opens and closes usually will not cause excessive turbulence. The schedule calls for an open lock if the water level is low, and the Clewiston Lock is often open for direct passage. Otherwise, the hours are: May 1 through September 30, 5 a.m. to 9 p.m., and October 1 through April 30, 5:30 a.m. to 8 p.m. NOAA Weather is on WX2/Belle Glade.

Dockage: Angler's Marina (for smaller boats), just inside to starboard, has a motel and marine store. Farther along the canal, Roland Martin's Marina, which has acquired Angler's Marina, is a popular spot for transients and boat clubs to spend a weekend or more, particularly bass fishing groups. The 700-foot face dock and covered slips for boats 35 feet or less have 30- and 50-amp shore power service and both gas and diesel fuel, plus a pumpout facility.

The main street of this town of more than 6,000 and a small grocery store and pharmacy are only three blocks away. The famous Clewiston Inn Motor Lodge, owned and operated by the U.S. Sugar Corporation, provides free transportation to and from the marina for dining or lodging. The marina, and indeed the whole area, suffered extensive damage from Hurricane Wilma. Repairs have been made, and all facilities are in full operation.

Clewiston to Moore Haven— Mile 65 to Mile 78

From Clewiston to Moore Haven and the entrance to the Caloosahatchee Canal, Mile 78, the Waterway is fairly wide and deep. Speeds obtainable on Lake Okeechobee by the fast boats are frequently matched along this route. Small-boat fishermen anchor or drift-fish in the cuts and channel, and wakes are a potential annoyance. The former appearance of this stretch has been altered by the Corps of Engineers' project to eradicate the exotic casuarina trees (Australian Pine) on the lake side of the route; this also eliminated a desirable windbreak and shelter.

Several dolphins on the channel's edge northwest of Clewiston can be used for making fast. Anchorage can be found lakeside of the channel, but swinging room is minimal, and wakes are a potential annoyance. The variety of growth ranges from grass to scattered clumps of remaining casuarina, bamboo, melaluka and cypress, plus a few small trees with a crown of lobulated leaves and melon-like fruit. This last is the female papaya with edible fruit. If it is a sunny day, have your camera ready because this canal is probably one of the best places to see alligators. They sun themselves on shore. You will lose count of the "gators" in this short stretch of Waterway.

■ CALOOSAHATCHEE CANAL

NAVIGATION: Use Chart 11428. The entrance to the Moore Haven Lock (Mile 78) is directly to port and easy to see and negotiate. The rim canal continues on well up the west side of Lake Okeechobee and provides some sheltered anchoring areas (again with limited swinging room). Several facilities for small fishing boats are along the way, and at times, fishing activity is intense.

The Moore Haven Lock, being in a protected canal, is even easier to pass through than the St. Lucie Lock, with equally capable lock tenders. It has been rebuilt and now has smooth walls that will no longer catch rails and fenders as the old timbered walls did for many years. However, if Hurricane Gate 1 is in use during discharge of high water, turbulence on the "down" side of the lock can be considerable. (If you arrive at the east side of the Moore Haven Lock late in the day and would prefer not to lock through until morning, you can proceed on past the turn into the lock and anchor in the canal, or you can make fast for the night between the dolphins located on the lake side of the Waterway, just before the canal turns into the lock.) Stay well back from the lock until the green light comes on, and enter carefully. Comments about hyacinths and manatees elsewhere in the text also apply here. Information about conditions farther on can usually be obtained from the lockmaster. Remember, you are now being lowered with the water level, so do not tie off your bow or stern lines, and be prepared for some surge as you drop. Wait for the gates to open completely before releasing the lines, and then proceed slowly out of the lock.

Caloosahatchee Canal & River, FL

CALOOSAHATCHEE CANAL & RIVER		Largest Vessel Accommodated	VHF Channel Monitored	Transient Berths / Total Berths	Approach / Dockside Depth (reported)	Floating Docks	Groceries, Ice, Marine Supplies, Snacks	Gas / Diesel	Repairs: Hull, Engine, Propeller	Lift (tonnage), Crane, Rail	1=110V, 2=220V, B=Both, Max Amps	Laundry, Pool, Showers	Pump-Out Station	Nearby: Grocery Store, Motel, Restaurant
				Dockage			**Supplies**				**Services**			
1. Moore Haven City Marina 78.2	863-946-0722	35		6/30	5/5		G		I		P	1/50	LS	MR
2. Moore Haven City Docks 78.4	863-946-0711	100			6/6							1/50	S	GMR
3. RiverHouse Marina 78.5	863-946-3300				15/15				I			B/50	S	GMR
4. The Glades Resort & Marina 89 🖵 🛜	863-673-5653	50	16	/26	12/8				IS			B50	LPS	P GMR
5. Port La Belle Marina 100	863-675-2261	70	16	10/08	6/6	F	GD		I				LS	P MR
6. Belle Hatchee Marina 102.6	863-675-4371	50		4/25	6/6	F			M			1/15		GMR
7. La Belle City Dock 102.6	863-673-1191	60	16	10/10	6/6							1/30		GMR
8. **RIALTO HARBOR DOCKS INC. 119** 🖵	**239-728-3036**	**100**	**16**	/12	8/8		**WEEKLY +**					B/50	LPS	**GMR**
9. Jack's Marine LLC 124.2 🖵 🛜	239-694-2708	200	16	15/15	23/8		GD	IMS	HEP	L10	B/50	LS		M
10. **OWL CREEK BOAT WORKS 125.5**	**239-543-2100**	**125**		6/48	7/7				**HEP**	**L150**	B/50	S		**GMR**
11. Sweetwater Landing 126	239-694-3850	100	16/09	5/65	9/5		G	IMS	EP		B/50	LS	P	GMR

Corresponding chart(s) not to be used for navigation. 🖵 Internet Access 🛜 Wireless Internet Access

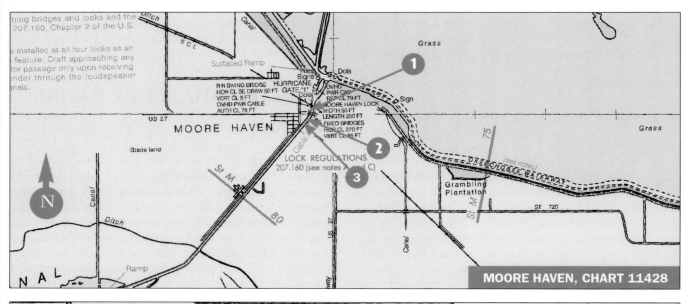

MOORE HAVEN, CHART 11428

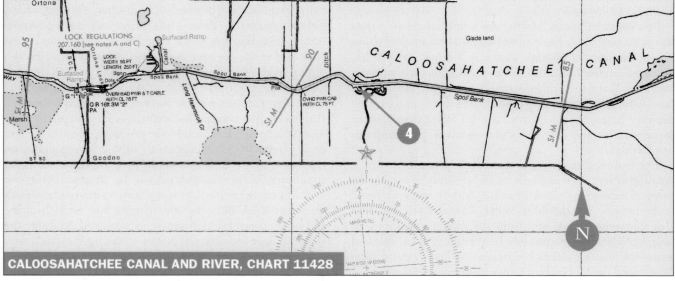

CALOOSAHATCHEE CANAL AND RIVER, CHART 11428

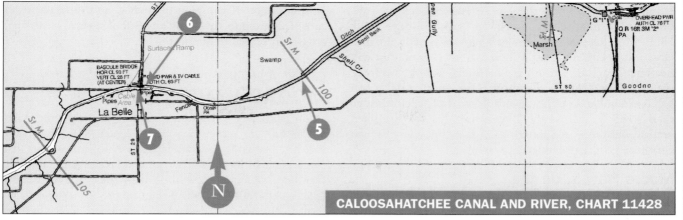

CALOOSAHATCHEE CANAL AND RIVER, CHART 11428

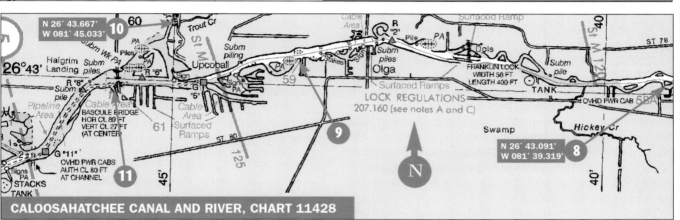

CALOOSAHATCHEE CANAL AND RIVER, CHART 11428

Calaosahatchee Canal, FL

Immediately beyond the Moore Haven Lock are two bridges. The first, the Moore Haven Railroad Bridge (Mile 78.3, 5-foot closed vertical clearance), is usually open; if closed, it opens on signal from 6 a.m. to 10 p.m., but will not open from 10 p.m. to 6 a.m. Signal before you leave the lock. The bridge is hand-operated, and the delay can be considerable. Use the eastern draw. The second bridge carries U.S. 27 across the Waterway. This bridge's fixed vertical clearance is charted at 55 feet, but there are no clearance gauges or fendering system.

Moore Haven, on the Caloosahatchee Canal

Dockage: On the west side of the Caloosahatchee Canal (the Waterway runs nearly north-south here), the city of Moore Haven (863-946-0711) has provided alongside dockage for visiting yachts. Normally, space is available, but during peak travel seasons, the early bird scores. The dock has been completely rebuilt and has a substantial rub rail on the outside of the pilings. Fenders will be needed, of course, to protect your boat from black marks. Use minimum space for tie-up so that the next boat will have room. Dockage fees may be paid at City Hall across the street, or to the dockmaster who calls in the early evening (and is a good source of local information). Showers are available behind City Hall during regular operating hours; get a key from the dockmaster.

The post office, a general store, a liquor store and other convenience stores are nearby on U.S. Route 27, the bridge road; a public library, with free wireless Internet, is across the street from the wharf, next to City Hall. (Between the bridges, a sign points up a side canal to the Moore Haven City Marina. This is open to the public, but is for small craft only; do not confuse this with the City Dock described above.)

Just beyond the City Dock is the Riverhouse Marina (863-946-3300) with additional dockage space. Showers and a guest laundry are available nearby; services of a marine mechanic are on call. Dockage fees are collected on the "honor system." In the morning, you will find an envelope on your deck, or where your power cord is plugged in, with information on the dockage rate; put cash or a check in the envelope, and deposit it in the marked locked box near the middle of the dock. If you are able to check in at the office, you will also find out that they have a golf cart available for use. At the far edge of these docks, there is now an overhead telephone or television cable (not a power line) crossing; clearance seems quite adequate, but specific height is not charted or known. A little farther along, at approximately Mile 90, there is another River Forest Yachting Center that is owned by the same people who own the River Forest Yachting Center on the St. Lucie River. This facility is just like the one on the eastern side of the lake except it is twice as large (at over 100,000 square feet). They also boast an 80-ton Travelift. This marina has been constructed to win the battles with hurricane winds. Transients are welcome with all of the amenities including showers, laundry, pump-out service and fuel.

Anchorage: If you plan to anchor, an overhead power cable (reported to have only an 18-foot vertical clearance) crosses the creek to the north.

GOIN' ASHORE:
MOORE HAVEN, FL

Moore Haven is an important trading and shipping point for produce and catfish, as well as a center for the sugarcane industry. Settled in 1915 by James A. Moore, it was the first real settlement in this Everglades and lake region. From the yachtsman's point of view, the nearby sugarcane fields are a mixed blessing. As part of the cutting process, the fields are burned, and (depending on the season, and wind direction and strength) your boat may end up covered with sooty black flakes. The Everglades Restoration Project, however, will change all this. Over the next decade or so, water from the Kissimmee River will be allowed to flood land at the southern end of Lake Okeechobee, thereby replenishing the flora and fauna of the Everglades. Despite opposition from farmers, cattlemen and the sugar industry, the project has wide support in Florida.

ADDITIONAL RESOURCES

■ Lake Okeechobee, **www.lakeokeechobee.org**

⚑ **NEARBY GOLF COURSES**
Glades Golf & Grill, 1682 Indian Hills Drive, Moore Haven, FL 33471, 863-983-8464

⚕ **NEARBY MEDICAL FACILITIES**
Hendry Regional Medical Center, 500 W. Sagamore Ave., Clewiston, FL 33440, 863-983-9121

Caloosahatchee Canal— Mile 82.5 to Mile 89

NAVIGATION: Use Chart 11428. Early-morning fog and mist sometime curtail an early departure, but normally the Caloosahatchee Canal is straightforward, wide and deep, with no surprises. At about Mile 82.5, the channel passes through shallow Lake Hicpochee, where again you may encounter small fishing boats anchored along the shore. Watch your wake as a matter of both prudence and courtesy.

Dockage: Just past Lake Hicpochee and the bend in the Caloosahatchee Canal, on the south bank, is Glades Marina. The basin is small and dockage is limited. Facilities ashore are sparse, but the marina offers excellent protection from the wakes of vessels passing by on the Waterway. You can also have your mast stepped here.

Anchorage: At Mile 91, just before Turkey Creek, there is a narrow canal that leads into Lollipop anchorage. It is small, but if you go all the way into the little lake, you will find ample room for anchoring in very protected water.

Ortona Lock—Mile 93.5

Before you get to Ortona Lock, several small canals lead off to the north into the Turkey Creek community. Most of its residents are boating types, and their docks usually are full of cruising boats of all descriptions—providing, of course, that these yachtsmen are not in the Bahamas or the Keys.

NAVIGATION: Use Chart 11428. Ortona Lock's smooth concrete walls are a vast improvement over its previous timbered sides that invariably caught fenders and rub rails. Tie-up dolphins are located outside both ends of the locks; boats normally make fast to the north side. The Ortona Lock operates the same way as the others; again, be prepared for some surge as the water is let out; the change in level varies, but 8 to 10 feet is normal depending on lake level. The lock operates from 6 a.m. to 9:30 p.m.

Dockage: At Mile 100, an entry channel leads off to the south into the Port La Belle Marina, with a restaurant, golf course, tennis courts, and horseback and bicycle riding. Although dockage is limited, you can anchor in 8-foot depths (at normal water levels).

Anchorage: Just east of the marina, there is another cove (known to some cruisers as Tranquility Cove) that is now being developed into an extension of the marina; this will greatly increase the availability of dockage. Slips have been built for boats of various sizes, and a wharf that has been constructed around the perimeter of about half the cove will provide alongside dockage for many craft.

La Belle—Mile 103

Dockage: The highway bridge at La Belle, (Mile 103.0, 28-foot closed vertical clearance), is closed from 10 p.m. to 6 a.m. Call 866-335-9696 for an opening during these hours; three hours notice is required. Additional restrictions prohibit openings during morning and afternoon rush hours (7 a.m. to 9 a.m. and 4 p.m. to 6 p.m.); at this time, no other bridge on the Okeechobee Waterway has such restrictions.

Just beyond the bridge, the town dock on the south side has free dockage (three-day limit, after which you must leave and not return for at least eight days), but it is exposed to the wake of passing boats. The small dock is usually full (six or seven boats can be accommodated if stern-in, Mediterranean mooring is used), and boats may be rafted or anchored. A library is just a few steps up from the dock. South along Bridge Street, within four blocks, are a hardware store, large supermarket, bank with ATM, coin laundry and post office. A&E Bait Shop sells ice in 25-pound blocks. A park is just across the highway at the foot of the La Belle Bridge.

Across the Waterway on the north shore is a longer dock with amenities, operated by the River's Edge Motel. Its overnight rates include use of the pool. A well-stocked convenience store is less than a block away. To the west, also on the north side, is a Hendry County Boat Ramp with a pier for small boats. No overnight docking is permitted.

GOIN' ASHORE: **LA BELLE, FL**

This quiet old river town dates back to the early 1800s. The Swamp Cabbage Festival is held in La Belle's boat-ramp park during the last full weekend in February. Swamp cabbage, also known as hearts of palm, is the growing part of the sable palm. Another local delicacy is alligator. La Belle also is known as the "Honey Capital." The Harold P. Curtis Honey Company is located near the beginning of the business district on the south side of the bridge. Worth a visit, the company maintains about 1,000 beehives and will permit you to sample different types of honey. A local restaurant, Flora and Ella's, famous for fresh catfish, hushpuppies and pie, is located west on Highway 80 a couple of miles from the La Belle Bridge.

ADDITIONAL RESOURCES

 Greater La Belle Chamber of Commerce,
www.labellechamber.com

 NEARBY GOLF COURSES
Admiral Lehigh Golf Resort, 225 E. Joel Blvd.,
Lehigh Acres, FL 33972, 239-369-2121

NEARBY MEDICAL FACILITIES
Hendry Regional Convenient Care Center,
450 S. Main, Suite 1, La Belle, FL 33935, 863-675-2356

■ CALOOSAHATCHEE RIVER

La Belle to Olga—Mile 103 to Mile 121

These are the scenic headwaters of the Caloosahatchee River, once a major transportation artery in the settling of Florida. Today, you will rarely encounter tugs and barges. Trucking has diminished the commercial importance of the river.

NAVIGATION: Use Chart 11428. Where once the Caloosahatchee River wandered, it is now a series of straight sections punctuated by gentle turns and numerous intriguing side loops (called oxbows) and streams. Still a beautiful Waterway, the water runs quite deep to the banks. Swinging room on the river, even at its widest points, is limited, and anchoring is not recommended unless you can keep your vessel from swinging into the channel. Some of the oxbows are deep enough if you feel adventurous, but snags or shoals, and possibly low-hanging power cables, are prevalent, and some property owners are not overly friendly. At about Mile 106.6, well out from the northern bank, red daybeacon "2" marks a shoal.

Bridges: Two bridges cross this section of the Caloosahatchee River. The Denaud Bridge, at Mile 108.2, is a swing bridge with a 9-foot closed vertical clearance. The bridge opens on demand, and arrows indicate which side of the draw to use. It is closed from 10 p.m. until 6 a.m. and requires a three-hour notice to open during those hours; call 863-675-2055. The Alva Bascule Bridge, at Alva at Mile 116, has a 23-foot charted closed vertical clearance and likewise opens on signal. Use VHF Channel 09 (same closed hours and advance notice required, call 239-278-2704).

Dockage: At Mile 119 is Rialto Harbor Docks, a small marina on a serene and picturesque oxbow off the south side of the river, east of the Franklin Lock. This marina is one-of-a-kind. You will have an individual dock, your own small deck area, barbeques that will be lit for you, a flower delivered to the ladies, as well as restrooms and showers that are almost like being at home. It is a truly enjoyable experience. Enter the oxbow at its west end, and keep to dockside when approaching and leaving. Nearby, there is a small convenience store and restaurants that deliver. Rialto Harbor is a seasonal dockage facility with on-site repairs.

Anchorage: Boats often anchor on the north side of the Caloosahatchee River in the wide spot across from the entrance to Rialto Harbor Docks. Anchor clear of the mooring.

W.P. Franklin Lock—Mile 121.4

The final lock on the Okeechobee Waterway is at Olga. The lock operates on demand from 6 a.m. to 9:30 p.m. daily.

Enter on the green light, and remember not to tie off your lines tightly, as the level will drop about 3 feet. Wait until the lock is fully open before casting off, and exit slowly. Sometimes eastbound boats are waiting nearby to enter. Immediately east of the lock and dam, on the north shore, is a small, but attractive Corps of Engineers marina consisting of eight slips (with shore power, water, showers and laundry) that can accommodate up to eight boats (not more

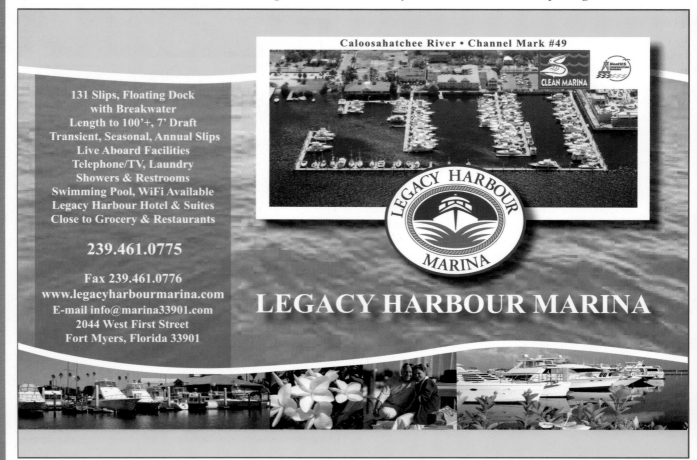

Fort Myers Area, FL

FORT MYERS AREA		Largest Vessel Accommodated	VHF Channel Monitored	Transient Berths / Total Berths	Approach / Dockside Depth (reported)	Floating Docks	Gas / Diesel	Groceries, Ice, Marine Supplies, Snacks	Repairs: Hull, Engine, Propeller	Lift (tonnage), Crane, Rail	1=110V, 2=220V, B=Both, Max Amps	Laundry, Pool, Showers	Pump-Out Station	Nearby: Grocery Store, Motel, Restaurant
		Dockage					**Supplies**				**Services**			
1. Prosperity Pointe 134 **WIFI**	239-995-2155	50	16	10/53	8/5	F		GIMS			B/50	LS	P	GMR
2. City of Fort Myers Yacht Basin 134.5 ⊑	239-321-7080	300	16/68	20/255	10/6		GD	GIMS			B/100	LPS	P	MR
3. Marinatown 135 ⊑	239-997-7711	68	16	40/139	5/5			IMS	EP		B/50	LPS	P	GMR
4. **Legacy Harbour Marina** 135 ⊑ **WIFI**	**239-461-0775**	**120**	**16/12**	**10/131**	**7/7**	**F**		**GI**			**B/100**	**LPS**	**P**	**GMR**
5. Royal Palm Yacht Club 136.5 ⊑	239-334-2176	80	16	/48	8/5						B/50	S	P	GMR
6. Paradise Yacht Club 139	239-997-1603	55	16	4/69	5/7						B/50	LPS	P	MR

Corresponding chart(s) not to be used for navigation. ⊑ Internet Access **WIFI** Wireless Internet Access

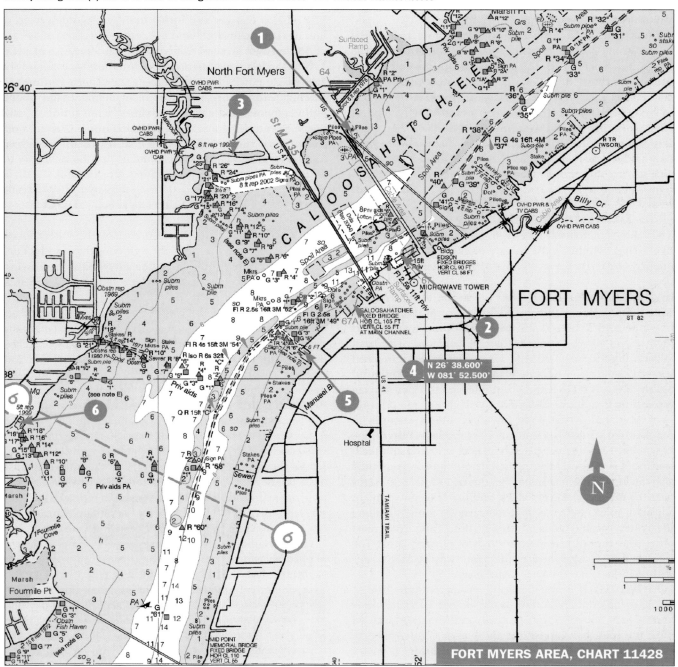

FORT MYERS AREA, CHART 11428

Fort Myers, FL

than about 35 feet long). Four of the slips are first-come, first-served, and advance reservations can be made for the other four slips (877-444-6777). Reservations must be made at least 72 hours before arrival. Another protected anchorage is just below the lock, next to the Corps of Engineers campground, with ample room and 10-foot depths.

Aids to Navigation: The Caloosahatchee River has many aids to navigation, beginning with red daybeacon "2" just downriver from the W. P. Franklin Lock. Although this is a navigable river coming in from the Gulf of Mexico, it is not marked with the conventional "red-right-returning" system with numbers increasing as one proceeds inland. The daybeacons, lights, etc., are a continuing part of the Okeechobee Waterway system—numbers increase as you cruise westward, and the "reds" are on your right side even though you are going downriver. This can be confusing if you do not understand the system.

Dockage: Approaching Mile 125.5, just before the Olga Bascule Bridge, a channel leads off to the north. The Owl Creek Boat Works and Storage is a full-service yard, friendly and familiar to both local and cruising yachtsmen. It is a good place to leave your boat if you have a land trip to make; the freshwater storage area under cover offers good storm protection. Also, if you need to re-step a mast, this area might be the best place other than Fort Myers to do it. A little farther on is Sweetwater Landing, a full-service marina that accepts transients and has gas available.

Olga to Fort Myers— Mile 121.4 to Mile 135

The Caloosahatchee River now looks and winds more like a river. Homes with private docks appear more frequently the farther you travel along the river.

NAVIGATION: Use Chart 11428. **Use the St. Petersburg Tide Tables. For high tide, add 1 hour, 56 minutes; for low tide add 2 hours, 23 minutes.** From here to Fort Myers, you have several bridges to consider. The first, Wilson Pigott Bridge at Mile 126.3, has a 27-foot closed vertical clearance. The bridge is closed from 10 p.m. until 6 a.m. and requires a three-hour notice to open during those hours; call 239-656-7800.

At Mile 127.5, the scale of Chart 11428 changes to 1:40,000 for its final section, an inset marked "Fort Myers Extension." A Manatee Speed Zone here is strictly enforced; specific restrictions vary in the channel and outside, and also during different seasons. Beginning at Mile 128, signs near the overhead power cables, and the large power plant adjacent, mark the zone. Manatees can be found all along the Waterway, but as usual they seem to congregate most often near the warm-water outflows of power plants. The Interstate 75 Bridge crosses the Waterway at Mile 128.9 with a 55-foot fixed vertical clearance.

At Mile 129.9 is the Beautiful Island Railway Bridge, normally open unless a train is due. Closed vertical clearance is only 5 feet, so signal or call, and then hold well off until the train has passed and the bridge is fully opened. (Note that the overhang is 55 feet when the bridge is open.)

Beautiful Island lives up to its name, but do not get in too close, here or from this point on. There are some areas, particularly on the south side, where you can leave the channel, but do so very cautiously after examining your chart. Because the Caloosahatchee River is more than a mile wide, it can get rough in nasty weather, so anchoring, although possible, could become unpleasant.

Dockage: Just west of flashing green "37," a marked channel leads south off the Okeechobee Waterway to Fort Myers Yacht, a large full-service storage and repair facility with a 55-ton lift and 300-ton railway.

Watch your wake as you pass through the two Edison Bridges (Mile 134.6, 56-foot vertical clearances). Note that the Waterway does not pass through the highest span of either bridge. The City of Fort Myers Yacht Basin is immediately to port as you clear the second bridge. The marina has gas and diesel fuel, pump-out service, a laundry, pool, showers and restroom.

Anchorage: Across from flashing green "13," at Mile 128, is the last good anchorage before Fort Myers. Locally known as Power Plant Slough, the western channel is reached by entering southwest of the manatee sign, about halfway between the sign and shore. Continuing in, the deepest water (7-foot plus depths) is about 100 feet off the western shore. The eastern channel of the slough is narrower, shallow and more difficult to follow.

■ FORT MYERS—MILE 135

While not actually the western end of the Okeechobee Waterway, most cruisers might well consider it to be Fort Myers. Like most of Florida, the city boasts a growing population, especially if you include the Cape Coral area across the river on the north shore.

Dockage: The City of Fort Myers Yacht Basin, situated on the south shore of the Caloosahatchee River between the westernmost span of the Edison Bridges and the Caloosahatchee Bridge (Mile 135.0, 55-foot fixed vertical clearance), has 280 slips and is within walking distance of supplies. Well-known by the cruising yachtsman boater, the dockmaster and his staff have made the marina a noted layover for both long- and short-term cruisers. Reserve ahead to make sure of having a space available when you arrive. A small store at the marina sells basic food items, boating supplies and nautical clothing. Across the river at some distance are 10 moorings administered by the City Yacht Basin; access across the shallows is by a marked channel. These are available to liveaboards on smaller sailboats. Seahorse Marine, an international yacht broker with a friendly staff, is also located here.

Legacy Harbour Marina, next downriver (make your turn to port at flashing green "49"), has floating slips for vessels up to 100 feet that are well-protected from the wakes of river traffic, complimentary cable TV hook-ups and slip-side pump-outs. A well-equipped and very pleasant daytime lounge is available with dial-up Internet connections; there is wireless Internet coverage over all the dock area and adjacent waters. Adjacent is a motel with well-appointed rooms and a swimming pool; advance reservations are recommended. There is a supermarket within a half-mile walk, and it is convenient to downtown Fort Myers. Joe's Crab Shack is next door.

The Royal Palm Yacht Club, an original member of the Florida Council of Yacht Clubs, is located about a mile beyond the Caloosahatchee Bridge. It has its own marked channel on the south shore and is open only to members, their guests and members of other recognized yacht clubs.

A marked channel on the north side of the river, just past the Caloosahatchee high-level bridge, leads into Hancock Creek and then into the North Fort Myers community. Just beyond red daybeacon "26" is Marinatown, with many local boats, but little to offer transients.

GOIN' ASHORE: **FORT MYERS, FL**

The city is named for a fort established during the Seminole Indian War of 1841. It became the winter home of Thomas Alva Edison in 1884 and remained so for almost 50 years. Edison's 14-acre riverfront estate is situated along McGregor Boulevard, which is lined for 15 miles with 2,000 royal palms (the reason Fort Myers is known as the "City of Palms"). His house, laboratory and grounds are open to the public. When enjoying the gardens, visitors should note the tropical plants given to Edison by friends. The immense Australian fig tree was tiny when Henry Ford sent it, and the 400-foot banyan (a gift from Harvey Firestone) was only two inches in diameter when planted. An excellent historical museum, with exhibits dating from 1200 B.C. to the present, is housed in the Atlantic Coast Line railroad depot relatively close to the downtown area.

ADDITIONAL RESOURCES

■ Greater Fort Myers Chamber of Commerce,
www.fortmyers.org

⚑ NEARBY GOLF COURSES
Fort Myers Country Club, 3591 McGregor Blvd.,
Fort Myers, FL 33901, 239-321-7488

☤ NEARBY MEDICAL FACILITIES
Lee Memorial Hospital, 2776 Cleveland Ave.,
Fort Myers, FL 33901, 239-332-1111

Cape Coral—Mile 142

NAVIGATION: Use Charts 11428 and 11427. Southwest of Fort Myers, the Caloosahatchee River continues somewhat circuitously for another 15 miles. At Mile 138.6 is the Mid Point Memorial Bridge, with a 55-foot fixed vertical clearance. At Mile 142, the Waterway passes under the Cape Coral Bridge (charted at 55 feet, but do not count on more than 54 feet of fixed vertical clearance). Cape Coral began when the Rosens purchased 103 square miles of swampland known as Redfish Point. At 114 square miles, it is now the second largest city in Florida and hosts a winter festival in February. Cape Coral's canals total more mileage than those of Venice, Italy.

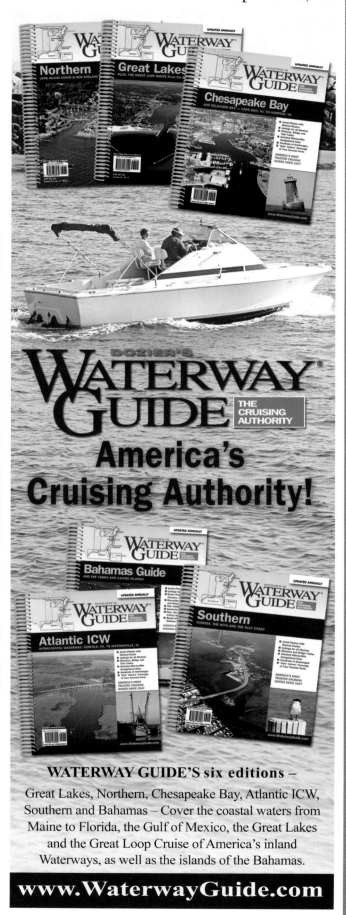

WATERWAY GUIDE'S six editions –
Great Lakes, Northern, Chesapeake Bay, Atlantic ICW, Southern and Bahamas – Cover the coastal waters from Maine to Florida, the Gulf of Mexico, the Great Lakes and the Great Loop Cruise of America's inland Waterways, as well as the islands of the Bahamas.

www.WaterwayGuide.com

Cape Coral, FL

CAPE CORAL		Largest Vessel Accommodated	VHF Channel Monitored	Approach / Dockside Depth (reported)	Transient Berths / Total Berths	Dockage Floating Docks	Gas / Diesel	Groceries, Ice, Marine Supplies, Snacks	Supplies Repairs: Hull, Engine, Propeller	Lift (tonnage), Crane, Rail	1=110v, 2=220v, B=Both, Max Amps	Services Laundry, Pool, Showers	Pump-Out Station	Nearby: Grocery Store, Motel, Restaurant
				Dockage				**Supplies**			**Services**			
1. The Landings Marina 142.5	239-481-7181	60	16	/193	5/		GD	IMS			B	S	P	
2. Fort Myers Boat Club 143	239-454-2629	60		/50	5/5		GD	IMS	EP	L20	B/50		P	
3. Gulf Harbour Marina 143.5 ⌨ WiFi	239-437-0881	101	16	10/186	6/5	F	GD	IMS			B/50	LS	P	R
4. CAPE CORAL YACHT BASIN 144 ⌨	**239-574-0809**	**55**	**16**	**4/93**	**5/5**		**GD**	**IS**	**EP**		**B/50**	**LPS**	**P**	**GMR**
5. St. Charles Yacht Club WiFi	239-466-2007	84	16/68	/65	5/5		GD				B/50	LPS	P	R
6. Sea Tow of Lee County 147	239-945-4820	150		TOWING SERVICE - CALL VHF CHANNEL 16 OR 11										
7. Tarpon Point Marina 147	239-549-8500	80	16	6/175	6/8		GD	IMS			B/50	PS	P	
8. The Marina at Cape Harbour 147	239-945-4330	60	16	16/76	6/6		GD	IMS		L11	B/50	LPS	P	GMR

Corresponding chart(s) not to be used for navigation. ⌨ Internet Access WiFi Wireless Internet Access

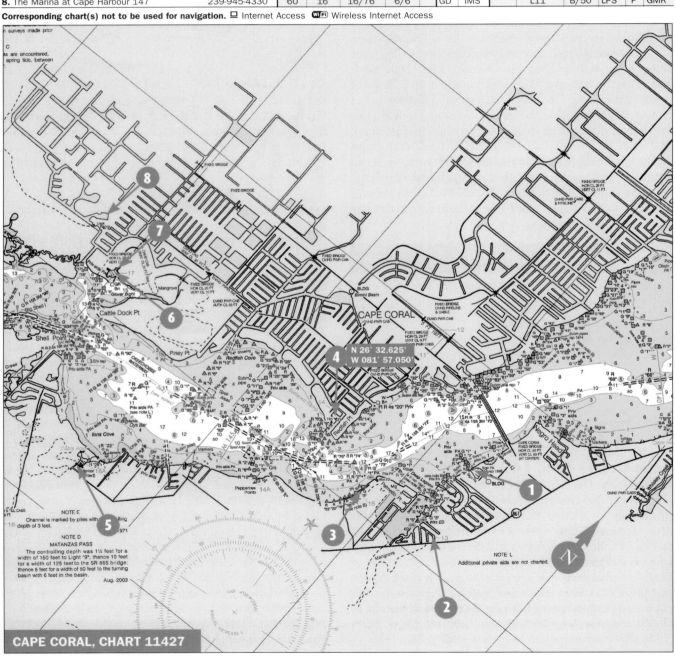

CAPE CORAL, CHART 11427

Note: West of Cape Coral, frequent groundings occur in the mouth of the Caloosahatchee River, an annual annuity for the towing firms and area boatyards. Follow the chart's magenta line, use the ranges front and rear, and it is easy. Lose track of markers or become careless, and you will have problems. Although the bay just west of red daybeacon "94" at Shell Point appears to be an attractive anchorage, the depths at the entrance have shoaled to 3 to 4 feet at mean low water.

Dockage: Between flashing red lights "70" and "72" on the south side of the river, a channel, marked near shore, leads into the Landings Marina, with gasoline and diesel fuel, but no transient dockage. Near quick flashing green "73," a well-marked channel leads southward to the Gulf Harbour Yacht and Country Club, a plush facility that welcomes transients. The Cape Coral Yacht Basin, offering many amenities, is north of red daybeacon "78" off a marked channel. Fuel is available at a separate facility located at the entrance. East of flashing green "89," a marked channel (starting with green daybeacon "1") leads southward to the St. Charles Yacht Club, another member of the Florida Council of Yacht Clubs; dockage, fuel and excellent shoreside facilities are available here in a completely protected harbor.

This is a boating-oriented area, and the traffic is reminiscent of downtown Fort Lauderdale. Exercise some care in transiting the remaining miles of the Okeechobee Waterway. Numerous shoal areas are outside the channel. If you have trouble, the local TowBoatU.S. and SeaTow boats are standing by. At red daybeacon "92," a channel leads behind Cattle Dock Point to the north, where markers guide you into the well-appointed Tarpon Point Marina.

Located just past Cattle Dock Point and Tarpon Point, signs will guide you to a small lock that provides access to the Marina at Cape Harbour. The marina offers transient dockage in a luxurious condominium setting. A laundry, pool, restrooms/showers and all fuels are available, as well as the upscale Rumrunner Restaurant on-site.

Anchorage: At Mile 145, there is a well-marked channel off to starboard that will lead you into Bimini Basin. You need to stay in this channel, and make a 90 degree turn to port when you get to green "25." Then keep the red markers on your port side (we know that this is different, but it is very important) until you come to the canal that will lead you into the anchorage. It is well-protected and is a handy spot to get to a couple of supermarkets and West Marine, as well as a variety of other services. There is also a dinghy dock at the park. You can anchor with confidence in 10 feet of water for up to 30 days. Glover Bight, just behind Cattle Dock Point at Mile 147, is another excellent, all-weather anchorage.

Cruising Options

In the following chapter, WATERWAY GUIDE explores the San Carlos Bay to Sarasota area past Sanibel and Captiva Island. San Carlos to Sarasota continues the journey northward up the Gulf Coast. ■

San Carlos Bay to Sarasota

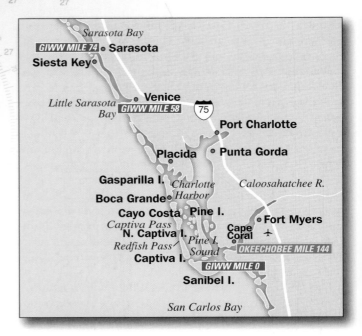

With its popular coastal barrier islands, including Sanibel, Captiva, North Captiva, Cayo Costa, Gasparilla Island, Little Gasparilla Island, Don Pedro Key and Manasota Key, fertile fishing grounds and one of Florida's great bodies of water (Charlotte Harbor), the 60-mile-long stretch from San Carlos Bay to Sarasota Bay and Sarasota itself is a mariner's paradise. The almost-tropical climate is kept comfortable by Gulf breezes much of the year, though some summer days can get very hot.

Traveling north from Fort Myers Beach, a skipper can choose between two passages from San Carlos Bay: outside up the Gulf of Mexico or inside along the Gulf Intracoastal Waterway (GIWW). Unless you must hurry to meet a deadline and are in a powerboat that can hit high double numbers, take the protected and infinitely more interesting GIWW route inside.

North, up the Gulf of Mexico (Outside)

NAVIGATION: Use Charts 11426, 11427 and 11425. Mariners running the Gulf of Mexico need only to choose their weather and go. The only complications along this route are the shoals and bars that extend out from many areas of the shoreline and form an integral part of virtually every pass and inlet on Florida's West Coast. Be sure you are standing sufficiently offshore to clear them. Staying three or four miles off the beach should get the job done.

To head north on the outside (this route is somewhat longer than cutting up Pine Island Sound because you have to skirt the shoaled southern end of Sanibel Island), one must first head south down a marked channel that goes underneath Sanibel Causeway Bridge. Once far enough south of the bridge, at the San Carlos Bay Morse (A) marker "SC," it is okay to turn west, but keep a sharp eye on your course and track as there are shoals to starboard.

Note the shoal area south of Sanibel where depths of 1 to 2 feet are reported. Once clear of the southern shore of Sanibel, lay a course west of the Boca Grande flashing red bell buoy "2" (roughly 4.5 nautical miles outside the entrance to Charlotte Harbor; GPS coordinates: N 26° 39.910'/W 082° 19.631'). You might find it convenient at this point to enter a target waypoint just offshore of your target destination. No matter where you choose to stop, you can always keep that waypoint to check distance to your final destination. Just make sure that waypoint keeps you far enough offshore to avoid shoal areas.

If you definitely plan to visit Sarasota, you may want to move inside at some point, and Venice is a good choice, if you are heading north (Venice has a clean, well-marked inlet). The two passes closest to Sarasota, New Pass and Big Sarasota Pass, (though substantially improved over the years), benefit from a lot of local knowledge to safely enter Sarasota Bay.

■ GULF INTRACOASTAL WATERWAY (GIWW)

NAVIGATION: Use Chart 11427 or 11426. The U.S. Army Corps of Engineers' project depth for the length of the 150-mile-long Gulf Intracoastal Waterway (GIWW) is purported to be 9 feet, but do not count on having that much water. Keep an eye on the depths here, especially in winter when northerly winds push the water out of bays and channels. Even under optimum conditions, in certain spots (noted in the text) shoaling is so chronic that boats should slow down and gently ease their way through.

Going north on the GIWW, leave red markers to starboard, green to port. As with the Atlantic Intracoastal Waterway, GIWW markers are green or red with small yellow triangles on red markers and squares on green markers (and an occasional yellow stripe), in addition to the numbers and/or letters. Another way to remember this is that the red marks delineate the mainland side of the GIWW channel.

A number of bridges cross the Waterway. Some open on signal; others are restricted. WATERWAY GUIDE gives the bridge schedules with each bridge (in the Skipper's Handbook section in the front of this book), but to stay on the safe side, verify information locally or with the Coast Guard. Remember that Florida bridge tenders are required to monitor VHF Channel 09. The bridge tenders are in control of the bridge openings, so what anyone else says is pretty much moot anyway. Always talk to the person in charge.

San Carlos Bay

NAVIGATION: Use Chart 11427. If you come out of the Okeechobee Waterway, you will be in the GIWW at Shell Point. There is not so much as a bump to tell of the transition. To reach the GIWW from Fort Myers Beach, head west from Matanzas Pass. If your vessel's overhead clearance requirements are no more than 26 feet above the water, you can use the fixed span "C" of the Punta Rassa-to-Sanibel Causeway; if not, you will have to go through the span "A" bridge, which is on the Punta Rassa side of the bay. If you plan on transiting span "C" from Matanzas Pass, set a course of 265 degrees magnetic from flashing green "1" when leaving the Matanzas Pass channel, to flashing red "2" on the Sanibel Island side of the entrance to San Carlos Bay, a distance of about 2.75 nautical miles. From there, once under the "C" span and about 2.5 nautical miles up the well-marked channel, you will pick out quick flashing green "11" of the GIWW channel.

The Sanibel Causeway Bridge (span A) is now a reality and has a 70-foot fixed vertical clearance at mean high water. To reach the high span of the Sanibel Causeway from flashing green "1" at Matanzas Pass, steer a course of 282 degrees magnetic to flashing red "6," indicating the start of the channel to the Caloosahatchee River and the Okeechobee Waterway. Follow the channel from flashing red "6," through the bridge and then to flashing red "14," leaving it to starboard. Shortly past that red lighted aid watch for the green daybeacon "1" to the southwest and flashing green "101" to the northeast, which marks the end of the Okeechobee Waterway and the beginning of the GIWW (Mile 0). Turn to port, and carefully follow the well-marked channel southwest, until you reach the junction of the GIWW and the main channel coming into San Carlos Bay from the Gulf (via the fixed 26-foot "C" span of the Sanibel Causeway).

Punta Rassa

Dockage: Just north of the eastern end of the fixed bridge (span "A") west of Punta Rassa, you may find a berth at Sonesta's Sanibel Harbor Resort & Spa.

Anchorage: Vessels have been seen anchoring between span "A" and the GIWW in a couple of different places. One is in the deeper water slot between Kitchel Key and Fisherman Key in 7 to 11 feet and the other is just north of Punta Rassa Cove in 8- to 13-foot depths. Both places are fairly exposed, but will suffice in a pinch during settled weather for those wanting to make a early start in the morning through the Okeechobee, to go outside heading south or to head north on the inside in the GIWW.

GIWW Mile Zero

NAVIGATION: Use Chart 11427. Coming from the south, if you were able to use span "C" of the Sanibel Causeway, you join the GIWW at quick flashing green "11." If you had to use the tall span to the east, to reach Mile Zero, you must

head north from the fixed span at Punta Rassa to the mouth of the Caloosahatchee River. Just past flashing red "14" (to starboard) off to the northeast, you will spot quick flashing green "101," which marks Mile Zero, the official beginning of the GIWW—heading generally westward before turning northwest—and the official end of the Okeechobee Waterway coming in from the east. At this junction, boats from Florida's east coast, the Keys and the southwest coast all meet. (See the "Okeechobee Waterway" chapter for coverage of the passage to and from Florida's east coast.)

Sailors in auxiliary-powered sailboats know the stretch between Mile Zero and the southeastern tip of Pine Island as the Miserable Mile. Here, the tide sweeps in and out directly across the arrow-straight channel, and strong crosscurrents are likely. Allow for the set, and line up markers fore and aft. The channel is well-marked and easy to follow. Be a bit careful heading west just past flashing green "5" where the channel cuts off to the northwest; do not stray too far to the west into 2- to 3-foot depths at mean low water. Along this stretch, you will see many ospreys tending their large nests.

Be especially careful crossing south of Matlacha Pass. Around green daybeacons "5" and "9," the currents are very strong and the channel, running through shoals, is prone to silting. A mile farther west, near where the channel bends to the northwest south of Pine Island, the problem worsens. Northerly winds tend to build up silt in the area.

Anchorage: At the southern tip of Pine Island sits St. James City, central point for fishing on the lower sound. Fishing camps and "runabout marinas" abound here, along with shallow water and numerous private markers that can be confusing to the stranger.

You can anchor south of town by the mangroves in 8 to 9 feet of water and dinghy to shore. A restaurant is a short block away.

Matlacha Pass (Chart 11426) carries a marked, but shallow, crooked channel north between Pine Island and the mainland to Charlotte Harbor. Controlling depth is about 3 feet, and a 32-foot-high power cable and a bascule bridge cross the pass. This passage is not recommended, but Matlacha Pass can be safely explored from the northern entrance. An anchorage with 7-foot depths is southeast of the bridge. Restaurants are within dinghy range. Note that the power cables (formerly at 56 feet of vertical clearance) have been raised to a 75-foot height.

Pine Island Sound

Liberally dotted with small islands and protected from the open Gulf by a string of barrier islands, Pine Island Sound runs about 15 miles to the mouth of Charlotte Harbor at Boca Grande Pass. Many of the small islands in the sound are part of the Pine Island National Wildlife Refuge, closed to all public access to protect the wildlife.

NAVIGATION: Use Chart 11427. The channel runs a jagged course, often at an angle to the swift current, through pools of relatively deep water interspersed with great shallow

SANIBEL MARINA
the islands only deepwater, full service marina

Nestled on the Southern tip of Sanibel Island sits the charming, tranquil Sanibel Marina. Its ideal location grants many boaters traveling up and down the Intercoastal direct access to the Gulf. Its many amenities include:

- 6' Depth at Low Water
- Transient Docks
- 86 Boat Slips
- Shower & Laundry Facilities
- Ship's Store
- Beverages, Snacks & Ice
- Full Service Department
- Yacht & Engine Sales
- 120' Fuel Dock-Gas & Diesel
- Boat Rentals
- Fishing Tackle & Bait
- Fishing Charters
- Gramma Dot's Restaurant

Gramma Dot's

Over 40 years ago, while cruising in her motor yacht, Marjella, Gramma Dot discovered Sanibel Island and fell in love. This love transcended through three generations and her name now adorns the most charming spot on the island - Gramma Dot's award winning Seaside Saloon, now serving the finest seafood, chowder, gourmet burgers, specialty salads - and Gramma Dot's own famous desserts.

Come to Sanibel Marina and discover the charm of Sanibel Island for yourself. But let us warm you just like Gramma Dot, you may fall in love with this tropical paradise and never want to leave.

IRELAND YACHT SALES
GRAMMA DOT'S

634 North Yachtsman Drive • Sanibel Island, Florida 33957 • Between the Causeway and the Lighthouse
(239)472-2723 • Open Daily • We monitor Radio Watch 16 • 7am - 5pm • Sanibelmarina@gmail.com

Sanibel Island, Punta Rassa, FL

SAN CARLOS BAY		Dockage					Supplies			Services			
		Largest Vessel Accommodated	VHF Channel Monitored	Transient Berths / Total Berths	Approach / Dockside Depth (reported)	Floating Docks	Gas / Diesel	Groceries, Ice, Marine Supplies, Snacks	Repairs: Hull, Engine, Propeller	Lift (tonnage), Crane, Rail	1=110V, 2=220V, B=Both, Max Amps	Laundry, Pool, Showers	Pump-Out Station	Nearby: Grocery Store, Motel, Restaurant
1. Sanibel Marina 0 💻	239-472-2723	120	16	15/86	6/6		GD	IMS		EP		B/50	LS	P	R
2. Sanibel Harbour Resort & Spa 0	239-466-4000	50	16	10/15	12/5	F		I				B/50	PS		GMR
3. Sanibel Harbour Marina 0	239-489-2969	30	16	PRIVATE											
4. Port Sanibel Marina 0	239-437-1660	65	16	10/100	5/8		GD	IMS				B/50	LS	P	R

Corresponding chart(s) not to be used for navigation. 💻 Internet Access **(WiFi)** Wireless Internet Access

SANIBEL ISLAND, SAN CARLOS BAY, CHART 11426

Sanibel Island, FL

Looking east from Sanibel Island over San Carlos Bay. (Not to be used for navigation.) WATERWAY GUIDE PHOTOGRAPHY.

bays. Exercise caution. Stay to mid-channel, take navigational aids in order, and do not try any shortcuts. In Pine Island Sound, between flashing green "23" and red daybeacon "24" at about Mile 8, power lines cross the channel with a charted vertical clearance of 95 feet at the main channel.

Anchorage: J.N. "Ding" Darling National Wildlife Refuge offers an excellent anchorage possibility during settled weather in the cove due south of flashing red "16" (situated south of York Island). Holding is excellent in sand and mud close to Sanibel Island's mangrove shoreline in 5 to 6 feet of water.

Chino Island in Pine Island Sound offers protection from easterly and northerly winds with good holding. Leave the Waterway at flashing green "23," and you will find 7- to 8-foot depths almost to the shore. A number of anchorages are located off the Miserable Mile, to both the north and south as the deep water is indicated, and in the deep pockets of Matlacha Pass, north of the Miserable Mile area.

■ OFFSHORE ISLANDS

A line of barrier islands—Sanibel, Captiva, North Captiva and Cayo Costa—separate Pine Island Sound from the Gulf of Mexico. Together, the islands form a shallow crescent lying at an angle to the currents. That accident of shape and location causes what are said to be the world's most prolific shell deposits and the resultant "Sanibel stoop" of the island's visitors.

More than 300 varieties of shells have been found on these beaches. A Sanibel Island law prohibits collectors from taking live shells, living starfish and sand dollars. The best shelling is at low tide after a storm, when winds and waves have washed a new supply up on the beaches. Sanibel Island can have as many as four tides a day. In March, the annual Shell Show attracts collectors from all over the world.

Facilities for transient mariners on Sanibel and Captiva islands range from rather simple overnight stops, to full-service marinas and resorts. Be careful making your approach, however. The sandy bottom is always shifting, and you are best advised to enter these basins at half-tide or better, and to call ahead for the latest local information.

Sanibel Island

The only public landing on the island, other than dropping the hook and landing by dinghy, is at Sanibel Marina.

NAVIGATION: Use Chart 11427. Plot a course for flashing red "2" south of span "C" of the Sanibel Causeway and about half a nautical mile due east of the coast of Sanibel. A little less than a nautical mile to the northwest-by-west, you will see red daybeacon "2" marking the entrance to the channel to Sanibel Marina. Enter the channel, take a sharp turn to port, then to starboard, avoid the obvious shoal to port and you will arrive at Sanibel Marina's fuel dock.

Once ashore, your best bet may be to rent a bike to explore the island. Heading southeast from the marina, you will come to the historic Sanibel Lighthouse at Point Ybel (circa 1884), the Lighthouse Beach Park and a fishing pier.

Heading northwest from the marina, the tree-lined main thoroughfare, Periwinkle Way, takes you to the Sanibel Historical Village and Museum (239-472-4648), which showcases the island's history with pioneer-vintage island residents and 1920s versions of a general store, post office and tearoom. The Bailey-Matthews Shell Museum (239-395-2233) houses shells from around the world, as well as special Florida exhibits. For provisioning, Jerry's Foods is along the way.

The 6,354-acre J.N. "Ding" Darling National Wildlife Refuge takes up much of this 12-mile long island, mainly along the northern, Pine Island Sound side. The refuge also serves as headquarters for several small wildlife refuges on nearby islands. During the nesting season, mariners are asked not to land on these rookery islands. If pelicans are frightened off their nests by human intruders, they leave their eggs exposed to fish crows. The refuge offers nature walks, canoe trips, a wildlife drive and an interpretive center. Even the most casual visitor here will inevitably see numerous Florida alligators, anhinga "snakebirds," roseate spoonbills, snowy egrets, wood storks, turkey vultures and great blue herons. Even pink flamingos are seen quite often. It is open daily and hours are 10 a.m. to 4 p.m. For more information, call 239-472-1100.

Dockage: A snug harbor is available at Sanibel Marina, which, as mentioned before, is essentially the only marina on the island. The marina monitors VHF Channel 16 and has transient slips to accommodate 6-foot drafts in an unhurried, palm-fringed setting. Once past the shoaling area, there is plenty of good water. Fuel, showers, laundry, bag and block ice and a pump-out facility at the fuel dock are all available. As an added treat, there is a complimentary early morning delivery of the local newspaper, The News-Press, and fresh muffins to your boat.

There is a ship's store that is expanding with a large inventory of boat necessities and clothing. Also, stop at the award-winning Gramma Dot's Seaside Saloon for some tasty Seafood Caesar, a local favorite, homemade potato chips and grouper sandwiches. South of the marina, and within walking distance, is Huxter's Market and Liquor Store (239-472-2151), a complete deli with some fruits and vegetables and an excellent beer assortment. The Lazy Flamingo restaurant and Dairy Queen are across the street from the market.

Depending on direction, it is a half-mile to either one of the world's most famous shelling beaches or two supermarkets. Sanibel Island has miles of bicycle paths (rental bikes are readily available) for easy access to all parts of the island. With the recent addition of a reverse osmosis water-treatment system, Sanibel Island has some of the best water in the area.

Anchorage: You can anchor with good protection in San Carlos Bay. When you enter from the Gulf of Mexico, proceed to flashing red "6" northeast of Pt. Ybel and turn toward the fixed bridge to port (span "C"), on the Sanibel Island side of the Punta Rassa-Sanibel Causeway. Good holding is available past the fishing pier on Sanibel Island, although the tidal current may call for a Bahamian moor.

Captiva Island

NAVIGATION: Use Chart 11427. Just to the north of Sanibel is Captiva Island, about six miles long and separated from Sanibel Island by Blind Pass, which is crossed by a 7-foot fixed vertical clearance bridge. Heading north up Pine Island Sound at red daybeacon "38," a course of about 215 degrees magnetic brings you back through shoal water to the little village of Captiva, where transients will find facilities.

Dockage: Honor the red markers (controlling depth is 6.5 feet) to reach 'Tween Waters Marina tucked in behind Buck Key. Here, you will find the 'Tween Waters Inn and its renowned dining room. The resort is complete, but unpretentious with a pool complex, tennis courts and lively pub-style bar (bands on weekends).

In addition to the usual marina amenities (gas and diesel are available here) and ships store, 'Tween Waters' superb private beach on the Gulf side is but steps away. Guided kayak tours of adjacent Buck Key are available, as are rental kayaks and canoes for private exploration of the local mangrove areas and Buck Island.

A channel marked with daybeacons leads from the GIWW just west of flashing green "39" to South Seas Island Resort (formerly South Seas Plantation). The channel leading into the marina is well-marked, but has been changed in late 2009. A call to the South Seas Island Resort's harbormaster (VHF Channel 16 or 239-472-7628) for local conditions and guidance is highly recommended. This has been an elegant and elaborate vacation complex with superb facilities for mariners, often regarded as one of the finest resorts on Florida's West Coast. Hurricane Charley (2004), the strongest hurricane to hit southwest Florida since Hurricane Donna in 1960, made some permanent changes here. It scored a direct hit. The marina has been entirely rebuilt since then, but some of the shade trees that were so delightful to sit under on a hot day are gone forever.

Redfish Pass, recommended only with local knowledge, has gained some depth and width with past hurricane activity. Reasonably well-marked, this channel has been recently changed and remarked with mean low water depths of 8 to 13 feet.

Anchorage: One anchorage is still available near 'Tween Waters Marina. However, the marina no longer offers dinghy docking privileges to anchored boats. Another anchorage area is located north of 'Tween Waters off the Green Flash Restaurant's dock. The only ATM in this area is down near the entrance to South Seas Island Resort. Take your dinghy to McCarthy's Marina and ask to tie up. This will reduce your hike for groceries, cash and the local liquor store.

North Captiva Island

NAVIGATION: Use Chart 11427. Shifting, shoaling Redfish Pass divides Captiva Island from North Captiva Island. This pass should only be used with local knowledge. If

Captiva Island, FL

Captiva Pass, looking southwest. (Not to be used for navigation.) Photo Courtesy of Sam Harris.

Looking southwest over Redfish Pass. (Not to be used for navigation.) Photo Courtesy of Sam Harris.

Useppa Island, looking west. (Not to be used for navigation.) Photo Courtesy of Sam Harris.

you choose to exit or enter the Gulf of Mexico here, call the South Seas Island Resort Marina for advice. Remember that currents are strong in this area. Also remember that free advice is worth what you pay for it.

Although used by fishermen with local knowledge, Captiva Pass, between North Captiva Island and Cayo Costa, is unmarked and subject to change. North Captiva Island is accessible only by boat. There are many private and rental homes here and a few restaurants in the Safety Harbor area. Stilt houses guard the entrance. Boca Grande Pass, a good exit to the Gulf of Mexico, is only six miles away to the north. Hurricane Charley cut the south end of the island in two in 2004, but the cut was shallow in nature and has been filling in.

Anchorage: A marked channel runs north from Captiva Pass across the GIWW toward Charlotte Harbor, but do not use it as a shortcut unless yours is a shallow-draft boat. This channel depth shoals in its upper reaches to about 5 feet. In the rest of the channel, depths run 7 to 13 feet with occasional spots for anchoring. The channel leads to Pineland, where there is a small marina with 3-foot controlling depths that services North Captiva Island. Off the southeast tip of Cayo Costa, an anchorage is within a dinghy-pull of the beaches at both North Captiva Island and Cayo Costa in 9 and 10 feet respectively.

Cayo Costa

Spanish fishermen from Havana gave Cayo Costa its name (translated as "Coastal Key"). Six miles long and located

at the north end of Pine Island Sound on the south side of Boca Grande Pass, this almost-uninhabited island (it does have feral pigs living on it) is accessible only by boat.

Anchorage: At Mile 22.5, at the southern tip of Punta Blanca, is a slice of deep water that provides an attractive anchorage. The adventurous skipper can take up to a 6-foot draft vessel completely around the point where there is an exceptionally cozy anchorage. The downside of the equation is that this anchorage has atrocious ventilation and is best in winter months.

At Mile 25, at the northern end of Punta Blanca Island (between Punta Blanca and Cayo Costa), is Pelican Pass and Pelican Bay. Although the Pelican Pass entrance may at first appear a bit dicey, the anchorage beyond is well worth the effort. Both Punta Blanca Island and Cayo Costa are part of the Cayo Costa State Park.

The park headquarters are located on Cayo Costa, just inside Pelican Pass. Here, you will find daytime dockage and some overnight dockage (no hookups). The park extends to the Gulf side of the island where there are not only beautiful beaches, but also cabins and camping. Transportation across the island is by foot, tram or rental bike.

With caution, a little help from the tide and a reliable depth sounder, boats drawing up to 5 feet can normally get through Pelican Pass into Pelican Bay. From red daybeacon "74," travel southwest toward the tip of the beach on Cayo Costa. Stay to within about 75 feet of the sand beach, and just past the little sign in the water, turn slightly to port

Pine Island Sound, FL

PINE ISLAND SOUND		Largest Vessel Accommodated	VHF Channel Monitored	Transient Berths / Total Berths	Approach / Dockside Depth (reported)	Floating Docks	Gas / Diesel	Groceries, Ice, Marine Supplies, Snacks	Repairs: Hull, Engine, Propeller	Lift (tonnage), Crane, Rail	1=110v, 2=220v, B=Both, Max Amps	Laundry, Pool, Showers	Pump-Out Station	Nearby: Grocery Store, Motel, Restaurant
				Dockage			**Supplies**		**Services**					
1. 'Tween Waters Marina 11.0	239-472-5161	100	16/72	41/41	6/6		GD	GIMS			B/50	LPS	P	GMR
2. Jensen's Twin Palm Resort & Marina 12 🖥 WiFi	239-472-5800	25	16		5/5		G	IS						GMR
3. South Seas Island Resort & Marina 13.6 🖥 WiFi	888-777-3625	120	16		6/4		GD	GIMS			B/50	LPS	P	GMR
4. Cabbage Key 21.14	239-283-2278	85	16	25/25	8/6			IS			B/50	LS		MR
5. Useppa Island Club 22 🖥 WiFi	239-283-4227	100	16	/50	10/10			GIMS			B/200	LPS		GMR
6. Four Winds Marina 6 NE of 19	239-283-0250	40	16	/89	3.5/4	F	G	IMS	HEP	L5	B/50	S		GMR

Corresponding chart(s) not to be used for navigation. 🖥 Internet Access WiFi Wireless Internet Access

(east) and follow the beach up into Pelican Bay. You will find 5 to 6 feet of water in the pass. When inside Pelican Bay, pay attention to your depth sounder as there are several very shallow areas. You can anchor in 7 to 8 feet with plenty of swing room. This is a very popular anchorage so it can get crowded on weekends.

Useppa Island

Opposite Cayo Costa, north of the GIWW, at about flashing red "60," is the private island of Useppa. This lovely, 100-acre island stands 37 feet above the water due to the numerous shell mounds here. The dunes are covered with more than 200 varieties of tropical trees, plants and flowers.

Legend claims the pirate José Gaspar kept a Spanish noblewoman prisoner here, and the island's name is a corruption of her name, Joseffa de Mayorga. A small museum on Useppa Island, open for a few hours a day, presents the history of the island and surrounding area in wonderful detail. It is a must-stop for all visitors.

Accessible only by water, Useppa Island has been established as a private club that has preserved the authentic flavor of the past. The cottages erected in 1912 by Barron Collier for his tarpon fishing friends have been rebuilt, and his mansion now serves as the clubhouse and restaurant.

Amenities consist of a fitness center and clay tennis courts, pool, hot tub and a horseshoe court on the beach.

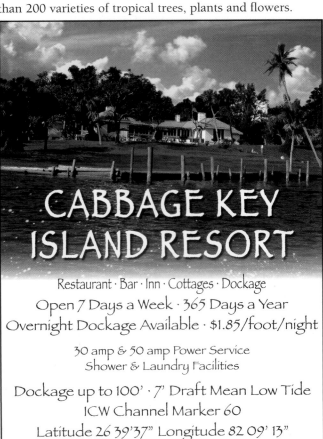

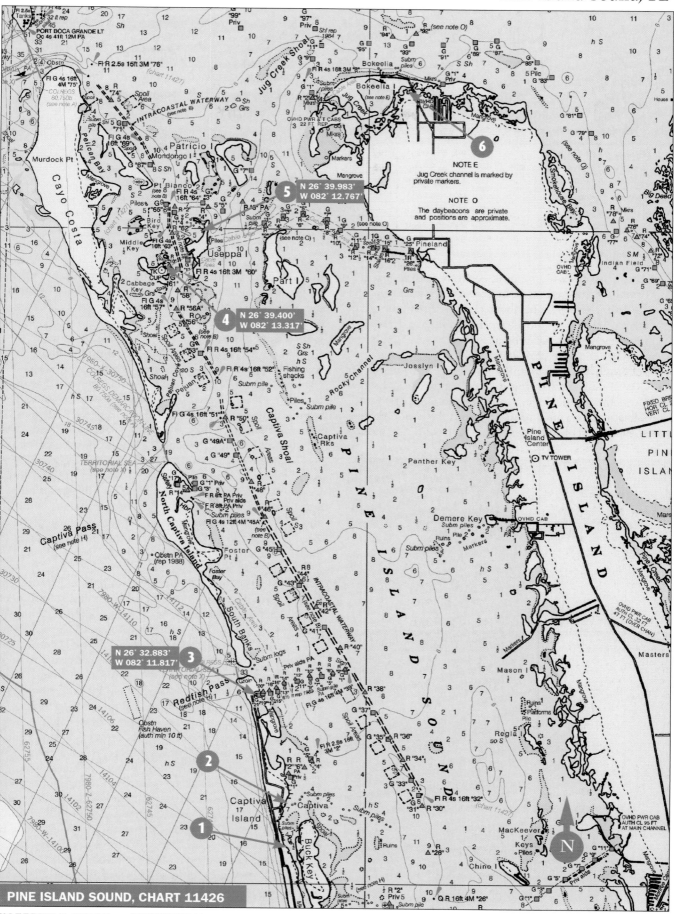

NOTE E
Jug Creek channel is marked by private markers.

NOTE O
The daybeacons are private and positions are approximate.

5 N 26° 39.983' W 082° 12.767'

4 N 26° 39.400' W 082° 13.317'

3 N 26° 32.883' W 082° 11.817'

PINE ISLAND SOUND, CHART 11426

Charlotte Harbor, FL

CHARLOTTE HARBOR, MYAKKA RIVER		Largest Vessel Accommodated	VHF Channel Monitored	Approach / Dockside Depth (reported) Transient Berths / Total Berths	Floating Docks	Gas / Diesel Groceries, Ice, Marine Supplies, Snacks	Repairs: Hull, Engine, Propeller	Lift (tonnage), Crane, Rail	1=110V, 2=220V, B=Both, Max Amps	Laundry, Pool, Showers Pump-Out Station	Nearby: Grocery Store, Motel, Restaurant
				Dockage		**Supplies**			**Services**		
1. BURNT STORE MARINA ⌨ WiFi	941-637-0083	100	16	30/525	7/6	GD	GIMS	EP		B/50	LPS	P	GMR
2. Fishermen's Village Yacht Basin WiFi	941-575-3000	120	16	97/111	7/7	GD	IMS			B/200	LPS	P	GMR
3. Laishley Park Municipal Marina	941-575-0142	80	16	20/85	7/7	F	IMS			B/50	LS	P	R
4. Punta Gorda Marina	941-639-2750	60	16		4/4	G	M	HEP	LC				MR
5. Charlotte Harbor Yacht Club	941-629-5131	65	16/68		4/6	GD	I			B/50	S	
6. ALL AMERICAN COVERED BOAT STORAGE	941-697-9900	50	16/68	12/32	6/7		M	HEP	L35,C	1/30		
7. Charlotte Harbor Boat Storage	941-828-0216	55							L37	1/30		

Corresponding chart(s) not to be used for navigation. ⌨ Internet Access WiFi Wireless Internet Access

Period touches include the pink concrete path that winds past cottages covered with latticework, a small gazebo and a 16-by-16-foot chessboard with three-foot playing pieces. Useppa Island is a private club, and inquires regarding membership can be answered by contacting the Membership Director (239-283-4227).

Anchorage: A large, popular anchorage is available off the GIWW between flashing red "60" and red daybeacon "62" near the west side of Useppa Island. This anchorage can sometimes be uncomfortable from wakes of passing boats, especially on weekends, but the scenery is beautiful. The advantages of this anchorage far outnumber the disadvantages. Cabbage Key, across the GIWW channel to the west, is a short dinghy ride away.

Cabbage Key

Just west of the Waterway channel at Mile 21, Cabbage Key lies in the lee of Cayo Costa. This delightful and unspoiled island offers ample opportunity for observing nature in all its forms. Here, reached by the marked entry channel just west of green daybeacon "61," is the classic old Florida island retreat, the Cabbage Key Inn. This special inn (with cottages and rooms available) is the former home of the son of Mary Roberts Rinehart, the famous mystery novelist. The marina is tucked into the foot of the 38-foot-high Indian shell mound that sites the Old House Restaurant and Inn. It is protected by a huge grass flat on the north and is accessible by a channel with an approach depth of 7 feet at mean low water. There is 6 to 8 feet of water at dockside. Space is limited, especially on weekends, so call for reservations (239-283-2278).

For years, visiting fishermen, passing to and from local tarpon-fishing hot spots, have taken rest and refreshment here. The story goes that to guarantee a cold beer on their return, they started the tradition of posting signed dollar bills on the bar and restaurant walls. The accumulated currency has piled up dollars deep over every square inch of wall and ceiling space, now adding up to more than $50,000. In addition to the expensive décor, the fresh shrimp, grouper and mahi-mahi are prepared to order.

For bird and nature enthusiasts, a bird-watching and nature walk should not be missed here. It is best begun at the top of the inn's walk-up water tower for an overview of the island. Easily followed trails traverse Cabbage Key's connected shell mounds, revealing representative varieties of subtropical trees, shrubs, plants and bird life. Nesting ospreys are abundant, as are telltale signs of the Florida gopher tortoise. Dockage is somewhat tight here, but is energetically assisted by the colorful resident harbormaster. For reservations, call ahead on VHF Channel 16.

A great side trip by dinghy gives you access to the front beach, by way of The Tunnel. If you are anchored northeast

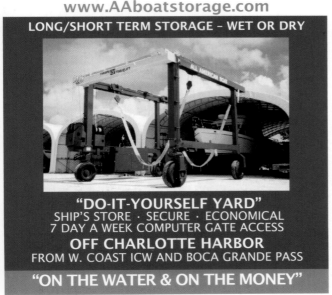

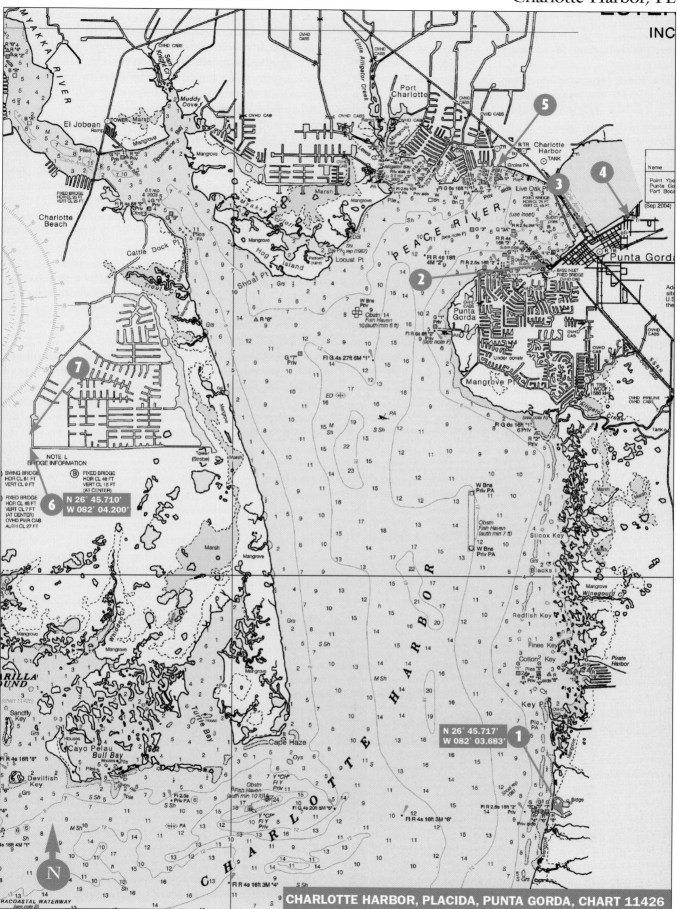

N 26' 45.710'
W 082' 04.200'

N 26' 45.717'
W 082' 03.683'

CHARLOTTE HARBOR, PLACIDA, PUNTA GORDA, CHART 11426

Charlotte Harbor, FL

of flashing red "60," proceed south around Cabbage Key to Murdock Bayou. Go almost to the end of Murdock Bayou and you will see a small, open area in the mangroves on the west side. There is enough room to tie a couple of dinghies to the mangroves. Walk through the tunnel of mangroves to the path that leads to the beach (watching out for alligators). It is a great place to picnic and enjoy the white sandy beach. In north winds, depths through The Tunnel and Murdock Bayou may be too shallow even for dinghies.

Bokeelia

On the north end of Pine Island, the small settlement of Bokeelia on Bokeelia Island offers some repairs and marine facilities—a marina and condo development here include a restaurant, clubhouse and swimming pool.

■ CHARLOTTE HARBOR

About 60 miles southeast of Tampa Bay, Charlotte Harbor is a wide, elbow-shaped bay carrying 9-foot depths to Punta Gorda at the mouth of the Peace River. Stretching 20 miles long and 10 miles wide, Charlotte Harbor offers a lot for the cruising boater.

Charlotte Harbor is formed by the confluence of the Peace and Myakka rivers. Tidal range averages 2 feet, but winds from the west reportedly can increase water levels as much as 5 feet. The open sweep and relatively uniform depths of water in Charlotte Harbor provide a welcome change from the narrow, shoal-bordered Waterway. The high sandbars that protect the shoreline limit opportunities for gunkholing, but both the Peace and Myakka rivers compensate for that weakness by offering opportunities for scenic dinghy trips.

It is a good place for daysailing and has variable winds. Yacht clubs in the area are involved year-round in sailboat racing and offer privileges to members of reciprocating clubs. When entering any marina in Charlotte Harbor, be sure to stay inside the marked channels; the water can be very shallow outside of them.

CHARLOTTE HARBOR PASS
WATERWAY GUIDE PHOTOGRAPHY

Dockage: Opposite Boca Grande Channel, and midway up the eastern shore of Charlotte Harbor, Burnt Store Marina is a justly popular stop. Flashing red "6" leads off the approach from Charlotte Harbor, and is then followed by flashing red "2" and a series of daybeacons into the protected harbor. The service is friendly, and the amenities are tops. It also offers discounts in the off-season. Here, you will find gas and diesel fuel, a laundry, pool, showers/restrooms, limited marine supplies, a restaurant and a gift shop—all laid out in a resort-style setting. Taxis are available for the relatively lengthy ride to Punta Gorda for any extensive re-provisioning.

Quiet anchorage off the GIWW. Photo Courtesy of Susan Landry.

Boca Grande, FL

Myakka River

Wandering through dense woodland, the Myakka River runs from the northwest from Myakka Lake to Charlotte Harbor. Boats drawing 3 feet or less and armed with local knowledge can travel about 17 miles up the Myakka River. A 25-foot fixed vertical clearance bridge three miles up limits overhead clearance; the railroad bridge just beyond is open and abandoned. Protected anchorages lie between the bridge and green daybeacon "9" in the river and Tippecanoe Bay. Myakka State Park, in the upper reaches of the Myakka River, preserves a wilderness reminiscent of the Everglades. There are big alligators, feral hogs, eagles, deer and rattlesnakes up there and even the very rare Florida panther.

At the mouth of the Myakka River past green daybeacon "9" on the south shore of the river is a set of daybeacons that lead to an automated lock and the Santa Cruz Waterway, which has 6.5-foot depths.

Dockage: Six miles down the Waterway in Placida are a couple of marine facilities, most notably All American Covered Boat Storage. The facility has a 37-ton lift, unique aircraft hanger dry storage for yachts of all sizes and a do-it-yourself yard. It is popular with boat owners looking for a safe and secure place to leave their boats in the off-season and to do repairs and maintenance.

Peace River

The Peace River enters Charlotte Harbor from the northeast. Marked for only about six miles, its channel is navigable to Hull, 15 miles up. Offering 3-foot depths, this stretch calls for local knowledge, and the snags and heavy growths of hyacinths in the upper river require caution as well. Two 45-foot fixed vertical clearance bridges and a 12-foot fixed vertical clearance bridge, 14 miles up, cross the Peace River. The first 45-foot bridge is the Interstate 75 Bridge. If you own a pocket cruiser and can get under the bridge, there is a lot of adventure ahead. You need to be resourceful for this out-of-the-comfort-zone kind of travel, but you will come back with some colorful stories.

Punta Gorda

Punta Gorda is a charming boating community made up of 60 miles of canals that meander through its neighborhoods and lead to Charlotte Harbor. The city has a historic district with 157 significant historical residential and commercial structures along its brick-lined streets. Its designation as a Florida Main Street Community, together with a revitalization that has been going strong since Hurricane Charley in 2004, has resulted in many new or renovated amenities now available to boaters.

Along the Punta Gorda coastline of Charlotte Harbor is the Harborwalk, a scenic pedestrian and bicycle friendly river walk lined with palm trees, brick pavers and park amenities. The Harborwalk currently extends from the eastern side of the town, through Laishley Park Municipal Marina to the site of the Best Western Hotel - the future home of the city's second mooring field.

The Harborwalk is planned to meander southwesterly to Fishermen's Village Marina and connect into the City's Linear Park and bicycle trail.

Dockage: Fishermen's Village Yacht Basin is located on upper Charlotte Harbor with no bridges or other restrictions to the Gulf of Mexico and is within walking distance of Historic Punta Gorda. Fishermen's Village Yacht Basin offers 111 slips enclosed by a breakwater, 31 courtesy docks for day trippers and a long dinghy dock. Daily and long-term slips are available to the public, and liveaboards are welcome. Vessels up to 120 feet can be accommodated. Each slip has a trash box, dock box, potable water, cable TV, wireless Internet service, 30- and 50-amp shore power (100-amp available) and holding tank pump-outs.

Fishermen's Village Yacht Basin is a Florida "Clean Marina" and offers spotless restrooms, showers and a laundry. Other shore facilities include an air-conditioned boater's day room, tennis courts, heated swimming pool, picnic areas with propane and charcoal grills, free loaner bicycles and a ship's store offering boating supplies, clothing items, fax and copying service. The 120-foot-long fuel dock offers gas and diesel fuel, ice and bait.

Laishley Park Municipal Marina, opened in 2007, consists of 85 slips, a sailor's day room with restrooms, showers and laundry facilities, a ship's store and a community room. A 40-ball mooring field has been proposed, but in spring 2010, permits had not been issued. The hope is that it will be constructed within the next year. Also, they are trying to get permits to construct 20 day-use docks. The existing boat ramp was renovated with two 90-foot adjacent loading docks and upland parking for vehicles and trailers. The marina is situated in Laishley Park, which hosts many festivals and activities throughout the year, including the nationally broadcast ESPN Redfish Tournament each spring. In the park is the 16,000 square foot Laishley Crab House restaurant and assorted shops. The Park and Marina sit adjacent to downtown Punta Gorda, which is home to the Charlotte Harbor Event & Conference Center, several hotels, many restaurants and boutique type shops.

■ BOCA GRANDE TO SARASOTA

When you leave Boca Grande for the northward push to Sarasota, or farther to Tampa Bay, you can choose to go outside to run north up the Gulf of Mexico or continue on the GIWW.

Outside Run

NAVIGATION: Use Chart 11425. From Boca Grande Pass, local knowledge permits use of the shortcut route (known locally as "The Swash Channel"), primarily of value to shoal-draft boats (5-foot drafts or less). The channel leads to deep water well inshore of the end of the big-ship route, the main ship channel. To follow The Swash Channel around the tip of Gasparilla Island, proceed west in Boca

Gasparilla Sound, Boca Grande, FL

GASPARILLA SOUND, BOCA GRANDE		Dockage					Supplies					Services			
		Largest Vessel Accommodated	VHF Channel Monitored	Transient Berths / Total Berths	Approach / Dockside Depth (reported)	Floating Docks	Gas / Diesel	Groceries, Ice, Marine Supplies, Snacks	Repairs: Hull, Engine, Propeller	Lift (tonnage), Crane, Rail	1=110v, 2=220v, B=Both, Max Amps	Laundry, Pool, Showers	Pump-Out Station	Nearby: Grocery Store, Motel, Restaurant	
1. Boca Grande Marina 28.5 💻 WiFi	941-964-2100	100	16/14	15/15			GD	GIMS			B/50	LS	P	GMR	
2. The Gasparilla Inn & Culb 29.5	941-964-2201	50		2/24	6/4.5	F	GD	IM	P	L	B/50			GMR	
3. The Innlet On The Waterfront 29.5	941-964-2294	35		/23	6/5			I			1/30		P	G	
4. Uncle Henry's Marina 32.8 WiFi	941-964-0154	90	16	40/58	6/9		GD	GIMS			B/50	LS	P	GMR	
5. Gasparilla Marina 34	941-697-2280	80	16	/225	6/6	F	GD	IMS		L70	B/50	LS	P	GMR	

Corresponding chart(s) not to be used for navigation. 💻 Internet Access WiFi Wireless Internet Access

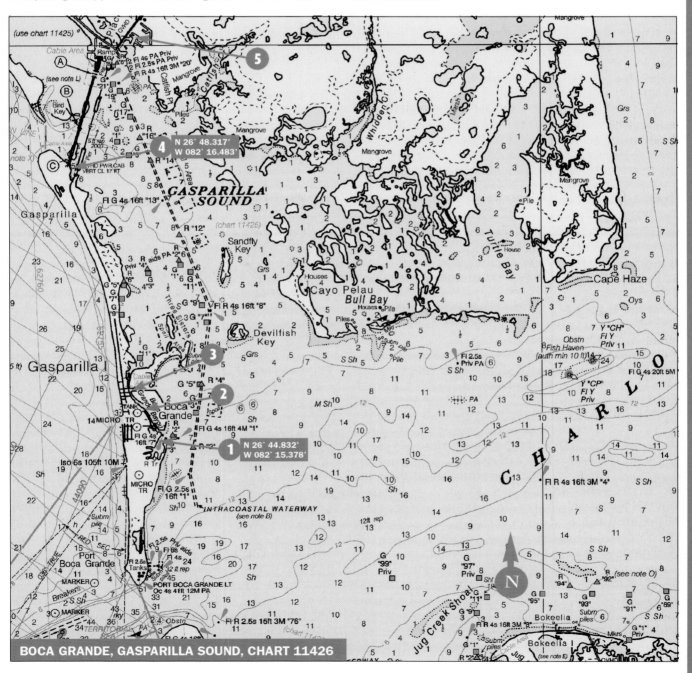

BOCA GRANDE, GASPARILLA SOUND, CHART 11426

Boca Grande, FL

Looking southwest over Boca Grande Pass. (Not to be used for navigation.) Photo Courtesy of Sam Harris.

GIWW

UNCLE HENRY'S MARINA

Little Gasparilla Island

Gasparilla Island

Gulf of Mexico

Looking east over Gasparilla Pass and the Gasparilla Causeway Bridge. (Not to be used for navigation.) Photo Courtesy of Sam Harris.

Grande Pass until the end of the dilapidated commercial pier, bearing 340 degrees magnetic. Pass the pier about 50 to 100 feet out in 7- to 8-foot depths (mean low water), avoiding the long shoal that runs off to the south-southeast. Once clear of the shoal, you will find 10- to 11-foot depths at mean low water.

Note, however, that if you are returning to Charlotte Harbor from the Gulf of Mexico in a brisk northwesterly with an outgoing tide, the longest way around is the shortest way home. Under such conditions, Boca Grande Pass can appear reasonably docile until you are almost next to the piers. Then you can be in breaking waves before you know it (the waves break away from you and are hard to recognize). So, the wise avoid The Swash Channel in such conditions, because there is no "wiggle room" there.

The more prudent, safer approach, or without local knowledge and particularly if the water is rough, is to enter via the ship channel. The shoals along the ship channel, particularly on the northwest side, need to be monitored carefully as the charted channel runs very close to them. If entering Boca Grande Channel when coming from the north, take care to come all of the way green buoy "3" and red nun buoy "4" to avoid them entirely. You will be at about the three nautical mile line and can then turn safely toward the northeast. Deeper water lies to the south side of the channel if you need to get out of the way of commercial vessels. Inexperienced skippers have lost their vessels on this shoal, so take heed.

Inlets

NAVIGATION: Use Chart 11425. From Charlotte Harbor to Sarasota, and even on to Tampa Bay, the coastline is nearly all straight sand beach and low, wooded shore broken by a few inlets. Most of these inlets are subject to frequent changes and should only be attempted with local knowledge.

The first one reliable enough for strangers is Venice Inlet, 26 miles northwest of Boca Grande. Carrying about 7-foot depths at mean low water, it passes between jetties to join the GIWW. In recent years, there was some shoaling from the Venice Inlet west to the GIWW and north beyond the Albee Road drawbridge. Observe the Idle-Speed/No-Wake Zone in Venice Inlet.

In Sarasota Bay, there are three inlets: Big Sarasota Pass (12 nautical miles from Venice Inlet), New Pass (three nautical miles north from Big Sarasota Pass) and Longboat Pass (about eight nautical miles north from New Pass).

Between Charlotte Harbor and Sarasota, only Venice and Longboat passes are unarguably recommended for use without local knowledge. And Venice is by far the better of the two.

Big Sarasota Pass is also passable without local knowledge, but only marginally so. Sarasota County has installed new markers in Big Sarasota Pass, making it passable for vessels with approximately 5-foot drafts. The data provided by the county is "not to be used for navigation," but it does indicate the location of each marker and course. The markers start at about the point of the old markers (discontinued by the U.S. Coast Guard some years ago because of consistent shoaling) somewhat south of Sarasota Point.

Reduce your speed and watch the markers carefully, as well as your depth sounder. Having your binoculars out is a must. The markers here are generally the floating type, cans and nuns. Know exactly where you are going before you get there, and do not run this channel in bad weather. Once "inside," green daybeacon "15A" is particularly confusing, because—when one is inbound in this channel—right behind "15A" is red daybeacon "16." This would indicate that the two together form a kind of gate that you will have to pass through. There is an indication of shoaling between these two close-together marks.

You may have more room and more depth when you are inbound if you leave green daybeacon "15A" to starboard and forget about red daybeacon "16" entirely. The next mark is green daybeacon "17," which you can leave to port, as you would normally. It has been suggested that you call TowBoatU.S. or another reliable source to get local information. After leaving green daybeacon "19" to port, your next mark will be flashing red "8," which puts you back in the GIWW heading for Ringling Causeway Bridge. Use the center span. There is some rubble on the bottom, to starboard, away from the center span.

NEW PASS BRIDGE

WATERWAY GUIDE PHOTOGRAPHY

New Pass continues to shoal on the north side. A bascule bridge (23-foot closed vertical clearance) crosses New Pass between Lido and Longboat keys. Buoys are moved frequently, and you can keep abreast of the moves through Local Notice to Mariners (available online at www.navcen.uscg.gov/lnm). Boats drawing more than 3 feet should use Longboat Pass as opposed to New Pass. Better still, if you have a boat that is challenged by shallow water, go inside at Venice, and stay inside all the way to Tampa Bay. These passes are not to be attempted in poor visibility or bad weather. On a good day, with little wind and with the sun overhead or behind you, they are okay. And even while they get an "okay" rating in the best of times, mistakes have been made here. A sailor with a steel-hulled boat lost his boat here when it hit the shallows and sank. Then, months and months later, a guy new to big powerboats managed to hit the sunken sailboat and sink his own brand-new-right-out-of-the-box power yacht on the second time out on the water. The loss of the second boat came to more than one million dollars.

Longboat Pass has a 17-foot closed vertical clearance bascule that opens on signal. Lightly powered boats should be aware of the strong currents that run through Longboat Pass.

The Coast Guard is no longer responsible for marking either the Big Sarasota Pass or the New Pass entrances to Sarasota Bay and advises boaters to use Venice Inlet to the south or Longboat Pass to the north. The West Coast Inland Navigation District (941-485-9402) offers several useful publications and can keep you advised of any changes in depths and buoys. Utilize every available resource to be informed, and keep you and your vessel out of harms way.

■ GIWW ROUTE

The inside route from Charlotte Harbor to Sarasota Bay is relatively clean, well-marked and not too heavily congested with manatee or boating safety areas with their Slow-Speed/Minimum-Wake or Idle-Speed/No-Wake Zones. The 25-mph speed zone in the Waterway channel (Slow-Speed/Minimum-Wake within a specified distance from the shore) is more the rule than the exception. Pay close attention to posted signs in order to ascertain exclusion or inclusion of the GIWW channel in these slow-speed restriction areas

Gasparilla Island (Boca Grande)—Mile 28

The waters around Boca Grande Pass are one of the world's great tarpon fishing grounds. Boca Grande, on the south end of Gasparilla Island, located about halfway between Fort Myers and Tampa, makes a good stop. In a bygone era, Boca Grande was a winter resort and fishing retreat for Northern socialites and tycoons (J.P. Morgan died here). For the most part, the gracious old homes they once occupied have been faithfully maintained, preserving the elegance of the past. There is old and new money here and lots of it. "Names" in the entertainment business seem to favor the Gasparilla Inn for its privacy and good manners.

In 1969, Boca Grande was the fourth busiest port in Florida, primarily because of the phosphate trade. Ten years later, the phosphate trade moved to Tampa, and the railroad serving the port was abandoned.

BOCA GRANDE BRIDGE

WATERWAY GUIDE PHOTOGRAPHY

NAVIGATION: Use Chart 11425. **Use the St. Petersburg Tide Tables. For high tide, subtract 1 hour, 12 minutes; for low tide, subtract 1 hour, 56 minutes.** The Boca Grande Channel from the Gulf runs between Cayo Costa and Gasparilla Island, forming the entrance to Charlotte Harbor. Easy to navigate, well-marked and lighted, it is one of the best passes on the stretch between Naples and Tampa.

To cross Boca Grande Channel from the GIWW inside, coming from the south, leave flashing red "76" to starboard off the northeast point of Cayo Costa. Take a bearing of about 350 degrees magnetic to cross the channel and pick up flashing green "1" off the eastern shore of Gasparilla Island. This is the start of the well-marked GIWW heading north.

Dockage: The landlocked Boca Grande yacht basin (not a business, but a designation on some charts), located about a quarter of the way up Gasparilla Island when you are headed north, offers secure berths or anchorage and a full range of amenities for visiting boaters. Sixteen-foot flashing green "1" must be kept to port; then turn west at red daybeacon "2" and pick up the channel markers into the harbor. On entering the Boca Grande Bayou, flashing green "7" should be given a wide berth because of the encroaching sandbar. Controlling depths are 6 feet at mean low water, both in the entrance channel and in Boca Grande Bayou.

Boca Grande Marina, located a half-mile from downtown inside the yacht basin, has renovated its floating slips to include shore power, wireless Internet access, portable slip-side pump-out service and good fendering. Heads and showers have been refurbished, and a coin-operated laundry is available. Plans call for a new restaurant and bar.

GOIN' ASHORE:
BOCA GRANDE, FL

The restored and upscale old Florida town is at the south end of Gasparilla Island. It is a charming place, with some of the feel of old Key West in the 1950s and '60s, before the tourist boom.

Hudson's Grocery (941-964-2621) on Park Avenue sells fresh produce, meat, fish, cheese and wine (closed on Sunday) and will deliver orders of more than $25 to your boat. The old railway depot in the center of town has been converted into a mini-mall with a variety of shops, including the well-regarded Loose Caboose Restaurant (941-964-0440).

Nearby are two banks, a hardware store, a health center, the post office (on Fourth Street), various boutiques and a bookstore. Favored by many for dining, the Pink Elephant (941-964-4540, closed Mondays) is located just across the street from an anchorage and private docks (rented by the elegant Gasparilla Inn) on Boca Grande Bayou, about a quarter-mile north of the harbor entrance. The Gasparilla Inn may also have dining space available (941-964-4535, by reservation only). Arrangements for an overnight tie-up may be possible through the Gasparilla Inn.

Boca Grande's most famous landmark is an 1890 lighthouse at the south end that was built to mark the entrance to Charlotte Harbor. It is open to the public the last Saturday of every month. As a point of interest, "Boca Grande" means "big mouth" in Spanish, referring to the deep Boca Grande Pass, one of Florida's deepest natural inlets.

One of Gasparilla Island's prime attractions is the community bike path, which runs almost the entire length of this seven-mile island, from the lighthouse at Boca Grande Pass to the Courtyard near Gasparilla Pass at the northern end of the island.

The beautiful vistas and accessible beaches along the way make this trek—by foot, bike or golf cart—well worth the effort. All manner of human- and battery-powered conveyances for this purpose, as well as various beach items, can be rented. And no tour of the island is complete without a walk along Banyan Street, south of the depot.

ADDITIONAL RESOURCES

■ Boca Grande Area Chamber of Commerce,
   www.bocagrandechamber.com

⚑ **NEARBY GOLF COURSES**
   Rotonda Golf & Country Club, 100 Rotonda Circle,
   Rotonda West, FL 33947, 941-697-2414,
   www.rotondagolf.com

⚕ **NEARBY MEDICAL FACILITIES**
   Boca Grande Health Clinic, 320 Park Ave.,
   Boca Grande, FL 33921, 941-964-2276

Little Gasparilla Island
NAVIGATION: Use Chart 11425. Those running north on the Waterway will find the bays beginning to narrow somewhat. Shores are closer and more developed, and you should watch the markers carefully.

From Boca Grande and deep Charlotte Harbor, heading north, the channel winds sufficiently to maintain interest. Channel depths average 7 to 11 feet at mean low water, although depths are extremely shallow outside the marked channel, where the birds are often able to walk.

Moving up the GIWW from the south, traversing Gasparilla Sound, at the town of Placida, Mile 34.3 (green daybeacon "19"), the Waterway channel doglegs to port. Pass through the permanently-opened railway bridge just past green daybeacon "21," then leave green daybeacon "1" to port before approaching the Boca Grande Swing Bridge (Mile 34.3, 9-foot closed vertical clearance; Monday through Friday, opens on the hour and half-hour from 7 a.m. to 6 p.m.; weekends and holidays, from 7 a.m. to

Cape Haze to Englewood, FL

LEMON BAY		Largest Vessel Accommodated	VHF Channel Monitored	Transient Berths / Total Berths	Approach / Dockside Depth (reported)	Floating Docks	Gas / Diesel	Groceries, Ice, Marine Supplies, Snacks	Repairs: Hull, Engine, Propeller	Lift (tonnage), Crane, Rail	1=110V, 2=220V, B=Both, Max Amps	Laundry, Pool, Showers	Pump-Out Station	Nearby: Grocery Store, Motel, Restaurant
1. Palm Island Marina 38.5 🖥	941-697-4356	70	16	27/96	7/6		GD	IM	EP	L50	B/50	LPS	P	GMR
2. Cape Haze Marina 39	941-698-1110	70	71	4/100	6/9		GD	I	P	L10	B/50	LPS		GR
3. Stump Pass Marina 40.8	941-697-4300	65	66	6/20	4.5/5	F	GD	IMS	HEP	L	B/50	PS	P	GMR
4. Thunder Marine 44.5	941-681-3400	46	08	/15	6/6	F	GD		HEP	L20	B/50			G
5. Royal Palm Marina 45.8	941-475-6882	65	16	/240	6/10		GD	IMS	HEP	L50	B/50	LS	P	GMR

Corresponding chart(s) not to be used for navigation. 🖥 Internet Access 📶 Wireless Internet Access

6 p.m., the bridge opens on the hour and at 15, 30 and 45 minutes past the hour). Of course, all that is subject to change. Use your VHF radio to get in touch with the bridge tender.

When approaching from the Gulf, buoys are not charted through Gasparilla Pass, an access used by local fishermen, but not recommended without thorough local knowledge. Take the long way around—it is smarter. The area around the pass is riddled with charted 2- to 3-foot spots, and the entire north side of the pass has a 1-foot bar on its border.

Dockage: At flashing red "20," a channel leads off to starboard (east) past the mouth of Coral Creek to Gasparilla Marina, which has about 20 transient slips in an enclosed basin. Arriving at this northern tip of Gasparilla Island, along the GIWW from the south, transients can put in at Uncle Henry's Marina. Entrance to the marina is on your port side just after passing the open railroad bridge and before reaching the swing bridge. Uncle Henry's Marina leads off to port at green daybeacon "1." The entrance has a 5.5-foot depth at mean low water and a 1.5- to 2-foot tidal range. With a wind out of the north, depths will be less. Pay attention to the tide tables; deep-draft skippers should call Uncle Henry's for a current report. There has been some silting along both sides of this access passage, so honor all markers, and stay as close to center channel as possible.

Uncle Henry's is a quiet, peaceful marina. The restaurant next to the marina is called Boca Bistro, an excellent,

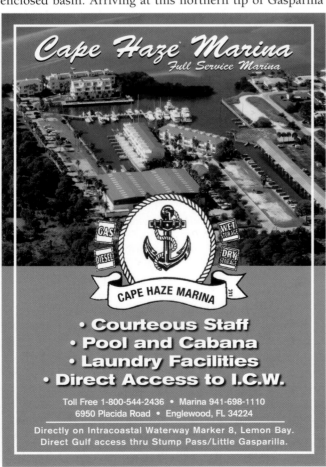
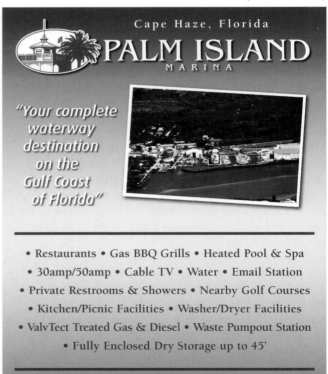

Lemon Bay, FL

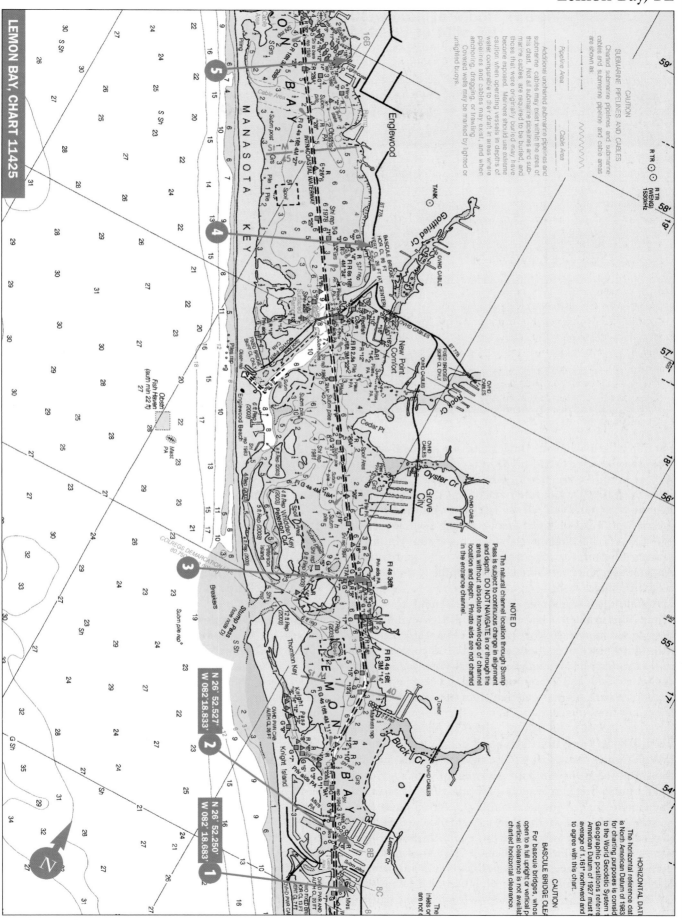

LEMON BAY, CHART 11425

Venice , FL

Looking east over Stump Pass. (Not to be used for navigation.) Photo Courtesy of Sam Harris.

top-notch establishment. Downstairs is a bar with a good wine selection and wood-fired-oven pizza to go. There is a grocery store a couple of doors away from the marina office, and laundry and other amenities are available. The marina rents golf carts for the five-mile or so trek to the pretty little town of Boca Grande proper (see above). If you plan on checking out the town, make sure you make a reservation for a cart well in advance, as the marina only has four available. More are available in the town, but it is a cab ride to get there.

Anchorage: Anchorage is limited around Gasparilla Island, and available space is often filled with locals on permanent moorings. At Mile 36, Cape Haze offers a nice, quiet anchorage northeast of red daybeacon "30" in 9-foot depths surrounded by private homes. Set your anchor carefully as the bottom is mucky. This is a pleasant anchorage with more protection from the Waterway than is evident from the chart.

Lemon Bay—Mile 40

NAVIGATION: Use Chart 11425. Beyond Placida Harbor, the Waterway turns south and threads through a series of small islands to a narrow 2.25-mile straight stretch called The Cutoff, leading into Lemon Bay. At green daybeacon "7" toward the end of The Cutoff, watch for the car ferry that crosses the Waterway. This is a real boat, not a valet parking service. Once into Lemon Bay, the Waterway swings to the northeast shore (starboard going north) and opens up for a 7.5-mile narrow straightaway through shallow water to the end of the bay. Shortly after green daybea-

con "17A," daybeacons will indicate a channel turning off to port, leading to Stump Pass, which opens to the Gulf. Stump Pass was reportedly dredged a few years ago, but charts indicate that no one should navigate in or through the area without absolute knowledge of the channel's location. It carries no official aids to navigation.

Dockage: Two marinas are located near Mile 38 before the GIWW enters Lemon Bay at Englewood Beach or at Englewood on the mainland shore.

The Palm Island Marina, located on the mainland near green daybeacon "7," offers showers, a swimming pool, ice and fuel. Marine supplies are available next door at MarineMax, a well-stocked ship's store.

Take the marina launch (it runs hourly) across the GIWW to Knight Island (aka Don Pedro Key) and visit the wide white beach. The marina's restaurant, bar and general store are open to visiting mariners. If your timing is good, you will arrive during one of the barbecues and enjoy the tangy ribs and sunset entertainment.

Just to the north is the Cape Haze Marina, a Texaco StarPort with a narrow, dredged channel. The friendly marina has transient dockage in a protected basin just off the ICW, pump-out service, a 10-ton lift, on-site repairs, a laundry, pool, showers/restrooms and 50-amp shore power and dockside cable television. There is a restaurant within walking distance.

Marinas in Lemon Bay tend to be small, unpretentious and friendly, but are geared to handle cruising boats. At green daybeacon "17A," right at the entrance to the Stump Pass Channel and just off the GIWW, is the large, full-

Venice Area, FL

VENICE AREA		Largest Vessel Accommodated	VHF Channel Monitored	**Dockage** Transient Berths / Total Berths	Approach / Dockside Depth (reported)	Floating Docks	**Supplies** Gas / Diesel	Groceries, Ice, Marine Supplies, Snacks	**Services** Repairs: Hull, Engine, Propeller	Lift (tonnage), Crane, Rail	1=110V, 2=220V, B=Both, Max Amps	Laundry, Pool, Showers	Pump-Out Station	Nearby: Grocery Store, Motel, Restaurant
1. Marine Max of Venice 55.1	941-485-3388	68	16	2/90	12/9		GD	IM	HEP	L	B/50	LS	P	GMR
2. Fisherman's Wharf/Marker 4 Marina 57	941-484-9246	120	16	12/44	8/7	F	GD	IM	E		B/100	S	P	GMR
3. Venice Yacht Club 57.5	941-483-3625	100	16	/49	10/10		GD	I	PRIVATE CLUB		B/50	PS		GMR
4. Crow's Nest Marina & Restaurant 58 ⌨	**941-484-7661**	**140**	**16**	**24/34**	**12/12**		**GD**	**IMS**			**B/50**	**LS**		**GMR**
5. Pop's Sunset Grill 59	941-488-3177	60			12/8			GIS			/30			GMR
6. Gulf Harbor Marina 59	941-488-7734	45	16		10/6		GD	IMS	HEP	L	/30			GMR
7. Pelican Alley Restaurant 59	941-485-1893	70			6/4			I						GMR

Corresponding chart(s) not to be used for navigation. ⌨ Internet Access 📶 Wireless Internet Access

VENICE AREA, CHART 11425

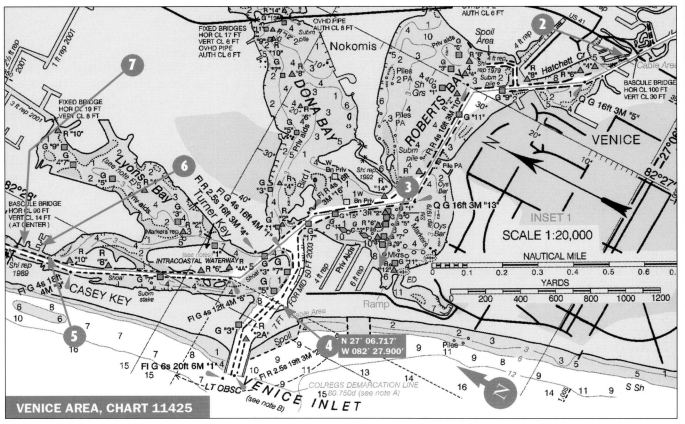

VENICE AREA, CHART 11425

Venice Inlet, looking east. (Not to be used for navigation.) Photo Courtesy of Sam Harris.

service Stump Pass Marina with overnight dockage for boats up to 65 feet. It offers electricity, showers, telephone and cable. A towering rustic lighthouse identifies the marina. At about Mile 43.5, the Tom Adams Bridge (26-foot closed vertical clearance bascule bridge) crosses the Waterway and opens on signal.

Anchorage: At Mile 43.5, on the west side of the Waterway, is a large, quiet anchorage with 7- to 10-foot depths at mean low water. The anchorage is reached by heading southwest between lighted red "22" and the Tom Adams Bridge. Buildings around the anchorage help to protect visiting yachts from buffeting winds. If you continue south, hugging the mangroves, you will be sheltered from all directions. Watch depths closely. You can dinghy to a nearby dock and restaurant. A convenience store and souvenir shop, dive shops, restaurants and the beach are across the street.

Past Lemon Bay, at Mile 53, the Waterway becomes a long, high-banked land cut, which runs through a corner of the Venice Municipal Airport. Watch for water-soaked debris in the cut; there is little tidal flushing action to move it out, and it can be a nuisance.

At Mile 54.9 and Mile 56.6, bascules with 25- and 30-foot closed vertical clearances, respectively, cross the channel. The first (Circus Bridge) opens on signal; the second (Venice Avenue Bridge) has restricted hours between 7 a.m. and 4:30 p.m., Monday through Friday, year-round, opening at 10, 30 and 50 minutes past the hour; note that it does not open between 4:35 p.m. and

Little Sarasota Bay, FL

LITTLE SARASOTA BAY		Largest Vessel Accommodated	VHF Channel Monitored	Approach / Dockside Depth (reported)	Transient Berths / Total Berths	Groceries, Ice, Marine Supplies, Snacks	Gas / Diesel	Floating Docks	Repairs: Hull, Engine, Propeller	Lift (tonnage), Crane, Rail	1=110V, 2=220V, B=Both, Max Amps	Laundry, Pool, Showers	Pump-Out Station	Nearby: Grocery Store, Motel, Restaurant
			Dockage					**Supplies**			**Services**			
1. Turtle Beach Marina 66	941-349-9449	40	16	/25	4/4	G	IMS		HEP		L	B/50	S	R
2. Coasters Restaurant 68.2	941-925-0300	32		8/8	6/6							1/30		R

Corresponding chart(s) not to be used for navigation. 🖳 Internet Access 📶 Wireless Internet Access

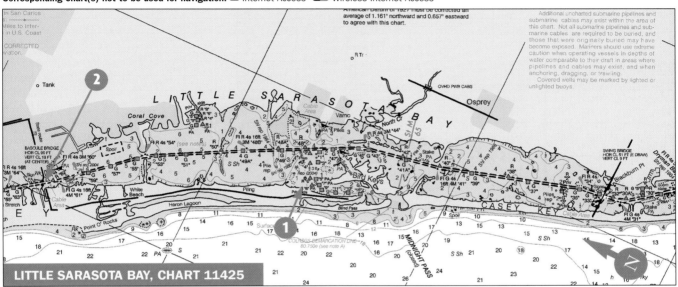

LITTLE SARASOTA BAY, CHART 11425

5:35 p.m. The bridges on Lemon Bay at Manasota Key and Englewood do not have any restrictions.

Venice—Mile 57

About 15 miles south of Sarasota, Venice is one of Florida's younger towns. One nice place to visit is the Historic Spanish Point on North Tamiami Trail. Call 941-966-5214 for more information. Warm Mineral Springs is located 12 miles south of Venice. Known as Florida's Fountain of Youth, its waters are 87 degrees year-round. Call 941-426-1692 for details.

NAVIGATION: Use Chart 11425. Entering Venice waters, the first bridge is the Hatchett Creek (Route 41) Bascule Bridge at Mile 56.9 (30-foot closed vertical clearance), with restricted openings year-round. Monday through Friday, from 7 a.m. to 4:20 p.m., it opens on the hour and at 20 and 40 minutes past the hour, and closes between 4:25 p.m. and 5:25 p.m.; on weekends and holidays, from 7:30 a.m. to 6 p.m., it opens on the hour and at 15, 30 and 45 minutes past the hour. Remember to call ahead and tell the bridge tender you are coming.

After leaving the land cut, the Waterway runs through Roberts Bay. Lightly powered vessels should be cautious of the strong currents flowing in and out of Venice Inlet, which cross the route and create some navigational challenges. Shoaling is a recurrent condition, although the

Corps of Engineers advises that 9-foot depths are maintained in Venice Inlet.

Dockage: Fisherman's Wharf-Marker 4 Marina is at red daybeacon "4," approaching Venice from the south. The marina has both gas and diesel fuel, a tackle shop and a boutique. Also located in the marina complex is the Oyster Bar Restaurant.

At Mile 58, between quick flashing green "13" and red daybeacon "14," a privately marked channel leads west toward the Venice Yacht Club (with reciprocal privileges for members of the Florida Yacht Council only). Also, there is a small city dock that five or six boats could tie up to for the day, but you must vacate the dock by midnight. The dock is located just opposite the Venice Yacht Club docks.

Venice Inlet is jettied and easily navigable (9-foot depths), except when strong westerly winds oppose an ebbing tide. Conveniently situated inside the inlet, the Crow's Nest Marina can accommodate deep-draft boats with slips that include electricity, water and access to showers and laundry. The rightly popular on-site Crow's Nest Restaurant and Tavern serves a full range of moderately priced entrees, with fine foods upstairs and a tavern menu downstairs.

The dockmaster or his helpful staff will assist you in tying up, either alongside at the dock or at the fuel dock. Both block and bag ice is available, as are courtesy bikes

Sarasota, FL

SARASOTA		Largest Vessel Accommodated	VHF Channel Monitored	Transient Berths / Total Berths	Approach / Dockside Depth (reported)	Floating Docks	Groceries, Ice, Marine Supplies, Snacks	Gas / Diesel	Repairs: Hull, Engine, Propeller	Lift (tonnage), Crane, Rail	1=110V, 2=220V, B=Both, Max Amps	Laundry, Pool, Showers	Pump-Out Station	Nearby: Grocery Store, Motel, Restaurant
		Dockage					**Supplies**				**Services**			
1. Marina Jack 73.5 ⌨ WiFi	941-955-9488	175	16/71	30/316	8/8	F	GD	IMS	HEP		B/100	LS	P	GMR
2. Hyatt Regency Sarasota 74.0 WiFi	941-953-1234	55		25/25	8/8	F		IS			B/50	LPS	P	GMR
3. Sara Bay Marina 1.5 N of 78.5 WiFi	941-359-0390	60	16	20/60	4/4		GD	M	HEP	L5	B/50	LPS	P	MR
4. Sarasota Cay Club 1.5 N of 78.5 ⌨ WiFi	941-355-2781	70	16	6/70	4/6	F	GD	IS	EP		B/50	LPS	P	GMR
5. Longboat Key Club Moorings 2.5 NW of 76 ⌨ WiFi	800-858-0836	145	16/08	30/287	8/20		GD	IMS	HEP		B/50	LPS	P	GMR
6. The Dock on the Bay 2 SW Of 80	941-383-3716	50		6/20	7/6						B/50	LPS		GMR
7. Field Club	941-924-1201			RECIPROCAL		PRIVILEGES -		CALL	AHEAD					
8. Cannons Marina 83.5	941-383-1311				5/5		G	IMS	HEP					
9. Moore's Stone Crab Restaurant & Marina Inc. 85	941-383-1748	60		15/	10/10			I			1/30			

Corresponding chart(s) not to be used for navigation. ⌨ Internet Access WiFi Wireless Internet Access

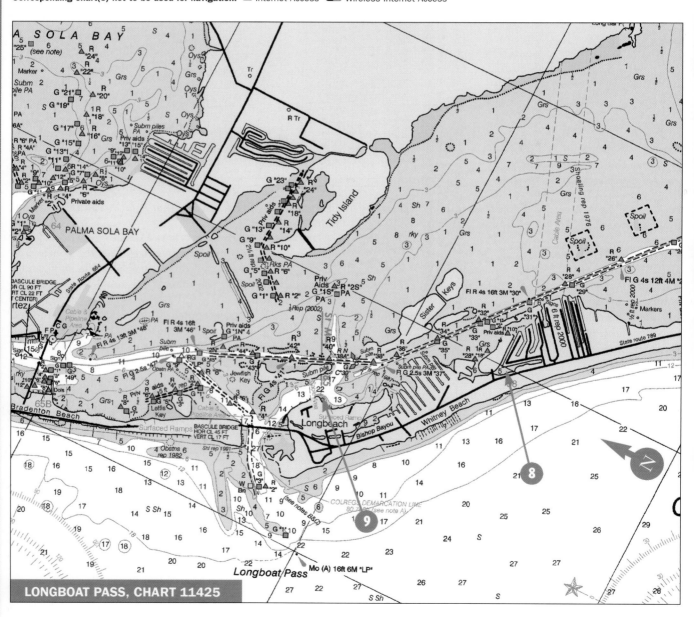

LONGBOAT PASS, CHART 11425

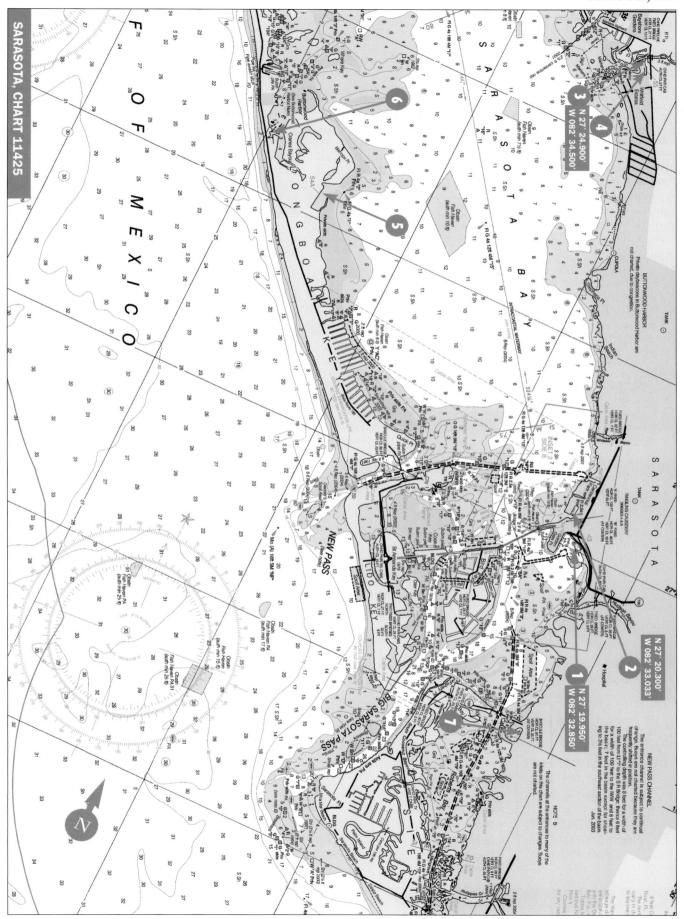

Sarasota, FL

Big Sarasota Pass, looking north. (Not to be used for navigation.) Photo Courtesy of Sam Harris.

for the 1.5-mile ride to town (well worth the trouble). Around a central green, and amidst the ambience of a small Florida town, are many stores of all varieties, from high-fashion clothing stores to drug and food stores. Many restaurants, including an excellent sidewalk extension of an Irish pub (where the ship's dog is welcome), offer a variety of foods.

From the marina, it is but a short walk to one of the widest and loveliest beaches on Florida's west coast. Fossilized sharks' teeth—either gray or black and have a triangular shape—are abundant here. Transient space is usually available but it is a good idea to call ahead.

GIWW to Sarasota

NAVIGATION: Use Chart 11425. North of Venice, the Waterway continues its sheltered path behind Casey Key—some huge names in the entertainment or sports business live here—through the Albee Bascule Bridge (Mile 59.3, 14-foot closed vertical clearance) to the Blackburn Point Swing Bridge (Mile 63, 9-foot closed vertical clearance) in Osprey. (There was a wild dolphin that frequented the north side of the Albee Bridge and cadged handouts from fishermen. Feeding this critter was a no-no. The townies called it "Beggar" and it was known to bite.) Both bridges open on signal. Passage through them is on an angle in tight quarters (51-foot horizontal clearance), and little maneuvering room is available on either side of the bridge; use caution here.

South Bay Marina is on the east side of the channel south

of the Blackburn Point Bridge, while the Blackburn Point Marina is immediately south of the bridge on the west side of the channel. Other marinas are north of the bridge on the east side of the channel.

Blackburn Bay, outside the GIWW, is very shallow. Proceed with caution, and definitely do not attempt transiting this area at night. Boaters who need to have the Albee Road Bridge (14-foot closed vertical clearance) opened should radio ahead on VHF Channel 09 before entering the channel. The course crosses Little Sarasota Bay, the approach to Sarasota.

Always a prime source of Waterway shoaling, Midnight Pass, at Mile 65, which separates Casey Key from Siesta Key, has been closed for years by the action of nature. Despite continuing attention, the Waterway channel both north and south of the inlet tends to silt in at some point. Keep an eye on your depth sounder throughout this area. Overall, the channel is well-marked and maintained, and, if you keep to the middle of the channel, you should encounter no problems.

■ SARASOTA/SARASOTA BAY

Mile 65 to Mile 86

At Siesta Key, off to port heading north, after clearing Little Sarasota Bay, the Sarasota area officially begins and then continues for about 18 miles. The passage starts with a well-marked stretch through the shoals of Roberts Bay and ends with the exit through Longboat Key Pass to the north of Sarasota Bay. This section of the Waterway traverses a sophisticated, fast-growing region and is a popular layover spot for cruising boats.

As such, facilities are plentiful, ranging from fishing camps to marina resorts, and all manner of boating needs and repairs can be handled here. As the mainland's focal point for a cluster of offshore island resorts (linked to it by causeways), Sarasota acts as the hub of an important agricultural and cattle-ranching district, but is proudest of its cultural image. Strangely, the one event that has consistently brought the most tourists and tourist money to town has been offshore powerboat races, which are to culture about what pickup trucks are to a Rolls-Royce show. They happen in the summer, when all the cultured people have left town for cooler climes.

NAVIGATION: Use Chart 11425. **Use the St. Petersburg Tide Tables. For high tide, subtract 1 hour, 38 minutes; for low tide, subtract 58 minutes.** Behind Siesta Key, the narrow, dredged Waterway runs up the center of Little Sarasota Bay until the bay narrows to the north. At the Stickney Point Bascule Bridge (Mile 68.6, charted 18-foot closed vertical clearance, but may be as much as 20 feet), the route moves over to the western shore, then swings out

into the middle again at Roberts Bay. The Stickney Point Bascule Bridge operates on a restricted opening schedule: Monday through Friday, from 6 a.m. to 10 p.m., the bridge opens on the hour and every 20 minutes thereafter. At the northern end of Siesta Key is the Siesta Key Bridge (Mile 71.6, 25-foot closed vertical clearance), with year-round restrictions. The bridge opens on signal from 7 a.m. to 11 a.m., thereafter opens on the hour and at 20 and 40 minutes past the hour until 6:00 p.m.

After traversing Roberts Bay, the Waterway widens amidst a variety of marine facilities, and then passes under the Ringling Causeway, with a fixed vertical clearance of 65 feet at Mile 73.6. From flashing green "13" north of the causeway, and opposite New Pass to the west, Sarasota Bay opens up, both in width and in certain areas in depth.

Farther north from the Ringling Causeway, Longboat Key shields Sarasota Bay from the Gulf of Mexico and opens wide with central controlling depths of 7 to 12 feet at mean low water. The low purple building on the east side of Sarasota Bay, just north of the causeway, is the Van Wezel (pronounced Vann WAY-zull) Theatre of Performing Arts. At about Mile 77, also on the east side, you can see the coral-colored mansion of John Ringling.

In this area, the GIWW runs a straight line down the middle of Sarasota Bay, with markers along this stretch spaced about two miles apart. At flashing green "17" (near the midpoint of Longboat Key, at Mile 80), the route turns

Sarasota, FL

Large Siesta Key, looking north. (Not to be used for navigation.)
WATERWAY GUIDE PHOTOGRAPHY.

sharply west, Sarasota Bay narrows, and you must observe all aids to navigation very carefully. Along this stretch, the Waterway follows a dredged path through shoal water (1- and 2-foot depths outside the channel).

Dockage: Many of Sarasota's marine facilities are on the mainland near the Ringling Causeway, in Whittaker Bayou and clustered around New Pass. Repairs and service are readily available.

Tucked in behind Island Park, Marina Jack is at the doorstep to downtown Sarasota. This large, 315-slip marina, with the dinner cruise boat at the outer dock, completed a major expansion only a few years ago, adding more than 100 floating concrete slips with shore power, cable TV, telephone, wireless Internet and dial-up Internet access and slip-side pump-out service. Plus, a courtesy van is available to take you into town for provisioning and other errands. A floating fuel dock offers gas and diesel and pump-out service, with easy access to the GIWW or the Gulf. You will find showers and restrooms here also.

The downstairs, open-air bar is a big attraction for Sarasotans. It has a casual atmosphere and serves good bar food. The upstairs dining room, however, offers a more upscale menu.

Hyatt Regency Sarasota is just a mile farther north with resort amenities and facilities, but no marine services.

At red daybeacon "16" in Sarasota Bay, steering a course of 038 degrees magnetic for 1.5 nautical miles will bring you to the entrance markers to the Sarasota Cay Club Resort and Marina (this facility used to be the Holiday Inn Airport Marina). It has slips, a restaurant and a swimming pool.

Adjacent to the ICW on Sarasota Bay, across from Longboat Key, Sara Bay Marina offers all the amenities of the resort to transients, including lodging, a pool, restaurant, Tiki bar, laundry, cable and wireless Internet. Gas and diesel, pump-out, repairs and a lift are also available.

To get farther away from the crowd, try the Longboat Key Club Moorings on Longboat Key. This elegant marina offers transients complete marine services, deli, ship's store, pool, sauna and courtesy van service to lovely shopping areas nearby. To reach its channel, steer 255 degrees true from flashing green "15." On this course, steer for the farthest south of the three high-rise condominiums. Just to the south of the three condominiums, you will encounter the privately maintained entrance channel to the Moorings. In addition to gas and diesel, the Moorings offers fuel dock pump-out service (no charge if you are fueling) and slip-side pump-out with a portable vacuum system. You will not want for much here. It is a physically attractive marina and is run immaculately.

Anchorage: Many transient and local boats anchor in Sarasota Bay. If you are heading north, enter by turning right at marker "8A," southeast of the Ringling Causeway. In the cove just north of Marina Jack, there is enough room for six or more boats to anchor with good holding in 9 to 10-foot depths, but it can be rather noisy due to automobile traffic. During the Christmas season, a once-a-year night boat parade of lights here has become quite an attraction.

The main anchorage around Island Park, south of Marina Jack, provides depths of 8 to 12 feet at mean low water, with fair holding in soft mud. Do not leave your dinghy on the park beach; city officials may remove it. The dinghy beach is on the eastern side of Island Park near O'Leary's Sailing School. O'Leary's charges a nominal fee for dinghy dockage. Its small restaurant also sells block ice.

At the newspaper boxes near O'Leary's, pick up a Sarasota Visitors Guide, which includes a map of Sarasota's attractions and shopping centers.

Sarasota's efficient bus system will get you around town at bargain prices. There is a grocery store less than a half-mile away and a lot of shopping on Main Street within just a couple of blocks. Many excellent restaurants are within walking distance of the dinghy beach. Give them a try. You won't be disappointed.

Ringling Causeway, Mile 73.6, crosses three Sarasota Bay keys (Bird, Coon and St. Armands) to link Lido Key to the mainland. The span between Bird and Coon keys is fixed, with only a 10-foot vertical clearance.

Near the northern end of Longboat Key and Sister Keys, watch for strong crosscurrents to and from Longboat Pass. Just before red daybeacon "40," a good anchorage in 13-foot depths lies behind the tip of Longboat Key just off Longbeach. To enter the anchorage, leave the GIWW just south of red daybeacon "40," stay about 15 feet off the south side of Jewfish Key, and aim at the dock behind Moore's Stone Crab Restaurant. The Mar Vista Dockside Restaurant is also within dinghy range of this anchorage. You can also take your dinghy across the Longboat Pass Inlet, secure it to the dock next to the city boat ramp, and then catch a free trolley into Bradenton Beach. Here, you will find the quant old Florida feel with shopping, shoreside restaurants and beaches. The Whitney Beach Plaza can be reached by taking the dinghy almost all the way down Bishop Bayou and tying up to the cement wall on the left side. The plaza offers a grocery, liquor store, restaurant and post office.

GOIN' ASHORE: **SARASOTA, FL**

Back in 1929, John Ringling chose the city as winter headquarters for his Greatest Show on Earth circus. Although the circus has moved on, the Ringling legacy lives on at the Museum of the Circus, where circus memorabilia—from ancient Roman relics to contemporary carnival props—are on display.

A major art center, Sarasota plays host to two important museums, including the Ringling Museum of Art, a Renaissance-style palace that the circus king built to house his art collection. On permanent display is an important collection of Baroque art and a grouping from Reuben's *Triumph of the Eucharist* series. The New Wing Gallery presents changing exhibits, and a contemporary gallery shows 20th-century art.

Next to his museum, Ringling reconstructed an 18th-century Italian theater with stones, brought piece by piece from Asolo. Throughout the year, visitors can see plays and operas in the playhouse built for Queen Catherine. A state-of-the-art theater and teaching center is housed on the New College campus.

Music lovers also find refuge in Sarasota during the spring. On par with Tanglewood in the Berkshires, the Sarasota Music Festival is held annually in June. Concerts, lectures and seminars are open to the public. For program information, contact the Sarasota Convention and Visitors Bureau at 941-957-1877. Other musical events are held every weekend, as well as a jazz festival at Island Park.

At City Island Park, Mote Marine Science Aquarium and Pelican Man's Bird Sanctuary make interesting stops. Anchor off City Island, south of the channel into New Pass, just beyond the Sarasota Sailing Squadron's mooring field. Dinghy down the channel, and tie up at the Salty Dog, a pleasant beer and burger place directly across from Mote Marine. Sarasota's extensive bus system will make shopping at major grocery stores possible.

ADDITIONAL RESOURCES

 Sarasota Convention and Visitors Bureau, www.sarasotafl.org

 NEARBY GOLF COURSES
Bobby Jones Golf Club, 1000 Circus Blvd., Sarasota, FL 34232, 941-955-8097
www.bobbyjonesgolfclub.com

NEARBY MEDICAL FACILITIES
Sarasota Memorial Hospital, 1700 S. Tamiami Trail, Sarasota, FL 34239, 941-917-9000

Siesta Key

Writers and artists congregate on the slender, six-mile-long, heavily-wooded Siesta Key, which boasts large private estates and deluxe condos with their own docks. A favorite among people from all over the world, Siesta Beach's sand is soft and cool. The beach facilities include picnic areas, restrooms, concession stands, a playground, trails and tennis and volleyball courts. If you want to enjoy some of this, you could anchor near Siesta Key's northerly point and dinghy ashore. The currents are strong here, however, so keep that all in mind.

Cruising Options

Continuing north, cruisers next encounter Anna Maria Island and the popular Tampa-St. Petersburg area. Beyond that, Clearwater and its famous resort beaches beckon. ■

WATERWAY GUIDE advertising sponsors play a vital role in bringing you the most trusted and well-respected cruising guide in the country. Without our advertising sponsors, we simply couldn't produce the top-notch publication now resting in your hands. Next time you stop in for a peaceful night's rest, let them know where you found them—WATERWAY GUIDE, The Cruising Authority.

Ship passing on the Gulf of Mexico. Photo Courtesy of Susan Landry.

Anna Maria Island to Tarpon Springs

CHARTS 11411, 11412, 11415, 11416, 11424, 11425

Lovely Anna Maria Island is noted for its white sandy beaches, good tarpon fishing in nearby waters and a premium restaurant, the Beach Bistro, on the beach at 66th Street. Just north of Longboat Key, which is separated by Longboat Pass with its bascule bridge (closed vertical clearance 17 feet), the island lies between Sarasota Bay on the south, Anna Maria Sound (separating the island from the mainland at the towns of Cortez and Bradenton) and Tampa Bay on the north. Cruisers can reach Tampa Bay and the north either directly from the Gulf of Mexico or via the inside Gulf Intracoastal Waterway (GIWW) route from Sarasota Bay.

The Approach to Anna Maria Island

NAVIGATION: Use Chart 11425. Traveling north from Sarasota Bay, there is no "quick" route north by going out into the Gulf of Mexico at Longboat Pass. Just stay on the inside. Even with a couple of bascule bridges that will have to open for you, you will save time and fuel. The inside route will bring you out in Tampa Bay at red daybeacon "68." Anna Maria Island is the barrier island that has been on your port side, heading north, since Longboat Pass.

Two bascule bridges cross the Waterway on this stretch before reaching Tampa Bay: the Cortez Bridge (Mile 87.4, 22-foot closed vertical clearance) and the Anna Maria Island Bridge (Mile 89.2, 24-foot closed vertical clearance). Both have year-round restrictions, and these have been changed so often that even the locals don't know for sure when they open. Suffice it to say, call the bridge tender on your VHF radio—they monitor channels 16 and 09, but 09 requires less effort—and get the latest scoop.

The GIWW channel cuts through shoals in much of Anna Maria Sound, and at red daybeacon "52" starts swinging toward Perico Island just south of the Anna Maria Bridge.

A back range at Mile 90 helps you stay on the magenta line until you reach the sand bar charted as "The Bulkhead," which is marked by flashing red "64" at Mile 92. After leaving red daybeacon "68," the water is deep, and you can head into Tampa Bay, go up the Manatee River to the east, or turn due west for about half a nautical mile to pick up green daybeacon "1." Leave it to port, and head in to the channel through Key Royale Bar to Bimini Bay on Anna Maria Island.

Dockage: Shortly after flashing red "48" and the Cortez Bridge, on the eastern shore is the Seafood Shack, a popular restaurant and marina with transient slips. The Seafood Shack's downstairs is open for sandwiches, fried clams and the like.

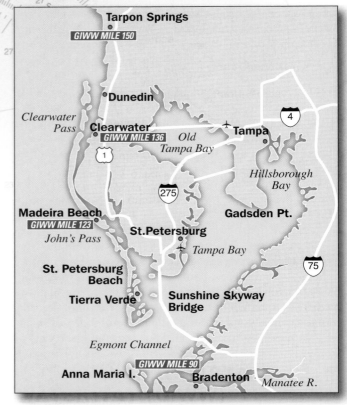

There is a bar inside, too. Some people prefer to sit outside and dine al fresco. You can do that, too, but not in the summer, though. With a western setting sun, it is like a furnace out there. The upstairs is not open for business. The helpful dockmaster answers on VHF Channel 16. A 24-hour Winn-Dixie supermarket is several miles to the east, at 75th Street.

Cortez Market, within walking distance, is just up the road, along with a post office and laundry. The Nautical But Nice gift store is nearby, and shares space with Gulf Coast Canvas. Several fish markets are located near the Cortez Coast Guard Station. To the west side of the Cortez Bridge is the Bradenton Beach Marina, which permits do-it-yourself work.

On Anna Maria Sound, to the northwest, Galati Yacht Basin, in Bimini Bay, offers slips and services for boats up to 60 feet, including fuel, pump-out, a ship's store with an excellent parts department and a laundry. If you are coming in here for the first time, it is easy to get confused by marina markers that seem to serve no useful purpose other than confusing visiting yachtsmen. There really is a scheme to everything, even if it is not easily discernible. Move slowly and get your bearings. Rotten Ralph's Bar and Restaurant is located next door to the marina.

To enter the basin, go out of Anna Maria Sound northbound past quick flashing green "67," hang a sharp left

Bradenton Beach, Anna Maria Sound, FL

ANNA MARIA SOUND		Largest Vessel Accommodated	VHF Channel Monitored	Transient Berths / Total Berths	Approach / Dockside Depth (reported)	Floating Docks	Gas / Diesel	Groceries, Ice, Marine Supplies, Snacks	Repairs: Hull, Engine, Propeller	Lift (tonnage), Crane, Rail	1=110V, 2=220V, B=Both, Max Amps	Laundry, Pool, Showers	Pump-Out Station	Nearby: Grocery Store, Motel, Restaurant
				Dockage				**Supplies**			**Services**			
1.	Bradenton Beach Marina 87.2 ▢	941-778-2288	70	16/07	15/40	6/8	GD	IM	HEP	L77	B/50	LS	P	GMR
2.	Seafood Shack 87.4	941-794-1235	100	16	10/80	10/8		IS			B/50	LS		GMR
3.	Galati Yacht Basin 1 W of 91.8	941-778-0755	105	16	2/56	7/7	GD	IMS		L55	B/50	LS	P	

Corresponding chart(s) not to be used for navigation. ▢ Internet Access (WiFi) Wireless Internet Access

ANNA MARIA SOUND, CHART 11425

SCALE 1:40,000

Manatee River, FL

MANATEE RIVER		Largest Vessel Accommodated	VHF Channel Monitored	Approach / Dockside Depth (reported)	Transient Berths / Total Berths	Floating Docks	Groceries, Ice, Marine Supplies, Snacks	Gas / Diesel	Repairs: Hull, Engine, Propeller	1=110V, 2=220V, B=Both, Max Amps	Lift (tonnage), Crane, Rail	Laundry, Pool, Showers	Pump-Out Station	Nearby: Grocery Store, Motel, Restaurant
			Dockage				**Supplies**				**Services**			
1. Snead Island Boat Works Inc.	941-722-2400	65		/75	8/8		MS		HEP	L70		B/50	S	
2. Bradenton Yacht Club	941-722-5936		16				GD							
3. REGATTA POINTE MARINA 🖥️📶	**941-729-6021**	**100**	**16**	/350	9/8		GD	IMS	HEP			B/100	LPS	P GMR
4. Riviera Dunes Marina Resort 🖥️📶	941-723-9595	120	16/68	20/220	10/18	F	GD	GIMS	HEP			B/50	LPS	P MR
5. Twin Dolphin Marina 🖥️📶	941-747-8300	80	16/72	25/225	12/9	F	GD	IMS				B/50	LPS	P GMR

Corresponding chart(s) not to be used for navigation. 🖥️ Internet Access 📶 Wireless Internet Access

heading west for a little more than a half nautical mile to flashing green "1," and on your left you will see the markers to Bimini Bay, which are privately maintained.

■ TAMPA BAY

One of the great natural harbors of the world, Tampa Bay extends about 25 miles north to south and about 10 miles east to west. It has two important cities and several large rivers that meander in from the east and north. Fringing the west side of the coast and extending northward is a pencil-thin chain of barrier islands with resort communities famous for their Gulf beaches.

For the cruising skipper, Tampa Bay is a welcome change from the confines of the GIWW channel. Here, there are some 300 square miles of cruising waters, Gulf of Mexico fishing, interesting ports, pleasant anchorages, good yacht facilities and superb sailing. After crossing The Bulkhead, the mariner faces about 4.5 nautical miles of open water across lower Tampa Bay to the continuation of the GIWW on the north side of the bay after crossing the main shipping channel. Commercial shipping traffic has the right-of-way, so be careful. Accidents (big ones) have happened here.

On January 28, 1980, the Coast Guard buoy tender *Blackthorn* was hit by an inbound tanker, *Capricorn*, then rolled over and sank. Twenty-three Coast Guard personnel died that night, most because they were trapped inside their ship and drowned.

Five months after the *Blackthorn* accident, on May 9, 1980, a bulk carrier by the name of *Summit Venture* hit the Sunshine Skyway Bridge, dropping 1,400 feet of the steel cantilevered southbound span into the water. Thirty-five people died, all of them either motorists or passengers in a Greyhound bus.

With its long fetch, this stretch can kick up an uncomfortable chop. Flashing red "70," near Mile 95, is a useful checkpoint on this open-water run.

On clear days, the Sunshine Skyway Bridge, the span of which forms a 15-mile-long highway across lower Tampa Bay, is clearly visible from The Bulkhead. The span is 425 feet high at the top of the two cable towers. At a charted fixed vertical clearance of 175 feet at the center, it has 25 more feet of vertical clearance than the old bridge and is located 1,000 feet farther east. Small man-made islands—they are called dolphins and their function is to deflect ships that might wander out of the channel—flank the 12 columns that support the Sunshine Skyway Bridge nearest the shipping channel. Half of the old southbound span, damaged when struck in 1980, remains as fishing piers on both sides.

Bradenton

The Manatee River's main city, Bradenton is a popular lay-over port for those who want to explore the river and other waters. The protected marina basin, described below, has decent depths and includes slips for liveaboards. There is a lot of history and beautiful scenery for the visitor to enjoy.

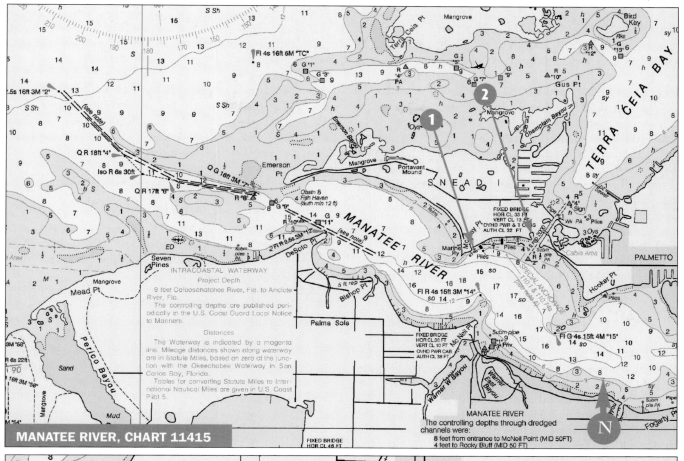

MANATEE RIVER, CHART 11415

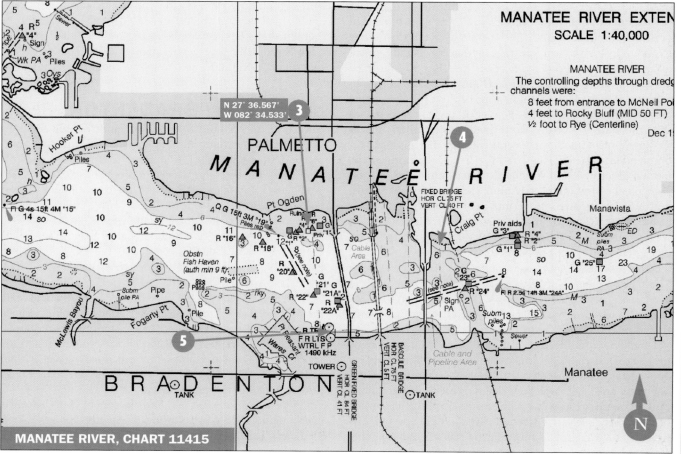

MANATEE RIVER, CHART 11415

Manatee River, FL

To Manatee River/Bradenton

NAVIGATION: Use Charts 11425 and 11415. **Use the St. Petersburg Tide Tables. For high tide, subtract 1 hour, 24 minutes; for low tide, subtract 55 minutes.** From the exit at The Bulkhead in Anna Maria Sound, a sharp turn to the east, around red daybeacon "68," leads to the mouth of the lovely Manatee River, one of Tampa Bay's finest cruising and gunkholing areas. The almost-tropical Manatee River has a well-marked, deep channel (8-foot depths), interesting side streams to explore by dinghy and friendly towns to visit. The entrance channel threads through shoals, but a series of ranges are strategically placed to keep the mariner from finding those shoals. However, as you head in, honor quick flashing red "4," even to the point of going on the wrong side. There is a shoal building out directly to its east. Locals stay away from that shoal.

To enter the Manatee River, first head for flashing red "2" northeast of The Bulkhead. When traveling in from the north, be aware of the shoal that is north of quick flashing red "4," and also be sure not to shortcut flashing red "2." Follow the markers closely until you are past DeSoto Point, marked by flashing red "12," where there is ample water. Continuing up the river, be aware of flashing red "14" and green "15" as there are shoals growing in and around the markers. Give them a wide berth.

Between Snead Island and Palmetto, a land cut beside the Bradenton Yacht Club leads into Terra Ceia Bay. This entrance offers channel depths of about 5 feet and a fixed bridge with a 13-foot vertical clearance.

At Bradenton, three bridges cross the Manatee River within one mile of each other. The first is a 41-foot fixed vertical clearance bridge. The second is a railway bridge (5-foot closed vertical clearance) that is usually open, except from 11 a.m. to 1 p.m. The third is a 40-foot fixed vertical clearance bridge (U.S. Highway 41). The upper Manatee River, east of these three bridges, offers some cruising options and holds depths of 10 feet or better to the Interstate 75 Bridge at Ellenton. After that, depths shallow considerably, and venturing up there is not recommended. Two miles beyond the last of the bridges, the Braden River opens to starboard. A lush and scenic stream with plenty of wildlife, it is unmarked and full of shoals, but nonetheless offers some fine gunkholing by dinghy.

Dockage: Conveniently located on the Manatee River west of the U.S. Business Highway 41 Bridge is the well-equipped and well-appointed Regatta Pointe Marina, which accommodates transient guests at its 350 wet slips. The marina features a full-service fuel dock with gas and diesel fuel, a well-stocked ship's store, an on-site restaurant, wireless Internet service, a laundry and air-conditioned restroom/shower facilities.

Directly across the river, Twin Dolphin Marina is close to the downtown Bradenton attractions and offers transient dockage at floating docks, with fuel, all amenities including pool and spa, cable television, water and electricity plus an on-site restaurant. The marina is on the south side of the Manatee River at green daybeacon "21" and red daybeacon "22." Twin Dolphin Marina has a single-opening entrance configuration through its breakwaters; sound your horn going in or coming out. From red daybeacon "22" to marker "41," there is an Idle-Speed/No-Wake Zone between the channel and the south shoreline.

Farther east, after the three bridges, on the north side of the Manatee River, Riviera Dunes Marina offers transient dockage with 10-foot depths, power connections, fuel, pump-out service, repairs and full amenities, including restaurant, pool and concierge. The 40-foot clearance on the two auto bridges constitutes the limiting factor for sailboats getting to Riviera Dunes. On Seventh Street you will find a Sweetbay supermarket and an ATM at a nearby Bank of America.

Before we completely leave the Manatee River, you need to know about Snead Island Boat Works, which is located on the north bank of the river, opposite red flashing "14." Snead Island Boat Works offers excellent repair service that is locally renowned.

Anchorage: Follow the channel past flashing red "12," then turn west into the cove behind DeSoto Point, being mindful of the charted shoal in the center of the cove. You can land your dinghy on shore to visit the DeSoto National Memorial. DeSoto Point offers a good anchorage regardless of the shoal. There is still plenty of room for several boats to anchor. It is protected except from the east and carries 9 to 10 feet of water.

There is another anchorage which is located in front of the Bradenton Yacht Club east of McKay Point, north of red daybeacon "14." Depths range from 4 to 9 feet, but protection is good only from north winds. Farther upriver, boats anchor just west of the bridge on either the Bradenton or Palmetto side. Of the two, the one near the Bradenton Yacht Club is the better. It is a "designated anchorage," meaning that one does not have to display an anchor light here.

GOIN' ASHORE: **BRADENTON, FL**

Ashore, visitors should stop by the South Florida Museum to see its planetarium and the Indian and aquatic exhibits. Snooty the Manatee is a great favorite with visitors. Bradenton offers some excellent dining. Fisherman Joe's (941-746-3077), a casual spot for lunch or dinner, and the Lost Kangaroo Pub (941-747-8114), with a vast assortment of imported beers, are on Old Main Street (12th Street).

Within taxi distance of the Ellenton waterfront is the Gamble Mansion. Built in 1845, it is the oldest house on Florida's west coast. It once served as the manor house for a big sugar plantation and, at the end of the Civil War, sheltered Confederate Secretary of State Judah Benjamin. Restored to its former glory, it has a fine collection of antebellum furnishings. Exhibits include Confederate money, stamps and uniforms, several fine four-poster beds with delicate antique bedspreads and Jefferson Davis' wedding bed. Here, the Civil War is often referred to as The War of Northern Aggression. Some things just have tradition going for them.

On DeSoto Point, you will find a National Park dedicated to Hernando DeSoto, a 16th century Spanish Explorer. Don Hernando DeSoto landed here in 1539 to begin the 4,000-

mile trek into the interior that led to his discovery of the Mississippi River. Every spring, DeSoto's landing is re-enacted as part of a weeklong festival. Since there is no dock at the park, those who want to look around must go in by dinghy and "beach it." The park also features a nature walk with recorded information that tells the history surrounding DeSoto Point and an air-conditioned theater showing a movie that depicts the landing of Hernando DeSoto. In 1987, archeologists in Tallahassee uncovered Indian and European artifacts—beads, ironware and a pig bone—identifying the site as DeSoto's 1539 winter encampment.

Also ashore is a large concrete cross that belongs to the Archdiocese of Venice. The cross is said to commemorate the first Catholic mass given on these shores.

ADDITIONAL RESOURCES

■ City of Bradenton, **www.cityofbradenton.com**

■ DeSoto National Monument, **www.nps.gov/deso**

NEARBY GOLF COURSES
Manatee County Golf Course, 6415 53rd Ave. W,
Bradenton, FL 34210, 941-792-6773
www.co.manatee.fl.us/golf.html

NEARBY MEDICAL FACILITIES
Manatee Memorial Hospital, 206 Second St. E,
Bradenton, FL 34208, 941-746-5111
www.manateememorial.com

■ TO TAMPA

Tampa Bay comprises three vast bodies of water—Tampa Bay proper, Old Tampa Bay to the northeast and Hillsborough Bay to the northwest—most providing good cruising. Lower Tampa Bay opens on the Gulf of Mexico, but enjoys the protection of the barrier islands. Old Tampa Bay reaches northwest from Tampa Bay to the shoal water around Safety Harbor and Mobbly Bay. Hillsborough Bay branches off to the northeast between Interbay Peninsula and the mainland, to serve the city of Tampa, Ybor City and Davis Islands, with their extensive shipping and industrial areas.

From the open mouth of Tampa Bay, St. Petersburg lies due north, with metropolitan Tampa to the northeast. Each dominates one of the two big peninsulas that pierce the bay.

Pinellas, to the west, extends about 45 miles from the southern edge of St. Petersburg almost to Tarpon Springs. MacDill Air Force Base occupies the southern tip of Interbay, the second peninsula (about three miles wide and 10 miles long). This is home to CENTCOM, the military entity that was strategically responsible for Desert Shield, Desert Storm and the current operations in the Middle East. The rest is given over to the bustling city of Tampa and its seaport.

NAVIGATION: Use Chart 11415 and 11416. **Use the St. Petersburg Tide Tables. For high tide at Davis Island, add 3 minutes; for low tide, add 32 minutes.** To get to Tampa from The Bulkhead, at the exit of Anna Maria Sound, set a course of 022 degrees magnetic for flashing red "70" well out in Tampa Bay at Mile 95. Continue on the same heading until you pick up quick flashing red buoy "26" at Mullet Key Channel, the big-ship route up Tampa Bay. Go under the center spans of the Sunshine Skyway Bridge (175-foot fixed vertical clearance), and you may follow the big-ship channel the 20 to 25 nautical miles all the way northeast to the city of Tampa.

Dockage: The Inn at Little Harbor and its marinas offer a range of dockage choices, including full amenities, three restaurants, lodging, a ship's store and a high and dry facility. The Little Harbor marinas, located on the eastern side of Tampa Bay (north of the Little Manatee River), give easy access to the entire area. Heading north, the cruising boater will find several dockage choices in northern Hillsborough Bay, including two yacht clubs and a municipal marina.

Nearly all of the dockage at Harbour Island, which is in downtown Tampa, is private. A few restaurants are located in the Harbor Island complex and at the hotel. Marjorie Park Marina, which also handles the Tampa Convention Center Transient Docks, is a full-service facility, with gas and diesel fuel, complimentary pump-out service, floating docks, shore power and easy access to mass transit. Bayshore Marina nearby offers monthly slips only (contact Marjorie Park Marina for details).

Anchorage: Square in the middle of the entrance to Tampa Bay lies Egmont Key, three miles off the tip of Anna Maria Island. And while it is 20-plus miles back out to Egmont Key from downtown Tampa, we had to cover it someplace. So, here it is. Egmont is a popular daytime anchorage that gets crowded on the weekends in the summer. You can anchor close to shore on the southeast end of the island and dinghy in. You used to be able to wander all over the island, but now it is a bird sanctuary, and unfettered wandering is proscribed. Check out the ruins of Fort Dade. The still-functioning Egmont Lighthouse has been there since before the Civil War. Fort Dade, or what is left of it, is an old military outpost on Egmont Key. It is a relic from the Spanish-American War. Gun emplacements are still evident, as are powder magazines, brick roads and a lot of mosquitoes. Before being host to a military detachment, the island was used to imprison Seminole Indians who were scheduled for trans-shipment to the Oklahoma Territories.

During World War II, the island was occupied by the Army, probably to keep Nazi subs from sliding through the gap between the island and the mainland in southern Pinellas County. You will see a lot of gopher tortoises on Egmont Key. (Note that these turtles are on the endangered species list.) All the rest of the gopher tortoises in Florida carry a respiratory disease that will probably kill them. Egmont's tortoises, quarantined as they are, are disease-free. As an overnight anchorage, the waters on the east side off Egmont may be uncomfortable when an evening land breeze kicks in and creates a lee shore. The bottom is hard sand and holds well, but if you are anchored close to others whose skills you are not so sure of, move.

Tampa, FL

Tampa Area, FL

TAMPA AREA		Largest Vessel Accommodated	VHF Channel Monitored	Transient Berths / Total Berths	Approach / Dockside Depth (reported)	Floating Docks	Gas / Diesel	Groceries, Ice, Marine Supplies, Snacks	Repairs: Hull, Engine, Propeller	Lift (tonnage), Crane, Rail	1=110V, 2=220V, B=Both, Max Amps	Laundry, Pool, Showers	Pump-Out Station	Nearby: Grocery Store, Motel, Restaurant
				Dockage			**Supplies**			**Services**				
1. Little Harbor Resort Marina 🖥WiFi	813-645-2411	60	16/68	20/	6/6		GD	IMS	HEP	12	B/50	LPS	P	MR
2. Little Harbor Village Marina 🖥	813-645-2411	70	16/68	20/99	6/6		GD	IMS	HEP		B/50	LPS	P	MR
3. Little Harbor Antigua Cove 🖥WiFi	813-645-2411	60	16/68	20/326	6/10	F	GD	GIMS	HEP	L12	1/30	LPS	P	MR
4. Shell Point Marina	813-645-1313	60		2/40	6/9		GD	IMS	HP	L	1/30	S	P	
5. Tampa Convention Center Transient Docks	813-259-1604	90		27/27	19/19	F					1/30			GR
6. Bayshore Marina	813-259-1604	50		4/37	19/4						1/30			GR
7. The Westin Tampa Harbour Island	813-229-5000	60		2/2	/6						B/50			
8. Marjorie Park Marina	813-259-1604	90	16	18/54	21/9		GD	GIMS			B/50	LPS	P	GR
9. Davis Island Yacht Club	813-251-1158	55		10/114	10/8			M		R	1/30	PS		R
10. Tampa Yacht & Country Club	813-831-1611	65	68	5/	10/4	F	GD	GIMS			B/50	S		GMR

Corresponding chart(s) not to be used for navigation. 🖥 Internet Access WiFi Wireless Internet Access

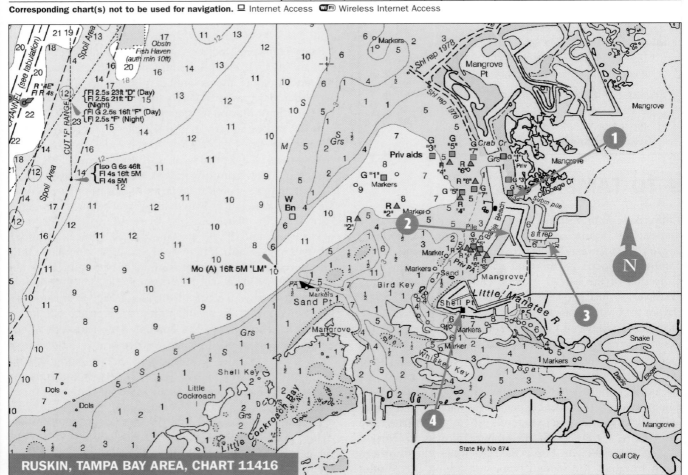

RUSKIN, TAMPA BAY AREA, CHART 11416

GOIN' ASHORE: **TAMPA, FL**

Originally an Army fort back in 1823, Tampa has grown to become Florida's third largest city. Its harbor enjoys the distinction of being the state's most important, and its cigar industry, which produces about 800 million cigars annually, makes Tampa the nation's cigar capital.

The city is a leading citrus-processing center and an important tourist destination. Busch Gardens, an extraordinary entertainment complex, does its part in attracting visitors to the area. The Dark Continent and Adventure Island, an outdoor water park, are part of the Busch Gardens complex, as is Montu, one of the southeast's largest inverted roller coasters. SheiKra, the nation's only dive coaster, is set among the jungle ruins of a once-mighty African civilization.

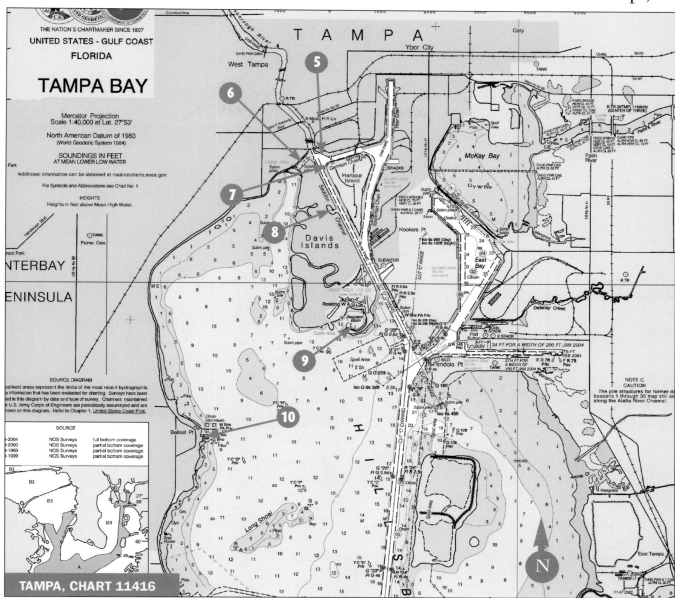

THE NATION'S CHARTMAKER SINCE 1807

UNITED STATES - GULF COAST

FLORIDA

TAMPA BAY

Mercator Projection
Scale 1:40,000 at Lat. 27°53'

North American Datum of 1983
(World Geodetic System 1984)

SOUNDINGS IN FEET
AT MEAN LOWER LOW WATER

Additional information can be obtained at nauticalcharts.noaa.gov.

For Symbols and Abbreviations see Chart No. 1

HEIGHTS
Heights in feet above Mean High Water.

TAMPA, CHART 11416

SheiKra begins by carrying riders up 200 feet then, hurtling them 70 mph straight down at a 90-degree angle. It is the first coaster of its kind in North America and only the third in the world.

Tampa's historic Latin Quarter, Ybor City, was once the cigar-making center, but only one cigar manufacturer remains. This section of town is home to numerous restaurants, shops and a nightlife that hops.

Not far from Ybor City, on Tampa's waterfront, is the Florida Aquarium, open daily from 9 a.m. to 5 p.m. A walk around downtown Tampa takes you past beautiful churches, historic Tampa Theatre, the public library and the Tampa Museum of Art, overlooking the Hillsborough River. Just across the Hillsborough River, the unusual building with 12 silver minarets is the old Tampa Bay Hotel, built in 1891 by railroad magnate Henry Plant to attract visitors to the west coast. It is now the main building of the University of Tampa.

Another worthwhile attraction, the Museum of Science and Industry, is open daily. Tampa's Gasparilla Festival, held in February, is also worth a visit. The Lowry Park Zoo includes a free-flight bird aviary, a primate center housing chimpanzees and woolly monkeys and the Florida Wildlife Center, a sanctuary for native species such as alligators, panthers, bears and red wolves.

ADDITIONAL RESOURCES

■ Tampa Bay Convention and Visitors Bureau,
www.visittampabay.com

⚑ **NEARBY GOLF COURSES**
Rocky Point Golf Course, 4151 Dana Shores Drive,
Tampa, FL 33634, 813-673-4316,
www.rockypointgc.com

⚕ **NEARBY MEDICAL FACILITIES**
Memorial Hospital of Tampa, 2901 Swann Ave.,
Tampa, FL 33609, 813-873-6400

Tampa, FL

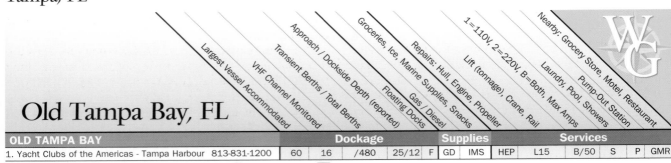

Old Tampa Bay, FL

OLD TAMPA BAY	Largest Vessel Accommodated	VHF Channel Monitored	Transient Berths / Total Berths	Approach / Dockside Depth (reported)	Floating Docks	Gas / Diesel	Groceries, Ice, Marine Supplies, Snacks	Repairs: Hull, Engine, Propeller	1=110V, 2=220V, B=Both, Max Amps	Lift (tonnage), Crane, Rail	Laundry, Pool, Showers	Pump-Out Station	Nearby: Grocery Store, Motel, Restaurant
			Dockage				**Supplies**			**Services**			
1. Yacht Clubs of the Americas - Tampa Harbour 813-831-1200	60	16	/480	25/12	F	GD	IMS	HEP	L15	B/50	S	P	GMR

Corresponding chart(s) not to be used for navigation. 🖥 Internet Access 📶 Wireless Internet Access

OLD TAMPA BAY, CHART 11416

■ TO ST. PETERSBURG

Abundant services, yachting or recreational, are available in St. Petersburg. The only two questions you need ask are, where in the city do you want to stay, and what kind of accommodations would you like? Facilities of one kind or another line all sides of the peninsula. Boaters heading up Tampa Bay reach those at the south end first, but there are others downtown on the east side of the peninsula and in Boca Ciega Bay on the west side.

NAVIGATION: Use Charts 11416, 11415 and 11411. Use St. Petersburg Tide Tables. Two routes, both clearly marked on Chart 11416, lead from Anna Maria Sound to St. Petersburg. You start, as you would going to Tampa, from The Bulkhead, setting a course of 022 degrees magnetic for flashing red "70" well out in Tampa Bay at Mile

95. Continue on the same heading until you pick up quick flashing red buoy "26" at Mullet Key Channel, the big-ship route up Tampa Bay.

The GIWW follows Mullet Key Channel eastward through the Sunshine Skyway Bridge, then turns north, (to port) at quick flashing green buoy "5A" and quick flashing red buoy "6A" at about Mile 102, leaving the main channel to Tampa for the well-marked route to St. Petersburg.

The alternate route to St. Petersburg, though longer, is more protected in easterly winds. This same route also represents a shortcut for crossing Tampa Bay via the GIWW. The route crosses Mullet Key Channel and runs northward along the Sunshine Skyway Bridge causeway in the Sunshine Skyway Channel, paralleling the bridge to the east, where depths average more than 8 feet. (Note that surveys from 2008 show that this channel only carries 6 feet at mean low water. Check locally before taking this route if you draw over 5 feet.) It picks up the GIWW again in Boca Ciega Bay.

At green daybeacon "13A," you meet the GIWW: Here you either turn to starboard and follow the Waterway eastward under the 65-foot fixed vertical clearance bridge, which is locally known as the Meissner Bridge, until it converges with the northbound channel to St. Petersburg. St. Petersburg (often called St. Pete by locals) is located on a peninsula, so water is everywhere, but unfortunately for boaters, much of it isn't very deep. Watching your charts is critical to avoid the shoals, which are often difficult to see. Unless you know the waters, stay in the well-marked channels to avoid bumping the sandy bottom. Also keep an eye out for large ships heading to the ports of Manatee and Tampa. To bypass the Tampa area and proceed to Clearwater, continue north on the Sunshine Skyway Channel, bear west at the north end in the GIWW channel, and proceed toward Pass-a-Grille.

Be advised that if you are trying to avoid easterly winds out in Tampa Bay, you will have them right on your nose when you turn to starboard at green daybeacon "13A." It is several miles to the northbound channel, and it is not much fun in easterlies.

Dockage: In downtown St. Petersburg, the St. Petersburg Municipal Marina has excellent transient facilities, a full-service fuel dock with gas and diesel fuel, pump-out service, a laundry, restrooms/showers and a courtesy dock for boats up to 60 feet in length (6 a.m. to 2 a.m., 6-hour maximum stay).

Other marinas in the area that have transient slips are the Vinoy Resort Marina, near the big pink historic Vinoy Hotel, and the St. Petersburg Yacht Club (membership in a reciprocal yacht club required).

If you are coming up the channel to St. Pete from Tampa Bay, you can turn to port at flashing green (2+1) "S" to get into Bayboro Harbor, the Port of St. Petersburg, and the Harborage Marina at Bayboro. The Harborage Marina is around the bend from downtown, but close to a trolley stop so you can get around if you need to. Coast Guard ships and cruise ships come in here, so the water is deep. The marina offers all fuels, repairs, pump-out, laundry, pool, restrooms/showers and a skipper's lounge.

Just east of the Maximo Point Bridge is the Holiday Inn Sunspree Resort with full amenities, including saltwater swimming, a couple of swimming pools, tennis, Scuba diving and boat rentals. This Holiday Inn has a small marina associated with it, and it offers a fine place to tie up if you are tired of anchoring out.

Anchorage: Anchoring in the North Basin (N 27° 46. 550'/W 082° 37. 740') gets you into the heart of downtown St. Petersburg. Also known as the Vinoy Basin, the holding can be tenuous, especially with a strong easterly wind. There appear to be a lot of "liveaboard" vessels here, some of which are anchored and some on private moorings, which makes anchoring difficult because of swing room.

Sunshine Skyway Bridge. Photo Courtesy of Susan Landry.

St. Petersburg, FL

ST. PETERSBURG AREA		Largest Vessel Accommodated	VHF Channel Monitored	Transient Berths / Total Berths	Approach / Dockside Depth (reported)	Floating Docks	Gas / Diesel	Groceries, Ice, Marine Supplies, Snacks	Repairs: Hull, Engine, Propeller	Lift (tonnage), Crane, Rail	1=110V, 2=220V, B=Both, Max Amps	Laundry, Pool, Showers	Pump-Out Station	Nearby: Grocery Store, Motel, Restaurant
		Dockage					**Supplies**				**Services**			
1. Renaissance Vinoy Resort & Golf Club	727-824-8022	100	16	15/74	16/12	F		I			B/100	LPS	P	GMR
2. St. Petersburg Municipal Marina 🖥️ WiFi	**727-893-7329**	110	16/68	/660	10/12		GD	IMS			B/100	LS	P	G
3. Marina Pt. Ship's Store, St. Petersburg Yacht Charter/Sales	727-823-2555	160	16		12/12		GD	IMS	HEP				LS	P	GMR
4. St. Petersburg Yacht Club	727-822-3227	150	16/69	13/80	10/10						B/50	PS	P	MR
5. The Harborage Marina at Bayboro WiFi	727-821-6347	200	16	15/300	24/12	F	GD	IMS			B/100	LPS	P	GMR
6. Sailor's Wharf Inc. 🖥️	800-879-2244	80		1/23	10/9	F		M	HEP	L60,C	B/50		S	GMR
7. Embree Marine	727-896-0671			7/7					HEP	L55				R

Corresponding chart(s) not to be used for navigation. 🖥️ Internet Access WiFi Wireless Internet Access

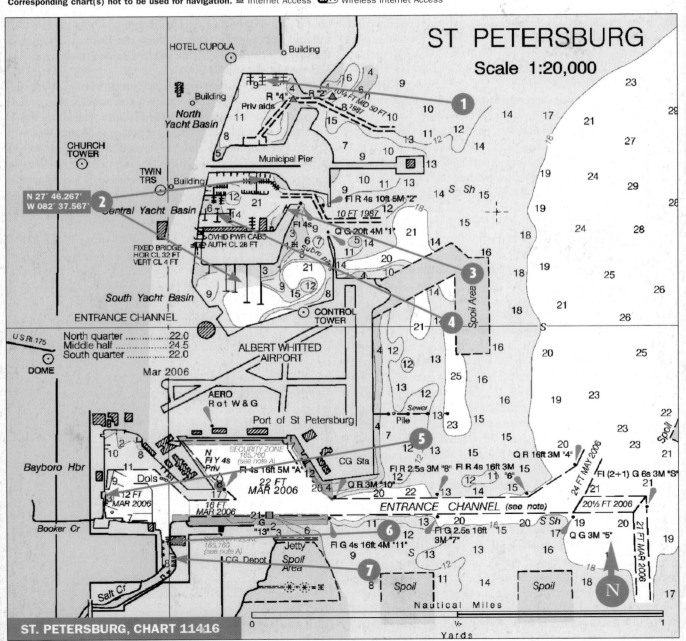

ST. PETERSBURG, CHART 11416

Chart Your Course
St. Petersburg Municipal Marina

Florida's largest city marina welcomes you.

- *Within footsteps of the docks, miles of downtown waterfront parks, world renowned museums and galleries, first class hotels, restaurants, shopping, the famous St. Petersburg Pier, Major League Baseball, Broadway and live theater, and more.*

- *650 slips, accommodating vessels up to 100'.*

- *500-foot transient dock (10' depth).*

- *Electric, water, phone, cable TV hook-ups, laundry, showers, 24-hour security, Sailing Center, boat ramps.*

- *Picnic shelters and playground.*

- *Eight courtesy docks for short-term docking downtown (up to six hours, $1/hour, accommodates vessels up to 60' long, open daily from 6 a.m. to 2 a.m. No overnight stays, please).*

- *Marina Store with commodities, gas, diesel. Now under marina management.*

st.petersburg
www.stpete.org

St.Petersburg
MUNICIPAL MARINA

For a free brochure or more information call 1-800-782-8350 or visit our website: www.stpete.org

St. Petersburg, FL

The depths are 14 to 16 feet. The concrete seawall offers little comfort, but many boats enjoy a comfortable stay here. The city had allowed yachts in transit two weeks anchorage, but this restriction should no longer apply. There has been talk by the city of installing a mooring field—stay tuned. Electric Marina, within the basin, offers a dinghy dock for a daily fee.

When taking the GIWW along its western leg beginning at Mile 104, you can anchor at the northeast corner of Boca Ciega Bay just east of the Sunshine Skyway Causeway. The area is exposed to winds from the southeast and the wakes of passing vessels, but can serve in a pinch. Depths are 7 to 10 feet.

GOIN' ASHORE:
ST. PETERSBURG, FL

Entering Tampa Bay from the Gulf of Mexico or the Intracoastal Waterway is pretty straightforward if you stay in the marked channels. As you cross under the magnificent yellow Sunshine Skyway Bridge, you are in Tampa Bay.

If you are entering Tampa Bay from outside the United States, St. Petersburg has a U.S. Customs office at the St. Pete/Clearwater International Airport. (There is also one in nearby Tampa.) Additionally, you can also use the U.S. Customs Local Boater Option and clear with a phone call. (www.cbp.org)

Known as the "Sunshine City" because of its climate and great weather, the city boasts a large variety of activities from professional sporting events, to performing and visual arts, to shopping and dining. St. Petersburg has the largest public waterfront park system of any U.S. city and the parks host many city festivals, music events and celebrations. These include First Night on New Year's Eve, the Festival of States in March, the Blues Festival and many more. (www.stpete.org)

St. Petersburg is an easy city to negotiate by foot or public transportation. Streets run north-south; avenues run east-west and Central Avenue separates North and South. You don't have to go far to get anything and everything you might need for your cruising journey.

Hopefully you will choose to get off the boat and enjoy some of the area's entertainment venues. You won't be at a loss for things to do. There are movies at Baywalk (a shopping/dining/movie complex on 2nd Avenue between 1st and 2nd Street); the largest collection of Salvador Dali works at the Salvador Dalí Museum, open daily except Thanksgiving and Christmas, with its display of paintings, sculpture, holograms and art glass. This museum is the only attraction on Florida's west coast that holds the Michelin Guide's top rating; and performing arts from the symphony to travelling Broadway plays at the Mahaffey Theater. Seasonal sports in the area include spring training baseball and Tampa Bay Rays baseball in St. Pete; Buccaneer football and Tampa Bay Lightning Hockey in nearby Tampa. The Honda Grand Prix races through the city streets of downtown St. Petersburg in April; and many classes of sailboat races take place in the Bay year round. Visit the city's Web site for maps and calendars of events (www.discoverdowntown.com).

There are several museums in addition to the Dali. The Museum of Fine Arts, History Museum, Holocaust Museum and Great Explorations Children's Museum. Many smaller galleries and performance centers including American Stage, Studio 620 and Florida Craftsmen are located in downtown.

The inverted triangle building jutting out into the Bay is the famous St. Petersburg Pier. It often hosts the replica of the HMS Bounty for tours and trips for a fee. The Pier houses a small aquarium, restaurants, shops and entertainment.

Great boat provisioning can be had at a weekly Saturday farmer's market in the Al Lang Stadium parking lot (1st Avenue and 1st Street South) from October through May from 9 a.m. to 2 p.m. A nearby Publix grocery store can cover you for the remainder of your supplies year-round. A post office, banks/ATM machines, Internet and just about anything you need can be found in downtown St. Petersburg.

There are many dining options indoors or at sidewalk cafes. You can enjoy a few drinks and music on the first Friday night of each month when a portion Central Ave. is shut down for the festivities. Latin dance lessons are a regular feature at Baywalk. Many events fill the parks along the waterfront throughout the year.

If you are in need of repairs, maintenance or haul-outs, the nearby Salt Creek marine area has many facilities. West Marine has a downtown chandlery and JSI has a facility in south St. Petersburg with spar, canvas and rigging, sails, upholstery and a chandlery.

Getting around downtown is easy. It is a great walking town. The downtown "Looper" trolley stops at many of the tourist spots and downtown locations for a minimal charge. The public bus service (PSTA) also can get you around the rest of the city and most lines run through downtown near Williams Park. Two airports serve the area: Tampa International and St. Pete/Clearwater. Super Shuttle services are available and run 24 hours a day seven days a week.

ADDITIONAL RESOURCES

- St. Petersburg/Clearwater Area Convention and Visitors Bureau, www.visitstpeteclearwater.com
- NEARBY GOLF COURSES
  Twin Brooks Golf Course, 3800 22nd Ave. S., St. Petersburg, FL 33711, 727-893-7445 www.stpete.org/golf/
- NEARBY MEDICAL FACILITIES
  Edward White Hospital, 2323 Ninth Ave. N., St. Petersburg, FL 33713, 727-323-1111

■ TAMPA BAY TO CLEARWATER

The GIWW runs from Tampa Bay to Anclote Key, at the mouth of the Anclote River leading to Tarpon Springs. There it ends and does not continue until you pick it up at Carrabelle, past the Big Bend or Nature Coast territory. From Carrabelle it runs west all the way to Brownsville, TX, with a U.S. Army Corps of Engineers project depth of 12 feet.

There are six bridges in the Pinellas Bayway bridge system (two of which are draw spans, the other four are fixed). When contacting the two bascule bridges by radio, use the alphabetical designation, either "C" or "E," rather than the bridge's name.

Two routes reach boating facilities on the west side of the Pinellas Peninsula. Those that can clear an 18-foot fixed vertical clearance bridge can use the shortcut past Cats Point off the straight-line extension of the Sunshine Skyway Channel. Otherwise, follow the Waterway channel through the Pinellas Bayway Structures "E" and "C" (both with 25-foot closed vertical clearances), and then behind Long Key into Boca Ciega Bay. Structure "E" (state Route 679) opens daily, from 9 a.m. to 7 p.m., on the hour and then every 30 minutes thereafter. Structure "C" (Vina del Mar) opens on the hour, and every 20 minutes thereafter, from 7 a.m. to 7 p.m. year-round. Call ahead on your VHF radio and get the latest scoop, making certain you know which bridge you are calling. Were you to call them "Structure Charlie" and "Structure Echo," you would not be confused between "C" and "E," which sometimes sound the same.

At the northern end of the GIWW, approaching Clearwater, the Waterway tends to narrow and bridges and shoaling become more frequent. Boats with significant draft should be very cautious. Marine services run the gamut from small fishing camps and motel and restaurant docks to large, elegant marina complexes.

From Tampa Bay to Clearwater, any one of three inlets affords easy access from the GIWW to and from the Gulf of Mexico (in good weather and daylight): North Channel (aka Pass-a-Grille Channel), Johns Pass and Clearwater Pass. North Channel, just north of Tampa Bay, leads from the Gulf to Pass-a-Grille Channel; Johns Pass, about 6.5 nautical miles north, connects with the Waterway between Mitchell and Sunshine beaches and is crossed by a bascule bridge (20-foot closed vertical clearance, opens on demand); and Clearwater Pass, about 13 miles farther to the north, which leads right into the heart of Clearwater proper. A 74-foot fixed vertical clearance bridge spans the pass.

Construction began in fall 2005 on a new Johns Pass twin-bascule bridge. It will have a closed vertical clearance of 27 feet at the center of the channel and horizontal width will be expanded from 60 to 100 feet. The expected completion date is still early 2011, at a cost of $76.6 million. (Call 727-343-3100 for details.)

Pass-a-Grille Channel to The Narrows

NAVIGATION: Use Chart 11411. At the start, the GIWW is a well-marked, dredged channel winding through shallows inside the barrier islands. From Pass-a-Grille Channel, it meanders northward inside the barrier islands referred to as the Holiday Isles: St. Petersburg Beach, Treasure Island and Sand Key. It threads around a maze of man-made islets pierced by canals.

The route begins where the main Waterway channel intersects Pass-a-Grille Channel near Mile 114. If you explore Pass-a-Grille Channel, watch for shoaling, and keep clear of the north side.

Dockage: Loggerhead Club & Marina is located in Frenchman Creek at Maximo Pt. Loggerhead's St. Petersburg location can accommodate vessels up to 60 feet and also provides Category 4 rated dry storage. Additionally, they provide a captain's lounge, ships store and easy access to restaurants, shopping and activities.

Just North of Cats Point is Maximo Marina. Two blocks from Maximo Marina is a shopping center with a large, well-stocked West Marine, a grocery store, a post office and an excellent Italian restaurant. The Tierra Verde Marine Center, located to the west of Structure "E" of the Pinellas Bayway, has an easy-to-reach fuel dock and transient slips. Take the current into consideration when you maneuver into your slip.

At Mile 114.5, just north of the Pinellas Bayway Bridge (Structure "C," 25-foot closed vertical clearance, opens on the hour and every 20 minutes thereafter from 7 a.m. to 7 p.m.), is a shoal spot that sometimes catches the unwary. It is well-marked, but do not be confused by the markers for the beginning of a side channel to Gulfport on the mainland. Red daybeacon "2," flashing red "26" and red daybeacon "26A" lead past the shoal. To continue north, leave all three to starboard, but to go to Gulfport and its boating facilities, turn to starboard at red daybeacon "2." The red flashing light marks the shoal itself. Gulfport Municipal Marina is located here with a full complement of transient facilities in its well-protected basin.

Johns Pass Marina is conveniently located right inside the inlet with gas and diesel fuel, transient slips, full-service prop and engine repairs and full shoreside facilities. From here north to Sand Key are full-service municipal marinas and facilities on both shores, including motels and on-the-water restaurants, all with dockage. Just north of Madeira Beach, on the mainland, is the Florida Holocaust Memorial Museum (727-820-0100). The museum, open daily, pays tribute to those who perished in the camps; exhibits include art, photography and artifacts.

Several bridges cross the GIWW, and while openings are usually prompt, delays can occur. When approaching bridges in this section, bide your time, and leave ample room for maneuvering while waiting. On the north side, there is no room outside the channel.

Anchorage: A number of anchorages can be found in Boca Ciega Bay just north of Mile 115. Proceed west between green daybeacon "31" and red daybeacon "30" from flashing red "32" then anchor where the chart shows 7- to 8-foot depths. Proceed between the last two No Wake markers to find the best depths. Or, proceed east at red daybeacon "32" in Cats Point Channel and anchor anywhere you can find sufficient depth and wind protection between Cats Point and Gulfport. Depth in the area are generally 7 to 10 feet, with 5 to 6 closer to shore.

Just north of the Treasure Island Bridge at green daybeacon "17," turn west, and stay north of the charted spoil area for a well-protected anchorage. Mean low water depths around the spoil are roughly 4 to 6 feet, and the

Boca Ciega Bay, FL

BOCA CIEGA BAY		Largest Vessel Accommodated	VHF Channel Monitored	Transient Berths / Total Berths	Approach / Dockside Depth (reported)	Floating Docks	Groceries, Ice, Marine Supplies, Snacks	Gas / Diesel	Repairs: Hull, Engine, Propeller	Lift (tonnage), Crane, Rail	1=110V, 2=220V, B=Both, Max Amps	Laundry, Pool, Showers	Pump-Out Station	Nearby: Grocery Store, Motel, Restaurant
Dockage							**Supplies**				**Services**			
1. Holiday Inn Sunspree Resort 110.3 🖳	727-867-1151	55	16	7/33	5/8			I			B/50	LPS		MR
2. **LOGGERHEAD CLUB & MARINA - ST. PETERSBURG** (WiFi)	**727-867-2600**	**60**	**16**	**470/470**	**5/5**		**GD**	**IMS**			**B/50**	**LPS**	**P**	**GMR**
3. Maximo Marina 1.5 NE of 115	727-867-1102	72	16	/320	8/8	F	GD	IMS	HP	L9	B/50	LS	P	GMR
4. **GULFPORT MUNICIPAL MARINA 1.5 NE OF 115** 🖳(WiFi)	**727-893-1071**	**45**	**16**	**6/250**	**7/6**	F	**GD**	**IMS**	**P**		**B/50**	**S**	**P**	**R**
5. Pasadena Yacht & Country Club 116.5 🖳	727-341-2628	100	16/69	6/82	8/12			IS			B/100	PS		GMR
6. Pasadena Marina 116	727-343-4500	55		1/125	6/6			GI			B/50	LPS	P	GMR
7. Tierra Verde Marina 113	727-866-0255	60	16	10/81	20/15	F	GD	GIMS	HEP	L10	B/50		P	GMR
8. Tierra Verde Resort & Marina 113	727-866-1487	130	16/71	20/107	12/12		GD	GIMS	P		B/100	LPS	P	GR
9. The Pass-A-Grille Marina 113.8	727-360-0100	50	16	10/	12/15	F	GD	GIMS	HEP	L15	B/100	LS	P	G
10. Isla Del Sol Yacht Club Marina 114.5 🖳(WiFi)	727-867-3625	100	16/68	3/73	20/20			I			B/50	LPS	P	R
11. Blind Pass Marina 118.5	727-360-4281	55	16/69	4/106				I			1/30	LS	P	GR
12. John's Pass Marina 1 S of 121.4 🖳	727-360-6907	125		12/20	10/5	F	GD	IMS	EP	L7	B/200	LS	P	GMR
13. Snug Harbor Marine Inc. 1 S of 121.4	727-398-7470	55		/7	6/5			M	HP	L25				GMR
14. Madeira Beach Municipal Marina 122.2 🖳	727-399-2631	100	68	6/80	6/11	F	GD	GIMS	HEP		B/50	LS	P	GMR
15. Bay Pines Marina 1.5 NE of 120.5	727-392-4922	50	16	/360	5/7	F	G	I	E		B/50		P	R

Corresponding chart(s) not to be used for navigation. 🖳 Internet Access (WiFi) Wireless Internet Access

bottom is sand. Highly visible west of the GIWW on St. Pete Beach is the renovated Don CeSar Hotel, a longtime landmark for mariners.

Bridge Restrictions: The opening times for the Corey Causeway, Treasure Island Causeway and the Madeira Beach Causeway may change every few months due to local pressure. Call ahead on VHF Channel 09 if you are in doubt of the opening schedule. The Corey Causeway Bridge (Mile 117.7, 23-foot closed vertical clearance) has restricted

openings Monday through Friday from 8 a.m. to 7 p.m., when it opens on the hour and every 20 minutes thereafter. On weekends and holidays from 10 a.m. to 7 p.m., the bridge opens on the hour and every 20 minutes thereafter. The Treasure Island Causeway (Mile 118.9, 21-foot closed vertical clearance) is restricted from 7 a.m. to 7 p.m. daily, when it opens on the hour and every 15 minutes thereafter, and from 11 p.m. to 7 a.m. daily, a 10 minute advance notice is required to open the span. The Madeira Beach

Looking west over Treasure Island and Johns Pass. (Not to be used for navigation.) JOHNS PASS MARINA

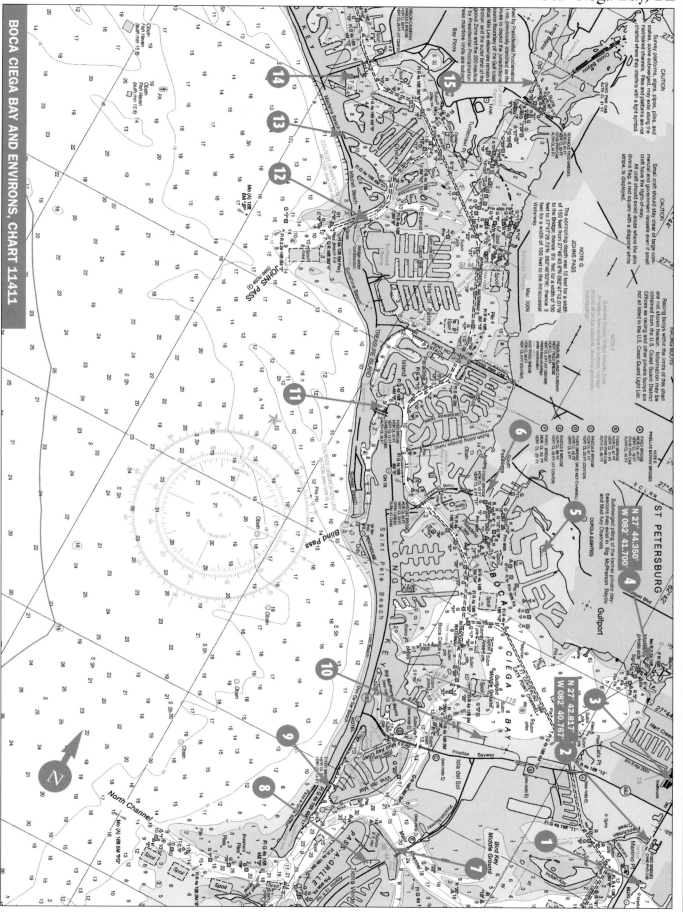

Clearwater, FL

Causeway (Mile 122.8, 25-foot closed vertical clearance) is restricted on weekends and holidays year-round from 9:30 a.m. to 6 p.m., when the bridge opens on the hour and every 20 minutes thereafter.

The Narrows—Mile 126

Nine miles south of Clearwater, the GIWW enters the well-named Narrows, a deep, but narrow channel, connecting Boca Ciega Bay to Clearwater Harbor, which is comparatively broad and open.

Dockage: Park Boulevard Bridge at Mile 126.0 has a 26-foot closed vertical clearance and opens on demand. South of Conch Key green daybeacon "27A" are two restaurants and a deli with docks. The Indian Rocks Beach Bascule Bridge at Mile 129.3 has a 25-foot closed vertical clearance and opens on demand. Near

the bridge is the Holiday Inn Harbourside Hotel and Marina, offering fuel, transient slips, a lively pool, tiki bar and restaurant. For a tasty dock-and-dine experience, The Pub Water-front Restaurant is located on the west side of The Narrows near red daybeacon "26."

The Belleair Causeway Bridge at Mile 131.8 is now a 75-foot (fixed vertical clearance) span. The old bridge has been completely removed so there is no restriction at this location.

■ CLEARWATER—MILE 136

Although divided by the GIWW channel, Clearwater and Clearwater Beach constitute one very boat-minded community. The seat of Pinellas County and one of Florida's fastest-growing resort cities, Clearwater extends across the upper end of the Pinellas Peninsula.

Boaters are finding it an increasingly important port of call, both as a base of operations from which to enjoy the nearby resort attractions, and also as a layover stop. The yacht services and elegant marinas here are mostly deep-water and capable of handling the largest boats that travel the GIWW. Marinas and repair installations are busy, but transient berths are generally available.

NAVIGATION: Use Chart 11411. The best access to Clearwater from the Gulf of Mexico is through Clearwater Pass, just south of Clearwater. A 74-foot fixed vertical clearance bridge crosses Clearwater Pass. This is one of the west coast's better daytime passes, and it is easy to use in good weather.

Just north of Clearwater Pass, the Clearwater Memorial Causeway Bridge (Mile 136.0, 74-foot fixed vertical clearance) crosses the GIWW. The bridge, which in 2005 replaced the old bascule bridge, has cleared the traffic jams between Clearwater and Clearwater Beach and eased congestion on the GIWW. North of the causeway the channel has shoaled; proceed with caution.

Dockage: Clearwater's biggest concentration of marinas is on the beach side between the Clearwater Pass and Clearwater Causeway. They can be approached either via a clearly marked and easy-to-navigate channel off the Clearwater Pass entrance channel, if you are coming from the Gulf of Mexico, or by a channel from the GIWW, if you are traveling by the inside route.

From the Clearwater Pass, once you are in the channel just after passing flashing red "8" and passing under the 74-foot fixed vertical clearance bridge, you will spot quick-flashing red "10," then flashing red "14" as you follow the channel. At flashing red "14," turn to port into the channel marked by red daybeacon "2" (leave to starboard) and green daybeacon "3." A well-marked channel will take you to green daybeacon "9," where you will turn to port into the channel leading in from the GIWW to the municipal marina.

From the GIWW, heading north, after passing flashing red "12," look for green daybeacon "1" just short of the

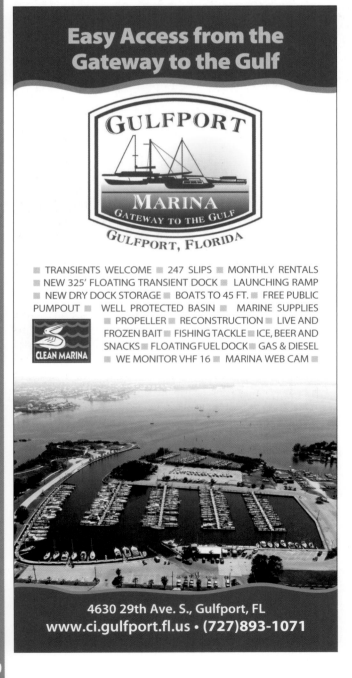

Sponge diver, Tarpon Springs. (Visit Florida)

Clearwater Causeway. Turn to port, and then follow the well-marked channel parallel to the causeway to green daybeacon "9," where that channel merges with the one coming in from Clearwater Pass. At this point, you can continue on to the marina of your choice.

The Chart House Suites and Marina, the closest marina to Clearwater Pass, offers 27 slips with cable TV and shoreside accommodations. The Best Western Sea Stone Resort offers transient slips, water view rooms/suites and a private beach. There is an Enterprise Car Rental agency on-site and a good Italian ice shop next door. Toward the end of the canal on the port side is the Clearwater Yacht Club.

Approaching from the GIWW channel, the Clearwater Municipal Marina is at green daybeacon "11." A sizable charter boat fleet is berthed here, as well as tour and fishing boats of all sizes. The Clearwater Municipal Marina takes reservations and the helpful marina staff can usually accommodate transients. A post office, ATM and nautical gift store are in the marina complex. Within about a half-hour walk is the Island Way complex, containing a Publix and some other small clothing stores.

A variety of restaurants are within a short walk. Frenchy's is a casual Jimmy Buffett-style restaurant, known for its fish sandwiches. The Island Way Grill and Bobby's Bistro are two good choices close by. Clearwater Downtown Boat Slips also offers overnight dockage with all amenities, as well as a courtesy dock during the day.

The Jolly Trolley stops in front of the marina complex and provides a convenient ride to the grocery store. "Sunsets at Pier 60", a daily celebration similar to Key West's Mallory Square, includes music, entertainment, food and crafts for sale.

■ DUNEDIN TO TARPON SPRINGS

About three miles north of Clearwater, the barrier islands fall away and the GIWW enters unprotected St. Joseph Sound and the approach to Anclote Key. After this final stretch on the GIWW, boaters continuing north beyond Anclote Key and the Anclote River have two choices. They may cross the open Gulf of Mexico for about 140

Indian Shores/ Clearwater, FL

W G

INDIAN SHORES/CLEARWATER	Phone	Dockage — Largest Vessel Accommodated	VHF Channel Monitored	Transient Berths / Total Berths	Approach / Dockside Depth (reported)	Floating Docks	Supplies — Gas / Diesel	Groceries, Ice, Marine Supplies, Snacks	Repairs: Hull, Engine, Propeller	Services — Lift (tonnage), Crane, Rail	1=110V, 2=220V, B=Both, Max Amps	Laundry, Pool, Showers	Pump-Out Station	Nearby: Grocery Store, Motel, Restaurant
1. The Pub Waterfront Restaurant 128.3	727-595-3172	70		50/50	7/5	F		S						GMR
2. Largo InterCoastal Marine 129.6	727-595-3592	35		3/381	4/4	F	G	IMS	HEP		B/50	S	P	GMR
3. Holiday Inn Harbourside 129.4 ⬚ 📶	800-726-0865	70	16	6/50	8/6			IMS	HEP		B/50	LPS		GMR
4. Indian Springs Marina 129	727-595-2956	40		/48	4.5/4.5	F	G	IM	HP	L30	1/30			GMR
5. CLEARWATER MUNICIPAL MARINA 136 ⬚	**727-462-6954**	**125**	16	23/220	6/12		GD	IS			B/50	LS	P	GMR
6. Days Inn Clearwater Beach 136	727-441-1722	70		10/10		F					1/30	LPS		GMR
7. Clearwater Yacht Club 136	727-447-6000	70	16	6/42	7/7	F		I			B/50	PS		GMR
8. CLEARWATER DOWNTOWN BOAT SLIPS	**727-462-6954**		16	/130		F	GD				B/50	PS		GMR

Corresponding chart(s) not to be used for navigation. ⬚ Internet Access 📶 Wireless Internet Access

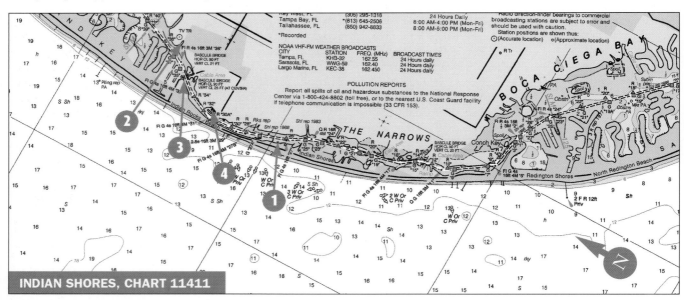

INDIAN SHORES, CHART 11411

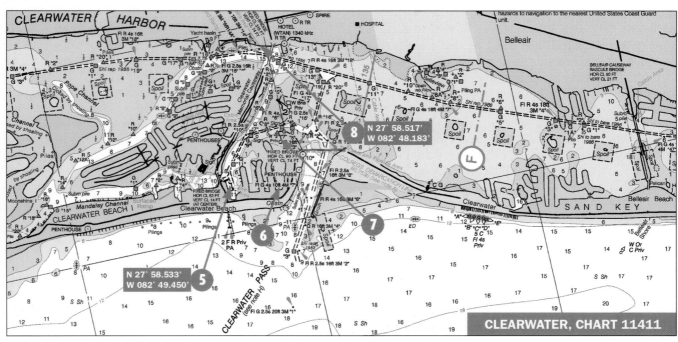

CLEARWATER, CHART 11411

nautical miles to Carrabelle, or they can follow a series of several markers relatively close in-shore around the Big Bend section of Florida for about 160 or 165 miles to Carrabelle.

Dunedin

Dockage: Dunedin (Mile 139) is a nice stop. The municipal marina has transient docks, showers and is within walking distance to Dunedin's restaurants and shopping. The Bon Appetit restaurant is next to the municipal marina and has docks for mariners who want to dine ashore (727-733-2151). Check to see if they are offering service for those who want to eat aboard their boats. Marker 1 Marina, immediately south of the Dunedin Causeway Bridge, offers transient dockage, gas and diesel fuel, shore power and pump-out service.

Caladesi State Park is off to the west with a wonderful isolated marina. To get there, turn west just south of the Dunedin Bridge (green daybeacon "17") and then follow the Honeymoon Island Channel to a separate buoyed channel into Seven Mouth Creek. There are 90 slips, but only three are wider than 11 feet. There are three "T" docks for larger boats. Average depths on the approach and dockside are reported at 4 feet so you need to travel at high tide, go slowly and obtain up-to-date local knowledge. Call 727-469-5918 for reservations. The beach at Caladesi Island is rated one of the best beaches in the United States.

Anchorage: A popular anchorage is Three Rooker Bar, a narrow C-shaped island located between Honeymoon Island and Anclote Key about 2.5 miles offshore from Tarpon Springs. Three Rooker's white sand beaches line the north and seaward sides of the island and offer some of the best shelling and beachcombing. The bay side of the island's shallow water teems with fish and birds. It is a well-protected anchorage from all but east winds. Enter around the north end of the bar, dropping anchor in the crescent near the beach in 4- to 8-foot depths over a soft mud bottom. Use the depth sounder and line-of-sight navigation, avoiding the white sand bars that run out from the beach. On holiday weekends, this normally placid anchorage becomes a maelstrom of activity, with jet skis, small outboards and a floating hamburger stand all vying for space.

Anclote River

NAVIGATION: Use Chart 11411. A range helps you through the big offshore shoal around the entrance to the Anclote River. But if you cannot see the onshore light, locate quick-flashing green "1." Channel markers are no more than three-quarters of a mile apart. For help in orienting, you will see a tall, strobe-lighted power plant chimney on the north side of the Anclote River entrance, visible from 25 miles at sea on a clear day. The chimney, illuminated by flashing lights at night, is plotted on Chart 11411 ("STACK") and mentioned in the U.S. Coast Pilot.

Dunedin, FL

DUNEDIN		Dockage				Supplies			Services			
1. Beso Del Sol 139.5	727-734-8851	21		/100	6/8				1/30	LPS		M
2. Dunedin Municipal Marina 139	727-298-3030	70	16	11/194	5/4.5				B/50	S	P	GMR
3. Marker 1 Marina .5 E of 141.5 🖵	727-733-9324	75	16/14	/144	6/6	GD	IMS		B/50	LPS	P	GR

Corresponding chart(s) not to be used for navigation. 🖵 Internet Access (WiFi) Wireless Internet Access

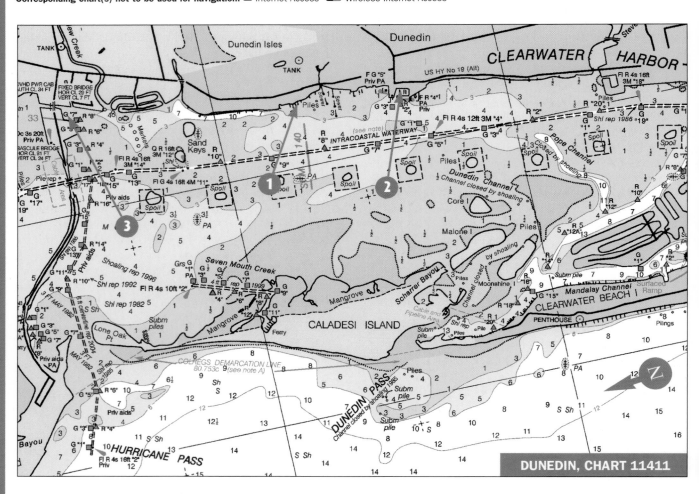

DUNEDIN, CHART 11411

Respect the shoal south of Anclote Key. When entering the GIWW south of Anclote Key, or entering the Anclote River, give flashing green "7" near Mile 150 its due respect. Older charts may not show the extension of the shoal southward.

Tarpon Springs

Tarpon Springs marks the end of the Florida GIWW at Mile 150. (The GIWW picks back up in Carrabelle, FL, where mileages are measured east and west of Harvey Lock, LA.) Beyond, from Anclote Key at the mouth of the Anclote River, lie the intriguing Big Bend (or Nature Coast) and the Florida Panhandle. Take it easy going upriver the three miles to Tarpon Springs, and observe

the posted IDLE-SPEED/NO-WAKE ZONE. There are many boats at slips in the river, and your wake can cause serious damage. The Cut C range's eastern mark is partially obscured by trees—favor the southern side of the channel to avoid the shoal.

Tarpon Springs is still the "Sponge Capital of the World" and has managed to diversify without losing its old-time flavor. While a large shrimp fleet and a lively boat-building industry make their homes in Tarpon Springs, colorful spongers still ply the waters as well. Along the picturesque sponge docks, you will find Greek restaurants galore, each vying with the other for the best broiled octopus and tastiest saganaki.

Dockage: Transient dockage in Tarpon Springs is readily available. Just as you enter the river, on the northeast side (to port) is a relatively new facility, Anclote Village Marina. With some transient slips available, and "high and dry" storage for small boats, the marina offers a convenient stopping place if you do not have the time to go upriver.

Farther up the river, opposite green daybeacon "39" on the northeast side (to port entering the river), Port Tarpon Marina has a convenient fuel dock just off the river channel, a limited number of transient slips and an on-site restaurant.

Just past flashing green "39," Anclote Harbors Marina, next door to Port Tarpon Marina, offers all hull, engine and propeller repairs, a 40-ton lift and welcomes cruising boats up to 60 feet to its well-maintained piers, with water, cable TV, laundry and showers.

Staying at any of the marinas on the north side of the river means you will need to arrange for transportation if you wish to get to the sponge docks and restaurants, most of which are on the south side of the river.

At the end of the navigable portion of the river, to starboard, right next to the sponge docks and the Sponge Museum is the Tarpon Springs City Marina. It retains an old-time flavor and offers transient slips, along with restrooms and showers; reservations are a must. Its location at the east end of the sponge docks is ideal for exploring Tarpon Springs, with its sponge-diving trips, the aquarium and its many excellent Greek restaurants.

Opposite the City Marina, across the river, is the Tarpon Landing Marina facility, offering five transient docks. Thirty- and 50-amp electrical hookups are available, as well as gas and diesel fuels and a high-speed pump-out service at the fuel dock. As evening approaches, the night is redolent with the sounds of live music and laughter from crowded Capt. Jack's full-service restaurant and bar at the head of the slips. Sponge docks and Greek restaurants are a short walk across the fixed highway bridge (state Road Alternate 19) to the south side of the river.

For cruisers with their dogs aboard, a 10-minute walk from either marina leads to a dog park, with two separate fenced-in play areas, where the dogs can romp without leashes.

Anchorage: An anchorage with 6-foot depths is located by the river's entrance east of green daybeacon "17" and just beyond the stack. There is a nearby park with a boat ramp and restrooms. Up the river in Tarpon Springs, some boats anchor in front of the city marina, but shoaling and traffic may be a problem, and it is not recommended.

GOIN' ASHORE:
TARPON SPRINGS, FL

In reality, there are two Tarpon Springs. Both are intimately interrelated and well worth a visit. The sponge docks, the unbroken string of Greek restaurants along Dodecanese

Boulevard and the marinas are one aspect, while the other—historic downtown Tarpon Springs—is a charming complement to the docks. Be sure to stop at the visitors center at the City Marina to pick up a map of the area.

A casual walk along the Dodecanese Boulevard waterfront includes a visit to the Sponge Factory (727-938-5366), where a brief movie tells the story of the original Greek sponge divers who made Tarpon Springs the "Sponge Capital of the World" and left an indelible mark on the city. Included in the theater is a museum, featuring sponge-diving exhibitions and exhibits of authentic sponging ships of bygone years; a 90-foot "mother" ship and a 38-foot diving boat. There you can also buy from a broad range of sponges of all sizes, shapes and types. You can then take an hour-long trip on an authentic sponge boat and watch a diver go through his paces.

No visit is complete without sampling the Greek food on Dodecanese Boulevard. When you have worked up an appetite from a hard day of sightseeing, stop in at one of the restaurants lining the main street. If you do not go for the flaming saganaki (flaming cheese appetizer) or the broiled octopus, their authentic Greek salads and lamb dishes are particularly noteworthy. After dinner or at snack time, sample some of the pastries sold at the bakeries inside each of the restaurants, especially the baklava. If you have had enough Greek food, try the Caribbean flavors at the Lime-N-Coconut Grill (118 ½ Arafaras Blvd., 727-945-0602) or Paul's Shrimp House (80 W. Live Oak St., 727-937-1239) for their generous portions of fresh seafood. For outdoor deck dining and entertainment, visit Capt. Jack's at the Landings Marina. You may also go downtown to historic Tarpon Springs for a bite at an authentic Irish pub.

There are no conventional grocery stores on the Greek side of town; however, a service station with a convenience store and a package store/bar with limited supplies are located near the bridge at the intersection of Dodecanese Boulevard and U.S. 19.

The second Tarpon Springs, historic Tarpon Springs, is a 10-minute cab ride from the sponge docks or you can catch a ride on the free City trolley or municipal bus. Both have stops close by the city marina. This is an unusual and charming area, well worth the cruiser's stop. Houses, shops and restaurants have an old-world look, and a walk through the moss-hung streets reveals several fine Greek Orthodox churches and shrines. On the south side of town there is a colorful flag store where you can buy flags for future cruising destinations. It also carries decorative flags and cocktail signals.

Two fine parks, Howard Beach Park and Sunset Beach, are near town and accessible by water. A short taxi ride takes you to A.L. Anderson Park, one of the South's prettiest and cleanest. A sure cure for a bad case of cabin fever, it has cool shady forests and an abundance of birds. You can take a nature walk and make use of the picnic and boating facilities.

From November to early spring you will find manatees that make their home in the shallow Spring Bayou close to

Tarpon Springs, FL

TARPON SPRINGS		Largest Vessel Accommodated	VHF Channel Monitored	Transient Berths / Total Berths	Approach / Dockside Depth (reported)	Floating Docks	Gas / Diesel	Groceries, Ice, Marine Supplies, Snacks	Repairs: Hull, Engine, Propeller	Lift (tonnage), Crane, Rail	1=110v, 2=220v, B=Both, Max Amps	Laundry, Pool, Showers	Pump-Out Station	Nearby: Grocery Store, Motel, Restaurant
				Dockage				**Supplies**				**Services**		
1. Anclote Village Marina	727-937-9737	45	16	2/20	5/7		GD	IMS	E		1/30			R
2. Port Tarpon Marina	727-937-2200	65	16	10/60	9/9	F	GD	IMS	HEP	L50	B/50	S		R
3. Anclote Harbors Marina	727-934-7616	40	16	4/30	9/6	F		I	HEP		B/50	LS		GMR
4. Anclote Isles Marina	727-939-0100	75	16	5.5/6							B/50			GMR
5. Neptune Marine	727-934-2370	45			10/6			M	HEP	L	B/50			R
6. F & Y Inc.	727-937-4351	200	16		12/12		GD				B/50			GR
7. Gulf Marine Ways	727-937-4401	100			10/10			IM	HEP	R	B/50			GMR
8. Tarpon Springs City Marina	727-937-9165	50	16	6/21	11/10			IS			B/50	S		GMR
9. The Landing at Tarpon Springs 🖥 📶	727-937-1100	65	16	5/50	5/6		GD	IMS	HEP		B/50	LS	P	GMR

Corresponding chart(s) not to be used for navigation. 🖥 Internet Access 📶 Wireless Internet Access

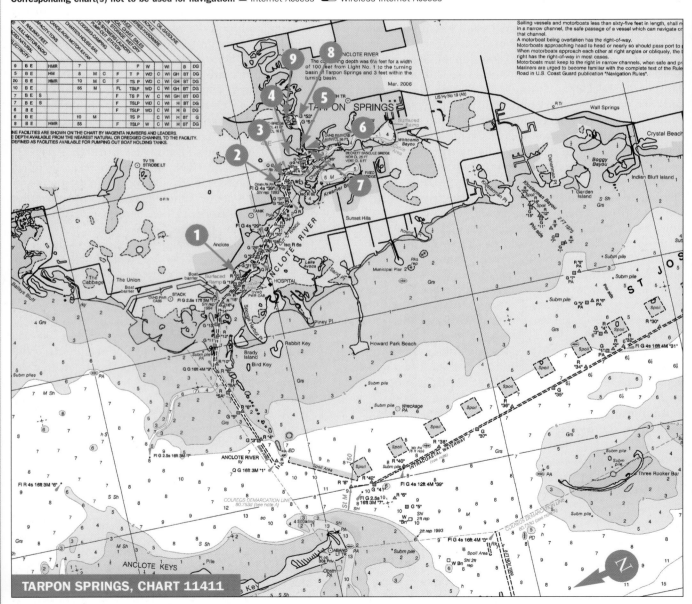

TARPON SPRINGS, CHART 11411

downtown. It only takes a short dinghy ride to get to the Bayou, but it becomes a non-motorized area so you will need to row in and around the bayou to view the manatees.

ADDITIONAL RESOURCES

- City of Tarpon Springs, **www.ctsfl.us**

NEARBY GOLF COURSES
Tarpon Springs Golf Course, 1310 S. Pinellas Ave., Tarpon Springs, FL 34688, 727-937-6906
www.ctsfl.us

NEARBY MEDICAL FACILITIES
Helen Ellis Memorial Hospital, 1395 S. Pinellas Ave., Tarpon Springs, FL 34689 727-942-5000

Cruising Options

From here, northbound skippers may continue on toward the Florida Panhandle. The outside run of 140 miles to Carrabelle's East Pass can be daunting if the weather is foul, so choose your weather carefully, and watch the depth sounder. Otherwise it can be an exciting and interesting run.

Or if fishing is your game, head on up the coast to Big Bend country with its many rivers and swamps, where fishing (salt and freshwater) is the thing. Remember you will be handling tricky shoals, so travel with up-to-date charts and a GPS to help. At press time, the disastrous effects from the oil rig explosion and subsequent leak offshore were just beginning to become apparent, and may have an effect on the ecology of Florida's West Coast ecosystem for some time to come. ■

Waterway Guide is always open to your observations from the helm. E-mail your comments on any navigation information in the guide to: editor@waterwayguide.com.

Waterway Guide advertising sponsors play a vital role in bringing you the most trusted and well-respected cruising guide in the country. Without our advertising sponsors, we simply couldn't produce the top-notch publication now resting in your hands. Next time you stop in for a peaceful night's rest, let them know where you found them—Waterway Guide, The Cruising Authority.

Tarpon Springs sponge boat. Photo Courtesy of Susan Landry

Florida's Upper Gulf Coast

■ THE BIG BEND
■ THE PANHANDLE: APALACHICOLA TO PENSACOLA

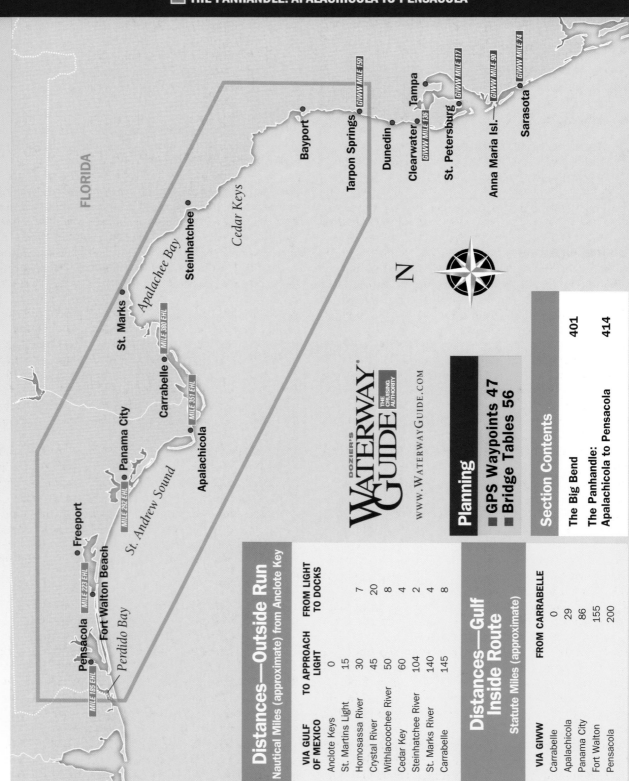

N

DOZIER'S WATERWAY GUIDE THE CRUISING AUTHORITY
WWW.WATERWAYGUIDE.COM

Planning
■ GPS Waypoints 47
■ Bridge Tables 56

Section Contents

The Big Bend	401
The Panhandle: Apalachicola to Pensacola	414

Distances—Outside Run
Nautical Miles (approximate) from Anclote Key

VIA GULF OF MEXICO	TO APPROACH LIGHT	FROM LIGHT TO DOCKS
Anclote Keys	0	
St. Martins Light	15	7
Homosassa River	30	20
Crystal River	45	8
Withlacoochee River	50	4
Cedar Key	60	2
Steinhatchee River	104	4
St. Marks River	140	8
Carrabelle	145	

Distances—Gulf Inside Route
Statute Miles (approximate)

VIA GIWW	FROM CARRABELLE
Carrabelle	0
Apalachicola	29
Panama City	86
Fort Walton	155
Pensacola	200

Florida's Upper Gulf Coast

Florida's Upper Gulf Coast stretches from Tarpon Springs on the eastern end to Pensacola and Perdido Bay on the west. It offers two distinct cruising regions: the fascinating swampy marshland and wilderness of the Big Bend/Nature Coast and the stretches of blazing white sand beaches, spiked by high-rise condominiums, of the dazzling coastline that is Florida's Panhandle. The coast, with its sandy barrier islands of sugar-white sands, has different names in different locales. In Panama City, the coastline is known as the "Redneck Riviera." In Destin and Fort Walton, it is called "The Emerald Coast." Nearer to Pensacola, they call it "The Miracle Strip."

Thus, skippers visiting Florida's Upper Gulf Coast for the first time find a very different kind of cruising, first from Anclote Key to Carrabelle across the Big Bend (or Nature Coast), then into the true Florida Panhandle, from Apalachicola to Pensacola and the Alabama line. The first part of this 350-mile stretch, known as the Big Bend area (but officially called Florida's Nature Coast), has no protected inside route, so mariners must make the trip across the open Gulf of Mexico. For the second half, from Carrabelle on to Florida's Panhandle, you can either pick up the Gulf Intracoastal Waterway (GIWW) or continue outside, weather permitting, with several serviceable cuts to move inside should you (or the weather) change your mind.

The effects of higher latitude are another major difference. With the exception of the northeastern coast of Florida, from Fernandina Beach to St. Augustine, the Upper Gulf Coast of Florida is the only coastal section of the state that experiences a noticeable winter. For example, whereas "Season" in South Florida runs generally from November to April, "Season" in the Upper Gulf Coast, depending on the marine facility and location, may run from Memorial Day to Labor Day. And it does get chilly in the winter.

But in the halcyon days of summer and even in the relatively milder weather of winter, it has much to offer boaters. There are relatively uncrowded, clear waters, award-winning beaches yet to be discovered by Northern snowbirds and interesting landfalls at charming, boating-oriented communities. Spacious natural harbors and bayous abound with birds, fish and wildlife, while bays and sounds are protected by long barrier islands.

Hurricanes and the Oil Spill

Much of the area's natural beauty and serenity has been rudely interrupted over the last seven years. In the late summer and early fall 2004, two killer hurricanes, Charley in August (Charlotte Harbor and Punta Gorda) and Ivan in September (Pensacola and the Panhandle), slammed directly into the Gulf of Mexico, and two more in August, Frances and Jeanne, swept across the mainland of Florida and caused additional damage to the west coast and Panhandle. In 2005, both Dennis (Navarre Beach) and Katrina (New Orleans) had strong effects on the Panhandle. Overall damage extended from Captiva Island in the south, to Pensacola and the Gulf Shores of Alabama in the northwest, leaving destroyed marinas along with the disaster they left farther inland. Most marinas planning to stay in business were up and running by the end of 2005, while other, more severely damaged facilities predicted (hopefully) that they would be "up and running soon," on a monthly basis.

The other disruption to the area has been the explosion and subsequent leak of the Deepwater Horizon rig. At press time, 500 miles of Gulf Coast beaches had seen oil come ashore, and ongoing efforts were being made to cap the spill. Visit our Web site at www.waterwayguide.com for the latest information on the spill and clean-up efforts. Hopefully by the time you transit the area, the clean-up efforts will be successful, and the Gulf will be restored to its former beauty.

The Coastal Cruiser

Along the west coast shore of the Big Bend/Nature Coast, from Anclote Key almost to Carrabelle, the Gulf of Mexico is relatively shallow and the coastline low and indistinct. Running along the shore calls for watching the depth sounder closely. Powerboats may cruise at any speed (there isn't a speed limit on the Big Bend), but they should slow down when meeting or passing other vessels. This is a fine sailing area, but boats with deep draft should be wary of the shoals.

Skippers with time to spare and a taste for exploring an area not yet swarming with cruising tourists shouldn't ignore the rivers of the Lonesome Leg. But remember, only an able, shallow-draft boat with a reliable depth sounder should attempt to cruise in this territory.

Visit Florida

The long rivers, some only a few miles apart, offer splendid gunkholing and excellent fishing, but go in carefully, and follow the approach and channel markers. Since many of these streams are loaded with weeds, be sure you have got strainers on all seawater intakes. The ubiquitous crab traps present another hazard, so give their floats a wide berth. This is brown pelican country—not only do they deface buoy numbers, but a pelican perched on a can buoy will, from a distance, change the outline to that of a nun buoy. Get in the habit of checking floating marks carefully.

Offshore Crossing

If you don't plan to cruise the Big Bend area, running the 130- to 140-nautical-mile rhumb line directly from Tarpon Springs or Clearwater to the St. George Island East Pass Entrance Buoy to Carrabelle can save a lot of time, but only an able boat enjoying good weather should attempt this passage. Many cruisers prefer to follow a route closer to the coastline. There used to be markers, called the Big Bend markers, which provided for shorter hops along the coastline. These were discontinued, but there are still several that can be used to keep the course closer to shore (i.e. no more than about 15 to 20 miles offshore) with 8- to 32-foot depths.

Before setting out, make sure your boat is seaworthy and your engine sound. Know your compass error. Along the route, plot your courses carefully and stick to them. Always know your position, by dead reckoning and by two or more bearings where possible. GPS provides accurate fixes, and a registered Emergency Position Indicating Radio Beacon (EPIRB) is an excellent addition to your safety equipment. The Yankeetown radio beacon used in conjunction with the Egmont Key beacon gives an additional Radio Direction Finder (RDF) fix capability. Let's face it though, if you think that an RDF fix is the "bee's knees," then you probably shouldn't venture out of sight of land in the first place.

Those choosing the direct route, particularly in the Big Bend area, should leave a float plan with a friend or relative. If trouble occurs, rescue units will arrive much faster if they know your route. Unless you are very experienced, run only in daylight. Most important: Watch the weather, because it can change quickly. NOAA weather radio or local commercial AM or FM radio stations and satellite weather services, such as XM Weather, should be monitored regularly for the latest information. Keep your eye on the sky, too.

Upper Gulf Inside Route—
Carrabelle to Pensacola/Perdido Bay

From Carrabelle, Florida's Panhandle curves around southwest, then northwest, west and again southwest to the Perdido River and the Alabama line. You can travel outside quite simply by following the coastline all the way to Pensacola. The more interesting GIWW route connects big bays and sounds that are protected by narrow, wooded barrier islands. From Carrabelle to Pensacola, there are 200 statute miles of inside cruising with frequent passes through to the Gulf of Mexico, but fixed bridge heights of 50 feet will prevent most sailboats from using some of the inside route.

On the east, the Florida Panhandle extends north beyond Carrabelle to inland Tallahassee, the state capital. To the west, the Panhandle extends to Pensacola, once an outpost of the Spanish colony of New Orleans, and later the capital of British West Florida during the American Revolution. Midway along the route is Panama City, a well-equipped sportfishing and boating center surrounded by pure white beaches. Other worthwhile stops include Apalachicola, Destin and Fort Walton Beach. A fixed 49-foot bridge at Destin will dictate whether or not you can access the inner route to Fort Walton. ■

The Big Bend

CHARTS 11404, 11405, 11406, 11407, 11408, 11409, 11411, 11412

From Anclote Key, the Big Bend, or Nature Coast, territory begins. Floridians call it the Big Bend. The state government and chambers of commerce call it the Nature Coast. Pick one. This is the area for cruisers interested in lovely, but sometimes lonely, wilderness grounds. Most cruising is done in the rivers entering the Gulf of Mexico, and there is no inside Intracoastal Waterway (ICW) protected route to take. Fishing and hunting are the name of the game here. But sharpen up your navigation skills and cruise carefully. You will be a long and expensive distance from commercial assistance if you make a mistake.

■ THE BIG BEND/ NATURE COAST

North of Anclote Key and Tarpon Springs, as far as Carrabelle to the west, the coastline presents cruising skippers with a very different kind of Florida cruising. Shoaling normally extends so far out that cruisers are basically in open, though shallow, Gulf of Mexico waters. These are fishermen's waters, both fresh and saltwater. The rivers are shallow and tricky, but loaded with fish of all types. Some are home to sturgeon.

Most of the coast is low and marshy—perfect duck hunting and fishing country. Fishing camp towns and facilities that cater to cruising boats are beginning to open along the many shallow rivers and creeks. The countryside is still undeveloped, even primitive in spots, and any place you put in will offer navigational challenges, but make for some interesting side trips.

Before starting out, make sure you have up-to-date charts, and pay close attention to compass headings to obtain regular position fixes while traveling between markers. To lose track of your position could mean running aground and having to call for assistance.

The Coast Guard station on the Withlacoochee River, at Yankeetown, about 17 nautical miles southeast of Cedar Key, covers this area and monitors VHF Channel 16. This station also operates and maintains three vessels, including a 41-foot utility boat, for emergency search and rescue. In addition to VHF, the station can be reached by telephone at 352-447-6900.

NAVIGATION: Use Chart 11400. The route around the Big Bend is well-marked, and the mariner can choose to follow markers that lie close to shore or farther out, as dictated by personal preference, weather conditions or vessel draft. Starting at flashing red "10," designated on some charts as St MARTINS, which is located about 14 nautical miles north-northwest of Anclote Key, a course of 322 degrees magnetic will carry you the 110 nautical miles to flashing red buoy "24" in Apalachee Bay. Although a lengthy passage, you will never be more than about 20 miles offshore. You can plot a course even closer to shore by using entrance buoys to the various river channels. The only caveat here is to make sure when plotting the course that your bearing does not carry you over shoals your vessel cannot handle. At that point, if you decide to enter St. George Sound to go to either Carrabelle or Apalachicola, alter course to 255 degrees magnetic for roughly 26 nautical miles to pick up flashing red bell "2" at the entrance to East Pass between St. George Island and Dog Island.

If weather is fair, winds are 10 to 15 knots (or less) out of the east, northeast or southeast; seas should be 2 to 3 feet or less. If your vessel is powered for cruising between 15 and 20 knots, the direct crossing from Anclote Key to Carrabelle, about 130 nautical miles, can be quite pleasant, brief and certainly shorter than the shoreside route.

For vessels that cruise in the 8-knot range and wish to get around the Big Bend, perhaps through a weather window and with a minimum of sightseeing, the trip can be broken up rather nicely into three days as follows: Day One, Anclote anchorage to Cedar Key; Day Two, Cedar Key to St. Marks; Day Three, St. Marks to Carrabelle or Apalachicola. The longest leg, just over 100 statute

Hernando Beach, FL

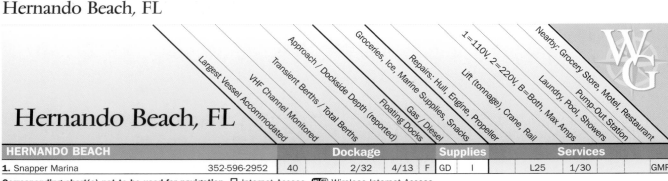

HERNANDO BEACH		Largest Vessel Accommodated		VHF Channel Monitored	Transient Berths / Total Berths	Approach / Dockside Depth (reported)	Floating Docks	Groceries, Ice, Marine Supplies, Snacks	Gas / Diesel	Repairs: Hull, Engine, Propeller	Lift (tonnage), Crane, Rail	1=110V, 2=220V, B=Both, Max Amps	Laundry, Pool, Showers	Pump-Out Station	Nearby: Grocery Store, Motel, Restaurant
			Dockage					Supplies			Services				
1. Snapper Marina	352-596-2952	40			2/32	4/13	F	GD	I		L25	1/30			GMR

Corresponding chart(s) not to be used for navigation. ⌨ Internet Access (WiFi) Wireless Internet Access

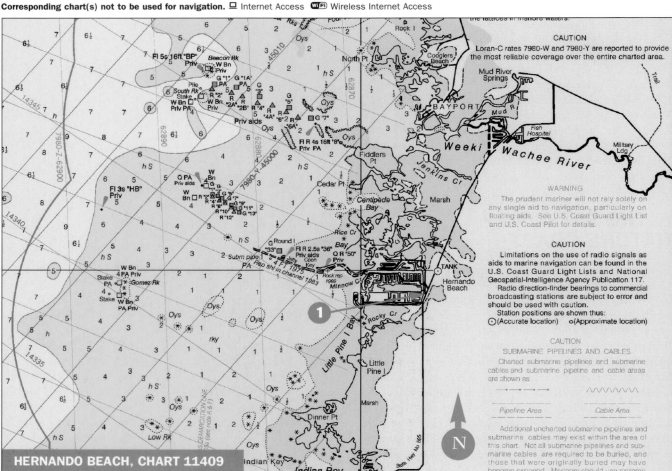

HERNANDO BEACH, CHART 11409

miles, is from Cedar Key to the town of St. Marks, but anchoring near the mouth of the St. Marks River would cut about 10 statute miles off this leg.

Slower vessels can also make the trip between Anclote Key and St. George's East Pass in an easy overnight passage, again with a good weather window. Get a good night's sleep, leave midday, and arrive at your destination in the morning with good light.

Exploring the Coast

Those intending to explore inland from the coast should get local information ahead of time. The river currents can be strong for lightly powered vessels. While tidal range is about 2.5 feet, prolonged offshore winds can drive the water out of the streams, and an onshore wind will increase charted depths.

Crystal & Homosassa Rivers, FL

CRYSTAL & HOMOSASSA RIVERS		Largest Vessel Accommodated	VHF Channel Monitored	Transient Berths / Total Berths	Approach / Dockside Depth (reported)	Floating Docks	Gas / Diesel	Groceries, Ice, Marine Supplies, Snacks	Repairs: Hull, Engine, Propeller	Lift (tonnage), Crane, Rail	1=110V, 2=220V, B=Both, Max Amps	Laundry, Pool, Showers	Pump-Out Station	Nearby: Grocery Store, Motel, Restaurant
1. Pete's Pier Inc.	352-795-3302	80	68	4/85	8/5	F	GD	IMS			B/50	S	P	GMR
2. Aquamarina Twin Rivers ☐ WiFi	352-795-3552	60	16	6/54	5/8	F	GD	IMS	HEP	L35	B/50	S		GM
3. MacRae's of Homosassa	352-628-2602	35	16/68	/10	6/3		G	IMS	P		1/30	L		GMR

Corresponding chart(s) not to be used for navigation. ☐ Internet Access WiFi Wireless Internet Access

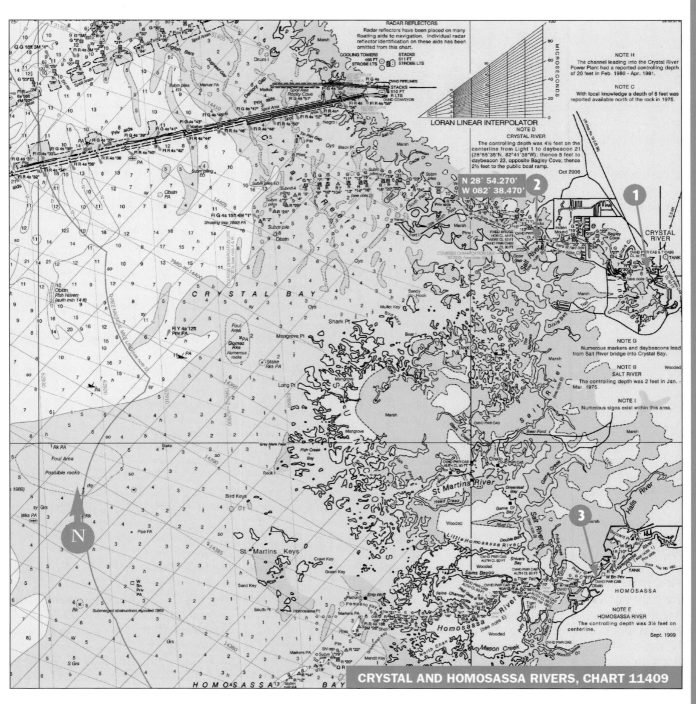

CRYSTAL AND HOMOSASSA RIVERS, CHART 11409

Withlacoochee River/ Yankeetown, FL

WITHLACOOCHEE RIVER/YANKEETOWN		Approach / Dockside Depth (reported)	VHF Channel Monitored	Transient Berths / Total Berths		Dockage			Supplies	Groceries, Ice, Marine Supplies, Snacks	Gas / Diesel	Floating Docks	Repairs: Hull, Engine, Propeller	Lift (tonnage), Crane, Rail	Services	1=110V, 2=220V, B=Both, Max Amps	Laundry, Pool, Showers	Pump-Out Station	Nearby: Grocery Store, Motel, Restaurant
1. Yankeetown Marina	352-447-5959	50	16	1/50		6/6			GD	GIMS					B/50				GMR

Largest Vessel Accommodated

Corresponding chart(s) not to be used for navigation. ☐ Internet Access 🛜 Wireless Internet Access

WITHLACOOCHEE RIVER/YANKEETOWN, CHART 11408

Even though well-marked, the rivers inside from the Big Bend route are often tricky to enter and sometimes too shallow for deeper-draft boats and therefore are best attempted during daylight hours only. The controlling depths vary. Some streams are prohibitively shallow, while others are deep enough for large commercial craft. However, communities on these rivers make an effort to take care of cruising boats.

Anclote Key

Just outside the entrance to the Anclote River and Tarpon Springs is Anclote Key, a favorite picnic spot and fishing area for local boaters, but also marking the start of the northwesterly corner coast of Florida called the Big Bend or Nature Coast. Anchor well off with plenty of scope; holding ground is only fair. The ground farther off the Key, charted "Anclote Anchorage," offers fine holding and a quiet, undisturbed night's sleep. Depths average 8 to 9 feet.

The town of Gulf Harbors, just northeast of Anclote Key, has an excellent seafood restaurant with dockage for patrons. Use the North Channel, holding as near to center as possible, then follow the dredged channel to its head.

Homosassa River

The Homosassa River is a comparatively narrow and shallow Waterway with winding channels and unforgiving oyster bars and rock beds. But it supplies some great fishing for both salt and freshwater species. The fishing village of Homosassa on the Homosassa River provides an interesting excursion for shallower draft boats.

NAVIGATION: Use Chart 11409. From St Martins flashing red "10" (about 12 miles north of Anclote Key), set a northeasterly course for the flashing red, 16-foot-high "2" southwest of the entrance to Homosassa Bay, about 17 nautical miles away.

From here, the Homosassa River Channel is about 3.5 nautical miles to the northeast, over 4- and 5-foot-deep shoals. Keep a sharp eye out for navigational aids on this run; orange fish haven beacons, which can easily be mistaken for red markers, may lure you off course. Flashing red "4" marks the channel entrance toward the Homosassa River.

With few exceptions, the channel is well-marked. The route twists and turns its way to the fishing village of Homosassa, about four miles upriver. In some reaches, you may encounter shallow depths between two consecutive marker numbers. Currents in the river are strong, so keep a firm hand on the helm and stay mid-channel. Depths are adequate for many small powerboats; 3-foot depths can be carried all the way to the village. This is, however, probably not an optional stopping-over spot for sailboats.

In Homosassa, an attractive fishing center that grows more popular each year, more than a 20 fishing guides operate year-round. Fishermen should remember that because the river qualifies as freshwater, a license is required.

Several marinas welcome transients. Do not venture beyond the marina area, as depths become uncertain in the upper reaches of the river. The Yulee Sugar Mill Ruins Historic State Park is worth a visit (352-795-3817). Once a thriving sugar plantation, the 5,100 acres supplied sugar products to the Confederate Army during the Civil War. A pathway leads visitors around the ruins to interpretive plaques that explain how the mill worked. This area more than repays the effort of the long trip in from the open Gulf. Those who know only the resort cities and sandy beaches farther south and north along the Gulf coast would never suspect Florida could look as it does along the Homosassa River.

Only an occasional fish camp breaks the river's narrow and tortuous channel, banked by jungles of palmetto, mangrove, yucca and palm. The gin-clear water teems with fish, and shore birds abound. Brown pelicans, egrets and anhinga (snakebird) are everywhere, and monkeys reside on the small island where a tiny lighthouse stands. The monkeys are not native to Florida and resentment at being captured some other place and brought here still runs in their genes. Left to their own, the monkeys have been inbreeding for generations. Some have lost all semblances of good manners and they bite. Don't go ashore. Instead, watch them from the Riverside Crab House.

Crystal River

Crystal River, fed by some 30 natural streams, is a manatee sanctuary. As the largest manatee haven on the west coast of Florida, this area is home for about 200 of the endangered mammals. Keep an eye out for them, and throttle down in restricted areas.

Since shoaling may affect the 6-foot projected depth of Salt River, keep to mid-channel, and get local information on depths. At the junction of the Salt and Crystal rivers

you will find the full-service Aquamarina Twin Rivers. Use caution approaching the marina on the Salt River, and check your height; the charted overhead power cables have only a 47-foot vertical clearance.

Marsh grass grows well back on the broad banks of the Crystal River, and the open vista provides a decided contrast to the tangle of foliage along the Homosassa River, just 15 miles south. As you cruise along, look over the side to understand how the Crystal River came by its name. As you near the headwaters, the river opens out, revealing both shores lined with elaborate vacation homes.

King's Bay, at the head of Crystal River, is a winter home of the manatee, and mariners should watch for signs designating SLOW- and IDLE-SPEED ZONES all along the river. Call the Chassahowitzka National Wildlife Refuge (352-563-2088) in Crystal River for information packets and maps before visiting.

NAVIGATION: Use Chart 11409. The entrance channel to the Crystal River lies about 12 nautical miles almost due north of flashing red "4" at the entrance to the Homosassa River. Fifteen-foot-high flashing green "1" marks the entrance to the Crystal River. If you draw more than a foot, you cannot steer directly to the Crystal River from the Homosassa entrance because of 1- and 2-foot shoals that pepper the area.

If your draft can clear 3-foot depths, head west from flashing red "4" at the Homosassa River entrance, go to the three-mile limit indicated on your chart, and then head north to N 26° 54.700'. From here, steer due east to N 26° 54.700'/ W 082° 44.900', where you will pick up flashing green "1," marking the entrance channel to the Crystal River. Your landmarks are two charted, strobe-lighted 500-foot nuclear power plant stacks up the coast, two miles north of the Crystal River. They are visible for about 15 miles except in hazy weather, when the range can be considerably less. This entire area is relatively shallow, so watch your depth sounder attentively.

Follow the markers through oyster bars and across some 5-foot spots on Crystal Reefs. Stay well south of the power plant channel, which has visible spoil banks well out into the Gulf of Mexico. Be careful entering the approach channel, as twin hard-sand shoals flank the entrance. Boats with drafts exceeding 5 feet should wait for half-tide or higher. Once in the channel, if you keep red to starboard and green to port, the channel should pose no problems.

Dockage: The only complete full-service boatyard in Crystal River, Aquamarina Twin Rivers offers transient dockage, a full-service fuel dock with gas and diesel fuel, full marine services and restrooms/showers. In 2010, the management at Aquamarina had plans to rebuild and expand by 60 slips. They were also in the process of getting the permits for some extensive dredging. Although not geared to transient mariners in 2010, upon completion of the renovations, they will be open for transients. A waterside resort on King's Bay, at the head of the Crystal River, has a good restaurant. Its docks are for guests only. Do not leave this area without checking out the spectacular cav-

Cedar Key, FL

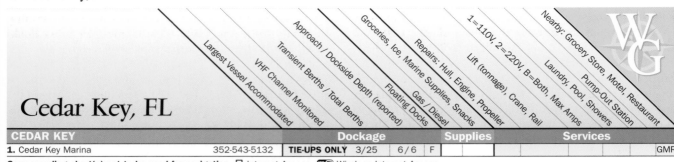

CEDAR KEY		Dockage				Supplies		Services	
1. Cedar Key Marina	352-543-5132	TIE-UPS ONLY	3/25	6/6	F				GMR

Corresponding chart(s) not to be used for navigation. ☐ Internet Access (WiFi) Wireless Internet Access

CEDAR KEY, CHART 11408

erns nearby. You can look down from King's Bay and see springs 60 feet under the surface. The people at the resort will give you directions to the caverns. You can also rent a small boat or Scuba gear, if you are dive-qualified.

The village of Crystal River is a small town on Florida Highway 19. Pete's Pier Marina is the only transient marina near downtown Crystal River. A grocery store, a fish market, a liquor store and a laundry are all about a mile from the waterfront.

This is the only place where you can legally swim with manatees in the wild in the U.S. Please be respectful of the manatees. You are in their waters. We recommend going with a local guide who can take you to the manatee "hot spots" and who will also educate you about them, giving you a more full experience and a greater understanding of these gentle creatures. Contact Sunshine River Tours at 352-682-3450 or check out their Web site at www.sunshinerivertours.com.

Anchorage: If your draft is shoal enough to allow you access to the Crystal River, you may find a secure anchorage in Kings Bay in 6 to 7 feet at mean low water north of the island in the middle of the harbor.

Cedar Key

Roughly a third of the way between Anclote Key and Carrabelle, about 22 nautical miles north of Crystal River and about 9.5 nautical miles northwest of the entrance channel to the Waccasassa River, Cedar Key makes a convenient stopping place for skippers who want to break the long open-water Gulf crossing. The charm of the village here, not to mention the superb seafood available at several waterside restaurants, more than compensates for the limited services.

Named for the stand of cedar trees that once grew here, today the island is all logged out, and the town subsists on fishing, both commercial and sport, with tourism playing an increasingly important role. Cedar Key is the top U.S.

producer of farm-raised clams. The annual arts festival in April draws 25,000 visitors to the village of 800 residents.

A stroll through the village will take visitors back 50 years or more. Frame houses and overhanging trees line the main street, and at the two-story hotel, local fishermen congregate in the bar to swap fish stories. Visit the Cedar Key Historical Museum (corner of Second Street, 352-543-5549) for a look at its history from the Seminole Indians through commerce, war and hurricanes.

NAVIGATION: Use Chart 11408. The approach to Cedar Key begins with 16-foot flashing green "1" (N 29°04.000'/W 083°04.500') at the start of the charted Main Ship Channel south of Seahorse Key (10 nautical miles northwest of flashing green "3" at the entrance to the Withlacoochee River).

Depths in the Main Ship Channel are at least 7 feet, but you must follow the well-marked channel carefully. Study an up-to-date chart in detail (use the inset on Chart 11408 or, better yet, obtain a print-on-demand updated chart) before you enter, and you should have no difficulty.

The shoal between red daybeacons "10" and "12" is building out into the channel. When transiting this area, give red daybeacon "12" a wide berth, favoring the Seahorse Key side of the channel to port. Be careful: Legions of unwary visitors seeking a shortcut have been grounded by the S-curve in the winding channel. Also, pay close attention at the junction of Ship and Northwest channels, just past Grassy Key. Sorting out the maze of shoals and lights demands serious concentration. Go slowly, attempt no shortcuts, and be aware of the currents.

Dockage: The City Marina is the only feasible place to tie up at Cedar Key. This dock, in reasonably good repair and located in the middle of the village, offers no services except that one of the omnipresent fishermen may offer to help with your lines. They also may not; be ready to do it on your own. The city would like to become more cruiser friendly so look for improvements to the City Marina in coming years, to include a pump-out. A mooring field is also in the discussion phase in 2010.

Depths are good (10 to 15 feet at mean low water) at the end of the pier on the face dock. The dock is particularly exposed to winds from the southeast and southwest. Currents here are very strong on both ebb and flood, so be especially alert to tide and wind when docking. Use long spring lines. The strong current and a 3-foot tide require close attention to your lines.

Anchorage: When conditions are too hazardous to dock, you might anchor in the charted 7- to 14-foot area north of Atsena Otie Key, but if you try it, feel your way in cautiously. Fuel is normally not available, but in an emergency, it may be trucked in at a premium price.

Another alternative to using the City Marina is to anchor just southwest of the dock (out of the channel), and then dinghy in under the bridge to the small-boat docking area in the basin. Because of the strong tidal current in the anchorage, you may want to use a two-anchor Bahamian moor.

When leaving northbound, take Northwest Channel,

which leaves the Main Ship Channel at quick flashing red "30" about one nautical mile from the town dock, off Grassy Key. Do not attempt Northwest Channel on a low tide if your draft exceeds 4 feet, or during darkness or rough water conditions. Shoaling is particularly acute between green daybeacon "17A" and flashing red "18," and also between flashing green "19" and red daybeacon "20." Two daybeacons have been added to the channel, green daybeacon "21" and red daybeacon "22." These daybeacons do not appear on older charts but are on Edition 29, dated July 2008 (the most recent chart at press time in summer 2010).

GOIN' ASHORE:
CEDAR KEY, FL

North or southbound shoal draft vessels, who are not in a hurry, will not want to miss this quaint, friendly little village. If you like to visit places that have not yet been overrun with cruising boats, then Cedar Key is for you. There are quality bed and breakfasts in town that will pamper you or your guests, great restaurants, scenic strolls and top-notch, gallery quality pottery and artwork. You won't have to walk far to find all of the above as downtown Cedar Key is only a few square blocks. It is a miniature version of a larger seaside village.

Aptly named Cedar Key Bed & Breakfast, this well-appointed and comfortable home will pamper you and treat you like family from the moment you arrive. You will also have access to the "Bottomless Cookie Jar" during your stay (810 3rd Street, 877-543-5051, www.cedarkeybandb.com). Just across the street at 3rd and G St. is the Faraway Inn. These small, but adequate rooms put you steps from the waterfront and beach-combing. They are also pet friendly (888-543-5330, www.farawayinn.com).

You will want to grab a bite after strolling along the quiet streets of Cedar Key. Try Tony's Seafood Restaurant (597 2nd St., 352-543-0022) for outstanding seafood. Tony's clam chowder has won The Great Chowder Cook-off held in Rhode Island. His dishes also get rave reviews from Senator Bill Nelson, Bon Appetit Magazine and our Editor. The Old Fish House Café recently opened on the waterfront in Cedar Key and is recommended by City Hall. The chef is a Yankee who adds a Southern flavor to his menu selections (352-543-9800).

Walk off your meal by visiting one of the many shops. Curmudgeonalia (352-543-6789) has an eclectic collection of books, touristy items and handcrafted pieces. Also stroll along the waterfront and visit the Dilly Dally Gally for souvenirs of your trip to Cedar Key. Don't forget to stop at Island Arts and Barefoot Artist Gallery, both on 2nd St. They have so many beautiful items that you won't be able to make up your mind.

ADDITIONAL RESOURCES

■ City of Cedar Key, cityofcedarkey.org
409 2nd Street, Cedar Key, FL 32625

Suwannee River, FL

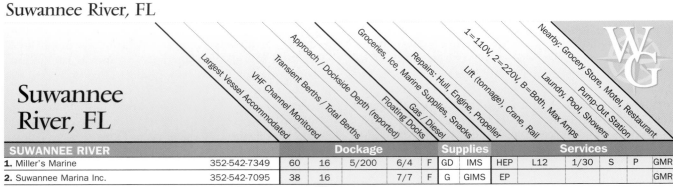

SUWANNEE RIVER		Dockage				Supplies		Services					
		Largest Vessel Accommodated	VHF Channel Monitored	Approach / Dockside Depth (reported)	Transient Berths / Total Berths	Floating Docks	Groceries, Ice, Marine Supplies, Snacks	Gas / Diesel	Repairs: Hull, Engine, Propeller	Lift (tonnage), Crane, Rail	1=110V, 2=220V, B=Both, Max Amps	Laundry, Pool, Showers	Pump-Out Station	Nearby: Grocery Store, Motel, Restaurant
1. Miller's Marine	352-542-7349	60	16	5/200	6/4	F	GD	IMS	HEP	L12	1/30	S	P	GMR
2. Suwannee Marina Inc.	352-542-7095	38	16		7/7	F	G	GIMS	EP					GMR

Corresponding chart(s) not to be used for navigation. 🖥 Internet Access 📶 Wireless Internet Access

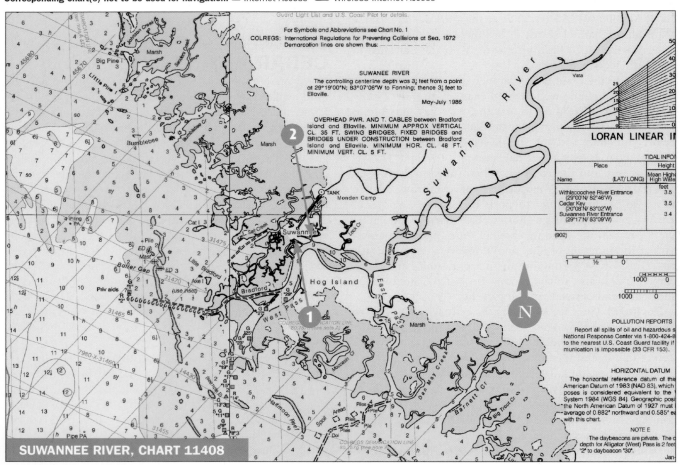

SUWANNEE RIVER, CHART 11408

Suwannee River

About 12 nautical miles north of Northwest Passage leading from Cedar Key is flashing red "2," which marks the entrance to the channel into Stephen Foster's "Suwannee River" from "Old Folks at Home," Florida's official state song. The U.S. Army Corps of Engineers tries to maintain the channel to 6-foot depths at mean low water, but with little success. Unfortunately, the river and the town of Suwannee will remain a mystery to most cruisers who draw 3 feet or more. Controlling depths can be as little as 2.5 to 3.5 feet.

Steinhatchee River

The interesting fishing village of Steinhatchee ("Stein" rhymes with "bean"), supports several seafood plants. Found about four nautical miles from flashing green "1," which marks the entrance to the Steinhatchee River, Steinhatchee's dock space is limited, but locals try their best to make room for everyone.

NAVIGATION: Use Chart 11407. Flashing green "1" marks the entrance to the channel to the Steinhatchee River. From flashing green "1," an alternating row of daybeacons and flashing aids to navigation leads across Deadman Bay to the Steinhatchee River, which itself is well-marked. The fixed bridge across the river has a 28-foot fixed vertical clearance at normal tides, but is officially charted with a 25-foot fixed vertical clearance. Controlling depth is 4 feet at mean low water.

Dockage: The marinas just upstream of the bridge are the only marinas with adequate depths for most cruising vessels. Only boats drawing under 4 feet which can clear a

Steinhatchee River, FL

STEINHATCHEE RIVER		Dockage					Supplies		Services					
		Largest Vessel Accommodated	VHF Channel Monitored	Transient Berths / Total Berths	Approach / Dockside Depth (reported)	Floating Docks	Groceries, Ice, Marine Supplies, Snacks	Gas / Diesel	Repairs: Hull, Engine, Propeller	Lift (tonnage), Crane, Rail	1=110V, 2=220V, B=Both, Max Amps	Laundry, Pool, Showers	Pump-Out Station	Nearby: Grocery Store, Motel, Restaurant
1. Sea Hag Marina (WiFi)	352-498-3008	45	09	6/20	5/8	F	GD	GIMS	HEP	L7	B/50	S		GMR
2. Gulfstream Motel & Marina	352-498-8088	60	16/09	3/50	9/9	F	GD	GIMS	P		1/30			GMR
3. River Haven Marina & Motel (Internet) (WiFi)	352-498-0709	70	09	4/51	3.5/8	F	GD	GIMS	HEP	L15,C	B/50	LS	P	GMR
4. Steinhatchee Landing Resort	352-498-3513	25		12/12	8/5	F		S			1/30	LPS		GMR

Corresponding chart(s) not to be used for navigation. ⌨ Internet Access (WiFi) Wireless Internet Access

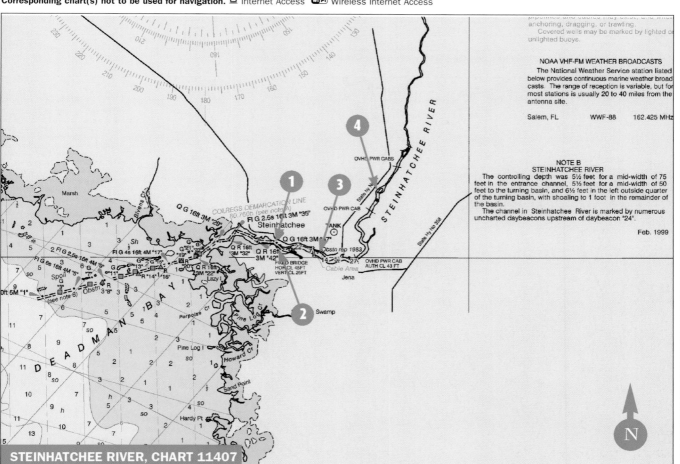

STEINHATCHEE RIVER, CHART 11407

Text within the chart image:

NOAA VHF-FM WEATHER BROADCASTS
The National Weather Service station listed below provides continuous marine weather broadcasts. The range of reception is variable, but for most stations is usually 20 to 40 miles from the antenna site.

Salem, FL   WWF-88   162.425 MHz

NOTE B
STEINHATCHEE RIVER
The controlling depth was 5½ feet for a mid-width of 75 feet in the entrance channel, 5½ feet for a mid-width of 50 feet to the turning basin, and 6½ feet in the left outside quarter of the turning basin, with shoaling to 1 foot in the remainder of the basin.
The channel in Steinhatchee River is marked by numerous uncharted daybeacons upstream of daybeacon "24".
Feb. 1999

bridge with 25-foot charted fixed vertical clearance should consider the Steinhatchee Landing Resort's marina for a one-of-a-kind Florida experience. They can handle boats up to 25 feet in length. Those in need of supplies can borrow the resort's courtesy car. To ensure space on the weekends, call ahead (352-498-3513).

Steinhatchee got some national notoriety in 1973 when nine tons of marijuana was found stacked neatly on shore near the mouth of the Steinhatchee River. The miscreants were named "The Steinhatchee Seven," and high-priced Houston attorney Percy Foreman showed up at the Dixie County courthouse with an entourage to represent the destitute commercial fishermen who had been captured by law enforcement.

Before the dust settled, the federal government attempted to seize a Baptist church in Horseshoe Beach because it had been built with drug money. A local stretch of highway, County Road 361, had been renamed Horseshoe Beach International Airport because so many planes had landed there in the dark of night and, after a quick turnaround, had evaporated up into the night sky.

Anchorage: An anchorage is located on the outside of the bend, several hundred feet beyond red daybeacon "36," in 6- to 7-foot depths. The holding is soupy, but protection from all directions is excellent.

St. Marks River to Carrabelle, FL

ST. MARKS RIVER TO CARRABELLE		Largest Vessel Accommodated	VHF Channel Monitored	Transient Berths / Total Berths	Approach / Dockside Depth (reported)	Floating Docks	Gas / Diesel	Groceries, Ice, Marine Supplies, Snacks	Repairs: Hull, Engine, Propeller	Lift (tonnage), Crane, Rail	1=110V, 2=220V, B=Both, Max Amps	Laundry, Pool, Showers	Pump-Out Station	Nearby: Grocery Store, Motel, Restaurant
				Dockage			**Supplies**				**Services**			
1. St. Marks Yacht Club	850-925-6606	50		1/25	7/7						B/50	LPS		GMR
2. Shields Marina	850-925-6158	70	16	2/100	12/10		GD	GIMS	HEP	L	B/50	LS	P	GMR
3. Riverside Marina	850-925-6157	60	06	1/55	12/8	F	GD	IM	H	C	B/50			GR
4. Alligator Point Yacht Basin	850-349-2511	45	16	3/45	4/5	F	GD	IMS			B/50	S		
5. Picketts Landing 380 EHL WiFi	850-566-6761	65	16	10/20	8/7						B/100	P		GMR
6. The Moorings at Carrabelle 380 EHL 🖥 WiFi	850-697-2800	150	16	15/150	15/9		GD	IMS			B/50	LPS	P	GR
7. Carrabelle Marina 380 EHL	850-697-3351	28	16	/8	10/6		G	IM		L	1/50	L		GMR
8. C-Quarters Marina 380 EHL	850-697-8400	100	16	15/68			GD	IMS			B/50	LS	P	GMR

Corresponding chart(s) not to be used for navigation. 🖥 Internet Access WiFi Wireless Internet Access

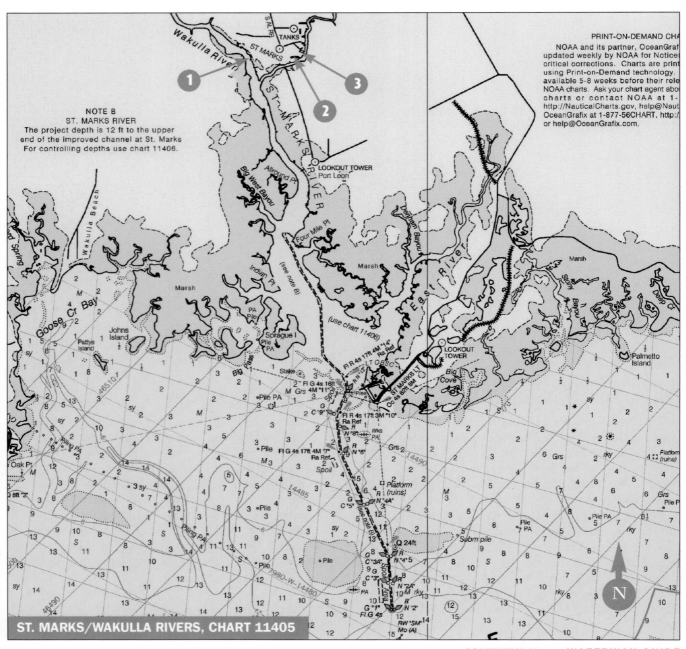

NOTE B
ST. MARKS RIVER
The project depth is 12 ft to the upper
end of the improved channel at St. Marks
For controlling depths use chart 11406.

PRINT-ON-DEMAND CHA
NOAA and its partner, OceanGraf
updated weekly by NOAA for Notices
critical corrections. Charts are print
using Print-on-Demand technology.
available 5-8 weeks before their rele
NOAA charts. Ask your chart agent abo
charts or contact NOAA at 1-
http://NauticalCharts.gov, help@Naut
OceanGrafix at 1-877-56CHART, http://
or help@OceanGrafix.com.

ST. MARKS/WAKULLA RIVERS, CHART 11405

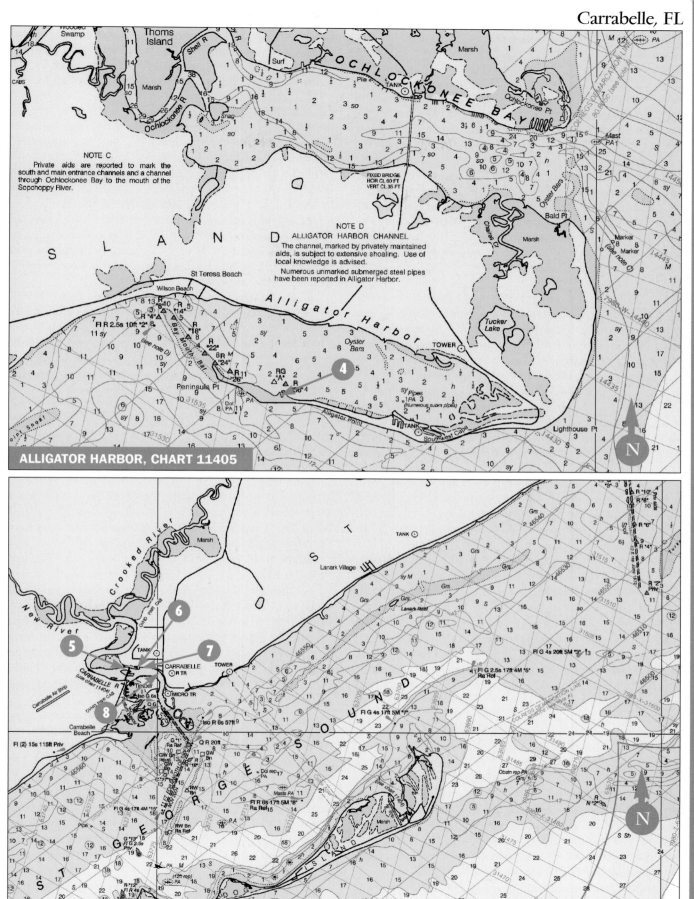

ALLIGATOR HARBOR, CHART 11405

CARRABELLE, CHART 11405

St. Marks River

From the hamlet of St. Marks, about eight nautical miles up the St. Marks River, Tallahassee, the state capital, is less than 20 miles north. Wakulla Springs is less than 10 miles away. This immense freshwater spring reaches a maximum depth of 185 feet, and more than 600,000 gallons flow from the spring every minute, literally creating the Wakulla River.

A number of films have been made at Wakulla Springs, including several of the original "Tarzan" films starring Johnny Weissmuller. The St. Marks National Wildlife Refuge, with 300 species of birds, is also near the town. In addition to extensive nature trails, observation points, abundant wildlife and a visitors center, the refuge also includes the historic St. Marks Lighthouse (still in use, but no longer open to the public).

NAVIGATION: Use Charts 11406, 11407 and 11405. From 30-foot flashing green "1," marking the entrance to the Steinhatchee River channel, set a course of 285 degrees magnetic for approximately 37 nautical miles to flashing red buoy "24" in Apalachee Bay leading to the channel into St. Marks. To enter the St. Marks River, steer due north for about 10 nautical miles to red and white Morse (A) buoy "SM" marking the entrance to the St. Marks River proper. Well before arriving at Morse (A) buoy "SM," you will see the 82-foot-high St. Marks Lighthouse (no longer lighted) on shore, but do not shortcut this leg. The well-marked entry channel twists and turns through a maze of shoals. Daylight passage should present no problems, but avoid going in at night. The single orange range marker is used in conjunction with the St. Marks Lighthouse—lining both up will keep you in mid-channel from flashing green "1" to the first dogleg at green can buoy "3A."

Dockage: In St. Marks, about eight miles upriver, Shields Marina, a friendly, full-service marina in freshwater, welcomes visitors. Shields Marina has showers, laundry, sells both gas and diesel fuels, has water, shore power and a pump-out service at the fuel dock. They have also built a nice ship's store that is very complete, including some limited snack and beverage items. A courtesy vehicle will be provided if needed for provisioning. Lynn's Riverside Marina, a few miles upriver from Shields, has gasoline and diesel fuel and shore power, but no pump-out facility.

Nearby is a general store with limited groceries and restaurants featuring local seafood. Locals recommend St. Marks River Cantina and the Riverside Café as restaurants they like, both close by. Fort San Marcos, within walking distance of the marinas, is located on a site first explored by a Spanish company in 1528, 10 years before the famous Hernando DeSoto expedition visited the same area. A state historic site, the fort offers a museum and nature walks. You may anchor off the state-maintained beach above the fort and take the dinghy ashore.

Anchorage: The St. Marks River, about a mile above the marinas, offers an anchorage completely different from the usual Gulf Coast beaches. Tropical plants line both riverbanks, wildlife abounds and you can anchor in complete solitude. Be sure to install your screens and apply plenty of insect repellent. You should have minimum 9-foot depths around the first bend past the industrial area of St. Marks.

St. Marks to Carrabelle

NAVIGATION: Use Chart 11405. There are shoals to skirt between St. Marks and Carrabelle, but two protected, full-service boating stops are along this stretch. Both have rather tricky entrance channels; obtain local knowledge to ensure a safe entry.

The entrance to Shell Point Harbor is reportedly now conventionally buoyed. Some report that if directions are followed faithfully, the channel carries 6-foot depths at half-tide or higher. The marina channel entrance is still marked with a white PVC pipe and carries 4-foot depths. Transient slips are available.

Alligator Harbor is correctly charted on Chart 11405. To reach Alligator Point Yacht Basin, take your departure from flashing red bell buoy "26" south of South Shoal. From there, take a course of 312 degrees magnetic to flashing green "1" at the northeast end of Dog Island Reef. At this point, you can alter course to 350 degrees magnetic. After just more than three nautical miles, you will pick up red flashing "2," marking the entrance to Alligator Harbor. Then you can follow the daybeacons all the way to the marina. A restaurant there, the Tiki Hut, offers good food and drinks at reasonable prices.

If you want to make the nonstop run from St. Marks to Carrabelle, go south from the St. Marks River entrance 10 nautical miles to flashing red bell buoy "24," then southwest almost 10 nautical miles to flashing red bell buoy "26." From there, it is about 17 nautical miles to the Carrabelle East Pass sea buoy, flashing red bell buoy "2."

Alternatively, from flashing red bell buoy "26," you can swing northwest up Duer Channel to pass north of Dog Island through St. George Sound. From flashing red bell buoy "26," make sure you plot your course to avoid Dog Island Reef, which is located to the northwest and marked by flashing green "1." Also, some aids to navigation have been changed, and older charts may not reflect this. The current edition (29 at press time in 2010) of Chart 11405 shows the aids to navigation here properly, although this chart is from 2003.

After negotiating Dog Island Reef heading west, your first marker is flashing green "3," which should be left to port when entering the St. George Channel via Duer Channel. About 2.5 nautical miles along a bearing of 245 degrees magnetic, you will come upon flashing green "5" (leave to port). About 3.5 nautical miles along the same course, you will encounter an added marker, flashing green "7." After rounding flashing green "7," alter your course to 218 degrees magnetic, and after a little more than two nautical miles, you will encounter flashing red "8," which should be left to starboard.

From flashing red "8," steer a course to flashing green buoy "13," which starts you out on the path north into the Carrabelle River entrance channel. Make sure you honor the red and white daybeacon marking the shoal to the northeast of flashing green buoy "13" on your way in from the east. The well-marked channel leads up the river. Make sure you follow the green daybeacons that bring you well over to the east side as you move through town.

If you are approaching Carrabelle from the Gulf, East Pass is your natural and best bet. As you approach East Pass from the southeast, your landmarks are the sand dunes on Dog and St. George islands and the Crooked River Light (115 feet high) on the north shore of St. George Sound, about two miles west of Carrabelle. East Pass, one of the better Florida west coast passes, leads five miles through St. George Sound to the Carrabelle River.

If possible, do not make this passage after dark; the lights from across Dog Island are so confusing that you might run down an unlighted buoy. Also, take time to study the chart before entering Carrabelle for the first time. It can be confusing. Many of the marks that may show up on older charts are not present and have been replaced with a completely different marking system.

Carrabelle

Carrabelle, close to where the GIWW resumes, heading west, is a strategic port for yachts heading in either direction. Locals call it "the best jumping-off spot in the Panhandle."

Dockage: One mile north of the GIWW on the Carrabelle River near marker "17," the large, modern Moorings at Carrabelle can accommodate drafts from 6 to 10 feet and vessels up to 150 feet. Services include gas and diesel fuel, plus a pump-out station on the fuel dock, laundry, restrooms/showers, a ramp, marine supplies and an on-site motel or condo. A cruisers lounge has been set up for transients, with TV and a computer for Internet access. Courtesy bikes are available; several restaurants, an IGA supermarket and a hardware store are a short walk away.

C-Quarters Marina, up the Carrabelle River at green daybeacon "9," also provides transient dockage for vessels up to 100 feet, with 10- to 15-foot dockside depths, fuel, restrooms, showers, pump-out and laundry. A ship's store, groceries, a motel and a waterfront restaurant are within walking distance. Just a few minutes' walk from either marina, you can stock up on provisions at the IGA supermarket and spruce up your wardrobe at the coin-operated laundry.

Anchorage: Just inside the hook of the west end of Dog Island, you can put down the anchor at an excellent spot in deep water (charted at 17 to 20 feet). The island's hospitable owner allows cruising mariners to explore the beaches. A portion of the island is a bird breeding area, posted with KEEP OUT signs. Please honor them. The posted section does not include the beach.

The bay at the northeast end of Dog Island offers protection from all but northwest winds. The 6-foot-plus channel leading to the small ferry dock is narrow, but well-marked. Stay in the center, and watch for the abruptly shoaling edges. You may anchor in 7-foot depths just off the dock among several permanently moored boats.

GOIN' ASHORE:
CARRABELLE, FL

Southbound and westbound skippers congregate here to wait out the weather and replenish supplies, or to take a respite from the rigors of the sometimes-lumpy cross-Gulf trip. To the advantage of locals and visitors alike, some seafood restaurants and icehouses are easily accessible in this small rural community along the U.S. Route 98 main thoroughfare through town.

A fishing port, as well as a stopover for cruisers, Carrabelle is completely water-oriented. Its principal industry is seafood processing, and one of the gustatory delights available here is shrimp bought directly from boats just returning from the Gulf. Pigging out on shrimp is an acceptable indulgence.

ADDITIONAL RESOURCES

- Carrabelle Area Chamber of Commerce, www.carrabelle.org

- **NEARBY GOLF COURSES** St. James Bay Golf Course, 151 Laughing Gull Lane, Carrabelle, FL 32322, 850-697-9606, www.stjamesbay.com/golf.html

- **NEARBY MEDICAL FACILITIES** Weems Medical Center East, N.E. Fifth St., Carrabelle, FL 32322, 850-697-2223

WATERWAY GUIDE is always open to your observations from the helm. E-mail your comments on any navigation information in the guide to: editor@waterwayguide.com.

WATERWAY GUIDE advertising sponsors play a vital role in bringing you the most trusted and well-respected cruising guide in the country. Without our advertising sponsors, we simply couldn't produce the top-notch publication now resting in your hands. Next time you stop in for a peaceful night's rest, let them know where you found them—WATERWAY GUIDE, The Cruising Authority.

WATERWAY GUIDE Bahamas Edition

Based on the popular Mathew Wilson Guide, WATERWAY GUIDE Bahamas Edition is your complete reference guide to the Bahamas and the Turks and Caicos Islands — with Aerial Photography, Marina Listings, Tide Tables, Route Planning, Waypoints, Courses, Distances, and Shoreside Information with Maps

Order Yours Today at www.WaterwayGuide.com or call 800-233-3359

The Panhandle: Apalachicola to Pensacola

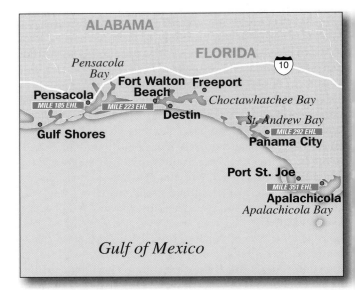

Florida's Panhandle

The Panhandle can be reached three ways: From the east and south (directly across 140 to 170 miles of Gulf of Mexico water); skirting the Big Bend area just offshore; or from the west from Mobile Bay, AL, from which many Midwestern cruisers come, down the river route.

Depending upon the amount of time you have, your personal inclination for offshore or inland cruising and the forecasted weather, you can take either the outside route or the inside (if you require less than 50-foot overhead vertical clearance) route all the way along the Florida Panhandle from Carrabelle, to the east, to Pensacola or even Perdido Bay, or vice versa. Also, the Gulf Intracoastal Waterway (GIWW) is much more intriguing and enjoyable than many other segments of the ICW. The reason is that the GIWW meanders along for a couple of hundred miles and real estate development is not as dense as you will find farther south and east.

Offshore Run

NAVIGATION: Use Chart 11400. Those making the long run nonstop to Carrabelle face about 170 nautical miles of travel from Tampa Bay or 140 nautical miles from Anclote Key. Either can be a pleasant offshore passage if your vessel is seaworthy and you pick the right weather. Using a professional weather forecasting service might be worth every cent you invest, because there are precious few places to put into to get out of adverse weather conditions. Once you have made the commitment, you are pretty much going to have to tough it out.

Your course will range from 300 to 310 degrees magnetic, depending on whether you depart from Tampa Bay or Anclote Key, respectively. In the winter months, prevailing winds are out of the north or northeast. In such cases, the seas will typically be on your nose or on your starboard bow heading northwest, making a tough ride for powerboats and a beat for sailboaters. In the summer, prevailing winds are southeasterly or southwesterly, bringing a following sea heading west, which can be much more comfortable under power if the wind pipes up, or can provide an interesting run or broad reach for sailors. Frontal systems are prevalent in the winter, and local thunderstorms are nearly always present during the summer.

In lieu of a straight-line course, you may plan instead to follow navigational aids that will keep you closer to shore around the Big Bend. Despite the greater length—150 to

160 nautical miles, total—some skippers prefer this route because they feel safer as opposed to cutting directly across the Gulf of Mexico. The Big Bend route keeps you somewhat closer to shelter if the weather turns bad and gives you occasional marks to shoot for, yet puts enough water under your hull to eliminate the worry of dodging shoals. On the debit side of the ledger, a run for a safe harbor in the Big Bend section of Florida will have to be decided upon very early, because the narrow channels that lead to protection cut through some very shoal water.

The Outside Route

NAVIGATION: Use Charts 11404, 11405 and 11401. At the eastern end of the Panhandle, the most frequently used pass to or from the Gulf of Mexico and the west coast of Florida is East Pass between Dog Island and St. George Island. This is normally a safe all-weather entrance, but some navigation aids have been moved, so be sure to have a current edition of Chart 11404 on board, or better yet, order a new print-on-demand (POD) chart, corrected through the previous week's Local Notice to Mariners.

Another option to East Pass for crossing over between the Gulf and Apalachicola Bay is Government Cut, a few miles west of East Pass. Government Cut is a dredged channel that cuts right through St. George Island and leads the mariner pretty much straight in to Apalachicola. It isn't a hard channel to navigate, because it has range markers, but there are not a lot of channel markers. You get a flashing red and a flashing green set of markers at the entrance in the Gulf and then one red and one green daybeacon inside. This is a fair weather entrance, because, though straight, it is as narrow as the cutting edge of a sword.

The charted depth is 8 feet and will be lower in the troughs of waves. If that number gives you pause, use East Pass, a much less nerve wracking entrance.

As indicated on the chart, the third apparent option, West Pass, is "unreliable for navigation." If you look at this pass at all on your chart, please note the symbols for wrecks on the shoals near this pass. There are three outside, one inside. You don't want to add to the collection.

Navigating outside, up the Gulf of Mexico, is not difficult. But as in most of Florida, keep well enough offshore to avoid shoal areas. For example, off Cape San Blas at the tip of St. Joseph Peninsula, water depths as little as 4 to 5 feet are charted at about two miles offshore.

The Inside Route—GIWW

The GIWW picks up in St. George Sound slightly west of East Pass after dropping off at Anclote Key, ending its trek up the west coast of Florida from where it connects with the Okeechobee Waterway. From East Pass, it then winds through five states and 1,000 miles to its western terminus at Brownsville, TX. Mileage is measured in statute miles east or west of Harvey Lock at New Orleans (expressed as EHL or WHL). East Pass is located at Mile 375 EHL.

Depths often range from 10 to 12 feet (the U.S. Army Corps of Engineers project depth is 12 feet), but shoaling in places can make the depth much shallower than that, so be sure to keep an eye on your depth sounder, and be alert to where you are at all times. Minimum vertical clearance at fixed bridges is 50 feet, except for a 48-foot fixed bridge at Aransas Pass, TX, where there is also an alternate bypass route with no bridges. The GIWW bridges at Destin (and the Destin Pass Bridge at Destin) are shown on the charts with 49- and 50-foot fixed vertical clearances, but some reports put the actual fixed vertical clearance at 48 feet or less at high water. If you are sporting anything more than 45 feet, these bridges bear careful consideration.

An Overview

The segment of the Waterway from East Pass to Pensacola covers 200 statute miles of relatively pleasant inside cruising, punctuated by the availability of frequent passes into the Gulf of Mexico for those seeking open waters and a little more space, or—going the other way—a respite from pending heavy weather. There is very little white-knuckle cruising here. The GIWW passage along the Florida Panhandle ranges in ambience from lovely and lonesome, narrow channels winding through swamp and bayou areas to "Northern" settings of deciduous trees and modern housing, connecting big, clear bays, bayous and sounds. Narrow barrier islands protect the entire passage. The Waterway undulates around like an anaconda—southwest, then northwest, west and again to the southwest to cross the entrance to Perdido Bay and on to Mobile Bay in Alabama.

From East Pass on the GIWW's eastern end and Carrabelle—a strategic port for yachts heading in either direction—the Florida Panhandle extends north to inland Tallahassee, the state capital. At the Panhandle's western end, the bustling, historic city of Pensacola was ruled at

times by Spain and France and was used as a military base by the British during the Revolutionary War. Legendary Apache chief Geronimo was confined here for a spell.

A worthwhile layover along this stretch of the Waterway is Apalachicola, with its quaint, village-like atmosphere, excellent local oysters and shopping within walking distance of the marinas. At the midway point is Panama City, a well-equipped sportfishing and boating center in the midst of the sparkling white sand beaches of the "Miracle Strip." Farther along, in Choctawhatchee Bay, the boating-oriented towns of Destin and Fort Walton Beach are also well worth investigating. And finally, at the end, is the welcome goal of Pensacola, the cradle of naval aviation and home to the Navy's Blue Angels. Pensacola's waterfront is architecturally rich and worth a look.

Carrabelle to Apalachicola

NAVIGATION: Use Chart 11404. If you go into Carrabelle, it is axiomatic that you will have to come back out. After exiting the Carrabelle River and retracing your course into

ST. GEORGE ISLAND BRIDGE
Mile 361 EHL
WATERWAY GUIDE PHOTOGRAPHY

St. George Sound, pick up flashing red "2" (Mile 374 EHL) just inside East Pass. From there, flashing red "6" becomes visible, about two nautical miles to the southwest. From flashing red "6," the GIWW is clearly marked as it jogs south by southwest at quick-flashing red "20" for about two nautical miles to quick-flashing red "28" (Mile 365 EHL), where it resumes its southwest direction. From that point, it is a straight shot southwest for about 7.5 nautical miles under the St. George Island Bridge (Mile 361.4 EHL, 65-foot fixed vertical clearance) over Apalachicola Bay at Bulkhead Shoal (red nun buoy "48"). The bridge is the boundary of demarcation between St. George Sound and Apalachicola Bay. After traversing much of Apalachicola Bay, at quick-flashing red "76," make a 90-degree turn to starboard, and follow the Waterway about 3.5 nautical miles to red nun buoy "24," marking the entrance to the Apalachicola River and the town of Apalachicola.

Dockage: After passing red nun buoy "24," and just south of the John Gorrie Memorial Bridge (Mile 351.4 EHL, 65-foot fixed vertical clearance), is the easily sighted Apalachicola Municipal Marina. A few transient slips accommodating yachts up to 50 feet are available on the outboard end, with 6-foot depths at dockside. This facility is open to wakes left by passing boaters transiting the GIWW, so be sure to use ample spring lines and fenders.

There is a complimentary pump-out facility on the inboard end of the dock. Marine supplies are available here also.

JOHN GORRIE MEMORIAL
BRIDGE Mile 351.4 EHL
WATERWAY GUIDE PHOTOGRAPHY

Apalachicola, FL

APALACHICOLA		Largest Vessel Accommodated	VHF Channel Monitored	Transient Berths / Total Berths	Approach / Dockside Depth (reported)	Groceries, Ice, Marine Supplies, Snacks	Gas / Diesel	Floating Docks	Repairs: Hull, Engine, Propeller	Lift (tonnage), Crane, Rail	1=110V, 2=220V, B=Both, Max Amps	Laundry, Pool, Showers	Pump-Out Station	Nearby: Grocery Store, Motel, Restaurant
		Dockage				**Supplies**		**Services**						
1. Apalachicola Municipal Marina 351 EHL	850-653-7274	50		15/	6/6						B/50			R
2. Apalachicola Marina, Inc. (formerly Miller Marine) 351 EHL	850-653-9521	100	16	3/6	15/12	IMS	GD				B/50	S		GMR
3. Apalachicola River Inn 351 EHL	850-653-8139	90	16	17/17	6/6	I					B/50	S		GMR
4. Water Street Hotel & Marina 351 EHL (WIFI)	850-653-3700	60	16	6/20	12/8			F			B/50	PS		GMR
5. Ganders Marine 351 EHL	850-653-8880	150			9/9		D							GMR
6. Scipio Creek Marina 351 EHL	850-653-8030	100	16	6/14	12/10	IMS	GD			L	B/50	LS	P	GMR

Corresponding chart(s) not to be used for navigation. 🖳 Internet Access 📶 Wireless Internet Access

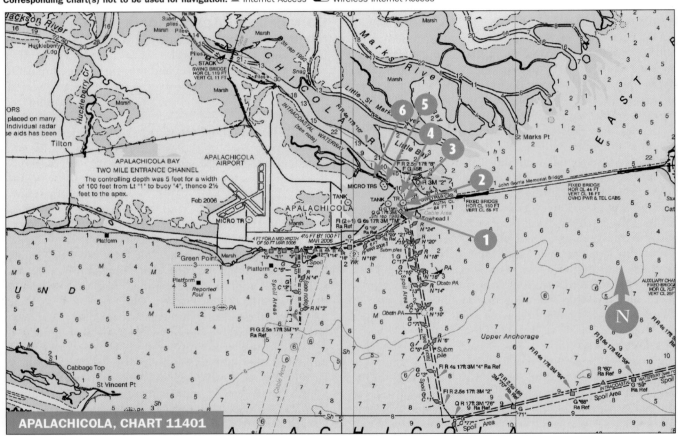

APALACHICOLA, CHART 11401

Besides the Municipal Marina, other dockage north of the bridge includes Apalachicola Marina, Inc. (formerly Miller Marine), which has gas, diesel and dockage, with 10-foot depths dockside. A supermarket, drug store and restaurants are within easy walking distance. Dredging was underway as of spring 2010.

Next is the Apalachicola River Inn complex, featuring recently renovated rooms, with transient slips to 50 feet and a dockside depth of 8 feet at mean low water. Caroline's River Dining restaurant, with its upstairs bar, is located here, as is Boss Oyster Restaurant.

Most of the other transient facilities are located on the north side of the bridge, along with various fuel docks, a boatyard and a waterfront motel with ample dock space.

Take care while docking, because the Apalachicola River can have a strong current depending on tidal flow.

If you want to get away from GIWW traffic, Scipio (the "c" is silent) Creek Marina is a popular stopover for cruisers. It has less tidal current than facilities located directly on the Apalachicola River. Scipio Creek Marina (located to the northwest of the river at green-red can "A"), just seven blocks from the center town, has gasoline and diesel fuel, a pump-out facility, a ship's store, maintenance facilities, restrooms, showers, laundry and a riverfront restaurant called Papa Joe's Oyster Bar & Grill. There is transient dockage for vessels up to 100 feet long. Motels, restaurants and provisions are within a three-block walk.

If you are headed for the grocery store, a dock cart would be in order. The store is about a dozen blocks from the marinas in this area, as is a large self-service laundry. That said, you won't have to wait for the next port if your dirty laundry has grown into an unacceptably large pile. Bring your own quarters and detergent. There are also several ATM machines available near the center of town, and a handy store is located at the Oasis Lounge.

GOIN' ASHORE:
APALACHICOLA, FL

This charming town, with its preserved historic buildings, has a variety of seafood specialties for the hungry boater and several places to tie up for a visit. In July 2008, a new Veterans Memorial Park was dedicated. The park features a bronze replica sculpture and is Apalachicola's dedication to the many men and women who served our country from the many towns in the southeast United States.

While taking a rest from the rigors of the sea, a walk around town as the shadows fall and the heat subsides will be like a time-travel trip to yesteryear. Many of the older buildings and homes are in the Victorian style, and a number of the restored antebellum houses have been turned into picturesque bed and breakfasts.

The fully-restored and expanded Gibson Inn (850-653-2191), just a block from the municipal pier, is an early 1900s structure, boasting one of the many area restaurants that specialize in seafood—especially the renowned local Apalachicola oysters brought fresh from the bay's shell beds.

Happy hour at the various bistros draws an interesting hodgepodge of oystermen, artists and naturally, cruisers. Locals and transients keep an eye on the weather fronts via the Weather Channel on the River Inn's television while quenching thirsts.

Caroline's River Dining and Boss Oyster are at the Apalachicola River Inn (850-653-8139). Boss Oyster (850-653-9364) has a casual atmosphere with charm and character, serving oysters prepared 17 different ways. You will also find restaurants by the names of The Apalachicola Seafood Grill (850-653-9510) and Tamara's Café Floridita (850-653-4111) close by.

Several art galleries worth browsing have blossomed in recent years, thanks to the influx of artists and tourists to this riverside town.

A visit to the John Gorrie State Museum might be in order, as it is just two blocks from the municipal pier. Dr. John Gorrie in the 1830s and '40s invented a machine that made ice. He doesn't get much recognition for his discovery today, but he was granted the first U.S. patent for mechanical refrigeration in 1851. A replica is on display in Apalachicola. The bridge over the Apalachicola River is named after him. Dr. Gorrie was honored by Florida, when his statue was placed in Statuary Hall in the U.S. Capitol. In 1899, a monument to Dr. Gorrie was erected by the Southern Ice Exchange in Apalachicola. He had been mayor in 1837. While Dr. Gorrie's invention was originally designed to help yellow fever patients, it changed the world by making southern climes more habitable. Real estate agents in Florida consider him a deity.

An annual feature during the first week of November is the Seafood Festival at Battery Park, a short walk from the municipal pier. The Antique Boat Show in April is also a popular and well-attended event.

ADDITIONAL RESOURCES

Florida Vacation and Beach Guide
www.awesomeflorida.com/florida-cities/apalachicola.htm

NEARBY GOLF COURSES
St. James Bay Golf Course, 151 Laughing Gull Lane, Carrabelle, FL 32322, 850-697-9606
www.stjamesbay.com/golf.html

NEARBY MEDICAL FACILITIES
George E. Weems Memorial Hospital, 135 Ave. G, Apalachicola, FL 32320, 850-653-8853

Apalachicola to White City

The GIWW leaves Apalachicola Bay and the Gulf of Mexico at Mile 350 EHL, and then winds along on the scenic Apalachicola River, undulating generally northwest to the Apalachicola Northern Railroad Bridge at Mile 347.0 EHL (11-foot closed vertical clearance, usually open). Keep a sharp eye out for tree limbs and other floating debris. After-dark passages are not recommended.

Northwest-bound, just before the railroad bridge, to port, is a promontory called Old Woman's Bluff. We are not certain of how this piece of land garnered its name, but the story might be interesting.

NAVIGATION: Use Charts 11401, 11402 and 11393. From the mouth of the Apalachicola River, the Waterway is well-marked. Past red daybeacon "30," the Apalachicola River turns north, and the Waterway continues along the Jackson River (named for Stonewall Jackson when he was governor of the territory) to Lake Wimico at Mile 340 EHL.

Boaters seeking a side trip can follow the Apalachicola River upstream through a few miles of heavily wooded swampland to the St. Marks, East and Brothers rivers, also from red daybeacon "30." There is ample depth of water here for smaller vessels (controlling depths of 9 and 10 feet are available to St. Marks Island on the St. Marks River). The really adventurous can navigate the river up to the Jim Woodruff Dam at Chattahoochee, but be advised to obtain local knowledge, and be sure of your source before setting out. A grounding up here that requires commercial assistance will take a large amount of money, especially if you don't have unlimited towing.

Back on the Jackson River, you will soon take a hairpin turn to the south past flashing green "9," just west of Mile 345 EHL, and about one nautical mile later, take a sharp curve to the west and proceed to Lake Wimico

White City, FL

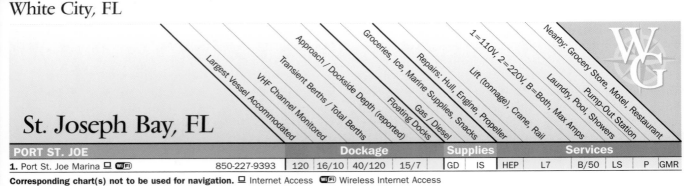

St. Joseph Bay, FL

					Dockage				Supplies			Services				
	Largest Vessel Accommodated	VHF Channel Monitored	Transient Berths / Total Berths	Approach / Dockside Depth (reported)	Floating Docks	Groceries, Ice, Marine Supplies, Snacks	Gas / Diesel	Repairs: Hull, Engine, Propeller	Lift (tonnage), Crane, Rail	1=110v, 2=220v, B=Both, Max Amps	Laundry, Pool, Showers	Pump-Out Station	Nearby: Grocery Store, Motel, Restaurant			

PORT ST. JOE

		Dockage				Supplies		Services				
1. Port St. Joe Marina 🖥 📶	850-227-9393	120	16/10	40/120	15/7	GD	IS	HEP	L7	B/50	LS	P	GMR

Corresponding chart(s) not to be used for navigation. 🖥 Internet Access 📶 Wireless Internet Access

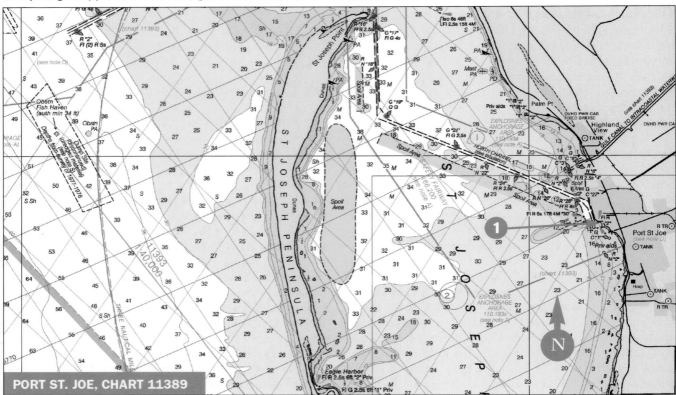

PORT ST. JOE, CHART 11389

at Mile 340 EHL and green daybeacon "3" and red daybeacon "4." The course for the straight 2.5-nautical-mile shot across the lake is about 310 degrees magnetic. At flashing green "15," enter Searcy Creek at the end of Lake Wimico (Mile 335 EHL).

Anchorage: Just after the Jackson River splits off from the Apalachicola, at Saul Creek (Mile 345 EHL) there is a hurricane hole. An excellent protected anchorage in 8 feet of water is located at the junction of Saul Creek and the Saul Creek Cutoff. Depths exceed 30 feet in this lovely spot; for optimum holding, use your depth sounder to find an appropriate spot to set the hook.

After exiting Lake Wimico into Searcy Creek, the chart indicates shoal in the oxbow, but the oxbow around the island at Mile 334 EHL normally carries 10 feet of water or better and provides an excellent secluded anchorage.

White City (Central Standard Time Begins)

From this point until you reach Wetappo Creek at Mile 315 EHL, there are virtually no aids to navigation, as none are

needed. The Waterway is relatively wide, relatively deep and there is little to intrude on an enjoyable view from all sides as you traverse swamp country (described on the charts as "impenetrable," "cypress" and "low swampy area").

About six miles from Lake Wimico is White City, where Central Standard Time meets Eastern Standard Time, so you gain an hour heading west (turn your clocks back) or lose an hour heading east.

Dockage: At White City, a 65-foot fixed vertical clearance bridge crosses the Waterway at Mile 329.3 EHL, and a rustic dock without amenities is accessible immediately off the GIWW at this location. If there is adequate berthing space, this could be a welcome respite in bad weather or if daylight is running short. You may get to White City earlier than you thought—get ready to set your clocks to Central Standard Time, which is an hour earlier than Eastern Standard Time. It is requested that you only remain here for 24 hours. Water is available from a nearby spigot, and trash may be left at the cans provided in the park. You may have friendly locals stop by for a chat.

White City to Panama City

For power vessels or sailing vessels, the subsequent 40 or 45 statute-mile trip on the Waterway to Panama City is a pleasure. This is something that both powerboat folks and sailing folks will be able to agree upon. The controlling vertical clearance on this section is 50 feet, defined by the DuPont Bridge leading out from the mainland to Tyndall Air Force Base, which is on a long and somewhat isolated peninsula.

White City to Panama City, via the Gulf of Mexico

NAVIGATION: Use Charts 11401, 11393 and 11389. About 1.5 nautical miles from White City on the GIWW, at about Mile 328 EHL, the Gulf County Canal cuts off 90 degrees south and extends five nautical miles southwest from the Waterway to Port St. Joe on St. Joseph Bay. The turn to port comes upon you with little warning or fanfare. The controlling depth is 12 feet, and there is a 75-foot fixed bridge near the exit to St. Joseph Bay.

Port St. Joe, which is a little southwest of White City, is on Eastern Time. You will have to switch your watch back and forth a bit if you don't continue on in the GIWW and instead, come out into St. Joseph Bay.

Exiting into St. Joseph Bay, if you are heading for the exit to the Gulf of Mexico, the ship channel from Port St. Joe to the Gulf is clearly marked and lies a half-mile straight ahead. You will have been coming southwestward on the canal. When you intersect the ship channel, you will turn to the northwest and, later, north to get around St. Joseph Point at the tip of St. Joseph Peninsula and out of St. Joseph Bay. You will be doing this incrementally, with the last straight run to the southwest until you get into the Gulf of Mexico and 30-plus feet of water. To get to the entrance buoy (RW "SA") off Panama City, steer northwest. The distance is 21 miles. The "SA" stands for either St. Andrew or St. Andrews. In Panama City, the appellation is a mixed bag. The chart you use will probably call it St. Andrew Bay. Locals will call it St. Andrews Bay. Be flexible. Dead ahead, a bit to the northeast, across the bay, you will spot the Panama City Municipal Marina.

Dockage: Port St. Joe can be a convenient stopover point, regardless of the direction you are traveling. A supermarket, liquor store and restaurants are only a short walk from the marina. Port St. Joe Marina is located just south of the paper mill in Port St. Joe. Follow the deep, well-marked channel into the harbor. Approach depths are around 12 feet at mean low water, and dockside depths average 6.5 to 7 feet at mean low water. The 120-slip facility can accommodate vessels up to 100 feet and has a café, ship's store, pump-out station, diesel, gasoline, air-conditioned restrooms/showers and a laundry.

White City to Panama City, via the GIWW

NAVIGATION: Use Charts 11390, 11391 and 11393. From White City, the Waterway continues to run clean, rela-

tively wide and relatively deep, with no need for navigational aids. At about Mile 318 EHL, it becomes the South Prong of Wetappo Creek and continues beneath Overstreet Bridge (Mile 315.4, 65-foot fixed vertical clearance) to about Mile 314 EHL, where it joins the North Prong and becomes Wetappo Creek.

At that point, aids to navigation appear again, starting with green daybeacon "1" at about Mile 313 EHL, and continuing down the Wetappo Creek and into Big Cove. At that same green daybeacon "1," eastbound vessels stay alert, as the channel turns north here and the small bay to starboard can be confused with the Waterway.

During strong southerlies, the narrow channel leading west to the sharp turn at Mile 310 EHL (quick flashing red "28") can pose serious difficulties to barge traffic. If meeting a tow along this stretch, be sure to coordinate on VHF Channel 13 to clarify your intentions. If you know the "lingo" the towboat traffic uses, so much the better. As a matter of practical concern, if you have your VHF radio cycling between Channel 16 and Channel 13 on this section of the GIWW, you will be in great shape. The GIWW channel runs southwest from Raffield Island and down around Murray Point. Near Mile 306 EHL, favor the southwestern side of the channel to avoid oyster reefs on the northeast side (generally marked with DANGER signs).

On this part of your journey, you will be passing a bay whose genesis is generally northwesterly. This bay leads to Sandy Creek just past Mile 310 EHL.

From that point, the Waterway runs into East Bay through well-marked, but relatively narrow channels. Watch your markers carefully in this area, as some very shoal water can be found out of the channel. For example, at red daybeacon "38" off Piney Point (Mile 300.75), there is a 4-foot-deep shoal charted just northeast of the channel.

Just past Long Point is the Dupont Bridge (Mile 295.4, 50-foot fixed vertical clearance). From there, all the way to Panama City, the GIWW runs through relatively deep water (25 to 35 and even 40 feet).

THE FOLLOWING AREA REQUIRES SPECIAL ATTENTION DUE TO SHOALING OR CHANGES TO THE CHANNEL

Study the chart carefully, however, for the run up East Bay to Panama City. Starting with flashing green "29" (Mile 294.2 EHL) off Parker Bayou, flashing green "29" should be left to starboard because the GIWW buoy system gives way to the Panama City buoy system (red-right-returning from the Gulf). This can be confusing, as red buoys are now on your port side as you travel west, switching back to red on the right with flashing red buoy "6" off Buena Vista Point past Panama City.

END SPECIAL CAUTION AREA.

Anchorage: Between White City and Panama City on the GIWW, a pleasant, protected overnight anchorage is located at Wetappo Creek (Mile 314.5). Just around the first bend

Panama City and Environs, FL

PANAMA CITY AND ENVIRONS		Largest Vessel Accommodated	VHF Channel Monitored	Transient Berths / Total Berths	Approach / Dockside Depth (reported)	Gas / Diesel	Floating Docks	Groceries, Ice, Marine Supplies, Snacks	Supplies	Repairs: Hull, Engine, Propeller	Lift (tonnage), Crane, Rail	1=110v, 2=220v, B=Both, Max Amps	Laundry, Pool, Showers	Pump-Out Station	Nearby: Grocery Store, Motel, Restaurant
1. PANAMA CITY MARINA 290 EHL ☐ WiFi	850-872-7272	110	16	20/240	10/10	GD		GIMS				B/100	LS	P	GMR
2. ST. ANDREWS MARINA 287 EHL ☐	850-872-7240	200	16/10	15/102	15/8 F	GD		IMS				B/50	LS	P	GMR
3. Sun Harbour Marina 287 EHL ☐ WiFi	850-785-0551	60	16	/80	12/12	GD		IMS				B/50	LS	P	GR
4. Bay Point Marina 280 EHL ☐ WiFi	850-235-6911	120	16/78A	20/205	6/7	GD		IS				B/100	LPS	P	MR
5. Lighthouse Marina 280 EHL	850-234-5609	70	16/11	6/50	7/8	GD		IMS	HEP	L55		B/50	S		GMR
6. Treasure Island Marina 280 EHL	850-234-6533	75	16	6/80	8/6	GD		GIMS	HEP	L35		B/50	LS	P	GMR
7. Pirates Cove Marina 280 EHL	850-234-3939	60	16	25/	6/8	G		GIMS	HEP	L50		B/50	S		GMR

Corresponding chart(s) not to be used for navigation. ☐ Internet Access WiFi Wireless Internet Access

of the creek (North Prong), you can safely anchor over a soft mud bottom in about 10 feet of water. Because of the current, a Bahamian moor might be appropriate here, preferably on the side of the river by the marshlands.

Panama City—Mile 290 EHL

Panama City boasts a large year-round charter fishing fleet, party boats, fishing piers, diving and surf fishing. Gulf fishing has greatly improved in the area, thanks to conservation efforts, and inshore light-tackle catch-and-release fishing on the bay has become very popular. Snapper, grouper and scamp are plentiful, and offshore fishing is considered magnificent.

For the past 26 years, Panama City Beach has held the Bay Point Billfish Tournament with a cash purse running into the hundreds of thousands of dollars. (The 2010 tournament was cancelled due to the oil spill.) Boaters can also enjoy the area's sparkling white sand beaches, rated as some of the finest in the country.

NAVIGATION: Use Chart 11389. Shell Island, the barrier island forming the southern side of the main pass from the

Panama City Marina

St. Andrews Marina

Panama City Marina
Gateway to the Gulf
1 Harrison Avenue
850-872-7272
Buoy Marker Green
Flashing 17
MM 290

St. Andrews Marina
A Historic Seaport
3151 West 10th Street
850-872-7240
Buoy Marker Red 6
MM 287

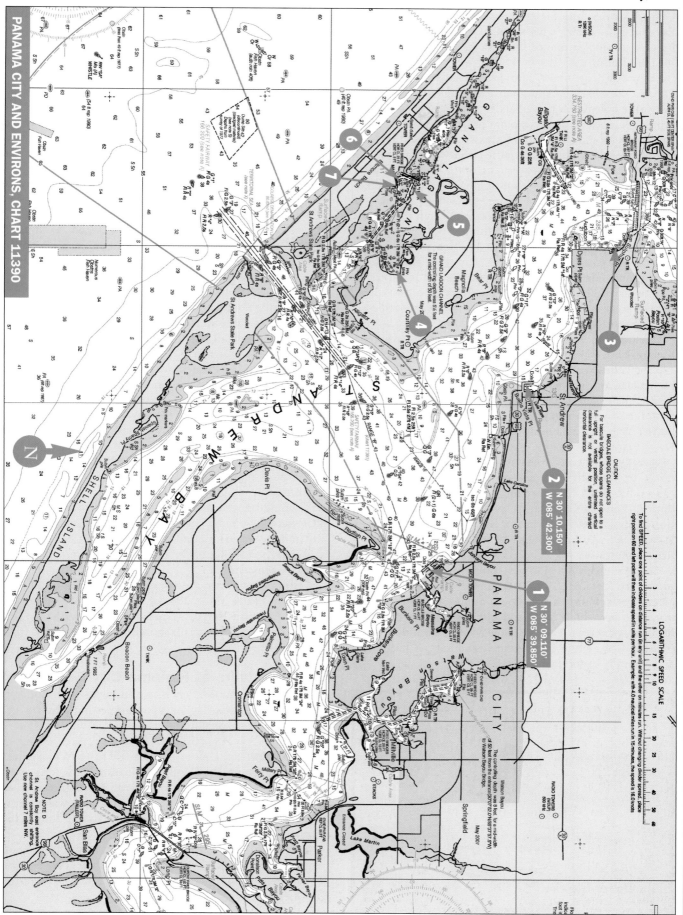

Panama City, FL

Gulf of Mexico into St. Andrew Bay, provides shelter for Panama City—a major harbor for transient yachts. The cut itself is considered one of the best deepwater channels on the Gulf Coast.

St. Andrew Bay, one of Florida's finest bays and home to Panama City, is deep and almost landlocked. It is a good hurricane hole for larger vessels, but cruising boats should, if possible, seek shelter in a more protected bayou.

The bay's exit to the Gulf of Mexico, a land cut through St. Andrews Park, is marble-jettied and well-marked. The Navy operates a lab on the west end of the bay and south of the Hathaway Bridge; you will frequently see helicopters, hovercraft and some very esoteric "special ops" equipment here. It is said that Navy SEALs rotate through this facility in the course of some of their training.

Under no circumstances should cruisers attempt to navigate the entrance to St. Andrew Bay at the eastern tip of Shell Island, labeled LANDS END on the chart. It is unmarked and, with the bottom continually shifting, is considered unsafe. Boats fishing or anchored in this area arrived from St. Andrews Bay, not the Gulf.

Dockage: As Panama City is probably the best-equipped harbor north of Tampa and St. Petersburg, berths are usually available except on holiday weekends. It is a good idea, particularly during the season, to call ahead and reserve a berth. There are facilities throughout the area, beginning from the east at Watson Bayou (due north of flashing green buoy "25") and extending west to flashing red "14" off Dyers Point.

Directly northeast of the pass from the Gulf, and due north of Redfish Point and quick flashing green buoy "17" (Mile 290.5 EHL) are the office, ship's store and fuel dock of Panama City Marina, one of two marina facilities owned by the city of Panama City. The city purchased St. Andrews Marina at Buena Vista Point and conducted a major renovation.

The Panama City Marina's transient docks are to the east of the fuel dock. This 240-slip full-service marina has amenities including a fuel dock, pump-out station, laundry, showers, ship's store and gift shop and a data port for Internet access. The marina is a block from downtown Panama City, with several fine restaurants, a post office and a variety of services.

Banks, delis, bookstores, the public library, theaters and performing arts centers all lie within a perimeter of about 10 blocks from the marina. Unique local and traveling exhibits are on display at the nearby Visual Arts Center.

Marine parts are available, but you will need transportation to get to West Marine. Consult local boaters for the best places to get repairs. Virtually all of the boatyards and several of the marinas have fallen prey to "condominiumization," though the trend appears to be slowing since the cooling of the housing market.

West of Watson Bayou, and just east of Panama City Marina, you will find some dockage and restaurants in Massalina Bayou. The drawbridge at the entrance (7-foot closed vertical clearance) opens on demand 24 hours a day. Transient spots are rare here, but you can anchor in 7 feet of water or more. If you are hungry, tie up at Bayou Joe's they serve breakfast, lunch and dinner daily.

Moving westward up the Waterway, Buena Vista Point is half a mile north of flashing red buoy "6." Once primarily known as a workboat marina, St. Andrews Marina has always been owned by the city of Panama City. It was, however, leased out to a commercial company that ran it as a private investment. Several years back, the city reclaimed the marina, put about $2.5 million into renovations and now operates the marina as its own source of income. St. Andrews Marina has 102 floating slips. The breakdown of the slip tenants comes to about 20 percent commercial workboats, 30 percent charter boats and about 40 percent private vessels. Fuel service is available 24 hours a day, seven days a week. Nearby are Uncle Ernie's Bayfront Grill & Brew House, a historic home with home-brewed beer and lighted docks, and Pappy's, a German-style pub. There is also Granite Café, a martini bar and bistro. The affable dockmaster at St. Andrews said that the townies eat at a place called Captain's Table, a seafood restaurant.

Continuing west on the Waterway, just south of the new Hathaway Bridge (Mile 284.6 EHL, 65-foot fixed vertical clearance) is Sun Harbor Marina. Transient berths for vessels up to 100 feet are available, with dockside depths from 6 to 10 feet.

Grand Lagoon, at Panama City Beach

Grand Lagoon, immediately inside and west of St. Andrews Inlet, off St. Andrew Bay, offers an interesting side trip and some superior hospitality.

NAVIGATION: Use Charts 11390 and 11391. When entering Grand Lagoon, you will benefit from some long overdue dredging recently performed on its entrance from St. Andrews Inlet. At one point, the channel was narrow and risky, but now it is an easy pass; simply follow the markers.

Dockage: Four marinas, along with a variety of good restaurants, are located inside the protected lagoon. They are Bay Point, Treasure Island, Lighthouse Marina and Pirates Cove.

Grand Lagoon and the St. Andrew Bay Inlet at Panama City Beach. (Not to be used for navigation.) Photo Courtesy of Army Corps of Engineers

At flashing green "5," private markers lead to Bay Point Marina off to starboard. The marina is an impressive facility in the Marriott Hotel complex, sheltered and completely updated. It is considered the premier transient yacht facility in the area. The tradition of flying weather flags is still honored there, and cruisers are definitely welcome. Look for cable television, telephone, water and 30- and 50-amp power connections at the dock.

A new office, air-conditioned restrooms, showers, laundry and a new swimming pool went in with the renovation. There also is Internet access. A well-stocked grocery store is one-and-a-half miles from the marina. Added attractions include tennis courts, three 18-hole golf courses in the vicinity and also a Jack Nicklaus-designed 18-hole course, the only one in the Panhandle. If you are into sybaritic delights, the Serenity Spa at Bay Point might have a package you will never forget.

Treasure Island Marina, Pirates Cove Marina and Lighthouse Marina are about a mile farther into Grand Lagoon. All have approaches and dockside depths of 6 to 7 feet. Treasure Island Marina, on the south side of the lagoon, is one of the few facilities offering 24-hour fuel, bait and ice. It can accommodate vessels up to 70 feet. Besides gas and diesel, the marina has a pump-out station and full repair services, along with restroom facilities and showers. Restaurants and shops are within walking distance.

Pirates Cove Marina, also on the south side, can take transient vessels up to 50 feet and sells gasoline only. The marina has restrooms and showers, a ship's store, full-service repairs and a restaurant.

Lighthouse Marina, on the north side, has restrooms, showers, The Boatyard restaurant and a full repair service and lift. The marina provides transient dockage for vessels up to 80 feet in length. Motels, restaurants and stores are within walking distance.

Some of the restaurants on the north side of the Grand Lagoon include 30 Degree Blue and Butler's Pantry, while within the Marriott complex are Club 19, Lime's Dockside and Kingfish Restaurant. Also out on nearby Panama City Beach is the perennially popular Capt. Anderson's restaurant, considered one of the top dining places in Florida, and Schooners, an equally delightful choice.

Anchorage: Along this stretch of the Waterway, from the Dupont Bridge to Panama City, virtually any cove well away from the channel offers good anchorage. Pearl Bayou is not only a nice anchorage, but could be considered a hurricane hole. Just west of the Dupont Bridge (Mile 295.4 EHL, 50-foot fixed vertical clearance), if you are westbound, turn to port (south) and continue on the well-marked channel. Be sure to use only the west branch, because the Air Force has appropriated the east branch for search-and-rescue craft moorings.

Farther west on the Waterway, Redfish Point or Smack Bayou offer protection from southerly winds. There are numerous places on St. Andrew Bay to anchor. Watson Bayou near the 9-foot fixed bridge offers 360 degree protections and good holding in 8 to 10 feet. It is a short walk to the store from a landing near the bridge.

Shell Island has some excellent anchorages off the beach, over a hard sand-and-shell bottom. If boat wakes from the

Panama City, FL

channel bother you, head farther east on the island, being wary of the charted sandbars between Davis Point and Shell Island. En route, if your depth sounder shows less than 7-foot depths, you are in the wrong place; you are either too close to the island or too far north over the Camel Humps.

Panama City to Choctawhatchee Bay

From Panama City, westbound cruisers will find about 12 nautical miles of relatively trouble-free transit through West Bay, then about 16 miles of transit through a land cut known to some as the "Grand Canyon," ending up in Choctawhatchee Bay, about 30 nautical miles long and three to five nautical miles wide.

NAVIGATION: Use Charts 11390 and 11385. When westbound from Panama City and approaching the Hathaway Bridge (Mile 284.6 EHL, 65-foot fixed vertical clearance), stay well to port of flashing red "14" off Dyers Point (Bird Island), as shoaling off the small island reaches into the marked channel. Beyond Hathaway Bridge, the Waterway opens up, heading north past the shoals at Shell Point (keep flashing green "5" well to port). From there, the Waterway curves northwest through West Bay, cuts under the West Bay Creek Bridge (Mile 271.8 EHL, 65-foot fixed vertical clearance) and then enters the relatively narrow channel of West Bay Creek, the start of the land cut known as the "Grand Canyon." For purposes of careful navigation, however, you may assume that you are in narrow circumstances at quick flashing green "15."

While in the "Grand Canyon," watch aids to navigation and your course carefully, as shoal water with depths of 2 to 4 feet runs very close to either side of the channel. The narrow channel persists past green daybeacon "39," and then aids to navigation cease; they are not needed. The channel runs relatively wide and deep. This situation continues for about 16.5 statute miles to Mile 254.5 EHL, entering Choctawhatchee Bay.

In the event of strong crosswinds, make it a point to check with any tows (VHF Channel 13) in the channel east of the Choctawhatchee Bay Bridge (Mile 250.4 EHL, 65-foot fixed vertical clearance), as the narrow channel may require coordinated meeting or passing. Barges, especially empties, are exceptionally difficult to handle for towboat operators in heavy wind and current.

While the cut is frequently dredged to 10.5-foot depths, shoaling is chronic, so hold to the center except when passing, and realize that hugging the shore while passing will likely run you aground in soft mud. Also use particular caution when transiting after strong winds or heavy rain, as large pine trees frequently break away from the nearly vertical banks. From time to time, when high winds are expected on Choctawhatchee Bay, be prepared to find westbound barges waiting inside the "Grand Canyon" at about Mile 254 EHL for better conditions. Cautious mariners might consider the example of the big guys and follow suit. Tying up to a commercial barge is entirely possible, if you make a proper approach to the towboat's skipper.

Choctawhatchee Bay

NAVIGATION: Use Chart 11385. As you travel into Choctawhatchee Bay from the east, the water deepens from about 9 feet to 38 feet, but is generally shallow along its southern shore. Be cautious passing Tucker Bayou (Mile 254 EHL), as it sometimes shoals to 3-foot depths or less at its mouth.

The route is closely pegged with markers for the first five or six nautical miles, but as the bay broadens and deepens, buoys thin out. Markers are used mainly to indicate shallows to the south, and these should be given a wide berth because of the possibility of shoaling. There is room to roam on this big open bay, but be aware that it can get rough in hard easterly or westerly blows because of the 20-mile east-west fetch. Just after flashing green "47," when you are westbound, a bay will open up to port. This bay, called Hogstown Bayou, is a great place to anchor, but there is one caveat: there are submerged iron pipes within the area delineated by a dotted line. If you picked your way in and out carefully, close to the shoreline, you might be rewarded with a lovely place to enjoy a peaceful time, out of any winds or waves.

If you need it, you can find anchorage in 7 feet of water over good holding ground in the lee of the causeway on either side of the Choctawhatchee Bay Bridge (Mile 250.4 EHL, 65-foot fixed vertical clearance). The Mid-Bay Bridge's (Mile 234.2 EHL, 64-foot fixed vertical clearance) east and west approaches are well-marked with buoys.

Dockage: Near the center of the long Choctawhatchee Bay, south of Mile 239 EHL in Horseshoe Bayou, is the full-service Baytowne Marina, part of the large Sandestin resort community that stretches from the bay to the beach. The gated community offers marina guests many amenities, including 63 holes of golf, 10 tennis courts, a health club, swimming pool and two waterfront restaurants. Courtesy transportation is available to the beach, hotels, golf courses and restaurants. A small ferry runs between the marina and the Village of Baytowne Wharf, or you can take a walk on the boardwalk built over the marshland. The Village of Baytowne Wharf has many charming shops and boutiques, restaurants, nightclubs, art galleries and other facilities.

To approach the marina, head south once clear of Fourmile Point and line up for flashing green "1" and flashing red "2" at the beginning of the entrance to the facility. Be careful to avoid the shoal depths when approaching shore to the east. Restrooms, a ship's store, the marina office and a tiki hut selling soft drinks are grouped adjacent to the dock and slips. The fuel dock and a pump-out station are located at the southwest corner of the dock/slip complex.

Captain Ron's Cove, about a half-mile west of the main marina complex, is used for docking small vessels (26 feet or less).

Located at the southeastern foot of the Mid-Bay Bridge (Mile 234.2 EHL, 64-foot fixed vertical clearance) is Legendary Marina, which offers dockage with power, water and a pump-out station. The marina, which is two miles south of the GIWW (Mile 235 EHL, flashing green buoy "51"), is in a dredged channel leading to a 500-foot concrete dock.

Choctawhatchee Bay entrance and the city of Destin. (Not to be used for navigation.) Photo Courtesy of Scott Jackson-PhotosFlorida.com

Approach and dockside depths are 6 feet. The marina has gas and diesel fuel, a ship's store, pool, restrooms and showers.

Wards Cove, Rocky Bayou

Dockage: To the northwest of flashing red "58," after passing under the Mid-Bay Bridge, at a distance of a little more than three miles, you will find flashing green "1," and that means you are on course for Rocky Bayou. Inside, in Wards Cove, is The Bluewater Bay Marina, with approach depths of 8 to 10 feet and 8 feet at dockside. Bluewater Bay Marina offers transient space with resort-style amenities. Wards Cove is to starboard as you approach Rocky Bayou on the north side of Choctawhatchee Bay. Locate flashing red "2" and green daybeacon "1," which mark the entrance to Wards Cove and Bluewater Bay Marina.

The marina has gas and diesel fuel, plus restrooms, showers and a ship's store. This is a full resort complex with courtesy transportation to restaurants, stores and hotels. Golf and tennis are available.

Anchorage: The above-mentioned Rocky Bayou provides a scenic anchorage. To enter Rocky Bayou, follow the directions above for Bluewater Bay Marina, pass Wards Cove to starboard and turn right into Rocky Bayou. Be aware of the 20-foot fixed vertical clearance bridge shortly after turning to starboard. Alternatively, at Mile 230 EHL, a turn to the south will bring you to a marked entry to Joes Bayou, a 360-degree protected anchorage, with a soft mud bottom and depths of 10 feet or more.

Destin—Mile 227 EHL

A major sportfishing and recreational center on northwest Florida's Miracle Strip, Destin is renowned for its sparkling beaches, crystal-clear waters and seaside resort activities, which attract thousands of tourists and boaters year-round. This is possible because the Gulf Coast's temperatures are relatively moderate from October through March. The average air temperature is 67.3 degrees maximum, with a minimum average of 52.2 degrees, so winter visitors throng from the north by both boat and car for respite from the chill and snow. Destin lies just north and east of the Choctawhatchee Bay Entrance on the barrier peninsula sheltering Choctawhatchee Bay on the south. Full-service marinas, waterfront hotels and restaurants abound.

Destin sponsors a billfishing tournament each year, which was cancelled in 2010 due to the oil spill, while the month of October is mainly devoted to the more than 50-year-old Deep Sea Fishing Rodeo. Big game fish that ply the Loop Current that circulates clockwise in the Gulf of Mexico are the reason, and the current comes relatively close to shore near Destin. The rodeo draws thousands of expectant anglers who ply the offshore waters, inshore bays and bayous for prize-winning fish, worth thousands of dollars. The rodeo's fate was not known at press time 2010. Scuba divers get their chance for fun and games at the annual Destin Underwater Easter Egg Hunt in April. Great food and conviviality add to the attraction of these events.

Destin to Fort Walton Beach, FL

DESTIN TO FORT WALTON BEACH		Largest Vessel Accommodated	VHF Channel Monitored	Approach / Dockside Depth (reported)	Transient Berths / Total Berths	Dockage	Gas / Diesel	Groceries, Ice, Marine Supplies, Snacks	Supplies	Repairs: Hull, Engine, Propeller	Lift (tonnage), Crane, Rail	Services	1=110V, 2=220V, B=Both, Max Amps	Laundry, Pool, Showers	Pump-Out Station	Nearby: Grocery Store, Motel, Restaurant
						Floating Docks										
1. Fisherman's Cove Marina 249 EHL	850-835-2035					15/10	G	MS				1/		P	GR
2. Sandestin's Baytowne Marina 240 EHL 🖥 WiFi	850-267-7773	140	16	20/99	8/7		GD	GIS	HEP		B/100	LPS	P	GMR
3. Bluewater Bay Marina 232 EHL 🖥 WiFi	850-897-2821	110	16	10/300	8/8		GD	GIMS	HE		B/50	LPS	P	GMR
4. North Light Yacht Club WiFi	850-678-2350	65	16	10/60	15/8		GD	IMS	EP		B/50	LPS	P	MR
5. Destin Marina	850-837-2470	40		6/10	6/6		GD	GIM						GMR
6. Harborwalk Marina 230 EHL	850-337-8250	65	16	7/52	10/6	F	GD	GIMS			B/50		P	GMR
7. Destin Fisherman's Co-op 230 EHL	850-654-4999	100		/40	8/8		D	IM			1/30			MR
8. Marina Café Yacht Club 230 EHL	850-837-7960	100		10/30	5/4						B/100			GMR
9. Legendary Marina 234 EHL	850-337-8200	40	16	/350	8/	F	GD	GIMS	HEP	L	B/50	S	P	GMR
10. Shalimar Yacht Basin 225 EHL	850-651-0510	100	16	6/134	32/8		GD	IMS	HEP	L35	B/50	LS	P	GMR
11. Leeside Inn/Deckhands Marina 224 EHL 🖥	850-243-1598	60	16	94/94	8/8			I	HEP	L35	B/50	LPS	P	GMR
12. Brooks Bridge Marina 223 EHL	850-243-7861	40	16	10/15	30/5	F	GD	IS			B/50	S		GMR
13. Brooks Bridge Bait & Tackle Inc. 223 EHL	850-243-5721	130	16		8/8		GD	IS					P	GMR
14. Ft. Walton Beach City Dock	850-833-9500	50		6/	6/								P	GMR
15. Fort Walton Beach Yacht Basin 222 EHL	850-244-5725	50	16	4/94	9/7		G	IS			B/50	S	P	GMR

Corresponding chart(s) not to be used for navigation. 🖥 Internet Access WiFi Wireless Internet Access

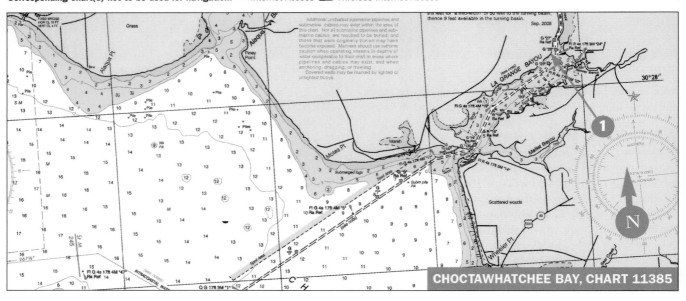

CHOCTAWHATCHEE BAY, CHART 11385

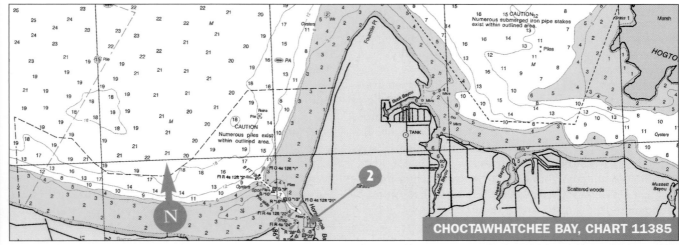

CHOCTAWHATCHEE BAY, CHART 11385

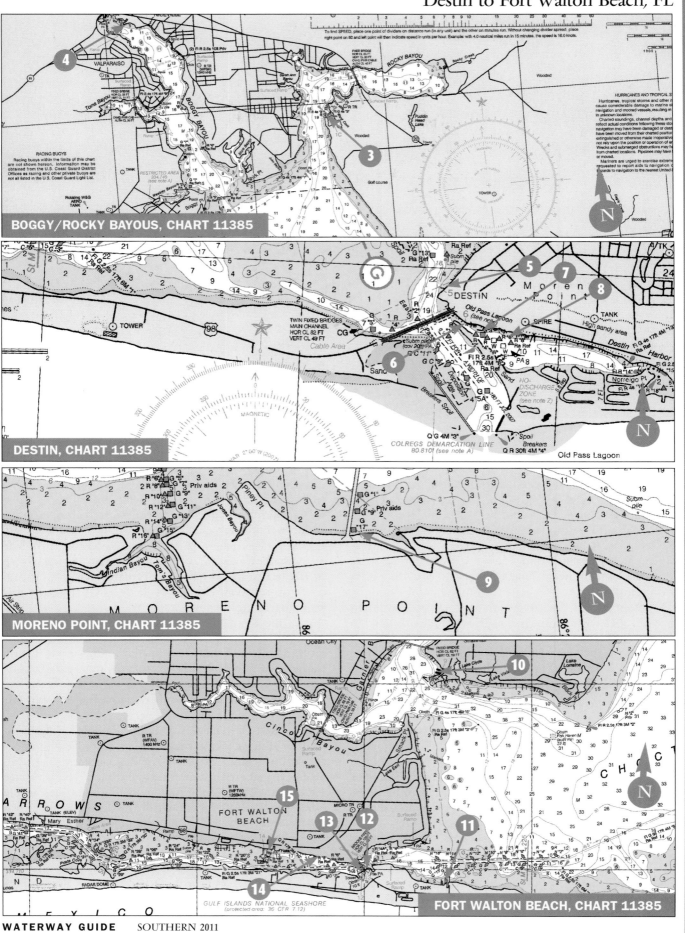

BOGGY/ROCKY BAYOUS, CHART 11385

DESTIN, CHART 11385

MORENO POINT, CHART 11385

FORT WALTON BEACH, CHART 11385

Destin to Fort Walton Beach, FL

Fort Walton Beach (note Brooks Bridge crossing the ICW route). (Not to be used for navigation.) Photo Courtesy of Scott Jackson-PhotosFlorida.com

NAVIGATION: Use Chart 11385. The main docking area in Destin is immediately south and east of the twin fixed bridges over the Choctawhatchee Bay entrance from the Gulf (south of the GIWW). The charted vertical bridge clearance is 49 feet, but there have been reports that 48 feet is closer to reality, so sailors should use caution if their vessel's mast height is more than 48 feet.

To enter the main Destin Harbor, commonly known as Old Pass Lagoon, from Choctawhatchee Bay to the north, turn sharply to port (east) after passing under the bridges. The channel into the large harbor is narrow, but well-marked with daybeacons. It runs between the mainland to the north and the protective sandbar to the south. Many facilities line the northern shore of the harbor. The pristine beaches and dunes of Santa Rosa Island are located across the peninsula on the Gulf side. Because of the substantial development along the beach, you will have to search for a spot with public access.

If entering the pass from the Gulf, care should be taken when crossing the bar if there is a swell running. Also note that buoys are not charted in the Choctawhatchee Bay Entrance channel, as constant shoaling necessitates frequent relocation. This is a pass that needs to be negotiated in flat water, daylight, good visibility and during reasonable tides.

Dockage: Along the north shore of the harbor are Destin Marina, Destin Fishermen's Co-op and Harborwalk Marina. Many locally popular eating establishments also offer dockage along with everything from snacks to gourmet meals.

Destin Marina, at the Destin North Channel (northeast side of the fixed twin U.S. Route 98 Bridges), has gas and diesel and limited transient dockage for two boats to 40 feet and five boats to 20 feet, with dockside depths at 6 feet. Marine supplies are available, and the marina is within walking distance of downtown.

Destin Fishermen's Co-op is located on the north side of the harbor and can accommodate transient vessels up to 100 feet in length. Diesel is available, but there are no dockside restroom or shower facilities. Restaurants and shopping are nearby.

Gas, diesel and limited transient dockage for vessels up to 60 feet are available at Harborwalk Marina, located southeast of the bridge and on the north side of Destin Harbor. The approach carries 6-foot depths, with dockside depths of 8 feet. There are restrooms, a pump-out station, a ship's store and motels, while restaurants and provisions are within walking distance.

For a first-class meal, tie up at the Marina Café Yacht Club or dinghy to the beach (restaurants lacking dockage still welcome customers coming ashore in their dinghies). If you are into more casual dining, you can have a great time just dinghy-hopping from one bistro to the other; try Al's Hotdogs and Grille, the Lucky Snapper and the Boathouse Oyster Bar, all with outdoor music. Harbor Docks and Harry T's also have excellent cuisine and feature bands indoors. McGuire's Irish Pub and Brewery, the legendary Pensacola bistro, now has a Destin counterpart just across the road near the bridge. Florida law requires that a dinghy carry a life jacket (with whistle attached) for every passenger. If you don't want a flashing blue light from a law enforcement boat from the Florida Fish and Wildlife Conservation Commission (FWC) approaching you, make certain you pay attention to this decree. It is actively enforced and not negotiable.

Anchorage: Destin Harbor (Old Pass Lagoon) provides excellent anchorage with no surge, and wakes are strictly controlled. Note that the harbor is a No-Discharge Zone. Inside, the channel splits to avoid a shoal down the center and then converges past the shoal. You can anchor on the south side of the harbor or just off Harbor Docks Restaurant. A municipal water taxi service is available during the summer months.

Fort Walton Beach—Mile 224 EHL

Fort Walton Beach combines the many charms of a major seaside resort and is well worth a cruising layover. Besides the swimming and snorkeling in crystal-clear water (locals swear you can see a quarter on the bottom at 30 feet), the area is an angler's delight.

This captivating town is a shopper's bonanza with its many antiques stores, novelty shops, boutiques, upscale dress shops and bookstores. Golf and tennis facilities abound, and there is an eclectic variety of restaurants and nightclubs.

Dockage: Transient space may be found north of the GIWW in Shalimar, on the eastern shore of the entrance to Garnier Bayou, and before the 19-foot fixed vertical clearance bridge. Shalimar lies approximately two nautical miles northwest of Mile 225 EHL on the GIWW and has a well-marked channel entrance with a tall cylindrical water tower as a beacon. This is a comprehensive area with all the amenities and services you might expect. While Cinco and Garnier bayous offer a number of anchorages and marine facilities, access to both is limited by 19-foot fixed vertical clearance bridges.

The Shalimar Yacht Basin offers transient slips. Approach depth is 18 feet, while the harbor depth is 8 feet. Gas and diesel are here, along with a pump-out station at the fuel dock, restrooms, showers, laundry, a computer with Internet access, a ship's store and full repair services, including a 35-ton Travelift.

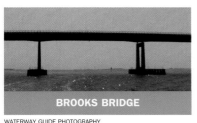

BROOKS BRIDGE

WATERWAY GUIDE PHOTOGRAPHY

At Mile 225 EHL, the Waterway narrows down considerably, and you will come across a series of floating marks that will get that point across to you quite well. On the southern shore after passing Mile 225 EHL, and approaching Fort Walton Beach and The Narrows, are the Leeside Inn and Marina and Brooks Bridge Marina and Storage. Brooks Bridge Bait and Tackle, on the west side of the Brooks Bridge, offers pump-out service at their dock or they can also come to you.

You can put into Leeside Inn and Marina from the GIWW by exiting south of Mile 224 EHL between green can buoys "13" and "15," just east of the Brooks Bridge (Mile 223.1 EHL, 50-foot fixed vertical clearance—but watch your tides). The marina has transient berths to 60 feet, with dock-side depths of 6 feet. There are restrooms, showers, a laundry and a full-service repair center with a 35-ton lift. The marina also has a ship's store and, at the connected Leeside Inn, there is a dockside bar plus two others inside, a heated pool and a restaurant. Brooks Bridge Marina is a full-service repair facility with a lift.

To reach the Fort Walton Yacht Basin (Mile 222), which offers full services, exit the GIWW between red daybeacons "16" and "20." Proceed to the marina by going north across the bar between the private channel green daybeacon "1" and red daybeacon "2." The marina has gas and diesel and limited transient dockage up to 50 feet. There is a pump-out station, plus restrooms, showers and a restaurant on-site. Other services are within walking distance.

Additionally, Fort Walton Beach offers a free pump-out station at a city park about a block west of Brooks Bridge, on the north side, where you can also stay overnight after obtaining approval by calling the city manager's office at 850-833-9500.

Fort Walton Beach has been and continues to be an Air Force town. The linchpin is Eglin Air Force Base, a military facility that's larger than the entire state of Rhode Island. The Air Force has, in its consummate wisdom, constructed a hangar about the size of a city block wherein it subjects bombers to sub-arctic conditions for weeks at a time. Why the Air Force built this facility in Florida as opposed to Alaska has never been explained. It was at Eglin that Jimmy Doolittle's Tokyo Raiders trained in absolute secrecy for their World War II raid on the Japanese home island of Honshu. Doolittle's famous raid, made in B-25 bombers, was launched April 18, 1942, from the carrier *Hornet*. It is also in Eglin's piney woods and dark swamps that the United States Army conducts part of its punishing Ranger training.

At Mary Esther, you will be close to the north-south runway at Hurlburt Field, so look for planes coming and going. They won't get in your way and you won't be in theirs, but you may see some esoteric aircraft. Hurlburt is home base for the Air Force's First Special Operations Group. These are the people in the Air Force who pull off the "black ops" missions that don't get any publicity.

Choctawhatchee Bay to Pensacola

From the southwestern terminus of Choctawhatchee Bay, west of Fort Walton Beach, the GIWW enters a section known as The Narrows. This Waterway, which is actually the eastern end of Santa Rosa Sound, is appropriately named.

Though well-marked, the channel twists back and forth through shallows for about six nautical miles before it widens somewhat as it approaches Santa Rosa Sound proper. As the Waterway winds through Santa Rosa Sound to Pensacola Bay, you will see an abundance of attractive homes along the mainland side, with beach communities dotting the barrier side. Santa Rosa Sound, which is almost as narrow as The Narrows, has numerous

Pensacola, FL

coves and good anchorages along its shores. However, check your depths, and remember the effect of the wind on tides, because the anchorages could be somewhat shallower than charted.

NAVIGATION: Use Charts 11385 and 11378. At Mile 206.7 EHL, the Navarre Causeway may have only a 48-foot fixed vertical clearance due to tide conditions, in spite of a charted fixed vertical clearance of 50 feet. East of the bridge, between flashing green "87" and quick-flashing red "88," is a shoal into the channel, so favor the green (south) side.

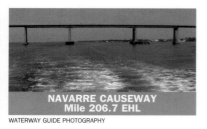

NAVARRE CAUSEWAY
Mile 206.7 EHL

WATERWAY GUIDE PHOTOGRAPHY

At Mile 205 EHL, the Waterway emerges from shoal territory into Santa Rosa Sound. Though the GIWW does move through some shoal areas in Santa Rosa Sound (5- and 6-foot depths at mean low water), for the most part it carries respectable depths of 13 to 17 feet.

While transiting The Narrows, monitor VHF Channel 16 and Channel 13 for barge traffic to avoid a "squeeze" when meeting with an oncoming behemoth. If you have already had contact with this type of barge traffic, you know the drill. "Passing one whistle" means that you both agree to alter course to starboard and pass port-side-to-port-side. "Two whistles" means that you are altering course to port and will pass starboard-to-starboard. If you are clever enough to ask the skipper of the tow what is best for him, you will get cooperation you never thought existed in this modern age. Remember, barges are not maneuverable like your pleasure craft, so give the barge traffic the benefit of the doubt. There isn't a pleasure boat yet that has ever won a close encounter with commercial traffic.

In your westward journey near Mile 200 EHL, past the Navarre Bridge, note that red daybeacon "124" (between flashing green lights "123" and "125") marks a shoal encroaching into the channel. Some charts do not show this marker. At this point, you should switch to Chart 11378 for your approach to the Pensacola Beach Twin Bridges (Mile 189.1 EHL, 65-foot fixed vertical clearances).

Dockage: Just past the Pensacola Beach Twin Bridges, if you turn south and parallel the Pensacola Beach Twin Bridges, you will see channel markers for Little Sabine Bay. Beach Marina is the first marina on the port side after entering Little Sabine Bay. It provides transient dockage, gas and diesel, restaurants and a grocery store.

Immediately east of the bridge (Mile 190) on the north side of Santa Rosa Sound is the Santa Rosa Yacht Club, offering limited transient dockage for vessels up to 60 feet, along with restrooms, showers, laundry and dry storage. Dockside depth is 8 feet.

For westbound skippers, as you enter Pensacola Bay, note that after passing flashing green "145" (at about Mile 184.2 EHL) the buoys shift to that of the Pensacola

Ship Channel (red-right-returning for vessels inbound from the Gulf to Pensacola). Thus, traveling the GIWW from this point, all the way across Pensacola Bay to the Pensacola Landcut and re-entering the GIWW at about Mile 179.5, you should leave red markers to port and green to starboard (these markers carry the appropriate small yellow triangles and squares indicating their dual role as GIWW route markers). When you get to the Gulf inlet between Fort McRee and Fort Pickens, pick up quick flashing red buoy "14," head northwest by west to green can buoy "1" and then turn left to transit the land cut, leaving quick-flashing red buoy "2" to starboard. Or if you turn north and exit Santa Rosa Sound to visit Pensacola, following the main ship channel, you will leave red markers to starboard and green to port.

GOIN' ASHORE: **PENSACOLA, FL**

Hurricane Ivan in 2004 hit the marine industry in this sprawling, cosmopolitan city and deepwater port at Mile 184 EHL harder than most any Florida community. Besides offering numerous marinas (most rehabbed after the hurricane), repair facilities, hotels, motels and restaurants, Pensacola has a long history that is worth knowing.

In 1513, world explorer Juan Ponce de Leon landed at what is presently known as Pensacola Beach and promptly named it after the now-extinct Indian tribe living there, the Panzacola. King Ferdinand VI later changed the name to Pensacola. During its sometimes turbulent history, Pensacola was the capital of British West Florida during the Revolutionary War with jurisdiction west and north to Natchez, MS. The Spanish finally settled Pensacola in 1559, left it two years later and returned in 1698.

The city changed hands 17 times over the years, alternately with Spain, France, England, the Confederacy and the United States. Pensacola is today a Navy town—in fact, it has been since construction of a Navy shipyard began in 1825, later evolving into an air station. The city is also a flourishing center for tourism and recreation, and a fine layover port for cruising mariners.

Also of historical note are Fort Pickens, Fort McRee, Fort Barrancas, the Pensacola Lighthouse (complete with the ghost of a past keeper) and the recently restored Seville Square Historical District. Architecture of the district reflects the five nations that have laid claim to it. Real estate prices in the district reflect modern-day reality.

There is little, if anything, left of Fort McRee. Isolated, as it was, at the tip of Perdido Key, it had little to no military significance, not even during the Civil War, when it was occupied by Confederate soldiers and gunners. On the other hand, Fort Pickens, which remained in federal hands throughout the war, was used to shell Fort McCree and, later, served as a compound where Geronimo was imprisoned for a while—more as a tourist attraction than anything else—after surrendering to the Army out West. Geronimo and some other Chiricahua Apache braves arrived in Pensacola in 1886, 10 years after General George Armstrong Custer's slight miscalculation at the Little Bighorn in Montana. They were housed at Fort Pickens until May 1888, when they were sent to Mount Vernon Barracks, north of Mobile, AL. In 1894, the tribe was moved to Fort Sill, OK. Geronimo died there in 1909 and is buried there. The rest of the Chiricahua Apaches were freed in 1913.

The National Museum of Naval Aviation at the Pensacola Naval Air Station is known throughout the nation for its collection of military aircraft dating from the earliest Navy plane to the latest jet fighters. The museum exhibits more than 150 aircraft, ranging from the Curtis Triad (1911) to the F/A-18 Hornet jet fighter used by the world-famous Blue Angels flying team. The museum registers some one million visitors a year. To find out more call 850-452-3604 or go online at www.navalaviationmuseum.org.

Pensacola is home to the Blue Angels, and the team does at least one home show a year, out at Pensacola Beach. There isn't a living soul in Pensacola who will admit publicly to not liking the Blue Angels, and rabid enthusiasm for the team is universal. One Navy pilot said he liked flying jets better than kissing his girlfriend because it lasted a darn sight longer and was infinitely more exciting. That may not go down in the naval history books with, "Don't Give Up The Ship!" but it is accurate.

ADDITIONAL RESOURCES

■ Pensacola Bay Area Chamber of Commerce
www.visitpensacola.com

⚑ **NEARBY GOLF COURSES**
Creekside Golf Course, 5555 Esperanto Drive,
Pensacola, FL 32526, 850-944-7969
www.thegolfcourses.net

☤ **NEARBY MEDICAL FACILITIES**
Gulf Breeze Hospital, 1110 Gulf Breeze Parkway,
Gulf Breeze, FL 32562, 850-934-2000
www.ebaptisthealthcare.org/gulfbreezehospital/

Pensacola Bay

Pensacola Bay, west of Deer and Fair points, has always been considered one of Florida's largest and safest harbors. It has served as a heavy weather refuge for commercial and Navy ships, as well as for smaller craft. Hurricane Ivan proved in fall 2004, however, that nothing is completely safe from severe weather. In Pensacola, there was pretty much nowhere to hide.

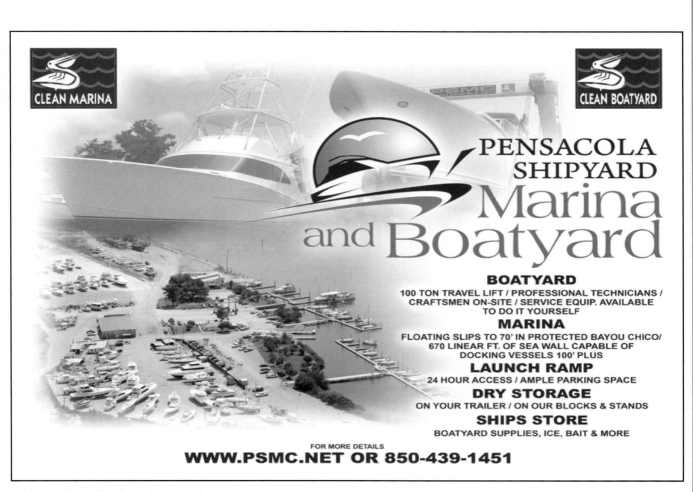

Pensacola Beach & Pensacola, FL

WG

PENSACOLA BEACH & PENSACOLA	Phone	Largest Vessel Accommodated	VHF Channel Monitored	Transient Berths / Total Berths	Approach / Dockside Depth (reported)	Floating Docks	Gas / Diesel	Groceries, Ice, Marine Supplies, Snacks	Repairs: Hull, Engine, Propeller	Lift (tonnage), Crane, Rail	1=110V, 2=220V, B=Both, Max Amps	Laundry, Pool, Showers	Pump-Out Station	Nearby: Grocery Store, Motel, Restaurant
				Dockage			**Supplies**		**Services**					
1. Santa Rosa Yacht & Boat Club 189 EHL ▢	850-934-1005	60	16	5/40	8/8		GD	I			B/50	LS	P	GMR
2. The Beach Marina 189 EHL	850-932-8466	100	16	4/30			GD	GIMS			B/50		P	GMR
3. Sabine Marina 189 EHL	850-932-1904	100	16	10/75	7/12			I			B/50	S		MR
4. Flounder's Chowder House 189 EHL	850-932-2003	45		20/	6/5			GIS						GMR
5. PENSACOLA SHIPYARD 185 EHL (WiFi)	**850-439-1451**	**250**	**16**	**4/60**	**15/7**	**F**		**IMS**	**HEP**	**L100,C**	**B/100**	**LS**	**P**	
6. Island Cove Marina 185 EHL	850-455-4552	75	16	6/94	6/6			IMS			B/50	LS		G
7. Bell Marine Service 185 EHL	850-455-7639	48		/20	5/6						B/30			G
8. Pelican's Perch Marina & Boatyard 185 EHL (WiFi)	850-453-3471	50		1/55	15/6	F			HEP	L50	1/30	S		
9. Palm Harbor Marina 185 EHL	850-455-4552	70	16	10/46	6/6.5	F		I			B/50	S	P	
10. Yacht Harbor Marina 185 EHL	850-455-4552	60	16	8/48	6/6.5	F		IMS			B/50	L	P	
11. Bahia Mar Marina 185 EHL	850-432-9620	65	16/09	6/60	8/6.5	F	GD	IMS	HEP	L50	B/50	LS	P	GR
12. Pensacola Yacht Club 185 EHL ▢	850-433-8804	100	16	/58	8/8						B/50	LPS		R
13. Palafox Pier & Yacht Harbor 186 EHL	850-432-9620	230	16/09	10/97	17/14	F	GD	IM			B/100	LS	P	MR
14. Seville Harbour 186 EHL	850-432-9620	No Transients												GMR

Corresponding chart(s) not to be used for navigation. ▢ Internet Access (WiFi) Wireless Internet Access

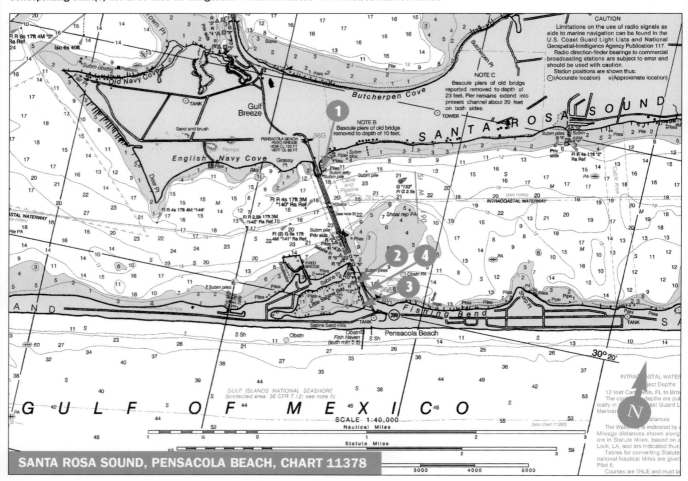

SANTA ROSA SOUND, PENSACOLA BEACH, CHART 11378

Visit our newly designed Web site to order WATERWAY GUIDE publications, get updates on current conditions, find links to your favorite marinas, and view updated fuel pricing reports. www.waterwayguide.com

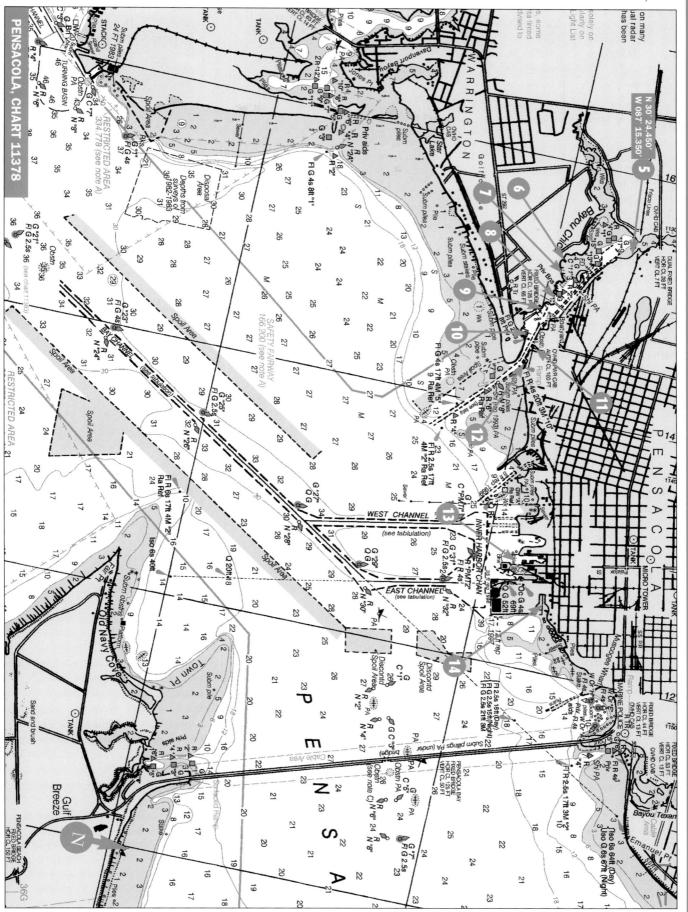

NAVIGATION: Use Chart 11378. Keep within all channel markers if you are entering the bay from the Gulf of Mexico. This good, all-weather passage is subject to shoaling. Encroaching shallows, however, are well-marked.

The old battleship *USS Massachusetts*, sunk for target practice during World War II, lies with turrets awash off Caucus Shoal. It is marked by quick flashing red bell buoy "WR2."

Dockage: Pensacola marinas, as a whole, were arguably the hardest hit of any concentration of marinas in Florida by Hurricane Ivan in 2004. Not everything marine in Pensacola came back together after the storm.

The Marina Management Group operates two major marinas in downtown Pensacola and one on Bayou Chico. The three facilities are listed under a single 24-hour telephone number (850-432-9620). Bahia Mar Marina in Bayou Chico was the least damaged and the first back in operation.

The Palafox Pier Yacht Harbor facility is six miles northeast of the GIWW, on the west side of the Commercial Port of Pensacola. The inner channel offers deep water (30 feet) and harbor depths from 10 to 12 feet. All facilities are post-Ivan; they are floating docks and have electrical stanchions and cable hookups. There is a pump-out facility, fuel, a laundry and showers/restrooms.

Seville Harbour Marina, also located six miles northeast of the GIWW, on the east side of the Port of Pensacola, in summer 2010 was not accepting transient boaters. It sustained serious damage from past hurricanes and has not yet been fully rebuilt.

The Barracks Street Fish House Restaurant is on the western edge of Seville Harbor. Very popular locally, the Fish House has deck dining and an outdoor bar, as well as inside dining. When the weather is right, this is the place to be. Check out the award-winning wine list. Fish House manager Brian Wielhouwer is rather proud of it. Next door, and under the same ownership, is the Atlas Oyster House, featuring Apalachicola oysters. If you didn't fill up in Apalachicola, eat them until you are stuffed in Pensacola.

There are literally hundreds of "best" spots to eat within the city, but just a few blocks up Palafox Street from Palafox Pier you can find any number of restaurant choices, including the upscale (but canine-friendly) Jackson's Steakhouse, serving beef and seafood with sidewalk café service.

BAYOU CHICO BRIDGE
WATERWAY GUIDE PHOTOGRAPHY

Bayou Chico

Dockage: One nautical mile southwest of the Port of Pensacola is a channel running northwest to Bayou Chico, which has a yacht club, full-service boatyards with facilities to handle most repairs and a number of full-service marinas.

To enter Bayou Chico proper you go under a 65-foot fixed vertical clearance bridge. Before the bridge to starboard are the Bahia Mar Marina and the adjacent Pensacola Yacht Club. Bahia Mar offers transients wet and dry slips and full boatyard services, with a 50-ton lift, contractors on-site for service and repair, a ship's store, covered wet slips and dry storage, gas and diesel, showers, laundry facilities and a pump-out station. There are restaurants nearby, plus a bed-and-breakfast near the marina. Pensacola Yacht Club is private.

Also before reaching the high-rise Bayou Chico Bridge near the mouth of the bayou, Palm Harbor Marina is a relatively new facility with floating docks.

Yacht Harbor Marina is located virtually next door to Palm Harbor Marina on Barrancas Avenue on the bay side, with quick access to Pensacola Bay and the Gulf.

Beyond the Bayou Chico high-rise bridge on the port side, full-service repairs and limited transient dockage for vessels up to 70 feet are available at Pelican's Perch Marina and Boatyard in Bayou Chico, located on the west side of the marked channel and immediately north of the bridge. There is a 50-ton lift that can accommodate boats with up to a 20-foot beam.

Past Pelican's Perch Marina and Boatyard, is Island Cove Marina. This full-service marina has restrooms, showers, laundry, a pump-out boat, a clubhouse, a barbecue area and a community kitchen. They have recently shut down their fuel dock and provide no fuel.

A little farther up Bayou Chico, to starboard, is the former Pensacola Marine Complex. Now the Pensacola Shipyard Marina and Boatyard, it is a full-service facility. They have a well-stocked ship's store and all of the amenities that transients need. The boatyard has a 100-ton Travelift and a 40-ton crane. The new floating docks have 9 to 10 feet of depth. Within 1.5 to 2 miles, shopping and restaurants are available.

Troendle Marine, located in the complex at Pensacola Shipyard Marina and Boatyard, can make repairs to any of your boat's systems. They also do structural and cosmetic work.

Perdido Key, FL

		Largest Vessel Accommodated	VHF Channel Monitored	Transient Berths / Total Berths	**Dockage** Approach / Dockside Depth (reported)	Floating Docks	Gas / Diesel	**Supplies** Groceries, Ice, Marine Supplies, Snacks	Repairs: Hull, Engine, Propeller	Lift (tonnage), Crane, Rail	1=110V, 2=220V, B=Both, Max Amps	**Services** Laundry, Pool, Showers	Pump-Out Station	Nearby: Grocery Store, Motel, Restaurant
PERDIDO KEY														
1. Holiday Harbor Marina & Grill 172 EHL	850-492-0555	125	16/14	3/60	7/7	F	GD	GIMS	HEP	L19	B/50	LS	P	R
2. Perdido Key Oyster Bar/Marina 172.5 EHL	850-492-5600	150	16	20/50	10/12		GD	IS			B/50	S		R

Corresponding chart(s) not to be used for navigation. 🖳 Internet Access 📶 Wireless Internet Access

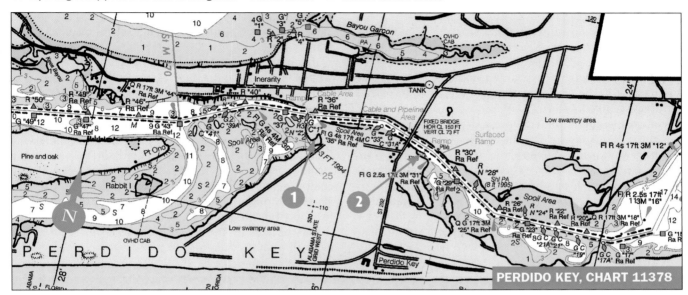

PERDIDO KEY, CHART 11378

To the Alabama Line

It is a run of about eight to 10 nautical miles from Fort McRee at Pensacola's Gulf entrance to the Alabama line at about Mile 170 EHL. Ahead on the GIWW are some fabulous anchorages, great waterfront restaurants and fine repair facilities.

Big Lagoon

From Pensacola Bay to get to the continuation of the GIWW, head out as though you were cruising for Caucus Channel, also called the Pensacola Ship Channel, which provides access to and from the Gulf of Mexico.

NAVIGATION: Use Chart 11378. Traffic here can get confusing, as the markers change to red-right-returning for vessels inbound from the Gulf to Pensacola; thus, major channel markers are red on the south and east, while green markers are to the north and west. Keep your chart handy here for easy reference.

After flashing green buoy "15," in the middle of the Caucus Channel between Forts Pickens and Barrancas, head west-southwest to green can buoy "1" (leave to port) and quick-flashing red buoy "2" (leave to starboard) to transit the short and narrow, but well-marked, passage known locally as the Pensacola Landcut (about Mile 178 EHL to Mile 179 EHL) leading to Big Lagoon.

Be careful not to confuse green can buoy "1" with green can buoy "13" just to its south, which is a marker for the

Caucus Channel. You can also line up the range markers to get to the land cut, which leads into Big Lagoon. As you enter, keep an eye out for shoaling caused by strong tidal currents through the Caucus Channel. The shallows are easily seen on sunny days, but if it is overcast, they will be harder to make out, so stay to the center except to pass. If you see a barge entering the pass, wait. There is not much room in there.

Anchorage: There is a good anchorage at the eastern end of Big Lagoon, south of the Waterway, and it is well-protected in most weather. This is known as Redfish Point. Turn south before flashing red "10," which marks a very shallow shoal; you can anchor as close to shore as your draft permits. You can also continue to flashing green "15" and double back toward the beach in 12-foot depths. For a bit of shoreside recreation, you can either swim or dinghy to the beach. The Gulf beach is a short walk across the dunes, which are part of the Gulf Coast Island National Seashore Park. This is a favorite weekend getaway for locals, but there is a bothersome chop during a northerly.

Perdido Bay

From Big Lagoon it is a short trip to Perdido Bay, down the middle of which runs the state line separating Florida from Alabama. Perdido Bay offers a variety of enticements for the cruising yachtsman.

Perdido Key, FL

NAVIGATION: Use Chart 11378. Leaving either the anchorage or the marinas, as you approach the left turn at the west end of Big Lagoon, be careful not to short-cut the channel, as flashing red "12" is way up in the cove and hard to see. The area southeast of green can buoy "11" is shallow—you will realize this when you see pelicans walking on the bar—so favor the center of the channel to avoid joining the many who have run aground here. Follow the markers because this entire area is surrounded by shoal water. After a turn at flashing red "16" and green daybeacon "15," you will see the Gulf Beach Bridge at Mile 171.8 EHL with a 73-foot fixed vertical clearance.

There is an interesting, but sad story associated with this bridge, the Perdido Key Bridge. Major Stephen Pless (USMC) was killed here in July of 1969 when the bridge was a bascule bridge. Pless, a Marine helicopter pilot in Vietnam, won the Medal of Honor for his heroic rescue of three wounded American soldiers on August 19, 1967. President Lyndon B. Johnson presented the decoration to Pless in a ceremony held at the White House on January 16, 1969. Seven months later, the two leaves of the draw at this bridge were rising when Pless, southbound and riding a motorcycle at a high rate of speed, tried to jump the widening gap. He hit the southern span, was probably killed immediately and fell into the GIWW.

After flashing green "35," enter the open but shoaled area between Perdido Key (FL) and Ono Island (AL, Mile 170 EHL). The GIWW is well-marked as it extends along the northern side of Ono Island and Inerarity Peninsula. From there at flashing green "57," the GIWW swings north into Perdido Bay. At this stage, right around Statute Mile 170, you are kind of betwixt and between. The last of Florida, Interarity Point, is now north of you and the first part of Alabama, Ono Island, is now to the south. Not all of Alabama is west of Florida.

Dockage: Immediately before the bridge on your left is the Perdido Key Oyster Bar Restaurant & Marina. The marina has new slips, fuel, water and overnight dockage. The Oyster Bar Restaurant offers both inside and outdoor accommodations, with not only oysters, but a full-fare, excellent seafood menu. Call ahead for reservations if you plan to stop.

If you are in need of repairs or a break, just a half-mile west of the bridge and immediately past flashing green "35," you can turn south (to port if westbound) and follow the private markers a short distance to Holiday Harbor Marina (closed Mondays). This sizable and growing marina offers transient dockage to 125 feet, gas and diesel, with pump-out facilities at the fuel dock (and portable slip-side pump-out facilities), restrooms, showers and laundry, plus a well-equipped ship's store and forklift dry storage. The Holiday Harbor Ship's Store and Grill offers beer and wine, fried fish, "po' boys," shrimp and hamburgers. They are either the last marina in Florida heading west, or the first marina in Florida heading east. ∎

Gulf Coast

Photo Courtesy of Mobile Bay Convention & Visitors Bureau and Susan Landry.

Gulf Coast

☐ **PENSACOLA BAY TO LOUISIANA** ☐ **LAKE PONTCHARTRAIN, NEW ORLEANS**
☐ **NEW ORLEANS TO FREEPORT** ☐ **FREEPORT TO BROWNSVILLE**

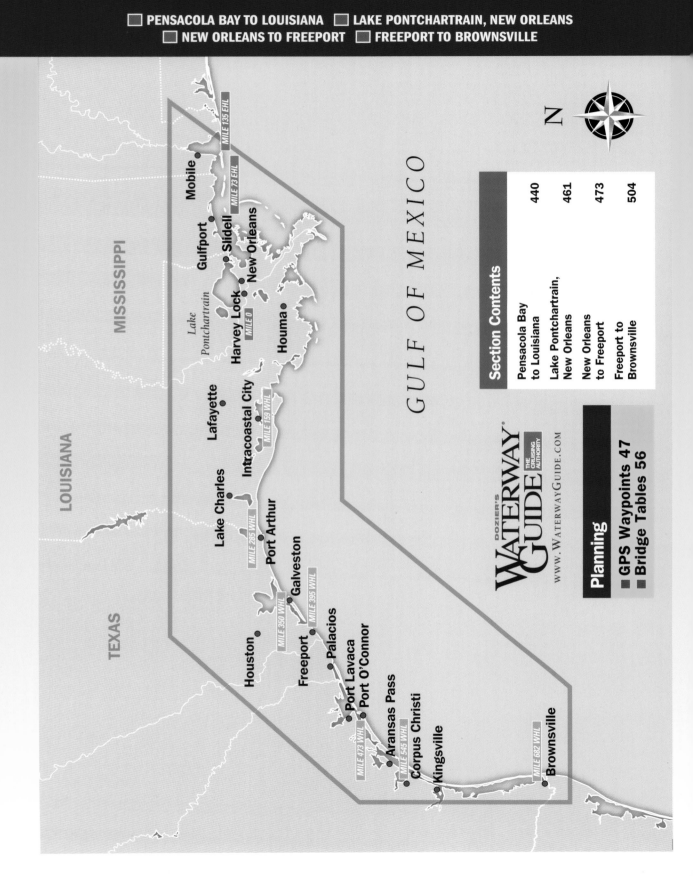

N

GULF OF MEXICO

MISSISSIPPI

LOUISIANA

TEXAS

Mobile

MILE 135 EHL

MILE 73 EHL

Gulfport

Slidell

New Orleans

Lake Pontchartrain

Harvey Lock

MILE 0

Houma

Lafayette

Intracoastal City

MILE 159 WHL

Lake Charles

Port Arthur

MILE 285 WHL

Galveston

MILE 395 WHL

Houston

MILE 350 WHL

Freeport

Palacios

Port Lavaca

Port O'Connor

Aransas Pass

MILE 473 WHL

Corpus Christi

MILE 545 WHL

Kingsville

Brownsville

MILE 682 WHL

WATERWAY GUIDE
DOZIER'S
THE CRUISING AUTHORITY
WWW.WATERWAYGUIDE.COM

Planning
■ **GPS Waypoints 47**
■ **Bridge Tables 56**

Introduction

Alabama to Mexico

The area west from Florida along the Gulf Coast historically has been described as the playground of the South. The region is known for its miles of pure white beaches, scenic landscapes and historic towns. This trip can challenge your boating skills. Expect to encounter a variety of conditions, ranging from open water on Mobile Bay and Mississippi Sound to narrow, sometimes cramped, canals and waterways. Lagoons and bayous often alternate with long and sometimes tedious land cuts. The route runs past historic Southern cities rich in antebellum history, as well as others, like Mobile and Biloxi, that have come to represent the New South.

The protected route, the Gulf Intracoastal Waterway (GIWW), arcs 870 miles from Pensacola to the Rio Grande. Distances are measured in statute miles east and west of Harvey Lock at New Orleans (given as EHL and WHL). The route is well-marked and charted, with well-maintained depths.

Weather

The Gulf of Mexico creates warm, moist air flowing generally northward from spring to fall, bringing relatively high temperatures and rain. New Orleans can be soggy and humid, while coastal waters in Texas often experience strong gales. Winters are usually mild, but occasionally northerners will bring temperatures down to 30 degrees.

Hurricane season runs from June through November, with the peak danger period being the months of August, September and October. Every few years, when one of these powerful storms comes ashore, the effects are usually devastating. The effects of wind in the Gulf are usually magnified due to the relatively shallow water. Even minor winds can kick up a nice chop. Monitor weather forecasts frequently, and have a plan to move inland via the numerous rivers and back bays along the coast in case a hurricane threatens.

Fog is occasionally a problem in the Mississippi Delta region in springtime. In these cases, be cautious of the commercial traffic that is more frequent in this area than in other parts of the Gulf Coast.

Tides

Tides are mostly diurnal, with one high and one low each day. They are easily affected by winds and pressure. Prolonged northerlies drop tides while southerlies raise

them. Generally, the range is 1 to 2 feet. Local tidal currents are usually weak—less than 2 knots—except near shoals, through certain cuts and at harbor entrances.

Commercial Traffic

Many commercial ships run offshore in the Gulf of Mexico, heading from port to port or serving offshore oil rigs. And the GIWW is often crowded with tugs and barges. Gulf Coast waters are also worked intensively by large fishing and shrimping fleets, as well as by the ever-present sport-fishermen running in and out of the many Gulf passes.

Commercial craft expect yachts to stay clear. Barge rigs can be gargantuan in size, exceeding 1,000 feet long in some cases. Vessels of this size must swing wide in turns and need up to a quarter mile to stop. Moreover, they usually travel in packs. The recreational boat must give way under all circumstances. On the other hand, most of the professional captains working these waters are valuable sources of information, and normally happy to help visiting boaters.

It is hard to overestimate the importance of VHF radio. Contact with towboats makes the journey easier. Call captains to find out when it is safe to pass, what traffic lies ahead and the best way to pass. Know the whistle signals; you will be told to pass on one whistle, two whistles or not at all. Call towboats on VHF Channels 13 or 16. In areas with heavy commercial traffic, you may want to leave your VHF on Channel 13.

Dockage

In many areas, marinas and fuel stops are scarce and often operate on bankers' hours. Keep a sizable reserve in your tanks, and call ahead to fuel docks as soon as you are in range. Since the GIWW was once strictly a commercial Waterway, many facilities are geared to commercial vessels.

Oil Spill

The explosion of the Deepwater Horizon rig and subsequent sinking and leak was an ongoing concern at press time. It was hoped that the leak would be capped by August 2010 and that continuing efforts to clean the water shorelines on the Gulf Coast could continue. Check our Web site www.waterwayguide.com for the latest updates. ∎

Distances—GIWW
Statute Miles (approximate)

East of Harvey Lock	
LOCATION	**MILES**
Pensacola	185
Mobile Bay Channel	134*
Dauphin Island	128
Pascagoula	104*
Biloxi	88*
Gulfport	73*
Pass Christian	65*
Rigolets	34
New Orleans West End	11
West of Harvey Lock	
LOCATION	**MILES**
Houma	58
Morgan City	95
Intracoastal City	160
Calcasieu River	241
Sabine River	266
Port Arthur	282
Galveston	354
Freeport	395
Port O'Connor	474
Aransas Pass	533
Corpus Christi	542
Port Mansfield	632
Port Isabel	667
Port Brownsville	684

* Distance to junction of GIWW and Ship Channel

Pensacola Bay to Louisiana

CHARTS 11367, 11368, 11369, 11371, 11372, 11373, 11374, 11375, 11376, 11377, 11378, 11382

Along this stretch of the Gulf Intracoastal Waterway (GIWW), you cross into Alabama waters. The Waterway route to Mile 160 EHL (East of Harvey Lock) is a wonderland of excellent protected anchorages, including Perdido Bay, Terry Cove, Cotton Bayou, Soldier Creek, Roberts Bayou, Ingrams Bayou and Wolf Bay. Check your charts, and pick any one of these places for a pleasant, protected overnight stop.

There are plenty of marinas in the area, along with repair facilities, restaurants and other amenities. Until you get to Mobile, the only water-accessible town is Orange Beach, AL, named for the orange groves that once were plentiful here. You can still find a few orange trees, thanks to city leaders who handed out free orange tree saplings a few years ago. Orange Beach, long known as the "Fishing Capital of Alabama," has a large charter fleet and boasts a variety of restaurants offering everything from Cajun cuisine to seafood specialties.

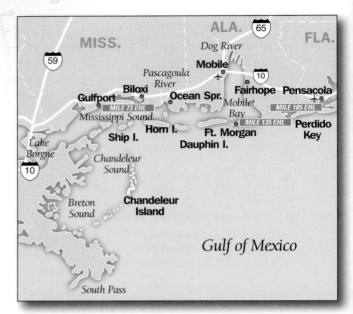

Orange Beach

At Mile 170 EHL, heading west on the GIWW, the tip of private Ono Island appears to port as you cruise the straight westward line of the GIWW to the entrance to Perdido Bay. When in this country, it is best to understand the esoteric language of the area. Ono Island, a private community across the border in Alabama, is explained as "Oh no, you can't go there." (Contact the Perdido Area Chamber of Commerce at 800-328-0107 or 850-492-4660 for more information, including a glossary of terms.) At flashing green "57," turn north to explore Perdido Bay or southwest to explore Bayou St. John.

NAVIGATION: Use Chart 11378. From flashing green "57" on the GIWW, there is a marked channel extending from the GIWW through Bayou St. John to Perdido Pass to the Gulf of Mexico. The pass has a 9-foot controlling depth (mean low water) and a bridge with a 54-foot fixed vertical clearance.

A number of restaurants and marinas are located in the bays and bayous on the way to Perdido Pass. To visit here, turn southwest off the GIWW at flashing green "57," then head for green daybeacon "17." Note that at the beginning of this channel, there are several private markers to a small cut into Ono Island to the south. Ignore them. Remember, if you are approaching from the east, as you enter Bayou St. John, you are no longer on the GIWW and are encoun-

tering the buoy system from Perdido Pass Inlet from the Gulf (red-right-returning); leave green to starboard (i.e. leave green daybeacon "17" to starboard and quick flashing red "18" to port).

If you want to explore marinas and facilities in Cotton Bayou, Terry Cove or Johnson Cove, turn to starboard at green daybeacon "1," short of the Perdido Pass Bridge, and parallel the bridge running west, on the bridge's north side.

At the western end of the bridge there are two channels, one going farther west into Cotton Bayou, the other going north from red daybeacon "8" and green daybeacon "9." This will take you into the body of water holding both Terry Cove and Johnson Cove.

If you choose to enter Cotton Bayou, be careful of shoal water. Downtown amenities can be reached from the bayou. You will see the marked channel just past green daybeacon "1" to starboard (it once marked the channel leading back northeast to Perdido Bay and the GIWW), and just past red daybeacon "8" to starboard, returning to Johnson Cove from the Gulf. There is a moderate current here as you pass the inlet, so be careful. Boaters with deep-draft vessels should use caution in Cotton Bayou; keep an eye on your depth sounder. There are generally 6-foot depths here during normal tides.

Dockage: On the south side of Cotton Bayou, Zeke's Landing Marina primarily handles charter fishing boats and is no longer heavily involved with transients. When available, Zeke's offers transient berths for vessels up to 65 feet, with a dockside depth of 6 feet at mean low water. Gas and

Orange Beach, AL

Orange Beach and Perdido Pass Inlet, looking east. (Not to be used for navigation.) Photo Courtesy of Orange Beach Marina.

diesel fuel are available, along with restrooms, showers, laundry, marine supplies and groceries. A forklift can handle vessels with displacements up to 10 tons and a 10-foot beam. Boat and engine repairs are available on-site.

Either from Cotton Bayou or Perdido Pass, if you are heading up to Terry Cove for Orange Beach Marina or Johnson Cove for Sportsman Marina, north of red daybeacon "10" (leave to starboard) and green daybeacon "11" (leave to port), you will pass a boat ramp on the west headland (port side). Just past this boat ramp is flashing red "12" to starboard.

For Orange Beach Marina, look due west (about 150 to 200 yards) to see green daybeacon "1" and red daybeacon "2." This marked channel curves southward and then westward along private docks and residences. Follow them, keeping red to starboard, and at the very end you will see Orange Beach Marina's private channel, running due south.

The full-service Orange Beach Marina is fully operational. With 20 of their 160 slips devoted to transients, they have plenty of transient dockage with depths averaging 8 feet at mean low water. Orange Beach Marina has a pump-out station at the fuel dock, new restrooms, showers, laundry and a full-service boatyard, Saunders Yachtworks. Saunders is equipped with a 60-ton lift that can accommodate vessels up to 70 feet with a 21-foot beam. The boatyard handles repairs from minor to extensive. Also on-site are two restaurants, Palms Bar & Grille for casual waterfront dining and Calypso's featuring Caribbean cuisine.

Sportsman Marina is fully operational after a substantial increase in wet slips and dry storage capacity. Located on the north shore of Johnson Cove or eastern end of Terry Cove, Sportsman Marina is easy to reach. At flashing red

"12" in Johnson Cove, carefully proceed north by northeast, but give flashing red "12" a wide berth to avoid shoals lying east of the marker. Approach depths to the marina are between 10 and 12 feet, with 8-foot depths at dockside. Gas and diesel are available, along with restrooms, showers, laundry and a pump-out station. The marina can handle transient dockage to 120 feet. There is a ship's store and an excellent waterfront restaurant, the Shipp's Harbour Grill.

GOIN' ASHORE:
ORANGE BEACH, AL

Spanish Explorer Carlos Sequenza was looking for a permanent base when he stumbled upon Perdido Bay, which means lost, hidden, perdition or Hell in Spanish. Presumably Perdido Bay was named "lost" because of its narrow entrance. Pirates reportedly once favored the bay and the many coves and bayous in the area because they made good hiding places.

Citizens using picks and shovels opened the Perdido Pass Inlet from the Gulf in Orange Beach proper in 1906. A breakwater has since been built. Previously, the only entry was at the Pensacola Inlet. A high-rise bridge with a fixed vertical clearance of 54 feet now spans Perdido Pass.

In the early 1800s, the area now known as Pleasure Island, where Orange Beach and the adjacent city of Gulf Shores are located, produced oranges and strawberries, but the crops failed commercially because of winds off the bays. However, soldiers from historic Fort Morgan, located at the entrance to Mobile Bay, were said to depend upon Orange Beach for fresh fruits and vegetables to supplement their Army rations.

Since 1979, when Hurricane Frederick scoured the south Alabama coast, the tourism industry and resultant building have flourished. As a result, Orange Beach is now a year-round tourist haven. There are churches of most denominations, numerous restaurants, bars, repair services, grocery stores and a seafood market that is also a gourmet specialty food shop.

Right at the Orange Beach Marina, Palms Bar & Grille (251-981-1416) and Calypso Joe's Caribbean Grille (251-981-1415), two of the area's most popular eateries, offer fine or casual dockside dining. Blalock's (251-974-5811), open all week and conveniently located on Canal Road (Highway 180), offers a daily seafood catch, plus succulent oysters and delicious shrimp, from local waters, as well as crawfish from Louisiana.

Some other waterside restaurants of note in Cotton Bayou include Tacky Jacks (251-981-4144) and Geno's Fresh Catch Grill (251-981-4044) with its lower-level eatery, Downunder. Several restaurants are at SanRoc Cay Marina, including Louisiana Lagniappe (251-981-2258), Café Grazie (251-981-7278) and North Shore Grill & Deli (251-981-8466). All are either on the water or immediately accessible. Franco's Italian Restaurant (251-981-9800) is at the other end of the Zeke's Landing parking lot, just off Perdido Beach Boulevard (Highway 182), which runs along the Gulf of Mexico and over the nearby Perdido Pass Bridge.

A mile down Perdido Beach Boulevard to the west of Cotton Bayou is Hazel's Seafood Restaurant (251-981-4628), a favorite for tourists and locals. Its varied cuisine includes breakfast, lunch and dinner buffets or a full-service menu.

Fatback's (251-974-3238), located at Sportsman Marina in Johnson Cove is the place for a drink, wonderful meal and the perfect end to the day. There are too many of these fine restaurants to name, but all are at the heart of Orange Beach.

The town's popular and famous Flora-Bama Lounge, Package/Oyster Bar (251-980-5118), at the Alabama/Florida line, is known affectionately as the "Ultimate Dive." The "bistro" has several local and visiting bands in various parts of the bar, playing a variety of music. The bar's owners are originators and major sponsors of the 10-day Frank Brown Songwriters' Festival, held every November. Songwriters from throughout the nation participate.

The watering hole also is internationally famous for its annual Mullet Toss, held the last full weekend in April (participants toss the fish across the state line). The very loosely held competition generally begins with a mullet toss by a celebrity, and thousands attend the event. On New Year's Day the Flora-Bama holds an annual "Southern-style" Polar Bear Swim and a foot race.

The Alabama Gulf Coast Area Chamber of Commerce coordinates the annual Shrimp Festival on the second weekend in October, drawing more than 200,000 people to Pleasure Island at the Gulf Shores Beach Boardwalk for four days of entertainment, savory foods and numerous booths featuring arts and crafts of all kinds. This beachside community of Gulf Shores shares Pleasure Island with Orange Beach and has numerous restaurants, nightclubs and shopping comparable to its neighboring city.

Relatively new to Orange Beach is the construction of a major multi-use development called The Wharf. This 222-acre development contains a 200-slip full-service marina on the GIWW (opened Memorial Day 2006 as part of Phase One of the development), a 10,000-seat amphitheater, a record-height Ferris wheel, several groups of condominiums, restaurants and other resort-style features.

Gulf State Park, on the fringe of the Gulf Shores city limits, has the largest freshwater lake nearest to saltwater in the nation. The park has hotel accommodations, cabins and campsites.

ADDITIONAL RESOURCES

■ Alabama Gulf Coast Convention and Visitors Bureau
www.gulfshores.com

⚑ **NEARBY GOLF COURSES**
Gulf State Park Golf,
20115 State Hwy. 135., Gulf Shores, AL 36542
251-948-7275, **www.alapark.com/GulfState/Golf/**

☤ **NEARBY MEDICAL FACILITIES**
South Baldwin Regional Medical Center,
1613 N. McKenzie St., Foley, AL 36535, 251-949-3400
www.southbaldwinrmc.com

Bear Point to Portage Creek

There are even more "must-see" spots off the GIWW, particularly for gunkholers. Many cruisers have a problem when they visit this bountiful area; they do not want to leave. Some who plan to stay for a week or so can only tear themselves away after several weeks. Some stay permanently.

NAVIGATION: Use Chart 11378. Reversing course toward the GIWW, as you leave Bayou St. John, you can safely cut across from green daybeacon "17" (which will now be on your port side) to GIWW flashing red "58" (leave to starboard, as you are back on the GIWW westbound).

The channel around Mill Point is well-marked, but it is narrow and shallow on the edges; a sharp watch is required here. Once in Arnica Bay, the channel opens up, particularly to starboard, before it closes down again off Hatchett Point at flashing red "68." From flashing red "68" to red daybeacon "90," the Waterway is relatively open through Bay La Launch, past Sapling Point and through the straight shot across Wolf Bay to red daybeacon "90," the entrance to Portage Creek.

Dockage: Curving around the green buoys off Bear Point into Arnica Bay, you will soon find Bear Point Marina (Mile 165 EHL) south of green daybeacon "65." This has traditionally been a favorite stopover for cruising boats, with 74 slips, 400 feet of alongside dockage outside the marina and 200 feet inside. Six-foot depths

Perdido Key, FL to Bon Secour Bay, AL

PERDIDO KEY TO BON SECOUR BAY		Dockage				Supplies					Services				
		Largest Vessel Accommodated	VHF Channel Monitored	Transient Berths / Total Berths	Approach / Dockside Depth (reported)	Floating Docks	Gas / Diesel	Groceries, Ice, Marine Supplies, Snacks	Repairs: Hull, Engine, Propeller	Lift (tonnage), Crane, Rail	1=110v, 2=220V, B=Both, Max Amps	Laundry, Pool, Showers	Pump-Out Station	Nearby: Grocery Store, Motel, Restaurant	
1. Pirates Cove Marina & Restaurant 165 EHL	251-987-1224	65		/16	10/10			I			1/30	LS	P	R	
2. Bear Point Marina 165 EHL 📶	251-981-2327	100	16	10/75	14/9		GD	GIS			B/50	LS	P	R	
3. Barber Marina 163 EHL 💻 📶	251-987-2628	125	16	30/155	12/12	F	GD	GIMS	HEP	L110	B/100	LS	P	
4. Sportsman Marina 167 EHL 💻 📶	251-981-6247	140	16/19	30/104	9/8		GD	GIMS	HEP	L25	B/50	LS	P	GMR
5. ORANGE BEACH MARINA 167 EHL 💻 📶	**251-981-4207**	130	16/69	30/170	9/8		**GD**	**GIMS**	**HEP**	**L80**	**B/100**	**LS**	**P**	**GMR**
6. SAUNDERS YACHTWORKS 167 EHL 📶	**251-981-3700**								HEP	L60	B/50			R
7. SanRoc Cay Marina 167 EHL	251-981-6167	150	16	75/75	5/5		GD	GIS			B/50	S	P	GMR
8. Zeke's Landing Marina 167 EHL	251-981-4044	100	69	4/50	7/7		GD	GIMS		L	1/50	LS	P	GMR

Corresponding chart(s) not to be used for navigation. 💻 Internet Access 📶 Wireless Internet Access

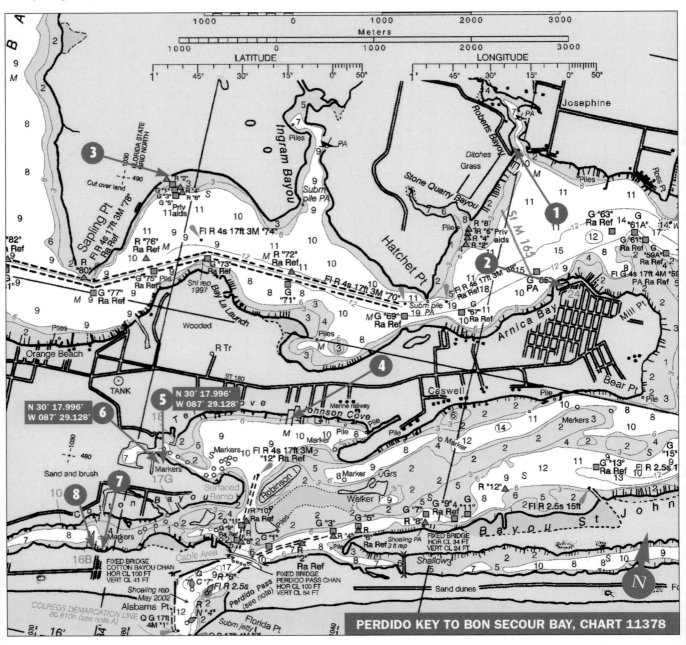

PERDIDO KEY TO BON SECOUR BAY, CHART 11378

Your Service Solution

The Saunders family has been in the marine service business since 1959, and operates **Yachtworks** at Orange Beach Marina. With 60 ton drydocking capacity, this yard offers a full array of factory authorized mechanical services and traditional boatyard crafts. Hundreds of customers, from Tampa to New Orleans, have discovered **Yachtworks'** professional attitude and capability is the solution to all their service needs.

800-392-2487
251-981-3700
saundersyacht.com

SAUNDERS
Yachtworks

MEMBER
ABYC
Setting Standards for Safer Boating

Gulf Shores, AL

GULF SHORES		Dockage					Supplies		Services				
		Largest Vessel Accommodated	VHF Channel Monitored	Transient Berths / Total Berths	Approach / Dockside Depth (reported)	Floating Docks	Gas / Diesel	Groceries, Ice, Marine Supplies, Snacks	Repairs: Hull, Engine, Propeller	Lift (tonnage), Crane, Rail	1=110v, 2=220v, B=Both, Max Amps	Laundry, Pool, Showers	Pump-Out Station	Nearby: Grocery Store, Motel, Restaurant
1. HOMEPORT MARINA 155 EHL ☐ WiFi	251-968-4528	100	16	15/76	7/7	F	GD	IS			B/100	LS	P	MR
2. The Marina at the Wharf 158.8 EHL WiFi	251-224-1900	150	16/68	30/210	10/10	F	GD	GIMS			B/100	P	P	GMR

Corresponding chart(s) not to be used for navigation. ☐ Internet Access WiFi Wireless Internet Access

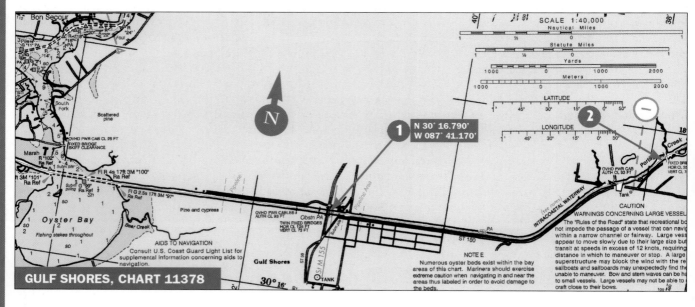

GULF SHORES, CHART 11378

N 30° 16.790'
W 087° 41.170'

prevail at dockside during normal tides. Gas and diesel fuel are available. There are restrooms, showers, laundry, a ship's store and a pump-out station. Mechanics and boat refinishers are available. You can anchor just to the west of the marina if you prefer and dinghy in.

A newer marina, Barber Marina, had its grand opening in 2009. Barber is located north off the GIWW (Mile 162.5) at red daybeacon "74."

Anchorage: Almost due north from Bear Point Marina, on the other side of Arnica Bay, is Roberts Bayou, commonly known both to cruisers and locals as "Pirates Cove." There is a narrow entrance with private markers leading to the bayou. While the narrow entrance may seem intimidating, a local sailing charter boat, the 50-foot former world cruiser, *Daedelus*, often transits the channel under sail. There is a spot at the mouth of Roberts Bayou and the end of the entrance channel that narrows to one boat width, so plan ahead.

You can dinghy to the Pirates Cove Marina Restaurant or tie up temporarily at a vacant dock next to the restaurant. It is very shallow at the gas dock; inquire before you try it. You will see the entrance to the marina docks and boatyard off to port as you approach the narrow cut into Roberts Bayou. There is a full-service boatyard with haul-out facilities, and some transient berths. Most of the

marinas in the Orange Beach/Bear Point area (and there are several small ones not listed here) welcome transients. Note that these are the last recreational boat marinas located on or near the GIWW east of New Orleans. Full-service marinas at Mobile, AL; Biloxi, MS; Gulfport, MS and Slidell, LA, all require side trips of up to 20 miles from the GIWW proper.

Roberts Bayou is also a popular anchorage for cruisers and locals, with about 8 feet of water and good holding ground. As in any anchorage that is or might be crowded, it is a good idea to buoy your anchor with a trip line, not only so someone will not drop their hook over your rode, but to prevent snarling and tangling in tight quarters. Permanent mooring lines are no longer permitted.

Ingram Bayou (Mile 164 EHL, due north of red daybeacon "72") is a true getaway for cruisers and locals who enjoy anchoring out. The bayou is about 1.5 miles west on the GIWW from Roberts Bayou. Turn right at red daybeacon "72," and then go straight into Ingram Bayou, right down the center. There is shoaling on either side of this excellent, all-weather anchorage, but 9-foot depths hold most of the way in.

Larger boats can find 8-foot depths just past the sharp bend to the left at the head of Ingram Bayou. You can anchor just about anywhere inside the bayou at around the same depths, but this is a favorite spot. Once inside, you will be surrounded by total greenery and quiet (except on a busy weekend), and there is usually a breeze to keep most of the bugs away.

There are also plenty of places to anchor in 5- to 8-foot depths at Wolf Bay, north of red daybeacon "84." This is a busy thoroughfare, so anchor appropriately.

Portage Creek

NAVIGATION: Use Chart 11378. At the western end of Wolf Bay, you will soon enter Portage Creek just after Mile 160 EHL. From here, proceed approximately seven nautical miles to Bon Secour Bay, which adjoins Mobile Bay.

At Mile 158.7 EHL is the Foley Beach Express Bridge and highway, the southern half built by the private sector as a hurricane escape route, and to allow easier automobile access to and from the Alabama Gulf Coast beaches. The northern half was built by the city of Foley, using a federal grant. This high-rise bridge, similar in appearance to Destin's Mid-Bay Bridge, has a 73-foot fixed vertical clearance.

Dockage: At this point, activity increases on the GIWW. Heading west, just past the Foley Beach Bridge at Mile 158.8 EHL, is the 200-slip Marina at The Wharf. In addition to the 200 floating slips, a variety of restaurants, shopping centers and condominiums are here.

Just about four nautical miles farther west on the GIWW, Homeport Marina is located at Mile 155.0 EHL just under the Highway 59 Bridge (73-foot fixed vertical clearance) with plenty of room for transients at its floating docks, along with gas and diesel fuel. LuLu's restaurant, operated by Lucy Buffett (Jimmy's sister), is located on-site. There is a 120-foot-long dock in front of the restaurant where you can tie up to if you are stopping to eat. Call 251-967-5858 to check availability. Plans call for the construction of three condominium buildings on the east, north and west sides of the marina.

A motel with slips for small boats is right on the canal's south side, directly east of the bridge, but if you should pull in there, be aware that there may be a strong current broadside (from either direction, depending on the tide) as you turn in.

A tugboat crew-change station and supply store is east of the bridge at Mile 154.9. There is an Idle-Speed/No-Wake Zone along this stretch. Shrimp boats and barges sometimes tie up to both banks east of the bridge to wait out inclement weather.

A note on communicating with barge tows: In virtually any marked channel, common courtesy, as well as safety, urges you to communicate with tows when you plan to pass. A common problem is that tugs often do not have their names on their transom, or anywhere a trailing vessel can identify a hailing name. In those cases, hail the tug on VHF Channel 13, and identify it by the direction, east or west, and the approximate mile marker or other identifying feature of the Waterway where you plan to pass, and identify yourself. Remember, the tug has a

much better view ahead, and experience with predicting and identifying a safe course. They appreciate the courtesy; you will, too. An (Automatic Identification System) AIS linked in with your chartplotter is very handy in the GIWW as it helps you see towboats pushing barges before they suddenly appear.

Bon Secour Bay

Immediately as you enter Bon Secour Bay, a well-marked channel leads north to the Bon Secour River and small Nelson's Marina, catering to shrimp boats and some pleasure craft. There is a haul-out facility there, but few amenities for cruisers. Watch out for several dangerous pilings immediately south of flashing green "135." Study your chart carefully before entering Mobile Bay, as there are numerous charted hazards.

The Waterway tracks west across lower Mobile Bay and crosses the Main Ship Channel at Mile 133.75 at flashing red buoy "26" on the channel. This is where the cruising sailor with plenty of time might want to change course, head north and sample some of the breezy bay's delights.

Dockage: Gulf Shores Yacht Club & Marina, located near Fort Morgan at the southeastern end of Mobile Bay, offers transient dockage, dry storage a fuel dock and an on-site restaurant, Tacky Jacks 2.

◼ MOBILE BAY

NAVIGATION: Use Chart 11376. The city of Mobile is a metropolis with a recently expanded and updated commercial waterfront, and since the completion of the Tennessee-Tombigbee Waterway in 1985, heavy barge traffic has greatly increased in the area, especially on the northern end near the mouth of the Mobile River. Opening of a cruise ship terminal has increased waterfront traffic and provided substantial financial support to historic downtown Mobile.

Cruisers should keep a sharp eye out for fast-moving tankers and cargo ships using the Mobile Bay Ship Channel. If you anchor out, be sure to stay well away from the buoyed channel and its traffic. The best and safest way to taste Mobile's ample pleasures is to stop at an outlying marina and tour the area by rental car or marina courtesy car (e.g. at one of the Dog River marinas, about 10 statute miles from downtown Mobile, or Fly Creek by Fairhope on the eastern shore).

There are numerous marinas around Mobile Bay. The bay itself can be roughly divided into the western shore and the eastern shore. Generally, western shore marinas are work-a-day marinas with good basic facilities but fewer frills, within convenient reach for a visit to downtown Mobile, either by rental car or marina courtesy car.

Eastern shore marinas, on the other hand, are more self-contained resort-type facilities (such as Marriott's Grand Hotel Resort & Golf Club at Point Clear) in more historic venues, such as the Fairhope area.

Mobile Bay—Western Shore

Dockage: Working clockwise around Mobile Bay from the southwest corner, Fowl River Marina appears first. The Fowl River Marina approach is three miles west of the Mobile Ship Channel from quick-flashing green "49." The channel entrance is between 17-foot flashing red "2" and green daybeacon "1." The channel is well-marked into the Fowl River. The marina is located half a mile upriver on the north side at red daybeacon "16," but before a 24-foot fixed vertical clearance highway bridge. Approach and dockside depths are 5 to 6 feet. Gas and diesel fuel are available at the floating fuel dock, with transient dockage for vessels up to 50 feet. There are restrooms, showers and a ship's store. Also, the on-site Pelican Reef Restaurant serves fresh seafood from its own boats daily.

The Dog River Channel (Chart 11376) leading from the Main Ship Channel normally carries 6-foot depths. Enter the channel at green daybeacon "1" and red daybeacon "2," between flashing green lights "63" and "65" in the Upper Reach of the Main Ship Channel. Hold dead center between Dog River Channel green daybeacon "1" and red daybeacon "2," steering 305 degrees magnetic. After clearing green daybeacon "5" and flashing red "6," alter course to 272 degrees magnetic, following markers to the high-rise bridge (73-foot fixed vertical clearance) at the entrance to the Dog River.

There is a cluster of four marinas on Dog River, off the west shore of Mobile Bay, roughly two-thirds of the way up the Ship Channel from the pass entering Mobile Bay and the city of Mobile. Two marinas are on each side of the river within 100 yards of the Dog River Bridge (73-foot fixed vertical clearance). Each has fuel and transient slips, and three of them have lifts. The approach depths to the marinas are 20 feet, and dockside depths range from 8 to 10 feet.

Beachcomber Marina is the first marina to port (south) after the bridge. It has transient dockage for vessels up to 100 feet (call ahead), restrooms, a 40-ton lift, full-service repairs and marine supplies.

Turner Marine Supply is about 150 yards past the bridge to starboard (north). It has transient dockage for vessels up to 150 feet (call ahead), restrooms, showers, laundry and a full-service boatyard.

Grand Mariner Marina, the second marina to port (south) after passing under the bridge, heading upriver, offers gas and diesel fuel, a pump-out station, an excellent restaurant and lounge (The Marina Restaurant) above the dockmaster's office, transient dockage for vessels up to 150 feet (call ahead), restrooms, showers, laundry, marine supplies and a 35-ton lift. The marina also has a 72-foot schooner, *Joshua*, for crewed charters on Mobile Bay. A courtesy car is also available. This is a really laid-back marina that has friendly staff.

Full-service Dog River Marina, to starboard (north), offers gas and diesel fuel, transient dockage (call ahead), restrooms, showers, laundry and a pump-out station. The marina has a 70-ton Travelift, which can handle a 22-foot beam. They also provide full-service repairs, a very complete West Marine store on the premises and a courtesy vehicle. This is a popular stop for transients so be sure to call ahead for reservations.

If you plan to transit north up the Tennessee-Tombigbee Waterway, a worthwhile marina is Winters Marina, north of the city on the Mobile River. This unique facility, which also serves as a secure hurricane hole, is about eight nautical miles up the river at the northwest end of the bay. You will find it 3.5 nautical miles off the Twelvemile Island channel by way of Bayou Sara and Gunnison Creek. (For complete and detailed navigation, dockage and anchorage information on the Tennessee-Tombigbee Waterway, see Waterway Guide's Great Lakes edition.)

Enter Sara Creek by holding to the right hand bank (northeast) at the swing bridge, which has a 3-foot closed vertical clearance, and go another three miles to Gunnison Creek, the third cut on the right after a set of power (lines 55-foot vertical clearance). Go a half mile to Winters Marina (there is no sign), where you will have about 20 feet of water. The marina has gas and diesel fuel, transient dockage (call ahead), restrooms, showers, engine and propeller repairs, marine supplies and groceries. A courtesy car is available and there is lodging nearby.

Mobile Bay—Eastern Shore

Resort-type marinas predominate Mobile Bay's eastern shore, a bit farther afield from the city of Mobile. These

Mobile Bay to Dauphin Island, AL

MOBILE BAY TO DAUPHIN ISLAND		Largest Vessel Accommodated	VHF Channel Monitored	Approach / Dockside Depth (reported) Transient Berths / Total Berths	Floating Docks	Gas / Diesel	Groceries, Ice, Marine Supplies, Snacks	Repairs: Hull, Engine, Propeller	Lift (tonnage), Crane, Rail	1=110V, 2=220V, B=Both, Max Amps	Laundry, Pool, Showers	Pump-Out Station	Nearby: Grocery Store, Motel, Restaurant
				Dockage			**Supplies**			**Services**			
1. Gulf Shores Yacht Club & Marina 135 EHL	251-540-2628	30	16	6/40	4/4	GD	GIMS		L10	1/30	LS		GR
2. Dauphin Island Marina 127.8 EHL	251-861-2201	65	16	5/150	6/8	GD	IMS			B/50		P	GMR
3. Marriott's Grand Hotel Resort & Golf Club	251-928-9201	115	16	8/34	6/5	GD	GIMS			1/50	PS	P	GMR
4. Fly Creek Marina 🖳 📶	251-928-4868	70	16	10/115	9/9		I			B/50	LS	P	GMR
5. Eastern Shore Marine Inc. 🖳	251-928-1283	80	16	7/65	8/7	GD	IM	HEP	L35	B/50	LS	P	GMR
6. Fowl River Marina	251-973-2696	50	16	3/60	5/5	F	GD	GIMS			B/50	S	P	R
7. **GRAND MARINER MARINA/RESTAURANT** 🖳 📶	**251-443-6300**	**155**	**16**	**15/85**	**15/9**	**GD**	**IMS**	**HEP**	**L30**	**B/50**	**LS**	**P**	**GR**
8. Beachcomber Marina	251-443-8000	100		15/70	9/16		IMS	HEP	L40	1/50			R
9. Turner Marine Supply Inc. 🖳	251-476-1444	100	16	20/150	9/9		M	HEP	L50, C2	B/30	LS	P	R
10. Dog River Marina 🖳 📶	251-471-5449	150	16	50/100	8/10	GD	IMS	HEP	L70	B/100	LS	P	GMR
11. Scenic Yacht Basin	251-479-5998	70		75/75	6/6					B/50	LS		

Corresponding chart(s) not to be used for navigation. 🖳 Internet Access 📶 Wireless Internet Access

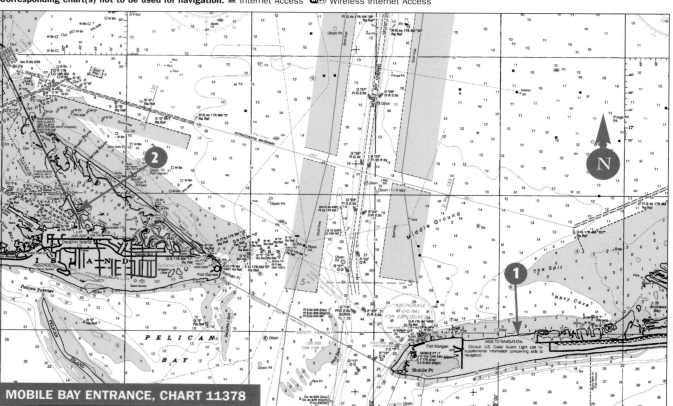

MOBILE BAY ENTRANCE, CHART 11378

are located from Seacliff to Point Clear near Mobile Bay's bluffs near Fairhope, which was originally founded by a gaggle of Marxists who were experimenting in communal living, but is now a quiet upscale residential community. It is a charming, quaint town with an impressive view of the bay and a lively arts scene. An annual arts and crafts show reportedly draws more than 200,000 people to the still-growing community, and is held in May each year.

Dockage: Fly Creek Marina is located at the entrance to Fly Creek at the town of Seacliff. Follow the Fly Creek Channel from Mobile Bay, holding to the south side until you are inside the breakwater; it is the first marina on the southeast side (to starboard on entering the creek). This 108-slip marina, similar to other eastern shore marinas, is heavily populated by sailboats. It is a neat, clean marina in a lovely wooded area, with an approach depth of 8 feet and dockside depths from 4 to 6 feet. There is transient dockage up to 80 feet, plus restrooms, showers and the Fly Creek Café, but no fuel dock or pump-out station.

Eastern Shore Marina is on the north side of the channel from Fly Creek Marina (to port on entering the channel). Eastern Shore Marina has 65 slips (45- and 60-foot covered

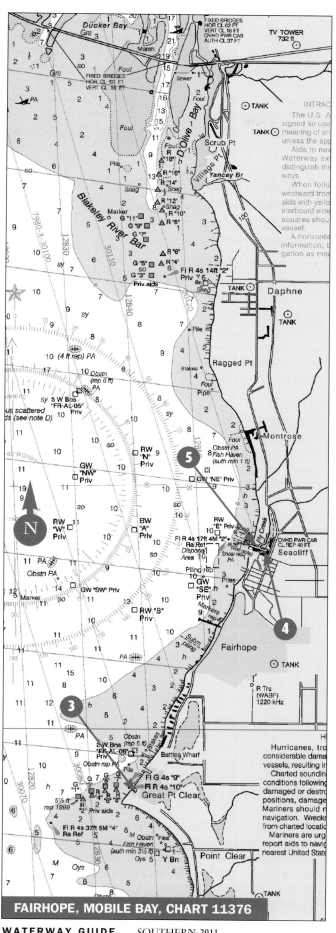

FAIRHOPE, MOBILE BAY, CHART 11376

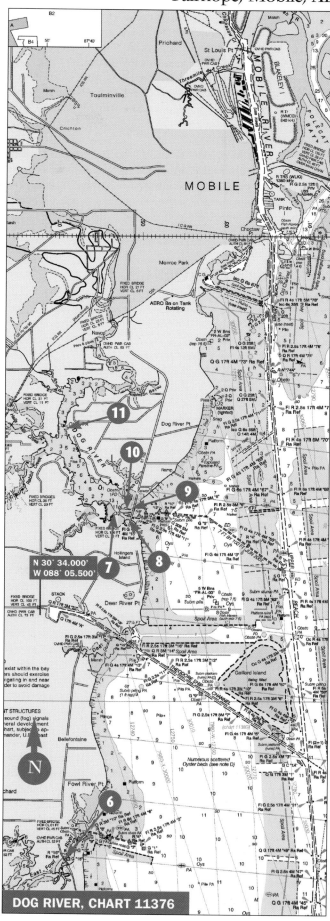

DOG RIVER, CHART 11376

Dauphin Island, AL

slips), a fuel dock with gas and diesel fuel, pump-out facilities and a courtesy car. They also have a 15-ton hydraulic crane as well as a full-service yard. The approach and dockside depths are 8 feet at mean low water.

The Fairhope Yacht Club is on the south side of the entrance. It welcomes transients of recognized yacht clubs and offers reciprocal privileges. The entire Yacht Club facility has been rebuilt and was reopened in August 2008 (call 251-928-3276).

To get to the Marriott's Grand Hotel Resort, Golf Club & Spa, use the charted Point Clear approach, and follow the daybeacons that line the entrance channel. The depth in the channel and in the harbor is at least 7 feet. Gas and diesel fuel, transient dockage for vessels up to 75 feet and courtesy transportation are available.

GOIN' ASHORE: **MOBILE, AL**

Mobile is a beautiful, historic port city. It is also a Coast Guard base for both sea and air. Upon arriving in Mobile, make Fort Conde Museum and Welcome Center your first stop so you can plan your itinerary. (Call 251-208-7304 for directions to the Welcome Center.)

The city of Mobile, on the western shore near the head of Mobile Bay, is a worthwhile tourist destination. A French nobleman, Pierre Le Moyne d'Iberville, established a settlement as the capital of the French colony of Louisiane (now the state of Louisiana) near the site of present Mobile. The settlement was abandoned a decade later, but Mobile ("moveable" in French) eventually sprang up to evolve into the significant and historic port it is today.

You can tour downtown Mobile by car, by foot, or by LoDa moda, an all-electric trolley. The city has charming old streets, ancient moss-draped live oaks and handsome French colonial architecture.

Mobile's historic houses, museums and theaters are very popular, and one of the major tourist attractions in the area is the splendid Bellingrath Gardens and Home, a 20-minute drive from the city. The site was the home in 1918 of Coca-Cola founder Walter Bellingrath. While initially utilized as a fishing camp, in 1935, Bessie Bellingrath transformed the estate into a garden that now covers 65 acres.

Step back in time as you tour the 15-room house, complete with period furniture, oriental rugs and other antique treasures acquired during a tour of Europe. Also included in the tour is a nature walk on a boardwalk through Southern Bayou where birds, fish, turtles, deer and even alligators appear. In addition, you can enjoy a cruise on the Fowl River aboard the Southern Belle River Cruiser. (Note that in summer/fall 2010, these cruises were cancelled as the owner was helping in the Gulf clean-up effort.)

Other attractions of note are the Mobile Museum of Art, the largest art museum along the Gulf Coast from New Orleans to Tampa, and the USS Alabama Battleship Memorial Park where you can tour the World War II battleship, USS Drum submarine, a Vietnam river patrol boat and historic aircraft. And do not forget famous, historic Dauphin Street, with its many restaurants ranging from fine dining to Cajun, to Tex-Mex and seafood. Some of the fine clothing stores have closed, but such progressive moves as the establishment of the Cruise Ship Center may help refurbish this historic area.

Mobile has sponsored Mardi Gras celebrations since 1703, longer than the more famous Mardi Gras in New Orleans.

In the spring during the annual Azalea Festival, you can take an "Azalea Tour" through the 37 miles of beautiful, blooming flora that abounds throughout the city's historic area.

ADDITIONAL RESOURCES

■ Mobile Bay Convention and Visitors Bureau
   www.mobile.org

 NEARBY GOLF COURSES
   Gulf Pines Golf Course, 167 Old Bay Front Dr.,
   Mobile, AL 36615, 251-431-6413

 NEARBY MEDICAL FACILITIES
   South Baldwin Regional Medical Center,
   1613 N. McKenzie St., Foley, AL 36535, 251-949-3400
   www.southbaldwinrmc.com

Dauphin Island—Mile 130 EHL

On the west side of the entrance to Mobile Bay, Dauphin Island, with its long sandy spit to the west, is the first of the barrier islands running from Mobile Bay to New Orleans. Of the many recreational and boating centers in the Mobile area, Dauphin Island is the closest to the GIWW. Dauphin Island is a pleasant and interesting stopover, with a sizable marina, anchorages along the entire length of the island and excellent beaches.

The island, now a scenic destination and bird sanctuary, was originally called "Massacre" by the French, who found a number of human skeletons there when they first landed; their origin remains a mystery.

Dauphin Island is now home to Fort Gaines, once a Confederate stronghold used to defend the east entrance to Mobile Bay. Now a historic site and museum, it can be explored daily, except Thanksgiving and Christmas. Every year, Fort Gaines hosts a variety of theme weekends, such as Civil War reenactments. Call for details: Dauphin Island Park and Beach Board (251-861-3607).

The island is also home to Dauphin Island Sea Lab, Alabama's marine education and research center. The lab operates the Estuarium, an extensive public aquarium, displaying features of coastal Alabama's ecosystems: the Delta, Mobile Bay and the Gulf of Mexico. For more information call 251-861-2141.

NAVIGATION: Use Chart 11378. Heading west, about 4.5 nautical miles after the GIWW crosses the Main Ship Channel entering Mobile Bay, you will pass under the Dauphin Island Bridge (Mile 127.8 EHL, 83-foot fixed vertical clearance), which replaced the original bridge destroyed by Hurricane Frederick in 1979.

Dauphin Island. Photo Courtesy of Mobile Bay Convention & Visitors Bureau.

Dockage: The only marina here, Dauphin Island Marina, is a 150-slip, full-service facility welcoming transients. The marina has gas and diesel fuel and a ship's store. Nearby there are restaurants, a post office, a bank and groceries. The marina has two approaches.

From the east, go south on the Mobile Ship Channel (south of the GIWW) to flashing green buoy "23," then steer 236 degrees magnetic for about one nautical mile, where you will pick up quick flashing green "1" and red daybeacon "2" marking the entrance to the Fort Gaines/Pelican Point Channel, known locally as "Billy Goat Hole." The U.S. Coast Guard station is located here, as is the terminal for the Dauphin Island/Fort Morgan Ferry.

The Coast Guard station and ferryboat dock are just inside the entry. The winding two-mile route to the marina is privately marked and maintained and hugs the southwest side of Dauphin Bay; birds walk in the middle among 1- to 2-foot depths. Channel depths are charted at 5 feet, with a dockside depth of 6 feet. The marina provides transient dockage for vessels up to 65 feet, restrooms, motels, restaurants, provisions and supplies. (It would be prudent to call ahead for reservations and the latest information on markers and water depths.)

From the west on the GIWW, if you can clear a bridge with a fixed vertical clearance of 25 feet, Dauphin Island Marina is reportedly reached by leaving the Waterway at Mile 126 EHL (just before entering Pass Aux Herons Channel), and turning south at flashing green "21," marked on the chart as 2+1, on a course of about 120 degrees magnetic.

After less than a mile, pick up green daybeacon "1" (leave to port) and flashing red "2" (leave to starboard) indicating the channel to Dauphin Island. After green daybeacon "3," watch for green daybeacon "1," the start of the channel, and then head toward the 25-foot fixed vertical clearance bridge. Carefully follow the daybeacons to the bridge, as the channel is in the middle of an extensive shoal area. Immediately past the bridge, after entering Dauphin Bay, turn to starboard to the privately maintained markers leading half a nautical mile to the marina.

Anchorage: Dauphin Island has many fine anchorages along its whole length, which are protected from southerly winds, but not from the north. The anchorage on the eastern end of the island, while well-protected and marked, is usually occupied by commercial boats, whose lights and noise can disturb your sleep. It is, however, within dinghy distance of a store and restaurant and bar. Hurricane Rita broke through the middle of Dauphin Island, leaving a breach in the island. Keep this in mind when deciding where to anchor.

■ MISSISSIPPI GULF COAST

West of Mobile Bay, the GIWW opens up to the Mississippi Sound, a bay-like expanse of water between the mainland and a string of barrier islands known as the Gulf Islands National Seashore. Navigating this part of the GIWW is much more like being in a large bay or perhaps even offshore—land on each side is barely visible. While shoreside facilities in this area are limited, the number and quality of destinations is growing rapidly, both from the popularity of the area as well as the rebuilding effort from hurricanes Ivan and Katrina. Anchorage is often available in the lee of the Gulf Islands during warm weather months when a South wind prevails.

Pleasure boaters should keep in mind that traveling west from this point will increase the frequency of encounters with commercial vessels, most often towboats. Give these vessels a wide berth at idle speeds, particularly in shallower

Biloxi, MS to Bay St. Louis, MS

BILOXI TO BAY ST. LOUIS		Largest Vessel Accommodated	VHF Channel Monitored	Transient Berths / Total Berths	Approach / Dockside Depth (reported)	Floating Docks	Groceries, Ice, Marine Supplies, Snacks	Gas / Diesel	Repairs: Hull, Engine, Propeller	Lift (tonnage), Crane, Rail	1=110V, 2=220V, B=Both, Max Amps	Laundry, Pool, Showers	Pump-Out Station	Nearby: Grocery Store, Motel, Restaurant
				Dockage				**Supplies**				**Services**		
1. Jackson County Small Craft Harbor 88 EHL	228-872-5754	60		12/178	8/8			GD			/30			GMR
2. Schooner Pier Complex 88 EHL	228-435-6320					F	I				B/100		P	GMR
3. Point Cadet Marina 88 EHL	228-436-9312	100	16	20/300	12/10	F	IMS	GD			B/100	LS	P	MR
4. D & H Three Rivers Marine 73 EHL (WiFi)	228-863-2700	200		/90	13/9	F	GIMS	GD	HEP	L70,C	/30	LS	P	GMR
5. Bay Marina/RV Park/Lodging 55 EHL [internet]	228-466-4970	50	16	10/75	5/5		IMS	GD	HEP		/30	LS	P	GMR

Corresponding chart(s) not to be used for navigation. [icon] Internet Access (WiFi) Wireless Internet Access

OCEAN SPRINGS, BILOXI, CHART 11372

waters and narrow channels. As suggested earlier, it is advisable to monitor both VHF Channels 13 and 16.

NAVIGATION: Use Charts 11378 and 11372. From Mobile Bay, the GIWW passes through Pass Aux Herons Channel and then enters Mississippi Sound. When leaving the channel at Mile 124 EHL, most markers are lighted and elevated, although some are as many as four miles apart. The GIWW is about five miles from the shoreline, which is often out of sight. Pay close attention to compass headings and position fixes on the long run between markers. The next 70 or more miles are a long and only partially protected passageway. Also, in sharp contrast with the GIWW to the east, there is a rapid change from crystal clear water and white sand beaches to the murky water and brown sand of the Mississippi coastline. The 60-foot depth line, which is within a few miles of the Alabama and Florida coast, is many miles offshore of Petit Bois and Horn islands and then takes a southern swing to the mouth of the Mississippi River.

A difficult area is the dogleg between Mile 98 (as the channel turns northwest) at quick flashing green "3" and flashing red "2" and Mile 96 (where the channel turns west again) at flashing green "5." Watch your depth sounder or follow a commercial vessel through this narrow channel with a hard bottom. This is between Round Island to the northeast and Middle Ground shoals to the southwest.

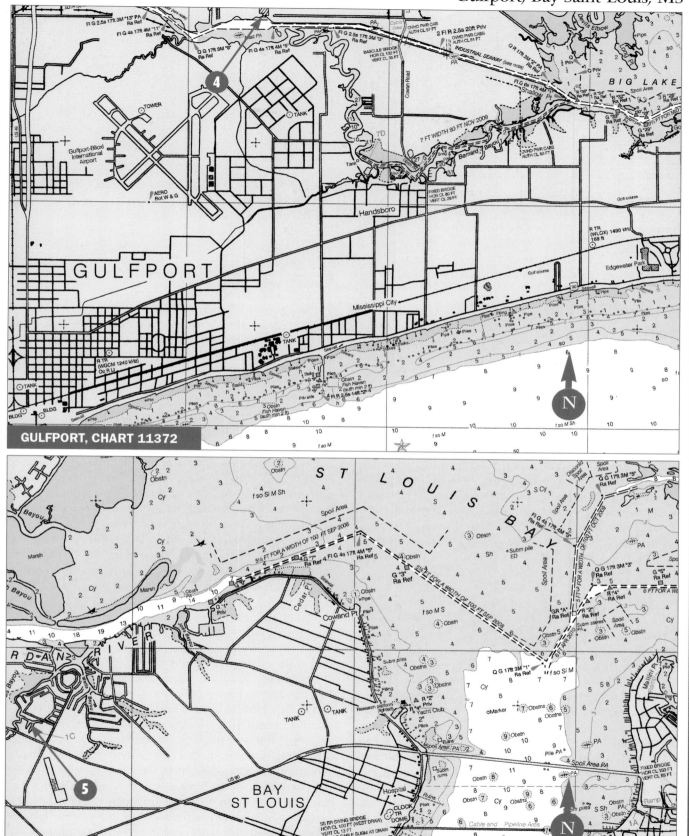

GULFPORT, CHART 11372

BAY SAINT LOUIS, CHART 11372

A sailboat and a powerboat docked at a pier in Biloxi, Mississippi on a calm overcast day. ©IstockPhoto/DenGuy

Pascagoula Area

Pascagoula is primarily a commercial shipping port, but recreational interest has grown in recent years. A marina was added to this area in 2006—the River City Harbor Marina in Moss Point (228-475-9200)—about 15 miles north of the GIWW along the Pascagoula River. The facility has fuel (gas and diesel), pump-out and an on-site restaurant. Also off of the Pascagoula River is the Mary Walker Marina (228-497-3141), catering mostly to sport-fishermen, but welcoming to transients of all kinds. Mary Walker Marina has 200 slips, a fuel dock with gas and diesel pumps, and ship store. Two seafood restaurants are on-site as well. The marina is located on Mary Walker Bayou one mile northwest of the Highway 90 bridge crossing at the Escatawpa River. Depths in the river can go as low as 7 feet at mean low tide—deep keel sailing vessels are urged to take caution.

■ BILOXI, MS

Ocean Springs

The Mississippi resort coast begins at Biloxi Bay. Ocean Springs is on the eastern shore, with Biloxi to the west. Biloxi is only two miles away across Biloxi Bay. Ocean Springs is noted for its art galleries that line the streets, several museums, boutique shops, restaurants and outside cafes, a few of which are walking distance from the marina.

Dockage: Jackson County Small Craft Harbor welcomes transient boaters and is one of the few facilities in coastal Mississippi to survive Hurricane Katrina. Note that entrance channel depths can go down to 6 feet at low tide. Adjacent to the harbor is Harbor Landing, which houses a fuel dock (gas and diesel), a restaurant, and a ship's store. For dinner or lunch try Alberti's for fine Italian dining, a complete wine list and a full-service bar. For more information on upcoming events, call the Oceans Springs Chamber of Commerce at 228-875-4424.

Across the ship channel from Ocean Springs is Biloxi, a world-class vacation destination with Las Vegas-style gambling resorts, restaurants, continuous nightlife and entertainment of all types. These amenities are within walking distance of several full-service marinas. Marine supplies, groceries, a post office and a library are nearby.

NAVIGATION: Use Charts 11378 and 11372. At Mile 88 EHL, follow the Biloxi Ship Channel into Biloxi Bay, and turn to port at green daybeacon "35" and quick flashing red "26." Do not drift outside the channel, as the water depth is 2 to 4 feet on the edges with an oyster shell bottom. Deer Island is south of the channel. Heading west-southwest, the channel opens up to the Biloxi waterfront and many marine facilities at red daybeacon "26."

Eastbound cruisers can return to the GIWW along the Biloxi Ship Channel as mentioned above. Westbound cruisers can save some time by continuing along the Biloxi Channel extending east to west along the city and then changing direction to the south toward the GIWW. From the Biloxi waterfront, travel west to flashing red "12," and then turn south to green daybeacon "5" and flashing red "6." This section of the channel is 150 feet wide and 6 feet deep with a soft mud bottom.

Dockage: Casinos are located all along the coast from Biloxi to Bay St. Louis; one of the newest and most opulent is the Beau Rivage Resort and Casino. Along with full-service amenities, you can enjoy casual and fine dining in several theme restaurants, world-class entertainment, a swimming pool, health spa, fitness center and, of course, around-the-clock gambling. Hurricane Katrina heavily damaged Beau Rivage, completely destroying the marina. The hotel and casino have been reopened and expanded, including a new Tom Fazio-designed golf course. A decision is still pending with Beau Rivage management on the reopening of the marina.

The Biloxi Small Craft Harbor is operational with 141 slips and a newly dredged harbor and fuel dock offering both gas and diesel.

The Point Cadet Marina, at the eastern tip of Biloxi, offers transient berths for vessels up to 65 feet. The marina building was destroyed during Hurricane Katrina, but was going to reopen by June 2010. When the renovation is completed, the marina will have expanded capacity of 270 fixed docks, including newer, larger slips for vessels up to 65 feet plus showers and laundry facilities.

The Schooner Pier Complex, half a mile west of Point Cadet, was constructed in June 2006 and includes a dozen or more transient slips as part of the Maritime & Seafood Industry Museum facility. It includes a laundry, restrooms, a small gift shop and two pavilions on a pier extending from the beach. Free wireless Internet access is also offered to guests. This complex is walking distance to several casinos and will be directly adjacent to the new Margaritaville Casino and Resort scheduled to open in 2012. It is also the home base of the two historic Biloxi Schooners—replicas of turn-of-the-century oyster ships that make daily sails around Mississippi Sound.

Back Bay of Biloxi

NAVIGATION: Use Chart 11372. The Biloxi Ship Channel continues north into Back Bay of Biloxi and three bridges cross the channel. The first is the Interstate 90 Highway Bridge with a fixed 90-foot vertical clearance. (This much higher span replaced the bascule bridge destroyed by Katrina in 2005.) The second is an abandoned bridge (now used as a fishing pier) with channel sections removed, and the third is a railroad swing bridge with a 14-foot closed vertical clearance, which opens on signal. The Back Bay of Biloxi is an excellent, protected anchorage, but has few marinas with transient service.

GOIN' ASHORE: BILOXI, MS

Originally inhabited by American Indians known as Biloxis ("first people"), the French first occupied and governed Biloxi in 1699. In 1763, the French ceded its territory east of the Mississippi River to the English, who controlled the territory until 1779. Spain took over soon after and governed the Mississippi coast until 1810. During a revolution against the Spaniards, the Anglo-Americans took control of Biloxi, which then became part of the short-lived Republic of West Florida. Most of the early settlers planted crops, built boats, raised cattle and lived a fairly peaceful co-existence with the native Indians.

From 1815 to 1850, Biloxi slowly evolved from an undeveloped area into a summertime resort community for affluent Southerners. In 1969, Hurricane Camille devastated the Mississippi coastline and destroyed much of Biloxi. Years of rebuilding followed, and in 1992, the state of Mississippi legalized dockside gaming. Since Biloxi was already a popular waterfront vacation spot, major casinos were built, and the local economy exploded.

Biloxi is one of the largest processors of shrimp and oysters in the world. Testaments to its fishing history are found in the Maritime and Seafood Industry Museum with special exhibits such as boatbuilding, net making, sailmaking and marine blacksmithing. The Biloxi Seafood Museum (228-435-6320) offers a film on Hurricane Camille and takes you back to a time when Biloxi was home to the largest seafood industry in the world. Visit the Maritime and Seafood Industry Museum Web site at www.maritimemuseum.org for more information.

The Biloxi Visitor Center (228-374-3105), located near the Biloxi Small Craft Harbor in the Brielmaier House (circa 1895), is open Monday through Friday, 8 a.m. to 4:30 p.m., and 9 a.m. to 5 p.m. on Saturday. This quaint center offers a walking tour, which takes less than an hour, or you can stay longer in the museums, shops and restaurants, which wind through the city's history dating back to 1699. The friendly, knowledgeable visitor center staff will direct you to many interesting sites along the tree-lined streets of Biloxi. A trolley travels along the scenic streets and makes many stops along the way. Visitors who want a little exercise should try the walking tour, which visits 17 historic sites, including Biloxi's Main Street District; the tour starts at the Biloxi Visitor Center. Don't forget the spectacular waterfront fireworks every Friday night during the summer.

Another popular visit is the Ohr-O'Keefe Museum of Art (228-374-5547), which houses a permanent collection of pottery by George E. Ohr, the "Mad Potter of Biloxi." The museum is also home to the Lila Wallace Gallery, featuring national and international art exhibits, and the Jambalaya Galley, which showcases local artists.

A treat for history buffs, Beauvoir, the Jefferson Davis Home & Presidential Library, allows a visit to a bygone era. The estate includes a library, antebellum home, Confederate museum and veteran's cemetery on 50 landscaped acres fronting the Gulf of Mexico. Beauvoir is located at 2244 Beach Blvd. It is open 9 a.m. to 5 p.m., March through October, and 9 a.m. to 4 p.m., November through February. There is a charge for admission.

Mississippi ranks third in gambling in the United States, trailing only Nevada and New Jersey. Casinos are open 24 hours a day, seven days a week, and offer a variety of dining experiences, along with excellent entertainment. The newest addition is the Jimmy Buffett/Harrah's joint project, Margaritaville Casino and Resort, located between the Schooner Pier Complex and Point Cadet on Beach Blvd, scheduled to open in 2012. A shuttle bus makes a continuous loop around the Biloxi casinos for a fare of $1 per person.

Though not created by Mother Nature, the Biloxi Beach is covered with beautiful white sand, which is brought in yearly from other sources to improve the "beach experience." For complete information about the tourist attractions, contact the Mississippi Gulf Coast Convention & Visitors Bureau (800-237-9493).

ADDITIONAL RESOURCES

■ **Mississippi Gulf Coast Convention & Visitors Bureau**
800-237-9493, www.gulfcoast.org

⚑ **NEARBY GOLF COURSES**
Gulf Hills Golf Course, 13700 Paso Road, Ocean Springs, MS 39564, 228-872-9663
www.gulfhillsgolf.com

⚕ **NEARBY MEDICAL FACILITIES**
Biloxi Regional Medical Center, 150 Reynoir St., Biloxi, MS 39530, 228-432-1571

Gulfport, MS

Ship Island—South of Mile 76 EHL

Located about 4.5 miles south of the GIWW at Mile 76 EHL, Ship Island is an attractive destination for history, recreation and relaxation. Its white sandy beaches are the best east of New Orleans, and offer great swimming and shelling. USA Today has named the beach areas here among the top 10 beaches in the United States.

Many colonists took their first steps on American soil at Ship Island. During the War of 1812, British troops and warships used the island as a staging area before their attempt to capture New Orleans, and in 1862, the Union fleet used the island to stage battles to capture New Orleans and Mobile during the Civil War. Fort Massachusetts, named in honor of a Union warship, has been reconstructed much as it was remembered from over 100 years ago. Guided tours are available.

In 1969, Hurricane Camille's 200-mph winds and 30-foot tides cut Ship Island in two, creating what is now known as East and West Ship islands. The latter is nearly four miles long with a natural white sand beach where the Mississippi Sound meets the Gulf of Mexico. This is a popular tourist destination, with boats from the coast making daily trips from March through October. The charter boats have priority at Ship Island's only pier, so space is limited.

Anchorage: The best anchorage is on either side of the Ship Island pier in 5 to 15 feet over a sand bottom, secure in east to southwesterly winds, with temporary daytime dockage at the pier. Transient vessels should note signs on the pier designating space reserved for ferry vessels. During the summer months, an open cold-water shower, and a snack bar are available at the concession stand near Fort Massachusetts. Picnic tables, a shade shelter, and umbrellas are available on the island, which was the target of substantial refurbishment in 2010. A newly constructed boardwalk will lead from the pier to the South side of the island—the beach facing the open Gulf. Pets must be on a leash when ashore and glass containers are prohibited. Overnight dockage is not allowed on the island pier, but overnight camping is allowed on the adjacent island to the East (these used to be connected before Katrina).

■ GULFPORT TO LOUISIANA

Gulfport—North of Mile 73 EHL

Located 13 miles west of Biloxi, Gulfport features casinos, restaurants, museums and the ferry to Ship Island—all near marinas. Take a bus or taxis to the mall and outlet stores on Interstate 49, about 3.5 miles north of the harbor.

NAVIGATION: Use Charts 11372 and 11367. At Mile 73 EHL, travel northwest for six miles until you reach Gulfport. Pass between flashing green "43" and flashing red "44," and then travel along Gulfport Shipping Channel to flashing red "62." From here, follow the channel markers into the Gulfport Small Craft Harbor, just east of the commercial harbor.

Dockage: D & H's Three Rivers Marina is a full-service marina and boatyard that offers gas and diesel fuel, floating docks, showers, ship's store, wireless Internet access and a pump-out station. Reconstruction of the floating docks and shoreside facilities was completed. There is also an adjacent restaurant. Three Rivers is located in the Back Bay at the end of the Industrial Seaway one mile due north of Gulfport Regional Airport. Gulfport Small Craft Harbor, also known as Bert Jones Yacht Basin, was devastated by Hurricane Katrina. Plans are underway to rebuild the entire marina and port complex to include additional slips, shops and restaurants.

Pass Christian—North of Mile 60 EHL

NAVIGATION: Use Chart 11372. From GIWW Mile 54 EHL, at the junction of Marianne Channel and the Grand Island Channel, travel five miles north to flashing red "2" (west side of Square Handkerchief Shoal) and then 2.5 miles to the railroad swing bridge (13-foot closed vertical clearance), which is followed by the Interstate 90 Highway Bridge (85-foot vertical clearance). The original bascule bridge was another casualty of Hurricane Katrina in 2005.

Dockage: Pass Christian Small Craft Harbor has completed numerous repairs since Hurricane Katrina. Shore power and water have been restored. Approximately eight slips are available for transients, for vessels up to 50 feet. The new fuel dock has been completed, offering both gas and diesel fuel. Ice is also available. A restaurant has been opened next to the harbor, The Harbor View Cafe.

Officials in Pass Christian have announced plans to construct a brand new harbor just east of the existing Small Craft Harbor. This new harbor will have capacity for 420 floating slips for vessels up to 60 feet in length.

Bay St. Louis—North of Mile 55 EHL

At the western entrance to St. Louis Bay, the town of Bay St. Louis is the last of the Mississippi coastal resorts. In Bay St. Louis, visiting shallow-draft vessels will find many suitable anchorages and fine fishing.

The John C. Stennis Space Center (where NASA does research work) offers free tours, but you will need ground transportation to get there. It is well worth the trip for those who are interested in the technical side of space travel.

Dockage: The Bay St. Louis Yacht Club (founded in the early 1950s) is located on the west side, just north of the bridge. The Bay Marina is located just north of the casino on Edward's Bayou, offering 18 transient slips for vessels up to 50 feet (15-foot beam and under) and gas and diesel fuel. Groceries and restaurants are nearby. Courtesy transportation to the two nearby casinos-—The Hollywood Casino and The Silver Slipper—is also available. The marina also hosts a ship store, laundry, restrooms, showers, and free wireless Internet access. Shore power consists of dual 30-amp connections at each post. A full service marine repair facility is situated on the property.

The city of Bay St. Louis announced plans in 2009 to construct a new marina near the Old Town district.

Mississippi River to Venice, LA

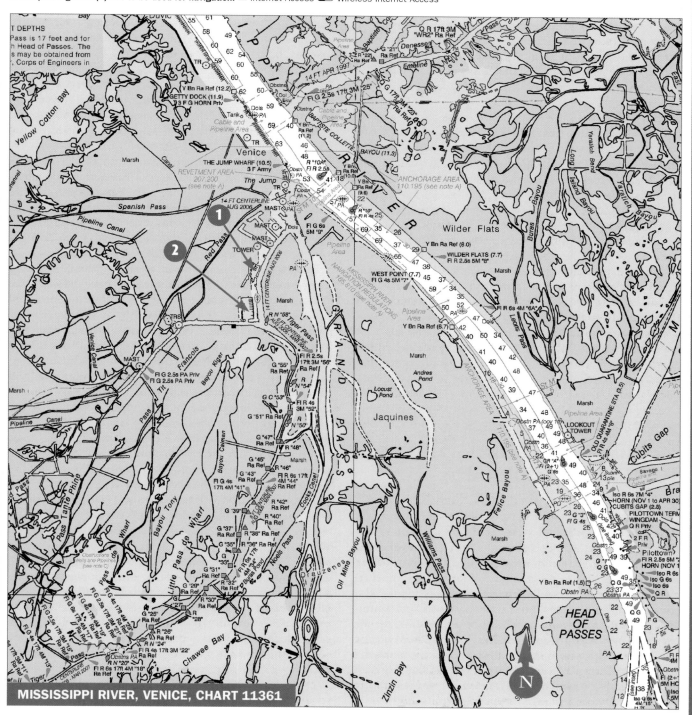

MISSISSIPPI RIVER TO VENICE		Dockage					Supplies		Services				
		Largest Vessel Accommodated	VHF Channel Monitored	Transient Berths / Total Berths	Approach / Dockside Depth	Floating Docks	Gas / Diesel	Groceries, Ice, Marine Supplies, Snacks	Repairs: Hull, Engine, Propeller	Lift (tonnage), Crane, Rail	1=110V, 2=220V, B=Both, Max Amps	Laundry, Pool, Showers	Pump-Out Station	Nearby: Grocery Store, Motel, Restaurant
1. Cypress Cove Marina Inc. ⌨	504-534-9289	120	16	40/150	8/10	F	GD	GIMS	HEP		B/50	L	P	GMR
2. Venice Marina ⌨	504-534-9357	100	16	30/110	10/8	F	GD	GIMS		C	B/50			

Corresponding chart(s) not to be used for navigation. ⌨ Internet Access 🛜 Wireless Internet Access

MISSISSIPPI RIVER, VENICE, CHART 11361

Venice, LA

This is on the West bank of the bay near the base of the railroad bridge. Plans call for 190 slips accommodating vessels to 60 feet in length. Restrooms and a fuel dock are also planned at the site. Construction began in 2010 with no estimated date of completion.

Bayou Caddy, located along the shoreline just a few miles west of Bay St. Louis and Waveland, is mostly a commercial fishing port. Carefully follow the 50-foot-wide channel (5.5-foot depths) into the bayou, which itself has 6-foot depths. The atmosphere is very friendly toward visiting pleasure boaters. Many interesting hours can be spent watching the commercial and private fishermen as they come and go.

Heron Bay, just northwest of Lighthouse Point and north of flashing green "3," may look like a good anchorage or fishing hole, but note its shallow depths. The many fishing boats you see are of the Lafitte skiff type, which draws less than 2 feet.

Pearl River

NAVIGATION: Use Chart 11367. The Pearl River can be entered from the GIWW just east of Mile 40. The entrance marks start with flashing green "1," which also serves as a borderline between Mississippi and Louisiana. At last report, the railroad swing bridge (14-foot closed vertical clearance) at Baldwin Lodge operated on horn signal only. The Pearl River offers many anchorage opportunities, but you need to choose carefully. Old Pearl River branches into two different Middle Rivers and provides numerous quiet, isolated anchorages and scenic cruising. Pearl River extends past the state Route 90 Swing Bridge (10-foot closed vertical clearance) and the Interstate 10 Bridge (73-foot fixed vertical clearance). The river depth is a reported 12 feet. Little Lake and East Pass, which divert from the Pearl River at quick-flashing green "21," return to the Rigolets and become part of the Lake Ponchartrain/New Orleans chapter.

■ OFFSHORE RUN— MISSISSIPPI SOUND TO VENICE, LOUISIANA

(Editor's Note: At the time this Guide was going to press in summer 2010, the long-term effects of the oil rig explosion offshore were only beginning to be felt. You will want to check our Web site, www.waterwayguide.com, before transiting this area.)

For those wishing to bypass New Orleans for the fast run to the west, an offshore run from Mississippi Sound to a stopping point in Venice may be a viable option for those cruisers with ranges of at least 200 miles. Venice is strategically situated at the head of several passes of the Mississippi River as it empties into the Gulf of Mexico, allowing both a protected anchorage and a shortcut to the Gulf of Mexico west of Mississippi.

There are two possible routes. First, in good weather, from Mobile Bay at red and white Morse (A) buoy "M," set a heading of 228 degrees to the sea buoy "NO," a distance of about 62 nautical miles. This will place you in the safety fairway for the entire route—recommended, as there are numerous oilfield structures as you enter Louisiana state waters. From Morse (A) buoy "NO," pick up the first set of red and green markers ("2" and "1," respectively) off the Mississippi Gulf Outlet Channel, which will direct you to the northwest. This channel ultimately meets up with the GIWW just east of the Industrial Canal.

The second alternative route can be used in more challenging weather conditions, although no routes are completely immune from swells caused by strong onshore flows common to this part of the Gulf. Stay in the GIWW until the western end of Horn Island. Head south to green can "3" and a series of markers directing you past Horn Island, visible off your port side via Dog Keys Pass. Head southwesterly on a course to the head of Baptiste Collette. You will travel in the lee of the Chandeleur Islands in depths of 10 to 15 feet. Look for the head markers of the Baptiste Collette Bayou, markers "1" and "2," which will lead a southwesterly direction to the Mississippi River. The bayou is well-marked and has good depths due to its primary use as a channel for commercial traffic. This route is strewn with oil platforms and wrecks and should only be attempted with good daylight and the latest charts and navigational equipment.

Dockage: One mile downstream in the Mississippi River to starboard is the entrance to Tiger Pass and the center of Venice, which is considered one of the finest sportfishing centers in the United States. In Venice there are two marina choices: The Venice Marina was reopened in fall 2006 after Katrina, offering fuel (gas and diesel) and a restaurant. The other is Cypress Cove Marina, adjacent to a small hotel, which also includes a restaurant. Both of these marinas are on the west bank of Tiger Pass and can accommodate large (50-foot and greater) vessels.

Next, coverage begins back on the GIWW at Mile 34 EHL and leads on into New Orleans with the Lake Pontchartrain/New Orleans section. ■

WATERWAY GUIDE is always open to your observations from the helm. E-mail your comments on any navigation information in the guide to: editor@waterwayguide.com.

WATERWAY GUIDE advertising sponsors play a vital role in bringing you the most trusted and well-respected cruising guide in the country. Without our advertising sponsors, we simply couldn't produce the top-notch publication now resting in your hands. Next time you stop in for a peaceful night's rest, let them know where you found them—WATERWAY GUIDE, The Cruising Authority.

Lake Pontchartrain, New Orleans

CHARTS 11352, 11367, 11368, 11369, 11370, 11371

The most popular route for recreational boaters westbound for a stay in New Orleans is to depart the Gulf Intracoastal Waterway (GIWW) just prior to Mile 35 EHL (East of Harvey Lock), enter the Rigolets ("rig-o-lees") via the railroad swing bridge (11-foot closed vertical clearance) and follow this passage to Lake Pontchartrain. The Rigolets (from the French word "rigolet," meaning "little canal") is not hard to traverse, with mostly deep water and plenty of width—but strong currents can be a problem at times. The distance from the GIWW to the marinas at West End, New Orleans is 35 miles, with other marinas along the route and on the north side of Lake Pontchartrain.

The GIWW route to New Orleans is the preferred route if proceeding west on the Waterway, or if the weather in Lake Pontchartrain is dubious. The distance to West End New Orleans is about the same as via the Rigolets.

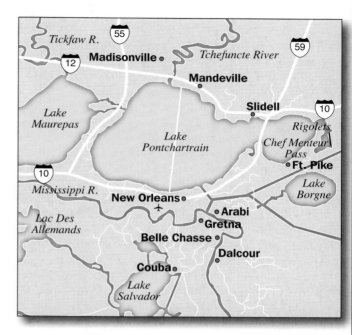

GIWW Route

This 26-mile-long land cut is without facilities except at Chef Menteur Pass, a deepwater pass between Lake Borgne and Lake Pontchartrain.

The brick remains of Fort McComb are near the west end of the Chef Menteur Bridge (closed to auto traffic since Hurricane Katrina). Built between 1820 and 1828, it was manned by both Confederate and Union troops during the Civil War. Inconspicuously hidden behind the crumbling fort is an older marina containing only covered sheds. It has a narrow, shallow entry flanking the crumbling brick walls. There is no on-site management and no transient facilities are available.

NAVIGATION: Use Chart 11367. The GIWW route starts at Catfish Point at Mile 34 EHL. Pass between flashing green "25" and quick flashing red "26." Follow the markers, and stay well inside the channel for the first half mile, as shoaling is prevalent here. The channel carries good depths from Mile 34 EHL to Mile 26 EHL. As you continue, stay in the center of the channel up to Mile 19 EHL due to shallow depths along both banks. When entering the Michoud shipping area at Mile 15 EHL, be aware of large commercial vessels and severe water turbulence in the narrow Waterways. This is also a guard-enforced No-Wake Zone. The Paris Road Bridge at Mile 13 has a 137-foot fixed vertical clearance. This portion of the Mississippi Gulf Outlet has 20- to 26-foot depths.

At Mile 14, the Michoud Bridge is where the VHF frequency for commercial vessels changes from VHF Channel 16 on the West side to VHF Channel 13 on the East side. VHF Channel 13 remains the commercial frequency for the GIWW from this point to the Galveston Causeway Bridge, where it changes back to VHF Channel 16. (Due to the high volume of commercial traffic in this area, recreational boaters should always monitor the same frequency as commercial traffic.)

The merging of the GIWW at Mile 7.5 EHL with the Inner Harbor Navigational Canal, and further coverage of the passage through the Industrial Locks, is covered later in this chapter under the "Locking Out of New Orleans" section.

Dockage: Hurricane Katrina destroyed the two marinas in this area—Venetian Isles Marina and Gulf Outlet Marina. The closest marinas to this point will be at the South Shore (see the "Lake Pontchartrain" section below).

The Rigolets—Mile 34 EHL

This route is deep and wide but plagued with strong currents. Use extra caution around the railroad bridge and the Interstate 90 Bridge at the western end. Fishing is popular in the Rigolets at the trestles of both bridges and at the mouth of the pass where its deep water meets the shallow lake. Cruisers should slow down and proceed at no-wake speeds as a courtesy to the fishermen.

Near Sawmill Pass along Interstate 90 is Fort Pike. The large stonework fort was built in the early 1800s, after the Battle of New Orleans, to protect the Lake Pontchartrain

The Rigolets, LA

approach to the city. Seek local knowledge to determine current depths in the approach channel to the small marinas in the area. Along Fort Pike Channel, Chef Harbor Marina is in the process of being rebuilt, but does offer fuel (gas and diesel) and restrooms for boats 25 feet in length and less. No transient dockage is available as of publication. The approach and dockside depths are 4 to 5 feet.

NAVIGATION: Use Chart 11367 and 11369. Entering the Rigolets at Mile 34, two bridges require passage. The railroad swing bridge (11-foot closed vertical clearance) will open when you call ahead on VHF Channel 13. When addressing the railroad bridge operator for an opening, use the name "CSX Rigolets Railroad Bridge" to prevent confusion with other nearby bridges. The fixed bridge for I-90 has a 66-foot vertical clearance. Passage through the Rigolets I-90 Bridge brings you to the 17-foot-high Rigolets flashing green "5," which is about 90 feet from the abandoned West Rigolets Lighthouse (built in 1854 and moved to its present location after storm damage in 1869). The entrance to Lake Pontchartrain is marked by flashing red "6."

You now enter one of the few shallow areas of Lake Pontchartrain, named Middle Ground, with some depths of 5 feet or less. From here, travel northwest past green daybeacons "3" through "9" in the 7-foot-deep channel. After a westerly turn and a two-mile run, you will pass under the Interstate 10 Bridge (65-foot fixed vertical clearance) and head for the Highway 11 Bascule Bridge and a railroad bridge (13- and 4-foot closed vertical clearances, respectively) less than two miles away. When addressing the railroad bridge for an opening, use the name "NS Highway 11 bridge."

Once you are west of the highway and railroad bridges, you have a choice of heading southwest to New Orleans or northwest around the northern rim of Lake Pontchartrain.

Dockage: Oak Harbor Marina has 96 50-foot-long wet slips. The marina entrance is located on the east side of the north shore between the Interstate 10 Bridge and the Highway 11 Bridge. Three slips are allocated for transient boaters, and the property has a restaurant, restrooms, showers, ice, laundry and swimming pools (a second restaurant is a dinghy ride across the marina). A convenience store is within walking distance, and rental car pickups are available at the marina. Fuel (gas and diesel) is available across the basin at The Dock at Slidell.

Anchorage: Whether heading on to New Orleans via the GIWW or Lake Pontchartrain, overnight anchorage can be had either in the oxbow behind Catfish Pt. or in the Blind Rigolets on the side closest to the GIWW. When anchoring in the oxbow, the northern side has better anchoring depths with 14- to 16-foot depths. The anchorage in the Blind Rigolets is a comfortable overnight anchorage in 15-foot depths with the occasional rumble from a passing train.

Lake Pontchartrain

Lake Pontchartrain is an almost ideal body of water for sailing. The oval-shaped lake is nearly 40 miles from east to west and 24 miles from New Orleans to the north shore.

It is consistently 10 to 12 feet deep, and tidal range is normally less than a foot. Lake Pontchartrain deserves a high level of respect when storm winds blow, especially when north winds prevail. A vessel losing power near the New Orleans lakefront could run into trouble anywhere along 10 miles of concrete bulkheads and sea walls that guard the city. Keep a sharp eye out for numerous crab traps that seem to be randomly scattered across the lake, usually indicated by a small round white buoy.

Efforts to preserve Lake Pontchartrain and its ecology have had positive effects. Dredging for commercial shell from the lake bottom and drilling for oil and gas were stopped many years ago, but several production platforms still stand west of the Causeway. (Unfortunately, oil from the Deepwater Horizon leak had found its way into the Lake at press time summer 2010.)

The Causeway first opened in 1969 amid much publicity as the longest bridge in the world (nearly 24 miles). A twin bridge system, the Causeway connects the south shore at Metairie to the north shore at Lewisburg. Before the entire highway can be seen, its raised support sections appear like islands.

NAVIGATION: Use Chart 11369. Five openings (four fixed and one twin bascule) raise the Causeway span to elevations of 22 to 50 feet. Prior notice must be given before the bascule bridge will open. Check your chart for the openings and their vertical clearances before proceeding.

There are no buoyed channels in Lake Pontchartrain, but some underwater obstructions are marked. Privately maintained race buoys are located in the area north of the Southern Yacht Club and New Orleans Yacht Club.

While the tidal range is negligible, storm winds can alter the water level as much as 4 feet.

◼ NEW ORLEANS

"The Big Easy" offers the cruising yachtsman a wide and varied choice of activities. There are so many events, tourist sights, hotels, motels and restaurants that WATERWAY GUIDE's humble attempt at a "Goin' Ashore" section to help cruisers enjoy their visit to New Orleans barely scratches the surface of the magnificent city. Whether you stay a few days or a few weeks, your visit to New Orleans will be a memory maker.

Note: New Orleans residents and businesses continue to feel the after-effects of Hurricane Katrina, even in summer 2010. Please check locally to verify if businesses are operational and to confirm their hours.

NAVIGATION: Use Chart 11369. From the Rigolets to New Orleans, head southwest for 10 miles after clearing the U.S. Highway 11 and railroad bridges (13- and 4-foot closed vertical clearances, respectively), and you should spot the New Orleans Lakefront Airport runway lights, some four miles away. Be careful of crab-trap floats strewn through the lake. If going to the South Shore Harbor Marina, you will keep the runway lights to starboard to enter the harbor at the east side of the airport. Follow the lighted buoys at the entrance to the harbor. The passage to the marinas and other facilities, at what is known as West End, is another five miles west of the runway light structures, which extend more than a half mile into Lake Pontchartrain from the airport itself. Follow flashing green "1" and flashing red "2" into the canal basin.

If you are heading back to the GIWW via the Inner Harbor Navigational Canal (which most locals refer to as the Industrial Canal), keep the runway lights to port, and turn to the south after passing them. The Industrial Canal is described toward the end of this chapter.

Dockage: The Coast Guard lighthouse (west of the airport) marks the entry into the twin basins of West End, the home of the Southern Yacht Club, the New Orleans Yacht Club, the New Orleans Municipal Yacht Harbor and the Orleans Marina.

The Municipal Yacht Harbor, Southern Yacht Club and New Orleans Yacht Club remain closed with no estimate of a reopen date. Orleans Marina, in the summer of 2010, was accepting transients and has amenities such as shore power and water, restrooms and showers, laundry and pump-out service. Markets and other shopping is only a block away. A bus stop is conveniently located at the corner.

Several restaurants are within walking distance of Orleans Marina along the east bank of the New Basin Canal and the west side of the harbors. The cuisine is excellent, varying from fine to casual dining, including New Orleans cuisine, local seafood, Italian, Chinese and some of the best steaks from Texas. Day docks at some of the waterfront restaurants are popular, but subject to shoaling, wind, waves and "party boat" wakes. Landry's Restaurant is located at the south shore at the mouth of the New Basin Canal. Boaters are welcome to tie up at the Landry's bulkhead while dining. There is a West Marine Store on Harrison Avenue, 10 blocks south of the orleans Marina. Fuel (gas and diesel) is available at Shubert's Marine at the entrance to Orleans Marina in the New Basin Canal.

A shopping center just east of the marinas offers a supermarket (Robért Fresh Market), bank with ATM, a drugstore, a video store, a mail service center, cleaners and other businesses. Groceries can be delivered to your boat from Robért Fresh Market (504-282-3428). For breakfast or a light lunch, try the Coffee Café. RTA bus service to the downtown area and the French Quarter is available from the shopping center. Call RTA Rideline (504-248-3900) for a bus schedule. Taxi service is also available for pickup at any of the marinas.

A large park with acres of landscaped waterfront along Lakeshore Drive separates the two basins. The park serves as a city playground on weekends, ideal for joggers and bikers alike. With several covered pavilions available, this is a great place for a picnic.

The East Basin, which is just east of the Lakefront Airport, is home to the South Shore Harbor Marina. This marina re-opened April 2009 with shore power, water, restrooms and showers. Situated next door to Lakewood Airport, South Shore is not within walking distance to restaurants.

GOIN' ASHORE:
NEW ORLEANS, LA

New Orleans is also known as the "Big Easy" due to its "laissez-faire" nature and laid-back, easy style of living. It is a city of streetcars, courtyards, iron balconies and delectable cuisine. With Mardi Gras, Jazzfest and voodoo ceremonies drawing people from near and far, the excitement of the city is contagious. Mardi Gras is always scheduled 47 days before Easter, which includes the 40 days of Lent (Catholic) plus seven Sundays. If you enjoy a good party with great music, food, parades and entertainment of all types, Mardi Gras is an event to behold. Fortunately, most of New Orleans' famed French Quarter was spared by the storms.

You don't want to rush in this wonderful city. The city tour is a good place to start, before exploring the French Quarter, the Riverwalk, the Garden District and the famous cemeteries. Jackson Square is the perfect place to gather historical facts and watch people. A "Good Times Guide" has valuable coupons redeemable at local establishments (visit online at www.neworleansonline.com).

In 1738, against all odds and in the midst of doubters, Sieur de Bienville, a French Canadian, and John Law, a Scottish Minister for Finance of France, mapped out the French Quarter, knowing it could survive without sinking. The fire of 1788, started by gas lamps in New Orleans, crumbled the city into a smoky pile of rubble, leaving nothing erect. New Orleans rebuilt itself into the "true grit" community that it is today. St. Charles streetcars, with 35 electric cars, still travel the city past Creole cottages and shotgun houses. The city lives in a time warp, still unique and yet not totally discovered.

HISTORY OF THE PEOPLE
A New Orleans Creole is a descendant of an early French or Spanish settler born in this country, not in Europe. The late-coming Anglo-Saxons, arriving after the Louisiana Purchase (1803), were considered "foreigners" and called "Les Americaines." Canal Street marked the divide between French Creoles and the alien "American Side." Creoles are not Cajun; both are French by descent, but the distinction ends there. Creoles are cosmopolitan city dwellers; Cajuns are bucolic, self-sufficient country dwellers.

HOW TO GET AROUND
The RTA Bus System located at 6700 Plaza Drive (504-248-3900) offers an RTA VisiTour Pass including streetcars and mass transit (in 2010 - 1-day pass/$5, 3-day pass/$12). Passes are available at the transit office and at major hotels. Cabs are also very easy to catch from any location in this busy tourist city.

From Orleans Marina, you can catch Line 40 or 41 RTA Bus Stop from Lakeshore Drive, next to Walgreen's Shopping Center. This bus does make several stops. You can also catch or call a cab and head for Bourbon Street (about 20 minutes from the marina) to enjoy the flavor of the city.

New Orleans, LA

New Orleans, LA

NEW ORLEANS		Largest Vessel Accommodated	VHF Channel Monitored	Transient Berths / Total Berths	Approach / Dockside Depth (reported)	Floating Docks	Gas / Diesel	Groceries, Ice, Marine Supplies, Snacks	Repairs: Hull, Engine, Propeller	Lift (tonnage), Crane, Rail	1=110V, 2=220V, B=Both, Max Amps	Laundry, Pool, Showers	Pump-Out Station	Nearby: Grocery Store, Motel, Restaurant
				Dockage				**Supplies**			**Services**			
1. M.G. Mayer Yacht Services	504-282-1700	120		4/16	8/8				HEP	L110,C35	B/50	S		GR
2. Orleans Marina 💻	504-288-2351	110	16	15/353	8/10						B/100	LS	P	GMR
3. Schubert's Marine 💻	504-282-8136	100	16		10/10		GD	IMS	HEP	C	B/50			GR
4. Seabrook Harbor/Seabrook Marine 💻	504-283-9801	120		17/17	15/10	F	GD	S	HEP	L77,C	B/50	S		R

Corresponding chart(s) not to be used for navigation. 💻 Internet Access 📶 Wireless Internet Access

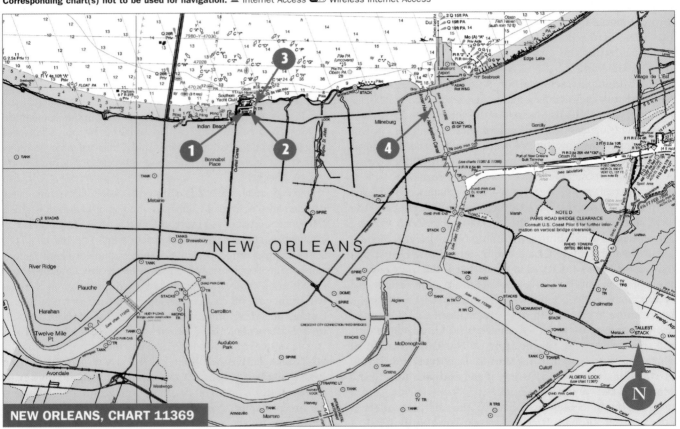

NEW ORLEANS, CHART 11369

SHOPPING

When uptown, go to Magazine Street and Charles Avenue to find an array of shops from trendy boutiques to CD warehouses that buy, trade and sell, to wine cellars and tattoo parlors. The wildly popular French Quarter offers five blocks of shopping and dining. Shop along Canal Street, and visit the Cigar Factory (415 Decatur St., 504-568-1003) where you can watch the making of a cigar.

Riverwalk Marketplace (1 Poydras St., 504-522-1555) is an upscale mall with more than 140 stores and restaurants lining the Mississippi River. Information is available online at www.riverwalkmarketplace.com. Tax-free shopping is available for international visitors; just present a passport.

The Shops at Jax Brewery (Jackson Square, 504-566-7245), with four floors of stores, restaurants and bars, is located on the Mississippi River. And don't forget to visit the JAX Beer Museum.

DINING

Dining opportunities are endless. Since the 1860s, Cafe Du Monde (800 Decatur St., 504-525-4544), open 24 hours a day, has been the city's original French market coffee stand. Hot beignets, coffee and iced coffee are their specialties. The Gumbo Shop has a sampler of different New Orleans specialties (630 Saint Peter St., 504-525-1486) and is open 11 a.m. to 11 p.m. daily, with a moderate price range. For another taste of Southern fare, try Bubba Gump Shrimp Co. located in the French Quarter (429 Decatur St., 504-522-5800). For Jimmy Buffet fans, visit Margaritaville Café (1104 Decatur St., 504-592-2565) for casual Gulf Coast dining and live entertainment. You can eat just about anything, anywhere, anytime in this city. Just walk around and see what suits your fancy.

NIGHTLIFE

New Orleans is a city that doesn't sleep. Jazz clubs abound, and nightclubs go from upscale to funky. Visit www.bigeasy. com for a listing of many different choices. Harrah's casino on Canal Street near the riverfront offers high-energy music shows that run nightly at 9 p.m. except Sunday and Wednesday (504-533-6600). Check the Web site at www.harrahs.com. The House of Blues (225 Decatur St., 504-310-4999) was opened by original Blues Brother Dan Aykroyd, Aerosmith and others. The club offers live music and a restaurant.

TOURS/ATTRACTIONS

New Orleans is full of interesting attractions to please your personal tastes. In the French Quarter, call 800-673-5725 to get the latest festival schedule to coincide with your visit. The French Quarter Festival in mid-April is a three-day music extravaganza by local musicians, with rhythm and blues, Dixieland jazz, contemporary brass bands, gospel and New Orleans funk all represented. You can sample New Orleans cuisine, enjoy fireworks along the river and attend art shows. The Satchmo Summer Fest honoring Louis "Satchmo" Armstrong occurs in early August and features the "music of the man who spread the language of jazz around the world." During the Christmas season, don't forget Christmas New Orleans Style, with famed New Orleans chefs preparing culinary delights and sharing a few of their secrets. Public concerts, bonfires, riverboat cruises and restaurants serving Reveillon, a Creole dining custom, fulfill the holiday season. The New Orleans Wine and Food Experience is held Memorial Day Weekend.

For history buffs, visit the National D-Day Museum, which relives World War II in a chilling audio/video presentation. Andrew Jackson Higgins was a New Orleans shipbuilder who helped the Allies win the war with his design of a flat-bottomed boat that could maneuver up on the banks, then off again, under its own power. The Eureka boats—similar to a Louisiana swamp boat—helped the New Orleans economy and the war effort. Thirty thousand people were employed (including "Rosie the Riveter") and produced 20,000 of the specialized boats. Higgins became a national hero, receiving present-day honors in the museum. Call 504-528-1944, or visit the Web site at www. ddaymuseum.org.

The Aquarium of the Americas (1 Canal St.) displays wildlife from Louisiana and the Gulf of Mexico. The Audubon Zoo (6500 Magazine St., 504-581-4629) features a rare white alligator and the endangered Sumatran tiger among the 1,500-animal display. The aquarium underwent a dramatic recovery after Katrina.

Much of Southern Louisiana is swamp and marshland, which acts as a filter for the Mississippi River and the Gulf of Mexico. This nature estuary is a fertile area for crawfish, oysters and shrimp. To better appreciate Mother Nature at her best, take one of many swamp tours in an airboat or pontoon boat (504-587-1719). (The residual effects of the oil rig explosion and subsequent spill will likely be felt here for some time.) Another choice is to visit the Louisiana Swamp at the Audubon Zoo. The swamps are fun to explore for their natural beauty and abundant wildlife. Alligators, egrets, herons, turtles, nutria and other creatures rule the swamp. Life in the swamps is harsh for most people, but proved very successful for pirates such as Jean Lafitte, who suc-

cessfully hid riches from captured Spanish merchant ships. The infamous Lafitte was such a threat to the American forces that Gen. Andrew Jackson worried Lafitte would aid the British in the Battle of New Orleans. Jackson offered amnesty for Lafitte and his men in exchange for his help in defeating the British at Chalmette Battlefield.

French Quarter cemetery walking tours of the macabre are offered all around town. Another popular tour is Le Monde Creole at 624 Royal St., at the rear of the courtyard. This tour relives five generations of one New Orleans family through the journal of Laura Locoul, a Creole woman and plantation mistress. For tour information call 504-568-1801, or visit the Web site at www.mondecreole.com. Architectural tours of New Orleans are available through the Preservation Resource Center (923 Tchoupitoulas St., 504-581-7032). These tours are arranged by appointment with 24-hour notice.

ADDITIONAL RESOURCES

■ **New Orleans Convention and Visitors**
Bureau, 800-672-6124, **www.neworleanscvb.com**

⚑ **NEARBY GOLF COURSES**
City Park New Orleans North Course
1051 Filmore Ave., New Orleans, LA 70124,
504-483-9410, **www.cityparkgolf.com**

⚕ **NEARBY MEDICAL FACILITIES**
Tulane Medical Center,
1415 Tulane Ave.,
New Orleans, LA 70112, 800-588-5800

North Shore of Lake Pontchartrain

The North Shore of St. Tammany Parish (22 miles north of New Orleans) offers everything from quaint bed and breakfast inns to antiques stores, fine restaurants and must-see swamp tours. One of the most pristine swamps in America is Honey Island. Pirates such as Jean Lafitte, who captured Spanish merchant ships in the Gulf of Mexico, took refuge from the authorities at Honey Island. Legends of buried treasure persist wherever Jean Lafitte came ashore. While the North Shore may be only 22 miles from New Orleans, it is worlds apart—a much more relaxed area with the feel of the country. Many visiting boaters are attracted to the North Shore's peacefulness with ready access to central New Orleans and its cuisine and nightlife.

NAVIGATION: Use Chart 11369. Coming into Lake Pontchartrain from the east at the Rigolets and after clearing the U.S. Highway 11 and railroad bridges (13- and 4-foot closed vertical clearances, respectively), the common entrance of Bayou Bonfouca and Liberty Bayou is two miles west-northwest. Enter at flashing red "2" and follow the well-marked channel (8-foot depths) to the bayou junction. Bayou Bonfouca, to the northeast, extends some six miles to the town of Slidell. To the west, Liberty Bayou is shallow (3.5-foot controlling depth).

Lake Pontchartrain North Shore, LA

LAKE PONTCHARTRAIN NORTH SHORE		Dockage					Supplies			Services				
Marina	Phone	Largest Vessel Accommodated	VHF Channel Monitored	Transient Berths / Total Berths	Approach / Dockside Depth (reported)	Floating Docks	Gas / Diesel	Groceries, Ice, Marine Supplies, Snacks	Repairs: Hull, Engine, Propeller	Lift (tonnage), Crane, Rail	1=110v, 2=220v, B=Both, Max Amps	Laundry, Pool, Showers	Pump-Out Station	Nearby: Grocery Store, Motel, Restaurant
1. The Dock @ Slidell	985-645-3625	90					GD	IS		L12		S		GMR
2. Oak Harbor Marina 🖥️ Wifi	985-641-1044	110	16		8/12			I			B/50	LPS	P	GMR
3. Prieto Marina LLC	985-626-9670	50		/158	10/5						1/30	S		R
4. Northshore Marine Sales & Services Inc.	985-626-7847	48		2/11	10/9			M	HEP	L25,C	B/50	S	P	R
5. Mariners Village Marina	800-360-3625	45	16	10/160	4/6		GD	IM	E		B/50		P	GMR
6. Marina Beau Chene	985-845-3454	62	16	/140	20/8						B/50	LS	P	
7. Bent Marine	985-845-4654	50		6/12	15/8			MS	HEP	L35		LS		GR
8. Marina Del Ray	985-845-4474	260	16	50/380	10/8	F	GD	GIMS			B/100	LPS	P	GMR
9. Salty's Marina	985-845-8485	40	16	5/100	14/12	F	G	IS			1/30			GR

Corresponding chart(s) not to be used for navigation. 🖥️ Internet Access Wifi Wireless Internet Access

Dockage: A New Orleans-based repair service, M.G. Mayer Yachts, now operates Maritime Services, just west of Slidell on Bayou Bonfouca.

Lacombe Bayou (farther west) has no marinas for pleasure craft, but does have a boatyard that caters mainly to large commercial craft. The entrance channel is short and shallow, and skippers entering or leaving should keep flashing red "2" and green daybeacon "5," with red daybeacon "4" midway, in sight. The channel has a depth of 6 feet and the bayou carries 7-foot depths.

Mandeville

This town on Bayou Castine is the sister port to Madisonville (see Tchefuncta River) in terms of ambience, amenities and popularity. Its shoreline and streets are landscaped with majestic oak, magnolia and sycamore trees, which augment the Southern charm and blend in with an array of fine dining houses and pubs.

Dockage: To the north on Bayou Castine (5-foot depths) is the Pontchartrain Yacht Club just across the street from the municipal docks. Established in 1967, the Pontchartrain Yacht Club has a classic clubhouse that blends with the many charming Mandeville homes. The latest building was completed in June 2007.

Northshore Marine has a full-service boatyard with a 25-ton lift, engine and hull repair and transient dockage for vessels up to 48 feet. A restaurant, groceries and a motel are nearby.

Prieto Marina sits along Bayou Castine, approximately two miles east of the Causeway. Green daybeacon "1" and flashing red "2" sit at the entrance to Bayou Castine. Transients tie up along the bulkhead, with shower and restroom facilities nearby. The marina is adjacent to the beautiful Fontainebleau State Park and the Tammany Trace Bike Trail.

Lewisburg

The Lewisburg Harbor is located in the northeast corner of Lake Pontchartrain at the foot of the Causeway bridge. The harbor entrance has about 10-foot depths.

Dockage: Mariner's Village is located just east of the Lake Pontchartrain Causeway. The marina was heavily damaged in Hurricane Katrina, but has since been partially restored. Groceries, a restaurant and a motel are within 15-minute walking distance, as is a West Marine store. There are restrooms, a small ship's store and a fuel dock with gas and diesel on the property. The channel, which had a silting problem, was (in spring 2010) dredged to a minimum depth of 8 feet. Call ahead for the latest channel depths and slip availability.

Tchefuncta River

The Tchefuncta ("cha-funk-ta") River, four miles west of Lewisburg and eight miles northwest of the Lake Pontchartrain Causeway, is Lake Pontchartrain's most popular weekend destination. This beautiful deep river has clean water, great anchorages, golf, tennis, country clubs, residential areas, marinas and miles of undeveloped shores.

NAVIGATION: Use Chart 11369. The entrance to the Tchefuncta River from Lake Pontchartrain is well-marked, but take care to enter properly. Follow the marked channel (7-foot depths) north from flashing red "2" toward the old lighthouse, and then turn to the east and use red daybeacons "6," "8" and "10" to the river entrance. Keep the red daybeacons to starboard, as cutting across the doglegged entrance has caused many vessels to go hard aground. The 40-foot-high Tchefuncta River Lighthouse, built in 1838, is still in service, although it is now automated. A black vertical stripe makes it easy to see as a daytime range mark. At the Tchefuncta River entrance, a heavily used launch ramp is on the west bank. The river depth is 10 feet from the entrance upstream for two miles, and then decreases to 4 feet. A No-Wake Zone extends northward from the southern tip of Marina Del Ray.

Dockage: The welcome mat is always out for pleasure boaters at Madisonville (1.5 miles up the Tchefuncta River), where dockage is usually available either north

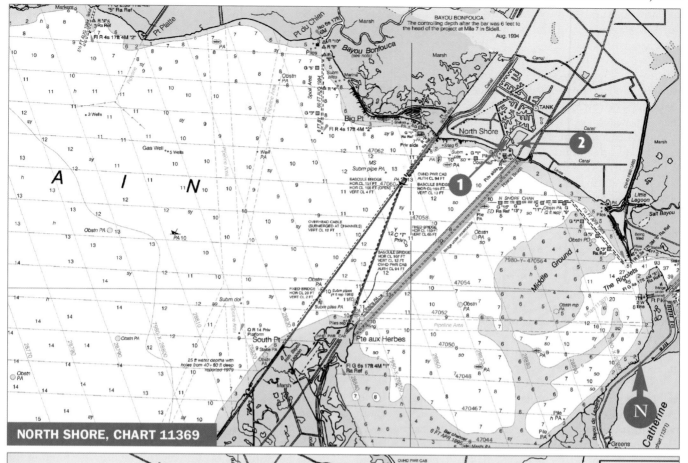

NORTH SHORE, CHART 11369

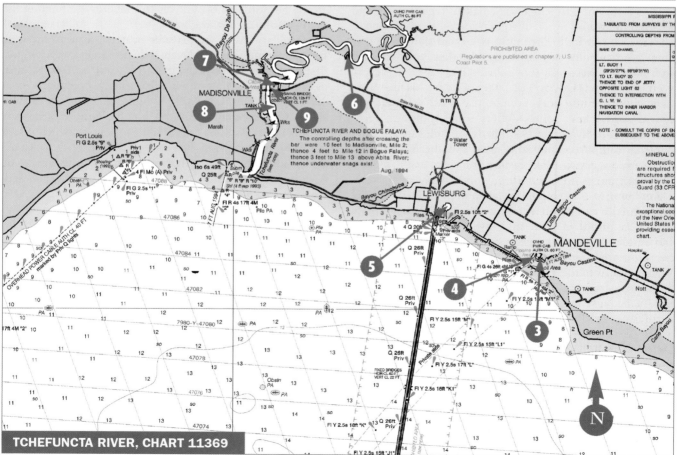

TCHEFUNCTA RIVER, CHART 11369

or south of the Highway 22 Swing Bridge (1-foot closed vertical clearance) on the west side. The docks become crowded with small boats during the shrimp season, and the town stays lively on weekends, so sleeping may be a challenge. A grocery store, post office, a local maritime museum and other shops and services are within walking distance. The town is famous for its Wooden Boat Festival, held every October.

On the east side of the Tchefuncta River is Marina Del Ray, located just south of the Highway 22 Swing Bridge. With an entrance depth of 10 feet and dockside depths of 8 feet, the marina has transient dockage for vessels up to 60 feet. Restrooms, showers, wireless Internet access and a laundry are located in a unique two-story marina building above the restaurant and cocktail lounge. A large swimming pool is located in a barge between the marina and the river, and a covered picnic area and party facilities are also featured. A ship's store lies next to the marina building.

After passage through the Highway 22 Swing Bridge, a trio of fine restaurants lines the bulkhead, offering German and New Orleans-style cuisine in addition to Cajun and Creole seafood. Complimentary dockage at the bulkhead is allowed for diners and visitors, and shore power is available in certain locations along the wharf.

Around the bend to the east in a basin on the south bank, is a small but popular marina named Salty's. This friendly well-run marina stays full most of the time with regular rentals, but will try to make room for transients in temporarily empty slips. A commercial area next to Salty's houses a marine brokerage and marine repair shop, and condominium and other business offices. Bent Marine, a service facility with a 35-ton lift, is located right in downtown Madisonville and can accommodate your hauling and service needs.

North of the Highway 22 Swing Bridge, Marina Beau Chene—a country club community with homes, golf courses and tennis courts—offers some transient dockage; it is probably one of best hurricane holes in the Lake Pontchartrain area. Transients must call ahead and make a reservation. A pump-out facility is located at the marina entrance (tokens for use must be purchased at the office).

Anchorage: A very popular anchorage is just past the beach to the east upon entering the river. A small state park, a multitude of great anchorage spots, country clubs and residential areas ranging from cottages to Southern mansions are located upriver.

Six miles from the mouth is the Interstate 12 Bridge (the direct route from the Mississippi Gulf Coast to Baton Rouge and Interstate 10 West). Cruising and anchorage are limited north of the bridge, as river depths decline rapidly.

Lake Maurepas, Tickfaw River

NAVIGATION: Use Chart 11369. On the western shore of Lake Pontchartrain, Pass Manchac provides a seven-mile-long entrance into Lake Maurepas. The north and south entrances to the pass from Lake Pontchartrain are well-marked with lighted platforms and buoys. Vessels with more than 3-foot drafts prefer the south channel, which has

6.5-foot depths. Follow flashing green "1" to green daybeacons "3" and "5," and then to flashing green "7." From here, steer east into Pass Manchac (23-foot minimum depths). An abandoned lighthouse marks what was once the north bank, but it is now a shoal area protected by rocks.

Watch your wake while traveling the seven miles to the bridges at the western end of Pass Manchac. As you pass the houses with small boats moored to their docks, be aware of the small skiffs and fishing trawlers anchored in Pass Manchac. Trawlers use the currents to usher the catch into their nets.

At the entrance to Lake Maurepas from Pass Manchac are a railroad bascule bridge (56-foot closed vertical clearance), fixed highway bridges (50-foot vertical clearances) and a 64-foot-high power line. On the north bank is a boat landing and a well-known seafood restaurant, Mittendorf's, famous for its catfish dinners.

The four-mile-long northwest run across the shoreline from flashing red "6" will bring you to the mouth of the Tickfaw River. The channel to the river entrance has 5-foot depths. Stumps on the east side and shallow water to the west require a straight-in entrance from the lake. Flashing green "1" guides you into the river toward green daybeacon "3." Often referred to as "Bikini Beach," the sandy and shallow shoreline on the west side is popular with swimmers and sunbathers. Dinghies and jet skis are plentiful. Once inside the Tickfaw River, depths increase to a controlled depth of 12 feet, with observed depths of 25 feet or more. An anchorage can be found near almost every bend.

The beautiful Tickfaw River is a favorite destination for high-performance powerboats, so be alert. Officials patrol the river for "BWIs" (intoxicated boaters), as weekend traffic from Baton Rouge and New Orleans can get wild. On the first Saturday of every May, this area hosts the Tickfaw 200, one of the largest powerboat poker runs in Louisiana.

Dockage: Upriver, within a couple of miles, are various small marinas, play spots and popular restaurants, such as Sun Buns, Tin Lizzy's and the Prop Stop (which offers a locally famous drink called a "worm bucket"). Only on the Tickfaw River would anyone drink a beverage out of a worm bucket, while feasting on a "gator" burger, and treasure the moment.

At the seven-mile point, just before the highway bridge near Springfield, is the Tickfaw Marina, and just beyond the bridge on the Blood River are Warsaw Marina and Vacajun Marina. Fuel is available at the Tickfaw and Warsaw marinas, and all offer limited transient dockage. The Blood River Landing and King's Point Marina are private facilities.

Locking Out of New Orleans

The Inner Harbor Navigational Canal, followed by the Industrial Canal, is the route from Lake Pontchartrain to the Mississippi River. Time your trip with the morning and evening bridge curfews in mind.

NAVIGATION: Use Chart 11369. Currents during flood or ebb tide through the Inner Harbor Navigational Canal can be strong, and are amplified when a strong north wind in

SKIPPER BOB PUBLICATIONS

Tickfaw River, LA

TICKFAW RIVER		Largest Vessel Accommodated	VHF Channel Monitored	Transient Berths / Total Berths	Approach / Dockside Depth (reported)	Floating Docks	Gas / Diesel	Groceries, Ice, Marine Supplies, Snacks	Repairs: Hull, Engine, Propeller	Lift (tonnage), Crane, Rail	1=110V, 2=220V, B=Both, Max Amps	Laundry, Pool, Showers	Pump-Out Station	Nearby: Grocery Store, Motel, Restaurant
				Dockage			**Supplies**				**Services**			
1. Tickfaw Marina	225-695-3340	60		/80	10/2		GD	GIMS			B/50		P	GR
2. Blood River Landing	225-235-7505	60		2/30	6/6						B/50			R
3. Warsaw Marina	225-294-3854	50		/35	12/12		G	GIS				S		G
4. Vacajun Marina	225-294-3105	55			10/6			I			B/	S		R

Corresponding chart(s) not to be used for navigation. 🖥 Internet Access 📶 Wireless Internet Access

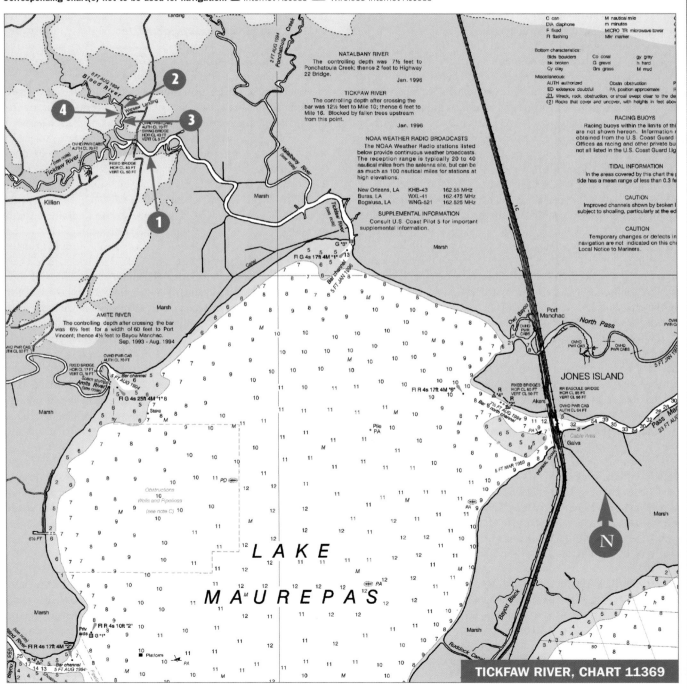

TICKFAW RIVER, CHART 11369

New Orleans Locks, LA

Lake Pontchartrain is countering the flow. Keep a good distance from tugboats off the bow, as the prop wash from these vessels can make holding position in the harbor or lock a challenge.

The first of four bridges on the Inner Harbor Navigational Canal (before it merges with the GIWW at Mile 7.5 EHL) is the Lakeshore Bridge, a bascule span with a normal clearance of 44 feet. The Lakeshore Railroad Bridge, sometimes referred to as the L&N Bridge, (1-foot closed vertical clearance), stays open until a train is approaching.

The next bridge traveling south is the Chef Menteur Lift Bridge, with a charted 50-foot closed vertical clearance, and a 120-foot vertical clearance in the open position. The Interstate 10 Highway Bridge (115-foot fixed vertical clearance) is just before a railroad bascule bridge that is usually left open (no vertical clearance when closed).

The Inner Harbor Navigational Canal then merges with the GIWW at Mile 7.5 EHL at the turning basin and continues toward the Mississippi River on what is commonly called the Industrial Canal. The Industrial Canal narrows to the dual-purpose Florida Avenue Bascule Bridge (Mile 7.5 EHL, zero-foot closed vertical clearance). Monday through Friday, there are no openings from 6:30 a.m. to 8:30 a.m. and from 3:30 p.m. to 6:45 p.m. Note that the bridges and the lock typically use separate radio channels. It is the responsibility of the boater to independently coordinate all lock and bridge crossings. It is a good idea to ask the master of the current crossing for the hailing frequency of the next crossing.

The last bridge before the Industrial Locks is the Judge Seeber Lift Bridge, more commonly known as the Claiborne Avenue Lift Bridge. The Judge Seeber Bridge has a clearance of 40 feet in the down position and 156 feet when up. Monday through Friday, there are no openings from 6:30 to 8:30 a.m. and from 3:30 to 6:45 p.m.

Dockage: Located less than one mile south of the Lakeshore Bridge, the marina on the west side of the canal is Seabrook Harbor, the only pleasure boat facility on the Inner Harbor Navigational Canal. There are approximately 10 wet slips available for transients, with shore power. Seabrook Harbor also has showers, a West Marine Express ship's store and a fuel dock (gas and diesel). A full-service boat repair facility is located on the property.

Industrial Lock

The Industrial Lock, five miles north of the Harvey Canal (GIWW Mile 0) on the Mississippi River, was built between 1918 and 1923 and measures 626 feet long by 75 feet wide. A Coast Guard station is on the west side, behind the guide wall on the canal side of the locks. Be aware that the Coast Guard occasionally conducts safety and documentation checks here. When locking through, the lockmaster will often direct you to hold position at "the dolphins," which are the large circular structures that extend outward along each edge of the canal. Do not attempt to tie up to the dolphins or any structure near the lock. Engines must be in idle, ready to make a move at any moment to maneuver through traffic.

NAVIGATION: Use Chart 11367. Contact the lockmaster on VHF Channel 14 while you are between Florida Avenue and the Judge Seeber Lift bridges. Have your boat name and registration number available and the length, beam and draft of your vessel. The lockmaster will inform you of the traffic lineup and provide instructions for entering the lock. Once inside, they will usually ask for one crew member wearing a personal flotation device (PFD) to stand ready on the bow with a line. A telescoping pole is very handy as well, keeping the boat away from the muddy concrete side walls of the chamber. "Red Flag" tows, carrying hazardous cargo, fly red flags on their barges and display a blue light at night. Regulations prohibit passenger and pleasure craft from sharing the lock with a "Red Flag" tow.

The usual lift at the lock is 3 to 6 feet, but during springtime, floods can be well over 10 feet. Tie-up procedures vary, and many times securing to the hip of a tug or barge is better than the normal wall position.

The St. Claude Avenue Bascule Bridge monitors the opening of the locks; it is not necessary to call for an opening. Once in the river, you are required to check in with the Gretna Light traffic service on VHF Channel 67 until you reach the next lock out point. Stay on VHF Channel 67 at all times while in the river.

Mississippi River, Algiers Lock

A decision about which westward route to take should be made before entering the Mississippi River. The choices are the Algiers Lock or the Harvey Lock. Algiers Lock is a longer route, but tends to have less traffic than Harvey Lock.

The Algiers Lock is four miles downriver, and the Harvey Lock is five miles upriver. Mississippi River currents are strong enough at times to make the Algiers Alternate Route the first choice, despite the heavy commercial traffic and occasional delays while waiting in the open river.

NAVIGATION: Use Chart 11367. The Algiers Alternate Route has three bridges. The first, a mile downstream from the Algiers Lock, is the General de Gaulle Bridge (100-foot fixed vertical clearance). A vertical-lift railroad bridge (100-foot clearance when raised, its normal position) is 3.5 miles farther downstream, adjoining the Belle Chasse Highway Bridge with a 40-foot closed vertical clearance. Openings are restricted during traffic rush hours.

The Algiers Alternate Route rejoins the GIWW at Barataria Bayou. There are no amenities for pleasure boats until reaching Lafitte and the Barataria Waterway.

Mississippi River, Harvey Lock

One reason to take the Harvey Lock route is the trip upriver itself. Along this route you will enjoy the full view of New Orleans: the French Quarter at Jackson Square and St. Louis Cathedral (the oldest active cathedral in the United States), the red brick Pontalbo apartments on either side of Jackson Square, the French Market, the Moon Walk and much more. Canal Street, where ferries still cross the river to the "west bank," downtown high-rise buildings and miles of wharves lined with oceangoing freighters and passenger cruise ships add to the scenery. You will also pass the site of the 1984 World's Fair, now a cluster of stores and restaurants called Riverwalk.

NAVIGATION: Use Chart 11367. The Harvey Canal and Lock are five miles upstream from the Industrial Lock off the Mississippi River. The preferred route upstream is to cross from the Industrial Canal outlet to the "west bank" (to the south by compass) at Algiers Point, and then make a 45-degree cut across the river to the "east bank" (to the west by compass) toward the French Quarter and the high-level bridges over the river. The Canal Street ferry crosses the Mississippi River north of Algiers Point.

Usually you will experience only short delays before locking through. When it is necessary to wait in the river, stay close to the bank on either side to stay out of the mainstream currents and traffic.

Harvey Lock represents Mile Zero on the GIWW. We will now start referring to miles west of Harvey Lock (WHL) through Louisiana and Texas to the Mexico border.

Dockage: Boomtown Casino in Harvey Canal allows visitors to tie up along the bulkhead. No power or water is available, but the casino welcomes visiting boaters. Tie up near the large bollard, and keep a sharp eye for construction debris. Depths of approximately 12 feet were reported at the wall. Have some robust fenders in place to guard against contacting the steel walls of the bulkhead. The entire canal is a No-Wake Zone, so disturbances from passing traffic should be at a minimum. Boomtown Casino offers several restaurants and a large gaming floor. Check in at the security desk upon arrival.

Baton Rouge

From New Orleans, Baton Rouge lies up the Mississippi River. This 100-mile section of the river, with limited transient facilities, strong currents and floating debris of major proportions, is not recommended, especially with underpowered vessels. A side trip from New Orleans to Baton Rouge, including a plantation tour along the river, should be reserved for a rental car. Dock your boat in New Orleans, and have a car rental company deliver a car to your marina.

GOIN' ASHORE:
BATON ROUGE, LA

Upriver from New Orleans is Baton Rouge, on the east side of the Mississippi River. Even though no marinas with transient accommodations are available in Baton Rouge, a side trip from your cruising schedule may be well worth the effort. Dock your boat in Lake Pontchartrain, and rent a car for a few days. Baton Rouge will reward you, maybe by winning at the casino, or more likely with great places to eat, to see and to shop. With more than 500 restaurants offering cuisine from around the world—especially local Cajun and Creole cuisine—it is unlikely that visitors will go hungry. The city is known for its beignets, crawfish étouffée, spicy crabmeat sauté, bourbon bread pudding and café au lait. If you like crawfish or alligator, local chefs can prepare it 10 different ways.

With its semi-tropical climate, golf courses, jazz clubs, gambling and food, Baton Rouge is authentic Louisiana. Places to see are limited only by the number of days of your visit. Baton Rouge offers antebellum plantations, swamp tours, botanical gardens, a world-renowned zoo, a symphony orchestra, museums, golf, tennis, sporting events and so much more. At night, the city rocks and rolls with the sounds of blues, jazz and rock at many nightclubs.

Baton Rouge was named on St. Patrick's Day in 1699, when French explorer Sieur d'Iberville led an expedition along the Mississippi River. According to local legend, wooden poles stained with the blood of fish and animals served as a dividing line between the Bayougoula and Houmas Indians. The city got its name from one of these poles—Baton Rouge means "red stick." Baton Rouge became the state capital in 1846 and fell to Union forces in 1862. Visit the State Capitol, built in 1932 by Louisiana's legendary governor, Huey P. Long. The tallest state capitol in the nation at 34 stories high, the building features beautiful Art Deco architecture.

Louisiana mud painting by native artist Henry Neubig is on display at his studio and gallery (16950 Strain Road, 225-275-5126). With pigments of local alluvial soils, Neubig captures the essence of life in Louisiana, especially summer living.

Traveling from New Orleans toward Baton Rouge, you will have an excellent opportunity to visit the largest community of antebellum plantations along the Mississippi River. Just south of Interstate 10, the plantations include: Destrehan, San Francisco, Evergreen, Whitney, Laura, Oak Alley, Tezcuco, Houmas House and Nottoway. Step back in time and savor the beauty, excitement and charm of the old South.

ADDITIONAL RESOURCES

- **Baton Rouge Convention & Visitors Bureau** 800-527-6843, www.bracvb.com

- **NEARBY GOLF COURSES** LSU Golf Course, Corner of Burbank and Nicholson Baton Rouge, LA 70893, 225-578-3394

- **NEARBY MEDICAL FACILITIES** Baton Rouge General Medical Center, 3600 Florida Blvd., Baton Rouge, LA 70806, 225-387-7000

WATERWAY GUIDE is always open to your observations from the helm. E-mail your comments on any navigation information in the guide to: editor@waterwayguide.com.

WATERWAY GUIDE advertising sponsors play a vital role in bringing you the most trusted and well-respected cruising guide in the country. Without our advertising sponsors, we simply couldn't produce the top-notch publication now resting in your hands. Next time you stop in for a peaceful night's rest, let them know where you found them—WATERWAY GUIDE, The Cruising Authority.

New Orleans to Freeport

CHARTS 11321, 11322, 11323, 11325, 11326, 11327, 11328, 11329, 11331, 11332, 11341, 11342, 11343, 11344, 11345, 11347, 11348, 11349, 11350, 11351, 11352, 11354, 11355, 11357, 11358, 11364, 11365, 11367, 11368, 11369, 11371

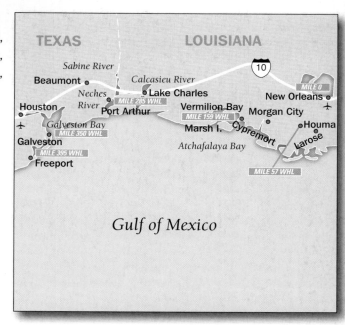

The western portion of the Gulf Intracoastal Waterway (GIWW) begins at the Harvey Lock (mileage is denoted as WHL, or West of Harvey Lock) on the Mississippi River at Mile Zero. This is the area where Acadians from Nova Scotia began settling in 1755, and you will hear commercial skippers on the VHF channels converse in English, French or a mixture of both. Vietnamese, spoken by the many Asian fishermen who have settled in southern Louisiana, is also prevalent in the area. Many bayous and rivers cross the Waterway, some navigable to the Gulf of Mexico. Towns may be only one street wide and a mile or more long, following the twisting Waterway.

Marinas, fuel stops, marine stores, provisions and restaurants are spaced far apart, so study the charts and plan for each day's run. Keep a close watch on the weather, as springtime fog is common in south Louisiana. This, coupled with strong currents and steady commercial traffic, can make for challenging navigation.

Louisiana Waterways retain much of the flavor of the past, when they were commercial ditches, the primary means of transporting goods and people to and from the Mississippi River at New Orleans. The Harvey Canal was originally a private enterprise, dug by hand in the early 1720s from the Mississippi River to the Barataria Waterway. Goods for New Orleans had to be unloaded on the Harvey Canal side, moved over the levee and then loaded on boats on the river.

■ NEW ORLEANS TO THE BARATARIA WATERWAY

Mile Zero to Mile 15 WHL

NAVIGATION: Use Chart 11367. This section of the GIWW is mostly straight, unmarked and runs deep up to the channel banks. Stay away from the banks since wrecks and cypress stumps are littered along them. Commercial traffic has increased each year from the Harvey Lock to Lake Charles; more large three- and four-deck tugs of the Mississippi River-type work these waters each year. You might see shrimp boats, oyster trawlers with two or more masts, petroleum supply vessels, shallow-water drilling barges and tows with as many as 12 or more barges. The wake turbulence can be troubling, even on large pleasure boats; do not follow too closely.

VHF radio is the accepted communication medium. Since using "one whistle" or "two whistles" in a radio conversation may be unclear, it is better to refer to the commercial vessel's starboard or port when you discuss passing. You can get valuable information readily if you request advice from commercial captains. Yield the right-of-way to commercial vessels. When meeting, crossing or overtaking a vessel, you should call the vessel (VHF Channel 13) by name and request instructions for safe passage. Pass barges with their tow at minimal wake. Wakes as small as 2 feet have caused tow cables to break loose.

Always use anchoring information with caution. The beautiful little inlet at mile so-and-so might have been deep with good holding a short time ago, but could be occupied by an abandoned barge or drilling rig today. Many inlets to drilling sites that were great spots to drop the hook are now barricaded at the entrance or have been filled in.

The Coast Guard Local Notice to Mariners says it best: "In addition to numerous bayous and natural canals, thousands of man-made canals have been dredged in the wetlands of the Eighth Coast Guard District. While the original purpose of these canals was for private access to pipelines, well locations or for other mineral-related activities, boaters are using some of them. These canals and bayous contain numerous obstructions including

New Orleans Area, LA

BARATARIA WATERWAY		Dockage				Supplies		Services					
		Largest Vessel Accommodated	VHF Channel Monitored	Transient Berths / Total Berths	Approach / Dockside Depth (reported)	Gas / Diesel	Groceries, Ice, Marine Supplies, Snacks	Repairs: Hull, Engine, Propeller	Lift (tonnage), Crane, Rail	1=110V, 2=220V, B=Both, Max Amps	Laundry, Pool, Showers	Nearby: Grocery Store, Motel, Restaurant	Pump-Out Station
1. Nautical Pointe	985-258-1941						IMS					GMR	
2. Lafitte C-Way Marina 15 WHL	504-689-3148	60	71	5/150	10/8	GD	GIMS	HEP	L20,R	1/30		GMR	
3. Lafitte Harbor Marina 15 WHL	504-689-2013	65	80	4/52	7/6	GD	GIMS		L7,C	B/50	LS	MR	

Corresponding chart(s) not to be used for navigation. 💻 Internet Access 📶 Wireless Internet Access

barriers, pipes, piles, construction debris, etc. Some of these structures are permanently maintained and have been suitably marked or lighted by their owners. Many others appear and disappear without notice and are uncharted, unlighted and unmarked. Even on marked structures, because of vandalism, etc., mariners cannot rely on the markings always being maintained in good condition. Therefore, all persons using canals and bayous must anticipate hazards posed by these obstructions and navigate with extreme caution, especially at night and in periods of reduced visibility."

Harvey Lock is the preferred lock used by pleasure craft. Always remember to have all crew members don PFDs before locking through and have (long) lines at the ready.

Locks west of the Harvey Canal and Locks, including the locks at Miles 93.3, 162.7, 238.5 and 441.5 WHL, are all designed to prevent saltwater intrusion into the marshlands and to assist in flood control. They were not designed for changing from one elevation to another, as on the rivers and the Tennessee-Tombigbee Waterway. The lockmaster normally is only needed for traffic control through the open lock. Call the lockmaster on VHF Channel 14 to receive instructions and permission to proceed through the lock. Note that all locks between New Orleans and Lake Charles use VHF Channel 14.

Twenty or more small-craft charts might be needed for the entire western Gulf voyage. Any offshore or inland ventures will require additional charts and information.

Traveling west from Harvey Lock, the GIWW is crossed by the Harvey Canal Twin Bridges (Mile 0.8 WHL, 95-foot fixed vertical clearance), and then the Lapalco Boulevard Bascule Bridge (Mile 2.8 WHL, 45-foot closed vertical clearance). The Lapalco Boulevard Bascule Bridge does not open Monday through Friday from 6:30 to 8:30 a.m. and 3:45 to 5:45 p.m. At Mile 6.3 WHL, the Harvey Channel joins the Algiers Channel at the flashing red (2+1) light to port (headed south). The Waterway then passes into Bayou Barataria.

Note that the Harvey Canal can be littered with debris. Most of the obstructions have been well-marked by authorities. (This channel saw the brunt of Hurricane Katrina's passage.) Use extreme caution, and watch for newly placed hazard markers in the Harvey Canal.

In the picturesque area from the town of Crown Point to Lafitte (Mile 10 to Mile 15 WHL), homes, businesses and parks line the Waterway. Most of them have boat docks and/or ramps. The Crown Point Bridge crosses the GIWW at Mile 11.9 WHL with a 73-foot fixed vertical clearance.

Transiting this area, the word to remember is "slow," as it is the playground of the west bank. Weekends bring high-speed sport boats, bright metal flake-painted fishing boats and a multitude of jet skis and ski boats; all seem to be running at full throttle.

■ BARATARIA WATERWAY

Mile 15 WHL

The town of Lafitte is named after Jean Lafitte, the most infamous pirate of the Gulf Coast. Legend has it that many of his treasures are buried along the Barataria Waterway. Pirates no longer use this passage to the Gulf of Mexico, but cruisers and fishermen enjoy its scenic bays, bayous and marshland.

NAVIGATION: Use Chart 11367. The 35-mile-long trip through scenic bayou country on the Barataria Waterway to Grand Isle on the Gulf of Mexico has an abundance of wildlife, especially alligators and mosquitoes. The Waterway offers a well-earned respite after maneuvering through the Mississippi River locks and the New Orleans waterfront. The channel is well-marked by lighted fixed markers as it meanders through the Barataria Waterway.

Dockage: There are few marina facilities along the first seven miles of the Barataria Waterway as you leave the GIWW. The Fleming Canal Store which used to be on the east bank just off the Waterway has closed. The space is now occupied by an airboat tour company.

Six miles south on the east side is the well-known Boutte's ("boot-ease") Bayou Restaurant, with dinghy docking and courtesy transportation. Across the Waterway, Joe's Landing has fuel and a ship's store with the adjoining "Lodge of Louisiana" hotel, but there is no transient dockage available.

A few miles from the GIWW, Lafitte Seaway Marina on the east side sells fuel and supplies, and has limited

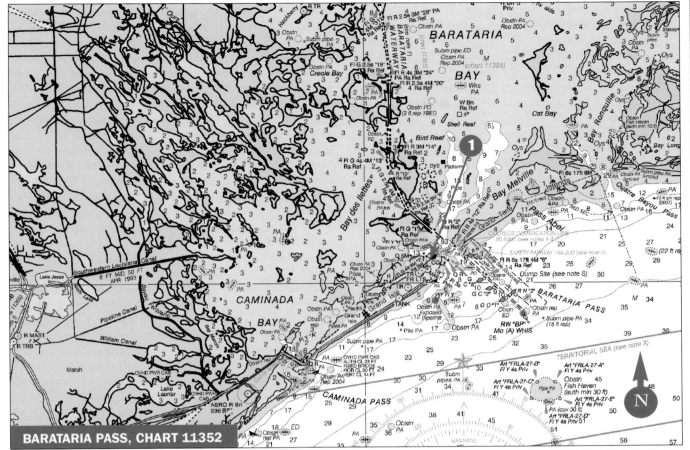

BARATARIA PASS, CHART 11352

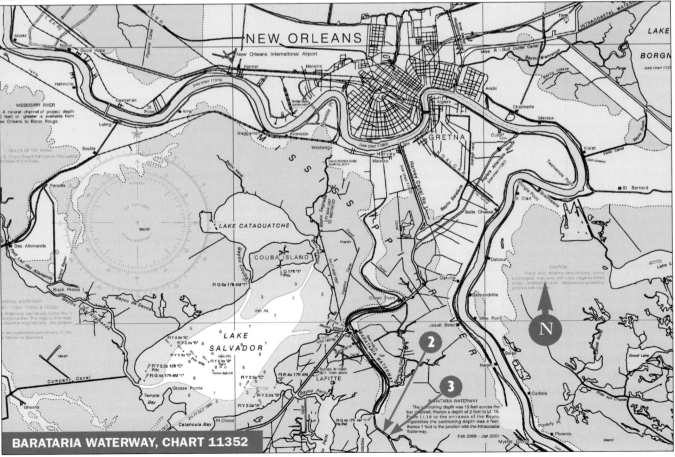

BARATARIA WATERWAY, CHART 11352

Barataria Waterway, LA

overnight dockage and a small motel. At the end of the road is Lafitte Harbor Marina, located on the C&M Bayou Fuel Dock. Fuel, dockage, groceries, marine supplies and a snack bar are available. Rental boats, lodging, repair service (do-it-yourself allowed) and lifts are located on-site.

Heading south, the remaining 28 miles of the Barataria Waterway lead through scenic and less-developed bayou country, ending at Grand Isle, Louisiana's offshore fishing capital and the entrance to the Gulf of Mexico. Here you will find Nautical Pointe Marina with wet slips available for purchase or lease. The Sand Dollar marina offers fuel, transient dockage, motel, restaurants and groceries.

Anchorage: It is possible to anchor just southwest of the airboat docks in 8 to 11 feet of water on the opposite side of the Waterway. Boat traffic dies down at night.

■ BARATARIA WATERWAY TO HOUMA

Mile 15 to Mile 60 WHL

At Mile 15 WHL, the GIWW passes through Lafitte and crosses the Barataria Waterway. The next 15-mile-long section is commonly called Stump Alley because the banks are closely lined with stumpy cypress "knees." Some of these are just below the water—be careful to stay in the center of the channel at all times. At Mile 35 WHL, the town of Larose marks the beginning of Cajun country.

NAVIGATION: Use Chart 11355. In the warmer months, hyacinths may be so thick that they impede the passage of pleasure vessels; large clusters sometimes hang on hidden debris. At Mile 20 WHL, pass by red daybeacons "2" and "4" to starboard, and be sure to stay in the channel near Lake Salvador.

Nearing Larose, do not become confused by the open water to the south where the chart indicates farms or swampland. This area, shown as Delta Farms, was inundated many years ago when broken levees caused the area to flood. Some markers remain from the channels to old drilling locales, but they are lined with rocks and pilings. The Larose Bridge at Mile 35.2 WHL has a 73-foot fixed vertical clearance.

The picturesque Acadian town of Larose straddles the intersection at Bayou Lafourche ("lah-foosh"). Small shipyards are located at both ends of town, while fishing trawlers and pleasure boats border the banks on both the GIWW and Bayou Lafourche. A No-Wake Zone extends for two miles until past the bend at Mile 37 WHL. Heed it, as small rafts are used for work platforms in the shipyards. Fuel may be available at one of the docks just south of the intersection. Overnight dockage is scarce and not charted.

Bayou Lafourche is navigable north to Thibodeaux (Tib-ah-dough), and 35 miles to the Gulf of Mexico, but there are many obstacles, four bridges and No-Wake Zones that are strictly enforced. The Larose-Bourg Cutoff Lift Bridge

at Mile 35.6 WHL, just west of Larose, has a 35-foot closed vertical clearance (73 feet open) and opens on signal.

Warning: At GIWW Mile 49.8 WHL is the Bayou Blue Pontoon Bridge, which opens on signal. A pontoon bridge is not a swing bridge (no vertical clearance) and can best be described as a barge that is pulled out of your way by cables, which hover just under the water where they cannot be seen. Get a clear go-ahead from the bridge tender before proceeding. Even experienced boaters have "gone to sleep at the helm" and started forward when they saw the "bridge" swing out of the way, only to wake up when the bridge tender snapped the cables enough to bring them out of the water. The bridge opens on signal—one long blast followed by a short blast.

Though this is a heavy commercial area, no fuel or other conveniences are available for pleasure craft. Just west of the industrial section is the Houma Bridge (Mile 54.4 WHL, 73-foot fixed vertical clearance). The GIWW then makes a left angle turn and enters Houma. The entire 10-mile-long section from Mile 52 to Mile 62 WHL should be considered a No-Wake area. In the spring months, be cautious of morning fog conditions.

Houma—Mile 57 WHL

Houma has become a popular destination for the transient boater. The city marina is truly Southern hospitality at its best. Houma has plenty of restaurants, attractions, shops and nightlife to entertain cruisers for a few days.

NAVIGATION: Use Chart 11355. The Park Avenue and Main Street bridges at Mile 57.6 and Mile 57.7 WHL, respectively, have 73-foot fixed vertical clearances. The Southern Pacific Railroad Lift Bridge at Mile 58.9 WHL has a 4-foot closed vertical clearance (70-foot clearance when open). The bridge opens on signal and ends just a few miles away, near the Houma Airport.

At Mile 59.5 WHL, the Houma Navigational Canal goes south from the GIWW to Cat Island Pass at the Gulf of Mexico, near the picturesque cities of Cocodrie and Chauvin. The Waterway makes a 45-degree turn to the west, so many skippers have inadvertently wandered southward into the wide-open canal; make sure you take the correct passage.

Many float planes operate from the hangars and ramps on the east side of the Waterway, from the Southern Pacific Railroad Lift Bridge at Mile 58.9 WHL to the Houma Navigational Canal diversion, but you usually will not see them until they roar overhead.

The last bridge going west is on the west side of Houma at Mile 59.9 WHL. The Bayou DuLarge Bridge (40-foot closed vertical clearance) does not open Monday through Friday, 6:45 a.m. to 8:30 a.m., 11:45 a.m. to 12:15 p.m., 12:45 p.m. to 1:15 p.m. and from 4:30 p.m. to 6 p.m.

Dockage: The Houma Downtown Marina, at Mile 58 WHL below the Park Avenue and Main Street bridges, is equipped with shore power, fresh water and pump-out facilities, but no restrooms or fuel. The dockmaster lives near the docks and can provide general information (their telephone number is posted on signs near the docks – call as soon as you get your vessel secure). Access to slips at Houma Downtown Marina is on a first-come, first-served basis. Many shops, banks, a hospital, churches and museums are within easy walking distance of this well-maintained marina. A laundry is located only a few blocks walk away down E. Park Ave. away from the Waterway. Fine dining is available at Café Milano on Belanger Street and Cristiano Ristorante on High Street, both walking distance from the waterfront. There are several restaurants, west of the marina in the Main Street area. Free wireless Internet access is available at the Coffee Zone, also on Main Street. A West Marine sits on the west side of town, but is not within walking distance. Friendly cabbies will come take you to Walmart or other stores for provisioning. The landscaped park offers a great place to relax and exercise and also includes a message board for local information.

Access to fuel in Houma is a challenge. With prior arrangement, gas or diesel fuel is available at Retif Oil and Fuel at the base of the Southern Pacific Railroad Lift Bridge on the north bank. It is recommended that transiting boaters take on fuel prior to reaching Houma.

■ HOUMA TO MORGAN CITY

Mile 57 to Mile 95 WHL

The most scenic section on the Louisiana GIWW is probably the area from Houma to Morgan City. Majestic cypress trees line the banks, their knee-like roots protruding from the water surface to breathe, and Spanish moss hangs from tree branches. Keep a lookout for eagles from Mile 80 to Mile 90 WHL. Anchorages are plentiful but should be used with caution, as a cozy hole reported last year might be unsuitable for the next trip.

NAVIGATION: Use Chart 11355. Beware of submerged pilings from Mile 65 to 75 WHL, and be sure to stay in the middle of the channel. At Mile 74 WHL, submerged pilings are along the northern half of the channel with Lake Hackberry to the north. During the summer, water hyacinths may cover the GIWW. Floating debris may be submerged underneath the hyacinths, so be careful. From Mile 76 through Mile 80 WHL is Lake Cocodrie, very shallow but well-marked. The Waterway becomes part of Bayou Cocodrie and Bayou Black into Morgan City.

The first 25 miles of Waterway, traveling west from Houma, pass through what appears to be a continuous oil and gas-producing field. Sunrise, Lake Hatch, Orange Grove and Hollywood are the charted areas.

Dockage: No marinas or fuel docks are located between Houma and Morgan City (approximately 40 miles); plan your trip accordingly.

Anchorage: Although there are many other possible anchorage areas, the best known is at Bayou Black just east of Mile 84 WHL. This is also a designated mooring area for large barges waiting for dock space; many times they arrive during the night. Your best bet is to proceed well past

the first bend, beyond the pipes lining the bayou. Show a bright anchor light and for added safety, you may want to tie stern-to the trees ashore to prevent you from swinging into the channel. The bayou is wider than the chart would have you believe depths of 11 feet or better are present.

Bayou Boeuf Locks—Mile 93 WHL

NAVIGATION: Use Charts 11355 and 11354. This is the time to check on the status of the Bayou Boeuf (buff) Locks. If the locks are closed for repairs, Bayou Chene (shen) Bypass route at Mile 85 WHL is available, but adds 10 miles to the travel distance. The Bayou Chene Bypass is located to the south of Morgan City and its Waterway-based industries, and offers pristine scenery with almost no evidence of mankind. It is also the route of choice for boaters who would rather not spend time going through Morgan City and its extended No-Wake Zone. This bypass route starts with Bayou Chene, which is 150 feet wide and 10 to 15 feet deep in the channel.

The first four miles of the bypass are unmarked until flashing green "15." Proceed along Big Horn Bayou to green can buoy "1" at the Atchafalaya (ah-chaff-ah-lie-ya) River. Stay in the channel and avoid submerged obstructions and pilings along the banks. When entering the Atchafalaya River, make sure that you pass green can buoy "1" to starboard to avoid shallow water in the east side of the riverbank. Steer north upstream, and follow the river through Sweet Bay Lake.

The well-marked river is wide and deep up to the GIWW at Mile 98 WHL (Atchafalaya River Mile 121). Currents during the spring months might be strong enough to warrant a second thought if you are westbound in a low-powered vessel. The area is also known for heavy fog in springtime. The entire Bayou Chene Bypass route is shown on Charts 11351, 11352, 11354 and 11355. Chart 11354 covers Morgan City to Port Allen and the Atchafalaya River. The route takes you through the delta of the Atchafalaya, some of the most pristine and beautiful swampland in the state.

Bayou Boeuf and the Lakeside Route to Port Allen and the Mississippi River join the GIWW at Mile 87 WHL. The route provides access to Lake Palourde, a shallow pleasure boat area, and then north to the Mississippi River. The Morgan City to Port Allen route, however, is the preferred way. Port Allen lies just across the Mississippi River from downtown Baton Rouge. However, there are no facilities en route or in the Baton Rouge area for recreational vessels.

Morgan City

Morgan City is a sampler of everything coastal Louisiana offers in a friendly and relaxed atmosphere—the heart of Cajun hospitality. If you can find transient dockage, Morgan City is a pleasant layover as you continue your way west on the GIWW. You may visit antebellum homes, plantations and historic communities here.

Morgan City is an island, homeport to more than a thousand fishing boats and what may seem to be an equal

Morgan City, LA

Houma to Morgan City, LA

HOUMA TO MORGAN CITY		Dockage			Supplies		Services			
		Largest Vessel Accommodated / VHF Channel Monitored	Transient Berths / Total Berths	Approach / Dockside Depth (reported) / Floating Docks	Gas / Diesel	Groceries, Ice, Marine Supplies, Snacks	Repairs: Hull, Engine, Propeller / Lift (tonnage), Crane, Rail	1=110V, 2=220V, B=Both, Max Amps	Laundry, Pool, Showers / Pump-Out Station	Nearby: Grocery Store, Motel, Restaurant
1. Downtown Marina of Houma 60 WHL	985-873-6428	140	5/5	8/5				B/50	P	MR
2. Retif Oil 60 WHL	985-872-3111				D					
3. Melvin's Restaurant 60 WHL	985-868-1594	DOCK & DINE								R
4. Shannon Hardware 95 WHL	985-385-2700					M				R
5. Morgan City Public Dock 95 WHL	985-385-1770	100	5/10	15/15	D	IM		1/30		
6. Lake End Park Marina 95 WHL	985-380-4623	55	/38	5/5				1/30	LS	P	GMR
7. Cajun Coast Visitors Bureau 95 WHL	985-395-4905	60	/1	10/10						GMR

Corresponding chart(s) not to be used for navigation. 🖥 Internet Access 📶 Wireless Internet Access

number of workboats. It has a unique waterfront with a concrete seawall to keep out the floodwaters. The downtown area is hard to miss: MORGAN CITY is actually spelled out in huge letters on the wall.

Residents of the area come out strong each Labor Day for the grand Shrimp & Petroleum Festival, held every Labor Day, a tribute to the region's two largest industries.

NAVIGATION: Use Charts 11355 and 11354. From Mile 85 to Mile 102 WHL the GIWW is mostly a No-Wake Zone. The Bayou Boeuf Locks at Mile 93.0 WHL have a depth over the sill of 13 feet, a width of 75 feet and a length of 1,150 feet. As you enter the locks, have your fenders ready, unless the lockmaster directs you to "float the chamber." Make sure you are secured to the wall before the lockmaster starts allowing water to move through the chamber. The timber walls are rough, with cleats widely spaced on huge horizontal beams. When leaving the locks, check in with Berwick Traffic on VHF Channel 11. They will request your name, type of vessel and destination, and then will give you instructions, traffic information and the checkpoints where you should make location reports between the locks and Mile 102, the western limit of Berwick Traffic for pleasure boats.

At Mile 94.3 WHL a ferry crosses the GIWW. Wait for a visual signal or three high-pitched blasts before passing the ferry station.

Dockage: Behind the seawalls are many marine-oriented businesses, a post office, banks, grocery, hardware stores and other shopping. Dockage for pleasure boats at Mile 95 WHL is with well-placed pilings, just under the twin spans on the Morgan City (east) bank of the Atchafalaya River; stern in for easier access to the Morgan City Pleasure Docks (30-amp and 50-amp power and water are available). The pilings will accommodate vessels with beams of 15 feet or less. An "honor payment" for the slip is made in a box hanging on a piling near the docks. During floodwater conditions (usually April and May), the docks may be submerged and the floodgates closed. The Pleasure Docks can be noisy from the traffic on the overhead bridge. Recent improvements in light-

ing and the addition of a covered pavilion make this a Spartan but comfortable dockage.

No marinas with transient amenities are present in Morgan City, and the next full-service marina will be in Lake Charles, 10 miles north of Mile 241 WHL.

Marine repairs and other cruising necessities are located north of the railroad lift bridge and the 50-foot fixed highway bridges on the east bank. Fuel (gas and diesel) is available 24-hours a day at Rio Fuel and Supply, a quarter-mile north of the Pleasure Docks. Look for a large Texaco sign nearby.

Rita Mae's Kitchen, offering authentic and hearty Creole fare, at 711 Federal Ave. is easy walking distance from the marina, as is a quiet public park and library.

GOIN' ASHORE:
ATCHAFALAYA SWAMP, LA

The coastal zone of the Atchafalaya Swamp extends from Bayou Terrebonne (Mile 50 WHL) to Avery Island (Mile 147 WHL). Here, the GIWW passes through several quaint towns and islands in the heart of Louisiana's Cajun/Creole country. Houma, Morgan City and Avery Island are each worth a visit, with each visit being uniquely different. Houma (Mile 57 WHL), with a population of 100,000, has maintained its small-town atmosphere.

Within walking distance of the city marina is Main Street, with quaint shops and nightclubs with live entertainment. For lunch, Clare's Café (531 Liberty St.) is the best in town. If Creole cuisine is your desire, then try Bayou Vue Café (7913 Main St.) overlooking Bayou Terrebonne. Jolly Inn (1507 Barrow St.) is a lunch café by day and a Cajun dance hall and bar by night. For more jazz music, try the Balcony on Main Street.

Houma has an interesting museum, Bayou Terrebonne Waterlife Museum (7910 West Park Ave.), which explores the ecological, cultural and industrial aspects of coastal life in the area. Houma also has excellent medical facilities located near the city marina. The elaborate Houma Public Library (151 Civic Center Blvd.), a few miles west of the marina, offers free public Internet access and a wealth of local information.

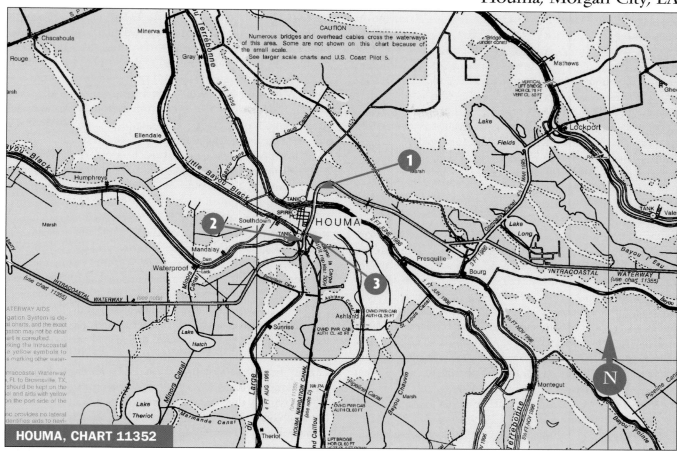

HOUMA, CHART 11352

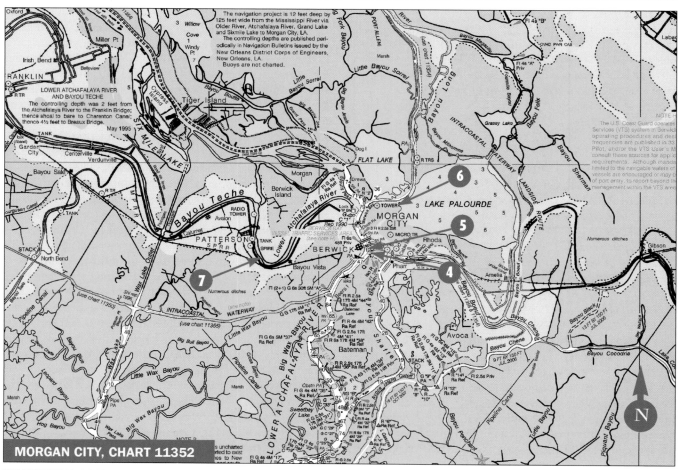

MORGAN CITY, CHART 11352

Atchafalaya River, LA

Morgan City (Mile 95 WHL) has a historic downtown Main Street with a variety of shops, restaurants and museums. Within walking distance of the public docks is Rita Mae's Kitchen (711 Federal Ave.), offering traditional Cajun cuisine. The International Petroleum Museum (111 First St., 985-384-3744) features an offshore drilling rig, affectionately named "Mr. Charlie." Turn of the Century House and Mardi Gras Museum (715 Second St., 985-380-4651) depicts life in the early 1900s, with guided tours through the Cypress Home. The annual Shrimp and Petroleum Festival, held in the downtown Historic District on Labor Day weekend, is one of the biggest events of the season.

If you can navigate to Avery Island, the effort will be well worth it. Located 18 miles north of the GIWW at Mile 145 WHL are Avery Island and the world famous Tabasco Pepper Sauce factory (800-634-9599). Avery Island, surrounded by marshland and water, is actually the top of a subterranean salt mountain extending a mile into the earth. Watch your depth sounder carefully after leaving the GIWW. Try to arrive at the day docks (call ahead for reservations) before 1 p.m., allowing plenty of time to tour the factory, sample different products and also to visit Jungle Gardens and Bird City. There is also a small general store and deli that serves lunch. Shortly after the Civil War, Edmund McIlhenny started to experiment with different types of peppers and recipes, and eventually invented the Tabasco pepper sauce found on kitchen tables throughout the world today. The McIlhenny family created Jungle Gardens in the late 1800s to help save the snowy egret from extinction. Today, the 200-acre garden is home to 20,000 of these and other water birds.

ADDITIONAL RESOURCES

■ **Houma Area Convention and Visitor Bureau**
985-868-2732, **www.houmatourism.com**

⚑ **NEARBY GOLF COURSES**
Atchafalaya Golf Course at Idlewild, 400 Cotten Road, Patterson, LA 70392, 985-395-4653, **www.atchafalayagolf.com**

☤ **NEARBY MEDICAL FACILITIES**
Terrebonne General Medical Center, 8166 Main St., Houma, LA 70360, 985-873-4141

■ ATCHAFALAYA RIVER TO VERMILION RIVER

The GIWW at the Atchafalaya River (Mile 98 WHL) extends westward to the Vermilion River and Intracoastal City (Mile 160 WHL). The Waterway is mostly straight, has no locks, and presents just one cable ferry and one swing bridge. Very limited dockage is available, but no fuel. Enjoy the pleasant scenery and be watchful of the commercial traffic.

NAVIGATION: Use Charts 11350, 11352 and 11355. South from Berwick Bay and Morgan City, the GIWW follows the Lower Atchafalaya River for three miles, and then turns to the southwest on Little Wax Bayou at flashing green "A," quick flashing red "2" and quick flashing green "1." At GIWW Mile 108 WHL, the route crosses Wax Lake Outlet, a deep drainage ditch from Bayou Teche and the Atchafalaya Basin. Strong currents, especially after heavy storms, can make towboat transit a "hair-raising" experience. Wait for oncoming tows to cross before proceeding.

Take care as you cross the swift north to south currents, which cause a few accidents each year; low power is a handicap at this point. Heavy debris becomes more plentiful during high-water periods. An estimated 40 percent of the flow from the Atchafalaya River is diverted through the Wax Lake Outlet Canal, representing roughly 12 percent of the Mississippi River's flow. You will find yourself crossing on a diagonal to make any headway in this extremely strong current.

The town of North Bend at Bayou Sale (sall-e) is a small commercial town with no transient services. The North Bend Bridge at Mile 113.0 WHL has a 73-foot fixed vertical clearance.

The first entrance into West Cote Blanche Bay and Vermilion Bay is through The Jaws just east of Mile 122.5 WHL, where the Charenton Drainage and Navigation Canal crosses the GIWW. Charenton Canal is the choice route north to scenic Bayou Teche. The area in the proximity of Mud Lake (Mile 121 to Mile 122 WHL between flashing green "9" and flashing green "11") is subject to shoaling just before the bend at the canal. Do not attempt to enter Mud Lake due to shoaling and submerged pilings.

If you are traveling west through West Cote Blanche Bay and Vermilion Bay, use Charts 11349 and 11351. This is an equidistant and much more open route to the Gulf of Mexico at Southwest Pass or back to the GIWW via Four Mile Cut (a dredged extension of the Vermilion River). Chart GPS coordinates before taking this route.

Dockage: Ten miles south of The Jaws (Mile 122), Cypremort (sip-ree-mow) Point (Chart 11349) offers a variety of marinas, a yacht club, ramps and repair facilities. Bayview Marina offers transient amenities, including restrooms, showers, a Travelift, shore power and slips that can accommodate vessels up to 60 feet in length. Nearby is a ship's store with a fuel dock for gas and diesel and a recently opened restaurant. Call ahead for reservations.

Anchorage: Just north of the GIWW on the Charenton Canal is a comfortable, overnight anchorage in 9 feet at mean low water. Proceed about .5 miles from the Waterway and anchor on the starboard side of the canal. You will have plenty of water close to shore, keeping you out of the way of commercial traffic.

Cypremort Cable Ferry—Mile 129.7 WHL

At Mile 129.7 WHL, a cable ferry operates across the Waterway. Cables may be at or near the water surface. After the ferry captain gives you a visual or horn signal, proceed cautiously at low speed.

A 73-foot vertical clearance fixed bridge is west of the ferry at Mile 134.0 WHL. This is the midway point between New Orleans and the Texas border. The area has become congested with loading platforms on both banks. Towboats with barges also use this area to make crew changes.

Weeks Island—Mile 137 to Mile 140 WHL

NAVIGATION: Use Chart 11350. At Mile 137 WHL is the Weeks Island Terminal, where workers are usually busy loading barges. At night, the run is difficult and confusing due to the great number of lights—some are moving and some are stationary. Just past Mile 137 WHL, the south bank is washed out, and at Mile 138 WHL, Weeks Bayou empties into Weeks Bay, creating swift currents during the tide changes and in southwesterly winds.

Rising 171 feet above the marsh to starboard, the huge salt dome of Weeks Island is the largest salt mine operation in Louisiana and the source of heavy barge traffic. Such a salt dome is actually a huge mound of salt that has risen from the ground over thousands of years; others are on Avery, Jefferson and Cote Blanche islands. Salt domes such as this usually cover huge deposits of oil and gas, hence the large number of barges for both salt and oil.

Between Mile 137 and Mile 140 WHL are many pipeline crossings, wellheads and storage tanks in side canals. They are protected by a limestone wall and idle barges. The area from Weeks Island to Intracoastal City is low marshland. If it is windy, be prepared for signals from tows indicating from which side they want you to pass.

Avery Island, Bayou Petit Anse— Mile 146 WHL

Avery Island offers a unique opportunity to visit the Tabasco Pepper Sauce factory, Jungle Gardens and Bird City. An on-site deli serves sundries and sandwiches. The security guard at the entrance gate can direct you to the visitors center.

NAVIGATION: Use Chart 11350. Across the GIWW from Avery Canal at Mile 146 WHL, Bayou Petit Anse (pet-E-onz) leads northeast to Avery Island. This area is not charted on the GIWW chart. The bayou leads north from the Waterway at Mile 146 WHL to its junction with the Delcambre (dell-comb) Canal, which has depths of 8 to 10 feet throughout. The canal then continues eastward and offers views of Avery Island.

Dockage: If you want to visit Avery Island, try to obtain advance information, as dockage and anchorage spaces are limited. Dockage (but no power) is available at the public dock at the head of the bayou, next to the boat launch. Do not dock at the private pier across from the launch adjacent to the security shack—this is owned by the Simmons family, who manage Avery Island.

Anchorage: Vessels may also anchor along the bayou, as this area is well-protected. One can anchor just off the public dock near Avery Island, in Bayou Petit Anse in 11 feet on the north side of the GIWW or south of the Waterway in the Avery Canal in 8 feet at mean low water.

Intracoastal City to Vermilion River— Mile 159 to Mile 160 WHL

The Vermilion River crossing at Mile 159 is a heavy commercial area, both from petroleum and fishing, 24 hours a day. Heavy wake action is the norm here, and pleasure craft seem to lose all claims to right-of-way, so all eyes (and clasped hands) are needed on watch.

NAVIGATION: Use Chart 11349 and 11350. To the south is the Four Mile Cutoff, which diverts the original riverbed from the GIWW to Vermilion Bay and the Southwest Pass onward to the Gulf of Mexico.

To the north on the Vermilion River (shown on the chart as the Vermilion River Extension), the interesting cities of Abbeville and Lafayette are located beyond the commercial area. Though the route is navigable to Lafayette, there are no transient facilities.

Dockage: One mile west of the Vermilion River crossing, on the north side of the GIWW at Mile 160 WHL, is a commercial facility that tries in every way to accommodate transient pleasure boats. Though it is a Texaco dealer, it is named the Shell Morgan Landing, a combination of family names. Dockage for vessels is first-come, first-served, whether you are a 30-footer needing 30 gallons of fuel, or a larger vessel needing 300 gallons; the fuel pumps for recreational boaters are located next to the red office building (fuel dock closes at 6 p.m.). Use your fenders (the dock is draped with huge black tires), and approach with caution, keeping an eye on any commercial traffic or wakes. You will find water and 30-amp shore power along the visitors dock. Showers and restrooms were added in 2007. The Maxie Pierce Grocery Store, located just east of Shell Morgan Landing, has all of the provisions needed for the transient boater. Homemade "po' boy" sandwiches are available at the store until 6 p.m. every day. Shell Morgan Landing is strategically located for those wishing accommodation on the GIWW with easy access to offshore routes (see Offshore Run—Intracoastal City to Galveston).

Danny Richard's (ree-shard's) Marina, on the Vermilion River just north of the GIWW, is often reported as having accommodations, but has not been open to transients for many years.

Note: The next "official" fuel stop is in the Lake Charles area, almost 100 miles away. The exception is at Mile 193, where Talen's Landing, a commercial facility, offers diesel fuel only to larger pleasure vessels.

Offshore Run—Venice to Intracoastal City; Intracoastal City to Galveston

Venice offers a good strategic stopover point for boaters traveling westbound from the Mississippi or Alabama coasts. From Venice to the west, Intracoastal City represents another good stopping point for those vessels with at least a 220-mile range. Tiger Pass moves to the southwest from Venice, putting you into the Gulf of Mexico at the end of its 12-mile run. Many of

Delcambre, Intracoastal City, Lake Charles, LA

WESTLAKE AREA & INTRACOASTAL CITY		Largest Vessel Accommodated	VHF Channel Monitored	Approach / Dockside Depth (reported)	Transient Berths / Total Berths	Floating Docks	Groceries, Ice, Marine Supplies, Snacks	Gas / Diesel	Repairs: Hull, Engine, Propeller	Lift (tonnage), Crane, Rail	1=110v, 2=220v, B=Both, Max Amps	Laundry, Pool, Showers	Pump-Out Station	Nearby: Grocery Store, Motel, Restaurant
		Dockage					**Supplies**				**Services**			
1. Port of Delcambre 146 WHL	337-685-2257	100		10/50	12/10		GD	GIMS	HEP	R	1/30	L		G
2. Danny Richard Marina 159.2 WHL	337-893-2157	65			8/5			GI	HP		1/30			
3. Shell Morgan Landing Inc. 160 WHL	337-893-1211	200		3/3	7/7		GD	GIMS		C	1/30	S		GM
4. Bridge Point Yacht Center 241 WHL	337-436-0803			12/12	F	GD	M	HEP	L35	B/50	LS		GM
5. L'Auberge du Lac Resort	337-395-7768	50		14/16	40/10			S			B/50	PS		GMR

Corresponding chart(s) not to be used for navigation. 🖳 Internet Access 📶 Wireless Internet Access

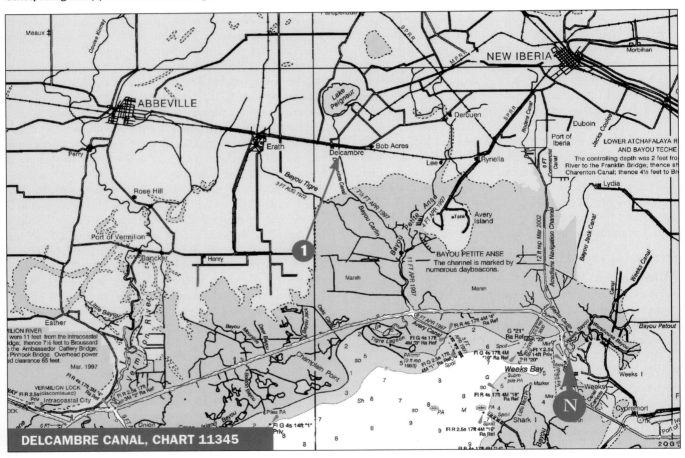

DELCAMBRE CANAL, CHART 11345

the navigation aids on Tiger Pass have been replaced in the last 5 years.

From the end of Tiger Pass' marked channel, it is nearly a straight course past Port Fourchon and Belle Pass on the mainland to starboard, 170 miles to the entrance to Vermillion Bay. The Vermillion Bay Channel will dogleg to port after reaching land and terminate at the GIWW less than a mile east of Shell Morgan Landing. Departing here to points west, you will want to take the Freshwater Bayou route through one set of locks, then on to the Gulf. From the sea buoy "FB" south of the locks, it is approximately 180 miles on a straight course to the jetties at Galveston Island.

◼ WEST FROM INTRACOASTAL CITY

NAVIGATION: Use Chart 11350. Heading west from Intracoastal City, from Shell Morgan Landing to Mile 161 WHL, both banks are lined with petroleum-related docks and wharves. Supply boats and crew boats move in and out both day and night.

The intersection of the GIWW with Freshwater Bayou to the Gulf of Mexico can be confusing. The GIWW turns 70 degrees to the northwest from Freshwater Bayou, and the turn is easy to miss. Many westbound cruisers have

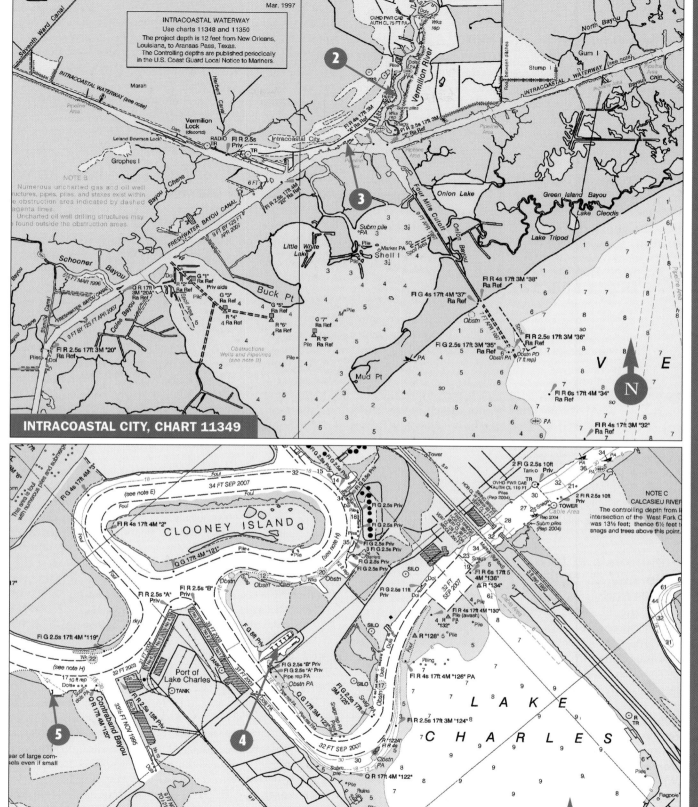

INTRACOASTAL CITY, CHART 11349

LAKE CHARLES AREA, CHART 11347

Lake Arthur, LA

proceeded straight ahead for a mile or more before realizing that the Leland Bowman Lock is nowhere in sight.

Leland Bowman Lock—Mile 163 WHL

This lock is part of the system that prevents the intrusion of saltwater into the farming areas of the Mermentau Basin. Together with the Calcasieu Locks and the Schooner Bayou Floodgates, they retain freshwater in Mermentau Basin at a predetermined level. The Leland Bowman Locks replaced the old Vermilion Locks on the north side of the newer structure.

NAVIGATION: Use Chart 11350. Contact the lockmaster after passing the Freshwater Bayou Canal; quite often the locks will be standing open, and you will be asked to pass through. Go slowly through the chamber, keeping good steerageway.

Schooner Bayou Alternate Route— Mile 161 to Mile 167 WHL

If the Leland Bowman Lock has a long backup of traffic or is closed for repairs, the alternate route shown on your chart may be preferable. Check first to be sure that it is open. It may be closed for the same reason as the Leland Bowman Lock.

NAVIGATION: Use Chart 11350. Go south four miles on Freshwater Bayou Canal before turning west into Schooner Bayou (5.5-foot depths). The Schooner Bayou Floodgate is two miles west of the canal and is open from 6 a.m. until 8 p.m., seven days a week. This is a saltwater control structure, so when the flow is minimal, the gates may be open for you to go right on through (with the lockmaster's permission). After passing the floodgate, steer north along the North Prong of Schooner Bayou (8-foot depths) for three miles to the GIWW at Mile 167 WHL.

Forked Island to Mermentau River— Mile 167 to Mile 202 WHL

NAVIGATION: Use Charts 11348 and 11350. The Forked Island Highway Bridge (Mile 170.3 WHL, 73-foot fixed vertical clearance) connects the towns of Abbeville and Lafayette with the Rockefeller Wildlife Refuge and westerly into Cameron and the Calcasieu River.

The next 30 miles to the Mermentau River is an isolated stretch through mostly swampy lowlands. It is a good time for bird-watching. A tractor-pulled cable ferry connecting the rice farms at Mile 178.4 WHL operates only when needed.

Dockage: For many years a local commercial fuel distributor maintained a service store (just past Mile 193 WHL), which offered groceries, ice and limited dockage for cruisers. The facility was closed to all pleasure boats in 1996. The landing is still for commercial use only.

The GIWW crosses the Mermentau River between Mile 201.5 and Mile 202.5 with flashing green "A" on the south bank marking the entrance and flashing green "7" marking the departure westward. A pipeline termi-

nal, with its numerous tanks, is located on the south side of the Waterway, one mile before arriving at the river entrance itself. Chart 11348 covers the river from the Gulf of Mexico to Lake Arthur. The mileage scale is reduced to one half of that on the GIWW, and the miles are measured starting with Mile Zero from the Gulf outlet, not from the GIWW.

Anchorage: A good anchorage was reported in the river on the west bank just north of green daybeacon "1A." Another good anchorage is north of GIWW can buoys "3" and "5" in a marshy cove at the Mermentau River mouth.

Mermentau River Side Trip—Lake Arthur to the Gulf of Mexico

The Mermentau River crosses the GIWW at Mile 202 WHL, about 37 miles north of the Gulf of Mexico. The friendly town of Lake Arthur lies 15 miles to the north of the GIWW. Lake Arthur has many summer visitors and is a destination for hunters during the winter.

NAVIGATION: Use Chart 11348. From the GIWW to Lake Arthur the river has a controlling depth of 9.5 feet, with greater depths generally found. Some uncharted islands, a sunken shrimp boat (marked by buoys) and anchored or beached barges are scattered about. Travel through in the center of the Narrows just prior to flashing red "20A" (Mermentau River Mile 50) due to the submerged vessel on the west shore.

The route south from the GIWW on the Mermentau River meanders for 37 miles through Grand Lake and upper and lower Mud Lake to a shallow Gulf inlet. The route is shown on Charts 11344 and 11348, but boaters should seek local knowledge before making this trip.

Dockage: Gasoline and diesel fuel may be available at Gary's Landing, Mermentau River Mile 40 (west bank), at the Lacassine Wildlife Refuge headquarters. A privately maintained (charted) flashing red marker signals the point for a west turn into Gary's Landing or an east turn on the Mermentau River. Another fuel stop (gas only) might still be located at Meyer's Landing and Lowry Dock at Mile 44 (west bank), seven miles north of the GIWW.

The Lake Arthur Yacht Club (12 miles north of the GIWW) has always been friendly to cruisers and will usually have space available for short visits. This is primarily a sailing club. Fuel can be trucked to the yacht club (minimum order 100 gallons).

Fuel, both gas and diesel, is available at the Lake Arthur town docks, but the docks are usually crowded with commercial and local fishermen. Dockage is scarce; anchoring off the docks is possible. Restaurants and stores are not within walking distance, but courtesy cars might be available.

Anchorage: Just past green daybeacon "5" on the Mermentau River, turn to starboard to anchor in the lee of the island marked "Stump PA" on the chart. You will have 8 to 10 feet of water and might even see an alligator swimming ashore.

Bayou Lacassine—Mile 205 WHL

Bayou Lacassine, a fine spot for bird- and alligator-watching, is part of the Lacassine Wildlife Refuge.

Anchorage: Many boaters have reported this area to be a fine anchorage. Depths of 5 to 8 feet off the GIWW on the north bank's east entrance prevail for at least 1,000 feet. Bayou Lacassine then turns sharply to the west with a depth of 5 feet or more.

Little Lake Misere—Mile 212 WHL

NAVIGATION: Use Chart 11348. The entrances to Little Lake Misere ("miz-air") are uncharted. Stay to the port side of quick flashing green "1" on the south bank of the GIWW at Mile 212.5 WHL. The open area, opposite the Bell City Drainage Canal (5.5-foot controlling depth), is not a charted entrance.

From GIWW Mile 217 WHL to the Gibbstown Bridge at Mile 219.8, stay clear of the uncharted, submerged rocks along the north bank extending up to 75 feet away from the bank.

Anchorage: The Bell City Drainage Canal, with a charted depth of 5.5 feet, is reported to be suitable for anchoring, but it does carry some workboat traffic.

Gibbstown (Creole Canal Bridge)—Mile 219.8 WHL

Snow geese are just one species of migrating waterfowl that populate the Cameron Prairie National Wildlife Refuge during the winter months. The most prominent feature in this area is the Creole Canal Bridge, remembered by many as the Gibbstown Ferry. The fixed bridge (73-foot vertical clearance), completed in 1976, is still called Gibbstown by most boat operators.

Sweet Lake—Mile 223 to Mile 224 WHL

NAVIGATION: Use Chart 11348. Sweet Lake is open on the north side. A tank farm on the north is followed by red daybeacons "2," "4" and "6." The lake is shallow, and depths are not charted.

Grand Lake Pontoon Bridge—Mile 231.5 WHL

NAVIGATION: Use Chart 11348. Remember, a pontoon bridge is not a swing bridge. It is a barge that is pulled open with cables that lurk under the surface even while the bridge is opening. Wait for visual or verbal instructions before moving. The Grand Lake Pontoon Bridge has no openings Monday through Friday from 6 a.m. to 8 a.m. and from 2 p.m. to 4 p.m.

Black Bayou Pontoon Bridge—Mile 238 WHL

NAVIGATION: Use Chart 11348. See the reminder above. The Black Bayou Pontoon Bridge is just before the Calcasieu Lock (Mile 238.2); do not go beyond this bridge without approval from the Calcasieu lockmaster. Westbound boaters must check with the lock on VHF Channel 14, obtain clearance, and then call the bridge on VHF Channel 13 for an opening. If you encounter a long delay, it is best to wait on the east side (where the Waterway is wider) than in the small area between the bridge and the locks. The Black Bayou Pontoon Bridge does not open Monday through Friday from 6 a.m. to 8 a.m. and from 2 p.m. to 4 p.m.

Calcasieu River—Mile 238 WHL

NAVIGATION: Use Charts 11331 and 11347. Once past the Black Bayou Pontoon Bridge, you are required to wait in the holding area between the bridge and the Calcasieu Lock. The north shore is shallow and lined by rocks. The south side near the lock has 7-foot depths, but no place to tie up or anchor. There is a warning sign, "DO NOT PASS THIS POINT UNTIL..," but it is a common practice when a tow is passing to gain increased maneuvering space. During low water, the lock gate might be open, and you may pass through if the green ball is hoisted. Contact the lockmaster if possible.

■ CALCASIEU RIVER TO LAKE CHARLES

Calcasieu River—Mile 241 WHL

North of the GIWW, the Calcasieu River extends 20 miles to the commercial port and casino gambling center of Lake Charles.

NAVIGATION: Use Chart 11347. Enter the Calcasieu River just northwest of Choupique Island. River depths range from 12 to 30 feet. Follow the well-marked channel as you pass through Moss Lake, and be sure to stay mid-channel. Change direction to the northeast, back to north, and then northeast. Follow the buoys until you get through Rose Bluff Cutoff and to the Interstate 210 Bridge (fixed 135-foot clearance). After the bridge, pass Contraband Bayou, and follow the buoys to the Port of Lake Charles. Traveling clockwise and then east around the port facilities, the channel enters Lake Charles.

Dockage: Coming through the locks westbound, you will pass Calcasieu Point Landing on your starboard side as you make the 280 degree turn to port toward the river. This facility has a convenience store, restrooms and launch ramps, but no fuel or overnight accommodations. On Contraband Bayou, three miles east of the Calcasieu River, Bow Tie Marina offers limited transient dockage with gas and diesel fuel available. A pump-out station and water are also situated next to the fuel dock. Full-service boat repairs are located nearby. The Inn on the Bayou motel and Bennigan's Bar and Grill are located just above the 15-foot fixed vertical clearance bridge and are accessible by dinghy or smaller boats. It is common practice to raft up with others docked along the wall. Just ask permission before you do. Free wireless Internet access is available at the hotel. (Call 337-474-5151.)

Lake Charles, LA

Going upriver, at a 120-degree turn to starboard around the Port of Lake Charles, are the remains of an old bridge whose base is still intact on the port bank. On the downriver side is the newly enlarged Bridge Point Yacht Center, offering transient dockage (at the end of the finger piers), marine repairs, a marine store and full amenities. Fuel is available (both gas and diesel) at Nalmar Landing on the upriver side of the bridge. There are no pump-out facilities here.

Anchorage: An excellent anchorage lies just a few miles upriver near the Haymark Terminal. Enter the oxbow across from flashing green "103" and proceed around to anchor in 16-foot charted depths. This is a quiet anchorage away from GIWW wakes. You may even see a roseate spoonbill in the marsh here.

Lake Charles

NAVIGATION: Use Chart 11347. Just northeast of the marinas is the lake that gave the city its name. Travel in the marked channel as you enter the lake and stay toward the west shore. If your draft is less than 4 feet, you can pass over the charted sand bar and explore the rest of the lake. The Calcasieu River extends north of the Interstate 10 Bridge (135-foot fixed vertical clearance) to the town of Sulfur and beyond.

Dockage: The floating gambling casinos are on the west side of the Calcasieu River just south of the Interstate 10 Highway Bridge. The floating casinos no longer leave their docks, so cruising by the casinos is not a problem. The casinos feature courtesy transportation to and from marinas, but check the regulations carefully before trying to dock there, either with your primary vessel or the dinghy.

The newest addition to the boating landscape in Lake Charles is the stunning 26-story L'Auberge du Lac Hotel and Casino at the southern mouth of Contraband Bayou as it empties into the Calcasieu River. The marina includes 16 double slips and can accommodate two 50-foot vessels and 14 30-foot vessels. Each slip has shore power and water, but the marina has no fuel or pump-out facilities. The resort boasts five restaurants, an ice cream parlor, an arcade, a swimming pool with a lazy river, a full-service spa, an RV park and an adjacent golf course.

It is not surprising that L'Auberge du Lac has become a popular destination, drawing boaters from New Orleans to Houston. For this reason, reservations for overnight dockage are strongly advised and may be booked through the spa (337-395-7768). Courtesy dockage is complimentary for dinner guests. The hotel owns an amphibious seaplane, which often docks nearby, so maintain a close watch as you come into the marina complex.

Anchorage: Lake Charles offers one of the finest anchorage spots along the Gulf coast, and it is the site of many celebrations and regattas throughout the summer. If you can cross the 5-foot bar into the lake, pick your location for the best wind protection in 7 to 9 feet at mean low water. Above Lake Charles, the Calcasieu River is navigable for many miles and offers scenic and remote anchorage opportunities.

GOIN' ASHORE:
LAKE CHARLES, LA

This "City by the Lake" has a great white sandy beach, clear water, exciting gaming and a wide variety of restaurants and shopping delights. You can visit the Imperial Calcasieu Museum, the Historic Charpentier District and the Mardi Gras Museum by taking a taxi downtown.

The Harrah's casino riverboat was heavily damaged by Hurricane Rita in 2005, as was the adjacent hotel and marina. The hotel has since been re-opened under a different name. On April 17, 2006, Pinnacle Entertainment (owner of L'Auberge du Lac) announced that it had signed a letter of intent to acquire all of the assets of Harrah's Lake Charles, including their coveted gaming license. In November 2006, voters approved the release of this license to Pinnacle, who will use it to develop Sugarcane Bay, a casino and golf resort lying just to the south of L'Auberge. Development was stalled due to the recession of 2008 and 2009.

Springtime at Lake Charles is a special time, but especially so during the Contraband Days Festival, which celebrates the legend of the famous pirate Jean Lafitte. The festival is usually held during the first two weeks of May. According to local folklore, Lafitte buried much of his treasure on the white, sandy shores of Lake Charles. The festival continues for two weeks with pirates making the mayor walk the plank; treasure hunting along the beach; and on-the-water concerts, food of all types, dancing, sailboat regattas, fireworks and many other events.

ADDITIONAL RESOURCES

■ **Southwest Louisiana Convention & Visitors Bureau**
800-456-7952, **www.visitlakecharles.org**

NEARBY GOLF COURSES
Mallard Cove Golf Course, 4300 Mallard Cove Dr., Lake Charles, LA 70602, 337-491-1204

NEARBY MEDICAL FACILITIES
Lake Charles Memorial Hospital, 1701 Oak Park Blvd., Lake Charles, LA 70601, 337-494-3000

Bayou Choupique

Anchorage: Back on the Waterway at Mile 242, this quiet bayou offers a secure anchorage with 9- to 12-foot depths. The entrance is one mile east of the Ellender Lift Bridge (Mile 243.8 WHL, 50-foot closed vertical clearance, 135-foot open vertical clearance) on the north side. As you move into the bayou and cross the bar, keep slightly to the west (starboard) of center. The port side may be filled with crab traps. Make a 90-degree turn to starboard, and then steer to the center of the next sharp left bend. You can go a bit farther upstream, as it does carry at least 9-foot depths for a good distance. As an added benefit, you won't be disturbed by workboat traffic here.

Ellender Bridge—Mile 243.8 WHL

NAVIGATION: Use Charts 11331 and 11347. The GIWW swings to the west after passing the Ellender Lift Bridge, a classic lift bridge with a 50-foot clearance down or 135 feet open. **Note:** This bridge requires four hours notice to open. (Call 800-752-6706.) Any vessel that requires more than 50 feet of vertical clearance should contact the Black Bayou Pontoon Bridge on VHF Channels 13 or 14. The Black Bayou bridge tender will then contact the Ellender Lift Bridge. You will receive instructions to contact them again when you are 30 minutes out from the Ellender Bridge. Eastbound, call 24 hours in advance, and make an appointment with the bridge. Leave some extra time in your schedule so you can arrive in advance and wait, rather than miss your opening. If you arrive early, they may open for you if commercial traffic is waiting as well.

West Port Calcasieu—Mile 244 WHL

From the Ellender Lift Bridge, it is a fairly boring (and almost perfectly straight) 20-plus-mile stretch to the Texas state line at Mile 266 WHL. The barge port of West Port Calcasieu is the last indication of civilization. Here, a large number of barges are stacked on the north and south banks. You may also encounter parked barge strings with no towboat, lighted at night with a flashing yellow light on both outboard corners. The water runs straight, wide and deep, and moss-draped trees give way to grass, low scrub and low marsh. This is excellent gator country. As you run to Mile 254.1 WHL, you will pass the abandoned Gum Cove Cable Ferry.

Pavell Island—Mile 265 to Mile 266 WHL

Anchorage: Exercise caution here, as the east side of Pavell Island is filled with wrecks of large and small boats, and a low wall of semi-submerged pilings blocks the upper end. However, the cut is excellent on the west side of the island. Be careful not to block the cut when you anchor. Some folks tie the bow up to a tree here and run a stern anchor, Mediterranean-style. Approach the bank with care; it shoals up quickly. This is a fairly quiet anchorage, but an occasional towboat moves through.

■ CROSSING INTO TEXAS

The Texas Gulf Coast offers a varied and slowly changing vista, from alligator-laden bayous to cactus-covered bird sanctuaries. It also offers full 75-foot vertical clearance at all fixed bridges. After the relatively short Alabama and Mississippi Gulf Coast segments and the Creole-flavored Louisiana GIWW run, the long Texas coastline slowly transforms the scenery and gradually shifts to the tropical. Passes between the extended low barrier islands are scattered about a day's run apart. Note, however, that not all passes are easily transited. The vast majority of the coast is made up of marsh islands that are sometimes little more than sandbars or shoals. Big, choppy bays run almost the entire length of the Texas coast. The bays are steeped in history and based on the waterborne commerce that created the Texas Gulf communities—especially the Galveston Bay area.

NAVIGATION: Use Chart 11331. The GIWW cuts through Texas bays, bayous and swampland in a wide and well-buoyed swath. Note that frequent changes to buoy numbers are made in all the bays, and charts may not show these new and altered numbers. Several buoys are missing in a few bays and are noted in subsequent navigation sections. The daybeacon numbers are usually more reliable. The upper half of the Texas coastline, from Sabine to Corpus Christi, has frequent and well-placed marinas and anchorages.

The lower Texas Gulf Coast (from Port Aransas to Port Isabel at the Mexican border) is more tropical and far less developed. Many anchorages are available, but most shoreline property is private. The top half of the Texas GIWW is well-traveled by barge and tug traffic, especially from Sabine to Freeport, where numerous petrochemical refineries are located.

Sabine River—Mile 265 to Mile 273 WHL

On the north side, the Texas border begins at the Sabine River just two miles downstream from Orange. However, Louisiana continues until Mile 272 WHL on the south side of the Waterway. Pavell Island is in Texas, while Cutoff Island (farther west) is in Louisiana.

NAVIGATION: Use Chart 11331. At Mile 265 just past Cutoff Island, the GIWW joins the Sabine River. After passing flashing red "22," head downstream toward Sabine Lake. The river is 200 feet wide and 30 feet deep in the center portion of the river. Follow the fixed flashing lights past Shell Island to the south as you enter Sabine Lake. This is a major ship channel.

There is an excellent anchorage on the Sabine River as it runs off the GIWW toward Orange. This is Adams Bayou at about Mile 266 WHL. You can enter the bayou on the northwest bank of the river in 15 to 20 feet of water. Depths remain steady until you reach the Dupont Barge Docks, about a mile up into the bayou.

Dockage: About another mile up Adams Bayou on the northeast shore is a yacht basin, which did not have a functioning marina at press time summer 2010. When you approach the basin, you will see two possible entry cuts. The first and best choice has 8-foot depths or more; the second is slightly shallower, with 6 to 7 feet of water, and passes a long dock and boathouse before it reaches the open area. If you choose to tie up here, be forewarned that the docks may not have been tended to in many years, so do so at your own risk.

Anchorage: There are many good anchorages in this area, from Adams Bayou to Shell Island. There is an excellent anchorage on the Sabine River as it runs off the GIWW toward Orange. This is Adams Bayou at about Mile 266 WHL. You can enter the bayou on the northwest bank of

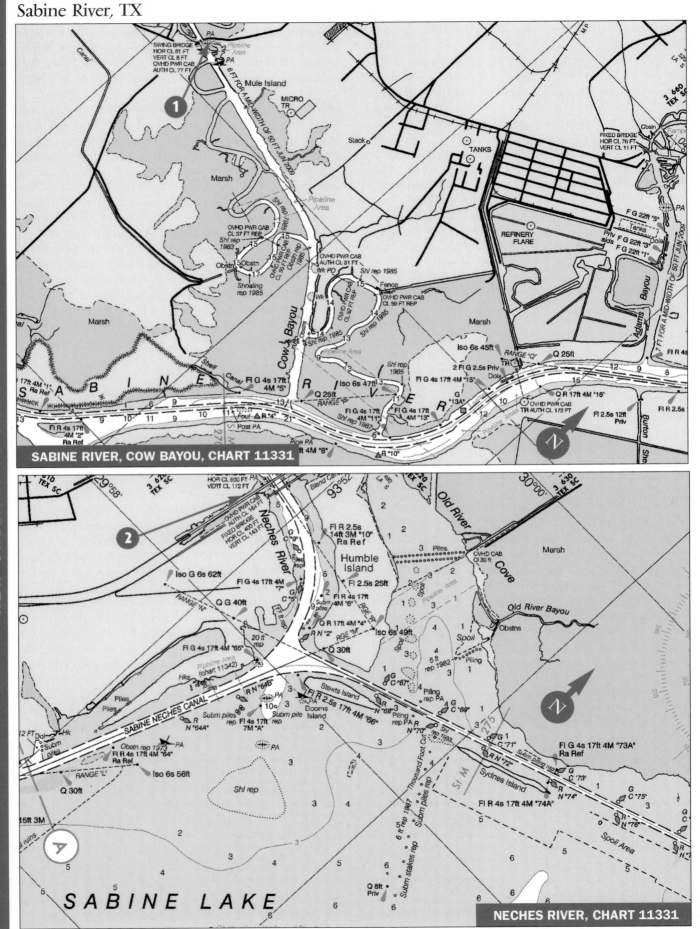

SABINE RIVER, COW BAYOU, CHART 11331

NECHES RIVER, CHART 11331

Sabine and Neches Rivers, Beaumont, TX

SABINE AND NECHES RIVERS		Largest Vessel Accommodated	VHF Channel Monitored	Dockage			Supplies			Services			
				Transient Berths / Total Berths	Approach / Dockside Depth (reported)	Floating Docks	Gas / Diesel	Groceries, Ice, Marine Supplies, Snacks	Repairs: Hull, Engine, Propeller	Lift (tonnage), Crane, Rail	1=110V, 2=220V, B=Both, Max Amps	Laundry, Pool, Showers	Pump-Out Station	Nearby: Grocery Store, Motel, Restaurant
1. Peggy's on the Bayou	409-886-1115			18/18	6/5		G	IS			1/50	LS		R
2. Rainbow Marina 276.5 WHL	409-962-9578	52	68	/30	4/4		G	GIMS			1/50			R
3. Beaumont Yacht Club	409-832-1456	50	16	2/81	5/6		GD	IS			B/30	LS	P	

Corresponding chart(s) not to be used for navigation. ⌨ Internet Access (WiFi) Wireless Internet Access

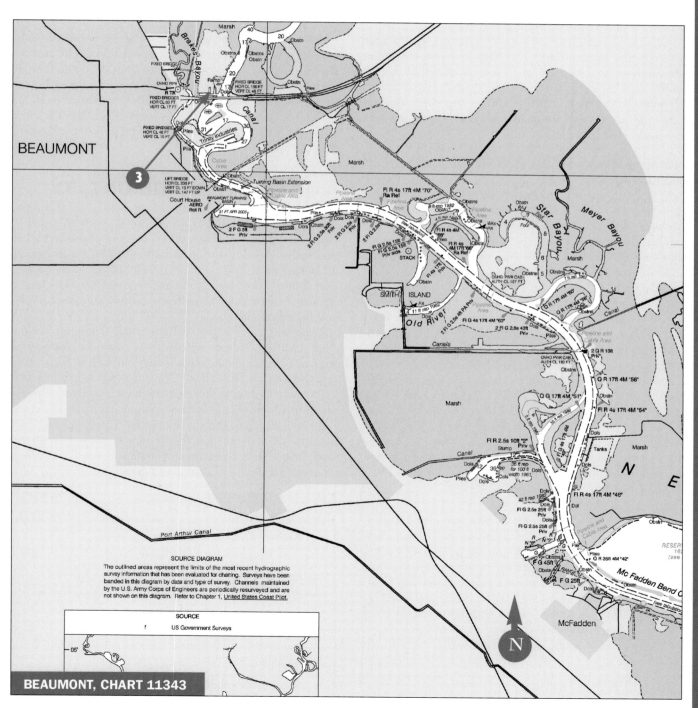

BEAUMONT, CHART 11343

Beaumont, TX

the river in 15 to 20 feet of water. Depths remain steady until you reach the Dupont Barge Docks, about a mile up into the bayou. You can continue up the bayou to just past the yacht basin and anchor in 8- to 9-foot depths. You can dinghy to shore in the basin and walk to the grocery store.

A wide bayou at the southeast corner of the anchorage area leads to Sabine Lake. This area is known as East Pass and has 7- to 11-foot depths up the lake's edge. This same channel has 7- to 12-foot depths as it runs into Black Bayou. There is a bar at the entry, so move over it slightly south of center where there is 6 to 7 feet of water. Once past the entry bar, there is 10 to 12 feet of water in an excellent, quiet anchorage. If a fall or winter northerly is predicted, avoid this anchorage; the water level could drop 3 to 4 feet, trapping you in the bayou behind the entry sandbar.

Another possible spot to drop the hook is found with a turn to the south at Mile 272 WHL to a spot charted as Middle Pass. It is as deep as 25 feet in spots, due to the strong tidal current that flows though the cut, so anchor accordingly. It does not offer the protection of East Pass or Black Bayou, so avoid the spot if there are strong south or southeasterly winds.

Neches River—Mile 277 WHL

NAVIGATION: Use Charts 11331 and 11343. The GIWW runs along the northern edge of Sabine Lake, past what is called the Thousand Foot Cut, to the mouth of the Neches River at Mile 277 WHL. The Neches River is navigable for 18 miles upriver from the Rainbow Bridge (172-foot fixed vertical clearance) to beyond the Interstate 10 Bridge at Beaumont. There is heavy barge and tug traffic here, servicing the center of a major petrochemical region. But the river is deep almost to its wide banks, so there is ample room. Chart 11343 shows complete Sabine River and Neches River details. Chart 11331 is good from the Louisiana border down Sabine River.

On the west bank of the Neches River under the old Rainbow Bridge (143-foot fixed vertical clearance) is a narrow channel (3- to 5-foot depths) more than a mile long, leading to Rainbow Marina and Esther's Restaurant, offering limited transient space and few amenities, yet Esther's remains a popular local seafood choice. There is shoaling both upriver and downriver of this channel. Move slowly, and watch your depth sounder. Beta Marine Services offers dry-docking, bottom work and boat repairs. There is an electronics facility next door.

Dockage: The 48-foot fixed Interstate 10 Highway Bridge, some 17 miles upriver, limits some sailboat access to the Beaumont Yacht Club, which welcomes visiting boats and offers fuel, ice, electricity, water, showers and the calm of a deep inland marina. As you come up to the bridge, you will see an oxbow on your port side; avoid the northwest shore as several old ships and barge hulks lurk just underwater. Stay to the east side of the Neches River in 20-plus feet of water, and then pass under the bridge. On the port side under the bridge lies another submerged wreck. The starboard side is fine. Since the current is fairly strong, especially in the spring, run a bit upstream

before turning to port and into the yacht club channel. Stay well to the center.

Anchorage: Frequent anchorages can be found along the Neches River banks in the lush marsh and cypress forests that line the river. The first easy anchorage is just two miles upriver in sight of the Rainbow Bridge. This is one of the many oxbows created by straightening out the curvy river. Here you will find 12-foot depths.

Off the first oxbow is Bird Island Bayou, which can offer an interesting side tour, depending on your draft. Another mile farther upstream is Port Neches Park. There are no facilities for large boats, but you can dinghy in to hunt for supplies. Ahead, before the next oxbow, is the narrow opening to the Bessie Heights Canal, marked by quick flashing red "30," which offers a good possible anchorage. The next feature running up the Neches River is the oxbow marked as Reserve Fleet on the north side. If the reserve fleet is not here, you may be able to drop the hook, though small outboards run through at all hours. Farther up where the ghost fleet is moored lies quite a remarkable sight: Dozens of huge sea-going ships moored side-by-side form the Reserve Fleet. The security force takes its job seriously, so look, but do not touch.

GOIN' ASHORE: **BEAUMONT, TX**

Beaumont, a charming town of more than 100,000 people, gained fame as the birthplace of the oil industry in 1901, when the famous Spindletop well blew, shooting crude oil hundreds of feet into the air. Texaco, Gulf, Exxon and Mobil all started here. The Golden Triangle, made up of Sabine, Port Arthur and Orange, is the true center of America's major petrochemical region. These refineries run along the GIWW and the Neches River.

Beaumont has "a little something extra," combining Bayou roots with pure Texas. Whether you enjoy the Texas two-step or Zydeco, entertainment is alive and well in Beaumont, especially on Crockett Street. This is downtown's dining and entertainment district, offering live music, outdoor festivals and much more. For breakfast or lunch, try Crockett Street Deli, and the Spindletop or the Texas Star Bar & Grill for a casual dinner. For dancing or music, walk over to the Dixie Dance Hall, The Hub or Antone's. Crockett Street is a 25-minute walk or a short cab ride from the waterfront.

ADDITIONAL RESOURCES

■ Beaumont Convention and Visitors Bureau
409-880-3749, **www.beaumontcvb.com**

⚑ **NEARBY GOLF COURSES**
Henry Homberg Municipal Golf Course, Babe Zaharias Drive, Beaumont, TX 77705, 409-842-3220

☤ **NEARBY MEDICAL FACILITIES**
Memorial Hermann Baptist Hospital, 3080 College St., Beaumont, TX 77701, 409-212-5000

Sabine Lake

NAVIGATION: Use Charts 11331 and 11342. If you choose to leave the GIWW, you can enter Sabine Lake at green can buoy "69" and red nun buoy "70" on the Thousand-Foot Cut with a turn to port (south) between Stewts and Sydnes islands. This private cut runs south-southeast into Sabine Lake. Go slow, watch your depth sounder and ease into the lake. Keep the private wood markers to starboard and the submerged pilings to port. You might also try the East Pass of the Sabine River, on your port side westbound as you come into Sabine Lake. Again, go slow and mind your depth sounder; it may carry 20 feet, or it may be shoaled over, depending on recent floodwaters. Sabine Lake is an undiscovered cruising area. Most charts show it with an average of 6 to 7 feet of water, but even with erosion, subsidence and river runoff, there seem to be 8-foot depths in most of the lake. Reports of severe shoaling may prevent access at the north end of the lake at Thousand-Foot Cut.

Dockage: On the west bank is Pleasure Island, with camping and picnic areas, an outdoor concert park, condominiums, public beaches, fishing piers and a beach club. Pleasure Island is not accessible directly from the GIWW—you will have to come in to the lake well north or south of this point.

Pleasure Island Marina, operated by the city of Port Arthur, is located about three miles southwest from the Thousand-Foot Cut channel on the Lake Sabine side of Pleasure Island. The marina offers 405 slips (approximately 20 are allotted to transients), a boatyard, a convenience store and sail repair and other supplies. The docks were heavily damaged in Hurricane Ike in 2008 and as of June 2010 remained closed. The restaurant here was destroyed in Hurricane Rita and has not yet reopened. The unmarked channel is maintained to 8-foot depths into the marina. As you enter the breakwater, there is a clear area of more than 200 yards where you can drop anchor or prepare for docking. Watch the depth sounder for some 3- and 4-foot spots bordering the channel and the approach as you enter. (The rebuilding of the marina was to begin in spring 2010 so hopefully transient slips will again be available.)

If you have a yacht club membership and wish to enjoy the gracious hospitality of the Port Arthur Yacht Club (PAYC), proceed to the end of Piers B and C, or along the dinghy dock in front of the PAYC clubhouse. The club offers power, ice, showers and the usual amenities, and also offers wireless Internet access.

The old swing bridge that used to occupy the southern entrance to Sabine Lake was replaced by a fixed bridge (63 foot vertical clearance) in November 2009. After passing through the bridge and under the overhead cables (72-foot vertical clearances), you will find 20 to 25 feet of water for a few hundred yards. Take a course of approximately 312 degrees magnetic for about 1.75 miles to the vicinity of two pilings marking a submerged wreck. About halfway to these pilings, you will note that the water is shoaling to 8 feet or less. Leave the pilings about 150 feet to port. Continue on a course that keeps you off the Louisiana side of Sabine Lake, where a lurking oyster reef awaits unwary

cruisers. Take note of the tidal current here, which can be strong. Despite what the chart shows, the old partially submerged wreck of a dredge is the only wreck now remaining in the area. Take care not to cut too close to Blue Buck Point. Then proceed on a more northerly course to Pleasure Island Marina.

From this point on, the lake is generally 6 to 9 feet deep and free of underwater obstructions. A good anchorage exists off Garrison Ridge, in 5- to 6-foot depths, along the east (Louisiana) shore, where you will see a high tree-covered ridge, visible from several miles away. Another possible anchorage is at Johnson Bayou, in 6- to 7-foot depths, is also on the eastern Louisiana shore past the marina.

Sabine Lake—South Entrance to Gulf of Mexico

NAVIGATION: Use Chart 11341 and 11342. Travel southeast from the state Route 82 Swing Bridge along the Sabine Pass Channel for six miles to Texas Point at the Gulf. The ship channel, 500 feet wide and 40 feet deep, is well-marked. As you enter the jetty channel, beware of submerged and exposed wrecks on both sides. After passing Sabine Pass East Jetty at flashing green "17" and red "18," the channel opens to the Gulf with water depths of 24 to 35 feet

Southbound from Sabine Lake, Louisiana is on your port side. A large designated big-ship anchorage area to port is filled with huge jack-up rigs. The small town of Sabine Pass on the starboard (Texas) side offers some interesting restaurants. Try the region's famous barbecued crabs, which are not really barbecued at all, but still delicious.

Dockage: The Sabine Pass Port Authority maintains a few slips for transient boaters. Water and power are provided, but no shoreside facilities exist. The fuel dock, open 24 hours a day, 7 days per week, offers both gas and diesel, and is one of the few such fueling facilities in the area. Be careful, though, because they are used for commercial boats and are lined with big black tires. The slips run across the tidal current flow, so a strong ebb or flood current may press you against the dock. Use a bow or stern line to warp you out and off the pilings. You can usually tie up alongside one of the many commercial docks, but ask permission first—the shrimp fleet may be due in at odd hours.

Anchorage: Just northwest of the town of Sabine Pass is a good anchorage lying between an island and town on an abandoned large-ship channel, now busy with clamorous shrimp boats. A strong current runs here at ebb or flood tide, so take that into account when anchoring. Be cautious, because there are a few wrecked hulks of old shrimp boats in the area.

The Coast Guard station is here, and the chart-designated anchorage is deep in the middle, carrying 8 to 10 feet of water all the way into shore. Ship and barge traffic is heavy, as are their wakes. Both of these anchorages and the town of Sabine Pass are six to eight miles south of the GIWW and do not appear on the GIWW charts, so use Chart 11342.

Sabine Lake—South Entrance to GIWW—Mile 289 WHL

From the state Route 82 Causeway Bridge, travel less than a mile south, and enter the Sabine-Neches Channel. Head northwest for 2.5 miles and then north-northwest for three miles to the intersection of the GIWW, the Sabine-Neches Canal and Taylor Bayou. The channel is 500 feet wide with 40-foot depths. Stay in the channel, and avoid the banks, which hide snags and wrecks.

West Port Arthur Bridge to Bolivar Roads Channel (Galveston)—Mile 289 to Mile 351 WHL

It is a 62-plus-mile run from the intersection of the GIWW, the West Port Arthur Bridge (Mile 288.8 WHL, 73-foot fixed vertical clearance) and the Sabine-Neches Canal to the wide-open and ship-filled Bolivar Roads Channel. The passage runs through marsh and pastureland and is dotted with walking-beam oil pumps until you reach Mile 335 WHL and the Stingaree Marina. You will see alligators swimming in the channel or basking on the shores during the day and, at night, their glowing red-orange eyes will reflect a spotlight aimed at the shore. They live in gator holes or crawls set into and alongside the shore and banks.

Taylor Bayou Outfall Canal— Mile 290.5 WHL

This is a good anchorage, which is better in the fall and winter than the spring and summer due to the extra-large salt grass mosquitoes. It has between 13 and 14 feet of water to the banks over soft, blue-black mud.

The Taylor Bayou Outfall Canal runs north from the Waterway for almost four miles to a lock that the Corps of Engineers has placed to stop saltwater from moving upstream. Despite its name, the outfall canal is a drainage canal that diverts the headwaters of the old Taylor Bayou. While it does not carry any sewage or chemical effluent, it does carry commercial traffic—both barges and shrimp boats.

An even better anchorage is available in the uncharted lateral canal that enters from the west, about three-quarters of a mile up the Taylor Outfall Canal. It is approximately 100 feet wide and 12 to 18 feet deep. This canal is within the Big Hill Bayou Wildlife Management Area and is alive with alligators, birds, fish and, unfortunately, mosquitoes.

The run to Galveston is an easy and quiet one, and since the GIWW runs in a favorable way in relation to the southeasterly trades, cruisers will find a welcome 15- to 20-knot wind boost for the journey. Each year, shore birds and waterfowl by the thousands fly down from Canada and stop here along the way, resting among the reeds and salt grass.

At Mile 305 WHL is Salt Bayou (known locally as Spindletop Gully). There is a dark, two-story building here, and less than a half-mile west is a harbor next to the Department of Energy Strategic Reserve Pump Station. Due to increased security concerns, this harbor is off-limits to recreational craft. Do not test the rules here; such an attitude will be met with a swift and decisive (armed) Coast Guard response.

High Island Bridge and Dome— Mile 319 WHL

At about the halfway point between Sabine River and Bolivar Roads, you will find the High Island Bridge (Mile 319.3, 73-foot fixed vertical clearance). The 40-foot-high mound of High Island to the south of the Waterway (an ancient salt dome) is the highest spot for nearly 100 miles and looks like a mountain compared to the flat surrounding landscape. As you go under the bridge, you will notice a wide, L-shaped cut into the north inside of the marsh grass. The cut holds 6- to 8-foot depths. You can drop anchor here, but on humid or foggy nights, the buzz and crackle of the overhead electrical lines may hinder a good night's rest.

Beyond the bridge, a long "S" turn takes three to four miles to unwind itself around Horseshoe Marsh and into East Bay Bayou. The towboat captains refer to it as the "High Island Wiggles." Down the line 100 miles, you will run into the "Freeport Wiggles." The High Island Bridge (Mile 319.3, 73-foot fixed vertical clearance) is the only hurricane escape route north for local residents of High Island and Bolivar Peninsula. It is a 66-mile run to Galveston and the Houston Ship Channel from High Island. The GIWW channel has been dredged to a depth of 12 feet and a width of between 125 and 300 feet here.

There are no recommended anchorages between Port Arthur and Galveston. The frequent side cuts that look so inviting were dug to service oil wells, and are often silted in at the mouth. If you have a good depth sounder, you might venture into a likely cut and find a good spot. Ease in slowly, and remember that mosquitoes make their home in the marshes here. Hurricane Ike in 2008 hit this area hard.

East Bay—Mile 325 to Mile 350 WHL

NAVIGATION: Use Chart 11331. At this point, the GIWW crosses a very shallow arm of East Bay (the southeast arm of Galveston Bay), and then crosses Rollover Bay. This first zone is known as the East Bay Washout by towboat captains. The banks of the Waterway are submerged here and marked with buoys on both sides—flashing green lights mark the east end and flashing red lights mark the west end. The cut through Rollover Bay is marked the same way, plus there is a set of range markers to help guide you through. The entire area is continuing to undergo substantial dredging, so be aware of dredging operations, and pass at idle speed.

This is the only outlet for the entire southeast section of Galveston Bay, so the crosscurrent can be fierce, up to 5 to 6 knots. There is an open pass to the Gulf of Mexico here, good only for shallow-draft fishing boats, and the current is strong with up to four tidal changes a day on the Gulf. Strictly avoid being near or passing any towboats or barge tows at Rollover Bay, as they can be forced completely across the channel into the opposite bank by the tremendous pressure of the tidal current flow. From the stern, you may see towboats churn up a six-foot rooster tail with their propellers as they attempt to power their way across the cut. Pay close attention to VHF Channels 13 or 16 as you near the area so you can hear towboat captains discuss the tidal flow and current strength. The slight turn in the east end of the cut can make the transit even more of a problem with a high current flow. Because of the strong current and misguided barges, the buoys can be pushed out of their charted position. Despite fairly constant dredging, the Waterway can shoal to 8 feet or less between red nun buoys "8" and "10." You will exit this area at 17-foot flashing red "14" at Mile 330.

Dockage: At Mile 336 WHL on the south side of the GIWW, opposite the channel to the western side of East Bay, is the Stingaree Marina. Gas is available at the fuel dock to port. The marina has two restaurants: Stingaree, upstairs with a screened balcony, specializing in seafood; and Little Chihuahuas, serving outstanding honey shrimp enchiladas and other Mexican favorites. There is also an RV park and commercial fishing center. Ice and limited supplies are available. Very limited transient dockage (with power and water) is available at the marina. Call ahead for fuel or dockage, and to check depths; there have been reports of shoaling at the marina entrance. At Mile 337 WHL, Steve's Landing had offered limited bulkhead transient dockage with water, electricity, restrooms and a restaurant. However, Steve's Landing was severely damaged in Hurricane Ike, and as of April 2010 had not re-opened.

From here, the GIWW is a land cut leading down the Bolivar Peninsula to Port Bolivar, a former small commercial port with a 116-foot abandoned lighthouse, now privately owned. The channel shoals along the north bank, so stay in the center. Port Bolivar overlooks Bolivar Roads, the entrance to Galveston Bay, which is the largest petrochemical port in North America. On the eastern side of the jetties, you may spot several oceangoing freighters and tankers anchored, waiting to enter port. Just offshore at the jetties is another holding anchorage for large ships. Then, 40 to 60 miles offshore, there is a major unloading anchorage for massive supertankers that are too huge to enter the ship channel. Lighter tankers constantly run in and out, carrying crude oil and refined products to the supertankers. In Bolivar Roads, ships and tugs are moving endlessly through this major intersection of the GIWW, the Houston Ship Channel, the Port of Galveston and the Texas City Ship Channel.

At Mile 343 WHL, near flashing red "4" and green can "3," the Bolivar Yacht Basin sits on the south side across from a large cut into Galveston Bay. (A small, shallow channel with private markers leads to the Galveston Bay fishing areas.) Gas, ice and limited supplies are available at the small marina dock, and transient dockage is very

limited. The marina caters to small fishing boats and commercial fishermen.

One mile past Bolivar Yacht Basin on the south shore is the development of Laguna Harbor. Laguna Harbor is a beautiful and well-protected private community just off the GIWW at Mile 345.5 WHL, which opened in Spring 2006. Slips with 50-amp shore power are available, and other shoreside amenities are being added. While Laguna Harbor is a private facility, some limited transient slips are available. Prior arrangements with Laguna Harbor must be made before entering the marina facility.

Dredges are frequently working the various channels in the Bolivar Roads area and the spoil areas of the Houston Ship Channel, trying to combat heavy shoaling caused by the ebb and flow of Galveston Bay's tide and tidal currents.

Throughout the Galveston Bay area, navigation lights blend in with those of ships, towboats, dredges and some of the world's largest petrochemical refineries to create a daunting light show. Picking out a slow-flashing red light in the midst of this kaleidoscope takes a keen and steady eye.

From Port Bolivar, the cruising skipper has a choice of destinations: Galveston, Offats Bayou, Clear Lake, Houston or the GIWW, southwest to the end of the line at Brownsville.

■ PORT ARTHUR/ SABINE TO GALVESTON

Offshore Run

NAVIGATION: Use Charts 11332, 11323 and 11324. On a nice day, it is a simple and easy 49-mile-long run from Sabine Pass to Galveston, jetty to jetty, on a 242-degree-magnetic course. Carefully check the tide tables for Sabine; a flood tide could add hours to the trip. Run out from the jetties for about a mile, and then turn to 242 degrees magnetic. This heading will keep you out of the shipping fairways and in 30 feet of water. You will be out of the sight of land, but a few water towers, radio towers and the mound of High Island provide good checkpoints. There are a few clusters of wellheads, "Christmas trees" and platforms, so keep the usual sharp lookout. If you run out a bit farther—three to five miles—you may hit deeper water.

The entrance to Galveston Bay is fairly straightforward. Stay in the shipping channel and avoid the spoil area along the north jetty and the shoaling along the south jetty. Stay well off the ends of the jetties, because huge rocks lie at their tips. The jetties, which run out for several miles, are more than a mile apart and, with a high tide, are often hard to see.

A strong ebb tidal current will slow you down, and combined with heavy following seas, can make for some serious rollers and cresting seas running in from the deep Gulf. Commercial traffic is constant and heavy here, so maintain a good watch. Note cautiously that shallows are indicated just inside the southwest side of the jetties.

If you are heading to the fuel dock at the Yacht Basin in Galveston, you can stay to the port (shore) side of the Inner Bar Channel with ample water (20 feet or more) just outside the channel markers all the way in. You will pass the Coast Guard station within 100 yards, and then the Galveston ferry docks. Keep a close lookout for the ferries, as four of them can be running at one time—in addition to cruise ships on weekends. Once past the ferry landing, it is a clear and easy shot of about 1.5 miles along Galveston Channel to the fuel dock on your port side. Seawolf Park, where a large WWII-era submarine is on display, lies to starboard as you enter Galveston Channel.

Galveston and Galveston Bay— GIWW Mile 350 WHL

NAVIGATION: Use Charts 11322 and 11326. Galveston Bay is one of the larger bays in the United States, but it is very shallow—just 6 to 10 feet deep, with a flat, smooth, muddy bottom. The bay is actually four bays in one, with East Bay and West Bay in the southern section, Galveston Bay itself on the south and northwest segments, and Trinity Bay in the northeast quadrant. Overall, it is more than 30 miles long from the GIWW north to Trinity Bay, 30 miles wide from Texas City to the and of East Bay and 17 miles across between Smith Point on the east and San Leon Point on the west. The shores are flat and marshy in some places, with very few distinctive features. On the western side, in sight from the GIWW, refineries and tank farms are plentiful in the Texas City area. To the northwest of the bay, the Houston Ship Channel is lined with more tank farms and petroleum loading docks at Baytown.

The normal tidal range on Galveston Bay is less than 2 feet with two to four tides a day. Small craft may anchor anywhere in the bay (outside of the channel markers), but must use caution when a weather front (a "northerly") is expected. Water levels may drop as much as 4 feet, and 5- to 6-foot waves in a sudden storm are not that unusual. Strong southerly winds, such as those prior to a cold front, may raise the water level as much as 3 to 5 feet.

Galveston is the oldest deepwater Gulf port west of New Orleans, and combined with the Port of Houston, tallies up to be the largest port area in the United States. There are only two marina facilities in Galveston that can be accessed via Galveston Channel. Although on the western side of the island itself, Offatts Bayou, with its many amenities, is entered from Mile 358 WHL just west of the Gulf Freeway Bridges (Mile 357.3, 74-foot fixed vertical clearances).

Dockage: Galveston Yacht Basin, located just west of the Bolivar Ferry landing and the Coast Guard Station (well-marked by a big Shell logo), offers transient powerboat slips, both open and covered, but space for sailing vessels is almost non-existent. The fuel dock is open from 6 a.m. to 6 p.m. every day. There is a swimming pool and cabanas. The Club portion is no longer operational since Ike. A drugstore, grocery, motel and eateries are within easy walking distance with the beach not much farther away.

QUICK FACT:

On September 13th, 2008, Hurricane Ike made landfall directly over Galveston Island in Texas. Hurricane Ike was a only a Category 2 storm, but it caused massive damage and destruction equivalent to a Category 4 storm. Hurricane Ike stretched over 500 miles and had howling winds up to 110 mph with a storm surge of 13-20 feet in most areas. It was the third most destructive hurricane to ever make landfall in the U.S. and was blamed for up to 200 deaths nationwide. Residents up and down the Texas and Louisiana coast were greatly effected by this hurricane, but Galveston Island and the Bolivar Peninsula were the hardest areas hit. The storm surge of up to 20 feet and flooding were the main culprits of most of the coastal damage. Unfortunately, homes, businesses, landmarks and even lives were lost due to Hurricane Ike.

It has been over 18 months since Hurricane Ike made landfall and Galveston Island is still rebuilding. Most everyone with any connection to Galveston knew that the rebuilding process would take years to achieve. Over 70 percent of the Islands homes and commercial buildings were either damaged or destroyed by Hurricane Ike. One major hospital closed, low income neighborhoods have vanished and the seawall and beaches were severely damaged. With all these issues, one would have thought Galveston was in major trouble. Galveston still has some issues to deal with, but overall residents and business owners are pleasantly surprised at the quick rate that Galveston is being rebuilt. There is still a long way to go for Galveston to get back to its pre Ike conditions, but everyday the Island looks better and better.

Part of the progress that Galveston Island has made is due to the many projects that have been completed and are still ongoing. The Galveston Bay clean-up started in January 2009, was completed in September 2009 and was a huge success. The Galveston bays are actually cleaner now than before Ike made landfall in September 2008. The land clean-up is almost complete in most areas. The beaches in front of the seawall are undergoing a huge sand restoration project and were to be finished by the end of May 2010. Business owners are seeing an increase in business and the hotels are starting to get booked again. The overall rebuilding progress has been better than expected in most areas.

Fishing in the bays of Galveston since Hurricane Ike has been good to outstanding. Anglers are catching good numbers of fish in all the three major bays systems. East Bay, West Bay and Trinity Bay have consistently produced limits of speckled trout, red fish, flounder and other species that are abundant in the bays. Fishing on the bays is actually better now than before Hurricane Ike. All this is excellent news and a sign that the Galveston bays are in great shape for the future. It is an ongoing process for Galveston Island with both positives and negatives. The Island is still rebuilding, recovering and starting over in many areas, and it will take some time for residents and business owners to feel totally comfortable again. Galveston Island continues to make progress.

The Harbor House complex in the Pier 21 area has a small transient-only marina. It is adjacent to the square-rigged vessel Elissa, which is on display and discussed in the "Goin' Ashore: Galveston" section. This location is very strategic, as it is only a few blocks from The Strand historical district, home to many art galleries and high end restaurants. The marina itself offers electricity and water, but no bath or shower facilities are available. The marina is nice, but very tight; enter and depart with caution. Watch the currents as you go into this small marina, as they can put you against the wall. Dockage is free if you get a room at the Harbor House Hotel, but it is usually booked well in advance for the weekends. Free wireless Internet access is available here.

If you are heading to the Moody Gardens Hotel and Marina, bear in mind that you cannot reach them from the Galveston Channel by water. The entrance for Offatts Bayou is from Mile 358 WHL on the GIWW, just west of the high-rise bridge from Houston to Galveston. The GIWW from Galveston Bay to Freeport is covered after the Galveston Bay section. Note that the Moody Gardens Marina was heavily damaged in Hurricane Ike, and was expected to open in the summer 2010. In the mean time, visiting boaters can anchor just off the beach (Offatts Bayou is an excellent anchorage), and land a dinghy at the dinghy dock.

Leaving the Galveston Channel, if headed west, the Pelican Island Railroad-Highway Bridge (12-foot closed and 75-foot open vertical clearances) returns you to the GIWW near Mile 356.0 WHL with the high-rise bridge in sight. The Pelican Island Railroad-Highway Bridge does not open Monday through Friday from 7 a.m. to 8:30 a.m., noon to 1 p.m. and 4:15 p.m. to 5:15 p.m. Note that just west of the bridge, the Offatts channel diverges from the GIWW, creating a "Y" channel confluence that is not well-marked. It is very shallow just off either channel, and many vessels run aground in this area as a result. Study the charts carefully before transiting this area. Commercial traffic monitors VHF Channel 16 west of this bridge, changing from VHF Channel 13 to the east.

Anchorage: A good anchorage is just east of the Galveston Yacht Basin. Anchoring in Galveston Channel is permissible and is suggested in the area of the concrete wall sheltering Galveston Yacht Basin. Tidal currents can be swift in either direction, so using two anchors (Bahamian-moor) is suggested. Though the commercial traffic is fairly heavy, the channel is wide, and riding "on the hook" is not uncomfortable. Offatts Bayou, just south of Interstate 45 on Galveston Island, is one big anchorage itself, particularly around and east of Moody Gardens, where 20-foot depths are the norm. Another option is off Pelican Island, a half-mile due north of Galveston Channel marker "2." This has the advantage of being somewhat within dinghy distance from the Pier 21 area, while offering some protection from passing tows and recreational craft.

GOIN' ASHORE: GALVESTON, TX

From the 1830s to 1900, Galveston was the biggest and most prosperous city in Texas. Its commercial center was then known as the "Wall Street of the Southwest," and its deep port made Galveston one of the world's preeminent shipping centers. The devastating hurricane of 1900 caused more than 6,000 deaths and brought the city to its knees. The glory days were over, and Galveston endured a long and steady decline throughout the first half of the 20th century.

Like many other cities, Galveston has enjoyed quite a reemergence, and many of the architectural gems of old have been restored. (Hurricane Ike took a heavy toll on the city, but Texans are resilient and have bounced back quickly.) Do not miss Ashton Villa, an Italian-style mansion built in 1893 by Samuel Williams, an early Texas banker and the financier of the Texas struggle for independence from Mexico. The old historic downtown strand is located one block south of Galveston Harbor at Harborside Drive between the north-south crossing of 19th to 25th streets. Gas lanterns line the streets, which can be toured by walking, or by catching a ride on a trolley or horse-drawn carriage. Visit the Old Peanut Butter Warehouse (20th Street and Harborside Drive), an 1895 building once used as a warehouse to store candy and peanut butter, now transformed into a unique shopping experience.

The Strand Landmark Historic District, with its charming Victorian-era buildings, has been restored and is now occupied with stores, restaurants, museums and outside cafés ideal for "people-watching." A local favorite is Colonel Bubbie's Strand Surplus Senter [sic], a government surplus store of huge dimensions. If you are hungry, try Fisherman's Wharf Seafood at Pier 21, Willie G's Seafood & Steaks or Landry's Oyster Bar. For fine dining, try Saltwater Grill in the heart of The Strand at 2017 Postoffice St. Galveston celebrates Mardi Gras in a big way, and Dickens on the Strand is a Christmas tradition.

Galveston has a maritime legacy, which can be best experienced with a trip along Pier 21 at Harborside Drive and 21st Street. Visit the Texas Seaport Museum and tour the 1877 tall ship, Elissa. The Texas Seaport Museum is a worthwhile stop for history buffs, and includes an immigration listing of those who came to America through this Texas port as early as the 1840s. Visit and view the architecture of the Grand 1894 Opera House (2020 Postoffice St.). The paddle wheel replica Colonel (a twin-screw vessel with false paddles) offers daily historic- or jazz-themed cruises with Creole dinners. Moody Gardens, with its aquarium and tropical rain forest, all under the roof of three gigantic glass pyramids, offers IMAX films, several restaurants and a mind-boggling ecotourism atmosphere. Next door to Moody Gardens is the Schlitterbahn Galveston Island Waterpark.

You can walk to the Downtown Visitors Center for information about local attractions and festivals. Stewart Beach and Pavilion are great places to cool off in the green water of the Gulf. The beach offers white sand and stretches for several miles, making it a favorite vacation place for Texans.

Galveston Area, TX

GALVESTON AREA		Largest Vessel Accommodated	VHF Channel Monitored	Transient Berths / Total Berths	Approach / Dockside Depth (reported)	Floating Docks	Gas / Diesel	Groceries, Ice, Marine Supplies, Snacks	Repairs: Hull, Engine, Propeller	Lift (tonnage), Crane, Rail	1=110V, 2=220V, B=Both, Max Amps	Laundry, Pool, Showers	Pump-Out Station	Nearby: Grocery Store, Motel, Restaurant
				Dockage				**Supplies**			**Services**			
1. Stingaree Marina 335.8 WHL	409-684-9530	50		8/32	7/6			IS			B/50			R
2. Galveston Yacht Club & Marina 350.8 WHL	409-762-9689	70	16	/500	10/8		GD	IMS	HEP	L70	B/50	LPS	P	GMR
3. Galveston Yacht Service Inc. 350.8 WHL	409-762-3835	75			10/8			M	HP	L				GMR
4. Harbor House Marina 350.8 WHL	409-763-3321	80	68	9/9	30/10	F		GIS			B/50			GMR
5. Payco Inc. 357 WHL	409-744-7428	65		5/260	5/6	F		IMS	HEP	L40,C	B/100	S	P	GR
6. Moody Gardens Marina 358 WHL	888-388-8484			DESTROYED BY IKE- RENOVATIONS SOON										
7. Harborwalk Yacht Club & Marina 362 WHL 🖵 Ⓦ️ⒾⒻ	409-935-3737	125	09	8/162	9/9	F	GD	GIMS			B/100	LPS	P	R

Corresponding chart(s) not to be used for navigation. 🖵 Internet Access Ⓦ️ⒾⒻ Wireless Internet Access

BOLIVAR PENINSULA, CHART 11331

A boardwalk extends along the beach for biking and walking, with restaurant and shopping stops along the way. The Galveston Chamber of Commerce has plenty of information (www.galvestoncc.com) and is conveniently located across from the beach walk. The beach is well-maintained, patrolled and has a beach wall with a wide sidewalk on top. Pedestrians, bicycles and electric and pedal carts are plentiful throughout the summer and on winter weekends.

ADDITIONAL RESOURCES

■ City of Galveston, 409-797-3500, **www.cityofgalveston.org**

⚑ **NEARBY GOLF COURSES**
Moody Gardens Golf Course, 1700 Sydnor Lane, Galveston, TX 77554, 409-683-4653

⚕ **NEARBY MEDICAL FACILITIES**
University of Texas Medical Branch (UTMB), 301 University Blvd., Galveston, TX 77555 409-772-2222, **www.utmb.edu**

Galveston Island From the GIWW— Mile 358 WHL

(West of the I-45 Gulf Freeway Bridges)

NAVIGATION: Use Chart 11322 and 11324. As you travel west through the Interstate 45 high fixed bridges, be aware that although the horizontal clearance through the highway bridges is now 300 feet (vertical clearance 73 feet), the railroad bridge's (monitors VHF Channel 10) horizontal clearance is still only 105 feet. Some say that this stretch of the GIWW is the most potentially hazardous in high winds and strong currents in the immediate area surrounding these bridges. It is best to transit this area in settled weather.

Dockage: The entry to the Payco Marina is along the west side of the Gulf Freeway Bridges (Mile 357.3 WHL, 74-foot fixed vertical clearances), though the rather narrow 6- to 8-foot deep channel is unmarked, so mind your depth sounder. Payco Marina offers slips for vessels up to 65 feet, has gas and diesel fuel available, 110/220-volt electricity, restrooms, showers, a pump-out station and a full-service marine facility. Snacks are available at the ship's store, and a restaurant is just a few blocks away.

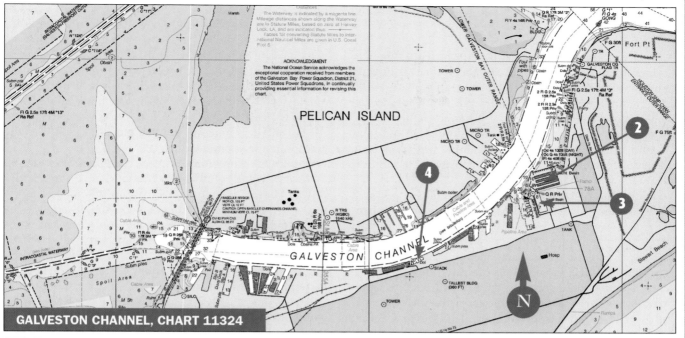

GALVESTON CHANNEL, CHART 11324

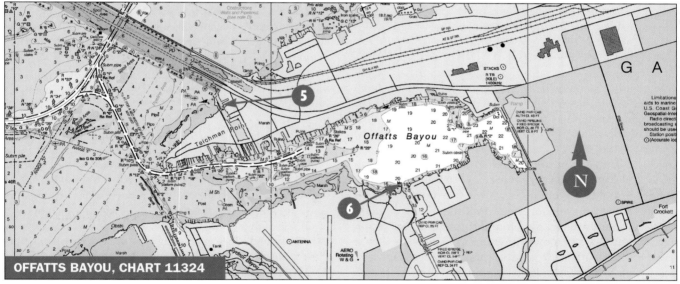

OFFATTS BAYOU, CHART 11324

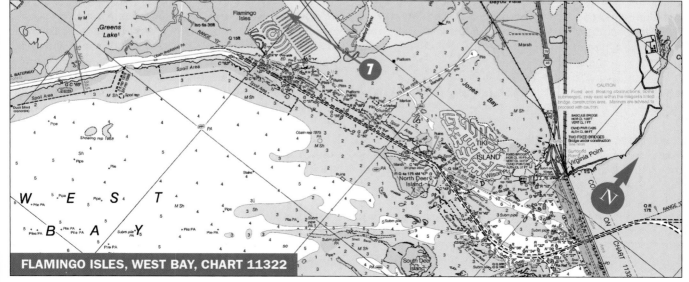

FLAMINGO ISLES, WEST BAY, CHART 11322

You will need transportation to go to town or get to the beach. Payco Marina is primarily a fishing center, not a resort-type marina.

Over on Tiki Island just west of the Gulf Freeway Bridges, the former Teakwood Marina entrance is directly opposite the Offatts Bayou Channel at Mile 357.5 WHL. The channel is almost a mile long and well-marked with red and green daybeacons. Charted depths to the marina show only 4 feet, but local information indicates 5-foot depths or more. Teakwood Marina was completely destroyed by Hurricane Ike. When it reopens, it will be a yacht club and condominium property.

Harborwalk Marina opened in March 2006 as part of a large planned community. The 600-yard entrance channel is located at Mile 362 WHL, west of Tiki Island just off of green can buoy "59." The facility has more than 150 slips, eight of which are open to transient boats. Shoreside facilities include fuel (gas and diesel), power, water, laundry, deli, showers, sundry and a ship's store. Free wireless Internet is available throughout the marina, and Starbucks Coffee is served in the deli. The community is also home to a fine dining restaurant (with a dress code) called Spoonbill's. Transient guests are granted access to the recently opened swimming pool facility.

Offatts Bayou—South of Mile 358 WHL

Offatts Bayou is the result of a major dredging that provided landfill to raise the west side of Galveston as much as 6 feet. After the dredging, it was opened as a small boat refuge and anchorage. It cuts into Galveston Island just south of the railway bridge and the Gulf Freeway (twin) Bridges (Mile 357.3 WHL, 73-foot fixed vertical clearances). Offatts Bayou offers charted depths ranging from 10 to 20 feet (local boaters report 20- to 25-foot depths) with good holding ground.

Sometimes your anchor might indicate a sand bottom, a far cry from the usual mud found throughout Galveston Bay. Offatts Bayou enjoys an almost constant sea breeze from the Gulf of Mexico. This popular anchorage can be crowded on weekends; it is popular with skiers and personal watercraft operators. It is big enough, however, and there always seems to be room for "just one more." It is the most popular destination for those coming from the northern part of Galveston Bay, and the only sheltered anchorage in the southern part of the bay.

NAVIGATION: Use Chart 11322. Entering from the GIWW after passing the Gulf Freeway Bridges (Mile 357.3 WHL, 73-foot fixed vertical clearances) westbound, wait until you can line up the channel markers, then head southeast on the well-marked channel. Shoals form on both sides of the channel, so use caution. As you pass Teichman Point and pick up the markers indicating the main channel east into Offatts Bayou, keep to port, and stay fairly close to the shoreline. There is an ever-expanding oyster reef on the south side. (Note: The current edition of 11322 - edition 32 dated November 2008 - has corrected the placement of red daybeacon "26." Previous editions put the aid

on the wrong side of the reef. Make sure you have the most recent edition when navigating Offatts Bayou.) Do not turn south until you are well past the last marker (red daybeacon "28") into the bay itself. It is difficult to see that "last marker" at night due to its easterly position in relation to the rest of the channel markers. If you turn south too quickly, you will run hard aground on the oyster reef, which is clearly visible at low tide. Once you have passed the last marker, your water depth increases rapidly to the 20-foot depths mentioned above.

Dockage: Along the entrance to Offatts Bayou (on Teichman Point) is Lakewood Yacht Club South. It is a private club with limited facilities, restrooms and a picnic area. Members of affiliated clubs should contact the Lakewood Yacht Club at Seabrook (on Clear Lake) for information. At the extreme southeastern end of Offatts Bayou is Boudreaux's on the Bayou, serving burgers, sandwiches and pizza. Newly built docks are available for patrons, with limited shore power. On the same property is Bayou Shores RV Park, and Boudreaux's on the Bayou guests are allowed access to the laundry and showers at the park. Free wireless Internet access is available across the property. (Call 409-744-2111.)

Anchorage: You have several options for your anchorage. The quickest and simplest location is toward Moody Gardens, easily recognizable with its large pyramid terrariums. Anchor in 12- to 15-foot depths. This is a great place to exercise your dinghy while viewing the many interesting homes along the shore.

Heading Clockwise Around Galveston Bay

From GIWW Mile 351 WHL, the Galveston Bay Entrance Chart 11324 and the Upper Galveston Bay Chart 11327 replace the small-craft chart. A better deal, however, is Galveston Bay small-craft chart 11326, which is a composite of all the Galveston Bay area. It includes special charts of Clear Lake and other interesting areas. The mileage scales on these charts are shown in nautical miles only, whereas the GIWW charts have both statute and nautical mile scales.

NAVIGATION: Use Chart 11326. Leaving the GIWW, head north on the Houston Ship Channel, which will be the reference point as we "go around" Galveston Bay. The channel is well-marked with flashing green and red lights. Although the ship channel has a project depth of 40 feet, recreational boats should use the "barge shelves" along the edges in 10- to 12-foot depths. Be on the lookout for dredging activity and the tugs and barges that may be working on the maintenance or relocation of the pipelines, which cross under the channel. The commercial vessels that traverse the ship channel seem to be moving slowly as they approach, but as they pass, you will realize their speed and their inability to "dodge" traffic. These vessels have the right-of-way, legally and physically. Monitor both the vessel-to-vessel channel (13) and the Houston Vessel Traffic Service on your VHF radio.

The Texas City Channel and protecting dike project five miles into Galveston Bay. The north side of the dike has become a sandy beach through the years, although it is charted as a spoil area. It is a popular area for sailboards, small catamarans and jet skis. The channel itself is strictly commercial.

Dickinson Bay is seven miles north of Mile 351 WHL along the Houston Ship Channel just past 17-foot flashing green "45" and flashing red "46." Steer southwest and follow the daybeacons and flashing lights in the bay (five miles from the ship channel). Dickinson Bay is navigable to the fixed highway bridge (45-foot vertical clearance) and the railroad swing bridge (8-foot closed vertical clearance) in Dickinson Bayou. Dickinson Bay is shallow, and, notably, the point on the southern tip of San Leon is aptly named "April Fool Point."

Dockage: The entrance to the old San Leon Marina is from the north. The entrance depth is reportedly 5 feet. The marina was a popular fishing center with transient slips before being destroyed by Hurricane Ike. It had not re-opened at press time 2010. On the southern tip at April Fool Point is the Topwater Grill, a popular seafood restaurant, adjacent to April Fool Marina, which caters to smaller fishing boats. Transient dockage is available, but power and water are limited. Note that Topwater Grill was destroyed in Hurricane Ike, and was re-opened in February 2010.

If you are in need of repairs or marine supplies, contact Hillman's Boatyard and Marine Supply just beyond the bridge (281-339-1546). A marina for small boats, Waterman's Harbor (no wet slips without lifts), is also in the bayou where you can purchase gas (281-339-1416).

Redfish Island

The Port of Houston and the Corps of Engineers have restored Redfish Island, once a popular boating destination, which eroded away more than a decade ago. The six-acre, U-shaped island protects boaters from south and southeast winds as well as from wakes from large cargo ships in the Houston Ship Channel, helping it once again become a favorite anchorage for both local and transient boaters, and the subject of a popular song by country music artist Kelly McGuire. A portion of the island is a bird habitat attracting barren-ground nesters like the black skimmer, Forester's tern, royal tern and gull-billed tern. Make sure that you bring your binoculars. Redfish Island is located just northwest of the intersection of the Trinity River Channel and Galveston Ship Channel.

Clear Lake

If you are traveling in Galveston Bay, Clear Lake is a popular visit, with its excellent marinas, marine services, restaurants, trendy shops and entertainment for the young and young at heart. Most of Clear Lake has recovered from Hurricane Ike.

NAVIGATION: Use Chart 11326. The Clear Lake approach was well-marked by 30-foot flashing red "2," a unique metal mesh tower above the wood platform. This tower

was lost in Hurricane Ike, and will be rebuilt in the future. The flashing reds "4" and "6" are 17 feet high, and green buoys mark the south side of the Clear Lake channel. Just south of green daybeacon "5" is the unmarked wreck of an old iron barge. The old warning markers were blown away and have not been replaced. When entering or leaving the channel, travel outside of 17-foot flashing red "4." This has become a common practice, causing traffic and high-speed wakes outside the channel, especially on the south side, to become more prevalent.

Entering Clear Lake at night is made easier by several 150-foot lights at the Kemah Boardwalk Marina. Take note that they are usually turned off by midnight on the weekends, and earlier during the week.

Dockage: Kemah on the south bank and Seabrook on the north bank of Clear Lake are joined by the state Route 146 Bridge (73-foot fixed vertical clearance). The Kemah Boardwalk on the south side of the entrance consists of a hotel, amusement park and many fine restaurants. The Kemah Boardwalk Marina is the only marina east of the highway bridge, offering more than 400 floating slips, with 10-foot depths and transient dockage for vessels up to 150 feet. This marina is full-service and has a swimming pool available to transient boaters.

Marinas west of the high-rise bridge are listed from east to west on Clear Lake. Check your depths, and watch your markers. Traffic is very heavy on weekends and holidays.

Portofino Harbor is located just past the bridge on the south side. Reminiscent of a yacht club, the marina has transient floating docks to 55 feet, restrooms, showers, a laundry, a clubhouse and a swimming pool. Reported approach and dockside depths are 7 feet. Gas and diesel fuel are nearby at the Three Amigos.

The Seabrook Shipyard is situated amid the Three Amigos' fuel dock, the Blue Dolphin Yachting Center and the Lakewood Yacht Club. The Seabrook Shipyard and Marina, a 55-acre island complex, offers complete transient amenities, floating slips (750 total), a full-service boatyard and a great swimming pool. Depths throughout the harbor are 8 feet, and transient vessels up to 80 feet are not unusual. Covered slips may also be available. This marina complex has a complete marine repair yard on-site, with haul-outs to 50 tons. The Lakewood Yacht Club facilities are not available without reciprocal membership or by prior arrangement. It is a large club with a swimming pool, tennis courts, a large restaurant (with bar) and a great attitude.

Opposite the entry to the above complex is another huge assortment of marinas, condominiums, restaurants and a shipyard. Watergate Yachting Center is a huge consortium of marine and other activity. Its name comes from a dammed creek in the locale that was dredged to make a harbor, before raising the "water gate" to let the lake in. South Texas Yacht Service is located at the "front door" of Watergate. The circular Marina Drive curves past the yacht brokers, charter boat operators, sailing schools, tennis courts, swimming pools, various other businesses

Clear Lake, TX

Clear Lake Area, TX

CLEAR LAKE AREA		Largest Vessel Accommodated	VHF Channel Monitored	Transient Berths / Total Berths	Approach / Dockside Depth (reported)	Floating Docks	Gas / Diesel	Groceries, Ice, Marine Supplies, Snacks	Repairs: Hull, Engine, Propeller	Lift (tonnage), Crane, Rail	1=110V, 2=220V, B=Both, Max Amps	Laundry, Pool, Showers	Pump-Out Station	Nearby: Grocery Store, Motel, Restaurant
				Dockage				**Supplies**			**Services**			
1. Seabrook Shipyard Marina Inc. 🖥 WiFi	281-474-2586	100	16	20/750	10/8	F	GD	GIMS	HEP	L50,C	B/100	LPS	P	GMR
2. Kemah Boardwalk Marina 🖥 WiFi	281-334-2284	145	16	/424	10/10	F		IS			B/30	LPS		GMR
3. Portofino Harbour Marina	281-334-6007	55	16	/212	7/7			I			B/50	LPS		GMR
4. Legend Point Marina	281-334-3811	50		/254	7/6						B/50	LPS	P	GMR
5. Watergate Yachting Center	281-334-1511	100	68	50/1200	8/7	F		MS	HE	L35	B/50	LPS		GMR
6. Waterford Harbor Marina 🖥 WiFi	281-334-4400	70	16	9/583	7/7	F		I			B/50	LPS		GMR
7. Marina del Sol WiFi	281-334-3909	65	16	10/331	8/6	F		IS			B/50	LPS		GMR
8. South Shore Harbour Marina	281-334-0515	120		/855	8/6	F	GD	IS			B/50	LPS	P	GMR
9. Bal Harbour Marina	281-333-5182	45		/133	5/5						1/30	PS		GMR
10. Clear Lake Marine Center	281-326-4426	45		/161	6.5/6.5				HE	L77,C	B/50	S		GMR
11. Lakewood Yacht Club	281-474-2511	100	78	/300	10/8	F	GD	IS	PRIVATE CLUB					GMR

Corresponding chart(s) not to be used for navigation. 🖥 Internet Access WiFi Wireless Internet Access

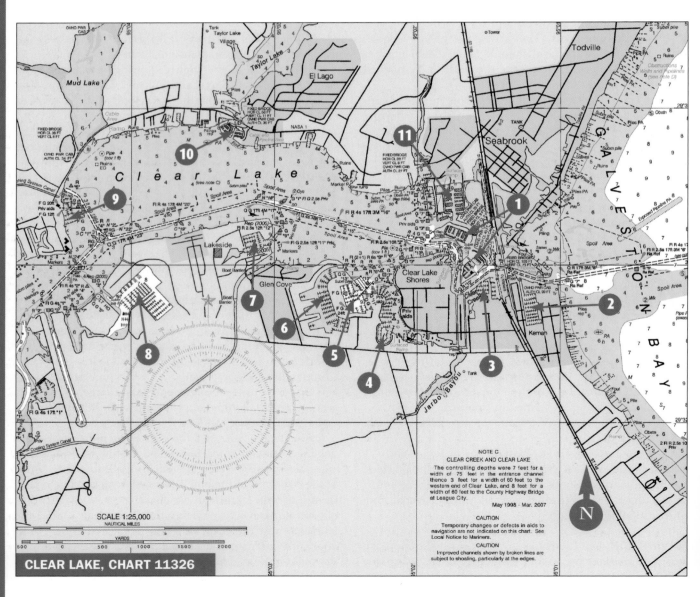

CLEAR LAKE, CHART 11326

and the marina office. On the west side is another bath and shower building, laundries and the liveaboard slips.

Legend Point is a rather unusual condominium marina with transient space available. The marina is built around an island, accessible from the gated and guarded entrance by a stone bridge. Parking, bathrooms, laundry and a clubhouse are located on the island. If you are going to stay awhile, look it over. Watergate Yachting Center and Legend Point comprise more than 1,500 boat slips in one small body of water.

You use the same entrance from Clear Lake, and then turn west to reach a fully dredged marina, the Waterford Harbor Yacht Club and Marina. The splendor begins with the Williamsburg-style yacht club featuring a waterfront restaurant, which offers fine dining or casual meals in the lounge or at poolside. There are four bathhouses, with private showers, dressing rooms and laundry rooms. More than 500 floating slips are available with 24-hour security.

One mile west (still on the south side) is Marina Del Sol, a quiet spot with transient dockage to 60 feet or more, prominent small-boat storage and a quiet harbor for those who are going to stay awhile. There are no restaurants or bars to disturb your peaceful surroundings.

The Nassau Bay Hilton is no longer a customary marina. Boat owners are not allowed to spend nights aboard. They may dock overnight or longer but must stay at the hotel or elsewhere. The Hilton is convenient to the NASA Johnson Space Center and all that it has to offer. Maximum vessel accommodations are to 45 feet with 4- and 3-foot approach and dockside depths, respectively. The Hilton features dining spots and lounges, and the pool is a great meeting spot.

Bal Harbour Yacht Club has more than 100 slips. It is a private club, but transients are sometimes able to make reservations through a club member. Tennis courts and a pool make it a great stopover for those who are able to make prior contact. Maximum vessel accommodation is 50 feet; harbor depth is 5 feet. There are some electric power limitations, so check first. The Hilton Hotel and other dining spots are nearby.

East of the Hilton Hotel on the north shore sits the Endeavour Marina, an indoor stack storage site whose blue and white building is easily visible from the center of Clear Lake. There are no transient facilities here, but there is a fuel dock offering both gas and diesel, along with a ship's store.

At the western end of the road is the last, but hardly the least, marina. South Shore Harbour Marina is part of a vast complex that includes a fine golf club, tennis courts, a fitness center and the beautiful South Shore Hotel. The marina itself has more than 1,000 floating slips with full power, telephone and TV cable hookups. The hotel, across the parking lot from the harbor, is a multi-story structure with parking under the building and around the perimeter. Restaurants and lounges are located in the hotel and on the lower floor adjacent to the marina. The swimming pool is almost beyond description and includes a swim-up bar, surrounding tropical trees and multiple sections. Food and beverages are served at the swim-up bar and at poolside. The marina is known as the local "hurricane hole." Dug out of dry land, it is protected by 12- to 15-foot banks. The fuel dock has a pump-out station (one of the few in the area) and dock store.

There are many other condominium and apartment marinas around the Clear Lake shore, and transient dockage may be available if you are able to make prior plans. Dockage at some restaurants might also be available, but local knowledge is needed.

GOIN' ASHORE: **CLEAR LAKE, TX**

Several coastal towns surround Clear Lake, Houston's boating capital: Clear Lake Shores, Kemah, Seabrook and League City. Seabrook, on the northeast section of the lake just east of the state Route 146 Bridge, is noted for its historic district, with commercial fishing vessels, the Old Seabrook Antique District, fresh seafood markets, hiking, biking and extensive birding trails (part of the Great Texas Coastal Birding Trails). League City and Clear Lake Shores on the south side of the lake are modern suburban areas with waterfront communities and marinas.

Kemah is an Indian word meaning "wind in my face." The name describes the coastal town, which offers a wonderful sea breeze coming from Galveston Bay. The quaint Kemah Boardwalk features entertainment, games, rides, shopping and restaurants of all varieties. The thrilling Boardwalk Bullet roller coaster is a special favorite among visitors. An authentic Tabasco Shop has souvenirs available in case you did not make it to the McIlhenny Tabasco Factory on Avery Island. The Kemah Inn and Shops overlook a courtyard displaying dancing water, which offers enjoyment for all ages. Thursday night offers "Rock the Dock," featuring live entertainment for family fun. Restaurants range from Starbucks Coffee Shop to Landry's Seafood House, Joe's Crab Shack, Chart House, the Flying Dutchman, the Aquarium, Saltgrass Steakhouse and the Cadillac Bar & Grill. The whole area is easily accessible to several marinas within walking/biking distance. Kemah Lighthouse Shopping District has an array of quaint shops and eateries where you can stroll leisurely and relax in a little lighthouse park. You can spend the day going from antiques and fudge shops to the Enchanted Christmas Cottage. Also, within walking/biking distance are Super Wal-Mart, Super Target, Home Depot, West Marine, the post office and several well-known chain restaurants.

A short drive away takes you to Houston Space Center, Battleship Texas and the Gulf Greyhound Park Racetrack. The Clear Lake Shuttle (281-334-3873) is available for transportation to local areas and also goes to and from Houston. From Clear Lake you can also take a car or cab to the Houston area, and hop on the electric bus system, which runs fast on its tracks down Main Street. You can stop in the theater district, museum district near Rice University or the restaurants for fine dining.

Freeport, TX

Galveston Bay—West Shore

NAVIGATION: Use Chart 11326. The Houston Yacht Club is situated on the west shore of Galveston Bay just four miles northeast, and then two miles northwest, of the Clear Lake entrance marker 30-foot flashing red "2." Stay well clear of Red Bluff Point by heading toward flashing green "73" on the Houston Ship Channel. A turn to the northwest, lining up green can buoy "1" and then 17-foot flashing green "3" to port on the Bayport Ship Channel, will put you in line to approach the enclosed harbor of the yacht club. But do not mistake the enclosed Bayport Shipping (restricted security zone) area with the Houston Yacht Club, which is a bit farther north.

Once clear of the charted 6-foot-deep shoals, turn north off the Bayport Ship Channel at flashing red "6" toward the yacht club. The glade of masts inside the breakwater and the magnificent Houston Yacht Club building are prominent landmarks. Steer directly toward the colorful Houston Yacht Club sign on the seawall, and then turn hard to starboard before you hit the sign. This beautiful yacht club, founded in the early 1900s, is private but offers reciprocal privileges to other yacht club members. A fuel dock with gas and diesel is available. The restaurant and lounge are located in the main club building.

Dockage: Up the Houston Ship Channel, the bustling city of Houston offers all the usual metropolitan sights and activities. Navigable all the way to the towering skyscrapers, Buffalo Bayou runs through the city from the ship channel and passes the restored Battleship *Texas* at San Jacinto Park. You can take a paddlewheel boat dinner cruise of the upper Houston Ship Channel and Buffalo Bayou, including Allen's Landing, where Houston was founded.

Bayland Park Marina is located just south of the Fred Hartman Bridge at the northern reaches of the Houston Ship Channel. It was severely damaged in Hurricane Ike and its status remains unknown.

Five-Mile Cut

The Five-Mile Cut is a maintained channel from Bayport Channel, crossing Houston Ship Channel into Trinity Bay just south of the charted spoil area at quick flashing red "76." Keep the red nun buoys to starboard, and stay in the center of the channel. It is the primary reliable entrance from the northern section of the Houston Ship Channel into Trinity Bay. The old cut, just three miles south, at flashing red "68," is no longer stable for travel. However, there are two other marked channels that cut across the Houston Ship Channel from the Clear Lake side to the Trinity Bay side. One, at flashing red "62" is charted. The other, at flashing red "72," is not.

Double Bayou, on the east side of Trinity Bay, is the anchoring messiah of the "let's anchor out" boaters. The entrance channel (7-foot depths) is marked by 17-foot flashing reds "2," "6," "10" and "16." Other daybeacons and buoys help direct you into Double Bayou itself (7-foot depths). The popular bar and eating spot is named Marker 17, even though there is no marker by that number (the menu is limited, but the beer is plentiful). Depending on your draft (your boat, not your beer), you can motor well up into Double Bayou and enjoy the beauty of the trees and countryside. Anchorage and bayou bank tie-ups are almost unlimited. Above, on the west fork, is a marine yard. The best shore tie-ups and anchorage are reported to be on the east fork. The only dockage facility on Double Bayou is the Beasons Park with space for transient dockage. It is located at the mouth of East Fork at the junction of the Double Bayou Channel. Power and water are available, and shower and laundry facilities are presently under construction. The local county has announced plans to construct a new marina adjacent to Marker 17.

Smith Point is roughly eight miles south-southeast of Double Bayou. It is accessible via Trinity Channel, which begins at the Houston Ship Channel near red "52" and ends at Smith Point, a distance of approximately six miles. All of the markers leading into the channel were destroyed during Ike so transit this area only with local knowledge. There, you will find the Spoonbill RV park, which offers transient dockage and limited shore power. The park has shower facilities and a small sundry store. Smith Point is a famous bird-watching center, most notably home to the beautiful native roseate spoonbill.

■ GALVESTON TO FREEPORT

Mile 360 to Mile 395 WHL

NAVIGATION: Use Chart 11322. It is a 35-mile-long run from the west side of Galveston at North Deer Island to Freeport, and the Freeport Harbor Channel to the Gulf of Mexico. Freeport Channel is the last offshore access point before reaching Port O'Connor, 80 miles to the west. Built around petroleum, chemical and Gulf fishing fleets, Freeport has few attractions for the traveler except Surfside Beach.

Freeport

Dockage: Just west of Mile 392 WHL, Oyster Creek leads north 2.5 miles to the Kirby Marina. Depths of 7 to 8 feet are charted both in Oyster Creek and the marina. Kirby Marina has gas and diesel fuel along with transient slips for vessels up to 44 feet. Electricity is limited to 110 volts. No restaurants are on-site. A small boat repair dock is located on the channel nearby.

Freeport, TX

FREEPORT		Dockage				Supplies			Services				
1. Kirby Marina 394 WHL	979-239-1081	60	16	/76	6/6	GD	M	HEP	L60	B/50	S		
2. Bridge Harbor Yacht Club 394 WHL	979-233-2101	100	68	8/300	10/8	GD	GIMS	HP	L70	B/100	LPS	P	GMR
3. Surfside Marina 394 WHL	979-230-9400	64	16	/38	12/8 F	GD	GIMS			B/100	LS		GMR
3. Freeport Municipal Marina	979-871-0100	Just opened Spring 2010											

Column headers: Largest Vessel Accommodated / VHF Channel Monitored / Transient Berths / Total Berths / Approach / Dockside Depth (reported) / Floating Docks / Gas / Diesel / Groceries, Ice, Marine Supplies, Snacks / Repairs: Hull, Engine, Propeller / Lift (tonnage), Crane, Rail / 1=110V, 2=220V, B=Both, Max Amps / Laundry, Pool, Showers / Pump-Out Station / Nearby: Grocery Store, Motel, Restaurant

Corresponding chart(s) not to be used for navigation. 🖥 Internet Access 📶 Wireless Internet Access

FREEPORT, CHART 11321

The Bridge Harbour Yacht Club offers a pleasant break and a convenient place to refuel along the long run to Matagorda Bay and beyond. The entrance to this well-protected marina is at Mile 393.5 WHL, just prior to rounding the bend to the Surfside Beach Bridge (Mile 393.8 WHL, 73-foot fixed vertical clearance). A three-story building marks the south side of the entrance channel, with the fuel docks just beyond. Bridge Harbour Yacht Club has gas, diesel, electricity, water, laundry facilities, a dock store, pump-out, showers, a swimming pool and repair facilities with a 70-ton lift. When entering the basin from the GIWW, the fuel dock is across the first side-channel, which branches off to port. Transient slips line the west side of this side-channel. Sportfishing boats dominate the marina, which hosts fishing tournaments and other summer events. Cruisers (especially those with sailboats or large powerboats that cannot use a covered slip) should make reservations ahead of time.

Gulf Coast Marina and Boat Storage sits at the south base of the Surfside Bridge, east side. It offers gas and diesel, ice,

and cold drinks. Showers and laundry are at transients' disposal. (Note: This is a dry-stack storage facility.)

The Surfside Marina opened in late 2007 at the base of the Surfside Bridge on the south side of the GIWW. A full-service facility, the marina has 260 stacked slips and 38 floating wet slips with 50-amp shore power, and caters especially to large offshore fishing boats up to 70 feet. The marina hosts a variety of amenities, including a ship's store, ice, restrooms and showers, a fuel dock with gas and diesel, and wireless Internet access. With the marina on the south end of the bridge, there is easy access to restaurants along the beach road, some within walking distance. Surfside did see some damage from Hurricane Ike but re-opened within a month of the storm.

In the Spring of 2010, the City of Freeport opened the brand new Freeport Municipal Marina, with floating slips accommodating vessels up to 60 feet in length. The marina is located downtown, behind an imposing hurricane floodgate, close to restaurants, parks and shops. A fuel dock is also planned. ■

Freeport to Brownsville

CHARTS 11301, 11302, 11303, 11304, 11306, 11307, 11308, 11309, 11311, 11312, 11313, 11314, 11315, 11316, 11317, 11319, 11321, 11322

This stretch of Texas coast offers remote anchorages, inexpensive marinas, miles of sandy beaches, a handful of tourist resorts and abundant birdlife. At the Gulf Intracoastal Waterway's (GIWW) end, South Padre Island and Port Isabel provide a great launching point to continue one's adventures into Mexico by either land or sea. First mapped by Spanish explorer Piñeda in 1519, the Texas barrier islands have been plied by the French explorer La Salle (1685), silver-laden Spanish galleons, the infamous pirate Jean Lafitte, frigates of the Texas Navy and Union gunboats.

From north to south, Matagorda Peninsula, Matagorda Island, San Jose, Mustang, Padre and South Padre islands form the low arc, known as the Coastal Bend, that protects the GIWW and separates the Texas bays from the Gulf of Mexico. From offshore, these barrier islands look like a long string of dune-backed beach. Only Mustang Island, the northern tip of Padre Island and the southern tip of South Padre Island are accessible by car and support large populations. Passage through this arc of islands between the Gulf of Mexico and the bays is provided at six jettied channels: the Freeport Ship Channel, the old Colorado River Channel (not recommended for cruising boats) the Matagorda Ship Channel (near Port O'Connor), Aransas Pass (near the town of Port Aransas), the Port Mansfield Channel and Brazos Santiago Pass (at the southern tip of South Padre Island).

From Freeport to its southern terminus in the Brownsville Ship Channel, the GIWW runs alternately through land cuts and open bays in mostly straight and angular lines. The volume of commercial traffic drops noticeably south of Freeport, decreases even more south of the Victoria Barge Canal at San Antonio Bay, and becomes nearly non-existent south of Corpus Christi Bay. Although three swing bridges and two sets of floodgates can slow travel between Freeport and Matagorda Bay, the remainder of the GIWW's course has nothing to hinder progress until the Port Isabel Swing Bridge just a few miles from the Waterway's end. Dredging along much of this stretch was scheduled for spring and summer 2010.

Offshore Run—Galveston to Corpus Christi

During periods of favorable weather, vessels with ranges exceeding 200 miles can use the offshore run from Galveston to Corpus Christi. There are two advantages of this offshore run as opposed to the Louisiana crossings:

First, the safety fairway runs much closer to the shore (10 to 20 miles), and second, there are many more points along the route to duck inside if the weather turns bad.

The distance from the sea buoy "GA" where the safety fairway meets the Gulf extent of the Bolivar Pass at Galveston to the sea buoy "AP" at Aransas Pass is approximately 180 miles and follows a dead straight course. Along the way, passage inside may be taken at Freeport or Port O'Connor.

■ MATAGORDA TO THE COLORADO RIVER

Via the GIWW—Mile 394 to Mile 441.5 WHL

NAVIGATION: Use Charts 11322 and 11319. In great contrast to the open nature of the Texas coast to the south, this narrow stretch of the Waterway has three swing bridges and two sets of floodgates to transit. Commercial traffic is fairly heavy, especially in the vicinity of Freeport and the Brazos River.

At Mile 395 WHL, the Freeport Harbor Channel (40 to 45 feet deep) crosses the GIWW from the Gulf of Mexico. Ships and trawlers entering from the Gulf, towboats transiting the GIWW and commercial vessels hopping between the commercial docks within the harbor converge here, creating challenging traffic situations. Listen closely to the VHF radio before reaching the intersection; ships entering from the Gulf often move fast and are hidden by a bluff until very near the intersection. (This is another place where that AIS comes in handy-you see them on the chartplotter before they suddenly loom before you.) Stay clear of the submerged vessel on the south side of the GIWW at Mile 395.5 WHL.

From the south side of its intersection with the Freeport Harbor Channel, the Waterway leads through a steep-sided land cut to the Freeport Bridge (Mile 397.6 WHL, 73-foot fixed vertical clearance). Three miles beyond the fixed bridge, the Brazos River crosses the GIWW between a pair of floodgates. Call the operator of the nearest gate (e.g. call the "East Brazos River Floodgate" if westbound) on VHF Channel 13 for an opening and check for traffic headed toward you. The floodgates usually open on signal, but may remain closed when river currents run strongly or while repairs are made. Strong currents and floating debris are common in the Brazos River. Give commercial vessels plenty of room, and proceed with caution.

The Brazos River (Mile 401 WHL) south to the Gulf is not navigable and is subject to shoaling at any time. The river to the north of the GIWW is 8 feet deep with fixed bridges (50- and 37-foot vertical clearances) and overhead power lines (57- and 47-foot vertical clearances) within the first four miles. Submerged pilings of unknown depths are at the first bridge.

Just beyond the Brazos River, the GIWW bends to port and follows the steep bank to the San Bernard River at Mile 405 WHL. Submerged pilings are charted to the north side of the Waterway from Mile 404 to Mile 406 WHL. In early 2009, the U.S. Army Corps of Engineers dredged the mouth of the San Bernard River to the Gulf of Mexico. This should allow for more stable water flows in and around the GIWW crossing with the river.

Plan ahead, and avoid being stuck between the San Bernard River (Mile 405 WHL) and Matagorda (Mile 440.5 WHL) when darkness approaches. This 35-mile-plus stretch has no reliable anchorages, few facilities for cruising boats and few navigational aids. The channel simply follows the shores of the land cut. At Mile 411 WHL, the Waterway passes to the north of Cedar Lakes, where depths are not charted. Do not enter the lakes south of the GIWW. A No-Wake Zone is present from Mile 413 to Mile 419 WHL due to residential waterfront properties on the north side of the Waterway. Remember that you are always responsible for your wake. The Farm Road 457 Pontoon Bridge, also referred to as the Caney Creek Swing Bridge (zero closed vertical clearance), crosses the GIWW at Mile 418 WHL and opens on signal. This bridge's closed horizontal clearance is only 13 feet and is only to be used by small fishing boats.

Just west of the entrance to Matagorda Harbor, the Matagorda Bridge (Mile 440.7 WHL, 73-foot fixed vertical clearance) crosses the GIWW. Once through the bridge, the east lock of the Colorado River stands plainly ahead. If proceeding west on the GIWW, contact the Colorado River East Lock on VHF Channel 13 to request an opening and to check for any oncoming traffic. The narrowness of the locks and the often-strong current of the Colorado River make passage across the river difficult for long tows, so stay well away from the locks until the lockmaster tells you to go ahead—even when slow currents allow the locks to remain open. Because the Colorado River Locks regularly close for repairs and during periods of strong currents, radio ahead in advance of your intended passage. You can anchor along the banks of the Colorado upstream of the locks when the current is light, but you will have to pick a wide spot away from the outside of a bend; tows transit the river as far north as Bay City. If you head up the river, tell the lockmaster ahead of time, or he will not open the far lock for you. Also, watch out for brush or whole trees floating in the Colorado River. Alligators here discourage swimming.

After passing between the locks at its intersection with the GIWW, the Colorado River discharges into Matagorda Bay. This diversion channel is not navigable. To reach the Gulf of Mexico from the GIWW, take the channel that branches south from the GIWW between the Matagorda Swing Bridge and the east lock of the Colorado River. This channel leads nearly six nautical miles from the GIWW to the jetty entrance at the Gulf of Mexico. Follow the daybeacons from green daybeacon "15" to flashing red "2" and flashing green "1" at the river's discharge into the Gulf of Mexico. The controlling depths at the entrance are as low as 2 feet, depths in the channel range from 12 to 15 feet. Dredging has been conducted fairly recently, and plans are underway for additional dredging and a rebuild of the jetties. Vessels exceeding a 2 foot draft are encouraged to contact the U.S. Army Corps of Engineers Galveston District Public Affairs for latest information (http://www.swg.usace.army.mil/pao/).

Dockage: Although there are no overnight facilities, the city of Sargent provides a rest stop for visiting boaters at Mile 419.5 WHL, just past the Farm Road 457 Pontoon Bridge (also referred to as the Caney Creek Swing Bridge). This bulkhead, however, is difficult to tie to and only offers 4 feet of water. There is a public park three-quarters of a mile west of the swing bridge that allows for transient dockage, although don't be confused by its looks—it appears to be a crew-changing zone for towboats. This is a safer and deeper alternative to the bulkhead adjacent to the swing bridge. No power or water is available, but a restaurant is located at the swing bridge on the north side, Tuttle's Krusty Pelican.

At Mile 440 WHL, Matagorda Harbor Marina has transient dockage with electricity, water, a fuel dock (gas and diesel), showers and restrooms. With a generous turning basin, the transient bulkhead can accommodate large boats. A friendly staff manages the well-protected marina. The harbor entrance is just east of the Matagorda Bridge (Mile 440.7 WHL, 73-foot vertical clearance). The harbormaster's office is in the two-story wooden building near the slips. Transients should tie alongside the bulkhead (with shore power outlets) between the

Colorado River, TX

harbormaster's office and the sailboat slips. Check in to get a combination for the restrooms and showers. Depths in the harbor are about the same as those of the GIWW. The building at the west end of the harbor has a pay phone and sells convenience-store items and gasoline. Next to the harbormaster's office is The Waterfront Restaurant, serving casual seafood fare and open every day except Wednesday. A self-service laundry, Texaco station (which sells automotive diesel), a pizza parlor and a café are within walking distance. Follow the road over the dike near the harbormaster's office, and turn left on the main road.

Private homes and fish camps line the channel's east bank. River Bend Marina, located adjacent to a pair of launch ramps about a mile down the Colorado River Channel from the GIWW, has a restaurant/tavern and lets patrons dock overnight. It sells gasoline but offers no other amenities. For boaters heading out the jetties into the Gulf, the dock offers a friendly and secure staging point.

Anchorage: Most local boaters who cruise in the 5- to 7-knot range anchor in the San Bernard River when making the two-day trip between Palacios, Port Lavaca or Port O'Connor and Galveston (it is also used extensively as shelter from passing storms). Although the San Bernard River is navigable for many miles north of the Waterway, towboats transit its narrow, meandering course, so anchoring south of the GIWW is preferred. Either drop a hook in the river just off the south side of the GIWW, or follow the river's steep east bank around the curve to anchor farther from the GIWW's traffic in 7-foot depths and within sound of the Gulf surf.

Colorado River Channel Offshore Approach

NAVIGATION: Use Charts 11316 and 11319. Considering all the maintained channels that link the Gulf of Mexico with the Texas GIWW, the Colorado River Channel is clearly the least desirable and most dangerous. No sea buoys or ranges mark the channel from offshore, and the surf often breaks between the short jetties through which the narrow channel passes. The channel is subject to frequent shoaling and is reported to only have 4-foot depths in summer 2010. The north jetty does not reach the shore and is connected to land by a footbridge. This arrangement allows water to flow between the north jetty and the beach, resulting in unpredictably swirling tidal currents at the channel entrance. Short beacons mark the seaward ends of the jetties (flashing green "1" and flashing red "2"), and a limited number of green daybeacons show the channel once through the jetties. From offshore, the most reliable landmarks are the bridge between the north jetty and shore, and the stilt houses, which back the beach and string north of the entrance. Passage from the Gulf of Mexico through the jetty entrance of the Matagorda Ship Channel farther to the south is much preferred.

COLORADO RIVER TO PORT O'CONNOR

Via the GIWW—Mile 442 to Mile 473 WHL

NAVIGATION: Use Chart 11319. South of the Colorado River, there are no more locks or floodgates and only two bridges until Port Isabel, the 48-foot fixed vertical clearance bridge at Aransas Pass and the 73-foot Kennedy Causeway Bridge at Corpus Christi. Commercial traffic decreases, and finally, less than 15 miles south of the Colorado River, the GIWW meets open bays and barrier islands. From Mile 445 to Mile 449 WHL, stay to the south side of the private broken wood daymarkers along the GIWW. Few navigational aids mark the channel's course from the Colorado River through the end of the land cut just past Mile 455.

Matagorda Bay from Statute Mile 460 to 470

> ⚠ **THE FOLLOWING AREA REQUIRES SPECIAL ATTENTION DUE TO SHOALING OR CHANGES TO THE CHANNEL**

NAVIGATION: Use Charts 11317 and 11319. The ICW channel markers end at quick flashing red "30" as you leave the charted spoil area to cross Matagorda Bay and pick up again across the Bay at green can "111." The ICW channel navigational aids in between have been removed with the exception of the old range markers near the Matagorda Peninsula. These ranges should only be used until reaching quick flashing red "30" and not again until picking up green can "111" on the Port O'Connor side of the Bay. The note on the latest edition of the chart (Edition 32, March 2009) states the following:

"Hurricanes, tropical storms and other major storms may cause considerable damage to marine structures, aids to navigation and moored vessels, resulting in submerged debris in unknown locations. Charted soundings, channel depths and shoreline may not reflect actual conditions following these storms. Fixed aids to navigation may have been damaged or destroyed. Buoys may have been moved form their charted positions, damaged, sunk, extinguished or otherwise made inoperative. Mariners should not rely upon the position or operation of an aid to navigation. Wrecks and submerged obstructions may have been displaced from charted locations. Pipelines may have been uncovered or moved. Mariners are urged to exercise extreme caution..."

The note on the marked channel across the bay reads as follows: "Due to strong currents, these aids to navigation are being established to temporarily mark an alternate channel for the intracoastal waterway through Matagorda Bay to the north of the existing channel. It has been established to accommodate vessels with no

Matagorda, Port Lavaca, Palacios, TX

MATAGORDA, PORT LAVACA, PALACIOS		Largest Vessel Accommodated	VHF Channel Monitored	Transient Berths / Total Berths	Approach / Dockside Depth (reported)	Floating Docks	Gas / Diesel	Groceries, Ice, Marine Supplies, Snacks	Repairs: Hull, Engine, Propeller	Lift (tonnage), Crane, Rail	1=110V, 2=220V, B=Both, Max Amps	Laundry, Pool, Showers	Pump-Out Station	Nearby: Grocery Store, Motel, Restaurant
				Dockage				Supplies			Services			
1. Matagorda Harbor 440 WHL	979-863-2103	100		5/222	10/8		GD	GIS			B/50	S	P	GMR
2. Nautical Landings 🖳	361-552-2615	50	16/68	/72	6/8	F					1/30	LS	P	GMR
3. Serendipity Bay Resort 🖳 WiFi	361-972-5454	45	16	/120	14/6	F		I			1/30	LPS	P	GMR

Corresponding chart(s) not to be used for navigation. 🖳 Internet Access WiFi Wireless Internet Access

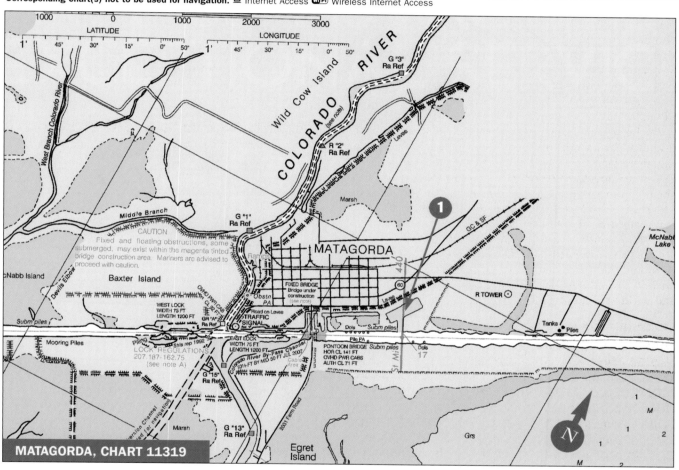

MATAGORDA, CHART 11319

greater than 10 feet draft, due to the presence of several pipelines crossing the channel at approximate positions 28° 27'31.2"N, 96° 22'59.2"W; 28° 27'30.3"N, 96° 22"59.6"W; and 28° 27'11.5"N, 96° 23'10.0"W. Mariners should be aware of the draft limitations in this alternate channel."

When heading southwest from quick flashing red "30," you will pass one or a pair of markers at approximately one mile intervals. The first will be flashing red "2," then "2A," "4" and "4A." Just before reaching quick flashing 17-foot red "6," you can turn north to head to Palacios in the marked channel or continue on toward Port O'Connor. At flashing red 17-foot "10," the channel makes a more southerly turn to then cross the

Matagorda Ship Channel leading to Port Lavaca just beyond green can "13A." Continuing on the same heading, the newer, temporary GIWW channel joins with the old channel at green can "121" at the Port O'Connor jetties. This entrance should not be confused with the "Matagorda Jetties" through which the Matagorda Ship Channel enters the Gulf of Mexico. Although the aids from green can "111" through "119" are still present, they would only be used if heading northeast to meet up with the Matagorda Ship Channel to run outside or return from the Gulf.

END SPECIAL CAUTION AREA.

Palacios, TX

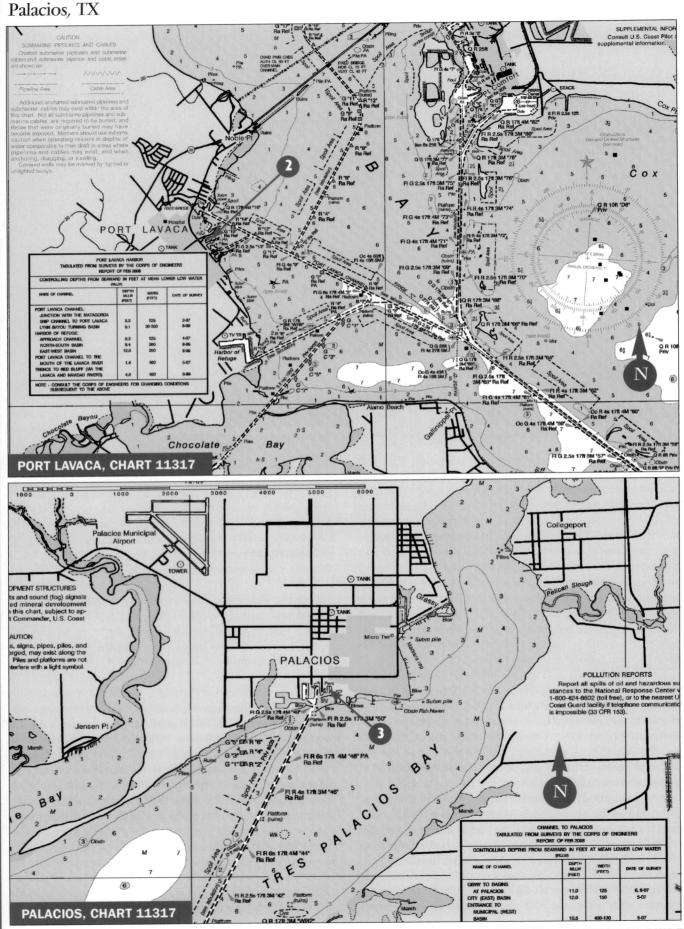

PORT LAVACA, CHART 11317

PALACIOS, CHART 11317

Commercial traffic is heavy. Be careful of shrimp boats working close to the GIWW. Continually shifting shoals render even the latest chart coverage inaccurate, and strong tidal currents can make running a course line difficult here.

Outside the marked channel at approximately Mile 466.5 WHL, the 1685 wreck of the Belle, one of French explorer René-Robert Cavelier, Sieur de La Salle's ships, was excavated in 1997. The excavation yielded a treasure trove of artifacts, including the hull of the ship, three bronze cannons, glass beads, bronze hawk bells, pottery and the skeleton of a crew member. Eventually, the ship will be reconstructed and, together with the artifacts, preserved at the Texas State History Museum in Austin.

Palacios

The small town of Palacios (pronounced locally as Pa-lash-us) is nestled along the Tres Palacios Bay, an inland bay of Matagorda Bay, and is considered by most folks as the "Shrimp Capital of Texas." Known as a winter resort town, Palacios makes a pleasant stop for a day or two. It offers haul-out facilities, a friendly sailing club and a well-protected, easily entered marina (with floating docks), laundry facilities, showers, a meeting room and a pool.

NAVIGATION: Use Chart 11316. The well-marked Palacios Channel meets the GIWW at Mile 466 WHL and leads north across Matagorda Bay, into Tres Palacios Bay and directly through the breakwaters of the harbor at Palacios. Westbound boaters can shorten the run to Palacios by exiting the red side of the GIWW anywhere along the stretch bound by red daybeacon "2A" and flashing red "4," and traveling across the 9- to 13-foot depths of Matagorda Bay to angle into the Palacios Channel (125 feet wide and 12 feet deep). When taking this shortcut, be certain to pass west of the charted Halfmoon Reef's 30-foot flashing light, which extends three miles into Matagorda Bay from Palacios Point. When traveling along the Palacios Channel, stay clear of the spoil areas north of the channel extending from the GIWW to Palacios.

Dockage: Palacios Channel passes through two parallel breakwaters and enters the harbor between flashing green "49" and flashing red "50." After passing through the outer rock breakwater, continue on a straight course past the short wooden breakwater that extends from the east side of the channel. Then turn to starboard, and follow the channel a short distance to the docks of Serendipity Resort and Marina to port. Pull into an empty slip on the central pier, but be aware that many of the slips lack adequate cleats and many boats in double slips have strung dock lines across the vacant slip next to them (thus barring entry).

Electricity, water and pump-out are available; showers and laundry facilities are located in the building next to the pool, and the marina office is located in the more distant building. Overnight transient slips are among the least expensive on the Texas coast. The number of boats at Serendipity Resort and Marina has increased noticeably, as the crowds and expense of Clear Lake have pushed more Houston-based sailors to the open bays down the coast. The Welded Boat, also on the harbor, has a 60-ton lift and repair facilities.

The Palacios Navigation District operates two marinas: South Bay Marina lies just east of Serendipity Resort next to the public boat launch. Turning Basin #3 is to just west of Serendipity adjacent to a large RV park and home to the shrimp fleet.

A quiet town with a large shrimp trawler fleet and a sizable Vietnamese population, Palacios has a lovely bayfront walkway around the seawall and a large pavilion extending into the bay. The picturesque and historic Luther Hotel, a short walk east of the marina, overlooks the bay near the pavilion and makes for a pleasant night off the boat. A bank, a hardware store with a good selection of marine supplies, a Mexican restaurant called PMR and propane refills are a few blocks east on the main road from the marina. Hilltop Marine Supply is located a few blocks west on the same road.

Port Lavaca

Known for its seafood—especially shrimp—Port Lavaca is the largest coastal town between Freeport and Rockport. The town has a protected marina with floating docks, electricity, showers and laundry. Port Lavaca also has the only hospital on the coast between Freeport and Corpus Christi. It is second only to Rockport's municipal marina as the region's most convenient place for boaters to provision. The arrival of visitors on weekends usually serves as the catalyst for a friendly potluck dinner.

NAVIGATION: Use Chart 11317. To travel the 17 miles to Nautical Landings Marina from the GIWW, take the deep, well-marked Matagorda Ship Channel into Lavaca Bay, and then follow the relatively short Lavaca Channel. Several anchorages also lie along this route (see "Anchorage: Matagorda and Lavaca Bays"). Although the Matagorda Ship Channel crosses the GIWW at Mile 471 WHL, westbound cruisers may shorten the run to Port Lavaca considerably by exiting the Waterway east of the Palacios Channel and heading across Matagorda Bay.

After leaving the GIWW and clearing the end of Halfmoon Reef, enter the open red side of the Palacios Channel, but leave its green side between the charted spoil deposits. Then plot a course across the open bay to quick-flashing green "45" and quick-flashing red "46" of the Matagorda Ship Channel. Because spoil borders most of the east side of Matagorda Ship Channel, entry from the open bay to the channel must be made through the 10-foot-deep cut just to the seaward side of flashing green "45" and flashing red "46." Eastbound boaters headed for Port Lavaca may shorten the run by cutting out of the GIWW just past Port O'Connor's north jetty and angling across Matagorda Bay to enter the open green side of the Matagorda Ship Channel at any point before flashing green "47."

Follow the Matagorda Ship Channel markers past Indianola and Magnolia Beach to the green over red intersection buoy "PL" just past markers "65" and "66."

Port Lavaca, TX

At this intersection, the well-lighted Matagorda Ship Channel angles to the north toward the industrial docks of Point Comfort, and the 6- to 8-foot-deep Lavaca Channel splits off to the west-northwest and leads to Port Lavaca. Every other green marker is lighted, making night entry less difficult. Foul ground lies immediately outside the line of red markers of the entrance channel; don't turn from the Lavaca Channel too late. The single piling (tacked with reflectors) between the last of the entrance channel's red markers and the end of the wooden breakwater may be passed on either side. A short wooden breakwater extends from the tall bulkhead just inside the basin and must be kept to starboard. Be careful of the exposed pilings and sunken vessels at the entrance to the harbor. Pull into any vacant slip. Visitors receive friendly welcomes here and are usually hailed on VHF Channel 16 if seen approaching from the bay.

Dockage: Maps of the town are available from the harbormaster, but most amenities are within a few blocks of the marina. A hardware store, two Mexican restaurants, the post office, the library, a bank, a coin-operated laundry and the county's museum of history are all within walking distance of Nautical Landings Marina. Nautical Landings is owned by the city of Port Lavaca and is also home to the Port Lavaca Yacht Club. It is a full-service, breakwater-protected marina with restrooms, shower facilities and pump-out. Diesel fuel only is available at the shrimp boat basin approximately a half-mile from the marina. Taxi service is available, and local boaters tend to be generous with rides. Many more businesses are clustered along Highway 35 (a short drive, but a long hike from the marina).

The city has constructed a stepped cement bulkhead around the shores of Bayfront Park, adjacent to the marina. Although wave reflection from the new bulkhead makes the final entry into Nautical Landings a bit rougher in southeast winds, the structure has greatly improved the attractiveness of the shoreline and provides a pleasant place to stroll, sit or fish at the water's edge.

A long walk on the road in front of the marina leads around the shrimp boat basin at the end of the Lavaca Channel to the Lighthouse Beach and Bird Sanctuary near the causeway. This park includes a man-made beach, the elevated Formosa Wetlands Walkway stretching over coastal wetlands and the tidal exchange basin, a bird-watching tower, a pier extending out into Lavaca Bay, playgrounds and picnic areas.

Anchorage (Matagorda and Lavaca Bays): In prevailing southeasterly winds, exit the green side of the GIWW almost anywhere between green buoys "25" and "89" to anchor in the lee of Matagorda Peninsula. The most popular spots along this stretch are just south of Mile 464 WHL near Greens Bayou between the tall back range (south of green "57") and shore, and off the bulkhead near the old Matagorda Club Airfield. Stilt houses and a wrecked plane on shore are visible along this stretch. Anchoring farther down the peninsula, nearer the inside of the jetties, is unwise because tidal currents run too swiftly, and the frequently shifting shoals are more abundant than suggested by even the latest chart. A few private moorings have been placed outside the green side of the Matagorda Ship Channel behind Decros Island. They are rarely occupied on weekdays, but should be used at your own risk.

For boats with drafts of less than 5.5 feet, Lavaca Bay has several easily entered anchorages. Although spoil banks line most of the red side of the Matagorda Ship Channel, the channel may be safely exited by heading northwest from red "56" to anchor off Sand Point in southeast to east winds, and off Rhodes Point in north to east winds. Boats with drafts of less than 5 feet can enter Keller Bay for a somewhat open anchorage, with nearly all-around protection from waves. Returning to the Matagorda Ship Channel from any of these anchorages, head toward the orange picnic shelters on the southeast shore of Lavaca Bay to find the cut beside marker "56" and re-enter the ship channel.

Magnolia Beach, reached by leaving the green side of the Matagorda Ship Channel between markers "57" and "64," makes an enjoyable day anchorage and overnight anchorage in settled weather. Although usually quiet, this fine shell beach draws crowds on spring and summer weekends. Anchor out from the two-story building in depths that shoal gradually from 6 feet. Cruisers can swim or dinghy ashore for a beer and burger at Bay Watchers. Hiking along the beach to the granite statue of La Salle and the site of the old town of Indianola is an enjoyable trip. Indianola rivaled Galveston as Texas' most important port before being devastated twice by hurricanes. The foundations of the buildings of old Indianola still lie beneath the surface of Lavaca Bay, as does the locomotive that sat on the long wharf during one of the 19th-century hurricanes. Bird-watching is spectacular along the wetlands adjacent to Indianola and Magnolia Beach.

Closer to Port Lavaca, Cedar Point offers a pleasant anchorage with excellent protection in southeast through southwest winds. To reach the anchorage, start into the Lavaca Channel from the intersection buoy in the Matagorda Ship Channel, but head southwest from the Lavaca Channel once past the low range marker. Head toward the house with the windmill, and drop anchor in 5- to 7-foot depths. The wreck of three scuttled shrimp boats marks the general vicinity of the anchorage. Dredging of the Lavaca Channel resulted in spoil being deposited in the bay between this anchorage and markers "1" through "5" of the Lavaca Channel, so you will have to leave this anchorage the same way you entered.

Lavaca River

NAVIGATION: Use Chart 11317. For vessels with drafts of no more than 3.5 feet and mast heights of less than 35 feet, the Lavaca River offers an interesting side trip with peaceful, protected spots to drop a hook. To reach the mouth of the Lavaca River, exit the Lavaca Channel near red "8" in 6-foot depths. Locate the distant red markers before exiting the Lavaca Channel. The markers are widely spaced, so frequently sight the markers ahead of (and behind) your position to monitor drift, and stay in the channel. Depths are quite shallow outside the channel, which turns sharply to port in Lavaca Bay before passing under the causeway, and then turns sharply to starboard en route to the Lavaca River's mouth. The fixed bridge for the Highway 35 Bypass has a 43-foot vertical clearance followed by a power line with a 69-foot vertical clearance. Just before reaching the last markers in upper Lavaca Bay, a bar with depths of less than 4 feet extends across the channel. Beyond the bar, depths range from 6 to 15 feet in the river. Before making this passage toward the Lavaca River, cruisers should check for local knowledge and with the U.S. Army Corps of Engineers for frequently changing conditions.

Anchorage: Although small cruising boats can nose into the bank for a quiet anchorage at several spots, the best anchorage lies by the twin bridges (one road and one railroad) that mark the end of the route for most vessels. Two sturdy dolphins by the bridge offer a convenient place to moor. Boats with heights of 10 feet or less (depending on river stage) can pass under the bridge and anchor in the 7-foot depths of the Navidad River, which enters the Lavaca River immediately beyond the railroad bridge, or they can anchor in the Lavaca River itself. When anchoring in the Lavaca River, stick well to the side and burn a bright anchor light. Outboard-powered ski and fishing boats often transit the river at high speeds.

■ PORT O'CONNOR TO CORPUS CHRISTI BAY

Mile 473 to Mile 523 WHL

The 50-mile-long run on the GIWW from Port O'Connor to Aransas Bay offers no marinas or other amenities, but does provide a beautiful cruise through the Aransas National Wildlife Refuge before entering Aransas Bay at Mile 515 WHL. Westbound boaters will notice the change at Port O'Connor right away—cleaner water and more abundant wildlife compared to the route immediately to the east. An evident advantage during the winter months, in addition to the great weather (you are now as far south as Tampa, FL) is the excellent fishing and abundance of whooping cranes. You need to see the whooping cranes to fully appreciate their majestic beauty. The decks of your boat make fine observation platforms. The birds seem to have their winter home roots in this area, and the tour boats from Rockport and Aransas Pass will be plentiful. As a bonus, you may see wild hogs, turkeys, coyotes and deer.

NAVIGATION: Use Charts 11319, 11315 and 11314. From Mile 475 to Mile 485 WHL, stay in mid-channel to avoid the shallow water along the banks, and strictly honor the line of red daybeacons starting at Mile 479 WHL. The daybeacons are placed in 2 to 3 feet of water along this stretch to avoid having them knocked down by commercial towboats.

At Mile 478 WHL, there is a well-marked 7-foot deep channel that extends southward from the GIWW and terminates six miles later at Matagorda Island State Park. A small dock with 5-foot depths can accommodate a handful of boats, but there is no shore power or other facilities. This is an unusual destination, both for its remote location and its features. Often referred to as the Army Hole, the park contains a massive WWII-era landing strip, an unspoiled (and mostly deserted) beach and a lighthouse built in 1852. It is a popular destination for local boaters. Contact the Texas Parks and Wildlife Department (979-244-6804) for tour information.

A small settlement at Mile 485 WHL has several private piers, a couple of boat ramps and dockage for shallow-draft vessels. On weekends, the area is often humming with small fishing and other pleasure boats as they cross the GIWW and disappear through a narrow cut in the spoil bank and into Espiritu Santo Bay. Space to tie up for transient pleasure boats is questionable at best. Just east of red daybeacon "10" to red "2E," be careful of submerged and exposed rocks along the north bank of the GIWW.

At Mile 501.5 WHL, on the north side of the channel, is a shallow canal leading to an Aransas National Wildlife ranger station. Some slips and docks are located near the small building at the channel end. Five-foot depths have been unofficially reported in the canal. This is a ranger station, so if you should need refuge, be prepared to explain why you are there.

Mile 503 to Mile 504 WHL is a "wiggle," so buoys are often knocked out of position. The wiggle is marked by 17-foot flashing red "48" and 17-foot quick flashing green "53," which are firmly located on the banks. A levee on the north bank prevents intrusion from the marshlands. In the vicinity of Mile 507 WHL, midway along Sundown Bay to the north, a privately maintained channel leads south from the GIWW into Mesquite Bay. The channel and Mesquite Bay are quite shallow, with charted depths of 4 feet or less. Fishing boats, park rangers and workboats, which maintain the petroleum production platforms south of the Waterway, use the channel. We would recommend you don't.

The GIWW is measured in miles west of the Harvey Lock (WHL), and actually changes from west to southwest and then to the south, as you head to Corpus Christi and Brownsville. Corpus Christi is as far south as Tampa, and South Padre Island is comparable to the Everglades with regard to latitude. We will refer to the northwest and southwest banks as we continue "west" on the GIWW.

At Mile 510 WHL, the GIWW leaves the wildlife refuge at 17-foot flashing green "1" and enters into Aransas Bay for a 10-mile-long, well-marked run to the Key Allegro and Rockport area. The bay and the spoil areas are well-marked. Stay in the channel; avoid the submerged pilings to the south and the shallow water to the north of the Waterway. Petroleum production platforms are numerous, well-marked and glow with white and amber lights.

Dockage: Transient dockage is available at Clark's Marina less than a mile west of the jetty tip on the north shore of the GIWW at Mile 474. The building exhibits a rounded wharf: follow this wharf around to the slips in the restaurant. The marina is tight, but should be able to accommodate vessels 40 feet and less. Also on the grounds is The Inn at Clark's, a summertime gathering for visiting "snowbirds." It is closed during the winter months and priority is given to Inn customers. The seafood restaurant is a popular favorite with locals and visitors alike.

■ ROCKPORT & KEY ALLEGRO

Mile 520 to Mile 525 WHL

NAVIGATION: Use Chart 11314. Keep on a heading toward Rockport until the opening between two spoil areas defined by daybeacons "1" and "2." Proceed through the cut, and set a heading of 270 degrees to the Rockport Harbor entrance.

At night, the lights from the multitude of homes on Key Allegro and the shopping center located to the north make the channel difficult to see. The other entrance to Key Allegro on the east, beneath the vehicle bridge, is only for small boats with a maximum height of 8 feet. Follow the channel, keeping the homes to starboard and the Rockport Beach Park to port. As you round the bend into the very shallow Little Bay, follow the channel markers that head directly toward the houses at the point next to the marina.

Dockage: The Rockport area has three outstanding marinas for transient boaters, the Key Allegro Island Marina, the Rockport Municipal Marina and The Fulton Harbor Marina, the latter two operated by the Aransas County Navigation District. When approaching from the east, the entrance to both marinas is through the spoil cut at Mile 521 WHL. Keep 17-foot flashing green "43" to port, and then steer northwest between green daybeacon "1" and red daybeacon "2." The entrance to Key Allegro is marked by 20-foot flashing green "1" and 20-foot flashing red "2."

The Key Allegro Island Marina has been under a complete renovation during the past few years. Dorado's Restaurant and Palapa's Lounge are delightful, with a great waterfront view and live entertainment on some evenings. The ship's store offers almost anything you might need. Gas and diesel fuel are dockside, and transient slips (covered and open) are available. Amenities, including restrooms, showers, a laundry room, a swimming pool and a snack bar are all available. Key Allegro Island itself is covered with large homes and condominiums bordering the many canals that provide water frontage and private docking. Tennis courts and beach access add to the resort feel of this facility. The Key Allegro Yacht Club is on the island, but is not accessible by water. The 5-foot depths around the small islands in Little Bay are favored for water skiing, jet boating and partying on tiki-hut barges equipped with bars, grills, entertainment and sunbathing platforms. If you have a rod and reel, try fishing at the docks or on Little Bay; fishing is excellent here, especially at night.

The Rockport Municipal Harbor is a favorite of the sail-ing crowd and popular with all boaters. The entrance is marked by 17-foot flashing green "1" and a series of green daybeacons leading into the harbor. Keep 17-foot flashing red "6" close to starboard when entering. First-timers should avoid a night entry if possible. The lights from the shopping center across the highway and downtown Rockport are imposing to say the least, but their proximity makes shore shopping and sightseeing an outstanding harbor asset. Proceed along the starboard side of the basin, and keep the recreational boat dock to port. The transient pier, amid the fishing boats, has a large sign to guide you in. Check in at the harbor office in the small brick building behind the arts building. The boater's building with showers, a laundry and restrooms is next door. Make slip reservations in advance to assure availability.

Rockport Municipal Harbor is also home to the Rockport Yacht Club, whose building is adjacent to the transient slip area. Yacht club members are friendly and will be happy to provide local knowledge to visitors. The harbor location in the center of town makes it a convenient place to take on provisions. The shops, stores and post office in downtown Rockport are just a few blocks away. Fresh seafood—oysters, crabs and shrimp—can be purchased right from the boats in the harbor. Right across the street is Latitude 28° 02, a local landmark serving seafood in a casual setting among works of art from the thriving local artist community. The Texas Maritime Museum is on-site, and the public beach and adjacent park playground adjoin the harbor to the east.

Fulton Harbor, also managed by the Aransas County Navigation District, is northeast of Key Allegro, and is home to many commercial fishing and shrimp boats. A transient boater facility building with showers and restrooms was added in late 2007. Fulton Yacht Yard is a service center with 15- and 70-ton lifts and complete ship's service and repairs. The channel (5 feet deep) is marked by 17-foot flashing reds "2" and "4" to starboard, and green daybeacons "3" and "5" to port. Less than a mile from the harbor, submerged pilings are marked by green daybeacon "1." The Fulton Mansion is charted as "CUPOLA (Old Mansion)" and should be on your sightseeing list while ashore. The Sandollar Marina & Restaurant (about a mile to the northeast) has a small, protected harbor, but offers no transient service. Sea Gun Marina is at the northeastern end of the highway causeway. A staked channel (3- to 5-foot depths) leads to the marina that is now, for the most part, a fishing resort, with no amenities for transient boaters. Just a block off the harbor sits Moondog Seaside Eatery, a popular local seafood café with excellent views of the water.

Anchorage: Anchorages in Aransas Bay are plentiful. The bight formed in the alcove at Pauls Mott, two miles southeast of 17-foot flashing green "31" at Mile 518 WHL, where it joins with Long Reef, is a favored anchorage, although open to northwest winds. Seven-foot depths can be carried fairly close to shore. A more popular spot, but equally exposed to northerly winds, is located in the bight formed by the tidal flats of Mud Island and San Jose Island. Anchor outside the two private channels in 7- to 8-foot depths.

ARANSAS BAY TO CORPUS CHRISTI BAY—GIWW

Mile 522 to Mile 540 WHL
NAVIGATION: Use Charts 11314, 11309 and 11312. The GIWW project, sometimes referred to as the Rockport Cut, takes the more direct route to Corpus Christi Bay and passes by the town of Aransas Pass. The alternative is the Aransas Channel, which passes through Port Aransas then continues on as the Lydia Ann Channel. The two routes rejoin at Mile 539.5 WHL before the GIWW enters Corpus Christi Bay through a narrow cut aptly named the "Eye of the Needle." Because the two routes differ so obviously, reasons for choosing either will vary. There tends to be less commercial traffic on the Lydia Ann route, and less residential and commercial development along its banks. For tall-masted sailboats, the ability to clear the 48-foot fixed vertical clearance highway bridge (Mile 533.1 WHL) at Aransas Pass is an obvious factor. The entrance from Aransas Bay into the GIWW channel (Rockport Cut) is marked by 17-foot flashing green "7" and is well-buoyed beyond that point. Stay in mid-channel, as shallow water is found outside the marked passage. Note again that we are referring to the right bank of the GIWW as the northwest bank and the left bank as the southeast bank. When traveling the GIWW, the compass itself is very seldom used.

Dockage: At the first bend to port at Mile 525.5 WHL, 17-foot, quick flashing red "12" marks the entrance to the House of Boats, Hooking Bull Boatyard and Captain Sally's Boating Center. In this service complex are a restaurant, fuel docks, marine supplies and other transient facilities. Full repair service is offered, and self-repairs are permitted.

Palm Harbor Marina (Mile 527.5 WHL) is located farther west on the northwest bank opposite 17-foot flashing green "13." Gas is available (no diesel) with transient dockage for vessels up to 60 feet. Restrooms, showers, a laundry and the Marker 13 Restaurant all add up to a fine overnight, or longer, stop. On-site lodging is also available for those who might enjoy a night off the boat with their feet on solid ground.

The Aransas Channel (Mile 533 WHL) to Port Aransas (five miles to the southeast) is busy with commercial trawlers and small fishing boats. The 48-foot fixed vertical clearance highway bridge is just south of the entrance to the Aransas Pass Turning Basin at Mile 533.1 WHL. To enter the basin, travel just past red nun buoy "36A," and then between 17-foot flashing green "23" and red daybeacon "24." The basin extends to Conn Brown Harbor; both the turning basin and the harbor have 14-foot depths. The Conn Brown Harbor is primarily a commercial port for Gulf trawlers and has nothing to offer the transient pleasure boats.

Back on the GIWW, just before 17-foot quick flashing green "41" is the channel to Hampton's Landing and Pelican Cove, a residential development. When entering from the GIWW, keep the TEXACO sign close to port, and head for the house on the corner bulkhead until the marina

on the port side becomes visible and the channel obvious. San Patricio County operates the slips in the fenced area. Privately operated Hampton's Landing is located to port as you enter the harbor. Gas and diesel fuel, a restaurant (serving breakfast, sandwiches and tacos), a ship's store and restrooms are available. The County Marina offers limited transient dockage, both covered and open, based upon availability. No slips are reserved exclusively for transients. A convenience store and a Chinese restaurant are within walking distance.

At Mile 535.5 WHL (17-foot quick-flashing red "50"), a commercial shipyard reportedly sells diesel fuel, and repair service is available to transients.

Corpus Christi Ship Channel
NAVIGATION: Use Chart 11308. From Mile 536.5 WHL (20-foot flashing red "A") to Mile 539 WHL (Corpus Christi Channel) the GIWW is marked only by green daybeacons, with the exception of 20-foot flashing red "A" at Mile 536.5 WHL. The Corpus Christi Channel has heavy traffic, inbound and outbound. Tows with long barge strings, Gulf-bound tankers and freighters, fast offshore supply boats, Navy and Coast Guard vessels and fishing trawlers are plentiful. Berthed tankers and large offshore production platforms under repair on the northwest bank at Port Ingleside sometimes impair visibility.

The channel to Corpus Christi and the continuation of the GIWW west are covered in the section following the GIWW Alternate Route, from Aransas Bay to Port Aransas and back to the Waterway again at Mile 539.

ARANSAS BAY TO CORPUS CHRISTI BAY— GIWW ALTERNATE ROUTE

Via Port Aransas: Mile 523 to Mile 540 WHL
NAVIGATION: Use Charts 11314 and 11308. The alternate route was originally the GIWW (Mile 522.5A) before the land cut was made between Rockport and Corpus Christi Bay through Aransas Pass. Though five miles longer than the GIWW route, it provides a great trip via the Lydia Ann Channel, many fine spots to anchor and access to the fishing and resort village of Port Aransas. It also bypasses the fixed 48-foot vertical clearance bridge on the GIWW for those with taller masts. Port Aransas offers miles of beaches, numerous restaurants, well-protected marinas, motels, condos and the only Gulf access between the Matagorda Ship Channel to the northeast and Port Mansfield to the southwest.

The alternate GIWW starts at Mile 522.5A (quick flashing green "49;" passes through Aransas Bay to Mile 531A, and then meets the Lydia Ann Channel, which extends to Corpus Christi Channel at Mile 531.5A). This alternate route is well-marked on both sides of the channel. Tidal currents from the Gulf entrance can slow your passage.

Aransas Bay Area, TX

ARANSAS BAY AREA		Largest Vessel Accommodated	VHF Channel Monitored	Transient Berths / Total Berths	Approach / Dockside Depth (reported)	Floating Docks	Gas / Diesel	Groceries, Ice, Marine Supplies Snacks	Repairs: Hull, Engine, Propeller	Lift (tonnage), Crane, Rail	1=110v, 2=220v, B=Both, Max Amps	Laundry, Pool, Showers	Pump-Out Station	Nearby: Grocery Store, Motel, Restaurant
					Dockage			Supplies			Services			
1. Fulton Harbor 520 WHL	361-729-6661	60	16	20/100	12/6			IMS	HEP	L49,C	B/50	LS	P	MR
2. Key Allegro Isle Marina 520 WHL ▫ⓦ	361-729-8264	120	16	3/159	8/7		GD	GIMS				LPS	P	GMR
3. Rockport Harbor 522.8 WHL	361-729-6661	70	16	10/175	11/7			GIM			1/50	LS	P	GMR
4. House of Boats 526 WHL ⓦ	361-729-9018	50		/3	12/12		GD	IMS	HEP	L50	1/30	S		R
5. Cove Harbor Marina and Drystack 526 WHL	361-790-5438	50	16	15/173	7/8	F	GD	IMS			B/50	S	P	R
6. Palm Harbor Marina 527.3 WHL	361-729-8540	50	16	10/55	7/6		G	GIMS			B/50	LS		R
7. San Patricio County Navigation Dist. #1 534 WHL	361-758-1890	50		18/157	10/12		G	S			1/30		P	GR
8. Port Aransas Municipal Marina 533 WHL	361-749-5429	150		38/250	10/10	F		I		C	B/50	LS	P	GMR
9. Fisherman's Wharf 533 WHL	361-749-5448	60	16		8/8		GD	IMS	FUEL DOCKS ONLY					GMR
10. Island Moorings Marina & Yacht Club 534 WHL	361-749-4100	100	16	50/350	8/8	F	GD	IMS			B/50	LPS	P	GMR

Corresponding chart(s) not to be used for navigation. ▫ Internet Access ⓦ Wireless Internet Access

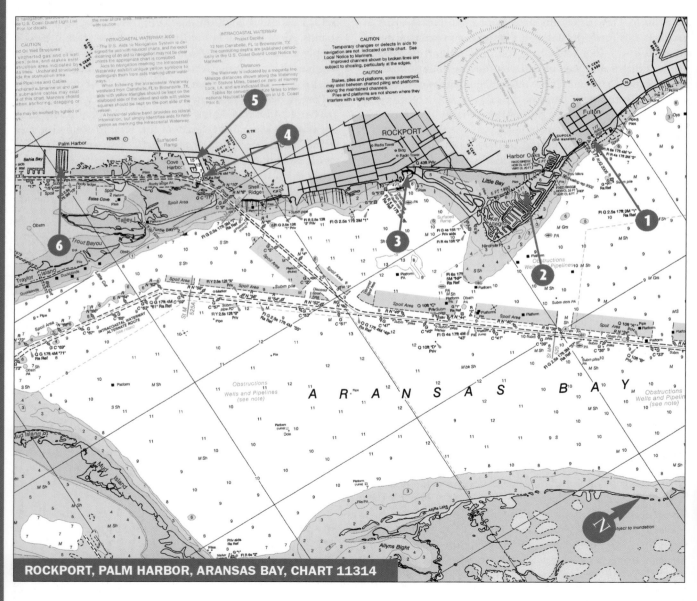

ROCKPORT, PALM HARBOR, ARANSAS BAY, CHART 11314

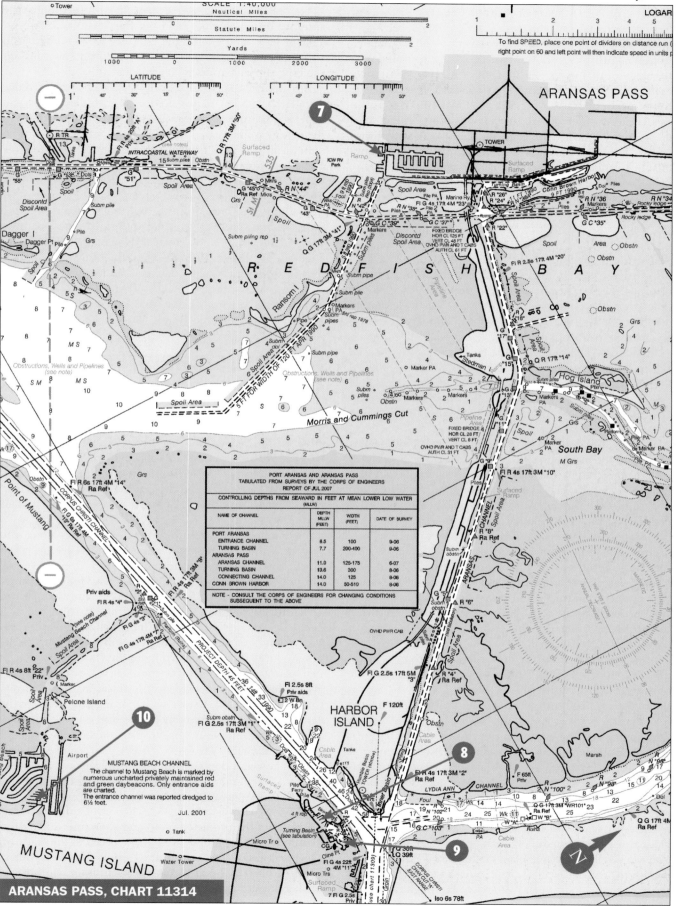

PORT ARANSAS AND ARANSAS PASS
TABULATED FROM SURVEYS BY THE CORPS OF ENGINEERS
REPORT OF JUL 2007

CONTROLLING DEPTHS FROM SEAWARD IN FEET AT MEAN LOWER LOW WATER
(MLLW)

NAME OF CHANNEL	DEPTH MLLW (FEET)	WIDTH (FEET)	DATE OF SURVEY
PORT ARANSAS			
ENTRANCE CHANNEL	8.5	100	9-06
TURNING BASIN	7.7	200-400	9-06
ARANSAS PASS			
ARANSAS CHANNEL	11.0	125-175	6-07
TURNING BASIN	13.6	300	8-06
CONNECTING CHANNEL	14.0	125	8-06
CONN BROWN HARBOR	14.0	50-510	8-06

NOTE - CONSULT THE CORPS OF ENGINEERS FOR CHANGING CONDITIONS
SUBSEQUENT TO THE ABOVE

MUSTANG BEACH CHANNEL
The channel to Mustang Beach is marked by
numerous uncharted privately maintained red
and green daybeacons. Only entrance aids
are charted.
The entrance channel was reported dredged to
6½ feet.

Jul. 2001

ARANSAS PASS, CHART 11314

Corpus Christi, TX

Just east of Port Aransas on Corpus Christi Channel, the ferry crossing is very busy with four ferryboats.

The GIWW Alternate Route crosses the Aransas Channel from the northwest: Aransas Pass (not to be confused with the town of that name) to the Gulf of Mexico, continuing east to the Corpus Christi Ship Channel. The alternate route meets the GIWW at Mile 539.5 WHL. The northeast corner is littered with the remains of old commercial docks that lie mostly under the surface. At the northwest corner is Harbor Island, with a petroleum tank farm, offshore drilling rig assembly center and other offshore operations. The southwest end of San Jose Island is barren and marked by a quick-flashing 38-foot-high tower. On Mustang Island is the town of Port Aransas, better known as "Port A" to the multitude of students who flock there for spring break.

If you are traveling to the Gulf of Mexico, strong currents may be encountered along the jetties at the entrance of Aransas Pass. The alternate GIWW at Mile 535A is two miles from the Gulf. Aransas Pass (600 feet wide and 45 feet deep) is well-marked, and several submerged wrecks are charted just north of flashing green buoy "9."

Dockage: The entrance to the Port Aransas City Marina (Dennis Dryer Harbor) is well-marked at the opening of the granite breakwater. The transient docks can handle vessels up to 100 feet (or more). Restrooms, a bathhouse and a laundry room are on-site. The marina is part of a large city park complex.

Both gas and diesel fuels are available at Woody's Sport Center on the mainland side of the harbor. The Sportsplex and Trout Street marinas have on-site restaurants, but very little transient dockage. The Back Porch on the waterfront next to Woody's serves cocktails and cold beer and has live music every day. For lunch or dinner, try Virginia's on the Bay Restaurant. Circle K is nearby for provisions.

Great seafood restaurants are plentiful throughout Port Aransas. Getting from the municipal marina to the downtown area requires a bus ride or a walk around the basin. Many motels and inns are also within the city confines. A stop at the chamber of commerce, across the street from the marina row, is worthwhile. They will provide you with a wealth of information.

After departure from the Port Aransas Harbor, a three-mile run up the Corpus Christi Ship Channel crosses the Mustang Beach Channel (17-foot flashing green "7" marks the ruins of a platform), which is well-charted with lighted 8-foot markers up to the Island Moorings Marina. Watch your sounder as you enter and run this channel. This great spot is the only marina in the area that offers everything outside of being "downtown." The Island Moorings Marina has wide floating docks, gas and diesel fuel, a dock store, pumpout, restrooms with showers, a pool and hot tub, a restaurant and bar and an airport next door. Beach access is less than a mile away, and a bus (made to look like a trolley car) provides transportation into Port Aransas just three miles away. You can watch the private planes take off and land from the airstrip that sits adjacent to the marina, and at night, watch the glow of the underwater lights placed throughout.

There had been a constant problem with shoaling at the entrance to the channel from the ship channel. However, a small jetty now guards the entrance to Mustang Beach Channel and Island Moorings. It is hoped the constant shoaling at the channel will be alleviated.

If a dredge is operating, call Island Moorings Dredge on VHF Channel 13 for advice and guidance. As you approach the marina, there are side canals that extend to the private home sites.

Returning to the Corpus Christi Channel, it is then just a five-mile run northwest to the GIWW before it threads the "Eye of the Needle" into Corpus Christi Bay at Mile 540 WHL.

Anchorage: Across from the lighthouse and just before quick-flashing green "97" is one of the area's most popular spots to anchor. A buoyed wreck is just beyond the light. High-speed offshore fishing boats throwing huge wakes may disturb your sleep at daybreak and your leisure hour at dusk. Aside from possible disturbances, this is an excellent anchorage with a clean sand beach and the Gulf of Mexico less than a mile away.

■ CORPUS CHRISTI BAY TO SOUTH PADRE ISLAND

Corpus Christi Channel to Ingleside and Corpus Christi

NAVIGATION: Use Charts 11308 and 11309. From Mile 540 WHL, the GIWW heads southwest into Corpus Christi Bay, as you thread the "Eye of the Needle," or take the Corpus Christi Ship Channel to Corpus Christi and all that it has to offer.

Two miles northwest of Mile 540 WHL, along the Corpus Christi Channel, the La Quinta Channel (five miles long, 300 feet wide and 45 feet deep) extends northeast toward Ingleside Cove. The La Quinta Channel entrance is marked by flashing green "1" and flashing red "2." After passing flashing green "1" and flashing red "2," enter the cove just north of 17-foot-high flashing red "8," and watch your depth sounder carefully. Transient facilities are located in downtown Ingleside On-the-Bay.

If you are traveling to Corpus Christi, truly a worthwhile destination, return to the well-marked Corpus Christi Channel, and steer west. Strong south or southeasterly winds are common in the afternoon, and wave action may cause your boat to drift outside the channel and into the spoil areas, so correct your course accordingly. The water depths throughout the bay average 10 to 12 feet. When approaching the enclosed basin protecting Corpus Christi's waterfront, stay in the channel until passing 17-foot flashing green "85." Then steer south between the rocks of the protected basin and shoreline. Stay in the middle at 8- to 10-foot depths, and proceed to the marinas. The breakwater's entrance to the Corpus Christi Marina is near the northeast end of the enclosed basin. Do not cut the breakwater entrance too sharply. Instead, enter in the middle between the marker and the wharf. Recreational vessels are restricted north of the Harbor Bridge.

Dockage: Heading north in the La Quinta Channel takes you to Ingleside Cove, which offers protected anchorage areas in 6- to 8-foot depths and the popular Bahia Marina, where temptation leads some to stretch an overnight stop into a longer, sometimes permanent home. The marina is a popular spot for boaters from Rockport, Port Aransas and Corpus Christi, when they want to get away for a few days. Bahia Marina has a dock store, a great pool, barbecue pits, showers, a laundry and a breezeway that overlooks the bird sanctuary. A word of caution: Do not cut the corner going into the marina channel. If your vessel draws over 5 feet, call the marina for a depth check before entering.

Across the Bay and inside the harbor at Corpus Christi, you might need a map to find the fuel dock, pump-out station, air-conditioned showers, restrooms and laundry, two restaurants (Landry's on Cooper's Alley L-Head and Joe's Crab Shack on Lawrence Street T-Head) and two yacht clubs (Corpus Christi Yacht Club and Bay Yacht Club). A special work area is provided where tenants may do their own maintenance and minor repairs. A boat repair facility, with a 15-ton Travelift, is available for contract repairs. More than 500 slips are available here.

The Corpus Christi Municipal Marina has received almost $7.5 million in updates and renovations in the last few years. A boater's facility building houses a library, meeting rooms and laptop Internet hookups (although free wireless Internet access covers the marina area). The marina has won numerous state and national awards, including Texas Marina of the Year, and is now the permanent home of the massive Texas International Boat Show, held every April. Corpus Christi is somewhat unique among major cities on the Gulf Coast, in that the downtown area is right along the water, only a few steps from the marina. The marina is part of a popular family walking and driving route, which includes the waterfront pathway of the city. On weekends, you will see a steady stream of "local tourists" out to see the boats.

GOIN' ASHORE:
CORPUS CHRISTI, TX

After a devastating hurricane in 1919 caused incredible damage and the loss of 287 lives, Corpus Christi, with the help of the federal government, completed a massive dredging project and rebuilt the city. With the increased port traffic, the city doubled its population in 10 years and today remains a major seaport on the Gulf of Mexico. This cosmopolitan city, with all the expected amenities, is becoming a choice destination for the GIWW cruiser.

Corpus Christi, a seaport at the mouth of the Nueces River, is the largest city on the South Texas coast and one of the nation's largest suppliers of natural gas. The city has much to offer within walking distance of several blocks and warrants more than a day's stay (maybe a week if you have the time).

Car rentals are very reasonable, and bus service is available throughout the city, with trolley service along the main streets. The Water Street Market is in the heart of Corpus Christi, with an open-air courtyard and a few little shops. The Water Street Seafood Co. (361-882-8683) and Water Street Oyster Bar (361-881-9448) offer a variety of seafood and Texas fare, while Aqua Java (361-882-0865) offers lighter fare, specialty coffees and teas and free wireless Internet access. A boardwalk extends along the bayfront where you can walk, jog and bike or rent a covered four-wheel bicycle for exploring. You can stop at the Selena Memorial located on the boardwalk or visit the Selena Museum (361-289-9013), a tribute to the life and contributions of the young Tejano singing star. The area usually has a delightful breeze that makes it an ideal place for windsurfing and sailing. Fishing is a popular pastime, and catches are plentiful. The white sandy beaches are easily accessible and open to the public. McGee Beach, about a mile south of the marina along Shoreline Boulevard, has just been replenished with clean, bright sand from recent dredging operations, extending the beach from 80 feet to over 200 feet.

A short bike ride or 20-minute walk from the marina, the Whataburger Field (opened in 2005) hosts baseball games for the Corpus Christi Hooks, the AA minor league affiliate team of the Houston Astros.

The second largest bridge in Texas, Harbor Bridge, goes from the port and connects Corpus Christi Beach to the downtown area. You can get there over land from the marina three ways: by taxi (less than $10); by ferry via the landing at the Arts Center Building, about a mile north of the marina; or by public bus, with a stop at the Cooper's Alley T-Head. Keep in mind that the buses do not run on Sundays. You can gather city information, current events and discount coupons for events and dining at the Corpus Christi Chamber of Commerce (120l N. Shoreline Blvd., 361-881-1800). The Central Library (805 Comanche St., 361-826-7000) is conveniently located, with Internet access available. The Texas State Aquarium, with Dolphin Bay as its newest addition (800-477-GULF), is a popular spot. Across from the aquarium, the USS Lexington Museum helps you imagine life aboard America's most famous aircraft carrier (2914 N. Shoreline Blvd., 361-888-4873).

You can stop for lunch or dinner in between these two sites at Pier 99 (2822 N. Shoreline Blvd., 361-887-0764) and enjoy a varied Texas menu of "po' boys," burgers and seafood. The Republic of Texas Bar & Grill at the Omni Bayfront Hotel (900 N. Shoreline Blvd., 361-886-3515) offers steak, seafood and pasta in a casual atmosphere where you can dine 20 floors above the city and enjoy a great view. For a little more nightlife, try Blackbeard's on the Beach with live music nightly (3117 Surfside Blvd., 361-884-1030).

The Corpus Christi Botanical Garden and Nature Center (361-852-2100) has exhibits, a water garden, bird and butterfly trails, a wetlands boardwalk and picnic areas (open 9 a.m. to 5 p.m. daily except on Mondays). Many homes are on the Texas Historic Landmark Tour, where history can be relived with a visit to nine restored homes from the turn of the 20th century. Tours are offered Thursday and Friday at 10:30 a.m. Located near the marinas, the Art Center of Corpus Christi (361-884-6406) is a pleasant spot to see artists practice their crafts, with

Corpus Christi Area, TX

SKIPPER BOB PUBLICATIONS

CORPUS CHRISTI AREA		Dockage					Supplies		Services				
		Largest Vessel Accommodated	VHF Channel Monitored	Transient Berths / Total Berths	Approach / Dockside Depth (reported)	Floating Docks	Gas / Diesel	Groceries, Ice, Marine Supplies, Snacks	Repairs: Hull, Engine, Propeller	Lift (tonnage), Crane, Rail	1=110v, 2=220V, B=Both, Max Amps	Laundry, Pool, Showers	Pump-Out Station / Nearby: Grocery Store, Motel, Restaurant
1. Bahia Marina 2NW of 540 WHL 🖥 WiFi	361-776-7295	50	16	6/56	6/6			IS			1/30	LPS	
2. North Shore Boat Works 2NW of 540 WHL	361-776-2525				18/10			M	HEP	L35	B		GMR
3. Corpus Christi Yacht Club	361-883-6518	60		3/	9/6			I			B/50	S	R
4. Corpus Christi Municipal Marina	361-826-3980	150	16/68	40/618	8/10	F		IMS	HEP	L15	B/100	LS	P	MR
5. Marker 37 Marina 553 WHL	361-949-8037	40	72	1/35	4/4		G	IMS					

Corresponding chart(s) not to be used for navigation. 🖥 Internet Access WiFi Wireless Internet Access

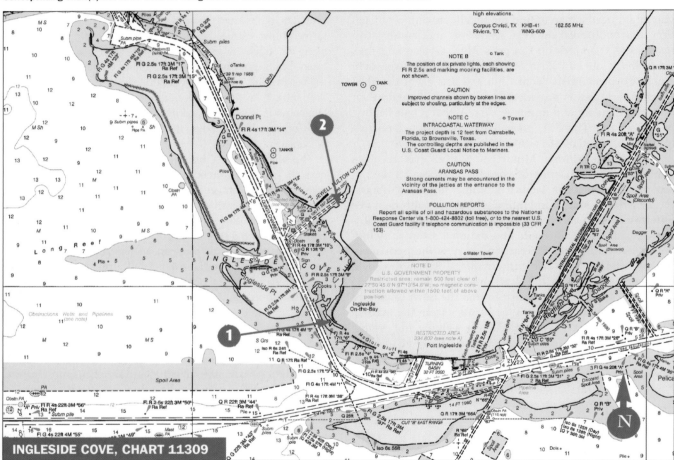

INGLESIDE COVE, CHART 11309

exhibits that change monthly. Grab a specialty lunch in the little restaurant, or visit the library and gift shop for an afternoon getaway. The Art Museum of South Texas (1902 N. Shoreline Blvd., 361-825-3500), allied with Texas A&M University, is open Tuesday through Saturday, 10 a.m. to 5 p.m., and Sunday, 1 p.m. to 5 p.m., with free admission on Thursday. The Museum of Science and History (1900 N. Chaparral, 361-826-4667) is home to replicas of Christopher Columbus' ships and artifacts of natural and cultural local history.

Take a ride along Ocean Drive, and head for Mustang Island State Park (361-749-5246) and Padre Island National Seashore (361-949-8068), which offers camping, fishing, sunbathing and beachcombing.

ADDITIONAL RESOURCES

■ Corpus Christi Convention and Visitors Bureau
800-678-6232, www.visitcorpuschristitx.org

NEARBY GOLF COURSES
Oso Beach Municipal Golf Course,
5601 S. Alameda St., Corpus Christi, TX 78412
361-826-8010

NEARBY MEDICAL FACILITIES
Christus Spohn Hospital Corpus Christi, 2606 Hospital Blvd.,
Corpus Christi, TX 78405, 361-902-4000
www.christusspohn.org

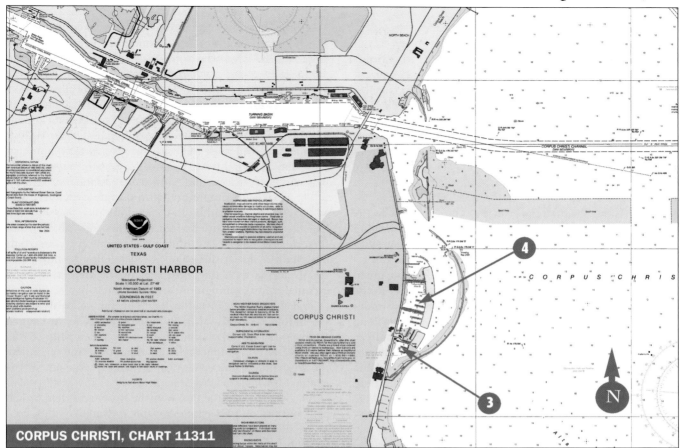

CORPUS CHRISTI, CHART 11311

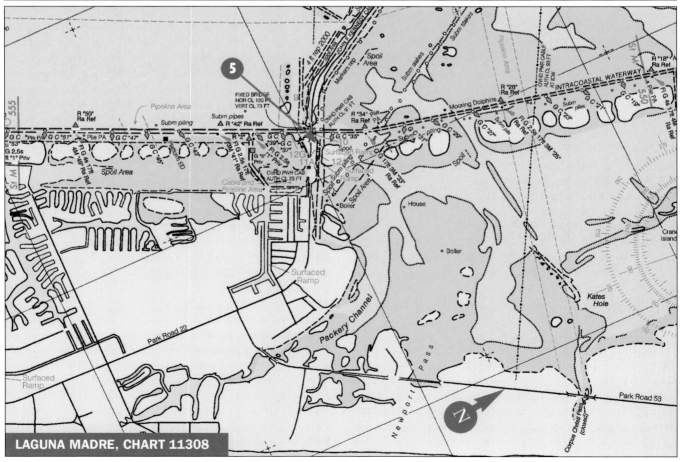

LAGUNA MADRE, CHART 11308

Port Mansfield, TX

Corpus Christi Bay via the GIWW: Mile 540 to Mile 555 WHL

NAVIGATION: Use Chart 11308. After crossing the Corpus Christi Ship Channel, the GIWW passes through a narrow cut (called "Eye of the Needle") into Corpus Christi Bay. Shoaling occurs on both sides of the cut, and tidal currents are sometimes strong. One vessel at a time should pass through this narrow cut. The cut can be detoured by following the Corpus Christi Ship Channel west from Mile 539.5 WHL for three miles into Corpus Christi Bay and then turning southeast just past flashing green "43" to return to the GIWW.

After passing through the "Needle" cut, stay close to the starboard side of the GIWW channel near quick-flashing red "66A" and green daybeacon "67." The GIWW passes uncomfortably close to the spoil area at Mile 540.5.

Channel markers, including 17-foot-high flashing green "71" and green daybeacon "79," identify the GIWW to the middle of Corpus Christi Bay before an open two-mile-long stretch to the marked channel at 17-foot flashing green "1" (with 17-foot Morse "C" just past the halfway mark of the stretch) and the start of a five-mile run to the 73-foot fixed vertical clearance JFK Causeway at Mile 552.7. Currents can be strong in this area. From flashing green "17" through Laguna Madre to green can buoy "35" near the bridge, stay in the channel; the depths shallow quickly outside the channel. The water is shallow to the southeast before crossing under the bridge.

Dockage: The Marker 37 Marina is located at green can "37," just to the southwest, and almost under the JFK Causeway Bridge. This is a shallow powerboat marina, with reported depths of only 3 to 4 feet at the fuel and transient dock. A store with ship and fishing supplies is at the gas-only fuel dock. A short walk around the boat ramp leads you to Snoopy's Restaurant and Ice Cream Parlor. Transient dockage is limited.

A private channel at green can "39" leads into a home subdivision and offers no transient facilities. Immediately past Mile 555 WHL (green can buoy "55"), a private channel leads to the Padre Island Country Club and the Padre Isles Yacht Club. Padre Isles Yacht Club welcomes visitors but has limited dockage.

Anchorage: Also at green can buoy "55" is an anchorage known as Sand Dune Lagoon or Spinnaker Hole (take your choice) has depths of 6 feet or more in the canals that were dug for homes yet to be built. Turn east into the channel and just past red daybeacon "14," turn to starboard into the undeveloped canals and find a spot to drop the hook.

Corpus Christi to Port Mansfield: Mile 553 to Mile 630 WHL

NAVIGATION: Use Charts 11308 and 11306. The 75-mile GIWW voyage to Port Mansfield through Laguna Madre is well-marked with green and red can buoys and an occasional 17-foot flashing light. There are no "wide spots" to relax in, so stay in the channel. Just before Mile 565, at green can buoy "119," a marked channel to North Padre Island brings fishermen and windsurfers into Laguna Madre from the last launching ramp on the island. Submerged pilings are located from Mile 564 to Mile 587 WHL on the east side of the GIWW. There are no mile markers between Mile 565 and Mile 590 WHL. The lack of facilities between Corpus Christi and Port Mansfield (this is King Ranch country - very sparsely populated) requires adequate fuel supplies and other provisions. Also note that Port Mansfield is the only offshore access from the GIWW between Port Aransas and South Padre Island.

The marked channel into Baffin Bay joins the GIWW at Mile 579.5 WHL. Although it may look promising, Baffin Bay has numerous uncharted shallows and no facilities for cruising boats. The numerous "stars" on your chart designate rocks. Baffin Bay is navigable for 15 miles to a small marina with the alluring name of Riviera Beach, a great spot for shallow-draft fishing craft.

Traveling south of Baffin Bay along the GIWW, cruisers should be aware of many uncharted rocks in Laguna Madre. Stay in the channel for safety. From Mile 587 to Mile 612 WHL, submerged and exposed pilings populate the west side of the GIWW, and then the east side of the channel through to Port Mansfield.

As you approach the Port Mansfield area, resident brown pelicans and dolphins are enjoyable to watch.

The Port Mansfield water tower is prominent and can be seen from miles away. The entrance from the GIWW to the Willacy County Port Mansfield Marina is just one mile west of the diamond-shaped intersection at Mile 629.5 WHL. Turn west at flashing red "PM," and then pass between green daybeacon "29" and red daybeacon "30." Farther on, after you pass green daybeacon "31" and red daybeacon "32," you will enter the harbor between green daybeacon "33" and red daybeacon "34." The channel and harbor both have 14-foot depths.

If traveling from the GIWW toward the Gulf of Mexico, start from the intersection at Mile 629.5 WHL, and travel east between red daybeacon "26" and green daybeacon "25" along the channel (200 feet wide and 7 to 10 feet deep). Continue along the channel for 8.5 miles to the jetties at flashing red "2" and flashing green "3."

Dockage: Port Mansfield has changed considerably during the last few years. El Jefe's Marina has expanded to include a restaurant area, a ship's store and extended service docks with gas and diesel fuel. The marina is located to port when entering the harbor. The Port Mansfield Marina offers a ship's store, snacks and fuel (both gas and diesel). There are two lodges, Fisherman's Inn and Casa Grande. The Willacy County Navigation District Marina is located to port at the end of the harbor. Both covered and open slips are available for transients. The harbormaster's office is located behind El Jefe's. Phone the office, or call "Port Mansfield Harbormaster" on the VHF radio to make sure that someone is on duty. Groceries, a café and tennis courts are just a few blocks away. This is usually a quiet and peaceful little town, but

Port Mansfield, TX

PORT MANSFIELD		Dockage				Supplies		Services				
		Largest Vessel Accommodated	VHF Channel Monitored	Transient Berths / Total Berths	Approach / Dockside Depth (reported)	Floating Docks	Gas / Diesel	Groceries, Ice, Marine Supplies, Snacks	Repairs: Hull, Engine, Propeller	Lift (tonnage), Crane, Rail	1=110V, 2=220V, B=Both, Max Amps	Laundry, Pool, Showers	Pump-Out Station	Nearby: Grocery Store, Motel, Restaurant
1. Port Mansfield Harbor/Willacy County Nav. Dist. 629.5 WHL 956-944-2325	60	16	/124	12/6		GD	GIMS		E			B/50	LPS	P	GMR
2. El Jefe's Marina 629.5 WHL 956-944-2876	60	68	23/	8/8		GD								GMR
3. The Port Mansfield Marina 956-944-2225						GD	I							

Corresponding chart(s) not to be used for navigation. ⌨ Internet Access **WiFi** Wireless Internet Access

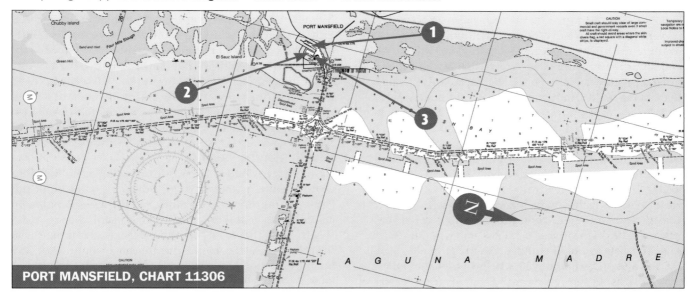

PORT MANSFIELD, CHART 11306

get ready for the weekends when it is a very popular spot for the folks from Raymondville and other inland areas. The massive King Ranch property dominates much of this remote area.

Port Mansfield to Queen Isabella Bridge—Mile 630 to Mile 665 WHL

NAVIGATION: Use Charts 11306, 11303 and 11302. A little more than a mile south of Port Mansfield, the "GIWW West" turns to a heading of about 150 degrees. It is sometimes hard to realize that you are now as far south as the Florida Everglades. At Mile 644 WHL, you are actually 400 miles west and 244 miles south of New Orleans.

Continuing from Port Mansfield along the GIWW, the channel (12-foot reported depths) remains well-marked with submerged pilings along the east side. At Mile 644 WHL, the forked entrance of the Arroyo Colorado Cutoff joins the GIWW from the west and marks the beginning of the Laguna Atascosa Wildlife Refuge and the channel to Port Harlingen.

Near Mile 650 WHL, where fishing camps line the east bank, and a large house stands prominently just west of the GIWW, the water tank and high-rise hotels of South Padre Island begin to emerge from the horizon off the port bow. The high arch of the Queen Isabella

Bridge comes into view. It connects Port Isabel on the mainland with the resorts and beaches of South Padre Island. A half-mile before the bridge, the marked channel leads west to the Port Isabel Small Boat Basin. Although the small boat basin is the most protected and convenient stopover, the entry from the GIWW can be a bit precarious. The marked channel shoals at times to about 2 feet near the GIWW according to local reports and enters the basin through a narrow and poorly marked cut. Deeper water is reported in the area from Mile 665 WHL, taking a heading of 265 degrees through uncharted waters, but still entered through the same narrow and poorly marked cut mentioned above. Seek local knowledge.

Dockage: The Port Isabel Small Boat Basin consists of several canals around a series of finger piers. It is linked to the GIWW again by a long canal, blocked by a fixed highway bridge, back to the GIWW near the South Point Marina. The Pelican Point Marina has 6-foot-plus depths, 50 slips up to 45 feet, 110-volt power, a bathhouse and a laundry room. The City Dock at the end of Pompano Avenue has dockage along the bulkheads up to 50 feet, unlocked restrooms and 120-volt electricity, but no other amenities. (Note that at press time 2010, the docks were under reconstruction after being destroyed during Hurricane Dolly in 2008.) Sea R Sea on the east side

South Padre Island, TX

has slips to 40 feet with 110-volt power. The office and store have a variety of supplies, and full repair service is offered. The Yacht Club Hotel is just across the street from Sea R Sea and offers fine dining, a lounge and rooms for those who want to get off the boat while it is under repair. You may also be able to find dock space at the White Sands Motel, Marina & Restaurant if their customers are not using all of the slips. (Call 956-943-6161.)

A walk down the main street (Highway 100) from the small-boat basin will take you past a liquor store, a minor emergency clinic, several restaurants, convenience stores, banks and the post office. This is also where the Port Isabel Lighthouse, built in 1852, is located. West from the small-boat basin is a large grocery store and a laundry. Some marine stores are located south of the highway: a canvas repair shop, a tackle shop and a few diesel and marine electrical service shops. To fully appreciate all that Port Isabel has to offer, a visit to the Chamber of Commerce office would be helpful.

Queen Isabella Bridge to the GIWW End—Mile 682 WHL

NAVIGATION: Use Charts 11303 and 11302. At Mile 665 WHL the GIWW passes under the Queen Isabella Bridge, connecting the causeway from Port Isabel to South Padre Island. The channel, which leaves the GIWW across from 17-foot quick flashing green "151," leads to the slips of many homes and condominiums. The remains of the storm-damaged Queen Isabella Marina have been removed, including the old breakwaters.

The Port Isabel Pontoon Bridge crosses the GIWW at Mile 666 WHL in the Port Isabella Channel. Monday through Friday, from 5 a.m. to 8 p.m., the bridge opens on the hour, but only opens by signal on weekends and holidays. It opens on signal for commercial vessels and allows recreational boats to go through with them. Past the pontoon bridge, a series of canals lead from the Waterway into a mobile home park on Long Island. Note that the depths of the GIWW do not extend to the bulkheads along the island. The GIWW continues along the Port Isabella Channel and the Cutoff Channel until the Waterway meets the Brownsville Ship Channel at Mile 668.5 WHL. The GIWW continues along the Brownsville Channel (250 feet wide and 45 feet deep). The Brownsville Fishing Harbor at Mile 677.5 WHL has some transient facilities, but limited dockage. The channel continues to the Brownsville Turning Basin at Mile 682 WHL.

If traveling to the Gulf of Mexico from the GIWW, at Mile 668.5 WHL, steer northeast along the Laguna Madre Channel. Pass 17-foot flashing red "28" and continue to red "4." Stay in the channel due to shoaling to the north and submerged pilings to the south of the channel (250 feet wide and 44 feet deep). At red "4," change course to due east and run for 1.5 miles to the Gulf through Brazos Santiago Pass. Expect strong currents just beyond the jetties.

Dockage: Southpoint Marina lies at the "Y" of the GIWW and the channel heading to the Port Isabel Small Boat Basin, which is restricted by a highway bridge with limited clearance. The largest and only full-service marina in Port Isabel is also the home of the Laguna Madre Yacht Club. The service dock is located at the first building off the GIWW. There is 30- and 50-amp electrical service, transient dockage to 100 feet and new floating docks have been completed. Restrooms, showers, a laundry and a ship's store are available. Full repair service, with a Travelift and forklift, are also on the premises (South Padre Boat Yard). South Shore Store nearby sells fuel.

South of the marina, at 17-foot quick flashing red "156," a turning basin for commercial vessels extends from the GIWW. The Waterway then makes a westerly turn to Port Brownsville and the end of the GIWW West, 682 miles from the Harvey Lock on the Mississippi River. The end of the GIWW is 400 miles west and 282 miles south of New Orleans, and as far south as the Everglades in Southern Florida.

South Padre Island

South Padre Island is famous for its white sand beaches, warm weather, superb fishing and proximity to the Padre Island National Seashore and the Mexican border. During college spring breaks and again during Holy Week, when thousands of affluent Mexican tourists visit, the island's hotels, motels, restaurants, nightclubs and beaches fill to capacity. Isla Blanca Park, adjacent to Sea Ranch Marina on the island's southern tip, and Andy Bowie Park, at the north end of the city, provide popular places to enjoy the beach. If traveling offshore, keep in mind that jetty swells can be substantial, particularly in the summer time; however, as soon as you move one mile out or north or south of the jetty wall, the effect is significantly reduced.

NAVIGATION: Use Charts 11303 and 11302. From Mile 668.5, travel northeast along Laguna Madre Channel to red "4." Steer north to the flashing green "1" and red daybeacon "2" to the entrance of Sea Ranch Marina. A shorter route from the Queen Isabella Bridge to South Padre Island, shown on your small-craft chart, is for shallow-draft vessels that can clear the charted 61-foot vertical clearance power lines at the end of the western section of the old causeway.

Dockage: The Sea Ranch Marina is located one mile north of the Laguna Madre Channel. The alternate route is charted from the Queen Isabella Bridge to the marina. Approach and dockside depths are reported to be 6 feet or more. The marina, located less than two miles from Brazos Santiago Pass, is the last marina and the last pass to the Gulf from the United States. The Sea Ranch Marina provides gas and diesel fuel and has transient dockage to 75 feet. Amenities include electricity service, restrooms, showers, a laundry, a ship's store and an adjoining restaurant with a lounge.

Port Isabel, South Padre Island, TX

PORT ISABEL/PADRE ISLAND		Largest Vessel Accommodated	VHF Channel Monitored	Transient Berths / Total Berths	Approach / Dockside Depth (reported)	Floating Docks	Gas / Diesel	Groceries, Ice, Marine Supplies, Snacks	Repairs: Hull, Engine, Propeller	Lift (tonnage), Crane, Rail	1=110v, 2=220v, B=Both, Max Amps	Laundry, Pool, Showers	Pump-Out Station	Nearby: Grocery Store, Motel, Restaurant
				Dockage				**Supplies**			**Services**			
1. Pelican Point Marina 668.5 WHL	956-943-6464	55	16	/46	13/5						B/30	LS		
2. Port Isabel City Dock 668.5 WHL	956-943-2682	50			7/6						B/50			
3. Sea Ranch II at Southpoint Marina 668.5 WHL	956-943-7926	60	68	10/30	8/8			GIMS	HEP	L50	B/50	LS		GMR
4. South Shore Ice & Fuel	956-943-1027						GD	I						
5. Sea Ranch Marina 668.5 WHL	956-761-7777	80	16	5/62	6/6		GD	GIMS	HP	L	B/250	LS		GMR

Corresponding chart(s) not to be used for navigation. 🖥 Internet Access 📶 Wireless Internet Access

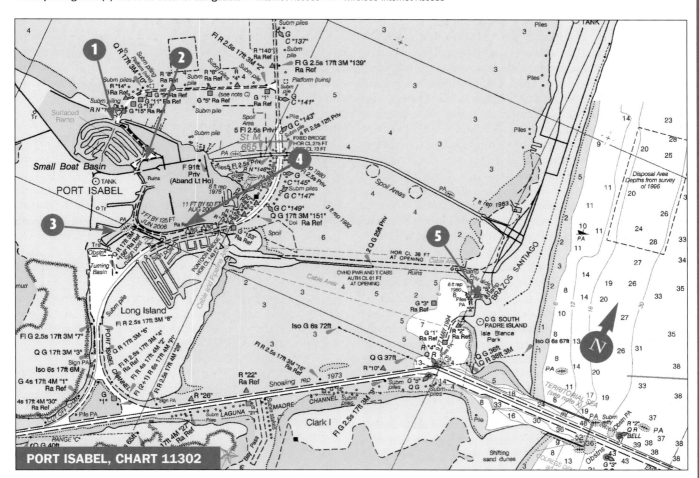

PORT ISABEL, CHART 11302

Anchorage: Anchorage outside the marked channel to Sea Ranch and the Coast Guard Station can be had in the lee of South Padre off of Isla Blanca Park or the marina entrance. Depths in this area range from 7 to 14 feet.

GOIN' ASHORE:
SOUTH PADRE ISLAND, TX

South Padre Island is truly a getaway to a relaxing, beautiful beach where resorts are plentiful, fishing is a positive experience and restaurants abound.

The history of South Padre Island dates back to 16th-century Spanish exploration. The Gulf of Mexico, Brazos Santiago Pass and Laguna Madre surround South Padre on three sides. Until the 1950s, the only way to get to South Padre was by ferry. The Queen Isabella Causeway brought prosperity to the area until 1966, when Hurricane Beulah hit and destroyed much of Port

South Padre Island, TX

Isabel, the gateway to the island. Today, its main industry is tourism, and international clientele own many of the businesses and private homes. During spring break, many college students migrate to its shores to enjoy the wonderful beaches and warm, sunny weather. The Schlitterbahn Beach Waterpark, at the southernmost tip of the island, offers more than a dozen attractions, from wave pools to tubing rivers.

Lovely beaches spread along the coast of South Padre Island, a resort community, and provide a scenic horizon with natural, protected sand dunes and fantastic sunsets. The beautiful green water coastline has been named one of the 10 best beaches in the world, a getaway place for many cultures. South Padre offers all the amenities of a resort island, with hotels, restaurants, t-shirt shops, mini-golf, water parks and water adventures for kids of all ages.

Restaurants feature fresh seafood brought in daily from the Gulf. Fishing (redfish, speckled and sand trout, sheepshead, flounder, croakers, skipjack and drum) is popular and plentiful, and the pier at Sea Ranch has great fishing (night and day). The natural coast has 75 percent of the world's turtle species, with many research projects in progress. Over the past 60 years, many sea turtles have nested on South Texas beaches. The Sea Ranch Restaurant & Bar (1 Padre Blvd., 956-761-1314) is the home of the Red Snapper and boasts the freshest prepared seafood in Texas. Enjoy the Sea Ranch Fishing Pier and Hooker's Upstairs Bar located in Sea Ranch Village on Laguna Madre.

The Visitors Center (600 Padre Blvd., 800-343-2368) is open from 9 a.m. to 4 p.m. daily and offers a 12-minute orientation program on the area. Laguna Madre is one of the top spots in the world for windsurfing because of its warm, shallow water and almost constant wind. A boat-launching ramp is also available. Worldwinds Windsurfing, located at Bird Island Basin, offers wind surfing rentals, lessons and sales. Birding is also a very popular activity on South Padre Island. Let's keep our fingers crossed that the oil spill offshore in the Gulf has been contained by press time in late summer 2010 with a minimal loss to sea life, the ecosystem and economy of the Gulf Coast.

ADDITIONAL RESOURCES

■ South Padre Island Visitors Guide, **www.sopadre.com**

⚑ **NEARBY GOLF COURSES**
South Padre Island Golf Club, 1 Golf House Rd., Laguna Vista, TX 78578, 956-943-5678

⚕ **NEARBY MEDICAL FACILITIES**
Island Family Practice, 3401 Padre Blvd., South Padre Island, TX 78597, 956-772-1911

Waterway Guide is always open to your observations from the helm. E-mail your comments on any navigation information in the guide to: editor@waterwayguide.com.

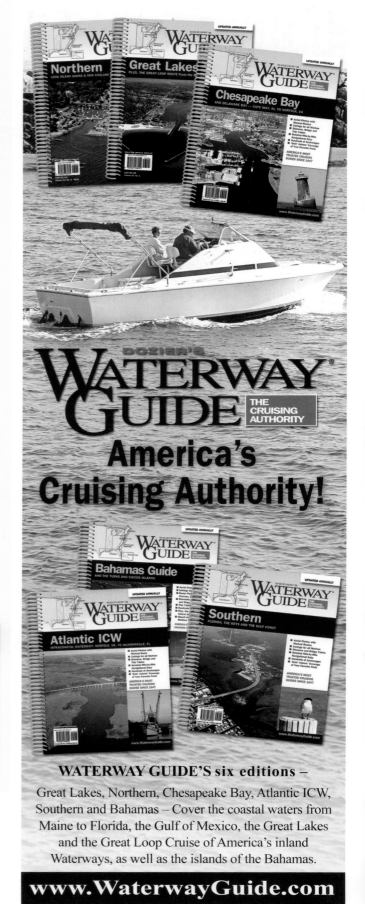

Extended Cruising

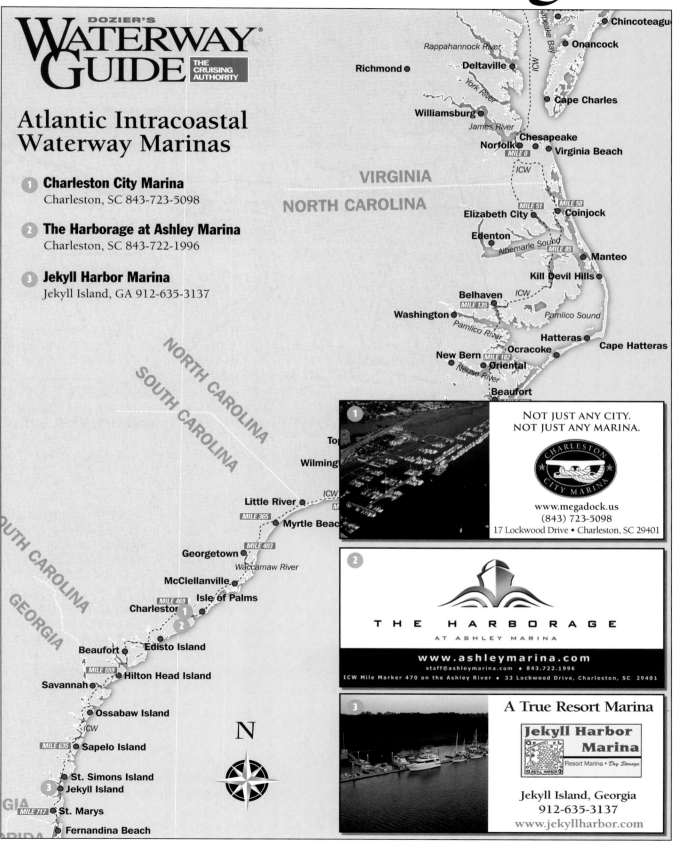

DOZIER'S WATERWAY GUIDE
THE CRUISING AUTHORITY

Atlantic Intracoastal Waterway Marinas

1 Charleston City Marina
Charleston, SC 843-723-5098

2 The Harborage at Ashley Marina
Charleston, SC 843-722-1996

3 Jekyll Harbor Marina
Jekyll Island, GA 912-635-3137

NOT JUST ANY CITY.
NOT JUST ANY MARINA.

CHARLESTON CITY MARINA

www.megadock.us
(843) 723-5098
17 Lockwood Drive • Charleston, SC 29401

THE HARBORAGE
AT ASHLEY MARINA

www.ashleymarina.com
staff@ashleymarina.com • 843.722.1996
ICW Mile Marker 470 on the Ashley River • 33 Lockwood Drive, Charleston, SC 29401

A True Resort Marina
Jekyll Harbor Marina
Resort Marina • Dry Storage

Jekyll Island, Georgia
912-635-3137
www.jekyllharbor.com

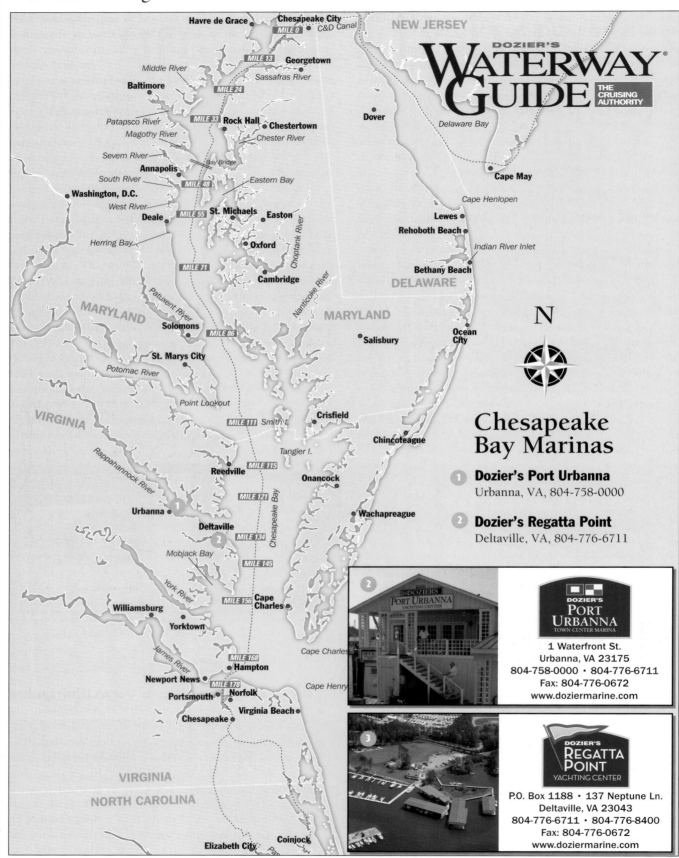

Chesapeake Bay Marinas

1 Dozier's Port Urbanna
Urbanna, VA, 804-758-0000

2 Dozier's Regatta Point
Deltaville, VA, 804-776-6711

Dozier's PORT URBANNA
TOWN CENTER MARINA

1 Waterfront St.
Urbanna, VA 23175
804-758-0000 • 804-776-6711
Fax: 804-776-0672
www.doziermarine.com

Dozier's REGATTA POINT
YACHTING CENTER

P.O. Box 1188 • 137 Neptune Ln.
Deltaville, VA 23043
804-776-6711 • 804-776-8400
Fax: 804-776-0672
www.doziermarine.com

For detailed navigational information, charts, and extensive marina coverage
see WATERWAY GUIDE, Chesapeake Bay Edition.
Purchase online: www.waterwayguide.com or call 800-233-3359.

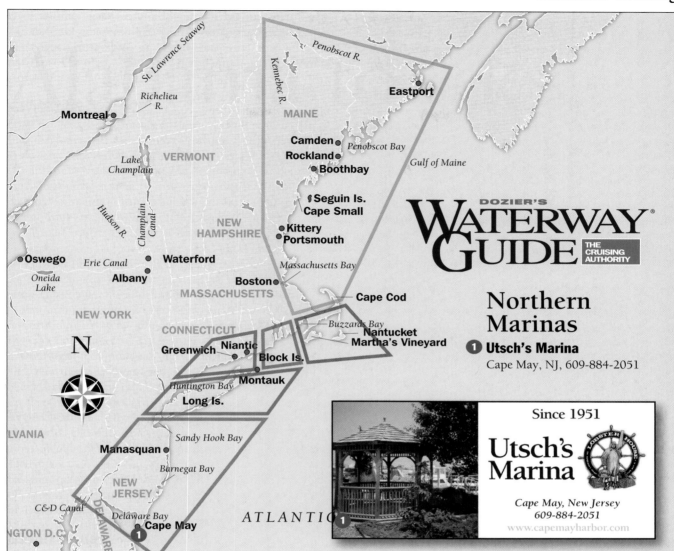

For detailed navigational information, charts, and extensive marina coverage see WATERWAY GUIDE, Northern Edition. Purchase online: www.waterwayguide.com or call 800-233-3359.

Skipper's Notes

Marina Index

Sponsors are listed in **BOLD**.

MARINA INDEX

Marina Index

MARINA INDEX

Subject Index

Subject Index

Subject Index

GOIN' ASHORES

SUBJECT INDEX

Skipper's Notes

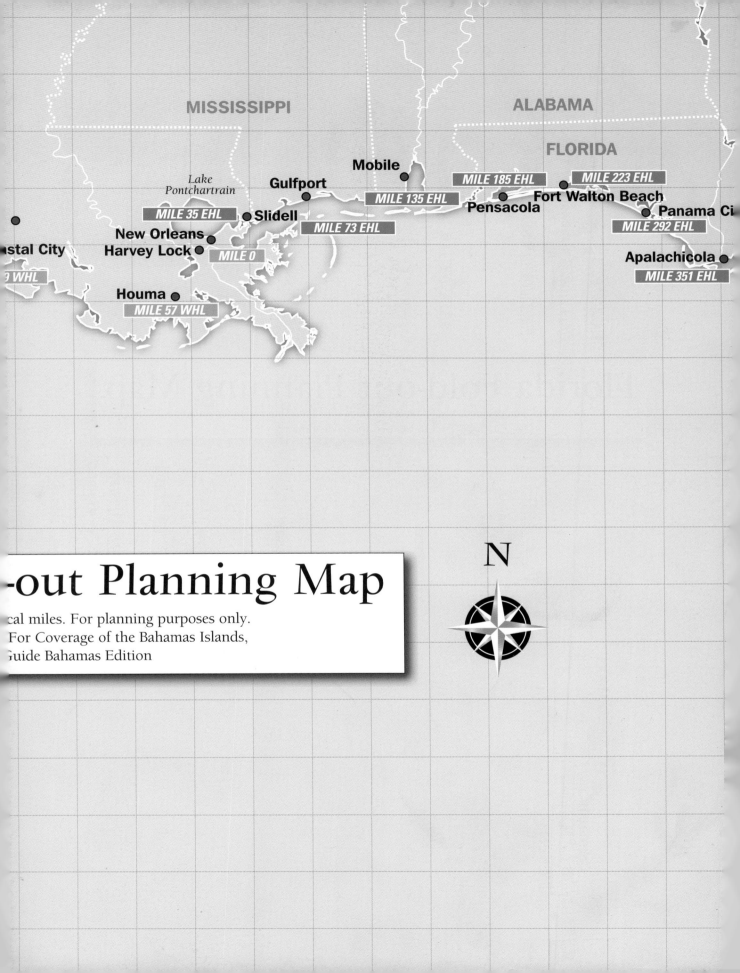

MISSISSIPPI

ALABAMA

FLORIDA

Lake Pontchartrain

Mobile

Gulfport

MILE 185 EHL

MILE 223 EHL

MILE 135 EHL

Fort Walton Beach

MILE 35 EHL

Slidell

Pensacola

Panama Ci

New Orleans

MILE 73 EHL

MILE 292 EHL

Harvey Lock

MILE 0

Apalachicola

stal City

MILE 351 EHL

9 WHL

Houma

MILE 57 WHL

-out Planning Map

cal miles. For planning purposes only.
For Coverage of the Bahamas Islands,
Guide Bahamas Edition

N

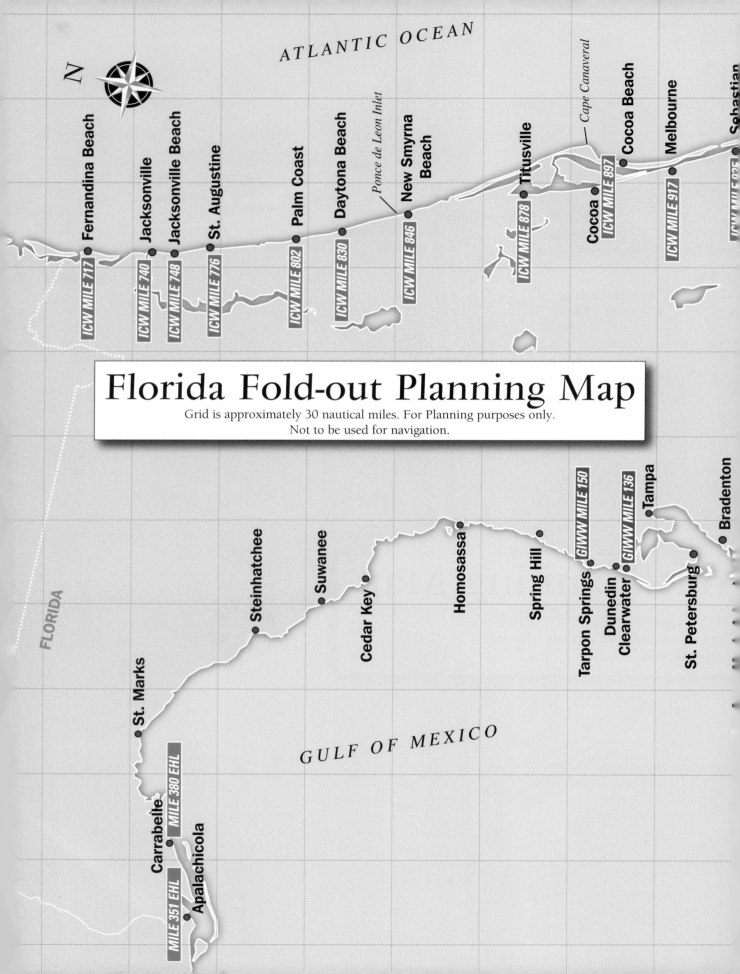

ATLANTIC OCEAN

N

Cape Canaveral

Fernandina Beach

Jacksonville

Jacksonville Beach

St. Augustine

Palm Coast

Daytona Beach

Ponce de Leon Inlet

New Smyrna Beach

Titusville

Cocoa

Cocoa Beach

Melbourne

Sebastian

ICW MILE 717

ICW MILE 740

ICW MILE 748

ICW MILE 776

ICW MILE 802

ICW MILE 830

ICW MILE 846

ICW MILE 878

ICW MILE 897

ICW MILE 917

ICW MILE 925

Florida Fold-out Planning Map

Grid is approximately 30 nautical miles. For Planning purposes only.
Not to be used for navigation.

FLORIDA

Tampa

Bradenton

GIWW MILE 150

GIWW MILE 136

Steinhatchee

Suwanee

Cedar Key

Homosassa

Spring Hill

Tarpon Springs

Dunedin

Clearwater

St. Petersburg

St. Marks

GULF OF MEXICO

Carrabelle

MILE 380 EHL

Apalachicola

MILE 351 EHL

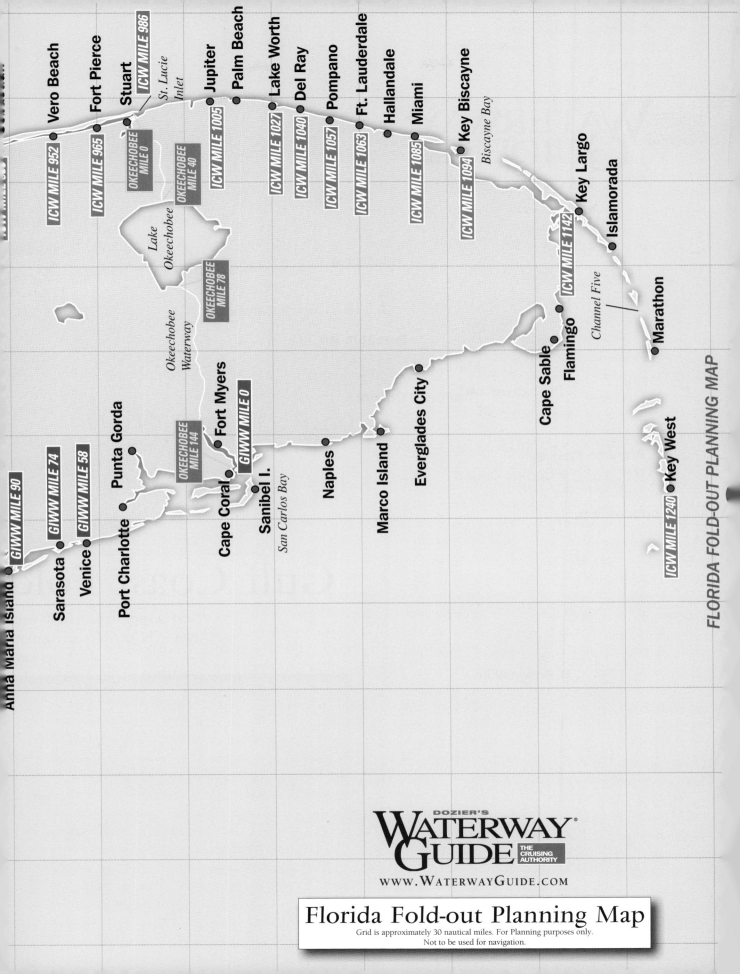

Florida Fold-out Planning Map

Grid is approximately 30 nautical miles. For Planning purposes only.
Not to be used for navigation.

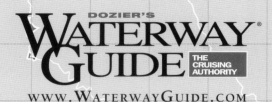

LOUISIANA

TEXAS

Lake Charles ●

Lafayette

Intracoa

Houston ●

`MILE 285 WHL` ● Port Arthur

`MILE 15`

`MILE 350 WHL` ● Galveston

Freeport ● `MILE 395 WHL`

Matagorda ●

`MILE 440 WHL`

Port Lavaca ● ● Port O'Connor

`MILE 473 WHL`

GULF OF MEXICO

Aransas Pass ●

`MILE 545 WHL` ● Corpus Christi

Kingsville ●

Gulf Coast Fold

Grid is approximately 40 nauti
Not to be used for navigation.
see Waterway (

`MILE 682 WHL`
● Brownsville

MEXICO

GULF COAST FOLD-OUT PLANNING MAP